Using Computers in the Law Office

Fifth Edition

FIFTH EDITION

USING COMPUTERS IN THE LAW OFFICE

Brent Roper, J.D., MBA

DELMAR
THOMSON LEARNING™

Australia Canada Mexico Singapore Spain United Kingdom United States

USING COMPUTERS IN THE LAW OFFICE, 5E

Brent Roper, J.D., MBA

Vice President, Career Education Strategic Business Unit:
Dawn Gerrain

Director of Learning Solutions:
John Fedor

Managing Editor:
Robert L. Serenka, Jr.

Acquisitions Editor:
Shelley Esposito

Senior Product Manager:
Melissa Riveglia

Editorial Assistant:
Melissa Zaza

Director of Content & Media Production:
Wendy A. Troeger

Technology Project Manager:
Sandy Charette

Director of Marketing:
Wendy E. Mapstone

Marketing Manager:
Gerard McAvey

Marketing Coordinator:
Jonathan Sheehan

Art Director:
Joy Kocsis

Cover Designer:
Dutton and Sherman Design

Cover Images:
© Getty Images, Inc.

Printed in Canada
1 2 3 4 5 XXX 11 10 09 08 07

For more information contact Delmar Learning,
5 Maxwell Drive, PO Box 8007, Clifton Park, NY 12065–2919.

Or find us on the World Wide Web at
http://www.delmarlearning.com.

Library of Congress Cataloging-in-Publication Data
Roper, Brent D.
Using computers in the law office / Brent Roper.— 5th ed.
p. cm. (West legal studies)
Includes bibliographical references and index.
ISBN-13: 978-1-4180-3312-5
ISBN-10: 1–4180–3312–X
1. Law offices--United States—Automation. 2. Information storage and retrieval systems—Law—United States. 3. Legal assistants--United States—Handbooks, manuals, etc. I. Title.

KF320.A9R66 2008
340.0285—dc22

2007020861

NOTICE TO THE READER

Publisher does not warrant or guarantee any of the products described herein or perform any independent analysis in connection with any of the product information contained herein. Publisher does not assume, and expressly disclaims, any obligation to obtain and include information other than that provided to it by the manufacturer.

The reader is notified that this text is an educational tool, not a practice book. Since the law is in constant change, no rule or statement of law in this book should be relied upon for any service to any client. The reader should always refer to standard legal sources for the current rule or law. If legal advice or other expert assistance is required, the services of the appropriate professional should be sought.

The Publisher makes no representation or warranties of any kind, including but not limited to, the warranties of fitness for particular purpose or merchantability, nor are any such representations implied with respect to the material set forth herein, and the publisher takes no responsibility with respect to such material. The Publisher shall not be liable for any special, consequential, or exemplary damages resulting, in whole or part, from the reader's use of, or reliance upon, this material.

The author and Delmar Learning affirm that the website URLs referenced herein were accurate at the time of printing. However, due to the fluid nature of the Internet, we cannot guarantee their accuracy for the life of the edition.

To Shirley, the love of my life

CONTENTS IN BRIEF

CONTENTS

PREFACE

The goal of *Using Computers in the Law Office,* Fifth Edition, is to educate legal assistants regarding computer use in legal organizations. Practically every task a legal professional now does is performed in some way with the assistance of a computer. The breadth of computer use in legal organizations continues to expand. When the first edition of the book was published in 1992 it was just over 450 pages and was in a much smaller format. The fifth edition is more than double this continues to expand.

The text assumes no prior experience with computer hardware or software. The focus of the text is on practical computer applications used in legal organizations and how computers can be used to make a legal assistant more productive and his or her job easier. I try to explain computer concepts simply and without jargon. Computer texts have a tendency to be esoteric, and for this reason I present step-by-step explanations, pictures of actual computer screens, and many practical ideas for using computers in a legal organization. The text encourages students to think independently and learn by participating. In addition, there are twenty separate tutorials in the text with step-by-step instructions.

After many years of performing legal tasks manually as a legal assistant, a law clerk, and finally an attorney, I was amazed to find how much a computer could increase efficiency and productivity, and at the same time, make these duties less difficult. The ultimate purpose of the text is to have the student feel this same amazement. Everything in the book is aimed at one goal: to help legal assistants solve real-life problems on the job.

TO THE STUDENT

Now, more than ever before, it is critical for legal assistants to have a broad and detailed working knowledge of technology as it relates to the modern law office. All legal services provided to clients now have a technological component to them. This includes drafting and filing documents, calendaring, billing, submitting and receiving discovery requests, research, evidence tracking, damage projections, trial preparation, deposition transcript management, client communication, and much, much more. Technology is now a major player in nearly every legal organization in the United States.

It is absolutely critical for legal assistants to go beyond having a basic understanding of a few programs. In the current legal environment legal assistants must have a detailed understanding of a wide variety of computer programs. Having this kind of knowledge allows the legal assistant to select the best type of program for a particular problem or need. Legal assistants need to be experts in word processing, litigation support, database management and other functions. Many successful and well-paid legal assistants have leveraged technology to get ahead in their career.

Become a technology expert. You probably already have a basic knowledge of Microsoft Office programs. That is not enough. My career advice to you is to read this text closely, install all of the sample software, and do every single tutorial, particularly the advanced ones, even if they are not assigned. This is one of the courses in your curriculum that cuts across all legal disciplines. Don't do these things because you want a good grade. Do them because it is great for your career and will help you get a job and get promoted. In addition, you'll make more money! In writing this book I have talked to many practicing legal assistants and they all roundly say that having advanced technology skills is absolutely required in the modern law office. Thank you, and good luck.

ORGANIZATION OF THE TEXT

This textbook is organized into thirteen chapters. The Microsoft Windows operating system is discussed in Appendix A on Disk 1. A sample deposition transcript appears in Appendix B on Disk 1. The first two chapters introduce the student to computers with a discussion of the importance of computers to the legal field and a review of computer hardware and software terms. The objective of these sections is to give students a rudimentary understanding of basic computer terminology and systems on which the rest of the book can build.

The next eleven chapters represent the heart of the book. They cover word processing, spreadsheets, databases, timekeeping and billing, case management / docket control, electronic discovery, litigation support, the Internet and electronic mail, computer assisted research and CD-ROM legal databases, the electronic courthouse / automated courtroom and presentation graphics, and specialized legal software. Each topic is

presented in a clear and organized manner and includes many examples of how the relevant software is actually used by legal assistants in a legal organization.

CHANGES TO THE FIFTH EDITION

Technology in the legal field continues to grow at an astounding rate. The level of effort it takes to update the book seems to grow with each edition. This edition represented a substantial rewrite and a complete overhaul of much of the book. Some of the changes included the following:

- A new chapter on electronic discovery has been added.
- New tutorials for Microsoft Office 2007, including Microsoft Word 2007, Excel 2007, Access 2007, and PowerPoint 2007, have been added.
- For the first time, the text comes with two CD-ROMs that include data files for Microsoft Word, Excel, Access, and PowerPoint and WordPerfect Office X3.
- A new tutorial for WordPerfect Office X3 has been added (on Disk 1).
- Appendix A, which covers Microsoft Windows, has been updated to include coverage of Vista. The Hands-on Exercises for Appendix A also includes coverage of Vista (on Disk 1).
- Every tutorial now includes a basic, intermediate, and advanced section. Most tutorials were greatly expanded to increase coverage of chapter content in the tutorials.
- Every tutorial includes a substantial increase in the number of screen shots. This was done to further increase the user friendliness of the tutorials.
- Every chapter includes more screen shots and explanations than ever before.
- Detailed installation instructions, including many screen shots, have been added to make installing the software more user-friendly.
- Increased coverage of technology and security topics, including metadata, various security issues, the virtual law office, and disaster recovery has been added.
- New, expanded sections on PDF files and document assembly were added to Chapter 3—Word Processing.
- Elementary word-processing concepts were deleted from Chapter 3 and replaced with more advanced technical concepts, including greater coverage of creating tables of authorities, comparing documents, styles, and other functionalities.
- Word and WordPerfect quick reference charts were included in Chapter 3.
- New sections entitled On the Web Exercises and Test Your Knowledge were included for each chapter.
- All charts, graphs, surveys, terminology, and research in the book have been completely updated.
- Every chapter has been completely updated to make the information as current and applicable as possible.
- An expanded tutorial has been included regarding using the Internet to find factual and legal research information.
- Full coverage of WESTLAW and LexisNexis has been added, including full tutorials for both.

LEARNING FEATURES

Chapter features include the following:

- **Chapter objectives** open each chapter to focus the student's attention on the main elements of the chapter.
- **Quotes** from legal professionals are used to make the text as practical as possible.
- **Internet sites** are referenced, and useful and pertinent ones appear near the end of each chapter.*
- **Key terms** are boldfaced in the body of the text and appear in the margin for easy review and reference. (A comprehensive glossary appears at the end of the book.)
- **Numerous illustrations,** including screen shots, legal documents, tables, and other graphics, are included throughout the text.
- **Ethical considerations** are included in each chapter.
- **On the Web exercises** have been added for each chapter.
- **"Test your Knowledge"** exercises have been added for each chapter.

---

*Please note that Internet resources are of a time-sensitive nature and URL addresses may often change or be deleted.

- **Questions and exercises** are included in each chapter to challenge the student to apply the information learned in the chapter.
- **Hands-on exercises** are included in nearly every chapter to give the student actual experience on a computer.

HANDS-ON EXERCISES / TUTORIALS

Tutorials are included at the ends of nearly all of the chapters, twenty in all. The tutorials assume that the student has access to a computer and to application software, but no prior computer experience is necessary to complete the tutorials.

The tutorials include step-by-step instructions that guide the student through the application. All of the tutorials are completely interactive, allowing the student to gain hands-on experience with software. In addition, all of the tutorials are specifically related to legal organizations and legal applications, so the student not only learns how to operate the computer and software, but also learns how to use them in the legal environment.

Full tutorials are included for the following applications:

- Microsoft Word 2007
- Microsoft Word 2003
- Corel WordPerfect X3 (on Disk 1)
- Microsoft Excel 2007
- Microsoft Excel 2003
- Microsoft Access 2007
- Microsoft Access 2003
- Microsoft PowerPoint 2007
- Microsoft PowerPoint 2003
- Legal and Factual Research Using the Internet
- Tabs3 (timekeeping and billing)
- AbacusLaw (case management and docket control)
- CT Summation iBlaze (litigation support)
- LexisNexis CaseMap 7
- LexisNexis TimeMap 4
- WESTLAW
- LexisNexis
- SmartDraw Legal
- Windows Vista (on Disk 1)
- Windows XP (on Disk 1)

EDUCATIONAL SOFTWARE

The following demonstration software is included with the text: (please note that many of the programs timeout, and will not work after a certain number of days from when the program was first loaded or have other limitations)

- **AbacusLaw.** AbacusLaw is a registered trademark of Abacus Data Systems, Inc. AbacusLaw timesout 90 days after it is first installed (Disk 1).
- **LexisNexis Case Map.** CaseMap is a registered trademark of CaseSoft, a division of LexisNexis. CaseMap times out 120 days after it is first installed (Disk 2).
- **Tabs3.** Tabs 3 is a registered trademark of Software Technology, Inc. Tabs3 does not timeout, but users are limited to 30 clients (Disk 1).
- **Summation iBlaze.** Summation and Summation iBlaze are trademarks of CT Summation, Inc. CT Summation, Inc. disclaims all responsibility for the content of this textbook, including but not limited to representations, instructions, and assertions about or relating to CT Summation, Inc. Summation timesout and will not work after February 1, 2010 (Disk 2).
- **SmartDraw.** SmartDraw Legal Edition is a registered trademark of SmartDraw.com. SmartDraw times out 120 days after it is first installed (Disk 2).
- **TimeMap.** TimeMap is a registered trademark of CaseSoft, a division of LexisNexis. TimeMap timesout 120 days after it is first installed.

SUPPLEMENTAL TEACHING AND LEARNING MATERIALS

The **Instructor's Manual with Test Bank** is available both in print and online at <http://www.delmarlearning.com> in the Instructor's Lounge. Written by the author of the text, the Instructor's Manual contains chapter outlines, teaching suggestions, class discussion ideas, answers to the exercises in the text, and transparency masters.

Computerized Test Bank—Features of the test bank include

- multiple methods of question selection
- multiple outputs – print, ASCII, and RTF
- graphic support (black and white)
- random question output
- special character support

Online Companion™—The Online Companion™ can be found at <http://www.delmarlearning.com> in the Resource section of the website. The Online Companion™ contains the following:

- Internet-related exercises
- Chapter-related exercises
- Websites related to chapter content
- Appendices

Website – Come visit our website at <http://www.westlegalstudies.com>, where you will find valuable information specific to this book, such as hot links and sample materials to download, as well as information about other West Legal Studies products.

Educational Demo Software—Software on the CD-ROMs packaged with the text includes AbacusLaw, Case Map, CT Summation iBlaze, SmartDraw Legal, Tabs3, and Time Map.

WESTLAW—West's online computerized legal research system offers students hands-on experience with a system commonly used in law offices. Qualified adopters can receive ten free hours of WESTLAW. WESTLAW can be accessed from computers running the Macintosh and Windows operating systems.

TO THE STUDENT

It is my hope that you will find this book useful in your professional career and that you will use some of the ideas in it to climb the ladder of success. I wish you the best of luck in your endeavors.

ACKNOWLEDGMENTS

This book was made possible by many individuals. Without their help and encouragement I would have been far too overwhelmed (not to mention depressed) to finish it. So, to all the people listed below who have worked on this project, *thank you for all your help.*

Reviewers

A special thanks goes to the reviewers of the text for their ideas and suggestions on how to improve it. Their help was critical in updating the text, and I am indebted to them for all of their assistance.

Eli Bortman, Babson College, Wellesley, MA
Stephanie Delaney, Highline Community College, Des Moines, WA
Scott Rokley, Lansing Community College, Lansing, MI
Julia Tryk, Cuyahoga Community College, Parma, OH

Thomson Delmar Learning

A special thanks goes to my editors, including Shelley Esposito, Melissa Riveglia, and Sandy Charette. All of them have been wonderful to work for and tremendously supportive. They worked long hours and sweated all the details to make sure we put out a quality product. I cannot say enough wonderful things about them. Thank you so much!

Research Materials

A special thanks goes to Professor John E. Christensen, Library Director of the Washburn University School of Law, for his help regarding this textbook's coverage of LexisNexis. Thank you, Professor Christensen, for your kindness and help going all the way back to the first edition. Washburn University School of Law's legal research website, <http://www.washlaw.edu>, was extremely helpful during the research phase of the book, and I find it to be one of the easiest and most comprehensive sites for conducting legal research on the Internet. It does not surprise me that this was done under Professor Christensen's careful eye. Thank you again, Professor Christensen.

Others

A special thanks goes to my wife, Shirley Phelps-Roper and our children, Samuel, Megan, Rebekah, Isaiah, Zacharias, Grace, Gabriel, Jonah, Noah, and Luke for their support and assistance. Without their love and patience I never could have seen this project through.

I would also like to thank my daughter Megan for copyediting every tutorial twice. This took hundreds of hours of work and she did it without complaining and met all of my impossible deadlines. Meg, I cannot thank you enough for your help and dedication! Thank you for being a wonderful daughter!

A special thanks goes to Zacharias and Isaiah for all of their work on copying the manuscript. It is a boring job, but one that had to be done. Thank you Zach and Zay, you were a huge help. I am proud of each of you!

I would also like to thank my sister-in-law Elizabeth for all of her help copyediting each chapter and helping me get my ideas across. Thank you Lizz, you are a jewel! I am truly lucky to have you as a sister-in-law!

Another thank you goes to Rebekah and Grace for cooking wonderful meals while I worked for hours and hours straight. They delivered room service to my office on a regular basis and were helpful in every way imaginable! Thank you, Beck and Grace.

Last but not least, I would like to thank the wife of my youth, Shirley. Thank you for your love, help, counsel, and support through life. And if I do not say it enough, I think it every day: Thank you for marrying me, and I love you.

Brent Roper
Topeka, KS 66604
broper@cox.net

*Please note that Internet resources are of a time-sensitive nature and URL addresses may often change or be deleted.

Contact us at westlegalstudies@delmar.com

> *Learning how to effectively use the Internet to do legal research, manage documents, and [access] other information is probably the clearest path for the would-be technology-savvy paralegal. Knowing how to weed through a lot of garbage to effectively gather a small amount of specific information is a valuable skill no longer overlooked by today's law firms.*[5]

Listservs and Electronic Mailing Lists Listservs are like electronic mailing lists. They send email messages to people whose names are on a list. They are a simple way for groups of people to communicate with one another through email. There are thousands of listservs on the Internet. Legal assistants use these to communicate with other legal assistants, to communicate with other legal professionals who practice in their legal specialty, and to communicate with others who have similar interests in other areas as well. Examples include:

LawTech—for legal professionals who want to discuss legal technology issues (see <http://www.abanet.org>)

Legal Assistant Today—specifically for legal assistants who want to share information about legal assistant issues, ideas, and experiences or who have questions about practice issues (see <http://www.legalassistanttoday.com>)

To find more listservs about the practice of law or the legal assistant profession, you can use an Internet browser and a general search engine to search for "legal assistant listservs," "paralegal listservs," or whatever specific topic you are interested in.

Blogs A "blog" is a website with information contained in posts that are arranged in reverse chronological order. Blogs resemble diary or journal entries, and they can contain links to other websites or articles. There are many law-related blogs on the Internet, including blogs on specific types of law, such as immigration or taxes.

Web Pages Some legal assistants design or update their legal organization's web page. This is typically done in smaller law firms, because the Internet offers law firms a relatively inexpensive way to market their firms to others.

Commerce The Internet allows legal assistants to research and purchase goods and services including law-related products, new technologies and software, law books, and much more.

Continuing Education Some legal assistants use computer-based learning strategies online and attend electronic seminars through distance learning programs.

Intranets and Extranets An **intranet** is an internal network designed to provide and disseminate information to internal staff using the look and feel of the World Wide Web. In short, it is a private "Internet" that is used only by a legal organization's internal staff. Typical information a legal organization might include on its intranet site would be office policies and procedures, training material, contact lists, legal research, and form files.

An **extranet** in a legal organization is an information distribution system for clients. It is a secure web-based site that allows clients to access information about their case and collaborate with the legal professionals that are providing legal services to them. A client with a web browser typically can access a legal organization's extranet by going through security and ID/password protections, and then access his or her case plans, documents, strategies, billing information, and other case data.

intranet
An internal network designed to provide and disseminate information to internal staff using the look and feel of the World Wide Web.

extranet
A secure web-based site that allows clients to access information about their case and collaborate with the legal professionals that are providing legal services to them.

Because the Internet changes so fast and connects so many people, the potential for legal assistants using the Internet in a productive and efficient manner is nearly limitless.

Drafting Documents: Computerized Word Processing

Most legal assistants draft documents on a regular basis. This task includes preparing summaries of deposition transcripts (i.e., transcripts of the oral examinations of witnesses), drafting correspondence, drafting interoffice memorandums regarding information gathered from witness interviews, drafting interrogatories, drafting legal research memorandums, correcting wills, and much more.

A word processor is a computer program that is used to edit, manipulate, and revise text (see Exhibit 1–6). Word-processing software is used overwhelmingly in all types of legal organizations. Word-processing programs are extremely powerful and allow text to be edited, manipulated, inserted, deleted, and moved with minimal effort. Word processors not only have useful general features such as spelling and grammar checking, tables, track changes, and footnotes, but may also have legal-specific features such as legal spell-checking dictionaries, legal-specific templates, and a table of authorities creation function, among others.

Exhibit 1–6
Word Processor Screen—Track Changes Feature
Microsoft product screen shot reprinted with permission from Microsoft Corporation.

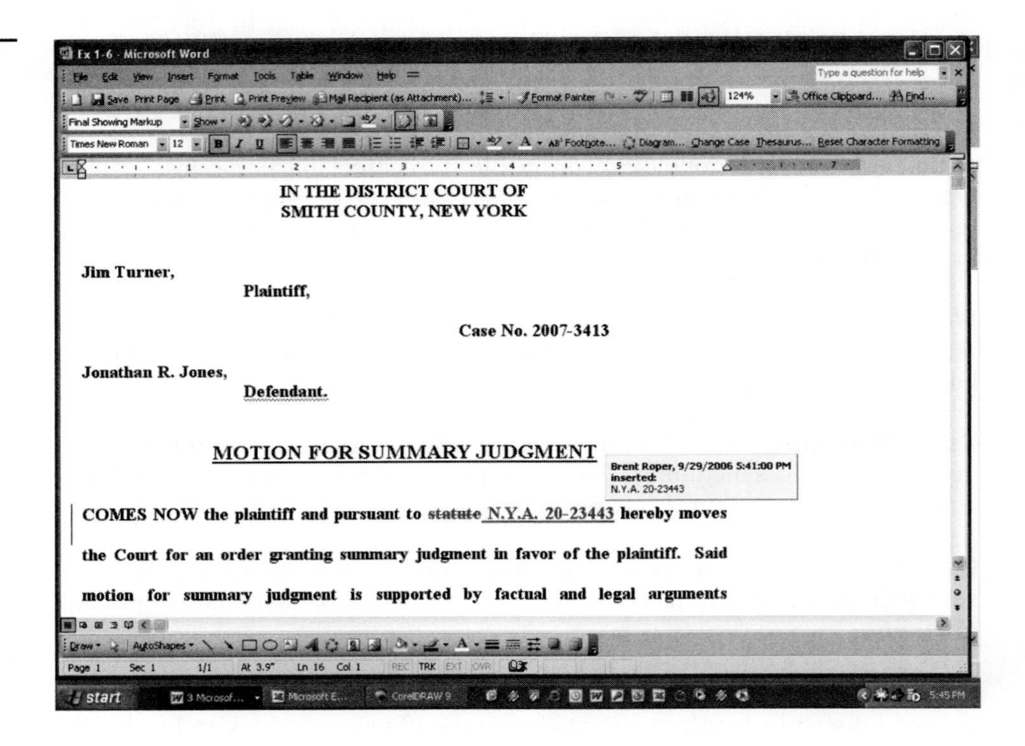

Electronic Discovery Software and Services

The increasing trends of storing electronic data and using software applications that maintain potentially discoverable information have rendered the process of obtaining and producing discovery a monumental task.[6]

electronic discovery software
Software that assists legal professionals in accurately assembling, producing, reading, converting, and searching electronic discovery requests.

Electronic discovery software is software that assists legal professionals in accurately assembling, producing, reading, converting and searching electronic discovery requests (see Exhibit 1–7). In years past, during litigation, parties would exchange hard-copy printouts of data related to a case. Now, many court rules,

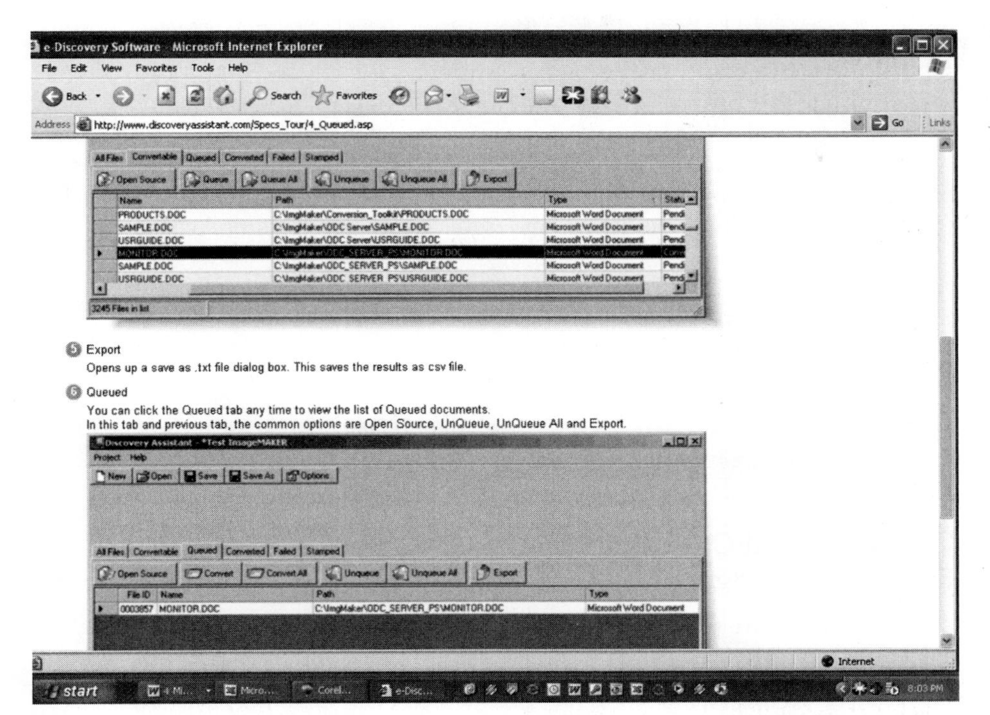

Exhibit 1–7
Electronic Discovery Software
Copyright ImageMAKER Development, Inc.

including the Federal Rules of Civil Procedure, require that parties exchange discovery information electronically. Because so much information is now maintained electronically, including electronic mail (and attachments thereto), word-processing documents, databases, spreadsheets, backup tapes, websites, accounting data, calendar information, presentations, schematics, graphics, and maps, producing the information can be extremely difficult. In addition, electronic data is stored in many file formats (such as *.doc*, *.xls*, *.pdf*, and *.jpg*) and in a variety of places (including desktop computers, laptops, network servers, backup tapes, email systems, storage media, and PDAs). Electronic discovery software and service providers assist legal professionals in both responding to electronic discovery requests from other parties and in strategizing and utilizing electronic information that has been produced by the opposing party. Some electronic discovery software reads multiple software formats and works across a variety of operating system platforms, converting the information so that it can be easily retrieved.

> *The traditional role of paralegals is vastly going by the wayside. You have to have a grip, or at least an understanding or knowledge, of the world of electronic discovery. [If paralegals do not] they are going to find themselves unemployed.*[7]

Litigation Support Software

Many legal assistants are involved in litigation support tasks. This means that they help attorneys organize, store, retrieve, and summarize the information that is gathered in the conduct of a lawsuit. Because numerous documents and pieces of information are gathered during the course of a lawsuit, these must be organized to be used at the time of trial. Documents that litigators often need immediate access to include deposition transcripts, deposition summaries, discovery documents (such as interrogatories and requests for admissions), motions, pleadings, and case exhibits (which can run into the tens of thousands), among others. For example, suppose you have a case with ten thousand documents in it and you are requested to find all the documents that refer to a

person named John Doe. Manual methods, such as looking through all ten thousand documents, could take weeks. Computerized litigation support software can automate this process so that you can do this search in seconds. In addition, your firm can make litigation support databases available to staff, clients, or co-counsel using the Internet or an extranet so that the information can be accessed from remote locations such as other offices, a courthouse, or a client's office. Litigation support software is crucial in large cases, but even small cases can benefit from this technology.

> *A short time ago, few technology skills were considered necessary requirements for paralegals. But in today's exceedingly digital legal industry, having a handle on business software like word processing or spreadsheet programs is no longer enough. For paralegals, a working knowledge of various types of litigation support and database programs is often expected by employers [and] are skills paralegals must possess.*[8]

Collecting and Organizing Data: Database Management Software

Legal assistants are often required to collect and organize data. For example, a legal assistant might be asked to prepare and track the names of witnesses and probable testimony in a case, generate a listing of documents in a case, prepare a chronological listing of major events in a case, or put together a current list of all the cases being handled by their firm, including name of client, adverse party, case number, court, and name of the presiding judge.

A database management system is a computer program that stores, searches, sorts, and organizes data (see Exhibit 1–8). Database management systems allow users to manipulate information in many different formats. For example, a legal assistant can easily create a current case list database that shows all active cases for the firm in alphabetical order. Once the data is entered, users can produce many different types of reports and formats without having to reenter the data. The legal assistant can then use the same database to produce a list of all the

Exhibit 1–8
Database Management Reports
Report B uses the same database of information as report A. The only difference is that to compile report B, only the cases in which Judge Alvin is the active judge were retrieved.

A. Current List of Cases Sorted by Client's Last Name

Client's Last Name	Client's First Name	Adverse Party	Case No.	Court	Judge
Casey	Charles	Shipley	00-6342	Dist. 10	Keith
Gonzalez	James	Gragg	01-2942	Dist. 12	Alvin
Lowell	William	Jenkins	02-2144	Dist. 10	Keith
Metzger	Jane	Maxon	02-9872	Dist. 7	Meek
Patterson	Don Q.	Cole	00-7481	Dist. 3	Owen
Schmanke	Ralph	Lawless	01-1138	Dist. 12	Alvin
Stewart	Mary	Ward	02-3352	Dist. 5	Williams
Turnkey	John	Patton	02-0234	Dist. 12	Alvin
Wallace	Andrew	Creamer	01-2342	Dist. 10	Keith

B. Current List of Cases Before Judge Alvin

Client's Last Name	Client's First Name	Adverse Party	Case No.	Court	Judge
Gonzalez	James	Gragg	01-2942	Dist. 12	Alvin
Schmanke	Ralph	Lawless	01-1138	Dist. 12	Alvin
Turnkey	John	Patton	02-0234	Dist. 12	Alvin

firm's cases in a specific court or before a particular judge or to produce a numerical listing by case number of all the firm's cases. In summary, a database management system allows users to store and retrieve information; arrange and rearrange information without affecting the information itself; update, change, and add information; organize and sort information; and search for data.

Performing Mathematical Calculations: Spreadsheet Software

Legal assistants may be required to perform mathematical calculations in their jobs. The calculations might be simple, such as adding up the amount of damages a party has asked for in a case or preparing a case budget for a client, or more complicated, such as calculating principal and interest payments in a real estate transaction, analyzing statistics for trends, or calculating lost wages in a workers' compensation case.

A spreadsheet program calculates and manipulates numbers (see Exhibit 1–9). Spreadsheet programs allow numerical data to be added, subtracted, multiplied, and divided automatically. They also allow users to edit, copy, and move numerical data; perform complex calculations easily; graph numerical data automatically; save and retrieve information; and recalculate totals if any numbers in the columns change.

Spreadsheet programs are easy to use and can greatly expedite work done with numerical data.

Post-Judgment Interest Calculator

Year	Judgment Awarded	Rate of Interest	Accrued Interest	Judgment Plus Interest
2007	$ 2,500,000.00	7%	$ 175,000.00	$ 2,675,000.00
2008	$ 2,675,000.00	7%	$ 187,250.00	$ 2,862,250.00
2009	$ 2,862,250.00	7%	$ 200,357.50	$ 3,062,607.50
2010	$ 3,062,607.50	7%	$ 214,382.53	$ 3,276,990.03
2011	$ 3,276,990.03	7%	$ 229,389.30	$ 3,506,379.33
2012	$ 3,506,379.33	7%	$ 245,446.55	$ 3,751,825.88
2013	$ 3,751,825.88	7%	$ 262,627.81	$ 4,014,453.69
	TOTAL		**$ 1,514,453.69**	**$ 4,014,453.69**

Exhibit 1–9
Spreadsheet
Microsoft product screen shot(s) reprinted with permission from Microsoft Corporation.

Performing Timekeeping and Billing Functions: Timekeeping and Billing Software

In some law firms, legal assistants record and track attorney and paralegal time and then send out bills to clients based on the amount of time recorded for a case. Using a word processor for timekeeping and billing functions is tedious and time-consuming. Manual billing methods are so slow, in fact, that billings are done infrequently and in most cases bills are late getting to clients. Both of these

consequences hurt the cash flow of a law office. In addition, the bills are more likely to have errors, since many must have numerous calculations performed.

When set up correctly, computerized legal timekeeping and billing programs are simple and easy to use. Information, such as the client's name, address, and billing rates, is entered into the system once. Then, as an attorney or legal assistant spends time on a case, the time is entered into the system. If all entries are accurate, at the end of a billing period—1 week, 2 weeks, 1 month, etc.—the invoices are automatically calculated and generated by the computer, so they are produced and mailed on time with no calculation errors (see Exhibit 1–10).

Exhibit 1–10
Timekeeping and Billing Software
Copyright 2007 Software Technology, Inc. www.Tabs3.com

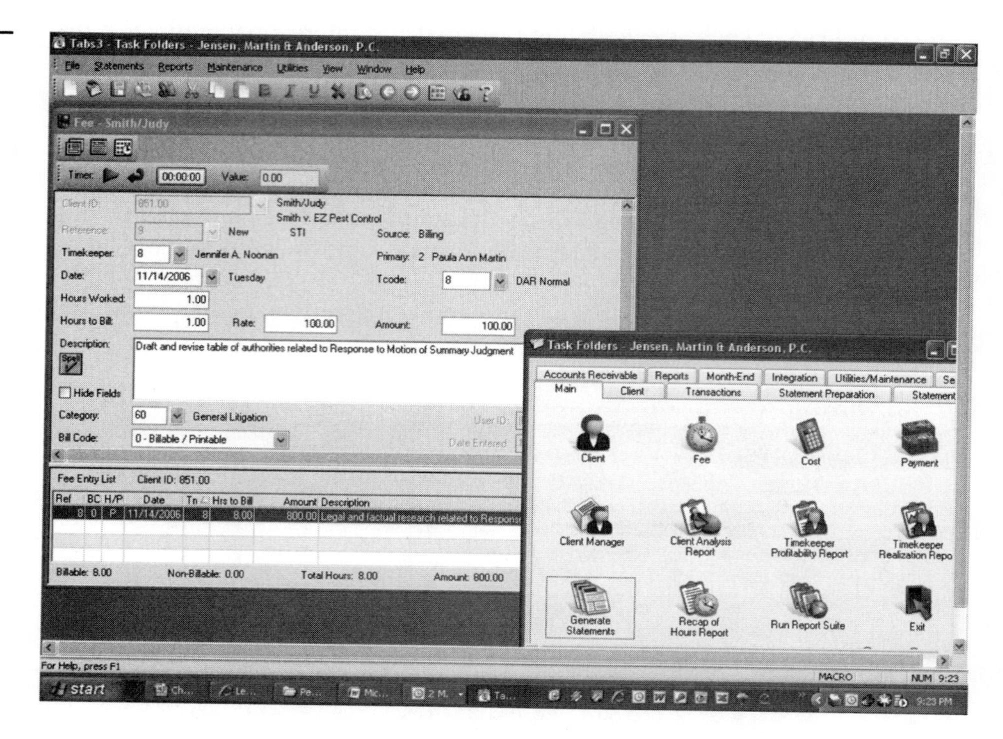

Tracking Appointments and Deadlines: Computerized Docket Control and Case Management Software

Some legal assistants must track appointments, deadlines, hearings, and other important dates to ensure that events get scheduled and then are not forgotten. This function is referred to as docket control, or sometimes as case management.

Notice in Exhibit 1–2 that approximately 62 percent of legal assistants use docket control programs on a daily or weekly basis. While scheduling and tracking appointments and deadlines in a legal organization may seem at first review like unimportant tasks, controlling an attorney's legal docket is, in fact, extremely important. Every year, thousands of ethical complaints are filed against attorneys. The number-one reason for a client filing an ethical complaint against his or her attorney is the attorney's failure to properly follow up on client matters. Many legal malpractice claims are also filed every year for the same reason. The importance of an effective docket control system in a legal organization should not be underestimated.

Most manual docket control systems use a calendaring system for writing down appointments and deadlines. Several problems arise with manual docketing systems. They are time-consuming; for example, one deadline that has three reminders—such as 3-, 5-, and 10-day reminders—must be written four times. Most manual docketing systems can record deadlines for only one year

at a time, even though attorneys must record deadlines that are two years or more in the future in some cases. Last, manual docketing systems can become confusing and hard to read when frequent changes must be made and can lead to missed deadlines.

> *A working knowledge of calendaring and docketing using databases and other software is critical and it can play a big role in advancing paralegal careers.*[9]

Computerized docket control programs (see Exhibit 1–11), on the other hand, allow for making entries quickly; in many cases each entry has to be made only once, because the program automatically enters reminders for the deadline. In addition, most computerized docketing programs have perpetual calendars and allow for entries many years into the future. Also, because they are entered into the computer, the docketing reports are printed neatly and can be reprinted when changes occur. Finally, docketing programs have other functions that manual methods cannot perform, such as the ability to print past due reports that show all the deadlines that have passed but have not yet been marked completed; print a free time report that shows a person's unscheduled hours (this is useful when scheduling other appointments); or produce a list of the future events that are scheduled for a particular case to see what the docket for that case looks like.

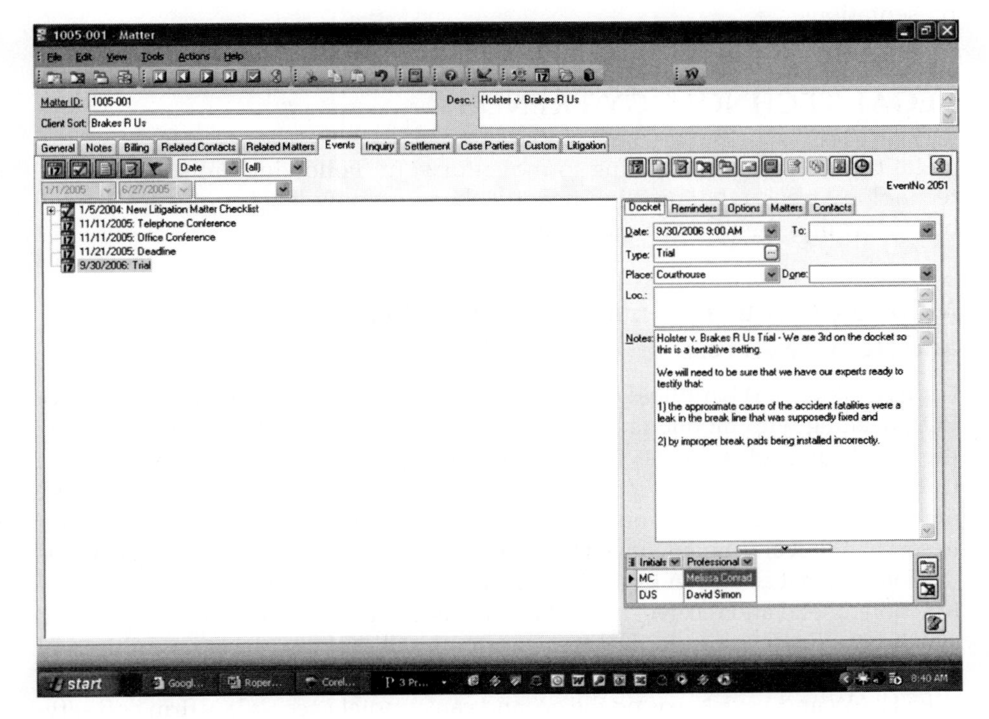

Exhibit 1–11
Docket Control and Case Management Software
Copyright 2007 Elite, a Thomson business

Docket control and case management are terms that are sometimes used interchangeably, but there is a difference. Docket control software is fairly limited in nature and primarily tracks appointments and deadlines in legal matters. Case management programs typically control the docket of a case, but they usually also help the legal professional track and control the entire case, not just the scheduling matters of a case. Many case management programs include the ability to track a client's name, address, and telephone numbers; make notes about each phone call a legal professional may have with the client; track appointments and deadlines by case; automatically schedule deadlines by type of case (typically where court rules

mandate deadlines); perform conflict of interest searches when new cases are entered; produce letters and notices depending on the type of case it is; and more.

Presentation Graphics/Trial Software

Courtrooms across the nation are seeing an explosion of technology, steadily changing the way evidence is presented, and what is expected of some paralegals. Paralegals can benefit by capitalizing on opportunities to learn about the technology taking hold in today's courtrooms. Many courtroom presentations now involve the bar coding of evidence and the scanning of documents so they can be brought up as images on a screen during trial.[10]

High-quality, professional presentations can be created using presentation graphics software. Legal assistants use presentation graphic programs to prepare charts, tables, video clips, evidence (including using barcodes to track scanned documents), and other information for juries and fact-finders; to present information to clients; and to present information to colleagues, such as an internal training program, law office marketing, budget presentation, or presentation on a new initiative. Each page of a presentation can include many elements such as color, images of documents, text, charts, shapes, video, clip art, photos, and sound. Presentation graphic programs can produce the information on paper, overhead transparencies, 35-mm slides, or electronic on-screen presentations.

LEGAL TECHNOLOGY TRENDS

Legal technology is continuing to move forward. Following are some general technology trends that are significantly changing how legal professionals will be performing their jobs in the future.

Mobile Computing, Instant Wireless Access, and Remote Access

Laptop, tablet, and handheld computers (also called personal digital assistants or PDAs), along with mobile phones and other wireless technologies, are changing the way legal professionals communicate. All of these technologies are merging to create small, extremely powerful, fully connected mobile machines. These machines, no matter what you call them, operate as a mobile phone, allow the user to send and receive email, have instant messaging features, act as a pager, access the Internet, act as a PDA (including calendaring, note-taking, and address book functions), send and receive faxes, allow the user to edit and send documents, and synchronize with a user's desktop system. Small laptops can store millions of pages of documents electronically, fully access online legal databases such as WESTLAW and LexisNexis on the go, and can remotely access law firm and service provider databases nearly globally. These types of mobile computers and remote access technologies can keep a legal professional connected with his or her office(s), client(s), and court(s) and give him or her access to information 24 hours a day, 7 days a week. Expanding technologies have created a "virtual law office" that exists electronically wherever the legal professional happens to be: At home, at court, in a hotel room, anywhere. Mobile printers, mobile scanners and wireless hotspots where users can connect to networks and the Internet allow a legal professional to access nearly all the same information and tools as if he or she was sitting at a desk in the office. This kind of mobile immediate access to information will continue to change and drive the way legal professionals practice law.

> *Handheld PCs can now access the web, research the U.S.Code, store and read the Federal Rules of Evidence and Civil Procedure, provide data for time and billing programs, allow one to receive and send email, handle personal finances, and edit legal documents, along with a host of other personal, business and legal applications. They can perform many other functions, including accessing electronic books, dictionaries and encyclopedias; faxing; paging; accounting; and calendaring. They can also run standard computer applications, including word-processing, spreadsheets and database applications.*[11]

Electronic Discovery

As discussed earlier, electronic discovery is the process of producing documents in litigation in an electronic format. Many court rules now provide for electronic discovery. This fact is forcing legal organizations to develop internal systems that can produce, store, search and handle the production of electronic information in a variety of formats and across multiple computing platforms (such as desktops, servers, laptops, and PDAs). Electronic discovery and the effective use of it will continue to have a profound impact on the practice of law for many years to come.

Electronic Filing

With **electronic filing,** courts accept electronic versions of legal documents via the Internet or other electronic means instead of requiring the hard copy of the document. While it sounds easy, in reality it is more complicated. Standardization, control, security, and the establishment of hardware and software systems to support electronic filing have all been issues that have had to be overcome. Many states, federal agencies, and other regulatory bodies have implemented electronic filing successfully and many others are currently in the implementation stage.

electronic filing
Where courts accept electronic versions of legal documents via the Internet or other electronic means instead of requiring the hard copy of the document.

The Paperless Office

Just as courts have been working to implement electronic filing and require electronic discovery, many law offices have begun to implement a **paperless office.** This refers to converting all information into an electronic form for storage, processing and distribution. Typically, this is done by scanning all hard-copy documents that come into the office and saving all computer-generated documents electronically without a hard copy. Some advantages of the paperless office include (1) significant reduction in paper usage and copying costs, (2) reduction of storage and lease space (the cost of office lease space now far exceeds the cost of electronic storage space), (3) increased portability, (4) increased collaboration (because digital information can be shared by multiple users via a network or Internet), and (5) quicker search and retrieval of documents than with manual methods. As with electronic filing, there are implementation issues regarding the paperless office, including putting the hardware and software systems in place to support it, training staff, and other issues. Some law offices have fully implemented this concept and many others are taking steps toward this goal.

paperless office
Refers to converting all hard-copy documents into an electronic form for storage, processing, and distribution.

automated courtroom
Sophisticated electronic equipment in the courtroom including evidence display systems, real-time court reporting, and others.

The Automated Courtroom

Many courts have installed sophisticated electronic equipment in their courtrooms, including evidence display systems (see Exhibit 1–12) and real-time court reporting. An **evidence display system** is a computerized system that displays evidence via monitors to the judge, jurors, counsel, and the public simultaneously. It also displays this information to the court reporter and clerk or clerks.

evidence display system
A computerized system that displays evidence via monitors to the judge, jury, counsel, and the public simultaneously.

Exhibit 1–12
The Automated Courtroom
© Guy Cali/Corbis

The master controls are located at the judge's bench so he or she can control all monitors, sound systems, and cameras in the courtroom. The attorneys and/or judge can use the evidence display system to display properly admitted evidence using cameras in the courtroom, whether by means of video images, animation, photographic images, hard copy, or other media types.

videoconferencing
A private broadcast between two or more remote locations, with live image transmission, display, and sound.

Internet depositions
Process that allows an attorney to join, monitor, or take a live deposition of a witness from any location with a personal computer, Internet connection, and an Internet deposition provider.

Many evidence display systems also support **videoconferencing** so that with the judge's approval, an out-of-state witness can testify at a trial without actually being present in the courtroom. Videoconferencing can also be used outside of the courtroom by law offices to take depositions of witnesses without traveling to the site where the witness is or to hold department or office conferences with staff in remote offices. A similar technology, **Internet depositions** allow an attorney to join, monitor, or take a deposition live from any location with a personal computer, an Internet connection, and an Internet deposition provider. The deposition can be monitored by co-counsel, expert witnesses, parties, or others. Participants see and hear the deposition via live streaming video and audio. Internet depositions can represent a tremendous cost savings, particularly if multiple participants must attend an out-of state deposition. Some Internet deposition providers also provide real-time text of the transcript in addition to the audio and video feeds.

> *Because trial technology will no doubt add some complexity to trial preparation . . . most trial teams are using paralegals, in-house technology managers or outside trial technology consultants to handle the presentation of evidence in the courtroom. If you are a techno-savvy paralegal, your experience in technology will be a definite benefit for your trial team.*[12]

real-time court reporting
A computerized court reporting system where witness's testimony is immediately converted from a court reporter's notes to a transcript in realtime.

Another type of courtroom technology is **real-time court reporting.** A witness's testimony is transcribed by a court reporter within a few seconds and can be displayed on the courtroom monitors or given to the judge, jurors, or attorneys on a real-time basis. This gives parties instant written and electronic access to witness testimony and can eliminate reading back a witness' testimony when

there is a question. Proponents of automated courtroom technology state that it cuts trial time by 25 to 35 percent.

Expanding Technology in Every Facet of Practicing Law

Over the past 25 years there has been a gradual but dramatic increase in the amount of technology it takes to practice law effectively. There is no reason to believe that this will change. Constantly more sophisticated hardware and software will continue to find its way into modern law offices of all sizes. Legal professionals will have to continue to adapt to the new technologies to compete in the twenty-first century legal field.

Increased Importance of Security and Confidentiality

The importance of security and confidentiality as it relates to technology in legal organizations cannot be understated. It is the "worm in the apple" of technology and it can provide disastrous results to legal organizations. Legal organizations of all sizes must continually purchase and maintain hardware and software infrastructure that can protect client confidentiality in the technology age. Legal professionals must also be extremely careful regarding security procedures, IDs, and passwords, and must maintain strict standards for how they share electronic information with others (see the next section). Protecting client information while still allowing legal professionals and clients access to data is a never-ending battle.

LEGAL ETHICS AND COMPUTER TECHNOLOGY

At first it may appear that legal ethics and computers have little to do with one another. In fact, the opposite is true. Many legal ethical issues arise out of the proliferation of computers in legal organizations. However, many of the ethical concerns revolve around two key issues, client confidentiality and competence/negligence of an attorney.

> *The electronic age is upon us. ...Increasingly, this means going online to do legal research, using email to communicate with clients, and posting World Wide Web pages that advertise legal services and provide client information. ...Yet all lawyers [and legal professionals] must beware; the computer age challenges practicing lawyers [and legal professionals] with numerous ethical and potential legal malpractice problems that have only begun to surface.*[13]

Client Confidentiality

Attorneys have a duty to keep client information completely confidential. Rule 1.6 of the American Bar Association *Model Rules of Professional Conduct* says that an attorney cannot disclose information about the representation of a client.

Attorneys have a duty to keep confidential all client-related information, including information that is contained on computers. The threat of releasing confidential client information either by mistake or by intrusion is real and can happen in a wide variety of ways including the following:

- interception of electronic mail by a third party
- interception of word-processing documents and other attachments to electronic mail by outsiders

- a breach of legal organization computer security, such as:
  - passwords not being appropriately maintained
  - computer hackers gaining access to confidential legal organization computers via the Internet or other online means
  - computer viruses deleting or accessing confidential client information
  - laptop and handheld computers being stolen or inadvertently left for third parties to find and access confidential client information
  - computer disks holding confidential client information being left or misplaced for third parties to find
  - computer hardware and storage devices not being sufficiently cleaned, so that client data is not destroyed before outdated equipment is disposed of

Attorney Competence

Attorneys have a duty to perform legal services in a competent manner. Rule 1.1 of the American Bar Association *Model Rules of Professional Conduct* says that:

> *An attorney will represent a client competently, including having the required skill, knowledge, and preparation.*

Computers, while incredibly helpful, can also be a vehicle for incompetence and legal malpractice. Computer-related legal malpractice and ethical breaches can take place in a variety of ways such as these:

- computer-related legal research being inadequate and being less than thorough
- prior word-processing documents being retrieved for a new client and old information (from the previous client) being left in the new document
- typographical errors being made
- inapposite or outdated law being cited (because legal research can be saved and retrieved, though it may not necessarily be current law any longer)
- improper computer forms being used
- a general failure to understand how a computer or a piece of software works, leading to failure to discover an error; and/or
- automated legal software being utilized with formula errors, logic errors, or lack of oversight or proofreading by attorneys or other legal professionals.

Attorneys are responsible for their work product, and if the end product has errors in it or is incompetently prepared, whether or not it was prepared by or with the assistance of a computer does not matter—the attorney is still ultimately responsible for the work product. If the error or incompetent work product causes harm to the client, the attorney may be subject to attorney discipline charges and a legal malpractice claim. Client confidentiality, competence, and other ethical issues related to using computers in legal organizations will be covered in more detail throughout the text.

SUMMARY

A few years ago, it was important that the legal assistant entering the competitive job market have computer skills. Now, it is imperative. Computer use in law offices has grown substantially and will continue to grow in the future. Computers are currently used in the legal field for a wide variety of purposes.

A computer is an electronic device that accepts, processes, outputs, and stores information. Information that is entered into a computer is called input. Information that comes out of a computer is called output. Hardware is the actual, physical components of a computer system. Software refers to instructions to the

INTERNET SITES

Internet sites for this chapter include the following:

General Legal Assistant/Legal Sites on the Internet

Organization	Product/Service	World Wide Web Address
American Bar Association	Many products and services for legal professionals	<http://www.abanet.org>
National Federation of Paralegal Associations	Products and information for practicing paralegals	<http://www.paralegals.org>
National Association of Legal Assistants	Products and information for practicing legal assistants	<http://www.nala.org>
Legal Assistant Management Association	Products and information for practicing legal assistants	<http://www.lamanet.org>
Legal Assistant Today magazine	Magazine for practicing legal assistants	<http://www.legalassistanttoday.com>
Technolawyer.com	Email newsletter regarding legal technology issues	<http://www.technolawyer.com>
American Bar Association Legal Technology Resource Center	A site devoted to legal technology issues	<http://www.lawtechnology.org>
The Center for Legal and Court Technology	Information related to improving technology in the practice of law and in the courtroom.	<http://www.legaltechcenter.net>
Findlaw's Legal Technology Events and Conferences Site	Upcoming legal technology-centered events, conferences, news, and white papers	<http://technology.findlaw.com>

computer hardware that make the computer function. An information system is a combination of the human involvement, computer hardware, and computer software that work together to perform a task.

Computers can be used to help legal assistants in many of the functions they must perform, including communicating with clients and other legal professionals using electronic mail, drafting documents using word-processing software, collecting and organizing data using database management software, performing mathematical calculations using spreadsheet software, performing timekeeping and billing functions using timekeeping and billing software, tracking appointments and deadlines using docket control and case management software, providing litigation support using litigation support software, preparing electronic discovery requests using electronic discovery software, conducting legal research using fee-based online computer-assisted legal research and the Internet, creating presentations with presentation graphics software, and using the power of the Internet to do factual research regarding cases.

Current and future technology trends that will impact the way legal professionals provide legal services to clients include mobile computer and instant wireless access, automated courtrooms, electronic filing of court documents, the paperless office, and the need to continously increase security.

KEY TERMS

Internet
computer
input
output
storage
hardware
software
information system
intranet
electronic discovery software
electronic filing
paperless office
extranet
evidence display system
videoconferencing
Internet depositions
real-time court reporting

TEST YOUR KNOWLEDGE

1. Why is it imperative for legal assistants to have an understanding of computers?
2. How many computer applications were widely used in law offices in 1978, 1988, and currently?
3. True or False: Solo and small law firms lag far behind large firms when it comes to using technology in the practice of law.
4. What are the top three types of computer applications used daily by practicing legal assistants?
5. A combination of human involvement, computer hardware and software, and raw information, all working together to perform a task is called an ________.
6. Some studies have shown that legal assistants can experience a ________ percent reduction in the time needed to perform a task by using computerized over manual systems.
7. True or False: The Internet has only had a mild impact on practicing legal assistants, because many of their day-to-day activities have not changed.
8. What kind of research can legal assistants do on the Internet?
9. True or False: Free legal research on the Internet and fee-based legal research on the Internet are pretty much the same.
10. Distinguish intranet, extranet, and Internet.
11. Software that assists legal professionals in assembling discovery requests is called ________.
12. True or False: Manual billing systems are typically slow and impede a legal organization's cash flow.
13. In the legal field another name for a calendaring system software is ________.
14. Name three trends in legal technology.
15. Name two ways that computer technology affects an attorney's ethical duty.

ON THE WEB EXERCISES

1. Using the Internet and a general search engine such as <http://www.yahoo.com> or <http://www.google.com>, or using one or more of the websites listed at the end of this chapter, research one of the following topics and write a one- to two-page paper on the topic. Update the information that is contained in the text and give a general overview of the topic.
   - Automated courtroom
   - Internet depositions
   - Real-time court reporting
   - Electronic filing
   - The paperless office
2. Using the Internet and a general search engine such as <http://www.yahoo.com> or <http://www.google.com>, or using one or more of the websites listed at the end of this chapter, research electronic mail tips and write a one-page report. What can users do to more efficiently use email and avoid email abuses and problems?
3. Using the Internet and a general search engine such as <http://www.yahoo.com> or <http://www.google.com>, identify at least one free source of online access to your state's statutes.
4. Using the Internet, write a two-page report on electronic discovery. Define what it is, why it is important, how it can be accomplished, and any problems that you see in responding to or using information obtained in an electronic discovery request. As a part of your report identify at least ten common file-saving protocols (such as *.doc*, used for saving Microsoft Word files).
5. Using the Internet, identify a minimum of three calendar, docket-control, or case-management programs and select which one you found to be the best. Write a one-page memorandum regarding your findings.
6. Using the Internet, identify a minimum of five potential security threats that could affect a law office. For each, identify ways that a legal organization can mitigate the threat.

QUESTIONS AND EXERCISES

1. In reviewing Exhibit 1–1, did you notice that any types of computer programs that you currently use were not on the list?
2. Even though the legal profession did not at first accept computers and technology, why has it implemented them so thoroughly now?
3. In reviewing Exhibit 1–2, were you surprised to see the extent to which legal assistants use computers in their jobs? What conclusions can you draw from Exhibit 1–2 regarding the legal assistant computer user?
4. Why is the concept of an information system important?
5. Knowing that some legal research is available free of charge on the Internet, while other information is best found using a fee-based system, what approach would you use in conducting legal research?
6. How do specific computer applications listed in Chapter 1 support and lead to the "virtual office"?
7. You work as a legal assistant for a small law firm that handles collection matters. The firm currently is representing a furniture store that loaned money to a number of customers who now have disappeared. Unless you find the whereabouts of the customers, the furniture store will not be able to collect the money. What computer resource (discussed in Chapter 1) would you use to try to find the customers, and why?

END NOTES

[1] Pamela S. Brown, "Step Up Your Game," *Legal Assistant Today*, July/August 2004, 37.
[2] Rod Hughes, "Knowledge Is Power," *Legal Assistant Today*, May/June 2002, 55.
[3] Rod Hughes, "Knowledge Is Power," *Legal Assistant Today*, May/June 2002, 54.
[4] Rod Hughes, "Peering Into the Future," *Legal Assistant Today*, May/June 2005, 58.
[5] John Caldwell, "Climbing the Technology Ladder," *Legal Assistant Today*, May/June 2001, 53.
[6] Ellisa A. Santo, "E-Discovery Explosion," *Legal Assistant Today*, July/August 2006, 58.
[7] Saran Cron, "Technology to Go," *Legal Assistant Today*, May/June 2006, 60.
[8] John Caldwell, "Climbing the Technology Ladder," *Legal Assistant Today*, May/June 2001, 71.
[9] John Caldwell, "Climbing the Technology Ladder," *Legal Assistant Today*, May/June 2001, 52.
[10] John Caldwell, "Climbing the Technology Ladder," *Legal Assistant Today*, May/June 2001, 52.
[11] Michael R. Arkfeld, Esq., *The Digital Practice of Law* (Phoenix: Law Partner Publishing, 2001), 2–23.
[12] Dwayne E. Krager, "Staying on Top of Courtroom Technology," *Legal Assistant Today*, January/February 2002, 30.
[13] Jeffrey E. Kirkey, "Legal Ethics in Cyberspace: Keeping Lawyers and Their Computers Out of Trouble," 18 *Cooley L. Rev.*, 37 (2001).

CHAPTER 2

COMPUTER HARDWARE AND SOFTWARE

CHAPTER OBJECTIVES

After completing chapter 2, you should be able to do the following:

1. Discuss the different types of storage devices.
2. Identify several different kinds of mobile computing devices.
3. Identify basic local area network concepts.
4. Explain what operating system software does.
5. Discuss the penalties for illegally copying software.
6. Understand basic legal organization security issues and why good security measures are imperative in a legal organization.

Computers are an integral part of how legal organizations go about providing legal services to clients. Computers are used in nearly every facet of how legal organizations provide services to clients and how they manage their business operations. The use of computer technology in the legal industry is continuing to grow. A recent survey found that on average, medium-sized law firms spend an average of $17,700 per attorney on technology, while large firms are spending $25,800 per attorney.[1] It is helpful for legal assistants to have a basic understanding of computer hardware and software so they can (1) comment or participate in computer purchasing decisions (if asked), (2) answer basic technology/compatibility questions if asked by clients, counsel, or others, and (3) have some background knowledge in case they must work with technical support or computer professionals to resolve their own hardware or software problems. This chapter explains basic computer hardware and software and also covers security and ethical issues related to computer hardware/software.

In a recent survey, 55 percent of the legal assistants surveyed indicated that they had input on technology decisions at their legal organization.[2]

A COMPUTER SYSTEM: AN OVERVIEW

A computer system is made up of hardware and software elements. Hardware consists of the physical elements of a computer system, including the monitor, keyboard, and computer itself. An example of computer hardware is shown in

Exhibit 2–1
A Microcomputer

Exhibit 2–1. **Computer programs,** also referred to as computer software or just software, are the step-by-step instructions that direct the computer to do certain tasks. Two types of computer programs make the computer function: operating system software and application software. An **operating system program** instructs the computer how to operate its circuitry and how to communicate with input and output devices. An **input device** (e.g., a keyboard) enters information into a computer, whereas an **output device** (e.g., a printer) feeds out information from a computer. Operating system software performs housekeeping and internal functions. **Application software,** on the other hand, instructs the computer to perform a specific application or task, such as word processing. Hardware and software are interdependent and cannot function without each other.

computer programs
Sets of instructions that direct a computer to perform a task.

operating system program
A computer program that directs a computer how to operate its own circuitry and to manage its components.

input device
A device that enters information into a computer.

output device
A device that feeds out information from a computer.

application software
Instructions to a computer to perform a specific application or task.

> *Several lawyers have lamented ... that they would like to spend their time practicing law instead of worrying about computers. They feel they constantly are maintaining their computer systems rather than performing legal work. Unfortunately, computer technology has become so entwined with the practice of law you simply can't turn the clock back.*[3]

SYSTEM UNIT COMPONENTS

A computer or system unit works together with peripheral devices such as auxiliary storage, input, output, and communication devices (hardware) to receive, process, store, and produce information. The system unit contains a central processing unit and a main memory.

central processing unit (CPU)
The part of a computer that contains the processor chip and main memory. The CPU organizes and processes information in addition to coordinating with peripheral devices.

Central Processing Unit

The **central processing unit (CPU)** organizes and processes information. It is the "brain" of the computer. It performs logical operations—in accordance with the operating system software—and coordinates and communicates with auxiliary storage devices and input, output, and communication devices (see Exhibit 2–2).

At the heart of the CPU is the processor chip (see Exhibit 2–2). One or more **processor chips** perform the actual arithmetic computations of the computer.

processor chip
The part of the CPU that performs the actual arithmetic computations of the computer.

Exhibit 2–2
Central Processing Unit (CPU)

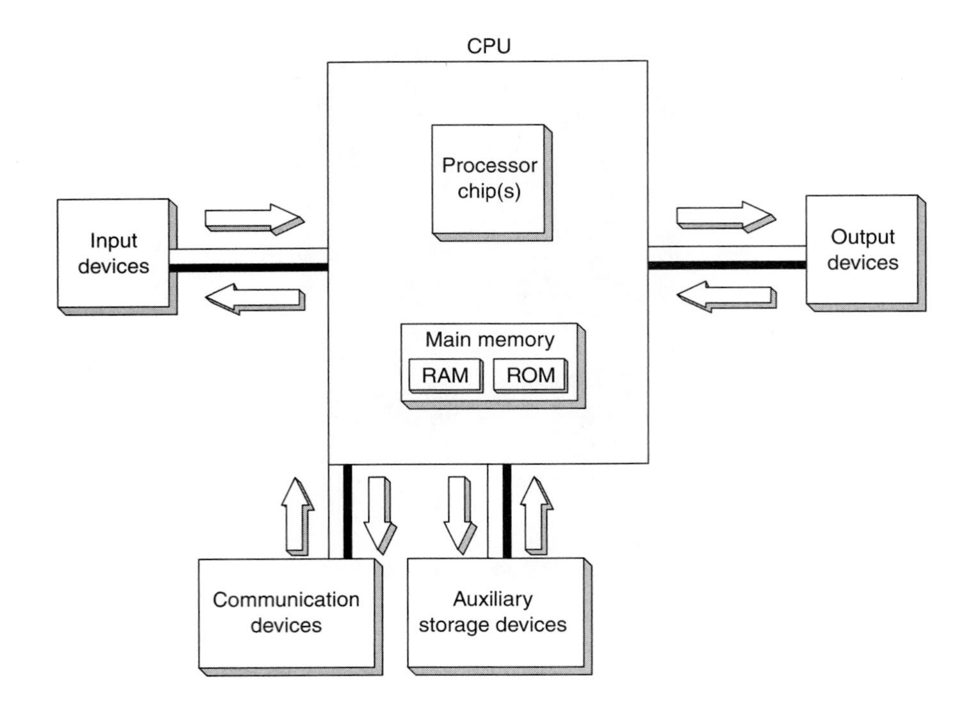

Common CPUs for microcomputers include the Core 2 Duo, Pentium D, Pentium IV, Celeron, and Athlon 64. Some computers now have multiple CPUs in one unit. The processor chips used in microcomputers are called **microprocessors.**

microprocessors
The processor chips found in microcomputers.

The speed of the processor, and in turn of the computer, is determined by how many bytes of information it can process at a time and how fast it acts to process the information. Some CPUs can process at 16, 32, or 64 bits at a time. This represents the amount of information that can be processed in one computer cycle. The more bits that can be processed in one cycle, the faster the computer will be. A processor that processes at 64 bits at a time is considerably faster than the one that processes at only 16 bits. How fast a computer works to process information is also characterized in **gigahertz (GHz),** which refers to the "clock speed" of a computer. The faster the clock speed is, the faster the computer processes information. A computer that has a clock speed of 4 GHz is considerably faster than a computer with a speed of only 1 GHz. Because computers become obsolete so fast in the current market, it is usually best to buy a computer with the latest CPU and fastest clock speed a user can afford.

gigahertz (GHz)
The clock speed of a computer.

Main Memory

The function of the **main memory** is to hold or store information that the computer is processing. This is accomplished through memory chips. **Memory chips,** like processor chips, are made up of tiny electronic circuits, but instead of processing information, they store or hold information. As information is entered into a computer, it is temporarily stored in memory locations, also called memory addresses, while the computer is processing it. This is similar to what happens in a post office that has a mail slot for each address on a route. The individual pieces of mail are temporarily stored in the mail slots until all the mail has been processed or sorted for the route.

main memory
The part of the CPU that stores information that the computer is processing. Main memory consists of read-only memory and random-access memory.

memory chips
Electronic circuits that store or hold information.

Main memory is made up of two types of memory: read only and random access.

Read-Only Memory **Read-only memory (ROM)** is permanent, unchanging memory that is used internally by a computer to operate itself. It is permanently

read-only memory (ROM)
A part of main memory that contains permanent information a computer needs to operate itself. ROM can be read from, but cannot be written to.

installed by the manufacturer and cannot be changed or altered, thus the name read only. A computer reads ROM, but you cannot enter information into it or change the data in it. The data contained in ROM is not lost when the computer is turned off. Practically speaking, you never realize ROM exists.

Random-Access Memory **Random-access memory (RAM)** is temporary memory that is used when the computer is turned on. Unlike ROM, it is erased when the computer is turned off. RAM is temporarily used to store programs "on the computer screen" when they are loaded. For example, when a word processing program is loaded so the user sees the word processor on his computer screen, the program is in RAM. As words are typed into the word processor, the words are also stored in RAM. In order to save the information when the computer is turned off, the user must save the information from RAM to an **auxiliary storage device,** such as a hard disk. An auxiliary storage device stores data so it can be retrieved at a later time. A frustrating experience occurs when a user has information in RAM and power is interrupted, as it is when the lights flicker. When power to the computer is interrupted, the computer turns off, and any information in RAM is lost.

The number of bytes a computer can hold is measured in *kilobytes* (K), *megabytes* (MB), *gigabytes* (GB), or *terabytes* (TB) (see Exhibit 2–3). Most microcomputers produced today have between 512 Mb and 4 Gb of RAM.

random-access memory (RAM)
A part of main memory that is temporary and volatile in nature and is erased every time the computer's power is turned off. Application programs and data are loaded into RAM when the computer is processing the data.

auxiliary storage device
A device that stores information so that it can be retrieved for later use. Auxiliary storage devices can hold data and retrieve it even after power to the computer has been turned off. Auxiliary storage devices include flash drives, hard disk drives, and others.

Exhibit 2–3
Storage Capacities

Kilobyte (K)	=	One thousand bytes
Megabyte (MB)	=	One million bytes
Gigabyte (GB)	=	One billion bytes
Terabyte (TB)	=	One trillion bytes

All application programs require a minimum amount of RAM to run. Newer application programs continue to require more and more RAM to run properly. Most computer manufacturers make it fairly simple to install additional RAM into their computers.

Cache Memory **Cache memory** is a high-speed buffer that is used to speed the processing operations of a computer. Accessing cache memory is faster than accessing main memory. When a computer executes an instruction, it will first look for the needed data in cache memory and if it is not found there the computer will then access main memory.

cache memory
A high-speed buffer that is used to speed the processing operations of a computer.

System Units in Legal Organizations

> *Legal technology has developed rapidly over the past decade—the pace of change keeps accelerating.... Technology seems to take a bigger bite out of the budget every year.*[4]
>
> *A survey found that on average legal organizations spend nearly 7 percent of gross revenue annually on information technology.*[5]

Legal organizations, like most businesses, may have a variety of computers/systems units running on employee desktops throughout the office at any one time. For example, one employee may be using a computer with a Pentium D microprocessor running at a clock speed of 3 GHz with 512 Mb of RAM, while another employee may be using a computer with a Core 2 Duo processor running at 4 GHz with 4 GB of RAM. Does the practicing legal assistant need to know the technical difference between the two computers/system units? The answer is "no," but it would explain why software on the second system runs much faster than on the first system, or why the second computer can do things the first

peripheral devices
Pieces of equipment that are connected to a computer to perform specific functions such as storing information (auxiliary storage devices), inputting information (input devices), outputting information (output devices), and communicating between computers (communication devices).

storage capacity
The maximum amount of data that can be stored on a device.

access time
The amount of time it takes to transfer data between a storage device and RAM.

sequential access
A device that records and reads back data in a sequence (like an audiocassette).

random (direct) access
A device that can go directly to a location of specific data without having to read through all of the data preceding it (like a CD).

floppy disk drive
An auxiliary storage device that stores data on a plastic magnetic disk called a floppy disk or a diskette.

system just cannot. Like most businesses, legal organizations try to use their computers/systems units as long as they can while still staying reasonably abreast of technology.

PERIPHERAL DEVICES

Peripheral devices are pieces of equipment that are connected to a computer to perform specific functions. They include auxiliary storage devices, input devices, output devices, and communication devices.

Auxiliary Storage Devices

An auxiliary storage device is used to permanently store information. Auxiliary storage devices and RAM are sometimes confused with one another. RAM is where information is stored temporarily, and it is erased every time the computer is turned off; an auxiliary storage device is where information can be stored permanently. The two are sometimes confused because they both use megabytes and gigabytes to refer to their respective storage capacities, and they both store information, albeit for different purposes.

In discussing auxiliary storage devices, there are several concepts to be aware of, including storage capacity, access time, and file design. **Storage capacity** refers to the maximum amount of data that can be stored on a device. **Access time** refers to the amount of time it takes to transfer data between a storage device and RAM. Auxiliary storage devices are either sequential-access or random-access devices. **Sequential access** describes a device that records and reads back data in a sequence. This is similar to an audiocassette or a VCR tape. **Random access,** sometimes called **direct access,** describes a device that can go directly to a location of specific data without having to read through all of the data preceding it. This is similar to a CD or a DVD.

Many different types of auxiliary storage devices are used, including floppy disks, hard disks, magnetic tape, removable drives, and optical storage devices. Most computer systems have several different auxiliary storage devices (see Exhibit 2–4).

Floppy Disk A **floppy disk drive** stores data on a plastic magnetic disk called a *floppy disk* or a *diskette*. Floppy disks are now a relatively outdated technology. They can write and read data. Writing data means saving information to the disk.

Exhibit 2–4
Comparison of Auxiliary Storage Devices

Storage Device	Capacity	Ability to Read & Write Data	Access Time	Sequential or Direct
Floppy disk	360 K–2.88 MB	Read & write data many times	Slow	Direct
Hard disk	Up to 1 TB	Read & write data many times	Fast	Direct
Magnetic tape	Up to 1 TB	Read & write data many times	Slow	Sequential
Removable drives	Up to 4 GB	Read & write data many times	Medium to Fast	Direct
CD-ROM	Up to 650 MB	Read data	Medium	Direct
CD-R	Up to 650 MB	Read & write data once	Medium	Direct
CD-RW	Up to 650 MB	Read & write data many times	Medium	Direct
DVD-ROM	Up to 10 GB	Read data	Medium	Direct
Recordable DVD	Up to 10 GB	Read & write data many times	Medium	Direct

Reading data means reading information previously stored on the disk back into the computer's main memory.

Floppy disk drives have relatively slow access times, so they have largely been replaced with other devices.

Hard Disk Data is stored on a rigid magnetic disk or **hard disk drive.** Hard disks are very reliable and have faster access times than floppy disks. They can also read and write data. It is possible, however, for them to "crash" if they are handled roughly (e.g., by dropping the computer) or if they are defective. A crash occurs when some or all of the information on a hard disk is lost or destroyed. Crashing often causes physical damage to the surface of the disk.

hard disk drive
A reliable and fast auxiliary storage device that stores data on a rigid magnetic disk.

Hard disks are usually mounted inside the computer and can be identified by a small light that turns on when information is either accessed from or saved to the drive. Most hard disks are permanently sealed and are fixed inside the drive; thus, they cannot be removed. A fixed hard disk, since it is immovable, should have the information on it periodically backed up or copied onto another source. Then, if the hard disk crashes, the data will not be lost, since it can be restored. Large hard disks are standard equipment on most computers produced today.

Removable Drives A large amount of data, up to 4 GB, can be stored using **removable drives.** Removable drives include zip drives and flash drives. Zip drives are about the size of an audio cassette and are somewhat slow. They are a somewhat dated technology. Flash drives have largely replaced them. Flash drives or "thumb" drives are about the size of your thumb, so they are extremely small and portable. A flash drive simply plugs into a computer's USB port and is immediately accessable by the computer once it has been loaded. Flash drives are also fairly fast and are typically used to move large files from one system to another. Many MP3 players also use this technology.

removable or flash drive
A storage device that allows a large amount of data, up to 4 GB to be stored.

magnetic tape system
Storage device that holds data on magnetic tape.

Magnetic Tape Data is stored on a reel of magnetic tape in a **magnetic tape system.** The magnetic tape can be stored either on large **tape reels** or in **tape cartridges.**

tape reels
Large reels of magnetic tape on which information is stored.

Magnetic tape systems store data sequentially. For this reason, they have slow access times. This is why magnetic tape is usually used only for making backup copies of information on other storage devices. However, while their access times are slow they have large capacities, up to a terabyte or more.

tape cartridges
Small cartridges of magnetic tape on which information is stored.

Optical Storage Devices By using laser beams, **optical storage devices** can store data on small laser disks. Optical storage devices can store hundreds of megabytes of data on a single disk. This has allowed manufacturers to store everything from music and video/multimedia presentations to large software programs on a single disk. Optical storage devices include compact disk–read-only medium (CD-ROM), compact disk-recordable (CD-R), CD-RW, digital versatile disk (DVD), and recordable DVD.

optical storage devices
Devices that use laser beams to store data on small laser disks. Optical storage devices can store hundreds of megabytes of data on a single disk.

CD-ROM Information stored on compact disks is read by a **CD-ROM drive.** CD-ROM drives can typically store up to 650 MB (250,000 pages of text or 15,000 document images) of data on a single disk. They can be purchased in several speeds and are quite affordable, but they still tend to be slower than hard disks. Many software programs that are purchased are stored on CD-ROM. Some law offices have drives, sometimes called jukeboxes, that can hold many CDs at the same time so users do not have to constantly take disks in and out of the drive.

CD-ROM drive
A device that reads information stored on compact disks. CD-ROM drives can typically store up to 650 MB of data on a single disk.

CD-R A **compact disk-recordable drive,** or **CD-R,** is a device that permanently stores information on a compact disk. Unlike CD-ROM, CD-R allows the user to store information on the disk. However, CD-R disks are not erasable, so any data recorded onto a disk is permanent and cannot be changed.

CD-R (compact disk-recordable) drive
A device that permanently stores information on a compact disk.

CD-RW (compact disk–Rewritable) drive
Device similar to a CD-R drive, but the data on the disk can be changed many times, much like a floppy disk or hard disk.

DVD-ROM (digital versatile disk) drive
Device that reads information stored on DVD-ROM or CD-ROM disks.

recordable DVD drive
Device that allows data to be recorded on DVD disks.

CD-RW A **compact disk–Rewritable,** or **CD-RW, drive** is similar to a CD-R drive, but the data on the disk can be changed many times, much like a floppy disk or hard disk. CD-R and CD-RW drives require special software to record data onto a CD-R or CD-RW disk. CD-R and CD-RW drives are often referred to generically as CD-ROM burners.

DVD-ROM A **digital versatile disk drive,** also known as **DVD-ROM,** reads information stored on DVD-ROM or CD-ROM disks. A DVD disk is similar in appearance to a CD-ROM disk, but it can store much more information due to different encoding techniques. A double-sided DVD disk can store up to 17 GB of data on a single disk. Like CD-ROM drives, DVD drives come in different speeds and are read-only devices. They can play DVD video disks and CD-ROM disks.

Recordable DVD (DVD+/R+RW) Data is recorded on DVD disks using a **recordable DVD drive.** Some recordable DVD drives are rewritable, so data can be changed on the disk. DVD burners offer an advantage over CD burners because they can hold up to 5 GB per side of data (versus 650 MB for CD-ROMs).

Auxiliary Storage Devices in Legal Organizations

A variety of auxiliary storage devices are found in most legal organizations depending on the specific needs of the office. Like many businesses, legal organizations use tape drives, removable drives, CD-ROM, CD-R, CD-RW, CD-ROM jukebox, and DVD drives for a variety of purposes including these:

- installing and updating software
- using CD-ROM legal libraries, which can contain hundreds and hundreds of published cases on one CD-ROM (whole state reporters can sometimes be stored on a handful of CD-ROM disks). Some firms use a central CD-ROM jukebox (which can hold up to 24 or more CD-ROMs) to house their CD-ROM legal library so that all staff can access it from their computers
- saving and retrieving litigation support documents (which can number in the tens of thousands for some cases), including images, evidence, pleadings, transcripts, summaries, and other case-related information
- storage of video including video depositions, video evidence, etc.
- backing up data

Input Devices

Input devices are used to enter information into a computer. Input devices include keyboards, mice, scanners (including bar code and imaging scanners), voice recognition devices, digital cameras, and others.

Computer Keyboard Most computer keyboards are similar to the keyboard of an ordinary typewriter with a few additions. They are made up of alphanumeric keys, function keys, cursor movement keys, special keys, and a numeric keypad. Keyboards are inexpensive and come in a variety of types and styles.

Scanner A scanner has the ability to scan hard copy documents into a computer. Many scanners look like small office copiers. Scanners reflect light on the document and translate the document into digital signals recognized by the computer. They can scan the image of a document, like a photograph or a microfilm image into a computer; this is called imaging. Scanners can also translate the text of the document into an electronic format; the text can then be electronically searched or brought into a word processor, for example. This is called optical character recognition.

Imaging refers to the ability to scan a document into a computer so the user can see the exact image of the document on the computer. Imaging is similar to taking a photographic image of a document—you can see the image of the document, but you cannot edit the text. To edit the text of a document the user would need optical character recognition software (see below). With document imaging, the paper is handled only once. Document images can be reviewed, copied, sorted, and filed electronically. Document imaging gives users immediate access to documents, saves on storage space, and means no lost originals. Imaging software allows law offices to track and manage scanned images. Imaging and OCR technology are used quite frequently in litigation support, discussed later in this text, to track and search for documents in litigation.

imaging
The ability to scan a document into a computer so the user can see the exact image of the document on the computer.

Using a scanner and **optical character recognition (OCR)** software, users can "read" printed material into a computer so the text of the document can be searched (like searching in WESTLAW or LEXIS databases) or be brought into a word processor to edit the text. Through the use of OCR technology, it is possible to scan printed information into a computer much faster than a keyboard operator could enter the information. Large OCR scanners can scan thousands of pages of text into a computer. OCR reflects light onto the printed text, compares the letters of the text to the letters in its memory, and writes the information into the computer. If the printed text that is being scanned does not exactly match the letters in the scanner's memory, an error will occur, and the right letter will not be entered. This potential for inaccuracy can be a problem. Even if a document is scanned in with 99 percent accuracy, that still leaves plenty of errors in the scanned version of the document. If a user scans in a 10,000-word document, that would leave 100 errors in the document. The accuracy rating drops dramatically if a document is not clear or has nonstandard type. OCR scanners can be very useful, but accuracy must be checked carefully.

optical character recognition (OCR)
A technology that allows the text of documents to be read or scanned into a computer so the text of the document can be searched or brought into a word processor to be edited.

Imaging and optical character recognition are similar yet different. Imaging allows the user to see the document's image in its original state, but the user cannot search for words using imaging. Optical character recognition allows the user to search for word patterns, but not to see an image of the document, only straight text.

Our firm has been paperless for six years now. Our electronic office has helped increase efficiency and productivity, with corresponding cost savings. We have eliminated the need for several full-time and part-time staff. Thanks to technology, our five-attorney firm has saved $100,000 a year... To start our paperless office, we installed two network copier/scanners. We implemented a policy for scanning, including how to handle paper until scanned... Because all documents are stored electronically, we have quick access to them.[6]

Imaging and OCR are a central part of many legal organizations' efforts to go completely paperless. Paperlessness offers many advantages to legal organizations, including the ability to access documents remotely anywhere in the world; cost savings, because electronic storage is far cheaper than storing hard copy; and the ability for multiple users to access the data at the same time or nearly the same time.

Some law firms use **bar code scanner** systems to track documents in litigation and to track law office furniture and equipment. The bar code scanner or reader can read the special lines on the bar codes. This is the same technology used in nearly all retail stores.

bar code scanner
Reads the special lines on bar codes. Can be used to track documents in litigation as well as office furniture and equipment.

There are also many multifunction devices currently on the market that include OCR scanning, imaging, faxing, copying, and printing. Because the prices of all of these technologies have fallen so much in recent years, these devices are extremely popular.

mouse
An input device that is used to move the cursor on the monitor. As the mouse is moved, the cursor correspondingly moves in the same direction.

trackball
Allows the user to control the cursor by rotating a ball that sits on top of the device.

trackpoint
Device that looks like a pencil eraser positioned in the middle of the keyboard. A finger is used to rotate the trackpoint in the direction the user wants the cursor to move.

touch pad
A small rectangular surface that the user slides a finger across. The cursor follows the finger's movement.

speech recognition
The ability of a computer to understand speech.

Mouse The cursor on a monitor is moved with a **mouse,** sometimes called a pointing device. It is approximately the same size as the palm of your hand. As the mouse is moved, it transmits to the computer a signal that correspondingly moves the cursor in the same direction. If the mouse is moved to the right, the cursor moves to the right, and so on.

Other Pointing Devices There are a variety of other pointing devices that perform functions similar to those of a mouse. These include a trackball, a trackpoint, and a touch pad. With a **trackball,** the user controls the cursor by rotating a ball that sits on top of the device. A **trackpoint** looks like a pencil eraser positioned in the middle of the keyboard. A finger is used to rotate the trackpoint in the direction the user wants the cursor to move. A **touch pad** is a small rectangular surface that the user slides a finger across. The cursor follows the finger's movement.

Speech Recognition The ability of a computer to understand speech is called **speech recognition.** The user speaks into a microphone that is connected to the computer. Using sophisticated software, the computer is able to interpret the speech and translate it into computer commands and into text for use with word processors, email, and other software. Most speech recognition software leads the user through exercises that are designed to teach the software the nuances of that particular person's voice. Voice input systems have a number of advantages. Most people can speak faster and more naturally than they can write or type and they need little or no training to use the system. It also allows the hands to be free to perform other tasks. Speech recognition systems are very popular in law offices where they can augment or take the place of some secretarial functions such as transcribing dictation. Some users also prefer to use speech recognition instead of typing, since it increases their productivity. While speech recognition accuracy is quite good, typically greater than 95 percent, it is still necessary to proofread information entered. For whatever reason, speech recognition to this point is not largely used in many legal organizations.

Digital Cameras and Camcorders Digital cameras and camcorders allow the user to take photographs or full motion video and sound and download or transfer them directly into a computer. They also allow the user to easily edit, enhance, and view the information. Many legal organizations are using these devices to cut and paste data directly into presentation graphic programs for presenting evidence to juries. Many legal organizations are discovering the old adage that "a picture is worth a thousand words." Video evidence can be extremely persuasive to juries and fact finders.

The use of digital cameras and graphic software programs such as Adobe Photoshop to enhance and manipulate photographs has also recently greatly expanded in legal organizations. All of these tools allow legal professionals the ability to better tell their story and to assist fact finders in discovering the truth.

> *A recent addition to the firm's trial preparation strategy is to videotape many of its depositions so the team has the ability to synchronize the video and transcript for both mediation and trial presentation. [Our paralegal] ... is, of course, the videographer.*[7]

Input Devices in Legal Organizations A keyboard and a mouse are two of the most prevalent input devices in legal organizations, although this is beginning to change. Legal assistants and attorneys have been waiting for voice recognition technology to mature for many years. According to a recent survey, only 17 percent of the participating legal organizations had voice recognition in their office.

However, this is an emerging technology that may shortly gain many followers as the technology becomes faster, more accurate, and easier to use. Scanners are currently being used in many legal organizations for imaging and optical character recognition. This is being driven by the desire to move to the paperless office and to convert documents, evidence, and case-file information to digital media for use at trial and for mobile computing.

Output Devices

Output devices provide a user with the data that a computer has generated. Like input devices, they come in many different types. The type you select depends on the application you are using.

Monitor Computer output is displayed on a **monitor.** There are two primary types of monitors; cathode-ray-tube (CRT) (a standard television display), and flat-panel monitors, which use liquid crystal display (LCD) technology. Flat-panel monitors take up less space on a desktop, are lighter, and use less electricity. Monitors vary in size from 14 to 30 inches or more. Picture quality of the monitor is determined by several factors including resolution, or sharpness, of the image. The display consists of a grid of thousands of pixels. A pixel is the smallest dot that a monitor can display. Generally, the more pixels the monitor can display, the better its resolution.

It is important to recognize that the quality of the picture on the monitor is also determined by the video adapter card. The **video adapter card** acts as an interface between the monitor and the computer. The number of colors that a color monitor can display is also dependent on the video adapter card. Because of the graphical nature of the Internet and the rise in multimedia and video, manufacturers now produce graphics accelerators, video card memory, and other hardware to make graphics appear on the monitor faster.

Printer Data is output on paper, sometimes called hard copy, with a **printer.** A tremendous number of printers are available. All have different methods, speeds, and print quality. Choosing a printer is a personal decision based on your specific needs.

Generally, there are two categories of printers, impact and non-impact printers. An **impact printer** prints data on paper by physically impacting or striking the paper, as a typewriter does. A **non-impact printer** prints data on paper without physically striking the paper.

A **dot-matrix printer** is an impact printer that prints data by forming rows and columns of dots. The dots are created when the pins or wires in the print head strike the paper through the ribbon. Dot-matrix printers have been nearly totally replaced by non-impact printers, such as laser printers and inkjet printers.

An **inkjet printer** is a non-impact printer that sprays very fine ink onto the page. The print quality is not quite as crisp as with laser printer, and they are also slower than laser printers. Inkjet printers are usually less expensive and weigh less than laser printers, and do not take up as much room. Inkjet printers are also reliable and very quiet.

A **laser printer** is a non-impact printer that uses a laser beam to form characters on a page. This process is similar to that of a copy machine. The print quality that laser printer produces is outstanding when compared to other methods. Laser printers are very fast and quiet, and are the most commonly used type of printer in legal organizations.

Color printers are typically non-impact printers that use inkjet or laser technologies to print text and graphics in a wide variety of colors. The cost of color

monitor
Displays computer output. There are several different types of monitors including cathode-ray-tube (CRT), which is similar to a television, and flat-panel (LCD).

video adapter card
Acts as an interface between the monitor and the computer.

printer
An output device that produces data from the computer on a piece of paper. Many different types and sizes of printers are available.

impact printer
Prints data on paper by physically impacting or striking the paper, as a typewriter does.

non-impact printer
Prints data on paper without physically striking the paper.

dot-matrix printer
An impact printer that prints data by forming rows and columns of dots.

inkjet printer
A non-impact printer that sprays very fine ink onto the page.

laser printer
A non-impact printer that uses a laser beam to form characters on a page.

color printers
Typically non-impact printers that use inkjet or laser technologies to print text and graphics in a wide variety of colors.

printers has fallen dramatically so that they are now widely available. Color inkjet printers are particularly popular due to their low cost. Color laser printers produce better quality but are still more expensive than their inkjet counterparts.

multi-function printer
A printer that includes printing capabilities as well as added functions such as faxing, scanning, or copying.

portable printer
A compact printer that can be connected to a laptop or handheld computing device for printing when the user is away from the office.

network copier/printer
A printer that combines the function of a traditional copy machine and a network printer.

A **multi-function printer** includes printing capabilities as well as added functions such as faxing, scanning, or copying. They typically use either inkjet or laser technologies. A **portable printer** is a compact printer that can be connected to a laptop or handheld computing device for printing when the user is away from the office. A **network copier/printer** combines the functions of a traditional copy machine and a network printer. Using one machine, a user can send a document to print or copy from his or her computer or use the machine as a walk-up copier. Some network copier/printers also fax and scan.

sound card
A device that enhances the sounds that come out of a computer. Nearly all computers now come with a sound card.

Sound Card Board Nearly all computers now come with a sound card and speakers. A **sound card** enhances the sounds that come out of the computer. Most software programs support sound.

portable projector
A projector that allows a user to display the image as a computer to an audience.

Portable Projector A portable projector allows a user to display the image as a computer to an audience. Portable projectors are often in trials in conjunction with laptop computers to display presentations and computer-generated evidence to juries.

Communication Devices

communication device
A device, such as a modem, that allows computers to exchange information.

A **communication device,** such as a modem, allows computers to exchange information. It is technically both an input and an output device, since it can receive data from other computers (input) and also send data to other computers (output).

modem
A device that allows computers in different locations to communicate using a telephone line.

A **modem** allows computers in different locations to communicate using a telephone line. It converts the digital signals that a computer produces into analog signals that can be transmitted over a standard telephone line (see Exhibit 2–5). This is necessary because normal telephone lines cannot transmit digital signals. The modem at the other end of a transmission does just the opposite, converting the analog signals back to digital signals. Modems can transmit data at a variety of different speeds. Most can transmit data at 56,000 bits per second (bps). Modems can be either external units, which usually sit next to the computer, or internal units, which are housed inside the computer itself.

While modems allow users to exchange information with each other over long distances using a dial-up connection, the connection is relatively slow when compared to other types of technology. This is particularly true regarding most World Wide Web sites on the Internet, since they are graphically based. ISDN, cable, T1, and DSL are alternatives to standard analog phone lines and modems that are being used to speed up communication. These and other technologies are making standard modems obsolete, particularly regarding access to the Internet. The main advantage dial-up connections have over cable, T1 and DSL is they are much lower in cost.

cable modem
A data modem that is designed to work over cable TV lines.

A **cable modem** is a data modem that is designed to work over cable TV lines. The primary advantage of cable modems over dial-up modems is that

Exhibit 2–5
How a Modem Works Over Traditional Analog Phone Lines

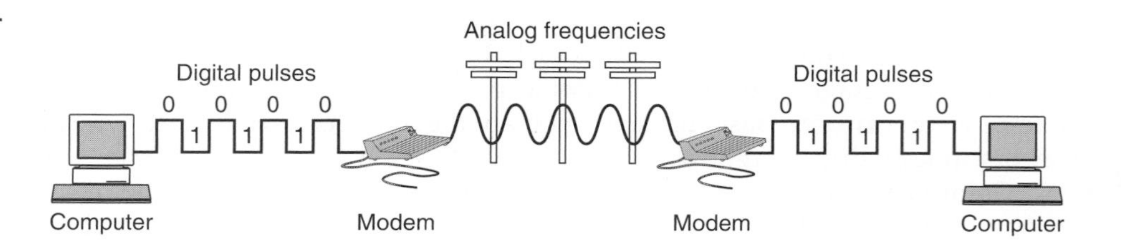

they can transmit data at much faster rate of speed since the bandwidth of co-axial cable is far greater than standard phone lines.

DSL (Digital Subscriber Line) is a type of digital phone line that is hundreds of times faster than a modem and a regular phone line and also allows data and voice to be transmitted on the same line (similar to ISDN, but much faster).

DSL (Digital Subscriber Line)
A type of digital phone line that is hundreds of times faster than a modem and also allows data and voice to be transmitted on the same line (similar to ISDN, but much faster).

Wireless Modem Many mobile phones and handheld computers now use **wireless modems** to connect to the Internet. A wireless modem typically slides into an open slot on a laptop or handheld computer and allows the user to access wireless email, the Internet, and other mobile technologies.

wireless modem
Modems that many mobile phones and handheld computers now use to connect to the Internet.

Fax Modem Many modems also come with facsimile (fax) capability. **Fax modems** can be used as both fax machines and modems. Using a fax modem, a user can prepare a document on the word processor and fax it directly from the computer to the recipient's fax machine. The downside of a fax modem compared to a stand-alone fax machine is that hard-copy documents cannot be faxed.

fax modem
A device that can be used as both a fax machine and a modem.

Videoconferencing **Videoconferencing** requires audiovisual equipment and special communication lines. Videoconferencing is very useful in a legal organization for meeting with clients, interviewing job candidates, meeting with co-counsel, taking depositions, and other applications.

For a videoconference to take place, all participants in the videoconference must have the proper videoconferencing equipment with an ISDN line or similar connection. Most legal organizations also have computer support staff to set up and troubleshoot videoconferences.

videoconferencing
Uses data communications to conduct long-distance, face-to-face meetings.

> *Be prepared for the unexpected. Dialing up a videoconference should be easy as dialing the phone, but it usually isn't. We ask our support staff to be there forty-five minutes early. A technician stays on hand for the first few minutes to make sure everything gets off to a good start. And when the unexpected happens, participants can dial an easy-to-remember four-digit extension to be connected with our videoconferencing bridging service.*[8]

Voice Over Internet Protocol (VoIP) **Voice Over Internet Protocol (VoIP)** allows users to make telephone calls using a broadband Internet connection instead of a regular (analog) phone line. Most VoIP service providers allow the user to call anyone who has a telephone number, including local, long distance, mobile, and international numbers. VoIP allows users to make a call directly from a computer, a special VoIP phone, or a traditional phone using an adapter (see Exhibit 2–6). Benefits include the ability to route calls over the Internet to remote locations such as hotel rooms or a client's location. Cost savings over long-distance telephone charges can be substantial because most providers charge a flat fee for unlimited call time. Some systems can support multiparty conference calls, and can integrate voice mail and faxes with email. Negatives include VoIP's dependence on electrical power—if the power goes out, so do the phones unless there is a backup system. VoIP is also dependent on both the broadband connection and the network being up; if they go down, so do the phones.

Voice Over Internet Protocol (VoIP)
Functionality that allows users to make telephone calls using a broadband Internet connection instead of a regular analog phone line.

Communication Devices in Legal Organizations

Most legal organizations have long since moved from slower, dial-up modems to faster communication technologies such as cable, DSL, and T1. This is primarily due to the overwhelming use of the Internet in law offices and the need for fast connections to email and legal and factual research sources on the Internet.

Exhibit 2–6
How Voice Over Internet Protocol (VoIP) Works
VoIP converts a voice signal from a telephone into a digital signal that travels over the Internet. The signal is then converted back at the other end.

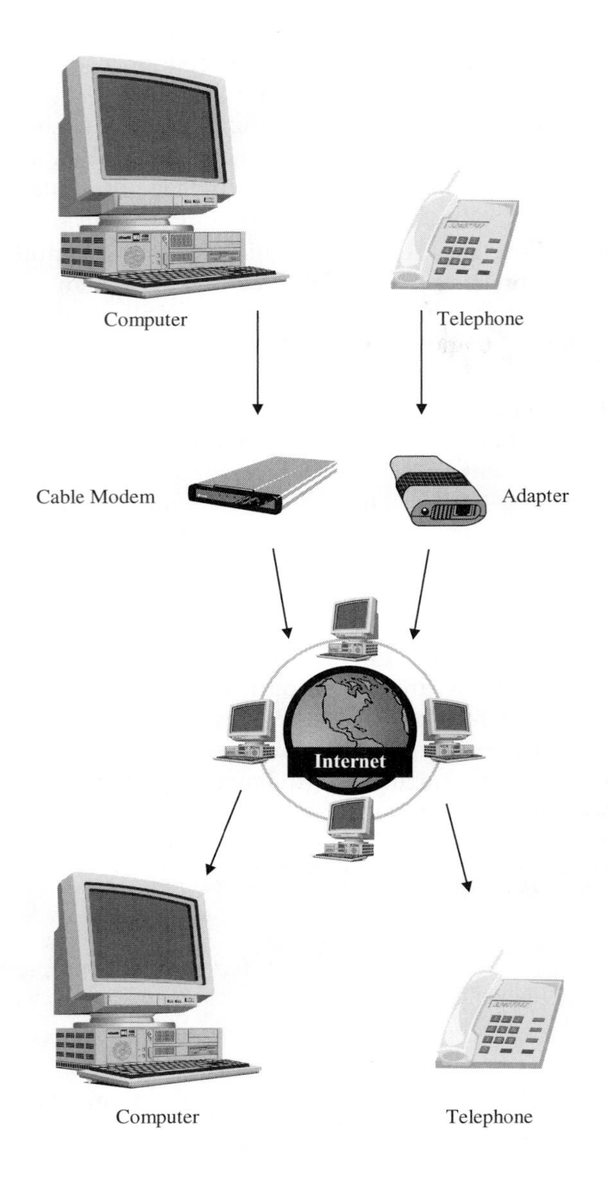

SIZE CLASSIFICATIONS OF COMPUTERS

Computers are used for a variety of purposes, both large and small. Computers with limited capabilities can support small applications, whereas computers that support large applications must have the ability to digest, store, and process tremendous quantities of data.

Computers are classified based on speed, main memory capacity, and auxiliary storage capacity. Computers generally come in two sizes: mainframe computers and microcomputers.

Mainframe Computers

mainframe computer
A large and powerful computer that can process and store large volumes of data. Mainframe computers are extremely expensive.

A **mainframe computer** is a large computer that is more powerful than a minicomputer and is capable of processing enormous volumes of data. At one time, mainframes were the only kind of computers available. Mainframe computers are very expensive. In addition, mainframe computers can support a large number of input and output devices and hundreds of users at the same time. Mainframe computers typically cost more than a million dollars. Drawbacks of

mainframe computers include the fact that they require specialized conditioning, such as heating and cooling systems, and a special power supply. Mainframes also require advanced software programs to operate the input and output devices they use. Finally, mainframes require a full-time operator or staff to operate them.

Organizations that need the computing power of a mainframe are typically large and need to store and use enormous quantities of information. For example, mainframe computers are used by the federal government for military purposes, by state governments for tax return processing, and so forth. Some very large law firms with thousands of attorneys use a mainframe computer system.

The largest, fastest, and most expensive computers in existence are special mainframe computers called **supercomputers.** Supercomputers represent the most advanced computer technology and are used for advanced research and mathematical calculations such as for weather forecasting, defense, and the space program.

supercomputers
The largest, fastest, and most expensive computers in existence.

Microcomputers

A **microcomputer** is a computer that is cheaper and less powerful than a mainframe computer and is generally referred to as a *personal computer* (see Exhibit 2–1). The microcomputers of today are more powerful than the mainframe computers of the early generations. The price of a microcomputer ranges from less than $500 to $5,000, depending on the size of the microprocessor, main memory, and auxiliary storage devices. Unlike mainframes microcomputers do not ordinarily need a professional computer operator to operate them.

microcomputer
A computer that is cheaper and less powerful than a mainframe computer and is generally referred to as a personal computer.

Microcomputers are popular because they are inexpensive, relatively powerful, and able to perform numerous and varied tasks. Many microcomputers have access to thousands of computer programs that can be used in a law office. Most microcomputers can also be upgraded to add a variety of different devices to meet practically any need. Microcomputers can be networked so that users in a law firm can exchange information.

Sizes of Microcomputers Microcomputers come in a variety of sizes and types including desktop, laptop/tablet, and handheld.

Desktop Computers A microcomputer that sits on a desk or on the floor is called a desktop computer. According to a recent survey, desktop computers still represent the primary computer for many legal assistants, but this is beginning to change.

> *It's now possible for an attorney or trial team to take all necessary trial case materials with them in one airline carry-on bag.*[9]

Laptop/Tablet Computers A **laptop computer** (sometimes called a portable, notebook, or tablet computer) is a microcomputer that is portable and easily moved but more powerful than a handheld. Laptop computers are convenient for people who travel frequently or need computing power wherever they go. They are used successfully in the courtroom as a means of accessing large quantities of data immediately, accessing the Internet remotely, or making presentations to juries. Laptops can also be used for interviewing witnesses or conducting legal research when not in the office, using either CD-ROM databases, online fee-based service providers such as WESTLAW and LexisNexis, or the Internet. Many portable computers now rival desktop computers in terms of processing power, RAM, hard disk space, and other features.

laptop computer
Sometimes called a portable, notebook, or tablet computer. A microcomputer that is portable and easily moved but more powerful than a handheld; can run on batteries or DC power.

A lawyer equipped with a PDA walked into court... The lawyer on the other side, in his argument, decided to cite the case of Smith v. Jones. Our lawyer signed onto WESTLAW [on his PDA], ran a citation history on Smith v. Jones and found the case was no longer good law.... Our lawyer simply handed his PDA up to the bench and said, "My learned friend cited the case of Smith v. Jones. The decision is no longer good law." The judge looked at the citation history on the Palm [Pilot] and—after saying, "Cool"—said, "Print that up, and you've just won your argument."[10]

handheld computer
Also called a personal digital assistant (PDA). An extremely portable computer that is small enough to be carried in a user's hand. Features may include email, Internet access, mobile phone service, faxing, and a wide variety of computer applications.

Handheld Computers/PDA A **handheld computer,** also called a personal digital assistant (PDA), is an extremely portable computer that is small enough to be carried in a user's hand. Handheld computing devices are extremely popular. Depending on the device, they provide users with email, mobile phone service, scheduling, address book, word processing, spreadsheets, databases, paging, Internet access, ability to send and receive faxes, and just about anything that can be done on a desktop or laptop computer. Also, many handheld computers can be synchronized with the user's desktop or laptop so addresses, email, to-do lists, and schedules are always in sync with each other.

I couldn't live without it [a PDA]. Our clients, in today's world, need to do business in real time, and when you consider how expensive lawyers [and legal professionals] are, clients understandably expect the same responsiveness in us.[11]
—A practicing legal professional

Common handheld computer brands include Palm Pilot, Blackberry, and many, many others. For many legal professionals, it's not whether to have a single desktop, portable, or handheld computer, but whether one should have all three.

I spend much of my time in the office and, therefore, want a powerful desktop with full-sized keyboard and large monitor. This is what makes me most efficient when I am creating documents, viewing exhibits stored in my litigation database or merely exchanging email with a client.... Notwithstanding [that]... I make presentations to clients...take depositions out of town or away from the office, and sometimes try to work on airplanes... for that, I need a lightweight notebook computer...But then there are other times...in the courtroom at a prehearing conference, or perhaps just traveling light on a day trip to meet a client. For that I need a handheld PDA with my portable calendar.[12]

The Virtual Law Office

The virtual law office is here! Many legal organizations are literally open 24 hours a day, 365 days a year in one way or another. The Internet, extranets, intranets, remote computing, laptops, handhelds, desktops, wireless networks, mobile phones, wide-area networks, the paperless office, and videoconferencing make the virtual law office a reality. Clients can access law firm websites via the Internet and firm extranets 24 hours a day, whether or not anyone is in the office. They can view marketing material, download a recent client training seminar/video, access discovery documents, complete a questionnaire, review recent

correspondence, look at a video deposition, review their current bill, examine the opposing party's recent motion, access court records, view a presentation that will be presented to a jury, and leave email and voice mail messages so when the legal professional arrives at work in the morning the messages are waiting for her in her in-box.

In many legal organizations nearly everything in the office already is or is moving to an electronic digital format. This means that attorneys and legal assistants now can access nearly everything in their office from a remote location. Word-processing files, databases, spreadsheets, litigation documents, deposition transcripts, video testimony, court records, photographs, sound, animation, drawings, billings, accounting records, and calendars now reside on a computer network in digital format. A legal professional can work from home, a client's office, or a hotel room across the country or on the other side of the world using the same tools and accessing the same electronic documents and records she would use in the office. The legal professional can access work product from the firm's satellite office located across the country as easily as she can access a document from a co-worker in the next cubicle. Legal professionals can access terabytes of information from their laptop, log on to WESTLAW or LexisNexis and do legal research, hop on the Internet and check out whether or not a witness knows what they are talking about, and do it all in real time right from the courtroom. Make no mistake about it, the virtual law office is here and it is here to stay.

Microcomputer Open Architecture and System Expansion Many microcomputers are built with an open architecture, which means that they can be easily expanded. Most of the components of a microcomputer are put on circuits that can be easily added to and removed from the computer or include slots where peripherals and other devices can be easily added. The motherboard contains the essential elements of the computer, including the CPU, main memory, and more. The boards fit into electrical slots. Most microcomputers come with at least three open slots, and several universal ports that can be used to install peripherals, so there is room to add things such as network cards, sound cards, additional RAM, digital cameras/camcorders, and scanners. This open architecture design makes it very easy to expand a microcomputer to the changing needs of the user.

Surge Protector and Uninterruptible Power Supply Computers should always be connected to a surge protector to protect them from electrical spikes or power surges, which can burn out the components of a computer. Most electrical strips come with a surge protector, and they should always be used.

Surge protectors protect only against power surges. If there is a total loss of power, even for a brief moment, such as when the lights flicker, the surge protector will do nothing to help. When this happens, the computer turns off, and RAM is cleared out. If the user did not happen to just save the document being worked on, data will be lost. An **uninterruptible power supply (UPS)** is a battery backup device that automatically supplies power to the computer in the event there is any loss of power, no matter how small. A UPS device can supply battery power to the computer for fifty to sixty minutes, giving the user sufficient time to save files and turn the equipment off. A small UPS for a microcomputer can be purchased for around $100.

uninterruptable power supply (UPS)
A battery backup device that automatically supplies power to the computer in the event there is any loss of power, no matter how small.

IBM-Compatible / Windows-Based Microcomputers These are based on the IBM personal microcomputer or PC that was released in 1981. IBM compatible microcomputers run the Microsoft Windows operating system. IBM-copatible microcomputers primarily use the Intel or AMD lines of microprocessors and run the Microsoft Windows (Windows) operating system. (The term "IBM-compatible" is a bit of a misnomer, as IBM sold its PC division to Lenovo group in 2004.) According to American Bar Association surveys, IBM-compatible machines are in 98 percent of the legal organizations in the United States.

Apple Macintosh Microcomputers In 1984, Apple Computers introduced the Macintosh (Mac). The Mac used a mouse, had a graphical interface, used icons (pictures) to accomplish computer commands instead of requiring users to remember long commands, and used pull-down menus. It gained an immediate reputation as being easy to use. For many years, Macintosh and Windows-based machines were not compatible. Software developed for Windows-based machines would not run on the Macintosh. That has now changed. Macintosh computers can run Windows-based software. Pricing is reasonably comparable between the machines. Macintosh computers are solid machines that some law offices swear by. However, the legal market is dominated by IBM-compatible/Windows-based machines.

Microcomputer Obsolescence Microcomputers are advancing at such a rapid pace that they become relatively obsolete within two to three years of purchase. Legal organizations use different philosophies and strategies to deal with this fact. Some legal organizations choose to upgrade their microcomputer systems every two to three years and buy the latest and fastest computers and peripherals possible. The obvious disadvantage of this is the high cost, particularly now, when nearly all members of a legal organization's staff have to have computers just to do their jobs. Another strategy is to periodically upgrade the CPU and internal parts of the computer. While this is less expensive than buying all new systems, it can lead to compatibility problems with existing software and systems and the overall effectiveness of the upgrades. A third strategy is to simply ignore current trends and continue to use existing computers and existing software as long as possible. Many firms wait four to five years between upgrades. While more cost effective, the strategy may not take advantage of increased features, productivity, and efficiency in new systems. Such a strategy can also be frustrating to a firm's corporate clients, which may upgrade more often. A final strategy is to buy more inexpensive systems with the intention of replacing them in a relatively short amount of time (not more than two years). Different legal organizations use different strategies and the answer will depend on the particular needs of each organization.

LOCAL AND WIDE AREA NETWORKS

The business world is rapidly adopting a technology model premised on "everybody is connected to everybody" and "everything is connected to everything." Almost all business computers in the United States [including those in legal organizations] are networked.[13]

In a recent survey 97 percent of legal assistants participating in the survey indicated that the computers they used were networked.[14]

Local Area Networks

single-user system
A system that can accommodate only one person at a time and is not linked to other systems or computers.

local area network (LAN)
A multiuser system that links microcomputers or minicomputers that are in close proximity for the purpose of communication.

Microcomputers started as single-user systems. A **single-user system** can accommodate only one person at a time and is not linked to other systems or computers. A **local area network (LAN)** is a multiuser system that links computers that are in close proximity for the purpose of communication. Two primary reasons for installing a LAN are to share data and software among multiple computers and to share peripheral devices such as expensive printers, optical storage devices, communication devices, and hard disks (see Exhibit 2–7). Consider how a LAN can be used in a law office. Suppose a law office has twenty staff members who need access to each other's word-processing files, docket control data, and time and billing information, and who also need to communicate via email with one another. Using stand-alone microcomputers, the staff members would not be able to share information effectively. However, using a LAN, each staff member has access to all the information from any

microcomputer on the network. Nearly all legal organizations now have a LAN and most software that is purchased for legal organizations is a networked version of the program. Primary network software used in a legal organization typically includes word processing, database management, spreadsheets, timekeeping and billing, accounting, calendar/docket control/case management, electronic mail, document management, litigation support, client files/records, and specialized legal-specific programs. Another advantage is that different types of computers (e.g., IBM-compatible machines, Apple Macintosh machines, and others) can be linked together to share data in many LAN configurations.

With a network, attorneys and legal assistants who are traveling can connect to the network and exchange messages, access files, and do other tasks.

To operate a network, typically all computers on the network must have a network card and cabling to connect the computers, and there must be network software to administer and run the network. Most networks also have **groupware** to help people on the network coordinate and manage projects. Groupware packages usually let the users exchange email, schedule meetings, manage files, and do much more.

groupware
Allows users on a network to coordinate and manage projects, exchange email, schedule meetings, and manage files.

Types of LANs There are several different types of LANs, including client/server and peer-to-peer networks.

Client/Server Networks **Client/server networks** use a server or servers to meet the needs of the other computers on the network. *Network servers* are computers that meet the needs of the other computers, which are called *workstations* or "clients" (see Exhibit 2–7). The server is used to store program files and data

client/server network
A network that uses a server to meet the needs of the other computers on the network.

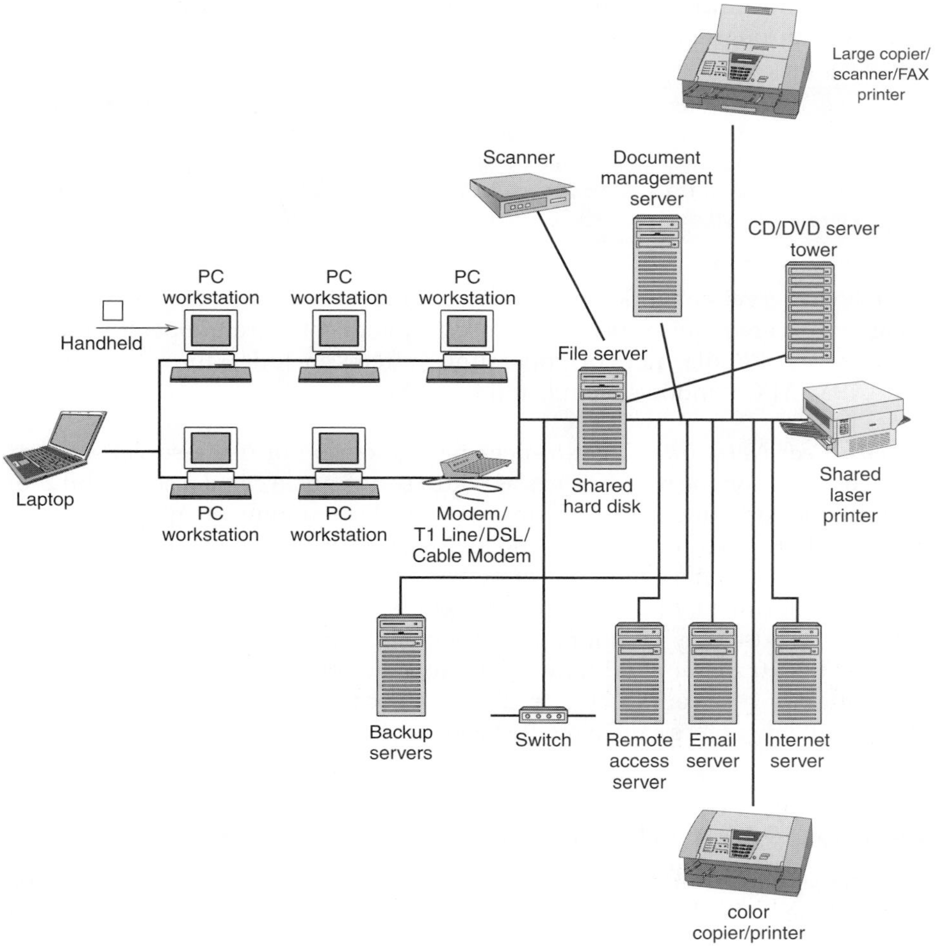

Exhibit 2–7
A Local Area Network Allows Users to Share Hardware and Software

files, host email and remote access platforms are used by the workstations, among other applications. Some servers are *dedicated,* meaning that they cannot be used for any other purpose. Other servers, depending on how the LAN is configured, are nondedicated, meaning that they can also be used as workstations. Client/server LANs use network interface cards that fit inside each workstation, cable or wireless antennas to connect the workstations and make the communications link to the server, protocol software to move data from computer to computer, interface software to connect the user and the network, and network operating software to meet users' needs for resources like files and printers. Most LANs in legal organizations are client/server.

Servers are generally high-powered machines that can support some of the computing needs of many workstations. Servers can be devoted to specific network operating functions and can be connected together on the network. For example, a legal organization could have a separate electronic mail server, file server, print server, web server, and remote access server (for giving staff access to the office network from remote locations such as a staff member's house, hotel room, or the courtroom).

wireless networking
Allows computers on the network to communicate with each other using wireless antennas coordinated through a wired access point.

In years past most networks were hard-wired. Today, an alternative to hard-wired networks that require cables is **wireless networking.** In a wireless network, each computer has a network card with an antenna. The computer transmits data from the antenna to an access point (typically another antenna that is fixed on or near the ceiling). The access point connects by wire to a network hub that transmits the data to the network. As long as the computer moves within the broadcast range, the user has access to the network (typically in or near the building where the access point is). Wireless networks are extremely popular in law offices, because they nearly eliminate the necessity to make long cable runs throughout an office.

> *The typical law office [in the 21st century] has multiple computers wired together to communicate, share data and access research resources. Local area networks (LANs) are the hallmark of the modern law office. They enable even a two-person firm to share information and access it in ways that were possible in the past only by using a "sneaker" network—data transferred on foot.*[15]

Client/server networks are now relatively affordable and are fairly fast and reliable. Servers require special operating system software to operate and run the network. Popular network operating systems include Linux, Novell Netware, IBM AIX, Windows Server, and Mac OS X.

peer-to-peer network
A computer network where each computer acts as both a server and a client.

Peer-to-Peer Networks **Peer-to-peer networks** do not use a server; instead, each computer on the network acts as both a server and a client (see Exhibit 2–8). Because the computers are performing two tasks—running an application program, such as a word processor, and acting as a server—they are not as fast as the workstations on a client/server network. However, they still offer the ability to share printers, files, and other resources. Peer-to-peer networks are inexpensive, because they do not require a server. Common peer-to-peer networks include LANtastic and Windows for Workgroups. Peer-to-peer starter kits, including network cards, cable, and software, can range from $350 to $800, so even small law offices can enjoy the benefits of a network.

Web-Based Networks—Internet, Intranet, and Extranet

Many legal organizations have expanded their networks to include intranets and extranets. As discussed in Chapter 1, an intranet is an internal network

designed to provide and disseminate information to internal staff using a web browser and using the look and feel of the World Wide Web. In much the same way the Internet provides information to the public, an intranet provides information to internal users (see Exhibit 2–9). An intranet can be walled off from the Internet to provide security from Internet users. An intranet is located on a

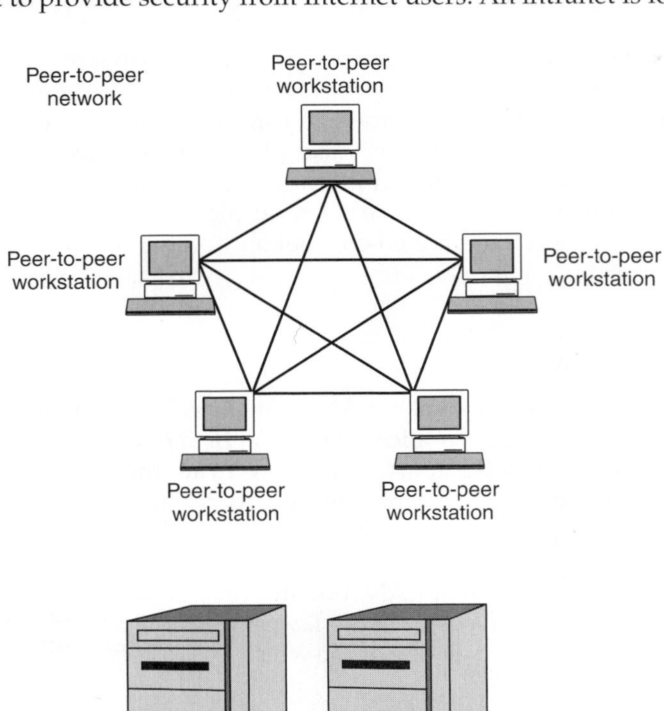

Exhibit 2–8
Peer-to-Peer Network

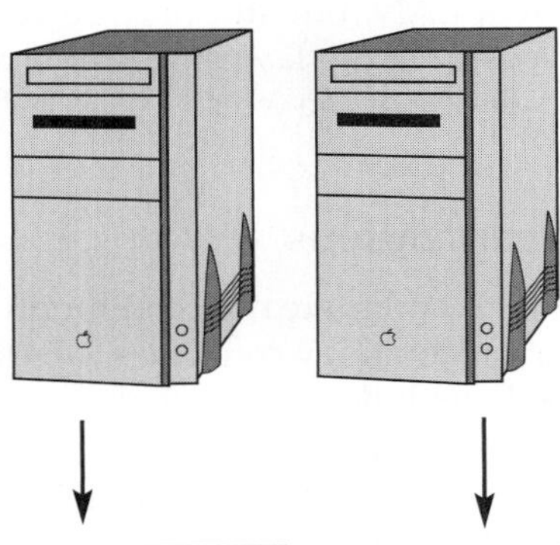

Extranet Server

SECURITY

Client:
- ID
- Password

FILES AND APPLICATIONS

Client File
- Case overview
- Case strategies
- Billing/invoices
- Legal forms
- Access to discovery documents
- Client material
- Web links

Intranet Server

SECURITY

Office Staff:
- ID
- Password

FILES AND APPLICATIONS

- Office policies and procedures
- Office training materials
- Office resources
- Office-wide contacts
- Expert witness database
- Benefits and compensation

Exhibit 2–9
Extranet and Intranet

legal organization's network computer system and in some cases the organization as a server dedicated to supporting the intranet. Typical information a legal organization might place on an intranet includes office policies and procedures, links to law-related websites, training materials, contact lists, and access to the firm's extranet. The use of intranets is growing substantially in legal organizations.

An extranet is a network designed to provide, disseminate, and share confidential information with clients. A client with a web browser can dial into the legal organization's extranet, go through security and ID/password protections, and access his or her case plans, documents, case strategies, billing information, and other information (see Exhibit 2–9). This is also extremely helpful when a law office has multiple clients to communicate with on one case or where there are co-counsel and others to coordinate strategy with on a case.

Wide Area Networks

wide area network (WAN)
A multiuser system that links microcomputers or minicomputers that may be located thousands of miles apart.

Wide area networks take up where LANs stop. A **wide area network (WAN)** is a multiuser system that links microcomputers or minicomputers that may be located thousands of miles apart. Large law firms that have several offices located across the country or across the world can use WANs to allow their offices to communicate with each other as if they were next door. LANs and WANs can also be used together. A law firm's offices located in New York and Los Angeles may each have a LAN, but still may be connected to each other using a WAN. LANs and WANs allow law offices to share information in the same location, across town, or across the world.

Networks in Legal Organizations

LANs, WANs, intranets, and extranets are now commonly found in legal organizations (see Exhibit 2–10). As technology continues to expand, so will the use of all types of networks in the legal industry. While it is not necessary for a legal assistant to have a working knowledge of the ins and outs of office networks, it is helpful to have a general overview of how important networks are to the practice of law in the twenty-first century.

Exhibit 2–10
Types of Networks Used in Law Offices
As seen in the May/June 2006 issue of Legal Assistant Today, Copyright 2006 James Publishing, Inc. Reprinted courtesy of LEGAL ASSISTANT TODAY magazine. For subscription information call (800) 394-2626, or visit http://www.legalassistanttoday.com

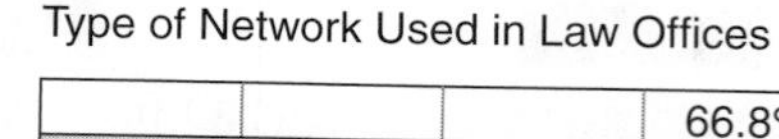

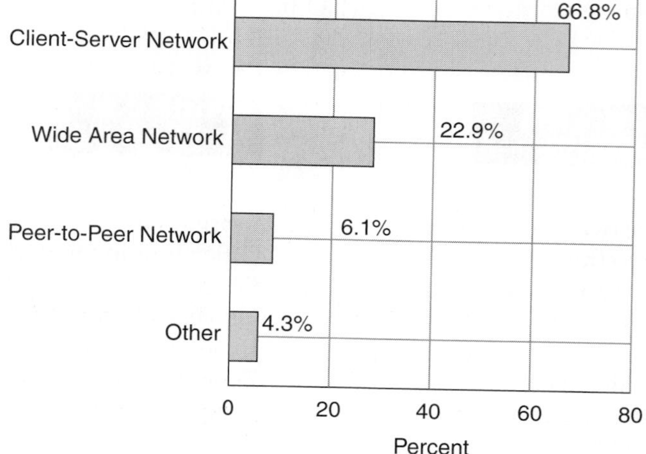

Hardware and Software in a Small to Medium-Sized Legal Organization

The hardware and software needs of a small to medium-sized legal organization are amazing, given that 25 years ago they were almost nil. A fifteen-attorney office with twenty support staff members might have something like the following system:

HARDWARE

- Thirty to thirty-five computers (a mixture of desktops with flat-screen monitors and laptops with docking stations) with network cards, DVD +R/RW drives/burners, speakers, and sound cards)
- Four to seven servers (file server, database/document management/backup, email server, fax server, Internet, intranet, and remote access server) with one uninterruptible power supply (UPS) per server and one tape backup machine per server
- Various PDAs, smart phones, and handheld computers
- One or two large network copier/printer/fax/scanner(s) with 10–15 or more standalone black-and-white laser or inkjet printers and at least one color printer
- Dedicated scanner
- One to two digital cameras / camcorders
- One DVD / CD tower server
- Various hardware hubs, routers, switches, cables, and wireless network hubs

COMMUNICATION

- One T1 or DSL (business class) line

HARDWARE AND SOFTWARE SECURITY/ETHICAL CONSIDERATIONS

While computers give tremendous benefits to legal organizations in terms of efficiency, productivity, and delivery of high-quality legal services to clients, they also create substantial ethical and security issues.

Your [law] firm is your castle—lock the doors, bar the windows, and dig a moat... Stress security practices the same way you would with a child—"stranger, danger!"[16]

Ethical Duty to Safeguard and Keep Client Data Confidential

Attorneys have a duty to safeguard and keep client information completely confidential. Rules 1.5 and 1.6 of the *Model Rules of Professional Conduct* speak to this issue. Every state has similar rules requiring attorneys to maintain the confidentiality of client information, including information that is maintained on all types of computers: handhelds, laptops, desktops, and servers.

This represents an enormous responsibility, given the technological advances in society and in legal organizations in particular. The threat of confidential client information being released either by mistake or by intrusion is very real.

Paralegals have a duty of confidentiality that extends to communications that might be more at risk of disclosure because of technology. Because of the dynamic nature of technology, we learn of new risks to confidentiality all the time. Paralegals and others in law firms need to keep up to date with the latest in this critical area.[17]

General Law Office Security Law office computer systems in general are vulnerable to ordinary security threats such as theft, sabotage, and natural disasters. It is important for all legal organizations to maintain adequate security

measures including having security and alarm systems to protect computer equipment from being stolen or damaged.

passwords
Codes entered into a computer system or software that act as a key and allow the user to access the system and the information it contains.

Passwords **Passwords** are codes entered into a computer system or software that act as a key and allow the user to access the system and the information it contains. Passwords are very important and are usually a first line of defense against intrusion into a computer system, but they are not invulnerable. It is important to choose strong passwords. Hacker software programs on the Internet contain tens of thousands of common passwords that can be used to break into a computer system. These are some rules for selecting and using strong passwords:

- Passwords should be a minimum of eight characters.
- They should be non-dictionary words.
- They should combine uppercase and lowercase characters.
- They should use at least one symbol (e.g., "$" or ":").
- They should use at least one number.
- They should be changed every ninety days.
- They should not contain personal information such as birthdates, names of family members, or other easily attainable pieces of information.

An example of a strong password would be something such as: RD10$Tk# or XP358LIN!.

access rights
Network security measure that limits a user's access to only those directories and programs that the user is authorized to access.

Access Rights All network operating systems for LANs and WANs and even some sophisticated application programs allow an administrator to limit the access rights of users. **Access rights** determine which computer directories, programs, or functions a user can access. A user should be given only the access rights he or she absolutely needs to have—never more than he or she needs. For example, if John needed to use only general word-processing and litigation support files, his access rights could be limited to only those files and directories and he would not be able to access other directories and programs. Limiting the access rights of users limits the number of people who can access computer files, information, and programs, so the exposure of the legal organization is less than it would be if everyone were given access to everything, even things they did not need. It is important that access rights be closely controlled and monitored regularly.

Backing Up

> *Permanently losing any data could be catastrophic for a law practice.... As we migrate toward scanning and imaging case files, losing that electronic file image data becomes the equivalent of a major office fire.*[18]

backing up
Making a copy of a user's computer files.

Backing up refers to making a copy of a user's computer files. A backup is absolutely necessary in case the legal organization's file server or other storage device crashes, files are accidentally deleted, files become corrupted, or fire, theft or a natural disaster strikes. If a legal organization has a good, timely backup of its data, and then a disaster happens, the data can be restored with no loss of information. Backing up data is easier than it ever has been before. There are a number of hardware tools available for performing backups, including high-capacity, highly reliable data backup units, having secondary servers that back up data throughout the day or at the end of the day, or using DVDs or CDs (typical in smaller offices). Also, there are Internet-based companies that will back up a legal organization's data automatically at predetermined times. Whatever the method, it is important that the information is maintained securely off-site, that backup is regularly done, and that the backup is reliable and usable. Legal organizations should verify on a regular basis that their backups are actually working by restoring some of the data saved to make sure it is usable.

While most firms already run tape backups, very few of them verify that their backups are actually good.[19]

Diligently backing up your systems every day and then standing by as the tapes melt in an office fire does not accomplish much.[20]

"Why should I take responsibility for backup at all when I can outsource it? Not only is data backup the single most boring technology, but it's even more excruciating to be responsible for actually getting it done. So why not outsource and automate database backup to Internet-based data protection service providers?"[21]

Minimizing the Threat of Disgruntled Employees

A six-member law firm that saw devastating consequences as a result of its failure to initiate security measures wanted to set itself apart from its competition and went completely paperless. When an email was sent among the lawyers about firing the firm's network administrator, the administrator intercepted it.... Between the time she intercepted the email and the time she was fired, the administrator was able to completely destroy the backup tapes, wipe the servers [clean] and then lock them out of their own system.... With no way to get back into the system and no paper backup, the partners had no alternative but to shut down the firm.[22]

When an employee leaves or if serious consideration is being given to terminating an employee, his or her network access should be immediately removed. According to a nationwide network security expert, "disgruntled employees are the greatest threat to any system's security." It is also very important for multiple staff members to understand all legal organization computer systems. If only one person knows the passwords, or only one person knows how to access the data or solve problems, once that person leaves or is unavailable a crisis is sure to occur. A recent survey conducted by the FBI found that 44 percent of the public and private businesses they surveyed had their computer system attacked in some way from within their own organization.

Mass Copying of Data by an Employee Even if a employee is not necessarily "disgruntled," some employees, for their own financial gain, may steal data including client lists, client files, and other work-related information. This is a rather common occurrence in legal organizations when associates or partners leave a firm to go start their own business. Because many of them may rely on existing clients to get their business off the ground, stealing firm assets and intellectual property can occur. While email poses the threat that an employee will send firm files to their home computer or another unauthorized location, many systems prevent sending more than a couple of gigabytes at a time. On the other hand, removable "flash" or "thumb" drives, which are extremely small and can hold multiple gigabytes of information, pose a real threat. CD and DVD burners pose the same threat because large amounts of data can be stored on these media as well. It is important to carefully watch computer assets and review computer logs when suspicious activity takes place.

The Dangers of Metadata

Metadata might include information about the authors of a document, dates and times of revisions, as well as the actual edits or comments made at various stages of editing, which could potentially put confidential, privileged, or damaging case or client information in the wrong hands.[23]

metadata
Electronically stored information that may identify the origin, date, author, usage, comments, or other information about a file.

Metadata **Metadata** is electronically stored information that may identify the origin, date, author, usage, comments, or other information about a file. Metadata is often described as "data about data." For example, in Microsoft Office files (such as Word or Excel files) you can see metadata that identifies the original author of a document, company name, subject, previous authors, date created, date last modified, editing time, and other information. You can do this by simply loading the file and clicking on File Properties. Metadata is usually not visible when a document is printed, but if one knows where to look it is often easy to find.

Other, more dangerous metadata includes things like the comments and tracked changes in a Word document. There have been several instances where Word files were produced and tracked changes or comments were enabled to show the various stages of revisions of the document, including who saw the document and when and exactly what changes were made to the document. This kind of metadata allows subsequent users to infer things about the original creators.

Metadata can be extremely harmful if it is not managed correctly. For example, in one instance, the United Nations released a report about the assassination of a world leader. The report was electronically made available to others, Track Changes was later enabled, and the recipients were able to view the names of people that had been deleted from the document as being involved. In another instance, Track Changes was used to show that a drug manufacturer knew of a potential side effect of a drug two years before marketing it. In another instance information in a Word document was improperly redacted and then converted to Portable Document Format (PDF). When the information was converted from the PDF file back to Word using Adobe Acrobat (a PDF file converter), pages and pages of previously redacted information appeared.

When producing documents electronically it is important to know exactly what metadata is in the document. Users should always check to see if Track Changes is enabled and if any previous changes or comments are visible when these features are turned on. Always view the properties of a file so you know what it contains. When sending a PDF file, be sure that that the options "Convert document information" and "Attach source file to Adopt PDF" are unchecked, and that password protection is set.

Electronic Mail Electronic mail is an incredibly popular means of communication. A recent study estimated that 135 million Americans use email and that they send approximately 500 million messages each day. Although it is extremely convenient, email can present a large security risk due to a lack of privacy and security. The problem is that email sent over the Internet is not secure and it may pass through many other networks before it gets to the intended recipient. As it passes through the networks, others have the potential to see or read the message. Email can be encrypted to ensure that no one except the recipient reads the contents of the message while it is in transit. **Encryption** runs the message through an encoder that uses an encrypting key to alter the characters in the message. Unless the person wanting to read the message has the encryption key needed to decode it, the message appears unreadable.

encryption
Running a message through an encoder that uses an encrypting key to alter the characters in the message. Unless the person wanting to read the message has the encryption key needed to decode it, the message appears unreadable.

There are many other security issues with email, including sending email to the wrong person, sending email to distribution lists (many email recipients) by mistake, and much more. These issues can be quite complicated when the message concerns confidential client information. Unless encryption or similar methods are used, it is safest not to send confidential client information over electronic mail, given the potential for abuse. These issues will be further discussed, later in the text, but generally electronic mail provides a reasonable level of confidentiality. However, if extremely sensitive information will be sent through email, legal professionals should use encryption.

Viruses Email also presents a threat because computer viruses can be attached to emails. A **computer virus** is a computer program that is destructive in nature. When the attachment is opened the virus is allowed into the user's computer system. Users should never open an attachment from an unknown source. Most legal organizations have antivirus programs that prevent or at least slow down viruses. However, because hackers are constantly updating their technology, legal organizations must regularly update their antivirus programs at least weekly, using the Internet. Most such software programs issue patches and updates to their programs to respond to new threats. In addition to updating virus patches regularly, many software companies update their software to include new security measures. Users should regularly update their operating system and application programs as well to take advantage of the latest security measures in them. In addition to actual viruses, there are a large number of virus hoaxes. These hoaxes usually arrive in the form of an email and contain bogus warnings usually intent only on frightening or misleading users.

computer virus
A computer program that is destructive in nature and can be designed to delete data, corrupt files, or do other damage.

In a recent survey 90 percent of the 2,500 companies surveyed indicated that in the past year they had been infected with a computer virus even though many had antivirus software installed.... One virus infected an estimated 350,000 servers over a 14-hour period, causing $2.6 billion in damages worldwide; another recent virus caused between $8 and $15 billion in damage worldwide.[24]

Antivirus programs act like the immune system for your PCs. They fight off infections as they occur, and sometimes help to prevent others. But the antibodies are only as good as the last update, so it's key to have them auto-update frequently.[25]

Spyware **Spyware** is a general term used for software that tracks your movement on the Internet for advertising and marketing purposes, collects personal information about the user, or changes the configuration of the user's computer without the user's consent. A common way spyware gets on a user's computer is when the user downloads or installs a program. Spyware may be included with the program software, although the user was not told about it or the information is buried in the licensing agreement. Whenever you install programs on your computer, it is important to carefully read the disclosures and the license agreements and privacy statement. A number of anti-spyware programs are available that can remove installed spyware.

spyware
A general term used for software that tracks a user's movement on the Internet for advertising and marketing purposes, collects personal information about the user, or changes the configuration of the user's computer without his or her consent.

Computer Hackers and Firewalls Nearly all legal organizations now provide access to the Internet for their staff. Many of these organizations use DSL, T1, cable modems, and other communication technologies that are "always connected" to the Internet. Computer hackers can use this connection to access the office's computer system unless there is a firewall that cuts off this access. A **firewall** allows users from inside an organization to access the Internet but keeps outside users from entering the LAN.

firewall
Allows users from inside an organization to access the Internet but keeps outside users from entering the LAN.

If you have a cable or DSL connection on your computer or network, a firewall is an absolute must to protect yourself from outside intruders.[26]

It's not difficult to imagine what could happen if just one ... [mobile] computing device containing sensitive information was compromised. Indeed, some news headlines have provided good examples, and disclosure of confidential information, private or public embarrassment, and potential loss of clientele are just the tip of the mobile risk iceberg. It's important to recognize that security is a process, not a product ... it's a mix of effective products and procedures, along with a security-minded culture and education that often supports a quality security approach.[27]

Mobile Computing and Wi-Fi Dangers The security threats associated with mobile computers and wireless networks are substantial. A report from the Federal Bureau of Investigation found that six hundred thousand laptop computers (about one in eight) are stolen annually. They estimated that only 3 percent of stolen laptops are recovered. In addition, laptops and handheld computers are highly susceptible to being lost or having information stolen from them.

Because laptop computers now rival the power and versatility of desktop computers, they can literally contain tens of thousands of client records. The potential for harm to come to a client cannot be exaggerated. One way to protect data on laptops and handheld computers is to install a power-on password. With a **power-on password** the computer immediately prompts the user to enter a password after the machine has been turned on, but before the computer has completely booted the operating system software. If the user does not know the password, the system will not start. Nearly all laptops and handhelds have this feature, but it must be activated. This type of system is very effective in the event a computer is stolen. Encryption software can also be loaded onto a laptop. If the user loses the laptop or it is stolen, the data on the laptop cannot be accessed without the encryption key.

power-on password
Password that the computer immediately prompts the user to enter after the machine has been turned on, but before the computer has completely booted the operating system software. If the user does not know the password, the system will not start.

> *Several months ago I was on the bus to work when I realized I had lost my Palm handheld computer. Talk about panic! I freaked out and ended up taking the bus back home and ransacking my apartment. After an hour, and half a pack of smokes, I found my beloved Palm in one of my old jackets. In one hour, I probably tripled the number of gray hairs on my head.*[28]

Wi-Fi computing allows users to access wireless local area networks. A Wi-Fi–enabled device allows a user to connect to the Internet when in proximity of an access point. These are sometimes referred to as "hotspots." The problem is that in crowded spaces, for example, there are risks including easier and anonymous hacking, reduced security, and hijacking of signals and access points. For example, in a hotel, using a Wi-Fi connection may let the person in the next room hack your computer. It would be better in these circumstances to use an Ethernet or other hardwired system.

"Delete" Does Not Mean Permanently Delete Many users mistakenly believe that when a file is "deleted," it is permanently deleted. This is usually not the case. Simply erasing or deleting files does not permanently delete files even if you have emptied the "recycle bin." In many instances, files can be retrieved by hackers and others from hard drives, floppy disks, and CD-ROMs even after they have been "deleted." It is critical to physically destroy the storage device such as a floppy disk or CD-ROM to ensure that data on it cannot be retrieved. In addition, in Windows, deleted files are typically not deleted at all, but are sent to the "recycle bin," so it is important to empty it from time to time.

Disaster Recovery Plans A **disaster recovery plan** is a plan of action that can be followed in case a disaster befalls the legal organization. For example, what would happen if a legal organization suffered a total loss to their computer systems from a fire, hurricane, flood, earthquake, tornado, bomb, power failure, theft, hard disk crash, or virus? Disaster recovery plans are prepared in advance of a disaster (typically multiple plans are prepared for different types of disasters) when there is plenty of time to think through alternative courses of action, anticipate problems, and design solutions.

disaster recovery plan
A prewritten plan of action in case a disaster befalls the legal organization.

A recent survey of legal organizations showed that only 42 percent of participants had disaster recovery plans. Despite this, the importance of a disaster recovery plan cannot be understated for a legal organization. For most legal

organizations, even the loss of information for two to three days could be a problem, let alone losing it for a week or a month. How could a law office survive for long without accounting records, payroll information, billing records, client data and so on? Some larger legal organizations may have a co-location site, or a satellite office where computer information is backed up. In the case of a disaster the satellite office could function as the primary computer site and allow access to data as needed.

Disaster recovery plans include a wide variety of information such as who will be in charge, what services are the most vital, what will each department require in terms of resources (computers, software, data, etc.), how to contact vendors, and how to contact employees. If a legal organization waits until a disaster occurs, it's too late. By that time, all could be lost. If everything is lost, can the firm recover? Can the law office continue as a business? If many instances, the answer would be no; that's why disaster recovery planning is so important.

Software Piracy: Illegally Copying Computer Software

> *As part of a wave of investigations into the use of unlicensed and illegally pirated software used in businesses and on the Internet, a software trade group has descended upon the legal industry.... A law firm with seven attorneys and more than 80 support staff based in Atlanta agreed to pay $108,679 to settle claims of unlicensed software.*[29]

software piracy
The unauthorized copying of computer programs.

Software piracy refers to the unauthorized copying of computer programs. Commercial, copyrighted software enjoys the protection of federal copyright laws. Ordinarily, when a software manufacturer sells a software program to a user, the manufacturer includes a licensing agreement with the program. The licensing agreement states how the user can use the product. In essence, the manufacturer is not selling the program to the purchaser, but simply allowing the user to use it as long as the user complies with the licensing agreement. There are different types of licensing agreements. When an individual user purchases a software program he or she is buying one individual license agreement for that program. When institutions such as law firms, governments, or other businesses purchase software they typically obtain site or network licenses. A site license allows the software to be used on a specific number of computers. A network license allows the software to be placed on a local area network server so that it can be accessed by the computers on the network.

Under federal copyright law, users are allowed to make one backup copy of a software product as long as it is for archival purposes only. The archive copy cannot be sold or given away. Thus, a purchaser can install a program on his or her computer in order to use it and can make a backup copy of it. Any copying in excess of this allowed copying, such as loading the program on more than one of the purchaser's computers (unless the purchaser has a proper site or network license), or making additional copies of the software to give to others, is unauthorized and may make the person liable for copyright infringement.

Legal organizations, like any other kind of business, are susceptible to employees illegally copying software onto their business computers. A person or business caught pirating software on its machines faces a variety of possible penalties including actual damages, statutory damages, additional penalties if the infringement was willful, paying the prevailing party's attorney's fees and costs, and possible criminal charges.

A software company or any one of several national software associations, such as the Business Software Alliance (BSA) or Software Industry and Information Association (SIIA), can bring an action against the infringer to protect the copyright in its programs. The BSA and SIIA both have toll-free hotlines

where members of the public can report organizations that are breaking software copyright law. Many times, organizations that have been reported will settle with the BSA or SPA before copyright lawsuits are brought.

> *If information technology departments in large law firms have any skeletons in the closet, they would be jangling their bones about software licensing... The world runs on software, and if any industry should be aware of the rules, it should be the legal industry. That is the oddest irony. The very industry that thrives on writing the detailed, complex, and confusing licensing agreements can be caught red-handed when it comes to software licensing.*[30]

The BSA reports that revenue losses due to software piracy are in excess of $11 billion annually, and that up to four out of every ten software applications are pirated. The BSA and SPA indicate that each receives more than thirty calls a day to their antipiracy hotlines, typically from disgruntled employees of businesses that are committing software piracy. Legal organizations and law office employees should be very careful not to illegally copy software. The BSA recommends the following for organizations to protect themselves from piracy/copyright legal proceedings:

- adopt an organization-wide policy on compliance with copyright laws
- regularly audit the number of computer programs against licenses
- document software purchases and keep license agreements
- read and fully understand licensing agreements
- educate management and employees on their obligation under copyright laws
- lock up software so it cannot be copied onto additional computers without permission.

INTRODUCTION TO COMPUTER SOFTWARE

Computer hardware is useless without computer software to make it operate. **Computer software** (i.e., computer programs) is step-by-step instructions that direct a computer to perform a task. Quality software is extremely important in determining how beneficial a computer will be to a user.

It is not necessary to understand how a computer program is written in order to use a program. A **programmer** is a person who writes computer programs. Most people who use computers are not programmers. Instead, they buy and use **off-the-shelf software** that someone else has developed.

Three basic types of software are available: operating system software, utility software, and application software. **Operating system software** instructs the computer hardware how to operate its circuitry and how to communicate with input, output, and auxiliary storage devices and allows the user to manage the computer. Operating system software ties the computer hardware and software together. Using operating system software, users can delete old or unwanted files, obtain a directory of the files on a disk, and manage the resources of a computer. Some type of operating system software comes free with nearly all computers.

Utility software helps users with the housekeeping and maintenance tasks that a computer requires. Thousands of utility programs are available. Utility programs can back up a hard disk, recover data that has been accidentally deleted, protect computers from viruses, and carry out many other tasks as well. **Application software** instructs the computer to perform a specific function or task, such as word processing. Practically speaking, when people use the word software, they are usually referring to application software. A word-processing program, a spreadsheet program, and a database program are all examples of application software, because they each tell the computer how to perform a specific task.

computer software
Step-by-step instructions that direct a computer to perform a task.

programmer
An individual who writes and develops computer programs.

off-the-shelf software
Software that has been developed by an individual other than the end user. A person can use off-the-shelf software while knowing nothing about how it was programmed.

operating system software
Instructions that tell the computer how to operate its circuitry and how to communicate with input, output, and auxiliary storage devices and that allow the user to manage the computer.

utility software
Instructions that help users with the housekeeping and maintenance tasks a computer requires.

application software
Instructions that tell the computer to perform a specific function or task, such as word processing.

OPERATING SYSTEM SOFTWARE

When the computer is turned on, or "booted up," the operating system is loaded into RAM. Operating systems are necessary to the operation of a computer, and computers cannot even turn themselves on properly without them.

Some operating systems are pleasant and easy to use; others are frustrating, slow, and cumbersome. Users communicate with an operating system using a keyboard, mouse, or voice. When a user loads or runs a program, he is communicating with the operating system. Thus, operating systems communicate with the hardware and with the end user.

Operating systems are usually unique to each type of computer. For example, an Apple Macintosh microcomputer uses a different operating system than do IBM-compatible microcomputers. The manufacturer of a computer usually supplies the operating system, although this is not always the case. Some microcomputers now offer a choice of what operating system can be used.

Duties of the Operating System

The operating system is a cross between a traffic officer who directs the flow of data between the computer and different input, output, and auxiliary storage devices and a housekeeper who organizes and maintains the system. Operating systems manage main memory; control input, output, and auxiliary storage devices (including adding new devices and deleting old ones); manage the CPU; give the user tools to perform maintenance of the computer; and manage the computer's files. From a user's viewpoint, managing the files of the computer is one of the more important things the operating system software does.

Managing Files File management includes copying files, deleting files, and renaming files. An operating system must also store files logically. Since hard disks and optical storage devices like CD-ROMs and DVDs can store gigabytes or billions of characters of data, it is important that the user can effectively manage the information in them.

Most operating systems allow users to group files together into folders or subdivisions (sometimes called subdirectories). Folders are used to store data of the same kind or nature. Think of a file cabinet with drawers containing separate folders for each kind of data, such as a folder for word-processing files, a folder for spreadsheet files, and so on.

THE WINDOWS OPERATING SYSTEM

A graphical operating system called **Windows** was developed by Microsoft for IBM-compatible microcomputers. There are various versions of Windows, including Windows XP, and Windows Vista. Every few years Microsoft updates Windows to add more features.

Windows
A graphical operating system that was developed by Microsoft for IBM-compatible microcomputers. There are various versions of Windows, including Windows XP and Windows Vista.

All versions of Windows use a graphical interface. The graphical interface allows users to enter commands and work with programs using a mouse, pull-down menus, and icons (pictures that appear on the screen to represent applications or documents) instead of requiring users to learn a complicated command structure. Windows is also a multitasking environment that allows users to run several programs at the same time. Tens of thousands of programs are currently available for the Windows operating system. It is the predominant operating system for IBM-compatible microcomputers, and it controls most of the microcomputer software market in the United States. Windows applications have similar menus and appearances, and can share information quite easily. This similarity among programs allows users to learn programs more quickly

than if they had to learn a new command structure for each program. Windows is explored in more detail in Appendix A.

More than 95 percent of all legal organizations use some version of the Windows operating system. The latest version is Windows Vista. Exhibit 2–11 shows the most common operating systems used by practicing legal assistants prior to the release of Windows Vista. It demonstrates that Microsoft Windows in its various versions dominates the legal market for computer operating systems. Notice in Exhibit 2–11 that only 1.7 percent of the market uses an operating system other than Windows. The "Other" category includes Linux and Apple's operating systems for its Macintosh computers.

Exhibit 2–11
Operating Systems Used on Legal Assistants' Computers
As seen in the May/June 2006 issue of Legal Assistant Today, Copyright 2006 James Publishing, Inc. Reprinted courtesy of LEGAL ASSISTANT TODAY magazine. For subscription information call (800) 394-2626, or visit http: //www.legalassistanttoday.com

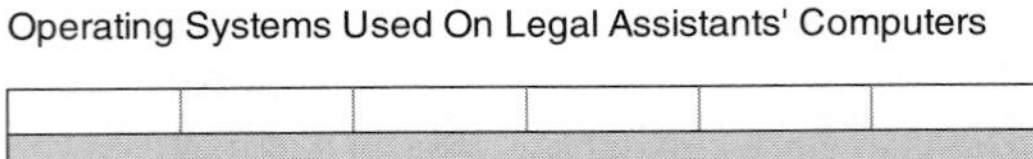

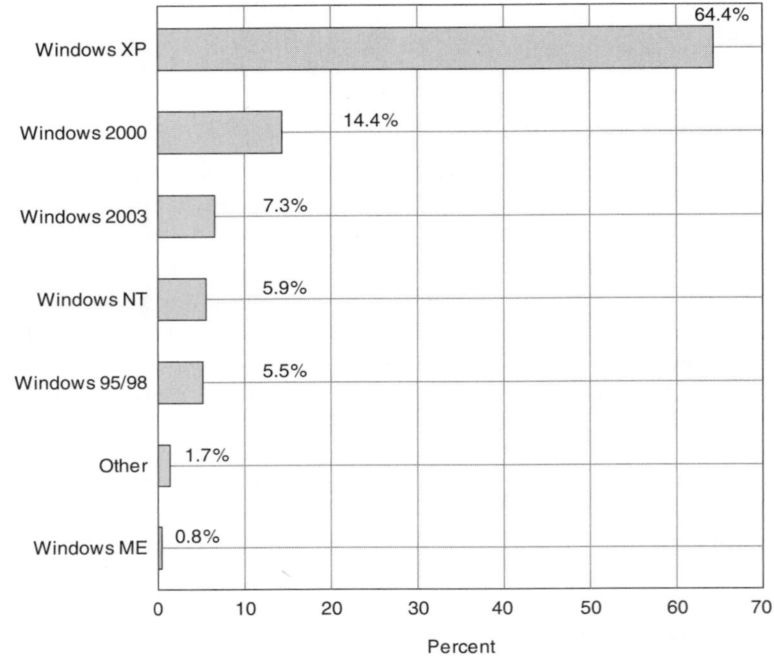

Network Operating Systems

network operating system
Handles the communication tasks between the computers on the network.

Local area networks (LANs) require special **network operating systems** to handle the communication tasks between the computers on the network. Regular operating systems such as Windows XP and Vista may work with file-server networks. However, more complex client-server networks require network operating systems such as Windows NT or Novell Netware.

Windows Server 2003 This operating system, designed primarily for networks and very powerful microcomputers, has an interface similar to that of Windows XP and Vista. Windows Server 2003 has network capabilities and security checks built into the operating system that make it suited for network applications.

Novell Netware Another type of network operating software, Novell Netware, offers many features and includes extensive security and tools to assist network administrators in controlling the network.

Linux Linux is a largely server platform based on UNIX that is distributed free. The source code is also distributed free. It has gained in popularity in recent years, but is not well known in the legal community.

UTILITY SOFTWARE

Utility software helps manage either the hardware or the software aspects of a computer. Some utility programs come as part of the operating system and some are separate programs. There are a number of utility programs including programs that compress files, back up files, and protect a computer from viruses.

utility software
Helps manage either the hardware or software aspects of a computer.

Compression Utilities

Compression utilities, such as WinZip, compress a file so that it takes up less room when it is saved. This is particularly important when a user has an extremely large file. For example, many large files that are downloaded from the Internet are routinely compressed.

compression utility
Compresses a file so that it takes up less room when it is saved. Many large files that are downloaded from the Internet are routinely compressed so that it takes less time to complete the download.

Backup Utilities

Backup utility programs create a copy of a user's hard disk or other storage device. The backup copy can be restored if the hard disk is damaged or lost. Some backup utilities allow users to back up files every Wednesday and Friday or on other specific days.

backup utility
Creates a copy of a user's hard disk or other storage device. The backup copy can be restored if the hard disk is damaged or lost.

Antivirus and Antispyware Utilities

Antivirus and antispyware utilities attempt to prevent virus and spyware programs from getting into the computer system and to locate and remove any viruses that do manage to get into the computer. Because new viruses and spyware are released almost daily, many antivirus software manufactures allow users to update their software from the Internet. Exhibit 2–12 shows a list of things that users can do to prevent or lessen the chance of getting a computer virus or spyware. Once a virus or spyware gets onto a user's computer system it can be extremely difficult, depending on the program, to completely remove it. The best solution is to prevent it from attaching to the computer to begin with.

antivirus and antispyware utility
Attempts to prevent virus and spyware programs from getting into the computer system and to locate and remove any viruses or spyware that do manage to get into the computer.

- Make backup copies of data regularly.
- Do not borrow DVDs or CD-ROMs from others—buy and use your own.
- Use passwords on your computer system.
- Turn your computer off when you are not using it.
- Do not let other people install programs on your computer or use your computer without expressly telling you how it will be used.
- Avoid downloading games, shareware, and other information from the Internet or other sources without knowing that the site is reputable and virus free.
- Do not loan or pass your software programs on to others.
- Install antivirus and antispyware programs and run them frequently.
- Update your antivirus and antispyware programs regularly.
- Do not open files that are attached to emails without knowing the sender of the email and that the file attached is safe.
- Read License Agreements and installation instructions carefully to prevent installing spyware.
- Try to restrict internet surfing to known reputable sites.

Exhibit 2–12
How to Protect Your Electronic Data from a Computer Virus

APPLICATION SOFTWARE

Application programs make a computer useful. They can be either programs custom-made for the particular needs of a specific user or generic off-the-shelf programs.

Custom-Made Application Software

Custom-made application software is written by a programmer for a specific user or company, usually to solve a specific, unique problem. It is typical for a large organization to have its own programming staff to write needed software. Small companies that need custom-made application software must hire independent software developers to write the programs they need. A large legal organization might have a custom-made program for timekeeping and billing or accounting, for example.

Off-the-Shelf or Packaged Application Software

Off-the-shelf software—sometimes known as packaged or generic software—can be purchased directly from software vendors. Most of the application software examined in this book falls into this category. The types of off-the-shelf software available depend on the type of computer the user has, because software is typically not interchangeable between different types of computers.

Thousands of off-the-shelf programs are written for IBM-compatible microcomputers. In fact, no matter how specific your interests or needs are, an off-the-shelf program suitable for the job has probably already been developed. Off-the-shelf programs include word processing, spreadsheets, databases, and many more.

Off-the-shelf programs have several advantages over custom-made software. The primary advantage is that they are inexpensive to purchase. Application programs for microcomputers can cost between $10 and $5,000, with most costing between $100 and $750. Development costs for many sophisticated off-the-shelf microcomputer programs, such as word processing and spreadsheets, can cost millions of dollars, so the user gets a multimillion-dollar program for a few hundred dollars owing to the large number of people who can buy the program. Another advantage of off-the-shelf programs is that they can be purchased and immediately put to use, and most companies provide customer support for their products. Finally, off-the-shelf programs are generally well tested and reliable and offer a greater selection than custom-made software.

The primary disadvantage to off-the-shelf software is that the programs are not made to a specific user's needs. Off-the-shelf software is basically "one-size-fits-all." Instead of a program being built to fit a user's needs—as with custom-made software—the user's needs must be altered to fit within the capabilities of a program.

When a software developer sells an off-the-shelf program, it does not give the user the actual code to the program. Although the program can run and work well without the source code, it cannot be altered or changed in any way, even if the user needs to update it. Finally, if the software developer updates the program, the user must usually pay another fee to receive the update.

KINDS OF APPLICATION SOFTWARE

Thousands of different kinds of application software have been developed. Chapter 1 introduced a number of software programs that are widely used in legal organizations including word processing, database management, spreadsheets, timekeeping and billing, docket control/calendaring/case management, electronic mail, electronic discovery, litigation support, computerized legal research, and presentation graphics/trial software. Each of these types of programs is covered in another chapter at length later in the text. This section covers a number of other types of software programs used in legal organizations that were mentioned in Chapter 1.

Integrated Programs and Office Suites

Integrated software combines several application functions into one. For example, an integrated program might include a word processing module, a spreadsheet module, and a database module all in one program. In an integrated program, the individual modules are not available separately. An **office suite** is a group of individual programs that are packaged together and have similar interfaces. For example, the professional version of Microsoft Office might come with Microsoft Word (word processor), Microsoft Excel (spreadsheet), Microsoft Access (database), Microsoft Power Point (presentation graphics), and Microsoft Outlook (email). The primary advantage to integrated software or an office suite is that the programs are highly compatible, so they are able to exchange information and have a common command structure.

In the past, the challenge was just getting new technology to work. Today, the challenge is adopting new systems to improve business, practice management and client service. Law firm managers guiding their firms' futures should consider technology-enabled opportunities along three dimensions—communications, practice management and business management.[31]

integrated software
Combines several application functions into one. For example, an integrated program might include a word-processing module, a spreadsheet module, and a database module all in one program. In an integrated program, the individual modules are not available separately.

office suite
A group of individual programs that are packaged together and have similar interfaces.

Browser

A **browser** is a software program that is used to access the World Wide Web (WWW) on the Internet. A browser connects a user to the World Wide Web (remote computers), opens and transfers files, displays text and images, and provides an interface to the Internet and WWW documents.

Common browsers include Microsoft Internet Explorer, Mozilla Firefox and Netscape. Microsoft Internet Explorer controls approximately 75 percent of the market.

browser
A software program that is used to access the World Wide Web (WWW) on the Internet. A browser connects a user to the World Wide Web (remote computers), opens and transfers files, displays text and images, and provides an interface to the Internet and WWW documents.

Project Management

Project management software uses the computer to track the sequence and timing of the separate activities of a larger project or task (Exhibit 2–13). Complex projects or jobs have many smaller activities that must be completed before they are finished. Some activities must be performed in a certain sequence, whereas others must be completed concurrently. Project management software tracks all of this information.

project management software
An application program that allows the user to track the sequence and timing of the separate activities of a larger project or task.

Exhibit 2–13
Project Management Software
Project management software allows users to break down a larger project into smaller components and to see a graphical representation of project.

Task Name	Duration	Start	End	Jan 1–5	Jan 6–10	Jan 11–15	Jan16–20	Jan 21–25	Jan 26–31
Talk to Client	10 days	Jan 3 08	Jan 13 08	■	■	■			
Read Client's File	14 days	Jan 3 08	Jan 17 08	■	■	■	■		
Perform Legal Research	4 days	Jan 11 08	Jan 15 08			■			
Draft/Dictate Brief	3 days	Jan 14 08	Jan 17 08			■	■		
Secretary Formats Brief	5 days	Jan 19 08	Jan 24 08				■	■	
Brief is Revised for Errors	2 days	Jan 25 08	Jan 27 08					■	■
Brief is Finalized	2 days	Jan 27 08	Jan 29 08						■
Brief is Copied	2 days	Jan 27 08	Jan 29 08						■
Brief is Filed	1 day	Jan 30 08	Jan 31 08						■

For example, an attorney might use a project manager to track all the things that need to be completed before a case is ready for trial, or a legal assistant might use a project manager to track concurrent projects and deliverables that are all coming due at one time.

Gantt chart
A timeline of projected begin dates and end dates.

Most project management software produces Gantt charts. A **Gantt chart** is a timeline of projected begin dates and end dates (see Exhibit 2–13. In short, project managers allow the user to see not only the big picture but also the specific tasks to complete a project. A spreadsheet program is also able to do some project management tasks, including creating simple Gantt charts.

Accounting

accounting software
An application program that tracks and maintains the financial data and records of a business or an individual.

Accounting software uses a computer to track and maintain the financial data and records of a business. Accounting information is crucial to any business or organization. It is required for income tax purposes, to obtain loans, to help in the operation and control of an organization, and more. Computerized accounting programs are often less time-consuming to use, are more error free, and usually produce final reports better and faster than manual methods. Such accounting software for legal organizations can include a general ledger, accounts payable, accounts receivable, payroll, and trust accounting.

The legal profession probably generates and maintains more paper than any other workplace.... Most studies show that businesses lose 15 percent of the documents they handle, and spend lots of money and time looking for them.

Even with word-processing applications, people can come up with some wacky naming conventions. A document management system can provide uniformity to your documents. So instead of looking for "mybrf2.wpd," you can find that important brief you were looking for.[32]

Document Management

document management software
Organizes, controls, distributes, and allows for extensive searching of electronic documents, typically in a networked environment.

Document management software organizes, controls, distributes, and allows for extensive searching of electronic documents typically in a networked environment. Document management software allows a legal organization to file documents electronically so they can be found by anyone in the organization, even when there are hundreds of users spread across offices located throughout the country. Document management software goes far beyond the file management capabilities in operating system software. It is the electronic equivalent of a file room with rows and rows of filing cabinets. As the legal community moves to "a paperless office," the legal organization will have to have a document management program to manage the electronic files. Document management software also provides for extensive searching capabilities and allows users to add a profile of every document, which can be easily searched on later.

Document Assembly

document assembly software
Software that creates powerful standardized templates and forms.

Document assembly software creates powerful standardized templates and forms. Instead of having to open an existing client's word-processing document and edit it for a new client, it allows the user to create a template that can be used over and over. Document assembly programs have more powerful commands and capabilities than templates found in word processing programs.

Imaging and Adobe Acrobat

imaging software
Converts an image of a hardcopy document (through scanning) into an electronic file such as a PDF (Portable Document Format) file.

Imaging software converts an image of a hard-copy document (through scanning) into an electronic file such as a PDF (Portable Document Format) file. A doc-

ument in a PDF file can be distributed over the Internet or other electronic means and read by another user typically as long as the user has a copy of a free PDF reader. The PDF file is typically read-only, so the user receiving the document can read the file but usually cannot electronically alter the file unless the user allows the receiver to change it. Many courts have moved to electronic filing and now require that documents sent to them for official filing be in a PDF file format. Other programs, such as Adobe Acrobat, can convert a word-processing file into a PDF file. PDF is a standard in the electronic distribution of text/image files. More information on Adobe Acrobat and PDF files is included in the next chapter.

> *With the proliferation of e-filing and the increased willingness of courts to accept documents on CD-ROM [and electronically], Adobe Acrobat has become the de facto standard for document exchange.*[33]

Graphic / Desktop Publishing Programs, Photo Editing, Video Editing, and Legal Drawing Programs Legal organizations are now using a wide variety of graphics and image-based programs. General graphics programs allow the user to draw, manipulate clipart and perform desktop publishing functions. These include programs such as CorelDRAW and Microsoft Publisher. Photo editing programs such as Adobe Photoshop allow the user to edit, enhance, zoom, and manipulate digital photographs. A number of programs allow the user to perform video editing as well. Finally, legal drawing programs such as Smart Draw Legal allow the user to draw legal diagrams such as crime scenes and accident scenes (see Exhibit 2–14).

Trial Software

A variety of **trial software** programs are emerging to help a litigator or a trial team prepare for and present a case to a jury or other fact finder. The programs include presentation graphic features, outlining and organization features, ability to organize information by legal issue, organize evidence and trial exhibits, and create complex timelines. This software is covered in more detail later in the text.

trial software
Programs that help a litigator or a trial team prepare for and present a case to a jury or other fact finder.

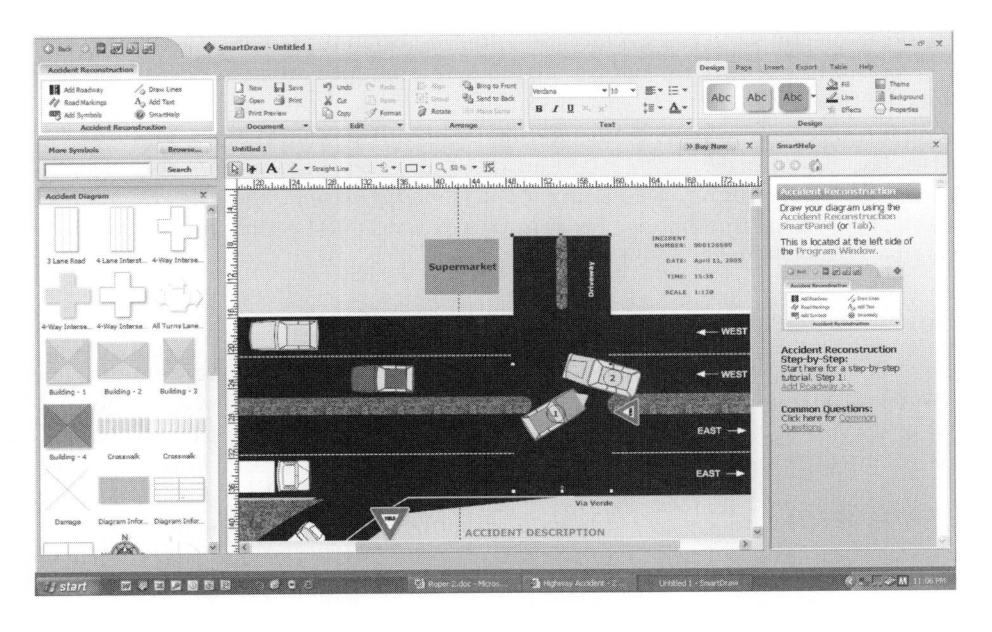

Exhibit 2–14
Legal Drawing and Diagram Programs
Screenshot created using SmartDraw Legal Edition software.

Application Service Providers and Internet-Based Programs (ASP)

application service provider (ASP)
A company that provides software or a service application through the Internet directly to the user's computer.

An **application service provider** is a company that provides software or a service application through the Internet directly to the user's computer. The software is not retained on the user's computer but instead resides on the software company's computer at a remote location and is "rented" to the user as needed. Two of the best known ASPs in the legal industry are WESTLAW and LexisNexis. The advantages of ASPs are that the user does not have to purchase the software, install the software, upgrade the software, or maintain it in any way, and globally, wherever there is an Internet connection. The user still has access to the software 24 hours a day, 7 days a week globally, wherever there is an Internet connection. Application service providers have not been widely utilized in the legal industry yet. Other common ASP applications (other than legal research) include timekeeping and billing, document management, and litigation support.

Specialized Legal Software

Specialized legal software is written to solve problems or address legal needs for a specific type of law practice. There are computer programs for nearly every type of law including business law, collection law, real estate, criminal law, general litigation, probate and estates, environmental law, and family law.

Groupware

Groupware is software that provides services to support group activities in a network environment including sharing documents, allowing groupwide scheduling, and other functions. This type of software allows two or more people to work on the information at the same time.

Artificial Intelligence

artificial intelligence or **expert programs**
Application programs that use a computer to provide analyses, make decisions, and solve problems based upon a known set of assumptions.

Artificial intelligence, also called **expert programs,** uses a computer to provide analyses, make decisions, and solve problems based upon a known set of assumptions. Programs that use artificial intelligence analyze factual situations and recommend that certain actions be taken to solve a problem. The systems ordinarily work by asking a series of questions and then, based on the answers to those questions, making a recommendation or analysis.

Computer programs that use artificial intelligence are being developed for specific types of law practices. For example, artificial intelligence could be used to determine what type of action should be filed and what type of claims or theories should be used given a certain fact pattern. Programs that use artificial intelligence are programmed using the knowledge base of known experts in the field. As artificial intelligence continues to expand and become more proficient, the use of it will grow.

Software Licensing

software license agreement
A software license agreement contains the rights and restrictions of how a piece of software can be used.

Most software that is purchased is done so under a **license agreement.** The license agreement allows the person or group to use the software. The software license agreement contains the rights and restrictions of the software's use. Some license agreements are based on the number of computers that software can be loaded on while others are based on the number of users that can utilize the software. Using software in a manner that violates the license agreements, such as copying software beyond the number of licenses that have been

purchased, can constitute copyright infringement which can subject the violator to civil litigation.

Shareware and Freeware

Shareware is a computer program that is distributed to users initially at no cost. If the user likes the software program, the user pays the author for it. Shareware is distributed on computer bulletin boards where users can download the shareware programs. Some shareware programs exist for law offices. **Freeware** is a computer program that is distributed to users free of charge for at least part of a program. Typically there is some cost involved if one desires full access to the program.

shareware
Computer programs that are distributed to users initially at no cost. If the user likes the software program, the user pays the author for it.

freeware
Computer programs that are distributed to users free of charge.

LAW FIRM INFORMATION SYSTEMS

Information is vital to a law firm; without it, a law firm cannot survive. However, law firms and attorneys do not want raw data. Raw data are facts or figures that have not been processed or organized. Many times, attorneys will have too much raw data. For example, when a matter is first being researched in a law library, too much material is often present—too many books, too many cases. What the attorney needs are the one or two cases that are directly relevant to the situation at hand. Information is data that are relevant and organized. A well-thought-out computerized information system can help manage this need for organized information.

A **law firm information system** is a combination of computer hardware, computer software, procedures, and human interaction that work together to solve problems in the law office. The emphasis is on this being a system, which means that all the separate components work together to achieve a common goal.

law firm information system
A systems approach that uses a combination of computer hardware, computer software, procedures, and human interaction to solve real-life problems in a law office.

A **system** is a group of interdependent parts that work collectively to accomplish a common task. Tracking information in a law firm is not the job of any one person or any one computer application. Instead, all the components must work together as a team. When the information system is developed, it is looked at and analyzed as a whole, and the effects of any one change on the entire system are examined.

system
A group of interdependent parts that work collectively to accomplish a common task.

Software is an integral part of a law firm information system. No one piece of software can solve all the problems of a firm. Instead, a collection of software, hardware, networks, security, communications, user support and training must combine to make up the law firm information system. The needs of each law office are separate and distinct, so no one information system is best for all firms. An effective law firm information system and technology staff produces organized, relevant information that is available to all who need it, when they need it, and how they need it.

Exhibit 2–15 shows some of the main components of many law firm information systems. This list is not meant to be exhaustive. Most law firms must be able to handle these types of problems and functions.

A saying in the information technology field is that the number-one reason for successful software/hardware implementations is training, and the number-one reason for failed implementations is lack of training.

An interesting fact is that the list in Exhibit 2–15 continues to grow each year. During the last five to seven years, the list of software products in a typical law firm information system has nearly doubled. Law office computerization continues to expand as computers are used in new and different ways to solve law office problems or to enhance services. Not only has the number of

Exhibit 2–15
Law Firm Information System / Information Technology Functions

	Functions	Description
	Hardware Support	Servers, computers, memory, laptops, handhelds, monitors, infrastructure, drives, printers, speakers, mice, storage, scanners
	Operating System and Back-Office Network Support	Windows, Windows Server 2003, cables, routers, network cards, wireless hubs, planning, drivers, maintenance
	Application Software	Word processing, spreadsheets, databases, timekeeping and billing, docket control/case management, litigation support, computerized legal research, presentation graphics/trial software, accounting, electronic mail, browsers, project management, document management, electronic discovery, document assembly, graphics, groupware, computerized legal research, transcript management, PDF creation, citation checking, upgrades
	Security	Backups, antivirus, antispyware, policies, procedures, passwords, IDs, access rights, computer monitoring, spam filters, encryption, firewalls
	Communications Support	Internet, extranet, intranet, VoIP, remote access, bandwidth, videoconferencing, fax, instant messaging, electronic mail
	User Support	Installation, troubleshooting, answering questions

software products grown, but the complexity of law office information systems has grown as well. Many law offices, including small, medium, large, corporate, and government law departments must have computer professionals on staff to maintain the growing list of software products used in law offices.

SUMMARY

Computers are used in nearly every facet of how legal professionals deliver legal services to clients. It is important that practicing legal assistants know the technology as well as the law.

Every computer has a system unit, which contains the CPU and main memory. The CPU is the "brain" of the computer. The CPU organizes and processes information in addition to coordinating with peripheral devices. The main memory is made up of ROM, which is permanent memory, and RAM, which is volatile memory.

Auxiliary storage devices store information so that it can be retrieved at a later time. They include devices such as hard disks and optical storage devices like CD-ROM and DVD drives. Removable drives such as flash or "thumb" drives are small and portable and can hold up to several gigabytes of information.

Input devices enter information into a computer. They include keyboards, mice, digital cameras and camcorders, scanners, and speech recognition tools. Scanning and imaging both refer to the ability of a computer to scan a hard-copy document into a computer. Making an image of a document is similar to taking a photograph of a document. A related functionality is optical character recognition (OCR). When a user scans a document into a computer using OCR the result is not an image, but rather a file that contains the text of the document so it can be brought into a word processor or other application to be edited.

Output devices provide the user with the data that the computer has generated. They include monitors, printers, portable projectors, and soundboards. Most printers now are non-impact printers and are either inkjet or laser. Many printers are multifunction printers that can fax, scan, and copy.

Communication devices allow computers to exchange information with other users over the Internet and other channels. Communication technology includes dial-up modems, cable modems, DSL and T1 lines, wireless modems, Voice Over Internet Protocol (VoIP), and videoconferencing.

Computers are generally available in two sizes: mainframe computers and microcomputers. Laptops and handheld computers are extremely common in the legal industry and are changing the way legal professionals deliver services to clients. The "virtual law office" is a reality. Clients and legal professionals can access law offices virtually via the Internet, viewing client files, billings, transcripts, legal research and other data from nearly anywhere in the country or the world.

A local area network (LAN) is a multiuser system that links mainframes or microcomputers that are in close proximity for the purpose of communication. LANs can be either client/server or peer-to-peer networks. Nearly all legal organizations are on a LAN. A wide area network (WAN) is a multiuser system that links computers that may be located thousands of miles apart.

There are many security and ethical issues pertaining to the use of technology in legal organizations. The underlying principle is that legal professionals must safeguard and keep client information confidential. Current security issues in the legal field include passwords, access rights to files, backing up data, sabotage by employees, mass copying of client information by employees, security surrounding electronic mail, viruses, spyware, firewalls, mobile computing issues related to lost or stolen laptops or handhelds, disaster recovery, software piracy, and metadata. Metadata is electronically stored information that may identify the

origin, date, author, usage, comments, or other information about a file. Metadata is often described as "data about data."

Operating system software instructs the computer hardware how to operate its circuitry and how to communicate with input, output, and auxiliary storage devices. It allows the user to manage the computer. Windows is the most common operating system in the legal environment.

Utility software helps to manage the hardware or software of a computer. Popular utility programs including antivirus and antispyware programs.

There are many types of application programs used in legal organizations. The list grows longer every day. Document management software organizes, controls, distributes, and allows for extensive searching of electronic documents, typically in a networked environment. Document assembly software creates powerful standardized templates/forms. A popular way of electronically filing court documents is by creating Portable Document Format (PDF) files using Adobe Acrobat. Acrobat has become a standard for filing electronic documents with many courts.

An application service provider is a company that provides software or a service application through the Internet directly to the user's computer.

A law firm information system is a combination of computer hardware, software, procedures, and human interaction that solve real-life problems in law offices. Technology functions in most legal organizations including hardware support, operating system and back office network support, application software, security, communications support, customer support, and training.

INTERNET SITES

Internet sites for this chapter include the following:

Computer Hardware

Organization	Product/Service	World Wide Web Address
AMD	Microprocessors	<http://www.amd.com>
APC	Uninterrupted power supplies and other peripherals	<http://www.apc.com>
Apple	Hardware and software for Macintosh computers	<http://www.apple.com>
Blackberry	Handheld computers	<http://www.rim.net>
Cisco	Network operating system peripherals	<http://www.cisco.com>
Compaq	All types of computer hardware and peripherals	<http://www.compaq.com>
Dell Computers	All types of computer hardware and peripherals	<http://www.dell.com>
Nuance	Dragon Naturally Speaking speech recognition	<http://www.nuance.com>
Hewlett-Packard	All types of computer hardware and peripherals	<http://www.hp.com>

INTERNET SITES (Cont.)

Organization	Product/Service	World Wide Web Address
Epson	All types of computer hardware and peripherals	<http://www.epson.com>
Gateway Computers	All types of computer hardware and peripherals	<http://www.gateway.com>
Lenovo	Computer hardware	<http://www.lenovo.com>
Iomega Corp.	Removable drives and other storage devices	<http://www.iomega.com>
Intel	Microprocessors	<http://www.intel.com>
Kodak	Digital cameras	<http://www.kodak.com>
Palm Pilot	Handheld computers	<http://www.palm.com>
NEC	All types of computer hardware and peripherals	<http://www.nec.com>
Sony	Handhelds and other computer hardware and peripherals	<http://www.sony.com>
Toshiba	Laptops and computer peripherals	<http://www.toshiba.com>
Xerox	Printers and other products	<http://www.xerox.com>
Adobe	PDF and photographic software and other application programs	<http://www.adobe.com>
Apple	Operating systems, application programs, and other products	<http://www.apple.com>
Business Software Alliance	Antipiracy information	<http://www.bsa.org/usa/>
Corel Corporation	Application programs and office suites	<http://www.corel.com>
Cisco	Network operating system solutions	<http://www.cisco.com>
LexisNexis	Legal and factual research databases and document assembly software	<http://www.lexisnexis.com>
Microsoft	Operating systems, application programs, office suites, utilities, and other products	<http://www.microsoft.com>
Mozilla	Browser software	<http://www.mozilla.com>
Netscape	Browser software	<http://www.netscape.com>
Network Associates	Antivirus and antispyware programs	<http://www.mcafee.com/us/>
Novell	Network operating systems	<http://www.novell.com>
Smart Draw	Legal diagram software	<http://www.smartdraw.com>
Software and Information Industry	Antipiracy information	<http://www.siia.com>
Symantec Corporation	Antivirus programs, utilities, and other application programs	<http://www.symantec.com>
Worldox	Document management software	<http://www.worldox.com>

KEY TERMS

computer programs
operating system program
input device
output device
application software
central processing unit (CPU)
processor chip
microprocessors
gigahertz (GHz)
main memory
memory chips
read-only memory (ROM)
random-access memory (RAM)
auxiliary storage device
cache memory
peripheral devices
storage capacity
access time
sequential access
random (direct) access
floppy disk drive
hard disk drive
removable or flash drive
magnetic tape
tape reels
tape cartridges
optical storage devices
CD-ROM drive
CD-R (compact disk–recordable) drive
CD-RW (compact disk–Rewritable) drive
DVD-ROM (digital versatile disk) drive
recordable DVD
imaging
optical character recognition (OCR)
bar code scanner
mouse
trackball
trackpoint
touch pad
speech recognition
monitor
video adapter card
printer
impact printer
non-impact printer
dot-matrix printer
inkjet printer
laser printer
color printers
multi-function printer
portable printer
network copier/printer
sound card
portable projector
communication device
modem
cable modem
DSL (Digital Subscriber Line)
wireless modem
fax modem
videoconferencing
Voice Over Internet Protocol (VoIP)
mainframe computer
supercomputers
microcomputer
laptop computer
handheld computer
uninterruptible power supply (UPS)
single-user system
local area network (LAN)
groupware
client/server network
wireless networking
peer-to-peer network
wide area network (WAN)
passwords
access rights
backing up
metadata
encryption
computer virus
spyware
firewall
power-on password
disaster recovery plan
software piracy
computer software
programmer
off-the-shelf software
operating system software
utility software
application software
Windows
network operating system
utility software
compression utility
backup utility
antivirus utility
integrated software
office suite
browser
project management software
Gantt chart
accounting software
document management software
document assembly software
imaging software
trial software
application service provider (ASP)
artificial intelligence or expert programs
shareware
freeware
law firm information system
system

TEST YOUR KNOWLEDGE

1. True or False: The central processing unit is the "brains" of a computer.
2. The memory that is cleared when a user turns the machine off is called ________.
3. Identify three auxiliary storage devices.
4. Differentiate imaging and optical character recognition.
5. What is VoIP?
6. What is a "virtual" law office?
7. True or False: Most legal organizations are not networked yet.
8. What is the difference between an extranet and an intranet?
9. Why are software access rights important?
10. What is an alternative to backing up software using hardware components such as tape backup and secondary servers?
11. Define metadata.
12. What are the ethical dangers of mobile computing?
13. What does document management software do?
14. Explain what a law firm information system is.

ON THE WEB EXERCISES

1. Using a general search engine on the Internet such as google.com or yahoo.com, write a one-page summary of what metadata is. If possible, list examples of how mistakes or problems arise from the use of metadata for unintended consequences.
2. Mobile computing involves many security risks for legal organizations. Using a general search engine on the Internet such as google.com or yahoo.com, list a minimum of five of tips that can improve the security of mobile computing.
3. Using a general search engine on the Internet such as google.com or yahoo.com, write a two-page disaster recovery plan that you could use if a disaster occurred at your current residence. What can you do now to plan for such a disaster, and what changes can you make currently that would greatly improve your ability to recover from the disaster quickly and seamlessly?
4. As a legal assistant in a small law office, you have been asked for your input regarding replacing your current IBM-compatible microcomputer, which is now outdated. Go to <http://www.pcmagazine.com>, <http://www.pcworld.com>, <http://www.practice.findlaw.com>, <http://www.dell.com>, <http://www.gateway.com>, <http://www.toshiba.com>, and <http://www.compaq.com> and research the following:
   (a) what common microprocessors are being used, (b) how much RAM is usually included with the machines, (c) how much hard disk storage is typically being included, (d) what type and size of monitors are common, (e) what common peripherals (such as CD-ROM or DVD burners) are sold with the computers, and (f) what choices you have among handheld, laptop, tablet, or desktop machines. What would you choose, and why?
5. As a legal assistant in a twenty-attorney office, you often talk to the network administrator responsible for the firm's network. The network administrator is leaving to take a new job and in the discussion she mentions that the backup units that the firm currently has are not working and, even when they were, the storage capacity of the units was too small. The firm currently has two servers that have 100 GB of storage. Concerned that the firm is not backing up adequately, you decide to do some research. Using the websites from the prior question, or from the list at the end of the chapter, or using other sites, decide what your options are and how you would replace the outdated backup system.
6. Using the Internet, determine what is the largest-capacity flash drives you can find and what it costs. Approximately how many hard-copy pages of documents could be stored on the flash drive by an employee who decided to steal documents from your law firm?
7. As a legal assistant in a corporate legal department, you are responsible for tracking hundreds of real estate transactions throughout the United States every year. Keeping track of the paperwork is beginning to overwhelm you as you try to stay organized. Because you work with attorneys and corporate staff all over the country, it would be nice to be able to forward electronic versions of real estate records, title searches, and other records. Because many of the documents are in hard-copy format, you would have to convert the documents to images. Using the <http://www.lawofficecomputing.com>, <http://www.lawtechnology.org>, <http://www.technolawyer.com>, and <http://www.practice.findlaw.com>, write a short paper on imaging. Answer the following questions: (a) How much do high-speed scanners cost? (b) How accurate is imaging? (c) Do many legal organizations use imaging? (d) In the end, would you recommend the move to imaging?
8. Recently, you were involved in car accident and your left hand was badly broken. It is currently in a full cast (you can barely move your fingers) and will be for approximately four to six months. As a legal assistant for a national association, you regularly review legislation being considered by state legislatures that might affect your association's members and draft long memos to your supervising attorney regarding the changes. This means doing a lot of typing. You do not have a secretary, so dictation is not an alternative. Using the websites in question 3 and those in the list at the end of the chapter, supplemented by other research on the Internet, discuss the pros and cons of speech recognition. Is this a reasonable alternative to use while your hand heals? Do you think the technology has matured to the place that it will be effective?
9. As a legal assistant in a solo practitioner's office, you have approached the attorney about purchasing handheld computers for both of you so that you can more easily communicate with each other and with clients. The attorney is concerned about security regarding handheld computers. He would like to know answers to the following questions: (a) If the device gets lost, can just anyone pick it up and have access to the information (and if so, is there any precautions that can be taken to reduce this risk)? (b) How secure is

information when using wireless services such as wireless email? (c) Assuming the security issues can be solved, what are the latest features being offered in these devices?

10. You are a legal assistant for a firm that specializes in product liability. Your firm is getting ready to file a large class-action lawsuit against an automobile manufacturer for negligence regarding the design of a recent car. The suit will involve working with up to ten separate co-counsels and hundreds of plaintiffs. The firm is considering using an extranet to help coordinate information and strategies with plaintiffs and co-counsel. Using a general search engine such as google.com or yahoo.com or the sites in Question 3 above, discuss what extranets are, whether an extranet might be useful in this case, and what benefits it would bring. Discuss any disadvantages you discover as well.
11. The twenty-attorney law firm you work for as a legal assistant is considering an intranet. However, the firm wants to implement it only if there will be a cost savings to the firm. By implementing an intranet, what cost savings might there be? Use the sites in Question 3 or a general search engine to assist you.
12. Microsoft is continually updating its Windows operating system software and Office application programs. Go to their website at <http://www.microsoft.com> and comment on the latest version(s) of the program that they are releasing.
13. You work in a legal aid society in a major city. Lately, the staff is frustrated because it has become increasingly difficult as the office has grown to find the office's word-processing documents with any degree of certainty. For example, you know that an attorney in the office recently represented a client regarding a landlord/tenant issue where the attorney filed an extensive brief on the matter. Your supervising attorney asked you to find the brief so she can use it to help a client who has recently come into the office, but you cannot locate it. The office files word-processing documents in a directory under the user's last name, but you can't seem to find it. What type of software might the office want to investigate? Using general search engines, the sites at the end of the chapter, or other sites, search for software that might help the office share files efficiently.
14. A friend of yours that you know from your local legal assistant association just told you about how his firm was attacked by an aggressive virus. The virus brought the computer systems to a halt and it took two days to finally get the computers back up. It was a nightmare. Your firm seems unconcerned with viruses and takes no precautions whatsoever to guard against them. Prepare a short memo to your supervising attorney about the threat. Include facts and figures from the Internet and other sources regarding this threat and make recommendations about how the firm might want to protect its network, electronic mail, and other computer systems.
15. Using the Internet, research the concept of the "paperless office." How does it work, and what technologies are involved? What policies and procedures must be put in place? Is it more or less expensive than hard copy? Write a two-page paper summarizing your results.
16. You just started as a new legal assistant at a small law firm with four attorneys. One of the reasons you were hired was because of your familiarity with computers and technology. While you have been given a number of cases to work on with your supervising attorney, she also has asked you if you know anything about VoIP and how it works. Prepare a two-page memorandum to her regarding the advantages and the disadvantages of VoIP.

QUESTIONS AND EXERCISES

1. What policies and procedures could be put in place that could limit an employee's ability to download and subsequently successfully use large amounts of client data when they leave a law firm to practice elsewhere?
2. Can you see any downside to the "virtual law office" keeping legal professionals connected to the office and to clients at all times?
3. Some law firms continue to use WordPerfect as their word processing program. Many corporate clients use Word. Because clients and legal professionals often exchange documents over email, what kind of problems do you think can occur? In the real world, do client expectations dictate what software a law firm can use?
4. Visit a law office, school, or other business in your area and ask what security precautions they have taken to secure the integrity of their data.
5. Assume that you have started working as a legal assistant at a judge advocate's office in the military.

You have noticed a general ambivalence toward other staff members copying software. Your supervising attorney has noticed it as well and asks you to do some research on the problem. Prepare a brief memo that explains the matter together with any liability risks the office might have. In addition to the liability issues, are there any ethical issues involved?

6. Write a two-page memorandum regarding the ethical rules in your state regarding a law firm's duty to safeguard client information that is stored electronically. What are the rules that might apply? Are there any exceptions for accidental disclosure?

ENDNOTES

[1] "Law Practice Benchmark," *Law Practice*, July/August 2005, 9.
[2] Sarah K. Cron, "Technology to Go," *Legal Assistant Today*, May/June 2006, 57.
[3] Dennis Kennedy, "Need a Newer Model," *Law Office Computing*, December/January 2006, 77.
[4] Eric H. Steele and Thomas Scharbach, "Planning Your Technology Future: Top Trends to Focus on Now," *Law Practice Management*, November/December 2001, 16.
[5] Karen Coleman, "Firm Technology Growth Continues," *Law Office Computing*, December/January 2002, 22.
[6] Thomas Baird, "Paperless and Loving it," *Texas Bar Journal*, July 2005, 591.
[7] Ari Kaplan, "A Formula for Success," *Legal Assistant Today*, July/August 2005, 60.
8 "Videoconferencing Success," *Law Technology News*, October 2005, 42.
[9] "4 Tech Attorneys Take on 5 Mobile Gadgets," *Law Office Computing*, April/May 2002, 63.
[10] "Technology in Practice," *Law Practice Management*, April 2002, 20.
[11] Tracie L. Thompson, "Twenty-Four Hours a Day, Seven Days a Week," *California Lawyer*, January 2002, 20.
[12] "Desktops v. Laptops v. Handhelds," *Law Office Computing*, April/May 2002, 14–15.
[13] Eric H. Steele and Thomas Scharbach, "Planning Your Technology Future: Top Trends to Focus on Now," *Law Practice Management*, November/December 2001, 16.
[14] David Whelon, "Welcome to the Wireless World," *Law Office Computing*, April/May 2002, 57.
[15] Sarah K. Cron, "Technology to Go," *Legal Assistant Today*, May/June 2006, 59.
[16] "Securing Your Computer Applications, Records and System," May 12, 2006, 2006 API Annual Conference on Prepaid Legal Services, ABA Legal Technology Resource Center.
[17] "Avoiding Technology Traps," *Legal Assistant Today*, May/June 2006, 12.
[18] Joseph L. Kashi and Thomas Boedeker, "Saving Private Data," *Law Office Computing*, December/January 2003, 26.
[19] Michael Tamburo, "Can Your Firm Survive a System Meltdown," *Law Practice Management*, January/February 2002, 13.
[20] Ross L. Kodner, "Bet-the-Firm Backups," *Law Practice Management*, April 2001, 21.
[21] Ross L. Kodner, "Covering Your Assets," *Law Office Computing*, October/November 2005, 67.
[22] Debra Levy Martinelli, "Security Warrior," *Law Office Computing*, August/September 2002, 75–76.
[23] Kathryn A. Thompson, "The World of Ethics and Technology Collide," *Legal Assistant Today*, September/October 2005, 60.
[24] Mark Rown, "Fending Off Viruses," *Law Office Computing*, February/March 2002.
[25] Jeff Beard, "Enhancing Mobile Security," *Law Office Computing*, February/March, 2006, 63.
[26] "What Legal Experts Are Saying," *Law Practice Management*, April 2002, 20.
[27] Jeff Beard, "Enhancing Mobile Security," *Law Office Computing*, February/March, 2006, 62.
[28] Kevin Lee Thomason, "The Handheld Law Firm," *Law Office Computing*, February/March 2001, 36.
[29] Brett Burney, "The Piracy Problem," *Law Office Computing*, August/September 2005, 85, 86.
[30] Ron Friedmann, "Technology Developments that Will Change Your Practice," *College of Law Practice Management News*, Spring 2005.
[31] Milton Hooper, "A Document Management System Can Be Your Most Valuable Player," *Law Office Computing*, October/November 2002, 70.
[32] "Flawless Functionality," *Law Office Computing*, June/July 2005, 54.

CHAPTER 

Word Processing, PDF File Creation, and Document Assembly

CHAPTER OBJECTIVES

After completing Chapter 3, you should be able to do the following:

1. Describe centralized and decentralized word processing.
2. Describe major features found in word-processing programs.
3. Explain how word processors are used by legal assistants.
4. Discuss ethical problems related to word processing.
5. Identify what a PDF file is and how PDF files are created.
6. Explain what document assembly is and how it works.

word-processing software
Program used to edit, manipulate, and revise text to create documents.

Portable Document Format (PDF)
A file format developed by Adobe Systems, Inc. for sharing files independently of the application that created the file or the application's operating system.

document assembly software
Software that creates powerful standardized templates and forms.

This chapter introduces the fundamentals of word processing, Portable Document Format (PDF) file creation, and document assembly. **Word-processing software** is used to edit, manipulate, and revise text to create documents. It is one of the most widely used types of application software in legal organizations. It is also one of the application programs most used by practicing legal assistants. Legal assistants use word processors to type memos, correspondence, form letters, deposition summaries, discovery documents, and other legal documents. **Portable Document Format (PDF)** is a file format developed by Adobe Systems for sharing files independently of the application that created the file or the application's operating system. The PDF file format is the de facto standard for digital document distribution, including for filing documents electronically with courts. **Document assembly software** creates powerful standardized templates and forms. Users create forms and templates and then respond to a series of questions and prompts. The document assembly program then merges the forms with the answers and builds completed documents. Many legal organizations incorporate document assembly into their practices, particularly in areas that have well-structured routine forms and templates to complete.

CENTRALIZED AND DECENTRALIZED WORD PROCESSING

Legal organizations use varied approaches to word processing, including centralized, decentralized, or a combination of both.

Centralized Word Processing

With a **centralized word-processing system**, a legal organization has a separate word-processing department where correspondence, memorandums, and other documents in the office are typed. For example, a large firm with a centralized word processing system might require its litigation, tax, and corporate law departments to send all their major word-processing requests to the word processing department.

centralized word-processing system
A system where all the word-processing documents for an organization are typed in one single location or by one department (i.e., a word-processing department).

Most word-processing departments, sometimes called word-processing centers, have a trained staff that does nothing but type documents. They use a standardized form for requesting their services. When a document has been typed and printed, it is then sent back to the originating party for corrections and for distribution. Such centralized word-processing departments are most often found in large firms.

Decentralized Word Processing

With a **decentralized word processing system**, individuals perform word processing for themselves, for another person, or for a small group. For example, it is common for legal assistants, law clerks, legal secretaries, and attorneys to perform some or all of their own word processing. Inexpensive microcomputers have made decentralized word processing possible. Many firms are able to place inexpensive microcomputers on the desks of most staff, thus creating a decentralized system. In the past, attorneys rarely, if ever, did their own word processing. Now it is very common.

decentralized word processing system
A system where individuals or separate departments in an organization perform their own word processing.

Today, many small law firms use a decentralized word-processing system. Large firms, which have traditionally used centralized word processing, now have a combination of the two. It is common for large firms to have a word-processing center while still allowing legal professionals to do some of their own word-processing.

LEGAL WORD-PROCESSING PROGRAMS—MICROSOFT WORD vs. COREL WORDPERFECT

The leading word-processing programs for legal organizations are Microsoft Word and Corel WordPerfect. Microsoft has two versions of Word that are popular in the legal field, Word 2007 and Word 2003. Word 2007 is the latest release. It represents a major change in the Word interface. Word 2007 uses a "ribbon" (see Exhibit 3–1) that is packed with tools that the user can change based on what the user is doing. There are eight different ribbon selections available (see Exhibit 3–1). Word 2007 also includes a "quick access toolbar" that the user can customize (see Exhibit 3–1). One of the major differences between Word 2007 and other versions of Word is that the drop-down menus that have been a staple of Word were eliminated. Word 2003, like earlier versions of Word, uses an interface that includes drop-down menus and a static toolbar (see Exhibit 3–1A).

Another major change in Word 2007 is that the file format in which documents are saved has been revised. The default file format in Word 2007 is ".docx" (e.g., "letter.docx"). For many years, Word has saved documents with the ".doc" file extension (e.g., "letter.doc). Word 2007 offers users the option of saving documents in the older ".doc" file format, but if this is done some Word 2007 options are not available.

Word 2007 documents saved in the newer ".docx" file format cannot be opened in previous versions of Word (including Word 2003) without a conversion utility. Because of the large change in the interface, file-saving issues, and

Exhibit 3–1
Microsoft Word 2007
Microsoft product screen shot reprinted by permission from Microsoft Corporation.

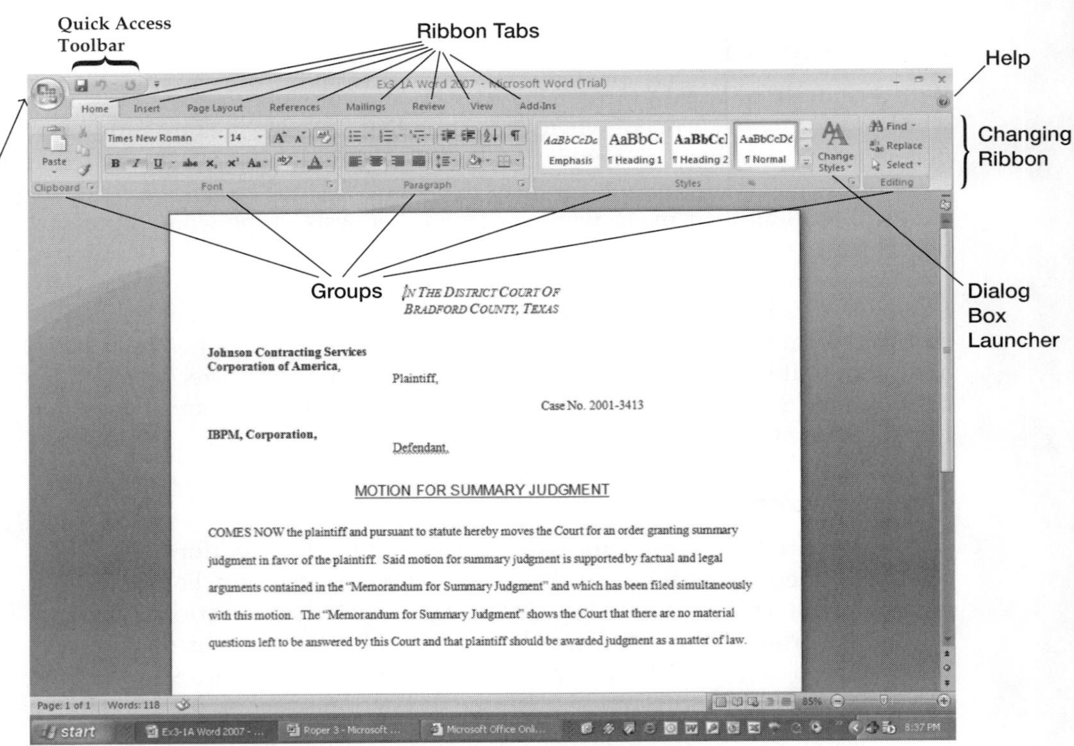

because law firms are sometimes notoriously slow in moving to expensive new software, particularly software that staff is trained on and accustomed to, both versions of Word will most likely be used by the legal industry for years to come.

Corel WordPerfect X3 is another word-processing program that is found in many legal organizations (see Exhibit 3–2). It uses a drop-down menu interface similar to that of Word 2003.

Exhibit 3–1A
Microsoft Word 2003
Microsoft product screen shot reprinted by permission from Microsoft Corporation.

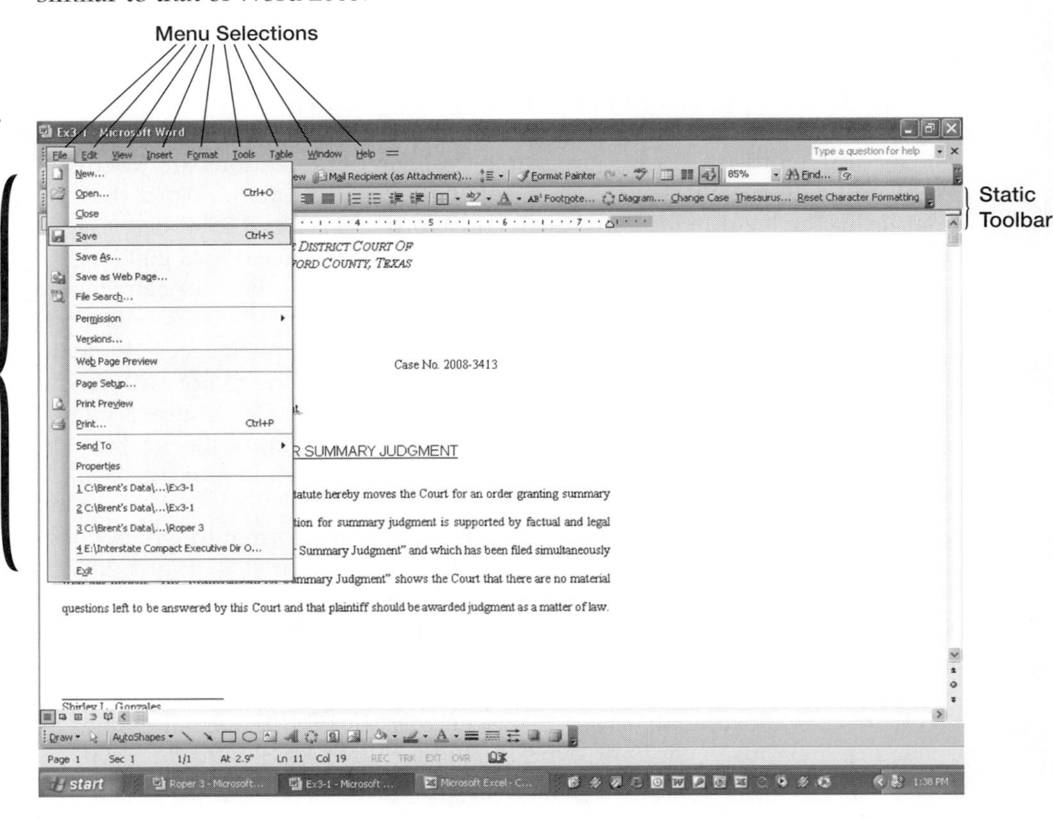

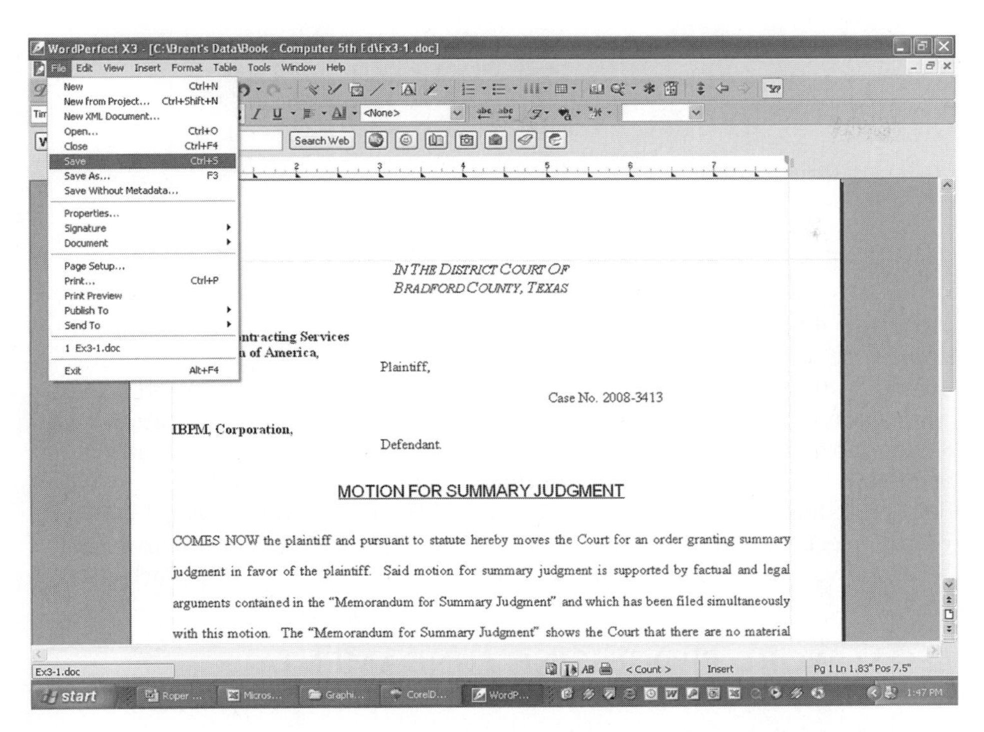

Exhibit 3–2
Corel WordPerfectX3

Extensive hands-on exercises are included for all three programs at the end of this chapter. The programs have somewhat similar features, including some designed specifically for the legal market. Word and WordPerfect are each sold as part of a suite of other products that are typically bundled with them, including a spreadsheet program, a database program, email and scheduling software, and a presentation graphics program. Screen shots from all three programs are used in this chapter.

According to a recent survey, approximately 53 percent of all legal organizations use Microsoft Word for word processing versus 47 percent using Corel WordPerfect (see Exhibit 3–3). Notice in Exhibit 3–4 that when legal assistants were recently surveyed that Microsoft Word was by far the overall winner by a large margin. Also, notice in Exhibit 3–4 that the totals add up to more than 100 percent, which indicates that some legal assistants are using both word-processing programs to some extent. This commonly occurs when a law office's primary word processor is Corel WordPerfect but corporate clients want to see word-processing file attachments in Word. Thus, in some legal organizations, it is necessary to have a working knowledge of both programs.

In the mid 1980s and early 1990s, before the dominance of Microsoft Windows, many legal organizations purchased and used WordPerfect because of its simple interface and ease of use. Some legal organizations have stayed with WordPerfect for these reasons and because their staff now know the program well and do not want to learn Word. Since the late 1990s, Microsoft Word has been the dominant word processor in the larger business community and many law offices have switched to Word because an overwhelming majority of their corporate clients use Microsoft Office products including Word. That said, both

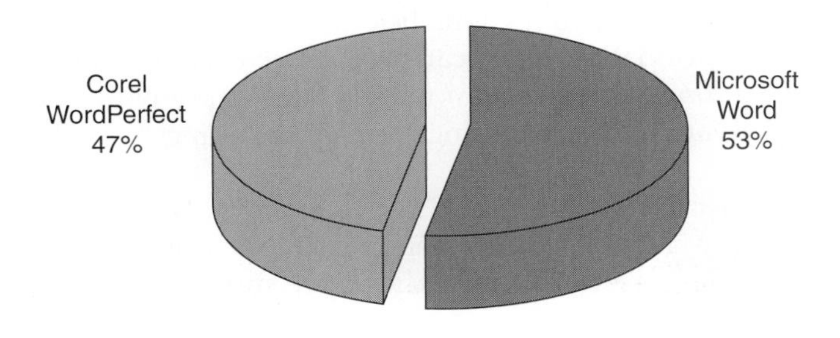

Exhibit 3–3
Word-Processing Legal Market Share
"11th Annual Readers' Choice Awards," *Law Office Computing, August / September* 2005, 61.

Exhibit 3–4

Legal Assistant Word-Processor Use

As seen in the May/June 2006 issue of Legal Assistant Today, Copyright 2006 James Publishing, Inc. Reprinted courtesy of LEGAL ASSISTANT TODAY magazine. For subscription information call (800) 394-2626, or visit www.legalassistanttoday.com.

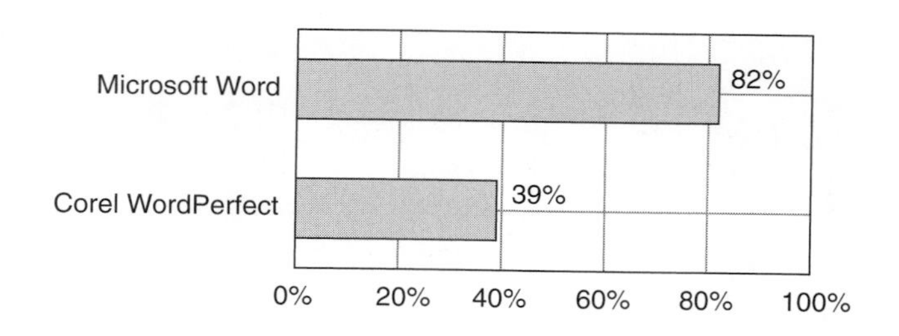

Word (no matter what version is used) and WordPerfect offer an incredible number of features and options and are capable of meeting the word-processing needs of just about any legal organization. Which program is used typically comes down to personal preference and whether the legal organization wants to standardize to Microsoft products for ease of use with their corporate clients. See Exhibits 3–5, 3–5A, and 3–6 for quick reference guides to Word and WordPerfect. Exhibit 3–7 shows a comparison of features between Word 2007 and WordPerfect X3 and how they can be accessed by each program, and Exhibit 3–7A shows a comparison of the features of Word 2003 and WordPerfect X3.

LEGAL WORD PROCESSING FUNDAMENTALS

Legal organizations use a variety of basic and advanced word-processing features and techniques. This includes basic editing functions such as copying, pasting, deleting, inserting, formatting text, and printing, among others. Legal organizations also use some basic functions such as page numbering, footnoting, and tables to the extreme. It is not uncommon for legal documents to be in the hundreds of pages, for a single footnote to run across several pages in a document, or for a table to be extremely complex. Legal organizations also use advanced word processing features such as tables of authorities, macros, and merges. A number of these types of features are covered in this section.

Automatic Paragraph Numbering

Most word processors have an automatic paragraph numbering feature that allows users to automatically number paragraphs and lists of information. This feature is used extensively in legal organizations because information is routinely presented in a hierarchical format (e.g., 1, 2, 3 or A, B, C). Using the automatic paragraph numbering feature, users can add or delete information on the list and the program will automatically renumber the list. If the list is entered manually, each time the user adds or deletes information from the list, the user needs to renumber the list. For example, notice in Exhibit 3–8 that the headings "A. Introduction" and "B. Jurisdiction" are in a hierarchical format as well as the list "1), 2) and 3)." If, for example after "A. Introduction," the user created a new topic, "B. Venue," the program would automatically renumber "Jurisdiction" to be "C. Jurisdiction." This can be a large time-saving feature in legal organizations where motions and briefs can be extremely long and complex and have many levels of hierarchical information. Users can even set up custom paragraph numbering schemes, including setting custom margins to comply with local court rules and employing a variety of numbering formats including "1.", "I.", "A.", "a)", and others.

style
A named set of formatting characteristics that users apply to text.

Styles A **style** is a named set of formatting characteristics that users apply to text. Using styles, users can quickly apply multiple formatting to text

Exhibit 3–5

Word 2007 Quick Reference Guide

HOME RIBBON

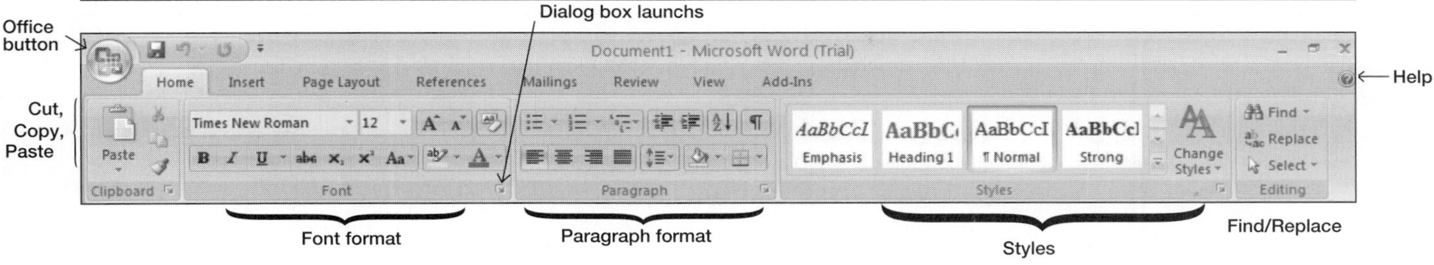

NAVIGATION

Up 1 Screen	[Page Up]	Beginning of Document	[Ctrl]+[Home]
Down 1 Screen	[Page Down]	End of Document	[Ctrl]+[End]
Beginning of a Line	[Home]	Go To	[F5]
End of a Line	[End]		

KEYBOARD SHORTCUTS

Copy Text	[Ctrl]+[C]	Undo a Command	[Ctrl]+[Z]
Paste Text	[Ctrl]+[V]	Redo / Repeat	[Ctrl]+[Y]
Cut Text	[Ctrl]+[X]	Print a Document	[Ctrl]+[P]
Bold Text	[Ctrl]+[B]	Save a Document	[Ctrl]+[S]
Underline Text	[Ctrl]+[U]	Select Everything	[Ctrl]+[A]
Italics Text	[Ctrl]+[I]	Open File	[Ctrl]+[O]
Find / Replace	[Ctrl]+[F]	New File	[Ctrl]+[N]
Go To	[Ctrl]+[G]	Reveal Formatting	[Shift]+[F1]
Spell, Grammar Check	[F7]	Hide Ribbon	[Ctrl]+[F1]

WORD FEATURE	COMMAND STRUCTURE
Attach Document to an Email	Office Button, Send, Email
Change Case of Text	Home, Font, Change Case
Clear all Formatting of Text	Home, Font, Clear Formatting
Clip Art from Internet (Inserting)	Insert, Illustrations, Clip Art, Clip Art on Office Online
Clip Art / Files / Charts, Shapes (Inserting)	Insert, Illustrations
Compare Documents	Review, Compare
Find / Replace	Home, Editing, Find / Replace
Font Control	Home, Font
Footnotes / Endnotes	References, Footnotes, Insert Footnotes
Header / Footer	Insert, Header & Footer, Header or Footer
Indent text	Home, Paragraph, Dialog Box Launcher
Line Spacing Changes	Home, Paragraph, Line Spacing
Macros	View, Macros
Mail Merge	Mailings, Start Mail Merge
Margins, Paper Orientation	Page Layout, Page Setup, Margins
Shading	Home, Paragraph, Shading
Styles	Home, Styles
Tables (Inserting)	Home, Insert, Tables
Tabs	Home, Paragraph, Dialog Box Launcher, Indents and spacing, Tabs
Track Changes	Review, Tracking, Track Changes
New Document	Office Button, New
Open (Existing) document	Office Button, Open
Save a document	Office Button, Save
Print and Print Preview	Office Button, Print
Table of Authorities	References, Table of Authorities

Exhibit 3–5A

Word 2003 Quick Reference Guide

STANDARD TOOLBAR

New Blank Document, Open, Save, E-mail, Print, Print Preview, Spell Check, Research, Cut, Copy, Paste, Format Painter, Undo, Redo, Insert Hyperlink, Tables and Borders, Insert Table, Insert Work sheet, Columns, Drawing, Zoom, Show / Hide, Reading View, Help, Style, Font, Font Size, Bold, Italic, Underline, Left, Center, Right, Justify, Numbering

NAVIGATION

Up 1 Screen	[Page Up]	Beginning of Document	[Ctrl]+[Home]
Down 1 Screen	[Page Down]	End of Document	[Ctrl]+[End]
Beginning of a Line	[Home]	Go To	[F5]
End of a Line	[End]		

KEYBOARD SHORTCUTS

Copy Text	[Ctrl]+[C]	Undo a Command	[Ctrl]+[Z]
Paste Text	[Ctrl]+[V]	Redo / Repeat	[Ctrl]+[Y]
Cut Text	[Ctrl]+[X]	Print a Document	[Ctrl]+[P]
Bold Text	[Ctrl]+[B]	Save a Document	[Ctrl]+[S]
Underline Text	[Ctrl]+[U]	Select Everything	[Ctrl]+[A]
Italics Text	[Ctrl]+[I]	Open (Existing) File	[Ctrl]+[O]
Find / Replace	[Ctrl]+[F]	New File	[Ctrl]+[N]
Go To	[Ctrl]+[G]	Reveal Formatting	[Shift]+[F1]
Spell, Grammar Check	[F7]	Task Pane	[Ctrl]+[F1]

WORD FEATURE	COMMAND STRUCTURE
Attach Document to an Email	File, Send to, Mail Recipient (as Attachment)
Change Case of Text	Format, Change Case
Character Spacing	Format, Font, Character Spacing
Clear All Formatting of Text	Edit, Clear, Formats
Clip Art from Internet (Inserting)	Insert, Picture, Clip Art, Clip Art on Office Online
Clip Art / Files / Charts (Inserting)	Insert, Picture
Compare Documents	Tools, Compare and Merge Documents
Find / Replace	Edit, Find or Replace
Font Control	Format, Font
Footnotes / Endnotes	Insert, Reference, Footnote
Header / Footer	View, Header / Footer
Indent Text	Format, Paragraph, Indent
Line Spacing Changes	Format, Paragraph, Spacing
Macros	Tools, Macro
Mail Merge	Tools, Letters and Mailings, Mail Merge
Margins, Paper Orientation	File, Page Setup
Shading	Format, Borders and Shading, Shading
Styles	Format, Styles and Formatting
Tables (Inserting)	Tables, Insert
Tabs	Format, Tabs
Text Effects (Blinking, Las Vegas, etc.)	Format, Font, Text Effects
Toolbar Selection	View, Toolbars
Track Changes	Tools, Track Changes
Widow Control, Orphan Control, Keeping Lines Together	Format, Paragraph, Line and Page Breaks, Widow / Orphan Control or Keep Lines Together

Exhibit 3–6

WordPerfect X3 Quick Reference Guide

STANDARD TOOLBAR

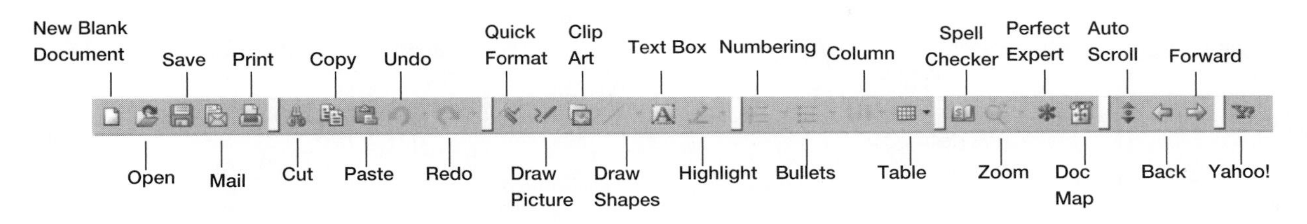

NAVIGATION

Up 1 Screen	[Page Up]	Beginning of Document	[Ctrl]+[Home]
Down 1 Screen	[Page Down]	End of Document	[Ctrl]+[End]
Beginning of a line	[Home]	Go To	[Ctrl]+[G]
End of a line	[End]	Page Up	[Alt]+[Page Up]
		Page Down	[Alt]+[Page Down]

KEYBOARD SHORTCUTS

Copy Text	[Ctrl]+[C]	Undo a Command	[Ctrl]+[Z]
Paste Text	[Ctrl]+[V]	Redo / Repeat	[Ctrl]+[Shift]-[Z]
Cut Text	[Ctrl]+[X]	Print a Document	[Ctrl]+[P] or [F5]
Bold Text	[Ctrl]+[B]	Save a Document	[Ctrl]+[S]
Underline text	[Ctrl]+[U]	Select Everything	[Ctrl]+[A]
Italics Text	[Ctrl]+[I]	Open File	[Ctrl]+[O]
Find / Replace	[Ctrl]+[F]	New File	[Ctrl]+[N]
Go To	[Ctrl]+[G]	Reveal Codes	[Alt]+[F3]
Spelling, Grammar Checker	[Ctrl]+[F1]	Symbol (Insert)	[Ctrl]+[W]
Font Change	[F9]	Margins	[Ctrl]+[F8]
Indent Paragraph	[F7]	Styles	[Alt]+[F8]
Double Indent	[Ctrl]+[Shift]+[F7]	Table (Create)	[F12]
Merge	[Shift]+[F9]	Delete to end of line	[Ctrl]+[Delete]
Change Case (Toggle)	[Ctrl]+[K]	Date [automatic - insert]	[Ctrl]+[Shift]+[D]

MENU COMMAND

PDF File (Create)	File, Publish to, PDF
Attach Document to an Email	File, Send to, Mail
Change Case of Text	Edit, Convert Case
Character Spacing	Format, Typesetting, Word / Letter Spacing
Clip Art (Inserting)	Insert, Graphics
Compare Documents	File, Document, Compare
Find / Replace	Edit, Find and Replace
Font Control	Format, Font
Footnotes / Endnotes	Insert, Footnote / Endnote
Header / Footer	Insert, Header / Footer
Indent Text	Format, Paragraph, Indent
Line Spacing Changes	Format, Line, Spacing
Macros	Tools, Macro
Mail Merge	Tools, Merge
Margins, Paper Orientation	File, Page Setup or Format, Margins
Highlighting / Shading Text	Tools, Highlight
Styles	Format, Styles
Tables (Inserting, Sorting, etc.)	Tables, Create
Track Changes	File, Document, Review

Exhibit 3–7
Comparing Word 2007 and WordPerfect X3 Features

MICROSOFT WORD 2007 FEATURE	COREL WORDPERFECT X3 FEATURE	TO ACCESS FEATURE IN WORD 2007	TO ACCESS FEATURE IN WORDPERFECT X3
AutoCorrect	QuickCorrect	Office Button, Word Options, Proofing	Tools, QuickCorrect
AutoShapes	Shapes	Insert, Illustrations, Shapes	Insert, Shapes
AutoText	QuickWords	Insert, Text, Quick Parts, Building Blocks Organizer	Tools, QuickWords
AutoRecover	Backup	Office Button, Word Options, Save, Save AutoRecover	Tools, Settings, Files, Doc
Break	New Page	Insert, Pages, Page Break	Insert, New Page
Bullets and Numbers	Bulleted, Numbered & Alphabetical Lists	Home, Paragraph	Insert, Outline / Bullets & Numbering
Change Case	Convert Case	Home, Font, Change Case	Edit, Convert Case
Character Spacing	Word and Letter Spacing	Home, Font, Dialog Box Launcher, Character Spacing	Format, Typesetting, Word / Letter Spacing
Charting	Chart	Insert, Illustrations, Chart	Insert, Chart
Comment	Comment	Review, Comments, New Comment	Insert, Comment, Create
Compare Versions	Document Compare	Review, Compare, Compare	File, Document, Compare
Drawing	Draw	Insert, Illustrations, Shapes, New Drawing Canvas	Insert, Graphics, Draw Picture
Find	Find and Replace	Home, Editing, Find	Edit, Find and Replace
Format Painter	QuickFormat	Home, Clipboard, Format Painter	QuickFormat Icon on Toolbar
Frame	Boxes	Insert, Illustrations, Shapes, New Drawing Canvas	Insert, Graphics, Custom Box
Go To	Edit, GoTo	Home, Editing, Find, Go To	Edit, Go To
Grammar	Grammatik	Review, Proofing, Spelling & Grammar	Tools, Grammatik
Header and Footer	Headers / Footers	Insert, Header and Footer	Insert, Header / Footer
Heading Numbering	Outlines, Bullets, and Numbering	Home, Paragraph, Multilevel List	Insert, Outlines / Bullets and Numbering
Hyperlink	Hyperlink	Insert, Links, Hyperlink	Tools, Hyperlink
Indentation	Indent	Home, Paragraph, Dialog Box Launcher, Indentation	Format, Paragraph, Indent
Index & Tables	Reference	Reference, Index	Tools, Reference, Index
Macro	Tools, Macro	View, Macros, Macros	Tools, Macro
Mail Recipient (As Attachment)	Emailing Documents	Office Button, Send, Email	File, Send To, Mail Recipient
Merge Documents or Mail Merge	Merge	Mailings, Start Mail Merge	Tools, Merge
Normal View	Draft and Page View	View, Document View, Draft or Print Layout, Full Screen, etc.	View, Draft or View, Page
Options	Setting	Office Button, Word Options	Tools, Settings
Page Alignment	Center Page	Page Layout, Arrange, Align	Format, Page, Center
Page Numbers	Numbering	Insert, Header & Footer, Page Number	Format, Page, Numbering
Paragraph Alignment	Justification	Home, Paragraph, General, Alignment	Format, Justification

Continued

Pleading Wizard	Pleading Expert Designer / Filler		Tools, Legal Tools, Pleading Expert Designer / Filler
Print Layout View	Page View	View, Document Views, Print Layout	View, Page
Replace	Find and Replace	Home, Editing, Replace	Edit, Find and Replace
Reveal Formatting	Reveal Codes	[SHIFT]+[F1]	View, Reveal Codes
Sorting	Sort	When Table is selected, click on "Layout" under "Table Tools" and then under "Data" click on "Sort"	Tools, Sort
Spelling	Spelling Checker	Home, Review, Proofing, Spelling & Grammar	Tools, Spell Checker
Styles	Format, Styles and Formatting	Home, Styles	Format, Styles
Table AutoFormat	Speed Format	When Table is selected, Table Styles	Table, SpeedFormat
Table of Authorities	Table of Authorities	Reference, Table of Authorities	Tools, Reference, Table of Authorities
Track Changes	Document Review	Review, Tracking, Track Changes	File, Document, Review
WordArt	TextArt	Insert, Text, WordArt	Insert, Graphics, Text Art

Exhibit 3–7A
Comparing Word 2003 and WordPerfect X3 Features

MICROSOFT WORD 2007 FEATURE	COREL WORDPERFECT X3 FEATURE	TO ACCESS FEATURE IN WORD 2007	TO ACCESS FEATURE IN WORDPERFECT X3
AutoCorrect	QuickCorrect	Tools, AutoCorrect Options	Tools, QuickCorrect
AutoShapes	Shapes	Insert, Picture, AutoShapes	Insert, Shapes
AutoText	QuickWords	Insert, AutoText	Tools, QuickWords
AutoRecover	Backup	Tools Options, Save, Save AutoRecover	Tools, Settings, Files, Doc
Break	New Page	Insert, Break	Insert, New Page
Bullets and Numbers	Bulleted, Numbered & Alphabetical Lists	Format, Bullets and Numbering	Insert, Outline / Bullets & Numbering
Change Case	Convert Case	Format, Change Case	Edit, Convert Case
Character Spacing	Word and Letter Spacing	Format, Font, Character Spacing	Format, Typesetting, Word / Letter Spacing
Charting	Chart	Insert, Picture, Chart	Insert, Chart
Comment	Comment	Insert, Comment	Insert, Comment, Create
Compare Versions	Document Compare	Tools, Compare and Merge Documents	File, Document, Compare
Drawing	Draw	Insert, Picture, New Drawing	Insert, Graphics, Draw Picture
Find	Find and Replace	Edit, Find	Edit, Find and Replace
Format Painter	QuickFormat	Format Painter Icon on Toolbar	QuickFormat Icon on Toolbar
Frame	Boxes	Insert, Picture, New Drawing	Insert, Graphics, Custom Box
Go To	Edit, GoTo	Go To	Edit, GoTo
Grammar	Grammatik	Tool, Spelling & Grammer	Tools, Grammatik
Header and Footer	Headers / Footers	View, Header and Footer	Insert, Header / Footer
Heading Numbering	Outlines, Bullets, and Numbering	Formats, Bullets and Numbering, Numbering	Insert, Outlines / Bullets and Numbering
Hyperlink	Hyperlink	Insert, Hyperlink	Tools, Hyperlink
Indentation	Indent	Format, Paragraph, Indentation	Format, Paragraph, Indent
Index & Tables	Reference	Insert, Reference, Index & Table	Tools, Reference, Index
Macro	Tools, Macro	Macro	Tools, Macro
Mail Recipient (As Attachment)	Emailing Documents	File, Sent To, Mail Recipient (as Attachment)	File, Send To, Mail Recipient
Merge Documents or Mail Merge	Merge	Tools, Letters and Mailings	Tools, Merge

Continued

MICROSOFT WORD 2007 FEATURE	COREL WORDPERFECT X3 FEATURE	TO ACCESS FEATURE IN WORD 2007	TO ACCESS FEATURE IN WORDPERFECT X3
Normal View	Draft and Page View	View, Normal or View, Print Layout	View, Draft or View, Page
Options	Setting	Tools, Options	Tools, Settings
Page Alignment	Center Page	File, Page Setup, Page Vertical Alignment	Format, Page, Center
Page Numbers	Numbering	Insert Page Number	Format, Page, Numbering
Paragraph Alignment	Justification	Format, Paragraph, Alignment, Justification	Format, Justification
Pleading Wizard	Pleading Expert Designer / Filler	File, New, Templates On My Computer, Legal Pleadings, Pleading Wizard	Tools, Legal Tools, Pleading Expert Designer / Filler
Print Layout View	Page View	View, Printout	View, Page
Replace	Find and Replace	Edit, Find or Replace	Edit, Find and Replace
Reveal Formatting	Reveal Codes	Format, Reveal Formatting	View, Reveal Codes
Sorting	Sort	Table, Sort	Tools, Sort
Spelling	Spelling Checker	Tools, Spelling and Grammer	Tools, Spell Checker
Styles	Format, Styles and Formatting	Styles	Format, Styles
Table AutoFormat	Speed Format	Table, Table AutoFormat	Table, SpeedFormat
Table of Authorities	Table of Authorities	Insert Reference, Index and Tables, Table of Authorities	Tools, Reference, Table of Authorities
Tabs	Tab Set	Format, Tabs	Format, Line, Tab Set
Track Changes	Document Review	Tools, Track Changes	File, Document, Review
WordArt	TextArt	Insert, Picture, WordArt	Insert, Graphics, Text Art

quickly. For example, notice in the Exhibit 3–8 "A. Introduction" and "B. Jurisdiction" have a style applied to them titled "Heading 2." Heading 2 is bolded, underlined, small caps, and is being automatically numbered. Instead of having to go to each section heading (e.g., "A. Introduction," "B. Jurisdiction," etc.), select the text, and then enter the Bold, Underline, and Small Cap format commands and the automatic numbering command, the user can simply use the Style command, click on "Style 2," and have all of the

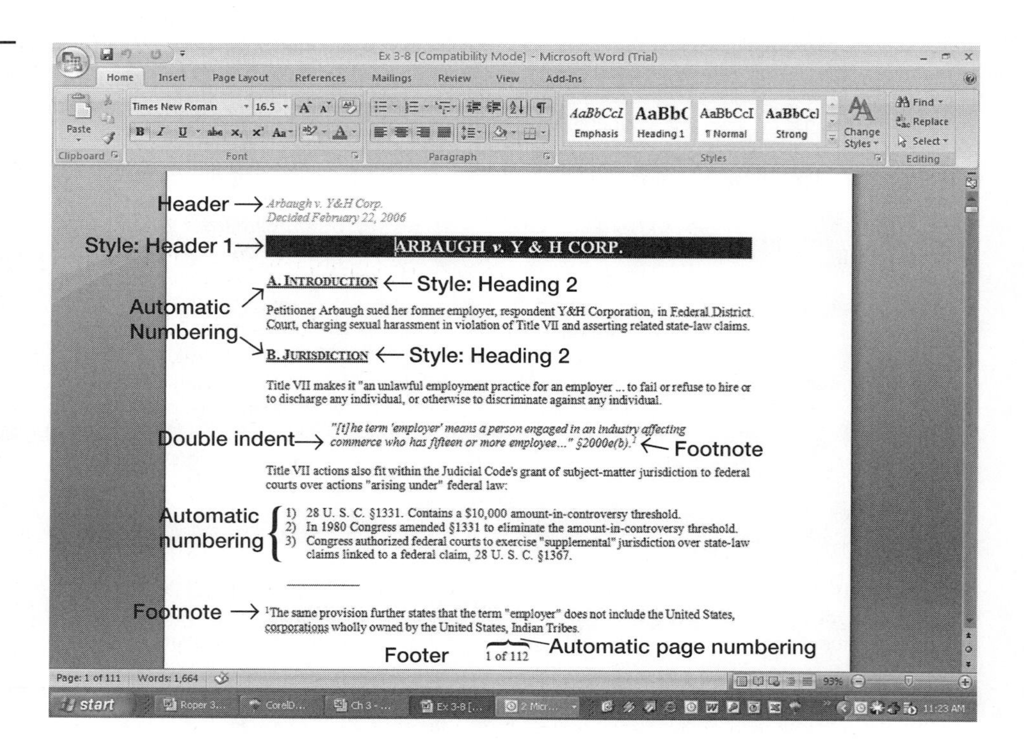

Exhibit 3–8

Word Processing: Header, Footer, Styles, Footnotes, Auto Number, Automatic Page Numbering in Word 2007

Microsoft product screen shot reprinted by permission from Microsoft Corporation.

formatting automatically applied. Styles can also be automatically changed and updated. Suppose that the user who created Exhibit 3–8 has forty section headings and now needs to change the format of all of these headings so that they are not underlined. If the user had not used the Style feature, he or she would have to go into each of the forty headings and delete the Underline command. Using the Style feature, the user can simply invoke the Style command, click on "Heading 2," use the Select All feature to automatically select all text with the "Heading 2" style, and then delete the Underline command. All "Heading 2" text is then automatically updated. The Style feature is particularly helpful in long and complex documents that have recurring elements where consistency is important. Styles are covered in detail in Lesson 6 of the Hands-On Exercises for Word 2007, Word 2003, and WordPerfect X3.

Headers and Footers A **header** is a title or heading that appears at the top of every page of a document. For instance, in Exhibit 3–8 the case name and date appear at the top of every page. A **footer** is text that appears at the bottom of every page of a document. For example, in Exhibit 3–8 a footer shows the current page number and the total number of pages of the document. Both the current page number and the total number of pages are automatically calculated by the program using an automatic page numbering feature.

header
A title or heading that appears at the top of the pages of a word processing or other type of document.

footer
Text that appears at the bottom of the pages of a document.

Automatic Page Numbering **Automatic page numbering** automatically calculates the appropriate page number on each page of a document (see Exhibit 3–8). In most word processors, you can specify where the page number should be placed on the page (e.g., centered at the bottom of the page in a footer or in the upper right corner of the header.) Using the automatic page numbering feature means that when text is added, moved, or deleted on a page, new page numbers are automatically recalculated and inserted.

automatic page numbering
A feature in a word processor that automatically numbers the pages of a document for the user.

Double Indenting Text is indented an equal distance from the left and right margins by using **double indenting** (see Exhibit 3–8). Legal assistants and attorneys use the double indent feature frequently to quote from books, cases, and other sources of reference. To use the double indent feature, go to where the double indent should start, enter the DOUBLE INDENT command, and type in the appropriate text. The text is automatically indented the same distance from the left and right margins.

double indenting
A feature in a word processor (also found in other types of programs) that indents text an equal distance from the left and right margins.

Footnotes and Endnotes A **footnote** is a numbered reference that is printed at the bottom of a page (see Exhibit 3–8). An **endnote**, like a footnote, is a numbered reference, but instead of appearing at the bottom of a page, it appears at the end of a chapter or document. Footnotes and endnotes are easy to produce in a word processor. Most word processors have an automatic footnote feature that tracks the current footnote number you are on and allows it to be printed at the bottom of the page where it is referenced. To enter a footnote, the user simply goes to the place in the text that is to be referenced. Then the user executes the footnote command. This command automatically enters the current footnote number and brings up a special footnote screen that allows the user to type the text of the footnote. When the user is done typing the footnote, the user exits the footnote feature, and the footnote is completed. Word processors automatically number the footnotes, and renumber them if necessary when footnotes are added or deleted. Footnotes and endnotes are used often in law office word processing, especially in legal briefs. Because lawyers and legal assistants must cite to the law when making an argument, footnotes and endnotes are common.

footnote
A numbered reference that is printed at the bottom of a page.

endnote
A numbered reference that is printed at the end of a chapter or document.

Electronic Distribution of Documents

Distributing documents, including word processing documents, in an electronic format is particularly important in the modern law office. For example, it is commonplace in many legal organizations to attach word-processing documents (particularly Microsoft Word documents) to emails sent to corporate clients. This allows clients to see and make revisions to legal work. Most legal organizations are also now filing documents electronically with court clerks. Most courts use the Portable Document Format (PDF) as the standard for filing documents electronically. PDF can be a secure format because recipients cannot edit the document sent (unless this functionality is enabled by the sender). As long as the recipient has a PDF viewer, the recipient can view the file on a different type or format of computer than the document was created on. PDF file creation is covered in depth later in this chapter. Some word processors can export to a PDF file from within the word processing program (see Exhibit 3–9). Users can also purchase a separate program to convert word-processing and other documents to a PDF file using a separate program, such as Adobe Acrobat (covered later in this chapter). Many word processors can also "print" to a fax machine if the necessary hardware has been installed on the user's computer.

Exhibit 3–9

Publishing Directly to PDF File in WordPerfect X3

Microsoft product screen shot reprinted by permission from Microsoft Corporation.

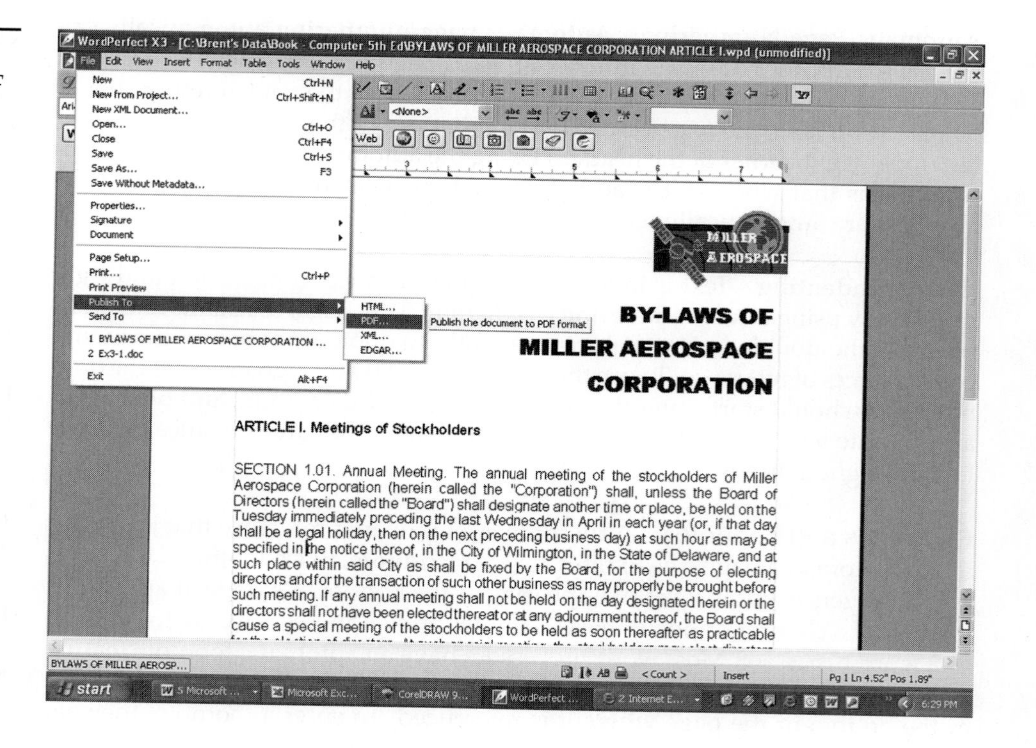

Printing

Even with the prevalence of electronic distribution of documents, printing hard copies of documents is still important. Word processors are extremely flexible when it comes to printing documents. Users can print single pages, whole documents, specific pages (e.g., 67 to 74), color, one- or two-sided pages, and much more. Many legal organizations have moved to digital printing, which allows users to access multifunction printers that can print, copy, scan, add tabs, collate, and staple. Most word processors also have a "print layout" view or a print preview command that allows the user to see the document exactly how it will be printed.

table
A word processing feature that allows the user to create a table of information using rows and columns.

Tables The **table** feature in word processors allows the user to create a table of information using rows and columns. The user can quickly organize information into columns and rows without using tabs. Exhibit 3–10 shows a somewhat complex table. Graphic lines divide the table into rows and columns. Tables can include text, numbers, and even formulas. Tables are very easy to set up in most word processors. The user simply enters the table command and tells the program how many rows and columns to start with. The user can also change the size of the columns or rows, add and delete columns or rows, split columns or rows, add color, add graphics, and include calculations. Notice in Exhibit 3–10 that graphic circles have been added to the table on the Parkinson's line. Tables are frequently used in legal word processing and have many uses. Tables are covered in detail in Lesson 4 of the Hands-On Exercises for Word 2007, Word 2003, and WordPerfect X3.

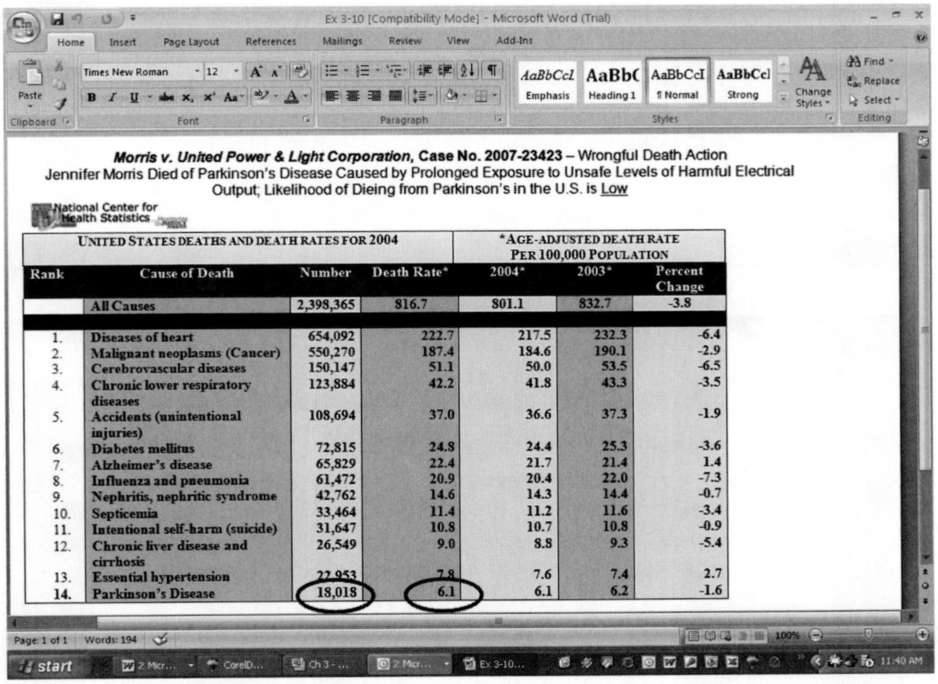

***Morris v. United Power & Light Corporation*, Case No. 2007-23423** – Wrongful Death Action
Jennifer Morris Died of Parkinson's Disease Caused by Prolonged Exposure to Unsafe Levels of Harmful Electrical Output; Likelihood of Dieing from Parkinson's in the U.S. is Low

National Center for Health Statistics

United States Deaths and Death Rates for 2004				*Age-Adjusted Death Rate per 100,000 Population		
Rank	Cause of Death	Number	Death Rate*	2004*	2003*	Percent Change
	All Causes	2,398,365	816.7	801.1	832.7	-3.8
1.	Diseases of heart	654,092	222.7	217.5	232.3	-6.4
2.	Malignant neoplasms (Cancer)	550,270	187.4	184.6	190.1	-2.9
3.	Cerebrovascular diseases	150,147	51.1	50.0	53.5	-6.5
4.	Chronic lower respiratory diseases	123,884	42.2	41.8	43.3	-3.5
5.	Accidents (unintentional injuries)	108,694	37.0	36.6	37.3	-1.9
6.	Diabetes mellitus	72,815	24.8	24.4	25.3	-3.6
7.	Alzheimer's disease	65,829	22.4	21.7	21.4	1.4
8.	Influenza and pneumonia	61,472	20.9	20.4	22.0	-7.3
9.	Nephritis, nephritic syndrome	42,762	14.6	14.3	14.4	-0.7
10.	Septicemia	33,464	11.4	11.2	11.6	-3.4
11.	Intentional self-harm (suicide)	31,647	10.8	10.7	10.8	-0.9
12.	Chronic liver disease and cirrhosis	26,549	9.0	8.8	9.3	-5.4
13.	Essential hypertension	22,953	7.8	7.6	7.4	2.7
14.	Parkinson's Disease	18,018	6.1	6.1	6.2	-1.6

Exhibit 3–10
A Table in Word 2007
Microsoft product screen shot reprinted by permission from Microsoft Corporation.

macro
A feature that records the keystrokes of a user, allows him to save those keystrokes, and then allows him to play those keystrokes back.

Macros A **macro** records the keystrokes of a user, allows him or her to save those keystrokes, and then allows him or her to play those keystrokes back. For example, a user might create a macro for the legal organization's name or to close a letter (see Exhibit 3–11). Notice in the top screen of Exhibit 3–11 that the user has created a macro entitled "LetterClosing." The macro includes the standard closing language of a letter and a signature block. From then on, the user never has to retype the closing language and signature block of a letter. At the end of a letter, such as the bottom screen of Exhibit 3–11, the user simply runs the macro and the macro does the rest. Macros increase productivity and efficiency, because users do not have to keep keying in repetitious material. Macros can also be created to perform word-processing commands. Macros can be created by invoking the new macro command and recording the new macro. The recording feature records the user's keystrokes and commands, and then saves them to the file name the user gives the macro. To play the macro, the user simply invokes the play macro command and enters the macro's name. Macros are an extremely handy and time-saving feature. Macros are covered in detail in Lesson 12 of the Hands-On Exercises for Word 2007, Word 2003, and WordPerfect X3.

Comments, Comparing Documents, and Track Changes Word processors allow groups of people to collaborate effectively using a number of features and

Exhibit 3–11

Macro in Word 2003

Microsoft product screen shot reprinted by permission from Microsoft Corporation.

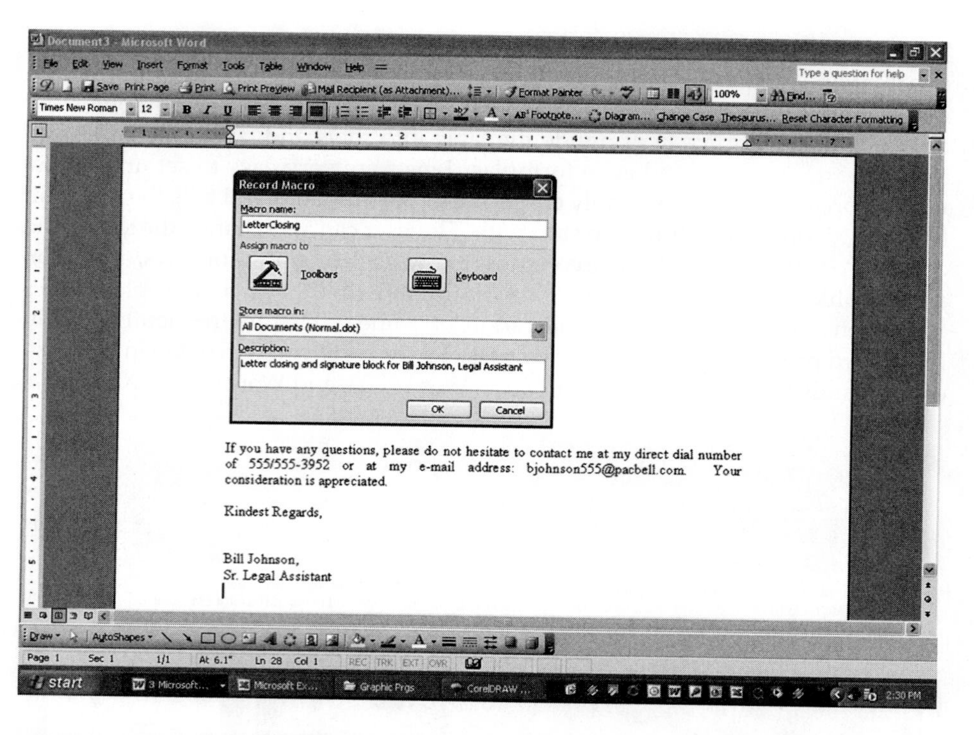

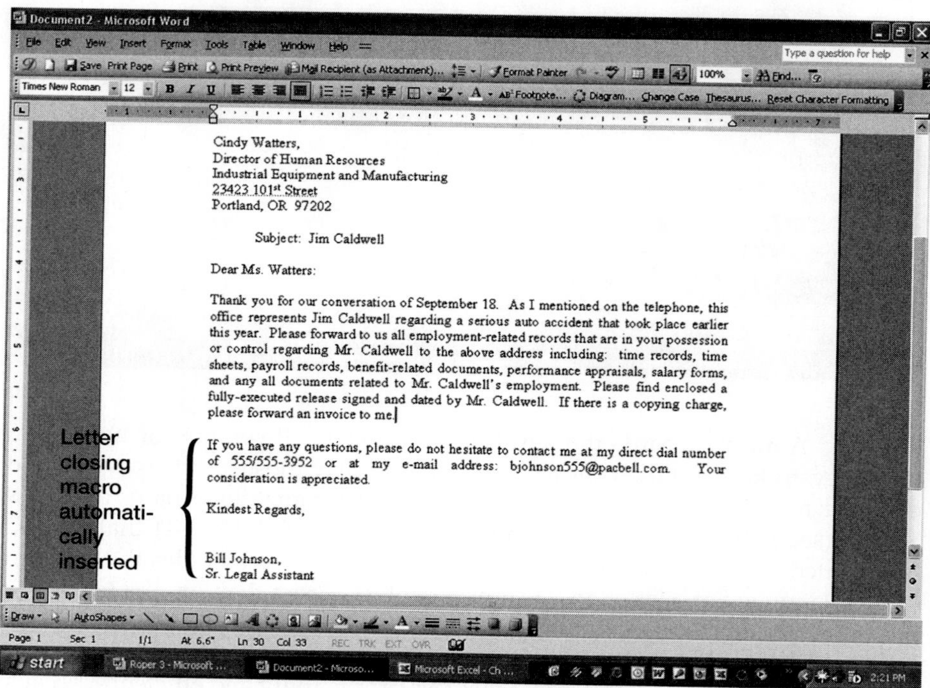

comment
The comment feature in a word processor allows a user to annotate and create notes in a document without changing the text of the document.

compare documents
The compare document feature in a word processor allows a user to compare and contrast two documents, either side by side or by blacklining.

tools, including comments, compare documents, and track changes. The **comment** feature allows a user to annotate and make notes or comments in a document without actually changing it. Notice in Exhibit 3–12 that the reviewer has made a comment, which includes several suggestions, to the user's document. The user can then make changes and delete the comment or respond to the reviewer by editing the comment with his or her own opinion.

The **compare documents** feature allows a user to compare two separate word processing files. Most word processors can do this a couple of ways, including allowing simultaneous viewing of the files or producing a third

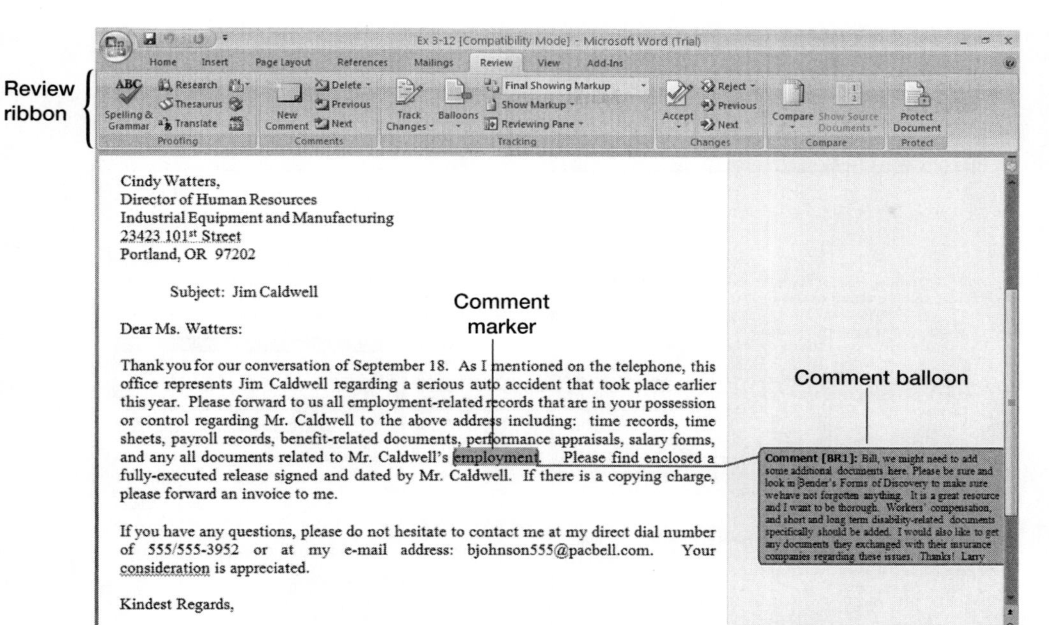

Exhibit 3–12
Adding a Comment to a Document in Word 2007
Microsoft product screen shot reprinted by permission from Microsoft Corporation.

document that shows the differences between the two versions. Notice in the first screen in Exhibit 3–13 that two similar but different documents are being viewed. The second document adds a paragraph at the beginning of the document, but other than that it is substantially similar. Using this method a user can view two documents at the same time to distinguish differences. The user can also set the word processor to synchronize the documents so they scroll side by side as the user moves through the documents.

Another way to compare documents is for the word processor to blackline the documents. Notice in the bottom screen of Exhibit 3–13 that the two documents have been compared but, this time, the word processor has placed them in a new document and has showed what was added to and deleted from the first document. The compare documents feature can be very useful in many legal organizations. The compare document feature is covered in detail in Lesson 8 of the Hands-On Exercises for Word 2007, Word 2003, and WordPerfect X3.

Another way for users to use word processors in a collaborative way is to use track changes. **Track changes** allows reviewers to make changes to the document that later can either be accepted or rejected by the user. For example, suppose an attorney asks a legal assistant to write a draft of a pleading. The legal assistant drafts the pleading; then the attorney turns on the track changes feature and makes changes right in the document itself (see Exhibit 3–14). Notice in Exhibit 3–14 that the user has received the changes back from the attorney with information inserted and deleted. The user can then accept all of the changes at one time, reject all of the changes at one time, or go through the changes one by one and accept or reject them. In some instances documents are reviewed by multiple people including attorneys, co-counsel, and clients. Most word processors can accommodate reviews by multiple parties by assigning different colors to each reviewer. The user can then easily determine who made each change. WordPerfect refers to track changes as Document Review. Track changes (and Document Review in WordPerfect) are covered in detail in Lesson 9 of the Hands-On Exercises for Word 2007, Word 2003, and WordPerfect X3.

track changes
Feature that allows reviewers to recommend changes to a word-processing document that later can be either accepted or rejected by the original author.

Exhibit 3–13
Comparing Documents—Simultaneous Viewing and Blacklining in Word 2003
Microsoft product screen shot reprinted by permission from Microsoft Corporation.

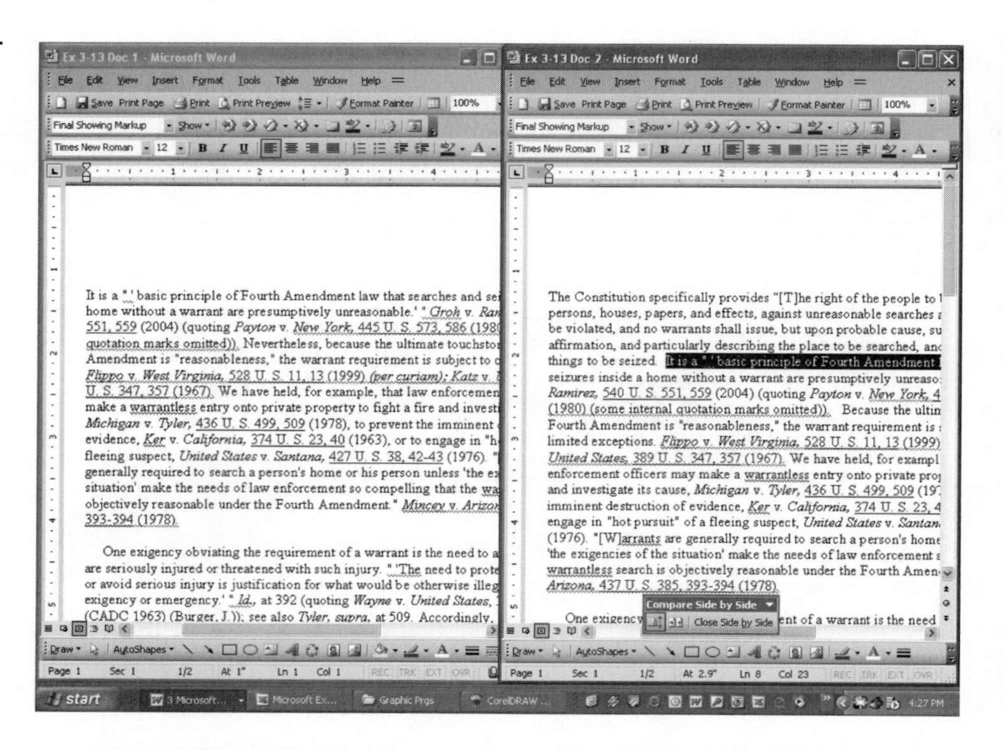

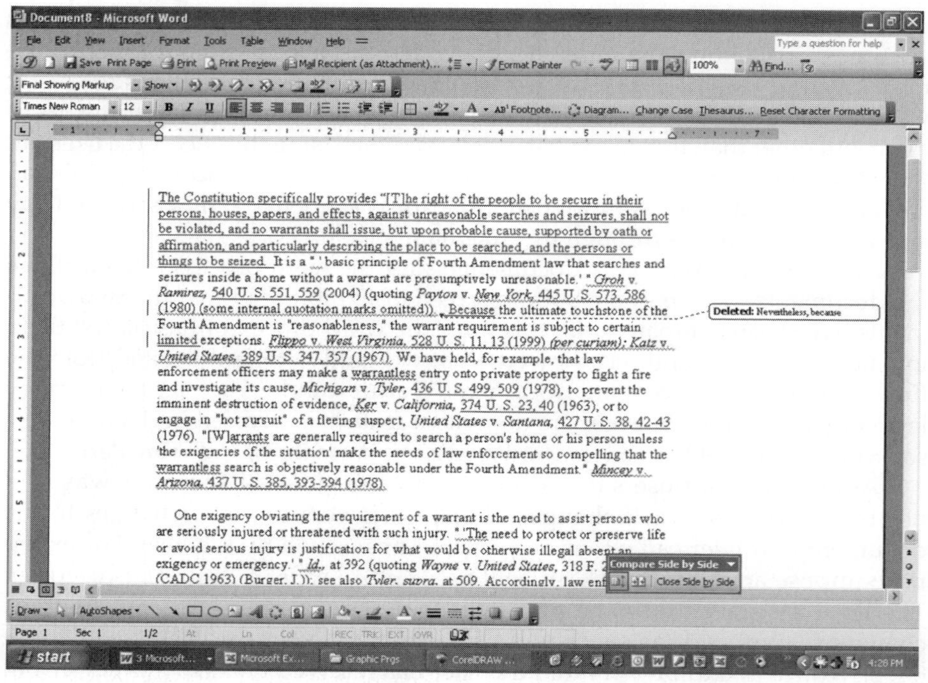

table of authorities
An automated feature in word processors that allows the program to generate an accurate table of authorities.

Table of Authorities Most word processors have automated features for creating a table of authorities (commonly referred to as TOA or TA). A **table of authorities** is a section in a legal document or brief that lists the cases, statutes, and other documents referenced in the legal document or brief. A table of authorities is similar to a table of contents except that instead of listing the contents of the document with page numbers, it lists cases and other reference material and page numbers that appear in the document. Tables of authorities are typically created by marking all of the case citations and then generating the table itself near the beginning of the document (see Exhibit 3–15). The table of

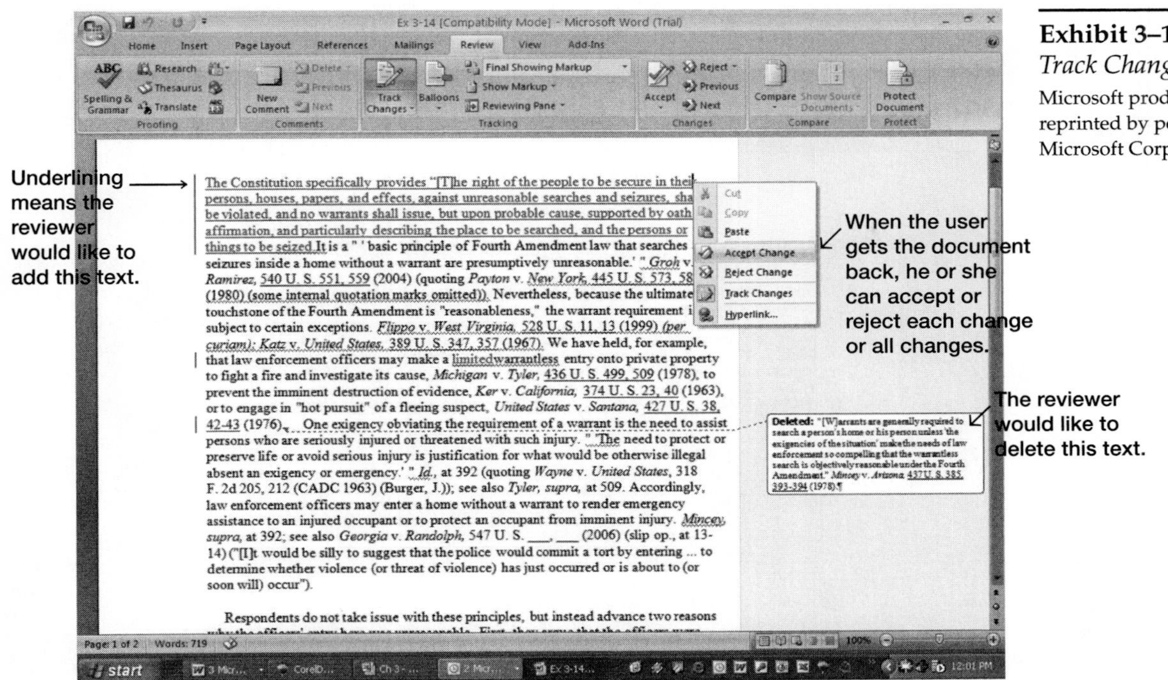

Underlining means the reviewer would like to add this text.

The reviewer would like to delete this text.

Exhibit 3–14
Track Changes in Word 2007
Microsoft product screen shot reprinted by permission from Microsoft Corporation.

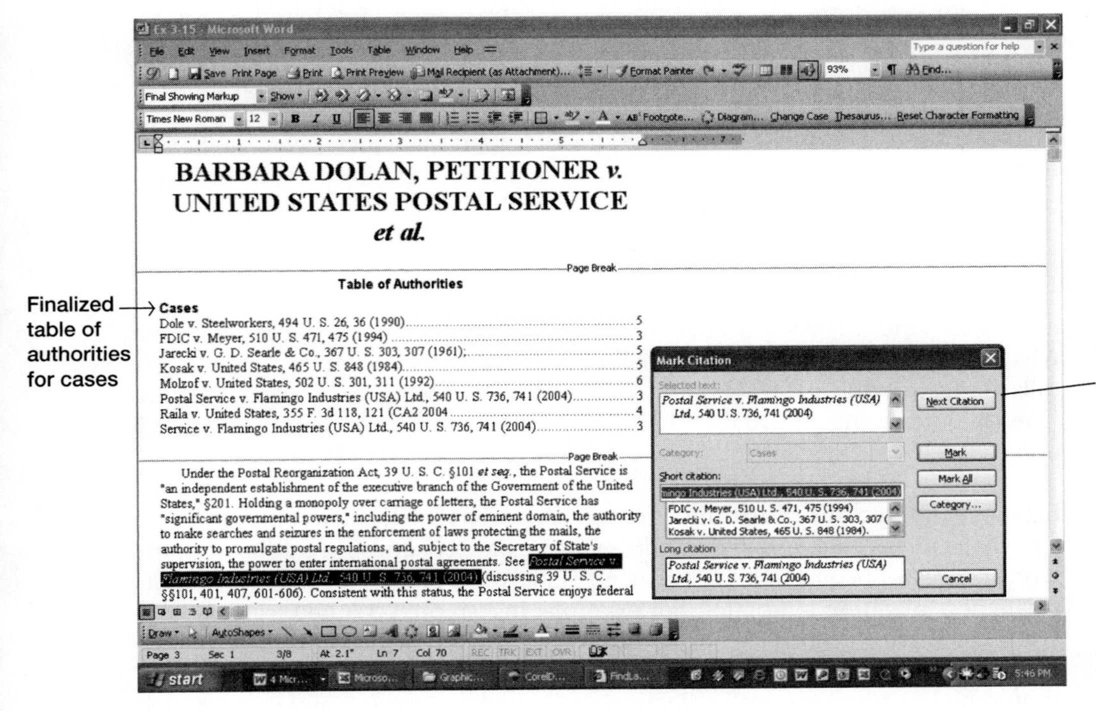

Finalized table of authorities for cases
Creating a table of authorities starts with the user highlighting or marking each item (case, statute, rule, etc.) in the document that is to be included in the table. Once the item is highlighted, the user then identifies the category of item it is (case, statute, etc.). Once all items have been marked and categorized the user then executes the Generate Table of Authorities command and the word processor automatically creates a table of all the items by category and includes the page number where the item appears.

Exhibit 3–15
Table of Authorities in Word 2003
Microsoft product screen shot reprinted by permission from Microsoft Corporation.

authorities feature in a word processor is very important because manually creating a table of authorities is an extremely time-consuming process, particularly if revisions are made after the table of authorities is generated. Even if changes are made to a document once a table of authorities has been created, there is no harm done because all the user has to do is to regenerate the table and it will automatically recreate the table with all of the new items and page numbers. Tables of authorities are covered in detail in Lesson 11 of the Hands-On Exercises for Word 2007, Word 2003, and WordPerfect X3.

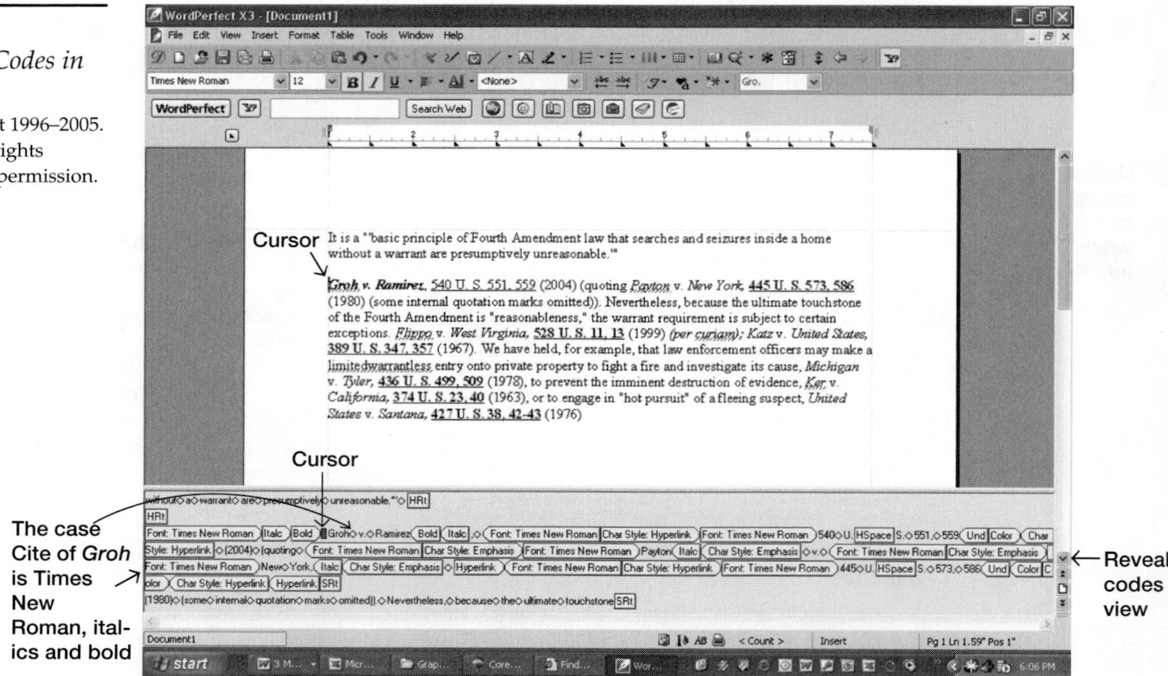

Exhibit 3–16
Revealing Hidden Codes in WordPerfect X3

Revealing Hidden Codes When text is typed into a word processor, all the user sees on the screen is the actual text. However, leading word processors have a command that allows the user to see the "invisible" codes that indicate format changes such as underlining, bold, and margin changes.

Revealing the hidden codes makes it easier to delete, edit, or change the formatting of a document (see Exhibit 3–16). For example, in Exhibit 3–16, when reveal codes is turned on, the user can plainly see that the case citation of *Groh v. Ramirez* has formatting codes of "Font: Times New Roman, Italics, and Bold." If the user wanted to delete one of these formatting codes they could use the Reveal Codes command to go to the spot in the document where the code is and delete it in the reveal codes view. The reveal codes command is helpful when trying to determine what formatting codes have been previously entered in a document. WordPerfect calls this feature "Revealing Hidden Codes" while Microsoft Word calls this feature "Reveal Formatting." Reveal codes / formatting is covered in detail in Lesson 5 of the Hands-On Exercises for Word 2007, Word 2003, and WordPerfect X3.

Pleading Wizard
A word processing feature that helps legal professionals quickly and easily create a legal pleading by having them answer questions about the pleading to be created.

Legal Templates and Pleading Wizard A variety of legal word-processing templates are available for many different legal specialties. In addition, some word processors come with a **Pleading Wizard** that helps legal professionals create new pleading templates. For example, in Exhibit 3–17 the Pleading Wizard gives the user a number of questions to answer, including things like the name of the court, what the layout of the page should be, and whether there should be line numbers on the document. Once the general template is created the Pleading Wizard then asks the user about the specific document that needs to be created, such as what the names of the parties are, the case number, and the attorneys involved. Based on the answers to these questions the Pleading Wizard then generates the document template (see Exhibit 3–17). In Microsoft Word 2003 the feature is accessed by selecting File, New, Templates on my computer, Legal Pleadings, Pleading Wizard. In WordPerfect the feature is called Expert Pleading Designer / Filler and is accessed by selecting Tools, Legal Tools, Expert Pleading Designer / Filler. The Pleading Wizard feature, no matter what it is called, can greatly speed up the creation of legal templates and forms.

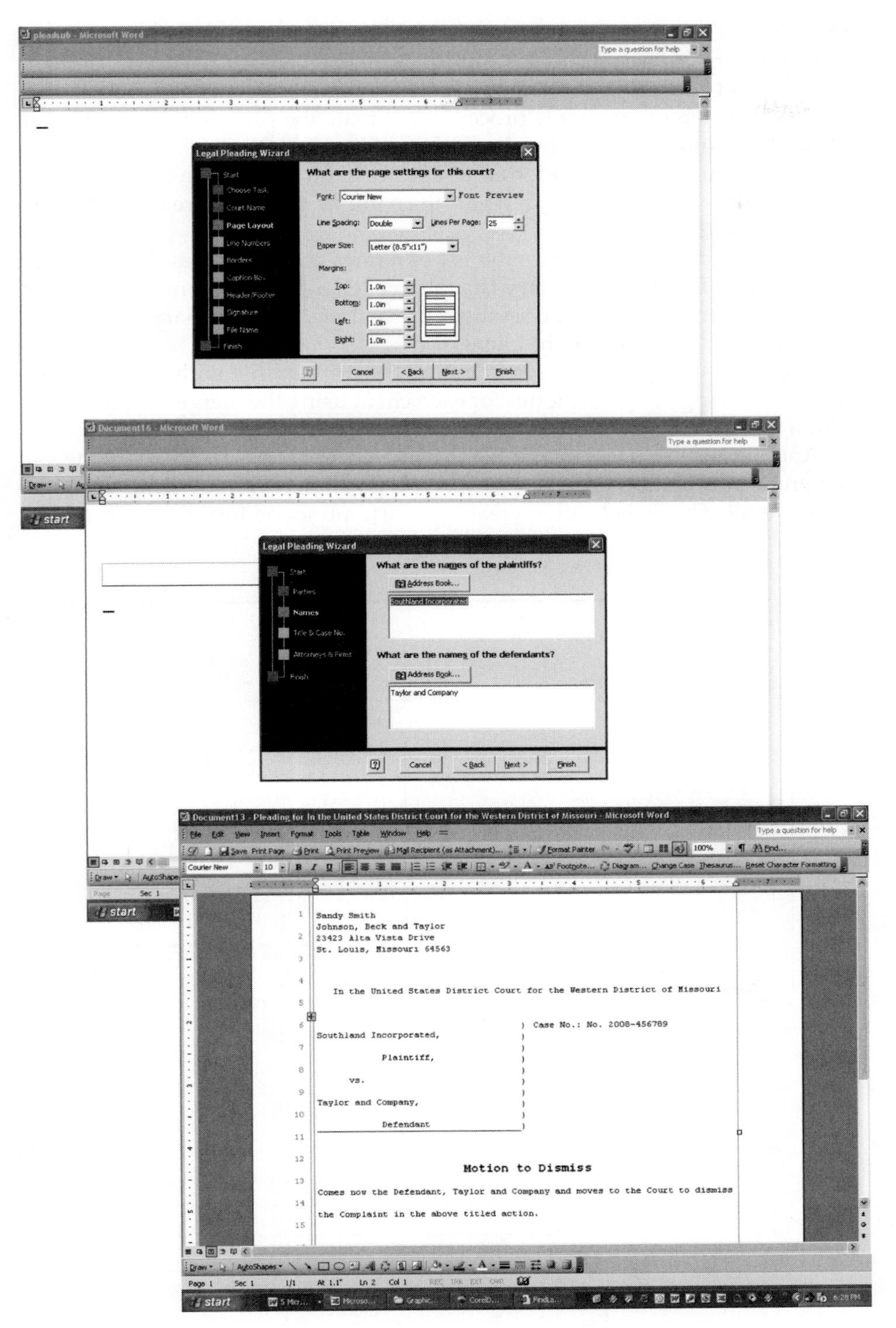

Exhibit 3–17
Legal Pleading Wizard in Word 2003

Merging / Document Assembly in Word Processors

Merging, sometimes called document generation or document assembly, is the process of combining a form with a list of variables to automatically produce a document. For instance, if you want to send the same letter to a number of clients, but you want each letter to be personalized, you can use the merge feature found in most word processors to do this quickly. The body of each letter remains the same; the only information that changes is the name and address

merging
The process of combining a form with a list of variables to automatically produce a document. Sometimes called document generation.

of the client. The information that remains the same in each letter (here, the body of the text) is called a constant. The information that changes in each letter (here, the name and address of the client) is called a variable.

primary file
A file that contains the constant information and is usually referred to as a form or template in a merge document.

secondary file
The file that contains the information that varies in a merge document.

The first step in the merge process is to create the primary file (see Exhibit 3–18). The **primary file** (also called a main document) contains the constant information and is usually referred to as a form or template in a merge document. In Exhibit 3–18, notice that where the name and address are to go, the variables F1 and F2 exist.

The second step is to create the list of names and addresses. This is called the secondary file. The **secondary file** (also called a data file) contains the information that varies in a merge document. In this case, the secondary file contains the names and addresses of the clients.

The third step is to merge or combine the primary file with the secondary file, thus creating a separate letter for each client using the merge command (see Exhibit 3–16). The final step is to print the document.

Another way to use a merge file is to create a primary file or template and then enter information into the form as you go along, without using a secondary file at all. This is helpful in creating short, mundane forms such as letters,

Exhibit 3–18
Merge File

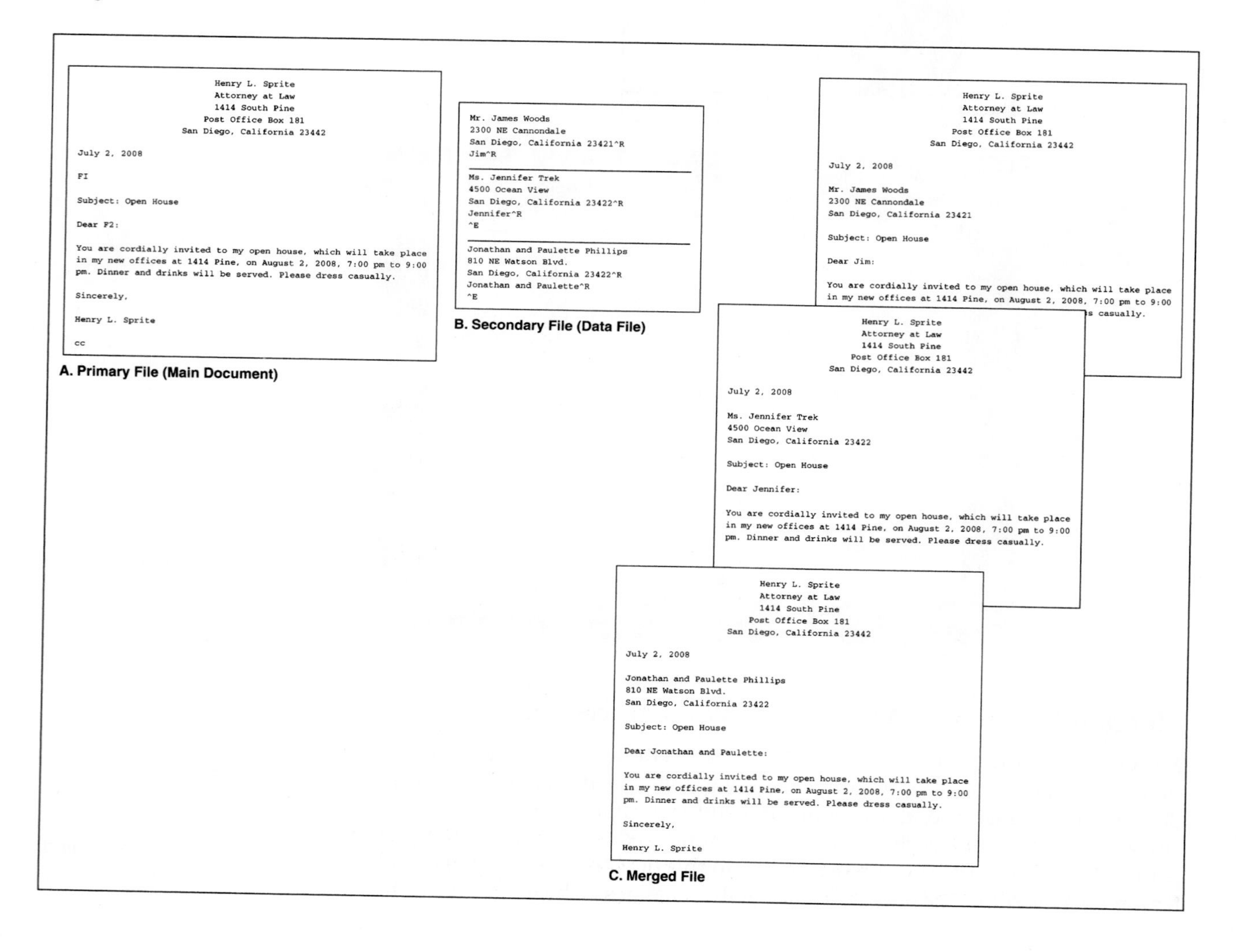

Henry L. Sprite
Attorney at Law
1414 South Pine
Post Office Box 181
San Diego, California 23442

July 2, 2008

FI

Subject: Open House

Dear F2:

You are cordially invited to my open house, which will take place in my new offices at 1414 Pine, on August 2, 2008, 7:00 pm to 9:00 pm. Dinner and drinks will be served. Please dress casually.

Sincerely,

Henry L. Sprite

cc

A. Primary File (Main Document)

Mr. James Woods
2300 NE Cannondale
San Diego, California 23421^R
Jim^R

Ms. Jennifer Trek
4500 Ocean View
San Diego, California 23422^R
Jennifer^R
^E

Jonathan and Paulette Phillips
810 NE Watson Blvd.
San Diego, California 23422^R
Jonathan and Paulette^R
^E

B. Secondary File (Data File)

Henry L. Sprite
Attorney at Law
1414 South Pine
Post Office Box 181
San Diego, California 23442

July 2, 2008

Mr. James Woods
2300 NE Cannondale
San Diego, California 23421

Subject: Open House

Dear Jim:

You are cordially invited to my open house, which will take place in my new offices at 1414 Pine, on August 2, 2008, 7:00 pm to 9:00 ...s casually.

Henry L. Sprite
Attorney at Law
1414 South Pine
Post Office Box 181
San Diego, California 23442

July 2, 2008

Ms. Jennifer Trek
4500 Ocean View
San Diego, California 23422

Subject: Open House

Dear Jennifer:

You are cordially invited to my open house, which will take place in my new offices at 1414 Pine, on August 2, 2008, 7:00 pm to 9:00 pm. Dinner and drinks will be served. Please dress casually.

Henry L. Sprite
Attorney at Law
1414 South Pine
Post Office Box 181
San Diego, California 23442

July 2, 2008

Jonathan and Paulette Phillips
810 NE Watson Blvd.
San Diego, California 23422

Subject: Open House

Dear Jonathan and Paulette:

You are cordially invited to my open house, which will take place in my new offices at 1414 Pine, on August 2, 2008, 7:00 pm to 9:00 pm. Dinner and drinks will be served. Please dress casually.

Sincerely,

Henry L. Sprite

C. Merged File

memos, and so forth. Once the primary file is created, use the merge command to retrieve it. Then, as you go along, fill in each variable that changes. Finally, when the document has been filled in, print it. Merge files greatly reduce the time it takes to perform repetitive tasks.

Many of the letters, pleadings, and other documents that law offices produce are essentially forms. In many cases, although the client names change from case to case, the letters and documents that are processed are generally the same. Merge files allow you to save these forms and simply retrieve them and quickly fill in the blanks. Merging is covered in detail in Lessons 7 and 10 of the Hands-On Exercises for Word 2007, Word 2003, and WordPerfect X3.

In addition to word processors with merge / document assembly capabilities, there are also separate document-assembly programs that work together with a word processor to perform this function. Document-assembly programs typically have more features and capabilities than word processors. Many legal organizations use document assembly programs to further automate correspondence, pleadings, contracts, and other legal documents. These programs are covered later in this chapter.

Word Processing File Formats

Most word processors such as Microsoft Word and Corel WordPerfect can save their word processing files in multiple file formats. Word 2007 for example can save files in several formats including Word 2007, Word 97–2003, plain text file, Rich Text Format, Web Page, and others. WordPerfect X3 can save files in multiple file formats including various versions of Microsoft Word. For WordPerfect users that need to send word processing files to clients using Microsoft Word, they can simply change the file format to a version of Microsoft Word that the client can open.

PDF FILE CREATION

The universality and acceptance of PDF and the free Adobe Reader have made PDF documents a commonplace in today's practice of law.[1]

Of all the software programs on the market, there is none more functional, versatile, and vital to paralegals and legal professionals than Adobe Acrobat.[2]

As noted earlier in this chapter, many courts now allow and in fact require legal organizations to file documents electronically. Most courts use the Portable Document Format (PDF) as the standard for filing documents electronically. The federal courts in particular have standardized around the PDF format. Twenty-seven million cases and more than two hundred thousand attorneys have filed documents using the federal courts' Case Management and Electronic Case File system.

The [Federal] Case Management and Electronic Case File system stores cases and related information as PDF files. Most legal professionals find the system easy to use—filers prepare a document using their word processor of choice, then save it to PDF for electronic filing with the court. Attorneys practicing in courts offering the electronic filing capability can file documents directly with the court via the Internet. When documents are filed electronically, the system automatically generates and sends a verifying receipt by electronic mail... Other parties in the case automatically receive notification of the filing. Litigants receive one free PDF copy of every document electronically filed in their cases, which they can save or print for their files.[3]

The PDF standard was created by Adobe Systems. PDF can be a secure format meaning that recipients cannot edit the document sent and the look and format of the document is locked and uniform. For filing documents with a court electronically, this is key. Another advantage of PDF is that as long as the recipient has a PDF viewer (which is free) the recipient can view the file on a different type or format of computer than the document was created on. Thus, if a court system used a UNIX-based operating system and an attorney used an Apple Macintosh computer, it wouldn't matter. As long as the attorney saved the document to be filed in PDF format, the court could still use and access the document even though it was on a completely different operating system. One PDF viewer that is free is the Adobe Reader program. Adobe states that the program has been downloaded more than five hundred million times worldwide and approximately 89 percent of all desktop computers have a version of Reader on them.

It is important to note that while the PDF reader (viewing software) is free, the software that converts a document, such as a Word document, to a PDF file must typically be purchased. For example, Adobe Acrobat is an extremely popular PDF file converter that must be purchased. As noted earlier, some word processors now can convert their files directly to PDF. Nonetheless, many legal organizations continue to use Adobe Acrobat for PDF file creation because the product has so many features and functionalities.

Adobe Acrobat

Adobe Acrobat is a PDF conversion utility. Acrobat can convert many types of files to PDF. Adobe Acrobat has several versions, which may be somewhat confusing. Acrobat has a Reader program that can be downloaded for absolutely free on the Internet. However, to create PDF files, the user needs either the Standard or Professional version of Adobe Acrobat.

For example, suppose in Exhibit 3–19 that the user has a file in Word that she would like to convert to a PDF file. Notice in Exhibit 3–19 that when Adobe Acrobat was installed it created a new menu item in Word entitled "Adobe PDF." The first step to convert the Word document to PDF is to select "Convert to Adobe PDF" from the "Adobe PDF" menu item (see Exhibit 3–19, screen 1) on the Word menu line. Acrobat then asks the user to enter the name of the new PDF file that is being created (Exhibit 3–19, screen 2). Acrobat then converts the file and opens it in the Adobe Acrobat program (see Exhibit 3–19, screen 3). Alternatively, the user can load Acrobat first and identify the file to be converted, in this case the Word file; then Acrobat will convert it and load the converted file into Acrobat. Acrobat can also convert multiple files into one PDF file. The conversion progress is typically easy and straightforward.

Acrobat has a number of features, including the bookmark feature. A bookmark is a navigation link to a specific location in the PDF file. Notice that in Exhibit 3–20 (the first screen) the user is creating a bookmark by right-clicking with the mouse on the page where the bookmark is to be created. Now, notice in Exhibit 3–20 (the second screen) that to the left of the page, next to the "bookmarks" tab, the user can see five bookmarks including Title Page, Section I, etc. By clicking on the Section II bookmark the user is immediately taken to Section II of the document (see Exhibit 3–20, second screen). This is a quick and convenient way to navigate in PDF files. Interestingly, if Microsoft Word users use the Styles feature to create their documents, including using Headings in the Style feature, Acrobat can actually convert all of these headings directly to bookmarks.

> *Licensed versions of Acrobat offer a variety of essential functions today's paralegal can't live without, such as the ability to create a Portable Document Format file from just about any document or Web page, creation of fill-in forms from paper or electronic documents, inserting bookmarks in documents, the ability to manipulate document pages, and collaborative document reviewing and commenting.*[4]

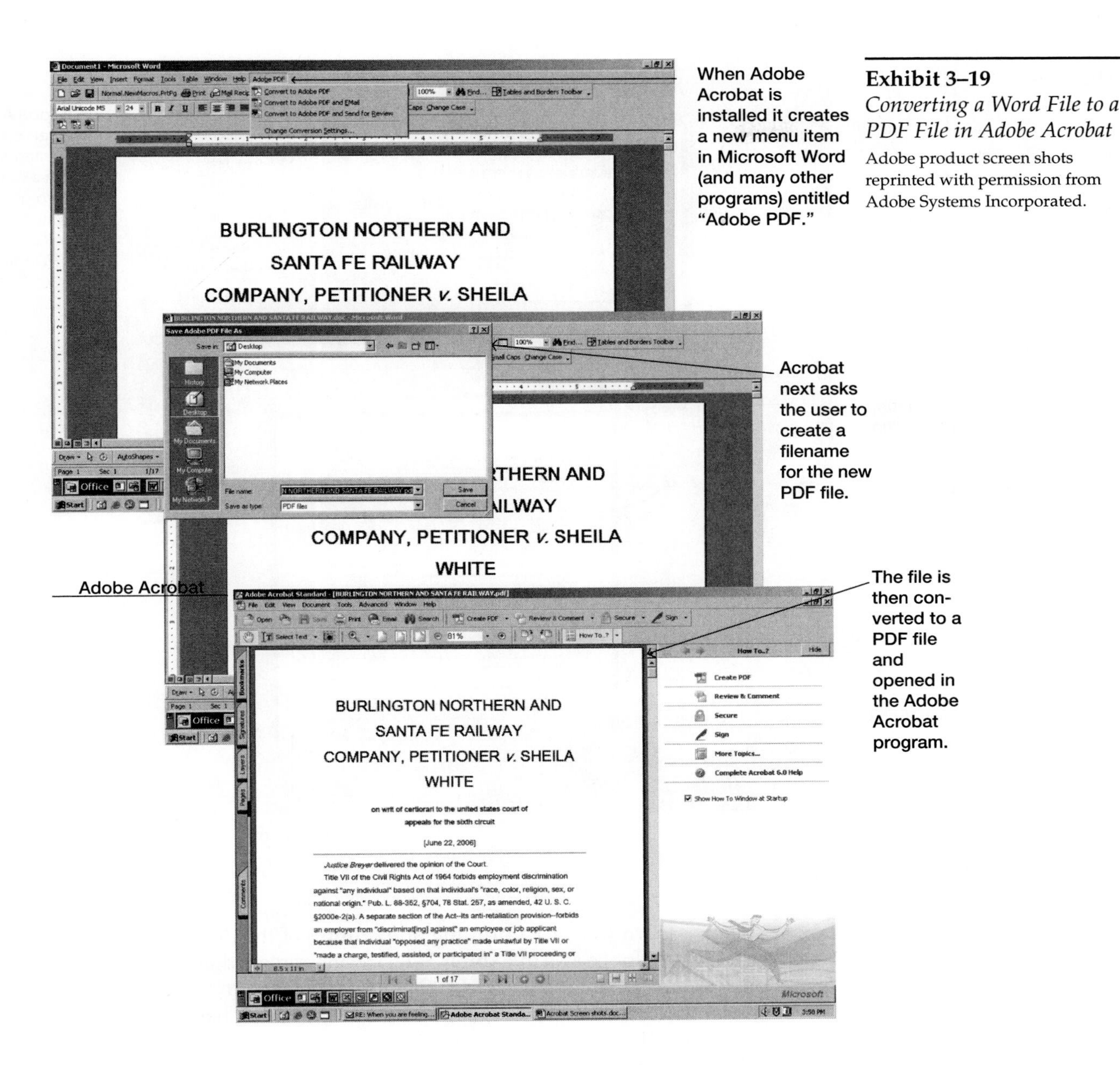
When Adobe Acrobat is installed it creates a new menu item in Microsoft Word (and many other programs) entitled "Adobe PDF."
BURLINGTON NORTHERN AND
SANTA FE RAILWAY
COMPANY, PETITIONER v. SHEILA
Acrobat next asks the user to create a filename for the new PDF file.
COMPANY, PETITIONER v. SHEILA
WHITE
Adobe Acrobat
The file is then converted to a PDF file and opened in the Adobe Acrobat program.
BURLINGTON NORTHERN AND
SANTA FE RAILWAY
COMPANY, PETITIONER v. SHEILA
WHITE

Exhibit 3–19
Converting a Word File to a PDF File in Adobe Acrobat
Adobe product screen shots reprinted with permission from Adobe Systems Incorporated.

Using Acrobat, users have tremendous control over how a PDF file will look. Users can create custom page numbers, include headers or footers, include multimedia links, create fill-in electronic forms, and much more.

Adobe Acrobat has many features, including the ability to create notes and comments (see Exhibit 3–21, first screen). Using this feature, people can collaborate using Acrobat even if they do not all use the same word processor. Notice in Exhibit 3–21 that the user has clicked on the "Pages" tab and page views of the document are being displayed to the left.

Adobe Acrobat allows users to attach a digital signature to a PDF file (see Exhibit 3–22, first screen). A digital signature not only validates the PDF file, but it also validates with Acrobat the identity of the person signing it. Using digital signatures is another security feature: once this is done, the recipient cannot alter the PDF file. Some courts require all PDF files to have a digital signature.

By default, new PDF files are NOT secure. This means that anyone receiving a PDF can open, view, print or make changes to the file. However, Acrobat has a number of security features that allow the user to completely lock down a PDF file. Notice, in Exhibit 3–22, second screen, that the user has checked the

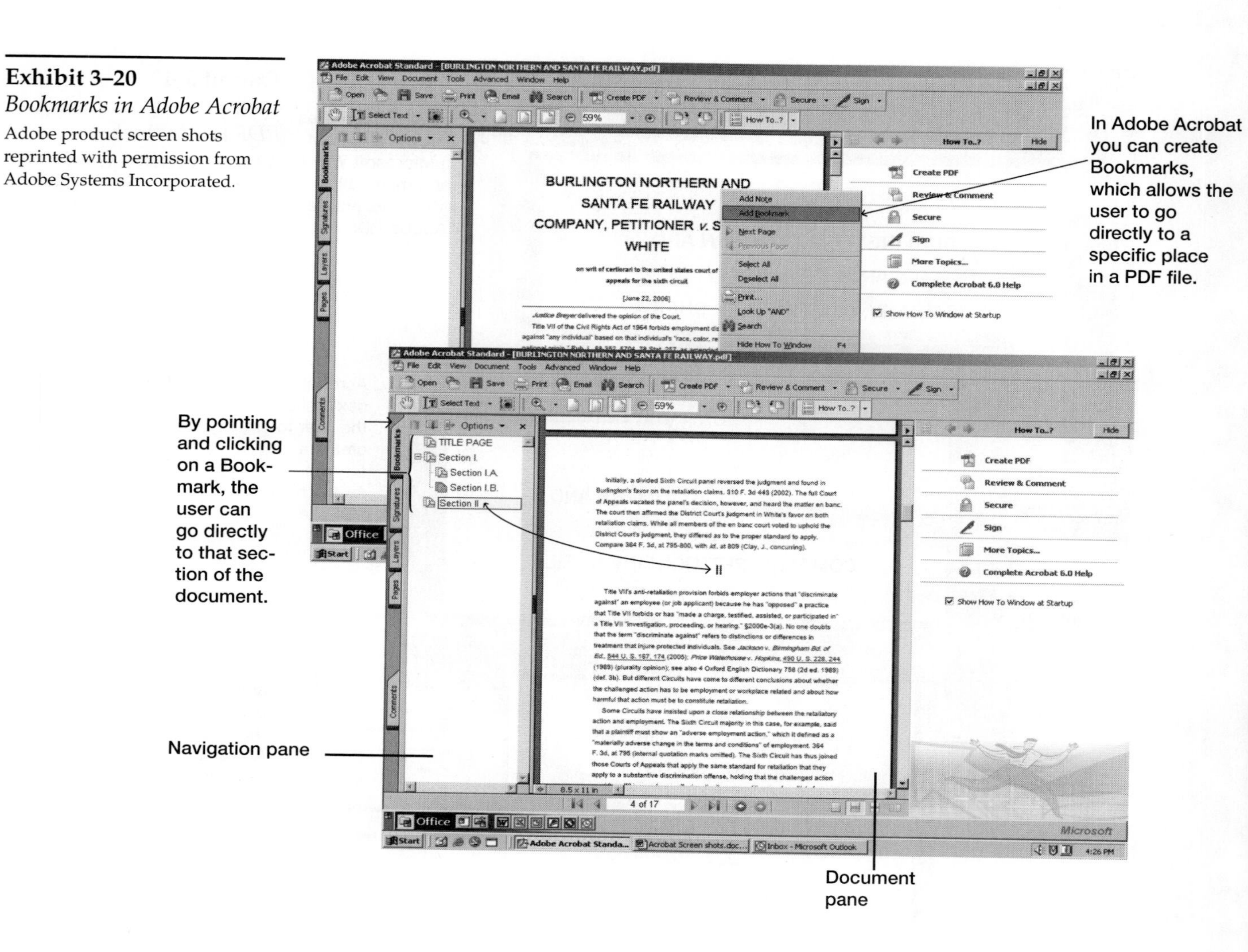

Exhibit 3–20
Bookmarks in Adobe Acrobat
Adobe product screen shots reprinted with permission from Adobe Systems Incorporated.

box "Use a password to restrict printing and editing of the documents and its security settings." Notice also in Exhibit 3–22, second screen, that next to "Printing Allowed" and "Changes Allowed," "None" is selected. In this instance the user has locked down the PDF file so that unless the recipient has the password, the recipient cannot print or change the PDF file.

In Adobe Acrobat, a PDF file can actually be exported to Microsoft Word as long as the user creating the file allows for it and turns the feature on. Adobe Acrobat is an incredibly powerful tool for information sharing and will most likely be an important part of legal word processing and document distribution for legal organizations for the foreseeable future.

DOCUMENT ASSEMBLY PROGRAMS

Document assembly software creates powerful standardized templates and forms. Users create forms and templates and then respond to a series of questions and prompts. The document assembly program then merges the templates and forms with the answers and builds completed documents. Document assembly programs work best when the user has well-structured and routine templates and forms that must be completed often. While word processors have some document assembly functions, stand-alone document assembly programs are much more powerful.

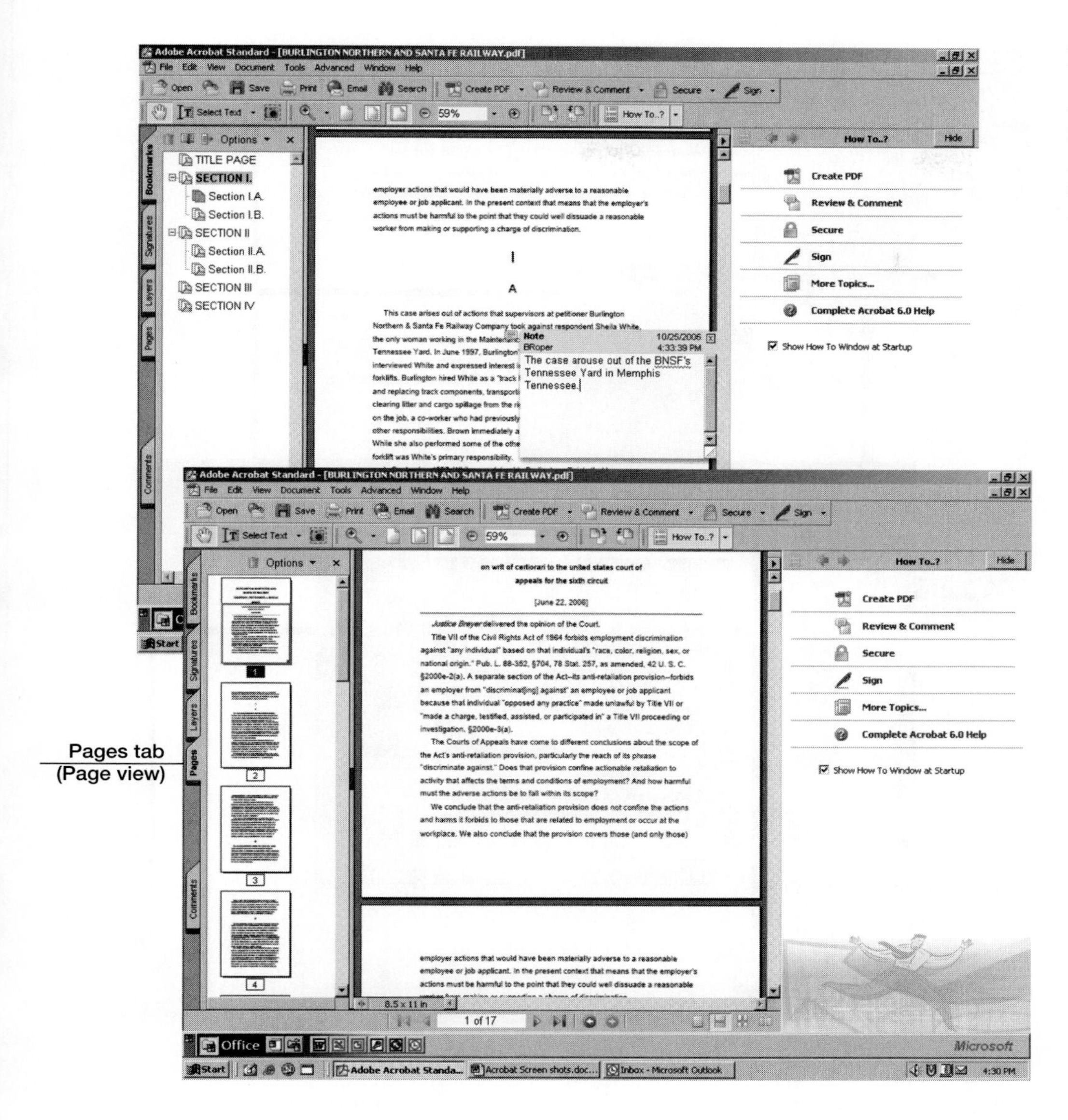

Exhibit 3–21

Notes and Page View in Adobe Acrobat

Adobe product screen shots reprinted with permission from Adobe Systems Incorporated.

For example, suppose a law firm routinely drafts employment contracts for a large client and, instead of using a word processor to slowly edit the document for every agreement, they would like to use a document assembly program to automate the process. Exhibit 3–23 shows a completed employment agreement. Everything that is bolded in the document is something that must be changed.

In Exhibit 3–24, the user has built a template for an employment agreement in a document assembly program. The document assembly program is running inside of the user's word processor; notice the special document assembly toolbar in Exhibit 3–24. Compare Exhibits 3–23 and 3–24. Notice that instead of "United Medical Association" being listed in Exhibit 3–24 as the employer, it now shows the variable <Company>. Notice that there are a number of variables listed in Exhibit 3–24 including <Company,> <Employee Name,> <Agreement Date,> and others.

A variable is something that will change in the document. Notice that the variable <Employee Name> in Exhibit 3–24 is included seven times in the document. The beauty of a document assembly program is that once the text for the variable <Employee Name> has been entered (e.g., "Cynthia Jones") the computer

Exhibit 3–22
Adobe Acrobat Security Features
Adobe product screen shots reprinted with permission from Adobe Systems Incorporated.

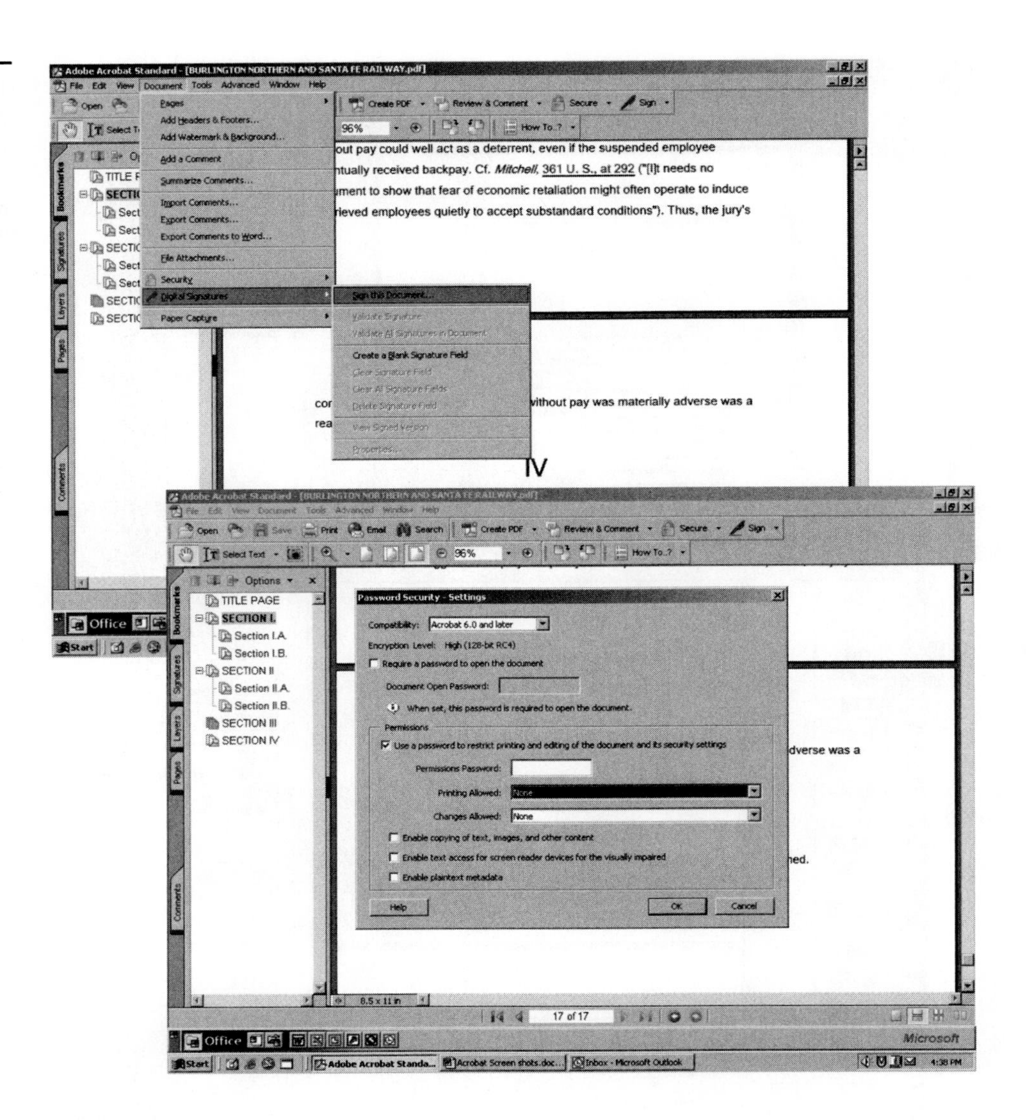

automatically fills it in anywhere the variable (e.g., <Employee Name>) is included.

In Exhibit 3–25, the user is creating the variable for <Company.> The user tells the document assembly program that the name of the variable is <Company> and that text will be stored in the variable. In Exhibit 3–26, the user is creating the variable for <Agreement Date>. Notice that the user has selected the variable type as "Date" and selected one of many different formatting options for how the date can be displayed.

In Exhibit 3–27 the user is creating a variable for <Monthly Salary>. Notice that the variable type is a Number and that the user has even told the document assembly program that the number entered must be a minimum of $3,000 and a maximum of $6,000 (see Exhibit 3–27).

In Exhibit 3–28 the user is creating a variable for <Yearly Salary>. Notice in Exhibit 3–28 that instead of entering this as a number, the user has selected the variable type as "Computation" and that the document assembly will take the <Monthly Salary> variable times 12 and automatically enter the correct number. Not only does this save on data entry time, but it also make the document less susceptible to errors. Document assembly programs have many advanced features like this.

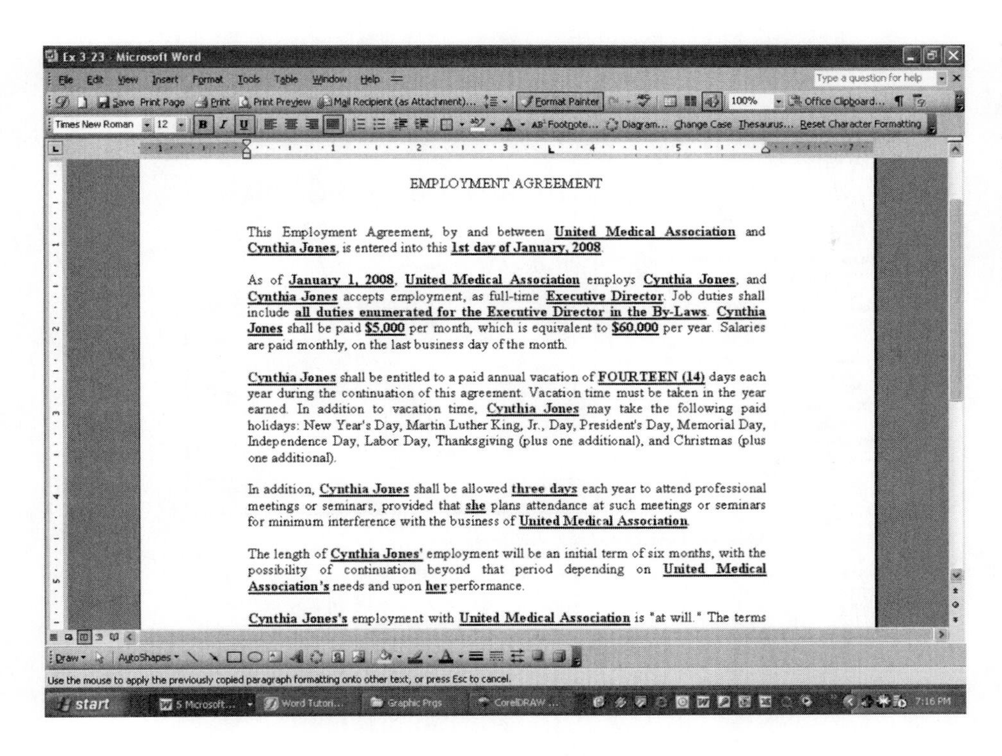

EMPLOYMENT AGREEMENT

This Employment Agreement, by and between **United Medical Association** and **Cynthia Jones**, is entered into this **1st day of January, 2008**.

As of **January 1, 2008**, **United Medical Association** employs **Cynthia Jones**, and **Cynthia Jones** accepts employment, as full-time **Executive Director**. Job duties shall include **all duties enumerated for the Executive Director in the By-Laws**. **Cynthia Jones** shall be paid **$5,000** per month, which is equivalent to **$60,000** per year. Salaries are paid monthly, on the last business day of the month.

Cynthia Jones shall be entitled to a paid annual vacation of **FOURTEEN (14)** days each year during the continuation of this agreement. Vacation time must be taken in the year earned. In addition to vacation time, **Cynthia Jones** may take the following paid holidays: New Year's Day, Martin Luther King, Jr., Day, President's Day, Memorial Day, Independence Day, Labor Day, Thanksgiving (plus one additional), and Christmas (plus one additional).

In addition, **Cynthia Jones** shall be allowed **three days** each year to attend professional meetings or seminars, provided that **she** plans attendance at such meetings or seminars for minimum interference with the business of **United Medical Association**.

The length of **Cynthia Jones'** employment will be an initial term of six months, with the possibility of continuation beyond that period depending on **United Medical Association's** needs and upon **her** performance.

Cynthia Jones's employment with **United Medical Association** is "at will." The terms

Exhibit 3–23

Completed Employment Agreement Using a Stand-alone Document Assembly Program

Microsoft product screen shot reprinted with permission from Microsoft Corporation.

In Exhibit 3–29 the user has created a variable <Employee Gender: he / she>. Notice that the variable type is multiple choice. This allows the form to correctly enter "he" or "she" depending on the gender of the employee. Again, this is an extremely powerful tool that is a large time-saver when it comes to accurately completing the form.

Once the template has been built, (see Exhibit 3–24) the user executes the template in the document assembly program (see Exhibit 3–30, first screen).

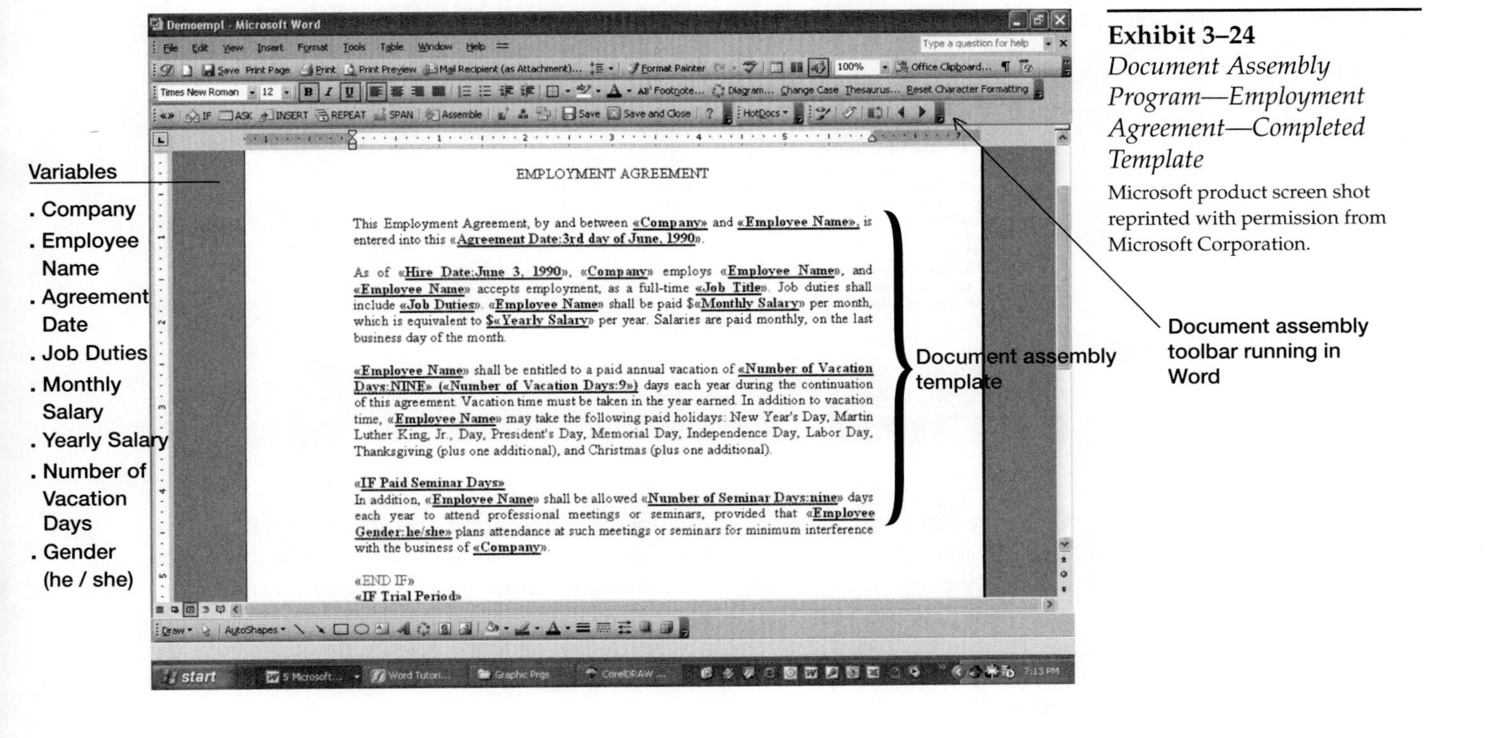

EMPLOYMENT AGREEMENT

This Employment Agreement, by and between «**Company**» and «**Employee Name**», is entered into this «**Agreement Date:3rd day of June, 1990**».

As of «**Hire Date:June 3, 1990**», «**Company**» employs «**Employee Name**», and «**Employee Name**» accepts employment, as a full-time «**Job Title**». Job duties shall include «**Job Duties**». «**Employee Name**» shall be paid $«**Monthly Salary**» per month, which is equivalent to $«**Yearly Salary**» per year. Salaries are paid monthly, on the last business day of the month.

«**Employee Name**» shall be entitled to a paid annual vacation of «**Number of Vacation Days:NINE**» («**Number of Vacation Days:9**») days each year during the continuation of this agreement. Vacation time must be taken in the year earned. In addition to vacation time, «**Employee Name**» may take the following paid holidays: New Year's Day, Martin Luther King, Jr., Day, President's Day, Memorial Day, Independence Day, Labor Day, Thanksgiving (plus one additional), and Christmas (plus one additional).

«**IF Paid Seminar Days**»
In addition, «**Employee Name**» shall be allowed «**Number of Seminar Days:nine**» days each year to attend professional meetings or seminars, provided that «**Employee Gender:he/she**» plans attendance at such meetings or seminars for minimum interference with the business of «**Company**».

«END IF»
«**IF Trial Period**»

Exhibit 3–24

Document Assembly Program—Employment Agreement—Completed Template

Microsoft product screen shot reprinted with permission from Microsoft Corporation.

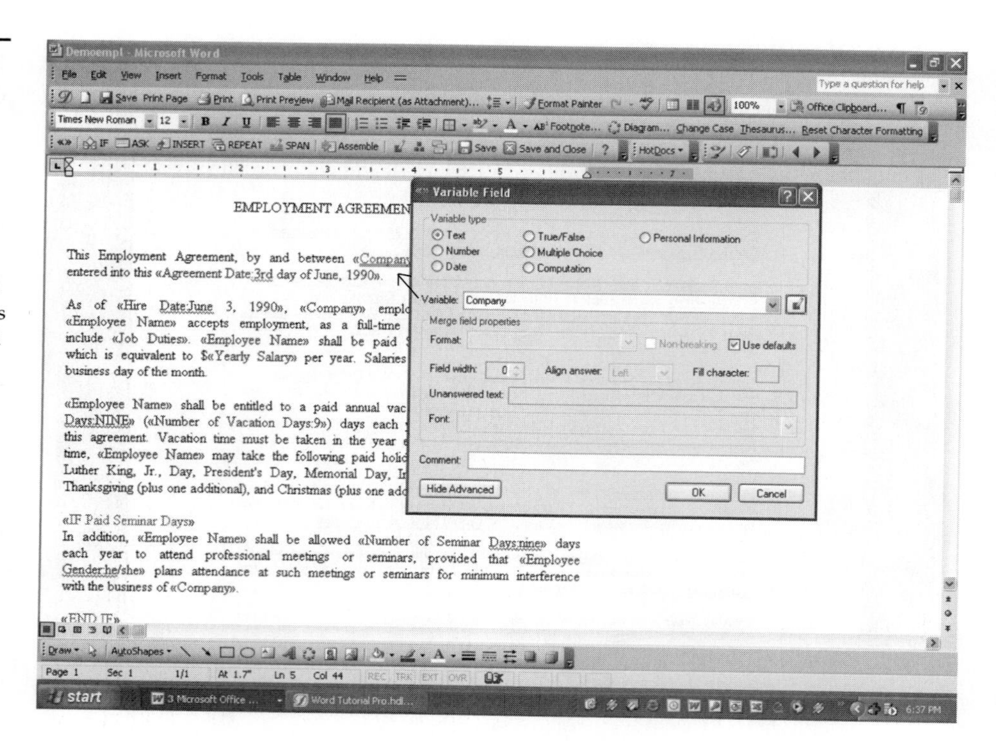

Exhibit 3–25

Creating the <Company> Variable (Text)

LexisNexis and the Knowledge Burst logo are registered trademarks of Reed Elsevier Properties Inc. HotDocs is a registered trademark of Matthew Bender & Company. TimeMap and CaseMap are registered trademarks of LexisNexis CourtLink, Inc. Used with the permission of LexisNexis.

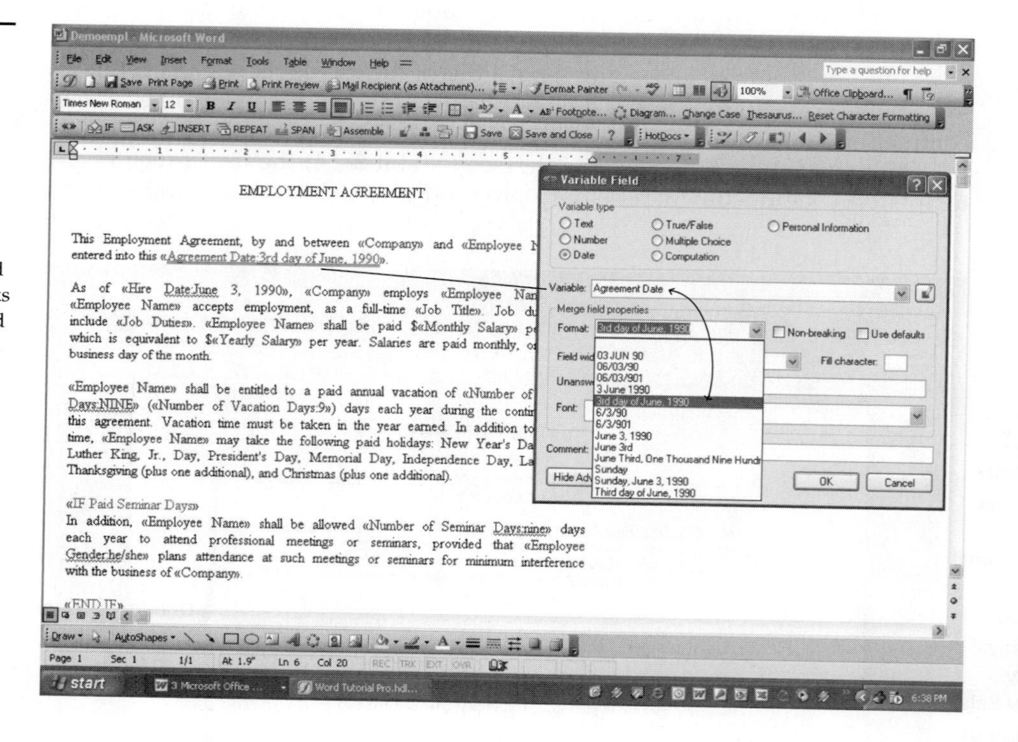

Exhibit 3–26

Creating the <Agreement Date> Variable (Date)

LexisNexis and the Knowledge Burst logo are registered trademarks of Reed Elsevier Properties Inc. HotDocs is a registered trademark of Matthew Bender & Company. TimeMap and CaseMap are registered trademarks of LexisNexis CourtLink, Inc. Used with the permission of LexisNexis.

Once the template is executed the document assembly program asks if a "New Answer File" should be created (see Exhibit 3–30, second screen). The document assembly program will take the answers the user gives and open a new word processing document.

The next step in the process is for the user to answer the questions the template asks. In Exhibit 3–31, notice that the program asks for a company name. The user types in "United Medical Association" and selects "Next." The

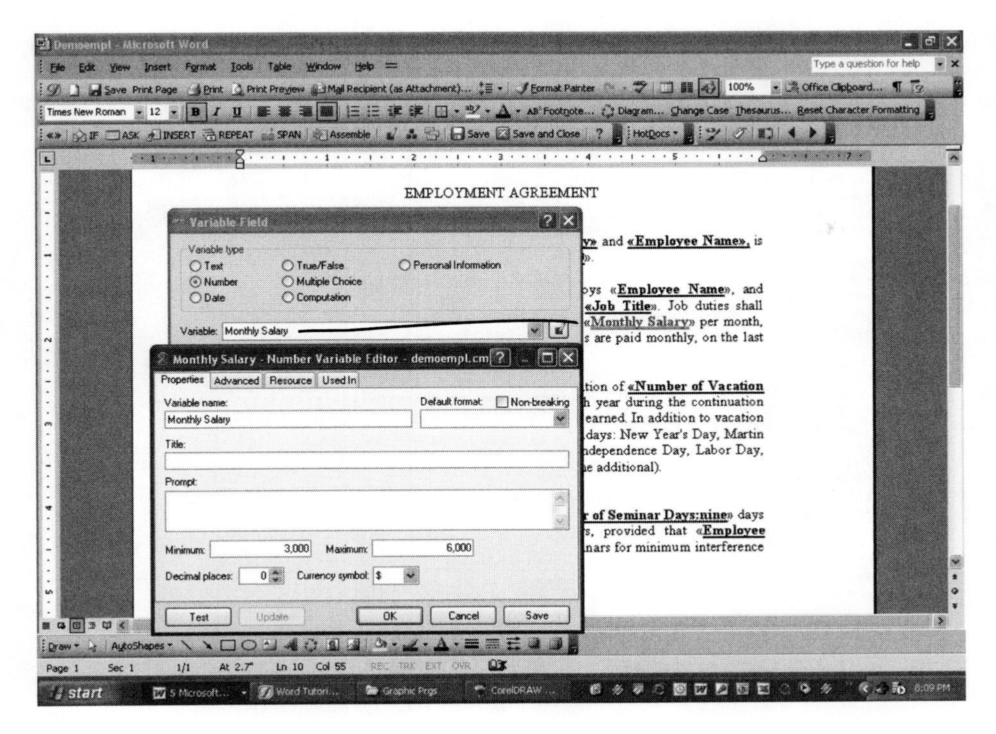

Exhibit 3–27

Creating the <Monthly Salary> Variable (Number)

LexisNexis and the Knowledge Burst logo are registered trademarks of Reed Elsevier Properties Inc. HotDocs is a registered trademark of Matthew Bender & Company. TimeMap and CaseMap are registered trademarks of LexisNexis CourtLink, Inc. Used with the permission of LexisNexis.

program then asks for "Employee Name," "Employee Gender," and so on. Once the user completes answering all of the questions, the program displays the finished document as shown in Exhibit 3–23. Notice in Exhibit 3–23 that the program accurately computed $60,000 as the yearly salary and that the correct gender pronoun "she" was used. Also, note in Exhibit 3–23 that the finished template document is displayed in the user's word-processing program so the finished document can be fully edited as needed.

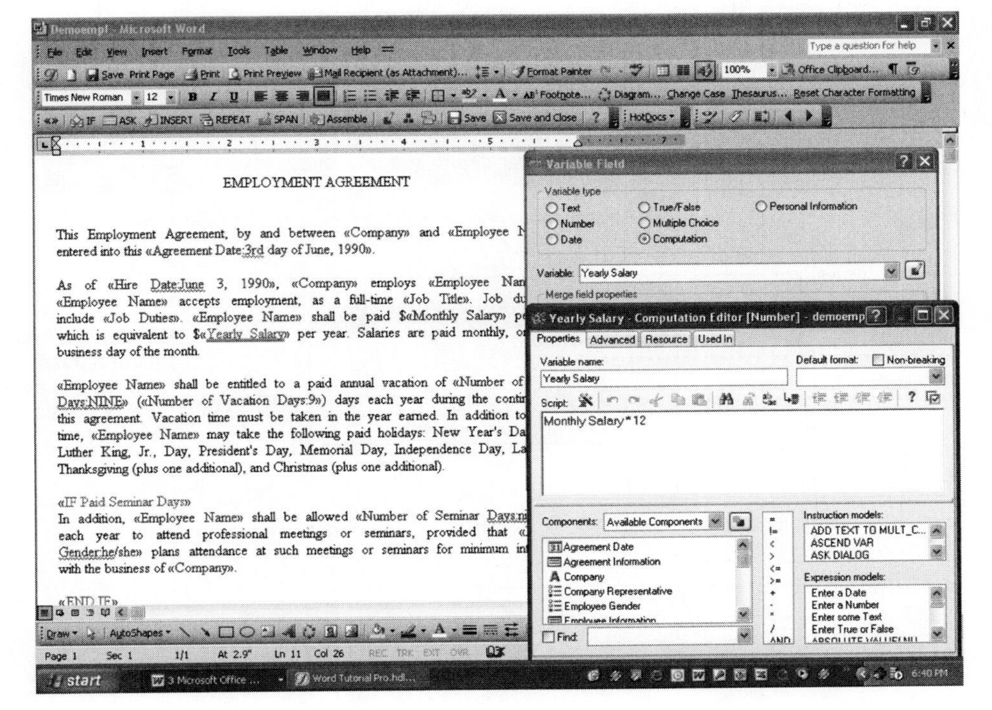

Exhibit 3–28

Creating the <Yearly Salary> Variable (Computation)

LexisNexis and the Knowledge Burst logo are registered trademarks of Reed Elsevier Properties Inc. HotDocs is a registered trademark of Matthew Bender & Company. TimeMap and CaseMap are registered trademarks of LexisNexis CourtLink, Inc. Used with the permission of LexisNexis.

Exhibit 3–29

Creating the <Employee Gender: he / she> Variable (Multiple Choice)

LexisNexis and the Knowledge Burst logo are registered trademarks of Reed Elsevier Properties Inc. HotDocs is a registered trademark of Matthew Bender & Company. TimeMap and CaseMap are registered trademarks of LexisNexis CourtLink, Inc. Used with the permission of LexisNexis.

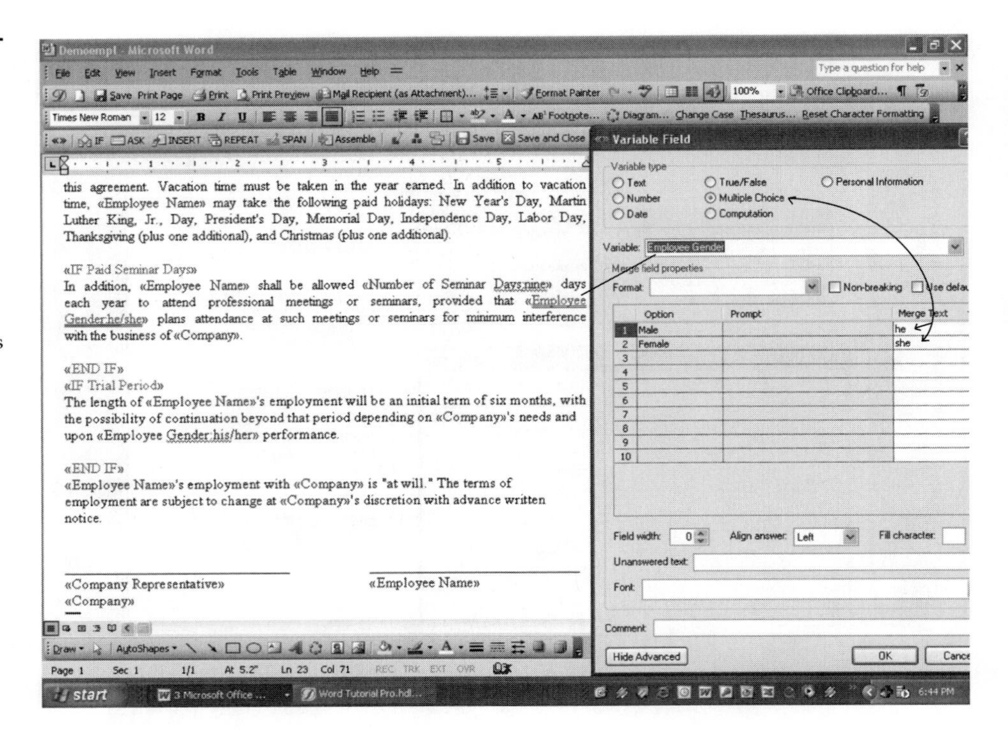

Exhibit 3–30

Executing the Employment Agreement Template in the Document Assembly Program

LexisNexis and the Knowledge Burst logo are registered trademarks of Reed Elsevier Properties Inc. HotDocs is a registered trademark of Matthew Bender & Company. TimeMap and CaseMap are registered trademarks of LexisNexis Courtlink, Inc. Used with the permission of LexisNexis.

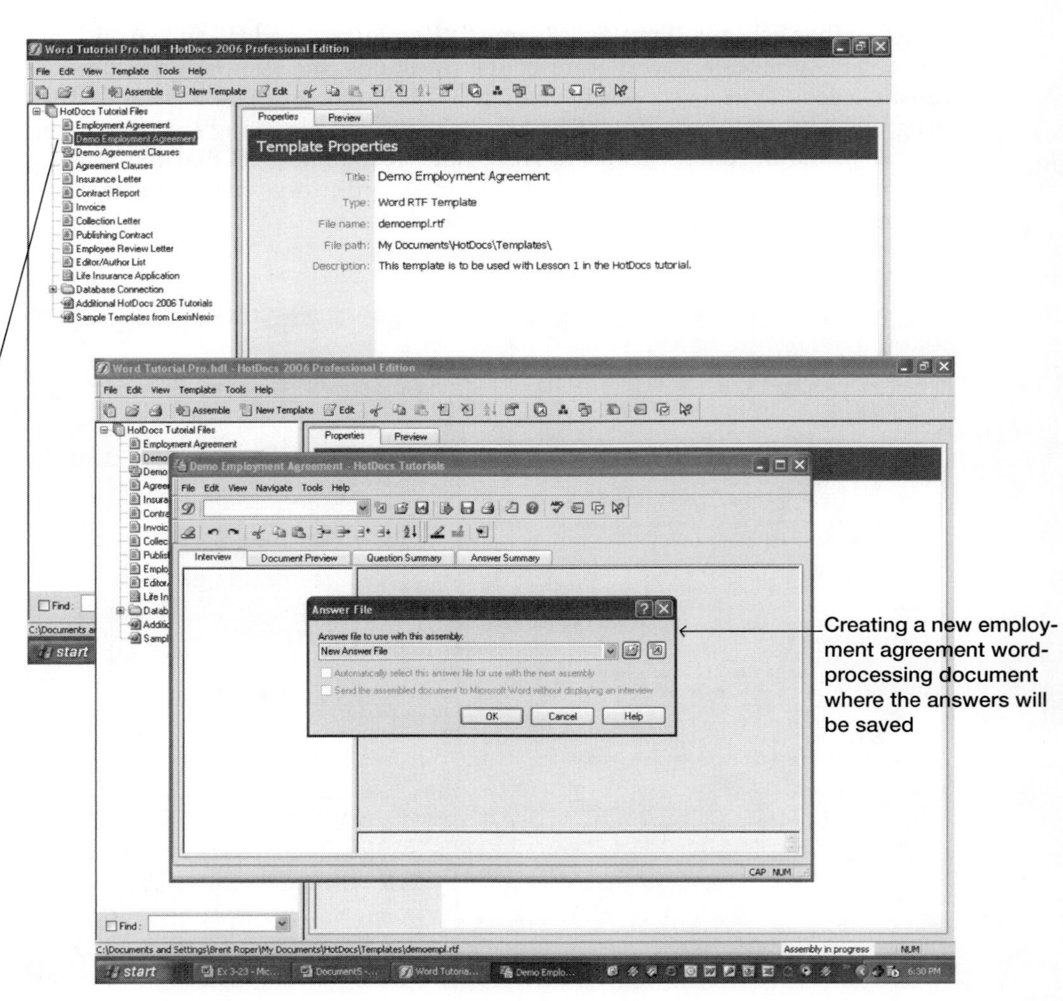

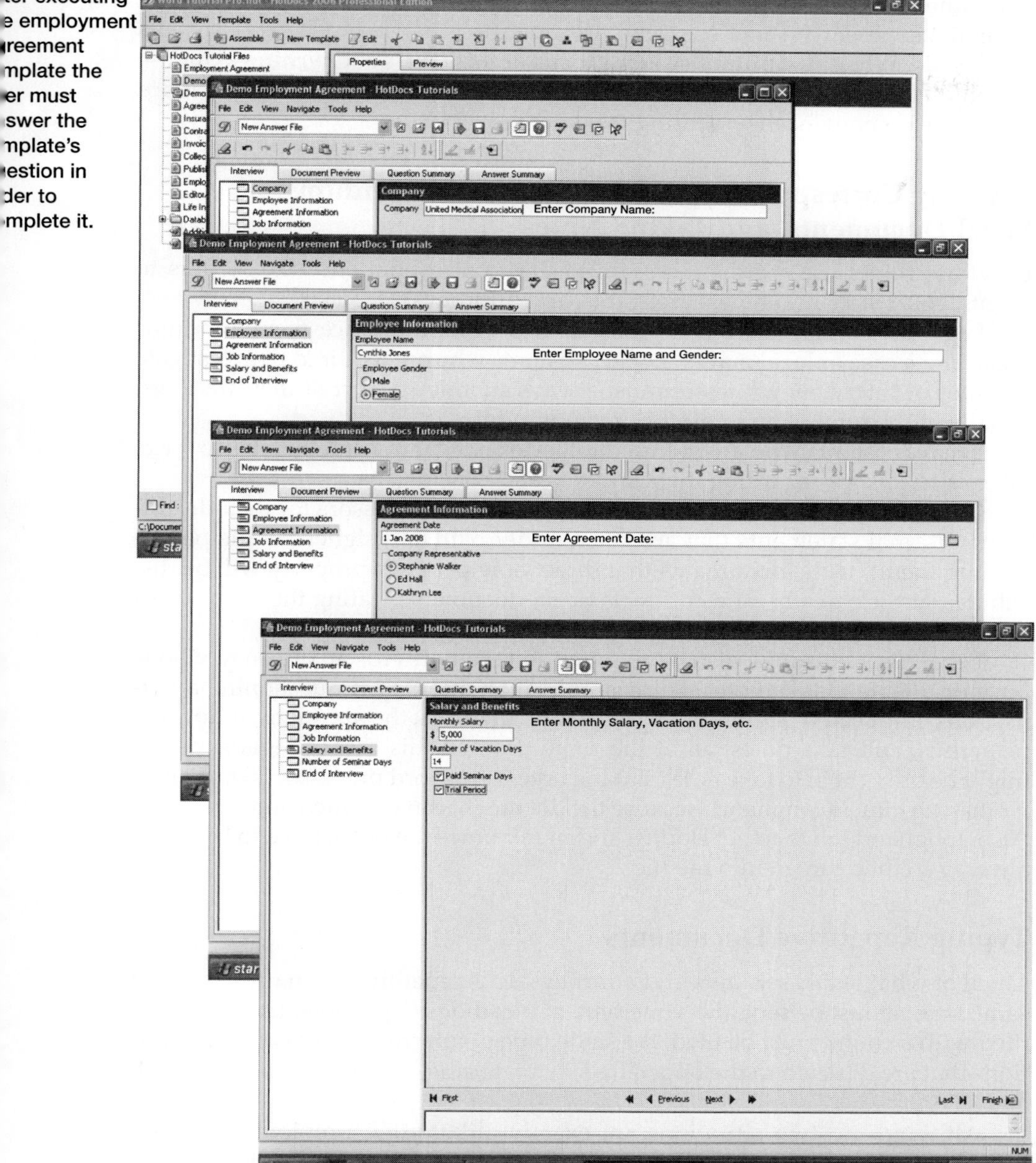

Exhibit 3–31
Answering Template Questions

LexisNexis and the Knowledge Burst logo are registered trademarks of Reed Elsevier Properties Inc. HotDocs is a registered trademark of Matthew Bender & Company. TimeMap and CaseMap are registered trademarks of LexisNexis CourtLink, Inc. Used with the permission of LexisNexis.

Document assembly programs are extremely powerful and have many advanced features that make them great time-savers in many legal organizations.

WORD PROCESSING IN THE LEGAL ENVIRONMENT

Many legal assistants effectively use a word processor to cut down on the time-consuming task of writing. Legal assistants routinely write correspondence, memorandums, court documents, and more.

The primary role of the legal assistant is to assist attorneys in all aspects of practicing law. Legal assistants must be able to do many things well. The specific duties of a legal assistant differ, because each legal organization practices its own specialty of law and has its own procedures. Nevertheless, the legal assistant's job almost always requires writing and organizing in one form

or another. The abilities to draft and write quality documents on their own and to analyze, research, and organize are qualities that make legal assistants invaluable. While computer use is the focus of this text, good writing skills are extremely important to any legal assistant. Legal assistants can use a word processor in many of their writing tasks.

Drafting Correspondence, Interoffice Memorandums, Legal Documents, and Taking Notes

Legal assistants use word processors to draft correspondence (i.e., letters to clients, court staff, other legal assistants, and attorneys).

Legal assistants may also be required to type interoffice memorandums regarding a case or legal matter. Legal assistants who are required to investigate a matter or interview witnesses must always submit a report of their findings, usually in the form of an interoffice memorandum.

Legal assistants who are required to perform legal research must also write interoffice memos regarding their findings and conclusions.

Other documents that legal assistants use word processors for include affidavits (formal statements that are taken under oath and signed by the people making them), wills (documents that direct how people's property will be distributed at their death), and contracts (legal documents stating the terms of an agreement).

Legal assistants may also be required to take notes for an attorney who is busy or unable to take notes. For example, if an attorney is questioning a witness on complicated matters, it might be difficult to ask the questions, follow the responses, and take notes, all at the same time. In this case, a legal assistant might be brought in to take notes. Taking notes on a word processor is much easier than writing in longhand, because the document can be edited and redrafted. Also, longhand tends to get sloppy, and many times the notes have to be typed anyway so they can go into the file.

Typing Repetitive Documents

Much of what legal assistants and attorneys do is repetitive. In many cases, the same letters must be sent, the same type of pleadings (legal documents that are filed with a court) must be filed, the same type of interrogatories (written questions that are directed to the opposing side regarding a case) must be prepared, and so on.

Although no two situations are exactly alike, often previously drafted documents have only to be edited to fit a new client or situation. It is common for attorneys and legal assistants to practice a particular type of law or have a specialty, such as personal injury law (which deals with people who have been injured in accidents), corporate law (which concerns the legal aspects of a corporation), or criminal law (which deals with preparing a defense for a person accused of a crime). Attorneys and legal assistants who practice a specialty almost always encounter the same situations over and over. Word processors are suited for repetitive documents, because a document can be saved and later retrieved and edited instead of being retyped from scratch each time.

Typing Form Letters

Legal assistants must sometimes type form letters. A form letter has standard or stock language that usually does not change. The only thing that changes is certain information such as the name and address of the addressee. When the

merge feature of a word processor is used, the text of a form letter has to be typed only once, and the information that changes can be merged into the form, thus saving considerable typing time. It is important to not overwrite the form or template with case-specific information about a client. Document assembly programs can also be used to effectively generate form letters.

Producing Legal Briefs

Legal assistants are sometimes asked to assist in drafting legal briefs. A legal brief is a formal document that is filed with a court and is usually full of both factual and legal arguments. A factual argument concerns a dispute over the facts or underlying events that led up to a case, whereas a legal argument concerns what the law is or how it should be applied to the case at hand. Most legal briefs must have a table of contents and a table of authorities. Many word processors are particularly suited to producing legal briefs, because they can automatically generate these tables quickly and more easily than one can by hand.

Preparing Drafts of Pleadings, Motions, and Discovery Requests

Many legal assistants prepare drafts of pleadings, motions, and discovery requests for their supervising attorney to review. With any kind of formal document that is to be filed with a court it is imperative that the legal assistant consult the court's local rules to make sure the format of the document complies with the rules. Tracking changes and revisions can be fairly painless when using the automated features of most word processors. Typically, the document is emailed to the supervising attorney, who revises the document online and then emails the document back to the legal assistant for final revisions and e-filing with the clerk.

Typing Documents That Require Footnotes

Some research assignments and other documents require a legal assistant to use footnotes. Footnoting on a standard typewriter is a long and difficult chore, because it is sometimes hard to judge how long a footnote will be. On the other hand, footnoting on a word processor is a simple task.

Drafting Deposition Summaries

Legal assistants who practice in the area of litigation must routinely summarize deposition transcripts. The summary or outline gives the attorney a quick digest of the testimony to remind the attorney of what a witness said previously and to allow the attorney to quickly refer back to particular pages of the transcript itself.

Preparing Litigation Support—Type Documents

Because of enhanced features that have been added to word processors, some firms have begun using their word processors to perform litigation support tasks. Litigation support refers to organizing, storing, retrieving, and summarizing information that is gathered in the litigation of a lawsuit.

For example, most word processors can search for words or phrases within a document. Thus, a legal assistant who prepared a deposition summary on a word processor would be able to use the search or find feature to search for

specific words or phrases, such as a person's name. Most word processors also have the ability to search for words or phrases through all of a user's word processing documents or files with one command. Thus, for example, if a legal assistant had twenty deposition summaries (i.e., twenty separate documents or files), she could instruct the word processor to look for a person's name through all the files with one command.

Note that although a word processor is better than nothing, it does not have the power and flexibility of a true litigation support program and is a poor substitute.

Preparing Database Management Documents

Most full-featured word processors can sort data (basic functions only) much like a database management system. For example, if you have a list of names or columns of information that need to be sorted in alphabetical order, many word processors have a sort function that will automatically do so. The sorting features of a word processor are not nearly as advanced as those of a database management system and, again, are a poor substitute for a full-featured database program.

Microsoft Word Online Training and Word Templates

Microsoft provides free online training courses for Microsoft Word 2007 and 2003 on their website. More than twenty courses are available for each product. To find the online training courses use a general search engine such as www.google.com or www.yahoo.com and use the search criteria: Microsoft Word 2003 Courses or Microsoft Word 2007 Courses.

Microsoft also provides a wide variety of free Word templates on their website. In Word 2007, the online templates can be accessed by selecting the Office Button, selecting New, and then clicking on any of the categories to the left of the screen under Microsoft Office Online. In Word 2003, the online templates can be accessed by selecting File, selecting New, and then selecting Templates on Office Online under the Templates heading.

ETHICAL CONSIDERATIONS

While word processing has done wonders for the legal profession in terms of efficiency and ease of use, it has a negative side as well that raises an important ethical issue. Word processors have the ability to make users lazy. For instance, users can misspell words because the spell checker will catch them. Users can use poor grammar, because the grammar checker will fix it. Users do not have to start from scratch to prepare a will or other legal document because form wills, templates, and other documents that can easily be modified are available on the computer or for purchase on the Internet. Users do not have to go back and do legal research over and over again every time a new legal document is filed, because they can cut and copy legal research from one client's documents to another.

Finally, even if a document's content is not very good, users can make it look pretty with fancy fonts, justified margins, tables, and many other features. And that is the problem—potential lack of content. An attorney has an ethical duty to provide competent representation. Lawyers and legal assistants must make sure that their word processing documents are competently and thoroughly prepared. That is, they should not only look good, but also be

proofread well, contain up-to-date and accurate cites, and be the best documents the attorney or legal assistant can produce.

The following are a few common problems with using word processors.

Leaving Metadata in Documents

As you may recall from Chapter 2, metadata is electronically stored information in files that may identify the origin, date, author, usage, comments, or other information about a file. Metadata is often described as "data about data." It is important that any document a legal organization prepares has the metadata from the document deleted from it before it leaves the firm. In Chapter 2, we discussed several instances were noted where metadata in word-processing documents and PDF files were accessed and used against the creators of the document. WordPerfect X3 allows the user to save documents without metadata. See Exhibit 3–2 and notice that on WordPerfect's File menu there is a specific command called Save Without Metadata. In Word 2007 a user can inspect all parts of a document for metadata (see Exhibit 3–31A). If metadata is discovered in the document, the user can choose to remove it. In addition, Adobe Acrobat now has

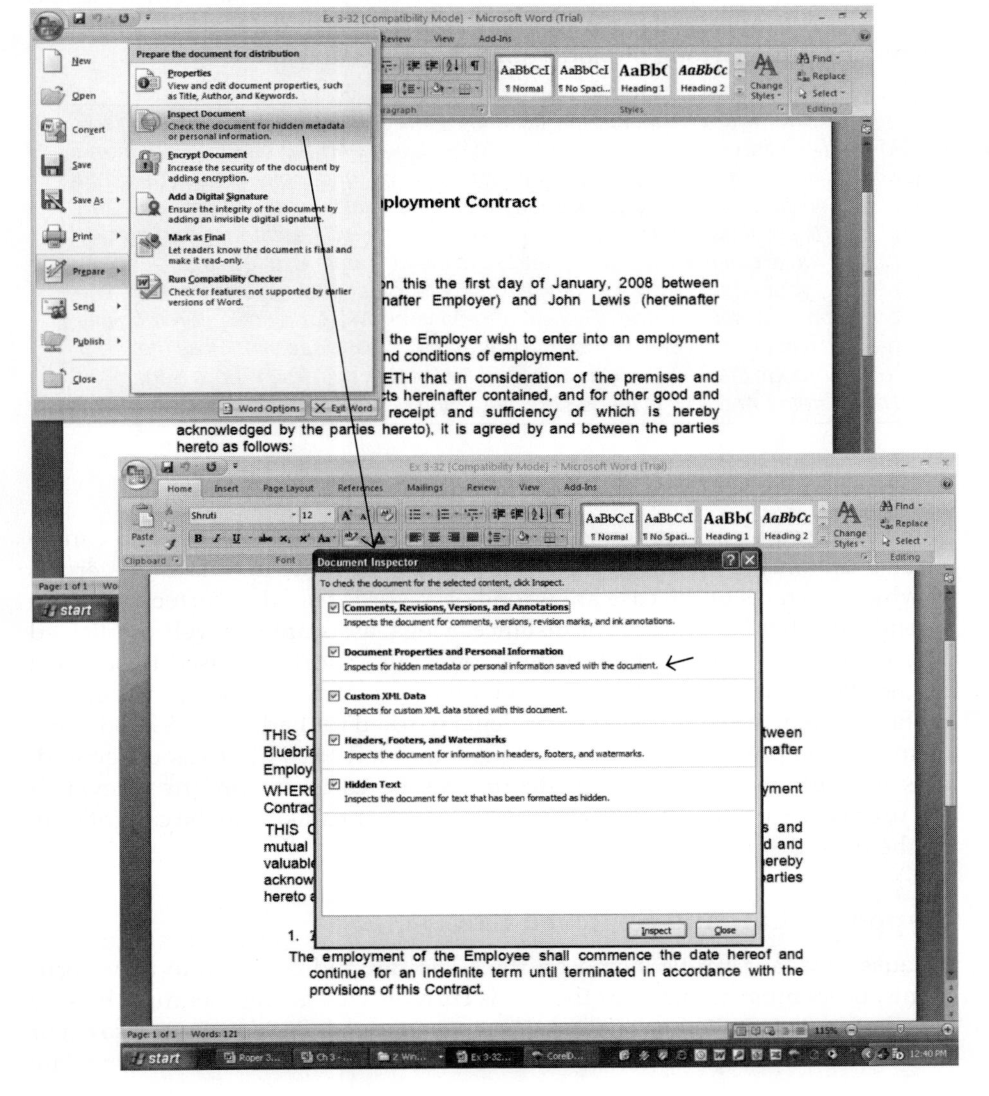

Exhibit 3–31A

Inspecting Documents for Metadata in Word 2007

Microsoft product screen shot reprinted with permission from Microsoft Corporation.

strong security enhancements that can remove metadata in PDF files and permanently remove information that has been redacted.

It should be noted that while legal organizations do not want word processing and other case related documents going out of the office with metadata, some courts have found that in the context of electronic discovery (documents that are produced in the discovery stage of a lawsuit), opposing parties are entitled to metadata. This will be discussed at length in Chapter 8. However, it is important to note that there is a major difference between documents prepared by attorneys for their clients (e.g., word processing documents), where security is of the utmost importance, and discovery documents produced by clients for the opposing parties, where some courts have said the parties have the right to see metadata, including the origin of documents and other information. Before a word-processing document leaves the legal organization is it important as a matter of practice to make sure the document has no metadata attached to it.

Old Client Data Left in New Document

It is common when preparing a new document to retrieve an old document. For instance, when preparing a new real estate contract, the user might pull up an old real estate contract from a few months ago as a place to start. The trouble is that it is easy to leave the old data (i.e., old property description, old client names, old prices, wrong pronouns) in the new document.

Imagine that you have just prepared a fancy will and estate plan for the elderly Mr. McMannion (who has one foot in Forest Lawn and the other on a banana peel). The will is double justified, with lots of fonts, and looks great. The client has been charged a goodly fee, even though the total time and talent consisted of the 10 seconds it took you to retrieve the master will / estate file and quickly fill it in. You are at the will signing, and so is the accountant, a few important witnesses, your supervising attorney, and several other attorneys of the firm. The occasion is a solemn one. The soon-to-pass-on McMannion is ceremonially handed a copy of his Last Will and Testament. There is dead silence as the client reads through the will. Then the testator McMannion speaks: "Who is Sugar Ray Rubenstein? And why is he getting everything I own?"

Typographical Errors the Spell Checker Will Not Catch

Some typographical errors will not be caught by a spell checker and can be picked up only by carefully proofreading a document. These are errors in which the facts of the case are wrong or a word is spelled correctly but the wrong word has been used. For instance, a legal assistant in a well-publicized case mistakenly left out the last three zeros on a mortgage used to secure a $92,885,000 loan to a company that eventually went into bankruptcy. Because of the mistake, the company the paralegal worked for had only a $92,885 lien. Going by the provisions of the mortgage, that left $92,792,115 as unsecured. It is absolutely critical that all documents be carefully proofread even if the user is using a word processor, because some mistakes can be caught only by the user.

Inapposite Law and Switched Law

Because case law can be stored on the computer and copied into new documents, users must be sure that the law is current. That is, the user must be sure that the law being cited has not now been overturned. Problems can also occur if case law that is copied is not relevant to the new client because the wrong law

is copied, the law does not apply to the new client's fact situation, or the case that is being cited is no longer good law.

Improper Form Selected, Leaving In or Deleting Wrong Paragraphs

It is very easy to select the wrong form when choosing documents. Unfortunately, this can have a devastating impact. Another very easy error is to either leave in or delete a wrong paragraph from the form. If you are using a form, it is important to know and understand every paragraph in the form so you can make appropriate decisions about what stays and what goes.

Not Following Court Rules

Many courts have rules regarding the kind of font or type used, the size of font, margin widths, and paper sizes. It is important that these rules be followed. In one case, a corporate legal department repeatedly filed appellate briefs using a 10-point Times New Roman font instead of using a 12-point Courier as required by court rules. The law department did this because another court rule limited briefs to thirty pages and so they could get 50 percent more verbiage using the smaller font. The court dismissed the appeal for not following court rules.

Preparing Legal Documents without the Supervision of an Attorney (The Unauthorized Practice of Law)

Most states have a criminal statute that prohibits a layperson from practicing law. Besides criminal prosecutions, there are ethical prohibitions as well that prevent a nonlawyer from practicing law. Simply put, legal assistants cannot draft legal documents such as wills, briefs, motions, pleadings, or contracts *without* the supervision of an attorney. Legal assistants routinely draft these types of documents; the distinction is that they do so properly under the direction and supervision of a member of the bar. The attorney is ultimately responsible for the legal documents. But what happens if an attorney does not look at a document a legal assistant has prepared using a word processor or document assembly program? Assume the legal assistant has been working hard on a motion and has taken cases and arguments from past documents prepared by the supervising attorney, but the document is due at 5:00 P.M. and there is no time for the attorney to review it. This is how unauthorized practice of law issues regarding word processing and drafting documents arise in real life.

> *It is the obligation of the legal assistant to make sure his or her work product is reviewed by the lawyer before it is filed with a court or agency or shown to a client or third party.*[5]

The reason for the rule is that legal documents affect the legal rights of clients and parties and therefore require the oversight of an attorney. As long as a legal assistant is actively working under the supervision of an attorney and the attorney maintains a relationship with the client, the legal assistant may interview witnesses or prospective clients, perform legal research, draft pleadings and briefs, and investigate the facts of cases without being accused of the unauthorized practice of law. However, the minute the legal assistant prepares a legal document on his or her own, without the review of an attorney, a breach of the rule has most likely occurred. No matter how routine the legal document is, always have an attorney review it. Never let an attorney approve your work

without reading it. If the attorney says "I do not have time to review it, I'll sign it and you just send it out, I trust you," bring the document back at another time or find a tactful way to suggest to the attorney that the document needs to be approved the right way.

Overlooking Prudent Practices

Use the Full-Function Spell and Grammar Checker While you should not just rely on the spell / grammar checker for your only review of documents you should by all means use these functions on every document you prepare. There is nothing more embarrassing than finding obvious typographical / grammar errors in a document that has gone out—particularly when it has been sent out under the signature of your supervising attorney. Never assume the automatic spell / grammar checking that occurs as you type your document (where problems are underlined with squiggly lines in color) is enough. It is not. It is extremely easy when drafting to forget to see these errors. Always go back and run the full-function spell / grammar checker to make sure you have not missed any obvious mistakes.

Always Validate Cases / Citations and Factual References Before a legal assistant cites an unfamiliar case or references a fact in a legal document that he or she is unsure about, it is imperative to double-check and validate the case or fact to make sure it is good law or that the "fact" actually happened. Never throw something down in a word processor with the thought that you will get back to it and verify it—what happens if you forget? The answer is that the client can be harmed, the attorney's reputation can be harmed, your reputation certainly will be harmed, and ethical ramifications could occur for your supervising attorney or the legal office. Do not take the chance; always double-check your work.

Password Protect Confidential Word Processing Documents That Will Be Emailed It is always a good idea, out of the abundance of caution, to password protect confidential documents that will be emailed through an Internet provider or over large networks. Most word processing programs have the capability to do this and it is very easy to do. It does not cost anything and it is just one more layer of protection to maintain the confidentiality of client / case related data.

Both Word and WordPerfect can password protect their word-processing files (see Exhibit 3–32).

SUMMARY

Word processors are computer programs that are used to edit, manipulate, and revise text to create documents. A centralized word-processing system has a separate word-processing department that types all correspondence for an organization, as opposed to a decentralized word-processing system where individuals perform word processing for themselves or a small group. The two word-processing programs that dominate the legal word-processing market are Microsoft Word and Corel WordPerfect.

Modern legal organizations use a variety of word processing functions and features including, among others, automatic paragraph numbering, styles, footnotes, tables, macros, making comments, comparing multiple documents, tracking changes, creating tables of authorities, and merging documents.

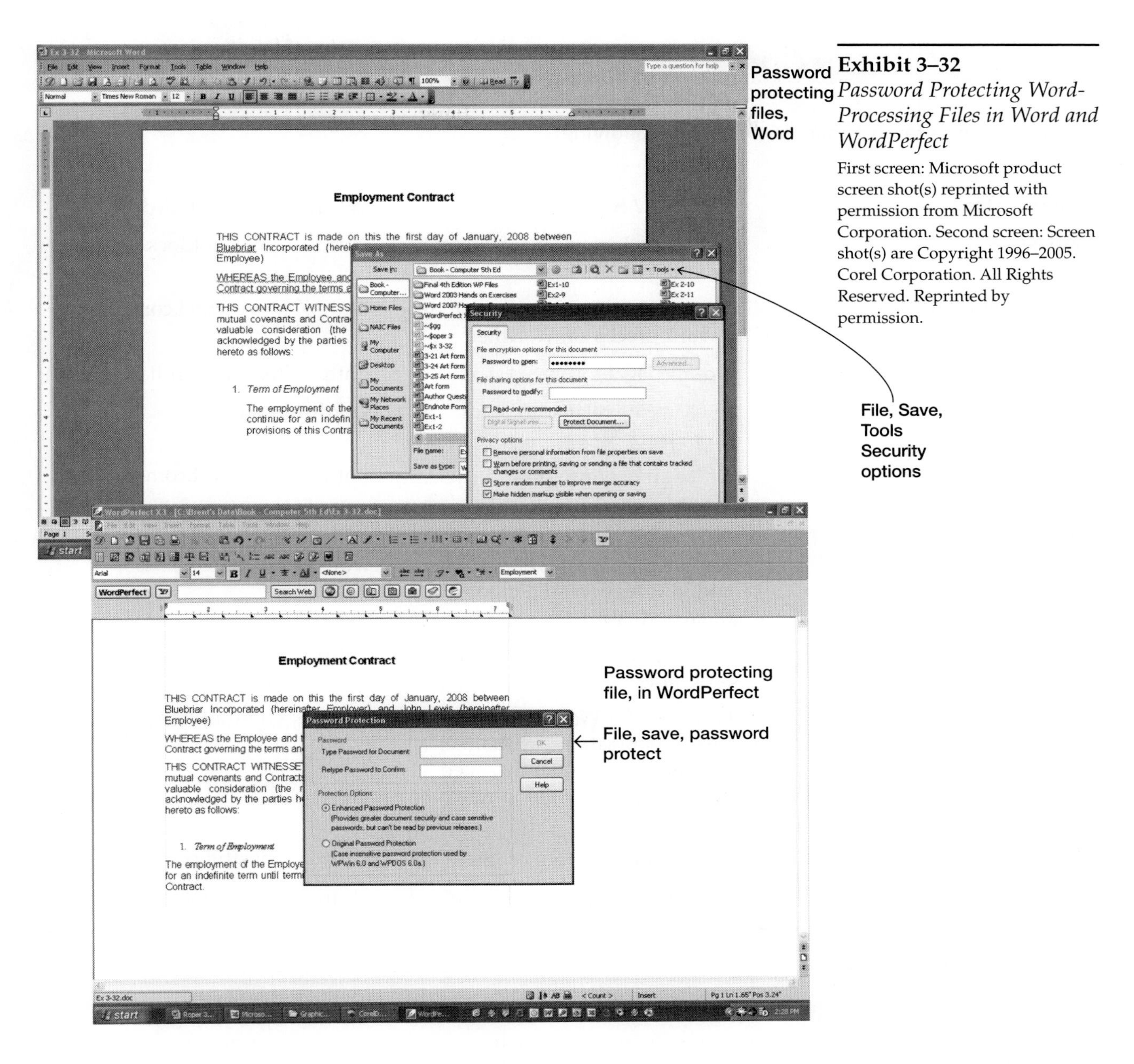

Exhibit 3–32
Password Protecting Word-Processing Files in Word and WordPerfect
First screen: Microsoft product screen shot(s) reprinted with permission from Microsoft Corporation. Second screen: Screen shot(s) are Copyright 1996–2005. Corel Corporation. All Rights Reserved. Reprinted by permission.

Creating Portable Document Format (PDF) files is an important part of document generation for many legal organizations because many jurisdictions require word-processing documents to be filed electronically in this format. Adobe Acrobat is one of the most popular programs used for converting files into PDFs.

Document assembly software creates powerful templates for form documents. Once the user answers the questions in the template, the answers are then merged with the template and a final document is prepared. Document assembly software is extremely sophisticated and has many functions in legal organizations.

When preparing legal documents it is important for users to carefully review their work to ensure old information is not left in documents, metadata is deleted, research is updated and current, and there are no typographical errors.

INTERNET SITES

Internet sites for this chapter include the following:

Organization	Product / Service	World Wide Web Address
LexisNexis	Hot Docs document assembly program	<http://www.hotdocs.com>
Corel Corporation	Office suite of programs including a word processor, WordPerfect	<http://www.corel.com>
Findlaw.com	On-line legal forms	<http://forms.lp.findlaw.com>
wordprocessing.com	Internet site related to word processing	wordprocessing.com
Microsoft	Office suite of programs including a word processor—Word	<http://microsoft.com>
Microsoft	Microsoft Word home page containing a wealth of tips, tricks, and information related to Microsoft Word	<http://www.microsoft.com/word>
ProDoc	Pro Doc document assembly program	<http://www.prodoc.com>
Web Resources for Microsoft Word	Large site for Word users in legal organizations, with links to templates, frequently asked questions, tutorials, and much more	<http://www.addbalance.com/word>
Ghostfill Technologies, Inc.	Document assembly program	<http://ghostfill.com>
Adobe Systems, Inc.	Adobe Acrobat PDF file creation	<http://www.adobe.com>

KEY TERMS

word processing software
Portable Document Format (PDF)
document assembly software
centralized word-processing system
decentralized word-processing system
style
header
footer
double indenting
footnote
endnote
table
macro
comment
compare document
track changes
table of authorities
Pleading Wizard
merging
primary file
secondary file

TEST YOUR KNOWLEDGE

1. What does PDF stand for?
2. Compare and contrast centralized and decentralized word processing.
3. What product was a leader in the legal word-processing market in the mid-1980s and early 1990s?
4. Many legal organizations use this word-processing program because many of their corporate clients use it.
5. True / False: The automatic paragraph numbering feature numbers the pages in a document.

6. True / False: A style is a named set of formatting characteristics that users apply to text.
7. Text that is indented an equal distance from the left and right margin is called _______.
8. True / False: A word-processing feature that combines a primary and secondary file is called a macro.
9. A word-processing feature that allows the reviewer to make annotations in the document without actually changing it is called a _______.
10. Distinguish between primary and secondary merge files.
11. What standard document type do most courts use to allow attorneys to file documents electronically?
12. True / False: Word-processing merge files have the same exact features as stand-alone document assembly programs.

ON THE WEB EXERCISES

1. Using the websites at the end of the chapter and a general Internet search engine (like google.com or yahoo.com), research the current versions of Microsoft Word and Corel WordPerfect. Prepare a summary of the differences, similarities, and reviews of the products. Which product would you rather use in the legal environment and why?
2. Using the websites at the end of the chapter and a general Internet search engine (like google.com or yahoo.com), research the Case Management and Electronic Filing System for the U.S. federal courts. Write a two-page summary of your findings including how it works, what the standard is, and other relevant information about the system.
3. Using the websites at the end of the chapter and a general Internet search engine (like google.com or yahoo.com), find a word-processing template for a general will (Last Will and Testament) for your state. How hard or easy was it to find? Were you able to find fee-based forms, free forms, or both?
4. Using http://forms.lp.findlaw.com/ find a recent United States Supreme Court opinion under "Laws: Cases and Codes." Copy and paste the opinion into your word processor. How easy was this to do? Can you manipulate and edit the document? Describe why using the Internet and your word processor in this way might be an important feature for a legal organization.
5. Using the websites at the end of the chapter and a general Internet search engine (like google.com or yahoo.com), research document assembly programs. What programs did you find? What features do they have? What are their advantages? How are they different from the merge capabilities in word processors? Do they have any disadvantages?
6. Using the websites at the end of the chapter and a general Internet search engine (like google.com or yahoo.com), research what a PDF file is and what advantages PDFs have over other file formats.

QUESTIONS AND EXERCISES

1. Contact a law office, legal organization, legal assistant, or attorney you know and ask what word processor they use and why. Ask what features they like about it, what features they wish they had, whether the program is fulfilling their basic needs, and whether they are looking to change word processors. Also, ask who does word processing at the firm, and if there is a centralized or decentralized system. Type a one-page summary of your conversations.
2. Word processors have developed over time so that they have hundreds of features and functions. Write a short paper on the top ten functions or features that you use when you do word processing. Explain what each function is and why you use it.
3. On your own computer open any word processing document in your word processor. Point and click on File and then on Properties. What metadata was included in the "Properties" section of the document, were you surprised at the amount of data given?
4. In Microsoft Word, open a new document and do the following:
   a. Type the following phrases: This is secret text no one should see. This is text that is open to the public.
   b. Turn on Track Changes by going to "Tools" on the menu bar and then on "Track Changes."
   c. Now, using the delete key, delete the sentence "This is secret text no one should see." Notice that to the right it now shows the text is deleted.

d. Point and click with your mouse on the down arrow next to "Final Showing Markup" in the "Display for Review" item on the Reviewing toolbar. Then click on "Final." Notice that you cannot see "This is secret text no one should see." Assume for this exercise that you sent this document to the opposing party in a case.
e. Now, assume you are the opposing party in the case. Select the down arrow next to "Final" in the "Display for Review" item on the Reviewing toolbar and select "Original." Notice that you can perfectly see the "This is secret text no one should see." Point and click with your mouse on the down arrow next to "Original" in the "Display for Review" item on the Reviewing toolbar and select "Original Showing Markup." You can now see all of the changes in the document.

END NOTES

[1] Dennis Kennedy, "Putting PDF and Adobe Acrobat in Your Tech Toolbox," *Law Practice* May 2004.
[2] "Kim T. Plonsky," "Learning to Fly," *Legal Assistant Today,* July / August 2005, 42.
[3] David Masters, "*Adobe Acrobat 8 For Legal Professionals,*" 2, Adobe Systems, Inc., 2007.
[4] "Kim T. Plonsky," "Learning to Fly," *Legal Assistant Today,* July / August 2005, 42.
[5] *The Legal Assistant's Guide to Professional Responsibility,* 2nd Edition, American Bar Association, 2004, 30.

HANDS-ON EXERCISES

WORD PROCESSING HANDS-ON EXERCISES

READ THIS FIRST!

1. Microsoft Word 2007
2. Microsoft Word 2003
3. Corel WordPerfect X3

I. DETERMINING WHICH TUTORIAL TO COMPLETE

To use the Word Processing Hands-On Exercises you must already own or have access to Microsoft Word 2007, Microsoft Word 2003, or Corel WordPerfect X3. If you have one of the programs but do not know the version you are using it is easy to find out (e.g. whether your version is Word 2007, Word 2003, WordPerfect X3, or some other version of these programs). For Word 2003 and Corel WordPerfect X3, load your word processor and then point and click on "Help" from menu and then on "About [name of the program]" (e.g., "About Microsoft Office Word.)" It should then tell you exactly what version of the program you are using. For Word 2007 you should point and click on the Office Button, and then click on "Word Options" and then look under the title "Resources." You must know the version of the program you are using and select the correct tutorial version or the tutorials will not work correctly. For example, if you have Word 2003 but try to use the Word 2007 tutorial, the tutorial will not work correctly.

II. USING THE WORD PROCESSING HANDS-ON EXERCISES

The Word Processing Hands-On Exercises in this section are easy to use and contain step-by-step instructions. They start with basic word-processing skills and proceed to intermediate and advanced levels. If you already have a good working knowledge of your word processor, you may be able to proceed directly to the intermediate and advanced exercises. To truly be ready for word processing in a legal environment you must be able to accomplish the tasks and exercises in the advanced exercises. Please note that the WordPerfect X3 tutorial is included on a disk that comes with the text.

III. ACCESSING THE HANDS-ON EXERCISE FILES ON THE CDs THAT COME WITH THE TEXT

Some of the intermediate and advanced Word Processing Hands-On Exercises use documents on Disk 1 of the CDs that come with the text. On some computers, to access the files all you need to do is put the disk in the drive, close it, and the directory will automaticaly be loaded. If the directory does not automatically load, follow the directions below. To access these files, in Windows XP, or Windows Vista put the CD in your computer select "Start," My Computer," then select the appropriate drive- and then double-click on the Word-Processing Files folder. To access the exercise files, then double-click on the appropriate folder (e.g., Word or WordPerfect). You should then see a list of word processing files that are available for each lesson. To access these files in Windows Vista, put the CD in your computer, select the Start button, select Computer and then double-click on the appropriate folder (e.g., Word or WordPerfect). You should then see a list of word processing files that are available for each lesson.

HANDS-ON EXERCISES

MICROSOFT WORD 2007 FOR WINDOWS

IV. INSTALLATION QUESTIONS

If you have installation questions regarding loading the word processing file from the data disk, you may contact Technical Support at 800/477-3692.

Basic Lessons

Number	Lesson Title	Concepts Covered
Lesson 1	Typing a Letter	Using word wrap, tab key, cursor keys, underline, bold, italic, saving and printing a document.
Lesson 2	Editing a Letter	Retrieving a file, block moving/deleting, and spell/grammar checking.
Lesson 3	Typing a Pleading	Centering, changing margins, changing line spacing, adding a footnote, double indenting, and automatic page numbering.
Lesson 4	Creating a Table	Creating a table, entering data in a table, using automatic numbering, adjusting columns in a table and using the table auto format command.

Intermediate Lessons

Number	Lesson Title	Concepts Covered
Lesson 5	Tools and Techniques (Using the "Lesson 5" file on Disk 1)	Editing an employment policy, using the Format Painter tool, revealing formatting, beginning of document command, clear formatting, change case, search and replace, go to command, creating a section break, and changing the orientation of the page to Landscape.
Lesson 6	Using Styles (Using the "Lesson 6" file on Disk 1)	Using, modifying, and creating styles to maintain consistent and uniform formatting of documents.
Lesson 7	Creating a Template (Office Letterhead/ Letter)	Finding ready-made templates in Word, creating a new office letterhead and letter template, filling in/completing a, template, and adding a command to the Quick Access Toolbar.
Lesson 8	Comparing Documents (multiple versions of an employment contract) (Using the "Lesson 8A and 8B" file on Disk 1)	Comparing documents using the simultaneous viewing method and merging the documents into a separate, annotated, blacklined document.
Lesson 9	Using Track Changes (Using the "Lesson 9" file on Disk 1)	Turning on track changes, making revisions, and then accepting and rejecting revisions.

Advanced Lessons

Number	Lesson Title	Concepts Covered
Lesson 10	Creating a Mail Merge	Creating and entering a list of recipients for a mail merge, creating a mail merge document, and merging the list with the document.
Lesson 11	Creating a Table of Authorities in a Brief (Using the "Lesson 11" file on Disk 1)	Finding and marking cases in a brief, and then generating an actual table of authorities for the brief.
Lesson 12	Creating a Macro (Pleading Signature Block)	Creating and executing a pleading signature block macro.

Number	Lesson Title	Concepts Covered
Lesson 13	Drafting a Will	Using Word to draft a will.
Lesson 14	The Pleading Wizard	Using the Pleading Wizard.
Lesson 15	Deposition Summary	Summarizing a deposition using Word.

GETTING STARTED

Introduction

Throughout these lessons and exercises, information you need to type into the program will be designated in several different ways:

- Keys to be pressed on the keyboard will be designated in brackets, in all caps, and in bold (i.e., press the: **[ENTER]** key).
- Movements with the mouse will be designated in bold and italics (i.e., ***point to "File" on the menu bar and click the mouse***).
- Words or letters that should be typed will be designated in bold (i.e., type: **Training Program).**
- Information that should be displayed on your computer screen is shown in the following style: ***Press ENTER to continue.***

OVERVIEW OF MICROSOFT WORD 2007

Below are some tips on using Microsoft Word that will help you complete these exercises.

I. General Rules for Microsoft Word 2007

A. *Word Wrap*—You do not need to press the **[ENTER]** key after each line of text like you would with a typewriter.

B. *Double-Spacing*—If you want to double-space, do not hit the **[ENTER]** key twice. Instead, change the line spacing by ***clicking on the Home Ribbon tab, then clicking on the Line spacing icon in the Paragraph group and selecting*** 2 (see Word 2007 Exhibit 1).

C. *Moving Through Already Entered Text*—If you want to move the mouse pointer to various positions within already entered text, ***use the cursor (arrow) keys, or point and click.***

D. *Moving the Pointer Where No Text Has Been Entered*—You cannot use the cursor keys to move the pointer where no text has been entered. Said another way, you cannot move any further in a document than where you have typed text or pressed the **[ENTER]** key. You must use the **[ENTER]** key or first type text.

E. *Saving a Document*—To save a document, ***click the Office Button in the upper left corner of the screen and then click Save*** (see Word 2007 Exhibit 1).

F. *New Document*—To get a new, clean document, ***click the Office Button, then click New, and then double-click on "Blank document"*** (see Word 2007 Exhibit 1).

G. *Help*—To get help, press **[F1]** or ***click on the ? icon in the upper right corner of the screen*** (see Word 2007 Exhibit 1).

HANDS-ON EXERCISES

Word 2007 Exhibit 1
Word 2007 Screen
Microsoft product screen shot reprinted with permission from Microsoft Corporation.

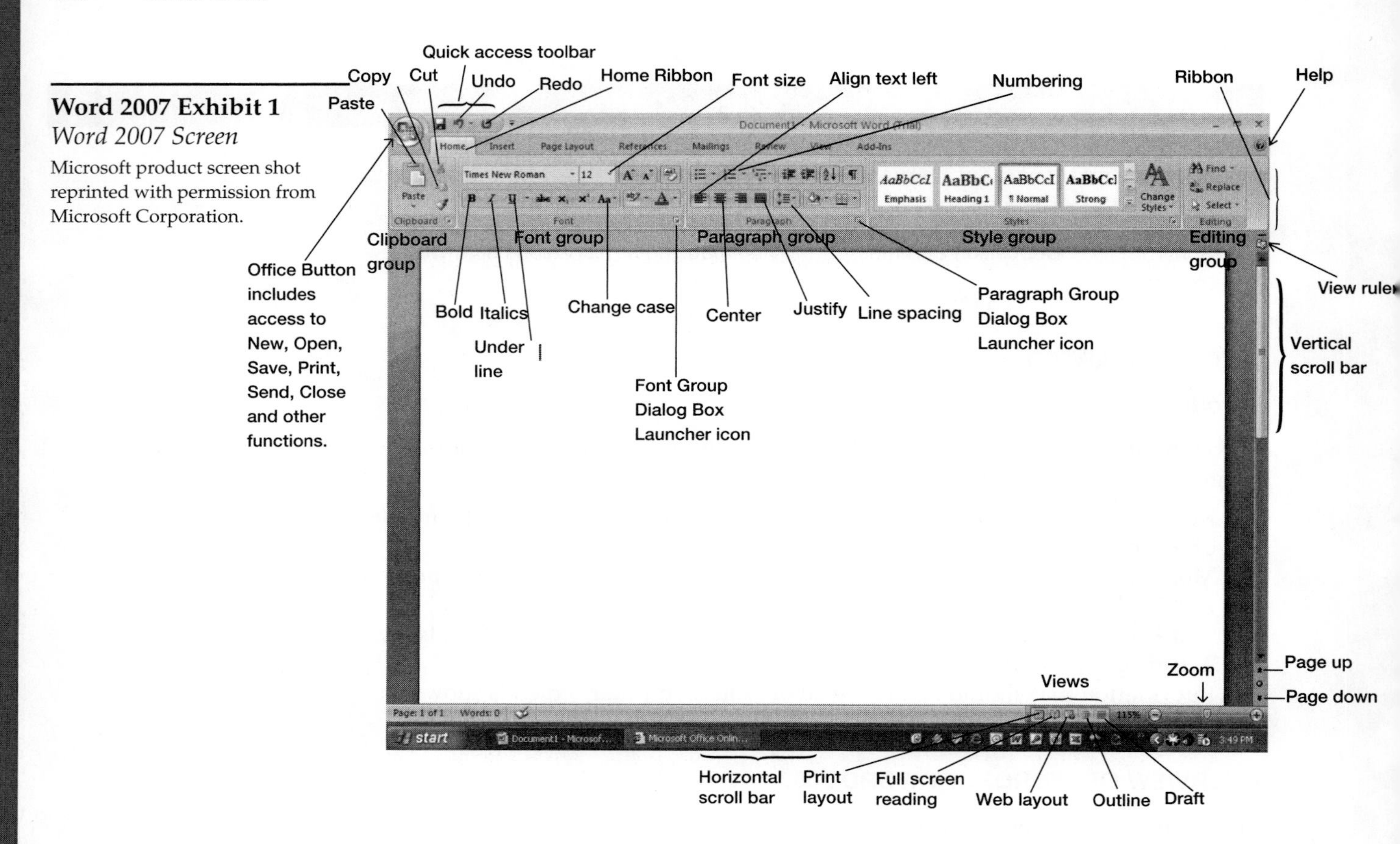

II. Editing a Document

A. *Pointer Movement*

One space to left	[LEFT ARROW]
One space to right	[RIGHT ARROW]
Beginning of line	[HOME]
End of line	[END]
One line up	[UP ARROW]
One line down	[DOWN ARROW]
One screen up	[PAGE UP]
One screen down	[PAGE DOWN]
Beginning of document	[CTRL]+[HOME]
End of document	[CTRL]+[END]

B. *Deleting Text*

Delete the text under the pointer or to the right	[DEL]
Delete the text to the left of the pointer	[BACKSPACE]
Delete the whole word to the left of the pointer	[CTRL]+[BACKSPACE]
Delete the whole word to the right of the pointer	[CTRL]+[DEL]

C. *Delete Blocked Text*—***Drag the mouse pointer to select or highlight text,*** and press **[DEL]**, or ***drag the mouse pointer, and then from the Home Ribbon tab, select the Cut icon from the Clipboard group*** (see Word 2007 Exhibit 1). Another way to select or highlight text is ***while pressing the [SHIFT] key, use the cursor keys to mark/highlight the desired text.***

D. *Undoing/Undeleting Text*—If you delete text and immediately want it back, ***click the Undo icon on the Quick Access Toolbar.*** This can also be done by pressing **[CTRL]+[Z]**. Press **[CTRL]+[Z]** or click the Undo icon until your

desired text reappears. The Undo feature works on many other activities in Word, but not all. So, if something goes wrong, at least try pressing **[CTRL]+[Z]** to undo whatever you did.

E. *Moving Text*—***Drag the mouse pointer to highlight or select the text. Then, from the Home Ribbon tab, select the Cut icon from the Clipboard group*** (see Word 2007 Exhibit 1), ***move the mouse pointer to where the text should be moved, and, from the Home Ribbon tab, select Paste from the Clipboard group.*** Another way to do this is to ***drag the mouse pointer to highlight the area and then right-click.*** This brings up a menu that includes the ***Cut, Copy,*** *and* ***Paste*** commands. Yet another way to do this is to use the drag-and-drop method. The user ***drags the mouse pointer to highlight the area, releases the mouse button, clicks the highlighted area, and drags the text to the new location, and releases the mouse button.***

F. Copying Text—***Drag the mouse pointer to highlight or select the area. From the Home Ribbon tab, click the Copy icon from the Clipboard group (see Word 2007 Exhibit 1). Then, move the mouse pointer to where the text should be copied, and from the Home Ribbon tab, click Paste.*** Another way to do this is to ***drag the pointer to highlight the area and then right-click Copy. Then move the cursor to where the text should be copied to and right-click Paste.*** Still another way to do this is to use the drag-and-drop method. ***The user drags the pointer to highlight the area, releases the mouse button, clicks the highlighted area*** while pressing **[CTRL]**, ***drags the text to the new location, and releases the mouse button.*** The text is then copied to the new location.

III. Formatting

A. *Centering Text*—Move the pointer to the line where the text should be centered. ***From the Home Ribbon tab, click the Paragraph Group Dialog Box Launcher icon (see Word 2007 Exhibit 1). In the Indents and Spacing tab, click on the down arrow key next to Alignment and select Centered, then click on OK and begin typing.*** If the text has already been typed, move the pointer to the paragraph where the text is and then issue the command. ***Alternatively, from the Home Ribbon tab, click the Center icon in the Paragraph group (see Word 2007 Exhibit 1).***

B. *Bold Type*—To type in bold, ***from the Home Ribbon tab, click the Font Group Dialog Box Launcher icon (see Word 2007 Exhibit 1), and then in the Font tab, click Bold under Font Style. Then, click on OK. Alternatively from the Home Ribbon tab, click the Bold icon in the Font group.*** Another way is to press **[CTRL]+[B]**.

C. *Underlining*—To underline, ***from the Home Ribbon tab, click the Font Group Dialog Box Launcher icon (see Word 2007 Exhibit 1). Then, in the Font tab, click the down arrow under Underline style, select the underline style you would like, and then click OK.*** Alternatively, ***from the Home Ribbon tab, click the Underline icon in the Font group.*** Another way is to press **[CTRL]+[U]**.

D. *Margins*—Margins can be set by ***clicking the Page Layout ribbon tab and then clicking on Margins from the Page Setup group.***

E. *Line Spacing*—Line spacing can be changed by ***clicking the Home Ribbon tab, and then clicking the Line Spacing icon in the Paragraph group (see Word 2007 Exhibit 1).***

F. *Justification*—Move the pointer to the line where the text should be justified, and then, ***from the Home Ribbon tab, click the Paragraph Group Dialog Box Launcher icon (see Word 2007 Exhibit 1). In the Indents and Spacing tab, click the down arrow key next to Alignment and select Justified, and then click on OK and begin typing.*** If the text has already been typed, move the cursor to the paragraph where the text is and then issue the command. ***Alternatively, from the Home Ribbon tab, click the Justify icon in the Paragraph group (see Word 2007 Exhibit 1).***

G. *Header/Footer*—***From the Insert ribbon tab, click Header or Footer from the Header & Footer group.***

H. *Hard Page Break* — To force the addition of a new page in the current document by using the hard page break command, press **[CTRL]+[ENTER]**, or ***from the Insert ribbon tab, click Blank Page from the Pages group.*** Page breaks also occur automatically when the current page is full of text.

I. *Indent* — ***From the Home Ribbon tab, click the Paragraph Group Dialog Box Launcher icon (see Word 2007 Exhibit 1). In the Indents and spacing tab under Indentation, click the up arrow next to Left or Right to set the indentation amount, and then click on OK and begin typing. Alternatively, from the Home Ribbon tab, point to the Decrease Indent or Increase Indent icon in the Paragraph group.***

IV. Other Functions

A. *Printing* — To print, ***click the Office Button, and then click Print*** (see Word 2007 Exhibit 1).

B. *Spell Check* — To turn on the spell checking function, ***from the Review ribbon tab, click Spelling & Grammar in the Proofing group. Additionally, a red squiggly line will appear under each word that is not recognized. If you right-click the word, the program will suggest possible spellings.***

C. *Open Files* — To open a file, ***click the Office Button, and then click Open*** (see Word 2007 Exhibit 1).

D. *Tables* — ***From the Insert ribbon tab, click Table from the Tables group.*** You can move between cells in the table by pressing the **[TAB]** and the **[SHIFT]+[TAB]** keys.

Basic Lessons

LESSON 1: TYPING A LETTER

This lesson shows you how to type the letter shown in Word 2007 Exhibit 2. It explains how to use the word wrap feature, the **[TAB]** key, the cursor (or arrow) keys, the underline, bold and italics features, the save document function, and the print document function. Keep in mind that if at any time you make a mistake in this lesson, you may press **[CTRL]+[Z]** to undo what you have done. Also remember that any time you would like to see the name of an icon on the ribbon tabs, just ***point to the icon for a second or two*** and the name will be displayed.

1. Open Windows. Then, ***double-click on the Microsoft Office Word 2007 icon on the desktop*** to open Word 2007 for Windows. Alternatively, ***click the Start button, point to Programs or All Programs, and then click on the Microsoft Word***

2007 icon (or point to Microsoft Office and then click Microsoft Office Word 2007). You should now be in a clean, blank document. If you are not in a blank document, ***click the Office Button, click New, and then double-click Blank document.***

2. At this point you cannot move the pointer around the screen by pushing the cursor keys (also called arrow keys). This is because text must first be entered before the pointer can be moved using the cursor keys. The pointer can only move through text. On the Home Ribbon tab, click the Paragraph Group dialog launcher. In the "Paragraph" window, click the down arrow below "Line spacing" and select "Single." Then, make sure the "Before" and "After" spacing are both 0 point. Then, click OK.

3. Press the **[ENTER]** key four times. (Watch the status line in the lower left-hand corner of the screen, which tells you what page of your document you are on.)

4. Type the date of the letter as shown in Word 2007 Exhibit 2. Notice as you type the word "October" that Auto Text may anticipate that you are typing "October" and give you the following prompt: October (Press ENTER to Insert). You can either press the **[ENTER]** key and Auto Text will finish typing the word for you, or you can ignore it and continue typing the word yourself.

5. Press the **[ENTER]** key three times.

October 1, 2008

Stephen Wilkerson, Esq.
Wilkerson, Smith & Russell
P.O. Box 12341
Boston, MA 59920

Subject: Turner v. Smith
Case No. 2008-1423

Dear Mr. Wilkerson:

In line with our recent conversation, the deposition of the defendant, Jonathan R. Smith, will be taken in your office on **November 15 at 9:00 a.m.** Please find enclosed a *"Notice to Take Deposition."*

I expect that I will be able to finish this deposition on November 15 and that discovery will be finished, in line with the Court's order by December 15.

I will be finishing answers to your interrogatories this week and will have them to you by early next week.

If you have any questions, please feel free to contact me.

Kindest Regards,

Shirley L. Gonzalez
For the Firm

SLG:db
Enclosures (As indicated)
cc

Word 2007 Exhibit 2
Letter
Microsoft product screen shot reprinted with permission from Microsoft Corporation.

6. Type the inside address as shown in Word 2007 Exhibit 2. Press the **[ENTER]** key after each line of the inside address. When you finish the line with "Boston, MA 59920," press the **[ENTER]** key three times.

7. Press the **[TAB]** key one time. (Word automatically sets default tabs every five spaces.) The pointer will move five spaces to the right.

8. Type **Subject:** and then press the **[TAB]** key. ***On the Home Ribbon tab, click on the Underline icon in the Font group*** (it looks like a "U"). Alternatively, you can press **[CTRL]+[U]** to turn the underline feature on and off, or ***point to the Font Group Dialog Box Launcher*** (see Word 2007 Exhibit 1) and select the Underline style. Then, type **Turner v. Smith**. ***On the Home Ribbon tab in the Font group, click the Underline icon*** to turn the underline feature off.

9. Press the **[ENTER]** key one time.

10. Press the **[TAB]** key three times, and then type **Case No. 2008-1423**.

11. Press the **[ENTER]** key three times.

12. Type the salutation **Dear Mr. Wilkerson:**

13. Press the **[ENTER]** key twice.

14. Type **In line with our recent conversation, the deposition of the defendant, Jonathan R. Smith, will be taken in your office on**. *Note:* You should not press the **[ENTER]** key at the end of the line. Word will automatically "wrap" the text down to the next line. Be sure to press the **[SPACEBAR]** once after the word "on."

15. ***Turn on the bold feature by clicking the Bold icon (a capital "B") in the Font group in the Home Ribbon tab*** (see Word 2007 Exhibit 1). Alternatively, you can press **[CTRL]+[B]** to turn bold on and off. Type **November 15 at 9:00 a.m.** Turn off the bold feature by either pressing **[CTRL]+[B]**, or ***clicking the Bold icon in the Font group in the Home Ribbon tab.*** Press the **[SPACEBAR]** twice.

16. Type **Please find enclosed a** and then press **[SPACEBAR]**.

17. ***Turn on the italics feature by clicking the Italics icon (it looks like an "I") in the Font group in the Home Ribbon tab*** (see Word 2007 Exhibit 1). Alternatively, you can press **[CTRL]+[I]** to turn italics on and off. Type **Notice to Take Deposition.** Turn off the italics feature by either pressing **[CTRL]+[I]**, or ***clicking the Italics icon in the Font group in the Home Ribbon tab.***

18. Press the **[ENTER]** key twice.

19. Type the second paragraph of the letter and then press the **[ENTER]** key twice.

20. Type the third paragraph of the letter and then press the **[ENTER]** key twice.

21. Type the fourth paragraph of the letter and then press the **[ENTER]** key twice.

22. Type **Kindest regards,** and then press the **[ENTER]** key four times.

23. Type **Shirley L. Gonzalez** and then press the **[ENTER]** key.

24. Type **For the Firm** and then press the **[ENTER]** key twice.

25. Finish the letter by typing the author's initials, enclosures, and copy abbreviation (cc) as shown in Word 2007 Exhibit 2.

26. To print the document, ***click the Office Button, and then click Print, and then click on OK.***

27. To save the document, ***click the Office Button and then click Save.*** Then, type **Letter1** next to File Name. ***Click Save to save the letter to the default directory.*** (*Note*: In Lesson 2, you will edit this letter, so it is important that you save it).

28. ***Click the Office Button and then Close*** to close the document, or, to exit Word 2007, ***click the Office Button and then click Exit Word.***

This concludes Lesson 1.

LESSON 2: EDITING A LETTER

This lesson shows you how to retrieve and edit the letter you typed in Lesson 1. It explains how to retrieve a file, perform block moves and deletes, and spell/grammar check your document. Keep in mind that if at any time you make a mistake in this lesson, you may press **[CTRL]+[Z]** to undo what you have done. Also remember that any time you would like to see the name of an icon on the Ribbon tab, just *point to the icon for a second or two* and the name will be displayed.

1. Open Windows. Then, ***double-click on the Microsoft Office Word 2007 icon on the desktop*** to open Word 2007 for Windows. Alternatively, ***click the Start button, point to Programs or All Programs, and then click the Microsoft Word 2007 icon. (You can also point to Microsoft Office and then click Microsoft Office Word 2007).*** You should now be in a clean, blank document. If you are not in a blank document, ***click the Office Button, click New, and then double-click Blank document.***

2. In this lesson, you will begin by retrieving the document you created in Lesson 1. To open the file, ***click the Office Button, and click Open.*** Then type **Letter1** and ***click Open.*** Alternatively, ***scroll using the horizontal scroll bar until you find the file, click on it, and then click Open.***

3. Notice in Word 2007 Exhibit 3 that some editing changes have been made to the letter. You will spend the rest of this lesson making these changes.

4. Use your cursor keys or mouse to go to the salutation line, "Dear Mr. Wilkerson:" With the pointer to the left of the "M" in "Mr. Wilkerson," press the **[DEL]** key thirteen times until "Mr. Wilkerson" is deleted.

5. Type **Steve**. The salutation line should now read "Dear Steve:"

6. Using your cursor keys or mouse, ***move the pointer to the left of the comma following the word "conversation" in the first paragraph.*** Press the **[SPACEBAR]**, then type **of September 30**. The sentence now reads:

In line with our recent conversation of September 30, the deposition of the defendant …

7. The next change you will make is to move the second paragraph so that it becomes part of the first paragraph. Although this can be accomplished in more than one way, this lesson uses the **Cut** command.

8. Using your cursor keys or mouse, ***move the pointer to the beginning of the second paragraph of Word 2007 Exhibit 3.***

9. ***Click and drag the mouse pointer*** (hold the left mouse button down, and move the mouse) ***until the entire second paragraph is highlighted, and then release the mouse button.***

Word 2007 Exhibit 3

Corrections to a Letter

Microsoft product screen shot reprinted with permission from Microsoft Corporation.

October 1, 2008

Stephen Wilkerson, Esq.
Wilkerson, Smith & Russell
P.O. Box 12341
Boston, MA 59920

Subject: Turner v. Smith
Case No. 2008-1423

Dear Steve ~~Mr. Wilkerson~~:

In line with our recent conversation of September 30, the deposition of the defendant, Jonathan R. Smith, will be taken in your office on **November 15 at 9:00 a.m.** Please find enclosed a *"Notice to Take Deposition."*

I expect that I will be able to finish this deposition on November 15 and that discovery will be finished, in line with the Court's order by December 15.

I will be finishing answers to your interrogatories next ~~this~~ week. ~~and will have them to you by early next week.~~

If you have any questions, please feel free to contact me.

Kindest Regards,

Shirley L. Gonzalez
For the Firm

SLG:db
Enclosures (As indicated)
cc

10. ***From the Home Ribbon tab, click the Cut icon in the Clipboard group (see Word 2007 Exhibit 1).*** An alternative is to right-click anywhere in the highlighted area, and then click **Cut**. The text is no longer on the screen, but it is not deleted—it has been temporarily placed on the Office Clipboard.

11. Move the pointer to the end of the first paragraph. Press the **[SPACEBAR]** twice. If the pointer appears to be in italics mode, from the Home Ribbon tab, ***click the Italics icon in the Font group,*** or press **[CTLR]+[I]** to turn the italics feature off.

12. ***From the Home Ribbon tab, click Paste from the Clipboard group (see Word 2007 Exhibit 1).*** Notice that the text has now been moved. Also, you may notice that a small icon in the shape of a clipboard has appeared where you pasted the text. Click the down arrow of the Paste Options icon. Notice that you are given the option to keep the source formatting or change the formatting so that the text matches the destination formatting (i.e., the formatting of the place you are copying it to). In this example, both formats are the same so it does not matter, but if the text you are copying is a different format, you may or may not want to change it to the destination format. Press the **[ESC]** key to make the Paste Options menu disappear.

13. Move the pointer to the line below the first paragraph, and use the **[DEL]** key to delete any unnecessary blank lines.

14. Using your cursor keys or mouse, ***move the pointer to what is now the second paragraph and place it to the left of the "t" in "this week."***

15. Use the **[DEL]** key to delete the word "this," and then type **next**.

16. We will now delete the rest of the sentence in the second paragraph. ***Drag the pointer until "and will have them to you by early next week." is highlighted.*** Press the **[DEL]** key. Type a period at the end of the sentence.

17. You have now made all of the changes that need to be made. To be sure the letter does not have misspelled words or grammar errors, we will use the Spelling and Grammar command.

18. ***Point on the Review Ribbon tab, then click Spelling & Grammar in the Proofing group.***

19. If an error is found, it will be highlighted. You have the choice of ignoring it once, ignoring it completely, accepting one of the suggestions listed, or changing or correcting the problem yourself. Correct any spelling or grammar errors. ***Click OK when the spell and grammar check is done.***

20. To print the document, ***click on the Office Button, click Print, and then click on OK.***

21. To save the document, ***click the Office Button, and then select Save As.*** Type **Letter2** in the **File name** box, ***and then click Save to save the document in the default directory.***

22. ***Click the Office Button, and then click Close*** to close the document, or ***click the Office Button, and then click Exit Word*** to exit the program.

This concludes Lesson 2.

LESSON 3: TYPING A PLEADING

This lesson shows you how to type a pleading, as shown in Word 2007 Exhibit 4. It expands on the items presented in Lessons 1 and 2. It also explains how to center text, change margins, change line spacing, add a footnote, double-indent text, and use automatic page numbering. Keep in mind that if at any time you make a mistake you may press **[CTRL]+[Z]** to undo what you have done.

1. Open Windows. Then, ***double-click the Microsoft Office Word 2007 icon on the desktop*** to open Word 2007 for Windows. Alternatively, ***click the Start button, point to Programs or All Programs, and then click the Microsoft Word 2007 icon. (You can also point to Microsoft Office and then click Microsoft Office Word 2007).*** You should now be in a clean, blank document. If you are not in a blank document, ***click the Office Button, click New, and then double-click on Blank document.*** Remember, any time you would like to see the name of an icon on the ribbon tabs, just ***point to the icon for a second or two*** and the name will be displayed.

2. You will be creating the document shown in Word 2007 Exhibit 4. The first thing you will need to do is to change the margins so that the left margin is 1½ inches and the right margin is 1 inch. To change the margins, ***click the Page Layout Ribbon tab and then click Margins in the Page Setup group. Next, click***

Word 2007 Exhibit 4
A Pleading
Microsoft product screen shot reprinted with permission from Microsoft Corporation.

IN THE DISTRICT COURT OF
ORANGE COUNTY, MASSACHUSETTS

Jim Turner,

Plaintiff,

-vs- Case No. 2008-1423

Jonathan R. Smith,

Defendant.

NOTICE TO TAKE DEPOSITION

COMES NOW the plaintiff and pursuant to statute[1] hereby gives notice that the deposition of Defendant, Jonathan R. Smith, will be taken as follows:

Monday, November 15, 2008, at 9:00 a.m. at the law offices of Wilkerson, Smith & Russell, 17031 W. 69th Street, Boston, MA.

Said deposition will be taken before a court reporter and is not expected to take more than one day in duration.

____
Shirley L. Gonzalez
Attorney for Plaintiff

[1] Massachusetts Statutes Annotated 60-2342(a)(1).

Page 1

Custom Margins at the bottom of the drop-down menu. In the Page Setup window, change the left margin to 1.5 inches and the right margin to 1 inch. Then, click OK. Also, on the Home Ribbon tab, click the Paragraph Group dialog launcher. In the "Paragraph" window, click the down arrow below "Line Spacing" and select "Single." Then, make sure the "Before" and "After" spacing are both 0 point. Then, click OK.

3. Notice in Word 2007 Exhibit 4 that there is a page number at the bottom of the page. Word will automatically number your pages for you.

4. ***Click the Insert Ribbon tab, and then click Page Number in the Header & Footer group*** (see Word 2007 Exhibit 5).

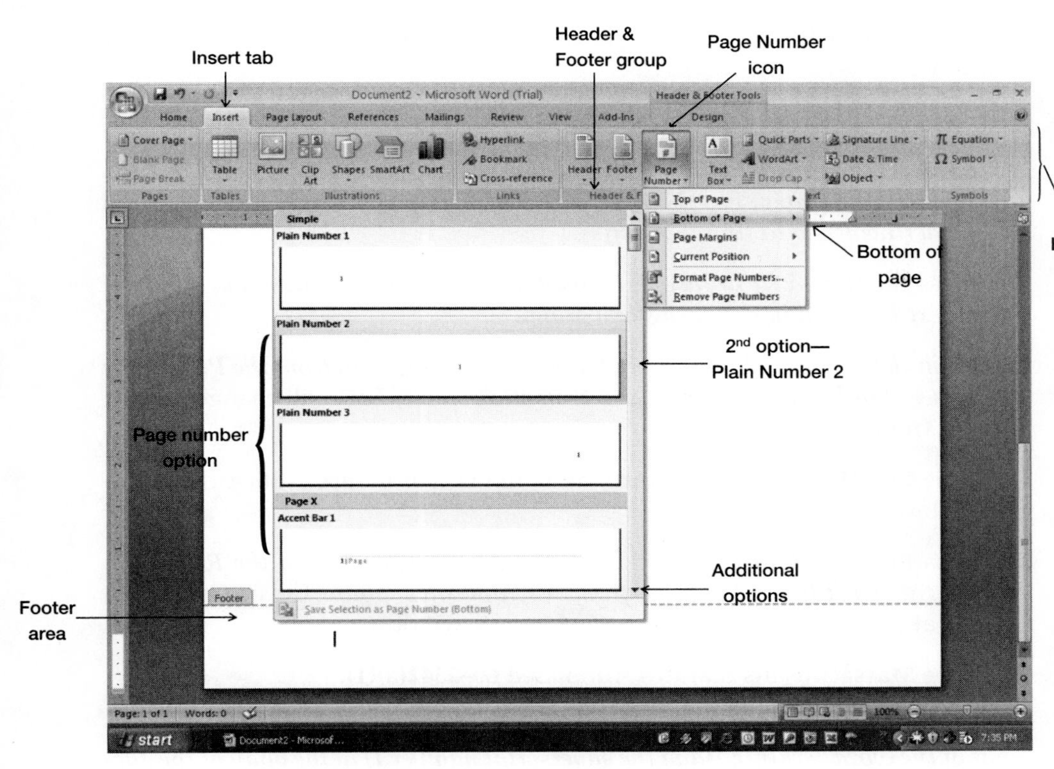

Word 2007 Exhibit 5

Adding A Page Number

Microsoft product screen shot reprinted with permission from Microsoft Corporation.

5. ***Next, point to Bottom of Page*** (see Word 2007 Exhibit 5) and notice that a number of options are displayed. ***Click the down arrow in the lower right for additional options*** (see Word 2007 Exhibit 5). Notice that many page number options are available. ***Scroll back up to the top of the option list and click the second option, Plain Number 2.***

6. Your pointer should now be in the area marked "Footer." Specifically, your pointer should be to the left of the number 1. Type **Page** and then press **[SPACEBAR].**

7. ***Click the Home Ribbon tab. Then, click the vertical scroll bar (see Word 2007 Exhibit 1) or use the [UP ARROW] key to go back to the beginning of the document.***

8. ***Point and double-click just below the header.***

9. On the first line of the document, ***from the Home Ribbon tab, click the Center icon in the Paragraph group***. Type **IN THE DISTRICT COURT OF**. Press the **[ENTER]** key. Type **ORANGE COUNTY, MASSACHUSETTS.**

10. Press the **[ENTER]** key five times. ***From the Home Ribbon tab, click the Align Text Left icon in the Paragraph group.***

11. Type **Jim Turner,** and press the **[ENTER]** key twice.

12. Press the **[TAB]** key three times and type **Plaintiff,** then press the **[ENTER]** key twice.

13. Type **–vs-**. Then, press the **[TAB]** key six times, and type **Case No. 2008-1423**.

14. Press the **[ENTER]** key twice.

15. Type **Jonathan R. Smith,** and press the **[ENTER]** key twice.

16. Press the **[TAB]** key three times and type **Defendant.** Press the **[ENTER]** key four times.

17. ***From the Home Ribbon tab, click the Center icon in the Paragraph group.***

18. ***From the Home Ribbon tab, click the Bold icon and the Underline icon, both found in the Font group.*** Type **NOTICE TO TAKE DEPOSITION**. ***Click the Bold and Underline icons to turn them off.***

19. Press the **[ENTER]** key three times. ***From the Home Ribbon tab, click the Align Text Left icon in the Paragraph group.***

20. ***From the Home Ribbon tab, click the Line Spacing icon from the Paragraph group (see Word 2007 Exhibit 1), and then click on 2.0.*** This will change the line spacing from single to double.

21. Type **COMES NOW the plaintiff and pursuant to statute**. Notice that a footnote follows the word *statute.*

22. With the pointer just to the right of the e in "statute," ***from the References Ribbon tab, click Insert Footnote from the Footnotes group.*** The cursor should now be at the bottom of the page in the footnote window.

23. Type **Massachusetts Statutes Annotated 60–2342(a)(1).**

24. To move the pointer back to the body of the document, simply ***click to the right of the word "statute" (and the superscript number 1) in the body of the document.*** Now, continue to type the rest of the first paragraph. Once the paragraph is typed, press the **[ENTER]** key twice.

25. To double-indent the second paragraph, ***from the Home Ribbon tab, click the Paragraph Group Dialog Box Launcher (see Word 2007 Exhibit 1).*** The "Paragraph" window should now be displayed. ***Under "Indentation," add a .5" left indent and a .5" right indent using the up arrow icons*** (or you can type it in). ***Click OK in the "Paragraph" window.***

26. Type the second paragraph.

27. Press the **[ENTER]** key twice.

28. ***From the Home Ribbon tab, click the Paragraph Group Dialog Box Launcher and, under Indentation, change the left and right indents back to 0. Then, click OK.***

29. Type the third paragraph.

30. Press the **[ENTER]** key three times.

31. The signature line is single spaced, so ***from the Home Ribbon tab, click the Line spacing icon from the Paragraph group, and then click 1.0.*** This will change the line spacing from double to single.

32. Press **[SHIFT]+[-]** (the key to the right of the zero key on the keyboard) thirty times to draw the signature line. Press the **[ENTER]** key. *Note*: If Word automatically inserts a line across the whole page, press **[CTRL]+[Z]** to undo the Auto Correct line. Alternatively, you can click the down arrow in the Auto Correct Options icon (it looks like a lightning bolt and should be just over the line that now runs across the page) and select Undo Border Line.

33. Type **Shirley L. Gonzalez**, and then press the **[ENTER]** key.

34. Type **Attorney for Plaintiff**.

35. To print the document, ***click the Office Button, click Print, and then click OK.***

36. To save the document, ***click the Office Button, and then select Save As.*** Type **Pleading1** in the File name box, ***and then click Save to save the document in the default directory.***

37. ***Click the Office Button, and then Close*** to close the document, or ***click the Office Button, and then Exit Word*** to exit the program.

This concludes Lesson 3.

LESSON 4: CREATING A TABLE

This lesson shows you how to create the table shown in Word 2007 Exhibit 6. It expands on the items presented in Lessons 1, 2, and 3 and explains how to change a font size, create a table, enter data into a table, add automatic numbering, adjust column widths, and use the Table AutoFormat command. Keep in mind that if at any time you make a mistake, you may press [CTRL]+[Z] to undo what you have done.

1. Open Windows. Then, ***double-click the Microsoft Office Word 2007 icon on the desktop*** to open Word 2007 for Windows. Alternatively, ***click the Start button, point to Programs or All Programs, and then click the Microsoft Word 2007 icon. (You may also point to Microsoft Office and then click on Microsoft Office Word 2007.)*** You should be in a clean, blank document. If you are not in a blank document, ***click the Office Button, click New, and then double-click Blank document.***

2. ***From the Home Ribbon tab, click the Center icon in the Paragraph group, and then click the Bold icon in the Font group.***

3. ***From the Home Ribbon tab, click the Font Size icon in the Font group*** and change the font size to 14 by either typing **14** in the box or ***choosing 14 from the drop-down menu.*** Alternatively, you can both turn on bold and change the font

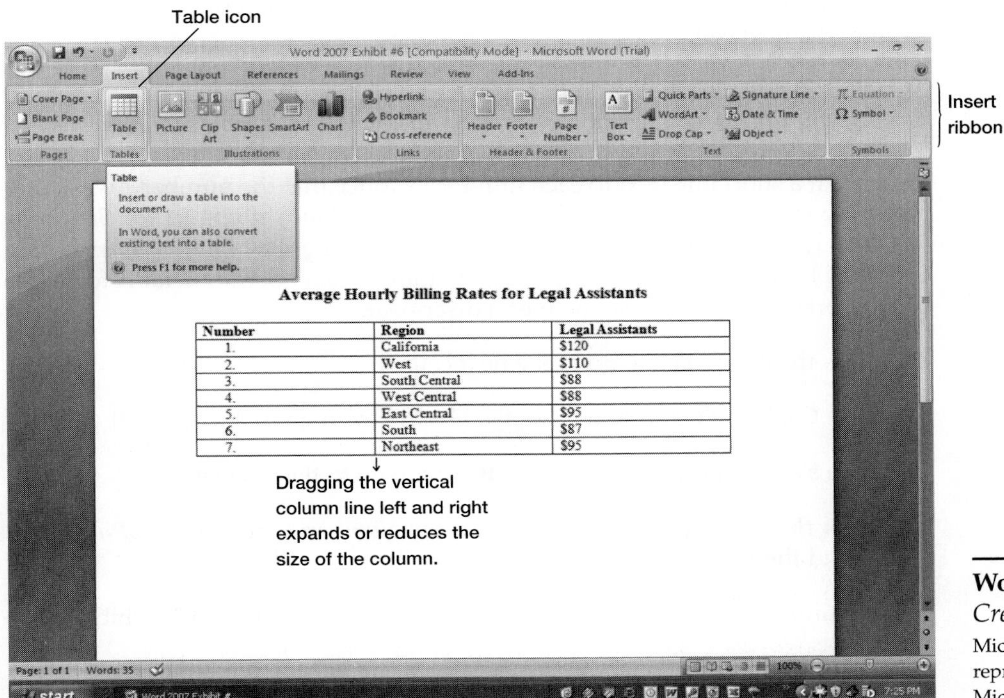

Number	Region	Legal Assistants
1.	California	$120
2.	West	$110
3.	South Central	$88
4.	West Central	$88
5.	East Central	$95
6.	South	$87
7.	Northeast	$95

Word 2007 Exhibit 6
Creating a Table
Microsoft product screen shot reprinted with permission from Microsoft Corporation.

size by *clicking the Font Group Dialog Box Launcher from the Home Ribbon tab (see Word 2007 Exhibit 1).*

4. Type **Average Hourly Billing Rates for Legal Assistants** (see Word 2007 Exhibit 6). Press the **[ENTER]** key once, and then *click the Font Size icon and change the type back to 12 point. Click the Bold icon to turn bold off.*

5. Press the **[ENTER]** key once.

6. *From the Insert Ribbon tab, click Table.* Notice that a number of columns and rows of boxes are displayed. This allows you to graphically depict your table.

7. *Point with in the Table menu so that three columns are highlighted, and then point and click so that eight rows are highlighted (e.g., 3 x 8 Table).* Notice that as you point, the table is temporarily shown in your document. This is called a "live preview." When you point and click on the cell that is three columns over and eight cells down, the table (as opposed to the live preview) will be displayed permanently in your document.

8. The blank table should now be displayed and the cursor should be in the first column of the first row of the table. *If the cursor is not in the first column of the first row, click in this cell to place the cursor there. Click on the Bold icon on the Home Ribbon tab.* Type **Number** and then press the **[TAB]** key once to go to the next cell in the table.

9. *Click on the Bold icon.* Type **Region** and then press the **[TAB]** key once to go to the next cell in the table. (*Note*: If you need to go back to a previous cell, you can either use the mouse or the cursor keys or you can press **[SHIFT]+[TAB]**. Also, if you accidentally hit the **[ENTER]** key instead of the **[TAB]** key, you can either press the **[BACKSPACE]** key to delete the extra line, or you can press **[CTRL]+[Z]** to undo it.

10. *Click on the Bold icon.* Type **Legal Assistants** and then press the **[TAB]** key to go to the next cell.

11. We will now use the automatic paragraph numbering feature to number our rows. *From the Home Ribbon tab, click on the Numbering icon in the Paragraph group* (see Word 2007 Exhibit 1—it is the icon that has the numbers 1, 2, 3 in a column, with a short line next to each number). Notice that the number 1 was automatically entered in the cell. *From the Home Ribbon tab, point on the down arrow next to the Numbering icon in the Paragraph group.* Under "Numbering Library," look at the different formats that are available. The default format is fine, so press **[ESC]** to make the menu disappear.

12. Press the **[TAB]** key to go to the next cell.

13. Type **California** and then press the **[TAB]** key to go to the next cell.

14. Type **$120** and then press the **[TAB]** key to go to the next cell.

15. *From the Home Ribbon tab, click on the Numbering icon in the Paragraph group,* and then press the **[TAB]** key to go to the next cell.

16. Continue entering all of the information shown in Word 2007 Exhibit 6 into your table.

17. *Put the pointer in the upper-most left cell of the table and drag the pointer to the lowest cell at the right of the table to completely highlight the table. Then,*

from the Home Ribbon tab, click on the Align Text Left icon in the Paragraph group. Now, the whole table is left aligned.

18. ***Put the pointer on the vertical column line that separates the Number column and the Region column, and then drag the line to the left (see Word 2007 Exhibit 6).*** Notice that by using this technique you can completely adjust each column width as much as you like. Press **[CTRL]+[Z]** to undo the column move, because the current format is fine.

19. ***Click on any cell in the table.*** Notice that just above the Ribbon tab new options are now shown; under the new heading "Table Tools" two more tabs, "Design" and "Layout," appear. ***Click on the Design Ribbon tab.*** Notice that the Ribbon tab now shows six table styles. ***Point (don't click) on one of the tables;*** notice that the Live Preview feature shows you exactly what your table will look like with this design. ***Point and click on the down arrow in the Table Styles group and browse to see many more table styles. Point and click on a table style that you like.*** The format of the table has been completely changed.

20. To print the document, ***click on the Office Button, click on Print, and then click on OK.***

21. To save the document, ***click on the Office Button, and then select Save As.*** Type **Table1** in the "File name" box, ***and then point and click on Save to save the document in the default directory.***

22. ***Click on the Office Button, and then on Close*** to close the document, or ***click on the Office Button, and then on Exit Word*** to exit the program.

This concludes Lesson 4.

Intermediate Lessons

LESSON 5: TOOLS AND TECHNIQUES

This lesson shows you how to edit an employment policy (from the data disk supplied with this text), use the Format Painter tool, reveal formatting, clear formatting, change the case of text, use Find and Replace feature, use the Go To command, create a section break, and change the orientation of a page from Portrait to Landscape. This lesson assumes you have completed Lessons 1 through 4 and that you are generally familiar with Word 2007.

1. Open Windows. Then, ***double-click on the Microsoft Office Word 2007 icon on the desktop*** to open Word 2007 for Windows. Alternatively, ***click on the Start button, point the pointer to Programs or All Programs, and then click on the Microsoft Word 2007 icon. (You also may point to Microsoft Office and then click on Microsoft Office Word 2007).*** You should be in a clean, blank document. If you are not in a blank document, ***click on the Office Button, click on New, and then double-click on "Blank document."***

2. The first thing you will do is to open the "Lesson 5" file from Disk 1 supplied with this text. Ensure that the disk is inserted in the disk drive, ***point and click on the Office Button, and then point and click on Open.*** The Open window should now be displayed. ***Point and click on the down arrow to the right of the white box next to "Look in:" and select the drive where the Disk 1 is located. Point and double-click on the Word-Processing Files folder. Double-click on the Word 2007 folder. Double-click on the "Lesson 5" file.***

3. The file entitled "World Wide Technology, Inc. Alcohol and Drug policy" should now be displayed on your screen. In this lesson, you will be editing this

Word 2007 Exhibit 7
The Format Painter Feature
Microsoft product screen shot reprinted with permission from Microsoft Corporation.

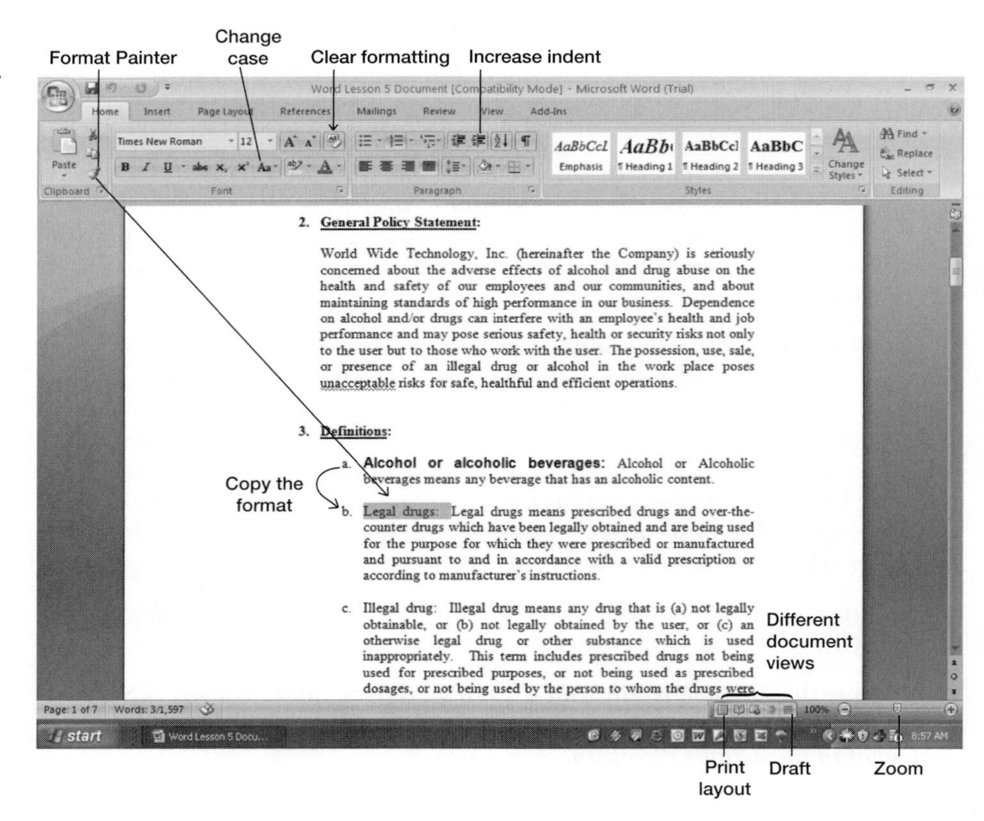

policy for use by another client. The next thing you need to do is to go to section 3, "Definitions," and change the subheadings so that they have all have the same format. You will use the Format Painter tool to do this.

4. Use the cursor keys or the mouse and the horizontal scroll bars to scroll to section 3, "Definitions" (see Word 2007 Exhibit 8). Notice that the first definition, "Alcohol or alcoholic beverages," is bold and in a different font from the rest of the definitions in section 3. You will use the Format Painter feature to quickly copy the formatting from "Alcohol or alcoholic beverages" to the other four definitions in section 3.

5. ***Point and click anywhere in the text "Alcohol or alcoholic beverages:"*** This tells the Format Painter feature the formatting you want to copy.

6. Next, ***from the Home Ribbon tab, point and click on the Format Painter icon in the Clipboard group.*** It looks like a paintbrush (see Word 2007 Exhibit 7.) Remember, if you hover your mouse pointer over an icon for a second or two the name of the icon will appear.

7. Notice that your mouse pointer now turns to a paintbrush. ***Drag the pointer*** (hold the left mouse button down and move the mouse) ***until the heading "Legal drugs:" is highlighted*** (see Word 2007 Exhibit 8), ***and then let go of the mouse button.*** Notice that the paintbrush on your cursor is now gone. ***Click the left mouse button once anywhere in the screen to make the highlight go away.*** Notice that "Legal drugs" now has the same formatting as "Alcohol or alcoholic beverages." The Format Painter command is a quick way to make formatting changes.

8. You will now use the Format Painter command to copy the formatting to the remaining three definitions, with one additional trick. ***Point and click anywhere in the text "Legal drugs."***

9. Next, ***from the Home Ribbon tab, double-click on the Format Painter icon in the Clipboard group. (Your pointer should now have a paintbrush attached to it.)*** The double-click tells Format Painter that you are going to copy this format to

multiple locations, instead of just one location. This is a great time-saving feature if you need to copy formatting to several places, because it keeps you from having to click the Format Painter icon each time you copy the same formatting to a new location.

10. ***Drag the pointer until the heading "Illegal drug:" is highlighted, and then let go of the mouse button.*** Notice that the paintbrush is still attached to your pointer.

11. ***Drag the pointer until the heading "Controlled substance:" is highlighted, and then let go of the mouse button.***

12. ***Drag the pointer until the heading "Prescription drug:" is highlighted, and then let go of the mouse button.***

13. To turn the Format Painter off, press the **[ESC]** button on the keyboard. ***Click the left mouse button once anywhere in the document to make the highlight go away.*** Notice that all of the headings are now uniform.

14. You will now learn to use the Reveal Formatting command. ***Point and click on the heading "Prescription drug:"***

15. Press **[SHIFT]+[F1]** on the keyboard. Notice that the Reveal Formatting task pane has opened on the right side of the screen. The Reveal Formatting task pane lists all format specifications for the selected text. The items are divided into several groups including Font, Paragraph, Bullets and Numbering, and Section. You can make formatting changes to the text directly from the Reveal Formatting task pane by simply clicking on the format setting you want to change (the links are shown in blue, underlined text). For example, ***point and click on the blue underlined word "Font" in the Reveal Formatting task pane.*** Notice that the Font window opens. You can now select a new font if you so desire. The Reveal Formatting task pane allows you to quickly see all formatting attached to specific text and, if necessary, to change it.

16. ***Point and click on Cancel in the Font window.*** To close the Reveal Formatting task pane, ***point and click on the "x" (the Close button) at the top of the Reveal Formatting task pane. It is just to the right of the words "Reveal Formatting."*** The Reveal Formatting task pane should now be gone.

17. Press **[CTRL]+[HOME]** to go to the beginning of the document.

18. You will now learn how to use the Clear Formats command. Notice under the heading "1. Objectives" that the sentence "The objectives of this policy are as follows:" is bold and italics; this is a mistake. ***Drag the pointer until this text is highlighted.***

19. Next, ***from the Home Ribbon tab, point and click on the Clear Formatting icon in the Font group*** (see Word 2007 Exhibit 7.) This icon looks like an eraser next to a capital "A" and a lowercase "a". Then, ***click the left mouse button once anywhere in the sentence to make the highlight go away.*** Notice that all of the formatting is now gone. The "Clear Formats" command is a good way to remove all text formatting quickly and easily.

20. To move the text to the right so it is under "1. Objectives," ***from the Home Ribbon tab, point and click three times on the Increase Indent icon in the Paragraph group*** (see Word 2007 Exhibit 8). This is the icon with a right arrow and some lines on it. The line should now be back in its place.

21. You will now learn how to use the Change Case command. Press **[CTRL]+[HOME]** on the keyboard to go to the beginning of the document.

22. ***Drag the pointer until "World Wide Technology, Inc." in the document's title is highlighted.***

23. ***From the Home Ribbon tab, point and click on the Change Case icon in the Font group. Point and click on UPPERCASE.*** Notice that the text is now in all capitals. ***Point and click anywhere in the document to make the highlighting disappear.***

24. ***Drag the pointer until the subtitle "alcohol and drug policy" is highlighted. From the Home Ribbon tab, point and click on the Change Case icon in the Font group. Point and click on "Capitalize Each Word."*** Notice that the text is now in title case. ***Click the left mouse button once anywhere in the document to make the highlighting go away.*** The Change Case command is a convenient way to change the case of text without having to retype it.

25. Notice that the *A* in *and* in "Alcohol And Drug Policy" is now capitalized, and that a green squiggly line is underneath it. This tells you that Word believes there is a grammar error. ***Point and right-click on the word "And" in the title. A menu will be displayed. Point and click on* and *(this is what Word is suggesting the correction should be).*** The word "and" in the title is now lower case.

26. Press **[CTRL]+[HOME]** on the keyboard to go to the beginning of the document.

27. You will now learn how to use the Find and Replace command. ***From the Home Ribbon tab, point and click on the Replace icon in the Editing group.*** Alternatively, you could press **[CTRL]+[H],** and then click on Replace.

28. In the Find and Replace window, in the white box next to "Find what," type **World Wide Technology, Inc.** Then, in the white box next to "Replace with," type **Johnson Manufacturing.** ***Now, point and click on the Replace All button in the Find and Replace window.*** The program will respond by stating that it made four replacements. ***Point and click on "OK."***

29. ***Point and click on the Close button in the Find and Replace window to close the window.*** Notice that World Wide Technology, Inc. has now been changed to Johnson Manufacturing.

30. You will now learn how to use the Go To command. The Go To command is an easy way to navigate through large and complex documents. Press **[F5].** Notice that the Find and Replace window is again displayed on the screen, but this time the Go To tab is selected. In the white box directly under "Enter page number," type **7** from the keyboard and then ***point and click on Go To in the Find and Replace window.*** Notice that page 7, "Reasonable Suspicion Report," is now displayed. (*Note:* If the Find and Replace window blocks your ability to see the text of the document, point at the blue box in the Find and Replace window and drag the window lower so you can see the document). ***Point and click on Close in the Find and Replace window.***

31. Suppose that you would like to change the orientation of only one page in a document from Portrait (where the length is greater than the width) to Landscape (where the width is greater than the length). In this example, you will change the layout of only the Reasonable Suspicion Report to Landscape while keeping the rest of the document Portrait. To do this in Word, you must enter a section break.

32. Your cursor should be on page 7 just above "Johnson Manufacturing Reasonable Suspicion Report." ***From the Page Layout ribbon tab, point and click on Breaks in the Page Setup group.***

33. ***Under "Section Breaks," point and click on "Next Page."***

34. In the lower right of the screen ***point and click on the Draft icon*** (see Word 2007 Exhibit 7). ***Press the [UP] arrow key 2 times.*** Notice that a double dotted line that says "Section Break (Next Page)" is now displayed.

35. The Word 2007 interface allows you to switch views by clicking on one of the view layouts in the lower right of the screen (see Word 2007 Exhibit 7). Print and Draft are two of the most popular layouts. In addition, the Zoom tool just to the right of the Draft view allows you to zoom in or out of your document.

36. With the Section Break in place, you can now change the format of the page from Portrait to Landscape without changing the orientation of previous pages.

37. ***With the cursor on the "Johnson Manufacturing Reasonable Suspicion Report" page, from the Page Layout ribbon tab, point and click on Orientation in the Page Setup group. Point and click on Landscape.*** Notice that the layout of the page has changed.

38. ***Point and click on the Print Layout icon in the lower right of the screen (see Word 2007 Exhibit 7).***

39. To confirm that the layout has changed, ***point and click on the Office Button, then point to "Print" and then click on "Print Preview."*** Notice that the layout is now Landscape (the width is greater than the length). Press the **[PAGE UP]** key until you are back to the beginning of the document. Notice that all of the other pages in the document are still in Portrait orientation.

40. ***Point and click on the Close Print Preview icon on the Print Preview ribbon tab (This icon is a red X at the far right of the ribbon tab.)***

41. To print the document, ***click on the Office Button, click on Print, and then click on OK***.

42. To save the document, ***click on the Office Button, point to Save As..., and then click on "Word 97—2003 Document."*** Under "Save in" select the drive or folder you would like to save the document in. Then, next to "File Name," type **Done—Word 2007 Lesson 5 Document** ***and point and click on Save to save the document.***

43. ***Click on the Office Button, and then click on Close*** to close the document, or ***click on the Office Button, and then on Exit Word*** to exit the program.

This concludes Lesson 5.

LESSON 6: USING STYLES

This lesson gives you an introduction to styles. Styles are particularly helpful when you are working with long documents that must be formatted uniformly.

1. Open Windows. Then, ***double-click on the Microsoft Office Word 2007 icon on the desktop*** to open Word 2007 for Windows. Alternatively, ***click on the Start button, point with the mouse to Programs or All Programs, and then click on the Microsoft Word 2007 icon. (You may also point to Microsoft Office and then click on Microsoft Office Word 2007).*** You should now be in a clean, blank document. If you are not in a blank document, ***click on the Office Button, click on New, and then double-click on "Blank document."***

2. The first thing you will do is to open the "Lesson 6" file from Disk 1 supplied with this text. Ensure that the disk is inserted in the drive, ***point and click on the Office Button, and then point and click on Open.*** The Open window should now be displayed. ***Point and click on the down arrow to the right of the white box next***

Word 2007 Exhibit 8
Styles
Microsoft product screen shot reprinted with permission from Microsoft Corporation.

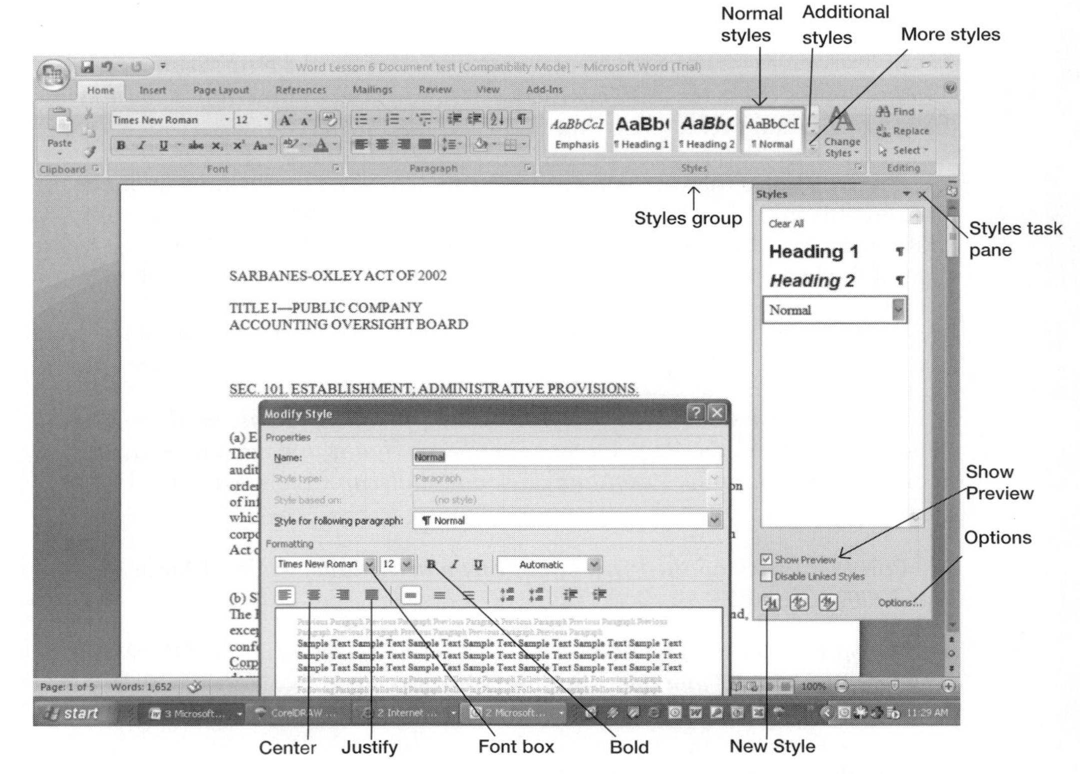

to "Look in:" and select the drive where Disk 1 is located. Point and double-click on the Word-Processing File folder. Double-click on the Word 2007 folder. Point and double-click on the "Lesson 6" file.

3. The text "Sarbanes-Oxley Act of 2002" should now be displayed on your screen (see Word 2007 Exhibit 8). In this lesson you will use styles to add uniform formatting to this document. In the Home Ribbon tab, notice the Styles group. ***Point and click on any text on the page.*** Notice in the Styles group on the Home Ribbon tab that the Normal box is highlighted in yellow (see Word 2007 Exhibit 8). Currently, all text in the document is in the Normal style.

4. Using your cursor keys or the horizontal scroll bar, scroll down through the document. Notice that all of the paragraphs are left aligned and that the right edge of all the paragraphs is jagged (e.g., not justified).

5. ***From the Home Ribbon tab, point and click on the Styles Group Dialog Box Launcher.*** Notice that the Styles task pane now appears on the right side of the screen (see Word 2007 Exhibit 8). In the Styles task pane, ***if the white box next to "Show Preview" is not marked, click on the box so a green check mark appears (see Word 2007 Exhibit 8).*** Notice that a few styles in the "Styles" task pane are currently being displayed (e.g., Heading 1, Heading 2, and Normal). Also notice that the Normal style has a blue box around it, indicating that your cursor is on text with the Normal style. Finally, notice that there is a paragraph sign after each of these heading names, indicating that these are paragraph styles.

6. Notice at the bottom of the Styles task pane the word *Options* in blue; ***point and click on Options. The Styles Pane Options window should now be displayed.***

7. ***In the Styles Pane Options window under Select styles to show, click the down arrow next to "In current document" and click on "All Styles." Then, in the Styles Pane Options window, click on OK.***

8. Notice that the Styles task pane is now full of additional styles. These are all of the styles that are automatically available in Word 2007. ***Point and click on the down arrow in the Styles task pane to see the full list of styles.***

9. To return to the list of just a few styles, ***point and click on "Options" in the lower right of the Styles task pan. Under "Select styles to show," click on the down arrow and click on "In current document." Then, in the Styles Pane Options window, click on OK.***

10. Notice that the short list of styles is again displayed. To access a longer list of styles from the Styles group on the Home Ribbon tab, ***point and click on the down arrow in the Styles group. If you select the More icon (the icon that shows a down arrow with a line over it) in the Styles group, you can see all of the styles at one time.*** Press the **[ESC]** key to close the list.

11. Styles are extremely useful. Assume now that you would like to have all of the text in the document justified. ***Point and right-click on Normal in the Styles task pane. Then, point and left-click on Modify.*** The Modify Style window should now be displayed (see Word 2007 Exhibit 8). Using the Modify Style window, you can completely change the formatting for any style.

12. ***Point and click on the Justify icon in the Modify Style window to change the Normal style from left aligned to fully justified*** (see Word 2007 Exhibit 8).

13. ***Then, point and click on the down arrow in the Font box in the Modify Style window and point and click on Arial (you may have to scroll through some fonts to find it). Next, point and click on the OK button in the Modify Style window.*** Notice that Word quickly changed the alignment of all of the text to fully justified and changed the font to Arial.

14. ***Drag the pointer until the full title of the document is highlighted*** (SARBANES-OXLEY ACT OF 2002 TITLE I—PUBLIC COMPANY ACCOUNTING OVERSIGHT BOARD).

15. ***Then, point and click on "Heading 1" in the Styles task pane.***

16. ***Point and right-click on "Heading 1" in the Styles task pane and select Modify. Then, point and click on the Center icon. Select the OK button in the Modify Style window.***

17. ***Click the left mouse button anywhere in the title to make the highlight disappear.*** Notice that the text of the title shows as Heading 1 in the Styles task pane.

18. ***Point and click anywhere in "Sec. 101. Establishment; Administrative Provisions." Then, point and click on "Heading 2" in the Styles task pane.*** Notice that the heading has now changed.

19. ***Point and click anywhere in the subheading "(a) ESTABLISHMENT OF BOARD." Then, point and click on the New Style icon at the bottom of the Styles task pane (see Word 2007 Exhibit 8).***

20. The Create New Style from Formatting window should now be displayed. Under Properties, next to Name, type **Heading 3A**, and then under Formatting, ***point and click on the Bold icon. Then, point and click on OK in the Create New Style from Formatting window.***

21. Now, go to the following subheadings and format them as Heading 3A by clicking on them and selecting "Heading 3A" from the Styles task pane:

(b) STATUS
(c) DUTIES OF THE BOARD
(d) COMMISSION DETERMINATION
(e) BOARD MEMBERSHIP
(f) POWERS OF THE BOARD

(g) RULES OF THE BOARD
(h) ANNUAL REPORT TO THE COMMISSION

Press **[CTRL]+[HOME]** to go to the beginning of the document. Your document is now consistently formatted. Using styles, your documents can also easily be uniformly changed. For example, if you read in your local rules that subheadings for pleadings must be in 15-point Times New Roman font, you could quickly change the subheadings in your document by modifying the heading styles, rather than highlighting each subheading and changing the format manually.

22. To print the document, ***click on the Office Button, click on Print, and then click on OK.***

23. To save the document, ***click on the Office Button, and point to Save As. Then click on "Word 97—2003 Document."*** Under "Save in" select the drive or folder you would like to save the document in. Then, next to "File Name," type **Done—Word 2007 Lesson 6 Document** ***and point and click on Save to save the document.***

24. ***Click on the Office Button, and then on Close*** to close the document, or ***click on the Office Button, and then on Exit Word*** to exit the program.

This concludes Lesson 6.

LESSON 7: CREATING A TEMPLATE

This lesson shows you how to create the template shown in Word 2007 Exhibit 9. It explains how to create a template of a letter, how to insert fields, and how to fill out and use a finished template. You will also learn how to add a command to the Quick Access Toolbar. The information that will be merged into the letter will be entered from the keyboard. Keep in mind that if at any time you make a mistake, you may press **[CTRL]+[Z]** to undo what you have done.

1. Open Windows. Then, ***double-click on the Microsoft Office Word 2007 icon on the desktop*** to open Word 2007 for Windows. Alternatively, ***click on the Start***

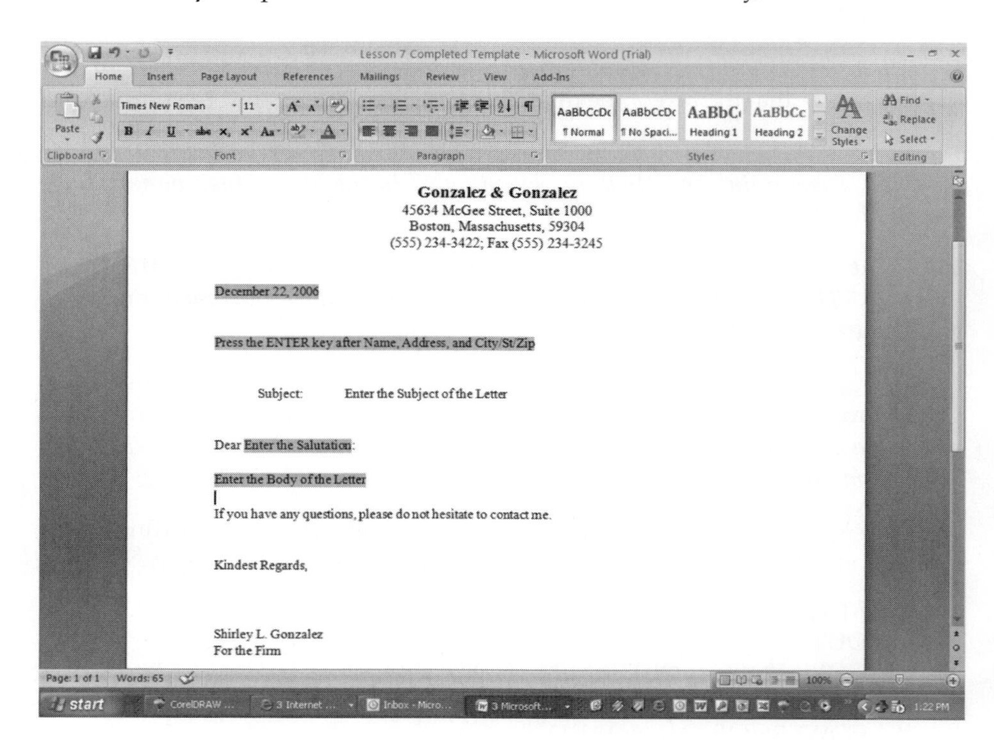

Word 2007 Exhibit 9
Office Letter Template
Microsoft product screen shot reprinted with permission from Microsoft Corporation.

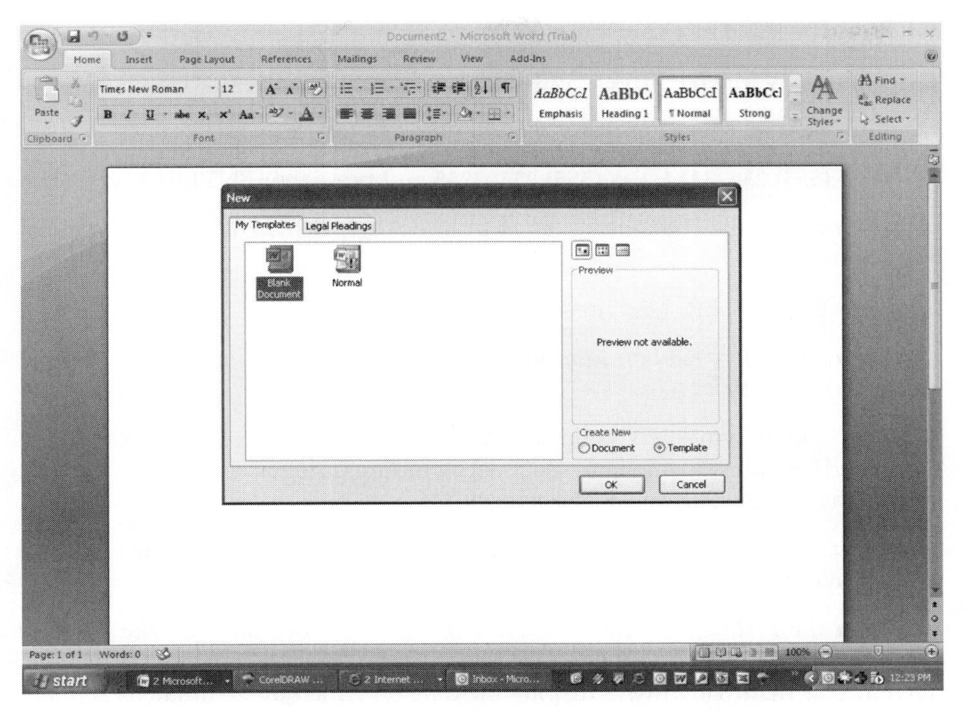

Word 2007 Exhibit 10
Creating a New Template
Microsoft product screen shot reprinted with permission from Microsoft Corporation.

button, point the pointer to Programs or All Programs, and then click on the Microsoft Word 2007 icon. (You can also point to Microsoft Office and then click on Microsoft Office Word 2007.) You should be in a clean, blank document. If you are not in a blank document, ***click on the Office Button, click on New, and then double-click on "Blank document."***

2. ***Click on the Office Button, then click on New, and then under Templates click on My templates.***

3. ***Click on Template under the Create New field in the lower right of the Templates window*** (see Word 2007 Exhibit 10).

4. ***Click on Blank Document.*** Blank Document should now be highlighted. ***Then, click on OK*** (see Word 2007 Exhibit 10).

5. You should now have a blank template on your screen. The Windows title should say "Template1—Microsoft Word" in the upper middle of the screen. You will now build the template shown in Word 2007 Exhibit 9.

6. ***Also, on the Home Ribbon tab, click the Paragraph Group dialog launcher. In the "Paragraph" window, click the down arrow below "Line Spacing" and select "Single." Then, make sure the "Before" and "After" spacing are both 0 point. Then, click OK.***

7. ***From the Home Ribbon tab, click on the Center icon in the Paragraph group. Then, from the Home Ribbon tab, click on the Bold icon in the Font group.***

8. ***Next, from the Home Ribbon tab, click on the Font Size icon from the Font group and select 14 from the list. Then, click on the Font and select Times New Roman.***

9. Type **Gonzalez & Gonzalez** and then ***from the Home Ribbon tab, click on the Font Size icon and select 12 from the list. Click on the Bold icon from the Font group to turn off bolding.***

10. Press the **[ENTER]** key.

11. Type **45634 McGee Street, Suite 1000** and press the **[ENTER]** key.

12. Type **Boston, Massachusetts, 59304** and press the **[ENTER]** key.

13. Type **(555) 234–3244; Fax (555) 234–3245** and press the **[ENTER]** key.

14. ***From the Home Ribbon tab, click on the Align Text Left icon in the Paragraph group.***

15. Press the **[ENTER]** key three times.

16. ***From the Insert Ribbon tab, point and click on Quick Parts from the Text group and then click Field.***

17. The "Field" window should now be displayed (see Word 2007 Exhibit 11). The "Field" window has several sections, including Categories and Field Names. Under Categories, (*All*) should be selected.

18. ***Point and click on the down arrow on the Field Names scroll bar until you see the field name Date*** (see Word 2007 Exhibit 11). ***Click on it.***

19. ***From the Field Properties list, click on the third option from the top (the date, the month spelled out, and the year).*** Notice that the current date is displayed. This field will always display the date on which the template is actually executed, so if the template is executed on January 1, January 1 will be the date shown on the letter. ***Then, click on OK in the "Field" window.***

20. Press the **[ENTER]** key three times.

21. ***From the Insert Ribbon tab, point and click on Quick Parts from the Text group and then click Field.***

22. ***Point and click on the down arrow on the Field names scroll bar until you see "Fill-In" in the Field Name area*** (see Word 2007 Exhibit 11). ***Click on Fill-In.***

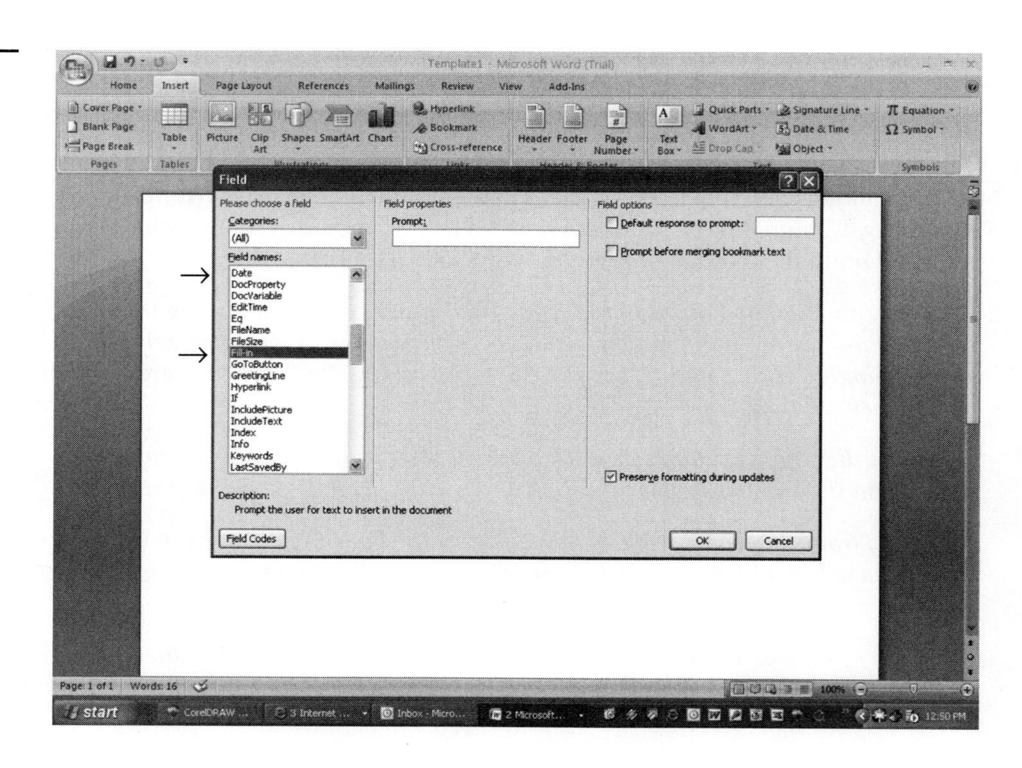

Word 2007 Exhibit 11
Inserting Fields in a Template
Microsoft product screen shot reprinted with permission from Microsoft Corporation.

23. In the Prompt: box under Field Properties, type **"Type the Name and Address of the Recipient."** *Note:* You must type the quotation marks.

24. ***Point and click on OK in the "Field" window.***

25. You will now see a window on your screen that says "Type the Name and Address of the Recipient." **Press the ENTER key after Name, Address, and City/St/Zip** (see Word 2007 Exhibit 12). ***Then, click on OK.***

26. Press the **[ENTER]** key three times.

27. Press the **[TAB]** key.

28. Type **Subject:**.

29. Press the **[TAB]** key.

30. ***From the Insert Ribbon tab, point and click on Quick Parts from the Text group and then click on Field.***

31. ***Point and click on the down arrow on the Field names scroll bar until you see Fill-In in the Field Name area. Click on Fill-In.***

32. In the "Prompt:" box under "Field Properties," type **"Type the Subject of the Letter."** *Note:* You must type the quotation marks. ***Point and click on OK.***

33. You will now see a window on your screen that says "Type the Subject of the Letter." Type **Enter the Subject of the Letter**. ***Then, click on OK.***

34. Press the **[ENTER]** key three times.

35. Type **Dear**, press the **[SPACEBAR],** then ***from the Insert Ribbon tab, point and click on Quick Parts from the Text group, and then click Field.***

36. ***Point and click on the down arrow on the Field names scroll bar until you see Fill-In in the Field Name area. Click on Fill-In.***

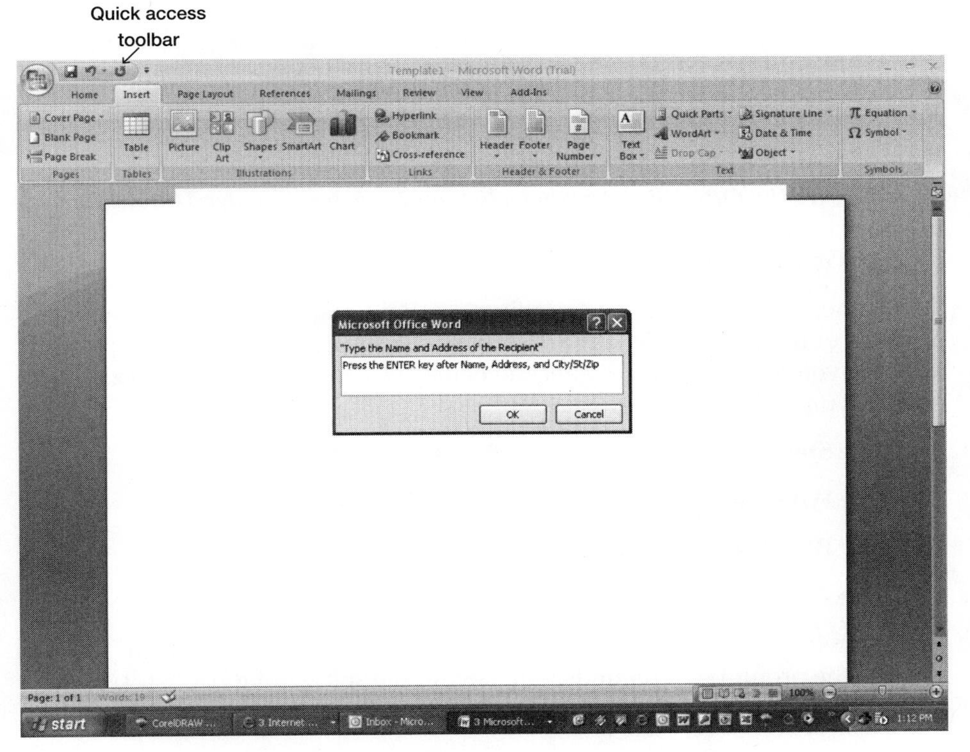

Word 2007 Exhibit 12

Entering a Fill-In field

Microsoft product screen shot reprinted with permission from Microsoft Corporation.

37. In the "Prompt:" box under Field Properties, type **"Salutation"** *Note:* You must type the quotation marks. ***Point and click on OK.***

38. You will now see a window on your screen that says "Salutation." Type **Enter the Salutation.** *Then, click on OK.*

39. Type **:** *(a colon).*

40. Press the **[ENTER]** key twice.

41. ***From the Insert Ribbon tab, point and click on Quick Parts from the Text group and then click Field.***

42. ***Point and click on the down arrow on the Field names scroll bar until you see Fill-In in the Field Name area. Click on Fill-In.***

43. In the "Prompt:" box under "Field Properties," type **"Body of Letter."** *Note:* You must type the quotation marks. ***Point and click on OK.***

44. You will now see a window on your screen that says "Body of Letter." Type **Enter the Body of the Letter**. *Then, click on OK.*

45. Press the **[ENTER]** key twice.

46. Type **If you have any questions, please do not hesitate to contact me.** Press the **[ENTER]** key three times.

47. Type **Kindest Regards,** and press the **[ENTER]** key four times.

48. Type **Shirley L. Gonzalez** and press the **[ENTER]** key once.

49. Type **For the Firm**.

50. ***Click on the Office Button, then point to Save As and click on Word Template (Note: If you do not save this as a Word Template you will not be able to finish the lesson).*** Then, next to File Name: type **Gonzalez Letter Template.** Word will save the template to a special template folder; if you save it to another folder you will not be able to run the template in the next portion of this exercise. ***Next to "Save as type:" point and click on the down arrow button, select Word 97–2003 Template, and then point and click on Save to save the document.***

51. ***Click on the Office Button and then on Close.*** You are now ready to type a letter using the template.

52. ***Click on the Office Button, then click on New. Next, under Templates click on My templates.*** In the "New" window, under the My Templates tab, ***double-click on Gonzalez Letter Template.***

53. The template letter is now running. You will see the "Type the Name and Address of the Recipient" field on the screen. You will also see the prompt that reminds you to press ENTER after the name, address, and city/state/zip. Type over this prompt.

54. Type **Stephen Wilkerson, Esq.** and press the **[ENTER]** key.

55. Type **Wilkerson, Smith & Russell** and press the **[ENTER]** key.

56. Type **P.O. Box 12341** and press the **[ENTER]** key.

57. Type **Boston, MA 59920** and then *click on OK.*

58. You will see the "Type the Subject of the Letter" field on the screen. You will also see the prompt that reminds you to enter the subject of the letter. Type over this prompt.

59. Type **Turner v. Smith, Case No. 2008-1423** and then *click on OK.*

60. You will now see the Salutation field on the screen. You will also see the prompt that reminds you to enter the salutation. Type over this prompt.

61. Type **Steve** and then ***click on OK.***

62. You will now see the Body of Letter field on the screen. You will also see the prompt that reminds you to enter the body of the letter. Type over this prompt.

63. Type **This will confirm our conversation of this date. You indicated that you had no objection to us requesting an additional ten days to respond to your Motion for Summary Judgment.** ***Click on OK.*** You are now through typing the letter. The completed letter should now be displayed. (*Note:* If another window is displayed prompting you for the name and address of the recipient, simply ***click cancel***; the completed letter should then be displayed.)

64. You are now ready to print the document. First, you will create a Quick Print icon on the Quick Access Toolbar. Instead of going to the Office Button each time to print, you will be able to print a document from the Quick Access Toolbar (see Word 2007 Exhibit 12).

65. ***Point and right-click anywhere in the Ribbon. Point and click on Customize Quick Access Toolbar.***

66. The "Word Options" window should now be displayed. ***Point and double-click on Quick Print on the left side of the screen (under Popular Commands.) Then point and click on OK in the "Word Options" window.***

67. Notice that a Quick Print icon is now displayed in the Quick Access Toolbar.

68. ***Point and click on the Quick Print icon on the Quick Access Toolbar,*** or ***click on the Office Button, click on Print, and then click on OK.***

69. To save the document, ***click on the Office Button, point to Save As, and then click on Word 97—2003 Document.*** Under Save in, select the drive or folder you would like to save the document in. Then, next to File Name, type **Done—Word 2007 Lesson 7 Document** ***and point and click on Save to save the document.*** *Note*: You just saved the output of your template to a separate file named "Done—Word Lesson 7 Document." Your original template ("Gonzalez Letter Template") is unaffected by the Lesson 7 Document, and is still a clean template ready to be used again and again for any case.

70. ***Click on the Office Button, and then on Close*** to close the document, or ***click on the Office Button, and then on Exit Word*** to exit the program.

This concludes Lesson 7.

LESSON 8: COMPARING DOCUMENTS

This lesson shows you how to compare documents by simultaneously viewing two documents and by creating a separate blacklined document with the changes. There are times in a law office when you send someone a digital file for revision, but when the file is returned, the revisions are not apparent. Using these tools in Word 2007, you can see what has changed in the document.

1. Open Windows. Then, ***double-click on the Microsoft Office Word 2007 icon on the desktop*** to open Word 2007 for Windows. Alternatively, ***click on the Start button, point the pointer to Programs or All Programs, and then click on the Microsoft Word 2007 icon. (You can also point to Microsoft Office and then click on Microsoft Office Word 2007.)*** You should now be in a clean, blank document. If you are not in a blank document, ***click on the Office Button, click on New, and then double-click on Blank document.***

2. For the purpose of this lesson, we will assume that your firm drafted an employment contract for a corporate client named Bluebriar Incorporated. Bluebriar is in negotiations with an individual named John Lewis, whom they would like to hire as their vice-president of marketing. Your firm is negotiating with John Lewis's attorney regarding the terms and language of the employment contract. The file "Lesson 8A" on Disk 1 for this text is the original document you sent to John Lewis's attorney. The file "Lesson 8B" on Disk 1 for this text is the new file sent to you by John Lewis's attorney.

3. You will now open both of these files from Disk 1 supplied with this text and then compare them side by side. Ensure that Disk 1 is inserted in the drive, ***point and click on the Office Button, and then point and click on Open.*** The Open window should now be displayed. ***Point and click on the down arrow to the right of the white box next to "Look in:" and select the drive where the Disk 1 is located. Point and double-click on the Word-Processing Files folder. Double-click on the Word 2007 folder. Point and double-click on the "Lesson 8A" file.***

4. Follow the same directions to open the "Lesson 8B"file.

5. ***From the View ribbon tab, point and click on View Side by Side in the Window group.*** Both documents should now be displayed side by side (see Word 2007 Exhibit 13).

6. Push the **[DOWN ARROW]** key to scroll down through the document. Notice that both documents simultaneously scroll.

7. From the View ribbon tab, notice that the Synchronous Scrolling icon in the Window group is highlighted (see Word 2007 Exhibit 13). To turn off this feature, you would click on this icon. The synchronous scrolling icon toggles synchronous scrolling on and off. If you turn off synchronous scrolling and wish to turn it back on, simply realign the windows where you want them, and ***point and click on the Synchronous Scrolling icon.*** (*Note:* If the View ribbon tab looks like Word 2007 Exhibit 13, with the Window group collapsed, ***point and click on the Window Group, and click Synchronous Scrolling.***)

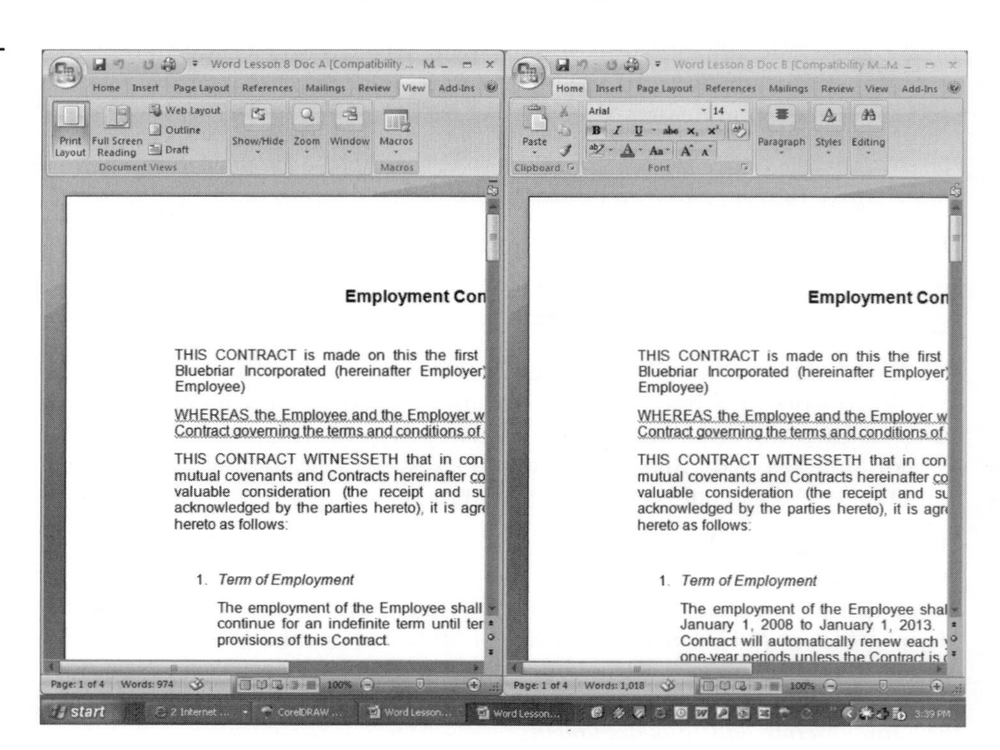

Word 2007 Exhibit 13
Comparing Documents Side by Side
Microsoft product screen shot reprinted with permission from Microsoft Corporation.

8. You will now learn how to merge the changes into one document. ***Point and click anywhere in Lesson 8A.doc; and then point and click on the Office Button and then on Close.***

9. ***Next, do the same for Word Lesson 8B.doc.***

10. You should now have no documents open.

11. ***From the Review ribbon tab, point and click with the mouse on Compare in the Compare group. Then, point and click on "Compare…."***

12. The Compare Documents window should now be displayed (see Word 2007 Exhibit 14). ***Under Original Document, point and click on the down arrow, use the Browse feature to find Lesson 8A.doc, and then double-click on it (see Word 2007 Exhibit 14).***

13. ***Next, under "Revised document," point and click on the down arrow, use the Browse feature to find "Lesson 8B.doc" and then double-click on it (see Word 2007 Exhibit 14).***

14. Next to "Label Changes with," type **John Lewis' Attorney** and then ***point and click on OK in the Compare Documents window.***

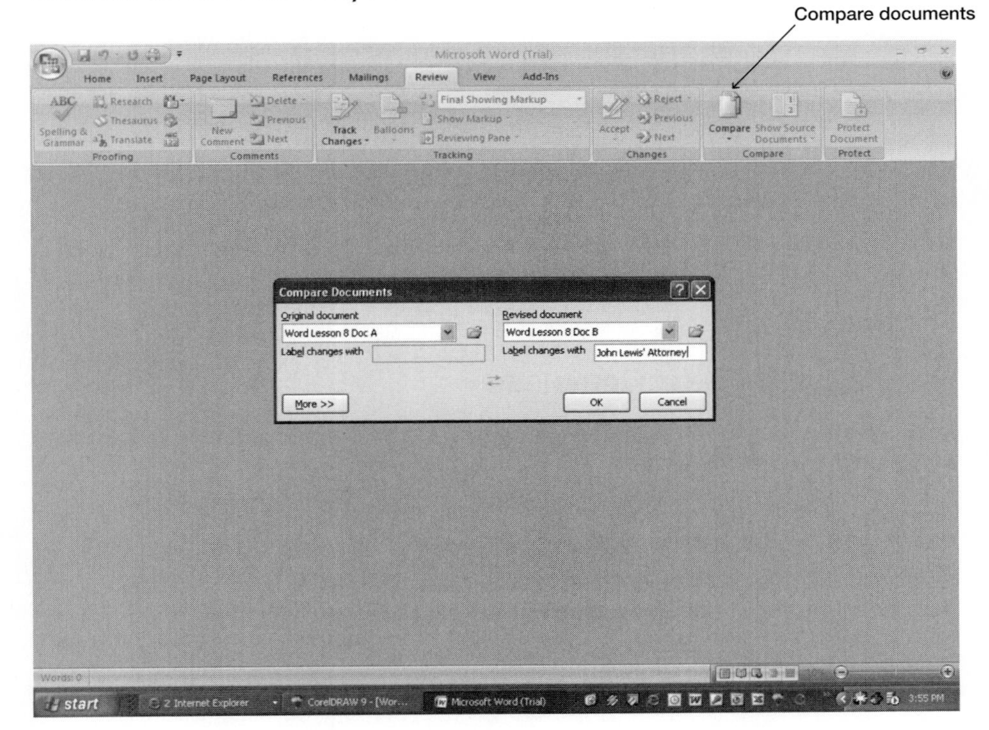

Word 2007 Exhibit 14
Comparing Document—Legal Blackline Settings
Microsoft product screen shot reprinted with permission from Microsoft Corporation.

15. Notice that a new document has been created that merges the documents (see Word 2007 Exhibit 15). Scroll through the new document and review all of the changes.

16. The Compare and Merge Document feature is extremely helpful when you are comparing multiple versions of the same file. By right-clicking on any of the additions or deletions, you can accept or reject the change. This is called Track Changes, and you will learn how to do this in more detail in the next lesson.

17. To print the document, ***point and click on the Quick Print icon on the Quick Access Toolbar,*** or ***click on the Office Button, click on Print, and then click on OK.***

18. To save the document, ***click on the Office Button, point to Save As..., and then click on "Word 97—2003 Document."*** Under "Save in" select the drive or folder

Word 2007 Exhibit 15
Completed Legal Blacklined Document
Microsoft product screen shot reprinted with permission from Microsoft Corporation.

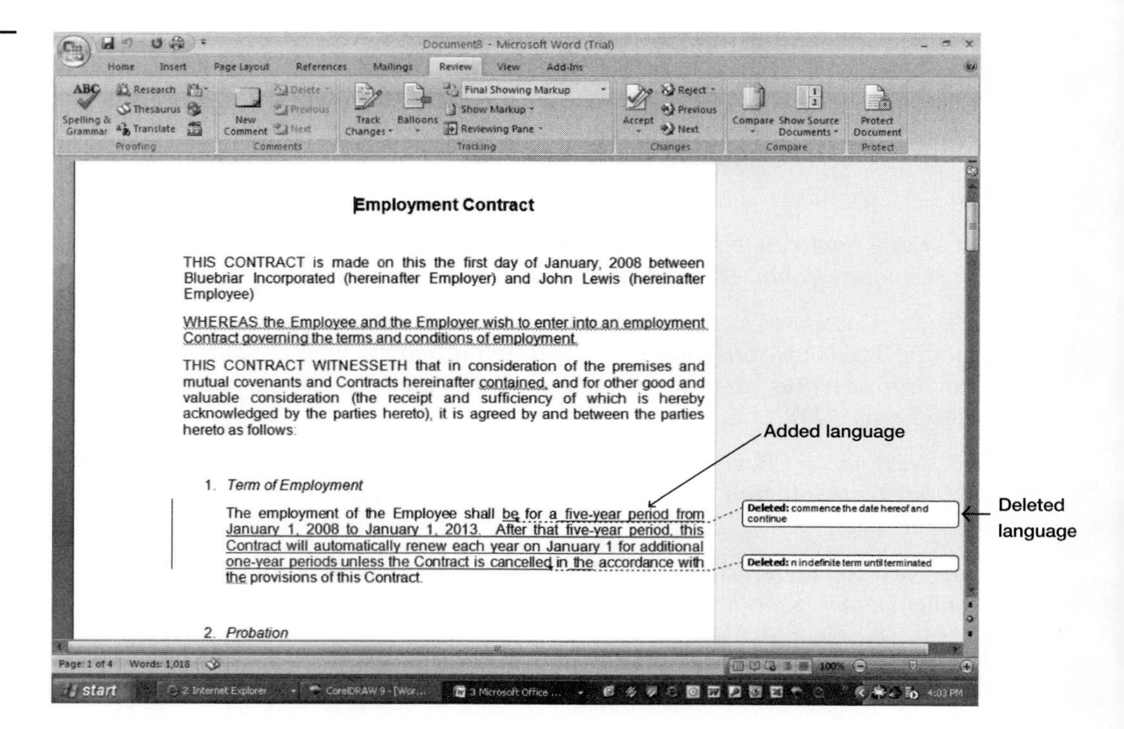

you would like to save the document in. Next to "File Name:" type **Done—Word 2007 Lesson 8 Merged Doc** and then ***click on Save to save the document.***

19. ***Click on the Office Button, and then on Close*** to close the document, or ***click on the Office Button, and then on Exit Word*** to exit the program.

This concludes Lesson 8.

LESSON 9: USING TRACK CHANGES

In this lesson, you will learn how to use the Track Changes feature by editing a will, and then accepting and/or rejecting the changes.

1. Open Windows. Then, ***double-click on the Microsoft Office Word 2007 icon on the desktop*** to open Word 2007 for Windows. Alternatively, ***click on the Start button, point the pointer to Programs or All Programs, and then click on the Microsoft Word 2007 icon. (You can also point to Microsoft Office and then click on Microsoft Office Word 2007).*** You should now be in a clean, blank document. If you are not in a blank document, ***click on the Office Button, click on New, and then double-click on Blank document.***

2. The first thing you will do is to open the "Lesson 9" file from Disk 1 supplied with this text. Ensure that the Disk is inserted in the drive, ***click on the Office Button, and then click on Open.*** The Open window should now be displayed. ***Point and click on the down arrow to the right of the white box next to "Look in:" and select the drive where Disk 1 is located. Point and double-click on the Word-Processing Files folder. Double-click on the Word 2007 folder. Double-click on the "Lesson 9" file.***

3. The text "LAST WILL AND TESTAMENT" should now be displayed on your screen (see Word 2007 Exhibit 16). Notice in Word 2007 Exhibit 16 that several revisions have been made to this document. Your client, William Porter, has asked you to use the Track Changes feature to show your supervising attorney the changes he would like to make. Mr. Porter is rather leery of the legal process and wants to make sure your supervising attorney approves of the changes.

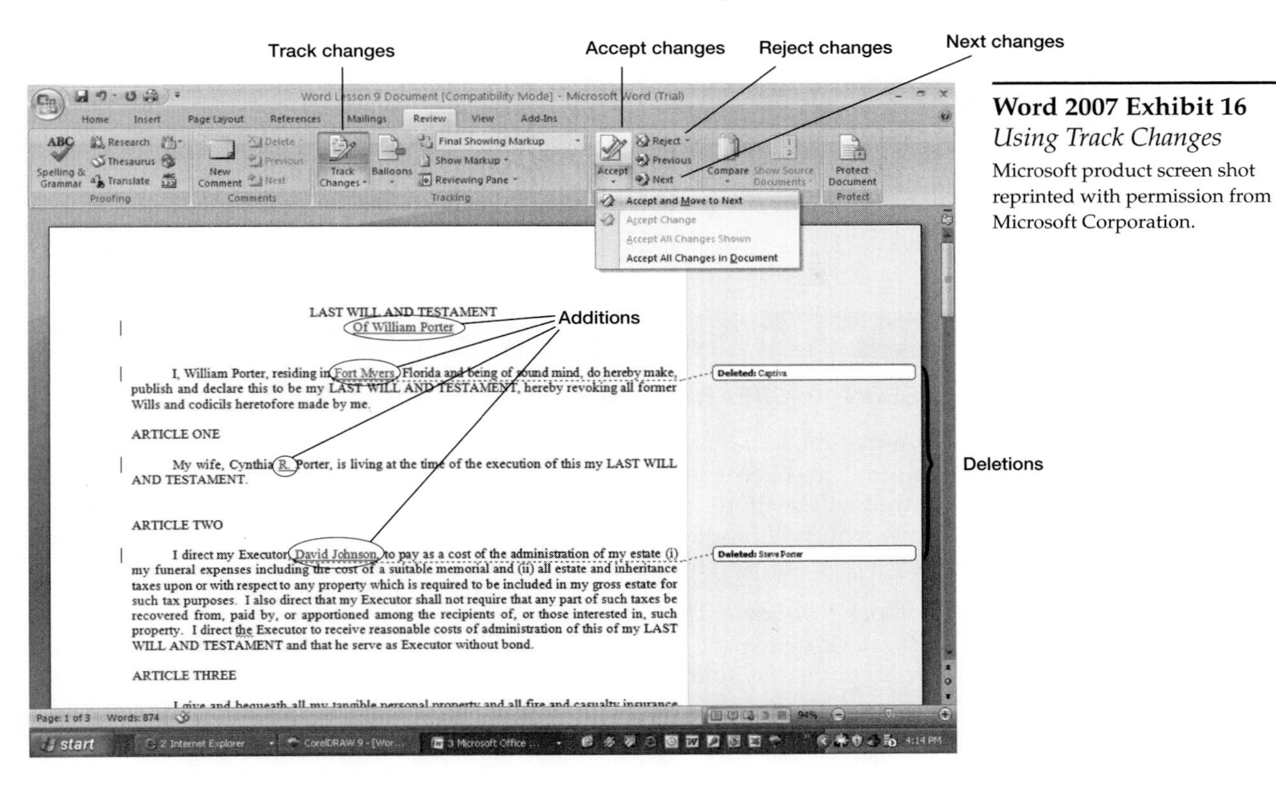

Word 2007 Exhibit 16
Using Track Changes
Microsoft product screen shot reprinted with permission from Microsoft Corporation.

4. ***From the Review ribbon tab, point and click on Track Changes from the Tracking group. Then, point and click on Track Changes from the drop-down menu*** to turn on Track Changes.

5. Make the changes shown in Word 2007 Exhibit 16. Everything that should be added is circled, and everything that should be deleted is shown at the right.

6. Assume now that you have shown the changes to your supervising attorney. ***From the Review ribbon tab, click on Track Changes, and then click on Track Changes on the drop-down menu*** to turn off Track Changes (see Word 2007 Exhibit 16). This allows you to make changes to the document without having them show up as revisions.

7. ***Point and right-click anywhere on the text, "Of William Porter," which you added just under "Last Will and Testament."*** Notice that a menu is displayed that allows you to accept or reject the insertion, among other actions. ***Point and click on Accept Change.*** The revision has now been accepted.

8. ***From the Review ribbon tab, point and click on Next in the Changes group (see Word 2007 Exhibit 16).*** This should take you to the next change. ***From the Review ribbon tab, point and click on Accept in the Changes group, then click on Accept and Move to Next (see Word 2007 Exhibit 16) to accept the change.*** Notice that one of the options is "Accept All Changes in Document." Do not select it. This is a quick way to accept all changes in a document without going through each one of them.

9. Use the Next feature, to continue to go to each change and accept the revisions. The only revision you will *not* accept is changing the executor from Steve Porter to David Johnson; reject this change. Assume that the supervising attorney has learned that Mr. Johnson is terminally ill and most likely will not be able to serve as executor, so the client has decided to keep Steve Porter as the executor.

10. To print the document, ***point and click on the Quick Print icon on the Quick Access Toolbar or click on the Office Button, click on Print, and then click on OK.***

11. To save the document, ***click on the Office Button, and then point to Save As.... then click on "Word 97—2003 Document."*** Under "Save in" select the drive or

folder you would like to save the document in. Next to "File Name," type **Done—Word 2007 Lesson 9 Document** *and then click on Save to save the document.*

12. *Click on the Office Button, and then on Close* to close the document, or *click on the Office Button, and then on Exit Word* to exit the program.

This concludes Lesson 9.

Advanced Lessons

LESSON 10: CREATING A MAIL MERGE DOCUMENT

In this lesson, you will create a merge document for an open house that you will send to three clients (see Word 2007 Exhibit 17). First, you will create the data file that will be merged into the letter. Then, you will create the letter itself, and finally, you will merge the two together. Keep in mind that if at any time you make a mistake, you may press **[CTRL]+[Z]** to undo what you have done.

1. Open Windows. Then, ***double-click on the Microsoft Office Word 2007 icon on the desktop*** to open Word 2007 for Windows. Alternatively, ***click on the Start button, point the pointer to Programs or All Programs, and then click on the Microsoft Word 2007 icon. (You may also point to Microsoft Office and then***

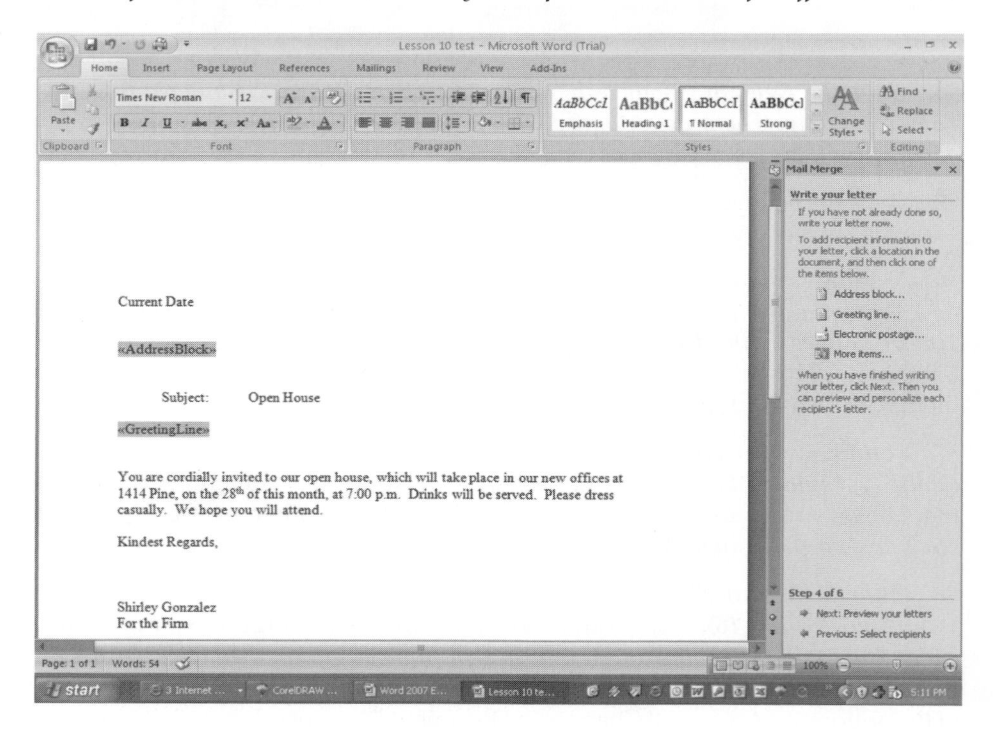

Word 2007 Exhibit 17
Mail Merge Letter
Microsoft product screen shot reprinted with permission from Microsoft Corporation.

click on Microsoft Office Word 2007). You should now be in a clean, blank document. If you are not in a blank document, ***click on the Office Button, click on New, and then double-click on Blank document.***

2. ***From the Mailings Ribbon tab, point and click on Start Mail Merge. Then, from the drop-down menu, select "Step by Step Mail Merge Wizard…."*** The Mail Merge task pane is now shown on the task pane to the right of your document.

3. The bottom of the Mail Merge task pane shows that you are on step 1 of 6. You are asked to "Select document type." You are typing a letter, so the default selection, "Letters," is fine. To continue to the next step, ***click on Next: Starting document at the bottom of the "Mail Merge" task pane under Step 1 of 6.***

4. The bottom of the "Mail Merge" task pane shows that you are on step 2 of 6. You are asked to "Select starting document." You will be using the current document to type your letter, so the default selection, "Use the current document," is fine. To continue to the next step, ***click on Next: Select recipients at the bottom of the Mail Merge task pane under Step 2 of 6.***

5. The bottom of the Mail Merge task pane shows that you are on Step 3 of 6. You are asked to "Select recipients." You will be typing a new list so ***click on Type a new list.***

6. ***Under the "Type a new list" section of the Mail Merge task pane, click on "Create...."***

7. The New Address List window is now displayed. You will now fill in the names of the three clients that you want to send your open house letter to.

8. Type the following. (*Note:* You can use the **[TAB]** key to move between the fields, or you can use the mouse.) Only complete the fields below; skip the fields in the New Address List window that we will not be using.

Title	
First Name	Jim
Last Name	Woods
Company Name	
Address Line 1	2300 NE Cannondale
Address Line 2	
City	Cambridge
State	MA
ZIP Code	55342
Country	
Home Phone	
Work Phone	
Email Address	

9. When you have entered all of the information for Jim Woods, ***click on the New Entry button in the New Address List window.***

10. Enter the second client in the blank New Address List window.

Title	
First Name	Jennifer
Last Name	Trek
Company Name	
Address Line 1	4500 Wheatley
Address Line 2	
City	Boston
State	MA
ZIP Code	55856
Country	
Home Phone	
Work Phone	
Email Address	

11. When you have entered all of the information for Jennifer Trek, ***click on the New Entry button in the New Address List window.***

12. Enter the third client in the blank "New Address List" window.

Title	
First Name	Jonathan
Last Name	Phillips
Company Name	
Address Line 1	8100 Watson Blvd
Address Line 2	
City	Boston
State	MA
ZIP Code	55983
Country	
Home Phone	
Work Phone	
Email Address	

13. When you have entered all of the information for Jonathan Phillips, ***click on OK in the "New Address List" window.***

14. The "Save Address List" window is now displayed. You need to save the address list so that it can be later merged with the open house letter. In the "Save Address List" window, next to "File Name," type **Open House List** and then ***click on Save in the "Save Address List" window to save the file to the default directory.***

15. The "Mail Merge Recipients" window is now displayed (see Word 2007 Exhibit 18). ***Click on the "Last Name" field in the "Mail Merge Recipients" window to sort***

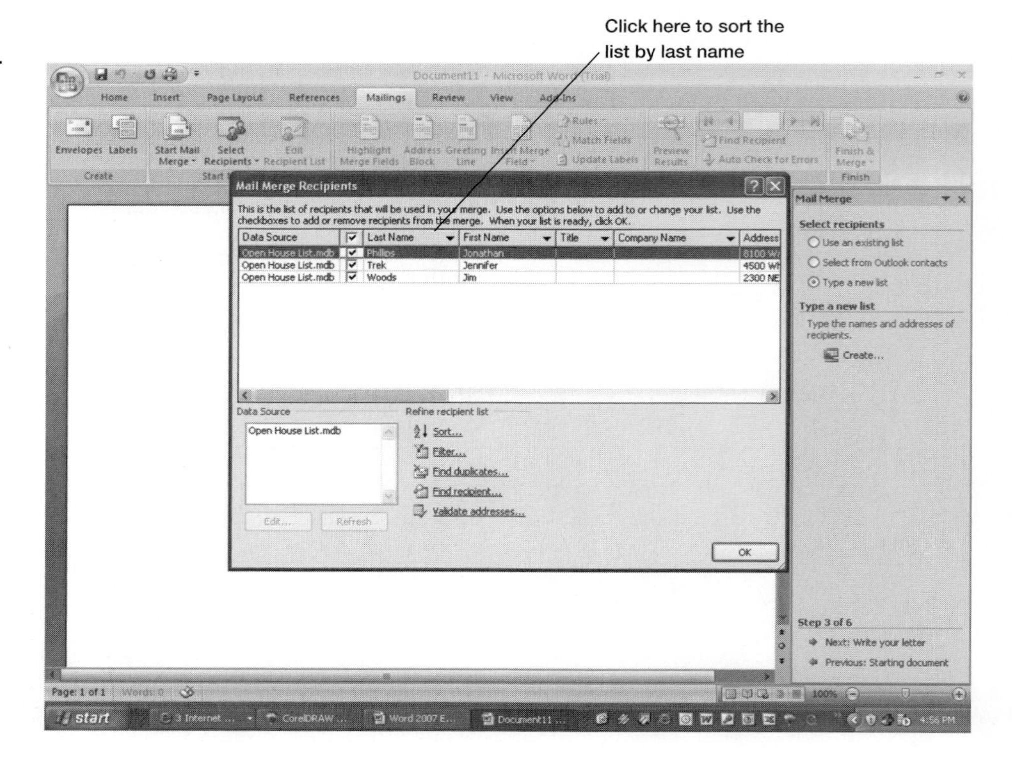

Word 2007 Exhibit 18
Entering Mail Merge Recipients
Microsoft product screen shot reprinted with permission from Microsoft Corporation.

the list by last name (see Word 2007 Exhibit 18). Notice that the order of the list is now sorted by last name.

16. ***Click on OK in the "Mail Merge Recipients" window.*** You are now back at a blank document with the Mail Merge task pane open to the right. The bottom of the Mail Merge task pane, indicates that you are still at step 3 of 6. ***Click on Next: Write your letter at the bottom of the Mail Merge task pane under Step 3 of 6*** to continue to the next step.

17. The bottom of the Mail Merge task pane indicates that you are on step 4 of 6. In the Mail Merge task pane, "Write your letter" is displayed. You are now ready to write the letter. On the Home Ribbon tab, click the Paragraph Group dialog launcher. In the "Paragraph" window, click the down arrow below "Line Spacing" and select "Single." Then, make sure the "Before" and "After" spacing are both 0 point. Then, click OK.

18. Press the **[ENTER]** key four times.

19. Type the current date and press the **[ENTER]** key three times.

20. ***Click on Address Block… in the Mail Merge task pane under "Write your letter."***

21. The "Insert Address Block" window is now displayed. You will now customize how the address block will appear in the letters.

22. ***In the "Insert Address Block" window, click on the second entry, "Joshua Randall Jr."*** Then, ***click on "Insert company name" to deselect because we did not include company names in our data list*** (see Word 2007 Exhibit 19).

23. Then, under "Insert postal address," ***click on "Never include the country/region in the address" (see Word 2007 Exhibit 19).***

24. ***Click on OK in the "Insert Address Block" window.***

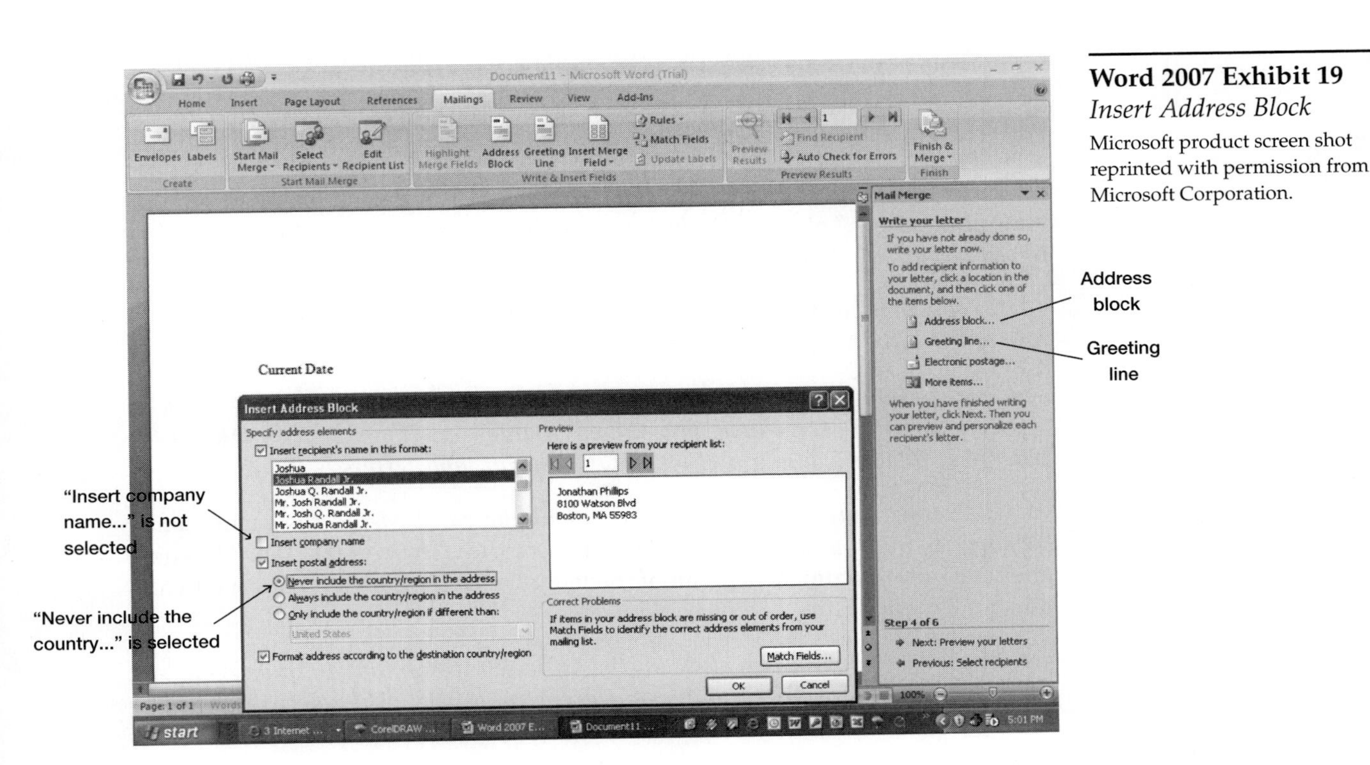

Word 2007 Exhibit 19

Insert Address Block

Microsoft product screen shot reprinted with permission from Microsoft Corporation.

25. The words "<<AddressBlock>>" are now displayed in your document.

26. Press the **[ENTER]** key three times.

27. Press the **[TAB]** key once and then type **Subject:**.

28. Press the **[TAB]** key and then type **Open House.**

29. Press the **[ENTER]** key twice.

30. ***In the Mail Merge task pane under "Write your letter" click on Greeting line... (see Word 2007 Exhibit 19).***

31. The "Insert Greeting Line" window is now displayed. You will now customize how the greeting or salutation will appear in the letter. In the "Insert Greeting Line" window, ***click on the down arrow next to "Mr. Randall" and then scroll down and click on "Josh." Then, click on OK in the "Insert Greeting Line" window.***

32. The words "<<GreetingLine>>" are now displayed in your document.

33. Press the **[ENTER]** key three times.

34. Type **You are cordially invited to our open house, which will take place in our new offices at 1414 Pine, on the 28th of this month, at 7:00 p.m. Drinks will be served. Please dress casually. We hope you will attend.**

35. Press the **[ENTER]** key twice.

36. Type **Kindest Regards**.

37. Press the **[ENTER]** key four times.

38. Type **Shirley L. Gonzalez**.

39. Press the **[ENTER]** key once and type **For the Firm**.

40. You are now done typing the letter. Your letter should look similar to Word 2007 Exhibit 17. The only thing left to do is to merge the recipient list with the form.

41. Under "Step 4 of 6" at the bottom of the Mail Merge task pane, ***click on "Next: Preview your letters"*** to continue to the next step.

42. Your first letter is now displayed. In the Mail Merge task pane under "Preview your letters," ***click on the button showing two arrows pointing to the right to see the rest of your letters.***

43. ***To continue to the next step, click on "Next: Complete the merge" at the bottom of the Mail Merge task pane under Step 5 of 6.***

44. The Mail Merge task pane now will display "Complete the Merge." ***Click on Print in the Mail Merge task pane under "Merge," and then click on OK. At the "Merge to Printer" window, click on OK to print your letters.***

45. ***Click on "Edit individual letters..." in the Mail Merge task pane under "Merge."*** In the "Merge to New Document" window, ***click on OK.*** Word has now opened a new document with all of the letters in it (*Note:* Here you can edit and personalize each letter if you would like).

46. To save the document, ***click on the Office Button, point to Save As..., and then click on "Word 97—2003 Document."*** Under "Save in" select the drive or

folder you would like to save the document in. Then, next to "File Name," type **Open House Letters** ***and then point and click on Save to save the document.***

47. ***Click on the Office Button and then on Close to close the personalized letters.***

48. You should be back at the mail merge letter. ***Click on the Office Button, point to Save As. Then click on "Word 97—2003 Document."*** Under "Save in" select the drive or folder you would like to save the document in. Then, next to "File Name:" type **Open House Mail Merge** ***and then point and click on Save to save the document.***

49. ***Click on the Office Button, and then on Close*** to close the document, or ***click on the Office Button, and then on Exit Word*** to exit the program.

This concludes Lesson 10.

LESSON 11: CREATING A TABLE OF AUTHORITIES

In this lesson, you will prepare a table of authorities for a reply brief (see Word 2007 Exhibit 22). You will learn how to find cases, mark cases, and then automatically generate a table of authorities.

1. Open Windows. Then, ***double-click on the Microsoft Office Word 2007 icon on the desktop*** to open Word 2007 for Windows. Alternatively, ***click on the Start button, point the pointer to Programs or All Programs, and then click on the Microsoft Word 2007 icon. (You may also point to Microsoft Office and then click on Microsoft Office Word 2007).*** You should now be in a clean, blank document. If you are not in a blank document, ***click on the Office Button, click on New, and then double-click on Blank document.***

2. The first thing you will do is to open the "Lesson 11" file from Disk 1 supplied with this text. Ensure that the disk is inserted in the disk drive, ***point and click on the Office Button, and then point and click on Open.*** The Open window should now be displayed. ***Point and click on the down arrow to the right of the white box next to "Look in:" and select the drive where Disk 1 is located. Point and double-click on the Word-Processing Files folder. Double-click on the Word 2007 folder. Point and double-click on the "Lesson 11" file.***

3. The text *In the Supreme Court of the United States–Ted Sutton, Petitioner v. State of Alaska, Respondent* should now be displayed on your screen.

4. In this exercise you will build the case section of the Table of Authorities for this reply brief. There are five cases to be included and they are all shown in bold so that you can easily identify them. Your first task will be to mark each of the cases so Word knows they are the cases to be included, and then you will execute the command for Word to build the table.

5. If you are not at the beginning of the document, press **[CTRL]+[HOME]** to go to the beginning.

6. You will now mark the cases. ***From the References ribbon tab, click on Mark Citations from the Table of Authorities group.***

7. The Mark Citation window should now be displayed (see Word 2007 Exhibit 20). Notice next to "Category:" that "Cases" is displayed. This indicates that you will be marking case citations. ***Point and click on the down arrow next to "Cases" to see that you can also mark citations to be included for statutes, rules, treatises, regulations, and other sources.***

Word 2007 Exhibit 20
Marking a Citation for Inclusion in a Table of Authorities

Microsoft product screen shot reprinted with permission from Microsoft Corporation.

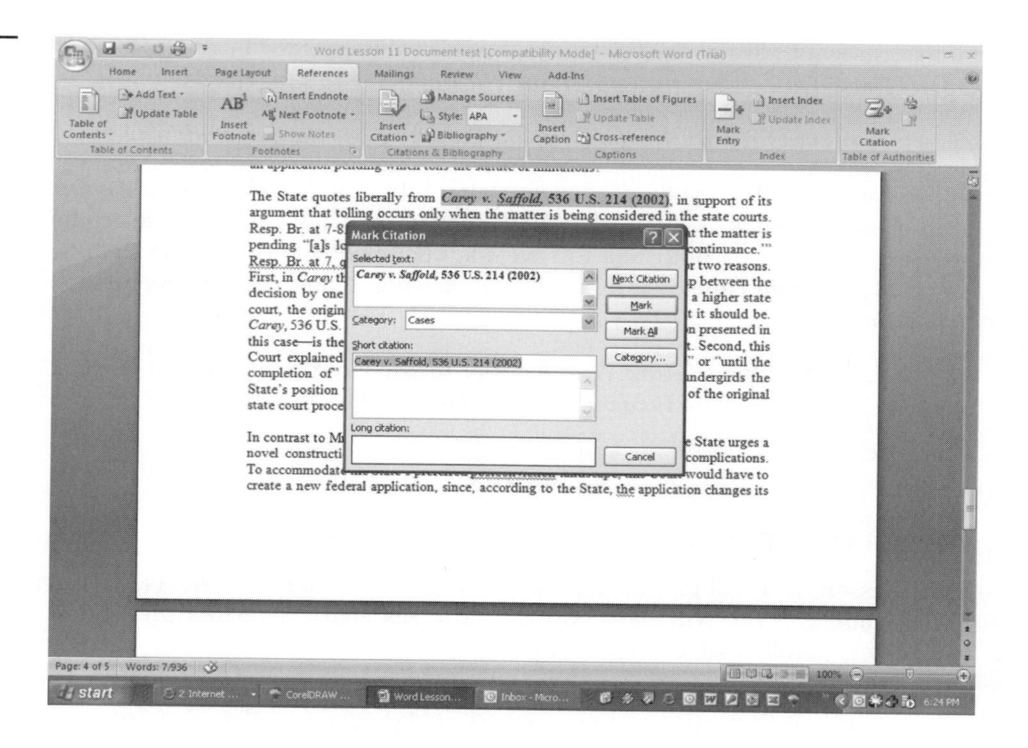

8. ***Point and click on "Cases" again because you will now start marking cases to be included in the table of authorities.***

9. In the Mark Citation window, ***click on "Next Citation."*** Word looks for terms such as "vs" or "v." when finding citations. The cursor should now be on the "v." in *Ted Sutton v. State of Alaska*. Because this is the caption of the current case, we do not want to mark it. *Note*: If the Mark Citation window gets in the way of your seeing the brief, put the pointer on the blue title bar of the Mark Citation window and drag it out of your way.

10. ***Click on "Next Citation" in the Mark Citation window.*** Again, this is the caption of the current case, *Ted Sutton v. State of Alaska,* so we do not want to mark it.

11. ***Click again on "Next Citation" in the Mark Citation window.*** Word has now found the case *Carey v. Saffold*. We want to mark this case so that it is included in the table of authorities.

12. ***Click once on the* Carey v. Saffold *case.***

13. ***Drag the pointer and highlight Carey v. Saffold, 536 U.S. 214 (2002) and then click in the white box under "Selected text:" in the Mark Citation window; the case is automatically copied there*** (see Word 2007 Exhibit 20).

14. ***Then, click on "Mark" in the Mark Citation window.*** *Note:* When you mark a citation, Word changes your view to the Show/Hide paragraph view. It shows you that you have embedded table of authorities formatting codes in the document. To switch out of Show/Hide view, from the Home Ribbon tab point on the Show/Hide icon in the Paragraph group. (It looks like a paragraph sign.)

15. ***Click on "Next Citation" in the Mark Citation window.***

16. *Click once on the* **Duncan v. Walker** *case.*

17. *Drag the mouse and highlight* "**Duncan v. Walker, 533 U.S. 167, 174 (2001)**" and then *click in the white box under "Selected text:" in the Mark Citation window.* The case is automatically copied there.

18. *Click on "Mark" in the Mark Citation window.* Notice under "Short Citation" in the Mark Citation window that the *Carey* and *Duncan* cases are listed. Again, if at any time the Mark Citation window prevents you from seeing the case you need to highlight, just click on the blue bar at top of the Mark Citation window and drag to the left or the right to move the window out of your way.

19. *To switch out of Show/Hide view, from the Home tab on the ribbon, point on the Show/Hide icon in the Paragraph group.*

20. *Click on "Next Citation" in the Mark Citation window.*

21. *Click once on the* **Bates v. United States** *case.*

22. *Drag the pointer and highlight* "**Bates v. United States, 522 U.S. 23, 29–30 (1997)**," *and then click in the white box under "Selected text:" in the Mark Citation window.* The case is automatically copied there.

23. *Click on "Mark" in the Mark Citation window.*

24. *Click on "Next Citation" in the Mark Citation window.*

25. *Click once on the* **Abela v. Martin** *case.*

26. *Drag and highlight* "**Abela v. Martin, 348 F.3d 164 (6th Cir. 2003)**" *and then click in the white box under "Selected text:" in the Mark Citation window. The case is automatically copied there.*

27. *Click on "Mark" in the Mark Citation window.*

28. *Click on "Next Citation" in the Mark Citation window.*

29. *Click once on the* **Coates v. Byrd** *case.*

30. *Drag the mouse and highlight* "**Coates v. Byrd, 211 F.3d 1225, 1227 (11th Cir. 2000)**," *and then click in the white box under "Selected text:" in the Mark Citation window. The case is automatically copied there.*

31. *Click on "Mark" in the Mark Citation window.*

32. *Click on Close in the Mark Citation window to close it.*

33. *Point and click on the Show/Hide paragraph icon to on the Home Ribbon tab make the paragraph marks disappear.*

34. *Using the cursor keys or the horizontal scroll bar, place the cursor on page 3 of the document two lines under the title "TABLE OF AUTHORITIES"* (see Word 2007 Exhibit 21). You are now ready to generate the table.

35. *From the References ribbon tab, click on the Insert Table of Authorities icon in the Table of Authorities group (see Word 2007 Exhibit 21).*

36. *The Table of Authorities window should now be displayed (see Word 2007 Exhibit 21). Click on Cases under Category and then click on OK.*

Word 2007 Exhibit 21
Inserting the Table of Authoritites
Microsoft product screen shot reprinted with permission from Microsoft Corporation.

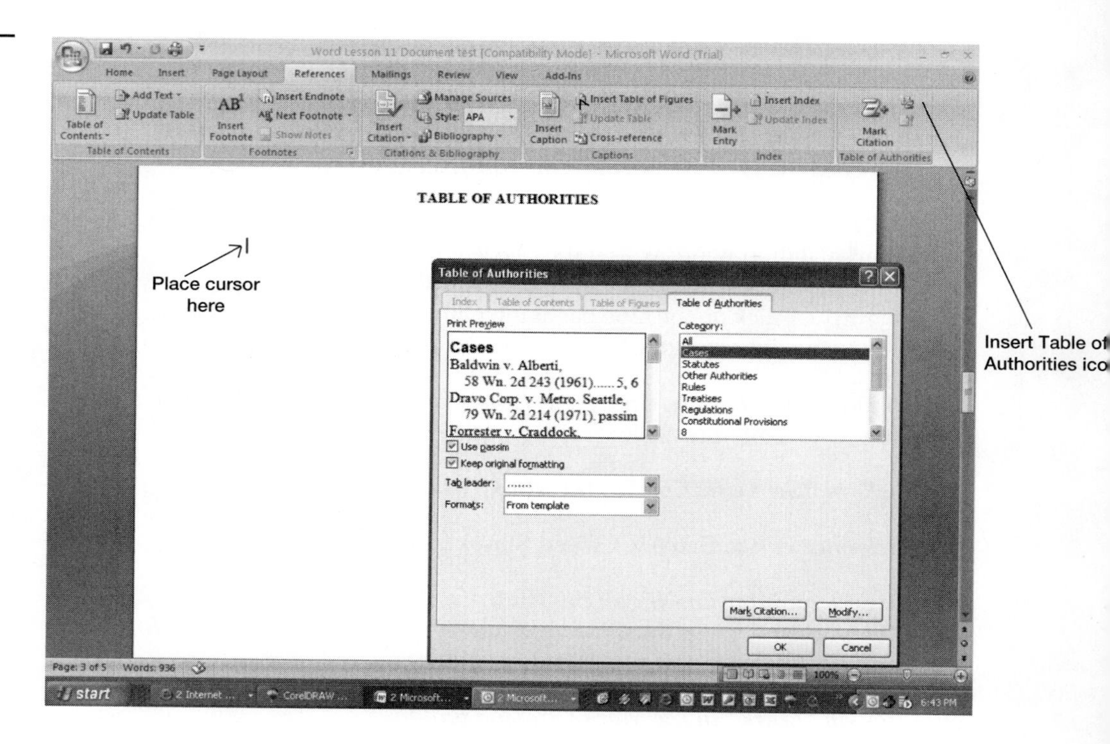

37. Notice that the table of authorities has been prepared and completed, and that the cases and the page numbers where they appear in the document have been included (see Word 2007 Exhibit 22).

38. To print the document, ***point and click on the Quick Print icon on the Quick Access Toolbar or click on the Office Button, click on Print, and then click on OK.***

39. To save the document, ***click on the Office Button and point to Save As…, then click on "Word 97—2003 Document."*** Under "Save in" select the drive or folder

Word 2007 Exhibit 22
Completed Table of Authorities
Microsoft product screen shot reprinted with permission from Microsoft Corporation.

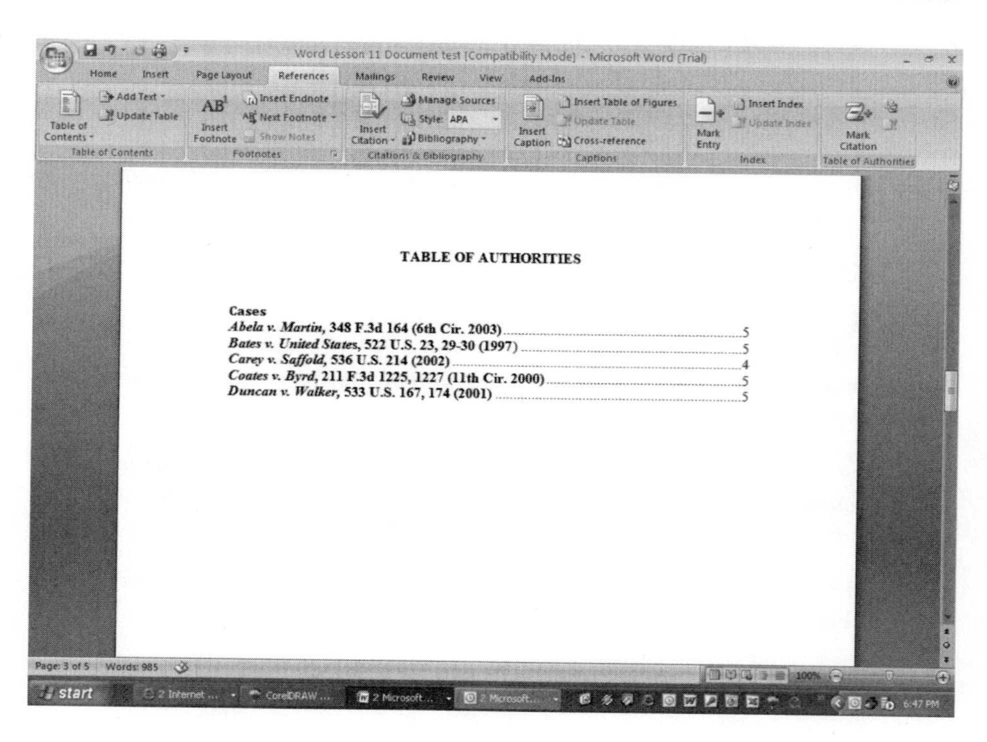

you would like to save the document in. Then, next to "File Name," type **Done—Word 2007 Lesson 11 Document** *and click on Save to save the document.*

40. ***Click on the Office Button, and then on Close*** to close the document, or ***click on the Office Button, and then on Exit Word*** to exit the program.

This concludes Lesson 11.

LESSON 12: CREATING A MACRO

In this lesson you will prepare a macro that will automatically type the signature block for a pleading (see Word 2007 Exhibit 23). You will then execute the macro to make sure that it works properly.

1. Open Windows. Then, ***double-click on the Microsoft Office Word 2007 icon on the desktop*** to open Word 2007 for Windows. Alternatively, ***click on the Start button, point to Programs or All Programs, and then click on the Microsoft Word 2007 icon. (You can also point to Microsoft Office and then click on Microsoft Office Word 2007.)*** You should now be in a clean, blank document. If you are not in a blank document, ***click on the Office Button, click on New, and then double-click on Blank document.***

2. The first thing you need to do to create a new macro is to name the macro and then turn on the Record function. ***From the View Ribbon tab, point and click on the down arrow under "Macros" in the Macros group (see Word 2007 Exhibit 23).***

3. ***Then point and click on "Record Macro..." on the drop-down menu.***

4. The "Record Macro" window should now be displayed (see Word 2007 Exhibit 23). In the "Record Macro" window under "Macro Name:" type **Pleadingsignblock** ***and then point and click on OK*** (see Word 2007 Exhibit 23).

5. Notice that your cursor has a cassette tape on it. The cassette tape on your cursor indicates that Word is now recording all of your keystrokes and commands.

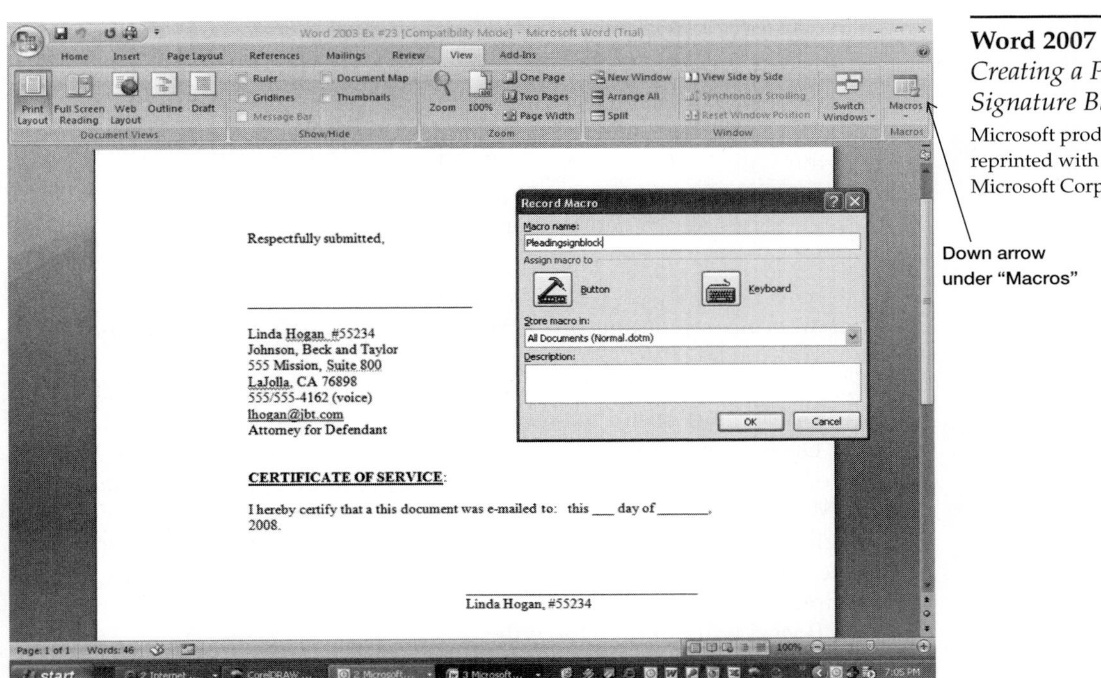

Word 2007 Exhibit 23
Creating a Pleading Signature Block Macro
Microsoft product screen shot reprinted with permission from Microsoft Corporation.

6. *Type the information in Word 2007 Exhibit 23.* When you have completed typing the information, *from the View Ribbon tab, point and click on the down arrow under "Macros" in the Macros group (see Word 2007 Exhibit 23).*

7. *Then point and click on "Stop Recording" on the drop-down menu.*

8. You will now test your macro to see if it works properly. *Click on the Office Button and then on Close to close the document.* At the prompt "Do you want to save the changes to Document?" *click on No.*

9. To open a blank document, *click on the Office Button, click on New, and then double-click on Blank document.*

10. *To run the macro, from the View Ribbon tab point and click on the down arrow* under *"Macros" in the Macros group (see Word 2007 Exhibit 23).*

11. *Then point and click on "View Macros."*

12. *In the Macros window, point and click on* **Pleadingsignblock** *and then point and click on Run.* Your pleading signature block should now be in your document.

13. To print the document, *point and click on the Quick Print icon on the Quick Access Toolbar or click on the Office Button, click on Print, and then click on OK.*

14. To save the document, *click on the Office Button, point to Save As, and then click on "Word 97—2003 Document."* Under "Save in" select the drive or folder you would like to save the document in. Then, next to "File Name," type **Done—Word 2007 Lesson 12 Document** *and point and click on Save to save the document.*

15. *Click on the Office Button, and then on Close* to close the document, or *click on the Office Button, and then on Exit Word* to exit the program.

This concludes Lesson 12.

LESSON 13: DRAFTING A WILL

Using the websites at the end of the chapter or going to a law library and using a form book, draft a simple will that would be valid in your state. You will be drafting the will for Thomas Mansell, who is a widower. The will should be dated July 1 of the current year. Mr. Mansell requests the following:
That his just debts and funeral expenses be paid.

- That his lifelong friend, Dr. Jeff Johnson, receive $20,000 in cash.
- That his local YMCA receive his 100 shares of stock in IBM.
- That all of his remaining property (real or personal) descend to his daughter Sharon Mansell.
- That in the event Mr. Mansell and his daughter die simultaneously, for all of his property to descend to Sharon's son Michael Mansell.
- That Dr. Jeff Johnson be appointed the executor of the will; if Dr. Johnson predeceases Mr. Mansell, that Mr. Joe Crawford be appointed executor.
- Mr. Mansell has requested that his will be double-spaced and have 1-inch margins. He would like the will to look good and be valid in his state.
- Three witnesses will watch the signing of the will: Shelly Stewart, Dennis Gordon, and Gary Fox.
- John Boesel will notarize the will.

Print out a hard copy of the will and email it to your instructor.

LESSON 14: THE PLEADING WIZARD

Use the Pleading Wizard in Microsoft Word 2007 to create the motion in Exhibit 3–17 to Chapter 3 of the text (the word-processing chapter). To bring up the Pleading Wizard, ***click on the Office Button, then click on New. Next, under "Templates," click on "My templates…." Click on the Legal Pleadings tab, click on "Pleading Template 1," and under "Create New" click on "Template." Finally, click on OK.*** (*Note*: If you are unable to find the Pleading Wizard, it may not have been installed. If this is the case, move to the next lesson.) The Pleading Wizard will guide you through creating a pleading form and completing the form. Use Exhibit 3–17 as a guide, but you do not need to copy the format exactly. When the document is completed, print out a hard copy and email the file to your instructor.

LESSON 15: DEPOSITION SUMMARY

In this exercise, you will prepare a summary of the deposition contained in Appendix B to this book. The deposition is in the case of *Judy Smith v. EZ Pest Control, Inc.* The Petition by Judy Smith alleges that the defendant, EZ Pest Control, Inc., breached their contract in that EZ Pest failed to adequately conduct effective termite inspections, and failed to control termites in accordance with its contract. The Petition also alleges that the defendant acted negligently and below a reasonable standard of care for providing such pest control services. The Petition requests $40,000 in damages.

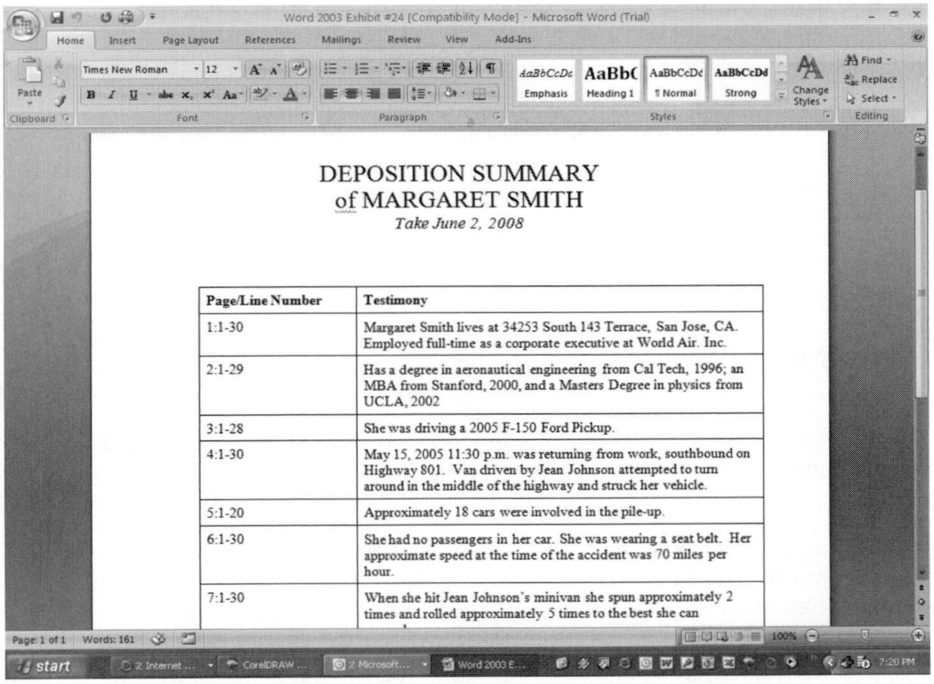

DEPOSITION SUMMARY
of MARGARET SMITH
Take June 2, 2008

Page/Line Number	Testimony
1:1-30	Margaret Smith lives at 34253 South 143 Terrace, San Jose, CA. Employed full-time as a corporate executive at World Air. Inc.
2:1-29	Has a degree in aeronautical engineering from Cal Tech, 1996; an MBA from Stanford, 2000, and a Masters Degree in physics from UCLA, 2002
3:1-28	She was driving a 2005 F-150 Ford Pickup.
4:1-30	May 15, 2005 11:30 p.m. was returning from work, southbound on Highway 801. Van driven by Jean Johnson attempted to turn around in the middle of the highway and struck her vehicle.
5:1-20	Approximately 18 cars were involved in the pile-up.
6:1-30	She had no passengers in her car. She was wearing a seat belt. Her approximate speed at the time of the accident was 70 miles per hour.
7:1-30	When she hit Jean Johnson's minivan she spun approximately 2 times and rolled approximately 5 times to the best she can

Word 2007 Exhibit 24
Deposition Summary
Microsoft product screen shot reprinted with permission from Microsoft Corporation.

As stated above, your job is to summarize the deposition of the plaintiff, Judy Smith. Word 2007 Exhibit 24 shows a sample of a deposition summary. You can use whatever format you would like, but a fairly standard approach is to use a table format of the table. Each row can represent a page of the deposition (see Word 2007 Exhibit 24); alternatively, a row can represent each separate topic on a page. (You may reference line numbers as well.) The purpose of a deposition summary is to summarize the essence of the deposition so the user does not have to read the whole deposition, and to create an index so the user can quickly go to the page they are looking for without having to wade through the whole deposition. When the document is completed, print out a hard copy and email the file to your instructor.

HANDS-ON EXERCISES

MICROSOFT WORD 2003 FOR WINDOWS

Basic Lessons

Number	Lesson Title	Concepts Covered
Lesson 1	Typing a Letter	Using word wrap, tab key, cursor keys, underline, bold, italics; saving and printing a document.
Lesson 2	Editing a Letter	Retrieving a file, Insert mode, Overtype mode, block moving/deleting, and spell/grammar checking.
Lesson 3	Typing a Pleading	Centering, changing margins, changing line spacing, adding a footnote, double indenting, and automatic page numbering.
Lesson 4	Creating a Table	Creating a table, entering data in a table, using automatic numbering, adjusting columns in a table and using the Table AutoFormat command.

Intermediate Lessons

Lesson 5	Tools and Techniques (Using the "Lesson 5" file on Disk 1)	Editing an employment policy, using the Format Painter tool, revealing document formatting, using the beginning of document command, clearing formatting, changing case, using Find and Replace, using the Go To command, creating a section break, and changing the orientation of the page to landscape.
Lesson 6	Using Styles (Using the "Lesson 6" file on Disk 1)	Using, modifying, and creating styles to maintain consistent and uniform formatting of documents.
Lesson 7	Creating a Template (Office Letterhead/Letter)	Finding ready-made templates in Word, creating a new office letterhead and letter template, and filling in / completing a template.
Lesson 8	Comparing Documents (multiple versions of anemployment contract) (Using the "Lesson 8A and 8B" files on Disk 1)	Comparing documents using the simultaneous viewing method and merging the documents into a separate annotated blacklined document.
Lesson 9	Using Track Changes (Using the "Lesson 9" file on Disk 1)	Turning on Track Changes, making revisions, and accepting and rejecting revisions.

Advanced Lessons

Lesson 10	Creating a Mail Merge	Creating and entering a list of recipients for a mail merge, creating a mail merge document, and merging the list with the document.

Number	Lesson Title	Concepts Covered
Lesson 11	Creating a Table of Authorities in a Brief (Using the "Lesson 11" file on Disk 1)	Finding and marking cases in a brief and generating an actual table of authorities for the brief.
Lesson 12	Creating a Macro (Pleading Signature Block)	Creating and executing a pleading signature block macro.
Lesson 13	Drafting a Will	Using Word to draft a will.
Lesson 14	The Pleading Wizard	Using the Pleading Wizard.
Lesson 15	Deposition Summary	Summarizing a deposition using Word.

GETTING STARTED

Introduction

Throughout these lessons and exercises, information you need to type into the program will be designated in several different ways:

- Keys to be pressed on the keyboard will be designated in brackets, in all caps, and in bold (i.e., press the: **[ENTER]** key).
- Movements with the mouse will be designated in bold and italics (i.e., ***point to File on the menu bar and click the mouse***).
- Words or letters that should be typed will be designated in bold (i.e., type **Training Program**).
- Information that should be displayed on your computer screen is shown in the following style: ***Press ENTER to continue.***

OVERVIEW OF MICROSOFT WORD

Below are some tips on using Microsoft Word that will help you complete these exercises.

I. General Rules for Microsoft Word 2003

A. *Word Wrap*—You do not need to press the **[ENTER]** key after each line of text, as you would with a typewriter.

B. *Double Spacing*—If you want to double-space, do not hit the **[ENTER]** key twice. Instead, change the line spacing (***click on Format from the menu bar and then click on Paragraph.*** In the Indents and Spacing tab under "Spacing—Line Spacing," ***click on the down arrow key and select Double and then click on OK.***

C. *Moving Through Already Entered Text*—If you want to move the cursor to various positions within already entered text, use the cursor (arrow) keys, or ***point and click.***

D. *Moving the Cursor Where No Text Has Been Entered*—You cannot use the cursor keys to move the cursor where no text has been entered. Said another way, you cannot move any further in a document than where you have typed text or pressed the **[ENTER]** key. You must use the **[ENTER]** key or first type text.

E. *Saving a Document*—To save a document, ***click on File from the menu bar, and then click on Save.***

F. *New Document*—To get a new, clean document, ***click on File from the menu bar, then click on New, and click on blank document*** (or choose another document).

G. *Help*—To get help, ***click on Help from the menu bar, and then click on Microsoft Office Word Help.*** In the "Search for" box, type the subject you would like to search for and then ***click on the green "Start searching" arrow to execute the search.***

II. Editing a Document

A. *Cursor Movement*

One space to left	**[LEFT ARROW]**
One space to right	**[RIGHT ARROW]**
Beginning of line	**[HOME]**
End of line	**[END]**
One line up	**[UP ARROW]**
One line down	**[DOWN ARROW]**
One Screen up	**[PAGE UP]**
One Screen down	**[PAGE DOWN]**
Beginning of Document	**[CTRL]+[HOME]**
End of Document	**[CTRL]+[END]**

B. *Insert v. Overtype*—The **[INSERT]** key toggles from Insert mode to Overtype mode. When text is added in Overtype mode, the new text is typed over the existing text. In Insert mode, the text is added before the existing text.

C. *Deleting Text*

Delete the text under the cursor or to the right of it	**[DEL]**
Delete the text to the left of cursor	**[BACKSPACE]**
Delete the whole word to the left of the cursor	**[CTRL] + [BACKSPACE]**
Delete the whole word to the right of the cursor	**[CTRL] + [DEL]**

D. *Delete Blocked Text*—***Drag the mouse to select or highlight text,*** and press the **[DEL]** key, or ***drag the mouse, and then select Edit from the menu bar and then Cut,*** or ***drag the mouse, and then right-click the mouse and select Cut.*** Another way to select or highlight text is to press and hold the **[SHIFT]** key while using the cursor keys to mark/highlight the desired text.

E. *Undo/Undeleting Text*—If you delete text and immediately want it back, ***click on Edit from the menu bar and then select Undo Typing.*** This can also be done by pressing **[CTRL]+[Z]**. Press **[CTRL]+[Z]** or ***click on Undo typing*** until your desired text reappears. The Undo feature also works on many other activities in Word, but not all. So, if something goes wrong, at least try pressing **[CTRL]+[Z]** to undo whatever you did.

F. *Moving Text (cutting and pasting)*—***Drag the mouse to highlight or select the text. Click on Edit from the menu bar and then click on Cut. Then, move the cursor to where the text should be inserted, and click on Edit from the menu bar and then click on Paste.*** Another way to do this is to ***drag the mouse to highlight the area and then right-click the mouse.*** This brings up a menu that includes the commands to Cut, Copy, and Paste text. Yet another way to do this is to use the drag-and-drop method. The user ***drags the mouse to highlight the area, releases the mouse button, clicks on the highlighted area, drags the text to the new location, and releases the mouse button.***

G. Copying Text—***Drag the mouse to highlight or select the area. Click on Edit from the menu bar, and then click on Copy. Then, move the cursor to where the text should be copied to and click on Edit on the menu bar, and then click on Paste.*** Another way to do this is to ***drag the mouse to highlight the area***

and then right-click the mouse and click on Copy. Then move the cursor to where the text should be copied to and right-click the mouse and click on Paste. Still another way to do this is to use the drag-and-drop method. The user ***drags the mouse to highlight the area, releases the mouse button, clicks on the highlighted area while pressing the [CTRL] key, drags the text to the new location, and releases the mouse button.*** The text is copied to the new location.

III. Formatting

A. *Centering Text*—Move the cursor to the line where the text should be centered, ***click on Format from the menu bar, and then click on Paragraph.*** In the Indents and Spacing tab, ***click on the down arrow next to Alignment and select Centered and then click on OK*** and begin typing. If the text has already been typed, move the cursor to the paragraph where the text is and then issue the command. Alternatively, you can use the Center icon on the toolbar.

B. *Bold Type*—To type in bold, ***click on Format from the menu bar, then click on Font. In the Font tab, click on Bold under Font Style. Then, click on OK.*** Alternatively, you can use the Bold icon on the toolbar or press **[CTRL]+[B]** from the keyboard.

C. *Underlining*—To underline, ***click on Format from the menu bar, then click on Font. In the Font tab, click on the down arrow under Underline Style and click on the type of underline you would like. Then, click on OK.*** Alternatively, you can use the Underline command on the toolbar or press **[CTRL]+[U]** on the keyboard.

D. *Margins*—Margins can be set by ***clicking on File on the menu bar and then Page Setup on the Margins tab.***

E. *Line Spacing*—Line spacing can be changed by ***clicking on Format on the menu bar and then on Paragraph.*** In the Indents and Spacing tab under "Spacing—Line spacing," change the line spacing.

F. *Justification*—Move the cursor to the line where the text should be justified. ***Click on Format from the menu bar and then click on Paragraph. In the Indents and Spacing tab, click on the down arrow next to Alignment and select Justified. Click on OK.*** Alternatively, you can use the Justify icon on the toolbar.

G. *Header/Footer*—***Click on View from the menu bar and then Header and Footer.***

H. *Hard Page Break*—To start a new page of text in the current document by using the hard page command, press **[CTRL]+[ENTER]**. A soft page break occurs when the program automatically creates a new page because the current page is full of text.

I. *Indent*—To indent a paragraph, ***click on Format from the menu bar and then select Paragraph. Change the indentation in the Indents and Spacing tab under Indentation.***

IV. Other Functions

A. *Printing*—To print, ***click on File from the menu bar, then on Print, and then on OK.*** Alternatively, you can select the printer icon from the toolbar.

B. *Spell Check*—To turn on the spell checking function, ***click on Tools from the menu bar and then click on Spelling and Grammar.*** Alternatively, a red squiggly line appears under a word when it is not recognized. You can ***right-click on the word to get the program to suggest possible spellings.***

C. *Open Files*—To open a file, ***click on File from the menu bar, and then select Open.***

D. *Tables*—To insert a table, ***click on Table from the menu bar, then on Insert, and then on Table.*** You can move between cells in the table by pressing the **[TAB]** and the **[SHIFT]+[TAB]** keys.

BEFORE STARTING LESSON 1—SETTING THE TOOLBAR AND MENU BAR

Before starting Lesson 1, complete the exercise below to adjust the toolbar and menu bar so that they are consistent with the instructions in the lessons.

1. Load Windows. Then, ***double-click on the Microsoft Office Word 2003 icon on the desktop*** to load Word 2003 for Windows. Alternatively, ***click on the Start button, point with the mouse to Programs or All Programs, and then click on the Microsoft Word icon (or point to Microsoft Office, and then click on Microsoft Office Word 2003).*** You should be in a clean blank document. If you are not in a clean document, ***click on File on the menu bar and then click on New, and then click on Blank document.***

2. ***Click on View from the menu bar and then point with the mouse to Toolbars.***

3. Only the "Standard" and "Formatting" toolbars should be checked, see Word 2003 Exhibit 1. If the "Standard" and "Formatting" toolbars are not checked, ***click on them to select them*** (the check mark indicates they have been selected). If another toolbar has been selected (marked with a check mark), then click on it to deselect it. Please note that you can only make changes to the toolbar one at a time, so it may take you a few steps to only have "Standard" and "Formatting" selected—or, your computer may already be set for this and you may not have to make any changes. If you do not have to make changes, just press the **[ESC]** key to exit the View menu.

4. We also want to make sure that the full menus are displayed when you select an item from the menu bar (Word normally will only show the most recent/commonly used selections), and that the toolbars are shown on two rows so that you can see all of the icons.

5. ***Click on View from the menu bar, then point to Toolbars, and then click on Customize.***

6. ***Click on the Options tab.*** Then, under "Personalized Menus and Toolbars," make sure that check marks are checked next to "Show Standard and Formatting Toolbars on two rows" and "Always show full menus" (see Word 2003 Exhibit 2). *Note:* If there is an option under "Personalized Menus and Toolbars" that says "Standard and Formatting Toolbars share one row," do not check the box (the toolbars are already on two rows). If there is an option that says "Menus show recently used commands first," again, do not check the box (full menus will already be displayed). ***Click on Close.***

You are now ready to begin Lesson 1.

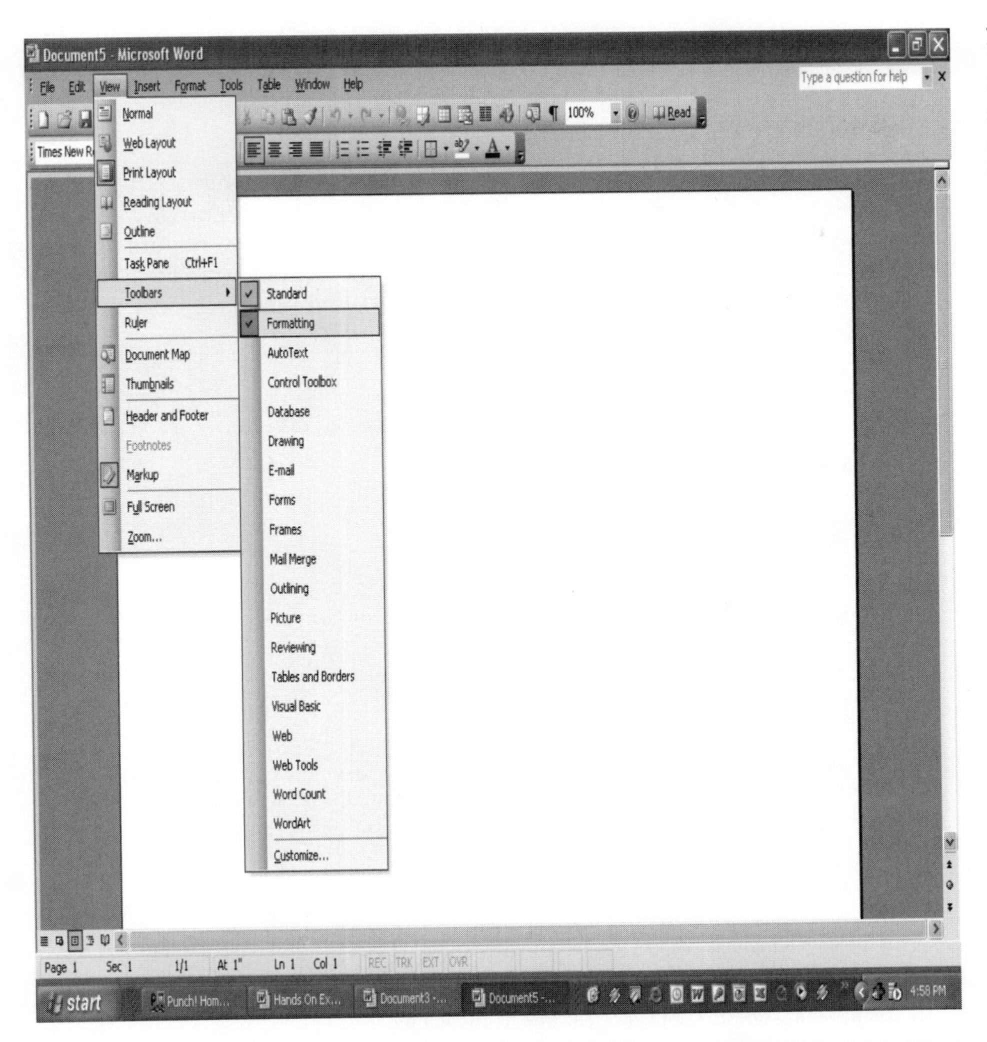

Word 2003 Exhibit 1

Setting the Toolbar

Microsoft product screen shot reprinted with permission from Microsoft Corporation.

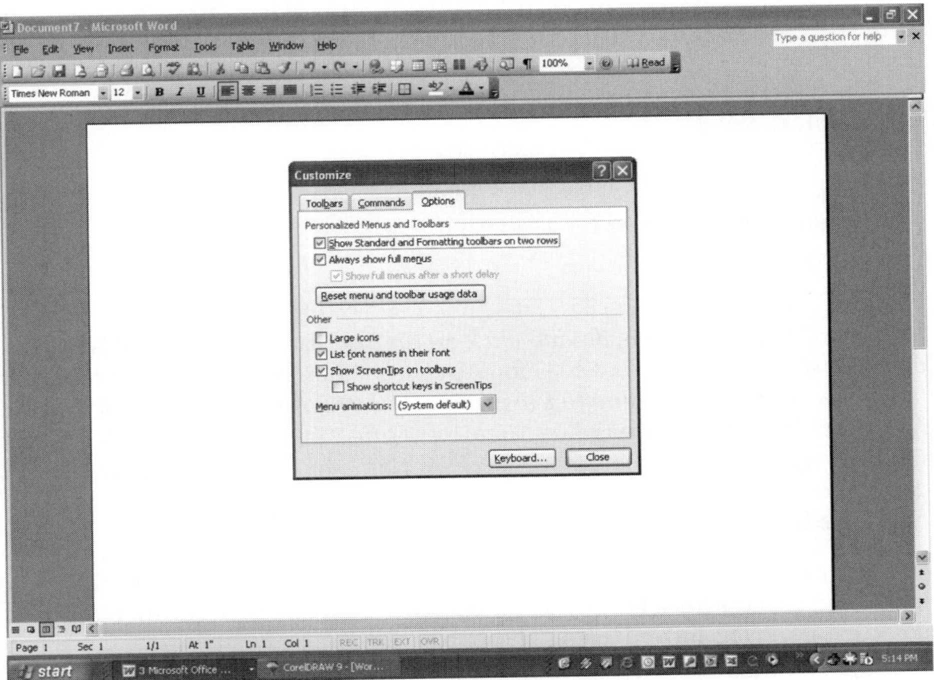

Word 2003 Exhibit 2

Customizing the Toolbar

Microsoft product screen shot reprinted with permission from Microsoft Corporation.

Basic Lessons

LESSON 1: TYPING A LETTER

This lesson shows you how to type the letter in Word 2003 Exhibit 3. It explains how to use the word wrap feature, the **[TAB]** key, the cursor (or arrow) keys, the underline, bold and italics commands, the save document function, and the print document function. Keep in mind that if at any time you make a mistake in this lesson you may press **[CTRL]+[Z]** to undo what you have done.

Word 2003 Exhibit 3
Letter
Microsoft product screen shot reprinted with permission from Microsoft Corporation.

October 1, 2008

Stephen Wilkerson, Esq.
Wilkerson, Smith & Russell
P.O. Box 12341
Boston, MA 59920

Subject: Turner v. Smith
Case No. 2008-1423

Dear Mr. Wilkerson:

In line with our recent conversation, the deposition of the defendant, Jonathan R. Smith, will be taken in your office on **November 15 at 9:00 a.m.** Please find enclosed a *"Notice to Take Deposition."*

I expect that I will be able to finish this deposition on November 15 and that discovery will be finished, in line with the Court's order by December 15.

I will be finishing answers to your interrogatories this week and will have them to you by early next week.

If you have any questions, please feel free to contact me.

Kindest Regards,

Shirley L. Gonzalez
For the Firm

SLG:db
Enclosures (As indicated)
cc

1. Open Windows. Then, ***double-click on the Microsoft Office Word 2003 icon on the desktop*** to open Word 2003 for Windows. Alternatively, ***click on the Start button, point with the mouse to Programs or All Programs, and then click on the Microsoft Word icon (or point to Microsoft Office, and then click on Microsoft Office Word 2003).*** You should be in a clean blank document. If you are not in a clean document, ***click on File on the menu bar and then click on New, and then click on Blank document.***

2. You cannot yet move the cursor around the screen by pushing the cursor keys (also called arrow keys). This is because text must first be entered before the cursor can be moved using the cursor keys. The cursor can only move through text.

3. Press the **[ENTER]** key four times. Watch the status line in the lower left-hand corner of the screen. The status line tells you what page of your document you are on, and the line number and position where your cursor is.

4. Type the date of the letter as shown in Word 2003 Exhibit 3. Notice that as you type the word "October" that Auto Text may anticipate that you are typing the word "October" and give you the following prompt: October (Press ENTER to Insert). You can either press the **[ENTER]** key and Auto Text will finish typing the word for you, or you can ignore it and continue typing the word yourself.

5. Press the **[ENTER]** key three times.

6. Type the inside address as shown in Word 2003 Exhibit 3. Press the **[ENTER]** key after each line of the inside address. When you finish the line with "Boston, MA 59920," press the **[ENTER]** key three times.

7. Press the **[TAB]** key one time (Word automatically sets default tabs every five spaces). The cursor moves five spaces to the right.

8. Type **Subject**: and then press the **[TAB]** key. ***Click on the Underline icon on the toolbar*** (It looks like a *U*. *Note*: If you point at any single icon on the toolbar for a few seconds, Word will show you a description of what the icon does). Alternatively, to turn the underline feature on and off you can press **[CTRL]+[U]**, or ***select Format from the menu bar and click on Font***. Then click on the down arrow under underline style, click on the type of underline, and click on ok.

9. Type **Turner v. Smith**. ***Click on the Underline icon on the toolbar again***. This will turn the underline feature off.

10. Press the **[ENTER]** key one time.

11. Press the **[TAB]** key three times, and then type **Case No. 2008-1423**.

12. Press the **[ENTER]** key three times.

13. Type the salutation **Dear Mr. Wilkerson:**

14. Press the **[ENTER]** key twice. (*Note*: If the animated assistant appears, right-click on it and click on "Hide" to make it go away).

15. Type the first paragraph of the letter. Do not press the **[ENTER]** key at the end of each line. Word will automatically "wrap" the text down to the next line. *Note*: To turn on the bold feature (e.g., for **November 15 at 9:00 a.m.**), press **[CTRL]+[B]** on the keyboard, or ***click the Bold icon on the toolbar***. To turn on the italics feature (e.g., for *"Notice to Take Deposition.")* press **[CTRL]+[I]** on the keyboard, or ***click the Italics icon on the toolbar***.

16. After you have typed the first paragraph, press the **[ENTER]** key twice.

17. Type the second paragraph of the letter, and then press the **[ENTER]** key twice.

18. Type the third paragraph of the letter, and then press the **[ENTER]** key twice.

19. Type the fourth paragraph of the letter, and then press the **[ENTER]** key twice.

20. Type **Kindest Regards**, and the press the **[ENTER]** key four times.

21. Type **Shirley L. Gonzalez** and then press the **[ENTER]** key.

22. Type **For the Firm** and then press the **[ENTER]** key twice.

23. Finish the letter by typing the author's initials, enclosures, and copy abbreviation (cc) as shown in Word 2003 Exhibit 3.

24. To print the document, ***click on File from the menu bar, click on Print, and then click on OK.*** Alternatively, click on the Printer icon on the toolbar.

25. To save the document so that you can retrieve it later (this letter will need to be retrieved to complete Lesson 2), ***click on File on the menu bar, and then select Save.*** Type **Letter1** in the "File name" box, ***and then click on Save to save the document in the default directory.***

26. ***Click on File on the menu bar, and then on Close*** to close the document, or ***click on File from the menu bar, and then on Exit*** to exit Word.

This concludes Lesson 1.

LESSON 2: EDITING A LETTER

This lesson shows you how to retrieve and edit the letter you typed in Lesson 1. It explains how to retrieve a file, use the Insert and Overtype modes, perform block moves and deletes, and spell/grammar check your document. Keep in mind that if at any time you make a mistake in this lesson, you may press **[CTRL]+[Z]** to undo what you have done.

1. Open Windows. Then, ***double-click on the Microsoft Office Word 2003 icon on the desktop*** to open Word 2003 for Windows. Alternatively, ***click on the Start button, point with the mouse to Programs or All Programs, and then click on the Microsoft Word icon (or point to Microsoft Office, and then click on Microsoft Office Word 2003).*** You should be in a clean blank document. If you are not in a clean document, ***click on File on the menu bar and then click on New, and then click on Blank document.***

2. In this lesson, you will begin by retrieving the document you created in Lesson 1. To open the file, ***click on File from the menu bar, and select Open.*** Then type **Letter1** and ***click on Open.*** Alternatively, ***scroll until you find the file using the horizontal scroll bar and then point and click on Open.***

3. Notice in Word 2003 Exhibit 4 that some editing changes have been made to the letter. You will spend the rest of this lesson making these changes.

4. Use your cursor keys or mouse to go to the salutation line, "Dear Mr. Wilkerson:" With the cursor left of the "M" in "Mr. Wilkerson," press the **[DEL]** key thirteen times until "Mr. Wilkerson" is deleted.

5. Type **Steve**. The salutation line should now read "Dear Steve:"

6. Using your cursor keys or mouse, ***move the cursor to the left of the comma following the word "conversation" in the first paragraph.*** Press the **[SPACE BAR]**, then type **of September 30**. The sentence now reads:

In line with our recent conversation of September 30, the deposition of the defendant,

Because Word is in the Insert mode (i.e., the default mode) when it is loaded, it allows you to add the words **of September 30** automatically. *Note:* When Word is in Insert mode, it is not specifically indicated on the screen. However, when Word is in the Overtype mode, the letters OVR appear in the center of the status line at the bottom of the screen.

October 1, 2008

Stephen Wilkerson, Esq.
Wilkerson, Smith & Russell
P.O. Box 12341
Boston, MA 59920

Subject: Turner v. Smith
Case No. 2008-1423

Steve
Dear ~~Mr. Wilkerson~~:

of September 30
In line with our recent conversation, the deposition of the defendant, Jonathan R. Smith, will be taken in your office on **November 15 at 9:00 a.m.** Please find enclosed a *"Notice to Take Deposition."*

I expect that I will be able to finish this deposition on November 15 and that discovery will be finished, in line with the Court's order by December 15.

next
I will be finishing answers to your interrogatories ~~this~~ week. ~~and will have them to you by early next week.~~

If you have any questions, please feel free to contact me.

Kindest Regards,

Shirley L. Gonzalez
For the Firm

SLG:db
Enclosures (As indicated)
cc

Word 2003 Exhibit 4

Corrections to a Letter

Microsoft product screen shot reprinted with permission from Microsoft Corporation.

7. The next change you will make is to move the second paragraph so that it becomes part of the first paragraph. Although this can be accomplished in more than one way, this lesson uses the opportunity to show you the Cut command.

8. Using your cursor keys or mouse, ***move the cursor to the beginning of the second paragraph of Word 2003 Exhibit 3.***

9. ***Click and drag the mouse*** (i.e., hold the left mouse button down, and move the mouse) ***until the entire second paragraph is highlighted, and then release the mouse button.***

10. ***Click on Edit from the menu bar, and click on Cut.*** An alternative is to right-click the mouse anywhere in the highlighted area, and then select Cut. The text is no longer on the screen, but it is not deleted—it has been temporarily placed on the Office Clipboard.

11. Move the cursor to the end of the first paragraph. Press the **[SPACEBAR]** twice. If the cursor appears to be in italics mode, click on the italics icon on the toolbar to turn it off.

12. ***Click on Edit from the menu bar, and select Paste.*** Notice that the text has now been moved. Also, you may notice that a small icon in the shape of a clipboard has appeared where you pasted the text. ***Click on the down arrow of the Paste Options icon.*** Notice that you are given the option to keep the source formatting or change the formatting so that the text matches the destination formatting (the formatting of the place you are copying it to). In this example, both formats are the same so it does not matter, but if the text you are copying is a different format, you may or may not want to change it to the destination format. Press the **[ESC]** key to make the Paste Options menu disappear.

13. Move the cursor to the line below the first paragraph, and use the **[DEL]** key to delete any unnecessary blank lines.

14. Using your cursor keys or mouse, ***move the cursor to what is now the second paragraph and place the cursor to the left of the t in "this week."*** You will change this to say "next week," using the Overtype mode.

15. Press the **[INS]** key. Notice that on the status line at the bottom of the screen, the letters OVR appear. This indicates that Word is now in Overtype mode. In Overtype mode, any characters entered will replace existing characters.

16. Type **next**. Notice how the word *this* is replaced with the word *next*. Press the **[INS]** key to return to Insert mode.

17. You will now delete the rest of the sentence in the second paragraph. ***Drag the mouse until "and will have them to you by early next week." is highlighted.*** Press the **[DEL]** key.

18. Type a period at the end of the sentence.

19. You have now made all of the changes that need to be made. To be sure the letter does not have misspelled words or grammar errors, you will use the Spelling and Grammar command.

20. ***Click on Tools from the menu bar, and then click on Spelling and Grammar.***

21. If an error is found, it is highlighted and you have the chance to ignore it once, ignore it completely, accept one of the suggestions listed, or change/correct the problem yourself. Correct any spelling or grammar errors. ***Click on OK when the spell and grammar check is done.***

22. To print the document, ***click on File from the menu bar, click on Print, and then click on OK.*** Alternatively, click on the Printer icon on the toolbar.

23. To save the document, ***click on File from the menu bar, and then select Save As...*** Type **Letter2** in the "File name" box, ***and then point and click on Save to save the document in the default directory.***

24. ***Click on File on the menu bar, and then on Close*** to close the document, or ***click on File from the menu bar, and then on Exit*** to exit Word.

This concludes Lesson 2.

LESSON 3: TYPING A PLEADING

This lesson shows you how to type a pleading, as shown in Word 2003 Exhibit 5. It expands on the items presented in Lessons 1 and 2. It also explains how to center text, change margins, change line spacing, add a footnote, double indent text,

and use automatic page numbering. Keep in mind that if at any time you make a mistake you may press **[CTRL]+[Z]** to undo what you have done.

1. Open Windows. Then, ***double-click on the Microsoft Office Word 2003 icon on the desktop*** to open Word 2003 for Windows. Alternatively, ***click on the Start button, point with the mouse to Programs or All Programs, and then click on the Microsoft Word icon (or point to Microsoft Office, and then click on Microsoft Office Word 2003).*** You should be in a clean blank document. If you are not in a clean document, ***click on File on the menu bar and then click on New, and then click on Blank document.***

IN THE DISTRICT COURT OF
ORANGE COUNTY, MASSACHUSETTS

Jim Turner,

Plaintiff,

-vs- Case No. 2008-1423

Jonathan R. Smith,

Defendant.

NOTICE TO TAKE DEPOSITION

COMES NOW the plaintiff and pursuant to statute[1] hereby gives notice that the deposition of Defendant, Jonathan R. Smith, will be taken as follows:

Monday, November 15, 2008, at 9:00 a.m. at the law offices of Wilkerson, Smith & Russell, 17031 W. 69th Street, Boston, MA.

Said deposition will be taken before a court reporter and is not expected to take more than one day in duration.

Shirley L. Gonzalez
Attorney for Plaintiff

[1] Massachusetts Statutes Annotated 60-2342(a)(1).

Word 2003 Exhibit 5
A Pleading
Microsoft product screen shot reprinted with permission from Microsoft Corporation.

2. You will be creating the document in Word 2003 Exhibit 5. The first thing you will need to do is to change the margins so that the left margin is 1½ inches and the right margin is 1 inch. To change the margins, ***click on File on the menu bar and then click on Page Setup. Change the left margin to 1.50" and the right margin to 1". Then, click on OK.***

3. Notice in Word 2003 Exhibit 5 that there is a page number at the bottom of the page. Word will automatically number your pages for you.

Word 2003 Exhibit 6
Creating a Footer
Microsoft product screen shot reprinted with permission from Microsoft Corporation.

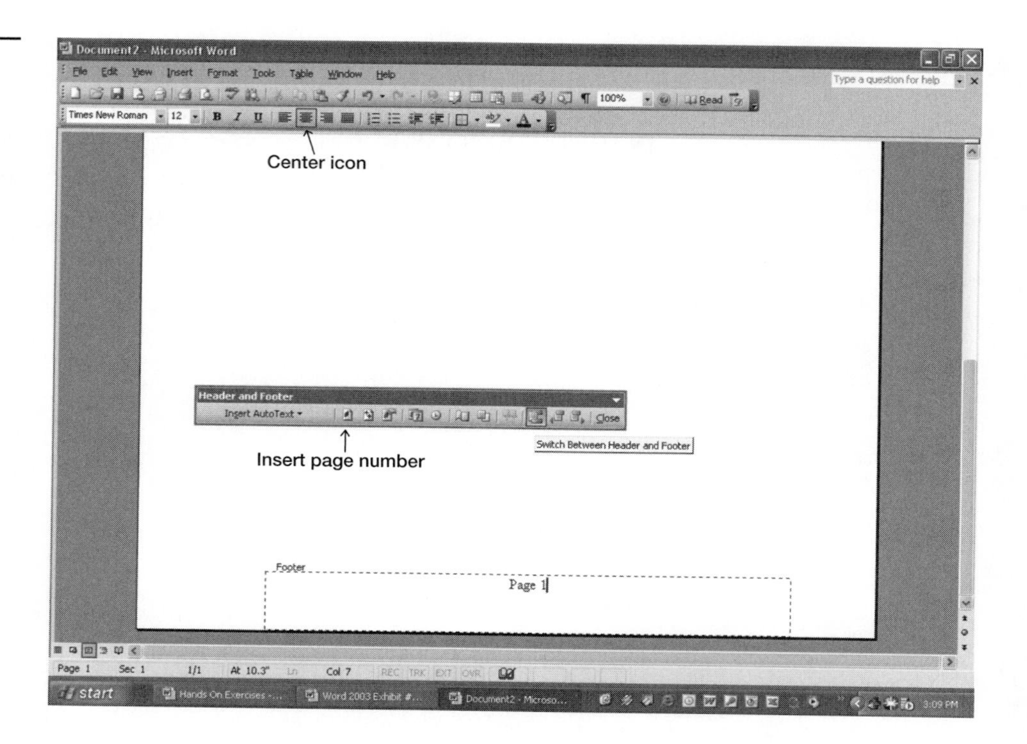

4. ***Click on View from the menu bar and then on Header and Footer.*** The "Header and Footer" window is then displayed (see Word 2003 Exhibit 6).

5. ***Click on the fourth item from the right (the Switch Between Header and Footer icon) in the Header and Footer window*** (see Word 2003 Exhibit 6). (*Note:* If you point at an icon with your mouse for a second, the description of the icon will be displayed.) Notice that the screen moved from the page header (at the top of the page) to the page footer (at the bottom of the page).

6. ***Click on the Center icon on the toolbar*** (see Word 2003 Exhibit 6). Notice that the line in the footer is now centered.

7. Type **Page** and press the **[SPACEBAR]** key.

8. ***Click on the Insert Page Number icon (it is the second item from the left, just to the right of the Insert Auto Text icon) in the Header and Footer window*** (see Word 2003 Exhibit 6). A "1" is then displayed on the screen. The footer should now read "Page 1."

9. Before closing the Header and Footer window, ***click on Insert Auto Text.*** Notice that Word can automatically print additional information in your header and footer including the file name, the author, the path, the last printed date,

Page X of Y, and many more. We do not need any of these selections for this document, so press the **[ESC]** key to exit the Insert Auto Text field.

10. *Click on Close in the Header and Footer Window to close the window.*

11. On the first line of the document, *click on the Center icon on the toolbar.* Type **IN THE DISTRICT COURT OF**. Press the **[ENTER]** key. Type **ORANGE COUNTY, MASSACHUSETTS**.

12. Press the **[ENTER]** key five times. *Click on the Align Left icon on the toolbar* (it is just to the left of the Center icon).

13. Type **Jim Turner**, and press the **[ENTER]** key twice.

14. Press the **[TAB]** key three times and type **Plaintiff,** and press the **[ENTER]** key twice.

15. Type **–vs-**. Then, press the **[TAB]** key six times, and type **Case No. 2008–1423**.

16. Press the **[ENTER]** key twice.

17. Type **Jonathan R. Smith,** and press the **[ENTER]** key twice.

18. Press the **[TAB]** key three times and type **Defendant**. Press the **[ENTER]** key four times.

19. *Click on the Center icon on the toolbar.*

20. *Click on the Bold icon on the toolbar, and then click on the Underline icon on the toolbar.* Type **NOTICE TO TAKE DEPOSITION**. *Click on the Bold and Underline icons on the toolbar to turn them off.*

21. Press the **[ENTER]** key three times and *click on the Left Align icon on the toolbar.*

22. *Click on Format on the menu bar, then on Paragraph, and then, under Spacing—Line Spacing, click on the down arrow and select Double. Click OK.* This will change the line spacing from single to double.

23. Type **COMES NOW the plaintiff and pursuant to statute**. Notice that a footnote follows the word *statute.*

24. With the cursor just to the right of the e in "statute," *click on Insert from the menu bar, point to Reference, then click on Footnote.* The "Footnote and Endnote" window is now displayed; the default options are fine so *click on Insert in the "Footnote and Endnote" window.*

25. Type **Massachusetts Statutes Annotated 60–2342(a)(1).**

26. To move the cursor back to the body of the document, simply *click just to the right of the word "statute" and footnote number 1 in the body of the document.* Now, continue to type the rest of the first paragraph. Once the paragraph is typed, press the **[ENTER]** key twice.

27. To double-indent the second paragraph, *click on Format in the menu bar, then click on Paragraph. Under "Indentation,"add a .5" left indent and a .5" right indent using the up arrow icons* (or you can type it in). *Click on OK.*

28. Type the second paragraph.

29. Press the **[ENTER]** key twice.

30. ***Click on Format from the menu bar, then click on Paragraph.*** Under Indentation, change the left and right indents back to 0". ***Then, click on OK.***

31. Type the third paragraph.

32. Press the **[ENTER]** key.

33. The signature line is single-spaced, so ***click on Format from the menu bar, then click on "Paragraph."*** Under "Spacing—Line Spacing," ***click on the down arrow and select Single. Then click OK. Press the [ENTER] key.***

34. Press **[SHIFT]+[-]** (the "_" is the underscore; it is the key to the right of the zero key on the keyboard) thirty times to draw the signature line. Press the **[ENTER]** key. *Note:* If Word automatically inserts a line across the whole page, press **[CTRL]+[Z]** to undo the Auto Correct line.

35. Type **Shirley L. Gonzalez**, and then press the **[ENTER]** key.

36. Type **Attorney for Plaintiff.**

37. To print the document, ***click on File from the menu bar, click on Print, and then click on OK.*** Alternatively, click on the Printer icon on the toolbar.

38. To save the document, ***click on File from the menu bar, and then select Save As....*** Type **Pleading1** in the "File name" box, ***and then point and click on Save to save the document in the default directory.***

39. ***Click on File on the menu bar, and then on Close*** to close the document, or ***click on File from the menu bar, and then on Exit*** to exit Word.

This concludes Lesson 3.

LESSON 4: CREATING A TABLE

This lesson shows you how to create the table shown in Word 2003 Exhibit 7. It expands on the items presented in Lessons 1, 2, and 3. It explains how to change a font size, create a table, enter data into a table, add automatic numbering, adjust column widths, and use the Table AutoFormat command. Keep in mind that if at any time you make a mistake, you may press **[CTRL]+[Z]** to undo what you have done.

1. Open Windows. Then ***double-click on the Microsoft Office Word 2003 icon on the desktop*** to open Word 2003 for Windows. Alternatively, ***click on the Start button, point with the mouse to Programs or All Programs, and then click on the Microsoft Word icon (or point to Microsoft Office, and then click on Microsoft Office Word 2003).*** You should be in a clean, blank document. If you are not in a clean document, ***click on File on the menu bar, then click on New, and then click on Blank document.***

2. ***Click on the Center icon on the toolbar. Click on th e Bold icon on the toolbar. Click on the Font size icon on the toolbar (just to the left of the Bold icon)*** and change the font size to 14 by either typing 14 in the box or ***choosing 14 from the drop-down menu.*** Alternatively, you can turn on bold and change the font size by ***clicking on Format on the menu bar, then on Font, and then selecting these options in the "Font" window.***

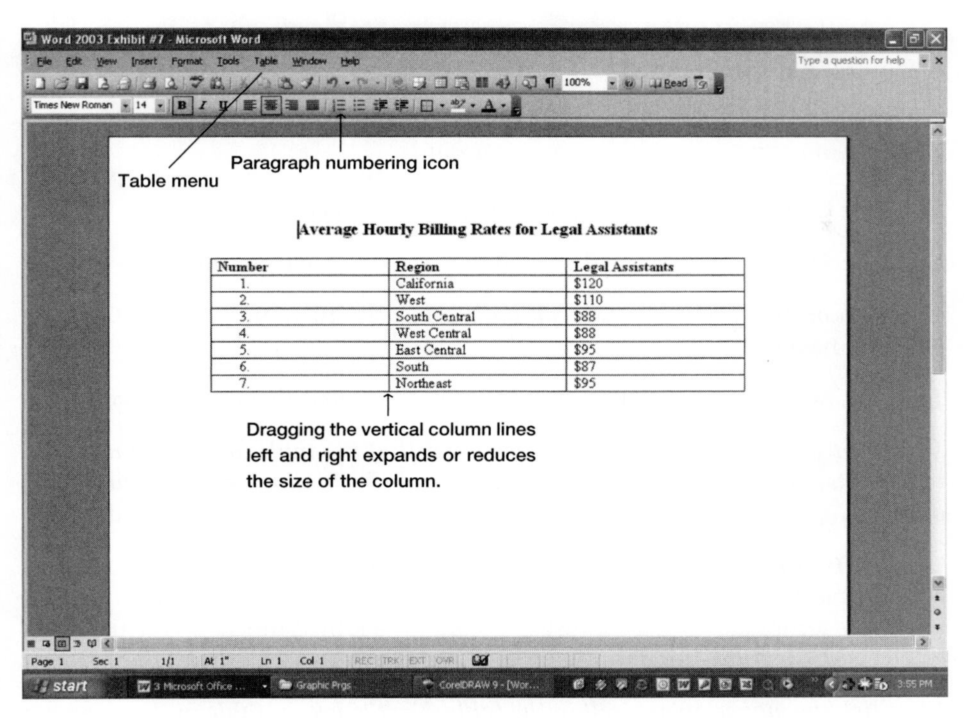

Average Hourly Billing Rates for Legal Assistants

Number	Region	Legal Assistants
1.	California	$120
2.	West	$110
3.	South Central	$88
4.	West Central	$88
5.	East Central	$95
6.	South	$87
7.	Northeast	$95

Word 2003 Exhibit 7
Creating a Table
Microsoft product screen shot reprinted with permission from Microsoft Corporation.

3. Type **Average Hourly Billing Rates for Legal Assistants** (see Word 2003 Exhibit 7). Press the **[ENTER]** key once, and then ***click back on the Font size icon on the toolbar and change the type back to 12 point. Click on the Bold icon to turn bold off.***

4. Press the **[ENTER]** key once.

5. ***Click on Table from the menu bar, then point to Insert, then click on Table.*** The "Insert Table" window is now displayed. Under Table Size, make the number of columns **3** and the number of rows **8**. Then, ***click on OK.***

6. The blank table should now be displayed and the cursor should be in the first column and in the first row of the table. ***If the cursor is not in the first column of the first row, click into this cell to place the cursor there. Click on the Bold icon on the toolbar.*** Type **Number** and then press the **[TAB]** key once to go to the next cell in the table.

7. ***Click on the Bold icon on the toolbar.*** Type **Region** and then press the **[TAB]** key once to go to the next cell in the table. *Note:* If you need to go back to a previous cell, you can either use the mouse or you can press **[SHIFT]+[TAB]**. Also, if you accidentally hit the **[ENTER]** key instead of the **[TAB]** key you can either press the **[BACKSPACE]** key to delete the extra line, or you can press **[CTRL]+[Z]** to undo it.

8. ***Click on the Bold icon on the toolbar.*** Type **Legal Assistants** and then press the **[TAB]** key to go to the next cell.

9. You will now use the automatic paragraph numbering feature to number your rows. ***Click on the Numbering icon on the toolbar*** (see Word 2003 Exhibit 7—it is the icon that has the numbers 1, 2, 3 in a column, with a short line next to each number). Notice that the number 1 was automatically entered in the cell. ***Click on Format on the menu bar, then on Bullets and Numbering, and then on***

Customize. You can completely customize your numbering if you wish. The default format is fine, so ***click on Cancel*** twice to make the "Bullets and Numbering" window disappear.

10. Press the **[TAB]** key to go to the next cell.

11. Type **California** and then press the **[TAB]** key to go to the next cell.

12. Type **$120** and then press the **[TAB]** key to go to the next cell.

13. ***Click on the Numbering icon on the toolbar*** and then press the **[TAB]** key to go to the next cell.

14. Continue entering all of the information in Word 2003 Exhibit 7 into your table.

15. ***Point with the mouse to the upper left cell of the table and drag the mouse to the lower right cell of the table to completely highlight the table. Then, click on the Align left icon on the toolbar.*** Now, the whole table is left aligned.

16. ***Point with the mouse to the vertical column line that separates the Number column and the Region column, and then drag the line to the left.*** Notice that by using this technique you can adjust each column width as much as you like. Press **[CTRL]+[Z]** to undo the column move, because the current format is fine.

17. ***Click the mouse on any cell in the table. Next, click on Table in the menu bar and then on Table AutoFormat, and then click on Table Colorful 1 (or any of the other options), and then click on Apply.***

18. The format of the table has been completely changed. Experiment with some of the other formats using the Table AutoFormat command. Press **[CTRL]+[Z]** to undo the format changes—if you tried a number of formats, just keep pressing **[CTRL]+[Z]** until your table is back to its original format.

19. To print the document, ***click on File from the menu bar, click on Print, and then click on OK.*** Alternatively, click on the Printer icon on the toolbar.

20. To save the document, ***click on File from the menu bar, and then select Save As...*** Type Table1 in the "File name" box, ***and then point and click on Save to save the document in the default directory.***

21. ***Click on File on the menu bar, and then on Close*** to close the document, or ***click on File from the menu bar, and then on Exit*** to exit Word.

This concludes Lesson 4.

Intermediate Lessons

LESSON 5: TOOLS AND TECHNIQUES

This lesson shows you how to edit an employment policy (from a file on Disk 1 supplied with this text), use the Format Painter tool, reveal formatting, clear formatting, change the case of the text, use the Find and Replace feature, use the Go To command, create a section break, and change the orientation of a page from portrait to landscape. This lesson assumes you have completed Lessons 1 through 4 and that you are generally familiar with Word 2003.

1. Open Windows. ***Double-click on the Microsoft Office Word 2003 icon on the desktop*** to open Word 2003 for Windows. Alternatively, ***click on the Start button, point the pointer to Programs or All Programs, and then click on the Microsoft***

Word icon (or point to Microsoft Office, and then click on Microsoft Office Word 2003). You should be in a clean, blank document. If you are not in a clean document, ***click on File on the menu bar, then click on New, and then click on Blank document.***

2. The first thing you will do is to open the "Lesson 5" file from Disk 1 supplied with this text. Ensure that the disk is inserted in the disk drive, ***point and click on File on the menu bar, and then point and click on Open.*** The Open window should now be displayed. ***Point and click on the down arrow to the right of the white box next to "Look in:" and select the drive where Disk 1 is located. Point and double-click on the Word-Processing Files folder. Double-click on the Word 2003 folder. Point and double-click on the "Lesson 5" file.***

3. The file entitled "World Wide Technology, Inc. Alcohol and Drug policy" should now be displayed on your screen. In this lesson, you will be editing this policy for use by another client. The next thing you need to do is to go to Section 3, "Definitions" and change the subheadings so that they have all have the same format. You will use the Format Painter tool to do this.

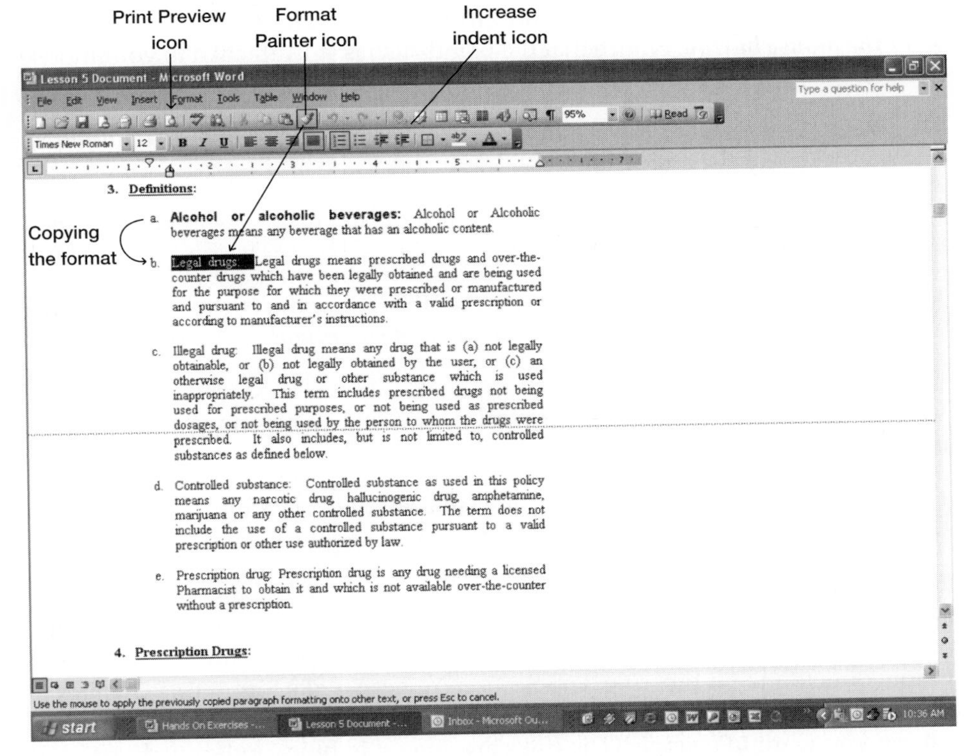

Word 2003 Exhibit 8

The Format Painter Feature

Microsoft product screen shot reprinted with permission from Microsoft Corporation.

4. Use the cursor keys or the mouse and the horizontal scroll bars to scroll to Section 3, "Definitions" (see Word 2003 Exhibit 8). Notice that the first definition, "Alcohol or alcoholic beverages," is bold and in a different font from the rest of the definitions in section 3. You will use the Format Painter feature to quickly copy the formatting from "Alcohol or alcoholic beverages" to the other four definitions in Section 3.

5. ***Point and click anywhere in the text "Alcohol or alcoholic beverages..."*** This tells the Format Painter feature the formatting you want to copy.

6. Next, ***point and click on the Format Painter icon on the toolbar.*** It looks like a paintbrush (see Word 2003 Exhibit 8—remember, if you hover your pointer over an icon for a second or two the name of the icon will appear).

7. Notice that your pointer now turns to a paintbrush. ***Drag the mouse*** (hold the left mouse button down and move the mouse) ***until the heading "Legal drugs:" is highlighted*** (see Word 2003 Exhibit 8), ***and then let go of the mouse button.*** Notice that the paintbrush on your cursor is now gone. ***Click the left mouse button once anywhere to make the highlight go away.*** Notice that "Legal drugs:" now has the same formatting as "Alcohol or alcoholic beverages." The Format Painter command is a quick way to make formatting changes.

8. You will now use the Format Painter command to copy the formatting to the remaining three definitions, with one additional trick. ***Point and click anywhere in the text "Legal drugs:."***

9. Next, ***point and*** **double-click** ***on the Format Painter icon on the toolbar. (Your cursor should now have a paintbrush attached to it.)*** The double-click tells Format Painter that you are going to copy this format to multiple locations, instead of just one location. This is a great time-saving feature if you need to copy the formatting to several places, because it keeps you from having to click the Format Painter icon each time you copy the same formatting to a new location.

10. ***Drag the pointer until the heading "Illegal drug:" is highlighted, and then let go of the mouse button.*** Notice that the paintbrush is still attached to your mouse pointer.

11. ***Drag the pointer until the heading "Controlled substance:" is highlighted, and then let go of the mouse button.***

12. ***Drag the pointer until the heading "Prescription drug:" is highlighted, and then let go of the mouse button.***

13. To turn the Format Painter off, press the **[ESC]** button on the keyboard. ***Click the left mouse button once anywhere to make the highlight go away.*** Notice that all of the headings are now uniform.

14. You will now learn to use the Reveal Formatting command. ***Point and click with the mouse on the heading "Prescription drug:."***

15. ***Point and click on Format on the menu bar, and then on Reveal Formatting....*** (Alternatively, you can press **[SHIFT]+[F1]** on the keyboard).

16. Notice that the Reveal Formatting task pane opened on the right side of the screen. The Reveal Formatting task pane lists all format specifications for the selected text. The items are divided into several groups including Font, Paragraph, Bullets and Numbering, and Section. You can make formatting changes to the text directly from the Reveal Formatting task pane by clicking on the format setting you want to change. (The links are shown in blue, underlined text.) For example, ***point and click on the blue underlined word*** Font ***in the Reveal Formatting task pane.*** Notice that the Font window opens. You could now select a new font if you so desired. The Reveal Formatting task pane allows you to quickly see all formatting attached to specific text and give you the ability to change it.

17. ***Point and click on Cancel in the Font window.*** To Close the Reveal Formatting task pane, ***point and click on the "x" (the Close button) at the top of the Reveal Formatting task pane. It is just to the right of the words "Reveal Formatting."*** The Reveal Formatting task pane should now be gone.

18. Press **[CTRL]+[HOME]** on the keyboard to go to the beginning of the document.

19. You will now learn how to use the Clear Formats command. Notice under the heading "1. Objectives" that the sentence "The objectives of this policy are as follows:" is bold and italics; this is a mistake. ***Drag the pointer until this text is highlighted.***

20. Next, ***point and click on Edit on the menu bar, and then point to Clear and then Formats.*** Then, ***click the left mouse button once anywhere in the sentence to make the highlight go away.*** Notice that all of the formatting is now gone. The "Clear Formats" command is a good way to remove all text formatting quickly and easily.

21. To move the text to the right so it is under "1. Objectives," ***point and click on the Increase Indent Icon three times*** (see Word 2003 Exhibit 8—it is the icon with a right arrow and some lines on it). The line should now be put back in its place.

22. You will now learn how to use the Change Case command. Press **[CTRL]+[HOME]** on the keyboard to go to the beginning of the document.

23. ***Drag the pointer until the title "World Wide Technology, Inc." is highlighted.***

24. ***Point and click on Format on the menu bar and then on Change Case.*** UPPERCASE should already be selected, but if it is not, ***click on UPPERCASE and then click on OK in the "Change Case" window.*** Notice that the text is now in all capitals.

25. ***Drag the pointer until the subtitle "alcohol and drug policy" is highlighted. Point and click on Format on the menu bar and then on Change Case. "Title Case" should already be selected, but if it is not, go ahead and click on "Title Case" and then click on OK in the "Change Case" window.*** Notice that the text is now in title case. ***Click the left mouse button once anywhere to make the highlight go away.*** The Change Case command is a convenient way to change the case of text without having to retype it.

26. Press **[CTRL]+[HOME]** on the keyboard to go to the beginning of the document.

27. You will now learn how to use the Find and Replace command. ***Point and click on Edit on the menu bar and then on Replace.*** Alternatively, you could press **[CTRL]+[H]**, or **[F5]** and then click on Replace.

28. In the "Find and Replace" window, in the white box next to "Find what:" type **World Wide Technology, Inc.** Then, in the white box next to "Replace with:" type **Johnson Manufacturing.** ***Now, click on the Replace All button in the "Find and Replace" window.*** The program responds by stating that it made four replacements. ***Point and click on OK in the "Microsoft Office Word" window.***

29. ***Point and click with the mouse on the Close button in the Find and Replace window to close the window.*** Notice that World Wide Technology, Inc. has now been changed to Johnson Manufacturing.

30. You will now learn how to use the Go To command. Press **[F5]** on the keyboard. Notice that the Find and Replace window is again displayed on the screen, but this time the Go To tab is selected. In the white box directly under "Enter page number," type **7** from the keyboard and then ***point and click on Go To in the "Find and Replace" window.*** Notice that page 7, "Reasonable Suspicion Report," is now displayed. The Go To command is an easy way to navigate through large

and complex documents. ***Point and click on Close in the Find and Replace window.***

31. Suppose that you would like to change the orientation of only one page in a document from Portrait (meaning the length is greater than the width) to Landscape (meaning the width is greater than the length). In this example you will change the layout of only the Reasonable Suspicion Report to Landscape while the rest of the document remains in Portrait. To do this in Word, you must enter a section break.

32. Your cursor should be on page 7 just above "Johnson Manufacturing Reasonable Suspicion Report." ***Point and click on View from the menu bar, and then on Normal. Point and click on Insert from the menu bar, and then on Break. Under Section break types, point and click on Next Page, and then click on OK in the "Break" window.*** Notice that a double dotted line that says "Section Break (Next Page)" is now displayed. You can now change the format of the page from Portrait to Landscape without changing the orientation of previous pages.

33. With cursor on the "Johnson Manufacturing Reasonable Suspicion Report" page, ***point and click on File from the menu bar, then on Page Setup. Then, point and click on Landscape under Orientation, and then on OK in the "Page Setup" window.*** Notice that the layout of the page has changed.

34. To confirm that the layout has changed, ***point and click on the Print Preview icon on the toolbar*** (see Word 2003 Exhibit 8). Notice that the layout is now Landscape (the width is greater than the length). Press the **[PAGE UP]** key on the keyboard until you are back to the beginning of the document. Notice that all of the other pages in the document are still in Portrait orientation.

35. ***Point and click on Close from the Print Preview toolbar. (It is the word Close just under Table on the menu bar).***

36. To print the document, ***click on File on the menu bar, click on Print, and then click on OK.*** Alternatively, click on the Printer icon on the toolbar.

37. To save the document, ***click on File from the menu bar, and then select Save As.... Under "Save in," select the drive or folder where you would like to save the document. Next to "File Name"*** type **Done—Word 2003 Lesson 5 Document,** ***then point and click on Save to save the document.***

38. ***Click on File on the menu bar, and then on Close*** to close the document, or ***click on File on the menu bar, and then on Exit*** to exit Word.

This concludes Lesson 5.

LESSON 6: USING STYLES

This lesson gives you an introduction to styles. Styles are particularly helpful when working with long documents that must be formatted uniformly.

1. Open Windows. ***Double-click on the Microsoft Office Word 2003 icon on the desktop*** to open Word 2003 for Windows. Alternatively, ***click on the Start button, point with the mouse pointer to Programs or All Programs, and then click on the Microsoft Word icon*** **(*or point to Microsoft Office, and then click on Microsoft Office Word 2003*).** You should be in a clean, blank document. If you are not in a clean document, ***click on File on menu bar, then click on New, then click on Blank document.***

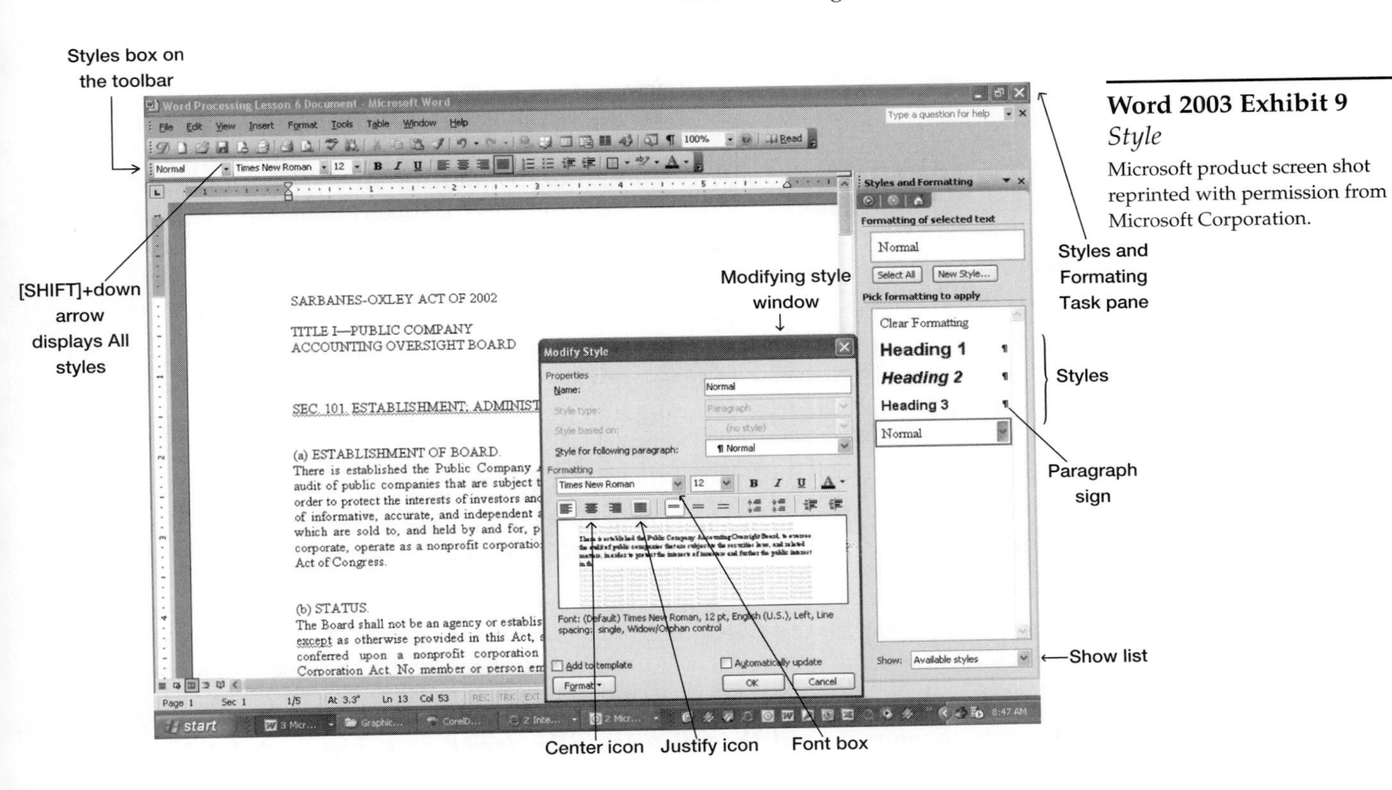

Word 2003 Exhibit 9

Style

Microsoft product screen shot reprinted with permission from Microsoft Corporation.

2. The first thing you will do is to open the "Lesson 6" file from Disk 1 supplied with this text. Ensure that the disk is inserted in the disk drive, ***point and click on File on the menu bar, and then point and click on Open.*** The Open window should now be displayed. ***Point and click on the down arrow to the right of the white box next to "Look in:" and select the drive where Disk 1 is located. Point and double-click on the Word-Processing Files folder. Double-click on the Word 2003 folder. Point and double-click on the "Lesson 6" file.***

3. The text "Sarbanes-Oxley Act of 2002" should now be displayed on your screen (see Word 2003 Exhibit 9). In this lesson you will use styles to add uniform formatting to this document. Notice the Style box on your toolbar (see Word 2003 Exhibit 9); it should say "Normal" in the box. This is telling you that the text where your cursor is located is formatted in the Normal style.

4. ***Point and click on any text on the page.*** Notice that "Normal" continues to be displayed in the Style box on the toolbar. Currently, all text in the document is in the Normal style.

5. Using your cursor keys or the horizontal scroll bar, scroll down through the document. Notice that all of the paragraphs are left-aligned and that the right edge of all the paragraphs is jagged (not justified).

6. ***Point and click on Format on the menu bar and then on Styles and Formatting.*** Notice that the Styles and Formatting task pane now appears on the right side of the screen (see Word 2003 Exhibit 9). Notice that a few styles are currently being displayed (Heading 1, Heading 2, Heading 3, and Normal). Also, notice that the "Normal" style has a blue box around it, indicating that your cursor is on text with the Normal style. Finally, notice that there is a paragraph sign after each of these heading names, indicating that these are paragraph styles.

7. Notice at the bottom of the Styles and Formatting task pane there is an option to "Show: Available Styles" (see Word 2003 Exhibit 9). ***Point and click on the down arrow next to "Available styles." Point and click with the mouse on "All styles."*** Notice that the Styles and Formatting task pane is now full of additional styles. These are all of the styles that are automatically available in Word. ***Point***

and click on the down arrow next to the styles in the Styles and Formatting task pane to see the full list of styles.

8. *Point and click on the down arrow next to "Show: All styles." Then point and click on "Available styles."* Notice that the short list of styles is again displayed. To access the longer list of styles from the toolbar, press the **[SHIFT]** key while *pointing and clicking on the down arrow on the Style box* (press the **[ESC]** key to close the list).

9. Styles are extremely useful. Assume now that you would like to have all of the text in the document justified. *Right-click on Normal in the Styles and Formatting task pane. Then left-click on Modify.* The Modify Style window should now be displayed (see Word 2003 Exhibit 9). Using the Modify Style window, you can completely change the formatting for any style.

10. *Point and click on the Justify icon in the Modify Style window to switch the Normal style from left-aligned to fully justified* (see Word 2003 Exhibit 9).

11. *Point and click on the down arrow in the Font box in the Modify Style window and point and click on Arial. Then, point and click on the OK button in the Modify Style window.* Notice that Word quickly changed the alignment of all of the text to fully justified and changed the font to Arial.

12. *Drag the mouse until the full title of the document is highlighted* (SARBANES-OXLEY ACT OF 2002 TITLE I – PUBLIC COMPANY ACCOUNTING OVERSIGHT BOARD).

13. *Point and click on Heading 1 in the Styles and Formatting task pane.*

14. *Point and right-click on Heading 1 in the Styles and Formatting task pane and select Modify. Then, point and click on the Center icon* (see Word 2003 Exhibit 9). *Select the OK button in the Modify Style window.*

15. *Click the left mouse button anywhere in the title to make the highlight disappear.* Notice that the text of the title shows "Heading 1" in the Styles and Formatting window.

16. *Point and click anywhere in "Sec. 101. Establishment; Administrative Provisions." Then, point and click on Heading 2 in the Styles and Formatting task pane.* Notice that the heading has now changed.

17. *Point and click anywhere in the subheading "(a) ESTABLISHMENT OF BOARD." Then, point and click on Heading 3 in the Styles and Formatting task pane.*

18. Now, go to the following subheadings and format them as Heading 3:

(b) STATUS

(c) DUTIES OF THE BOARD

(d) COMMISSION DETERMINATION

(e) BOARD MEMBERSHIP

(f) POWERS OF THE BOARD

(g) RULES OF THE BOARD

(h) ANNUAL REPORT TO THE COMMISSION

19. You will now create your own style. Press **[CTRL]+[END]** on the keyboard to go to the end of the document. *Point and click on New Style… in the Styles and Formatting task pane.*

20. The "New Style" window is now displayed. "Style 1" is currently highlighted in blue next to "Name." Type **Statutory Heading.** This will be the new name of the style you are creating. Next, change the font to Times New Roman, change the font size to 14 point, and change the color to red (the color icon is the letter A with a line under it).

21. ***Point and click on OK in the New Style window.*** Notice that the Statutory Heading style has now been added.

22. ***Point and click anywhere on 15 U.S.C. 7201*** and then ***point and click on Statutory Heading in the Styles and Formatting task pane.*** The text is now displayed in the Statutory Heading style.

23. Press **[CTRL]+[HOME]** on the keyboard to go to the beginning of the document. Your document is now consistently formatted. Using styles, your documents can also easily be uniformly changed. For example, if you read in your local rules that subheadings for pleadings must be in 15-point Times New Roman font, you could quickly change the subheadings in your document by modifying the heading styles, rather than highlighting each subheading and changing the format manually.

24. To print the document, ***click on File on the menu bar, click on Print, and then click on OK.*** Alternatively, click on the Printer icon on the toolbar.

25. To save the document, ***click on File from the menu bar, and then select Save As.... Under "Save in," select the drive or folder you would like the document in. Then, next to "File Name"*** type **Done—Word 2003 Lesson 6 Document** ***and then click on Save to save the document.***

26. ***Click on File on the menu bar, and then on Close*** to close the document, or ***click on File from the menu bar, and then on Exit*** to exit Word.

This concludes Lesson 6.

LESSON 7: CREATING A TEMPLATE

This lesson shows you how to create the template in Word 2003 Exhibit 10. It explains how to create a template of a letter, how to insert fields, and how to fill out and use a finished template. The information that will be merged into the letter will be entered from the keyboard. Keep in mind that if at any time you make a mistake you may press **[CTRL]+[Z]** to undo what you have done.

1. Open Windows. Then, ***double-click on the Microsoft Office Word 2003 icon on the desktop*** to open Word 2003 for Windows. Alternatively, ***click on the Start button, point to Programs or All Programs, and then click on the Microsoft Word icon (or point to Microsoft Office, and then click on Microsoft Office Word 2003).*** You should be in a clean, blank document. If you are not in a clean document, ***click on File on the menu bar, then click on New, and then click on Blank document.***

2. ***Click on File on the menu bar, click on New, then under Templates (to the right of the screen) click on "On my computer...."***

3. Notice that Word automatically provides you with a number of ready-made templates. ***Click on the Letters & Faxes tab;*** notice that there are a number of different letter styles, fax cover pages, and other documents. ***Click on the Memos tab;*** note that there are a number of different memo styles. ***Click on the Other Documents tab;*** note that there are several different resume styles presented. ***Click on the General tab.***

4. ***Click on Template Under Create field in the lower right of the "Templates" window*** (see Word 2003 Exhibit 11).

Word 2003 Exhibit 10
Office Letter Template
Microsoft product screen shot reprinted with permission from Microsoft Corporation.

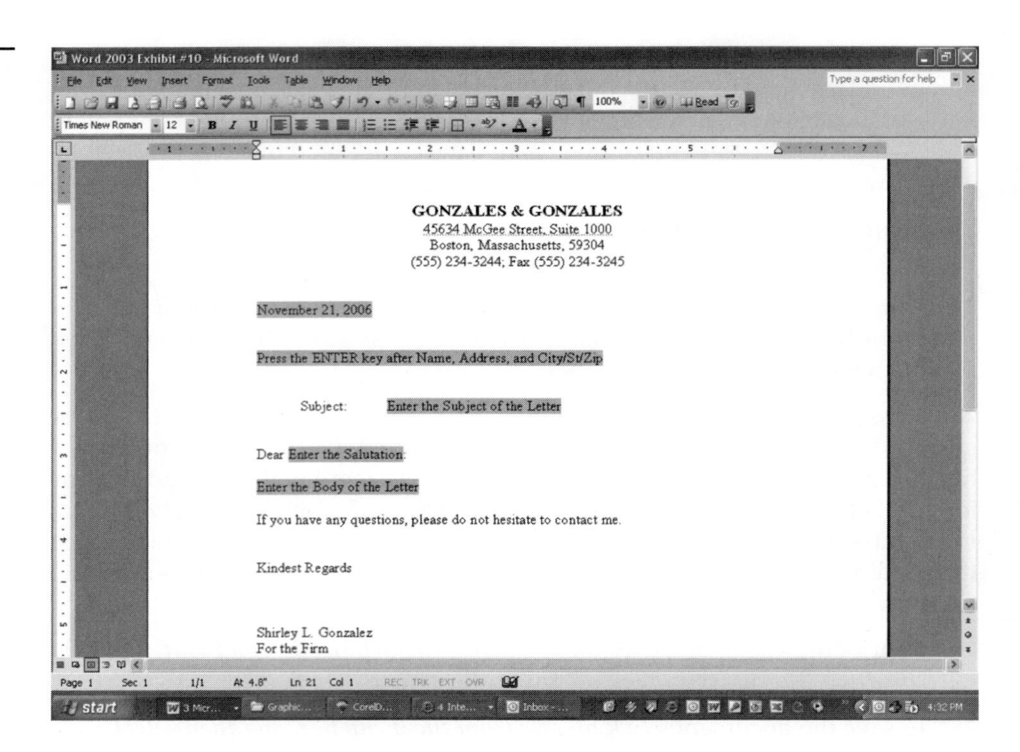

Word 2003 Exhibit 11
Create a New Template
Microsoft product screen shot reprinted with permission from Microsoft Corporation.

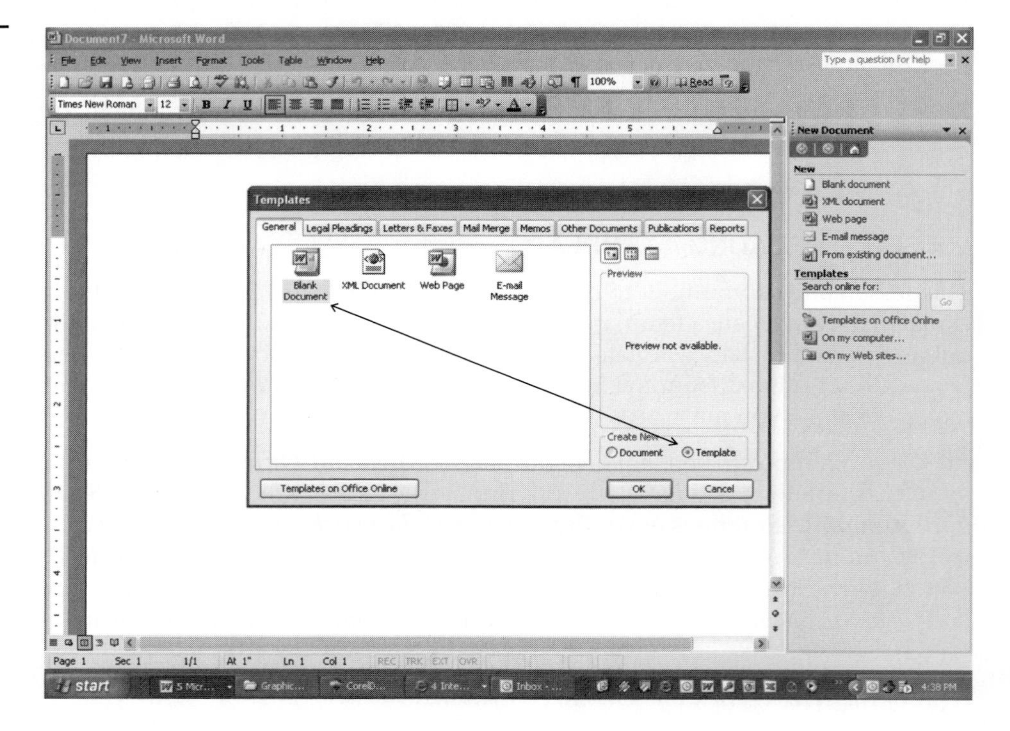

5. Under the General tab, ***click on Blank Document.*** Blank Document should now be highlighted. ***Then, click on OK*** (see Word 2003 Exhibit 11).

6. You should now have a blank template on your screen. The Windows title should say "Template1—Microsoft Word" in the upper left of the screen. You will now build the template shown in Word 2003 Exhibit 10.

7. ***Click on the Center icon on the toolbar. Then, click on the Bold icon on the toolbar. Then, click on the Font Size icon and select 14 from the list.***

8. Type **GONZALEZ & GONZALEZ** and then *click on the Bold icon on the toolbar to turn off Bold. Click on the Font Size icon and select 12 from the list.*

9. Press the **[ENTER]** key.

10. Type **45634 McGee Street, Suite 1000** and press the **[ENTER]** key.

11. Type **Boston, Massachusetts, 59304** and press the **[ENTER]** key.

12. Type **(555) 234–3244; Fax (555) 234–3245** and press the **[ENTER]** key.

13. *Click on the Align Left icon on the toolbar.*

14. Press the **[ENTER]** key three times.

15. *Point and click on Insert on the menu bar and then select Field.*

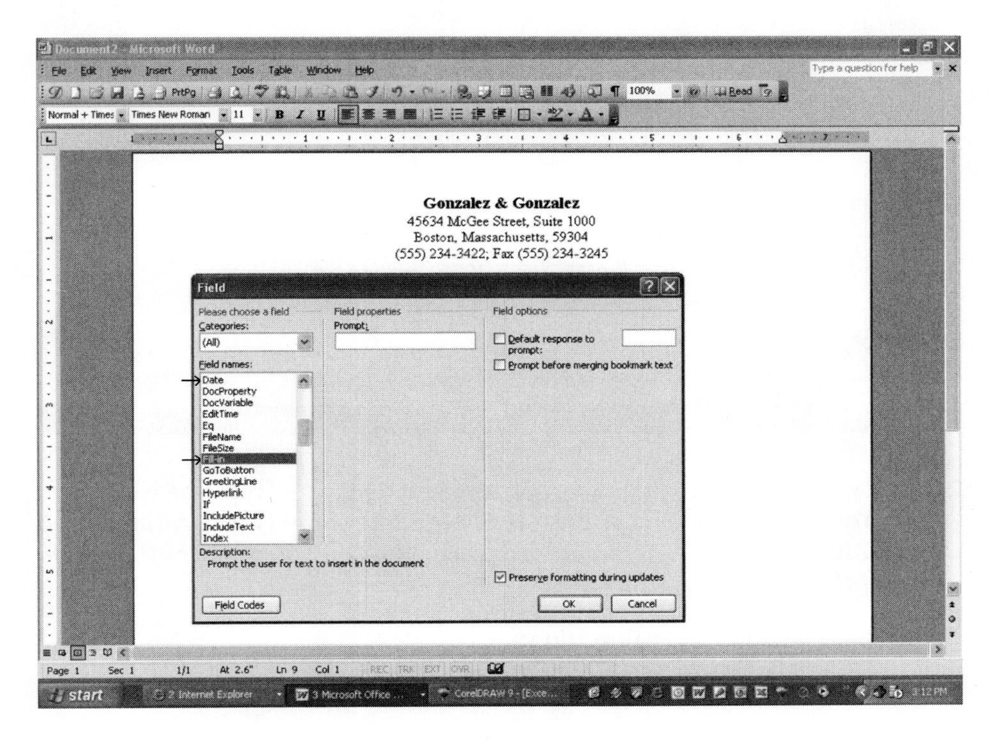

Word 2003 Exhibit 12
Inserting Fields in a Template
Microsoft product screen shot reprinted with permission from Microsoft Corporation.

16. The "Field" window should now be displayed (see Word 2003 Exhibit 12). The Field window has several sections, including Categories and Field Names. Under Categories, "All" should be selected.

17. *Point and click on the down arrow on the Field Names scroll bar until you see the field name "Date"* (see Word 2003 Exhibit 12). *Click on it.*

18. *From the Field Properties list, click on the third option from the top (the one with month, day of the month spelled out, and year).* Notice that the current date is displayed. (This field will always display the date that the template is actually executed, so if the template is executed on January 1, "January 1" will be the date shown on the letter.) *Then, click on OK in the "Field" window.*

19. Press the **[ENTER]** key three times.

20. *Click on Insert on the menu bar and then on Field.*

21. *Point and click on the down arrow on the Field names scroll bar until you see "Fill-In" in the Field Name area* (see Word 2003 Exhibit 12). *Click on Fill-In.*

22. In the "Prompt:" box under "Field Properties," type **"Type the Name and Address of the Recipient."** *Note*: **You must type the quotation marks.**

23. *Click on OK in the "Field" window.*

Word 2003 Exhibit 13
Entering a "Fill-In" Field
Microsoft product screen shot reprinted with permission from Microsoft Corporation.

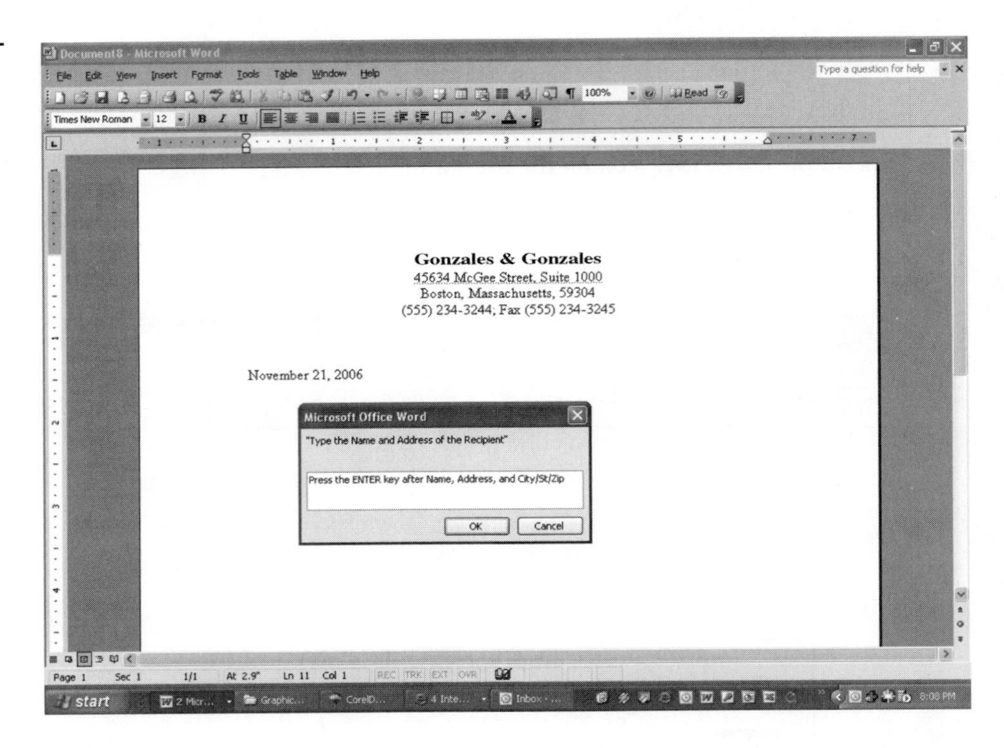

24. You will now see a window on your screen that says "Type the Name and Address of the Recipient." Type **Press the ENTER key after Name, Address, and City/St/Zip** (see Word 2003 Exhibit 13). *Then, click on OK in the bottom right corner of the window.*

25. Press the **[ENTER]** key three times.

26. Press the **[TAB]** key.

27. Type **Subject:.**

28. Press the **[TAB]** key.

29. *Click on Insert on the menu bar and then on Field.*

30. *Point and click on the down arrow on the Field names scroll bar until you see "Fill-In" in the Field Name area. Click on Fill-In.*

31. In the Prompt: box under Field Properties, type "Type the Subject of the Letter" (*Note*: **You must type the quotation marks.**) *Point and click on OK.*

32. You will now see a window on your screen that says "Type the Subject of the Letter." Type **Enter the Subject of the Letter.** *Then, click on OK in the bottom right corner of the window.*

33. Press the **[ENTER]** key three times.

34. Type **Dear** and press the **[SPACEBAR]**, select *Insert from the menu bar, and then select Field.*

35. *Point and click on the down arrow on the Field names scroll bar until you see "Fill-In" in the Field Name area. Click on Fill-In.*

36. In the "Prompt:" box under "Field Properties," type **"Salutation"** (*Note*: **You must type the quotation marks.)** *Point and click on OK.*

37. You will now see a window on your screen that says "Salutation." Type **Enter the Salutation**. *Then, click on OK at the bottom right corner of the window.*

38. Type: *(a colon).*

39. Press the **[ENTER]** key twice.

40. *Click on Insert on the menu bar and then on Field.*

41. *Point and click on the down arrow on the Field Names scroll bar until you see "Fill-In" in the Field Name area. Click on Fill-In.*

42. In the Prompt: box under "Field Properties," type **"Body of Letter" (***Note***: You must type the quotation marks.)** *Point and click on OK.*

43. You will now see a window on your screen that says "Body of Letter." Type **Enter the Body of the Letter.** *Then, click on OK in the bottom right corner of the window.*

44. Press the **[ENTER]** key twice.

45. Type **If you have any questions, please do not hesitate to contact me.** Press the **[ENTER]** key three times.

46. Type **Kindest Regards,** and press the **[ENTER]** key four times.

47. Type **Shirley L. Gonzalez** and press the **[ENTER]** key once.

48. Type **For the Firm**.

49. *Click on File on the menu bar and then on Save.* Type **Gonzalez Letter Template** and then *click on Save.*

50. *Click on File on the menu bar and then on Close.* You are now ready to type a letter using the template.

51. *Click on File on the menu bar, and then click on New.* Under Templates *click on On my computer....*

52. In the Templates window, under the General tab, *double-click on Gonzalez Letter Template.*

53. The template letter is now running. You will see the "Type the Name and Address of the Recipient" field on the screen. You will also see the prompt that reminds you to press ENTER after the name, address and city/state/zip. Type over this prompt.

54. Type **Stephen Wilkerson, Esq.** and press the **[ENTER]** key.

55. Type **Wilkerson, Smith & Russell** and press the **[ENTER]** key.

56. Type **P.O. Box 12341** and press the **[ENTER]** key.

57. Type **Boston, MA 59920** and then *click on OK.*

58. You will see the "Type the Subject of the Letter" field on the screen. You will also see the prompt that reminds you to enter the subject of the letter. Type over this prompt.

59. Type **Turner v. Smith, Case No. 2008–1423** and then ***click on OK.***

60. You will now see the "Salutation" field on the screen. You will also see the prompt that reminds you to enter the salutation. Type over this prompt.

61. Type **Steve** and then ***click on OK.***

62. You will now see the "Body of Letter" field on the screen. You will also see the prompt that reminds you to enter the body of the letter. Type over this prompt.

63. Type **This will confirm our conversation of this date. You indicated that you had no objection to us requesting an additional ten days to respond to your Motion for Summary Judgment.** ***Click on OK.*** You are now through typing the letter. The completed letter should now be displayed (*Note:* If another window is displayed prompting you for the name and address of the recipient, simply ***click Cancel***; the completed letter should then be displayed).

64. To print the document, ***click on File on the menu bar, click on Print, and then click on OK.*** Alternatively, click on the Printer icon on the toolbar.

65. To save the document, ***click on File from the menu bar, and then select Save As...*** Type Wilkerson Letter in the "File name" box. ***Click on the down arrow next to the Save as type: box and choose "Word document (*.doc)." Point and click on Save to save the document in the default directory.*** *Note:* You saved the output of your template to a separate file named "Wilkerson letter." Your original template ("Gonzalez Letter Template") is unaffected by the Wilkerson letter, and is still a clean template ready to be used again and again for any case.

66. ***Click on File on the menu bar, and then on Close*** to close the document, or ***click on File from the menu bar, and then on Exit*** to exit Word.

This concludes Lesson 7.

LESSON 8: COMPARING DOCUMENTS

This lesson shows you how to compare documents by simultaneously viewing documents and by creating a separate blacklined document with the changes. There are times in a law office when you send someone a digital file for revision, but when the file is returned, the revisions are not apparent. Using these tools in Word, you can see what has changed in the document.

1. Open Windows. Then, ***double-click on the Microsoft Office Word 2003 icon on the desktop*** to open Word 2003 for Windows. Alternatively, ***click on the Start button, point the mouse pointer to Programs or All Programs, and then click on the Microsoft Word icon (or point to Microsoft Office, and then click on Microsoft Office Word 2003).*** You should be in a clean, blank document. If you are not in a clean document, ***click on File on the menu bar and then click on New, and then click on Blank document.***

2. For the purpose of this lesson, we will assume that your firm drafted an employment contract for a corporate client named Bluebriar Incorporated. Bluebriar is in negotiations with an individual named John Lewis, whom they would like to hire as their vice-president of marketing. Your firm is negotiating with John Lewis's attorney regarding the terms and language of the employment

contract. The file "Lesson 8A" on Disk 1 for this text is the original document you sent to John Lewis's attorney. The file "Lesson 8B" on Disk 1 for this text is the new file sent to you by John Lewis's attorney.

3. You will now open both of these files from Disk 1 supplied with this text and then compare them side by side. Ensure that Disk 1 is inserted in the drive, ***point and click on File on the menu bar, and then point and click on Open.*** The Open window should now be displayed. Point and ***click on the down arrow to the right of the white box next to "Look in:" and select the drive where Disk 1 is located.*** **Point and double-click on the Word-Processing Files folder. Double-click on the Word 2003 folder.** *Double-click on the "Lesson 8A" file.*

4. Follow the same directions to open the "Lesson 8B" file. Then, point and click on Window from the menu bar and click on "Lesson 8A.doc (Read Only)."

5. ***Point and click on Window from the menu bar, and then click on "Compare Side by Side with Word Lesson 8B doc."*** Both documents should now be displayed side by side (see Word 2003 Exhibit 14).

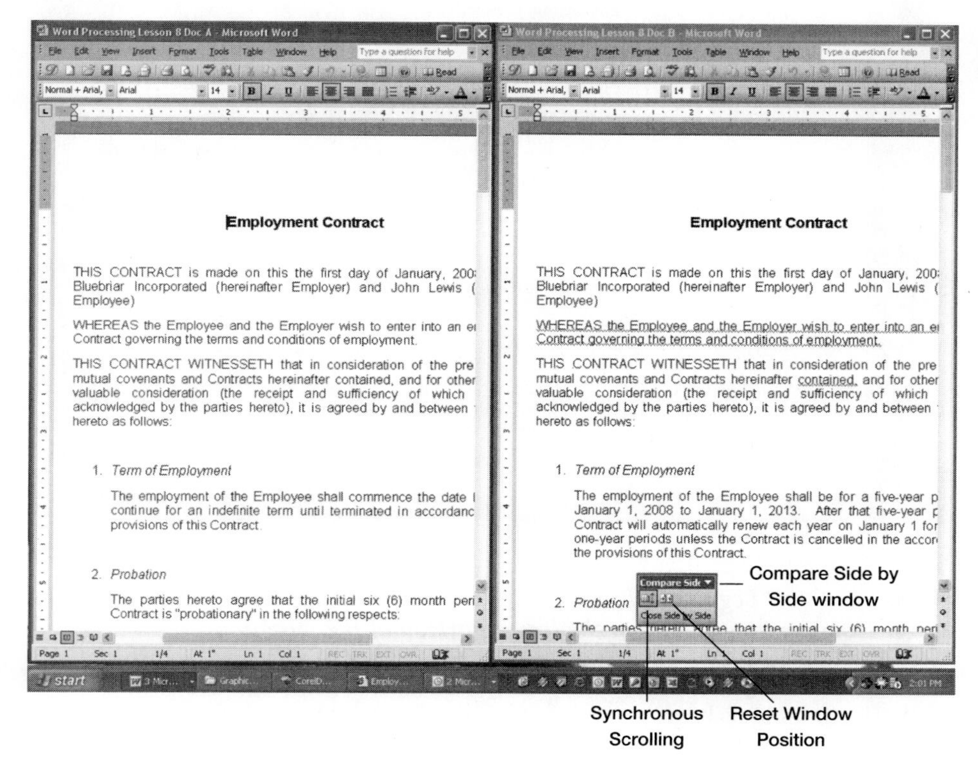

Word 2003 Exhibit 14
Comparing Documents "Side-By-Side"
Microsoft product screen shot reprinted with permission from Microsoft Corporation.

6. Push the [DOWN ARROW] key on the keyboard to scroll down through the document. Notice that both documents simultaneously scroll. Also, notice the Compare Side by Side window (see Word 2003 Exhibit 14). The Synchronous Scrolling icon toggles synchronous scrolling on and off. If you turn off synchronous scrolling and wish to turn it back on, simply realign the windows where you want them, ***point and click on the Reset Window Position icon on the Compare Side by Side window*** (see Word 2003 Exhibit 14), and then select ***the Synchronous Scrolling icon in the Compare Side by Side window.*** Using the "Compare Side by Side" feature, you can see the changes to the document paragraph by paragraph.

7. You will now learn how to merge the changes into one document. ***Point and click on "Close Side by Side" in the Compare Side by Side window.***

8. *Point and click on Window on the menu bar, and then point and click on Lesson 8A.doc.*

9. *Click on File from them menu bar and then on Close* to close this document.

10. Lesson 8B.doc should still be open. You will now create a separate file with the changes merged into one document so you can see everything that has been modified.

11. *Point and click on Tools on the menu bar, and then on Compare and Merge Documents. Point and click on "Lesson 8A.doc." Make sure there are check marks next to "Legal blackline" and "Find formatting" in the Compare and Merge Documents window in the lower portion of the window.*

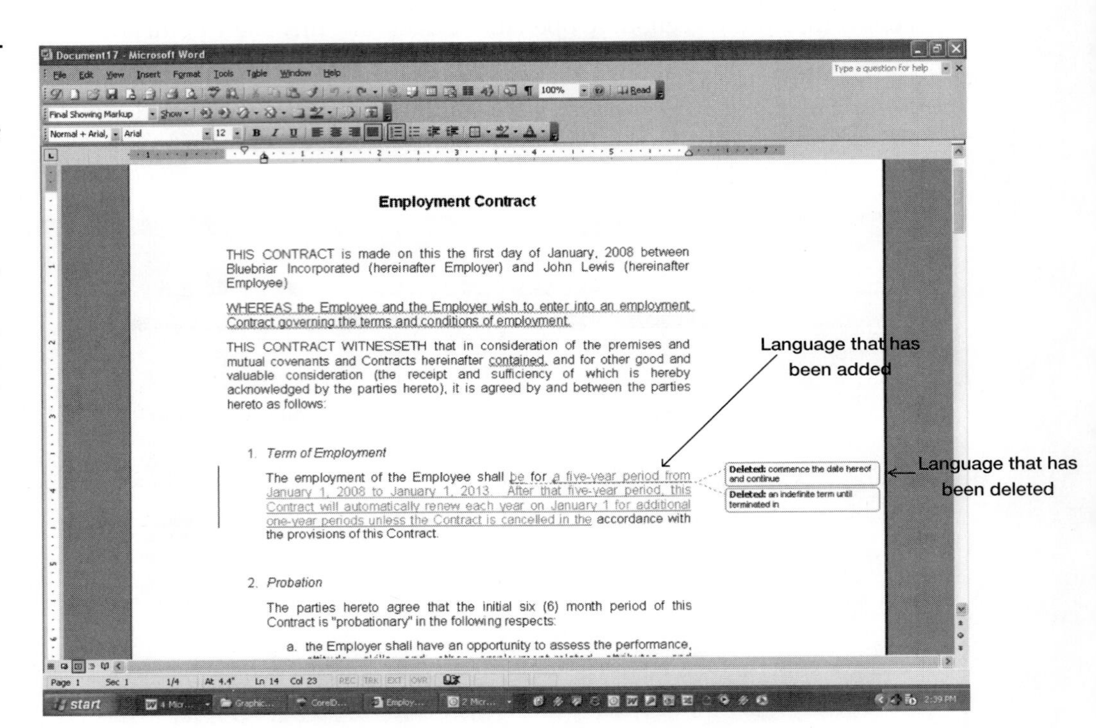

Word 2003 Exhibit 15
Compare and Merge Documents—Legal Blackline
Microsoft product screen shot reprinted with permission from Microsoft Corporation.

12. *Click on Compare in the Compare and Merge Documents window.* Notice that a new document has been created that merges the documents (see Word 2003 Exhibit 15). Scroll through the new document and review all of the changes.

13. The Compare and Merge Documents feature is extremely helpful when comparing multiple versions of the same file. By right-clicking on any of the additions or deletions, you can accept or reject the change. This is part of the feature called Track Changes, which you will learn about in the next lesson.

14. To print the document, *click on File on the menu bar, click on Print, and then click on OK.* Alternatively, click on the Printer icon on the toolbar.

15. To save the document, *click on File from the menu bar, and then select Save As.... Under "Save in" select the drive or folder you would like to save the document in. Then, next to "File Name"* type **Done—Word 2003 Lesson 8 Merged Doc** *and then click on Save to save the document.*

16. ***Click on File on the menu bar, and then on Close*** to close the document.

17. ***Click on File on the menu bar, and then on Close*** to close "Lesson 8B.doc."

18. ***Click on File from the menu bar, and then on Exit*** to exit Word.

This concludes Lesson 8.

LESSON 9: USING TRACK CHANGES

In this lesson, you will learn how to use the Track Changes feature by editing a will and then accepting and/or rejecting the changes.

1. Open Windows. ***Double-click on the Microsoft Office Word 2003 icon on the desktop*** to open Word 2003 for Windows. Alternatively, ***click on the Start button, point the mouse pointer to Programs or All Programs, and then click on the Microsoft Word icon (or point to Microsoft Office, and then click on Microsoft Office Word 2003).*** You should be in a clean, blank document. If you are not in a clean document, ***click on File on the menu bar, click on New, and then click on Blank document.***

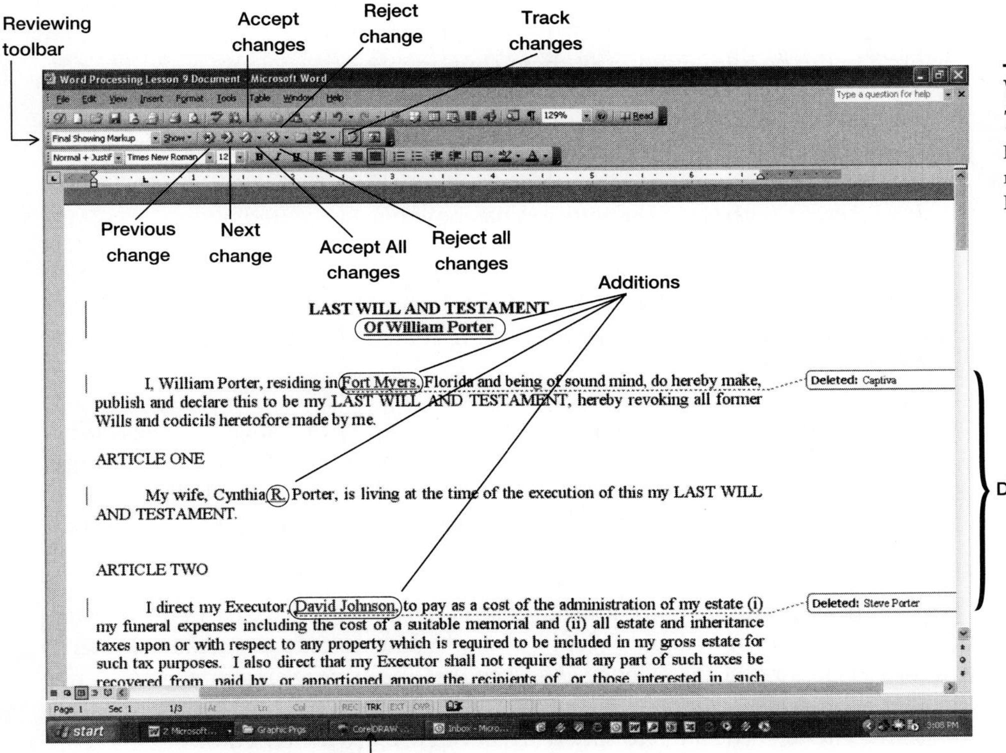

Word 2003 Exhibit 16
Track Changes
Microsoft product screen shot reprinted with permission from Microsoft Corporation.

2. The first thing you will do is to open the "Lesson 9" file from Disk 1 supplied with this text. Ensure that the disk is inserted in the drive, ***point and click on File on the menu bar, and then point and click on Open.*** The Open window should now be displayed. ***Point and click on the down arrow to the right of the white box next to "Look in:" and select the drive where Disk 1 is located.*** **Point and double-click on the Word-Processing Files folder. Double-click on the Word 2003 folder.** ***Point and double-click on the "Lesson 9" file.***

3. The text "Last Will and Testament" should now be displayed on your screen (see Word 2003 Exhibit 16). Notice in Word 2003 Exhibit 16 that several revisions

have been made to this Last Will and Testament. Your client, William Porter, has asked you to use the Document Review feature to show your supervising attorney the changes he would like to make. Mr. Porter is rather leery of the legal process and wants to make sure your supervising attorney approves of the changes.

4. ***Point and click on Tools on the menu bar and then on Track Changes.***

5. Notice on the status line at the bottom of the screen that the initials "TRK" for Track Changes are shown. This tells you that the Track Changes feature is now on (see Word 2003 Exhibit 16). Notice also at the top of the screen that the Reviewing toolbar has now been displayed (see Word 2003 Exhibit 16). This toolbar displays the commands to control Track Changes.

6. Make the changes shown in Word 2003 Exhibit 16. Everything that should be added is circled, and everything that should be deleted is shown at the right.

7. Assume now that you have shown the changes to your supervising attorney. ***Point and click on the Track Changes icon on the Reviewing toolbar*** to turn off track changes (see Word 2003 Exhibit 16). It is the second icon from the right on the Reviewing toolbar. *Remember that you can hover your cursor over an icon on the toolbar and the name will appear after a second or two).* This allows you to make changes to the document without them showing up as revisions.

8. ***Point and right-click anywhere on the revised text you added—"Of William Porter"—just under "Last Will and Testament."*** Notice that a menu is displayed that allows you to accept or reject the insertion, among other things. ***Point and click on Accept Insertion.*** The revision has now been accepted.

9. ***Point and click on the Next icon on the Reviewing toolbar (see Word 2003 Exhibit 16).*** This should take you to the insertion of "Fort Myers." ***Point and click on the Accept Change icon on the Reviewing toolbar (see Word 2003 Exhibit 16) to accept the change.***

10. ***Point and click on the down arrow next to "Accept Change" on the toolbar (see Word 2003 Exhibit 16).*** Notice that one of the options is "Accept All Changes in Document." (Do not select it now.) This is a quick way to accept all changes in a document without going through each one of them. Press the **[ESC]** key on the keyboard to close this menu.

11. Use the Next feature to continue to go to each change and to accept the revision. The only revision you will not accept is changing the executor from Steve Porter to David Johnson; reject this change. Assume that the supervising attorney learned that Mr. Johnson is terminally ill and most likely will not be able to serve as executor, so the client has decided to stay with Steve Porter as the executor.

12. To print the document, ***click on File from the menu bar, click on Print, and then click on OK.*** Alternatively, click on the Printer icon on the toolbar.

13. To save the document, ***click on File from the menu bar, and then select Save As....*** Type **Done**—Word 2003 Lesson 9 Document in the "File name" box, ***and then point and click on Save to save the document in the default directory.***

14. ***Click on File on the menu bar, and then on Close*** to close the document, or ***click on File on the menu bar, and then on Exit*** to exit Word.

This concludes Lesson 9.

Advanced Lessons

LESSON 10: CREATING A MAIL MERGE DOCUMENT

In this lesson, you will create a merge document for an open house that you will send to three clients (see Word 2003 Exhibit 17). First, you will create the data file that will be merged into the letter. Then, you will create the letter itself, and finally, you will merge the two together. Keep in mind that if at any time you make a mistake you may press **[CTRL]+[Z]** to undo what you have done.

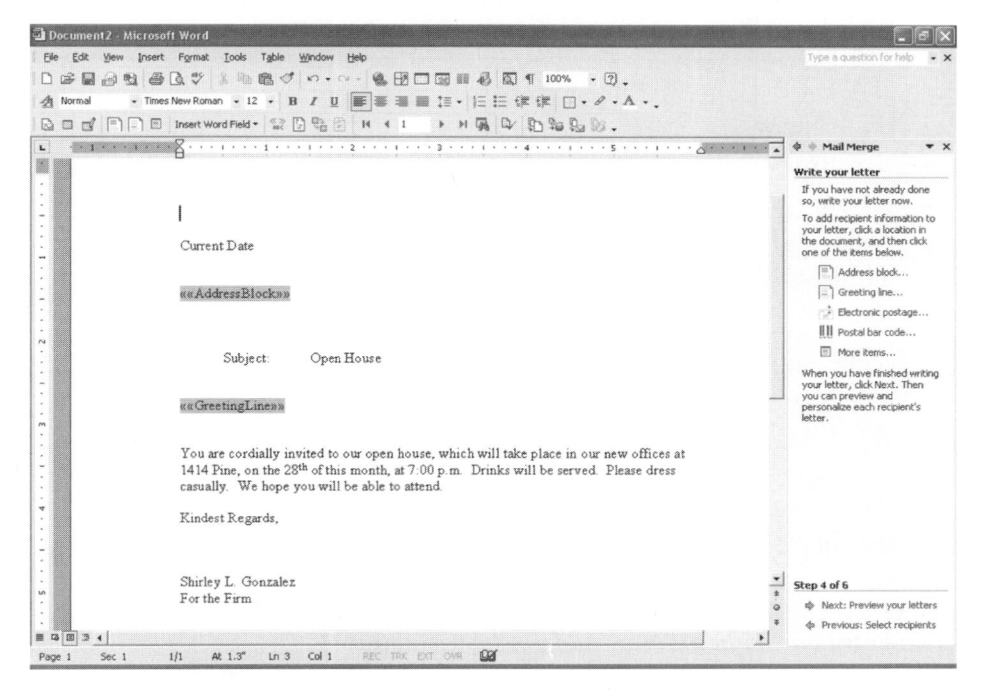

Word 2003 Exhibit 17
Mail Merge Letter
Microsoft product screen shot reprinted with permission from Microsoft Corporation.

1. Open Windows. Then, ***double-click on the Microsoft Office Word 2003 icon on the desktop*** to open Word 2003 for Windows. Alternatively, ***click on the Start button, point to Programs or All Programs, and then click on the Microsoft Word icon (or point to Microsoft Office, and then click on Microsoft Office Word 2003).*** You should be in a clean, blank document. If you are not in a clean document, ***click on File on the menu bar, click on New, and then click on Blank document.***

2. ***Click on Tools on the menu bar, then point to Letters and Mailings, and then click on Mail Merge.*** The Mail Merge task pane is now shown on the task pane to the right of your document.

3. The bottom of the Mail Merge task pane shows that you are on Step 1 of 6. You are asked to "Select document type." You are typing a letter so the default selection, "Letters," is fine. To continue to the next step, ***click on "Next: Starting document" at the bottom of the Mail Merge task pane under Step 1 of 6.***

4. The bottom of the Mail Merge task pane shows that you are on step 2 of 6. You are asked to "Select starting document." You will be using the current document to type your letter, so the default selection, "Use the current document," is fine. To continue to the next step, ***click on "Next: Select recipients" at the bottom of the Mail Merge task pane under Step 2 of 6.***

5. The bottom of the "Mail Merge" task pane shows that you are on step 3 of 6. You are asked to "Select recipients." You will be typing a new list so ***click on "Type a new list."***

6. ***Under the "Type a new list" section of the Mail Merge task pane click on "Create…."***

7. The "New Address List" window is now displayed. You will now fill in the names of the three clients that you want to send your open house letter to.

8. Type the following (*Note:* You can use the **[TAB]** key to move between the fields, or you can use the mouse pointer). Only complete the fields below (skip the fields in the "New Address List" window that we will not be using).

Title	
First Name	Jim
Last Name	Woods
Company Name	
Address Line 1	2300 NE Cannondale
Address Line 2	
City	Cambridge
State	MA
ZIP Code	55342
Country	
Home Phone	
Work Phone	
Email Address	

9. When you have entered all of the information for Jim Woods, ***click on the New Entry button in the New Address List window.***

10. Enter the second client in the blank New Address List window.

Title	
First Name	Jennifer
Last Name	Trek
Company Name	
Address Line 1	4500 Wheatley
Address Line 2	
City	Boston
State	MA
ZIP Code	55856
Country	
Home Phone	
Work Phone	
Email Address	

11. When you have entered all of the information for Jennifer Trek, ***click on the New Entry button in the New Address List window.***

12. Enter the third client in the blank New Address List window.

Title	
First Name	Jonathan
Last Name	Phillips
Company Name	
Address Line 1	8100 Watson Blvd
Address Line 2	
City	Boston
State	MA
ZIP Code	55983
Country	
Home Phone	
Work Phone	
Email Address	

13. When you have entered all of the information for Jonathan Phillips, ***click on Close in the "New Address List" window.***

14. The "Save Address List" window is now displayed. You need to save the address list so that it can be later merged with the open house letter. In the "Save Address List" window, next to File Name: type **Open House List** and then ***click on Save.***

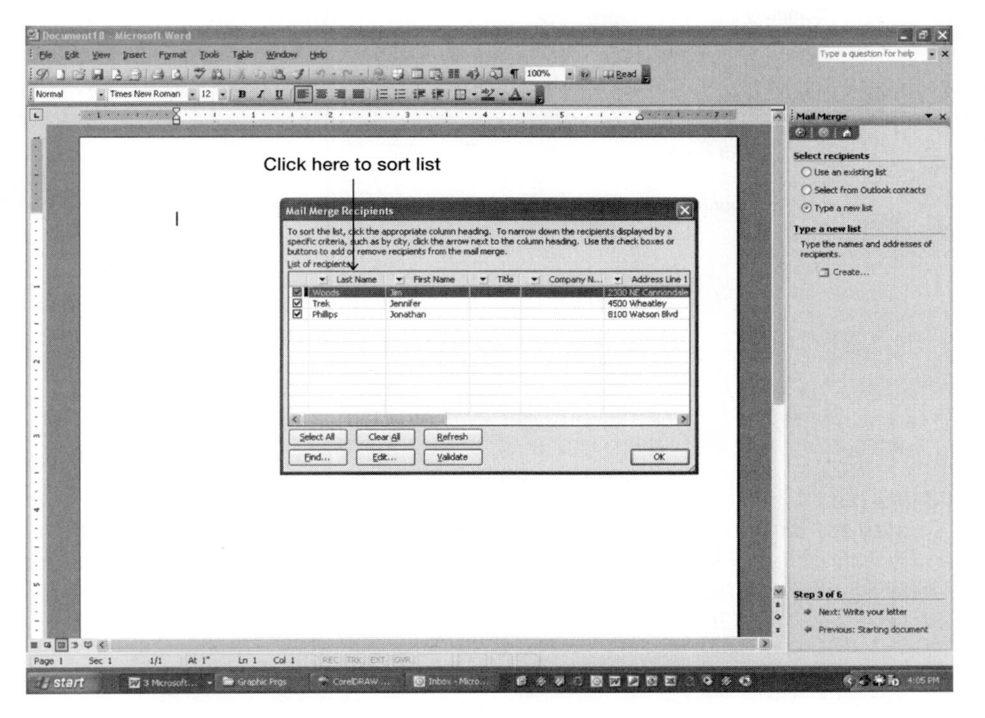

Word 2003 Exhibit 18
Entering Mail Merge Recipients
Microsoft product screen shot reprinted with permission from Microsoft Corporation.

15. The "Mail Merge Recipients" window is now displayed (see Word 2003 Exhibit 18). ***Click on the Last Name field in the Mail Merge Recipients window to sort the list by last name*** (see Word 2003 Exhibit 18). Notice that the order of the list is now sorted by last name.

16. ***Click on OK in the "Mail Merge Recipients" window.*** You are now back at blank document with the Mail Merge task pane open at the right. The bottom of the Mail Merge task pane indicates that you are still at step 3 of 6. ***Click on "Next: Write your letter" at the bottom of the Mail Merge task pane under Step 3 of 6*** to continue to the next step.

17. The bottom of the Mail Merge task pane indicates that you are on step 4 of 6. In the Mail Merge task pane, "Write your letter" is displayed. We are now ready to write the letter.

18. Press the **[ENTER]** key four times.

19. Type the current date and press the **[ENTER]** key three times.

20. ***Click on "Address Block..." in the Mail Merge task pane under "Write your letter."***

21. The "Insert Address Block" window is now displayed. You will now customize how the address block will appear in the letters.

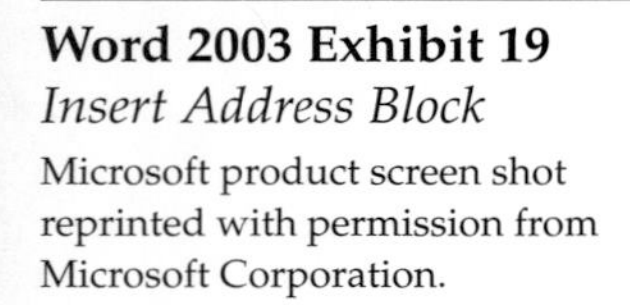

Word 2003 Exhibit 19
Insert Address Block
Microsoft product screen shot reprinted with permission from Microsoft Corporation.

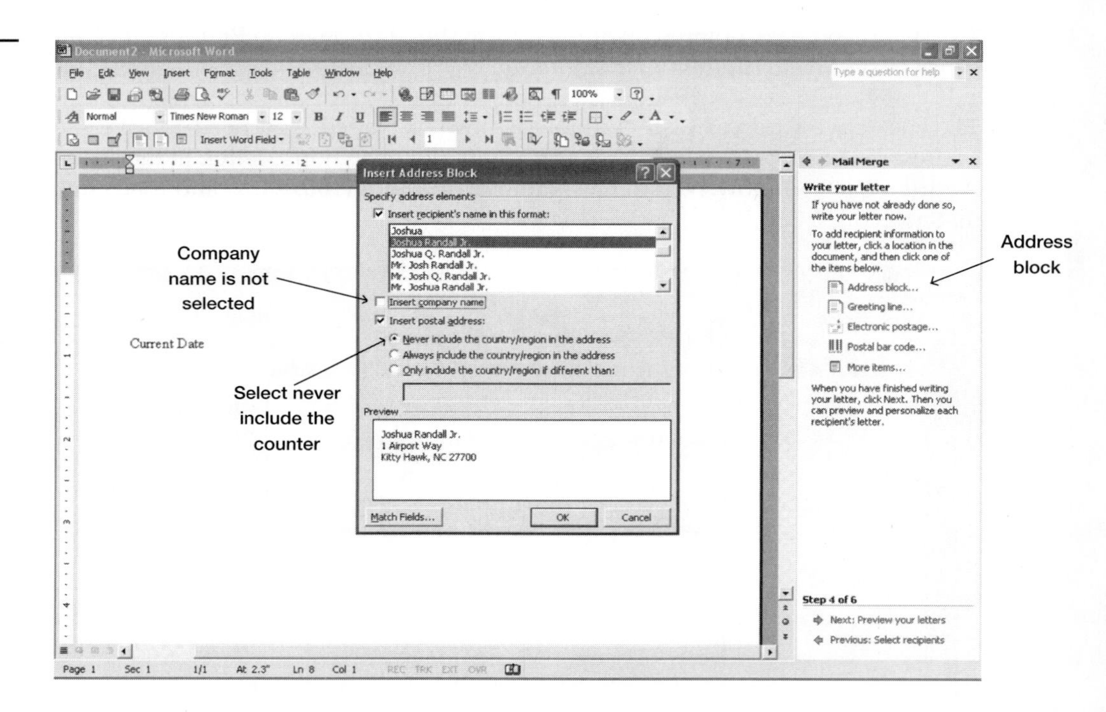

22. ***In the "Insert Address Block" window, click on the second entry, "Joshua Randall Jr."*** Then, ***click on "Insert company name" to deselect it,*** *because we did not include company names in our data list* (see Word 2003 Exhibit 19). Then, under "Insert postal address:" ***click on "Never include the country/region in the address"*** *(see Word 2003 Exhibit 19).*

23. ***Click on OK in the Insert Address Block window.***

24. The words "<<AddressBlock>>" are now displayed in your document.

25. Press the **[ENTER]** key three times.

26. Press the **[TAB]** key once and then type **Subject:**

27. Press the **[TAB]** key and then type **Open House.**

28. Press the **[ENTER]** key twice.

29. ***Under "Write your letter" in the Mail Merge task pane, click on "Greeting line…."***

30. The "Greeting Line" window is now displayed. You will now customize how the greeting or salutation will appear in the letter. In the "Greeting Line" window, ***click on the down arrow next to "Mr. Randall" and then scroll down and click on "Josh." Then, click on OK in the "Greeting Line" window.***

31. The words "<<GreetingLine>>" are now displayed in your document.

32. Press the **[ENTER]** key three times.

33. Type **You are cordially invited to our open house, which will take place in our new offices at 1414 Pine, on the 28th of this month, at 7:00 p.m. Drinks will be served. Please dress casually. We hope you will be able to attend.**

34. Press the **[ENTER]** key twice.

35. Type **Kindest Regards.**

36. Press the **[ENTER]** key four times.

37. Type **Shirley L. Gonzalez.**

38. Press the **[ENTER]** key once and type **For the Firm.**

39. You are now done typing the letter. The only thing left to do is to merge the recipient list with the form.

40. Under "Step 4 of 6" at the bottom of the Mail Merge task pane, ***click on "Next: Preview your letters"*** to continue to the next step.

41. Your first letter is now displayed. In the Mail Merge task pane under "Preview your letters," ***click on the button showing two arrows pointing to the right to see the rest of your letters.***

42. ***To continue to the next step, click on "Next: Complete the merge" at the bottom of the Mail Merge task pane under "Step 5 of 6".***

43. The Mail Merge task pane displays "Complete the Merge." ***Click on Print in the Mail Merge task pane under "Merge," and then click on OK. At the Merge to Printer window, click on OK to print your letters.***

44. ***Click on "Edit individual letters…" in the Mail Merge task pane under "Merge."*** In the "Merge to New Document" window, ***click on OK.*** Word has now opened a new document with all of the letters in it (*Note:* Here, you can edit and personalize each letter if you would like).

45. ***Click on File from the menu bar, and then on Save.*** Type **Open House Letters** and then ***click on Save*** to save the document in the default directory.

46. ***Click on File from the menu bar and then on Close to close the personalized letters.***

47. You should be back at the mail merge letter. ***Click on File from the menu bar and then on Save.*** Type **Open House Mail Merge** and then ***click on Save*** to save the document in the default directory.

48. ***Click on File on the menu bar, and then on Close*** to close the document, or ***click on File from the menu bar, and then on Exit*** to exit Word.

This concludes Lesson 10.

LESSON 11: CREATING A TABLE OF AUTHORITIES

In this lesson, you will prepare a table of authorities for a Reply Brief (see Word 2003 Exhibit 22). You will learn how to find cases, mark cases, and then automatically generate the table of authorities.

1. Open Windows. Then, ***Double-click on the Microsoft Office Word 2003 icon on the desktop*** to open Word 2003 for Windows. Alternatively, ***click on the Start button, point the mouse pointer to Programs or All Programs, and then click on the Microsoft Word icon (or point to Microsoft Office, and then click on Microsoft Office Word 2003).*** You should be in a clean, blank document. If you are not in a clean document, ***click on File on the menu bar, click on New, and then click on Blank document.***

2. The first thing you will do is to open the "Lesson 11" file from supplied with this text. Ensure that the disk is inserted in the disk drive, ***point and click on File on the menu bar, and then point and click on Open.*** The Open window should now be displayed. ***Point and click on the down arrow to the right of the white box next to "Look in:" and select the drive where Disk 1 is located. Point and double-click on the Word-Processing Files folder. Double-click on the Word 2003 folder. Point and double-click on the "Lesson 11" file.*** The text "In the Supreme Court of the United States – Ted Sutton, Petitioner v. State of Alaska, Respondent" should now be displayed on your screen.

3. In this exercise you will build the case section of the Table of Authorities for this Reply Brief. There are five cases to be included and they are all shown in bold so that you can easily identify them. Your first task will be to mark each of the cases so Word knows they are a case to be included, and then you will execute the command for Word to build the table.

4. If you are not at the beginning of the document, press **[CTRL]+[HOME]** on the keyboard to go to the beginning.

5. You will now mark the cases. ***Click on Insert from the menu bar, point to Reference, and then click on Index and Tables….***

6. ***Click on the "Table of Authorities" tab in the Index and Tables window.***

7. ***Click on "Cases" under "Category" and then click on Mark Citation*** (see Word 2003 Exhibit 20). This tells Word that you are going to mark a case, as opposed to a statute, rule, or other data type, because they have their own tables.

8. The Mark Citation window is now displayed. ***Click on "Next Citation" in the Mark Citation window.*** Word looks for words such as "vs" or "v." when finding citations. The cursor should now be on "v." in *Ted Sutton v. State of Alaska.* Because this is the caption of the current case, we do not want to mark it.

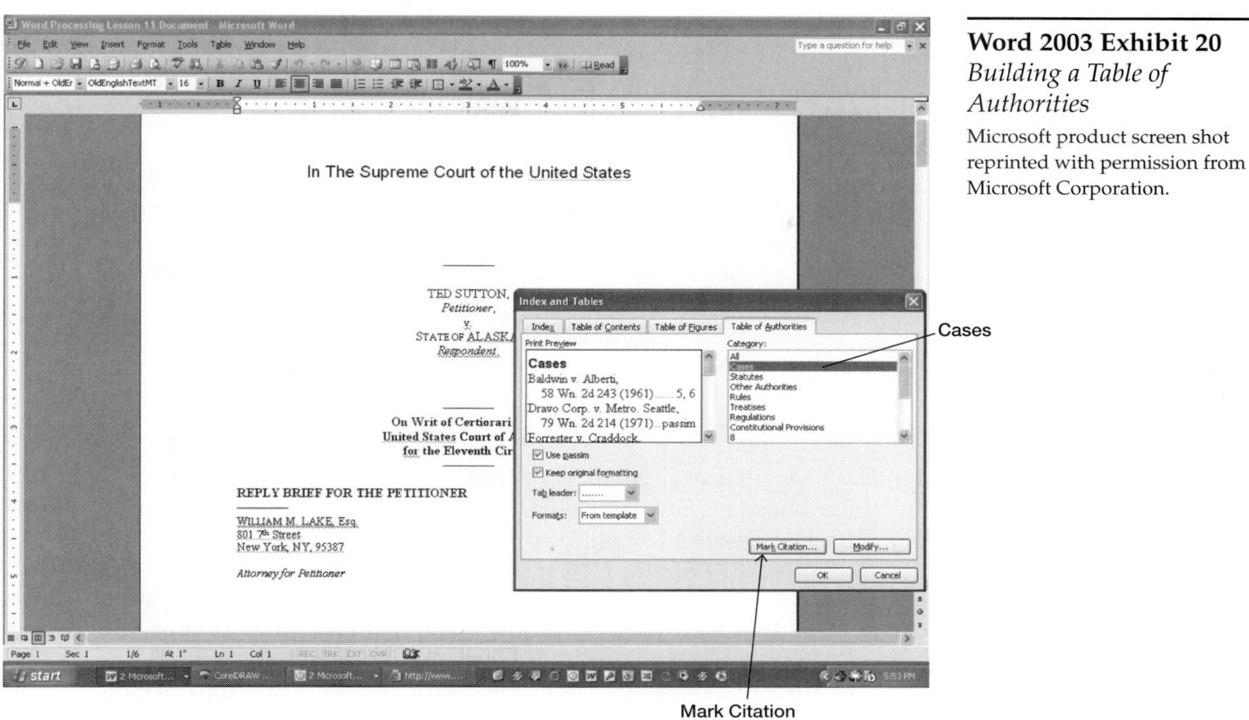

Word 2003 Exhibit 20
Building a Table of Authorities
Microsoft product screen shot reprinted with permission from Microsoft Corporation.

9. ***Click on "Next Citation" in the Mark Citation window.*** Again, this is the caption of the current case *Ted Sutton v. State of Alaska,* so we do not want to mark it.

10. ***Click on "Next Citation" in the Mark Citation window.*** Word has now found the case *Carey v. Saffold.* We want to mark this case so that it is included in the Table of Authorities.

11. ***Click the mouse once on the* Carey v. Saffold *case.***

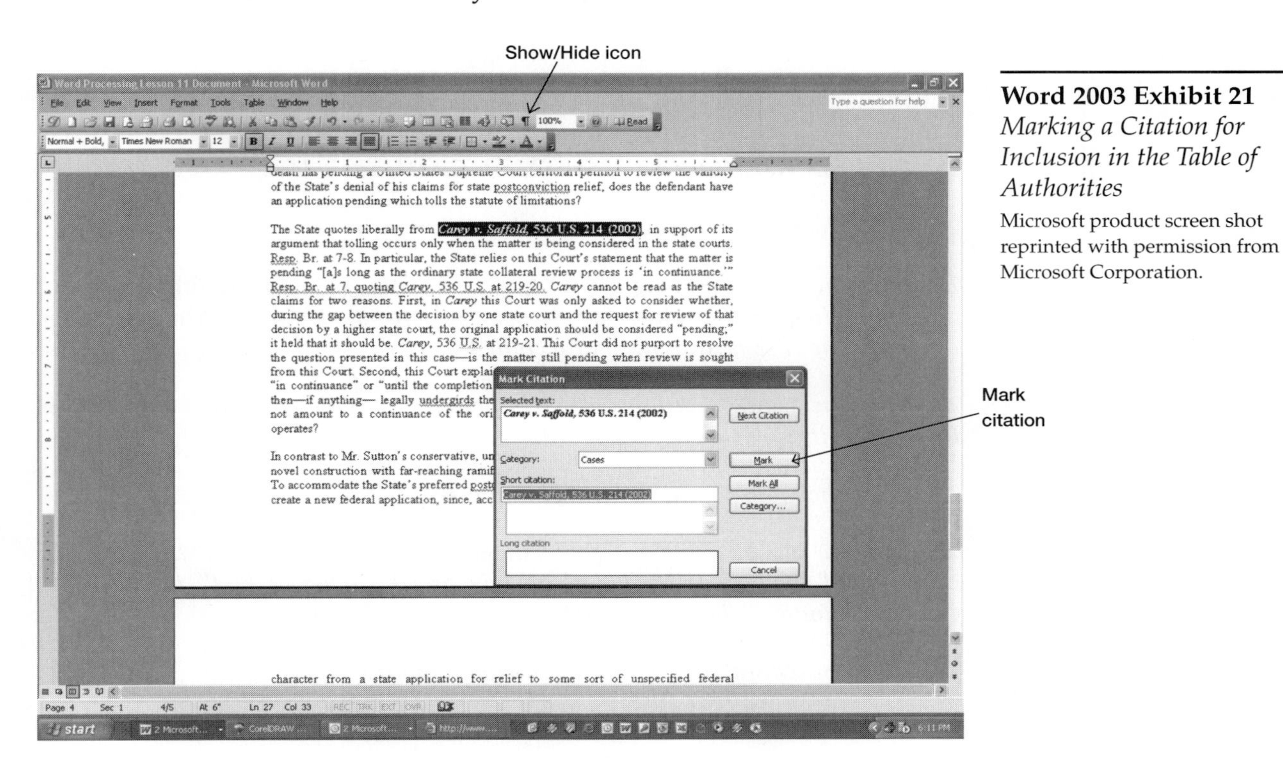

Word 2003 Exhibit 21
Marking a Citation for Inclusion in the Table of Authorities
Microsoft product screen shot reprinted with permission from Microsoft Corporation.

12. ***Drag the cursor to highlight "*****Carey v. Saffold*****, 536 U.S. 214 (2002)," and then click in the white box under "Selected text" in the Mark Citation window; the case is automatically copied there*** (see Word 2003 Exhibit 21).

13. ***Then, click on "Mark" in the Mark Citation window.*** *Note that when you mark a citation, Word changes your view to the Show/Hide paragraph view. It shows you that you have embedded table of authorities formatting codes in the document. To switch out of Show/Hide view, click on the "Show/Hide" icon on the toolbar (it looks like a paragraph sign and is just to the left of the Zoom view, which typically says "100%" See Word 2003 Exhibit 21).*

14. ***Click on "Next Citation" in the Mark Citation window.***

15. ***Click the mouse once on the "Duncan v. Walker" case.***

16. ***Drag the pointer to highlight "*****Duncan v. Walker**, 533 U.S. 167, 174 (2001)," and then ***click in the white box under "Selected text" in the Mark Citation window.*** The case is automatically copied there.

17. ***Click on "Mark" in the Mark Citation window.*** Notice under "Short Citation" in the Mark Citation window that the ***Carey*** and ***Duncan*** cases are listed.

18. If at any time the Mark Citation window prevents you from seeing the case you need to highlight, just click on the blue bar at the top of the Mark Citation window and drag the pointer to the left or the right to move the window out of your way.

19. ***Click on "Next Citation" in the Mark Citation window.***

20. ***Click once on the*** **"Bates v. United States"** ***case.***

21. ***Drag the cursor and highlight "*****Bates v. United States, 522 U.S. 23, 29–30 (1997),"** ***and then click in the white box under "Selected text" in the Mark Citation window.*** The case is automatically copied there.

22. ***Click on "Mark" in the Mark Citation window.***

23. ***Click on "Next Citation" in the Mark Citation window.***

24. ***Click the mouse once on the*** **"Abela v. Martin"** ***case.***

25. ***Drag the pointer and highlight*** "Abela v. Martin, 348 F.3d 164 (6th Cir. 2003)," ***and then click in the white box under "Selected text" in the Mark Citation window. The case is automatically copied there.***

26. ***Click on "Mark" in the Mark Citation window. Click on "Next Citation" in the Mark Citation window.***

27. ***Click the mouse once on the*** **"Coates v. Byrd"** ***case.***

28. ***Drag the mouse and highlight*** **"Coates v. Byrd, 211 F.3d 1225, 1227 (11th Cir. 2000),"** ***and then click in the white box under "Selected text" in the Mark Citation window. The case is automatically copied there.***

29. ***Click on "Mark" in the Mark Citation window.***

30. ***Click on Close in the Mark Citation window to close it.***

31. ***Point and click on the Show/Hide paragraph icon to remove the paragraph symbols*** (see Word 2003 Exhibit 21).

32. ***Using the cursor keys or the horizontal scroll bar, place the cursor on page three of the document two lines under the title "TABLE OF AUTHORITIES."*** You are now ready to generate the table.

33. ***Click on Insert on the menu bar, point to Reference, and then click on Index and Tables.... Click on Cases under Category and then click on OK.***

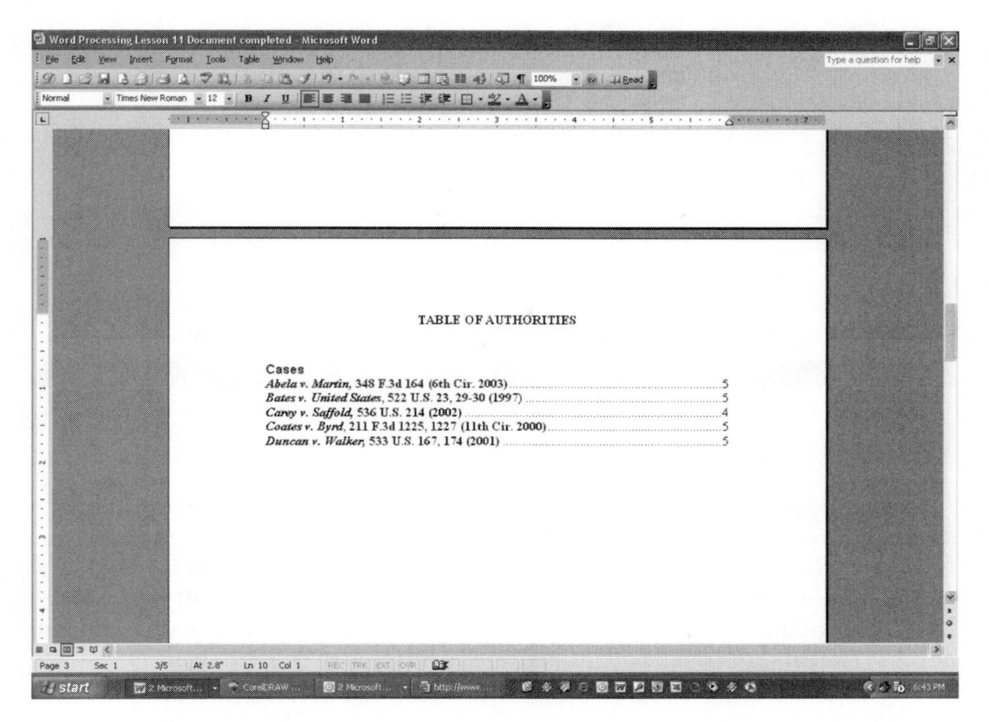

Word 2003 Exhibit 22
Completed Table of Authorities
Microsoft product screen shot reprinted with permission from Microsoft Corporation.

34. Notice that the table of authorities has been prepared and completed, and that the cases and the page number where they appear in the document have been included (see Word 2003 Exhibit 22).

35. To print the document, ***click on File on the menu bar, click on Print, and then click on OK.*** Alternatively, click on the Printer icon on the toolbar.

36. To save the document, ***click on File from the menu bar, and then select Save As.... Under "Save in" select the drive or folder you would like to save the document in. Then, next to "File Name"*** type **Done—Word 2003 Lesson 11 Document** ***and point and click on Save to save the document.***

37. ***Click on File on the menu bar, and then on Close*** to close the document, or ***click on File from the menu bar, and then on Exit*** to exit Word.

This concludes Lesson 11.

LESSON 12: CREATING A MACRO

In this lesson you will prepare a macro that will automatically type the signature block for a pleading (see Word 2003 Exhibit 23). You will then execute the macro to make sure that it works properly.

Word 2003 Exhibit 23
Creating a Pleading Signature Block Macro
Microsoft product screen shot reprinted with permission from Microsoft Corporation.

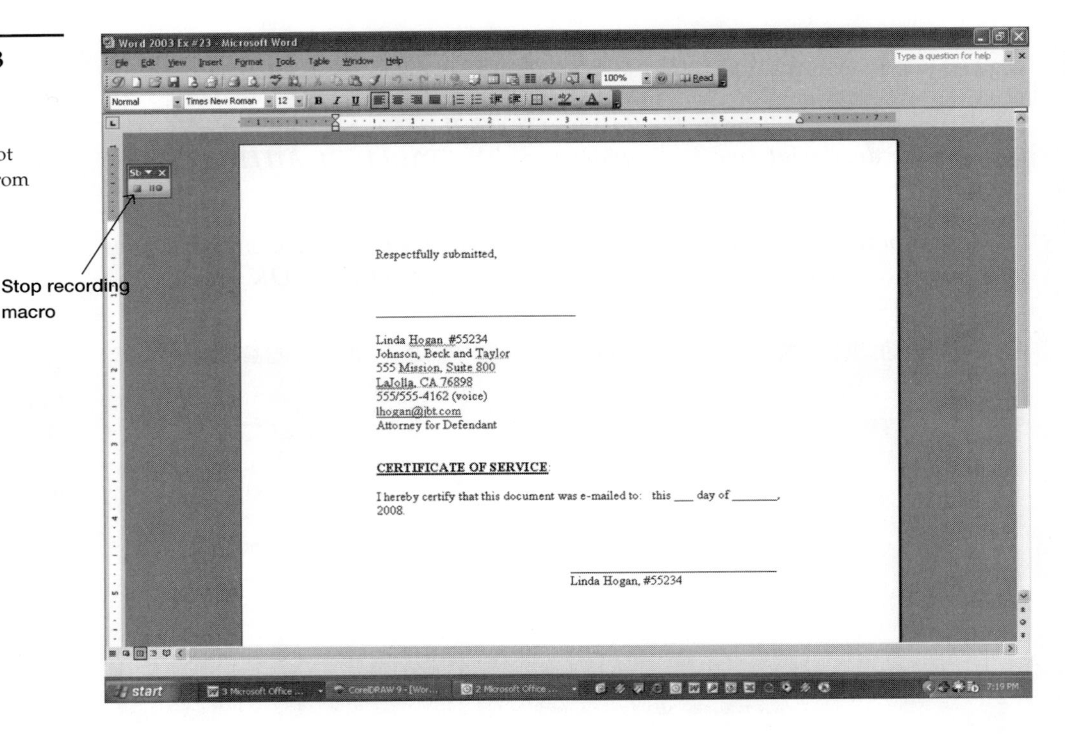

1. Open Windows. ***Double-click on the Microsoft Office Word 2003 icon on the desktop*** to open Word 2003 for Windows. Alternatively, ***click on the Start button, point with the pointer to Programs or All Programs, and then click on the Microsoft Word icon*** (***or point to Microsoft Office, and then click on Microsoft Office Word 2003***). You should be in a clean, blank document. If you are not in a clean document, ***click on File on the menu bar, click on New, and then click on Blank document.***

2. The first thing you need to do to create a new macro is to name the macro and then turn on the Record function. ***Point and click on Tools on the menu bar, and then on Macro, and then on Record New Macro.***

3. In the "Record Macro" window just under "Macro Name," type **PleadSign-Block** and then ***point and click on OK.*** Notice that your cursor now looks like a cassette tape and the "Stop Recording Macro" window has opened. The cassette tape on your cursor indicates that Word is now recording all of your keystrokes and commands.

4. ***Type the information shown in Word 2003 Exhibit 23.*** When you have completed typing the information, ***point and click on the "Stop Recording" button in the "Stop Recording Macro" window.***

5. You will now test your macro to see if it works properly. ***Click on File on the menu bar and then on Close to close the document.*** At the prompt "Do you want to save the changes to Document?" ***point and click on No.***

6. ***Point and click on the "New Blank Document" icon on the toolbar (it looks like a blank sheet of paper and is at the far left on the toolbar).***

7. ***To run the macro, point and click on Tools on the menu bar, then on Macro, and then on Macros.***

8. ***In the Macros window, point and click on PleadSignBlock and then point and click on Run.*** Your pleading signature block should now be in your document.

9. To print the document, ***click on File on the menu bar, click on Print, and then click on OK.*** Alternatively, click on the Printer icon on the toolbar.

10. To save the document, ***click on File from the menu bar, and then select Save As....*** Type **Done—Word 2003 Lesson 12 Document** in the "File name" box, ***and then point and click on Save to save the document in the default directory.***

11. ***Click on File on the menu bar, and then on Close*** to close the document, or ***click on File on the menu bar, and then on Exit*** to exit Word.

This concludes Lesson 12.

LESSON 13: DRAFTING A WILL

Using the websites at the end of the chapter or going to a law library and using a form book, draft a simple will that would be valid in your state. You will be drafting the will for Thomas Mansell, who is a widower. The will should be dated July 1 of the current year. Mr. Mansell requests the following:

- That his just debts and funeral expenses be paid.
- That his lifelong friend, Dr. Jeff Johnson, receive $20,000 in cash.
- That his local YMCA receives his 100 shares of stock in IBM.
- That all of his remaining property (real or personal) descend to his daughter Sharon Mansell.
- That in the event Mr. Mansell and his daughter die simultaneously, all of his property would descend to Sharon's son Michael Mansell.
- That Dr. Jeff Johnson be appointed the executor of the will; if Dr. Johnson predeceases Mr. Mansell, that Mr. Joe Crawford be appointed executor.
- Mr. Mansell has requested that his will be double-spaced and have 1-inch margins. He would like the will to look good and be valid in his state.
- Three witnesses will watch the signing of the will (Shelly Stewart, Dennis Gordon, and Gary Fox).
- John Boesel will notarize the will.
- Print out a hard copy of the will and email it to your instructor.

LESSON 14: THE PLEADING WIZARD

Use the Pleading Wizard in Microsoft Word 2003 to create the Motion in Exhibit 3–17 of Chapter 3 of the text. To bring up the Pleading Wizard, ***click on File on the menu bar, then click on New. Then, under "Templates," click on "On my computer..." Then, click on the Legal Pleadings tab, and under "Create New" click on "Document." Finally, double-click on the Pleading Wizard icon.*** The Pleading Wizard will guide you through creating a pleading form and with completing the form. Use Exhibit 3–17 of the text as a guide, but do not try to copy the format exactly. When the document is completed, print out a hard copy, and email the file to your instructor.

LESSON 15: DEPOSITION SUMMARY

In this exercise, you will prepare a deposition summary of the deposition contained in Appendix B to this book. The deposition is in the case of *Margaret Smith v. EZ Pest Control, Inc.* The Petition by Margaret Smith alleges that the defendant,

EZ Pest Control, Inc., breached their contract in that EZ Pest failed to adequately conduct effective termite inspections as the contract stated, and failed to control termites as the contact stated. The Petition also alleges that the defendant acted negligently below a reasonable standard of care for providing such pest control services. The Petition requests $40,000 in damages.

Word 2003 Exhibit 24
Deposition Summary
Microsoft product screen shot reprinted with permission from Microsoft Corporation.

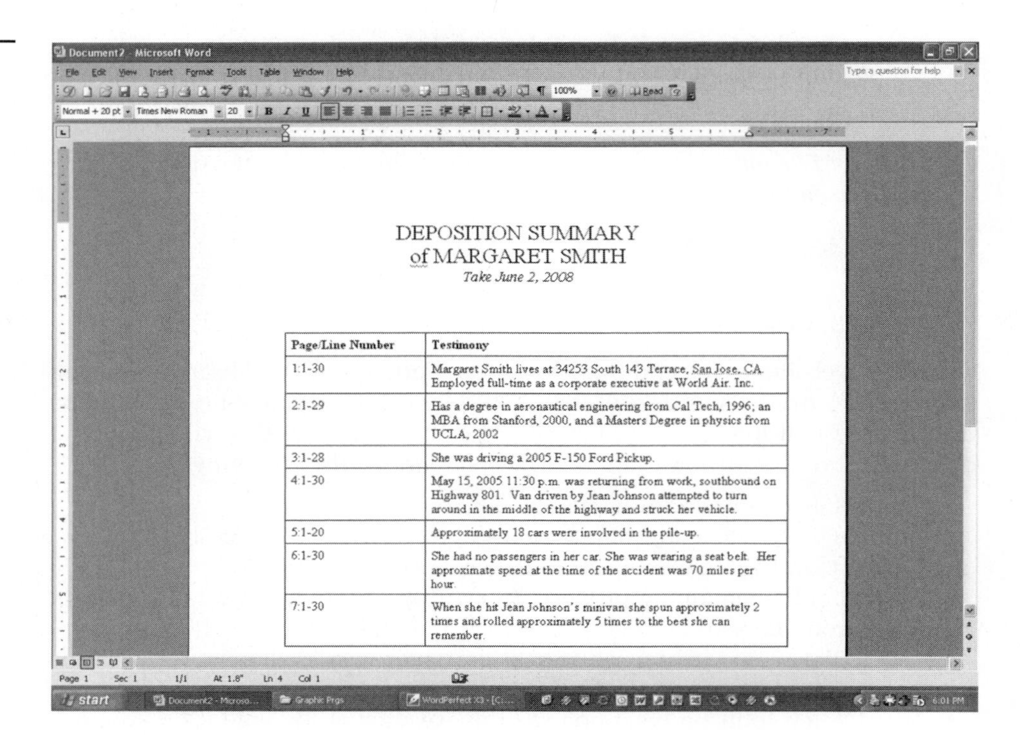

DEPOSITION SUMMARY
of MARGARET SMITH
Take June 2, 2008

Page/Line Number	**Testimony**
1:1-30	Margaret Smith lives at 34253 South 143 Terrace, San Jose, CA. Employed full-time as a corporate executive at World Air. Inc.
2:1-29	Has a degree in aeronautical engineering from Cal Tech, 1996; an MBA from Stanford, 2000, and a Masters Degree in physics from UCLA, 2002
3:1-28	She was driving a 2005 F-150 Ford Pickup.
4:1-30	May 15, 2005 11:30 p.m. was returning from work, southbound on Highway 801. Van driven by Jean Johnson attempted to turn around in the middle of the highway and struck her vehicle.
5:1-20	Approximately 18 cars were involved in the pile-up.
6:1-30	She had no passengers in her car. She was wearing a seat belt. Her approximate speed at the time of the accident was 70 miles per hour.
7:1-30	When she hit Jean Johnson's minivan she spun approximately 2 times and rolled approximately 5 times to the best she can remember.

As stated above, your job is to summarize the deposition of the plaintiff, Margaret Smith. Word 2007 Exhibit 24 shows a sample of a deposition summary. You can use whatever format you would like, but a fairly standard format is to use a table. Each row would represent a page of the deposition (see Word 2003 Exhibit 24) or, alternatively, use a row to represent each separate topic on a page (you may reference line numbers as well). The purpose of a deposition summary is to summarize the essence of the deposition without having to read the whole deposition, and to create a summary so someone can quickly go to the page they are looking for without having to wade through the whole deposition. When the document is completed, print out a hard copy and email the file to your instructor.

CHAPTER

SPREADSHEET SOFTWARE

CHAPTER OBJECTIVES

After completing Chapter 4, you should be able to do the following:

1. Explain what a spreadsheet is.
2. Describe how rows and columns make up the structure of a spreadsheet.
3. Explain what text, values, and formulas are.
4. Describe the common types of graphs found in spreadsheet programs.
5. Explain how copying formulas can simplify the use of a spreadsheet.
6. List and describe the ways spreadsheets can be used by legal assistants.

Spreadsheet software calculates and manipulates numbers using labels, values, and formulas. Legal organizations use spreadsheets to create department/firm budgets; to calculate child support and alimony payments in domestic relations cases; to prepare amortization schedules, Truth-in-Lending statements, and loan calculations in real estate matters; and to estimate taxes and help prepare tax returns for tax matters. These are just a few of the many uses of spreadsheets for law offices of all types. Spreadsheet software can automate all of these tasks. As word processors manipulate words, spreadsheets manipulate numbers. Instead of performing word processing, spreadsheets perform number processing. This chapter describes what a spreadsheet is and discusses "what if" analysis, the structure of spreadsheet programs, the fundamentals of spreadsheets, how to plan or create a spreadsheet, and how spreadsheets are used in the legal environment.

Spreadsheet software
Programs that calculate and manipulate numbers using labels, values, and formulas.

WHAT IS A SPREADSHEET?

A **spreadsheet** is a computerized version of an accountant's worksheet or ledger page. Spreadsheet software is used to create a spreadsheet, sometimes called a worksheet. Accounting professionals use ledger pages, also sometimes called worksheets, to track financial information (see Exhibit 4–1). They enter financial transactions across the rows and down the columns of the ledger paper. Each column is totaled using a calculator or an adding machine. This process can be cumbersome and time consuming if changes need to be made or if errors are found.

Spreadsheets, on the other hand, are flexible and easy to use. Exhibit 4–2 is a simple spreadsheet showing a small law firm's budgeted expenses for a

spreadsheet
A computerized version of an accountant's worksheet or ledger page.

Exhibit 4–1
Accountant's Worksheet (i.e., Ledger Paper)

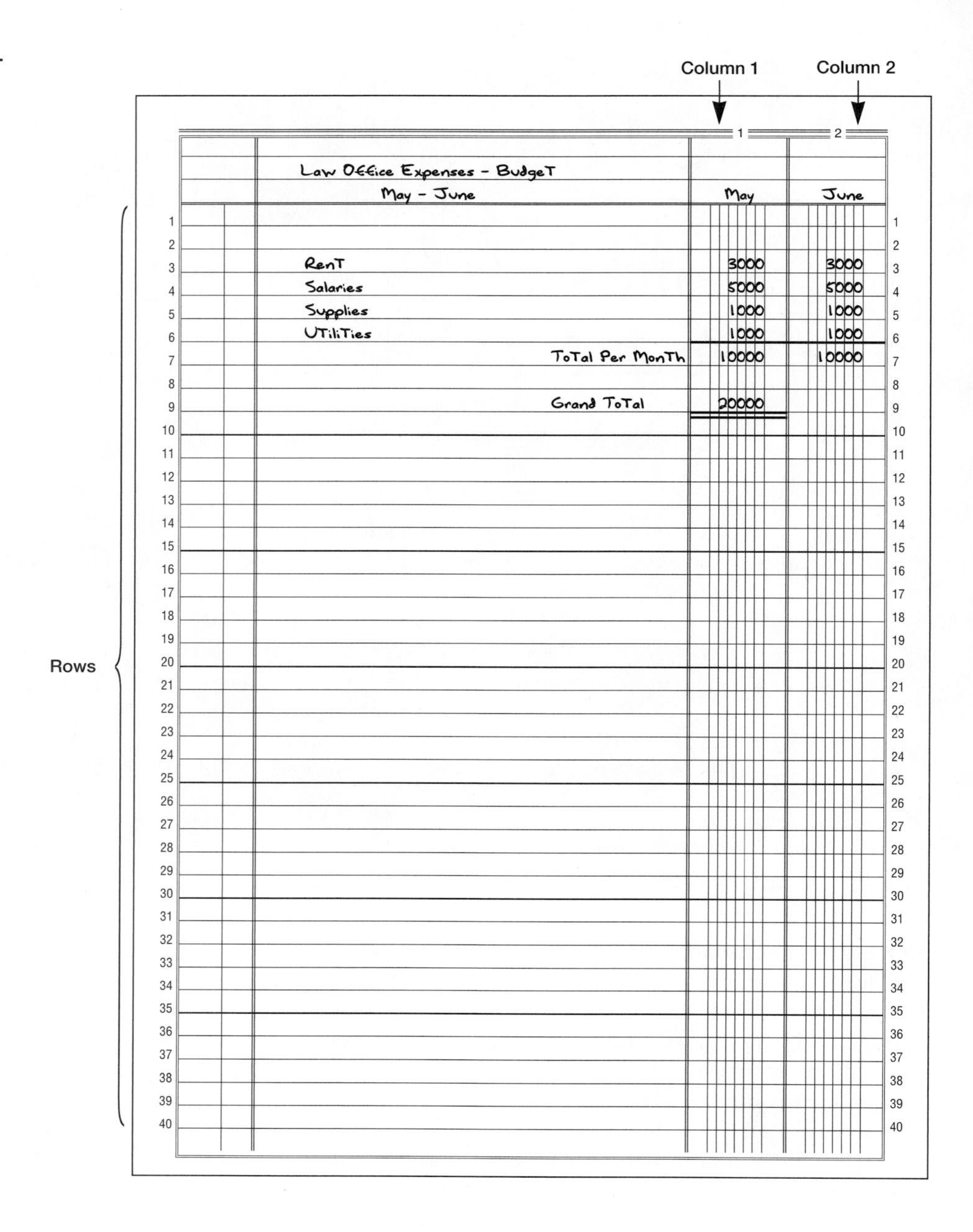

two-month period. This example introduces basic spreadsheet concepts. More sophisticated and more useful spreadsheets for the legal environment will be introduced later in this chapter.

Spreadsheet programs were among the first general business application programs designed to run on microcomputers. Spreadsheets are easier to use than manual worksheets, since the data in a spreadsheet can easily be edited and changed. In addition, spreadsheets can calculate totals and perform other mathematical functions automatically. When data is changed in a spreadsheet, the resulting totals automatically recalculate to reflect the changes made. Spreadsheets have greatly altered the way businesses and legal organizations track and keep numerical data. Reports and computations that once took hours or days now take minutes.

Firms in the legal environment are also enjoying the benefits of spreadsheets. Numerical data is critical in almost all areas of the law. For example, many cases

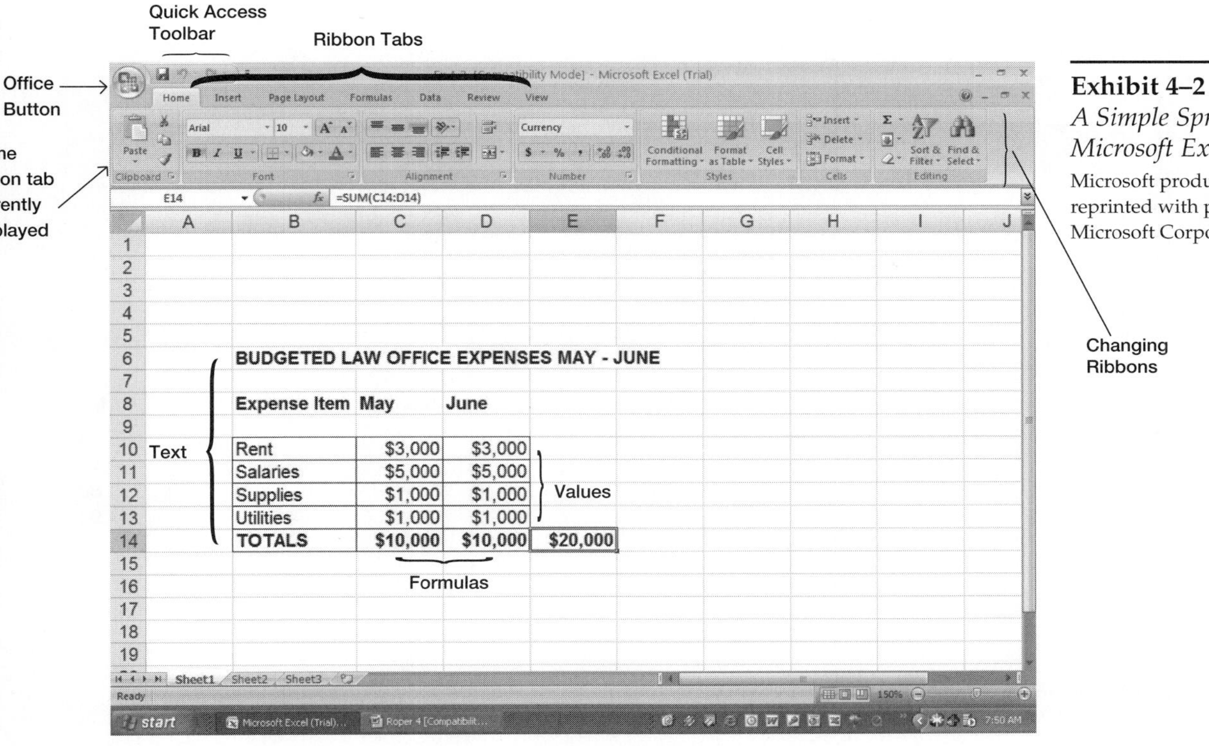

Exhibit 4–2

A Simple Spreadsheet in Microsoft Excel 2007

Microsoft product screen shot reprinted with permission from Microsoft Corporation.

that are filed in court include claims for damages; that is, people filing cases often ask for money or some type of monetary relief. Damages calculations can be complex and are often well suited for spreadsheets. Spreadsheets are also used in bankruptcy law, tax law, estate law, and other areas. Law firms use spreadsheets administratively to track income and expenses, create budgets, produce financial and accounting records, produce statistical reports about the business, and so on.

Spreadsheet software is easy and flexible to use because it does the following:

1. allows all entries to be edited, moved, or copied to other places in the spreadsheet
2. makes it easy to insert additional columns and rows, even after the spreadsheet has been created
3. multiplies, divides, adds, and subtracts one entry or many entries
4. performs complex calculations (e.g., statistical functions, such as standard deviations, averages, and square roots, and financial calculations, such as present value, future value, and internal rate of return)
5. allows totals and other calculations to be automatically recalculated when information in a column or a row changes
6. allows numerical information to be graphed using several different kinds of charts
7. allows information to be saved and retrieved for future use
8. allows information to be sorted or organized automatically
9. allows the information in the spreadsheet to be printed

Microsoft Excel is the spreadsheet program overwhelmingly used by most legal organizations. There are currently two versions of Excel that are widely used in the legal environment, Excel 2007 and Excel 2003. The programs are

Exhibit 4–3
Elements of Spreadsheet (Excel 2003)
Microsoft product screen shot reprinted with permission from Microsoft Corporation.

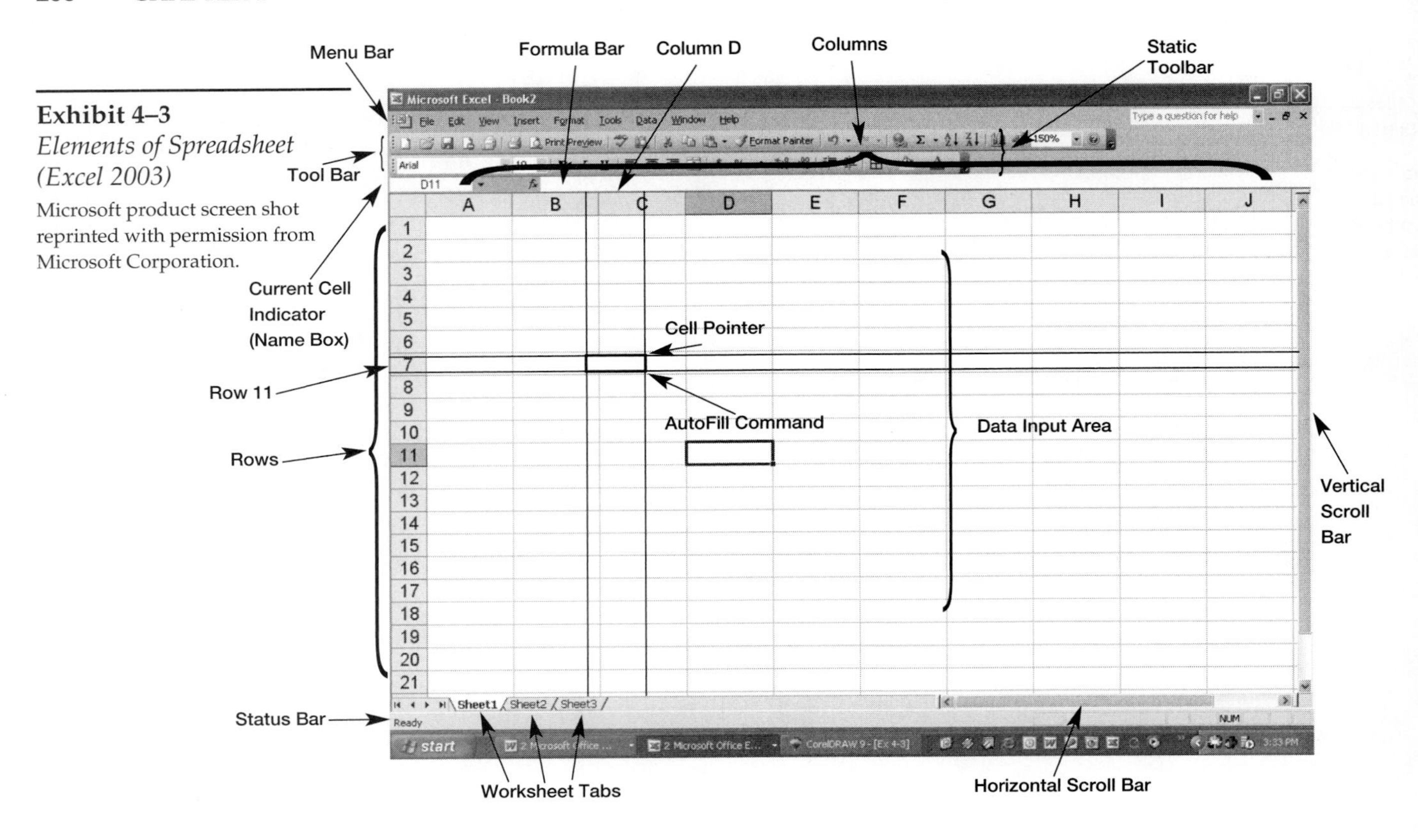

largely similar except that Excel 2007 uses a ribbon interface (see Exhibit 4–2) and Excel 2003 uses a largely menu-driven interface. Screen shots from both programs are used throughout this chapter.

"WHAT IF" ANALYSIS

"what if" analysis
A feature of spreadsheets that allows the user to build a spreadsheet and then change the data to reflect alternative planning assumptions or scenarios.

Spreadsheets can also be used for "what if" analysis. **"What if" analysis** refers to the ability to build a spreadsheet and then to change it to reflect alternative planning assumptions or scenarios. As mentioned before, when numerical data is entered into a spreadsheet and later changed, the totals automatically recalculate. Thus, it is possible to evaluate the effects of a change simply by changing a number. This allows users to hypothesize and evaluate the effects of possible changes easily. For example, in Exhibit 4–2, if the small law firm wanted to evaluate what would happen if rent doubled for the two-month period shown, it could simply change the "3000" rent figure to "6000" and the spreadsheet would automatically recalculate the total. Since most businesses are in a state of change at all times, this feature allows users to prepare for unexpected events.

SPREADSHEET STRUCTURE AND ORGANIZATION

Rows and Columns

row
An area that extends across a page horizontally.

column
An area that extends down a page vertically.

Like an accountant's worksheet, a spreadsheet has rows and columns. A **row** is an area that extends across a page horizontally, and a **column** is an area that extends down a page vertically. For example, in Exhibit 4–3, rows are designated by a number (row 1, row 2, etc.), and columns are designated by a capital letter

(column A, column B, etc.). Although only twenty-one rows and ten columns are shown on the screen in Exhibit 4–3, the spreadsheet actually extends all the way down several thousand rows and all the way across several hundred columns. The exact length of a spreadsheet depends on the spreadsheet program. When the columns go past column Z, the column letters double up (column AA, column AB, etc.). In Exhibit 4–3, row 11 is shaded all the way across the page, and column D is shaded all the way down the page to illustrate the difference between rows and columns.

Cells and Cell Addresses

A **cell** is an intersection between a row and a column (see Exhibit 4–3). Every cell has a cell address. A **cell address** is the row and column location of a cell. It is usually represented by the letter of the column and then the number of the row, such as cell D11 in Exhibit 4–3. Every cell in a spreadsheet has a cell address. Cells hold information such as values (numbers), formulas (mathematical calculations), and text.

cell
An intersection between a row and a column in a spreadsheet.

cell address
The row and column location of a cell.

The Elements of a Spreadsheet

Most spreadsheet programs have a user interface similar to the one in Exhibit 4–3. After a user loads a spreadsheet program, a blank spreadsheet is displayed. Exhibit 4–3 shows the various elements of a spreadsheet.

Cell Pointer All spreadsheets have a **cell pointer,** or cursor, that indicates what cell is currently selected. The cell pointer is moved by using the arrow or direction keys and can also be moved up and down pages or screens by using the [PAGE UP], [PAGE DOWN], and other keys, depending on the spreadsheet. Most spreadsheet programs also allow the cell pointer to be moved with a mouse. Finally, the cell pointer can be moved using the GO TO command. The GO TO command instructs the spreadsheet to "go to" a certain cell address. In Microsoft Excel 2003 and 2007, the [F5] key is the GO TO command.

cell pointer
The cursor in a spreadsheet program.

Current Cell Indicator and Formula Bar The current cell indicator, sometimes called the name box shows the address of the cell pointer (see Exhibit 4–3). The formula bar, which is just to the right of the current cell indicator, shows the contents of the current cell. Notice in Exhibit 4–3 that the current cell indicator shows "D11" and that there is nothing in the formula bar, because cell D11 is empty. When the cell pointer is on a cell containing text, a value, or a formula, the information in the cell will be shown in the formula bar. The text, value, or formula can be edited by placing the mouse in the formula bar. When the cell pointer is moved, the current cell indicator automatically displays the current cell address.

Data Input Area Data is entered into a spreadsheet in the data input area, which is made up of cells.

Status Bar The status bar signifies the current status of the spreadsheet. For example, in Exhibit 4–3, the spreadsheet is in the ready mode, which means that it is ready to accept instructions from a user.

Menus, Toolbars and Ribbons

Excel 2007 (see Exhibit 4–2) uses a changing ribbon as the interface with the user instead of menus. In Exhibit 4–2 the Home ribbon tab is shown. There are seven ribbons available: **Home, Insert, Page Layout, Formulas, Data, Review** and

View. The tools on the ribbon change depending on what tab is selected. Excel 2007 also has a small Quick Access Toolbar that does not change and that is customizable by the user (see Exhibit 4–2). Excel 2003 (see Exhibit 4–3) on the other hand, uses a static toolbar (which remains constant) and a series of drop-down menus (**File, Edit, View, Insert, Format, Tools, Data, Window**, and **Help**) as the interface with the user. Most of the other elements in Excel 2007 and 2003 operate in the same way.

Horizontal and Vertical Scroll Bars The user is able to see other parts of the spreadsheet by using the horizontal and vertical scroll bars.

Worksheets Most spreadsheet programs allow the user to have multiple worksheets in one spreadsheet file. Notice in Exhibit 4–3 that there are three sheets available (Sheet 1, Sheet 2, and Sheet 3). Many users find it convenient to have separate worksheets in one file. For example, if a law office had three locations, the user could have one spreadsheet file called "budget" with a separate worksheet for each location. The worksheets (Sheet 1, Sheet 2, etc.) can be renamed as anything the user wants, such as Location 1, 2, and 3.

Spreadsheets with WYSIWYG

Most spreadsheets offer a WYSIWYG (pronounced "wizzy-wig") screen. Exhibits 4–2 and 4–3 are examples of Windows spreadsheet programs with WYSIWYG. The WYSIWYG format allows the user to add different fonts or type styles to the spreadsheets and allows for boxes and other formatting options that can make a spreadsheet easier to read. In addition, all of the formatting appears on the user's screen exactly as it will print out.

SPREADSHEET FUNDAMENTALS

In this section, you will learn about spreadsheet menus and about inputting text, values, and formulas. Exhibits 4–4 and 4–4A show Quick Reference guides for Excel 2007 and Excel 2003.

Data Input

Data is usually entered into a spreadsheet using a keyboard. It can be entered more easily and faster if the keyboard has a separate numeric keypad in addition to the direction and cursor keys. This allows a user to move the cell pointer with the cursor keys and to enter values and formulas using the numeric keypad.

Three types of data can be entered into a spreadsheet: text, values, and formulas.

text
Descriptive data, including headings and titles, that is used for reference purposes in a spreadsheet.

Text Descriptive data, called **text**, is entered into a cell. It cannot be used in making calculations. It includes headings, titles, and so forth. For example, in Exhibit 4–2, the title "BUDGETED LAW OFFICE EXPENSES MAY - JUNE"; the column headings "Expense Item," "May," and "June"; and the row headings "Rent," "Salaries," "Supplies," "Utilities," and "TOTALS" are all text.

Text is usually an alphabetical character entry, but numbers can also be included, although no calculations can be performed on a number entered as text. For example, instead of writing out May and June for column headings in Exhibit 4–2, the numbers 5 and 6 could be substituted, showing that May and June are the fifth and sixth months of the year. The numbers could be entered as text, since no calculations would be performed on these cells, which are used only as column headings.

Function commands are entered in nearly the same way as arithmetic operator formulas. A user points to the cell where the total should be placed. Next, the user enters the "=" sign, followed by the name of the function command and an opening parenthesis. The user then enters the beginning cell address of the range followed by a colon (:) and the ending cell address of the range. Finally, the user closes the parentheses and presses the [ENTER] key to enter the formula into the cell.

A function formula may also be entered using the pointing method. The first step is to go to the cell where the total is to be placed. The next step is to enter the = (equal sign), followed by an opening parenthesis—for example, =SUM(. The next step is to point to the beginning of the range that is to be included and type a colon (:). The colon anchors the range (i.e., it tells the spreadsheet program where the range is starting). The next step is to point to the end of the range. The final step is to type the closing parenthesis and hit the [ENTER] key to execute the command (e.g., =SUM(C10:C13)). Using the pointing method is simpler than typing in the cell range for many people and is especially easy for beginning spreadsheet users. Entering formulas is covered in detail in the Excel 2007 and Excel 2003 Hands On Exercises at Lessons 1–4 and 6.

Entering Formulas Using Both Arithmetic Operators and Function Commands Arithmetic operators and function commands can also be used together. For example, if a user wanted to add cells C10, C11, C12, and C13 and then divide the total by 2, the formula would read =SUM(C10:C13)/2. This formula uses the SUM function to add the cells together and the division operator to divide the total by 2.

In any case, no matter how a formula is entered, whether it be by using arithmetic operators or using a function command, if the values change in the cells that are calculated, the totals will automatically recalculate.

Other Spreadsheet Features

Spreadsheets can perform many functions, including changing cell widths, copying data and formulas, moving formulas, and sorting data.

cell width
The number of characters that can be placed in any given cell in a spreadsheet program.

Changing the Cell Width Every cell has a cell width, sometimes called a column width. The **cell width** refers to the number of characters that can be placed in a cell. Cells in most spreadsheet programs have a starting value of nine. That is, a cell can hold nine characters or numbers.

Many times, a cell width will need to be changed to hold either large values (e.g., $200,000,000) or long labels. If a cell width is not large enough to hold a large value, the cell will be filled with asterisks (*) until you enlarge it. Cell widths can also be shortened if needed. Making cells smaller allows more information to be seen on a page or computer screen at a time. The cell width is easily changed by pointing to the column to be changed and then executing the **Column Width** command, entering the number of characters the column should hold, and then pressing [ENTER] or OK.

Another way to change the column width is to use the pointing method. The user points to the right border of the heading of the column to be changed. The mouse pointer changes to a double arrow. Then the user drags it to the right to expand the column or to the left to make the column smaller. When the mouse button is released, the column width is automatically changed (see Exhibit 4–8). Lesson 1 in the Hands-On Exercises at the end of the chapter cover changing column width in detail.

Copying Data Spreadsheets have a **Copy** command that copies information from one part of a spreadsheet to another part or from one spreadsheet to another, while leaving the original intact (see Exhibit 4–9). The user points to the cell to be copied and then clicks **Edit, Copy.** The user then moves the cell pointer to the location where the information is to be copied and presses [ENTER].

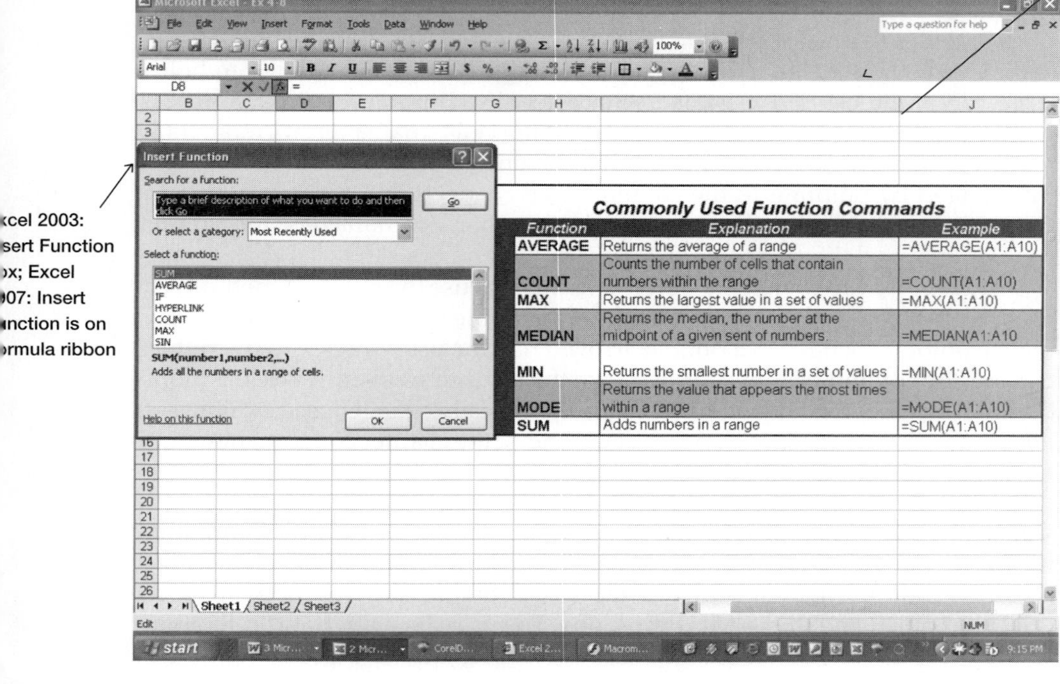

Exhibit 4–7
Entering Formulas with Function Commands
Microsoft product screen shot reprinted with permission from Microsoft Corporation.

Many different function commands are available in most spreadsheets programs (see Exhibit 4–8). Some of the function commands represent long, complex formulas and make them easy to use. Both the arithmetic operators and the function commands obtain the same results (compare the totals in Exhibits 4–5 and 4–7). However, for a long formula such as one that adds 100 cells together, to use the arithmetic operator method, a user would have to type addition signs between all 100 cell addresses. The function commands make calculating large ranges of cells easy.

To change a column's width, point to the right border of the column heading and drag it right to enlarge the column or left to make it smaller.

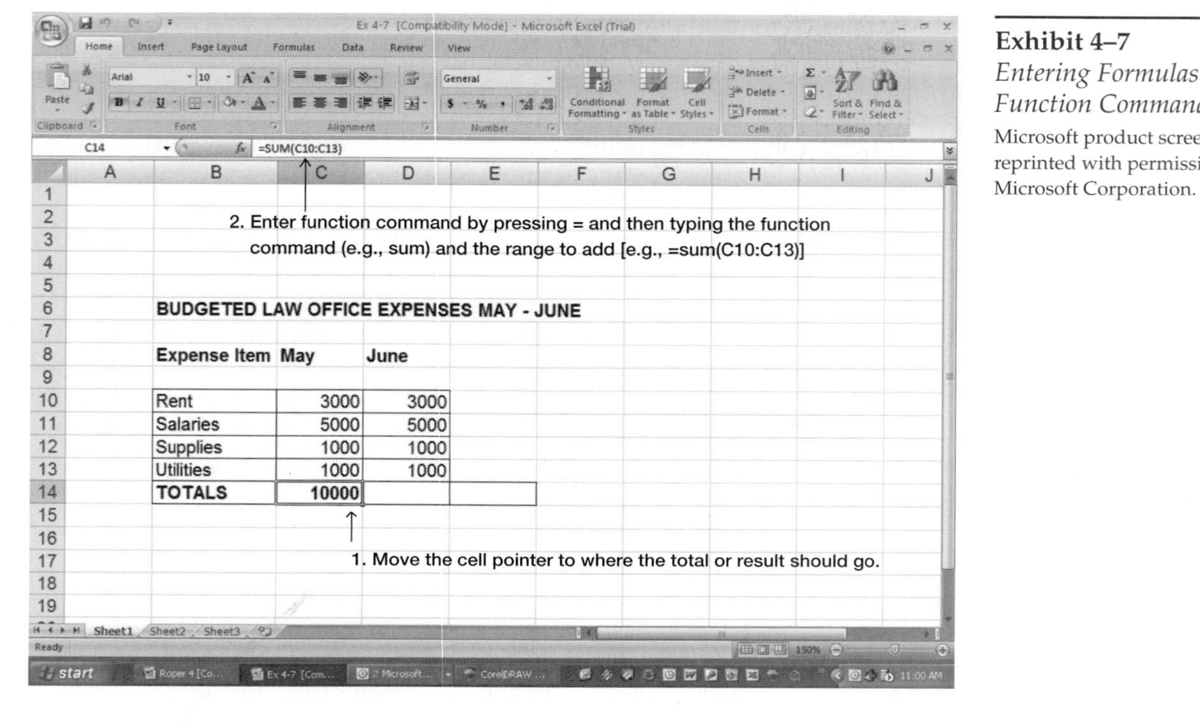

Exhibit 4–8
Commonly Used Function Commands in Excel
Microsoft product screen shot reprinted with permission from Microsoft Corporation.

You can also change a column width by selecting Format Column Width.

formulas
Expressions used in spreadsheet programs to automatically perform calculations on other values.

Formulas Calculations using the values in other cells are performed with **formulas**. For example, in Exhibit 4–5, the entry in cell C14 is a formula (=C10+C11+C12+C13) that adds the values of cells C10, C11, C12, and C13. Because the formula is placed in cell C14, the total is also placed there. The real power of a spreadsheet program is that formulas automatically recalculate if a cell value is changed. Thus, if any of the values in C10, C11, C12, or C13 were later changed, the program would automatically recalculate the total in C14.

Formulas can be entered using arithmetic operators or function commands or both.

arithmetic operators
Symbols that tell a spreadsheet how to compute values. Examples include addition signs, subtraction signs, and multiplication signs.

Entering Formulas Using Arithmetic Operators One way to enter formulas is to use arithmetic operators and list each cell to be computed separately (see Exhibit 4–5). **Arithmetic operators** tell a spreadsheet how to compute values (see Exhibit 4–6). With this method, a user points to the cell where the total should be placed. The user then begins by typing an = (equal sign) or a + (plus sign). These tell the spreadsheet that a formula will be entered. When the formula has been typed, the user presses the [ENTER] key or a cursor key to enter it.

Exhibit 4–6
Arithmetic Operators

Arithmetic Operator	Name	Formula Example
+	Addition	=C10+C11 or =100+10
–	Subtraction	=C10–C11 or =10–10
*	Multiplication	=C10*C11 or =100*10
/	Divsion	=C10/C11 or =100/10

In Exhibit 4–5, the formula in cell C14 uses the addition arithmetic operator (+) to tell the spreadsheet program to add the values in cells C10 through C13. This is an example of using an arithmetic operator. Spreadsheets also have arithmetic operators to subtract, multiply, and divide the contents of cells. For example, in Exhibit 4–5, if instead of adding cell C13 you wanted to subtract it, the formula would read =C10+C11+C12-C13, and the total would read 8000.

In most spreadsheets, the user has the option of either typing the cell addresses of the cells to be included in the formula (typing =C10+C11+C12+C13 in Exhibit 4–5) or using the cursor keys to point to the cells to be included in the formula. The second option could be accomplished by simply pointing to the C10 cell, adding an arithmetic operator (+ in this case), and then pointing to the next cell reference to be included in the formula (C11 in this case) until the formula is complete. Beginners to spreadsheets usually find the pointing method of entering formulas easier.

Arithmetic operators can also be used to add, subtract, multiply, and divide numbers in addition to cells. For example, in addition to a formula using an arithmetic operator to add, subtract, multiply, and divide the values entered into cells (=C10+C11), arithmetic operators can also be used in a formula to add, subtract, multiply, and divide numbers themselves (=100+10). See Exhibit 4–6.

function command
A predefined calculation used in a spreadsheet program to speed up the process of entering complex formulas.

Entering Formulas Using Function Commands Another way to enter formulas is by using function commands. A **function command** is a predefined or preprogrammed calculation that a spreadsheet can perform.

Function commands are designated by an = (equal sign) followed by the function name. For example, in Exhibit 4–7, the SUM function is used to add cells C10, C11, C12, and C13. Notice that the formula in Exhibit 4–7 reads =SUM(C10:C13). This means add the contents of cells C10 through C13. This process of dealing with a group of cells is called entering a range (a range is a group of cells). One powerful feature that spreadsheets can offer is working with a group or range of cells at one time.

When a character or letter is typed into a cell, most spreadsheets assume it is a text entry. Likewise, when a number is typed into a cell, most spreadsheets assume it is a value or number entry on which calculations can be performed.

The procedure to enter text into a cell is simple. A user moves the cell pointer to the cell where the text should be placed. Then the user begins typing the text. As the text is being typed, the characters are displayed in the formula bar and in the cell. After the characters have been typed, the user presses the [ENTER] key to enter the text into the cell. Most spreadsheets also allow the user to enter data into a cell by pressing either the [ENTER] key or any of the four arrow or direction keys.

Text can be edited later by using the edit command. The edit command differs among different spreadsheets programs, but it generally allows a user to correct or change the contents of the cell. The edit command in Microsoft Excel is [F2]. A user can also double-click on a cell to edit it.

Another way to change the contents of an existing cell is to point to the cell to be changed, type new content and enter the new text into the cell. This deletes the existing content and inserts the new content in the same cell. This procedure can be used for changing text, values, or formulas. A user is simply overwriting the old cell.

Values Numbers that are entered into a cell and that can be used in making calculations are **values.** In Exhibit 4–2, the amount listed for each expense item is a value. Values can be entered as either positive or negative numbers. Negative values are usually represented with parentheses around them or a negative sign before them. For example, if you wanted to enter negative 20,000, the spreadsheet would show either (20,000) or <–>20,000.

values
Numbers that are entered into a spreadsheet program for the purpose of making calculations.

Entering a value in a spreadsheet is similar to entering text. First, a user points to the cell where the value should be placed. Then the user types the value. As the value is being typed, the characters are usually displayed in the formula bar and in the cell. After the value has been typed, the user presses the [ENTER] key or a cursor key on the keyboard to enter the label into the cell. In Exhibit 4–5, notice that no commas or dollar signs are shown. A separate command is used to enter formatting codes. This will be covered later in this chapter.

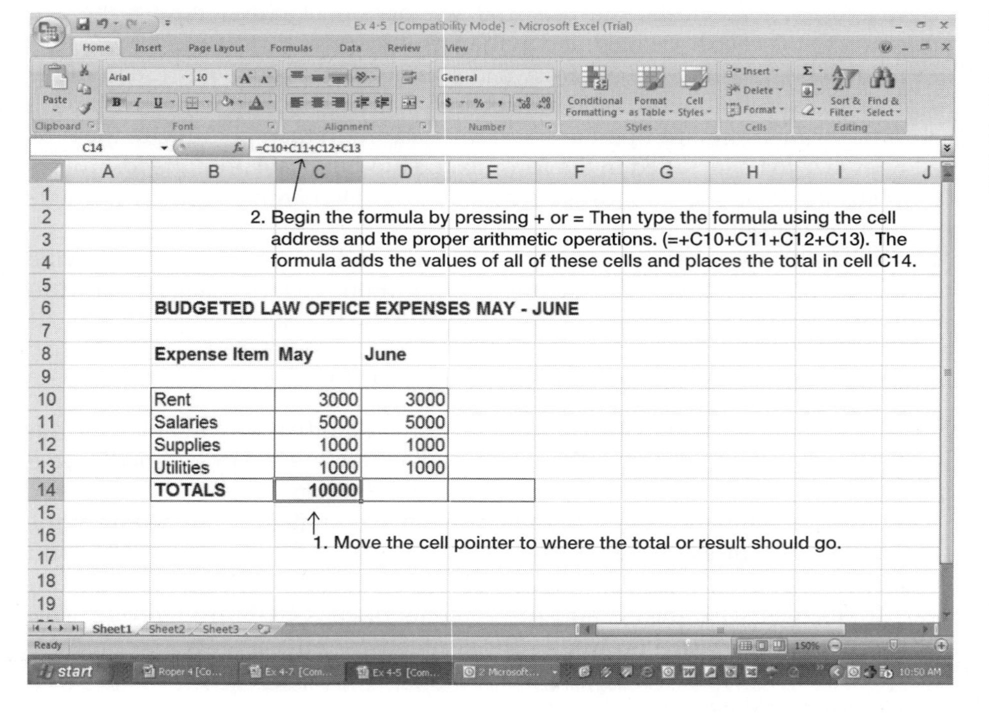

Exhibit 4–5
Entering Arithmetic Operator Formulas

Microsoft product screen shot reprinted with permission from Microsoft Corporation.

Exhibit 4–4A

Roper's Excel 2003 Quick Reference Guide

STANDARD TOOLBAR

NAVIGATION

Up 1 Screen	[Page Up]	To Cell A1	[Ctrl]+[Home]
Down 1 Screen	[Page Down]	To Last Cell With Data	[Ctrl]+[End]
Beginning of a Row	[Home]	Go To	[F5]
Cell Below Current Cell	[Enter]	1 Screen To The Left	[ALT]+[Page Up]
		1 Screen To The Right	[ALT]+[Page Down]

KEYBOARD SHORTCUTS

Copy Text	[Ctrl]+[C]	Undo a Command	[Ctrl]+[Z]
Paste Text	[Ctrl]+[V]	Redo/Repeat	[Ctrl]+[Y]
Cut Text	[Ctrl]+[X]	Print a Workbook	[Ctrl]+[P]
Bold Text	[Ctrl]+[B]	Save a Workbook	[Ctrl]+[S]
Underline Text	[Ctrl]+[U]	Open a Workbook	[Ctrl]+[O]
Italics Text	[Ctrl]+[I]	Find/Replace	[Ctrl]+[F]
Edit a Cell	[F2]	Absolute Cell Reference	F4

EXCEL FEATURES	COMMAND STRUCTURE
Absolute Cell Reference	(=B10*$A$1); $ signs represent an absolute cell reference; the [F4] key will insert the $ signs in a formula.
Adjusting Column Width or Row Height	Drag the right border of the column header or the bottom border of the row header. Double-click to auto fit the column/row.
Autofill	Point at the fill handle of the bottom corner of the cell(s), then drag it to the destination cells(s).
Chart	**Insert>Chart**
Clear Cell Contents	**[DEL]** or **Edit>Clear>Contents Del**
Clear Format	**Edit>Clear>Format**
Delete Row/Column	**Edit>Delete**
Edit a Cell	Select the cell and click the Formula Bar to edit the contents.
Find and Replace	**Edit>Find** or **Edit>Replace**
Fit to One Page	**File>Page Setup>Fit to 1 page**
Format Cells	**Format>Cells>(Number, Alignment, Font**, etc.)
Formula	Select the cell where you want the formula, press = (equal), and enter the formula, and press [Enter] when done (e.g., =A1+A2; =A1*10). Excel performs operations in this order: ( ), :, %, ^, * and /, + and -.
Freeze Pane	**Window>Freeze Pane**
Functions	**Insert>Function**
Hide/Unhide a Column	Right-click **Column Header>Hide**; right-click **Header>Unhide**
Insert a Row/Column	**Insert>Row** or **Insert>Column**
Macro	**Tools>Macro**
Page Breaks for Printing	**View>Page Break Preview>** drag page break indicator line to where you want the page break to occur. **View>Normal** when completed.
Password Protect	**File>Save>Tools>General Options>Password to Open**
Total a Cell Range	Click the cell where you want the total inserted, click the autosum icon on the toolbar, verify the range and press [Enter].
Worksheet Tab Name	Right-click on **Tab Name>Rename**
Wrap Text	**Format>Cells>Alignment>Wrap Text**

Exhibit 4–4

Roper's Excel 2007 Quick Reference Guide

HOME RIBBON

Home Button, Quick Access Toolbar, Font, Fill color, Font color, Font orientation, Wrap Text, Ribbon Tabs, Number Format, Insert cells, Autofill, Sum, Sort, Help, Cut, Paste, Copy, Find/Select, Format Painter, Bold, Italic, Underline, Borders, Format Cells Dialog Box Launcher, Left, Center, Right, Merge Center, Increase decimal, Decrease decimal, Delete cells, Format Rows/Columns, Clear

NAVIGATION

Up One Screen	[Page Up]	To Cell A1	[Ctrl]+[Home]
Down One Screen	[Page Down]	To Last Cell With Data	[Ctrl]+[End]
Beginning of a Row	[Home]	Go To	[F5]
Cell Below Current Cell	[Enter]		

KEYBOARD SHORTCUTS

Copy Text	[Ctrl]+[C]	Undo a Command	[Ctrl]+[Z]
Paste Text	[Ctrl]+[V]	Redo/Repeat	[Ctrl]+[Y]
Cut Text	[Ctrl]+[X]	Print a Workbook	[Ctrl]+[P]
Bold Text	[Ctrl]+[B]	Save a Workbook	[Ctrl]+[S]
Underline Text	[Ctrl]+[U]	Open a Workbook	[Ctrl]+[O]
Italics Text	[Ctrl]+[I]	Find/Replace	[Ctrl]+[F]
Edit a Cell	[F2]	Absolute Cell Reference	F4

EXCEL FEATURES	COMMAND STRUCTURE
Absolute Cell Reference	(=B10*a1); $ signs represent an absolute cell reference, the F4 key will insert the $ signs in a formula.
Adjusting Column Width or Row Height	Drag the right border of the column header or the bottom border of the row header. Double-click to Auto Fit the column/row. Or **Home>Cells>Format>Cell Size**
Autofill	Point to the fill handle of the bottom corner of the cell(s), then drag to the destination cells(s).
Chart	**Insert>Charts>**
Clear Cell Contents	DEL key or **Home>Editing** group>**Clear, Clear Contents**
Clear Format	**Home>Editing>Clear>Clear Formats**
Delete Row/Column	**Home>Cells>Delete**
Edit a Cell	Select the cell and click the Formula Bar to edit the contents or press F2
Find and Replace	**Home>Editing>Find & Select>Find or Replace**
Fit to One Page	**Page Layout> Scale to Fit Dialog Box Launcher>Fit To**
Format Cells	**Home>Font>Font Dialog Box Launcher>**or Right-click **Format Cells**
Formula	Select the cell where you want the formula, press = (equal), enter the formula, and press [enter] when done (e.g., =a1+a2; =a1*10). Excel performs operations in this order: ( ), :, %, ^, * and /, + and -.
Freeze Pane	**View>Window>Freeze Panes**
Functions	Click **Insert Function** icon next to the Formula Bar; or **Formulas> Function Library>Insert function**
Hide/Unhide a Column	Right-click **Column Header>Hide**; right-click **Header>Unhide;** or **View>Window>Hide**
Insert Row/Column	**Home>Cells>insert**
Macro	**View>Macros>Macros**
Page Breaks for Printing	**Page Layout>Page Setup>Breaks** or **View>Workbook Views> Page Break Preview;** Drag page break Indicator line to where you want the page break to occur.
Password Protect	**Office Button, Save>Tools>General Options>Password to Open**
Total a Cell Range	Click the cell where you want the total inserted, click the autosum icon (**Home**, **Editing, Sum** icon), verify the range, and press [Enter].
Worksheet Tab Name	Click Sheet1 name and type over it to rename
Wrap Text	**Format>Cells>Alignment>Wrap Text**

Exhibit 4–9
Copying Formulas
Relative Cell References
Microsoft product screen shots reprinted with permission from Microsoft Corporation.

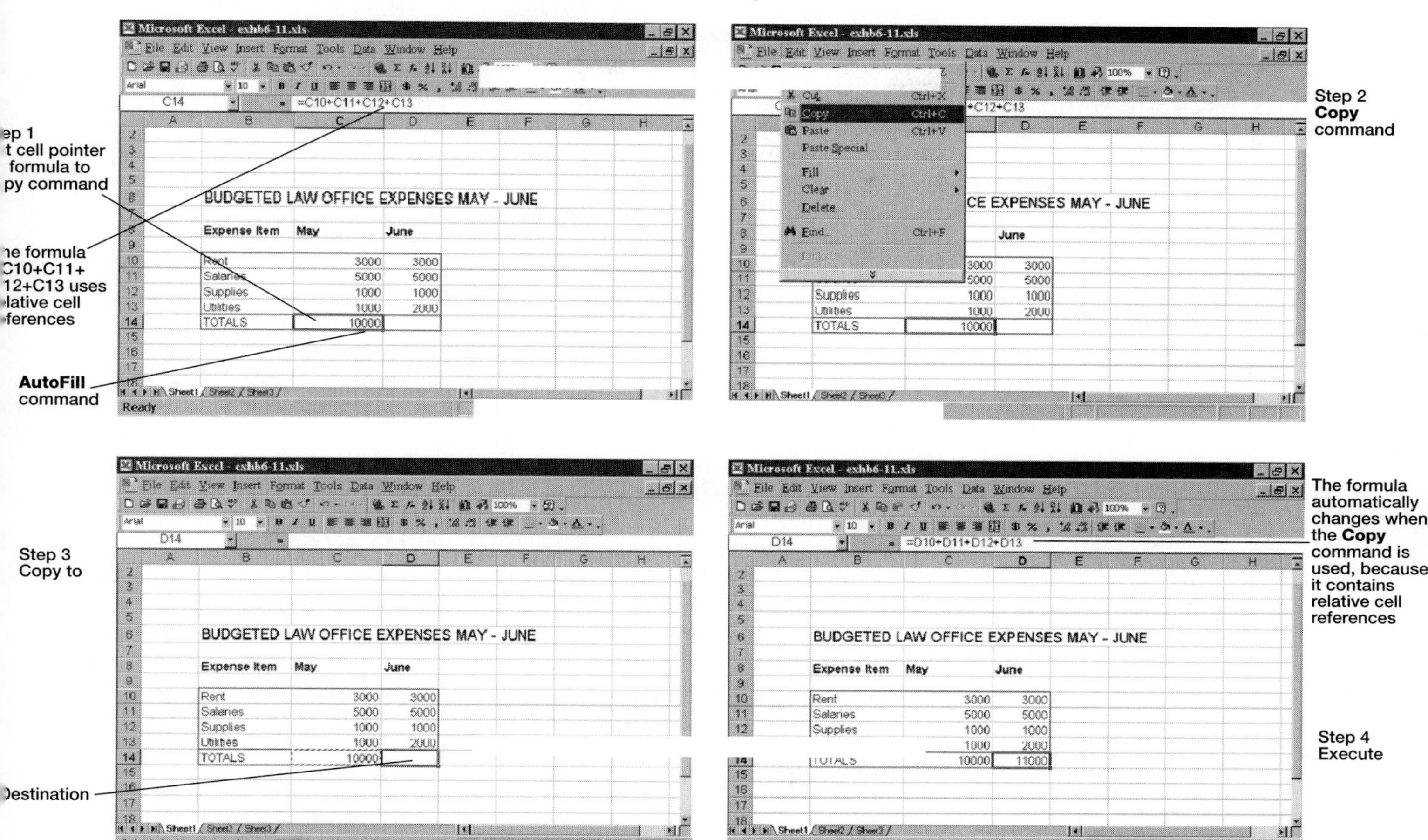

Another way to do this is to place the mouse over the information to be copied, right-click, and click **Copy.** The user then moves the pointer to the new location and presses [ENTER]. An even more convenient way to copy information (as long as the cells are adjacent to one another) is to use the AUTOFILL command. Notice in the first screen in Exhibit 4–9 that the pointer is on cell C14. Notice in the lower right corner of the pointer that there is a small box. To copy data, put the pointer on the cell you want to copy, position the pointer over the AutoFill box, drag it to the adjacent cells where the information is to be copied, and release the mouse button. The information is automatically copied. The AutoFill command also works with ranges of cells.

Copying Formulas Copying formulas is beneficial and a great time-saver. The process for copying formulas is exactly the same as for copying data generally, but it is important that a user understand *how* formulas are copied.

Exhibit 4–9 shows an example of copying a formula from C14 to D14. Notice that the utilities expense has been increased to 2,000 for the month of June (from 1,000 in May), thus making 11,000 the correct total for June expenses. Also note that even though the formula was copied from C14 to D14, the correct total of 11,000 is shown in D14.

Most new users assume that if the formula in C14, which is +C10+C11+ C12+C13, is copied to D14, the formula in cell D14 will read "+C10+C11+

absolute cell reference
A cell address in a spreadsheet program formula that does not change when it is copied to a new location.

relative cell reference
A cell address in a spreadsheet program formula that automatically changes to reflect its new location when it is copied.

C12+C13" and will put the wrong total of 10,000 in the cell. This would happen if a formula used absolute cell references. An **absolute cell reference** is a cell address that does not change when it is copied to a new location. Absolute references can be placed in a formula in most spreadsheets using the dollar sign (e.g., $D$10+$D$11+$D$12+$D$13). This would give the result most people expect.

However, most spreadsheets assume that users want a relative cell reference. A **relative cell reference** is a cell address that will automatically change to reflect its new location when it is copied. For example, look again at Exhibit 4–9. The formula in C14 is a relative cell reference. So, when it is copied to D14, the spreadsheet automatically changes it to read "+D10+D11+D12+D13." Thus, once a formula is entered, it can be copied time and time again instead of being entered from scratch each time.

Suppose a relative cell reference/formula of "=C10+C11" was placed in cell C12. C12 is where the total formula will go. The relative cell reference in C12 actually tells the computer to "go to the cell two rows up from C12 (which is C10) and add the value in it to the value in the cell one row up from C12 (which is C11)." Thus, when a relative cell reference is copied it is just telling the computer how many cells to go up and over. The only thing that has changed is where the formula will be copied to. So, in our example, if the user copied the formula in C12 to D12, the computer would go to the cell two rows up from D12 (which is D10) and add the value in it to the value in the cell one row up from D12 (which is D11). The formula in Exhibit 4–9 is a relative cell reference.

There are times when a user must use an absolute cell reference, such as in Exhibit 4–10. In Exhibit 4–10, the formulas in cells F7–F10 all use a combined relative cell reference and an absolute cell reference. To calculate cells F7–F10 (the 2008 salary) in Exhibit 4–10 the user must take the salary in cells E7–E10 (the 2007 salary) times the salary increase figure in E4 (104.50 percent). Notice in Exhibit 4–10 that cell G7 shows the formula for cell F7. The formula in F7 shows "E7" (which is a relative cell reference—meaning go one cell over to the left) "*" (times) "$E$4" (the dollar signs mean that this is an absolute cell reference—no matter where this formula is copied to, the application will go one cell over to the left and always multiply it times the value in the cell E4). If a relative cell reference were used for cell F7 it would read "E7*E4." This would tell the application to take the

Exhibit 4–10
Absolute Cell References
Microsoft product screen shot reprinted with permission from Microsoft Corporation.

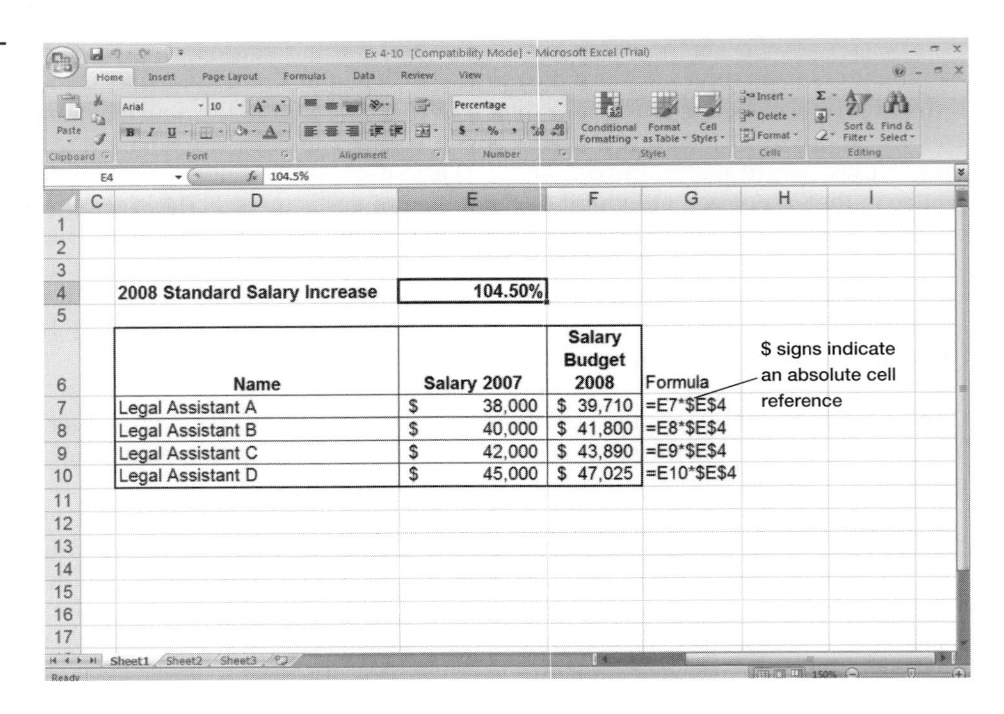

cell one row over to the left times the cell three rows up and one column over. This would work fine for cell F7. But if cell F7 were copied to cell F8 (or F9 or F10) the formula would not work anymore. This is because in cell F8 the computer would take the cell one row over to the left (which is E8–that is correct) times the cell three rows up and one column over (which is cell E5). Notice that there is nothing entered into cell E5; it is blank. The computer would enter $40,000 ($40,000 * 0 = $40,000). Thus, the only way for the second part of the formula to work is to always (absolutely) reference cell E4. By the time the formula got to cell F10, the results would be very bad. The formula would take cell E10 (one cell over to the left), $45,000 (which is correct) times cell E7 (three rows up and one column over), $38,000. The result would be $1,710,000 instead of the correct answer of $47,025. Copying formulas with relative cell references is covered in detail in Lesson 1 of the Hands-On Exercises at the end of the chapter. Copying formulas with absolute cell references is covered in Lesson 4.

Moving Data Moving data is similar to copying data. First, the user points to the cell to be moved, selects **Edit**, and then selects **Cut.** The user then points to the location where the information is to be moved and presses [ENTER]. Another way to do this is to point to the cell to be moved, right-click, and then select **Cut**. The user would then move the pointer to the new location and press [ENTER].

Inserting Rows and Columns It is sometimes necessary to go back and insert additional rows and columns into a spreadsheet. If, for example, a user wants to insert an expense item (such as an equipment expense item) in Exhibit 4–7 he or she can do this easily. To insert a row or a column, the user moves the cell pointer to where the new row or column should be inserted. Then the user executes the Insert Row or Insert Column command. One new row or column is inserted. To insert more than one row or column, drag the pointer down or over the number of rows or columns you want to add, right click and select Insert. Extreme caution should be used when inserting rows and columns after formulas have been created, because it is possible for the fomulas to not include the new row or column.

Sorting Data Sorting is the process of placing things in a particular order. Spreadsheets, like databases, can sort information. They can sort either values or text in ascending or descending order. In Exhibit 4–11, before sorting, the expense items are not in alphabetical order. To sort data, a user marks the data range of the information to be sorted, executes the Sort command (in Excel the user points to **Data** and clicks **Sort**), and then indicates which column to sort the data on and whether the information is to be sorted in ascending or descending order. In Exhibit 4–11, the data range must include not only the Expense Item column, but also the May and June columns. If the May and June columns were not included in the data range, the spreadsheet would put the expense items in alphabetical order, but would not move the corresponding dollar amounts. In Exhibit 4–11, with the data range properly selected, the user executes the **Sort** command, instructs the computer to sort the data by Column B, which is the Expense Item, in ascending order, and then selects **OK.** The spreadsheet responds by placing the expense items and corresponding dollar amounts in alphabetical order.

Formatting Cells Most spreadsheet programs allow a user to indicate which format or type of values has been entered. For example, in Exhibit 4–11, the values in the spreadsheet should be represented in dollars.

To change the format of the content of the cells to dollars, the user would drag the pointer over the cells to be changed and execute the format cells command (in Excel 2007 or 2003 the command is right click and then select Format Cells). In Exhibit 4–12, notice that when the format cells command is initiated the user

Exhibit 4–11
Sorting Data
Screen shot reprinted with permission from Microsoft Corporation.

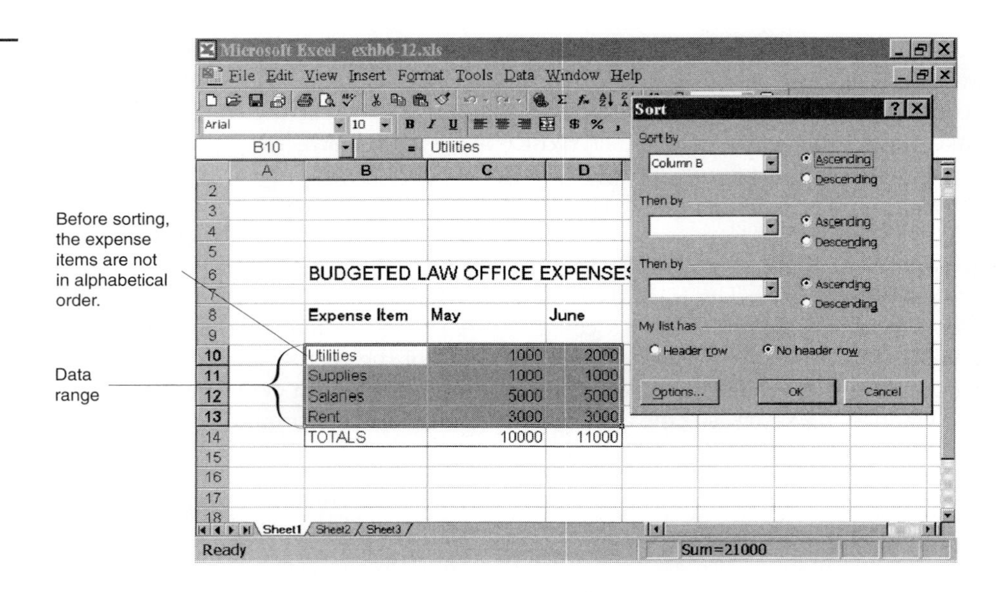

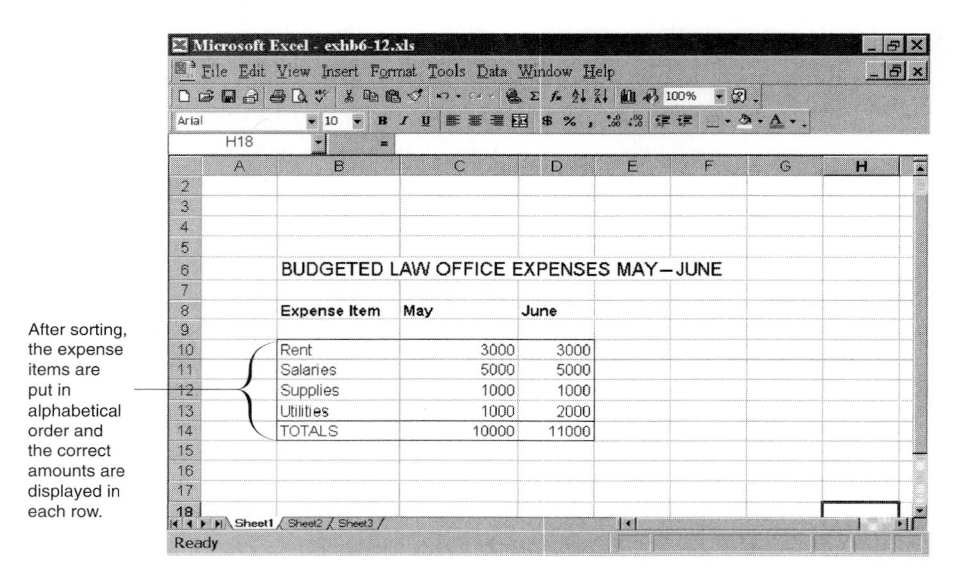

selects **Currency** and zero decimal places. The user then selects OK and the cell values automatically are changed to dollar signs. Also, notice in Exhibit 4–12 that numbers can be formatted as percentages and other expressions. Most spreadsheets can change the format of cells in many ways, such as alignment, fonts and type sizes, borders, and patterns or backgrounds. Formatting cells is covered in detail in all lessons of the Hands-On Exercises at the end of the chapter.

Saving and Retrieving Files Spreadsheets can be saved and retrieved for later use, just as word-processing files and database files can. When working with any program, users should save their work often.

Printing Reports All spreadsheet programs allow for the printing of spreadsheets. Printing large spreadsheets with many columns used to be difficult, because only a limited number of columns could be printed on a page. It often meant taping pages together. Now, however, most spreadsheets and printers allow pages to print in a condensed or compressed mode as well. This means

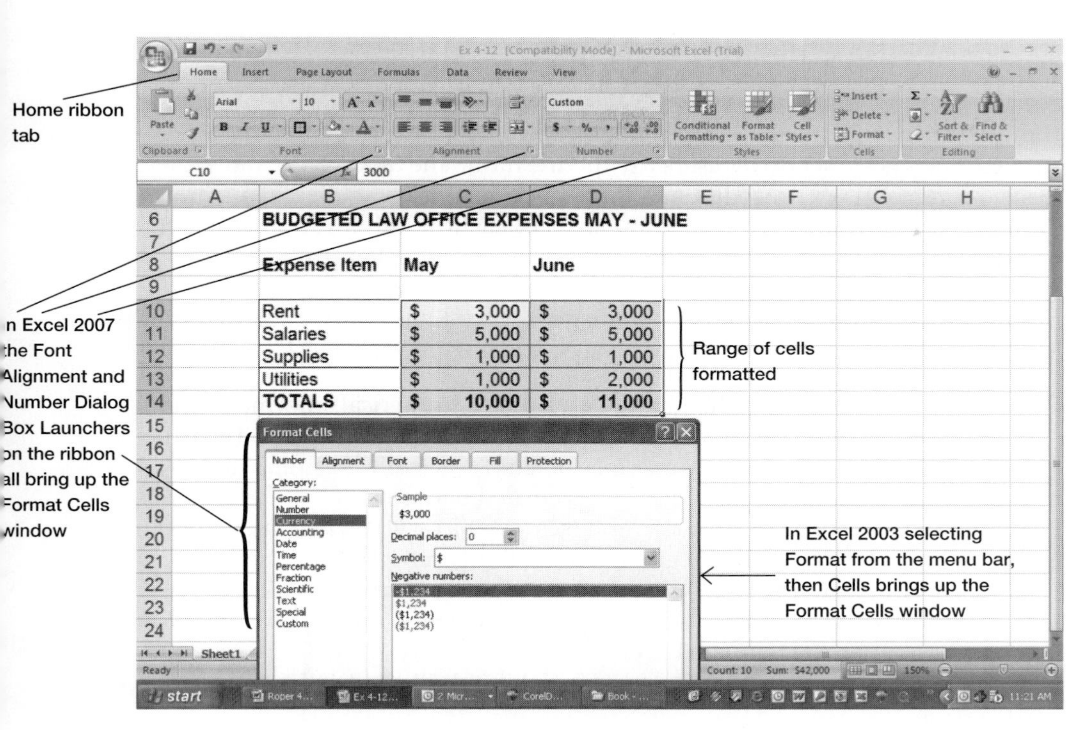
Home ribbon tab
n Excel 2007
he Font
Alignment and
Number Dialog
Box Launchers
on the ribbon
all bring up the
Format Cells
window
BUDGETED LAW OFFICE EXPENSES MAY - JUNE
Expense Item May June
Rent $ 3,000 $ 3,000
Salaries $ 5,000 $ 5,000
Supplies $ 1,000 $ 1,000
Utilities $ 1,000 $ 2,000
TOTALS $ 10,000 $ 11,000
Range of cells formatted
Format Cells
In Excel 2003 selecting Format from the menu bar, then Cells brings up the Format Cells window

Exhibit 4–12
Formatting Cells
Microsoft product screen shot reprinted with permission from Microsoft Corporation.

that the data is printed smaller than normal, and it allows more information to be printed on a page. In Exhibit 4–13 notice that one of the options is the **Fit to** command. This option allows the user to automatically compress a print selection into a certain number of pages, including being able to compress a print selection into one page.

Most spreadsheets allow the user to change margins, add headers or footers, indicate whether the page should be printed in portrait or landscape mode,

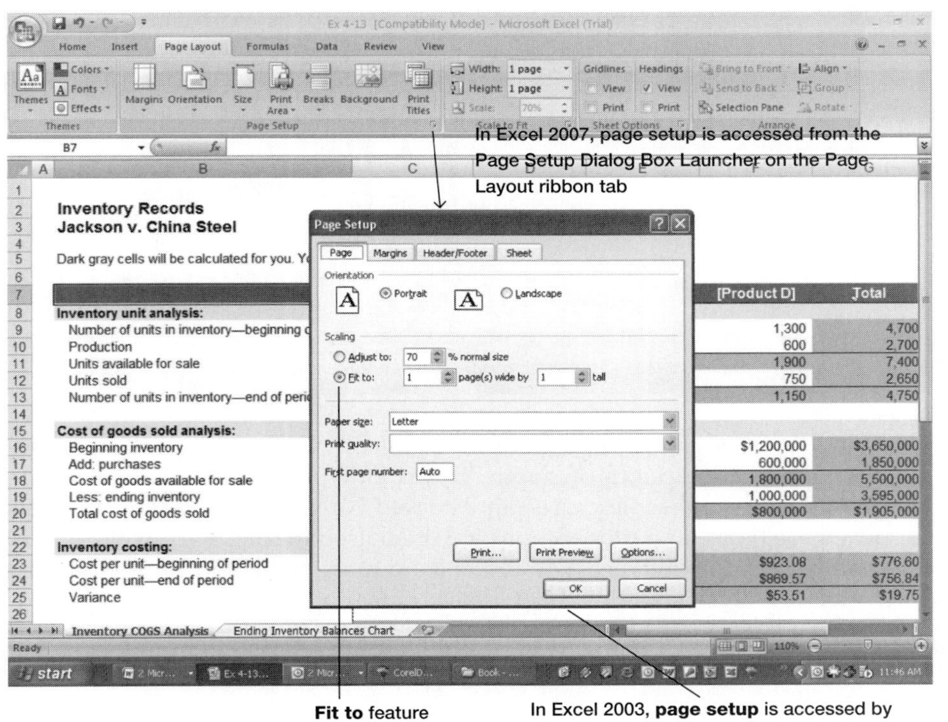
In Excel 2007, page setup is accessed from the Page Setup Dialog Box Launcher on the Page Layout ribbon tab
Inventory Records
Jackson v. China Steel
Page Setup
Fit to feature
In Excel 2003, page setup is accessed by choosing Page Setup from the File menu

Exhibit 4–13
Page Setup Print Options in Excel
Microsoft product screen shot reprinted with permission from Microsoft Corporation.

portrait
A method of printing that arranges data down the length of a page.

landscape
A method of printing that arranges data across the width of a page.

macro
A previously saved group of commands or keystrokes that, when invoked, replays those commands or keystrokes.

and so on. **Portrait** refers to printing down the length of the page, whereas **landscape** refers to printing across the width of the page. (See Exhibit 4–13).

Using Macros A **macro** is a previously saved group of commands or keystrokes. Macros are set up by users to expedite mundane tasks. They allow users to save commands or procedures so that they can be used again and again. For example, if you routinely print a spreadsheet each month a certain way, you could write a macro that would automatically save the keystrokes and commands it comprises. This way, you could print the spreadsheet by running the macro, instead of reentering the commands every time you wanted to print. Macros are a powerful tool that can be used to save time and work faster.

Charting and Graphing The ability to visualize numerical information in a spreadsheet is beneficial. Most spreadsheet programs have graphing and charting capabilities built into them. After a graph (or chart—we will use graph and chart interchangeably) has been created, a link is created between the numerical information in the spreadsheet and the graph (see Exhibit 4–14). When the values in the spreadsheet are changed, the graph automatically reflects those changes.

Most spreadsheet programs have a chart wizard feature that takes the user through a step-by-step process and gives the user many options on how to set up a chart. Creating a chart in an Excel spreadsheet is easy. First, drag the pointer over the data that you want charted (see Exhibit 4–14) and then click on the Chart Wizard.

Exhibit 4–14
Linking the Values in a Spreadsheet with a Graph (Column Chart)
Microsoft product screen shot reprinted with permission from Microsoft Corporation.

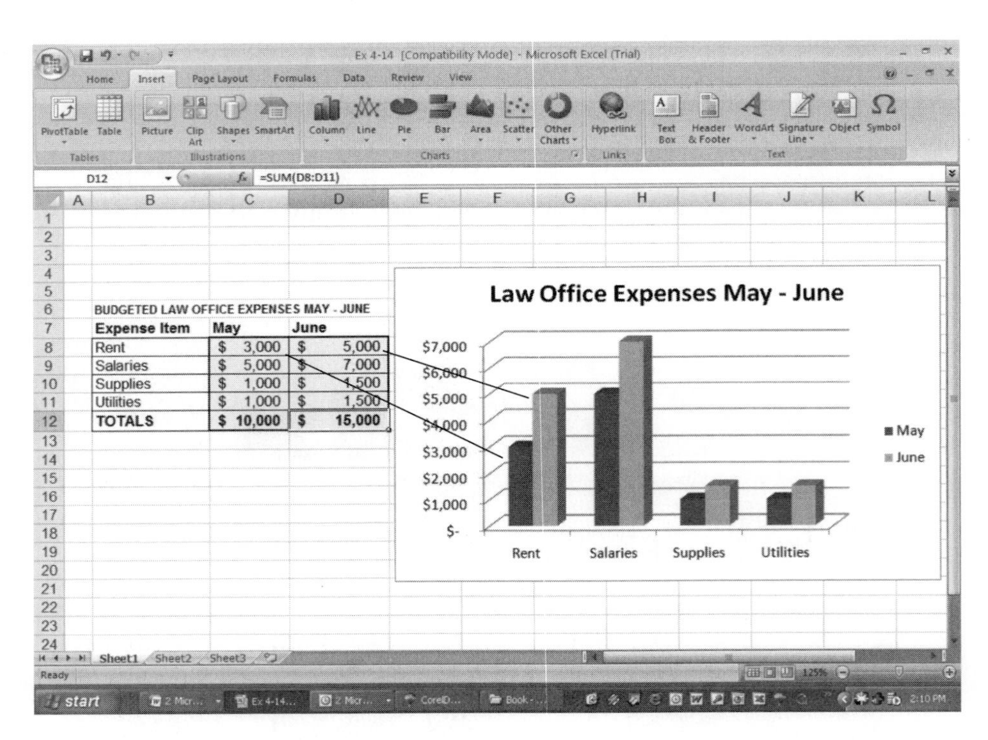

Many types of graphs and charts are available. Different spreadsheet programs support various kinds of graphs. The major types of graphs and charts are bar graphs, line graphs, pie charts, and stacked bar graphs. Most spreadsheets support these types of graphs. Graphs are often used in trials to convey complicated numerical data in an easy-to-understand manner. Lesson 2 in the Hands-On Exercises at the end of this chapter covers creating a chart.

bar/column graph
A graph that consists of a sequence of bars that illustrate numerical values.

Bar/Column Graph A **bar/column graph** consists of a sequence of bars that illustrate numerical values. Bar or column graphs are common and can be either

horizontal or vertical. Vertical bar or column graphs have bars that go straight up the page (see Exhibit 4–14), and horizontal bar graphs have bars that go across the page. Bar graphs are best used for comparing values at a specific point in time. For example, the bar graph in Exhibit 4–14 compares the office expenses for the months of May and June.

Bar graphs have many uses in legal organizations. A bar graph might be used in a personal injury case to illustrate the large earning potential of a person before an accident and their reduced earning potential after the accident. A bar graph might also be used in a breach of contract case to show the profits a business was making before the breach of contract compared with the reduced profits it made after the breach.

Line Graph A **line graph** plots the course of a value over time. In the line graph in Exhibit 4–15, each line represents a month's worth of expenses. Because line graphs plot changes over time, they are useful for plotting trends. For example, in Exhibit 4–15, notice that each expense item listed rose in the month of June. This is a trend.

line graph
A graph that plots numerical values as a time line.

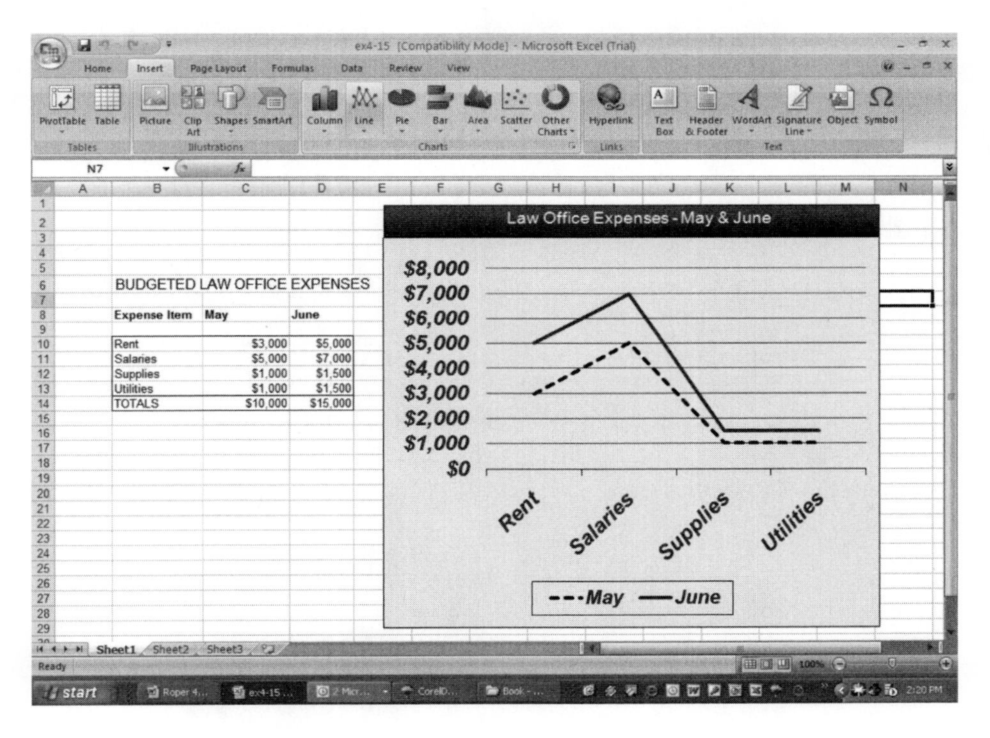

Exhibit 4–15
Line Graph
Microsoft product screen shot reprinted with permission from Microsoft Corporation.

Pie Chart A **pie chart** represents each value as a piece or percentage of a total pie. In Exhibit 4–16, each expense item represents a slice of the pie, with the whole pie representing the total amount of expenses for the month of May. This chart shows that salaries are the biggest piece (or expense) of the pie (or the firm's total expenses). Pie charts are best used for showing the relative contributions of various pieces that go to make up a whole.

pie chart
A chart that represents each value as a piece or percentage of a total "pie."

Stacked Bar Graph A **stacked bar graph** compares data by placing bars on top of one another. Like a pie chart, a stacked bar graph shows the relative contributions of various elements to a whole. The difference is that rather than showing only a single entity or a single pie, a stacked bar can show several. In Exhibit 4–17, each bar segment represents a month, and each stack of bars represents an expense item. The stacked bar allows a user to see the allocation of an expense item over two months.

stacked bar graph
A graph that depicts values as separate sections in a single or stacked bar.

Exhibit 4–16
Pie Chart Graph
Microsoft product screen shot reprinted with permission from Microsoft Corporation.

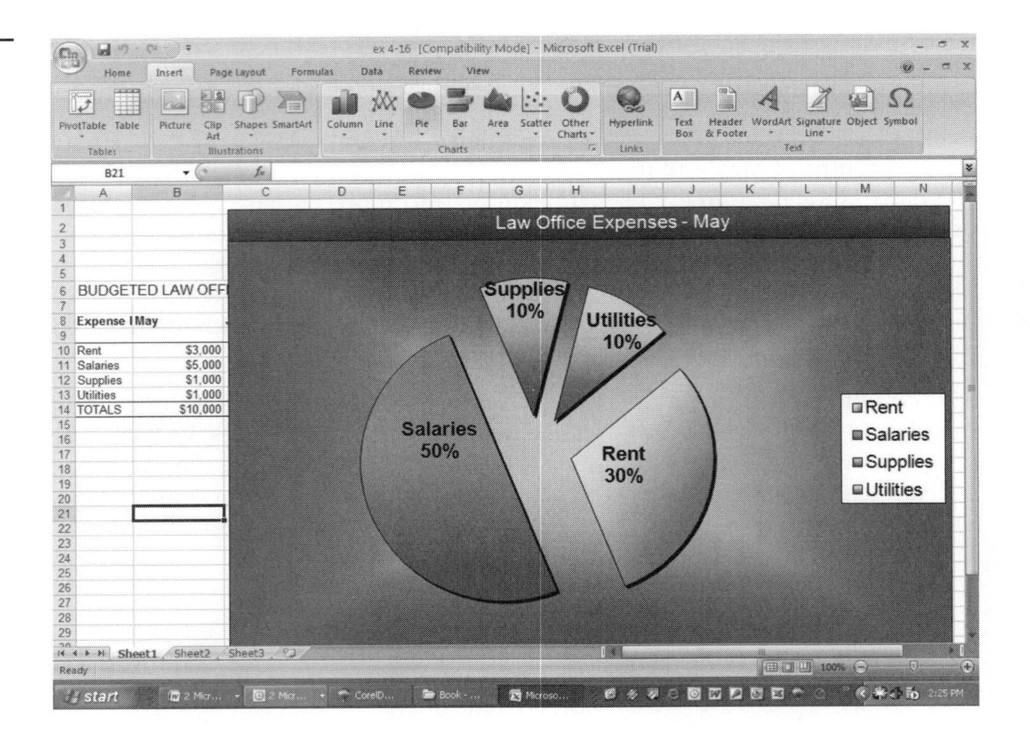

Exhibit 4–17
Stacked Bar Graph
Microsoft product screen shot reprinted with permission from Microsoft Corporation.

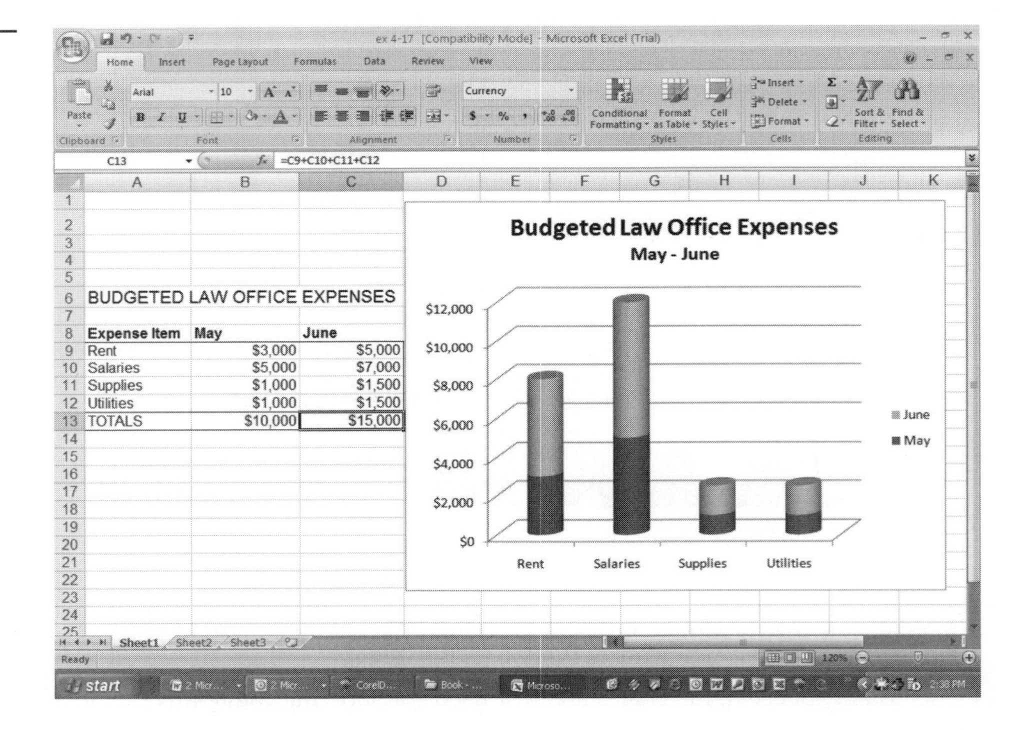

SPREADSHEET PLANNING

Planning is critical to developing a spreadsheet that accomplishes its intended purpose. Most spreadsheets are more complex than the law office expense spreadsheet that was previously used in this chapter. Most people find it helpful to draft a model of a spreadsheet on paper before actually beginning to enter it in the computer. Some of the most complex aspects of creating a spreadsheet

concern the use of formulas. Entering formulas can get complicated quickly, especially when a spreadsheet requires a lot of formulas. Take your time, and plan the formulas out carefully.

This section discusses a few rules to keep in mind when planning and using a spreadsheet.

Keep Your Spreadsheet Simple

Keep your spreadsheet as simple as possible. Complex spreadsheets are more likely to have errors. In addition, other people may have to use the spreadsheet, and a simple design will keep you from spending hours training others. It is also common for even the person who designed a spreadsheet to forget certain aspects of the spreadsheet if she has not worked with it for some time. Finally, use easy-to-understand headings and titles. Say what you mean, and mean what you say. It is confusing to read titles that do not make sense to everyone involved.

Always Document Your Spreadsheet

Always document your spreadsheet well, making notes and narrative statements right in the spreadsheet itself. Always include a section called "Notes" in your spreadsheet. It is common to make assumptions when designing a spreadsheet (such as when entering formulas) and then later forget why or how you made them. Another technique is to add a comment directly to a cell. In Excel and other spreadsheets you can add explanatory text to a cell itself. The Comment tool is a great way to add specific information about a cell, including any assumptions or justifications you have made regarding the value or formula entered. Users can show or hide comments as needed depending on their needs at the time (see Exhibit 4–18). Creating a comment is covered in Lesson 7 of the Hands-On Exercises at the end of the chapter.

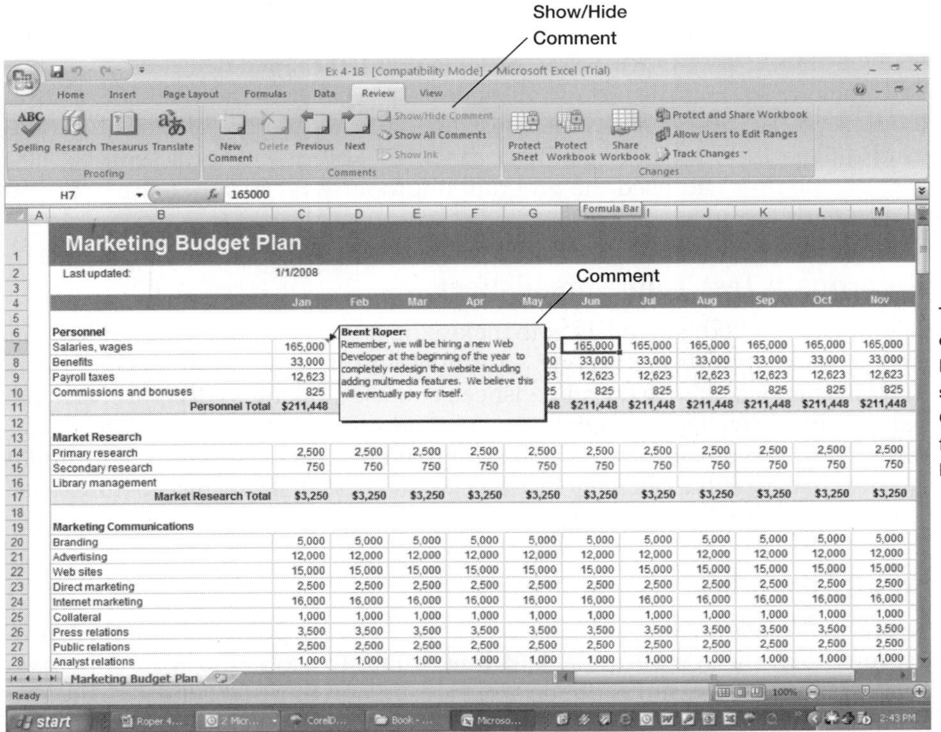

Exhibit 4–18
Adding a Comment to a Cell in Excel
Microsoft product screen shot reprinted with permission from Microsoft Corporation.

To create a comment in Excel 2003, select **Insert> Comment** from the menu bar.

To create a Comment in Excel 2007, select **Review>** New Comment from the menu bar.

Make a Template of Your Spreadsheet

A template is a blank spreadsheet that has had labels and formulas entered, but has no values filled in. Once a template is made and saved, copies of it can be made and given to other users; then the only thing they will have to do is enter the values. Some software companies also sell a variety of predefined templates. A template saves a user from having to rebuild the same spreadsheet over and over. Users can also access free templates online from software providers and other sources.

Leave Room in the Upper Left Corner

Do not start your spreadsheet at cell A1; always leave yourself some room to include additional labels and notes. Start your spreadsheet no closer to the upper left corner than cell C4. This gives you room to add notes, dates, and so forth later on.

Use Cell Widths Wisely

Cell widths should be used wisely. Some people make all their columns twenty characters wide; the problem with this is that they can then see and print only four columns at a time, which makes a spreadsheet difficult to work with. It is better to use narrow columns, which maximize the amount of information you can see and allow the spreadsheet to be printed on one page. For long labels, keep the column width the same size, but wrap the text down to the next line, using the wrap text feature found in most spreadsheets.

Be Careful Inserting Rows and Columns

If you must insert additional rows and columns after a spreadsheet has been designed and entered into the computer, be sure that the formulas you have already entered have been adjusted to take them into account. A celebrated lawsuit was filed against Lotus Development Corporation over this problem. A construction firm designed a spreadsheet to allow it to bid on jobs. Staff would enter job costs into the spreadsheet, and the spreadsheet would calculate what the bid on a job should be. Unfortunately, at some point, the spreadsheet user inserted additional rows, and the old formulas did not pick up, or add, the job costs in the new rows. Subsequently, the construction firm bid several hundred thousand dollars too low on a job. The firm sued Lotus, but Lotus won the suit because the user had used the program improperly. So be sure to go back and look at your formulas.

Rigorously Test Your Spreadsheet

Rigorously test your spreadsheet to make sure it is functioning as intended. It is easy to make a mistake entering a formula, but it is often difficult to find it. Always enter test data in the spreadsheet, and use a calculator to spot check that the formulas have been entered properly and are making the calculations correctly. Most spreadsheets have an option that allows a user to see the formulas entered instead of the calculations (see Exhibit 4–19). This is a nice feature when you are checking the logic and formulas of your spreadsheet.

Audit Formulas

To access this feature in Excel 2003, on the **Tools** menu, point to **Formula Auditing**, and then click on **Formula Auditing Mode**. To access this feature in Excel 2007, point to the **Formulas** ribbon tab, then click on **Show Formulas** in the **Formula Auditing** group.

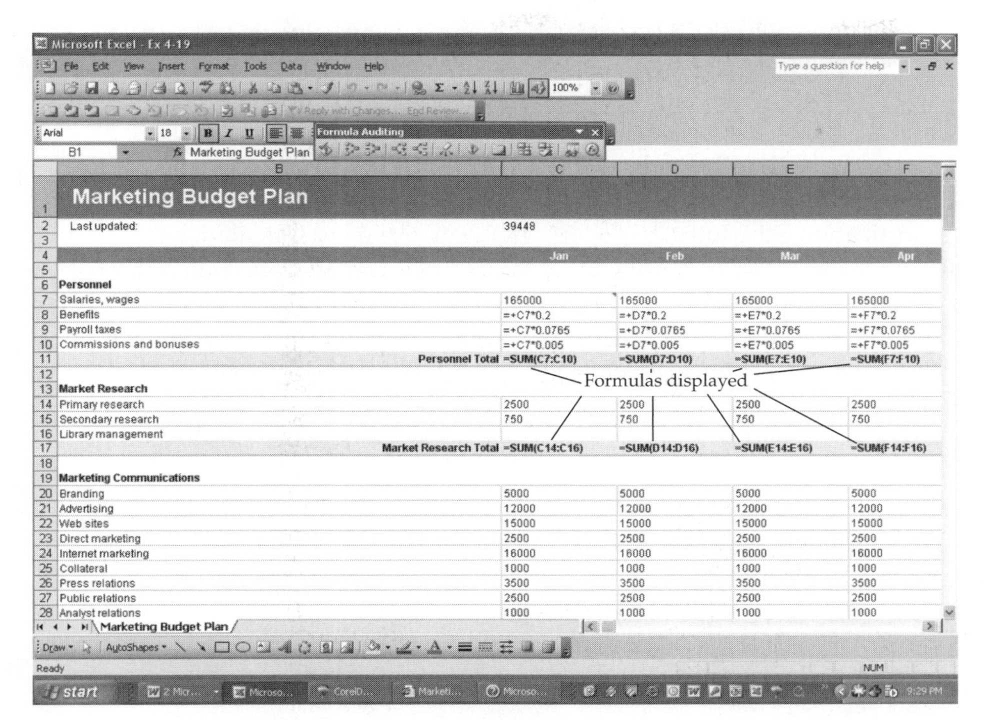

Exhibit 4–19
Formula Auditing Mode in Excel 2003
Microsoft product screen shot reprinted with permission from Microsoft Corporation.

Occasionally Read the Spreadsheet Documentation

Most spreadsheet users employ only a fraction of the commands, operators, and function commands that are available in most spreadsheets. Although the commands covered in this book will get you started with spreadsheets, you will find that as you grow more proficient, many sophisticated features will help you solve tough problems. Take the time occasionally to read the Help features and other documentation for your spreadsheet program to learn more about its functionalities.

SPREADSHEETS IN THE LEGAL ENVIRONMENT

Numerical data is important in the outcome of many types of cases. In some lawsuits, parties hire statisticians to research a matter in hopes that the final statistics or numerical data will support their case. Spreadsheets can be used to analyze statistical findings, look for trends, and so forth. Spreadsheet programs, like word processors and database management systems, are extremely flexible, so it is easy to use them to accomplish all types of tasks. One legal professional stated that the spreadsheet could affect the legal profession as dramatically as the polio vaccine affected medicine. Whether that is true remains to be seen, but spreadsheets undoubtedly have many uses in the legal environment.

The type of law that is practiced will dictate how much a spreadsheet is used and what it is used for. Exhibit 4–20 shows the diversity of how legal organizations use spreadsheets. Once a spreadsheet template has been designed for a given task and saved, it can be copied and used over and over again, with only new values having to be entered, not labels or formulas.

Legal assistants can use spreadsheet programs for calculating damages, budgeting, and so forth. Most of the uses are specific to a particular type of law practice.

Damages Calculations

In many cases, the plaintiff (the person bringing the lawsuit) alleges that he is entitled to money damages—that is, that he should be compensated for

Exhibit 4–20
How Legal Organizations Use Spreadsheets

Tax Planning	Tax Returns
Estate Planning	Calculations for Bankruptcy Actions
Child Support Calculations	Alimony Payments
Divorce Asset Distributions	Truth-in-Lending Statements for Real Estate Transactions
Amortization Schedules	Loan/Payment Calculations
Judgment and Post-Judgment Calculations	Calculations for Collection Actions Regarding Principal and Interest Due
Present Value and Future Value Calculations Regarding Damages	Lost Wages and Benefits Calculations for Worker's Compensation Claims
Budgeting	Accounting-Related Calculations
Litigation Support	Back Wages and Benefits Regarding Employment/Discrimination Actions
Antitrust Calculations Regarding Financial Impact Invoice Preparation	Insurance Actions Regarding the Extent of Losses Invoice Preparation

Exhibit 4—21
Simple Damages Calculation—Excel 2003
Microsoft product screen shot reprinted with permission from Microsoft Corporation.

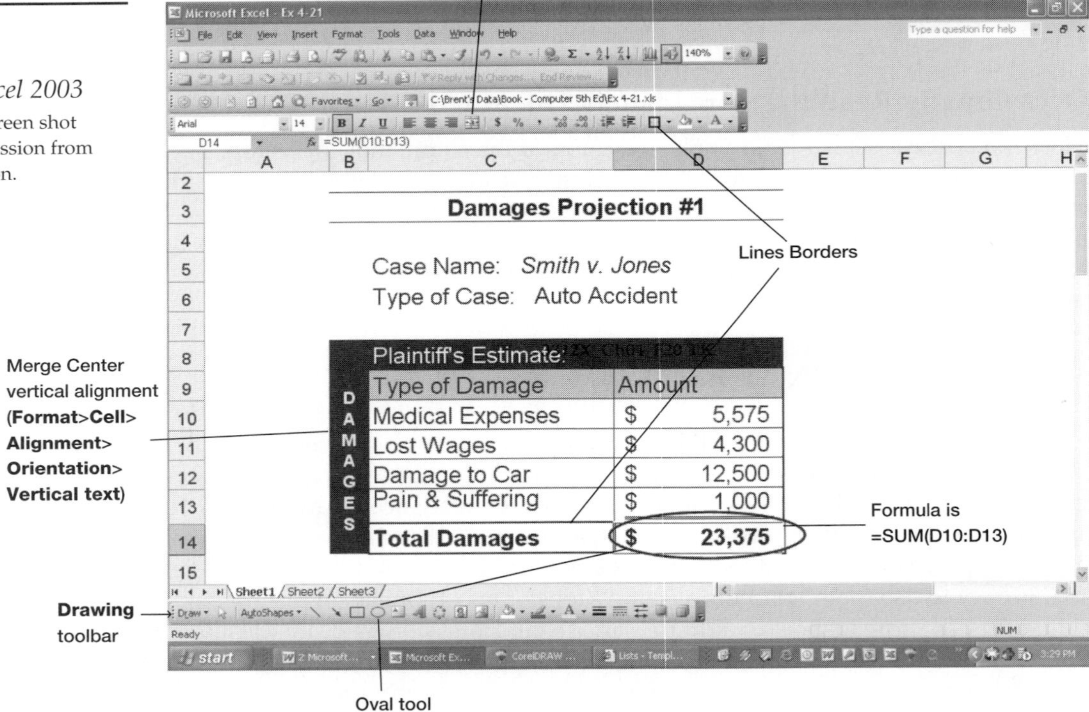

whatever injury was sustained. The amount of damages a person should receive is always in dispute. A spreadsheet allows a user to test different options or assumptions.

A Simple Damages Calculation Exhibit 4–21 is an example of an easy damages projection. Assume you represent the plaintiff, John Smith, in an automobile accident case and you must prepare an exhibit to the jury that shows the amount of damages the plaintiff is seeking. This spreadsheet simply lists the damage items, the amounts asked for, and a total (i.e., a formula using the SUM function).

A More Complex Damages Calculation (Net Present Value) Spreadsheets can handle complex damages calculations as well, as shown in Exhibit 4–22.

Assume Wendyl Jones suffered a severe injury on the job and your firm represents him on his workers' compensation claim. Jones is 59 years old and was going to retire at age 65. Assume that because he is totally disabled, he is entitled to six years of income from his employer. He was making $25,000 a year before he was injured, and on the average, he has received increases of about 2 percent every year. Therefore, in the first year following the accident, assume Jones would have received $25,000, and in every year after that, assume he would have received 2 percent increase. Exhibit 4–22 automatically calculates what his gross earnings would have been until retirement, for a total loss of wages of $157,703.

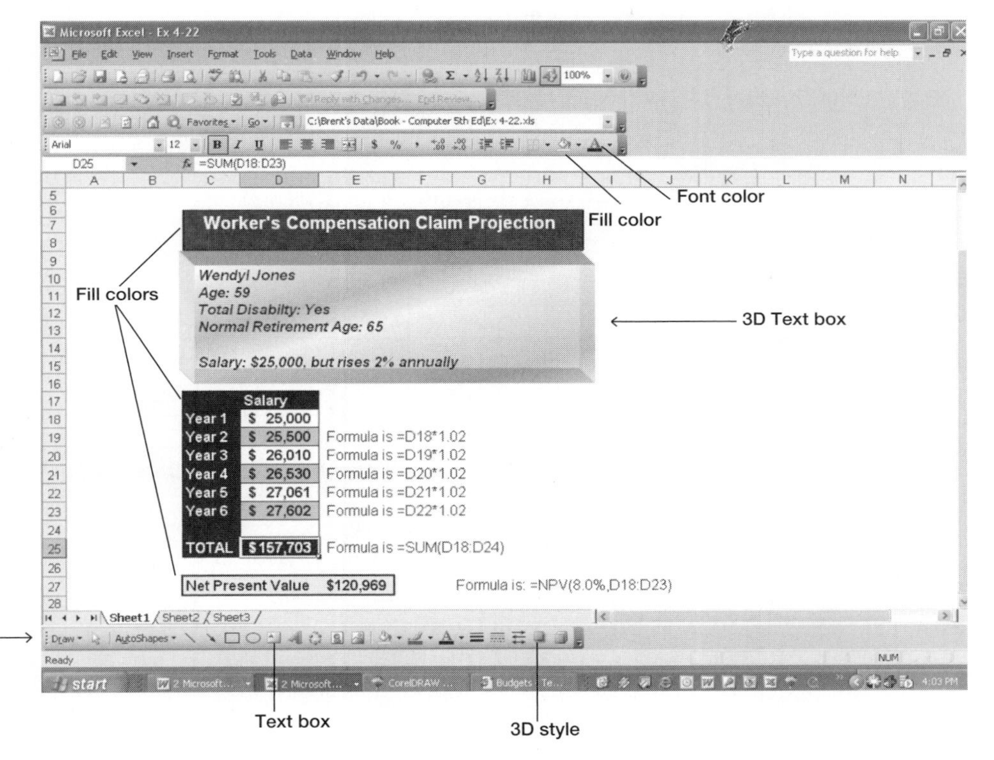

Exhibit 4–22
Complex Damages Calculation—Word 2003
Microsoft product screen shot reprinted with permission from Microsoft Corporation.

Unfortunately, Jones is not entitled to a lump sum payment of $157,703. This is because Jones could take the lump sum payment, invest it at 8 percent, and by the end of the six years, have more than $233,400. Thus, the future payments must be reduced to their present, or current, value. Nearly all spreadsheets have a present value function that accomplishes this task easily. The spreadsheet in Exhibit 4–22 calculates that Jones should be awarded a lump sum payment of $120,969 for future payments worth $157,703.

This type of calculation (reducing a payment schedule to a present value) is also useful when considering different settlement offers or options. Notice in Exhibit 4–22 that a number of graphic elements have been added to the spreadsheet. The spreadsheet includes a number of different fill (background) colors and textures, font sizes, styles, and colors. The spreadsheet also includes a text box that has been formatted in 3-D. These are all standard features in Excel and other spreadsheets. In Excel 2003 these tools can be found on the Standard and

Drawing toolbars (see Exhibit 4–22). In Excel 2007 these features can be found on the Insert ribbon tab. Notice in Exhibit 4-21 that an oval has been added to the spreadsheet around the total and that the word "Damages" appears vertically in the spreadsheet. All of these graphical features are extremely easy to use and can give spreadsheets added visual impact.

Legal Organization Budgeting

Many legal organizations prepare a yearly budget to track expenses and income. The budget is used as a planning tool and as a means of spotting potential problems. Exhibit 4–23 shows that a firm budgeted $12,600 in total expenses for January, but actually spent $12,400. The formula for the Budgeted Total Expenses cell (D28) is =SUM(D20:D27). The formula for the Actual Net Income/Loss cell (E30) is =E17–E28, which means to take the total income minus the total expenses. Some spreadsheet formats show a negative number by placing parentheses around it (see cell K30 in Exhibit 4–23).

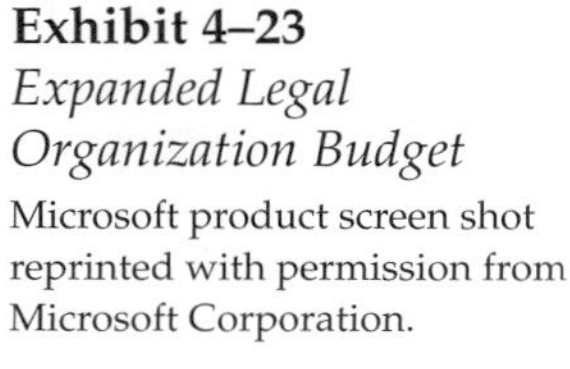

Exhibit 4–23
Expanded Legal Organization Budget
Microsoft product screen shot reprinted with permission from Microsoft Corporation.

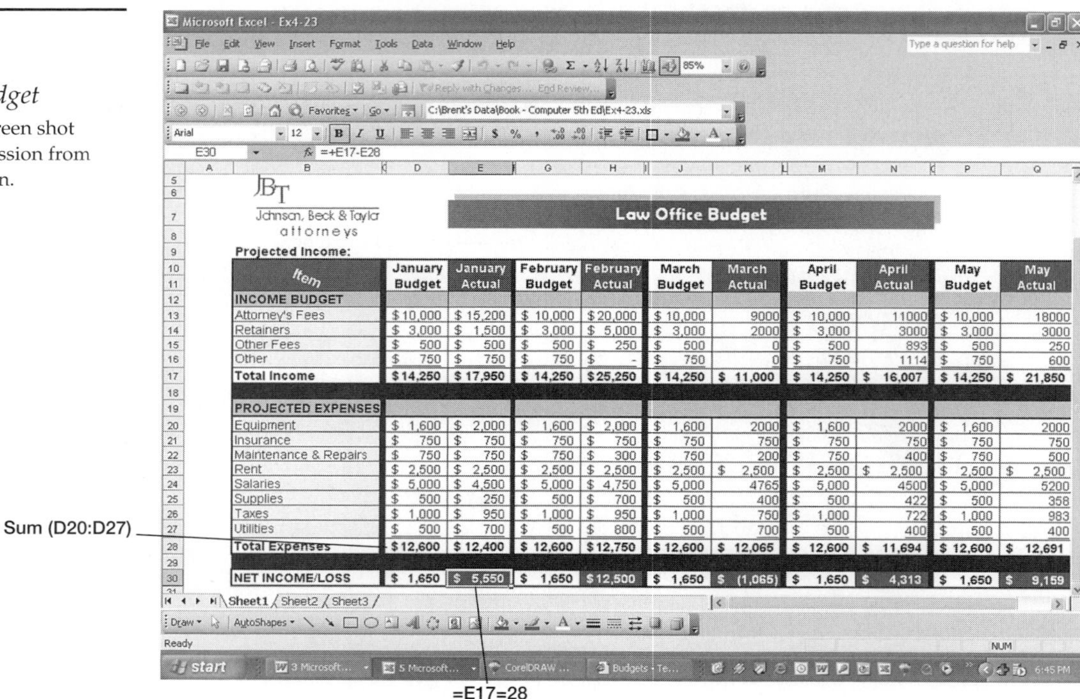

Johnson, Beck & Taylor attorneys

Law Office Budget

Projected Income:

Item	January Budget	January Actual	February Budget	February Actual	March Budget	March Actual	April Budget	April Actual	May Budget	May Actual
INCOME BUDGET										
Attorney's Fees	$10,000	$ 15,200	$ 10,000	$20,000	$ 10,000	9000	$ 10,000	11000	$ 10,000	18000
Retainers	$ 3,000	$ 1,500	$ 3,000	$ 5,000	$ 3,000	2000	$ 3,000	3000	$ 3,000	3000
Other Fees	$ 500	$ 500	$ 500	$ 250	$ 500	0	$ 500	893	$ 500	250
Other	$ 750	$ 750	$ 750	$ -	$ 750	0	$ 750	1114	$ 750	600
Total Income	$14,250	$ 17,950	$ 14,250	$25,250	$ 14,250	$ 11,000	$ 14,250	$ 16,007	$ 14,250	$ 21,850
PROJECTED EXPENSES										
Equipment	$ 1,600	$ 2,000	$ 1,600	$ 2,000	$ 1,600	2000	$ 1,600	2000	$ 1,600	2000
Insurance	$ 750	$ 750	$ 750	$ 750	$ 750	750	$ 750	750	$ 750	750
Maintenance & Repairs	$ 750	$ 750	$ 750	$ 300	$ 750	200	$ 750	400	$ 750	500
Rent	$ 2,500	$ 2,500	$ 2,500	$ 2,500	$ 2,500	$ 2,500	$ 2,500	$ 2,500	$ 2,500	$ 2,500
Salaries	$ 5,000	$ 4,500	$ 5,000	$ 4,750	$ 5,000	4765	$ 5,000	4500	$ 5,000	5200
Supplies	$ 500	$ 250	$ 500	$ 700	$ 500	400	$ 500	422	$ 500	358
Taxes	$ 1,000	$ 950	$ 1,000	$ 950	$ 1,000	750	$ 1,000	722	$ 1,000	983
Utilities	$ 500	$ 700	$ 500	$ 800	$ 500	700	$ 500	400	$ 500	400
Total Expenses	$12,600	$ 12,400	$ 12,600	$12,750	$12,600	$ 12,065	$ 12,600	$ 11,694	$ 12,600	$ 12,691
NET INCOME/LOSS	$ 1,650	$ 5,550	$ 1,650	$12,500	$ 1,650	$ (1,065)	$ 1,650	$ 4,313	$ 1,650	$ 9,159

Real Estate Law

Spreadsheets are particularly helpful for legal organizations that practice in the real estate field. Two examples of spreadsheets used in this field are a real esate closing statement and an amortization schedule.

Real Estate Closing Statement For legal assistants working in the real estate field, a template similar to Exhibit 4–24 could be made to calculate closing costs. In Exhibit 4–24, the cost of the real estate (payable to the seller) is $50,000. However, the buyer has already paid $10,000 down as earnest money. In addition, the buyer will have to pay off the first mortgage on the property and will pay the title insurance costs and reimburse the seller for taxes the seller has already paid through April. Because many of these costs are really the seller's costs, they will be credited to the buyer. Therefore, when all is said and done, the buyer will have

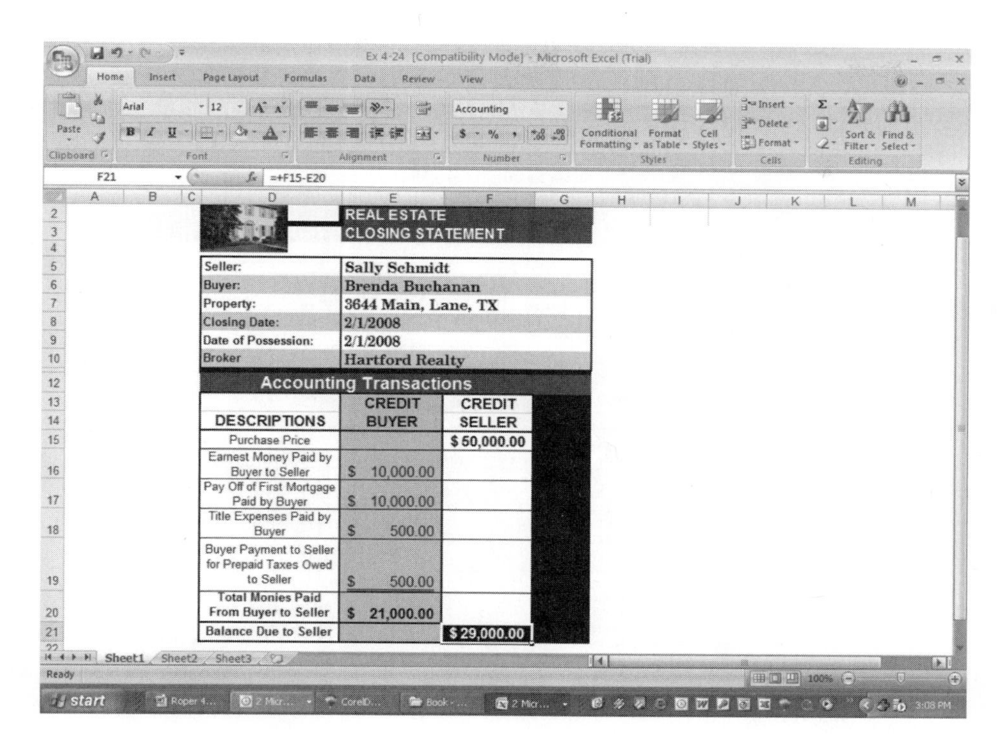

Exhibit 4–24

Real Estate Closing Statement—Excel 2007

Microsoft product screen shot reprinted with permission from Microsoft Corporation.

paid $21,000 of the $50,000 purchase price. Thus, a balance of $29,000 will be due the seller. Most real estate closing statements will be longer than Exhibit 4–24, but they will look much the same.

Monthly Payment and Amortization Schedules Spreadsheets can automatically calculate the monthly payment on a loan and produce an amortization schedule. The loan amortization schedule in Exhibit 4–25 is a template that comes free with Excel. The user simply fills in the data in the Loan Information section (cells F7–F12) and the spreadsheet does the rest. To access the template in Excel 2003, on the **File** menu click **New**, then click **Templates on my computer . . .**, **Spreadsheet Solutions**, and then **Loan Amortization**. In Excel 2007, click on the Office Button, New and then click under Templates.

Tax Planning

Tax planning allows clients and attorneys to test what the tax consequences of different investments are. Some investments have greater tax consequences than others, and a spreadsheet allows a planner to see the short-term or long-term tax effects of different investments.

Consider the investments and their tax consequences shown in Exhibit 4–26. Would you recommend to a client investment 1, corporate bonds (federal income taxes are payable on the income from this investment), or investment 2, in tax-free municipal bonds? (No federal income taxes are assessed on the income from municipal bonds). After taxes are taken into consideration, the tax-free municipal bonds (paying a low interest rate) are worth more than the corporate bonds (paying a higher interest rate). The second investment nets the client more after-tax dollars than the first. This is an example of tax planning.

Look at the formulas in Exhibit 4–26. The Amt. Invested cell (H12) has the formula = F12*G12; this is the quantity of bonds times the purchase price of each. The formula in the Interest Accum. at Maturity cell (K12) is H12*I12*J12; this is the amount invested times the interest rate times the number of years over which the interest will accumulate or accrue. Finally, the formula to figure the

Exhibit 4–25
Loan Amortization Schedule—Excel 2007
Microsoft product screen shot reprinted with permission from Microsoft Corporation.

A Ready-to-use Excel template

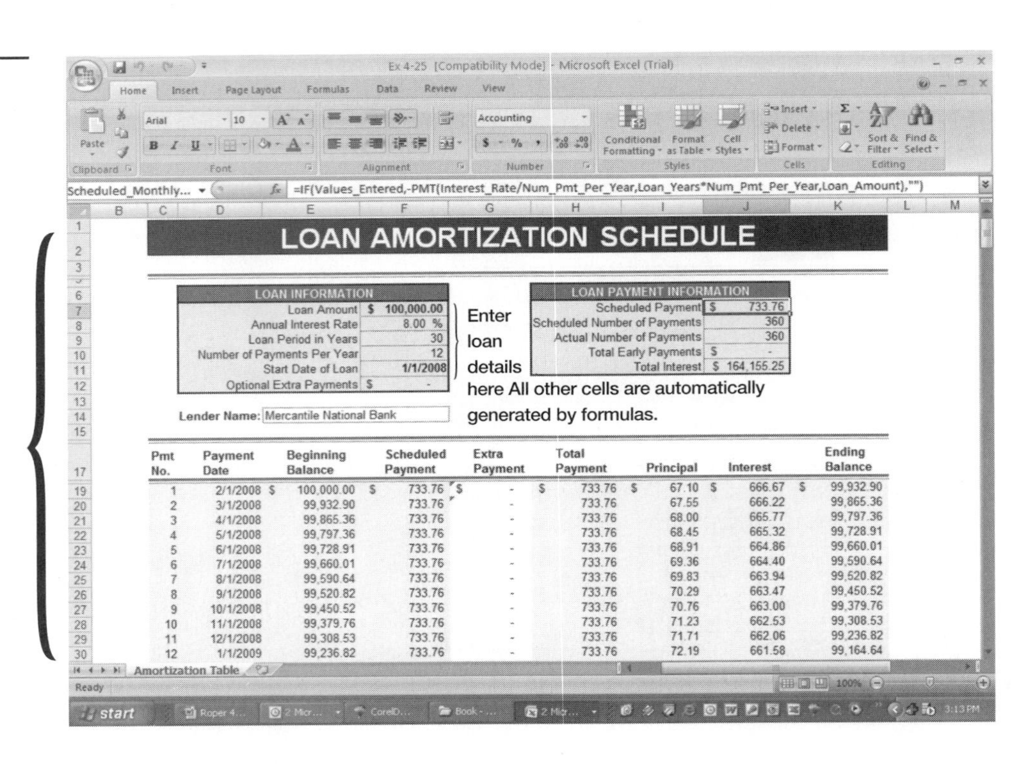

Pmt No.	Payment Date	Beginning Balance	Scheduled Payment	Extra Payment	Total Payment	Principal	Interest	Ending Balance
1	2/1/2008	$ 100,000.00	$ 733.76	$ -	$ 733.76	$ 67.10	$ 666.67	$ 99,932.90
2	3/1/2008	99,932.90	733.76	-	733.76	67.55	666.22	99,865.36
3	4/1/2008	99,865.36	733.76	-	733.76	68.00	665.77	99,797.36
4	5/1/2008	99,797.36	733.76	-	733.76	68.45	665.32	99,728.91
5	6/1/2008	99,728.91	733.76	-	733.76	68.91	664.86	99,660.01
6	7/1/2008	99,660.01	733.76	-	733.76	69.36	664.40	99,590.64
7	8/1/2008	99,590.64	733.76	-	733.76	69.83	663.94	99,520.82
8	9/1/2008	99,520.82	733.76	-	733.76	70.29	663.47	99,450.52
9	10/1/2008	99,450.52	733.76	-	733.76	70.76	663.00	99,379.76
10	11/1/2008	99,379.76	733.76	-	733.76	71.23	662.53	99,308.53
11	12/1/2008	99,308.53	733.76	-	733.76	71.71	662.06	99,236.82
12	1/1/2009	99,236.82	733.76	-	733.76	72.19	661.58	99,164.64

Exhibit 4–26
Tax Planning Spreadsheet—Excel 2003
Microsoft product screen shot reprinted with permission from Microsoft Corporation.

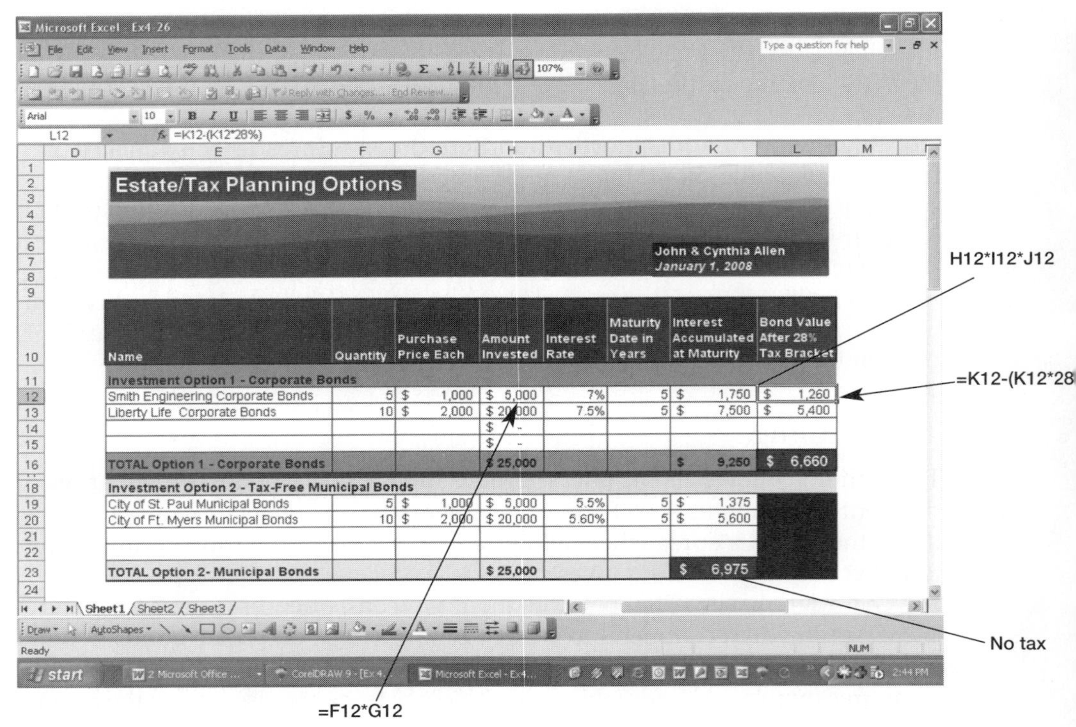

Name	Quantity	Purchase Price Each	Amount Invested	Interest Rate	Maturity Date in Years	Interest Accumulated at Maturity	Bond Value After 28% Tax Bracket
Investment Option 1 - Corporate Bonds							
Smith Engineering Corporate Bonds	5	$ 1,000	$ 5,000	7%	5	$ 1,750	$ 1,260
Liberty Life Corporate Bonds	10	$ 2,000	$ 20,000	7.5%	5	$ 7,500	$ 5,400
			$ -				
			$ -				
TOTAL Option 1 - Corporate Bonds			$ 25,000			$ 9,250	$ 6,660
Investment Option 2 - Tax-Free Municipal Bonds							
City of St. Paul Municipal Bonds	5	$ 1,000	$ 5,000	5.5%	5	$ 1,375	
City of Ft. Myers Municipal Bonds	10	$ 2,000	$ 20,000	5.60%	5	$ 5,600	
TOTAL Option 2- Municipal Bonds			$ 25,000			$ 6,975	

taxes in the Bond Value After Tax 28% Bracket cell (L12) is =K12-(K12*0.28%); this is the interest accumulated minus the tax. Spreadsheets are well suited for these types of financial calculations and comparisons.

Tax Return Preparation

Spreadsheets can also calculate tax returns. Once a template has been designed for a particular kind of tax form (such as the common Form 1040), a user fills in

the proper blanks, and the spreadsheet automatically performs the calculations. Although a spreadsheet program can calculate the proper tax amounts, it cannot usually fill in the tax form itself. Some tax programs can do both.

Graphs and Charts

Most spreadsheet programs can produce graphs. Charts and graphs are routinely used at law firms, especially when cases are going to trial, to help a judge or a jury visualize an important point. Recall that line graphs are useful in tracking data over time and for spotting trends. Suppose your firm represents an investor who was defrauded into investing money in a business. Shortly after the investor purchased stock in January at seventy-eight dollars a share, the executives at the company realized the business was headed down and sold a majority of their shares. By June the stock was worth only five dollars a share. Exhibit 4–27 graphically depicts the decline of the stock over the six-month period. Such a chart might be persuasive at the time of trial.

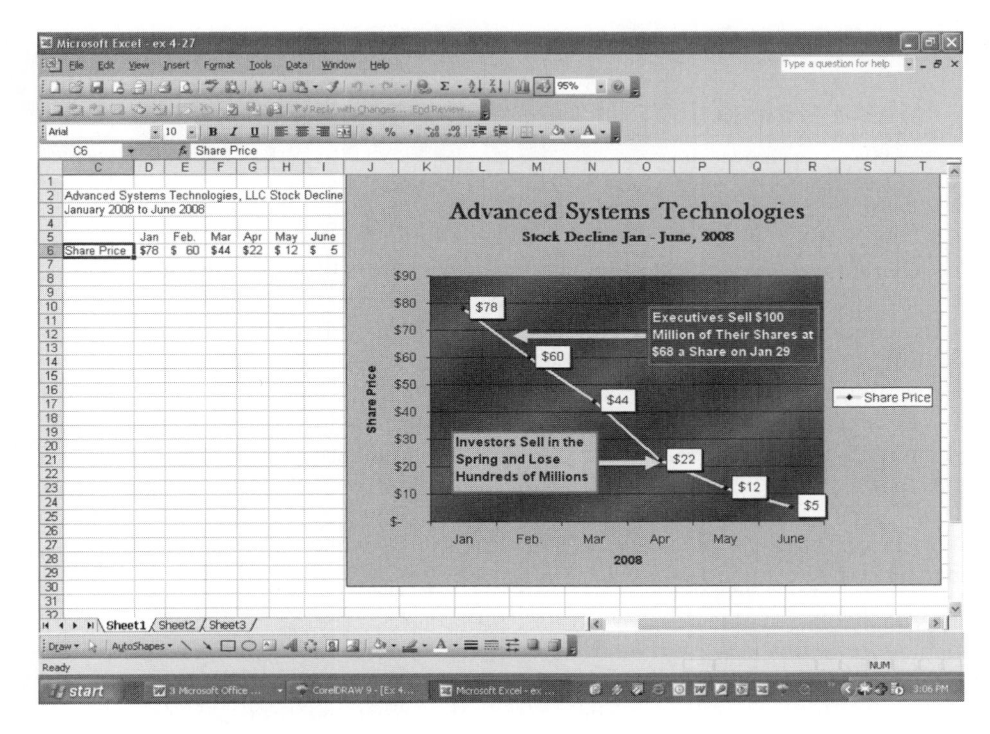

Exhibit 4–27

Line Graph as Evidence in a Case—Excel 2003

Microsoft product screen shot reprinted with permission from Microsoft Corporation.

Family Law Cases

Spreadsheets are commonly used to help divide assets in a divorce. When a marriage is dissolved, it is the duty of a court to try to fairly distribute or divide the assets the parties have gathered during the marriage so that neither party gets more than her or his fair share. Exhibit 4–28 represents a simple but effective example. A spreadsheet enables the user to lay out different division of asset scenarios or options for consideration. Spreadsheets can also produce lists of assets, family budgets, balance sheets, and income comparisons (such as between husband and wife). These documents are routinely prepared in many divorces.

Another way to use a spreadsheet program in a divorce action is to make a liabilities and assets worksheet that lists all of the liabilities and assets that the couple acquired during the marriage (see Exhibit 4–29). The list of assets includes the approximate value of each asset, the amount of any mortgages or loans outstanding on the asset, the date it was acquired or purchased (the date

Exhibit 4–28
Spreadsheet for Dividing Assets in Family Law—Excel 2003
Microsoft product screen shot reprinted with permission from Microsoft Corporation.

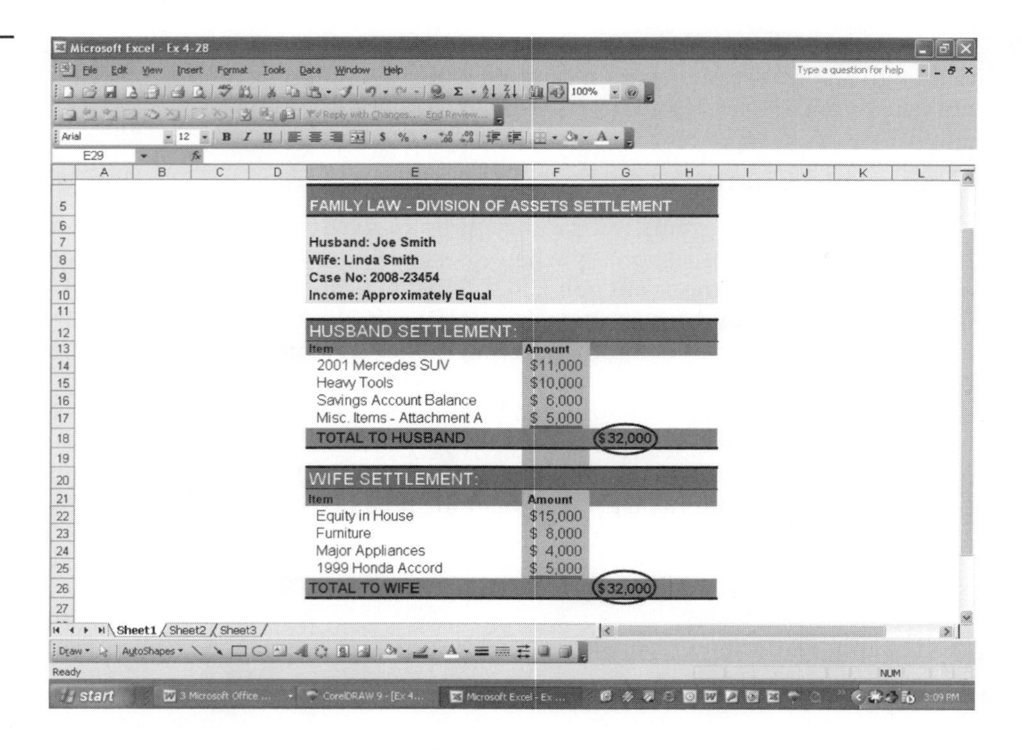

is pertinent when establishing whether the asset was brought into the marriage by one of the parties or was purchased during the marriage), and how the asset was acquired (whether it was a gift, a purchase, an inheritance, etc.). This type of spreadsheet is used early in the divorce action to organize the file and to determine how much is at stake.

Exhibit 4–30 shows a spreadsheet designed to track arrearages on child support, which is another common way spreadsheets are used in family law matters.

Statistical Analysis

Spreadsheets can also be used to analyze statistics. Most spreadsheets have statistical functions that can help a user analyze a group of values. Suppose your firm represents the plaintiff John Snow, a salesman, in an age discrimination suit against his former employer. The defendant company states that Snow was terminated because he did not sell enough units of its product. Snow must convince a judge that he was really terminated because the company wanted a younger workforce.

Exhibit 4–31 shows the names and ages of the company's salespersons and the units of product that were sold. Looking at the statistical analysis part of the exhibit, notice that the average age of salespersons is 30 (far below Snow's age of 56—it appears the company may be trying to hire young salespersons). This was arrived at by using the average function (AVG), which automatically totals up the values in a range and divides by the number of values.

Now, look at the Most Units Sold cell. The spreadsheet automatically placed the highest value here using the MAX function. Notice also that the minimum number of units was placed in the Least Units Sold cell using the MIN function. Also, look at the Avg. Units Sold cell, which was calculated automatically using the AVG function. (Snow was twenty units above the average units sold—it certainly seems he can make a strong argument for his case.)

Exhibit 4–29

Assets and Liabilities Worksheet in a Divorce

In the matter of the marriage of:
Denise Showsbury
and
John Showsbury

Case No.2008 D 234

List of Assets

Item	Source	Purchase Date	Fair Market Value	Amount Mortgaged
Trailer lot at 528 North Vine	Purchased	9/15/03	$1,100.00	
2002 Atlantic double-wide mobile home	15-year mortgage	11/30/02	49,490.80	$25,345.53
2002 Ford Explorer	3-year loan	01/05/02	9,495.36	2,345.54
Woodshed	Purchased	2000	200.00	
Sears washer and dryer	On credit	1/1/06	956.00	826.40
Dishwasher	Came with house	11/30/05	0.00	
China set	Mr. Showsbury's grandmother	1971	500.00	
Wedding china	Gift	6/20/05	500.00	
China set	Ms. Showsbury's great-aunt	1978	500.00	
Cedar chest	Purchased	08/02	100.00	
Portable DVD player	Purchased	8/06	200.00	
Couch	Gift	unknown	unknown	
Dresser	Gift to Mr. Showsbury	1981	unknown	
Child's bed	Auction	2003	75.00	
Three-piece bedroom set	Gift	unknown	unknown	
Nightstand	Purchased	2001	300.00	
Vacuum cleaner	Purchased	unknown	150.00	
Television	Purchased	2002	450.00	
Lawn mower	Purchased	2000	250.00	
Total			$64,267.16	
				$28,517.47

List of Liabilities

	Type	Loan Date	Left to Pay
2002 Atlantic double-wide mobile home	15-year	11/30/02	$25,345.53
2005 Chevy Tahoe	Mortgage 3 yr loan	01/05/05	2,345.54
Sears washer and dryer	On credit	01/01/06	826.40
Credit union loan	Loan	11/11/07	2,111.71
Total			$30,629.71

Bi-weekly Income

Ms. Showsbury	$1,466.00
Mr. Showsbury	$1,243.00

Notes:

1. Since September 1999 the parties have maintained separate bank account.
2. Unless otherwise noted, all assets were purchased during the marriage.
3. Date of marriage: 06/02/81

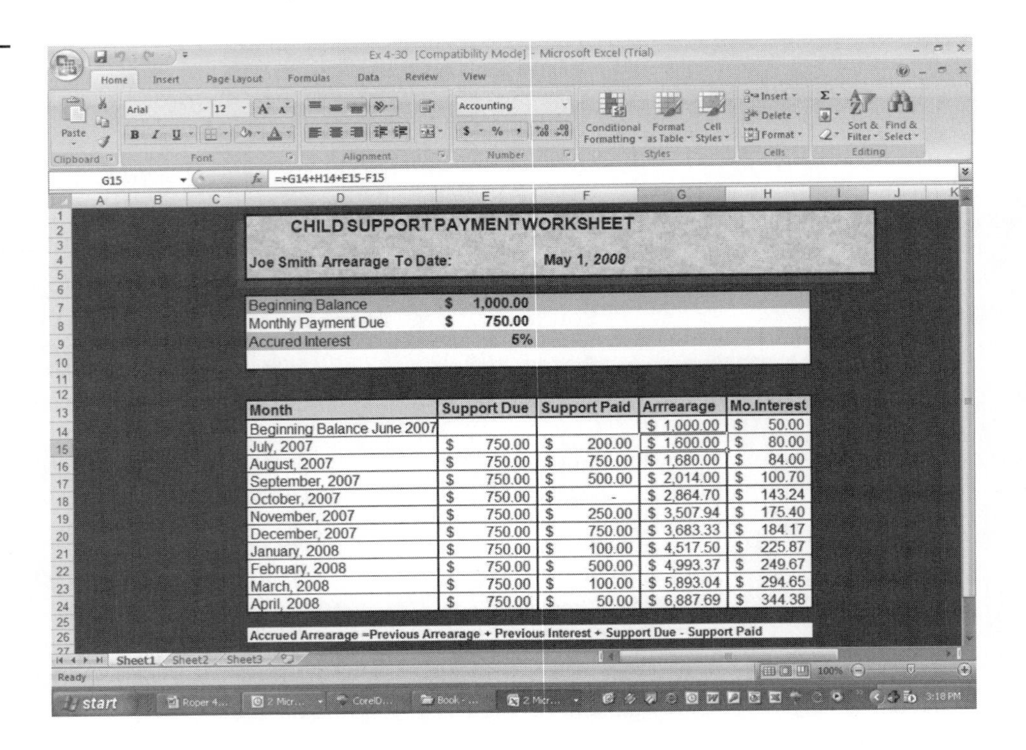

CHILD SUPPORT PAYMENT WORKSHEET

Joe Smith Arrearage To Date: May 1, 2008

Beginning Balance	$ 1,000.00
Monthly Payment Due	$ 750.00
Accured Interest	5%

Month	Support Due	Support Paid	Arrrearage	Mo.Interest
Beginning Balance June 2007			$ 1,000.00	$ 50.00
July, 2007	$ 750.00	$ 200.00	$ 1,600.00	$ 80.00
August, 2007	$ 750.00	$ 750.00	$ 1,680.00	$ 84.00
September, 2007	$ 750.00	$ 500.00	$ 2,014.00	$ 100.70
October, 2007	$ 750.00	$ -	$ 2,864.70	$ 143.24
November, 2007	$ 750.00	$ 250.00	$ 3,507.94	$ 175.40
December, 2007	$ 750.00	$ 750.00	$ 3,683.33	$ 184.17
January, 2008	$ 750.00	$ 100.00	$ 4,517.50	$ 225.87
February, 2008	$ 750.00	$ 500.00	$ 4,993.37	$ 249.67
March, 2008	$ 750.00	$ 100.00	$ 5,893.04	$ 294.65
April, 2008	$ 750.00	$ 50.00	$ 6,887.69	$ 344.38

Accrued Arrearage =Previous Arrearage + Previous Interest + Support Due - Support Paid

Exhibit 4–30
Child Support Payment Arrearage Spreadsheets—Excel 2007
Microsoft product screen shot reprinted with permission from Microsoft Corporation.

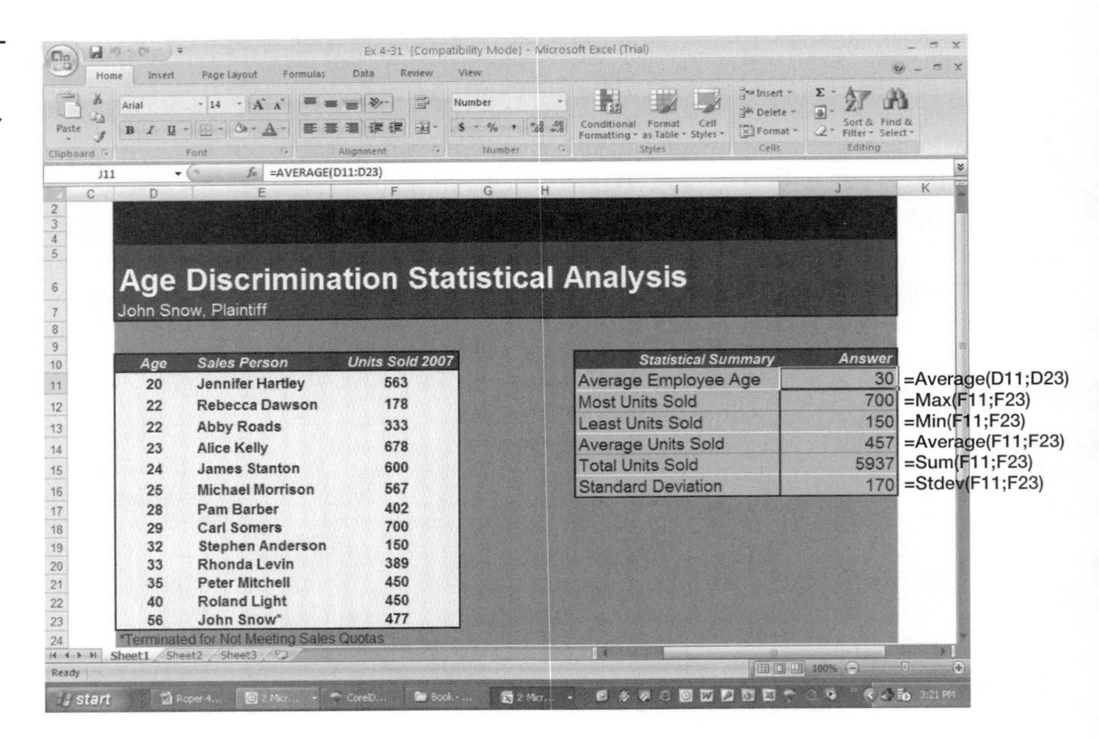

Age Discrimination Statistical Analysis

John Snow, Plaintiff

Age	Sales Person	Units Sold 2007
20	Jennifer Hartley	563
22	Rebecca Dawson	178
22	Abby Roads	333
23	Alice Kelly	678
24	James Stanton	600
25	Michael Morrison	567
28	Pam Barber	402
29	Carl Somers	700
32	Stephen Anderson	150
33	Rhonda Levin	389
35	Peter Mitchell	450
40	Roland Light	450
56	John Snow*	477

*Terminated for Not Meeting Sales Quotas

Statistical Summary	Answer	
Average Employee Age	30	=Average(D11;D23)
Most Units Sold	700	=Max(F11;F23)
Least Units Sold	150	=Min(F11;F23)
Average Units Sold	457	=Average(F11;F23)
Total Units Sold	5937	=Sum(F11;F23)
Standard Deviation	170	=Stdev(F11;F23)

Exhibit 4–31
Using Statistical Functions in Spreadsheets—Excel 2007
Microsoft product screen shot reprinted with permission from Microsoft Corporation.

Finally, the standard deviation of the values (i.e., the standard deviation from the average of each value) is high, showing that the data varies widely. The formula for calculating standard deviations is not simple, but a spreadsheet user can find it by issuing a function command and marking the range. This is an example of how spreadsheets can turn hard tasks into easy ones.

Importation of Spreadsheets into Other Programs

Sometimes it is necessary to include numerical information in a word-processing document. For example, a user might want to incorporate part of a spreadsheet or a graph into a brief or pleading. In most cases, it is simple to paste a spreadsheet or graph into a word-processing document.

Tracking of Investments for Trusts and Estates

Sometimes attorneys or law firms act as trustees or fiduciaries for trusts and estates. Part of this responsibility can be to invest money on behalf of a trust or an estate. Such fiduciaries have a duty not to waste or neglect the trust or estate and to make reasonable investments.

Exhibit 4–32 is an example of a spreadsheet that tracks the progress of stock market investments. By tracking the current prices of the stocks, the firm can get an idea of how the investments are doing and whether it should sell them and buy something else. Notice the formula in Exhibit 4–32. The market value formulas are obtained by taking the number of shares purchased times the current price of the stock. The dollar gain formulas are obtained by subtracting the total purchase price (the shares times the purchase price) from the market value. Finally, the percentage gain formulas are arrived at by dividing the dollar gain by the total purchase price.

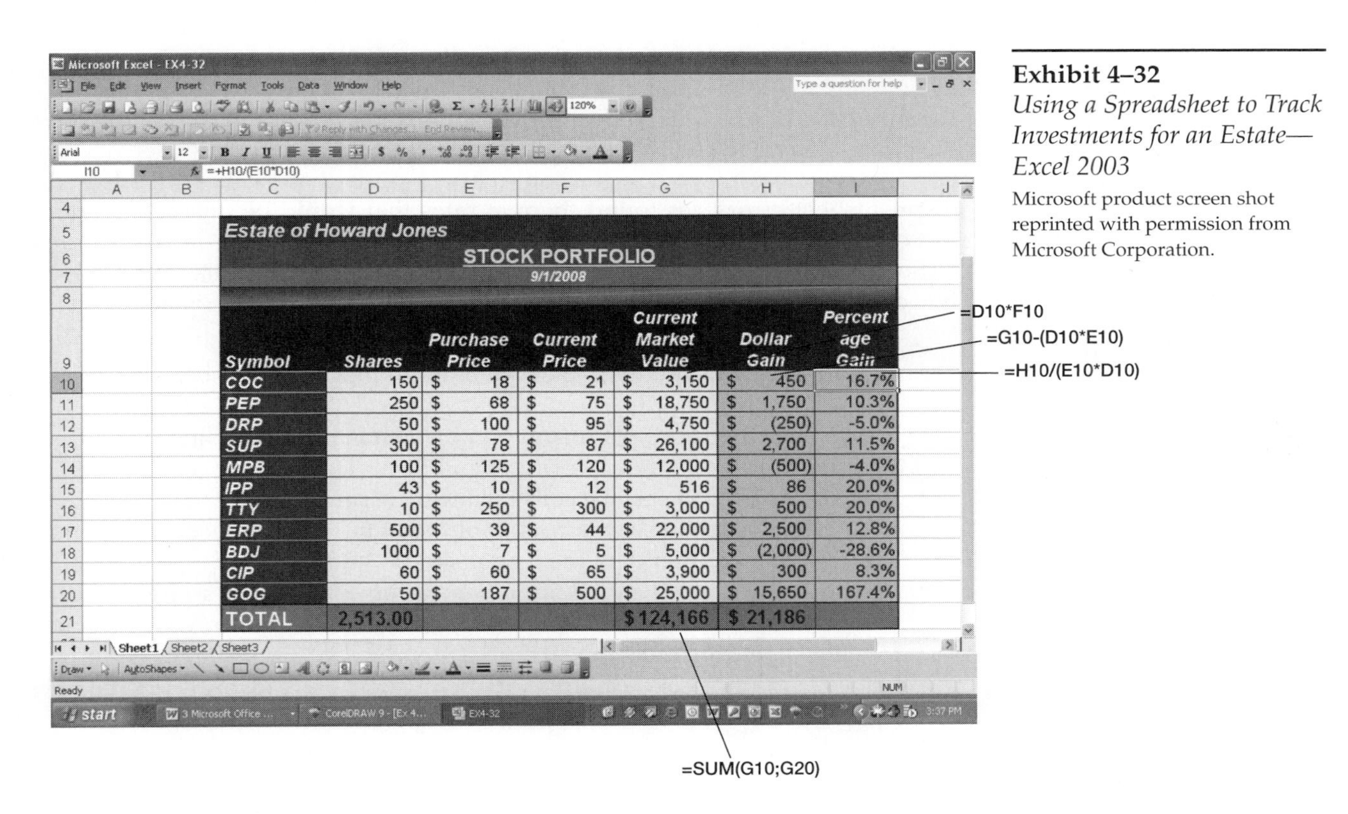

Estate of Howard Jones

STOCK PORTFOLIO

9/1/2008

Symbol	Shares	Purchase Price	Current Price	Current Market Value	Dollar Gain	Percent age Gain
COC	150	$ 18	$ 21	$ 3,150	$ 450	16.7%
PEP	250	$ 68	$ 75	$ 18,750	$ 1,750	10.3%
DRP	50	$ 100	$ 95	$ 4,750	$ (250)	-5.0%
SUP	300	$ 78	$ 87	$ 26,100	$ 2,700	11.5%
MPB	100	$ 125	$ 120	$ 12,000	$ (500)	-4.0%
IPP	43	$ 10	$ 12	$ 516	$ 86	20.0%
TTY	10	$ 250	$ 300	$ 3,000	$ 500	20.0%
ERP	500	$ 39	$ 44	$ 22,000	$ 2,500	12.8%
BDJ	1000	$ 7	$ 5	$ 5,000	$ (2,000)	-28.6%
CIP	60	$ 60	$ 65	$ 3,900	$ 300	8.3%
GOG	50	$ 187	$ 500	$ 25,000	$ 15,650	167.4%
TOTAL	2,513.00			$124,166	$ 21,186	

Exhibit 4–32
Using a Spreadsheet to Track Investments for an Estate—Excel 2003
Microsoft product screen shot reprinted with permission from Microsoft Corporation.

ETHICAL CONSIDERATIONS

Accuracy & Competence

The primary ethical consideration regarding spreadsheets is accuracy and competence. It is absolutely critical that the spreadsheets the legal assistant produces

be 100 percent accurate and well tested. If formulas do not add up all the data they are supposed to, if formulas have wrong numbers in them, if data is not updated, or if there are any other errors in the spreadsheet, disaster will occur. Unfortunately, often when legal assistants work with spreadsheets they are not just working with raw numbers, mathematics and research; they are working with spreadsheets that relate to actual money and financial projections that have a dollar impact. Thus, errors in a spreadsheet typically have a negative financial impact as well.

These problems are not as much an ethical issue (although this is a problem) as they are a malpractice risk. By way of example, imagine the following situations: (1) in the damages calculation in Exhibit 4–22 the net present value of the damages was not $120,969, but $150,969; (2) in Exhibit 4–24, the balance due to the seller was only $25,000, not $29,000, because an expense item paid by the buyer was left out of the spreadsheet; or (3) in Exhibit 4–26, the interest rate for the municipal bonds was only 4 percent and that the corporate bonds were the better investment. All of these errors raise ethical problems, but, more importantly, if any of these situations happened, it is clear that the client's interests would be damaged. If this happens, a malpractice claim against the law office is entirely likely. Most spreadsheet users fail to understand the likelihood of creating spreadsheet errors or the absolute importance of careful quality control of every spreadsheet, no matter how small.

So, how prevalent are errors in spreadsheets? A number of studies have shown that spreadsheet errors are relatively high. Cell error rates are typically around 5 percent. Thus, for every twenty cells you create, on average, you will have one error. As the total number of cells in a spreadsheet rises so does the propensity for errors. One auditing firm found that 90 percent of all spreadsheets that they reviewed that had 150 or more cells had one or more errors. In many cases the errors were serious ones. Every study that has been conducted on spreadsheet errors has found them at rates that would be unacceptable in most organizations.

So what can legal assistants do to minimize the potential for errors? They can:

- Double-check all numbers that are entered into a spreadsheet for accuracy.
- Triple-check every single formula in a spreadsheet, including using the Formula Auditing mode to print out all formulas.
- Make comments in specific cells regarding assumptions.
- Create a notes section at the bottom or top of the spreadsheets containing assumptions or other data the reader should be aware of.
- Be extremely careful when adding rows or columns to a spreadsheet where formulas already exist. Double-check each inserted row or column to make sure a formula appears in it.
- Have someone else carefully review your spreadsheet, including formulas.
- If a spreadsheet is outside of your knowledge base or comfort zone, ask your supervising attorney to get an expert such as an accountant or financial analyst to prepare and/or review the calculations. In the end, it is far cheaper to do this than to discover an error later.
- Before using a new function, you should completely understand exactly what it does and that it is working 100 percent correctly.
- Use a calculator to spot-check your spreadsheets to make sure the formulas are accurate.
- Use the Protect feature to protect cells, particularly formulas, from accidentally being changed (see below).

The American Bar Association recently conducted a study of more than eleven thousand malpractice claims, and found that approximately 27 percent (3,000 cases) were attributable to routine administrative errors.

Consider this recent case. Two attorneys were hired by a businessman to merge his insurance agency with another agency that was owned by two other individuals. During the merger the attorneys were to create a voting trust in favor of the two new principals. The intent was that, in the end, the businessman would own 50 percent of the new company, and the two new principals would together own 50 percent of the company as equal partners. Unfortunately, the attorneys miscalculated the amount of stock put into the voting trust. This gave the two new principals 51 percent of the new company, which meant that they had control of the direction of the company, if they wished. Approximately three weeks after the merger documents were executed, one of the attorneys discovered the mathematical error. They discussed it and decided among themselves to cover up the mistake by replacing two pages of their copy of the merger documents that contained the error with corrected ones. The parties to the merger were not told of the error. Later, the two new principals terminated the relationship with the businessman (who had now become disabled and was presumably relying on the business for financial support). The businessman sued the attorneys for legal malpractice. The case provides two important points. First, the mathematical error that was made was not great—it was a 1 percent error. Unfortunately, that 1 percent was absolutely crucial to the attorneys' client.

Errors do not have to be large to be important or substantial. This is why it is critical to put mathematical computations into spreadsheets, where they can be easily reviewed, where automatic formulas can be used, and where the calculations can be in a form that can be checked and rechecked. Second, the attorneys immediately should have notified the parties of the error instead of trying to cover it up. If you make a mistake, admit the mistake and then take action to correct it. A lawsuit might have been avoided, and harm to the client might have been avoided, if the attorneys had just done the right thing and admitted the problem up front.

Password Protection Passwords are an easy way to increase the security of your documents. Password-protecting spreadsheets is easy to do and should always be done if the spreadsheet is going outside of the firm. In Excel 2003, the command sequence is **File>Save>Tools>General Options>Password to Open**. In Excel 2007 the command sequence is **Office Button>Save>Tools>General Options>Password to Open**.

Protecting Cells and Spreadsheets When multiple people use a spreadsheet, it is common for formulas and other data to be accidentally deleted by users. If a formula, for example, is deleted and the recipient tries to correct the problem by writing a new formula, but makes an error, a large problem has been created that could go a long time without being noticed. One way to solve this problem is to use the Protect Cells feature found in most spreadsheets. Protection is a useful security tool when using spreadsheets.

In Excel, for example, to protect all or part of a spreadsheet, the user must turn on the Protection feature. In Excel 2003, protection can be turned on by pointing to the **File** menu, then clicking **Tools>Protection>Protect Sheet**. In Excel 2007, protection can be turned on from the Review ribbon tab by checking **Protect Sheet** in the Changes group. *Note*: Cells can be protected against accidental deletion by simply turning on the **Protect** command (which a user can turn off at a later time) or can be password protected, in which case unless the user has the password, protection cannot be turned off. For example, suppose a

creator of a spreadsheet wants to protect certain formulas in an Excel spreadsheet from being accidentally typed over. The creator of the spreadsheet does not want the user to have to type a password if they want to edit the spreadsheet; the creator just wants to protect the formulas from accidental deletion. The creator of the spreadsheet would use **Protect Sheet** and leave the password blank. The creator of the spreadsheet would mark all of the cells that were not locked and in Excel 2003, point to the **Format** menu, then click **Cells>Protection**, and uncheck the **Locked** feature. In Excel 2007 the command is right-click, **Format Cells>Protection**. If a user then wanted to change a formula, he or she could not but instead would get an error message stating that the cell is protected. However, all the user would have to do would be to click **Tools>Protection>Unprotect Sheet** to turn off the protection feature. The user would then be able to edit the formula. If the creator of the spreadsheet did not want the user to be able to do this, the creator could use the password feature to lock the spreadsheet cells he wanted to keep from being edited.

SUMMARY

Spreadsheet software calculates and manipulates data using labels and formulas. Spreadsheets use rows and columns, which look similar to those on an accountant's worksheet. A row is an area that extends across a page horizontally, and a column is an area that extends down a page vertically. A cell is an intersection between a row and a column.

The cursor, or cell pointer, in a spreadsheet indicates what cell is currently selected.

Three types of data can be entered into a spreadsheet: text, values, and formulas. Text is descriptive data, including headings and titles, that are entered into a cell and cannot be used in making calculations. Values are numbers that are entered into a cell and can be used in making calculations. Formulas perform calculations using the values in other cells. Arithmetic operations and function commands are used in making formulas and instruct a spreadsheet how to make the calculations.

Copying data places information from one part of a spreadsheet into another part while leaving the original intact. When copying formulas, an absolute cell reference does not change to reflect the new location of the cell pointer. A relative cell reference will automatically change to reflect the new location of the cell pointer.

A variety of graphing capabilities are provided in most spreadsheets. A bar graph consists of a sequence of bars that illustrate numerical values. A line graph plots the course of a value over time. A pie chart represents each value as a piece or percentage of a total pie. A stacked bar graph compares data by placing bars on top of one another.

Legal assistants can use spreadsheets to track all kinds of information, including damages calculations, budget plans and problems, and tax plans and tax return calculations.

INTERNET SITES

Internet sites for this chapter include the following:

Organization	Product/Service	World Wide Web Address
Microsoft	Microsoft Excel spreadsheet program	<http://www.microsoft.com>
Microsoft	Home page for Microsoft Excel containing a wealth of information, tips, and tricks	<http://www.microsoft.com/excel>
Corel Corporation	Quattro Pro spreadsheet	<http://www.corel.com>
The A to Z of Spreadsheets	General site offering tips and information on spreadsheets	<http://www.mathsnet.net/>
Matt H. Evans, CPA	Assorted free Excel spreadsheets	<http://www.exinfm.com>
About.com	General site about spreadsheets, with information and tips on how to use them	<http://www.spreadsheets.about.com>

KEY TERMS

spreadsheet software
spreadsheet
"what if" analysis
row
column
cell
cell address
cell pointer
text
values
formulas
arithmetic operators
function command
cell width
absolute cell reference
relative cell reference
portrait
landscape
macro
bar graph
line graph
pie chart
stacked bar graph

TEST YOUR KNOWLEDGE

1. An area on a spreadsheet that extends vertically up and down the page is called a _______.
2. An area on a spreadsheet that extends horizontally across a page is called a _______.
3. True or False: An intersection between a row and a column in a spreadsheet is called a location.
4. Descriptive data entered in a spreadsheet such as titles and headings is called _______.
5. Numbers entered in a spreadsheet are called _______.
6. Expressions used in a spreadsheet program to automatically perform calculations are called _______.
7. True or False: The plus sign, minus sign, multiplication sign, and division sign are examples of function commands.
8. Write two formulas for adding the following cells: A1, A2, and A3.
9. "=SUM," "AVERAGE," and "MAX" are examples of what kind of formulas?
10. Name two kinds of cell references.
11. Name three things that should be kept in mind when planning a spreadsheet.
12. True or False: It is difficult to make errors in spreadsheets due to templates, formulas, and function commands.
13. One way to keep formulas and cells from being accidentally deleted is to use which command?

ON THE WEB EXERCISES

1. Using the websites at the end of the chapter and a general Internet search engine like google.com or yahoo.com, research the issue of errors in spreadsheets. Write a two-page paper on your findings.
2. Go to http://www.microsoft.com/excel and, under the "Templates" section, view ten of the many ready-to-use templates for Excel.
3. Research legal-related Excel templates, including tax, real estate, child support, financial planning, estate planning, and related subjects. Write a two-page paper summarizing the types of free and fee-based sites and templates that you found.

QUESTIONS AND EXERCISES

1. Using the *Wall Street Journal* or a local paper that carries stock prices for the New York Stock Exchange, track the price of any four stocks that you have an interest in for one week using a spreadsheet. Show the daily beginning stock price, ending stock price, and difference. Calculate the stock's total per share movement for the week and calculate the stock's average price per share for the week.
2. Using a spreadsheet program, prepare an expense budget for a mythical start-up law firm for one year. Assume the law firm will have four attorneys (two of whom are partners and two of whom are associates), two legal assistants, and two secretaries. Be sure to include leased space, office equipment (computers, copiers, printers, phones, etc.), office supplies, utilities, and miscelaneous expenses.
3. Using a spreadsheet program, summarize the amount of time you spend attending class and studying for your classes for a week. Assume that you will be paid for the time spent studying or attending classes, but that you must present a detailed bill of your activities. The bill must be professional in appearance and be totaled. Assume that you will be paid sixty dollars an hour.
4. Using a spreadsheet program, enter the names, complete addresses, and phone numbers of twenty relatives or friends. The list must be professional in appearance and sorted alphabetically by last name.
5. You have requested a new computer from your law firm in next year's budget. Your managing attorney has asked you to provide a detailed, itemized list of the equipment and the price for each component of the system. Your managing attorney is very frugal, so include a one-page memorandum (with the itemized listing) summarizing why the system you have selected is appropriate.
6. The office manager in the law office where you work finds out that you have taken a class on law office computing and asks you to develop a spreadsheet that will automate the trust account checkbook. She has drawn a picture of what she would like and asks you to complete the formulas. Refer to the columns and rows (e.g., D1+C4).

	Column A	Column B	Column C	Column D
	Date	Payee	Check Amt.	Balance
Row 1	1/01/2008	Balance from Last Month		$10,000
Row 2	1/01/2008	Filing Fee – *Smith v. Steel*	$100	Formula?
Row 3	1/03/2008	Process Fee – *Smith v. Steel*	$200	Formula?
Row 4	1/04/2008	Expert Fee – *Smith v. Steel*	$3,000	Formula?
Row 5	1/05/2008	Attorney's Fees – *Smith v. Steel*	$1,000	Formula?

HANDS-ON EXERCISES

SPREADSHEETS

SPREADSHEETS HANDS-ON EXERCISES READ THIS FIRST!

1. Microsoft Excel 2007
2. Microsoft Excel 2003

I. DETERMINING WHICH TUTORIAL TO COMPLETE

To use the Spreadsheet Hands-On Exercises, you must already own or have access to Microsoft Excel 2007 or Excel 2003. If you have one of these programs but do not know which version you are using, it is easy to find out. For Excel 2003, load the program and point to the **Help** menu, then click **About Microsoft Office Excel**. It should then tell you what version of the program you are using. For Excel 2007 click the Office Button, and click **Excel Options>Resources**; it will tell you what version you are using. You must know the version of the program you are using and select the correct tutorial version or the tutorials will not work correctly.

II. USING THE SPREADSHEET HANDS-ON EXERCISES

The Spreadsheet Hands-On Exercises in this section are easy to use and contain step-by-step instructions. They start with basic spreadsheet skills and proceed to intermediate and advanced levels. If you already have a good working knowledge of Excel you may be able to proceed directly to the intermediate and advanced exercises. To truly be ready for using spreadsheets in the legal environment you must be able to accomplish the tasks and exercises in the advanced exercises.

III. ACCESSING THE DATA FILES ON THE CDs THAT COME WITH THE TEXT

Some of the intermediate and advanced Excel Hands-On Exercises use documents on Disk1 of the CDs that come with the text. To access these files in Windows XP, put the CD in your computer, select "Start," "My Computer," then select the appropriate drive and double-click on the appropriate drive, and then double-click on the Excel folder. You should then see a list of Excel files that are available. To access these files in Windows Vista, put the CD in your computer, select the Start button, select Computer and then double-click on the Excel folder. You should then see a list of Excel files that are available for each lesson.

IV. INSTALLATION QUESTIONS

If you have installation questions regarding loading the Excel data from Disk1 of the CDs included with the text you may contact Technical Support at 800/477-3692.

HANDS-ON EXERCISES
MICROSOFT EXCEL 2007 FOR WINDOWS

Basic Lessons

Number	Lesson Title	Concepts Covered
Lesson 1	Building a Budget Spreadsheet – Part 1	**[CTRL]+[HOME]** command, moving the pointer, entering text and values, adjusting the width of columns, changing the format of a group of cells to currency, using bold, centering text, entering formulas, using the Auto Fill/Copy command to copy formulas, and printing and saving a spreadsheet.
Lesson 2	Building a Budget Spreadsheet – Part 2	Opening a file, inserting rows, changing the format of cells to percent, building more formulas, creating a bar chart with the chart wizard, printing a selection, and fitting/compressing data to one printed page.
Lesson 3	Damages Projection	Changing font size, font color, and fill color, using the AutoSum feature, using the wrap text feature, creating borders, and setting decimal points when formatting numbers.
Intermediate Lessons		
Lesson 4	Child Support Payment Spreadsheet	Creating a white background, creating formulas that multiply cells, creating formulas that use absolute cell references, and using the AutoFormat feature.
Lesson 5	Loan Amortization Template Lesson 5 from Disk1	Using a template, protecting cells, freezing panes, splitting a screen, hiding columns, and using Format Painter.
Lesson 6	Statistical Functions “Lesson 6” from Disk1	Using functions including average, maximum, minimum, and standard deviation; sorting data; checking for metadata; using the format clear command; using conditional formatting; and inserting a picture.
Advanced Lessons		
Lesson 7	Tools and Techniques 1—Marketing Budget“ “Lesson 7” from Disk1	Creating and manipulating a text box, advanced shading techniques, working with a 3-D style text box, creating vertical and diagonal text, creating a cell comment, and using lines and borders.
Lesson 8	Tools and Techniques 2—Stock Portfolio “Lesson 8” from Disk1	Using the Merge and Center tool, using the Formula Auditing feature, using the oval tool, and password protecting a file.

GETTING STARTED

Overview

Microsoft Excel 2007 is a powerful spreadsheet program that allows you to create formulas, "what if" scenarios, graphs, and much more.

Introduction

Throughout these lessons and exercises, information you need to operate the program will be designated in several different ways:

- Keys to be pressed on the keyboard will be designated in brackets, in all caps and in bold (i.e., press the **[ENTER]** key).
- Movements with the mouse pointer will be designated in bold and italics (i.e., ***point to File and click***).
- Words or letters that should be typed will be designated in bold (i.e., type **Training Program**).
- Information that is or should be displayed on your computer screen is shown in the following style: **Press [ENTER] to continue**.
- Specific menu items and commands will be designated with boldface and an initial capital letter (i.e., click **Open**).

OVERVIEW OF EXCEL 2007

I. Worksheet

A. *Entering Commands: The Ribbon*—The primary way of entering commands in Excel 2007 is through the ribbon. The ribbon is a set of commands or tools that change depending on which ribbon is selected (see Excel 2007 Exhibit 1). There are seven ribbon tabs: Home, Insert, Page Layout, Formulas, Data, Review and View (see Excel 2007 Exhibit 1). Each tab has groups of commands. For example, on the Home tab, the Font group contains a group of commands that given font choice, font size, bold, italics, underlining, and others attributes (see Excel 2007 Exhibit 1).

B. *Office Button*—The Office Button (see Excel 2007 Exhibit 1) is where a user accesses commands such as **New, Open, Save**, and **Print.** The Office Button replaces the **File** menu in previous versions of Excel.

C. *Entering Data*—To enter data, type the text or number in a cell, and press the **[ENTER]** key or one of the arrow (cursor) keys.

D. *Ranges*—A *range* is a group of contiguous cells. Cell ranges can be created by ***clicking and dragging the pointer*** or holding the **[SHIFT]** key on and using the arrow (cursor) keys.

E. *Format*—Cells can be formatted, including changing the font style, font size, shading, border, cell type (currency, percentage, etc.), alignment, and other attributes by ***clicking the Home ribbon tab, and then clicking one of the Dialog Box Launchers in the Font Group, Alignment Group, or Number Group.*** Each of these Dialog Box Launchers brings up the same **Format Cells** window. Users can also enter a number of formatting options directly from the Home tab.

F. *Editing a Cell*—A user can edit a cell by ***clicking in the cell and then clicking in the formula bar.*** The formula bar is directly under the ribbon and just to the right of the **fx** sign (see Excel 2007 Exhibit 1). The formula bar shows the

Excel 2007 Exhibit 1

Excel 2007 Interface

Microsoft product screen shot reprinted with permission from Microsoft Corporation.

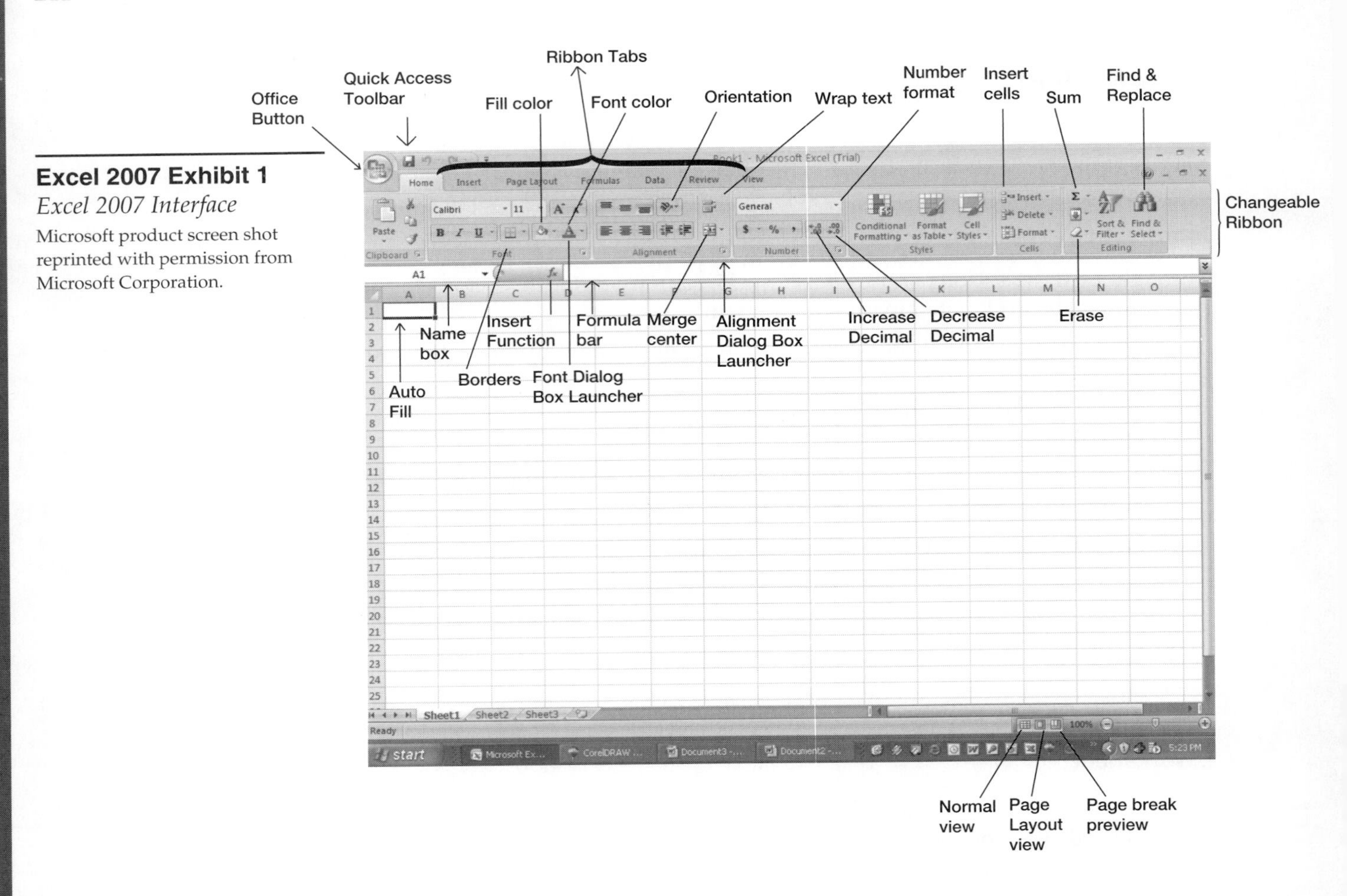

current contents of the selected cell, and it allows you to edit the cell contents. You can also edit the contents of a cell by ***clicking in the cell*** and then pressing the **[F2]** key.

G. *Column Width/Row Height*—You can change the width of a column by ***clicking the line to the right of the column heading***. (This is the line that separates two columns. When you point to a line, the cursor changes to double-headed vertical arrows.) ***Next, drag the pointer to the right or to the left to increase or decrease the column width, respectively.*** Similarly, you can change the height of a row ***clicking and dragging the horizontal line separating two rows***. You can also change the width of a column or height of a row by clicking somewhere in the column you want to change, ***clicking the Home tab, and then clicking Format in the Cells group.***

H. *Insert*—Users can insert one row or column by ***clicking the Home tab, then clicking the down arrow below the Insert icon in the Cells group, and clicking either Insert Sheet Rows, or Insert Sheet Columns.*** You can also insert a number of rows or columns by ***dragging the pointer over the number of rows or columns you want to add, clicking the Home tab, clicking the down arrow below the Insert icon in the Cells group, and then clicking either Insert Sheet Rows or Insert Sheet Columns.*** Finally, you can ***right-click and select Insert from the menu.***

I. *Erase/Delete*—You can erase data by ***dragging the pointer over the area*** and then pressing the **[DEL]** key. You can also erase data by ***dragging the pointer over the area, clicking the Home ribbon tab, and clicking the down arrow***

next to the Clear icon in the Editing group, and then click Clear All. You can delete whole columns or rows by ***pointing and clicking in a column or row, then clicking on the Home ribbon tab, clicking on the down arrow next to Delete in the Cells group, and then clicking either Delete Sheet Rows or Delete Sheet Columns.*** You can also delete whole columns or rows by ***pointing in the column or row and then right-clicking and selecting Delete.***

J. *Quit*—To quit Excel, ***click on the Office Button and then clicking Exit Excel.***

K. *Copy*—To copy data to adjacent columns or rows, ***click in the cell you wish to copy and then select the AutoFill command,*** which is accessed from the small black box at the bottom right corner of the selected cell. Then, ***drag the pointer to where the data should be placed.*** You can also copy data by ***clicking in the cell, right-clicking, clicking Copy, clicking in the location where the information should be copied,*** and pressing the **[ENTER]** key. Finally, data can be copied by ***clicking and dragging to highlight on the information to be copied, clicking the Home tab, and then clicking Copy in the Clipboard group.***

L. *Move*—Move data by ***clicking in the cell, right-clicking, selecting Cut, clicking in the location where the information should be inserted,*** and pressing the **[ENTER]** key. Data can also be moved by ***highlighting the information to be copied, clicking the Home tab and then clicking Cut in the Clipboard group.*** Then go to the location where the information should be moved, ***click the Home tab, and then click Paste in the Clipboard group.***

M. *Saving and Opening Files*—Save a file by ***clicking the Office Button, then clicking Save or Save As,*** and typing the file name. You can also save a file by ***clicking the Save icon*** (it looks like a floppy disk) on the Quick Access Toolbar (see Excel 2007 Exhibit 1). Open a file that was previously saved by ***clicking the Office Button, clicking Open,*** and typing (or clicking) the name of the file to be opened.

N. *Print*—You can print a file by ***clicking the Office Button, then Print, and then OK.***

II. Numbers and Formulas

A. *Numbers*—To enter a number in a cell, click in the cell, type the number, and press the **[ENTER]** key or an arrow (cursor) key.

B. *Adding Cells (Addition)*—You can add the contents of two or more cells by three different methods:

1) To add the contents of a range of two or more cells:

1. Click in to the cell where the total should be placed.

2. ***Click the Home tab, and then click the Sum icon in the Editing group (see Excel 2007 Exhibit 2).*** The Sum icon looks like an "E." *Note*: To see the name of an icon, point to the icon for a second and the name of the icon will be displayed.)

3. Excel guesses which cells you want to add. Press **[ENTER]** if the correct range is automatically selected, or select the correct range by highlighting it (i.e., ***clicking and dragging until the range of cells to be added is selected***). Then, press **[ENTER]**.

2) To add the contents of two cells, which need not comprise a range:

1. Click in the cell where the total should be placed.

2. Press = (the equals sign).

3. Type the address of the first cell to be added (e.g., B4), or alternatively, ***click in it***.

4. Press + (the plus sign).

5. Enter the address of the second cell to be added (or ***click in it***).

6. Press the **[ENTER]** key. (For example, to add the values of cells C4 and C5, you would type = **C4+C5**.)

3) To add the contents of a range of two or more cells:

1. Click in the cell where the total should be placed.

2. Type **=SUM(**.

3. Enter the address of the first cell to be added (or ***click in it***).

4. Press **[:]** (the colon).

5. Enter the address of the second cell to be added (or ***click in it***).

6. Press **[)]** (the closing parenthesis).

7. Press the **[ENTER]** key. (For example, to add the values of C4 and C5, the formula would read **=SUM(C4:C5)**.)

C. *Subtracting Cells*—To subtract the contents of one or more cells from those of another:

a. Click in the cell where the result should be placed.

b. Press **=.**

c. Enter the first cell address (or ***click in it***).

d. Press **–.**

e. Enter the second cell address (or ***click in it***).

f. Press the **[ENTER]** key. (For example, to subtract the value of C4 from the value of C5, you would type **=C5–C4**.)

D. *Multiplying Cells*—To multiply the contents of two (or more) cells:

a. Click in the cell where the result should be placed.

b. Press **[=]**.

c. Enter the first cell address (or ***click in it***).

d. Press **[*]** (**[SHIFT]+[8]**).

e. Enter the second cell address (or ***click in it***).

f. Press the **[ENTER]** key. (For example, to multiply the value in C4 times the value in C5, you would type **=C5*C4**.)

E. *Dividing Cells*—To divide the contents of two (or more) cells:

a. Click in the cell where the result should be placed.

b. Press [=].

c. Enter the first cell address (or ***click in it***).

d. Press [/] (the forward slash).

e. Enter the second cell address (or ***click in it***).

f. Press the **[ENTER]** key. (For example, to divide the value in C4 by the value in C5, you would type **=C4/C5**.)

Basic Lessons

LESSON 1: BUILDING A BUDGET SPREADSHEET—PART 1

This lesson shows you how to build the spreadsheet in Excel 2007 Exhibit 2. It explains how to use the **[CTRL]+[HOME]** command; move the cell pointer; enter text, values, and formulas; adjust the width of columns; change the format of cells to currency; use the bold feature, use the AutoFill and Copy features to copy formulas; and print and save a spreadsheet. Keep in mind that if at any time you make a mistake in this lesson, you may press **[CTRL]+[Z]** to undo what you have done.

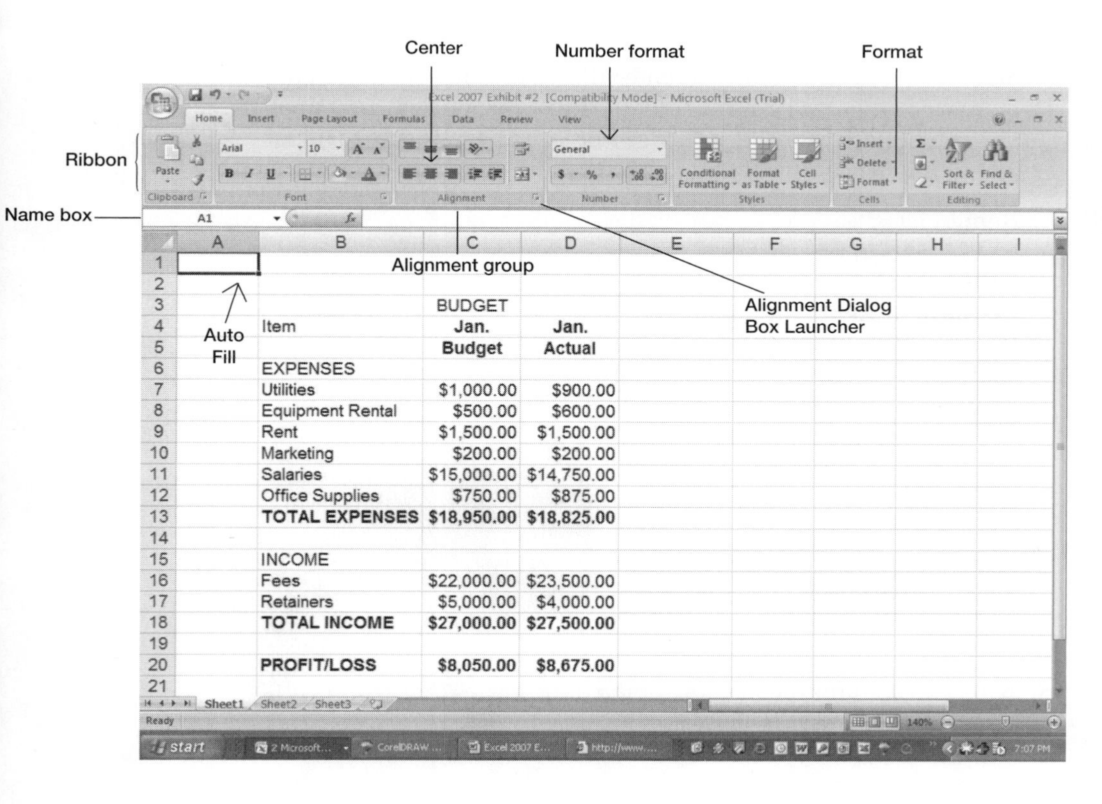

Excel 2007 Exhibit 2
Budgeting Spreadsheet
Microsoft product screen shot reprinted with permission from Microsoft Corporation.

1. Open Windows. Then, ***double-click the Microsoft Office Excel 2007 icon on the desktop*** to open the program. Alternatively, ***click the Start button, point to Programs or All Programs, to Microsoft Office, and then click Microsoft Office Excel 2007.*** You should be in a clean, blank workbook. If you are not in a blank

workbook, ***click the Office Button (see Excel 2007 Exhibit 1), click on New, and then double-click Blank Workbook.***

2. Notice that the pointer is at cell A1, and the indicator that displays the address of the current cell (called the name box in Excel) says A1. The name box is just under the ribbon and all the way to the left (see Excel 2007 Exhibit 2). Also, notice that you can move the pointer around the spreadsheet using the cursor keys. Go back to cell A1 by pressing the **[CTRL]+[HOME]** keys.

3. Go to cell C3 by ***clicking in cell C3*** or by pressing the **[RIGHT ARROW]** twice, and then pressing the **[DOWN ARROW]** twice.

4. You will now enter the title of the spreadsheet in cell C3. Type **BUDGET** and then press the **[ENTER]** key.

5. Notice that the pointer is now at cell C4.

6. Press the **[UP ARROW]** to go back to cell C3. Notice that BUDGET is left aligned. To center **BUDGET** in the cell, ***from the Home tab, click the Center icon in the Alignment group.*** It is the icon with several lines on it that appear centered (see Excel 2007 Exhibit 3). *Note*: If you hover the mouse over icons on the ribbon for a second, the name of the icon will be displayed. Alternatively, ***from the Home tab, click the Alignment Group Dialog Box Launcher. Next, on the Alignment tab, under the "Horizontal" field click the down arrow and select Center. Then click OK.***

7. You should now be ready to enter the budget information. First, move the cell pointer to where the data should go, then type the data, and finally enter the data by pressing the **[ENTER]** key or one of the arrow (cursor) keys. Type the remaining row labels as follows:

Item in B4.
EXPENSES in B6.
Utilities in B7.
Equipment Rental in B8.
Rent in B9.
Marketing in B10.
Salaries in B11.
Office Supplies in B12.
TOTAL EXPENSES in B13.
INCOME in B15.
Fees in B16.
Retainers in B17.
TOTAL INCOME in B18.
PROFIT/LOSS in B20.

8. Notice in column B that some of the data entries (such as "EXPENSES" and "Equipment Rental") actually extend into column C. To correct this, you must increase the width of column B. ***Put the mouse pointer in the cell lettered B at the top of the screen. Move the pointer to the right edge of the cell.*** The pointer should then change to a double-headed vertical arrow and the column width will be displayed in a small box. ***Drag the pointer to the right until the column width is 18.00.*** Alternatively, you can change the cell width by ***placing the cell pointer anywhere in column B, then from the Home tab, click Format in the Cells group, and then click Column Width. . .,*** type **18**, and ***click OK.***

9. Notice that all of the data entries now fit in the columns. Enter the following:

Jan. in C4.
Budget in C5.
Jan. in D4.
Actual in D5.

10. ***Click in cell C4 and drag the pointer over to cell D5*** (so that the whole cell range is highlighted)***; then, from the Home tab, click the Center icon in the Alignment group.***

11. You are now ready to enter values into your spreadsheet.

12. ***Move the pointer to cell C7.*** Type **1000.** Do not type a dollar sign or comma; these will be added later. Press the **[ENTER]** key to enter the value.

13. Enter the following:

500 in C8.
1500 in C9.
200 in C10.
15000 in C11.
750 in C12.
22000 in C16.
5000 in C17.
900 in D7.
600 in D8.
1500 in D9.
200 in D10.
14750 in D11.
875 in D12.
23500 in D16.
4000 in D17.

14. The values you entered do not have dollar signs or the commas appropriate to a currency format. You will now learn how to format a range of cells for a particular format (such as the **Currency** format).

15. ***Click in cell C7 and drag the pointer over to cell D20. From the Home tab, click the down arrow next to the Number Format box, which should say General. Then, click Currency.*** Notice that dollar signs have been added to all of the values. ***Click in any cell to deselect the cell range.***

16. ***Click in cell B13, drag the pointer over to cell D13, then from the Home tab, click the Bold icon in the Font group.*** This will make the TOTAL EXPENSES row appear in bold.

17. ***Click in cell B18, drag the pointer over to cell D18, then, from the Home tab, click the Bold icon in the Font group.*** This will make the TOTAL INCOME row appear in bold.

18. ***Click in cell B20, drag the pointer over to cell D20, then, from the Home ribbon tab, click on the Bold icon in the Font group.*** This will make the PROFIT/LOSS row appear in bold.

19. Your spreadsheet is nearly complete; all you need to add are the six formulas.

20. ***Click in cell C13.***

21. Type **=SUM(** and press **[UP ARROW]** six times until the cell pointer is at cell C7. Press **[.]** (a period) to anchor the range.

22. Press the **[DOWN ARROW]** five times, then press the **)** (a closing parenthesis), and then the **[ENTER]** key.

23. Go back to cell C13 and look at the formula in the formula bar. The formula should read =SUM(C7:C12). The total displayed in the cell should read $18,950.00. Note that you also could have typed the formula **=C7+C8+C9+C10+C11+C12.**

24. Enter the following formulas:

=SUM(D7:D12) in D13.
=SUM(C16:C17) in C18.
=SUM(D16:D17) in D18.

25. You now need to enter formulas for the PROFIT/LOSS columns. Enter the following formula in C20:
=C18–C13
(The total should read $8,050.00.)

26. ***Go to cell C20 and click the AutoFill command*** (it is the small black square at the bottom right of the cell—see Excel 2007 Exhibit 2). ***Drag it one column to the right and release the mouse button.*** Notice that the formula has been copied. The total should be $8,675.00. Alternatively, ***go to cell C20, right-click, click Copy, then move the pointer to cell D20,*** and press the **[ENTER]** key.

27. The spreadsheet is now complete. To print the spreadsheet, ***click the Office Button, then click Print, and then click OK.***

28. You will need to save the spreadsheet, because you will be use it in Lesson 2. To save the spreadsheet, ***click the Office Button and then click Save. Under Save in: select the drive or folder you would like to save the document in.*** Then, next to **File Name,** type **Budget1** and click **Save.**

29. To exit Excel, ***click the Office Button and then click on Exit Excel to exit the program.***

This concludes Lesson 1.

LESSON 2: BUILDING A BUDGET SPREADSHEET—PART 2

This lesson assumes that you have completed Lesson 1, have saved the spreadsheet in the lesson, and are generally familiar with the concepts covered in that lesson. Lesson 2 gives you experience in opening a file, inserting a row, formatting numbers as percentages, building additional formulas, creating a bar chart, printing selections, and fitting and compressing data on to one printed page. If you did not exit Excel after Lesson 1, skip steps 1 and 2 below, and go directly to step 3.

1. Open Windows. Then, ***double-click on the Microsoft Office Excel 2007 icon on the desktop*** to open the program. Alternatively, ***click the Start button, point to Programs or All Programs, point to Microsoft Office, and then click Microsoft Office Excel 2007.*** You should now be in a clean, blank workbook.

2. To retrieve the spreadsheet from Lesson 1, ***click on Office Button and then click Open. Next, click the name of your file*** (e.g., **Budget 1** – ***if you do not see it, click through the options under Look in: to find the file. When you have found it, click on Open.***

3. You will be entering the information shown in Excel 2007 Exhibit 3. Notice in Excel 2007 Exhibit 3 that a line for insurance appears in row 9. You will insert this row first.

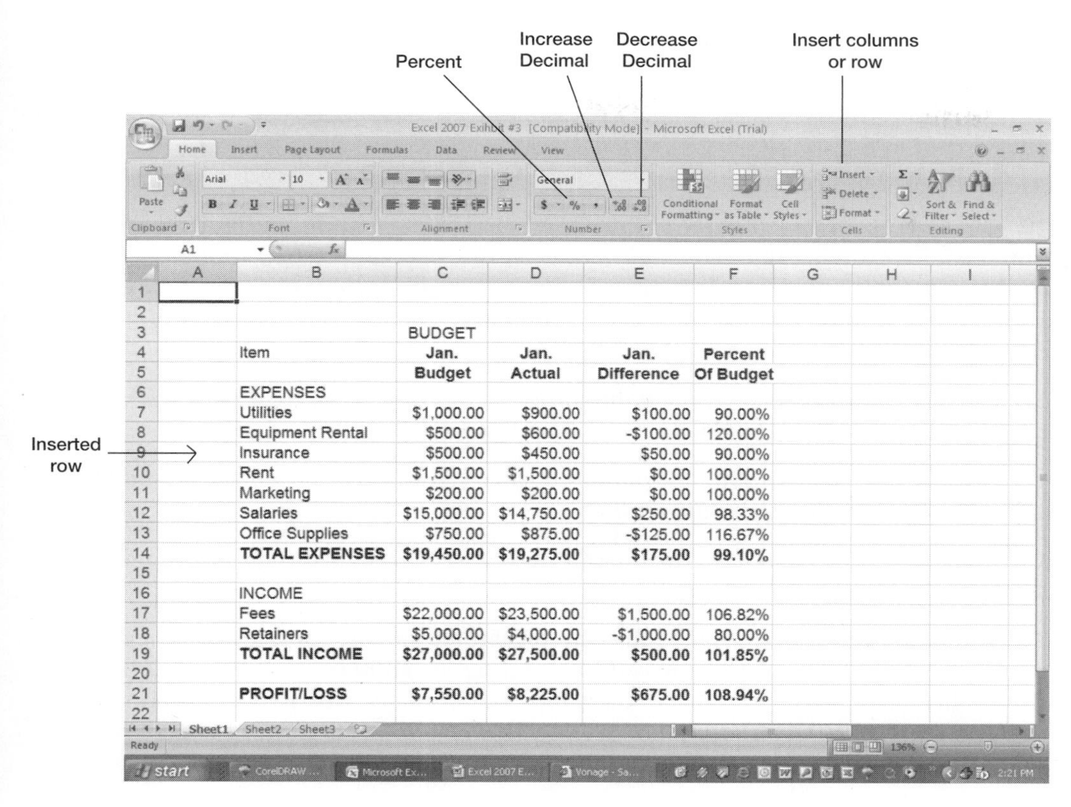

	A	B	C	D	E	F
1						
2						
3			BUDGET			
4		Item	Jan.	Jan.	Jan.	Percent
5			Budget	Actual	Difference	Of Budget
6		EXPENSES				
7		Utilities	$1,000.00	$900.00	$100.00	90.00%
8		Equipment Rental	$500.00	$600.00	-$100.00	120.00%
9		Insurance	$500.00	$450.00	$50.00	90.00%
10		Rent	$1,500.00	$1,500.00	$0.00	100.00%
11		Marketing	$200.00	$200.00	$0.00	100.00%
12		Salaries	$15,000.00	$14,750.00	$250.00	98.33%
13		Office Supplies	$750.00	$875.00	-$125.00	116.67%
14		TOTAL EXPENSES	$19,450.00	$19,275.00	$175.00	99.10%
15						
16		INCOME				
17		Fees	$22,000.00	$23,500.00	$1,500.00	106.82%
18		Retainers	$5,000.00	$4,000.00	-$1,000.00	80.00%
19		TOTAL INCOME	$27,000.00	$27,500.00	$500.00	101.85%
20						
21		PROFIT/LOSS	$7,550.00	$8,225.00	$675.00	108.94%
22						

Excel 2007 Exhibit 3
Expanded Budget Spreadsheet

Microsoft product screen shot reprinted with permission from Microsoft Corporation.

4. ***Click in cell B9. From the Home tab, click the down arrow below Insert in the Cells group. On the Insert menu, click Insert Sheet Rows.*** A new row has been added. You could also have ***right-clicked and selected Insert*** to open a dialog box with the option to insert another row.

5. Enter the following:

   Insurance in B9.
   500 in C9.
   450 in D9.

7. Notice that when the new values for insurance were entered, all of the formulas were updated. Because you inserted the additional rows in the middle of the column, the formulas recognized the new numbers and automatically recalculated to reflect them. Be extremely careful when inserting new rows and columns into spreadsheets that have existing formulas. In some cases, the new number will not be reflected in the totals, such as when rows or columns are inserted at the beginning or end of the range that a formula calculates. It is always prudent to go back to each existing formula, examine the formula range, and make sure the new values are included in the formula range.

8. Change the column width of column E to 12 by ***clicking the column heading (the letter E)*** at the top of the screen. ***Move the pointer to the right edge of the column.*** The pointer should change to a double-headed vertical arrow. ***Drag the pointer to the right until the column width is 12.*** Alternatively, you can change the cell width by ***placing the cell pointer anywhere in column E and, from the Home tab, clicking Format in the Cells Group and selecting Column Width. . . , and then typing 12 and clicking OK.***

9. Enter the following:

   Jan. in E4.
   Difference in E5.
   Percent in F4.
   Of Budget in F5.

10. *Click in cell E4 and drag the pointer over to cell F5* so that the additional column headings are highlighted. *Right-click. Notice that in addition to a menu, the Mini Toolbar appears. It has a number of formatting options on it, including Font, Font size, Bold and others. Click the Bold icon on the Mini Toolbar. Point and click the Center icon on the Mini Toolbar.*

11. *Click in cell E14 and drag the pointer over to cell F14. Then, right click with the mouse and click on the Bold icon on the Mini Toolbar.*

12. *Click in cell E19 and drag the pointer over to cell F19. Then, right-click and select the Bold icon on the Mini Toolbar.*

13. *Click in cell E21 and drag the pointer over to cell F21. Then right-click and select the Bold icon on the Mini Toolbar.*

14. You are now ready to change the cell formatting for column E to **Currency** and column F to **Percent**. *Click in cell E7 and drag the pointer down to cell E21. Right-click and select Format Cells. From the Number tab in the Format Cells window, click Currency and then OK. Click in any cell to get rid of the cell range.*

15. *Click in cell F7 and drag the pointer down to cell F21. From the Home tab, click the Percent (%) icon in the Number group (see Excel 2007 Exhibit 3). Then, from the Home tab, click the Increase Decimal icon twice.*

16. *Click in any cell to get rid of the cell range.*

17. All that is left to do is to enter the formulas for the two new columns. The entries in the Jan. Difference column subtract the actual amount from the budgeted amount for each expense item. A positive amount in this column means that the office was under budget on that item. A negative balance means that the office was over budget on that line item. The Percent of Budget column divides that actual amount by the budgeted amount. This shows the percentage of the budgeted money that was actually spent for each item.

17. You will first build one formula in the Jan. Difference column, and then copy it. Click in cell E7, type **=C7–D7**, and press the **[ENTER]** key.

18. Using the **AutoFill** command or the **Copy** command, copy this formula down through cell E14. (To copy, *right-click and then click Copy; highlight the area where the information should go; then right-click and select Paste.* Alternatively, you can use the **Copy** and **Paste** icons in the **Clipboard** group on the **Home** tab.)

19. Click in cell E17, enter **=D17–C17**, and press the **[ENTER]** key.

20. Using the **AutoFill** command, copy this formula down through cell E21. Delete the formula in cell E20 by *clicking in cell E20* and pressing the **[DEL]** key.

21. You will now build on the formula in the Percent of Budget column and copy it. Click in cell F7, enter **=D7/C7**, and press the **[ENTER]** key.

22. Using the **AutoFill** command, copy this formula down through cell F21. Delete the formula in cell F15, F16, and F20 by *clicking in the cell* and then pressing the **[DEL]** key.

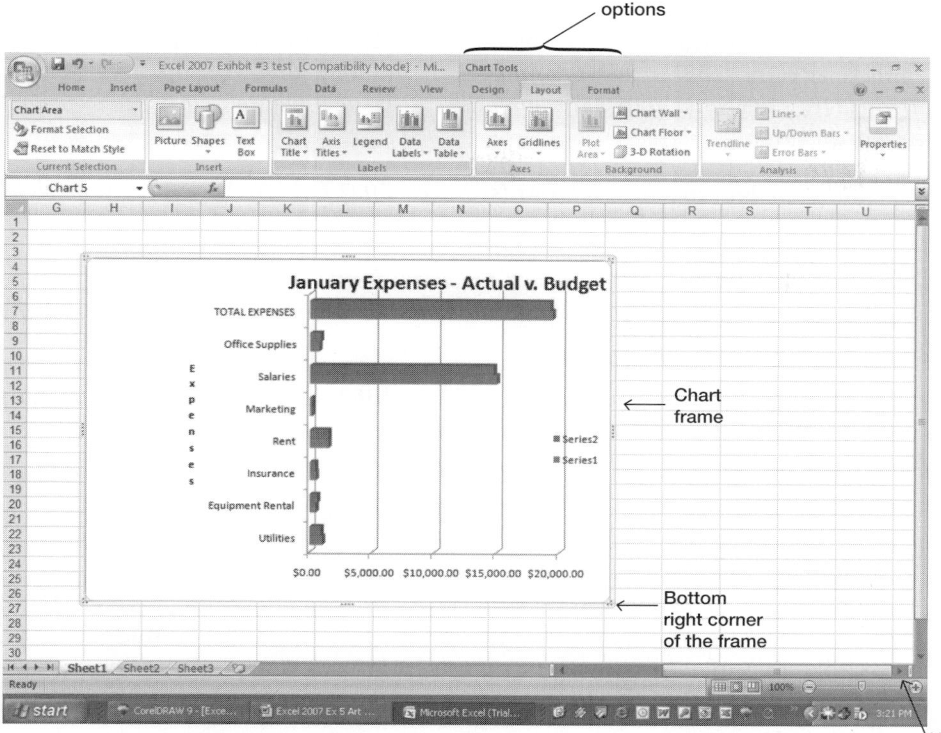

Excel 2007 Exhibit 4
Completed Bar Chart
Microsoft product screen shot reprinted with permission from Microsoft Corporation.

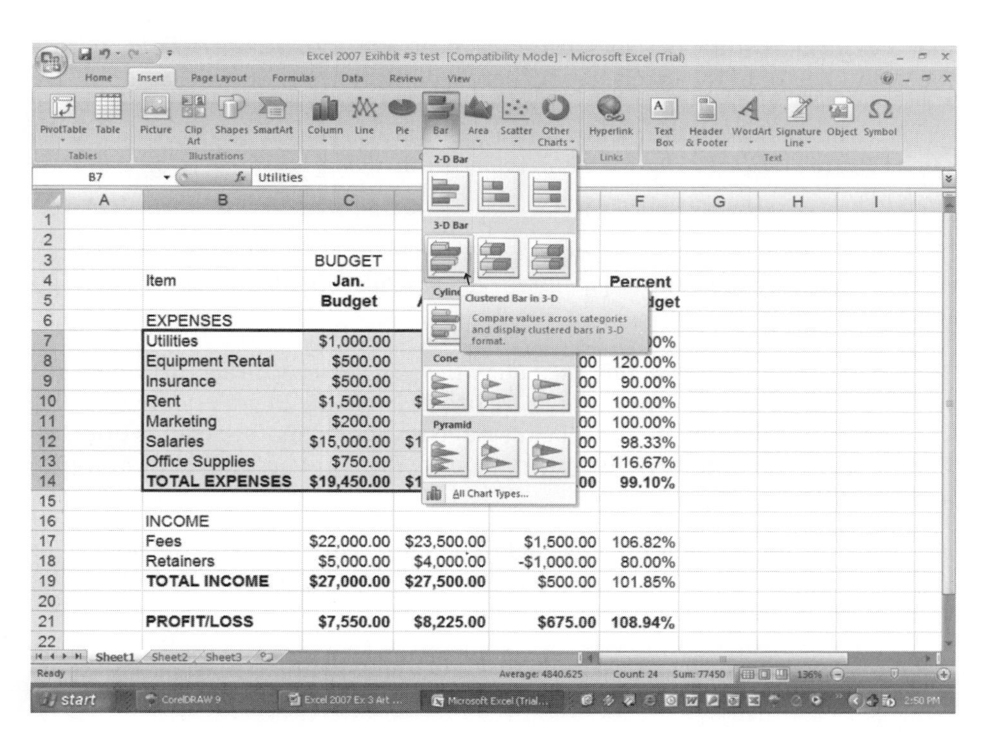

Excel 2007 Exhibit 5
Creating a Bar Chart
Microsoft product screen shot reprinted with permission from Microsoft Corporation.

23. The spreadsheet has now been built. We will now build a bar chart that shows our budgeted expenses compared to our actual expenses (see Excel 2007 Exhibit 4).

24. *Click in cell B7 and then drag the pointer down and over to cell D14.*

25. *From the Insert tab, click Bar from the Charts group. Under 3-D Bar, click the first option, Clustered Bar in 3-D* (see Excel 2007 Exhibit 5).

26. Notice that a draft bar chart has been created. *Click anywhere in the chart frame (see Excel 2007 Exhibit 4), and your pointer will turn to a four-headed arrow. Drag the chart across the spreadsheet so the upper left corner of the chart is near cell H4.*

27. *Using the horizontal scroll bar (see Excel 2007 Exhibit 4), scroll to the right so the chart is completely in your screen.*

28. *Click the bottom right corner of the chart frame. Your cursor should change to a two-headed arrow that is diagonal. Drag the chart so that the bottom right corner ends near cell P26 (see Excel 2007 Exhibit 4).*

29. Notice that new options have been added to the ribbon (e.g., **Chart Tools Design, Layout** and **Format**). *Click the Layout ribbon tab under Chart Tools.*

30. *Click Chart Title in the Labels Group, and then select Above Chart.* Notice that a title has been added, Chart Title.

31. *Point and click on the "Chart Title" text in the bar chart* and press the **[DEL]** key until the text is gone. Next, type **January Expenses—Actual v. Budget**. If you would like to move the title—for example, if it is off center—just click the title frame and drag it where you would like.

32. *From the Layout tab (under Chart Tools), click Axis Titles in the Labels Group. Click Primary Vertical Axis Title and then select Vertical Title.* Notice that a vertical axis title of "Axis Title" has been added. *Click Axis Title* and use the **[DEL]** key until the text is gone. Then, type **Expenses**.

33. *To print the chart, drag the pointer from cell G3 to cell Q27. Then click the Office Button, click Print, and then, under Print what, click Selection and then click OK.*

34. You will next print the spreadsheet and the chart on one page. *Click in cell B3 and then drag the pointer until both the spreadsheet and the chart are highlighted* (roughly cell B3 to cell Q27).

35. *Click the Page Layout tab, then click the Page Setup Dialog Box Launcher. (It is a little box directly under the Print Titles icon in the Page Setup group).* The **Page Setup** window should now be displayed. There is another way to bring up this window; *from the Page Setup group of the Page Layout tab, click Margins, and then click Custom Margins.*

36. *From the Page tab of the Page Setup window, click in the circle next to Fit To: and make sure it says "1 page(s) wide by 1 tall"* (it should default to one page). *Then, under Orientation click on Landscape.*

37. *Now, click Print and then click OK.* This will compress everything in the print area to one page.

38. To save the spreadsheet, *click the Office Button and then click Save As. Under Save in: select the drive or folder you would like to save the document in.* Then, next to **File Name,** type **Budget2** and click Save.

39. To exit Excel, *click the Office Button and then click Exit Excel.*

This concludes Lesson 2.

LESSON 3: BUILDING A DAMAGE PROJECTION SPREADSHEET

This lesson shows you how to build the damage projection spreadsheet shown in Excel 2007 Exhibit 6. It explains how to increase the size of type, how to wrap text in a cell, how to use the border features, how to use the font and fill color features, how to use the AutoSum feature, and how to change the decimal places for a number. This lesson assumes you have successfully completed Lessons 1 and 2. Keep in mind that if at any time you make a mistake in this lesson you may press **[CTRL]+[Z]** to undo what you have done.

1. Open Windows. Then, ***double-click the Microsoft Office Excel 2007 icon on the desktop*** to open the program. Alternatively, ***click on the Start button, point to Programs or All Programs, point to Microsoft Office, and then click Microsoft Office Excel 2007.*** You should now be in a clean, blank workbook. If you are not in a blank workbook, ***click the Office Button (see Excel 2007 Exhibit 1), then click New and double-click Blank Workbook.***

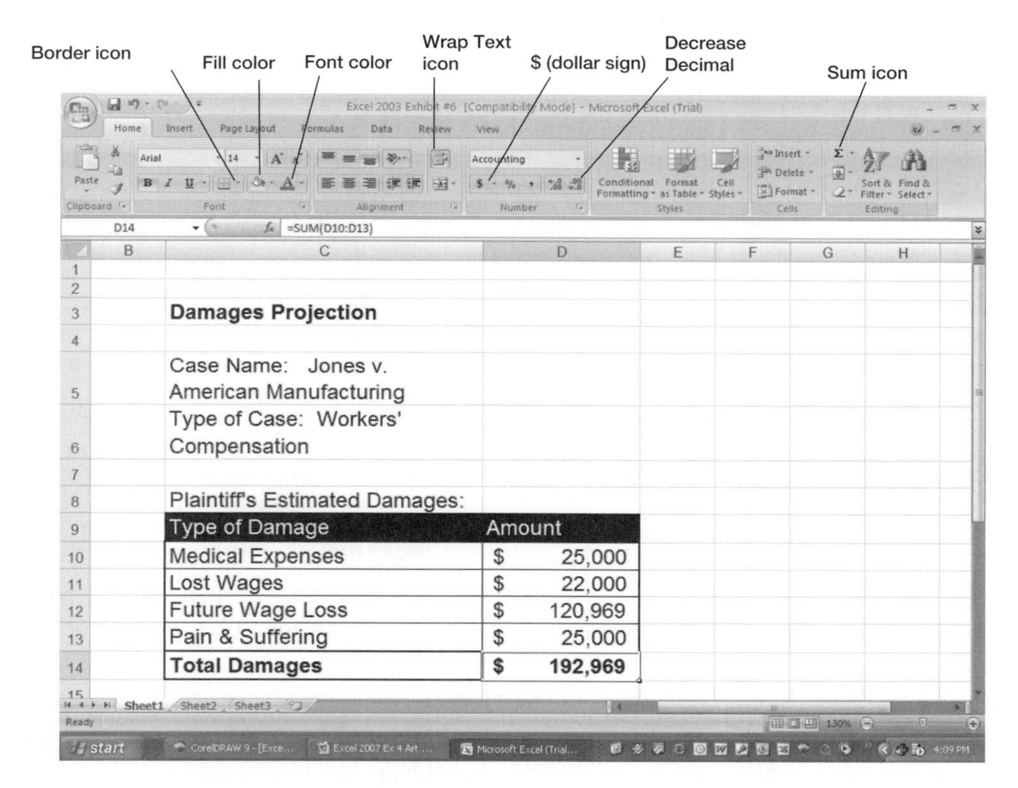

Excel 2007 Exhibit 6
Damages Projection
Microsoft product screen shot reprinted with permission from Microsoft Corporation.

2. To start building the spreadsheet in Excel 2007 Exhibit 6, begin by ***increasing the size of column C to a width of 37 (Home tab>Cells group>Format Column Width).***

3. In cell C3, type **Damages Projection.** With the pointer on C3, ***click the Bold icon from Font group on the Home tab. Then, change the size to 14 point by clicking the Font Size box in the Font group the Home tab and typing 14.***

4. Type the text shown in cell C5 (see Excel 2007 Exhibit 6). ***Click the Font Size box on the Home tab in the Font group and change the type to 14 point.*** Notice that the text goes into the next cell. To wrap part of the text down to the next line

within the current cell (see Excel Exhibit 6), ***from the Home tab, click the Wrap Text icon in the Alignment group (see Excel 2007 Exhibit 6).*** The text has now been wrapped down to the next line within the cell C5.

5. Type the text shown in cell C6, make the text 14 point, and wrap the text down so it does not go into cell D6.

6. Type the text shown in cell C8 and make the text 14 point.

7. Type the text and values shown in cells C9 to D13.

8. Type the text shown in cell C14.

9. To enter the formula in cell D14, ***click cell D14.*** Then, ***from the Editing group on the Home tab, click the Sum icon*** (see Excel 2007 Exhibit 6). Notice that **Sum** assumed you wanted to add the values in D10 to D13. You could adjust the range by pressing **[SHIFT]+[ARROW KEY],** but the range should be fine as is (i.e., D10 to D13). Press the **[ENTER]** key to enter the formula.

10. ***Click in cell C9, drag the mouse pointer to cell D14, and change the font size to 14 point.***

11. ***Click in cell C9 and drag the mouse pointer to cell D9. Right-click and on the Mini Toolbar, click the down arrow next to the Fill Color icon (the paint bucket) and select the black square.*** (You also could have clicked the **Fill Color** icon in the **Font** group on the Home tab.). The cells are all black; now you just need to change the font color to white to see the text.

12. With cells C9 and D9 still highlighted, ***on the Home tab click the down arrow next to the Font Color icon in the Font group, and click on the white square.***

13. ***Click in cell C10 and drag the mouse pointer to cell D14. From the Font group on the Home tab, click on down arrow next to the Border icon.*** (It is typically just to the left of the **Fill Color** icon—see Excel 2007 Exhibit 6). Then, ***click All Borders***—it looks like a windowpane. Notice that there is now a border around every square that was highlighted.

14. ***Click in cell C14 and drag the mouse pointer to cell D14. From the Font group on the Home tab, click the down arrow next to the Border icon again.*** Then ***click on the Thick Box Border*** (it looks like a heavy black window frame). Move the pointer and notice that there is now a heavy black border around cells C14 and D14.

15. ***Click in cell D10 and drag the pointer to cell D14. From the Number group or the Home tab click the dollar sign ($).*** Notice that two decimal places are shown (e.g., 25,000.00). It is not necessary to show two decimal places in our projection, so we will change it to zero decimal places. ***From the Number group on the Home tab, click the Decrease Decimal icon twice.*** Notice that whole dollars are now shown.

16. ***To print the spreadsheet, click the Office Button, then click Print and OK.***

17. To save the spreadsheet, ***click on Office Button and then click Save. Under Save in: select the drive or folder you would like to save the document in.*** Then, next to **File Name,** type **Damages Projection** and click **Save.**

18. To exit Excel, ***click the Office Button and then click Exit Excel to exit the program.***

This concludes Lesson 3.

Intermediate Lessons

LESSON 4: CHILD SUPPORT PAYMENT SPREADSHEET

This lesson shows you how to build the child support payment spreadsheet in Excel 2007 Exhibit 7. It explains how to create a white background, create formulas to multiply cells and formulas that use an absolute cell reference, and use the AutoFormat feature. This lesson assumes you have successfully completed Lessons 1–3. Keep in mind that if at any time you make a mistake in this lesson, you may press **[CTRL]+[Z]** to undo what you have done.

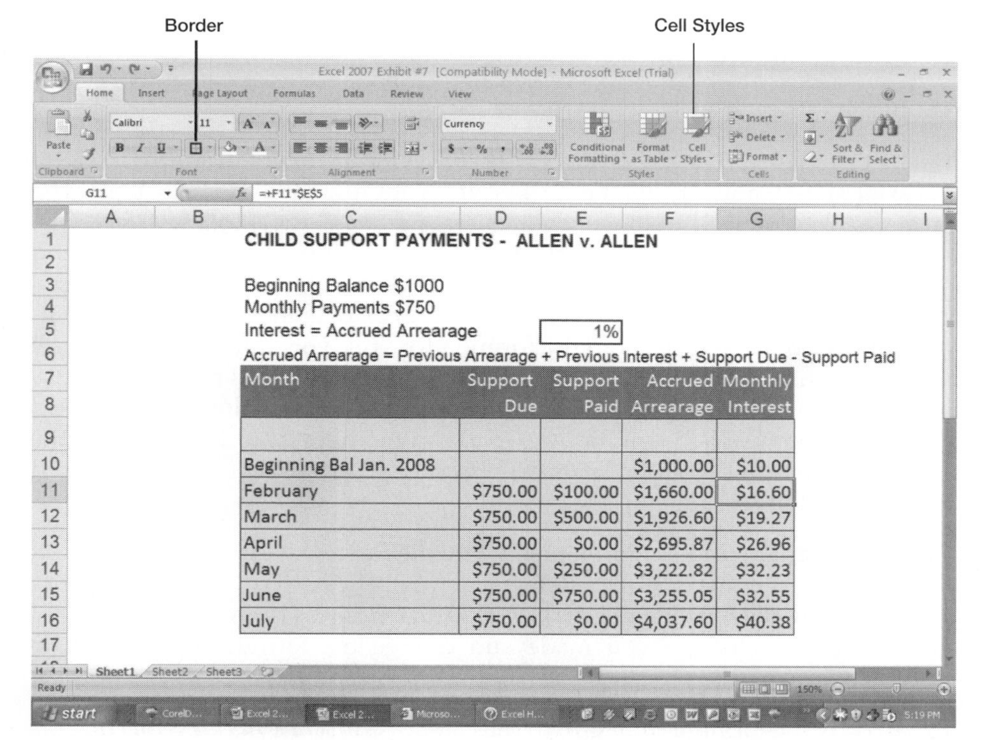

Month	Support Due	Support Paid	Accrued Arrearage	Monthly Interest
Beginning Bal Jan. 2008			$1,000.00	$10.00
February	$750.00	$100.00	$1,660.00	$16.60
March	$750.00	$500.00	$1,926.60	$19.27
April	$750.00	$0.00	$2,695.87	$26.96
May	$750.00	$250.00	$3,222.82	$32.23
June	$750.00	$750.00	$3,255.05	$32.55
July	$750.00	$0.00	$4,037.60	$40.38

Excel 2007 Exhibit 7
Child Support Payment Spreadsheet
Microsoft product screen shot reprinted with permission from Microsoft Corporation.

1. Open Windows. Then, ***double-click the Microsoft Office Excel 2007 icon on the desktop*** to open the program. Alternatively, ***click the Start button, point to Programs or All Programs, point to Microsoft Office, and then click Microsoft Office Excel 2007.*** You should now be in a clean, blank workbook. If you are not in a blank workbook, ***point and click the Office Button (see Excel 2007 Exhibit 1), then click New, and then double-click on Blank Workbook.***

2. When you start to build the spreadsheet in Excel 2007 Exhibit 7, notice that the background is completely white. A completely white background gives you a crisp, clean canvas on which to work and to which you can add colors and graphics.

3. Press **[CTRL]+[A].** The whole spreadsheet is now selected. ***From the Font group on the Home tab, click the down arrow next to the Fill Color icon, and then click the white square (it is all the way in the upper right corner). Click in any cell to make the highlighting disappear.*** Notice that the background of the spreadsheet is completely white.

4. Enter the text shown in cell C1, and change the font to **Bold** and the font size to 14 point.

5. Increase the width of column C to 20.

6. Enter the text shown in cells C3 to C6.

7. In cell E5, type **.01** and press **[ENTER].** Change the number format to **Percent** (zero decimal places).

8. Enter the text shown in cell C7 and in the cell range from D7 to G8.

9. Enter the text shown in the cell range from C10 to C16.

10. Enter the numbers (values) shown in cells in D11 to E16.

11. In cell F10, type **1000.**

12. In cell G10, press the = key, ***click in cell F10***, then press **[SHIFT]+[8]** (an asterisk will appear), then ***click in cell E5*** and press the **[F4]** key once. The formula **=F10*$E$5** should be on the screen; press the **[ENTER]** key. The formula multiplies the accrued arrearage (how much the individual is behind on payments) times the interest rate (which is 1 percent). The reason you pressed **[F4]** is that the formula needed to be an absolute cell reference; pressing [F4] simply put the dollar signs ($) into the formula for you. The dollar signs tell Excel that this is an absolute cell reference, rather than a relative cell reference. In this manner, when you copy the formula to other cells (see below), the accrued arrearage will always be multiplied by the value in E5. Said another way, the second half of this formula ($E$5) will not change when the formula is copied to other cells.

13. If you want to find out for yourself why the formula **=F10*E5** will not work once it is copied from cell G10 (where it will work fine), type **=F10*E5** in cell G10, and then copy the formula to cells G11 to G16. Once you have seen the effect of this, delete the changes you made and change the formula in cell G10 to **=F10*$E$5.**

14. To copy the formula from G10 to cells G11 to G16, ***click in cell G10, click the AutoFill handle*** (the little black box at the lower right corner of the cell) ***and drag the mouse pointer down to cell G16.***

15. In cell F11, type **=F10+G10+D11–E11**. The formula adds the accrued amount in the previous month with the previous month's interest and the current support due, and then subtracts the current amount paid.

16. To copy the formula from F11 to cells F12 to F16, ***click in cell F11, click the AutoFill handle, and drag the mouse pointer down to cell F16.***

17. ***Click in cell D10 and drag the mouse pointer to cell G16. Right-click, and then click Format Cells. Click the Number tab, click Currency; then click OK.***

18. Notice that the spreadsheet is very plain. We will use the **Cell Styles** feature to give the spreadsheet some color. ***Click in cell C7 and drag the mouse pointer to cell G8. From the Styles Group on the Home tab, click the down arrow next to the Cell Styles. Click Accent4 (it is solid purple with white letters).***

19. ***Click in cell C9 and drag the mouse pointer to cell G16. From the Styles group on the Home tab, click the down arrow next to the Cell Styles. Click 20%—Accent1. (It is light blue with black letters.) Click in any cell to make the highlighting disappear.***

20. To add borders to the spreadsheet, ***click in cell C9 and drag the mouse pointer to cell G16. Then, from the Font group on the Home tab, click the down arrow next to the Border icon. Next, click the All Borders icon (it looks like a windowpane).***

21. ***Click in cell E5. From the Font group on the Home tab, click the down arrow next to Borders. Then, click Thick Box Border.*** Press the **[ENTER]** key. The spreadsheet is now complete and should look like Excel 2007 Exhibit 7.

22. ***To print the spreadsheet, click the Office Button, then click Print and OK.***

23. To save the spreadsheet, ***click the Office Button and then click Save. Under Save in: select the drive or folder you would like to save the document in.*** Then, next to **File Name**, type **Child Support Payments** and click **Save.**

24. To exit Excel, ***click your mouse on the Office Button and then click Exit Excel to exit the program.***

This concludes Lesson 4.

LESSON 5: LOAN AMORTIZATION TEMPLATE

This lesson shows you how to open a loan amortization template and fill it in (see Excel 2007 Exhibit 8). Templates are a great way to simplify complicated spreadsheets. You will also learn how to protect cells, freeze panes, split a screen, hide a column, and use the Format Painter tool. This lesson assumes you have successfully completed Lessons 1–4. Keep in mind that if at any time you make a mistake in this lesson, you may press **[CTRL]+[Z]** to undo what you have done.

1. Open Windows. Then, ***double-click the Microsoft Office Excel 2007 icon on the desktop*** to open the program. Alternatively, ***click the Start button, point to***

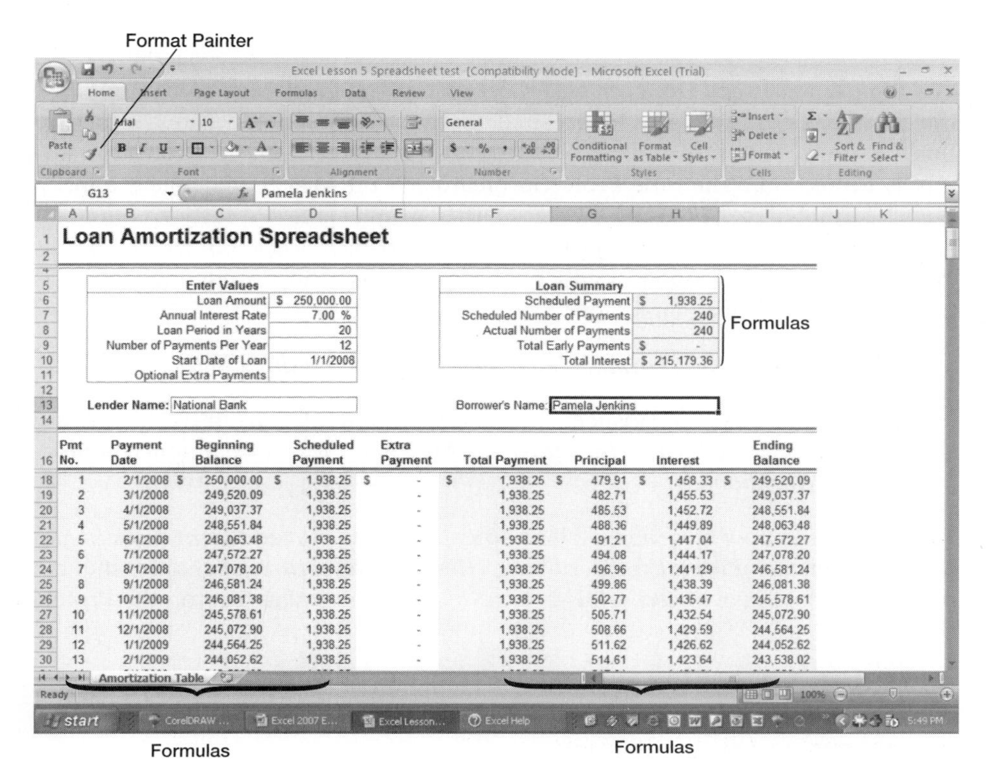

Excel 2007 Exhibit 8
Loan Amortization Template
Microsoft product screen shot reprinted with permission from Microsoft Corporation.

Programs or All Programs, point to Microsoft Office, and then click Microsoft Office Excel 2007. You should now be in a clean, blank workbook.

2. The first thing you will do to complete the template in Excel 2007 Exhibit 8 is to open the "Lesson 5" file from Disk 1 supplied with this text. Ensure that the disk is inserted in the disk drive, point and click on File on the Office button, and then point and click on Open. The "Open" window should now be displayed. Point and click on the down arrow to the right of the white box next to "Look in:" and select the drive where Disk 1 is located. Point and double-click on the Excel Files folder. Double-click on the "Lesson 5" file.

3. You should now have the loan amortization spreadsheet shown in Excel 2007 Exhibit 8 opened, except that your spreadsheet has no data yet.

4. Enter the following information as shown below:

Cell D6: **250000**
Cell D7: **7**
Cell D8: **20**
Cell D9: **12**
Cell D10: **1/1/2008**
Cell D11: **0**
(When you click in Cell D11 a note will appear regarding extra payments; just type a zero and hit **[ENTER]** and the note will disappear.)
Cell C13: **National Bank**
Cell G13: **Pamela Jenkins**

5. Notice that your spreadsheet now appears nearly identical to Excel 2007 Exhibit 8.

6. Notice in your spreadsheet that just about everything below row 16 is a formula. If a user accidentally deletes one of these formulas, the whole spreadsheet could be affected. You will now turn on the **Protection** feature and lock some of the cells so they cannot be accidentally deleted.

7. *Right-click in cell D6. Then click Format Cells. . . Click the Protection tab in the Format Cells window.* Notice that there is no green check mark next to **Locked.** Cells D6 to D13 and cell G13 are unlocked even when the **Protection** feature is turned on. When the **Protection** feature is off, you can change the lock/unlock format of cells by using the right-click, **Format Cells>Protection** command sequence. Interestingly, when a new blank spreadsheet is open in Excel, all cells default to "Locked," but this has no effect because the **Protection** feature is always turned off in a blank workbook.

8. *Click Cancel in the "Format Cells" window to close the window.*

9. Let's open a new spreadsheet so you can see that all cells in Excel start out with the format locked. *Click the Office Button, then click New, and then double-click Blank Workbook.*

10. You should now have a new blank spreadsheet displayed. *Right-click in any cell and then click Format Cells. . . Next, click the Protection tab.* Notice that the cell is locked. However, the cell is not truly locked until you turn on the **Protection** feature.

11. Now, *click Cancel in the Format Cells window in the new spreadsheet. Next, click the Office Button and then click Close to close the file.* You should now be back at your amortization spreadsheet.

12. To turn on the Protection feature, ***on the Review tab, click Protect Sheet in the Changes group.***

13. The **Protect Sheet** window should now be displayed (see Excel 2007 Exhibit 9). Make sure that the first two selections under **Allow all users of this worksheet to:** are selected (e.g., **Select locked cells** and **Select Unlocked Cells**). Notice that you could enter a password in the white box under **Password to unprotect sheet.** This would completely lock the spreadsheet (so only unlocked cells could be modified) to users that did not know the password. In this case this is not necessary; it is fine for someone to intentionally change the values at the top of the spreadsheet—we are just using this feature to prevent someone from accidentally changing the formulas below row 16.

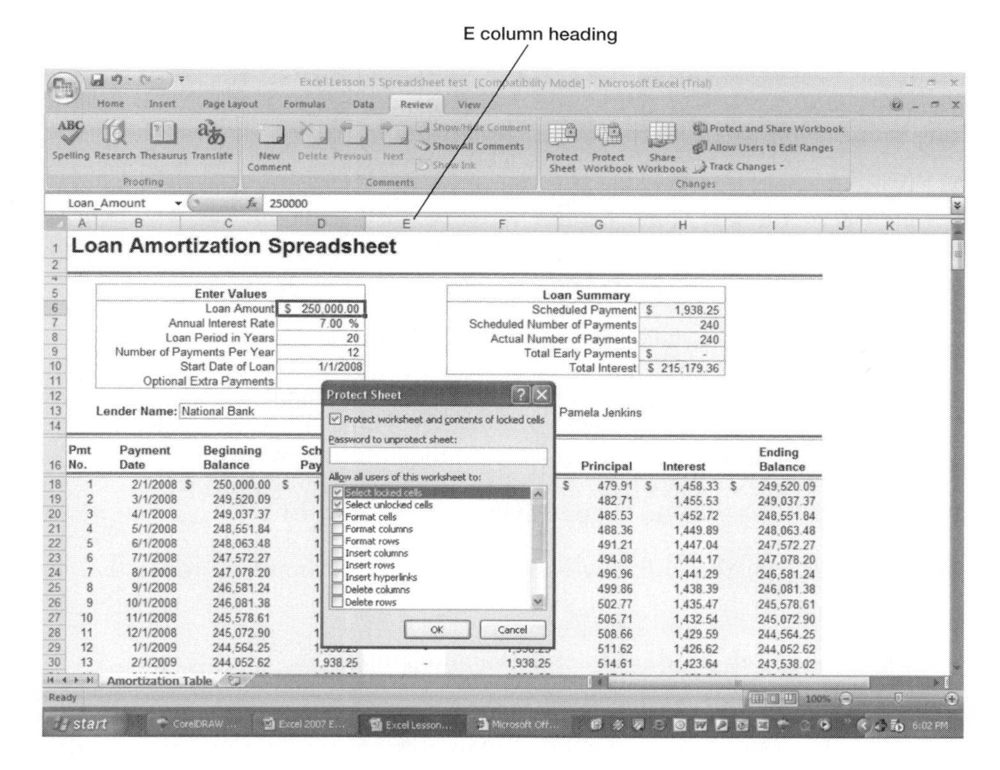

Excel 2007 Exhibit 9
Protecting Cells in Excel 2007

Microsoft product screen shot reprinted with permission from Microsoft Corporation.

14. After the first two items are check-marked under **Allow all users of this worksheet to,** *click OK.*

15. *Now, click in any cell other than D6 to D13 or cell G13 and try to type something in the cell.* You should get an error message that says **The cell** or **chart you are trying to change is protected and therefore read-only.** *Click OK to close the error window.*

16. The whole spreadsheet is now locked, except for cells D6 to D13 and cell G13, because these were not formatted as locked in the template.

17. Now you will turn off the Protection feature because you are still building the spreadsheet. ***On the Review tab, click Unprotect Sheet in the Changes group.***

18. You will now use the Format Painter tool to copy the formatting from one set of cells to another set of cells. Notice that cells F13 and G13 do not look like cells B13 and C13. You will copy the format from cells B13 and C13 to cells F13 and G13.

19. ***Point in cell B13 and drag the mouse pointer to cell C13. Next, on the Home tab, click the Format Painter icon in the Clipboard group. (It looks like a paintbrush).*** Your pointer now should have a paintbrush icon on it.

20. ***Click in cell F13, drag the mouse to cell H13, and then let go of the mouse button. Click anywhere to see the cell.*** Notice that the formatting has now been copied.

21. Column E in the amortization schedule of the spreadsheet is the "Extra Payment" column. Assume for this exercise that you will not have any extra payments and that you do not need this column, but you want to leave the column there in case you need it at a later date. For now, you can hide column E until you need it later.

22. ***Point and right-click on the "E" in the E column heading (see Excel 2007 Exhibit 9). From the drop-down menu, click Hide.***

23. ***Click in any cell.*** *The vertical line will disappear.* Notice that column E is no longer displayed. The column heading goes from D to F.

24. We will now Unhide column E. ***Point on the D column heading and drag the mouse to the F column heading so that both columns are highlighted. Right-click, then click Unhide on the drop-down menu.*** Notice that column E reappears.

25. ***Click in any cell to make the highlighting disappear.***

26. ***Click in cell D18.*** Use the **[DOWN ARROW]** key to go to cell D50. Notice that the some column titles, such as "Pmt No.," and "Payment Date," are no longer visible, so it is difficult to know what the numbers mean.

27. Press **[CTRL]+[HOME]** to go to the top of the spreadsheet.

28. ***Click cell A18.*** You will now use the **Split Screen** command to see the column titles.

29. ***On the View tab click Split in the Window group.***

30. Use the **[DOWN ARROW]** cursor key on the keyboard to go to cell A50. Notice that because you split the screen at row 18, you can still see column titles. Next, use the **[UP ARROW]** cursor key on the keyboard to go to cell A1. You now should see the top portion of your spreadsheet in both the top and bottom screens.

31. ***On the View tab, click Split again in the Window group.*** The bottom screen is now gone.

32. The **Freeze Panes** feature is another way to show the column headings when you scroll down a document. The **Freeze Panes** feature is a convenient way to see both column and row titles at the same time. ***Click in cell B18.***

33. ***On the View tab, click Freeze Panes in the Window group and then click the first option, Freeze Panes.***

34. Use the **[DOWN ARROW]** cursor key on the keyboard to go to cell B50. Notice that because you froze the screen at cell B18, you can still see column titles. Next, use the **[RIGHT ARROW]** cursor key on the keyboard to go to cell R50. You should still see the "Pmt No." column, including the payment numbers.

35. Press **[CTRL]+[HOME]** to go to the beginning of the spreadsheet.

36. ***On the View tab, click Freeze Panes in the Window group and then click the first option, Unfreeze Panes.***

37. ***To print the spreadsheet, click the Office Button, then click Print and OK.***

38. To save the spreadsheet, ***click the Office Button and then click Save As. Under Save in, select the drive or folder you would like to save the document in.*** Then, next to **File Name,** type **Excel Lesson 5 Spreadsheet DONE** and click **Save.**

39. Templates are a great way to utilize the power of Excel. There are many free templates available on the Internet. Microsoft alone offers more than 100 Excel templates on their website. To access them, ***click the Office Button, then New. They are listed to the left under Microsoft Office Online.***

40. To exit Excel, ***click on Office Button and then click Exit Excel to exit the program.***

This concludes Lesson 5.

LESSON 6: STATISTICAL FUNCTIONS

This lesson demonstrates how to use and enter statistical formulas such as average, maximum, minimum, and standard deviation. It also shows how to sort data, check for metadata in spreadsheets, to use the Format Clear command, how to use conditional formatting, and how to insert a clip art file. When the spreadsheet is complete, it will look like Excel 2007 Exhibit 10. Keep in mind that if at any time you make a mistake in this lesson, you may press **[CTRL]+[Z]** to undo what you have done.

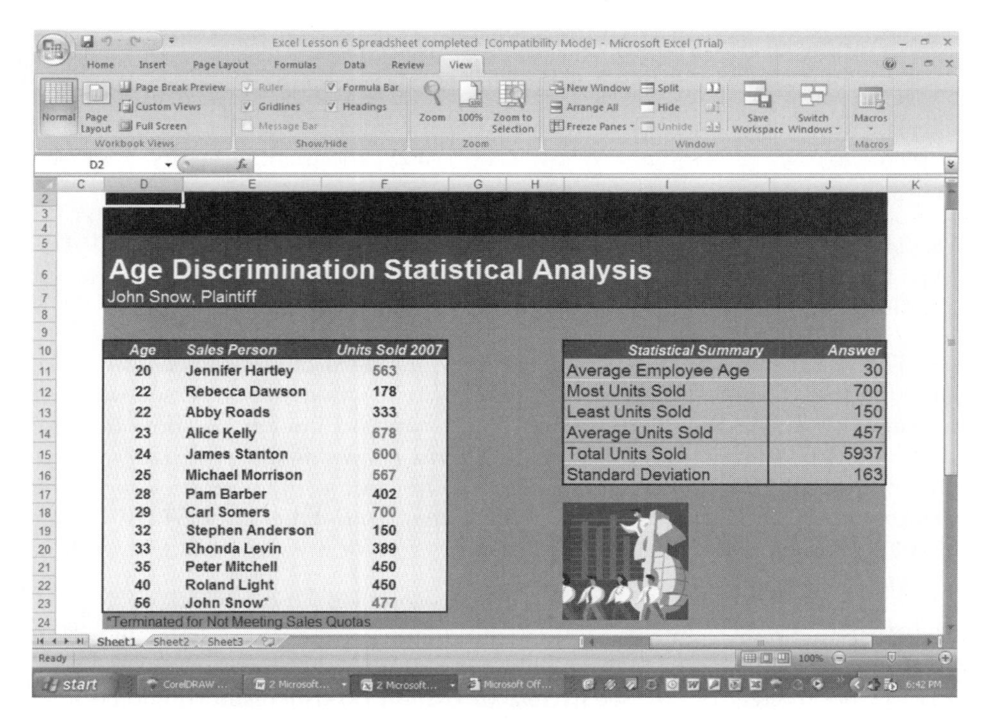

Excel 2007 Exhibit 10
Statistical Spreadsheet
Microsoft product screen shot reprinted with permission from Microsoft Corporation.

1. Open Windows. Then, ***double-click the Microsoft Office Excel 2007 icon on the desktop*** to open the program. Alternatively, ***click the Start button, point to Programs or All Programs, point to Microsoft Office, and then click Microsoft Office Excel 2007.*** You should now be in a clean, blank workbook. If you are not in a blank workbook, ***click the Office Button (see Excel 2007 Exhibit 1), then click New, and then double-click on Blank Workbook.***

2. The first thing you will do to complete the template shown in Excel 2007 Exhibit 8 is to open the "Lesson 6" file from Disk 1 supplied with this text. Ensure that the disk is inserted in the disk drive, point and click on File on the Office button, and then point and click on Open. The "Open" window should now be displayed. Point and click on the down arrow to the right of the white box next to "Look in:" and select the drive where Disk 1 is located. Point and double-click on the Excel Files folder. Double-click on the "Lesson 6" file.

3. You should now see the age discrimination statistical analysis spreadsheet shown in Excel 2007 Exhibit 10, except your spreadsheet has no formulas in the statistical summary section, the data has not yet been sorted, and there is no clip art yet.

4. You will now enter the formulas in the statistical summary section of the spreadsheet. The first formula will calculate the average age of employees of the company. ***Click in cell J11.*** Type the following formula: **=AVERAGE(D11:D23)** and then press **[ENTER]**. The result should be 30. *Note*: Another way to enter the average function would be to, on the **Formulas** tab, click **Insert Function** in the **Function Library** group; next to **Or select a category,** click the down arrow, then click **Statistical, average,** and **OK.**

5. The next formula will be to calculate the most units sold. ***Click in cell J12.*** Type the following formula: **=MAX(F11:F23)** and then press **[ENTER]**. The result should be 700.

6. The next formula will be to calculate the least units sold. ***Click in cell J13.*** Type the following formula: **=MIN(F11:F23)** and then press **[ENTER]**. The result should be 150.

7. The next formula will be to calculate the average units sold. ***Click in cell J14.*** Type the following formula: **=AVERAGE(F11:F23)** and then press **[ENTER]**. The result should be 457.

8. The next formula will be to calculate the total units sold. ***Click in cell J15.*** Type the following formula: **=SUM(F11:F23)** and then press **[ENTER].** The result should be 5937.

9. The last formula will be to calculate the standard deviation for units sold. The standard deviation is a measure of how widely values are dispersed from the average value (the arithmetic mean). Large standard deviations show that the numbers vary widely from the average. ***On the Formulas tab, click Insert Function in the Function Library group. Next to Or select a category, click the down arrow and select Statistical. Then, scroll down the list and click*** **STDEVP** (see Excel 2007 Exhibit 11). Notice there is a definition for this function. ***Click OK in the Insert Function window.***

10. The **Function Arguments** window should now be displayed. In the **Function Arguments** window next to **Number 1**, press **[DEL]** until the box is blank, type **F11:F23,** and then ***click OK*** (see Excel 2007 Exhibit 12). The result should be 163.

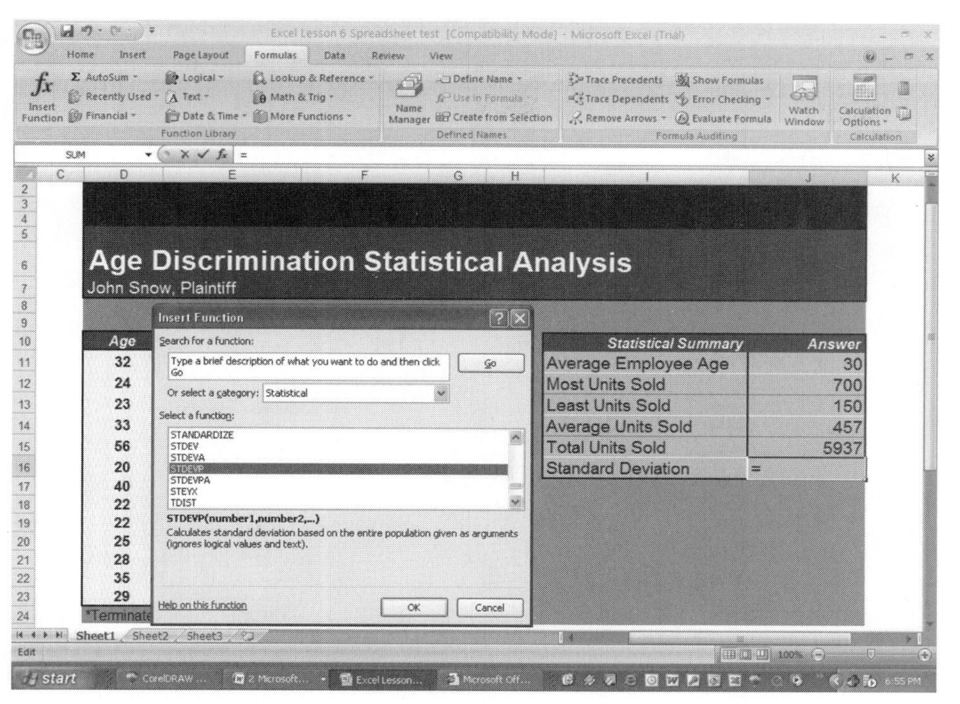

Excel 2007 Exhibit 11

Entering a Standard Deviation Formula Using the ***Insert Function*** *Command*

Microsoft product screen shot reprinted with permission from Microsoft Corporation.

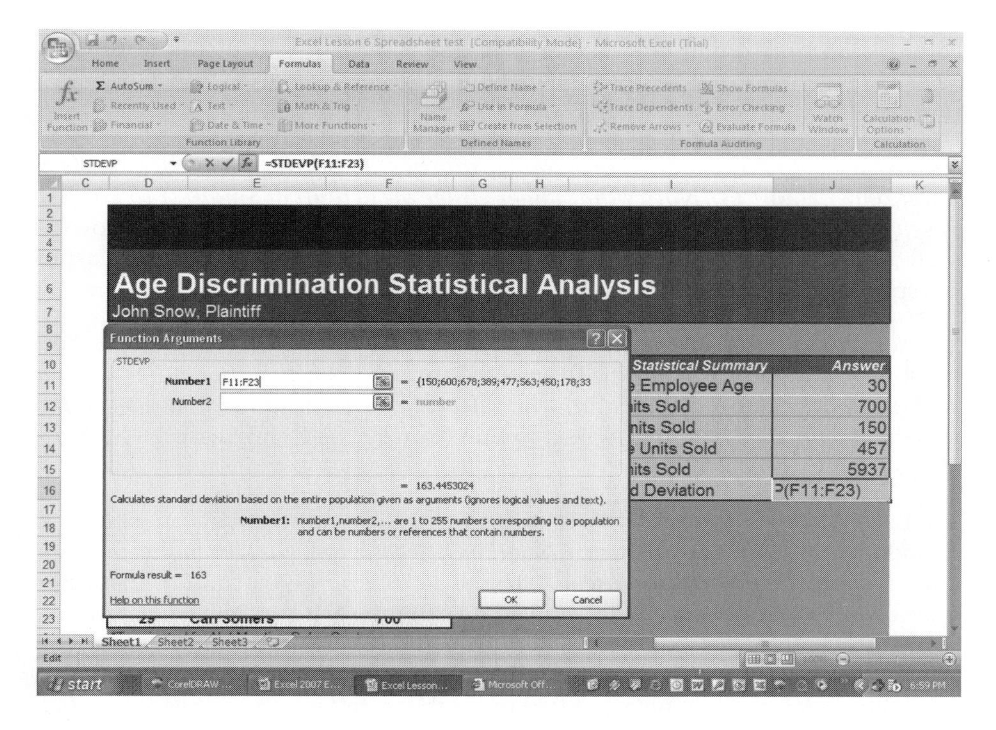

Excel 2007 Exhibit 12

Entering a Standard Deviation Formula—The ***Function Arguments*** *Window*

Microsoft product screen shot reprinted with permission from Microsoft Corporation.

11. You will now sort the data based on the age of the employees. ***Click in D11 and then drag the mouse down to F23. Then, from the Data tab, click Sort in the Sort and Filter group.***

12. The **Sort** window should now be displayed (see Excel 2007 Exhibit 13). *Note*: Even though you just want to sort by age, you must select the full data range that includes all of the information, or the age data will be sorted but the other

Excel 2007 Exhibit 13
Sorting Data
Microsoft product screen shot reprinted with permission from Microsoft Corporation.

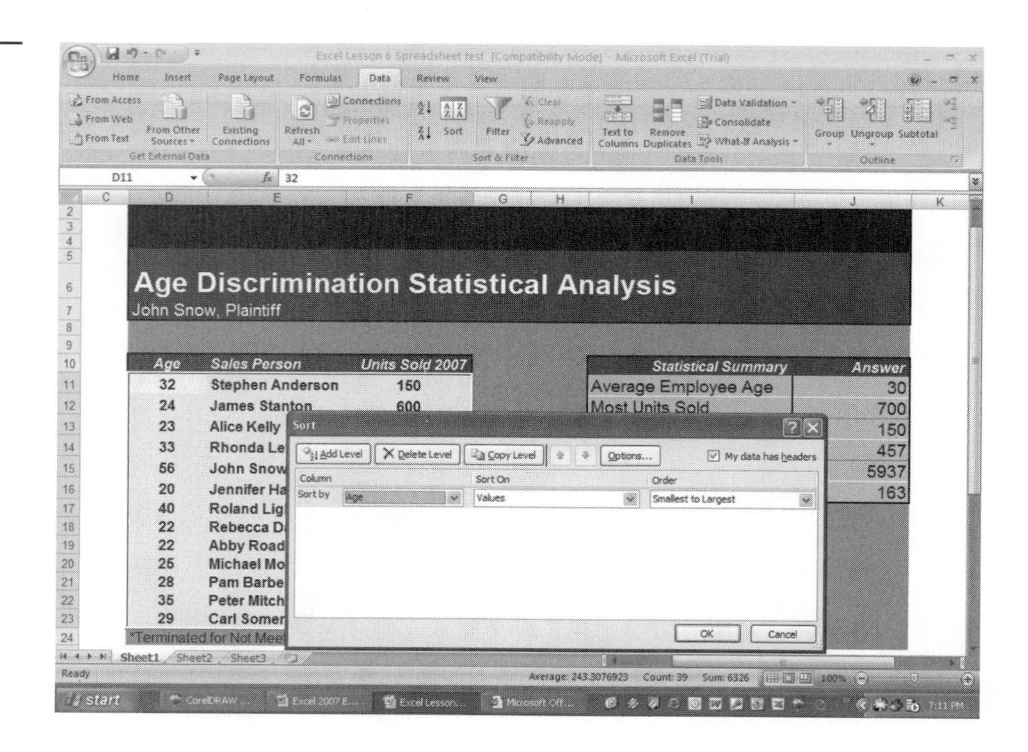

columns and rows will stay where they are. The data will therefore be mismatched (each age will not be matched with the correct person and number of units sold).

13. ***In the Sort window, click the down arrow next to Sort by, then click Age (see Excel 2007 Exhibit 13). Notice that under Order the default of Smallest to Largest is selected; this is fine, so click OK in the Sort window.*** The data should now be sorted according to the age of the individual, with John Snow appearing last in the spreadsheet.

14. You will now ensure that no metadata is included in your document. You must first save the spreadsheet. To save the spreadsheet, ***click the Office Button and then click Save As. Under Save in: select the drive or folder you would like to save the document in.*** Then, next to **File Name,** type **Excel Lesson 6 Spreadsheet DONE** and click **Save.**

15. Excel 2007 has a special feature called **Inspect Document** that can extract all metadata from your spreadsheet. ***Click the Office Button, click Prepare, and then click Inspect Document*** (see Excel 2007 Exhibit 14). In the **Document Inspector** window all of the possible places metadata can hide are checked. ***Click Inspect.*** Some of the categories may have a **Remove All** button. If you wanted to remove the metadata, you would just click on **Remove All** for each category. Because this is just an exercise, we do not need to remove the metadata, so go ahead and ***click Close*** to close the "Document Inspector" window.

16. Sometimes it is helpful to clear a cell or cells of all formatting information at one time. Notice that cell D6, the one titled "Age Discrimination Statistical Analysis," is elaborately formatted, including 24-point font, white letters, red background, and bold text. You will now quickly remove all of the formatting. ***Click in cell D6, then on the Home tab, click the down arrow next to the Clear icon in the Editing group (it looks like an eraser—see Excel 2007 Exhibit 15). Then, click Clear Formats.*** All of the formatting should be gone. Notice in Excel 2007

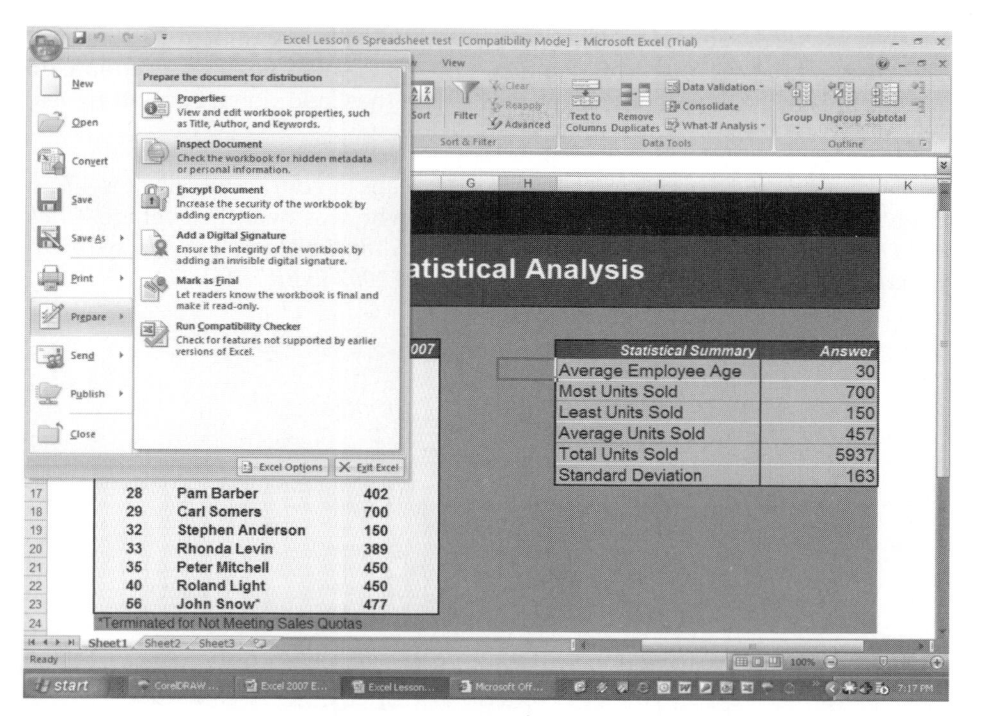

Excel 2007 Exhibit 14
Removing Metadata, the Inspect Document Command
Microsoft product screen shot reprinted with permission from Microsoft Corporation.

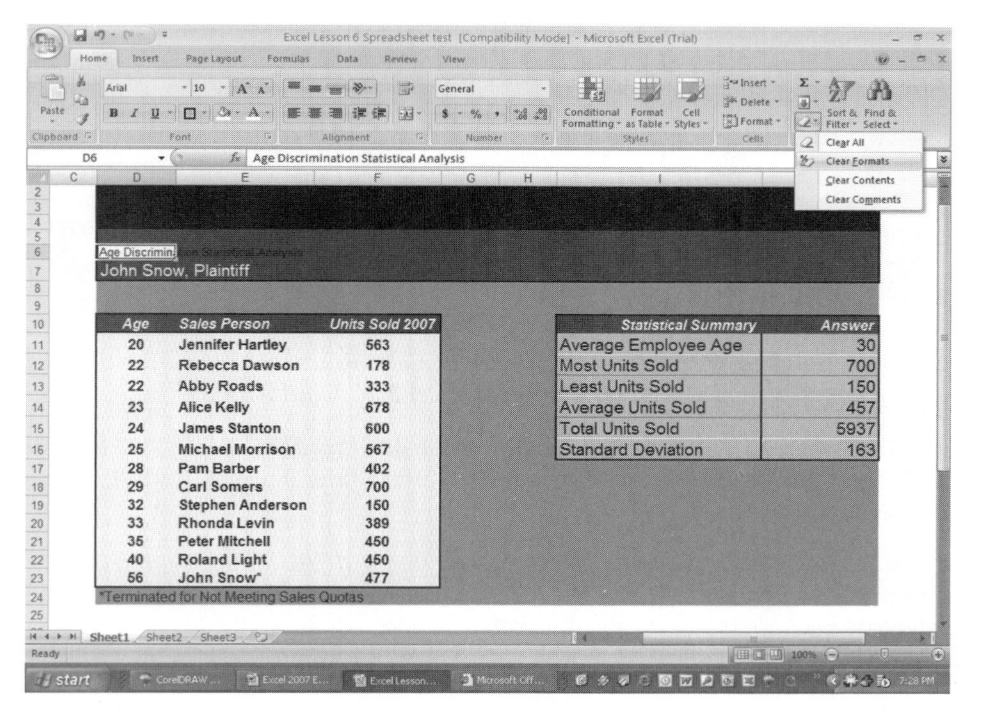

Excel 2007 Exhibit 15
Clear Command
Microsoft product screen shot reprinted with permission from Microsoft Corporation.

Exhibit 15 that one of the options when using the **Clear** command is **Clear All**. Clicking **Clear All** will not only clear the formatting, but will also clear the contents of the selected cell(s).

17. Press **[CTRL]+[Z]** (the **Undo** feature) to restore the original formatting to the cell.

18. Sometimes, particularly in large spreadsheets, it is helpful to have the formatting of a cell change if certain conditions are present. For example, in an

actual v. budget report, if an item goes over budget by more than 10 percent it might be helpful for that to be bolded so it catches the reader's attention. To accomplish this, you will now learn how to use the Conditional Formatting feature of Excel.

19. Notice that the average sales for the sales team in your spreadsheet is 457. It might be helpful to highlight any salesperson who was over the average. ***Click in F11 and then drag the mouse to F23. Then, from the Home tab, click Conditional Formatting in the Styles group (see Excel 2007 Exhibit 16).***

Excel 2007 Exhibit 16
Creating Conditional Formatting
Microsoft product screen shot reprinted with permission from Microsoft Corporation.

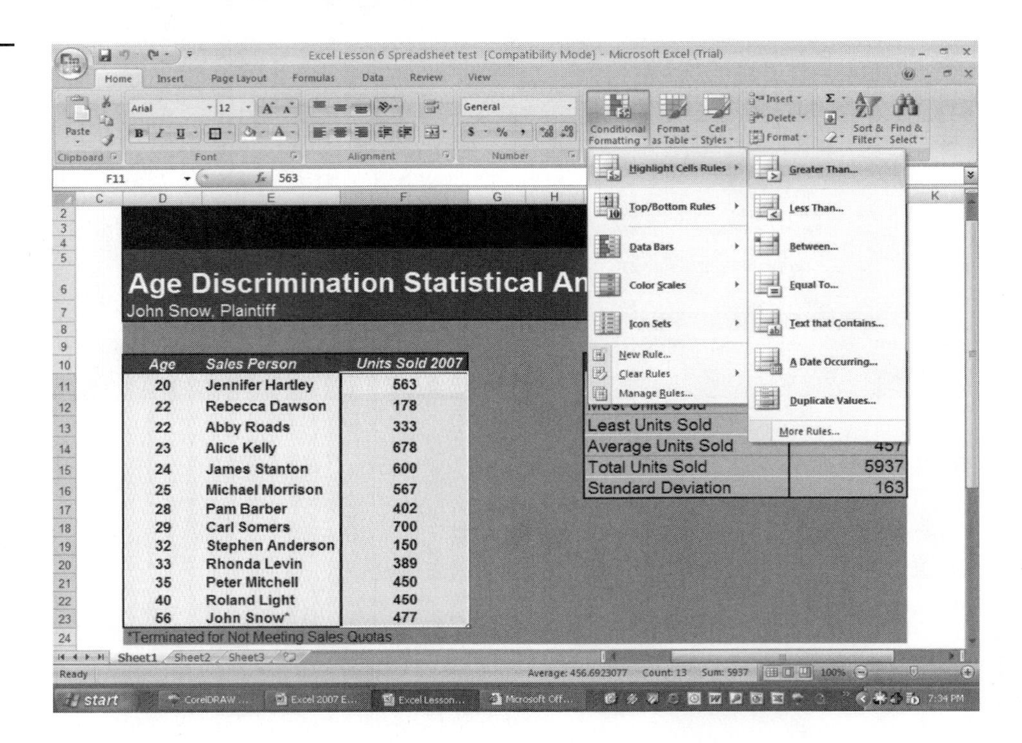

20. ***Now, point to the first option Highlight Cells Rules and then click the first option again, which is Greater Than (see Excel 2007 Exhibit 16).***

21. ***The Greater Than window should now be displayed (see Excel 2007 Exhibit 17).*** Press the **[DEL]** key to remove the value under **Format Cells that are GREATER THAN.**

22. ***Click cell J14 on the spreadsheet. Notice that cell J14 has been entered under Format Cells that are GREATER THAN.*** Dollar signs have been added to the cell reference because this is an absolute cell reference.

23. ***Click the down arrow next to Light Red Fill with Dark Red Text and select Red Text.*** Cells over the average will be shown in red text. ***Click OK in the Greater Than window.***

24. You will now add clip art to your spreadsheet (assuming clip art was included when Excel 2007 was installed). ***Click in cell I18. Next, from the Insert tab, click Clip Art in the Illustrations group.***

25. ***The Clip Art task pane will appear to the right of the screen.*** Under **Search For** type **Money** and then ***click Go. You may get a message that asks if you want to include clip art from Microsoft Office Online; click No.***

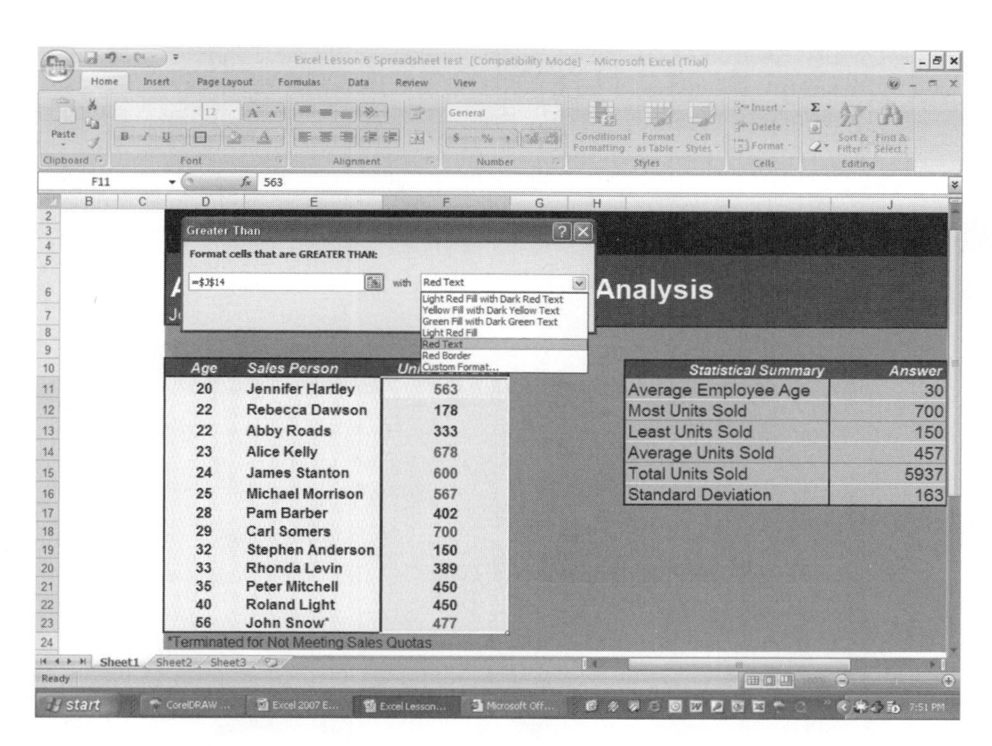

Excel 2007 Exhibit 17
Creating "Greater Than" Conditional Formatting
Microsoft product screen shot reprinted with permission from Microsoft Corporation.

26. ***Click on the clip art in Excel 2007 Exhibit 10 (a blue bar chart with people in it and a person climbing a dollar sign).*** The clip art has now been added to your spreadsheet. ***Position the clip art where you want it by clicking and dragging it into position.***

27. ***Click the "X" in the Clip Art task pane to close the task pane.***

28. ***To print the spreadsheet, click the Office Button, then click Print and OK.***

29. To save the spreadsheet, ***click the Office Button and then click Save As.*** Choose the directory where you want to save the file and ***click Save.***

30. To exit Excel, ***click the Office Button and then click Exit Excel to exit the program.***

This concludes Lesson 6.

Advanced Lessons

LESSON 7: TOOLS AND TECHNIQUES 1

In this lesson, you will learn how to create visual impact with spreadsheets. You will learn to create and manipulate a text box, use advanced shading techniques, create a 3-D style text box, create vertical text, create diagonal text, use lines and borders, and create a comment. When the spreadsheet is complete, it will look like Excel 2007 Exhibit 18. Keep in mind that if at any time you make a mistake in this lesson, you may press **[CTRL]+[Z]** to undo what you have done.

1. Open Windows. Then, ***double-click the Microsoft Office Excel 2007 icon on the desktop*** to open the program. Alternatively, ***click the Start button, point to Programs or All Programs, point to Microsoft Office, and then click Microsoft Office Excel 2007.*** You should now be in a clean, blank workbook.

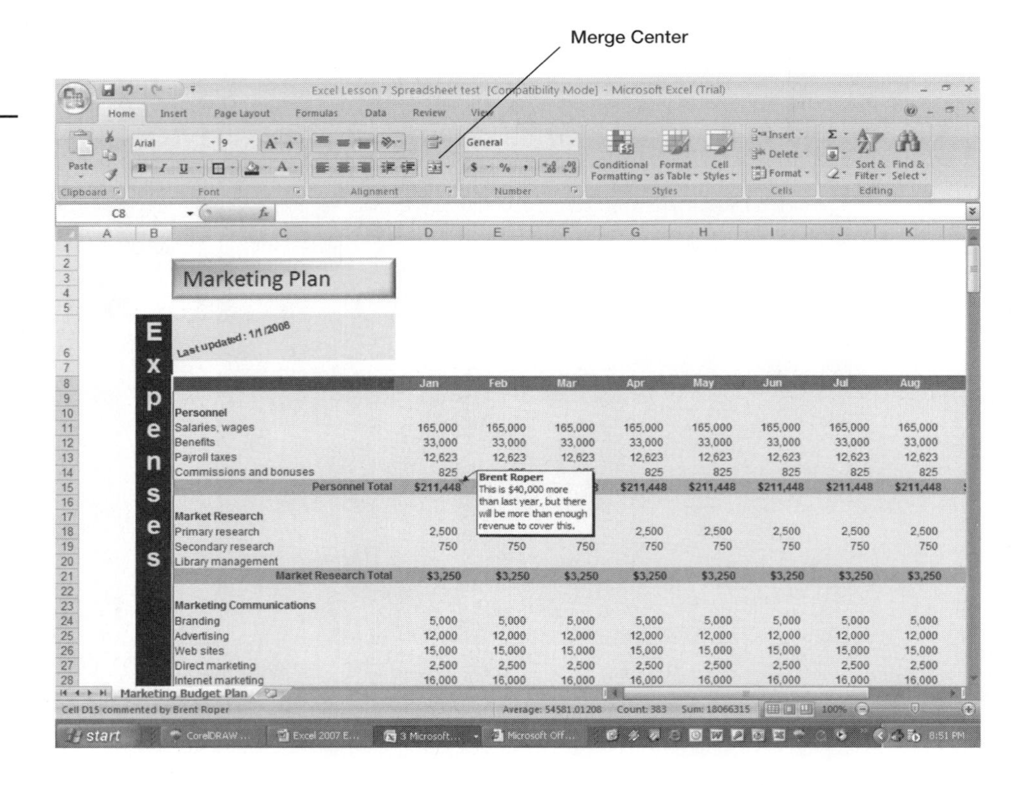

Excel 2007 Exhibit 18
Creating Visual Impact in Spreadsheets
Microsoft product screen shot reprinted with permission from Microsoft Corporation.

2. The first thing you will do to complete the spreadsheet in Excel 2007 Exhibit 18 is to open the "Lesson 7" file from Disk 1 supplied with this text. Ensure that the disk is inserted in the disk drive, point and click on File on the Office Button, and then point and click on Open. The "Open" window should now be displayed. Point and click on the down arrow to the right of the white box next to "Look in:" and select the drive where Disk 1 is located. Point and double-click on the Excel Files folder. Double-click on the "Lesson 7" file.

3. You should now have the Marketing Plan spreadsheet in Excel 2007 Exhibit 18 opened, except the spreadsheet is missing some of the formatting that gives it visual impact. You will add the formatting to the spreadsheet to make it more visually compelling.

4. You will first add the text box that holds the title "Marketing Plan," as shown in Excel 2007 Exhibit 18. ***From the Insert tab, click Text Box in the Text group.*** Notice that your mouse pointer just turned into an upside down letter "T."

5. ***Point to cell C2 and drag the mouse to about cell F4***. An outline of a box should now be shown from C2 to F4. This is a *text box*.

6. ***Click inside the text box. Click the Bold icon and change the font size to 20.***

7. Type **MARKETING PLAN.**

8. ***Point and right-click on the outline of the text box you just created. In the drop-down menu, click Format Shape.*** The **Format Shape** window should now be displayed.

9. ***In the Format Shape window, notice that Fill is currently selected. Click Gradient fill.***

10. ***Click the down arrow next to Preset Colors***. This will open a box with many colors; ***click Fog.***

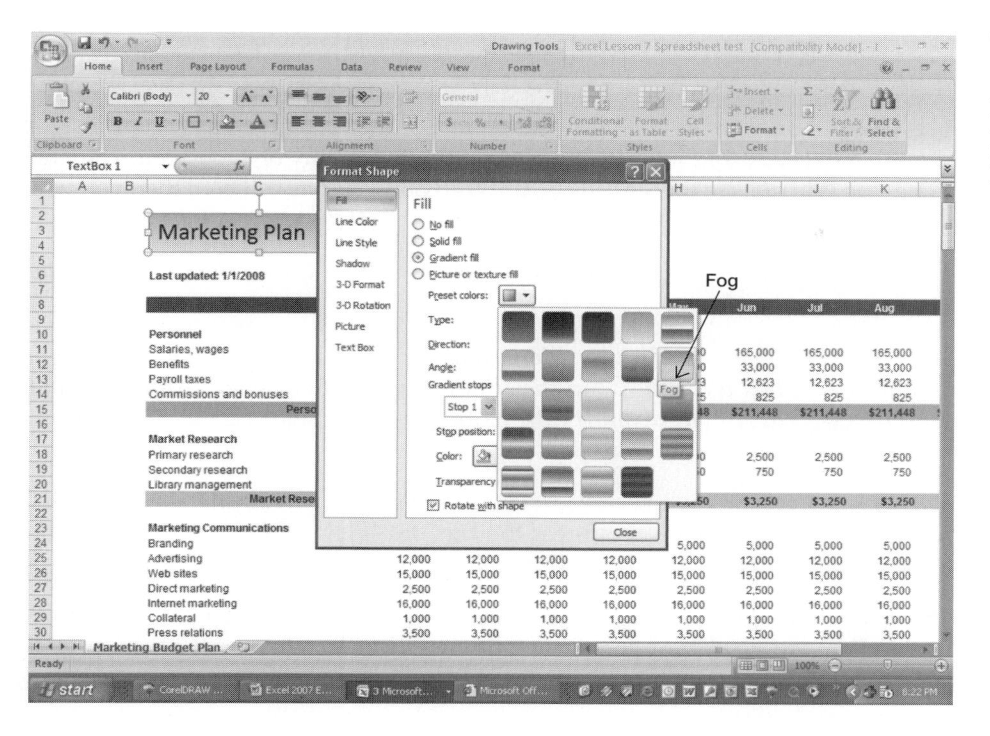

Excel 2007 Exhibit 19

Formatting a Shape

Microsoft product screen shot reprinted with permission from Microsoft Corporation.

11. ***Staying in the Format Shape window, point to the down arrow next to Direction and click the first option, which is Linear Diagonal.***

12. ***Still in the Format Shape window, click 3-D Format on the left side of the window.*** You will now add a 3-D style to the text box. ***When the 3-D style choices appear, under Bevel and next to Top, point to the down arrow and click the first selection under Bevel, which is Circle (see Excel 2007 Exhibit 20).***

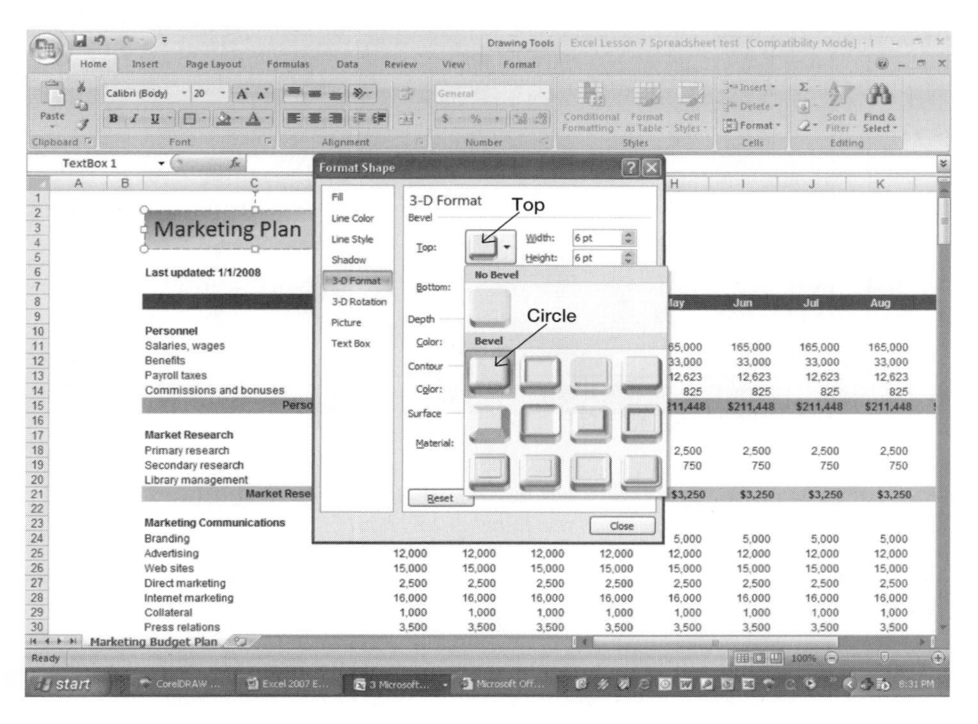

Excel 2007 Exhibit 20

Adding 3-D Effect to a Text Box

Microsoft product screen shot reprinted with permission from Microsoft Corporation.

13. ***Then, click Close to close the Format Shape window. Click in any other cell so you can see the effect.***

14. You will now create the vertical text in Column B that says "Expenses," as shown in Excel 2007 Exhibit 18. Notice that this is actually one long cell. The first thing you will do is to merge cells B6 through B53 into one cell, and then you will add the text and format it to be vertical.

15. ***Click in cell B6, drag the mouse down to cell B53, and then let go of the mouse.***

16. ***From the Home tab, click the Merge and Center icon in the Alignment group. It looks like a box with an "a" in the middle, with left and right arrows around the "a" (see Excel 2007 Exhibit 18).*** Notice that the selected cells have been merged into one cell now from B6 to B53.

17. With the cursor still in cell B6, ***change the Font Size to 22 and click the Bold icon.*** Now type **Expenses** and press the **[ENTER]** key. The text is shown at the bottom of the cell; you will now correct this.

18. ***Point and right-click anywhere in cell B6. Then, click Format Cells. The Format Cells window should now be displayed. Click the Alignment tab (see Excel 2007 Exhibit 21).***

Excel 2007 Exhibit 21
Creating Vertical Text in Excel 2007
Microsoft product screen shot reprinted with permission from Microsoft Corporation.

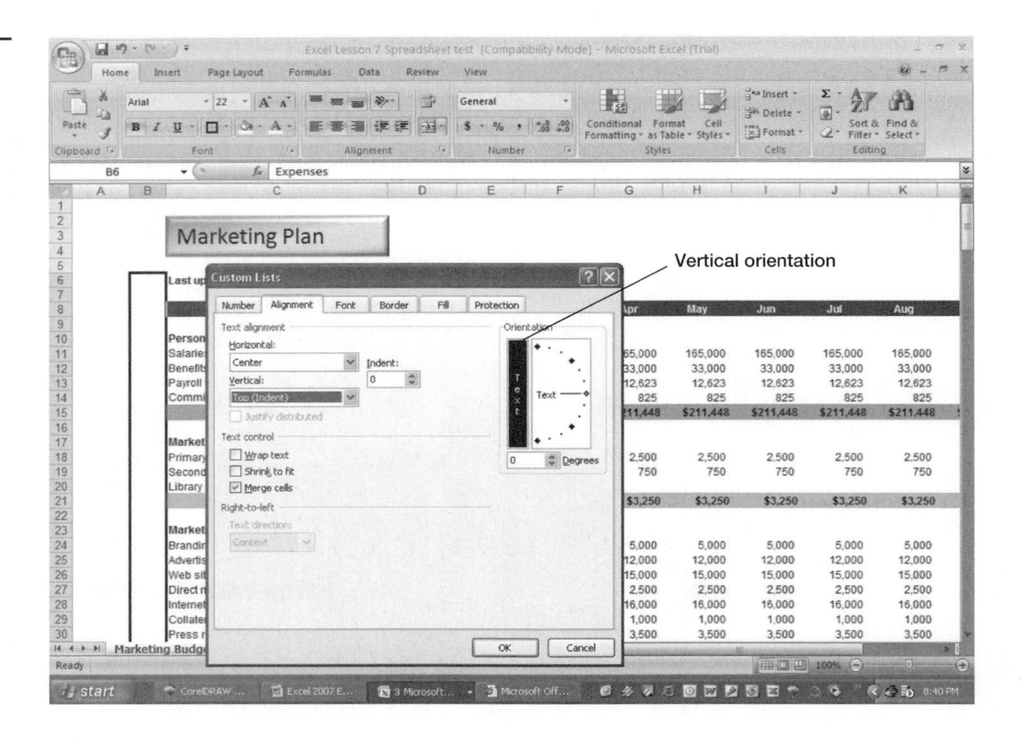

19. ***In the Format Cells window under Orientation, click the box that shows the word Text displayed vertically (see Excel 2007 Exhibit 21).***

20. ***In the Format Cells window under Vertical, click the down arrow and select Top (Indent).***

21. ***Click OK in the Format Cells window.*** The word "Expenses" should now be displayed vertically down the cell.

22. *With the pointer still in cell B6, on the Home tab, click the down arrow next to the Fill Color (a paint bucket) icon in the Font group and then select Black.*

23. *Next, on the Home tab, click the down arrow next to the Font Color icon and select Yellow.*

24. You will next make the text in cell C6 appear diagonally. *Right-click in cell C6. Then, click Format Cells.* The **Format Cells** window should now be displayed and the **Alignment** tab should be selected.

25. *In the Format Cells window under Orientation, click the up arrow next to Degrees until it reads "15 degrees."*

26. *In the Format Cells window click the Fill tab. Then, click the yellow square; then click OK.*

27. *Click in any cell to make the highlighting disappear.* The words "Last updated 1/1/2008" should now be displayed diagonally in black letters with a yellow background.

28. You will now add the Comment shown in Excel 2007 Exhibit 18. *Right-click in cell D15. On the drop-down menu, click Insert Comment.* Type **This is $40,000 more than last year, but there will be more than enough revenue to cover this.** *Click in any cell to exit the Comment box.*

29. *Hover your mouse over cell D15 so you can see the comment.*

30. You will now add borders to the spreadsheet. *Point to cell C53 and drag the mouse to cell P53. Then, on the Home tab, click the down arrow next to the Borders icon in the Font group and click All Borders.* The "Totals" row should now have borders around each cell.

31. *Click in cell C8 and drag the mouse to cell P53. Then, on the Home tab, click the down arrow next to the Borders icon in the Font group, and then click Thick Box Border.* A thick border now surrounds the data.

32. *To print the spreadsheet, click the Office Button, then click Print and OK.*

33. To save the spreadsheet, *click the Office Button and then click Save As. Under Save in, select the drive or folder you would like to save the document in.* Then, next to **File Name:** type **Excel Lesson 7 Spreadsheet DONE** and click **Save.**

34. To exit Excel, *click the Office Button and then click Exit Excel to exit the program.*

This concludes Lesson 7.

LESSON 8: TOOLS AND TECHNIQUES 2

In this lesson, you will continue to learn and apply helpful tools and techniques using Excel. This includes getting additional practice with using the Merge and Center tool, using the formula auditing feature, using the oval tool, and password protecting a file. When your spreadsheet is complete, it will look similar to Excel 2007 Exhibit 22. Some of these tools have been covered in previous lessons, and this lesson will help cement your ability to use them effectively.

This tutorial assumes that you have completed Lessons 1 through 7, and that you are quite familiar with Excel.

1. Open Windows. Then, ***double-click the Microsoft Office Excel 2007 icon on the desktop*** to open the program. Alternatively, ***click the Start button, point mouse to Programs or All Programs, point on Microsoft Office, and then click Microsoft Office Excel 2007.*** You should now be in a clean, blank workbook. If you are not in a blank workbook, ***click the Office Button (see Excel 2007 Exhibit 1), then click New, and then double-click Blank Workbook.***

Excel 2007 Exhibit 22
Stock Portfolio
Microsoft product screen shot reprinted with permission from Microsoft Corporation.

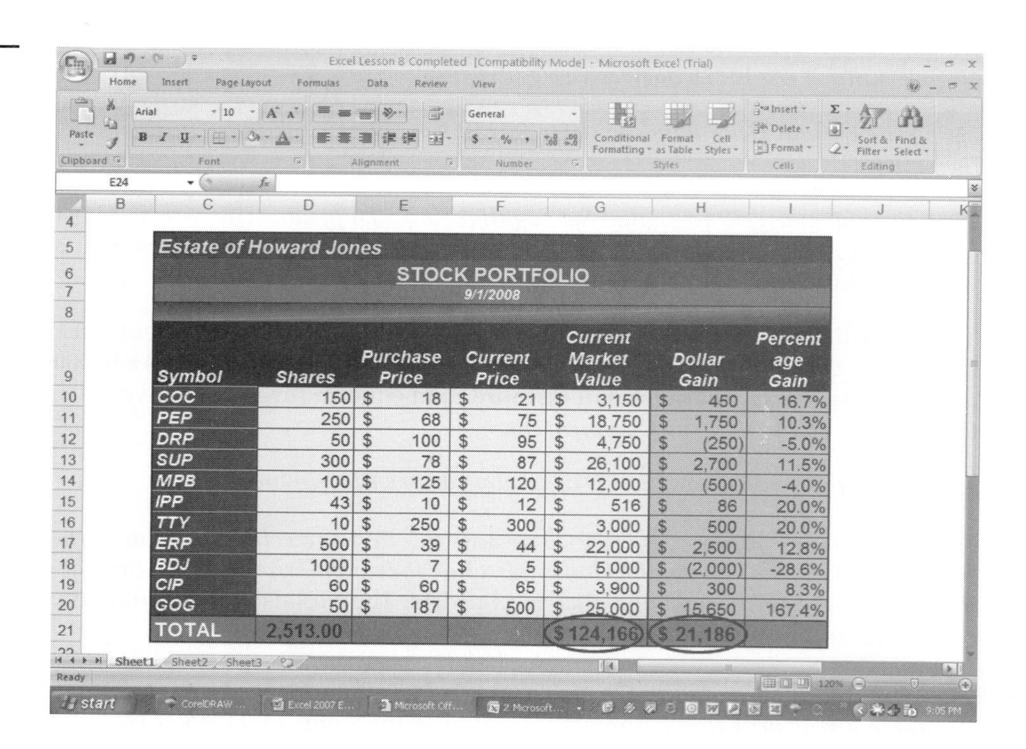

Estate of Howard Jones
STOCK PORTFOLIO
9/1/2008

Symbol	Shares	Purchase Price	Current Price	Current Market Value	Dollar Gain	Percentage Gain
COC	150	$ 18	$ 21	$ 3,150	$ 450	16.7%
PEP	250	$ 68	$ 75	$ 18,750	$ 1,750	10.3%
DRP	50	$ 100	$ 95	$ 4,750	$ (250)	-5.0%
SUP	300	$ 78	$ 87	$ 26,100	$ 2,700	11.5%
MPB	100	$ 125	$ 120	$ 12,000	$ (500)	-4.0%
IPP	43	$ 10	$ 12	$ 516	$ 86	20.0%
TTY	10	$ 250	$ 300	$ 3,000	$ 500	20.0%
ERP	500	$ 39	$ 44	$ 22,000	$ 2,500	12.8%
BDJ	1000	$ 7	$ 5	$ 5,000	$ (2,000)	-28.6%
CIP	60	$ 60	$ 65	$ 3,900	$ 300	8.3%
GOG	50	$ 187	$ 500	$ 25,000	$ 15,650	167.4%
TOTAL	2,513.00			$ 124,166	$ 21,186	

2. The first thing you will do to complete the spreadsheet in Excel 2007 Exhibit 18 is to open the "Lesson 8" file from Disk 1 supplied with this text. Ensure that the disk is inserted in the disk drive, point and click on File on the Office Button, and then point and click on Open. The "Open" window should now be displayed. Point and click on the down arrow to the right of the white box next to "Look in:" and select the drive where Disk 1 is located. Point and double-click on the Excel Files folder. Double-click on the "Lesson 8" file.

3. You should now have the stock portfolio spreadsheet shown in Excel 2007 Exhibit 22 opened, except the spreadsheet will be missing two rows of data and some of the formatting. You will add the rows and formatting to the spreadsheet.

4. ***Use the Merge and Center icon on the Home tab in the Alignment group to merge cells C5 to I5.***

5. ***Use the Merge and Center icon on the toolbar to merge cells C6 to I6.***

6. ***Use the Merge and Center icon to merge cells C7 to I7.***

7. ***Make sure the titles are aligned as shown in Excel 2007 Exhibit 22 (use the Left and Center Align icons on the Home tab in the Alignment group).***

8. *Use the Fill Color icon on the Home tab, in the Font group, to make the fill color for cell C5 dark blue (or any color you choose).*

9. *Use the Fill Color icon to make the fill color for cell C6 purple (any light purple is fine).*

10. *Use the Fill Color icon to make the fill color for cell C7 gray (any light gray is fine).*

11. *The cell range from C8 to I8 is a text graphic box (similar to a text box—it is just more difficult to see). Right-click the box, and select Format Shape. Then, in the Fill section, click Gradient fill and, next to Preset Color, click on the first one, Early Sunset (just hover your cursor over the colors and the name will be displayed). Under Direction click the first option, Linear Diagonal, and then click Close to close the Format Shape window.*

12. *Use the Borders icon on the Home tab, in the Font group, to give cells D10 to I21 a border of All Borders.*

13. *From the Insert tab, click Shapes in the Illustrations group. Under Basic Shapes click the Oval tool (it should be the second shape). Start in the upper left corner of cell G21 and drag the mouse to the lower right corner of G21 to make an oval around the total.* *Notes:* you can slightly move the oval by using the cursor keys on the keyboard to nudge them into place so they are centered in the cell.

14. The color of the oval must now be corrected. Notice that the ribbon has changed and the **Drawing Tools Format** ribbon is now displayed. *Click the down arrow next to Shape Fill in the Shape Styles group of the Drawing Tools Format tab. Then, click No Fill.* The oval is now surrounding the number but the line color of the oval must be changed.

15. *Right-click the oval and select Format Shape. On the left side of the Format Shape window, click Line Color. Then, click the down arrow next to Color, click Black, and then click Close in the Format Shape window. Make an oval in cell H21 identical to that in cell G21 using the same process.*

16. You will now use the Formula Auditing Mode to see the formulas that are in the spreadsheet to ensure they are accurate.

17. *On the Formulas tab, click Show Formulas in the Formula Auditing group.* Scroll over to the right and look at all of the cells in your spreadsheet. Notice that instead of seeing the result of the formulas, you see the formulas themselves. This is a great tool for checking the accuracy of your spreadsheets. Look at your formulas and make sure they are correct. When you are sure your formulas are accurate, *turn off the Formula Auditing mode by clicking on Show Formulas again.*

18. You will now learn how to password protect your spreadsheet files. *Click the Office Button and then click Save As. In the Save As window, click Tools (it is in the lower portion of the window) and then click General Options.* Under **File Sharing** and next to **password to Open,** type **A**, and click **OK.** At the **Confirm Password** window, type **A**, and then click **OK.** At the **Save As** window, *click Save* to save the file to My Documents (or the folder of your choice—you must remember where you save it). You will then get a prompt that asks you whether you want to increase the security of the document by conversation to Office Open XML Format. Because this is just an exercise, *click No.*

19. ***If you get a compatibility prompt, just click Continue.***

20. ***Click the Office Button, and then click Close to close the file.***

21. ***Now, click the Office Button, and under Recent Documents click on the file you just saved.***

22. The **Password** window should now be displayed. Type **A** in the **Password window.** (The password is case sensitive, so if you typed a capital A when you created the password, you must type a capital A to open the document.) Then ***click OK.*** The file should now be displayed.

23. You can turn off a password in the same way. ***Click the Office Button, and then Save As. In the Save As window click Tools and then on General Options.*** Under **File Sharing** and next to **Password to Open,** use the **[DEL]** key to remove the asterisk. ***Then, click OK and click Save.*** At the **Do you want to replace the existing file?** prompt, ***point and click Yes.***

24. ***If you get a compatibility prompt, just click Continue.***

25. Close the file and then reopen it, and you will see you no longer need a password to open it.

26. ***To print the spreadsheet, click the Office Button, then click Print and OK.***

27. To exit Excel, ***click the Office Button and then click Exit Excel to exit the program.***

This concludes the Excel 2007 Hands-On Exercises.

HANDS-ON EXERCISES

MICROSOFT EXCEL 2003 FOR WINDOWS

Basic Lessons

Number	Lesson Title	Concepts Covered
Lesson 1	Building a Budget Spreadsheet – Part 1	[CTRL] + [HOME] command, moving the pointer, entering text and values, adjusting the width of columns, changing the format of a group of cells to currency, using bold, centering text, entering formulas, using the Auto Fill/Copy command to copy formulas, and printing and saving a spreadsheet.
Lesson 2	Building a Budget Spreadsheet – Part 2	Opening a file, inserting rows, changing the format of cells to percent, building more formulas, creating a bar chart with the chart wizard, printing a selection, and fitting/compressing data to one printed page.
Lesson 3	Damages Projection	Changing font size, font color, and fill color, using the AutoSum feature, using the wrap text feature, creating borders, and setting decimal points when formatting numbers.

Intermediate Lessons

Number	Lesson Title	Concepts Covered
Lesson 4	Child Support Payment Spreadsheet	Creating a white background, creating formulas that multiply cells, creating formulas that use absolute cell references, and using the AutoFormat feature.
Lesson 5	Loan Amortization Template Lesson 5 from Disk1	Using a template, protecting cells, freezing panes, splitting a screen, hiding columns, and using Format Painter.
Lesson 6	Statistical Functions Lesson 6 from Disk1	Using functions including average, maximum, minimum, and standard deviation; sorting data; checking for metadata; using the format clear command; using conditional formatting; and inserting a picture.

Advanced Lessons

Number	Lesson Title	Concepts Covered
Lesson 7	Tools and Techniques 1—Marketing Budget Lesson 7 from Disk1	Creating and manipulating a text box, advanced shading techniques, working with a 3-D style text box, creating vertical and diagonal text, creating a cell comment, and using lines and borders.
Lesson 8	Tools and Techniques 2—Stock Portfolio Lesson 8 from Disk1	Using the Merge and Center tool, using the fit to page feature, printing selections, using the Formula Auditing feature, using the oval tool, and password protecting a file.

GETTING STARTED

Overview

Microsoft Excel 2003 is a powerful spreadsheet program that allows you to create formulas, "what if" scenarios, graphs, and much more.

Introduction

Throughout these lessons and exercises, information you need to operate the program will be designated in several different ways:

- Keys to be pressed on the keyboard will be designated in brackets, in all caps and in bold (i.e., press the **[ENTER]** key).
- Movements with the mouse or other pointing device will be designated in bold and italics (i.e., ***point to File on the menu bar and click New***).
- Words or letters that should be typed will be designated in bold (i.e., type **Training Program**).
- Information that is or should be displayed on your computer screen is shown in the following style: **Press [ENTER] to continue**.
- Specific menu item and commands will be designated with boldface and as initial capital letter (i.e., click **Open**).

OVERVIEW OF EXCEL

I. Worksheet

A. *Menus and Commands*—***Click the toolbar or the menu bar*** to access menus and/or execute commands.

B. *Entering Data*—To enter data, type the text or number, and press the **[ENTER]** key or one of the arrow (cursor) keys.

C. *Ranges*—A range is a group of cells. Cell ranges can be created by ***clicking and dragging the mouse*** pointer or holding the **[SHIFT]** key down while using the arrow (cursor) keys.

D. *Format*—Cells can be formatted, including changing the font style, font size, shading, border, cell type (currency, percentage, etc.), alignment, and other attributes by ***clicking Format on the menu bar, and then clicking Cells.*** Alternatively, ***right-click on the cell (or within a cell range) and then select Format Cells.***

E. *Editing a Cell*—You can edit a cell by ***clicking the cell and then pointing to the formula bar and editing the displayed content.*** The formula bar is directly under the toolbar and just to the right of the **fx** sign. The formula bar shows the current contents of the selected cell, and it allows you to edit the cell contents. You can also edit the contents of a cell by ***clicking in the cell*** and then pressing the **[F2]** key.

F. *Column Width/Row Height*—You can change the width of a column by ***clicking the line to the right of the column heading.*** (This is the line that separates two columns. When you point to a line, the cursor changes to double-headed vertical arrows.) ***Next, drag the pointer to the right or to the left to increase or decrease the column width, respectively.*** Similarly, you can change the height of a row by ***clicking and dragging the pointer on the horizontal line separating two rows.*** You can also change the width of a column by clicking somewhere in the column you want to change and ***clicking Format on the menu bar, then Column, and then Width***. You can change the height of a row by going to the row you want to change and ***clicking Format on the menu bar, then Row, and then Height***.

G. *Insert*—You can insert one row or column by ***clicking Insert on the menu bar and then clicking either Column or Row***. You can also insert a number of rows or columns by ***dragging the pointer over the number of rows or columns you***

want to add, clicking Insert on the menu bar, and then clicking either Column or Row. Finally, you can ***right-click and select*** **Insert** ***from the menu.***

H. *Erase/Delete*—You can erase data by ***dragging the pointer over the area*** and then pressing the **[DEL]** key. You can delete whole columns or rows by ***pointing to a column or row clicking Edit on the menu bar, and then Delete,*** and following the menus. You can also delete whole columns or rows by ***pointing to the column or row and then right-clicking and selecting Delete.***

I. *Quit*—To quit Excel, ***click File and then Exit.***

J. *Copy*—To copy data to adjacent columns or rows, ***click in the cell you wish to copy and then select the AutoFill command,*** which is the small black box at the bottom right corner of the selected cell. Then ***drag the pointer to where the data should be placed.*** You can also copy data by ***clicking in the cell, right-clicking and selecting Copy, moving the pointer to the location where the information should be copied,*** and pressing the **[ENTER]** key. Data can also be copied by ***clicking and dragging to highlight the information to be copied, clicking Edit on the menu bar, and then clicking Copy.*** Then go to the location where the information should be copied and ***click Edit and then Paste.***

K. *Move*—Move data by ***clicking in the cell, right-clicking, selecting Cut, clicking in the location where the information should be inserted,*** and pressing the **[ENTER]** key. Data can also be moved by ***highlighting the information to be moved, clicking Edit on the menu bar and then Cut, moving the pointer to the location where the information should be copied, and clicking Edit and then Paste.***

L. *Saving and Opening Files*—Save a file by ***clicking File and then Save,*** and typing the file name. You can also save a file by ***clicking the Save icon*** (a floppy disk) on the toolbar. Open a file that was previously saved by ***clicking File and then Open*** and typing (or clicking) the name of the file to be opened.

M. *Print*—You can print a file by ***clicking the Print icon*** on the toolbar or by ***clicking File on the menu bar, and then Print, and then OK.***

II. Numbers and Formulas

A. *Numbers*—To enter a number in a cell, click in the cell, type the number, and press the **[ENTER]** key or an arrow (cursor) key.

B. *Adding Cells (Addition)*—You can add the contents of two or more cells by three different methods:

1. To add the contents of two or more cells that are in a range (i.e., in adjacent rows and/or columns):
   - **a.** Click in the cell location where the total should be placed.
   - **b.** ***Click the AutoSum icon*** on the toolbar. This icon looks like an "E." (*Note:* To see the name of an icon, point to the icon for a second and its name will be displayed.)
   - **c.** Excel guesses which values you want to add. Press **[ENTER]** if the correct range is automatically selected, or select the correct range by highlighting it (i.e., ***clicking and dragging until the range of cells to be added is selected***). Then, press **[ENTER]**.
2. To add the contents of any two or more cells:
   - **a.** Click the cell where the total should be placed.

   b. Press [=].
   c. Enter the address of the first value to be added (e.g., B4. Alternatively, ***click in it***).
   d. Press [+].
   e. Enter the address of the second value to be added (or ***click in it***).
   f. Press the **[ENTER]** key. (For example, to add the values of cells C4 and C5, you would type **=C4+C5**.)

3. To add the contents of a range of two or more cells:
   a. Click in the cell where the total should be placed.
   b. Type **=SUM(**.
   c. Enter the address of the cell that defines the beginning of the range (or ***click in it***).
   d. Press [:] (a colon).
   e. Enter the address of the cell that defines the end of the range (or ***click in it***).
   f. Press [)] (the closing parenthesis).
   g. Press the **[ENTER]** key. (For example, to add the values of all cells between C4 and C6, the formula would read **=SUM(C4:C6)**.)

C. *Subtracting Cells*—To subtract the contents of one cell from those of another:

1. Click on the cell where the result should be placed.
2. Press [=].
3. Enter the first cell address (or ***click in it***).
4. Press [–].
5. Enter the second cell address (or ***click in it***).
6. Press the **[ENTER]** key. (For example, to subtract the value of C4 from the value of C5, you would type **=C5–C4**.)

D. *Multiplying Cells*—To multiply the contents of two or more cells:

1. Click in the cell where the result should be placed.
2. Press [=].
3. Enter the first cell address (or ***click in it***).
4. Press [*] (**[SHIFT]-[8]**).
5. Enter the second cell address (or ***click in it***).
6. Press the **[ENTER]** key. (For example, to multiply the value in C4 times the value in C5, you would type **=C5*C4**.)

E. *Dividing Cells*—To divide the contents of two cells:

1. Click in to the cell where the result should be placed.
2. Press [=].
3. Enter the first cell address (or ***click in it***).
4. Press [/] (the forward slash).
5. Enter the second cell address (or ***click in it***).
6. Press the **[ENTER]** key. (For example, to divide the value in C4 by the value in C5, you would type **=C4/C5**.)

Before Starting Lesson 1—Setting the Toolbar and Menu Bar

Before starting Lesson 1, complete the exercise below to adjust the toolbar and menu bar so that they are consistent with the instructions in the lessons.

1. Open Windows. Then, ***double-click the Excel icon on the desktop*** to open Excel for Windows. Alternatively, ***click the Start button, point to Programs or***

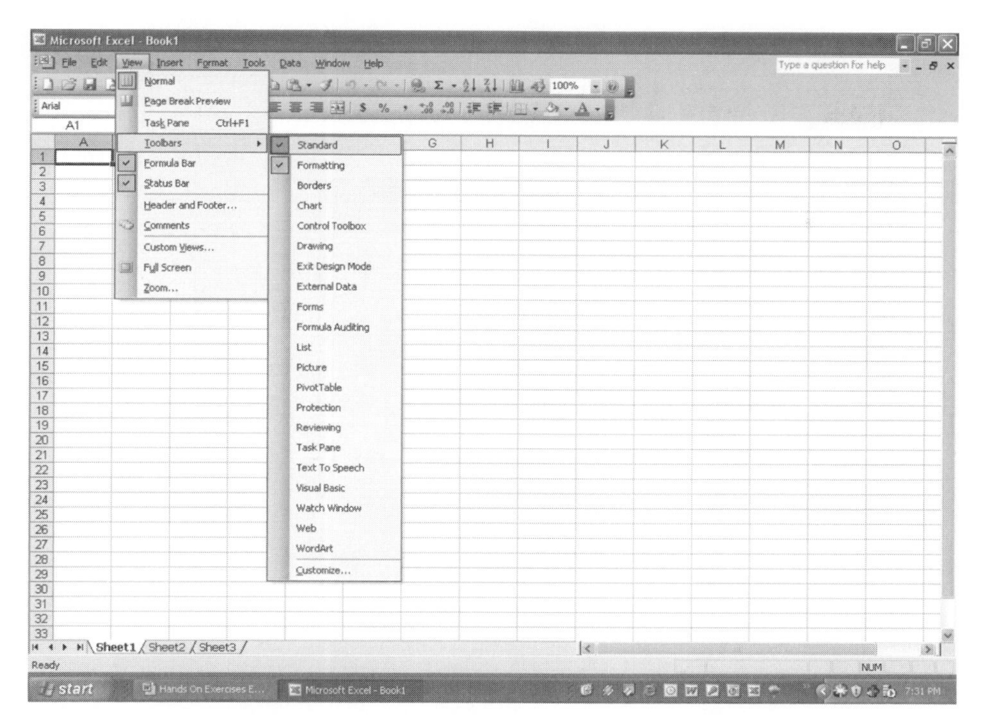

Excel 2003 Exhibit 1
Selecting Toolbars
Microsoft product screen shot reprinted with permission from Microsoft Corporation.

All Programs, click Microsoft Office, and then click on Microsoft Office Excel 2003. You should be in a clean, blank document.

2. ***On the View menu, point Toolbars.***

3. Only the **Standard** and **Formatting** toolbars should be checked (see Excel 2003 Exhibit 1). If the **Standard** and **Formatting** toolbars are not checked, click on them to select them (the check mark indicates they have been selected). If another toolbar such as the **Chart** toolbar, has been selected (marked with a check mark), then click it to remove it. Please note that you can only make one change of toolbar at a time, so it may take you a few steps to have only **Standard** and **Formatting** selected—or your computer may already be set for this and you may not have to make any changes. If you do not have to make changes, just push the **[ESC]** key twice to exit out of the **View** menu.

4. We also want to make sure (a) that the full menus are displayed when you select an item from the menu bar (Excel normally will show only the most recent and/or most commonly used selections), and (b) that the toolbar is shown on two rows so that you can see all of the options.

5. ***On the View menu bar, point to Toolbars, and then click Customize.***

6. ***Click on the Options tab.*** Then, under "**Personalized Menus and Toolbars,**" make sure that there are check marks next to "**Show Standard and Formatting Toolbars on two rows**" and "**Always show full menus**" (see Excel 2003 Exhibit 2). *Note:* if there is an option under "**Personalized Menus and Toolbars**" that says "**Standard and Formatting Toolbars share one row,**" do not check the box because the toolbars are already on two rows. If there is an option that says "**Menus show recently used commands first,**" again, do not check the box (full menus will already be displayed). ***Click Close.*** You are now ready to begin Lesson 1.

Excel 2003 Exhibit 2
Customizing the Toolbars
Microsoft product screen shot reprinted with permission from Microsoft Corporation.

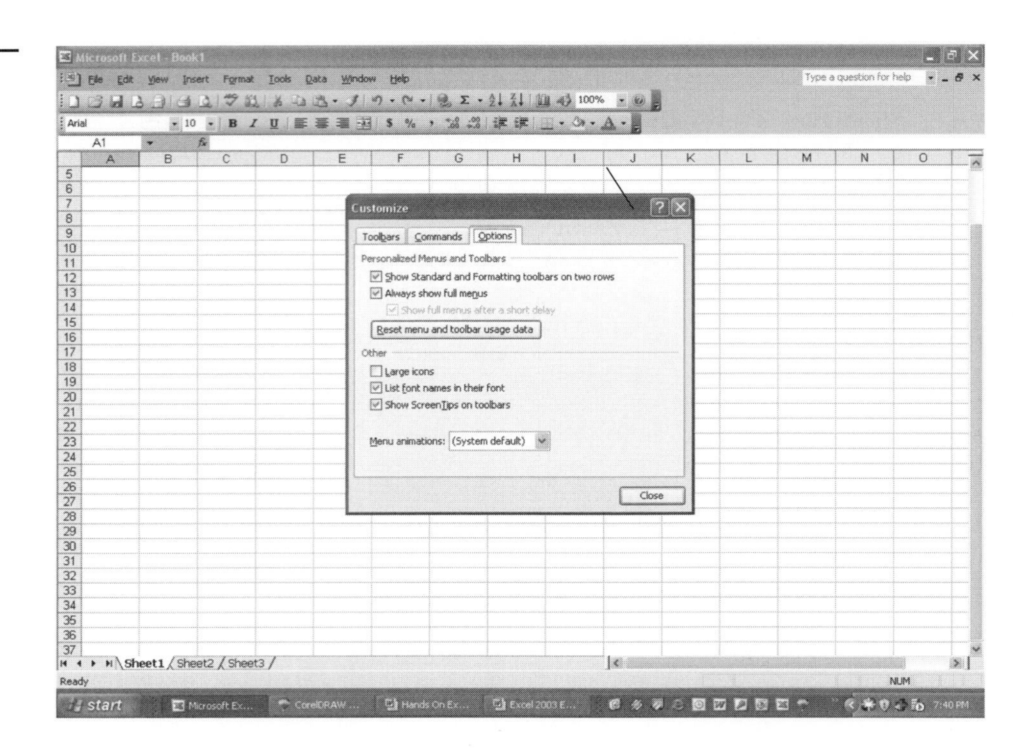

Basic Lessons

LESSON 1: BUILDING A BUDGET SPREADSHEET—PART 1

This lesson shows you how to build the spreadsheet shown in Excel 2003 Exhibit 3. It explains how to use the **[CTRL]+[HOME]** command; move the pointer; enter text, values, and formulas; adjust the width of columns; change the format of **Currency**, use the **Bold** command, use the **AutoFill** and **Copy** commands to copy formulas; and print and save a spreadsheet. Keep in mind that if at any time you make a mistake in this lesson, you may press **[CTRL]+[Z]** to undo what you have done.

1. Open Windows. Then, ***double-click the Excel icon on the desktop*** to open Excel for Windows. Alternatively, ***click the Start button, point to Programs or All Programs, point to Microsoft Office, and then click Microsoft Office Excel 2003.*** You should now be in a clean, blank document.

2. Notice that the pointer is at cell A1, and that the indicator that displays the address of the current cell (called the name box in Excel) says **A1**. The name box is just under the toolbar, all the way to the left (see Excel 2003 Exhibit 3). Also, notice that you can move the pointer around the spreadsheet using the cursor keys. Go back to cell A1 by pressing the **[CTRL]+[HOME]** keys.

3. Go to cell C3 by ***clicking in cell C3*** or by pressing the **[RIGHT ARROW]** twice, and then pressing the **[DOWN ARROW]** twice.

4. You will now enter the title of the spreadsheet in cell C3. Type **BUDGET** and then press the **[ENTER]** key.

5. Notice that the pointer is now at cell C4.

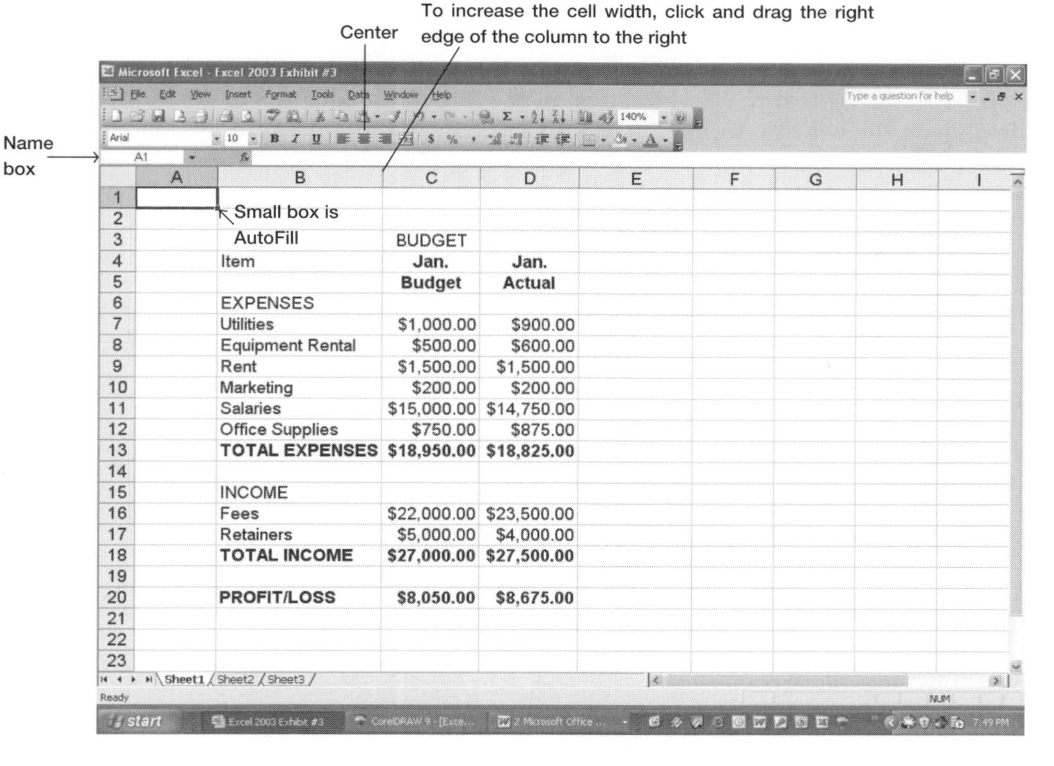

	A	B	C	D
1				
2				
3			BUDGET	
4		Item	**Jan.**	**Jan.**
5			**Budget**	**Actual**
6		EXPENSES		
7		Utilities	$1,000.00	$900.00
8		Equipment Rental	$500.00	$600.00
9		Rent	$1,500.00	$1,500.00
10		Marketing	$200.00	$200.00
11		Salaries	$15,000.00	$14,750.00
12		Office Supplies	$750.00	$875.00
13		**TOTAL EXPENSES**	**$18,950.00**	**$18,825.00**
14				
15		INCOME		
16		Fees	$22,000.00	$23,500.00
17		Retainers	$5,000.00	$4,000.00
18		**TOTAL INCOME**	**$27,000.00**	**$27,500.00**
19				
20		**PROFIT/LOSS**	**$8,050.00**	**$8,675.00**

Excel 2003 Exhibit 3
Budgeting Spreadsheet
Microsoft product screen shot reprinted with permission from Microsoft Corporation.

6. Press the **[UP ARROW]** to go back to cell C3. Notice that BUDGET is left aligned. To center BUDGET in the column, ***click the Center icon on the toolbar***. It is the icon with several lines on it that appear centered (see Excel 2003 Exhibit 3). If you hover the mouse over an icon on the toolbar for a second, the name of the icon will be displayed. Alternatively, you can ***click Format, then Cells; click on the Alignment tab, and then click Center in the Horizontal field. Then click OK.***

7. You should now be ready to enter the budget information. First, move the pointer to where the data should go; then type the data; and finally enter the data by pressing the **[ENTER]** key or one of the arrow (cursor) keys. Type the remaining row labels as follows:

Item in B4.
EXPENSES in B6.
Utilities in B7.
Equipment Rental in B8.
Rent in B9.
Marketing in B10.
Salaries in B11.
Office Supplies in B12.
TOTAL EXPENSES in B13.
INCOME in B15.
Fees in B16.
Retainers in B17.
TOTAL INCOME in B18.
PROFIT/LOSS in B20.

8. Notice in Column B that some of the data entries (such as "EXPENSES" and "Equipment Rental") actually extend into column C. To correct this, you must increase the width of column B. ***Point to the shaded cell with a letter B in it at the top of the screen. Move the pointer to the right edge of the cell.*** The pointer

should then change to a double-headed vertical arrow. ***Click and drag the pointer to the right until the column width is 18.00.*** (A small box should appear displaying the width.) Alternatively, you can change the cell width by ***placing the pointer anywhere in column B and clicking Format, then Column, then Width.*** Type **18**, and then ***click OK.***

9. Notice that all of the data entries now fit in the columns. Enter the following:

Jan. in C4.
Budget in C5.
Jan. in D4.
Actual in D5.

10. ***Click in C4 and drag the pointer over to cell D5*** (so that the whole cell range is highlighted)***, then click the Center icon and the Bold icon on the toolbar.***

11. You are now ready to enter values into your spreadsheet.

12. ***Move the cell pointer to cell C7.*** Type **1000.** Do not type a dollar sign or commas; these will be added later. Press the **[ENTER]** key to enter the value.

13. Enter the following:

500 in C8.
1500 in C9.
200 in C10.
15000 in C11.
750 in C12.
22000 in C16.
5000 in C17.
900 in D7.
600 in D8.
1500 in D9.
200 in D10.
14750 in D11.
875 in D12.
23500 in D16.
4000 in D17.

14. The values you entered do not have dollar signs or the commas appropriate for a currency format. You will now learn how to format a range of cells for a particular format (such as the **Currency** format).

15. ***Click in cell C7 and drag the pointer over to cell D20. On the Format menu, click Cells. On Number tab, click Currency.*** Notice that under **Decimal Places** it shows **2**. If you only wanted to show whole dollars (e.g., $1,000 and not $1,000.00), you could change this to zero. Leave the value as 2 for now. ***Click OK to close the Format Cells window.*** Notice that the cell format has now been changed. ***Click in any cell to deselect the cell range.***

16. ***Click in cell B13, drag the pointer over to cell D13, and click the Bold icon on the toolbar.*** This will make the TOTAL EXPENSES row appear in bold.

17. ***Click in cell B18, drag the pointer over to cell D18, and click the Bold icon on the toolbar.*** This will make the TOTAL INCOME row appear in bold.

18. ***Go to cell B20, drag the mouse over to cell D20, and click the Bold icon on the toolbar.*** This will make the PROFIT LOSS row appear in bold.

19. Your spreadsheet is nearly complete; all you need to insert are the six formulas.

20. ***Click in cell C13.***

21. Type **=SUM(** and press the **[UP ARROW]** six times until the cell pointer is at cell C7. Press **[.]** (a period) to anchor the range.

22. Press the **[DOWN ARROW]** five times, then press [)] (a closing parenthesis), and then the **[ENTER]** key.

23. Go back to cell C13 and look at the formula displayed in the formula bar. The formula should read =SUM(C7:C12). The total displayed in the cell should read $18,950.00. Note that you also could have typed the formula **=C7+C8+C9+C10+C11+12**.

24. Enter the following formulas:

=SUM(D7:D12) in D13.
=SUM(C16:C17) in C18.
=SUM(D16:D17) in D18.

25. We now need to enter formulas for the two PROFIT/LOSS columns. Enter the following formula:

=C18–C13 in C20.
(The total should read $8,050.00.)

26. ***Click in cell C20 and click the AutoFill command*** (the small black square at the bottom right of the cell). ***Drag it one column to the right and release the mouse button.*** Notice that the formula has been copied. The total should be $8,675.00. Alternatively, you could have ***clicked in cell C20 and, on the* Edit *menu, clicked* Copy, *moved the cell pointer to cell D20,*** and pressed the **[ENTER]** key.

27. The spreadsheet is now complete. You will need to save the spreadsheet as you will use it in Lesson 2.

28. To save the spreadsheet, ***on the* File *menu click* Save *and type* Budget1**. ***Click* Save *again.***

29. If you would like to print the spreadsheet, ***click the* Print *icon on the toolbar*** (it looks like a printer).

This concludes Lesson 1.

To exit Excel, ***click on* File *menu, click* Exit**.

To go to Lesson 2, stay at the current screen.

LESSON 2: BUILDING A BUDGET SPREADSHEET—PART 2

This lesson assumes that you have completed Lesson 1, have saved the spreadsheet from that lesson, and are generally familiar with the concepts covered in that lesson. Lesson 2 gives you experience in opening a file, inserting a row, formatting cells as Percent, building additional formulas, creating a bar chart, printing selections, and fitting and compressing data onto one printed page. If you did not exit Excel after Lesson 1, skip steps 1 and 2 below, and go directly to step 3.

Excel 2003 Exhibit 4
Expanded Budgeting Spreadsheet
Microsoft product screen shot reprinted with permission from Microsoft Corporation.

	A	B	C	D	E	F
1						
2						
3			BUDGET			
4		Item	**Jan.**	**Jan.**	**Jan.**	**Percent**
5			**Budget**	**Actual**	**Difference**	**Of Budget**
6		EXPENSES				
7		Utilities	$1,000.00	$900.00	$100.00	90.00%
8		Equipment Rental	$500.00	$600.00	-$100.00	120.00%
9		Insurance	$500.00	$450.00	$50.00	90.00%
10		Rent	$1,500.00	$1,500.00	$0.00	100.00%
11		Marketing	$200.00	$200.00	$0.00	100.00%
12		Salaries	$15,000.00	$14,750.00	$250.00	98.33%
13		Office Supplies	$750.00	$875.00	-$125.00	116.67%
14		**TOTAL EXPENSES**	**$19,450.00**	**$19,275.00**	**$175.00**	**99.10%**
15						
16		INCOME				
17		Fees	$22,000.00	$23,500.00	$1,500.00	106.82%
18		Retainers	$5,000.00	$4,000.00	-$1,000.00	80.00%
19		**TOTAL INCOME**	**$27,000.00**	**$27,500.00**	**$500.00**	**101.85%**
20						
21		**PROFIT/LOSS**	**$7,550.00**	**$8,225.00**	**$675.00**	**108.94%**
22						

Inserted Row → 9

1. Open Windows. Then, *double-click the* **Excel** *icon on the desktop* to open Excel for Windows. Alternatively, *click the* **Start** *button, point to Programs or All Programs, point to* **Microsoft Office**, *and then click* **Microsoft Office Excel 2003.** You should now be in a clean, blank document.

2. To retrieve the spreadsheet from Lesson 1, *click* **File** *on the menu, click* **Open.** *Then click on the name of your file (e.g.,* **Budget 1**) *and click* **Open.**

3. You will be entering the information shown in Excel 2003 Exhibit 4.

4. Notice in Excel 2003 Exhibit 4 that a line for insurance appears in row 9. You will insert this row first.

5. *Click in cell B9, right-click, and click* **Insert.** *Click* **Entire Row,** *and then click* **OK.** A new row has been added. You could also have gone to the *Insert menu and clicked* **Row.**

6. Enter the following:

Insurance in B9.
500 in C9.
450 in D9.

7. Notice that when the new values for insurance were entered, all of the formulas were updated. Since you inserted the additional rows in the middle of the column, the formulas recognized the new numbers and automatically recalculated to reflect them. Be extremely careful when inserting new rows and columns into spreadsheets that have existing formulas. In some cases, the new number will not be reflected in the totals, such as when rows or columns are inserted at the beginning or end of the range that a formula calculates. It is always prudent to go back to each existing formula, examine the formula range, and make sure the new values are included in the formula range.

8. Change the column width of Column E to 12 by ***pointing and clicking on the shaded cell containing the letter E,*** at the top of the screen. ***Move your pointer to the right edge of the column.*** Your pointer should change to a double-headed vertical arrow. ***Drag the mouse pointer to the right until the column width is 12*** (the width will appear in a small box). Alternatively, you can change the cell width by ***placing the pointer anywhere in column E, clicking*** **Format,** ***then*** **Column,** ***and then*** **Width,** and typing **12**. ***Click on OK.***

9. Enter the following:

Jan. in E4.
Difference in E5.
Percent in F4.
Of Budget in F5.

10. ***Go to cell E4 and drag the pointer over to cell F5*** (so that more column headings are highlighted). ***Click the*** **Center** ***icon and then the*** **Bold** ***icon on the toolbar.***

11. ***Click in cell E14 and drag the mouse pointer over to cell F14. Then click the*** **Bold** ***icon on the toolbar.***

12. ***Click in cell E19 and drag the mouse pointer over to cell F19. Then click the*** **Bold** ***icon on the toolbar.***

13. ***Click in cell E21 and drag the mouse pointer over to cell F21. Then click the*** **Bold** ***icon on the toolbar.***

14. You are now ready to change the cell formatting for column E to currency and column F to percent. ***Go to cell E7 and drag the mouse pointer down to cell E21. Click*** **Format** ***and then click*** **Cells.** ***On the*** **Number** ***tab, click*** **Currency** ***and then*** **OK.** ***Click in any cell to get rid of the cell range.***

15. ***Go to cell F7 and drag the mouse pointer down to cell F21. Click*** **Format** ***and then click*** **Cells.** ***On the*** **Number** ***tab, click*** **Percentage** ***and then click*** **OK.** ***Click in any cell to get rid of the cell range.***

16. All that is left to do is to enter the formulas for the two new columns. The entries in the January "Difference" column subtract the actual amount from the budgeted amount for each expense item. A positive amount in this column means that the office was under budget on that line item. A negative balance means that the office was over budget on that line item. The "Percent of Budget" column divides that actual amount by the budgeted amount. This shows the percentage of the budgeted money that was actually spent for each item.

17. You will first build one formula in the January "Difference" column, and then copy it. Click in cell E7, type **=C7–D7**, and press the **[ENTER]** key.

18. Using the **AutoFill** command or the **Copy** command, copy this formula down through cell E14.

19. Click in cell E17, enter **=D17–C17**, and press the **[ENTER]** key.

20. Using the **AutoFill** command, copy this formula down through cell E21. Delete the formula in cell E20 by ***clicking in cell E20*** and pressing the **[DEL]** key.

21. You will now build on the formula in the "Percent of Budget" column and copy it. Go to cell F7, enter **=D7/C7**, and press the **[ENTER]** key.

22. Using the **AutoFill** command, copy this formula down through cell F21. Delete the formula in cell F15, F16, and F20 by ***clicking in the cell*** and then pressing the **[DEL]** key.

23. The spreadsheet has now been built. We will now build a bar chart that shows our budgeted expenses compared to our actual expenses (see Excel 2003 Exhibit 5).

24. ***Click in cell B7 and then drag the mouse pointer down and over to cell D14.***

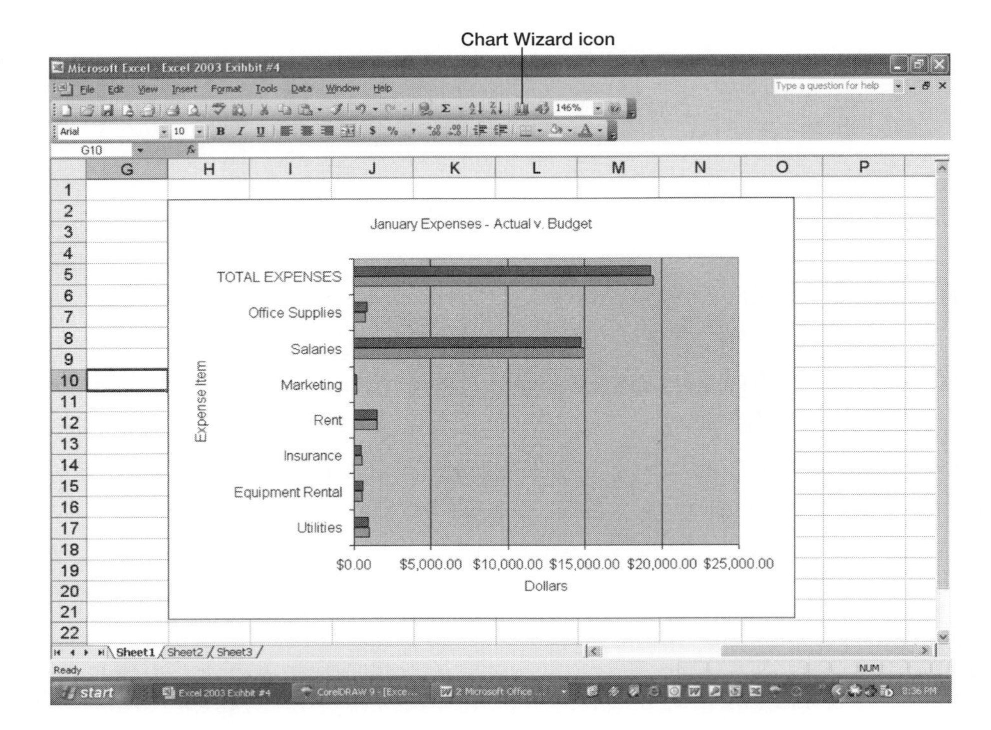

Excel 2003 Exhibit 5
Bar Chart
Microsoft product screen shot reprinted with permission from Microsoft Corporation.

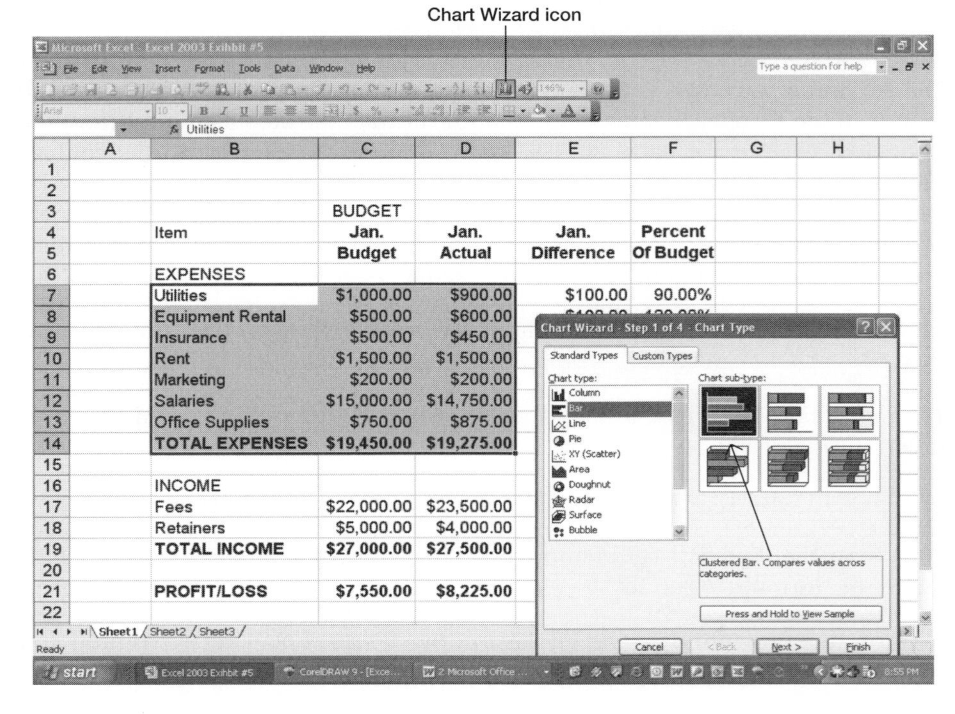

Excel 2003 Exhibit 6
Chart Wizard
Microsoft product screen shot reprinted with permission from Microsoft Corporation.

25. ***Click the Chart Wizard icon on the toolbar.*** (It looks like a multicolored column chart/vertical bar chart.) Alternatively, you can ***select Insert and then click Chart.*** The **Chart Wizard – Step 1 of 4 – Chart Type** window is displayed (see Excel 2003 Exhibit 6). This is where you will select the type of chart you want.

26. ***Click Bar from the Chart Type list.*** Six options will be displayed; the first (and default) option, **Clustered Bar,** is fine (see Excel 2003 Exhibit 6).

27. ***Click Next >.*** The **Chart Wizard – Step 2 of 4 – Chart Source Data** window will now be displayed. This is where you define where the data range will come from for the chart. The data range is correct.

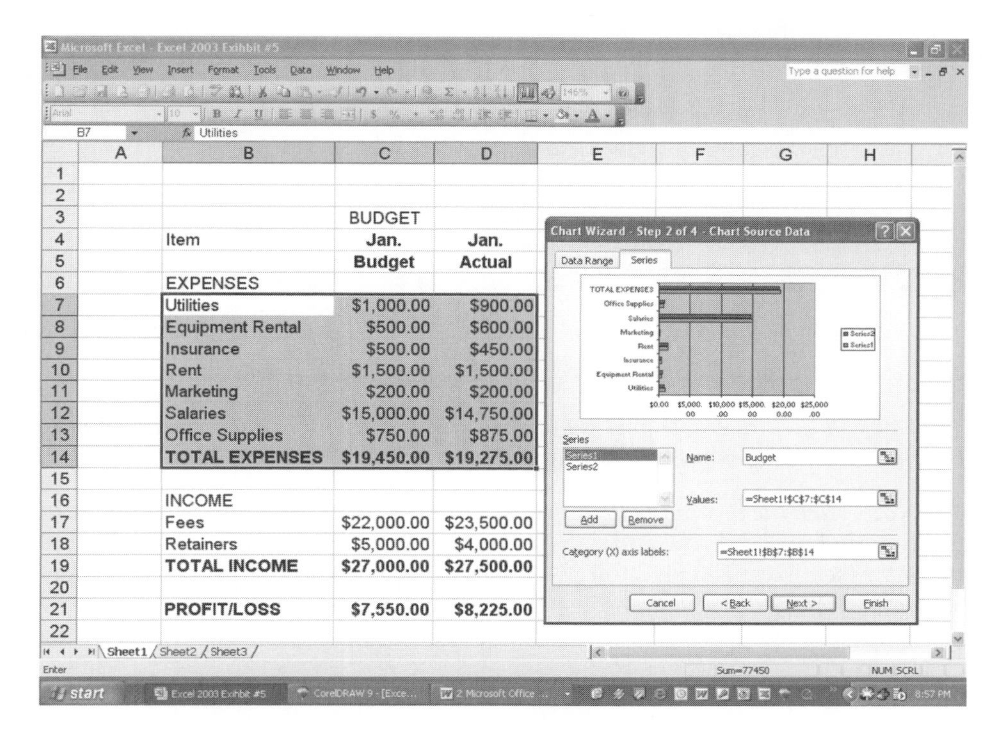

Excel 2003 Exhibit 7
Chart Wizard: Chart Source Data
Microsoft product screen shots reprinted with permission from Microsoft Corporation.

28. ***Click the Series tab in the Chart Wizard – Step 2 of 4 – Chart Source Data window.***

29. Under **(Series), (Series1)** is highlighted in blue. ***Click in the white box next to Name*** and type **Budget** (see Excel 2003 Exhibit 7).

30. ***Then, under Series, click Series2. Click in the white box next to Name and*** type **Actual**.

31. Then, ***click Next >.*** The **Chart Wizard – Step 3 of 4 – Chart Options** window is now displayed (see Excel 2003 Exhibit 8).

32. The **Title** tab should be displayed. In the **Chart Title** box, type **January Expenses – Actual v. Budget**. In the Category (X) axis box, type **Expense Item**. In the Category (Y) axis box, type **Dollars** (see Excel 2003 Exhibit 8). The default values for the other tabs are fine, so ***click Next >.***

33. The **Chart Wizard – Step 4 of 4 – Chart Location** window should now be displayed. The **As object in: Sheet1** option should be selected. ***Click Finish.***

Excel 2003 Exhibit 8
Chart Wizard: Chart Options

Microsoft product screen shots reprinted with permission from Microsoft Corporation.

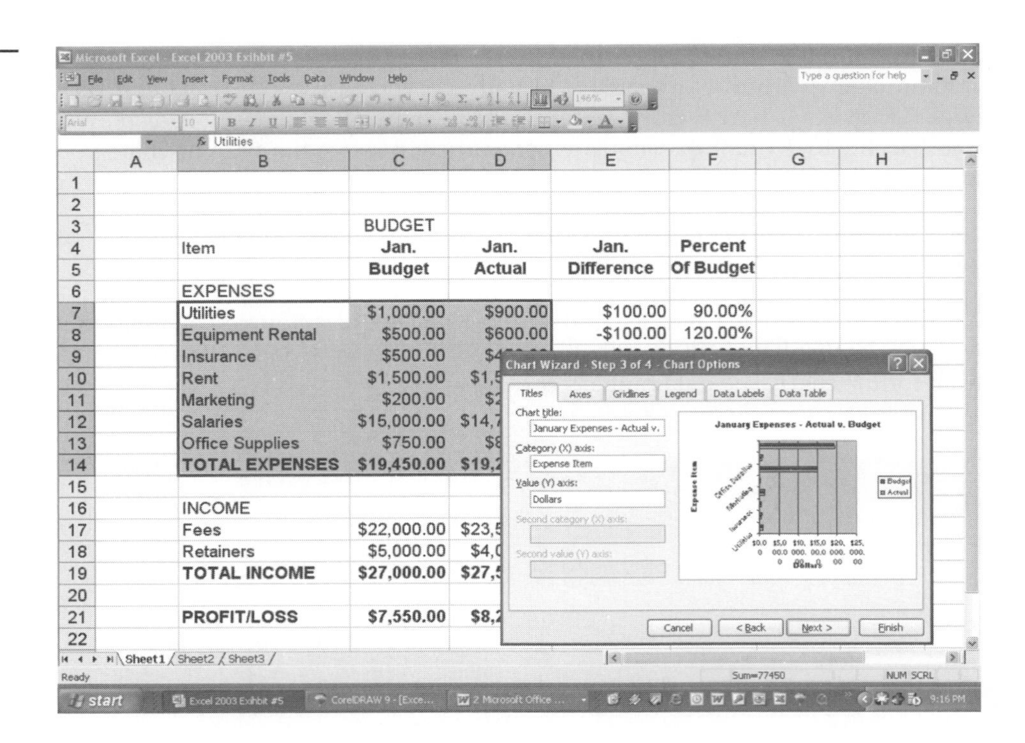

34. The chart is now superimposed over the top of your spreadsheet.

35. ***Click in the lower left portion of the chart (in a white space) and then drag the chart over to column H*** so the upper left portion of the chart starts at cell H2.

36. ***Now, click the box in the lower right corner of the chart.*** The cursor will turn to a double-headed arrow and will say "Chart Area." ***Drag the box down and to the right*** (see Excel 2003 Exhibit 5)—this will expand the chart proportionately and make it larger. Stop expanding the chart when you get to column O and row 21. You may have to use the scroll bars to get to the lower right corner of the chart.

37. The font size is too large, so next you will reduce the size of the font so all of the information fits in the chart. ***Right-click anywhere in the lower left portion of the chart (in a white space). Then, select Format Chart Area. In the Font tab, click 8 under Font Size. Then, click OK.***

38. ***Click in the chart and then click the Printer icon on the toolbar to print the chart.***

39. To print the spreadsheet, ***click out of the chart and click in one of the cells in the spreadsheet.*** Press **[CTRL]+[HOME]** to go to cell A1.

40. ***Click cell B3 and then drag the mouse pointer to cell F21.***

41. ***Click File, then click Print. In the Print window under Print What, click Selection. Then, click OK.*** This will print only the portion of the spreadsheet that is highlighted.

42. You will next print the spreadsheet and the chart on one page. ***Click on cell B3 and then drag the mouse pointer until both the spreadsheet and the chart are highlighted*** (roughly cell B2 to cell O21).

43. ***Click File and then click Page Setup. On the Page tab, click Fit to*** (it should default to one page). ***Then, click OK.*** This will compress everything in the print area to one page.

44. ***Click on File, then click Print, and in the Print window under Print What, click Selection. Then click OK.***

45. To save the document, ***click File and then click Save As.*** Type **Budget 2** next to **File Name.** ***Select Save to save the budget to the default directory.***

46. ***Click File and then click Close*** to close the document, or ***click File, and then click Exit*** to exit Excel.

This concludes Lesson 2.

LESSON 3: BUILDING A DAMAGE PROJECTION SPREADSHEET

This lesson shows you how to build the damage projection spreadsheet shown in Excel 2003 Exhibit 9. It explains how to increase the size of type, how to wrap text in a cell, how to use the border feature, how to use the font and fill color features, how to use the AutoSum features, and how to change the decimal places for a number. This lesson assumes you have successfully completed Lessons 1 and 2. Keep in mind that if at any time you make a mistake in this lesson, you may press **[CTRL]+[Z]** to undo what you have done.

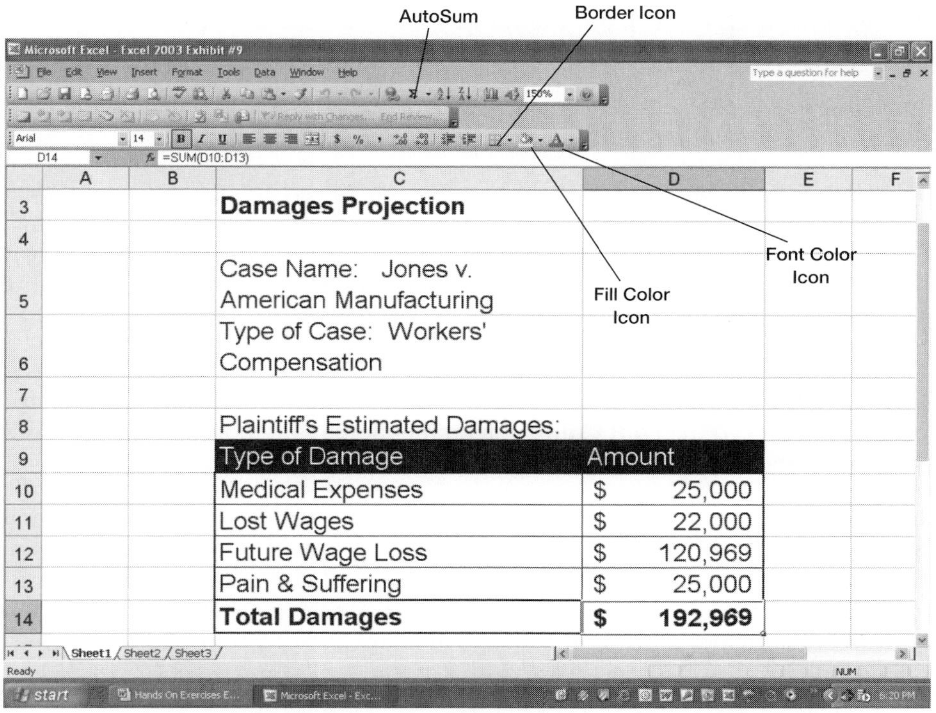

	C	D
3	**Damages Projection**	
4		
5	Case Name: Jones v. American Manufacturing	
6	Type of Case: Workers' Compensation	
7		
8	Plaintiff's Estimated Damages:	
9	Type of Damage	Amount
10	Medical Expenses	$ 25,000
11	Lost Wages	$ 22,000
12	Future Wage Loss	$ 120,969
13	Pain & Suffering	$ 25,000
14	**Total Damages**	**$ 192,969**

Excel 2003 Exhibit 9
Damage Projection
Microsoft product screen shot reprinted with permission from Microsoft Corporation.

1. Open Windows. Then, ***double-click the Excel icon on the desktop*** to open Excel for Windows. Alternatively, ***click the Start button, point to Programs or All Programs, point to Microsoft Office, and then click Microsoft Office Excel 2003.*** You should now be in a clean, blank document.

2. To start building the spreadsheet in Excel 2003 Exhibit 9, begin by ***increasing the size of column C to a width of 37 (Format > Column > Width).***

3. In cell C3, type **Damages Projection**. With the pointer on C3, ***click the Bold icon on the toolbar, and then click the Font Size icon on the toolbar and change the size to 14 point.***

4. Type the text in cell C5 (see Excel 2003 Exhibit 9). ***Click the Font Size icon on the toolbar and change the type size to 14 point.*** Notice that the text goes into the next cell. To wrap part of the text down to the next line within the current cell, ***click in cell C5, then click Format, and then click Cells. Click the Alignment tab, and then, under Text Control, click Wrap Text.*** Then, ***click OK.*** The text has now been wrapped down to the next line within cell C5.

5. Type the text in cell C6, make the text 14 point, and wrap the text down so it does not go into cell D6. *Note*: You can ***right-click in the cell, then click Format Cells*** to get to the window to wrap text.

6. Type the text in cell C8 and make the text 14 point.

7. Type the text and values in cells C9 to D13.

8. Type the text in cell C14.

9. To enter the formula in cell D14 ***click on cell D14.*** Then, ***click the AutoSum icon on the toolbar*** (see Excel 2003 Exhibit 9). Notice that AutoSum assumed you wanted to add the values in D10 to D13. You could adjust the range by pressing **[SHIFT]+[ARROW KEY]**, but the range should be fine as is (i.e., D10 to D13). Press the **[ENTER]** key to enter the formula.

10. ***Click in cell C9, drag the mouse pointer to cell D14, and then click the Font Size icon on the toolbar and change the point size to 14 point.***

11. ***Click in cell C9 and drag the mouse pointer to cell D9. Click Format, then click Cells.*** In the **Patterns** tab under **Color**, ***click the black square, and then click OK.*** (You also could have clicked the **Fill Color** icon on the toolbar to do this: it looks like a paint bucket.) The cells are all black; now you just need to change the font color to white to see the text.

12. With cells C9 and D9 still highlighted, ***click Format, then click Cells.*** In the **Font** tab under **Color**, ***click on the white square and then click OK.*** (You also could have clicked the **Font Color** icon on the toolbar—it looks like an "A" with a red box beneath it.)

13. ***Click in cell C10 and drag the mouse pointer to cell D14. Click the down arrow next to the Border icon on the toolbar.*** (It is typically just to the left of the **Fill Color** icon—see Excel 2003 Exhibit 9). Then, ***click the Borders icon*** which looks like a windowpane. (Remember, just put the mouse pointer over the icon for a second and the name of the icon will appear.) Now, notice that there is a border around every square that was highlighted.

14. ***Click in cell C14 and drag the mouse pointer to cell D14. Click the down arrow next to the Border icon on the toolbar.*** Then, ***click the Thick Box Border icon*** (it looks like a heavy black window frame). Move the pointer and notice that there is now a heavy black border around cells C14 and D14.

15. ***Click in cell D10 and drag the mouse pointer to cell D14. Right-click, and then click Format Cells. Click the Number, and then click Currency. Change decimal places to 0. Then, click OK.***

16. ***Click the Printer icon on the toolbar*** to print the spreadsheet.

17. To save the spreadsheet, ***click File, and then click Save.*** Then, type **Damages Projection** next to File Name. ***Select Save to save the file to the default directory.***

18. ***Click File and then click Close*** to close the document, or ***click File, and then click Exit*** to exit Excel.

This concludes Lesson 3.

Intermediate Lessons

LESSON 4: CHILD SUPPORT PAYMENT SPREADSHEET

This lesson shows you how to build the child support payment spreadsheet shown in Excel 2003 Exhibit 10. It explains how to create a white background, create formulas to multiply cells and formulas that use an absolute cell reference, and how to use the AutoFormat feature. This lesson assumes you have successfully completed Lessons 1–3. Keep in mind that if at any time you make a mistake in this lesson you may press **[CTRL]+[Z]** to undo what you have done.

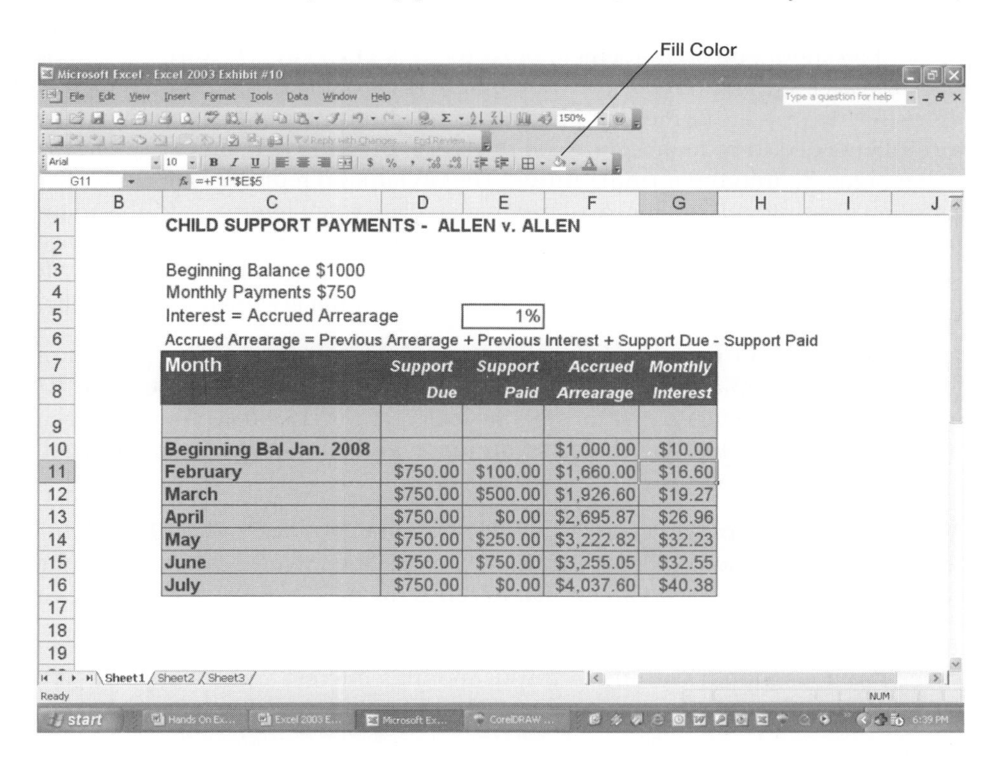

Month	Support Due	Support Paid	Accrued Arrearage	Monthly Interest
Beginning Bal Jan. 2008			$1,000.00	$10.00
February	$750.00	$100.00	$1,660.00	$16.60
March	$750.00	$500.00	$1,926.60	$19.27
April	$750.00	$0.00	$2,695.87	$26.96
May	$750.00	$250.00	$3,222.82	$32.23
June	$750.00	$750.00	$3,255.05	$32.55
July	$750.00	$0.00	$4,037.60	$40.38

Excel 2003 Exhibit 10
Child Support Payment Spreadsheet
Microsoft product screen shot reprinted with permission from Microsoft Corporation.

1. Open Windows. Then, ***double-click the Excel icon on the desktop*** to open Excel for Windows. Alternatively, ***click the Start button, point to Programs or All Programs, point to Microsoft Office, and then click Microsoft Office Excel 2003.*** You should now be in a clean, blank document.

2. In starting to build the spreadsheet in Excel 2003 Exhibit 10, notice that the background is completely white. A completely white background gives you a crisp, clean canvas on which to work and to which you can add colors and graphics.

3. Press **[CTRL]+[A]** on the keyboard. The whole spreadsheet is now selected. ***Click the down arrow next to the Fill Color icon on the toolbar. (The icon looks***

like a paint bucket.) Click the white square that is all the way in the lower right corner. Click in any cell to make the highlighting disappear. Notice that the background of the spreadsheet is now completely white.

4. Enter the text shown in cell C1, and change the font style to bold and the font size to 14 point.

5. Increase the width of column C to 20.

6. Enter the text shown in cells C3 to C6.

7. In cell E5, type **.01** and press **[ENTER]**. ***Click again in cell E5, then click the Percent Style icon on the toolbar.*** (The icon looks like a percent sign [%].)

8. Enter the text shown in cell C7 and in the cell range from D7 to G8.

9. Enter the text shown in the cell range from C10 to C16.

10. Enter the numbers (values) shown in cells in D11 to D16, and E11 to E16.

11. In cell F10, type **1000**.

12. In cell G10, press the **[=]** key, ***click in cell F10***, press **[SHIFT]+[8]** (an asterisk will appear), then ***click in cell E5*** and press the **[F4]** key once. The formula **=F10*$E$5** should be on the screen; press the **[ENTER]** key. The formula multiplies the accrued arrearage (how much the individual is behind on payments) times the interest rate (which is 1 percent). The reason you pressed **[F4]** is that the formula needed to be an absolute cell reference; pressing **[F4]** simply put in the dollar signs ($) into the formula for us. The dollar sign represents to Excel that this is an absolute cell reference, rather than a relative cell reference. In this manner, when you copy the formula to other cells (see below), the accrued arrearage will always be multiplied by the value in E5. Said another way, the second half of this formula ($E$5) will not change when the formula is copied to other cells.

13. If you want to find out for yourself why the formula **=F10*E5** will not work once it is copied from cell G10 (where it will work fine), type **=F10*E5** in cell G10, and then copy the formula to cells G11 to G16. Once you have seen the effect of this, delete the changes you made and change the formula in cell G10 to **=F10*$E$5**.

14. To copy the formula from G10 to cells G11 to G16, ***click cell G10, click the AutoFill handle*** (it looks like a little black box, in the lower right corner of the cell) ***and drag the mouse pointer down to cell G16.***

15. In cell F11, type **=F10+G10+D11–E11**. The formula adds the accrued amount in the previous month with the previous month's interest and the current support due, and then subtracts the current amount paid.

16. To copy the formula from F11 to cells F12 to F16, ***click in cell F11, click the AutoFill handle, and drag the mouse pointer down to cell F16.***

17. ***Click cell D10 and drag the mouse pointer to cell G16. Right-click, and click Format Cells. Click the Number tab, click Currency, and then click OK.***

18. Notice that the spreadsheet is very plain. You now will use the **AutoFormat** feature to give the spreadsheet some color. ***Click in cell C7 and drag the mouse pointer to cell G16.***

19. ***Next, click Format, and then click AutoFormat.*** The **AutoFormat** window should now be displayed. ***Click on the second spreadsheet format on the right***

(Classic 3) in the AutoFormat window. Then click OK. Click in any cell to make the highlighting disappear. The spreadsheet should now have a blue and gray background.

20. To add borders to the spreadsheet, ***click in cell C9 and drag the mouse pointer to cell G16. Then, click the right arrow next to the Borders icon on the toolbar. Click the All Borders icon (it looks like a windowpane).*** The spreadsheet is now complete and should look like Excel 2003 Exhibit 10.

21. ***Click the Print icon on the toolbar*** to print the spreadsheet.

22. To save the document, ***click File, and then click Save.*** Then, type **Child Support Payments** next to **File Name**. ***Select Save*** to save the file to the default directory.

23. ***Click File and then click Close*** to close the document, or ***click File, and then click Exit*** to exit Excel.

This concludes Lesson 4.

LESSON 5: LOAN AMORTIZATION TEMPLATE

This lesson shows you how to open a loan amortization template and fill it out (see Excel 2003 Exhibit 11). Templates are a great way to simplify complicated spreadsheets. You will also learn how to protect cells, freeze panes, split a screen, hide a column, and use the Format Painter tool. This lesson assumes you have successfully completed Lessons 1–4. Keep in mind that if at any time you make a mistake in this lesson you may press **[CTRL]+[Z]** to undo what you have done.

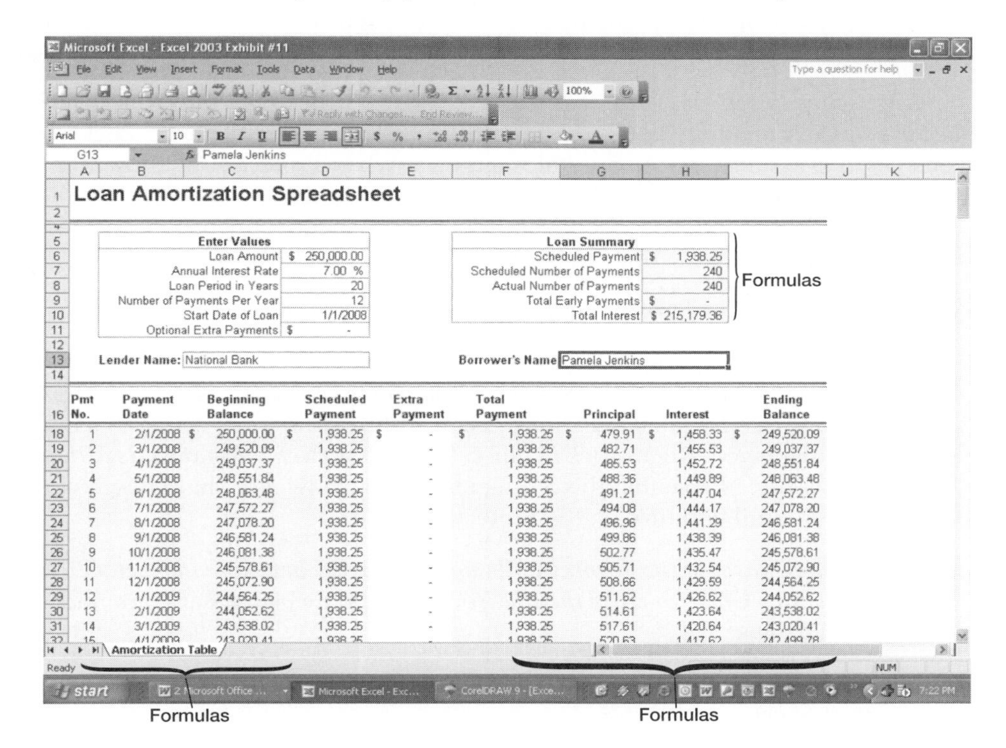

Excel 2003 Exhibit 11
Loan Amortization Template
Microsoft product screen shot reprinted with permission from Microsoft Corporation.

1. Open Windows. Then, ***double-click the Excel icon on the desktop*** to open Excel for Windows. Alternatively, ***click the Start button, point to Programs or All Programs, point to Microsoft Office, and then click Microsoft Office Excel 2003.*** You should now be in a clean, blank document.

2. The first thing you will do to complete the template shown in Excel 2003 Exhibit 11 is to open the "Lesson 5" file from Disk 1 supplied with this text. Ensure that the disk is fully inserted in the disk drive, point and click on File on the Menu Bar, and then point and click to Open. The "Open" window should now be displayed. Point and click on the down arrow to the right of the white box next to "Look in:" and select the drive where Disk 1 is located. Point and double-click on the Excel Files folder. Double-click on the "Lesson 5" file.

3. You should now have the loan amortization spreadsheet shown in Excel 2003 Exhibit 11 loaded, except your spreadsheet contains no data yet.

4. Enter the following information:

Cell D6: **250000**
Cell D7: **7**
Cell D8: **20**
Cell D9: **12**
Cell D10: **1/1/2008**
Cell D11: **0** (When you click in Cell D11 a note will appear regarding extra payments; just type a zero and hit **[ENTER]** and the note will disappear.)
Cell C13: **National Bank**
Cell G13: **Pamela Jenkins**

5. Notice that your spreadsheet now appears nearly identical to Excel 2003 Exhibit 11.

6. Notice in your spreadsheet that just about everything below row 16 is a formula. If a user accidentally deleted one of these formulas, the whole spreadsheet could be affected. You will now turn on the **Protection** feature and lock some of the cells so they cannot be accidentally deleted.

7. ***Right-click in cell D6. Then, click Format Cells. . . . Click the Protection tab in the Format Cells window.*** Notice that there is no green check mark next to **Locked**. Cells D6 to D13 and cell G13 are unlocked even when **Protection** is turned on. When **Protection** is off, you can change the locked/unlocked format of cells at will by using the **Format** > **Cells** > **Protection** command sequence. Interestingly, when a new blank spreadsheet is open in Excel, all cells default to **Locked**.

8. ***Click Cancel in the Format Cells window to close the window.***

9. Let's open a new spreadsheet so you can see that all cells in Excel start out with the Locked format. ***Click the New File icon on the toolbar; it is the very first icon on the left (see Excel 2003 Exhibit 12).*** You should now have a new blank spreadsheet displayed. ***Right-click in any cell and then click Format Cells. Click the Protection tab.*** Notice that the cell seems locked. However, the cell will not be truly locked until you turn on the **Protection** feature.

10. Now, ***click Cancel in the Format Cells window in the new spreadsheet. Click File and then click Close to close the file.*** You should now be back at your amortization spreadsheet.

11. To turn on the **Protection** feature, ***click Tools, point to Protection, and then click Protect Sheet.***

12. The Protect Sheet window should now be displayed (see Excel 2003 Exhibit 12). Make sure that the first two selections under **Allow all users of this worksheet to:** are selected (**Select locked cells** and **Select unlocked cells**). Notice that you can enter a password in the white box under **Password to unprotect sheet**. This would

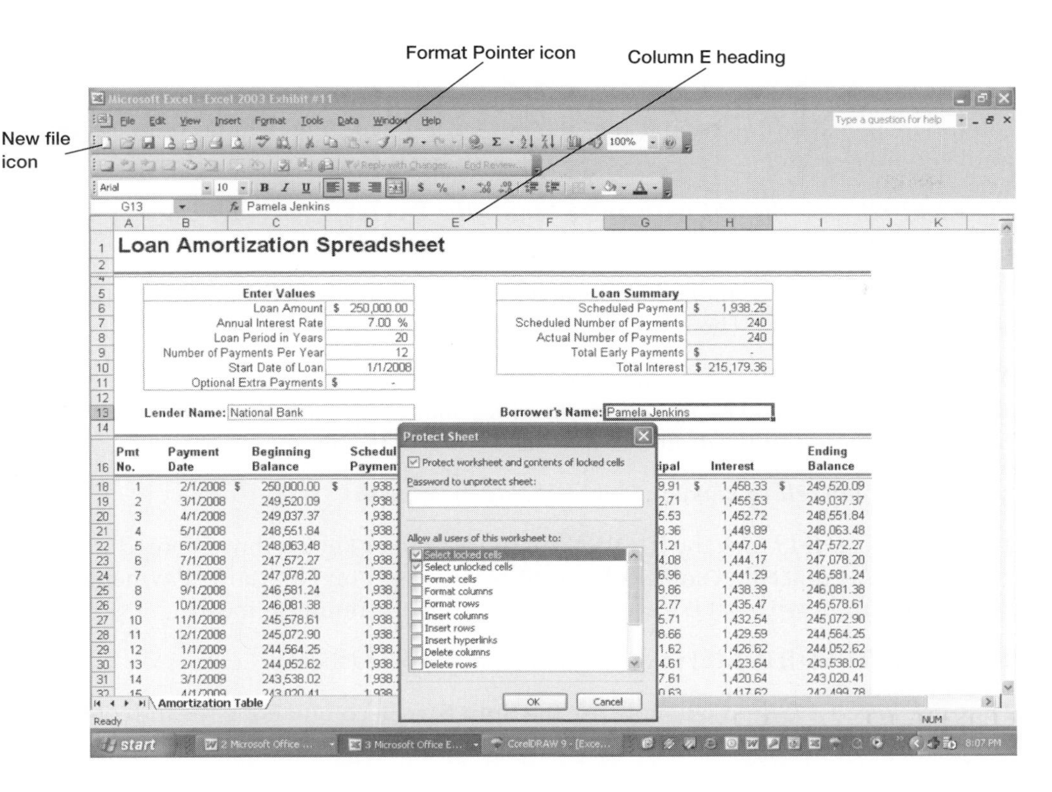

Excel 2003 Exhibit 12
Protecting Cells in Excel 2003
Microsoft product screen shot reprinted with permission from Microsoft Corporation.

completely lock the spreadsheet (only unlocked cells could be modified) to users that did not know the password. In this case this is not necessary; it is fine for someone to intentionally change the spreadsheet—you are just using this feature to prevent someone from accidentally changing information.

13. After ensuring the first two items are checked under **Allow all users of this worksheet to:** ***click OK.***

14. ***Now, click in any cell other than D6 to D13 or cell G13 and try to type something in the cell.*** Notice that you get an error message that says **The cell or chart you are trying to change is protected and therefore read-only.** ***Click OK to close the error window.***

15. The whole spreadsheet is now locked, except for cells D6 to D13 and cell G13, because in the template these were not formatted as locked.

16. We will turn off the "Protection" feature since we are still building the spreadsheet. ***Click Tools on the menu bar, click Protection, and then click Unprotect Sheet.***

17. You will now use the Format Painter tool to copy the formatting from one set of cells to another set of cells. Notice that cells F13 and G13 do not look like cells B13 and C13. You will now copy the format from cells B13 and C13 to cells F13 and G13.

18. ***Point to cell B13 and drag the mouse pointer to cell C13. Next, click the Format Painter icon on the toolbar (the icon that looks like a paintbrush—see Excel 2003 Exhibit 12).*** Your pointer now should have a paintbrush on it.

19. ***Click in cell F13 and drag the mouse pointer to cell H13, then let go of the mouse button.*** Notice that the formatting has now been copied.

20. Notice that column E in the amortization schedule of the spreadsheet is the "Extra Payment" column. Assume for this exercise that you will not have any

extra payments and that you do not need this column, but you want to leave the column there in case you need it at a later date. For now, you will hide column E until you need it later.

21. ***Right-click on the cell with an "E" in it (the E column heading) (see Excel 2003 Exhibit 12). Next, from the drop-down menu, click Hide.***

22. ***Click in any cell to make the vertical line disappear.*** Notice that Column E is no longer displayed. The next column heading has changed from D to F.

23. You will now unhide column E. ***Point on the "D" column heading, and drag the mouse pointer to the "F" column heading, and then right-click the mouse. Next, click Unhide on the drop-down menu.*** Notice that Column E reappears.

24. ***Click in any cell to make the highlighting disappear.***

25. ***Click in cell D18.*** Use the **[DOWN ARROW]** cursor key on the keyboard to go to cell D50. Notice that some column titles such as "Pmt No." and "Payment Date," are not shown, so it is difficult to know what the numbers mean.

26. Press **[CTRL]+[HOME]** to go to the top of the spreadsheet.

27. ***Click in cell A18.*** You will now use the **Split Screen** command to see the column titles.

28. ***Click Window on the menu bar and then click Split.*** Use the **[DOWN ARROW]** cursor key on the keyboard to go to cell A50. Notice that because you split the screen at row 18, you can still see column titles. Next, use the **[UP ARROW]** cursor key on the keyboard to go to cell A1. Notice that you now see the top portion of your spreadsheet in both the top and bottom screens.

29. ***Click Window on the menu bar and then click Remove Split.*** The bottom screen is now gone.

30. The **Freeze Panes** feature is another way to show the column headings when you scroll down a document. ***Click in cell B18.***

31. ***Click Windows on the menu bar and then click Freeze Panes.*** Use the **[DOWN ARROW]** cursor key on the keyboard to go to cell B50. Notice that because you froze the screen at cell B18, you can still see column titles. Next, use the **[RIGHT ARROW]** cursor key on the keyboard to go to cell R50. Notice that you can still see the "Pmt No." column, including the payment numbers. The **Freeze Panes** feature is a convenient way to see both column and row titles at the same time.

32. ***Click Window on the menu bar and then click Unfreeze Panes.***

33. ***Click the Print icon on the toolbar*** to print the spreadsheet.

34. To save the document, ***click File on the menu bar, and then click Save As.*** Under Save in, choose the location where you want the file to be saved. Then, type **Excel Lesson 5 Spreadsheet DONE** next to **File Name**. ***Select Save*** to save the file.

35. Templates are a great way to utilize the power of Excel. There are many free templates available on the Internet. Microsoft alone offers more than 100 Excel templates on its website. To access them, ***click File on the menu bar and then click New. Under Templates, click Templates on Office Online.***

36. ***Click File on the menu bar and then click Close*** to close the document, or ***click File, and then click Exit*** to exit Excel.

LESSON 6: STATISTICAL FUNCTIONS

This lesson demonstrates how to use and enter statistical formulas such as average, maximum, minimum, and standard deviation. It also shows how to sort data, check for metadata in spreadsheets, use the **format clear** command, use conditional formatting, and insert a clip art file. When the spreadsheet is complete, it will look like Excel 2003 Exhibit 13. Keep in mind that if at any time you make a mistake in this lesson, you may press **[CTRL]+[Z]** to undo what you have done.

1. Open Windows. Then, ***double-click the Excel icon on the desktop*** to open Excel 2003 for Windows. Alternatively, ***click the Start button, point to Programs or All Programs, point to Microsoft Office, and then click Microsoft Office Excel 2003.*** You should be in a clean, blank document.

2. The first thing you will do to complete the spreadsheet in Excel 2003 Exhibit 13 is to open the "Lesson 6" file from Disk 1 supplied with this text. Ensure that the disk is inserted in the disk drive, point and click on File on the Menu Bar, and then point and click on Open. The "Open" window should now be displayed. Point and click on the down arrow to the right of the white box next to "Look in:" and select the drive where Disk 1 is located. Point and double-click on the Excel Files folder. Double-click on the "Lesson 6" file.

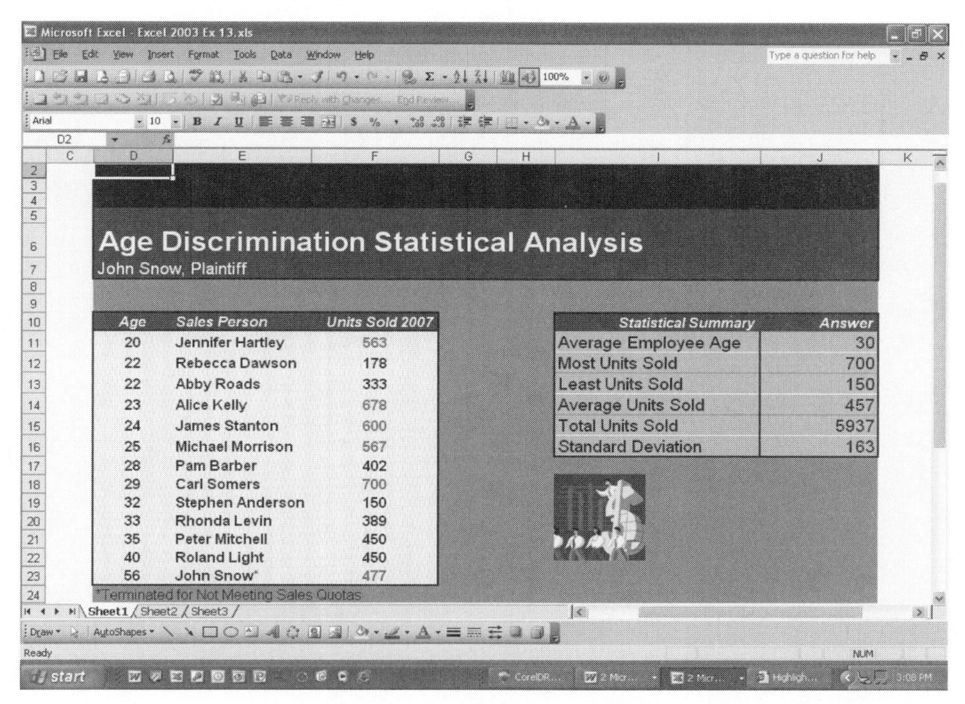

Excel 2003 Exhibit 13
Statistical Spreadsheet
Microsoft product screen shot reprinted with permission from Microsoft Corporation.

3. You should now have the age discrimination statistical analysis spreadsheet shown in Excel 2003 Exhibit 13 opened, except your spreadsheet has no formulas in the statistical summary section, the data has not yet been sorted, and there is no clip art yet.

4. You will now enter the formulas in the statistical summary section of the spreadsheet. The first formula will calculate the average age of employees of the company. ***Click in cell J11.*** Type the formula **=AVERAGE(D11:D23)** and then press **[ENTER]**. The result should be 30. *Note*: Another way to enter the average function would be to ***Click Insert on the menu bar and then click Function***. Next, under **Or select a category,** click the down arrow and select **Statistical**. Notice that **Average** is one of the functions listed.

5. The next formula will calculate the most units sold. ***Click in cell J12.*** Type the formula **=MAX(F11:F23)** and then press **[ENTER]**. The result should be 700.

6. The next formula will calculate the least units sold. ***Click in cell J13.*** Type the formula **=MIN(F11:F23)** and then press **[ENTER]**. The result should be 150.

7. The next formula will calculate the average units sold. ***Click in cell J14.*** Type the formula **=AVERAGE(F11:F23)** and then press **[ENTER]**. The result should be 457.

8. ***Point and click on cell J15.*** Type the formula **=SUM(F11:F23)** and then press **[ENTER]**. The result should be 5937.

9. The last formula will calculate the standard deviation for units sold. The standard deviation is a measure of how widely values are dispersed from the average value (the arithmetic mean). Large standard deviations show that the numbers vary widely from the average. ***Click Insert on the menu bar and then click Function.*** The **Insert Function** window should now be displayed. In the **Insert Function** window under **Or select a category**, ***click the down arrow and select Statistical. Scroll down the list and then click*** **STDEVP** (see Excel 2003 Exhibit 14). Notice there is a definition for this function. ***Next, click OK in the Insert Function window.***

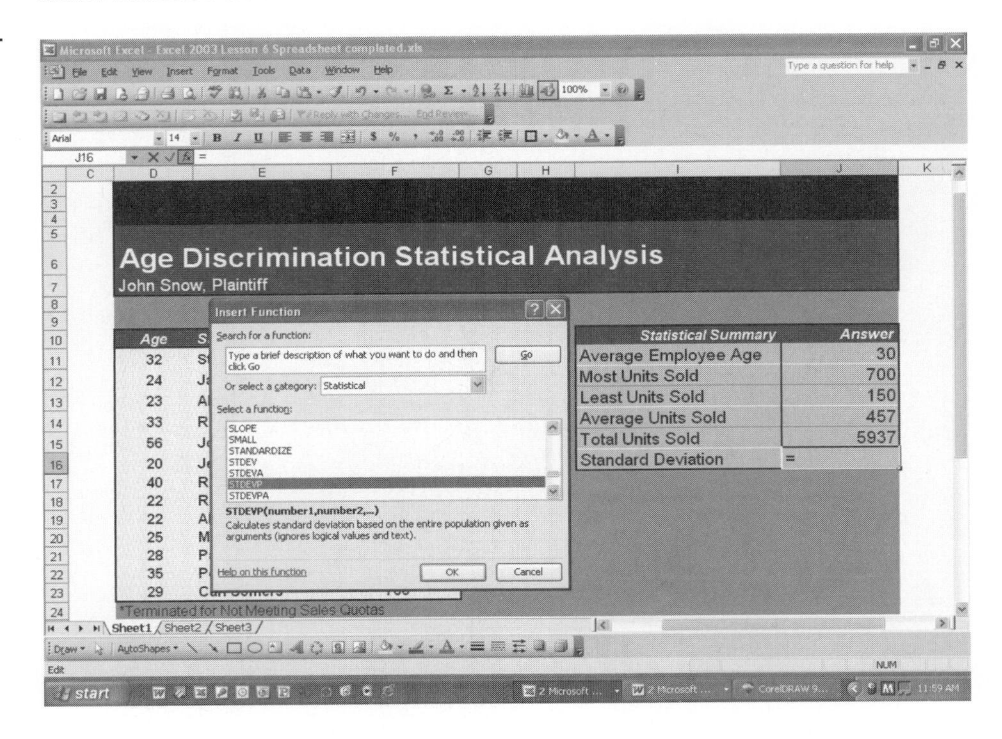

Excel 2003 Exhibit 14
Entering a Standard Deviation Formula Using the Insert Function Command

10. The **Function Arguments** window should now be displayed (see Excel 2003 Exhibit 15). In the **Function Arguments** window next to **Number 1** press **[DEL]** until the box is blank, type **F11:F23,** and then ***click OK*** (see Excel 2003 Exhibit 15). The result should be 163.

11. You will now sort the data based on the age of the employees. ***Click in cell D11 and then drag the mouse pointer down to F23. Then, click Data on the menu bar and then click Sort.*** The **Sort** window should now be displayed (see Excel 2003 Exhibit 16). *Note*: Even though you just want to sort by age, you must select the full data range, which includes all of the information, or the "Age" data will

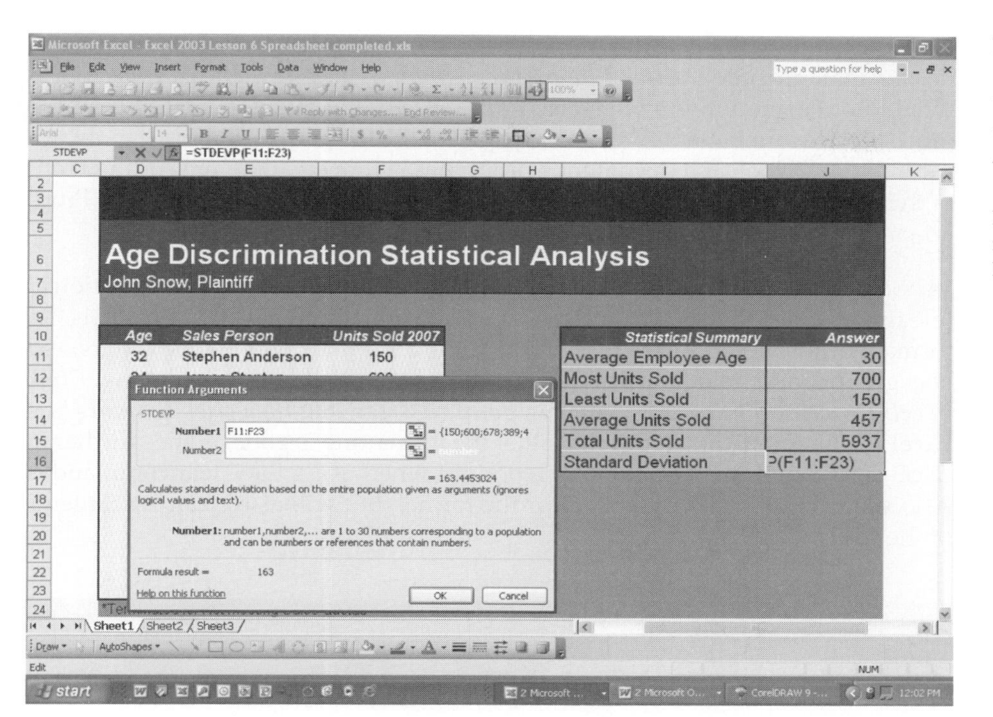

Excel 2003 Exhibit 15
*Entering a Standard Deviation Formula—The **Function Arguments** Window*
Microsoft product screen shot reprinted with permission from Microsoft Corporation.

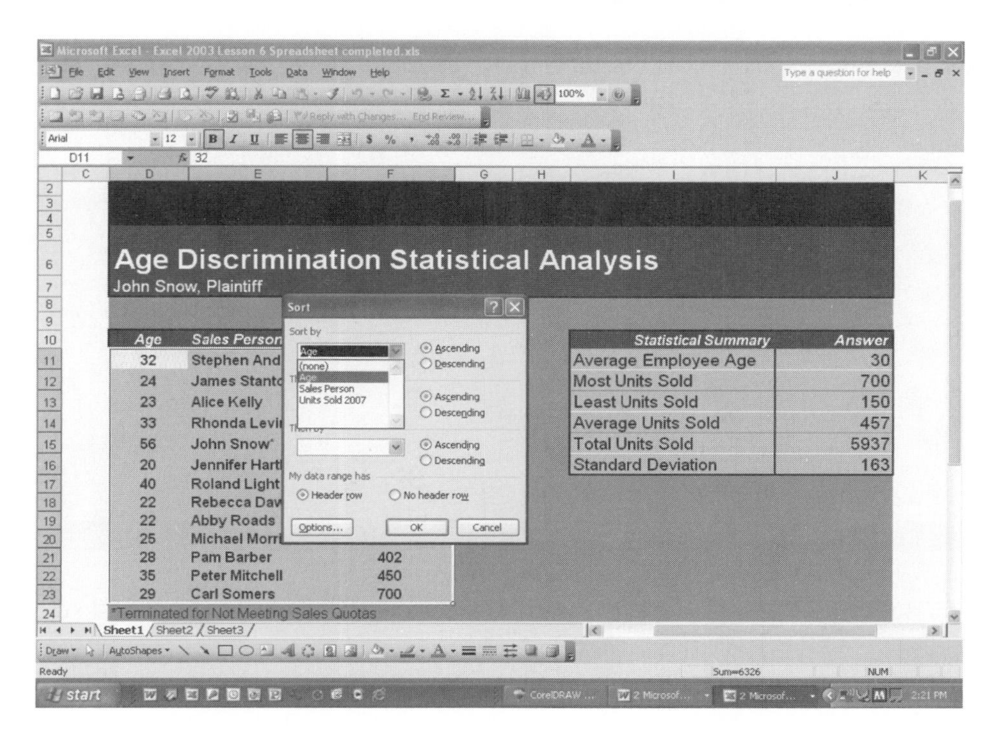

Excel 2003 Exhibit 16
Sorting Data
Microsoft product screen shot reprinted with permission from Microsoft Corporation.

be sorted but the other columns and rows will stay where they are. The data will then be mismatched (i.e., the age data will not be matched with the correct persons or number of units sold).

12. ***Click the down arrow under Sort by, then click Age. Notice that Ascending is selected; this is fine, so click OK in the Sort window.*** The data should now be sorted according to the age of the individual, with John Snow appearing last in the spreadsheet.

13. You will now look at the properties of the document to make sure there is no metadata included. ***Click File on the menu bar, and then click Properties.*** It would not be good if you were electronically sending this document out of the office, since a number of things are included in the **Properties** section. It is always a good idea to look at a document's properties before emailing or sending it out of the office. Use the **[DEL]** key to delete the information contained in the "Properties" Window. When you are done, ***click OK to close the window.***

14. Sometimes it is helpful to clear a cell or cells of all formatting information at one time. Notice that cell D6, titled "Age Discrimination Statistical Analysis," is formatted in several different ways, including 24-point type, white letters, red background, and bold. You will now quickly remove all of the formatting. ***Click in cell D6, click Edit on the menu bar, point to Clear, and then click Formats*** (see Excel 2003 Exhibit 17). Notice that all of the formatting is gone. Notice further in Excel 2003 Exhibit 17 that one of the options when using the **Clear** command is **All**. Selecting this will not only clear the format, but will also clear the contents of the selected cell(s).

Excel 2003 Exhibit 17
Clear Formatting/Contents of a Cell(s)

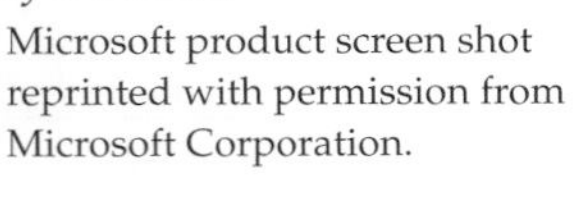

Microsoft product screen shot reprinted with permission from Microsoft Corporation.

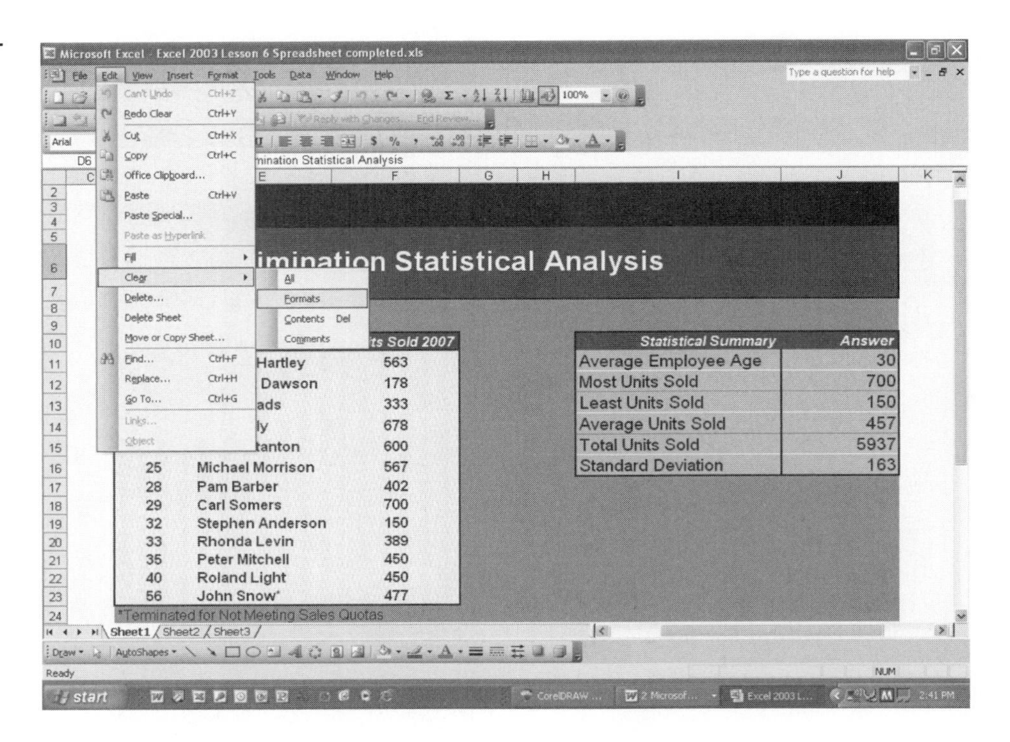

15. Press **[CTRL]+[Z]** (the Undo feature) to restore the original formatting to the cell.

16. You will now learn how to use the **Conditional Formatting** feature of Excel. Sometimes, particularly in large spreadsheets, it is helpful to have the formatting of a cell change if certain conditions are present. For example, in an actual vs. budget report, if an item goes over budget by more than 10 percent it might be helpful for it to be bolded.

17. Notice that the average sales for the sales team in your spreadsheet is 457. It might be helpful to highlight any salesperson who was over the average. ***Click in cell F11 and then drag the mouse pointer to F23. Click Format on the menu bar and then click Conditional Formatting.*** The **Conditional Formatting** window should now be displayed (see Excel 2003 Exhibit 18).

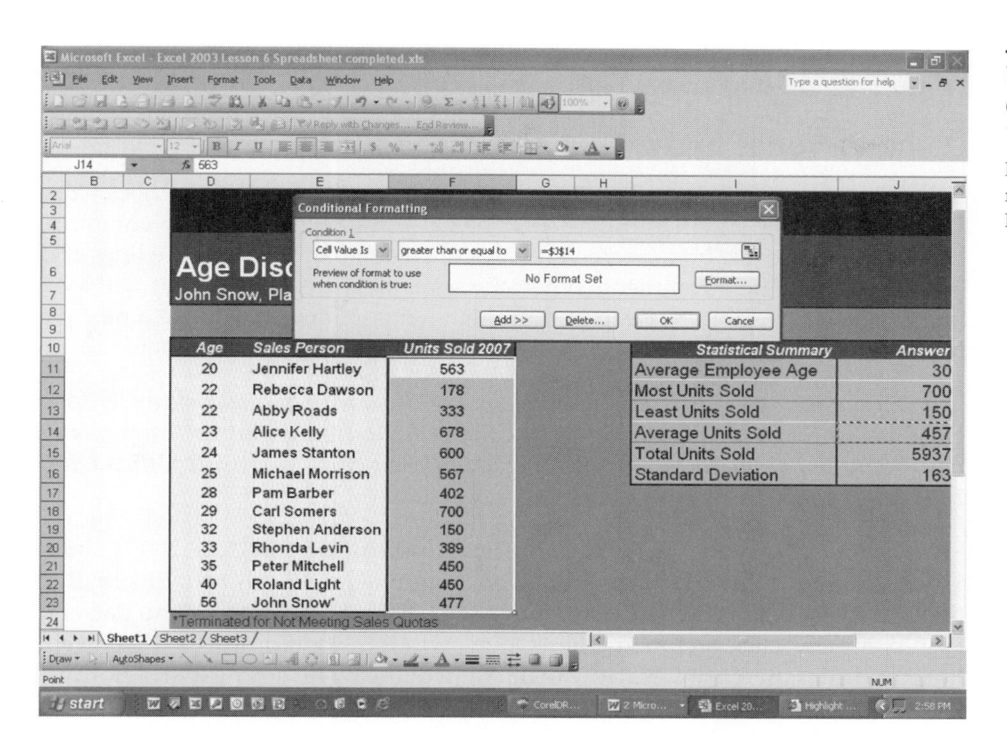

Excel 2003 Exhibit 18
Conditional Formatting Window

Microsoft product screen shot reprinted with permission from Microsoft Corporation.

18. Change the selections in the **Conditional Formatting** window so they match those in Excel 2003 Exhibit 18 (e.g., **Cell Value Is greater than or equal to =$J$14**). This will automatically format any cell greater than or equal to the sales average, no matter what that is.

19. ***Click Format in the Conditional Formatting window. Then, click the down arrow next to Color. Click the red square and then click OK in the Format Cells window.***

20. ***Click OK in the Conditional Formatting window. Next, click in any cell to make the highlighting disappear.*** Notice that any cell with a value greater than or equal to 457 now appears in red.

21. You will now add clip art to your spreadsheet (assuming clip art was included when Excel 2003 was installed on your computer). ***Click in cell I18. Next, click Insert on the menu bar, then point to Picture, and then click Clip Art.***

22. ***The Clip Art task pane will appear to the right of the screen.*** Under **Search For**, type **Money** and then ***click Go. Click the clip art shown in Excel 2003 Exhibit 13 (the image that has a blue bar chart with people in it and a person climbing a dollar sign).*** The clip art has now been added to your spreadsheet.

23. ***Click the red "X" in the Clip Art task pane to close the task pane.***

24. ***Click the Print icon on the toolbar*** to print the spreadsheet.

25. To save the document, ***click File on the menu bar, and then click Save As.*** Under **Save in**, choose the location where you want the file to be saved. Then, type **Excel Lesson 6 Spreadsheet DONE** next to **File Name**. ***Click Save*** to save the file.

26. ***Click File on the menu bar and then click Close*** to close the document, or ***click File, and then click Exit*** to exit Excel.

Advanced Lessons

LESSON 7: TOOLS AND TECHNIQUES 1

In this lesson you will learn how to create visual impact with spreadsheets. You will learn to create and manipulate a text box, use advanced shading techniques, create a 3-D style text box, create vertical text, create diagonal text, use lines and borders, and create a comment. When the spreadsheet is complete, it will look like Excel 2003 Exhibit 19. Keep in mind that if at any time you make a mistake in this lesson, you may press **[CTRL]+[Z]** to undo what you have done.

1. Open Windows. Then, ***double-click on the Excel icon on the desktop*** to open Excel for Windows. Alternatively, ***click the Start button, point to Programs or All Programs, point to Microsoft Office, and then click Microsoft Office Excel 2003.*** You should be in a clean, blank document.

2. The first thing you will do to complete the spreadsheet in Excel 2003 Exhibit 19 is to open the "Lesson 7" file from Disk 1 supplied with this text. Ensure that the disk is inserted in the disk drive, point and click on File on the Menu Bar, and then point and click on Open. The "Open" window should now be displayed. Point and click on the down arrow to the right of the white box next to "Look in:" and select the drive where Disk 1 is located. Point and double-click on the Excel Files folder. Double-click on the "Lesson 7" file.

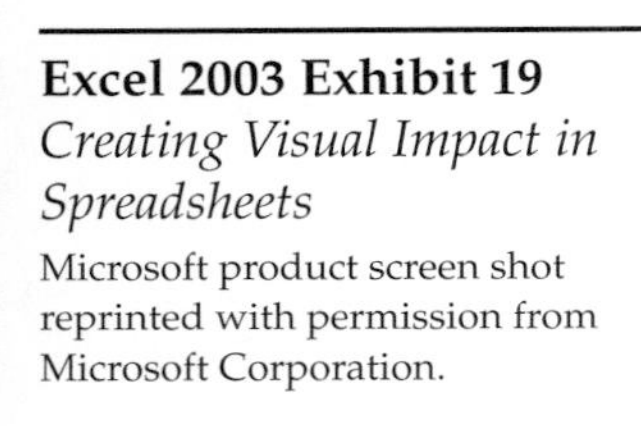

Excel 2003 Exhibit 19
Creating Visual Impact in Spreadsheets
Microsoft product screen shot reprinted with permission from Microsoft Corporation.

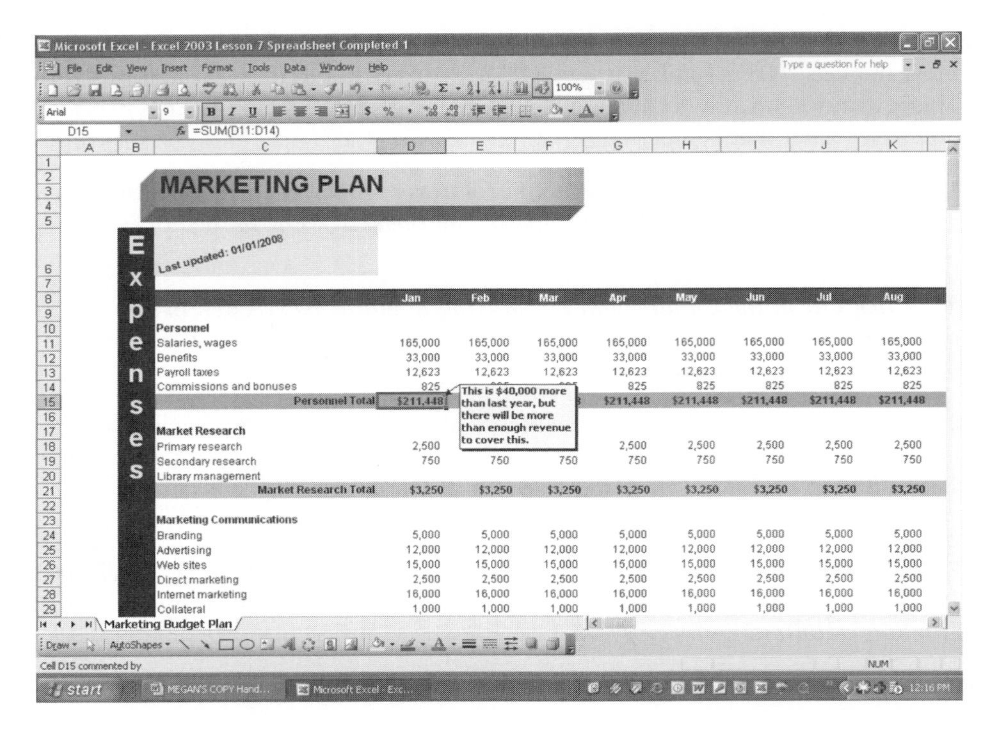

3. You should now have the marketing plan spreadsheet in Excel 2003 Exhibit 19 opened, except the spreadsheet is missing some of the formatting that gives it visual impact. You will add formatting to the spreadsheet to make it more visually compelling.

4. You will first add the text box that holds the title "Marketing Plan," as shown in Excel 2003 Exhibit 19. To do this, you need access to the Drawing toolbar. ***Click***

View on the menu bar, point to Toolbars, and then click Drawing. The Drawing toolbar should now be displayed at the bottom of the screen.

5. In the **Drawing** toolbar at the bottom of the page, *click the Text Box icon. (It looks like a rectangle with an "A" in it. It is NOT the icon with a large blue graphic "A." Remember that you can hover your mouse over any icon to see its name.)* Notice that your mouse pointer has turned into an upside down letter "T."

6. *Point to cell C2 and drag the mouse pointer to about cell F4.* An outline of a box should now be shown from C2 to F4. This is a text box.

7. *Click inside the text box. Click the Bold icon on the toolbar.*

8. *Click the down arrow next to the Font Size icon on the toolbar and select 20.*

9. Type **MARKETING PLAN.**

10. *Right-click on the outline of the text box you just created. In the drop-down menu, click Format Text Box.* The **Format Text Box** window should now be displayed.

11. *Click the Colors and Lines tab (see Excel 2003 Exhibit 20).* Under **Fill** and to the right of **Color**, *click the down arrow* (see Excel 2003 Exhibit 20). This will open a box with many colors; *click Fill Effects.* The **Fill Effects** window should now be displayed. The **Gradient** tab should be selected.

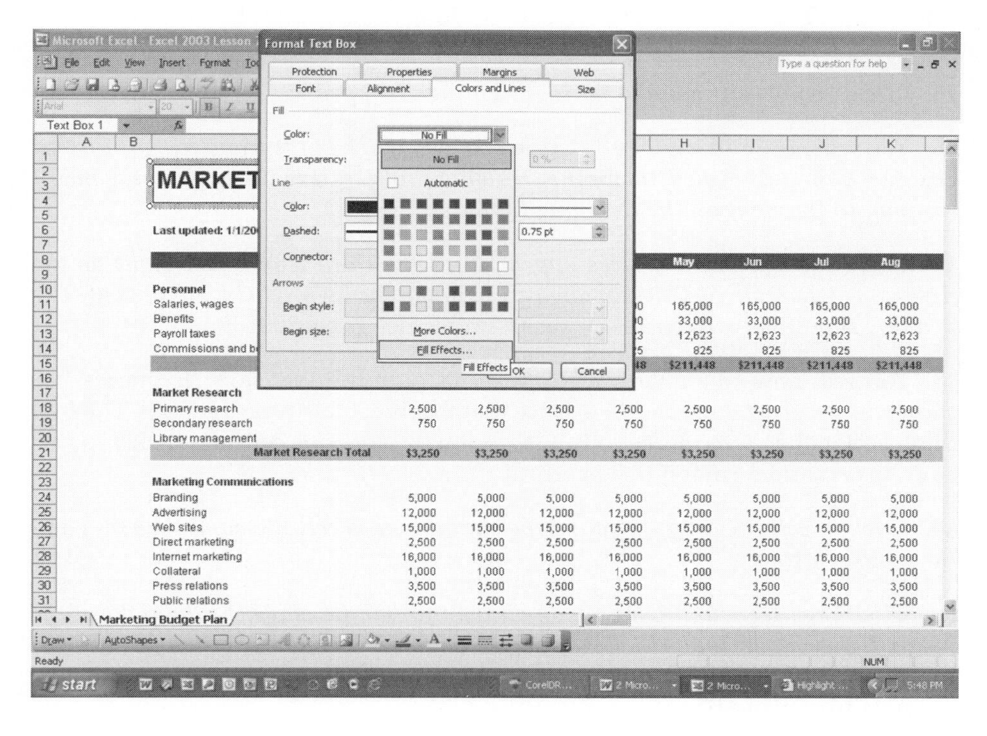

Excel 2003 Exhibit 20
Formatting a Text Box
Microsoft product screen shot reprinted with permission from Microsoft Corporation.

12. In the **Gradient** tab under **Colors**, *click Preset. Click the down arrow next to Present colors, and then scroll down and click Fog (see Excel 2003 Exhibit 21).*

13. *Now, still in the Fill Effects window and in the Gradient tab, click Vertical under Shading Styles (see Excel 2003 Exhibit 21).* Notice that four boxes under **Variants** appear. This gives you four additional styles you can select. *Select one of the four that you like.*

Excel 2003 Exhibit 21
Fill Effects in Excel 2003
Microsoft product screen shot reprinted with permission from Microsoft Corporation.

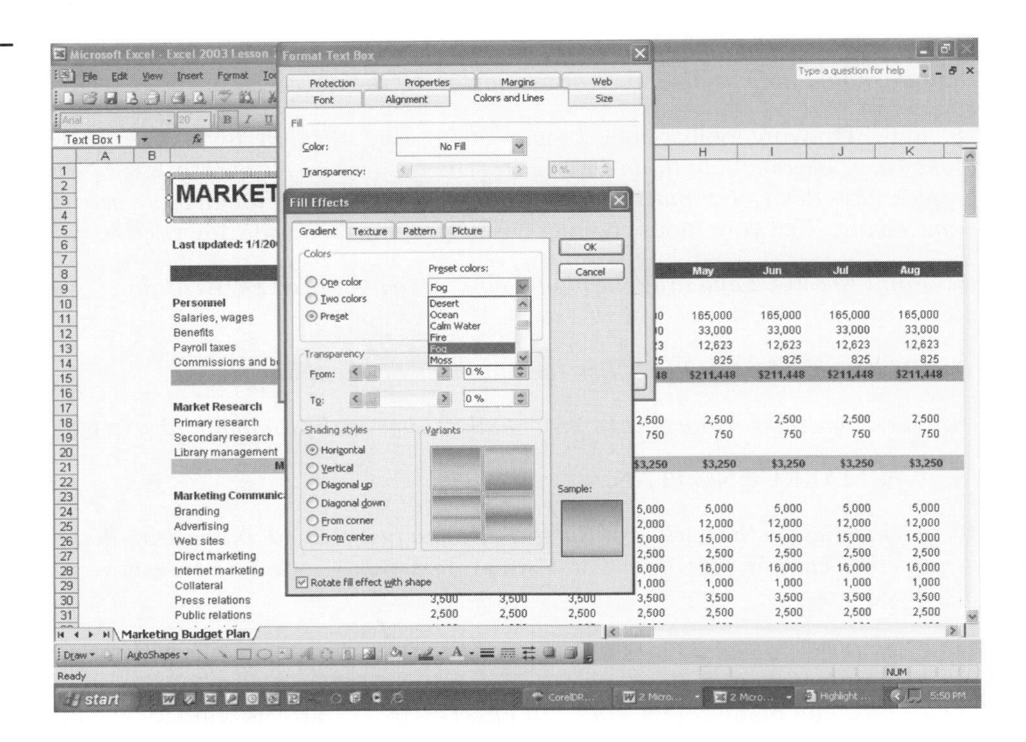

14. ***Click OK in the Fill Effects window. Then, click OK in the Format Text Box window.***

15. ***Click in any cell to make the highlighting disappear.***

16. You will now add a 3-D style to the text box. ***Click in the Marketing Plan text box. Click the 3-D Style icon on the Drawing toolbar (it is the very last icon, all the way to the right on the Drawing toolbar).***

17. ***When the 3-D style choices appear, click the third icon to the right on the first row (3-D Style 3). Click in any cell to make the highlighting disappear.*** The text box should now have a 3-D box around it (see Excel 2003 Exhibit 19).

18. You will now create the vertical text in Column B that says "Expenses," as shown in Excel 2003 Exhibit 19. Notice that this is actually one long cell. The first thing you will do is to merge cells B6 through B53 into one cell, and then you will add the text and format it to be vertical.

19. ***Click in cell B6, drag the mouse pointer down to cell B53, and then let go of the mouse button.***

20. ***Click the Merge and Center icon on the toolbar. (It is just to the right of the Align Right icon. It looks like a box with an "a" in the middle with left and right arrows around the "a.")*** Notice that the selected cells have been merged into one cell now from B6 to B53.

21. With the pointer still in cell B6, ***click the down arrow next to the Font Size icon and click 22. Next, click the Bold icon.*** Now type **Expenses** and press the **[ENTER]** key.

22. ***Right-click anywhere in cell B6. Then, click Format Cells. The Format Cells window should now be displayed, and the Alignment tab should be selected (see Excel 2003 Exhibit 22).***

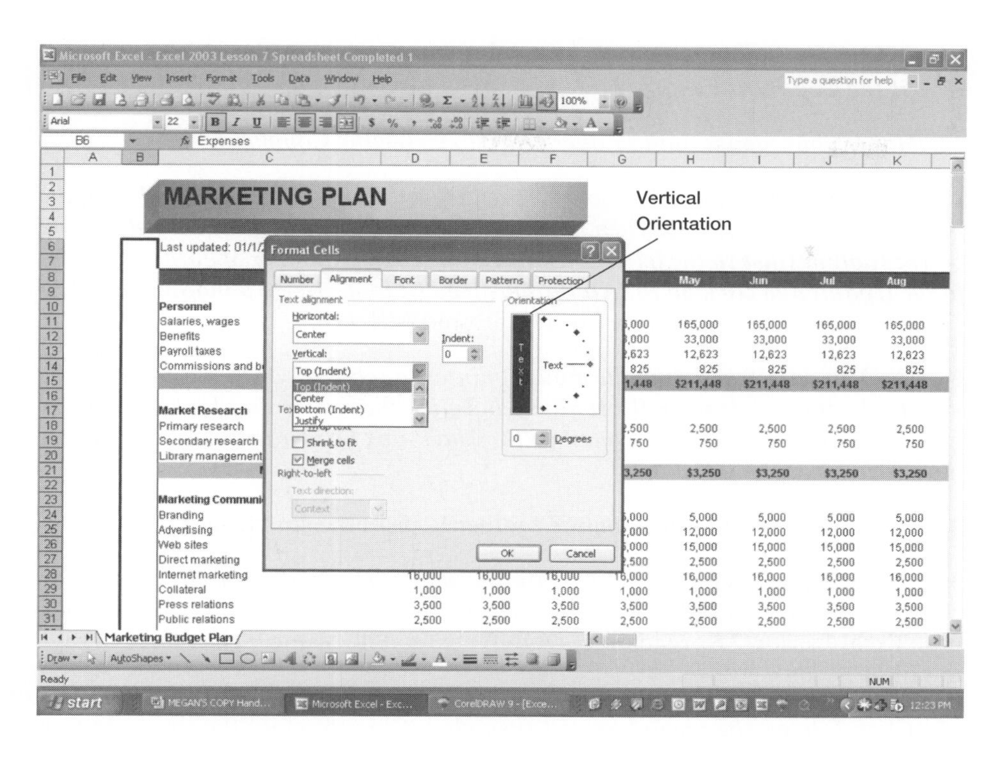

Excel 2003 Exhibit 22
Creating Vertical Text in Excel 2003
Microsoft product screen shot reprinted with permission from Microsoft Corporation.

23. ***In the Format Cells window under Orientation, click the box that shows the word "Text" displayed vertically (i.e., written from top to bottom, instead of from left to right—see Excel 2003 Exhibit 22).***

24. ***In the Format Cells window under Vertical, click the down arrow and select Top (Indent) (see Excel 2003 Exhibit 22).***

25. ***Click OK in the Format Cells window.*** The word "Expenses" should now be displayed vertically down the cell.

26. ***With the pointer still in cell B6, click the down arrow next to the Fill Color icon (it looks like a paint bucket with a color under it) on the toolbar and select black. Then, click the down arrow next to the Font Color icon (it looks like an "A" with a color under it) and select yellow.***

27. You will next make the text in cell C6 appear diagonally. ***Right-click on cell C6. Then, point and click on Format Cells.*** The **Format Cells** window should now be displayed and the **Alignment** tab should be selected (see Excel 2003 Exhibit 22).

28. ***In the Format Cells window under Orientation, click the up arrow next to Degrees until it says 15 degrees.***

29. ***In the Format Cells window, click the Patterns tab. Click the yellow square, and then click OK.***

30. ***Click in any cell to make the highlighting disappear.*** The words "Last updated 1/1/2008" should now be displayed diagonally in black letters with a yellow background.

31. You will now add the Comment shown in Excel 2003 Exhibit 19. ***Right-click in cell D15. On the drop-down menu, click Insert Comment.*** Press **[BACKSPACE]** twice to delete the colon, and then type **This is $40,000 more than last**

year, but there will be more than enough revenue to cover this. ***Click in any cell to exit the Comment box.***

32. ***Hover your mouse pointer over cell D15 to see the Comment.***

33. You will now add borders to the spreadsheet. ***Point to cell C53 and drag the mouse pointer to cell P53. Then, click the down arrow next to the Borders icon on the toolbar (just to the left of the Fill Color icon). A number of borders are displayed; point and click on the All Borders icon (it looks like a windowpane).*** The "Totals" row should now have borders around each cell.

34. ***Click in cell C8 and drag the mouse pointer to cell P53. Click the down arrow next to the Borders icon on the toolbar, and click the border that looks like a single box with a thick border around it (the Thick Box Border icon).*** A thick border now surrounds the data.

35. ***Click on the Printer icon on the toolbar*** to print the spreadsheet.

36. To save the document, ***click File the menu bar, and then click Save As.*** Under **Save in**, choose the location where you want the file to be saved. Then, type **Excel Lesson 7 Spreadsheet DONE** next to File Name. ***Select Save*** to save the file.

37. ***Click File on the menu bar and then click Close*** to close the document, or ***click File, and then click Exit*** to exit Excel.

LESSON 8: TOOLS AND TECHNIQUES 2

In this lesson, you will continue to learn and apply helpful tools and techniques using Excel. This includes getting additional practice using the Merge and Center tool, using the Fit to Page feature, printing selections, using the Formula Auditing feature, using the oval tool, and password protecting a file. When your spreadsheet is complete, it will look similar to Excel 2003 Exhibit 23.

Some of these tools have been covered in previous lessons, and this lesson will help cement your ability to use them effectively. This tutorial assumes that you have completed Lessons 1 through 7, and that you are quite familiar with Excel.

1. Open Windows. Then, ***double-click on the Excel icon on the desktop*** to open Excel for Windows. Alternatively, ***click the Start button, point to Programs or All Programs, point to Microsoft Office, and then click Microsoft Office Excel 2003.*** You should now be in a clean, blank document.

2. The first thing you will do to complete the spreadsheet shown in Excel 2003 Exhibit 23 is open to the "Lesson 8" file from Disk 1 supplied with this text. Ensure that the disk is inserted in the disk drive, point and click on File on the Menu Bar, and then point and click on Open. The "Open" window should now be displayed. Point and click on the down arrow to the right of the white box next to "Look in:" and select the drive where Disk 1 is located. Point and double-click on the Excel Files folder. Double-click on the "Lesson 8" file.

3. You should now have the stock portfolio spreadsheet shown in Excel 2003 Exhibit 23 opened, except your spreadsheet will be missing two rows of data and some of the formatting. You will add the rows and formatting to the spreadsheet.

4. ***Use the Merge and Center icon on the toolbar to merge cells C5 to I5.***

5. ***Use the Merge and Center icon on the toolbar to merge cells C6 to I6.***

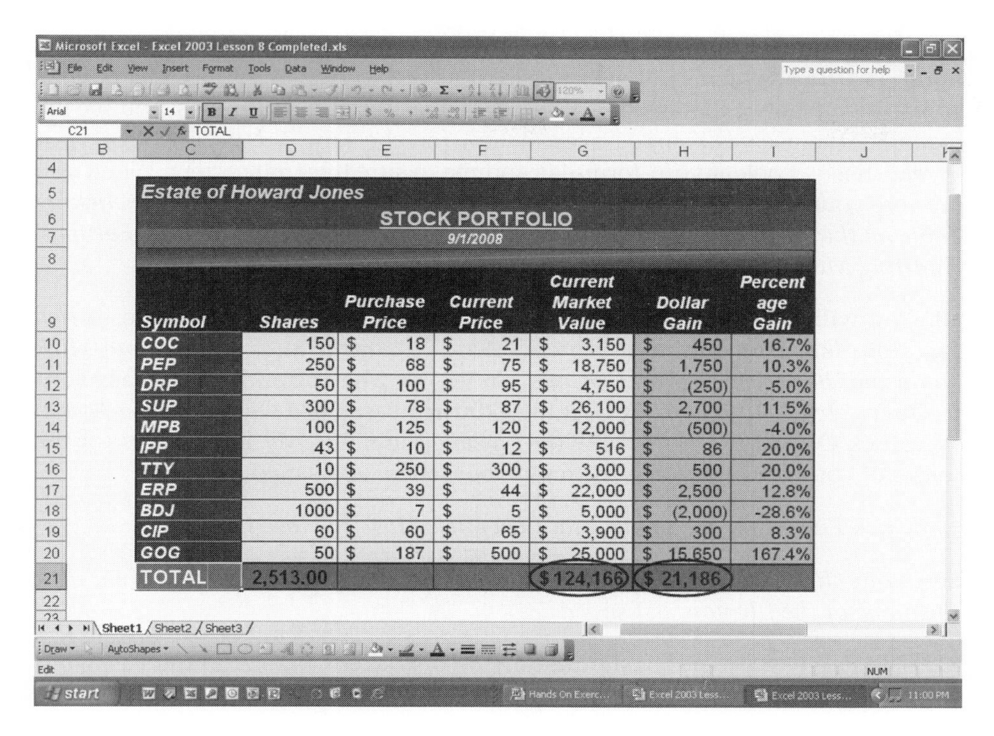

Estate of Howard Jones

STOCK PORTFOLIO

9/1/2008

Symbol	Shares	Purchase Price	Current Price	Current Market Value	Dollar Gain	Percentage Gain
COC	150	$ 18	$ 21	$ 3,150	$ 450	16.7%
PEP	250	$ 68	$ 75	$ 18,750	$ 1,750	10.3%
DRP	50	$ 100	$ 95	$ 4,750	$ (250)	-5.0%
SUP	300	$ 78	$ 87	$ 26,100	$ 2,700	11.5%
MPB	100	$ 125	$ 120	$ 12,000	$ (500)	-4.0%
IPP	43	$ 10	$ 12	$ 516	$ 86	20.0%
TTY	10	$ 250	$ 300	$ 3,000	$ 500	20.0%
ERP	500	$ 39	$ 44	$ 22,000	$ 2,500	12.8%
BDJ	1000	$ 7	$ 5	$ 5,000	$ (2,000)	-28.6%
CIP	60	$ 60	$ 65	$ 3,900	$ 300	8.3%
GOG	50	$ 187	$ 500	$ 25,000	$ 15,650	167.4%
TOTAL	2,513.00			$124,166	$ 21,186	

Excel 2003 Exhibit 23

Stock Portfolio

Microsoft product screen shot reprinted with permission from Microsoft Corporation.

6. ***Use the Merge and Center icon on the toolbar to merge cells C7 to I7.***

7. ***Make sure the titles are aligned as shown in Excel 2003 Exhibit 23 (use the Left Align and Center Align icons on the toolbar).***

8. ***Use the Fill Color icon on the toolbar to make the fill color for cell C5 Dark Blue.***

9. ***Use the Fill Color icon on the toolbar to make the fill color for cell C6 Indigo.***

10. ***Use the Fill Color icon on the toolbar to make the fill color for cell C7 Light Blue.***

11. ***The cell range from C8 to I8 is a text graphic box (similar to a text box). Right-click the box, select Format AutoShape, and change the fill color to a fill effect of Preset, Early Sunset, with a shading style of Diagonal Up.***

12. ***Use the Borders icon on the toolbar to give cells D10 to I21 a border of All Borders.***

13. ***On the Drawing toolbar, click the Oval tool, which looks like a circle. (If the Drawing toolbar does not appear, click View > Toolbars > Drawing). Start in the upper left corner of cell G21 and drag the mouse pointer to the lower right corner of G21 to make an oval around the total.*** *Note*: you can slightly move the ovals by using the cursor keys on the keyboard to nudge them into place so they are centered in the cell.

14. ***Right-click the oval and select Format AutoShape. Change the fill color to No Fill, and change the line weight to 1.75.***

15. ***Repeat the same process in cell H21.***

16. You will now use the Formula Auditing Mode to see the formulas that are in the spreadsheet and ensure they are accurate.

17. ***Click Tools on the menu bar, point to Formula Auditing, and then click Formula Auditing Mode.*** Scroll over to the right and look at all of the cells in your spreadsheet. Notice that instead of seeing the results of the formulas, you see the formulas themselves. This is a great tool for checking the accuracy of your spreadsheets. Look at your formulas and make sure they are correct. When you are sure your formulas are accurate, ***turn off Formula Auditing Mode by clicking Tools on the menu bar, pointing to Formula Auditing, and then clicking Formula Auditing Mode again.*** This will turn formula auditing off.

18. You will now learn how to password protect your spreadsheet files. ***Click File from the menu bar, and then click Save As. In the Save As window, click Tools and then click General Options.*** Under **File Sharing** and next to **Password to Open,** type **A**, and click **OK**. At the **Confirm Password** window, type **A**, and then click **OK**. At the **Save As** window, save the file to My Documents (or the folder of your choice—you must remember where you saved it).

19. ***Click File on the menu bar, and then click Close to close the file.***

20. ***Now, click File again, and then, at the bottom of the drop-down menu, click the name of the file you just saved.***

21. The **Password** window should now be displayed. Type **A** in the **Password window**, and then ***click OK.*** The file should now be displayed.

22. You can turn off a password in the same way. ***Click File, and then click Save As. In the Save As window, click Tools and then click General Options.*** Under **File Sharing**, next to **Password to Open**, use the **[DEL]** key to remove the asterisk. Then, click **OK**. At the **Do you want to replace the existing file?** prompt, click **Yes**.

23. Close the file and then reopen it and you will see you no longer need a password to open it.

24. Click the **Print** icon on the toolbar; the spreadsheet will most likely print on two pages.

25. You will now learn how to use the **Fit to** command to force Excel to print a spreadsheet on one page.

26. ***Click in cell C5 and drag the mouse pointer down to cell I21. Click File on the menu bar, and then click Page Setup. Then, under Scaling, click Fit to, select one page, and then click OK.***

27. ***With the cell range from C5 to I21 still highlighted, click File, and then click Print. Under Print What, click Selection, and then click Preview.*** Notice that the spreadsheet will print on one page. If you want to actually print the spreadsheet, ***click Print,*** or to close the **Print Preview** screen, ***click Close.***

28. ***Click in any cell to make the highlighting disappear.***

29. To save the document, ***click on File on the menu bar, and then click Save As.*** Under **Save in**, choose the location where you want the file to be saved. Then, type **Excel Lesson 8 Spreadsheet DONE** next to **File Name**. *Select Save* to save the file.

30. ***Click File, then click Close*** to close the document, or ***click File, and then click Exit*** to exit Excel**.**

This concludes the Excel 2003 Hands-On Exercises.

CHAPTER 

DATABASE MANAGEMENT SYSTEMS

CHAPTER OBJECTIVES

After completing Chapter 5, you should be able to do the following:

1. Define a database.
2. Explain what a field is.
3. Define a record and a table.
4. Explain relational and logical operators.
5. List how databases can be used in the legal environment.
6. Explain how to plan a database.
7. Define a relational database.
8. Discuss database management-related ethical considerations.

All businesses, including legal organizations, must maintain and track information. Businesses routinely use database management systems (DBMSs) to collect and analyze information. A **database management system** is application software that stores, searches, sorts, and organizes data. A **database** is a collection of pieces of related data. For example, a database can be anything from a list of appointments, to a card catalog in a library, to an address book. These databases, whether or not they are on a computer, contain related information: appointments, listing of books, and addresses, respectively. They are organized by the date of the appointment; by the subject, title, and/or author of the book; and by the name of the person. A DBMS allows users to track and organize this kind of information using a computer. This chapter explains what a database is and how one is structured, provides an overview of DBMS functions, introduces database management fundamentals, describes types of DBMSs, and discusses how a DBMS can be used in the legal environment.

database management system
Application software that manages a database by storing, searching, sorting, and organizing data.

database
A collection of related data items. Databases are created because the information contained in them needs to be accessed, organized and used.

> *A truism in the practice of law is that all attorneys [and all legal professionals], on a daily basis, are confronted with voluminous amounts of information, which need to be analyzed, studied, organized, recorded, catalogued and stored. This information needs to be readily available, which requires it to be easily located and retrieved when needed. Information is power and the ability to access that information in a database makes that information even more powerful.*[1]

WHAT IS A DATABASE?

DBMSs are used in millions of businesses to manage and track vital information. They are powerful and flexible and can be used for thousands of different

purposes. For example, a law firm might use a DBMS to track its clients' names and addresses, and a manufacturer might use a DBMS to track its inventory of parts and finished products. A DBMS can not only store or hold information but also organize that information in a relevant manner. For example, the law firm might need an alphabetical list of its clients' names and addresses to be used for reference purposes. The manufacturer, on the other hand, might use a DBMS to give it an inventory list of products by completion date. It is sometimes easy to think of databases as simply organized lists or catalogs of information.

Exhibit 5–1 is a database that shows a legal organization's client list. A client database tracks the name, address, and other information for each client that an attorney or law firm represents. Notice that a row exists for each individual client. Many things can be done with the client database in Exhibit 5–1.

Exhibit 5–1
Client Database Structure
The database has 1 table, 8 fields, 8 records, and 64 data values.

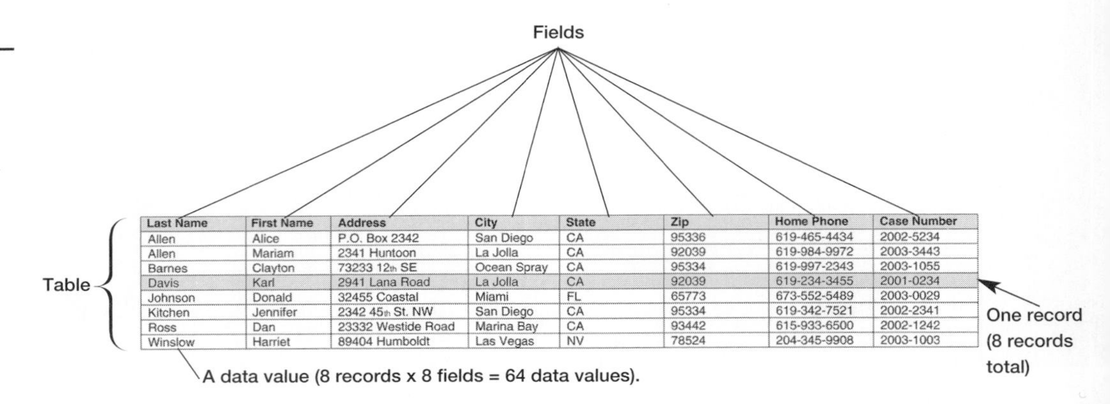

Last Name	First Name	Address	City	State	Zip	Home Phone	Case Number
Allen	Alice	P.O. Box 2342	San Diego	CA	95336	619-465-4434	2002-5234
Allen	Mariam	2341 Huntoon	La Jolla	CA	92039	619-984-9972	2003-3443
Barnes	Clayton	73233 12th SE	Ocean Spray	CA	95334	619-997-2343	2003-1055
Davis	Karl	2941 Lana Road	La Jolla	CA	92039	619-234-3455	2001-0234
Johnson	Donald	32455 Coastal	Miami	FL	65773	673-552-5489	2003-0029
Kitchen	Jennifer	2342 45th St. NW	San Diego	CA	95334	619-342-7521	2002-2341
Ross	Dan	23332 Westide Road	Marina Bay	CA	93442	615-933-6500	2002-1242
Winslow	Harriet	89404 Humboldt	Las Vegas	NV	78524	204-345-9908	2003-1003

1. A complete directory of the firm's clients, including names, addresses, and phone numbers, can be printed for the law office's staff to use when drafting correspondence and for general reference purposes. To make the directory easy to use, it can be sorted alphabetically by the clients' last names (as shown in Exhibit 5–1).
2. Information about new clients can easily be entered into the database.
3. Client data can be easily changed if a client moves or gets a new phone number.
4. Mailing labels can be printed for sending out firm newsletters, brochures, or other announcements. The labels can be sorted in numerical order according to zip code, so that all the pieces going to a single zip code are together (cheaper postal rates are available for mailings that are presorted).
5. Targeted mailings can be sent to clients in a specific state or area. If a multistate law firm wanted to send a mailing to only California residents, this could be done by searching for only CA in the State column of the database. The database would then retrieve only the names and addresses of clients who live in California.

Organizations in the legal environment use databases to track many kinds of information. Legal organizations use DBMSs to track specific information about a particular case, such as tracking many thousands of documents in large cases. This process is called litigation support. Each document is entered into a litigation support system, which is another kind of DBMS.

A DBMS allows users to manipulate data as they wish. For example, if a legal organization wanted a list displaying only its clients' names and home phone numbers on a report (and no other information), a new query report could be developed to display this information (see Exhibit 5–2) while still leaving the underlying data in Exhibit 5–1 unchanged. Even though a vast amount of information is entered into a database, that information does not have to be

printed out in every report. Information in a database is used as needed. Users have to use or print only the information they want at any given time. All the other information is still left intact, unharmed, in the database.

Database software is flexible, powerful, and convenient to use and operate because it allows users to do the following:

store and retrieve information easily
arrange and rearrange data over and over without affecting the data itself
update and change information
add information
search for information
sort and organize information
print information in many different formats

Legal organizations and legal assistants create databases for a wide variety of purposes in addition to litigation support, including opposing attorney databases, forms database, class action database, judges database, legal research database, conflict of interest database, factual database (for a specific case), expert witness database, library catalog database, active file database, inactive file database, licensed software database, marketing database, trial database, and many others.

According to a recent survey, Microsoft Access (a relational database program) controls approximately 76 percent of the legal database market. There are two versions of Access that are widely used today, Access 2007 and Access 2003. As in Word and Excel 2007, Access 2007 users issue commands by accessing tools on ribbons that change depending on which ribbon tab is selected (see Exhibit 5–2). In Access 2003 commands are issued using a combination of drop-down menus and toolbars. Access is a common database program used typically for "small" databases that may contain hundreds or even several thousand records. However, for large databases that contain millions of records, Access would not be used.

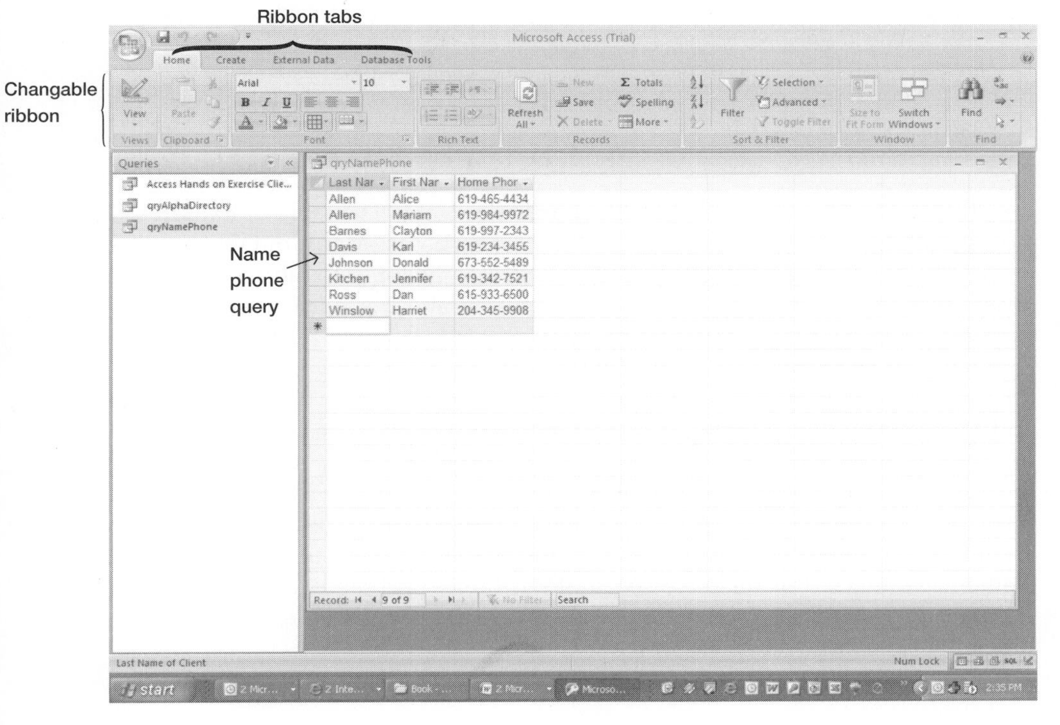

Exhibit 5–2
New Query and Report
This report shows only the clients' Last Names, First Names, and Home Phone Numbers. The underlying data (from Exhibit 5–1) remains unchanged. This is simply a different view of the same database.

Microsoft product screen shot reprinted with permission from Microsoft Corporation.

Depending on the size of the legal organization, legal assistants may be used in different roles as it relates to database management. For example, in a small legal organization a legal assistant might be completely responsible for the design and implementation of a complete database system whether it be for litigation support, for administrative purposes, or for some other reason. In larger legal organizations that have complex litigation support/database needs, legal assistants may answer questions and give assistance to a professional programmer who might be hired to actually design the database. In addition, in large legal organizations, legal assistants typically play a vital role in entering data into litigation support databases.

> *Are your paralegals computer literate and open to learning new things? If they aren't you will either have to abandon the [litigation support/database] project entirely or bring in new paralegals for the case.... The biggest stumbling block I have seen in the litigation-automation [database] process is the human skill and attitude component. It is critical to assess the computer literacy of the team members and stack computer-related tasks, objectives, and functions on those who have the right skills and attitude.*[2]

DATABASE STRUCTURE

Databases are organized into tables, records, fields, and data values.

Table

table
A collection of related information stored in rows and columns.

A database is made up of tables that contain related information and the tools necessary to manipulate the data. A **table** is a collection of related information stored in rows and columns. The entirety of the data in Exhibit 5–1 is a table.

> *A database table is fundamental to creating a database. Its function is to store information about a particular topic. Whenever you identify an additional "topic" for the database, it is wise to create another table in the database. Designing your table[s], might be the most complicated—and most important step in creating your database.*[3]

A table stores information about a particular topic. The table in Exhibit 5–1 stores contact information about a law office's clients. Many databases have more than one table. For example, the law firm database in Exhibit 5–3 has four separate tables. Each table contains information about a particular topic. For example, the Client table contains client contact information, the Case File table contains information about each case (case name, court, judge, case type, etc.), the Opposing Attorney table contains contact information for opposing counsel and the Case Evidence table contains a detailed listing of the pieces of the evidence in each case. Having additional tables simplifies and speeds up querying the database and in some ways makes the database easier to manipulate, since instead of having one file with everything dumped in it the user has broken up the information into smaller subunits while still having the various information elements connected or related to each other. Tables and table design are a crucial part of designing effective databases. There are usually at least thirty separate tables in a large database.

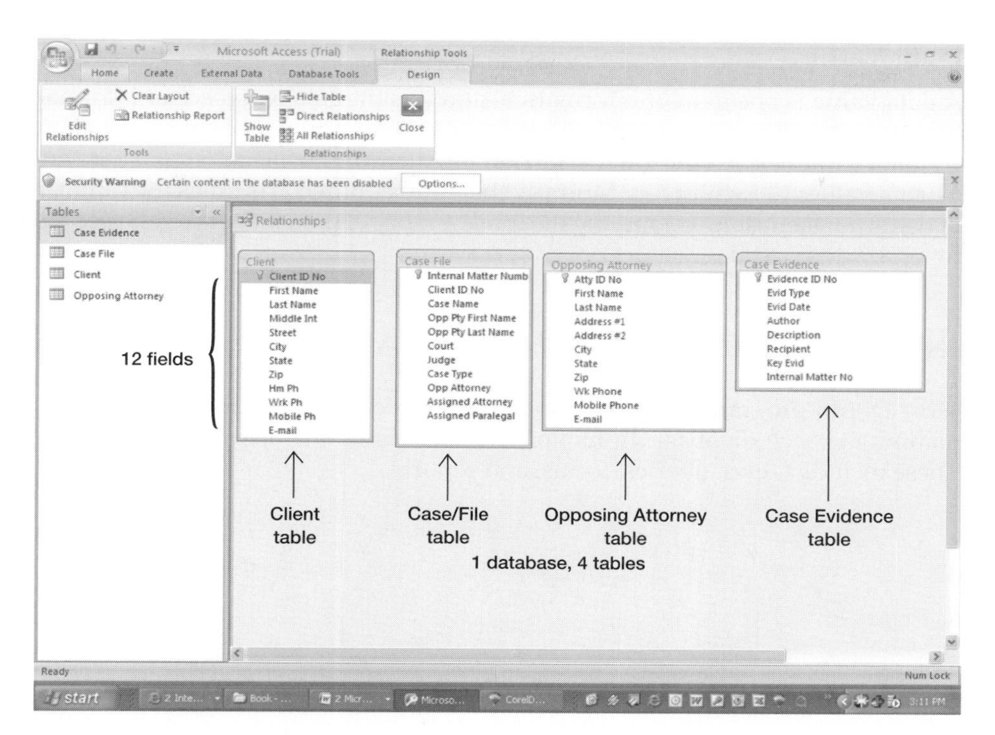

Exhibit 5–3

A Database With Multiple Tables—Access 2007

Microsoft product screen shot reprinted with permission from Microsoft Corporation.

Fields

A **field** is a column in a table that contains a category of information. For example, Exhibit 5–1 shows eight fields in the table:

field
A column in a table that contains a category of information.

1. Last Name
2. First Name
3. Address
4. City
5. State
6. Zip
7. Home Phone
8. Work Phone

In Exhibit 5–3 there are twelve fields in the Client table, eleven fields in the Case File table, eleven fields in the Opposing Attorney table, and eight fields in the Case Evidence table. The fields within any given database will be different. For example, in a docket control database used to control a legal organization's deadlines and appointments, the fields might include date of event, event description, case name, and place of event. All databases must have fields to input and collect the data. Large databases commonly have hundreds of fields in which to enter information. It is common for some DBMSs to refer to fields as columns.

Record

A **record** is a collection of fields treated as a unit. It is essentially one row in a table. In Exhibit 5–1, each record has all the information for one client entry—that is, the complete set of field data for one entry. A total of eight records, or clients, are entered in Exhibit 5–1. Large databases may have millions of records. For example, litigation support databases in large class action cases involving thousands of plaintiffs can easily have millions of records.

record
A collection of fields that are treated as a unit. It is essentially one row in a table.

Data Value

data value
One item of information, which is the smallest piece of information in a table.

A **data value** is one item of information, and it is the smallest piece of information in a table. For example, in Exhibit 5–1, each individual piece of information is a data value (e.g., "Winslow," "Harriett," "Allen," "San Diego" etc.). There are 64 data values in Exhibit 5–1. Multiply the number of records times the number of fields for each table to compute the total number of data values (e.g., 8 records times 8 fields = 64 data values).

INTRODUCTION TO DBMS PROGRAMS

Most DBMS programs use tools, sometimes called *objects*, that allow users to manipulate each database. In Exhibit 5–4 there are four tools or objects listed. These include tables, queries, forms, and reports.

Exhibit 5–4
Access 2007 Tools/Objects—Tables, Queries, Forms and Reports
Microsoft product screen shot reprinted with permission from Microsoft Corporation.

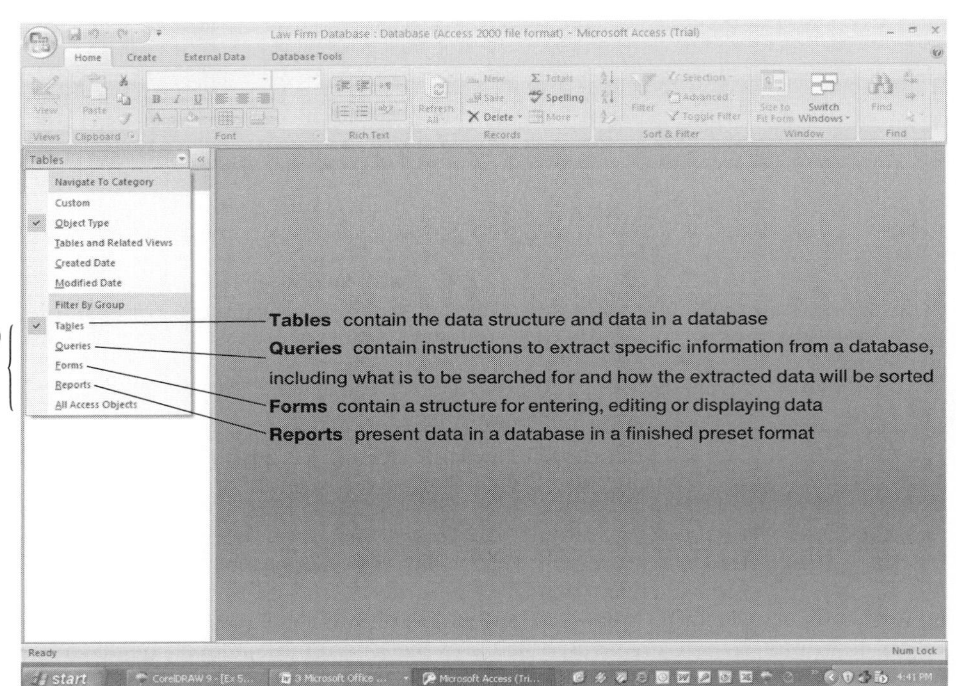

A table (sometimes called a *data table* or *datasheet*) stores the data in the database in row and column format similar to a spreadsheet (see Exhibit 5–5). Tables are the heart of a database program. Each database file can have more than one table. Exhibit 5–5 shows the Datasheet view of a table in Microsoft Access.

form
Allows a user to view, enter, and edit data in a custom format designed by the user.

A **form** allows a user to view, enter, and edit data in a special, or custom, format designed by the user. Notice in Exhibit 5–6 that the user created a special on-screen form in which to enter and view data. While information can be entered directly into a table in the Datasheet view (see Exhibit 5–5), many users find it easier to enter data into a form such as the one in Exhibit 5–6. Notice in Exhibit 5–5 that the client's last name comes before the first name. In Exhibit 5–6 the order was changed for data entry purposes, and First Name of Client comes before Last Name. This was done to make data entry easier and more logical. Also, notice in Exhibit 5–6 that the user can go to the next record by clicking on the next record arrow or go backward through the records.

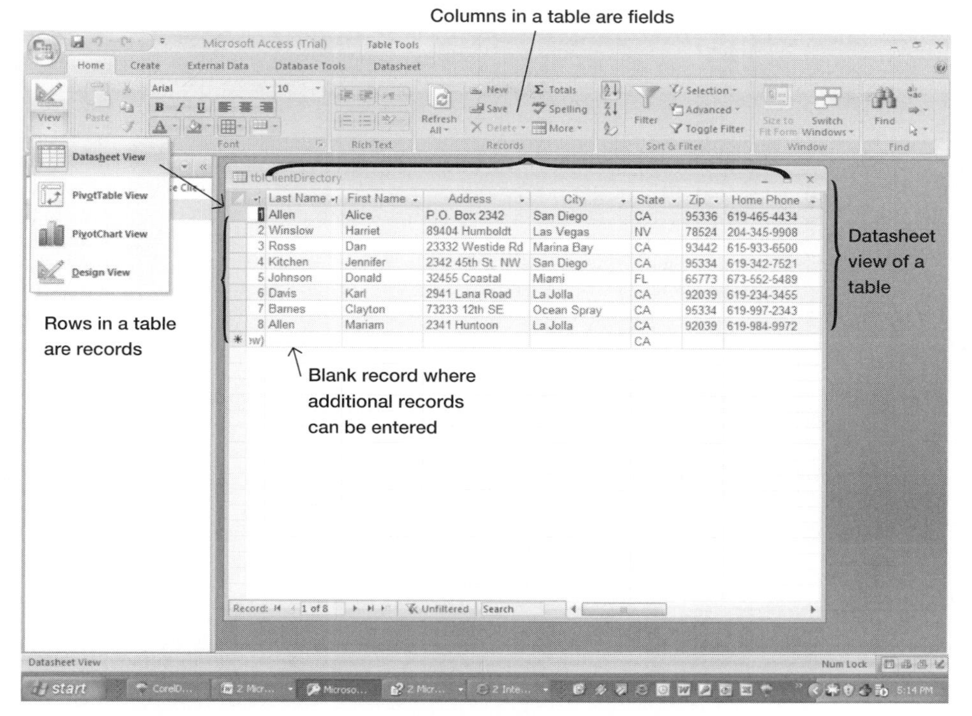

Exhibit 5–5

A Table in the Datasheet View in Access 2007

Microsoft product screen shot reprinted with permission from Microsoft Corporation.

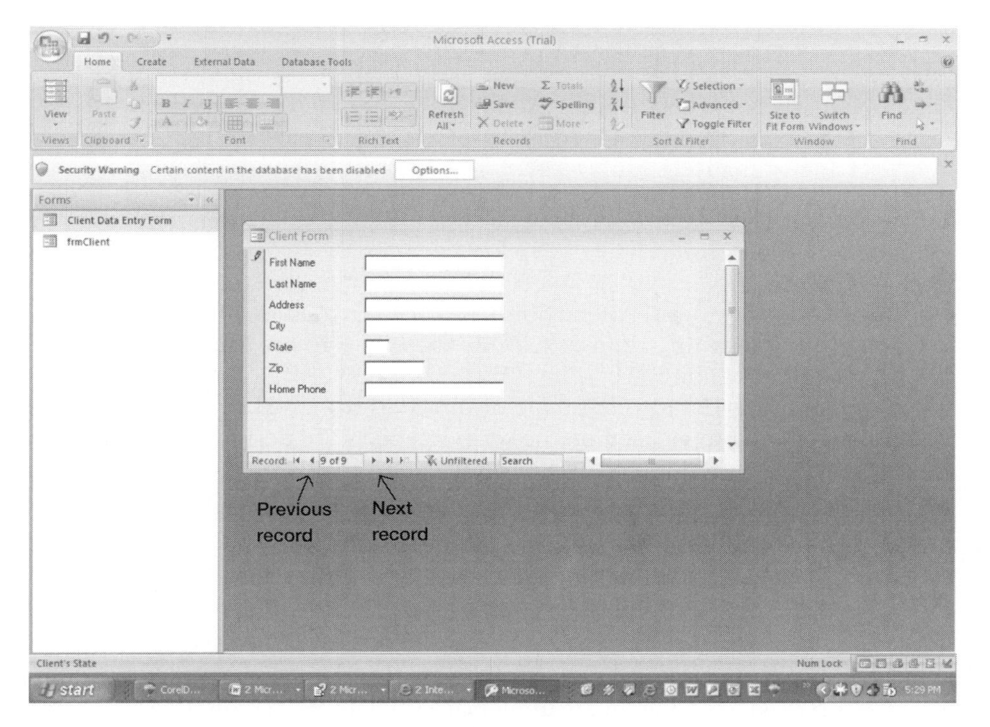

Exhibit 5–6

A Custom Designed Data Entry From

This form allows a user to enter data into the database in a particular order.

Microsoft product screen shot reprinted with permission from Microsoft Corporation.

A **query** extracts data from a table based on criteria designed by the user. A query allows a user to search for and sort only the information the user is looking for at that time. The first screen in Exhibit 5–7 shows a query in the design view and the second screen shows the results of the query. Queries create a specific view of data and allow the user to answer specific questions. In Exhibit 5–7 the question that is being answered by the query is "What clients of the law firm reside in San Diego?" Once a user creates a query, the user can save it and then

query
Extracts data from a table based on criteria designed by the user. A query allows a user to search for and sort only the information the user is looking for at that time.

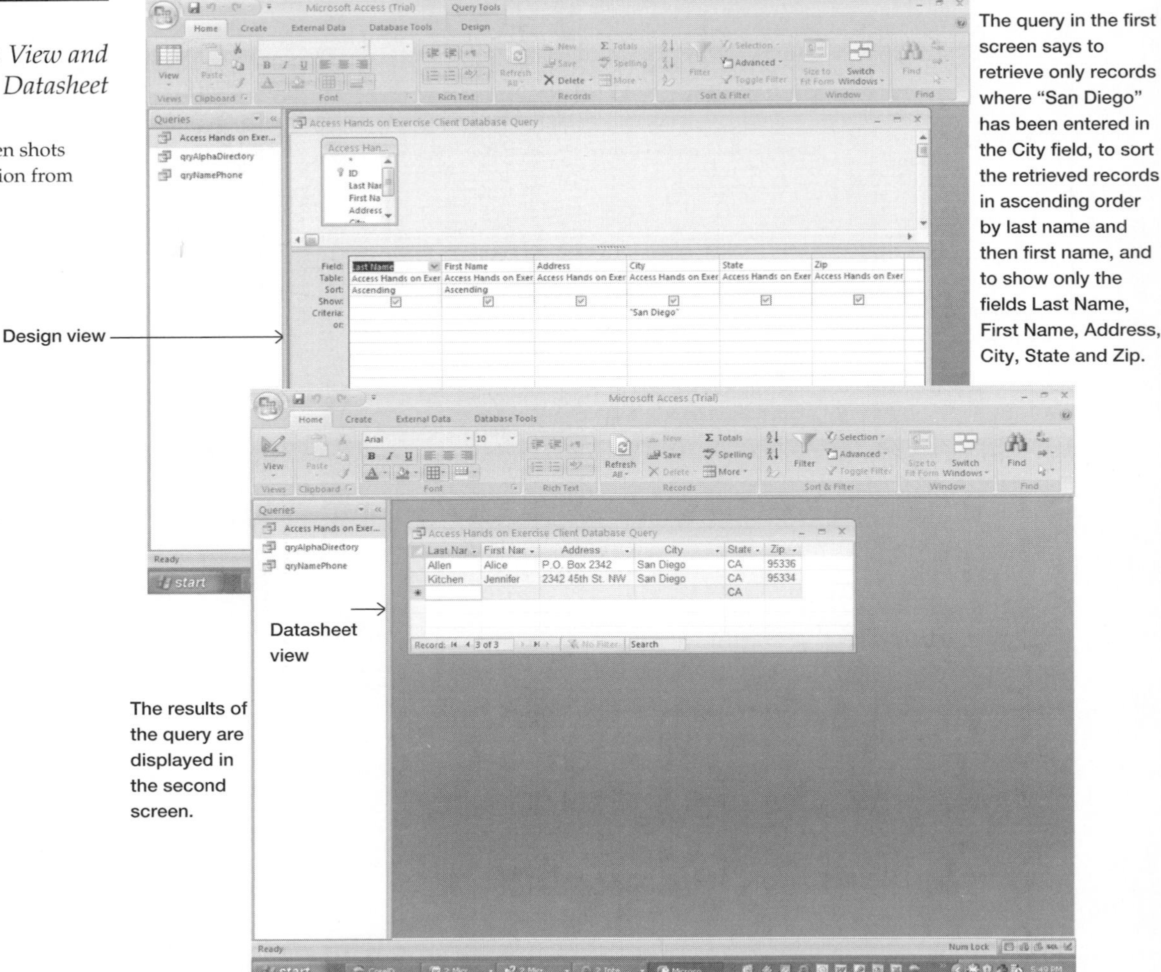
The query in the first screen says to retrieve only records where "San Diego" has been entered in the City field, to sort the retrieved records in ascending order by last name and then first name, and to show only the fields Last Name, First Name, Address, City, State and Zip.
Design view
Datasheet view
The results of the query are displayed in the second screen.

Exhibit 5–7
A Query in Design View and the Same Query in Datasheet View
Microsoft product screen shots reprinted with permission from Microsoft Corporation.

use it whenever they need. After a query has been created (see the first screen in Exhibit 5–7) the user must run or execute the query to see the results (see the second screen in Exhibit 5–7).

report
Prints data from a table or query as designed by the user. While forms are designed to be used on the screen, reports are designed to be printed.

A **report** prints data from a table or query as designed by the user. While forms are designed to be used on the screen, reports are designed to be printed (see Exhibit 5–8). A report consists of information that is pulled from tables or queries, as well as information that is stored with the report design, such as labels, headings, and graphics.

DBMS FUNCTIONS: AN OVERVIEW

Every DBMS program has its own set of commands and its own structure. However, the topics covered herein are universal to all DBMSs. These programs have been around since the inception of computers and contain hundreds of different commands and functions, but good database design is critical to all, from the simplest to the most complex database.

DATABASE PLANNING AND DESIGN

Database planning and design is a critical step in building an effective and competent database that meets the needs of the user. This section provides an

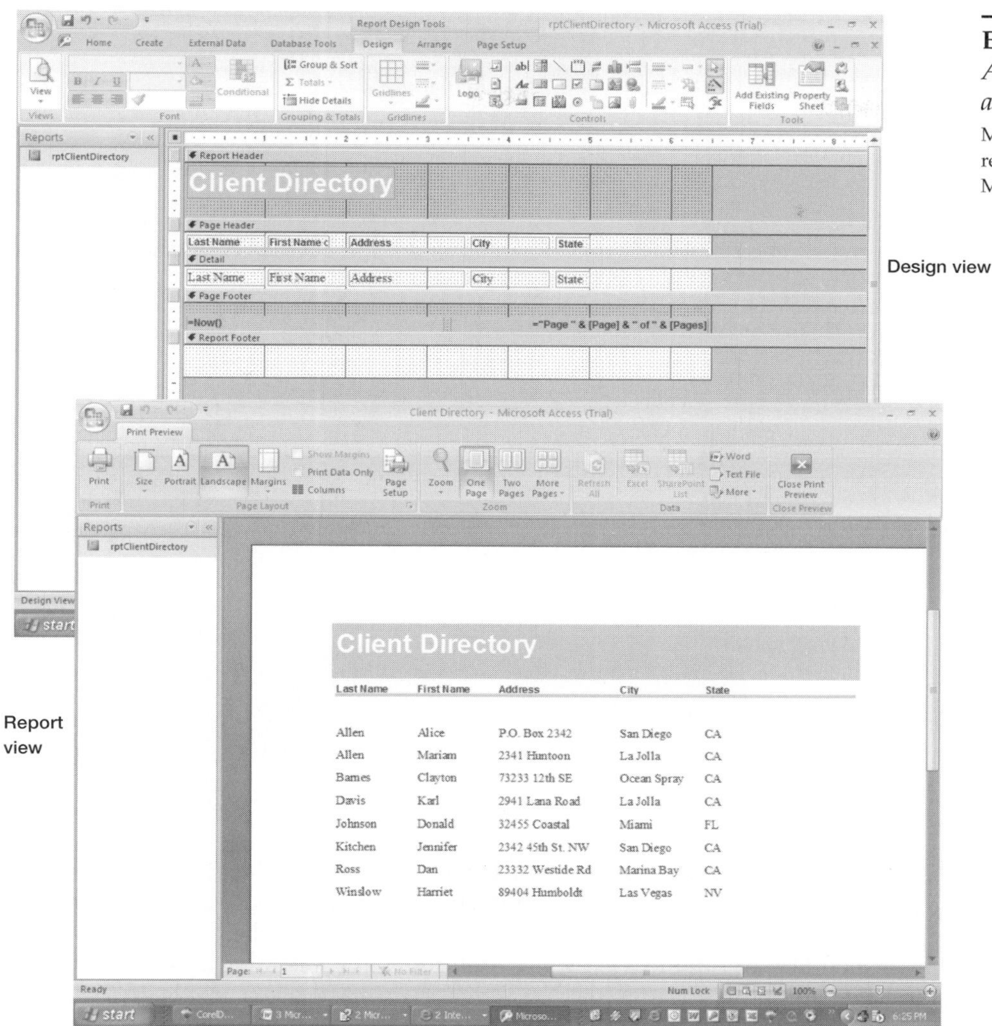

Exhibit 5–8

A Report in Design View and Report View

Microsoft product screen shots reprinted with permission from Microsoft Corporation.

overview of the design process and then goes into detail regarding database planning fundamentals.

Database Design and Implementation Process Overview

To design a database that is well-thought-out and truly meets the needs of the user, the steps shown in Exhibit 5–9 are recommended. Databases that are not carefully designed often contain logic mistakes and reasoning errors, causing the database not to meet the user's needs. They take much longer to complete, since the mistakes have to be corrected through trial and error. The larger the database, the more time and effort should go into its planning. It would be logical to assume that a database with tens of thousands of records might take months to plan, while a database with a few records, tables, queries, and reports might take a few hours to plan.

Identify the Problem A database is created to solve a problem or to fulfill a need. For example, before the client database in Exhibit 5–1 was created, a manual card file may have existed showing the names and addresses of all clients. Unfortunately, everyone in the office had to have his or her own card file. This was a problem, since any changes had to be entered on all the card files, which represented tremendous duplication.

Exhibit 5–9
Steps in the Database Design and Implementation Process
Microsoft product screen shot reprinted with permission from Microsoft Corporation.

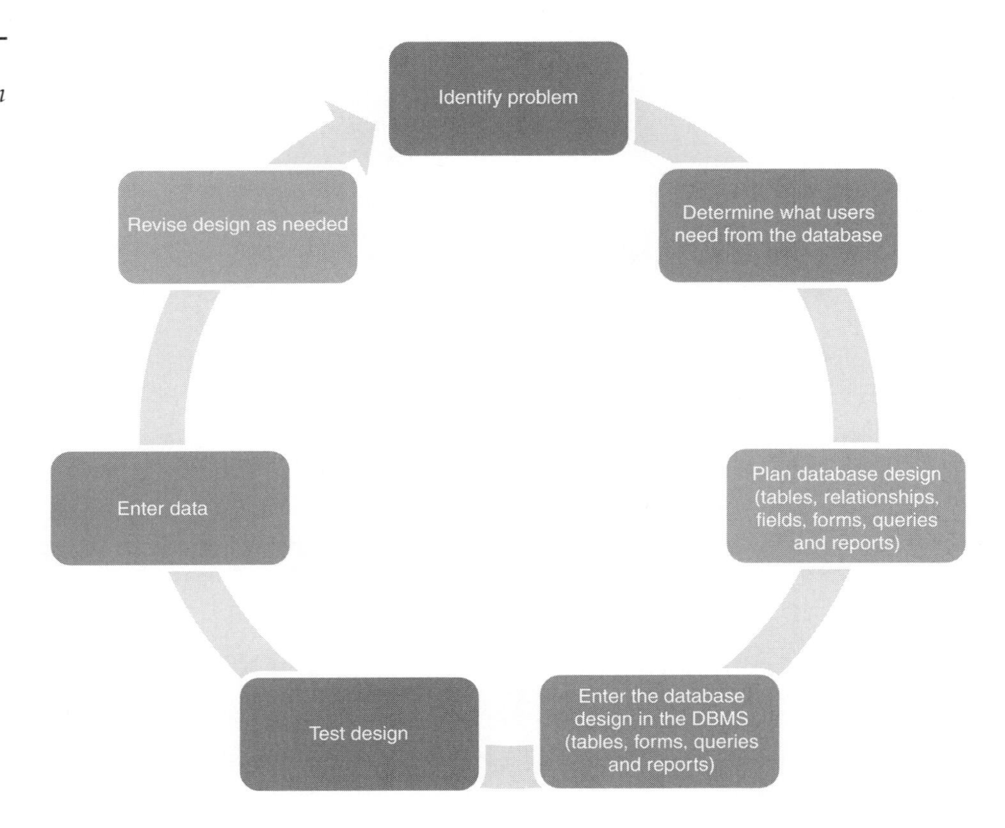

Determine What Users Need from the Database It is critical to accurately determine exactly how users will utilize the finished database and to accurately document what the users' needs are. To do this correctly the database designer must spend time with the end users to determine their existing and future needs. Possible alternatives need to be considered to meet the users' needs. In the client database example, a firm might determine that if a computerized database is created, the information could be kept by one person; any changes can be made by that one person; and the information could be accessed by all staff using a shared network directory that all staff have access to, or placed on a firm intranet.

> *Get together with as many team members as possible to flush out what you want the system to do.... Getting everyone involved from the beginning will prevent anyone from developing an "I-was-never-consulted-and-therefore-won't-cooperate attitude." Market your plan and get buy-in from the beginning. Get everyone to discuss what they want and need the system to do. The more you get on paper at the very beginning, the faster the development will be and the better the result.*[4]

It is also important to think in advance about who will be using the database. What problems does each of the users want to solve by creating the database? In analyzing and evaluating the problem, it is good to have the perspective of multiple people. A group of people tends to see problems and solutions from multiple angles, which greatly adds to the evaluation process and brainstorming new ideas and new answers. The importance of truly understanding the needs of the user cannot be overstated. If the end database does not meet the needs of the user, all the time and money in building and populating it has been wasted.

Plan the Database Design Many people outline the database design on paper or in a word processor before creating it directly in the DBMS. Among other things, you should think about the following:

- *What problems do I want to solve?* In thinking about a database design, it is a good idea to start at the end (what do I want the end product to look like?) and then work backwards.
- *What tables do I need and how will they be related to each other?* Decide how you will structure the data into groups and how will the groups be related so no information is duplicated from one table to the other.
- *What specific information do I want to track or store?* Decide what fields you need to include.
- *How will I want to see the data?* Determine what queries you will need to develop to search and sort the data to solve your problems.
- *How will I use the information?*—What are the different reports you will need to solve your problems?

Planning the database design includes carefully designing the fields needed for each table, the layout and design of each table, the relationships between the tables (discussed later in the chapter), and all of the forms, queries and reports the users will need for the finished system.

Enter the Database Design and Structure into the DBMS Once the user has an outline of a database design, it is time to actually begin creating or designing the database in the DBMS. The first task is to give the database a name. The database name should reflect exactly the kind of information that it will store. For example, Client Directory specifically identifies the type of database being stored in the example. Entering the database design, including creating tables, forms, queries, and reports, is included in detail later in this chapter.

> *Before actually creating your table, you should know in advance the name of each field you need to use in each table, as well as the type of data to be stored in each field. The criteria for determining the number, names and types of fields will depend on the information you intend to extract from the database. In short, you will need a field for any data you want to sort, query, compare, or relate, etc.*[5]

Test Design After a database design has been entered into the DBMS (including the tables, forms, queries, and reports), the user should test it. This can be done by entering a few records into the database and then executing the forms, queries, and reports to see if the database is producing the desired information. It is always a good idea to test the database before entering hundreds or thousands of records.

Enter Data Once the design of the database has been tested and put through its paces and the users have evaluated whether the design in fact meets their needs, it is time to enter the data. The data entry phase of the implementation process is critical. Data entry is covered in detail later in this chapter, but the old adage of "garbage in—garbage out" applies when entering data. If data is haphazardly entered in the database using inconsistent methods, then all searches and reports on the data will likewise be inconsistent and incomplete. It is crucial that all data be entered consistently and that careful planning go into the data entry process to minimize errors and problems later.

Revise Design as Needed Once the database design process has taken place, the structure entered, the testing done, and the data entered, any revising

should hopefully be very limited. It is extremely difficult and time consuming to revise a database, even a simple one, at this stage. However, as users utilize the system and time goes by, new queries, reports and uses may be identified, calling for changes to the system. For any database to continue to meet the needs of the user, the database should be reviewed and revised from time to time.

Why Should Paralegals Care about Databases?

By Rachel Levine

A "database" is just a fancy word for a collection of information. If you think about it, your job as a paralegal is all about information: getting it, filing it, finding it when you need it, and making sense of it. Any tool that can make all of the above faster and easier would probably be a good thing, wouldn't it? A database is that tool. And for that reason alone, paralegals should be interested in databases. But, there are more reasons:

1. CAREER ADVANCEMENT

Most paralegals can use a word processor, a spreadsheet, document imaging programs, and the like. How many understand databases? Not as many. Databases are not as easy to learn as other kinds of software and as a result, not as many people really learn them well enough to be useful to their firms. If you take the time to learn how to use database software, your career will surely benefit.

Inversely, since technology has been fully integrated into the practice of law, if you refuse to learn new technology, your career may suffer.

2. RESPECT IN THE WORKPLACE (A SUBSET OF THE ABOVE)

The paralegal who can pull together information and/or get answers to questions the quickest will get the most respect. People tend to be amazed at skills they don't possess (including attorneys).

For example, if you are working on a large medical malpractice case and are asked, "How many California complaints do we have?" you might be able to simply count them and come up with an answer in half an hour or less: "One hundred ten." Then you are asked, "How many of those California complaints include wrongful death?" Now you have to read through all 110 complaints, which will take much longer, and perhaps not be entirely accurate as you may have missed some.

If you had entered this kind of information into a database, you could have "asked" (or queried) the database how many California cases included "wrongful death" and gotten a response in under a minute. And, assuming the information had been entered correctly, the results of your query to the database would be entirely correct.

Getting such quick answers to ad hoc questions always impresses people.

3. TO HELP YOUR FIRM SUCCEED

Everything you do well contributes to the overall success of your firm. But sometimes you can do something that directly affects the outcome of a case. In the above example, it's easy to see the usefulness of a database. **In the following example, the database actually made some information so crystal clear that the other side couldn't refute it.**

It was a giant fraud case and, of course, proving "intent to defraud" is not always easy. Unless you're a mind reader, you can't know for sure exactly what someone else was intending. So, we have to rely on people's actions, words, relationships, and so on to prove the case. The database in question was dutifully collecting all kinds of information about the hundreds of "players" in the case when an attorney asked if it would be possible to use the data to *link each person involved in the case with every single organization, business, or institution they had ever been involved with in any capacity.* No one had bothered to enter this kind of information because the information itself was scattered in all kinds of documents, news articles, and other formats and it was time consuming to plow through it all just to find the little piece of information we needed. Still, we knew that if we took the time, the results would pay off. And they did.

Once the information was all in, it only took a few seconds to run a query and find out that Joe Defendant had been on five boards of directors, had been CEO of three different companies and trustee of four different organizations, and many of them were named in the suit. Bingo!

Of course, once the research was done it would have been possible to ascertain the above facts eventually without a database. But the key word

here is "eventually." And, you would risk missing something because humans are fallible and can get different results each time they attempt to solve the same problem.

4. A FEELING OF ACCOMPLISHMENT

Being involved in the legal profession, you will be presented with many opportunities to learn new things. The happiest and most successful paralegals I have met are those who welcome this challenge. That doesn't mean they never feel anxious about the next "new thing" that comes along. Rather, it seems they do not let their anxiety stop them. They know three secrets you should know:

1. it's perfectly normal to feel anxious about learning something new.
2. the utter confusion they feel at first *always* goes away, leading to…
3. a feeling of accomplishment and power when they finally "get it."

This is entirely true when learning database software. So stick with it and get to #3 so you can reap your reward.

5. TO MEET MORE OF YOUR COWORKERS

I'm actually only partly joking. In my own experience and in the experience of others, it has always been the case that once word is out that someone in the firm actually understands "this stuff," there will be a line at your office door (or cubicle as the case may be). People will want to know you. Or, more accurately, they will want *favors* from you. What you do with this newfound popularity is up to you!

Rachel Levine has been an independent database programmer, trainer, and consultant for the last 15 years. Having worked closely with paralegals on several complex litigations, she has seen some succeed wildly while others floundered. She has also written several articles about using databases for large litigations.

Database Planning Fundamentals

As indicated previously, planning and critical thinking about what a database is going to accomplish is very important. If, for example, you were planning the client database in Exhibit 5–1, you would write down all the information you wanted to track about a client. The particular information that is tracked depends on the legal organization and how it operates. In addition to tracking the name, address, phone number, and case number of a client, a firm might want to track information about the client's case. This might include the type of case (e.g., criminal, personal injury, etc.); whether the client paid a retainer and, if so, how much it was; and so forth. It is also a good idea to have others review your design. For example, if you are designing a database to track witnesses for a case, it is strongly recommended that the managing attorney on the case review the design to help troubleshoot it and to determine if there are any problems.

Example of a Poorly Planned Database Good design is critical to any database. Planning a database involves more than just writing down fields for information that must be tracked. You must think carefully about how the information will be used (i.e., how you want the information to be searched, sorted, and printed in the end). If this is not done well, the database will be error-ridden and will not work properly. For example, assume the client database is intended to be used to produce a list that is sorted using the client's last name. If the database were designed with only one name field, Name, and all 500 records were entered into the database as in Exhibit 5–10, with the first name first and then the last name (e.g., Harriet Winslow), the database would not accomplish the intended purpose, because most DBMSs use the first letters entered in a field to alphabetize or sort a list. Instead of having a list alphabetized by last name, you would have a useless client list that could be alphabetized only by first name. In this example, the database would have to be redesigned, and all the information would have to be reentered to solve the problem. Users must also be careful when designing a database with dates in it. If the DBMS can designate a field as a date field, then there is not much

Exhibit 5–10
Poorly Planned and Well-Planned Database
This database has only one name field. Many DBMS programs can only sort the names by the clients' first names, not by the clients' last names.

A. Poorly planned client database

Name	Address
Clayton Barnes	73233 12th SE
Harriet Winslow	89404 Humboldt
Jennifer Kitchen	2342 45th St. NW
Karl Davis	2941 Lane
Mariam Allen	2341 Huntoon

This database has two name fields: First Name and Last Name. Therefore, the DBMS can sort the names by the clients' first names or last names.

B. Well-Planned client database

Last Name	First Name	Address
Allen	Mariam	2341 Huntoon
Barnes	Clayton	73233 12th SE
Davis	Karl	2941 Lane
Kitchen	Jennifer	2342 45th St. NW
Winslow	Harriet	89404 Humboldt

problem. However, if the user enters a date, such as month/day/year (e.g., 07/03/2008), in a text field or tries to enter a date in a numeric field, it can cause problems. Many databases cannot sort or search dates properly using this design.

Rules for Planning a Database Keep the following rules or ideas in mind when planning a database:

1. ***Getting Started***—Many times, a computerized database design is based on a manual system or an outdated computer system. Start the process by enumerating what you like and dislike about the prior method. In the client database example, the legal organization might have previously used a manual card system for keeping track of clients. This would be a good starting point for designing the computerized version.
2. ***Plan Ahead***—Plan for the future. If you think you might need an extra field later, add it now for safety. For example, in the client database, if you think you eventually might want a field for a fax number, mobile phone number, Internet site or email address, include it now even though you might not use it right away. Some users enter two or three blank fields so they can go back, name them, and add information to them later. Try to anticipate your future needs. It is difficult to change a table's structure once it is filled with data.
3. ***Do Not Put Too Many Fields into One Table***—Each table should be simple and cover just one topic. A common mistake is to put too many fields and too much information into one table. Most databases, such as Access and others, are relational databases, which are covered later in the chapter. Relational databases can have multiple tables in one database with relationships among the fields in the different tables that operate as if they were in one table. Notice in Exhibit 5–3 that each of the four tables has a specific purpose and no one table has more than twelve fields in it. The tables in Exhibit 5–3 have been carefully designed so that no one table has too much information in it or contains unrelated information.
4. ***Do Not Repeat Fields***—Another common mistake is for users to try to make each table look like a stand-alone report. For example, if a user wanted to track the status of each case in the client database (e.g., whether the case is ready for

trial, in discovery, on appeal, etc.) it would not be necessary to recreate first name, last name, and case number in the new table. Since this information is already contained in the client database table, the user could relate the two tables together and thus easily create a report or form that includes this information any time (as long as each table had at least one common field in another table).

5. *Keep Fields in Logical Order*—When you create the table design and design the data entry form (the screen that you see when you enter the records), make sure the fields are put in a logical order that flows well. For example, in the client database, you would not want the last name field to be followed by the zip code field in the data entry form. Make sure the form corresponds to how you will be entering the information into the records. In Exhibit 5–5, the order of the fields is roughly the same as the information in a manual Rolodex system.
6. *Allow Plenty of Space for Each Field*—If you have to enter a maximum field length (i.e., the maximum number of characters you can enter into a field), leave plenty of space. For instance, if you allowed for only five digits in a zip code field, you would have a problem, since many businesses use the full nine-digit hyphenated zip code. Again, careful planning is critical.
7. *Separate Data into Small Fields*—It is almost always better to separate data into small fields, rather than place multiple kinds of information in large fields. The preceding example of a poor design that used one name field (Name) instead of two smaller name fields (Last Name and First Name) shows what can happen. Also, always separate city, state, and zip code. In the future, you might want to sort or search using these specific fields.
8. *Make Field Names as Small as Possible*—When you print data, large field names get in the way, especially when the data the field contains have only a few characters. While this can be adjusted, it is better to use smaller names whenever possible.
9. *Anticipate How the Database Will Be Used*—Before you design the database, think about how the information will be searched, how it will be sorted, and what format your reports and printouts will take. Most databases that fail do so because this rule was not followed.
10. *Always Test the Design*—No matter how good you think a design is, always test it before you put in hundreds of records, only to find out it is faulty.

Carpenters have a saying, "Measure twice and cut once," which means before you cut a board, measure the distance once and then measure it again for accuracy, so that when you actually cut the board, it is the right length. The same analogy applies here. Design and redesign the database; otherwise, the database may not do what you intend it to do.

CREATING A TABLE

Creating a table is the core of database management. Tables hold all of the data that users enter. Creating a table in most DBMSs is straightfoward. Tables that are efficient and meet all of the needs of the users take planning and attention to detail. Exhibit 5–11 shows a table being created in Design view for the client directory example. Users can switch between Design view (Exhibit 5–11) and Datasheet view (Exhibit 5–5) quickly and easily. Most DBMSs also have a wizard or automated feature that can help the user quickly and easily create a table. Many DBMSs come with a variety of standard templates, tables, and databases that have already been set up for users. These typically include time and billing, expense tracking, resource scheduling, and other applications. In addition, Microsoft Access has a direct link to a template website that has additional database templates. Looking at these designs is sometimes helpful in designing your own databases.

Exhibit 5–11
Creating a Table in Design View
Microsoft product screen shot reprinted with permission from Microsoft Corporation.

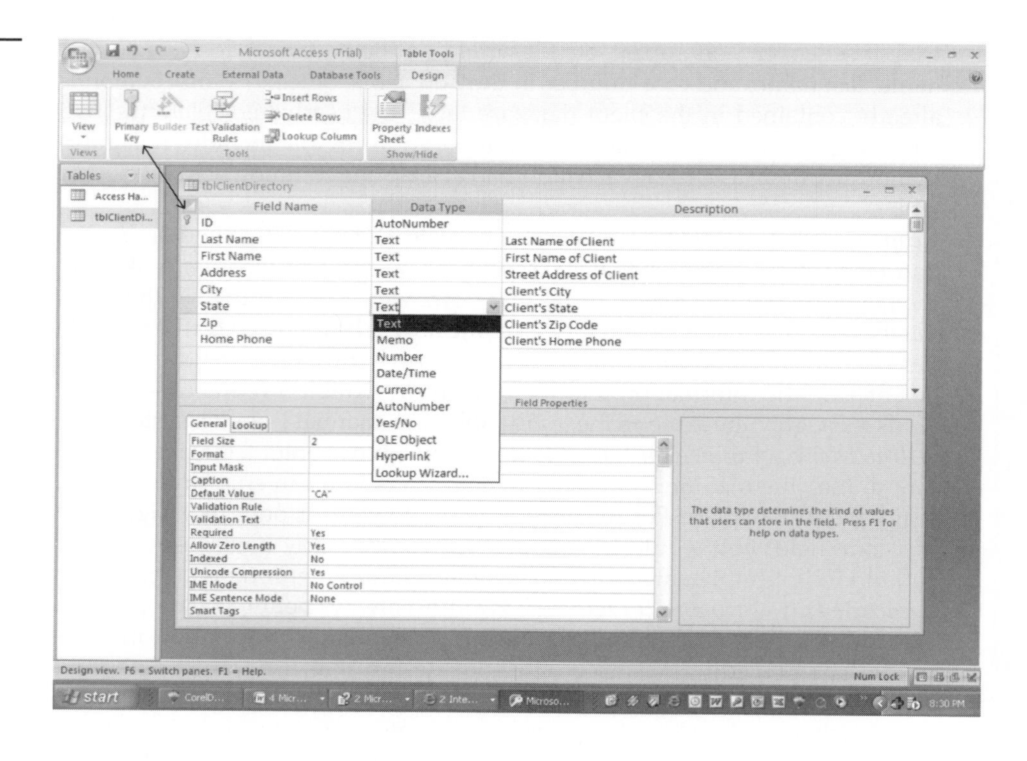

A recent *Legal Assistant Today* Paralegal of the Year winner won the award for, among other things, her design and implementation of a complex Microsoft Access database. *"Not many people, essentially self-taught in computers, could have designed and launched a new [complex caseload] database that stores 6,000 cases for the entire [Army's Tort Litigation Branch] division. It was supposed to be a temporary database, but is currently the main repository of case knowledge for all of the division's several branches.*[6]

Field Names

Each field in the database must have a field name. Each field name must be unique and should reasonably describe the information that will be placed in it. Exhibit 5–11 shows a listing of the fields in the client information database. To create a field in the database in Exhibit 5–11, and create some basic information for each field the user simply types the name in the Field Name box, enters the data type and description, and presses [TAB] to go to the next field. The user continues until all the fields are entered. In addition to entering the basic information, the user can also enter a number of types of highly customized information such as field size, default values, lookups, and whether a field is required.

Data Type

In all databases, the user must tell the DBMS what kind of information will be held in each field. Fields can hold several different kinds of data. In Exhibit 5–11, notice that a field can hold text, memo, numbers, dates and times, currency, an automatic number, Yes/No, and other types of information. The following is a description of the main data types.

Text Text fields hold text, numbers, and symbols. Notice in Exhibit 5–11 that most of the fields are shown as text in the data type.

Memo This type of field holds text but there is no maximum field length set, so the user can type an infinite amount of text in the field.

Number A number field contains only numbers. Most databases can perform complex mathematical computations on information entered into number fields; only numbers can typically be entered into number fields.

Dates/Times A date/time field holds dates and times, as the name implies. It is often necessary to sort information by date, and this feature makes it possible to do so. Some DBMSs require the user to indicate how the information should be formatted (e.g., 1/1/08, January 1, 2008, Jan 1, 08, etc.).

Currency The currency data type formats the numbers with dollar signs and treats the information as money. For example, if the client directory contained a field for the amount of retainer the client paid, this field would have a data type of currency.

AutoNumber An autonumber data type automatically generates a new consecutive number for the field when a new record is entered. For example, in Exhibit 5–11 notice that there is a field for a client ID number. It will be populated with a unique internal identification number (AutoNumber) that will be generated automatically by the DBMS for each client.

Yes/No A yes/no data type allows the user to indicate only yes or no in the field. In some DBMSs, this is represented by either a yes or a no appearing in the field or by a box that is checked if it is yes or not checked if it is no. There are other data types as well in some DBMSs.

Lookup Options A **lookup option** is a list of options that a user must choose from when entering information into a table (see Exhibit 5–11, "Lookup Wizard"). An example would be entering a client's state in the client database example; a list of state abbreviations will be displayed on the screen and the user can select from one of the fifty state abbreviation options. Lookup options are extremely helpful in trying to control accuracy and data integrity as data is being entered into the database. The process of trying to control what information is entered into a database is sometimes called **validation control.**

lookup option
A list of options that a user must choose from when entering information into a table.

validation control
The process of controlling and limiting what information is entered into a database for the purpose of ensuring accuracy.

Description

Description (see Exhibit 5–11) simply allows the user to enter additional information to describe what the field will hold.

General

The General tab in the lower area of Exhibit 5–11 has several options for defining the properties of each field. These include Field Size, Default Value, Required, and others.

Field Size Notice in Exhibit 5–11 that the State field is currently selected. Notice in the General tab at the bottom of Exhibit 5–11 that the user has entered a field size of 2. This means that the field can contain only two characters. This makes sense because the user wants the person entering the data to enter two-character state abbreviations instead of typing the Full Name of each state, which takes more time.

Default Value Default value means that a preset or standard value will be entered into the field unless it is changed by the user. This speeds up data entry. Notice in Exhibit 5–11 that the Default Value for the field is CA. This means that when a new client is being entered, CA will automatically be displayed in the State field. The user can either accept the default value or overwrite it.

Required This means that the field is mandatory and must be filled in for the record to be added to the database. In Exhibit 5–11, State is shown as a required field.

ENTERING AND EDITING DATA

The physical typing of data into databases is not difficult. However, entering the data so it is accurate, consistent, and in line with how the database was designed is more challenging. The larger the database, the more complex the database, and the more people entering the data, the more difficult it is to get information accurately entered into a database. Consider that even if the design of the database is brilliant (the tables, records, and fields will absolutely meet the users' needs), the queries are carefully crafted and designed, and the reports are beautifully formatted, if the data entry is poorly done (inconsistent, inaccurate, and haphazardly done)—nothing else will matter and the database will fail. The data entry must be done accurately, and in the end accuracy will play a significant role in whether the database accomplishes its purposes. The data entry must also exactly match how the queries will be performed, or the queries will come back incomplete and will fail to return all of the data they should.

> *Regardless of how well intentioned and careful data-entry people are, mistakes happen. Without a way of proofing the data routinely, you may never know that your information is incorrect.... You may run a query that asks for all the cases in California in which Company X is the defendant and get back a number that looks correct. Unfortunately, someone entered "Pennsylvania" accidentally for a case that should have been California.*[7]

Data can usually either be entered directly into the table in Datasheet view (see Exhibit 5–5) or be entered using a form (see Exhibit 5–6). To enter data, the user simply opens the table in Datasheet view or in a form and begins entering data. Most DBMSs allow users to go to the next field by either pressing the [TAB] key or using the mouse.

To edit or modify a field or record, the user goes to the record in either the table (Datasheet view) or in a form and edits the information. In large databases (with tens of thousands of records), finding a specific record may not be easy. To find a specific record, a user may want to use the Find icon, which in many DBMSs is the binoculars (see Exhibit 5–12). In Exhibit 5–12, the user has selected the binoculars, typed in "Barnes" in the Find What: field, selected a table in Look In, and chosen Any Part of Field in the Match field. The Match dropdown list allows the following options:

- *Whole Field*—This finds fields where the specified text is the only thing in that field. For example, "Barnes" would not find "Barnes and Noble."
- *Start of Field*—This finds fields that begin with the specific text. For example, "Barnes" would find "Barnes" and "Barnes and Noble," but not "J. Barnes."
- *Any Part of Field*—This finds fields that contain the specific text in any way. "Barnes" would find "Barnes," "Barnes and Noble," "Noble and Barnes" and "J. Barnes."

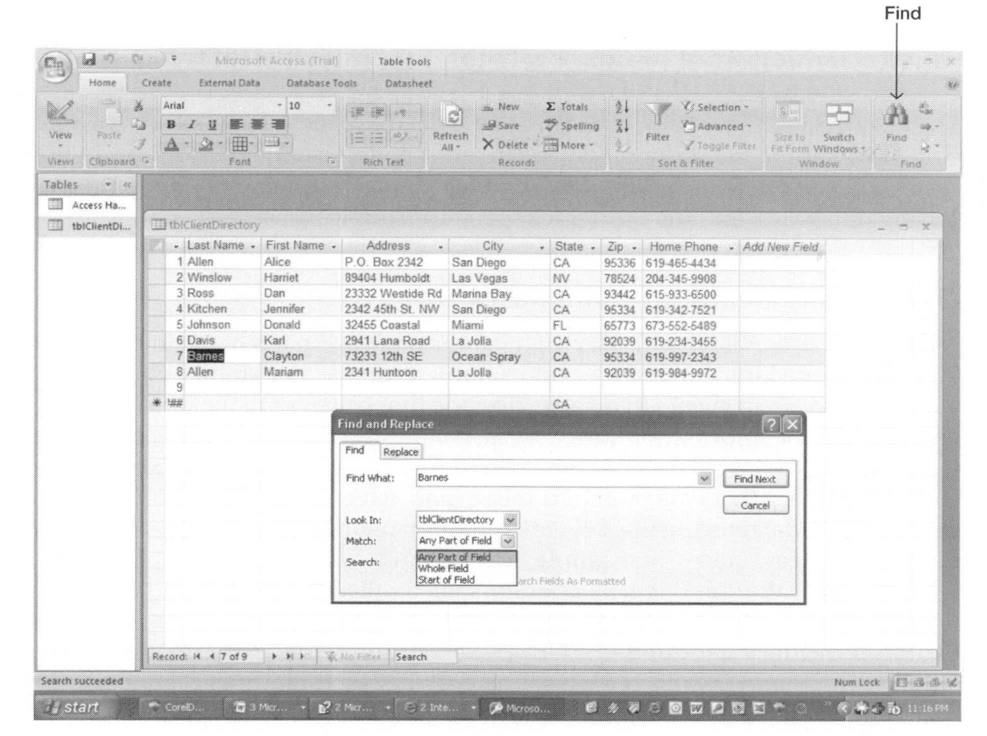

Exhibit 5–12
Using the Find Feature (Binoculars)
Microsoft product screen shot reprinted with permission from Microsoft Corporation.

It is typically easier to find something when Any Part of Field is selected because the DBMS will find the data in any part of a field and an exact match is not required. The down side is that Any Part of Field is more likely to find irrelevant fields as well.

Users can also delete entire records that are no longer needed and can copy and move information from one record to another.

CREATING FORMS

While it is possible to do all data entry using Datasheet view commands (see Exhibit 5–5), it is usually not the best way. Unless the field widths are set very wide, the entries probably will not be entirely visible and the user will frequently have to scroll horizontally while information is being entered. With a form (see Exhibit 5–6), data entry can be accomplished much more easily. The user can allot as much space as needed for each field, information can be entered into multiple tables, and it is easier to see what record is being worked on because only one record is shown at a time (see Exhibit 5–6). The Datasheet view is also cluttered with all of the previous records (see Exhibit 5–5). To create a form, the user simply indicates how the form should look and what fields to include in the form. Most DBMSs also have a wizard or automated feature that can help the user quickly and easily create a form.

> *Often, database tables contain too many fields for a meaningful display on a screen. Moreover, since the information for a record flows from left to right, viewing a record or entering information into a record can be difficult. Database forms can solve this problem. Forms let the lawyer [and legal assistant] display the fields of a record in an order that is logical and practical for a particular information need, without disturbing the actual order in which the fields in the table are arranged. Although the use of a form is not necessary, per se, its practical benefit makes it very important.*[8]

SEARCHING, SORTING, AND QUERYING THE DATABASE

The most powerful tools for manipulating a database include searching for specific information and sorting and organizing the information according to the specific needs of the user. This section gives you an overview of searching and sorting databases, and then provides specific examples.

Overview of Searching Databases

A user can ask a DBMS to display all the information or parts of the information that was entered into a database. For example, suppose in Exhibit 5–13 the user wanted to know all clients that had a zip code that began with the number 9, the user wanted the information sorted by last name and then first name, and these were the only fields the user wanted displayed. The first screen in Exhibit 5–13 shows the query that was built and the second screen shows the results. Users can query a database using several different methods including structured query languages, query by example, root expanders and wild card characters, relational operators, and logical operators (also called Boolean operators).

structured query language (SQL)
A database programming language used to search for and retrieve information in some DBMSs.

Structured Query Languages DBMSs search and retrieve information in different ways. Some DBMSs have a sophisticated structured query language for searching databases. A **structured query language (SQL)** uses words in proper syntax to search for and retrieve data in a database. In many ways, an SQL is much like regular programming languages. SQLs are somewhat complicated because the user must learn the proper command words and syntax, but they are also very powerful. SQLs are generally used in large, sophisticated DBMSs.

query by example (QBE)
A method of querying a database where the user interactively builds a query that will search and sort a database.

Query by Example Many DBMSs allow for a method of searching and retrieving data called **query by example** (**QBE**—see Exhibit 5–13). Using this method, a user interactively builds a query that will search and sort a database.

root expander
A search technique that increases the scope of a database search by searching for words with a common root.

wildcard character
A search technique that increases the scope of a database search by replacing one character in a word.

Root Expanders and WildCard Characters These are two methods used to enlarge keyword searches. A **root expander** allows a user to increase the scope of the search by searching for words with a common root. For example, some databases use the exclamation mark character (!) as a root expander. If a user wanted to search a database for the root of *litigation,* she could enter "litig!". This would search for words such as *litigation, litigate, litigates, litigated, litigator,* and *litigators.* Or, in the client database example, a user could search for all clients with case numbers starting with 2002 by entering "2002!". A **wildcard character** increases the scope of a search by replacing one of the characters in a word. A common wildcard character is the asterisk (*) (see Exhibit 5–13). For example, a user could search for *run* and *ran* by entering "r*n" in the search. Different databases use different symbols for root expanders and wild card characters, but the concepts are the same.

Root Expanders and Wildcard Characters
! Root expander: Retrieves all roots of the word
* Wildcard characters: Searches for all characters in the wildcard position

relational operator
A symbol that expresses data relationships in a database when performing searches. Examples include greater than, less than, and equal to symbols.

Relational Operators Data relationships are expressed by **relational operators**. For instance, if the client database included a field for the amount of retainer paid, and a user wanted to find all the clients who had paid a retainer fee of $999 or more, this could be done using a relational operator. The user would enter ">999" in the criteria part of the query in the "Retainer Amount" field. The ">" symbol is a relational operator that means *greater than.* The computer would respond by displaying the records that fit the search criterion.

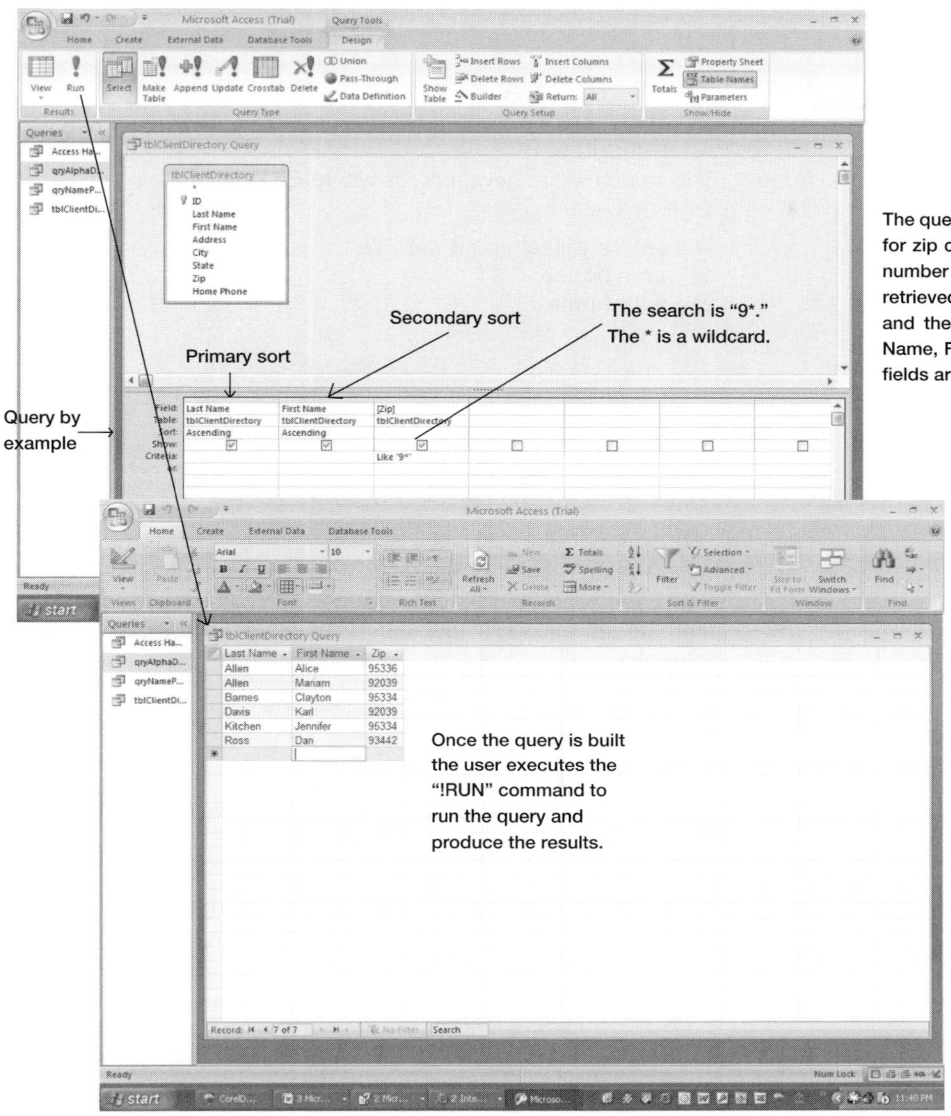
Secondary sort
Primary sort
The search is "9*."
The * is a wildcard.
Query by example
Like "9*"
Once the query is built the user executes the "!RUN" command to run the query and produce the results.

Exhibit 5–13

Creating a Query

Microsoft product screen shots reprinted with permission of Microsoft Corporation.

The query searches the database for zip codes that begin with the number 9. The query sorts the retrieved records by Last Name and then First Name. Only Last Name, First Name, and Zip Code fields are included in the query.

Relational operators include equal to, greater than, less than, greater than or equal to, less than or equal to, and not equal to. They are frequently used to search fields containing numbers and dates. For example, if the user wanted all dates greater than or equal to 6/1/2008 he would search using the following relational operators: ">=6/1/2008."

Relational Operators

>	Greater than
<	Less than
=	Equal to
<>	Not equal to
>=	Greater than or equal to
<=	Less than or equal to

Boolean/Logical Operators To instruct a database to look for more than one criterion, a **Boolean operator** (sometimes called a logical operator) is used. Boolean operators include: AND, OR, and NOT. Many database searches are

Boolean/logical operator
A symbol that instructs a DBMS to search for more than one criterion. Examples include AND, OR, and NOT.

Exhibit 5–14
Boolean/Logical Operators

Boolean/Logical Operators	Search Example	Description
OR	**House OR Home**	The search will retrieve records where EITHER of the search terms is present. The search will return the records: 1. Sam's **house** 2. Sam's **home** House / Home 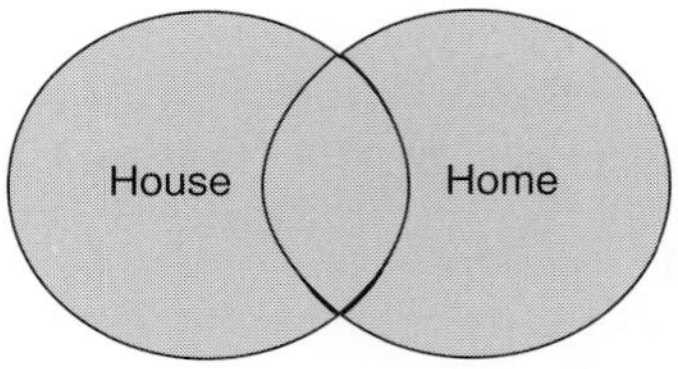 Since either "house" or "home" could be relevant to the search, both need to be included to make the search comprehensive. The more terms included in the search, the more records that will be retrieved.
And	**Real estate AND property**	The search will retrieve ONLY records where BOTH search terms are present. The search will return the record: 1. He owned personal **property** in Delaware and operated a **real estate** business in New Hampshire. 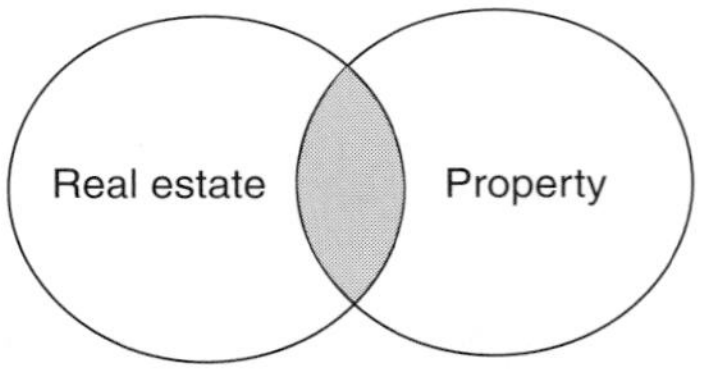 Real estate / Property The AND search logically states "I only want records that have BOTH search terms present." If only one search term is present the record will not be retrieved. The more search terms in an AND search, the fewer the records that will be retrieved.
NOT	**Property NOT Real estate**	The search will ONLY retrieve records where ONE term is present. The search will return the record: 1. He owned personal **property.** 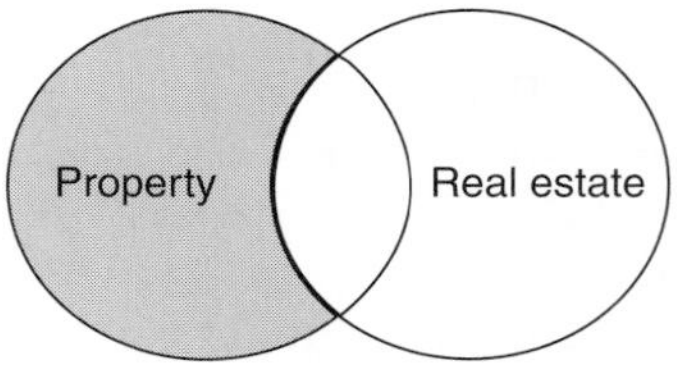 Property / Real estate The search logically stated "I only want to see records where property is used AND real estate is NOT." No records are retrieved in which the word "real estate" appears, even if the word "property" appears there too. NOT logic excludes records from the search.

based on the principles of Boolean logic. Boolean logic refers to the interrelationship between search terms and is named for the British mathematician George Boole. Exhibit 5–14 explains the general concepts of Boolean operators. Boolean operators expand or limit searches depending on the specific needs of the user at the time.

Overview of Sorting Databases

It is helpful for the data in a DBMS to be arranged or sorted in a specific manner. Several different sorting options are routinely used in DBMSs, including ascending and descending sorting, and primary and secondary sorting.

Ascending and Descending Sorts When data is sorted, the information must be placed in either ascending or descending order. **Ascending sorts** place data in ascending order from beginning to end, or from low numbers to high numbers. When words are sorted in ascending order, it means that they are placed in alphabetical order (i.e., from *A* to *Z*). When numbers are sorted in ascending order, it means that they are placed in numerical order, with smaller numbers coming before larger numbers (i.e., first *1*, then *2*, then *3*, etc.). Descending order is just the opposite of ascending order. **Descending sorts** place data in descending order from ending to beginning or from high numbers to low numbers. Words that are sorted in descending order are placed in reverse alphabetical order (i.e., from *Z* to *A*). Numbers that are sorted in descending order are placed with large numbers coming before small numbers (i.e., from *10* to *1*).

ascending sort
A sort criterion that places data in ascending order from beginning to end, from A to Z, or from low numbers to high numbers.

descending sort
A sort criterion that places data in descending order from end to beginning, from Z to A, or from high numbers to low numbers.

Primary and Secondary Sorts A **primary sort**, as the name implies, is the primary (or first) sort criterion that a DBMS executes. A **secondary sort** is the second sort criterion that a DBMS executes. For example, in Exhibit 5–13 in the client database, there are two clients with the name Allen—Alice Allen and Mariam Allen. To sort the database correctly (i.e., alphabetically), in Exhibit 5–13 the user must use a primary and a secondary sort. The primary sort criterion (which is ascending) is on the Last Name field. This tells the DBMS to sort the clients' last names alphabetically. If the user used only a primary sort (with, one sort criterion), then the DBMS could put Mariam Allen before Alice Allen, which would be incorrect (see Exhibit 5–13). To correct this problem, the user would include another, or secondary, sort on First Name. The primary and secondary sorts working together would then sort the data accurately.

primary sort
The first sort criterion that a DBMS uses to sort information.

secondary sort
The second sort criterion that a DBMS uses to sort information.

Examples of Searching, Sorting, and Querying Databases

DBMSs give users many options to search and sort the database including the Find feature, the filter feature, the ascending and descending sort features, and queries.

Find As indicated earlier to locate one specific record quickly, the Find feature (the binocular icon, see Exhibit 5–15), is the best way to locate the information.

Filter The Filter By Selection feature is a good way to quickly narrow down the records displayed. A filter is faster than building a query, because it can be executed directly in a table, but it cannot be saved. For example, in Exhibit 5–15, notice that the cursor is on the third record (Barnes, Clayton) in CA (the State field). To quickly display only the records with CA in the State field, click the Filter icon and only those records will be displayed (see the second screen in Exhibit 5–15). To remove the filter, click the mouse on the Toggle Filter icon and the data will be displayed in the original format (shown in the top screen in Exhibit 5–15).

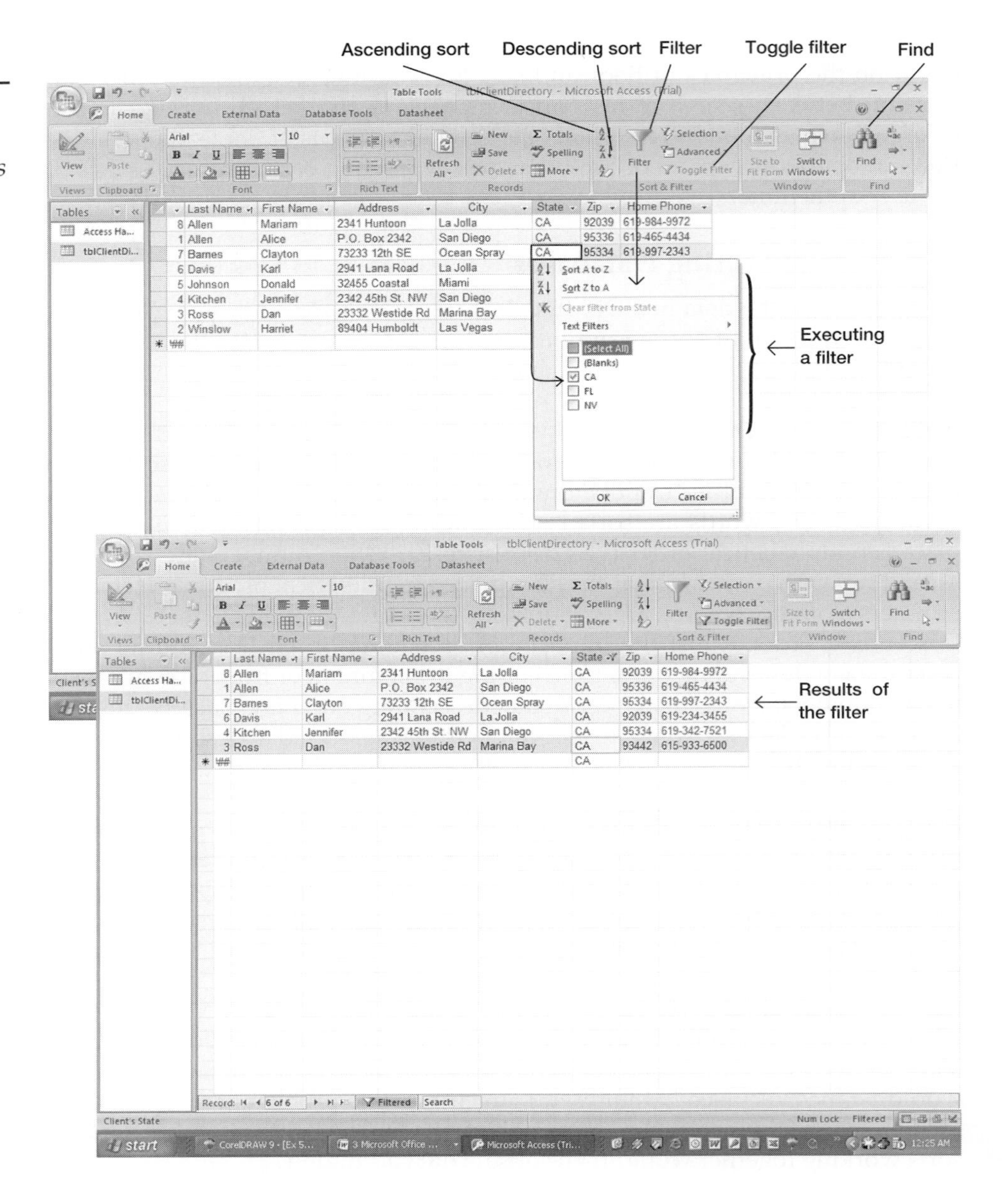

Exhibit 5–15
Find, Filters, and Ascending/Descending Sorts
Microsoft product screen shots reprinted with permission from Microsoft Corporation.

Ascending and Descending Sorts The ascending and descending sort icons work much like the Filter feature. For example, to see the data in Exhibit 5–15 sorted by city, alphabetically, simply click the mouse in any record in the City field and then click the Ascending Sort icon. The data would be sorted alphabetically in ascending order. The Descending Sort icon sorts the cities in descending order according to City when that feature is selected.

Queries Creating a query is the most powerful way of searching and sorting a database. A query allows a user to select or pull out only the information that she is looking for and to organize and sort the information any way she would like (see Exhibit 5–13). Queries are an extremely powerful and versatile way to manipulate databases. Most DBMSs have a wizard or automated feature that can help the user quickly create queries.

report writer
Allows the user complete control over how data in the database is printed without affecting the data in the database.

CREATING REPORTS

Most DBMS programs have a **report writer** feature that allows the user complete control over how data is printed, what information is printed (searched for,

selected, and retrieved), how that information is organized (sorted), and what format the data is printed in.

The top section of Exhibit 5–8 shows the Design view in Reports and the bottom section shows the report in Report view mode. To create a report, the user simply designs how the report should appear and what fields to include in the form. Most DBMSs have a wizard or automated feature that can help the user easily create a custom report. The user can also reference queries to control how the information is searched and sorted.

TYPES OF DBMSs

Several different types of DBMSs are available, including flat-file databases and relational databases. Each type of DBMS has its own unique capabilities and method of processing data.

Flat File

A **flat-file DBMS** handles data in one database or in a single file at a time and cannot link or merge data entered in one database with information in another database (see Exhibit 5–16). For example, if the client database was entered into a flat-file DBMS, you could not merge it with another database, such as a case list database that tracks information about the firm's active cases, including the

flat-file DBMS
A DBMS that can work with only one database table at a time.

Exhibit 5–16
Flat-File and Relational Databases

A. Flat-file database
In a flat-file database, files are separate.

Client list database

Data redundancy

Client's Last Name:
Client's First Name:
Client's Case Number:
Client's Address:
Client's City:
Client's State:
Client's Zip:

Case list database

Client's Last Name:
Client's First Name:
Client's Case Number:
Case Name:
Court:
Judge:
Status:

In a flat-file DBMS two separate databases would need to be created and maintained. Duplicate data would then be created (client's last name, first name and case number).

B. Relational database
In a relational database, files are related.

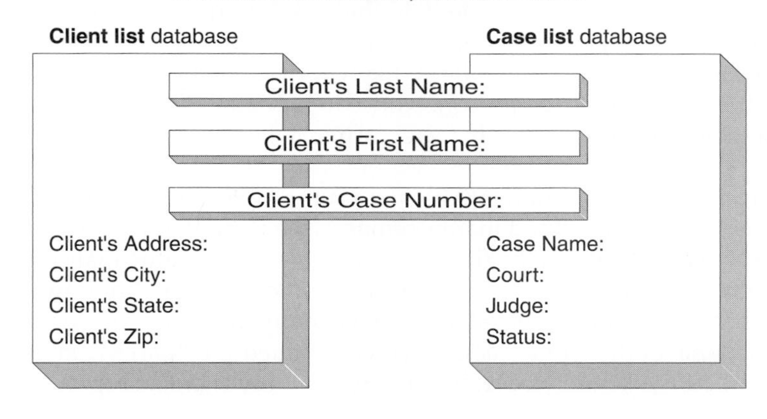

In a relational DBMS there is 1 database but there are 2 tables in the database. Data only needs to be entered and maintained in one place, because the tables are related to one another.

name of a case (e.g., *Johnson v. Sanders*), the case number, the client's first name and last name, the court where the case was filed, the judge assigned to the case, and the current status of the case. This is true even if some of the fields were the same in both databases (see Exhibit 5–16). If the firm wanted such a case list, it would have to be maintained separately from the client list. If, for example, a client's case number changed, the change would have to be entered into each of the databases separately.

Although a flat-file DBMS cannot link separate databases together, it is useful for small, less complex databases. Flat-file DBMSs are rare; most DBMSs on the market now, including Microsoft Access, are relational.

> *If the data collections are relatively small, a flat file database probably is adequate. However, for large collections of data, a flat file database would require too much space. Moreover, querying a flat file database cannot yield the kind of sophisticated information about stored data that querying a relational database would produce.*[9]
>
> *The purpose of "relating" tables in a relational database is to decrease the amount of space needed to store the data and to increase the speed of querying the database. In short, you should create another table [and relate it with the first] whenever you find you otherwise would duplicate data within the table.*[10]

Relational

relational DBMS
A DBMS that can work with multiple tables at a time, so long as at least one common field occurs in each table.

primary key
The primary key is a field that uniquely identifies each record.

one-to-one relationship
Each record in the first table contains a field value that corresponds and matches the field value in one record in the other table.

one-to-many relationship
One record in one table can have many matching records in another table. The table on the "one" side is called the "parent" table and the other is called the "child" table.

many-to-many relationship
One record in either table can relate to many records in the other table. The many-to-many relationship is not permitted in most relational databases.

A **relational DBMS** can handle data across multiple tables at the same time, so that the tables are connected, or related. Relational DBMSs allow users to remove data redundancy (duplicate data) from databases by dividing the data into many subject-based tables. Then, using relationships, the divided information is put back together. This is accomplished by placing common fields, called "keys," in tables that are related.

In Exhibit 5–3 the concept of having multiple tables in one database was presented. In that example a law office not only wanted to track client contact information, but also wanted to track case file information, case evidence, and information about opposing attorneys, all in one database. Instead of having all of the fields in one table, the fields were divided into four logical subject tables. Each table had a different subject matter. Exhibit 5–3, however, is incomplete because the tables are not linked together; they are all standing alone and as such they cannot share information.

Exhibit 5–17 shows the proper relationships among the tables. Notice in Exhibit 5–17 that each table has a small key symbol next to one field in the table. This is called a **primary key**. The primary key is a field that uniquely identifies each record. Exhibit 5–11 shows the primary key for the Client Directory database. Most tables have at least one field that is selected as the primary key. The data in the primary key field must be unique for each record. For example, a social security number would be a likely primary key in many databases because it is unique for each person. Notice in Exhibit 5–17 that the primary key for each table is different and that each primary key is a unique ID or internal number.

There are three types of relationships among tables in a relational database: one-to-one, one-to-many, and many-to-many (see Exhibit 5–18). In a **one-to-one** relationship each record in the first table contains a field value that corresponds and matches the field value in one record in another table. In a **one-to-many** relationship one record in one table can have many matching records in another table. The table on the "one" side is typically called the "parent" table and the other is called the "child" table. In a **many-to-many** relationship one record in

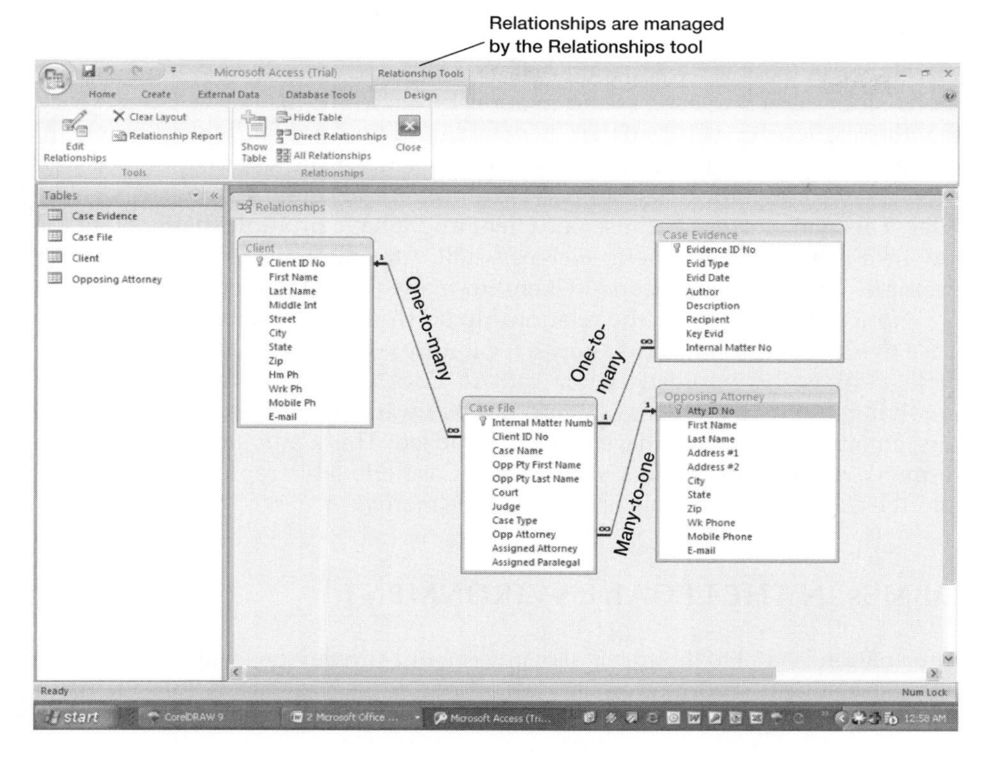

Exhibit 5–17
Creating Relationships Between Tables
Microsoft product screen shot reprinted with permission from Microsoft Corporation.

Exhibit 5–18
Three Ways to Relate Information in Tables

Relationship Type	Description
One-to-One	This is an association between two tables in which each record in the first table contains a field value that corresponds and matches the field value in one record in the other table. This relationship is more like a lookup tool, in which each record in one of the tables has a matching record in the other table.
One-to-Many	This is the most common type of relationship. One record in one table can have many matching records in another table. The table on the "one" side is typically called the "parent" table and the other is called the "child" table. To represent a one-to-many relationship in a database design, the primary key takes on the "one" side of the relationship and adds it as an additional field or fields to the table on the "many" side of the relationship.
Many-to-Many	This is an association between two tables where one record in either table can relate to many records in the other table. The many-to-many relationship is not permitted in relational databases as such; instead, a third table is used, called a "junction table," that serves as a bridge between the two tables.

either table can relate to many records in the other table. The many-to-many relationship is not permitted in most relational databases. If this type of design is needed, a third table, called a junction table, is used to be a bridge between the two tables. Advanced database relationships go beyond the scope of this text; suffice it to say that database relationships are complex and specific courses are taught in this one area of learning. This does, however, give you a brief overview of the subject.

Notice in Exhibit 5–17 that there is a small 1 and an infinity symbol (an "8" on its side) depicting each of the relationships. Notice further in Exhibit 5–17 that the relationship between the Client table and the Case File table shows a "1" on the Client side and an infinity symbol on the Case File side. This means that each client a law office has can have multiple (or an infinite number of) Case Files. This makes sense because one client might have multiple matters that the law firm is handling for them, such as a will, a tax matter, and an adoption for example. This represents a one- (Client) to-many (Case File) relationship.

Notice in Exhibit 5–17 the relationship between the Case File table and the Case Evidence table. Each case may have multiple types of evidence an attorney or legal assistant would need or want to track. For example, in any matter involving litigation there may be tens if not hundreds of pieces of evidence (letters, emails, reports, etc.) that need to be tracked. This again illustrates the one-to-many relationship. In this instance the Case File table represents the "one" and the Case Evidence table represents the "many."

DBMSs IN THE LEGAL ENVIRONMENT

Information is vital to the survival of any organization in the legal environment. Having relevant information at the proper time can mean the difference between winning and losing cases. A firm that manages information well always has an advantage. DBMSs manage information well because they are flexible to use, can store thousands of records, can retrieve and sort information precisely the way a firm needs it at any given time, and can print reports in many different formats.

The practice of law is information intensive. One role of a legal assistant is to assist attorneys in managing information. In any legal matter, information has a tendency to get backed up and out of control. In almost all cases, attorneys have a duty to share information (documents, witness testimony, etc.) with the other attorney or party in a lawsuit. The process of sharing information in a lawsuit is called *discovery.* During the discovery stage of a lawsuit, attorneys send written questions, called *interrogatories,* to the other party; take oral examinations, called *depositions,* of witnesses; and also request documents of the other party by filing a *request for production of documents.* Throughout the discovery stage and throughout the trial of a case, information is being distributed between the parties and must be tracked and organized. A database can be used to perform this litigation support process.

In addition to managing documents regarding cases, law firms must manage information about their clients, business, personnel, and so forth. Depending on the law firm, legal assistants may be required to set up and design databases, enter data into a database, perform searches and sorts, and print reports. They can use DBMSs to manage many types of information, ranging from legal research data to marketing data.

Legal Research Database

Every firm in the legal environment must at one time or another perform legal research. Since firms often handle certain kinds of cases and issues over and over, it is helpful to have an index showing what items have already been researched in prior cases and to have an index of unpublished opinions. Firms can easily keep an index of this information using a DBMS. For example, a firm's legal research database might contain fields such as these (see Exhibit 5–19):

1. Research Topic (to identify the general topic researched)
2. Subtopic (to further delineate and explain the specific issue involved)

Exhibit 5–19
Legal Research Database

Legal Research Database

Research Topic	Subtopic	Case Name	DOC Name	DOC Date
ANTITRUST	Generally	*Smith v. Jones*	Mot. Sum. Judg	4/3/2007
ANTITRUST	St. Act. Doct.	*Dunn v. Jones*	Mot. Sum. Judg	6/1/2006
APPEALS	Stnd. of Rev.	*Bud v. John*	Brief. Appell.	1/23/2007
APPEALS	Jurisdiction	*King v. Head*	Brief. Appell.	6/30/2006
DAMAGES	Present Value	*Copp v. USD 201*	Mot. New Trial	3/2/2008

3. Case Name (to identify what case the research was conducted for)
4. Document Name (to identify what document to look for in the file)
5. Document Date (also to help identify the appropriate document in the file)

A legal research database can help a legal assistant track often-used case law.

Conflict of Interest Database

Attorneys are bound by ethical rules not to participate in matters where they have a conflict of interest. For example, an attorney might have a conflict of interest if at one time the attorney represented a client's interest and then at a later time had to sue or take adverse action against the former client.

When attorneys represent a large number of clients, it is often difficult to remember every client. Thus, it is possible for an attorney to have a conflict of interest but simply not remember the former client. Some insurance companies that issue malpractice insurance to attorneys require that a conflict of interest database be maintained as a way to limit malpractice claims. A database can easily track such conflicts. A typical conflict of interest database might have fields such as the following:

1. Client's First Name
2. Client's Last Name
3. Client's Social Security Number
4. Client's Employer
5. Case Name or Matter
6. Date Case Handled
7. Adverse Party
8. Other Parties

When a new client comes into the office, the database can be searched for all possible conflicts against the new client, the new client's employer, adverse parties, or other parties, or for other possible conflicts.

Dead-File Database

All cases and legal matters must eventually come to an end. Cases that have been decided and are no longer being worked must be terminated or put on inactive status. In most offices, a terminated file will be shipped off to a storage facility or microfilmed. In any case, an index of what files have been terminated and where they have been stored must be kept so that the files can later be found and retrieved if necessary. Some legal assistants must track this information. A DBMS can easily handle this job.

A dead-file database usually contains fields such as these:

1. Case Name
2. Case Number
3. Location (where file is stored)
4. Dead-File Number (sometimes the files are stored by number instead of by case name)
5. Type of Case

Expert Witness Database

An expert witness is an individual who is a specialist or possesses a high degree of learning in a specific field or matter. Attorneys often hire expert witnesses to testify about a case or matter. Medical doctors often have a great deal of knowledge about specific types of injuries, depending on their specialty, and are sometimes called as expert witnesses to testify about a plaintiff's injuries in personal injury cases. In fact, a defendant in a personal injury case might also call an expert witness to try to attack the credibility of the plaintiff's expert.

Because attorneys regularly hire expert witnesses, it is sometimes necessary for legal assistants to keep a list of expert witnesses, what their specialties are, and how to contact them. When an attorney needs an expert for a case, all the legal assistant has to do is search for the particular specialty needed in the Specialty field, and the name of an expert will be displayed.

An expert witness database might contain fields concerning the expert witness such as the following:

1. Last Name
2. First Name
3. Address
4. City
5. State
6. Zip
7. Home Phone
8. Work Phone
9. Mobile Phone
10. Email Address
11. Specialty
12. Hourly Fee

Active Case List Database

An active case list is a list of all cases or matters that a firm or an attorney has pending. Usually the list will have fields such as these:

1. Client's Last Name
2. Client's First Name
3. Adverse Party's Last Name
4. Case Number
5. Attorney in Charge (i.e., for the office)
6. Court

An active case list database could also be used to give an attorney a list of all his cases. For example, a report could be generated that retrieved only the cases that had the initials "SLP" in the Attorney in Charge field. The attorney could then use this list to keep track of all his active cases.

Docket Control Database

Docket control means to handle and manage an attorney's appointments, meetings, deadlines, court appearances, and so forth (see Exhibit 5–20). Legal assistants often perform this task.

Exhibit 5–20
Docket Control Database

Docket Control Database

Date of Event	Event	Case Name	Place of Event	First Warning	Second Warning
01/13/2008	Trial	*Black v. Neal*	Court #3	01/02/2008	01/10/2008
01/24/2008	Appt/Sanders	*Smit v. Jones*	Office	01/02/2008	01/20/2008
01/30/2008	Depo/Defend.	*King v. Hill*	Def. Off.	01/15/2008	01/52/2008
02/01/2008	Setlmnt. Mtg	*Berg v. Rob*	J. Black's	01/20/2008	01/28/2008
02/03/2008	Deadin-MSJ	*Hope v. Hope*	Office	01/25/2008	01/30/2008
03/01/2008	Trail	*Doe v. Doe*	Court #12	01/02/2008	02/01/2008

A docket control database tracks this data using a DBMS. Most docket control databases will have fields such as the ones listed here:

1. Date of Event
2. Event
3. Case Name
4. Place of Event
5. First Warning (i.e., a reminder a few days *before* the event, notifying the firm of the approaching deadline or event)
6. Second Warning

In Exhibit 5–20, the events were sorted in ascending order according to their dates. The warning date fields are used to give the attorney a few days' notice before an event is to take place.

A report could also be generated that retrieved only a certain type of event, such as all the trials set for an attorney or office for a year. This could be accomplished by retrieving only those entries with the word *trial* in the Event field.

Library Catalog Database

Almost all offices in the legal environment have a library of law-related books. It is often necessary that the office have a card catalog to track the books in and out of the library and to keep inventory records. A firm's law library might want the collection sorted alphabetically by the titles of the books. It also would be helpful to produce an author index (by sorting the database alphabetically based on the authors' names) or a subject index (by sorting the database alphabetically based on the subjects).

A library catalog database typically has fields such as these:

1. Title
2. Author
3. Subject
4. Date Published
5. Library Number

Litigation Support Database

A litigation support database tracks documents and possible evidence in a particular case. A typical litigation support database will have the following fields:

1. Document Type
2. Document Name
3. Document Number (i.e., a number that the firm assigns to that document)
4. Document Date
5. Subject Matter
6. Document Author
7. Individual Who Received the Document
8. Notes

A litigation support database is used to search and retrieve whatever particular information an attorney needs at any given time. When thousands of documents are being tracked, a computerized database is almost a necessity for tracking down specific documents.

As indicated earlier in the chapter, databases and Microsoft Access in particular are used by legal assistants for litigation support purposes. Litigation support is an important task for which legal organizations use databases and legal assistants. A separate chapter on litigation support is included later in the text.

A database lets you transform data into usable information. When a discovery request yields a huge collection of documents, litigators need a means to store information about the document collection and retrieve meaningful answers to questions about it.[11]

Executing litigation is an organizational nightmare. Facts and figures, depositions and dockets can get lost in mountains of paper—or jumbled in an attorney's memory.... Firms use databases to manage litigation because they want quick and easy reports and information about a case.... These bits of information—and thousands of other facts—are key to success. Your attorneys just need to find the right piece.[12]

Collective Experience Database

Some firms have a database that contains the collective experience of the attorneys in the firm as it relates to judges the attorneys must appear before, expert witnesses, and others. Some judges have peculiar likes, dislikes, or requirements about certain types of cases or certain tendencies that a firm might want to remember when similar cases come up in the future. For example, a particular judge might like personal injury cases, but dislike labor law cases. If an attorney has a choice of where to file a case, this information might be important. An attorney might also like to have a database regarding expert witnesses, with information such as how to attack the credibility of certain experts and what prior cases the firm has encountered an expert in, so as to prepare for future encounters.

Lawyer Information Database

Some firms use a lawyer information database to track the names, addresses, telephone numbers, and areas of practice of other attorneys. Such a database can be helpful when returning phone calls or when trying to find a co-counsel in a case. Attorneys often bring in another attorney, called a co-counsel, who specializes in a particular area to help them represent a client. A database such as this makes tracking other attorneys' specialties easy and gives an ongoing list of attorney specialties.

Marketing Database

Many firms maintain a marketing database that tracks how clients are referred to them and where clients come from in an attempt to understand where they should be marketing their services. This information is usually gained from a questionnaire that is given to new clients. Such a questionnaire might ask how the client came to the attorney's office, whether by means of a referral from another attorney, from the firm's Internet site or banner ad, a referral from a past client, a newspaper article, the Yellow Pages, and so forth. This type of database allows firms to track which other attorneys or past clients are referring clients to them, so that the referring parties might be thanked or encouraged to keep doing this. This type of database also allows a firm to track which marketing efforts are working and which are not. Such a database might include fields about new clients such as the following:

1. First Name
2. Last Name
3. Address
4. City
5. State
6. Zip
7. Home Phone
8. Referral Source
9. Date
10. Other Comments

Trial Database

Trial databases are used to prepare for a trial. The purpose is to organize the file and documents in order to integrate every kind of evidence, including depositions, interrogatories, and documents, into one database. The following fields might be used:

1. Type of Evidence
2. Date of Evidence
3. Author
4. To (for documentary evidence)
5. Summary or Notes
6. Subject
7. Witnesses
8. Present Location of Evidence
9. Media Type (hard copy, image, etc.)

ETHICAL CONSIDERATIONS

Several ethical considerations arise when discussing database management in the legal environment, including checking for conflicts of interests when accepting new cases (DBMSs excel at checking conflicts), accurately and competently designing databases, accurately entering data, consistently and competently searching databases, and confidentiality.

Conflicts of Interests

An attorney and a law office have an ethical duty to avoid conflicts of interest. A conflict of interest occurs when an attorney or a legal assistant has competing personal or professional interests with a client's case that would preclude her

from acting impartially toward the client. Conflict of interest problems typically occur when a law office, attorney, or legal assistant previously worked for a client who is now an adverse party in a current case. See Rule 1.7 of the *Model Rules of Professional Conduct.*

Since many legal organizations and attorneys represent a large number of clients, it is often difficult for them to clearly identify the client or clients so that they can determine whether a conflict of interest actually exists. It is very possible for an attorney to have a conflict of interest but simply not remember a former client. For example, suppose an attorney represents a woman in a personal injury case and then eight years later the woman's husband comes in for representation in a divorce action against her. The attorney would arguably have a conflict of interest but simply not remember the prior representation of the woman. Thus, it is the responsibility of the legal organization and attorney to set up a system so the conflicts such as this do not happen. Many legal organizations use a conflict of interest database to do this (see earlier in the chapter for the design of such a database). They maintain a list of all of the organization's clients, former clients, and adverse parties and check the database before a new case is accepted to make sure there is no conflict.

> *Relying only on a good memory to identify potential adverse representation is probably the surest way for an attorney to become embroiled in a conflict of interest claim. As the complexity of litigation and commercial transactions increases, it has become increasingly difficult for the sole practitioner or law firm to conduct an adequate conflicts of interest check without the aid of a computerized conflict of interest system.*[13]

Design of Client Databases

As mentioned earlier, accurate design of client databases is critical to their success or failure. One of the ethics rules discussed earlier in this text states that attorneys and law offices must represent clients competently. See Rule 1.1 of the *Model Rules of Professional Conduct.*

If a legal assistant sets up a database with a poor design and bills the client for the amount of time it took to design and enter the information in it, and if the database then fails to produce the information needed due to poor design, this will probably hurt the client's case. Such a situation certainly brings up some ethics problems. The most powerful DBMS in the world will not solve a vague or poorly defined problem and will not prevent the failure of a poorly designed database. It is extremely important for the user to understand *exactly* what problem the database should solve *before* he begins to design it.

Data Entry Consistency and Errors

Data must be entered in a database with as much accuracy as humanly possible. Data entry errors are not just errors or misspellings in a database; they equate to the old adage "garbage in—garbage out" and also impact the ethical duty of competence. For instance, suppose a legal assistant is in charge of a client database project, including supervising three data entry operators who are entering information about evidentiary documents into a litigation support database for a case. Suppose one of the fields in the database is Document Type. Assume the legal assistant has not given the data entry operators any guidance

as to how to enter information. Suppose data entry operator 1 enters letters (correspondence) in the Document Type field as "LTR"; data entry operator 2 enters letters as "LT"; and data entry operator 3 enters letters sometimes as "Correspondence" (which is sometimes misspelled), sometimes as "LTS," sometimes as "Letters," and sometimes as nothing at all. Now, suppose the legal assistant is sitting in a courtroom, the lead attorney for the firm is cross-examining an important witness, and the witness refers to a crucial letter that the lead attorney must immediately have to effectively cross-examine the important witness. The legal assistant, sitting at the counsel table, searches the database for a list of all letters using the search criterion "LETTERS," and the database retrieves two records, neither of which is remotely close to the letter the witness is referring to. The lead attorney must continue with his examination as the legal assistant frantically searches for the document. The client's case suffers, the client is unhappy, the lead attorney is hampered in his cross-examination and is frustrated, and the legal assistant has failed to carry out an assignment properly. The point is that data-entry consistency and accuracy are extremely important, and if garbage is put into the computer, that is what it will output.

Search Criteria Accurately searching databases is as important as effectively designing the database and accurately entering the data. When entering search criteria, the user must be sure that the information is entered accurately and must understand how to search. Again, if the user enters a search criterion that will not retrieve what the attorney is looking for because the search is inaccurate or not well conceived, then the database is worthless, and all the time it took to develop it was wasted.

Confidentiality As with all client information a legal organization collects, the ethical duty to keep that information confidential is paramount. Client databases and the duty to keep those databases confidential represent a real ethical consideration for any legal organization. Consider that in one (litigation support) database, all of the evidentiary documents, summaries of the documents, and every piece of information about the client could reside on one CD-ROM. It is absolutely critical that any database with client-related information is securely maintained both from a physical standpoint in that only limited individuals have access to the computer, the CD-ROM, or the access rights (over a network) to the database, and that the database is adequately protected with passwords and other electronic security devices (firewalls for extranets, etc.). Consideration must also be given to adequately securing legal organization administrative databases. Think what would happen if a comprehensive client/case matter list for a large legal organization was backed up and the backup tape causally discarded and obtained by a competitor. Databases are wonderful for collecting, organizing, and searching information, but because they can contain so much useful information, legal professionals must clearly recognize the duty to keep the information absolutely confidential. They must also realize the catastrophic result if it is made public and take actions to make sure it never happens.

SUMMARY

A database is a collection of related items. A database management system is an application that manages a database by storing, searching, sorting, and organizing data. A table in a database is a collection of related information

stored in rows and columns. Many databases have more than one table. A field is a column in a table; each field contains a category of information. A record is a collection of fields that is treated as a unit. Large databases may have millions of records. A data value is the smallest piece of information in a table.

There are four tools or objects found in most DBMSs: tables, forms, queries, and reports. A table stores the information in the database. A form allows the user a custom format to view, enter, or edit the data. A query extracts specific data from a database and sorts the extracted data as required. A report prints data from a table or query in final format that can be used by the user.

The database design and implementation process includes (1) identifying the problem; (2) determining exactly what the user needs from the database; (3) planning the database design, including planning the tables, table relationships, and fields; (4) entering the database design in the DBMS; (5) testing the design; (6) entering the data; and (7) revising the design as needed.

Careful database planning includes not having too many fields in one table, not repeating fields, and not having redundant information. The job of entering data in the database in a uniform and consistent manner is crucial. Inconsistent data entry leads to searches, queries, and reports that are incomplete and error ridden. When searching databases, root expanders (!) and wildcard characters (*) can increase the scope of a search. Relational operators such as ">" greater than and "<" less than can be used in database searching. Boolean/logical operators such as "AND," "OR," and "NOT" can also be used in database searches.

When sorting data, the primary sort is the first sort criterion entered and the secondary sort is the second level of sorting. Ascending sorts manipulate the data so the data order is A to Z or 1 to 10. Descending sorts are just the opposite.

Relational databases handle and manipulate data across multiple tables. Using this method users can divide their data into many subject-based tables. Then, using relationships, the divided information is put back together into one coherent group of information. Most tables have a primary key designated that uniquely identifies each record. There are three data relationships in relational databases; one-to-one, one-to-many, and many-to-many. In the one-to-one relationship each record in the first table contains a field value that corresponds to and matches the field value in one record in the other table. In the one-to-many relationship one record in one table can have many matching records in another table. The table on the "one" side is called the "parent" table and the other is called the "child" table. In the many-to-many relationship one record in either table can relate to many records in the other table. The many-to-many relationship is not permitted in most relational databases.

KEY TERMS

database management system
database
table
field
record
data value
form
query
report
look up option
validation control
structured query language (SQL)
query by example (QBE)
root expander
wildcard character
relational operator
Boolean/logical operator
ascending sort
descending sort
primary sort
secondary sort
report writer
flat-file DBMS
relational DBMS
primary key
one-to-one relationship
one-to-many relationship
many-to-many relationship

INTERNET SITES

Internet sites for this chapter include the following:

Organization	Product/Service	World Wide Web Address
Microsoft	Microsoft Access database	<http://www.microsoft.com>
Microsoft Access home page	A wealth of information for Access users including database templates, tips, tricks, user group lists, and much more	<http://www.microsoft.com/office/access>
Corel Corporation	Paradox database	<http://www.corel.com>
IBM	Approach database	<http://www.IBM.com/Lotus>
About, Inc.	A general site that contains information about database design	<http://databases.about.com>

TEST YOUR KNOWLEDGE

1. True or False: An application program that stores and searches data is called a database.
2. A _______ is a collection of related information stored in rows and columns.
3. Typically relational databases have _______ table(s):
   a. Zero
   b. One
   c. Multiple
4. A _______ is a column in a table and contains a category of information.
5. A _______ is a row in a table and is treated as a unit.
6. The smallest individual piece of information in a database is called a _______.
7. True or False: A form holds the data in a database.
8. True or False: A query extracts data from a table.
9. Name the four tools or objects found in most DBMSs.
10. True or False: Good database design is about the person designing the system, not about the end user.
11. One of the single most important factors of having a good database is _______ data entry.
12. The old adage _______ is accurate when it comes to data entry. The data coming out of the system is only as good as what was entered.
13. Define what a lookup option in a database is.
14. What is validation control?
15. True or False: Uniform data entry is not important because queries can be written to make up for whatever deficiencies there are in data entry.
16. When using the Find tool, which search option is the most expansive: Whole Field, Start of Field, or Any Part of Field?
17. Name two relational operators.
18. Name one of three Boolean operators.
19. A _______ is a field that uniquely identifies each record.
20. When one record in one table can relate to many records in another table, the relationship is called _______.

ON THE WEB EXERCISES

1. Using a general Internet search engine (such as google.com or yahoo.com) or a general computing magazine, research the latest features in database management programs and write a one-page summary of your findings.
2. Using a general Internet search engine (such as google.com or yahoo.com) or the sites at the end of the chapter, research basic database design and write a three-page paper on what you found.
3. The business world literally runs on databases. Using a general Internet search engine (such as google.com or yahoo.com) research the largest databases in the world. What are they, what do they do, what would life be like if we did not have them, how important are they, and how complex are they? Write a two-page report on your findings.
4. Using a general Internet search engine (such as google.com or yahoo.com), research the database design process. Write a two-page paper on your findings.

QUESTIONS AND EXERCISES

1. Using a word processor or a legal pad, design your own contact database of addresses, phone, mobile phone, email, and other such information for friends and family. Include what tables and fields you would include in your design.
2. Using a word processor or legal pad, design a database that will track something that you collect, such as DVDs, CD-ROMs, MP3s, or other items. Design the table(s), fields, and at least one report you would like the system to output.
3. Using Exhibit 5–9, follow the steps in the process and design any database that will solve a problem that you have encountered. Document the design process in a paper that is at least three pages long and that explains how you worked through the design of the system.
4. Design a relational database for a legal organization that will track contact information for each client, the status of each client's case, a current list of upcoming events for each case, a list of witnesses for each case, and information on how to contact the witnesses. Prepare the database design on paper first by making a list of the fields for each table.
5. Design and implement your own expert witness database in a DBMS. Think of at least ten fields that your database can track.
6. Your supervising attorney asks you to type up a list of the documents in a case that he has to try. There are approximately fifty documents. The list must contain the date of each document, who it is to, the type of document it is, the subject of the document, and a short description of the contents. The attorney indicates it is up to you to decide whether you will use a word processor, a spreadsheet, or a DBMS. Discuss the strengths and weaknesses of using each and state which one you would use and why. Is there any additional information you would like from the attorney?
7. You have been asked to prepare a list of personal and real property in a complex divorce action. Approximately two thousand pieces of information will have to be entered. Key issues in the divorce include what the total value of the property is, how each piece of property was acquired (was it the husband's before marriage, the wife's before marriage, acquired during the marriage, given as a gift, etc.), when the property was acquired, whether there is a mortgage or loan on the item, whether your client is willing to give up the property or wants to keep it, and where the item is now. Plan and design a database to accomplish this.

END NOTES

[1] David B. Yavitz, "Database for Matrimonial Attorneys," *Fairshare*, January, 1998.
[2] Rachel Levine, "Is Microsoft Access the Magic Database Answer for Your Complex Litigation?" *Legal Management*, March/April, 2000, 49.
[3] John W. Barker Jr., "Litigation Support Tool—Creating Tables in Microsoft Access 95," *Lawyer's PC*, February 1, 1998.
[4] Rachel Levine, "Is Microsoft Access the Magic Database Answer for Your Complex Litigation," *Legal Management*, March/April, 2000, 49.
[5] John W. Barker Jr., "Litigation Support Tool—Creating Tables in Microsoft Access 95," *Lawyer's PC*, February 1, 1998.
[6] Lincoln Brunner & June D. Bell, "Being All They Can Be—*LAT's* 2002 Paralegal of the Year and Runners Up Make a Habit of Going the Extra Mile," *Legal Assistant Today*, September/October 2002, p. 48.
[7] Rachel Levine, "Is Microsoft Access the Magic Database Answer for Your Complex Litigation?" *Legal Management*, March/April, 2000, 49.
[8] John W. Barker Jr., "Using Microsoft Access for Litigation Support," *Lawyer's PC*, July 15, 1997, 3.
[9] John W. Barker Jr., "Using Microsoft Access for Litigation Support," *Lawyer's PC*, July 15, 1997, 3.
[10] John W. Barker Jr., "Litigation Support Tool—Creating Tables in Microsoft Access 95," *Lawyer's PC*, February 1, 1998, 7.
[11] John W. Barker Jr., "Using Microsoft Access for Litigation Support," *Lawyer's PC*, July 15, 1997, 3.
[12] Rachel Levine, "Is Microsoft Access the Magic Database Answer for Your Complex Litigation," *Legal Management*, March/April, 2000, 49.
[13] Jospeh A. Canillo, "Systems & Technology: Conflict of Interest Prevention," *Legal Malpractice Report*, 1990, 11.

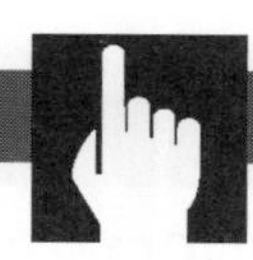

DATABASE HANDS-ON EXERCISES

READ THIS FIRST!

1. **Microsoft Access 2007**
2. **Microsoft Access 2003**

I. Determining Which Tutorial to Complete

To use the Database Hands-On Exercises you must already own or have available to you Microsoft Access 2007 or Access 2003. If you have one of the programs but do not know the version you are using, it is easy to find out. In Access 2003 load Access, and click "Help" on the menu bar and then click "About Microsoft Office Access." For Access 2007 you should click the Office Button, click "Access Options" and then look under the title "Resources." It should then tell you what version of the program you are using. You must know the version of the program you are using and select the correct tutorial version or the tutorials will not work correctly.

II. Using the Database Hands-on Exercises

The Database Hands-On Exercises in this section are easy to use and contain step-by-step instructions. They start with basic database skills and proceed to intermediate and advanced levels. To truly be ready for using databases in the legal environment you must be able to accomplish the tasks and exercises in the advanced exercises.

III. Accessing the Hands-On Exercises Files that Come With the Text

Lesson 6 of the Hands-On Exercises uses a document on Disk1 of the CDs that come with the text. To access the database in Windows XP, put the CD in your computer, select "Start," "My Computer," then select the appropriate drive and double-click on the appropriate drive, and then double-click on the Database Files folder. You will see one database file entitled Lesson 6 Law Firm Database. To access these files in Windows Vista, put the CD in your computer, select the Start button, select Computer, double-click on the appropriate drive, and then double-click on the Database Files folder. You will see one database file entitled Lesson 6 Firm Database. *Note:* In Access 2007, once the file is loaded you will need to immediately use the Save As command to save the file to another drive such as your hard drive. In Access 2003, you must copy the file to another drive such as your hard drive before you can even load it. Specific instructions are included in the hands-on exercises.

IV. Installation Questions

If you have installation questions regarding opening the Access database file contact Technical Support at 800/477-3692.

HANDS-ON EXERCISES

MICROSOFT ACCESS 2007 FOR WINDOWS

Basic Lessons

Number	Lesson Title	Concepts Covered
Lesson 1	Creating a Table—Client Database	How to create a new table/database, create and design fields, create a primary key, move between the Table Design view and the Datasheet view, enter a record, and save the database.
Lesson 2	Creating a Form/Entering Data—Client Database	How to create a form, enter data in the form, view the Datasheet view of the form, and close a form.
Lesson 3	Querying a Database—Client Database	How to use the Ascending Sort icon on the ribbon, create a query that searches and sorts the database, modify a query, use a primary and secondary sort option, run a query, and print a query.
Intermediate Lessons		
Lesson 4	Creating a Report-Client Database	How to create and print a report.
Lesson 5	Litigation Support Database	How to build a litigation support database that tracks documents in a case; creating the fields, entering the data, running helpful sorts and filters to search the data, running a query, running a report, and printing a report.
Advanced Lesson		
Lesson 6	Working with a Law Office Relational Database "Access Lesson 6 Law Firm Database" from Disk1	Working with a true relational database, including working with multiple tables, assigning relationships among tables, and writing queries and reports that access data from multiple tables.

Getting Started

Introduction

Throughout these lessons and exercises, information you need to type into the program will be designated in several different ways:

- Keys to be pressed on the keyboard will be designated in brackets, in all caps, and in bold (i.e., press the **[ENTER]** key).
- Movements will be designated in bold and italics (i.e., ***point to File on the menu bar and click the mouse***).
- Words or letters that should be typed will be designated in bold (i.e., type **Training Program**).
- Information that should be displayed on your computer screen is shown in the following style: ***Press ENTER to continue.***

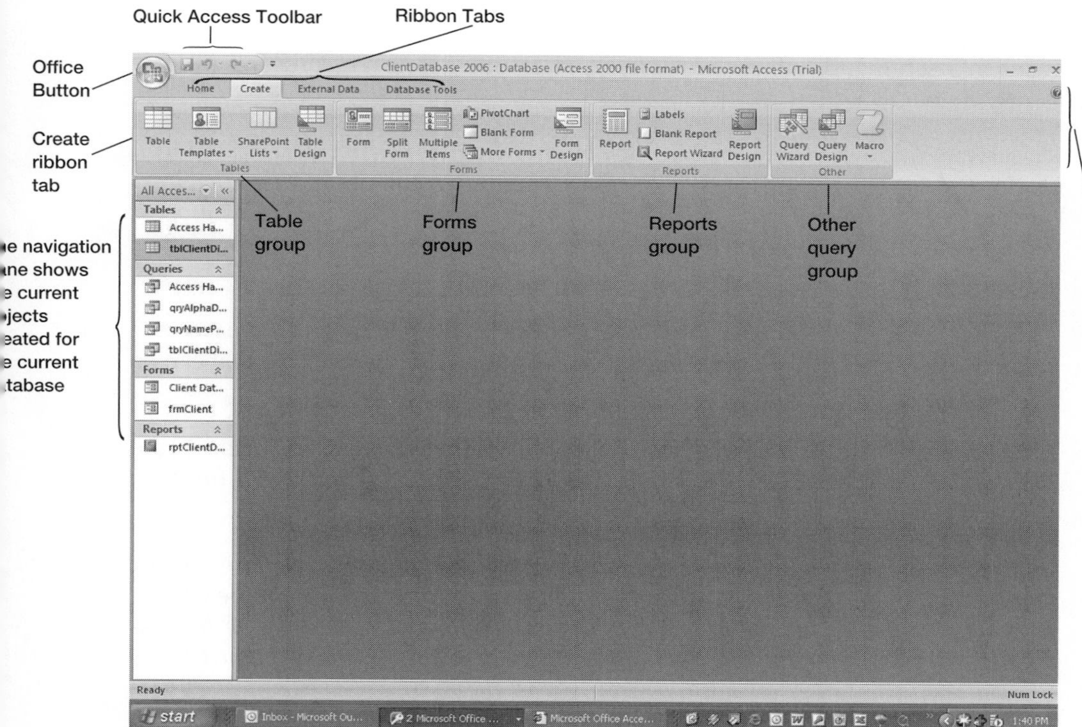

Access 2007 Exhibit 1
Access 2007
Microsoft product screen shot reprinted with permission from Microsoft Corporation.

Overview of Access 2007

Access 2007 is a relational database management application. Access 2007 Exhibit 1 shows the Access interface. Notice the ribbon across the top of the screen (see Access 2007 Exhibit 1). The ribbon has several tabs across the top; these are called "ribbon tabs" or sometimes just "tabs." When a different tab is selected, the tools and commands on the ribbon change. In Access 2007 Exhibit 1, the Create ribbon tab is selected. Notice that the Create ribbon tab in Access 2007 Exhibit 1 has four groups, including the Tables, Forms, Reports, and Other groups (which includes queries). At the very top to the left of the screen is the Quick Access Toolbar, this is a toolbar that can be customized by the user. In the top left of the screen is the Office Button. The Office Button allows the user to open files, save files, create new files, and print documents, among other things. On the left side of the screen is the Navigation Pane. The Navigation Pane can be configured in different ways, but in Access 2007 Exhibit 1 the user has all of the objects for the database displayed for easy access. This includes all of the user's tables, queries, forms, and reports.

Additional information about Access 2007 will be provided as you complete the exercises. By the end of the exercises you should have a good understanding of the basics of Access 2007.

Basic Lessons

Lesson 1: Creating a Table

This lesson shows you how to build the table shown in Access 2007 Exhibit 3. It explains how to create a new table/database, create new fields, create a primary key, move between the Table Design view and the Datasheet view, and save the database. Keep in mind that if you make a mistake in this lesson you may press **[CTRL]+[Z]** to undo what you have done, but note that in some

cases this command will not work (e.g., when you delete a record, it is permanently deleted).

1. Open Windows. Then, ***double-click on the Microsoft Office Access 2007 icon on the desktop*** to open Access 2007 for Windows. Alternatively, ***click on the Start button, point to Programs or All Programs, and then click on the Microsoft Access 2007 icon (or point to Microsoft Office and then click Microsoft Office Access 2007).***

2. When Access 2007 opens, the "Getting Started with Microsoft Office Access" screen is displayed. This screen offers the user a number of templates that can be accessed to speed the creation of databases in Access.

3. Just under the "Getting Started with Microsoft Office Access" title is the "New Blank Database" section. ***Click "Blank Database . . ." just under the New Blank Database section.***

4. Notice that the right side of the screen now says "Blank Database." ***Click under "File Name,"*** use the **[DEL]** key to delete the current title, and type **Client**. ***To save the new database in the default directory, click "Create." To browse where you would like to save the new database, click the Browse icon (it looks like open file folder with an arrow) just to the right of the file name. Then, select the directory or folder you would like to save the file to,*** type **Client** next to "File name," ***and then click OK. Finally, click Create.***

5. You should now have a blank table in Datasheet view displayed on your screen (see Access 2007 Exhibit 2). Notice that the Table Tools—Datasheet ribbon tab is currently shown (see Access 2007 Exhibit 2). From the Views group on the Datasheet ribbon tab, ***click the down arrow under View, and then click Design view.***

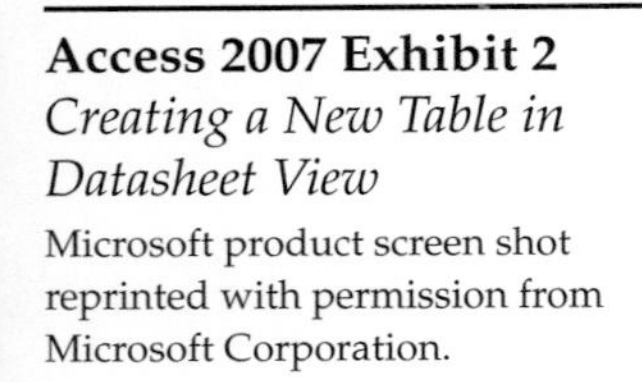

Access 2007 Exhibit 2
Creating a New Table in Datasheet View
Microsoft product screen shot reprinted with permission from Microsoft Corporation.

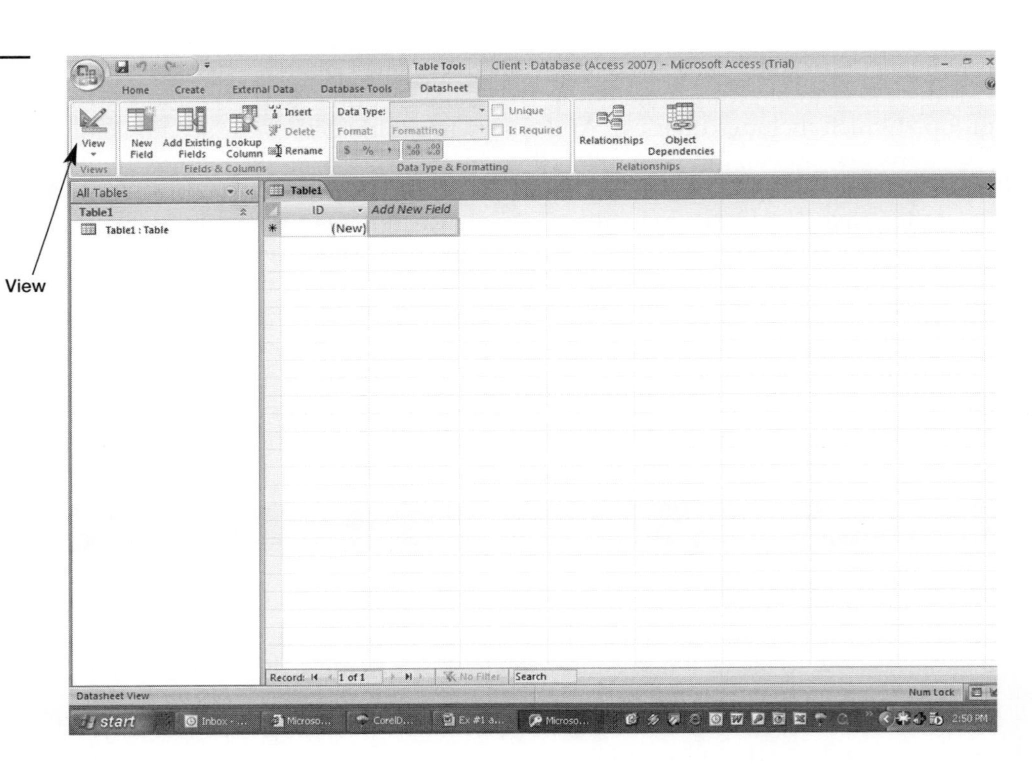

6. The "Save As" window should now be displayed. Type **tblClient** under Table Name and then ***click OK.***

7. The Design view of your table (tblClient) should now be on your screen. Your screen should be similar to Access 2007 Exhibit 3, except that the table on your screen will be blank. You will now begin to build the structure of a client database by entering the fields shown in Access 2007 Exhibit 3.

8. Notice that Access has entered a default field name of "ID" in the first row of your table (see Access 2007 Exhibit 3). It is useful to have an ID number for each client, so press **[TAB] three times** to move to the next row. Notice also in the ID field that the data type is "AutoNumber." This means that Access will automatically create a unique ID number for each client.

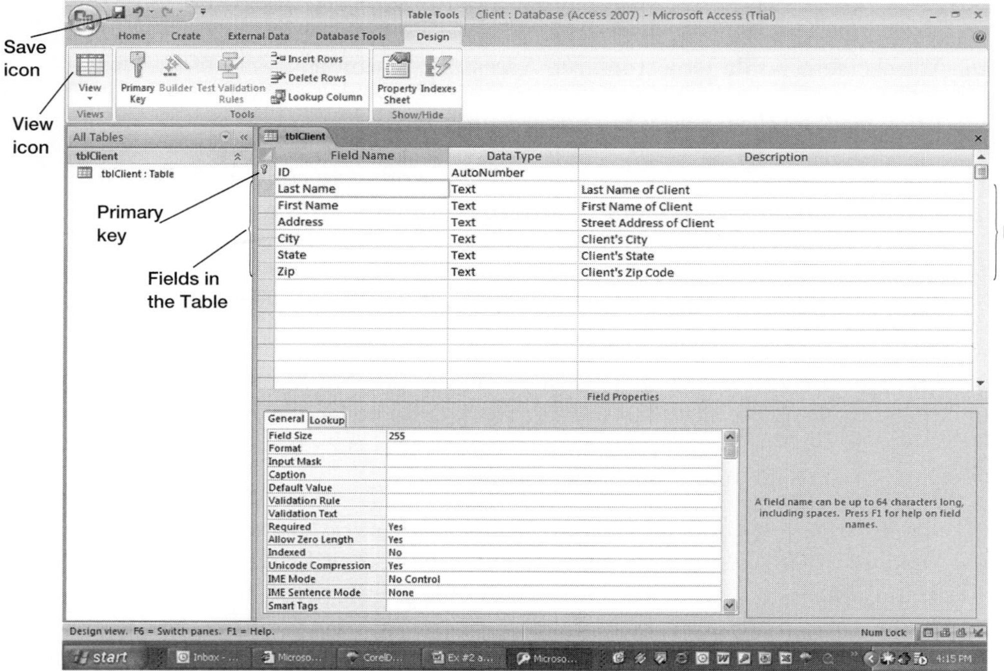

Access 2007 Exhibit 3
Creating Fields in a Table
Microsoft product screen shot reprinted with permission from Microsoft Corporation.

9. With your pointer in the second row of the first column, Field Name, type **Last Name** and then press **[TAB].**

10. Your pointer should now be in the Data Type column and "Text" should be displayed in the field. If you click the down arrow next to "Text" you can see the different data types that Access has. By selecting the data type, you tell Access what kind of information will be stored in the field. Since text will be stored in the Last Name field, press the **[TAB]** key to go to the Description column.

11. In the Description column, type **Last Name of Client.**

12. Notice at the bottom of the screen under Field Properties that there are two tabs, General and Look Up. The General tab should be displayed. It allows you to change the field size (the number of characters that may be entered into the field) and other items as well.

13. Next to the Required field under the General tab, ***click "No." Then, click the down arrow next to "No," and then click Yes.*** This will require the user to enter

this field when entering new data. The default field size and the other options are fine, so you do not have to change them.

14. The Last Name field is now complete. ***Click in the third row, directly under Last Name.***

15. Type the following information into the table:

Field Name	Data Type	Description	Field Size	Required
First Name	Text	First Name of Client	50	Yes
Address	Text	Street Address of Client	50	Yes
City	Text	Client's City	25	Yes
State	Text	Client's State	2	Yes
Zip	Text	Client's Zip Code	9	Yes

16. Your screen should look similar to Access 2007 Exhibit 3.

17. ***Click back on the General tab under Field Properties.***

18. Once all of the information has been entered, ***point and click on the Save icon (it looks like a floppy disk) on the Quick Access Toolbar to save your data.***

19. Notice that a small key icon is displayed next to the ID field. This indicates that the ID field is the primary key (the field that uniquely identifies each record) for this table.

20. You are currently in the Table Design view. Design view means that you are looking at the *design* of the table and not the data in the table itself. You will now change your view to Datasheet view. Once data has been entered into the table, you can see the data in the Datasheet view.

21. ***From the Views group on the Design ribbon tab, click the down arrow under the View icon*** (see Access 2007 Exhibit 3), ***and then select Datasheet view.*** *Note*: To see the name of any icon, just hover the mouse pointer over the icon for a second and the name of the icon will appear.

22. You should now see all of your fields displayed horizontally across the screen (see Access 2007 Exhibit 4). You can toggle back and forth between Design view and Datasheet view by clicking on the View icon.

23. Press the **[TAB]** key to go to the Last Name field.

24. Enter the following information (to go to the next field press the **[TAB]** key).

ID	Last Name	First Name	Address	City	State	Zip
	Allen	Alice	P.O. Box 2342	San Diego	CA	95336

25. While you can use Table Datasheet view to enter new records, it is not always the best way to enter data. In the next lesson, we will create a form to enter new records.

26. ***Click the Save icon on the Quick Access Toolbar to save your data.***

27. ***Click the Office Button and then click Exit Access to exit the program.***

This concludes Lesson 1.

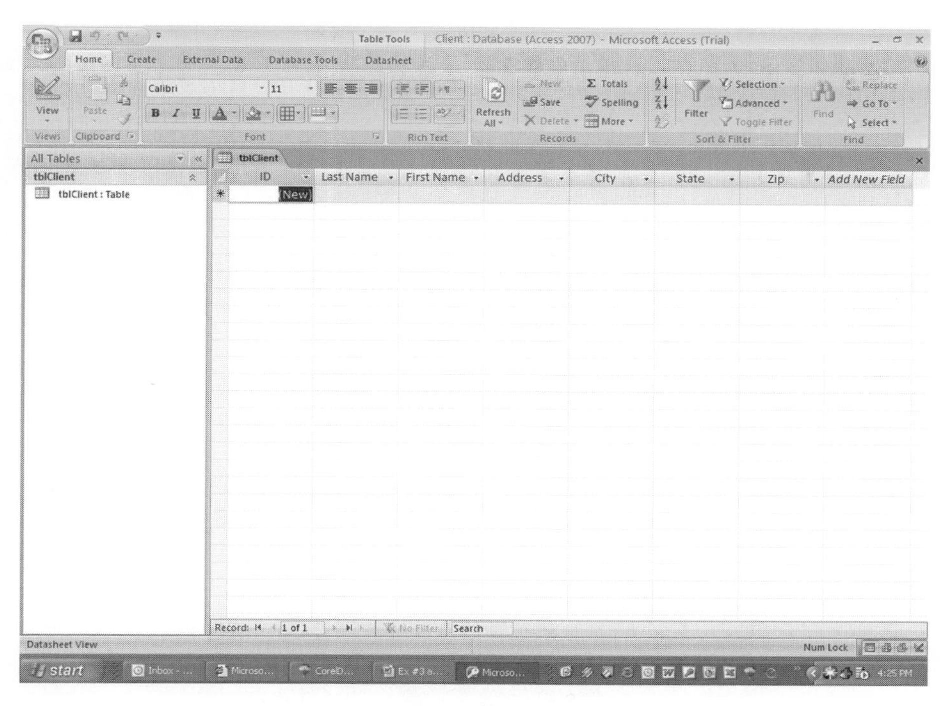

Access 2007 Exhibit 4
Table Datasheet View
Microsoft product screen shot reprinted with permission from Microsoft Corporation.

Lesson 2: Creating a Form and Entering Data

In this lesson, you will create a form from which you can enter data into the database. You will then enter the rest of the data into the client database using the form you created.

1. Open Windows. Then, ***double-click on the Microsoft Office Access 2007 icon on the desktop*** to open Access 2007 for Windows. Alternatively, ***click the Start button, point to Programs or All Programs, and then click the Microsoft Access 2007 icon (or point to Microsoft Office and then click on Microsoft Office Access 2007).***

2. ***Click the Office Button (see Access 2007 Exhibit 1). Then, under "Recent Documents," click the name of the client file you created in Lesson 1 (Client.accdb).***

3. If a security warning (for example, "Security Warning: Certain content in the database has been disabled") is displayed just under the ribbon, **click *"Options" next to the security warning. Then, in the Microsoft Office Security Options window, click Enable this Content and then click OK.*** There is no security problem, because you know the content came from a trustworthy source, as you are the one who created the file.

4. Notice that the file called "tblClient:Table" that you created in Lesson 1 is listed on the Navigation Pane.

5. You are now ready to create a data entry form that will assist you in entering the data into the "tblClient:Table" file.

6. ***Click the Create ribbon tab, then click Form in the Forms group.*** Access should return a default data entry form for you (see Access 2007 Exhibit 5).

7. Access gives you many options to easily format your form. Notice on the ribbon that a new tab appeared called "Form Layout Tools," and that "Form Layout Tools – Format" is selected. ***Click the down arrow in the AutoFormat group on the Format ribbon tab*** (see Access 2007 Exhibit 5) to look at the AutoFormat

Access 2007 Exhibit 5
Corrected Data Entry Form
Microsoft product screen shot reprinted with permission from Microsoft Corporation.

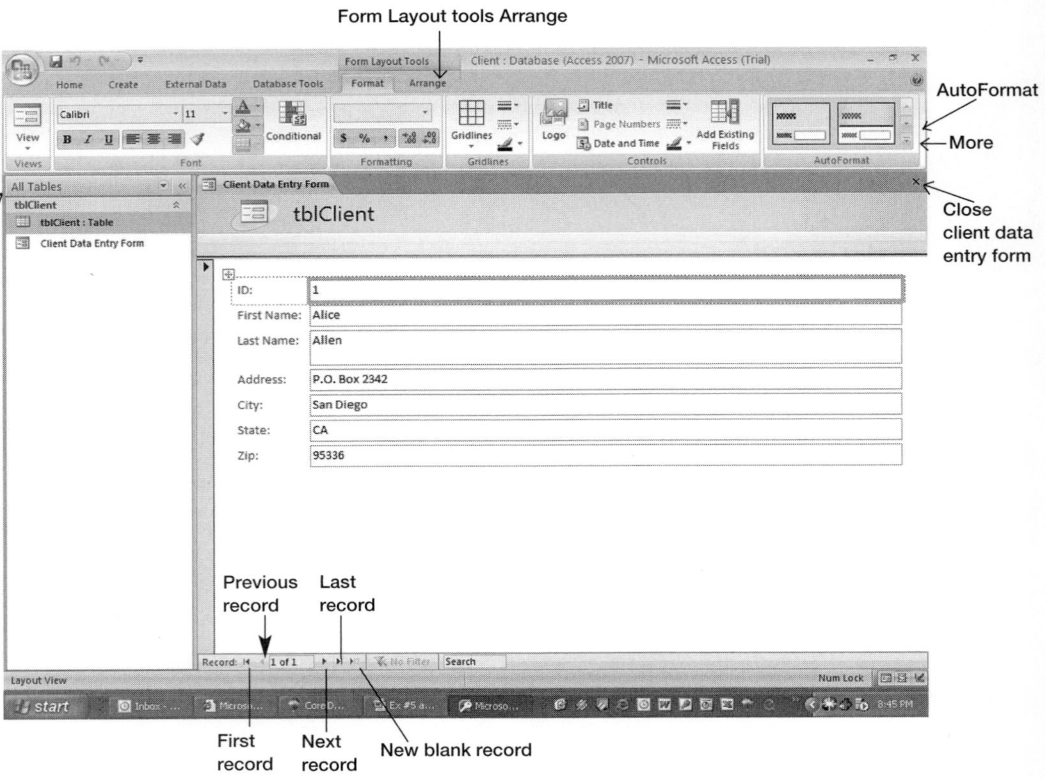

Form Layout tools Arrange
AutoFormat
More
Close client data entry form
All Tables in the Navigation Pane
Previous record
Last record
First record
Next record
New blank record

options for your form. You can click on the More icon in the AutoFormat group to see all of the options at one time (see Access 2007 Exhibit 5). ***Point and click on one of the AutoFormat options that you like.***

8. ***Point and click on the Save icon (it looks like a floppy disk) on the Quick Access Toolbar to save your form.*** In the Save As window, under Form Name, type **Client Data Entry Form** and then ***click OK.***

9. ***Click "All Tables" in the Navigation Pane (see Access 2007 Exhibit 5) and then, under "Navigate to Category," click "Object Type."*** Notice on the Navigation Pane that you can now see "tblClient" under Tables and "Client Data Entry Form" under Forms. Any time you add new objects to your database they will be shown in the Navigation Pane.

10. Notice that the first record you entered is now displayed (Allen, Alice).

11. Access placed the fields in the data entry form in the same way they were entered in the table. In this instance, Last Name is before First Name in the form. It would be more logical and easier for first name to be first. This is easy to correct.

12. ***Click anywhere in the First Name field of your form, then drag it (by holding the left mouse button) to just above the Last Name field and let go of the mouse button.*** The First Name field should now be shown above the Last Name field. While this corrected the physical layout on the screen, the tab order (where the pointer moves when you press the **[TAB]** key to go to the next field) must also be checked to make sure it changed as well.

13. ***Point and click on the "Form Layout Tools – Arrange" ribbon tab (see Access 2007 Exhibit 5). Then, point and click on Tab Order in the Control Layout Group. In the Tab Order window, make sure First Name is above Last Name.***

If it is, proceed to the next step. If it is not, ***point and click just to the left of First Name in the Tab Order window to select the First Name row, and then drag the line to just above the Last Name.***

14. ***Click OK to close the Tab Order window.***

15. To make the changes active, you need to save the form, exit the form, and then reopen the form. ***Click the Save icon on the Quick Access Toolbar. Then, click the Close Client Data Entry Form icon (the black X) to the right of the title "tblclient" (see Access 2007 Exhibit 5). Next, double-click the Client Data Entry Form (under Forms on the Navigation Pane) to reopen the form.***

16. Press the **[TAB]** key three times. Notice that the tab order is correct (ID, then First Name, then Last Name). (*Note*: If the order is not correct, you can right-click on Client Data Entry Form under Forms on the Navigation Pane, and click Layout view. Then you can click the Form Layout Tools—Arrange tab to once again readjust the tab order, and then save, exit, and reopen the Client Data Entry Form).

17. Press the **[TAB]** key four times, which will take you to the next record (Record 2). In addition, you can go to the next record or the previous record by ***clicking on the Greater Than and Less Than icons at the bottom of the page***, or by pressing the **[PAGE UP]** or **[PAGE DOWN]** keys on the keyboard (see Access 2007 Exhibit 5).

18. Enter the following records into the database. You can go between fields by pressing the **[TAB]** or **[SHIFT]+[TAB]** keys, or by ***clicking with the mouse.*** When you are on the last field you can go to the next record by pressing **[TAB].**

Record 2	
First Name	**Harriet**
Last Name	**Winslow**
Address	**89404 Humboldt**
City	**Las Vegas**
State	**NV**
Zip	**78524**

Record 3	
First Name	**Dan**
Last Name	**Ross**
Address	**23332 Westide Road**
City	**Marina Bay**
State	**CA**
Zip	**93442**

Record 4	
First Name	**Jennifer**
Last Name	**Kitchen**
Address	**2342 45th St. NW**
City	**San Diego**
State	**CA**
Zip	**95334**

Record 5	
First Name	**Donald**
Last Name	**Johnson**
Address	**32455 Coastal**
City	**Miami**
State	**FL**
Zip	**65773**

18. When you have finished entering all of the data, ***click the Save icon on the Quick Access Toolbar.***

19. ***Click the Close Client Data Entry Form icon (see Access 2007 Exhibit 5).***

20. ***Double-click tblClient under Tables on the Navigation Pane.***

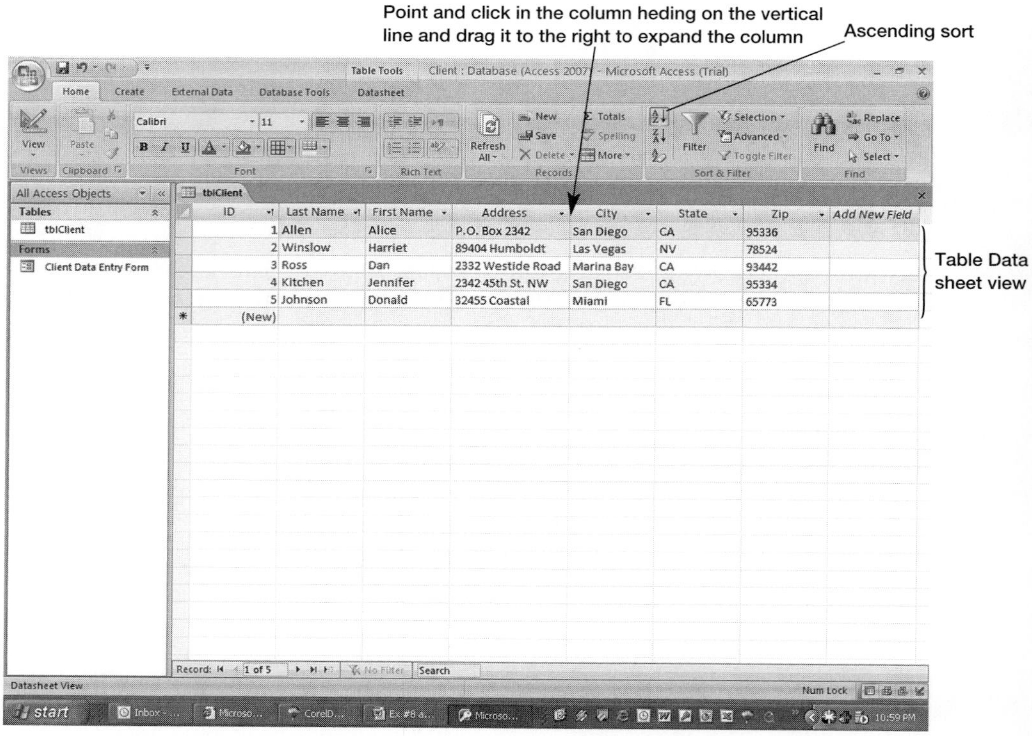

Point and click in the column heding on the vertical line and drag it to the right to expand the column

Ascending sort

Table Data sheet view

Access 2007 Exhibit 6
Datasheet View of the Table
Microsoft product screen shot reprinted with permission from Microsoft Corporation.

21. The Datasheet view of your table is now displayed (see Access 2007 Exhibit 6). You should now see all of your data displayed horizontally across the screen. *Note*: If you cannot see all of the data in a field, just point and click in the column heading on the vertical line that separates each field and drag it to the right to make the field larger (see Access 2007 Exhibit 6).

22. ***Click the Office Button, then click Print, and then click OK to print the document.***

23. ***Click the Save icon on the Quick Access Toolbar.***

24. ***Click the Office Button and then click Exit Access to exit the program.***

This concludes Lesson 2.

Lesson 3: Querying the Database

In this lesson, you will learn how to use the Ascending Sort icon on the toolbar, create a query that searches and sorts the database, modify a query, use a primary and secondary sort option, run a query, and print a query using the database you created in Lessons 1 and 2.

1. Open Windows. Then, ***double-click the Microsoft Office Access 2007 icon on the desktop*** to open Access 2007 for Windows. Alternatively, ***click the Start button, point to Programs or All Programs, and then click the Microsoft Access 2007 icon (or point to Microsoft Office and then click on Microsoft Office Access 2007).***

2. ***Click the Office Button (see Access 2007 Exhibit 1). Then, under "Recent Documents," click name of the client file you created in Lessons 1 and 2 (Client.accdb).***

3. If a security warning (for example, "Security Warning: Certain content in the database has been disabled") is displayed just under the ribbon, ***click Options next to the security warning. Then, in the Microsoft Office Security Options window, click Enable This Content and then click OK.*** There is no security problem, because you know the content came from a trustworthy source, as you are the one who created the file.

4. Notice that the "tblClient:Table" file you created in Lesson 1 and the Client Data Entry Form you created in Lesson 2 are listed on the Navigation Pane.

5. ***Double-click on "tblClient" under Tables in the Navigation Pane.***

6. You should now see your data displayed in the Datasheet view.

7. Notice that the data is not sorted. To quickly and easily sort the data, ***point and click on any record in the Last Name field and then, on the Home ribbon tab, click the Sort Ascending icon in the Sort & Filter group. (The icon looks like the letter "A" on top of the letter "Z" with a down arrow next to them—see Access 2007 Exhibit 6).*** *Note:* Point to any icon for a second and the name of the icon will be displayed. Your records should now be sorted alphabetically by last name.

8. ***Click the Save icon on the Quick Access Toolbar.***

9. ***Click the Close tblClient icon (the black "X").***

10. ***Click the Create ribbon tab, and then click Query Wizard in the Other group.***

11. ***In the New Query window, the Simple Query Wizard selection should be highlighted, so click OK.***

12. You should now have the Simple Query Wizard window on your screen (see Access 2007 Exhibit 7). ***Point and click ">>" (two "greater than" signs).*** This will select all of the fields for the query (see Access 2007 Exhibit 7).

13. ***Click on "Next."***

14. You will then be asked "What title do you want for your query?" Type **San Diego Query**. ***Then, click "Modify the query design," and then click on Finish.***

15. The query is then displayed on your screen (in Query Design view). You will now make the modifications shown in Access 2007 Exhibit 8. You will use the Query Design view mode to make the revisions. Notice that each column shows one of the fields in the table.

Access 2007 Exhibit 7
Creating a Query with the Query Wizard
Microsoft product screen shot reprinted with permission from Microsoft Corporation.

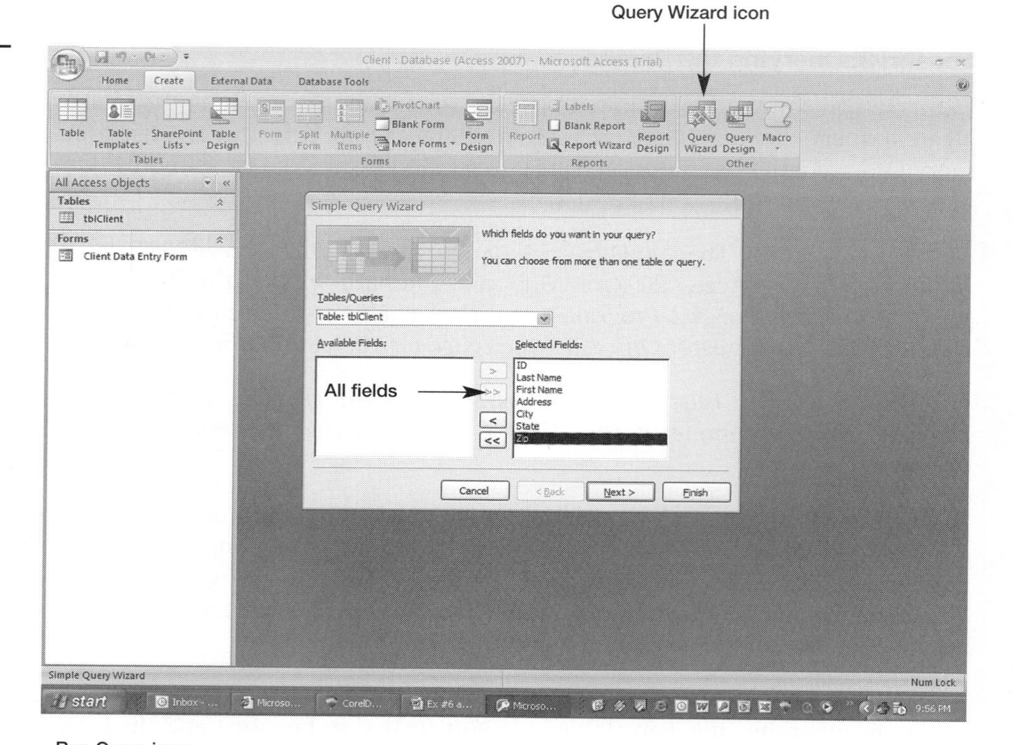

Access 2007 Exhibit 8
Modifying a Query in Design View
Microsoft product screen shot reprinted with permission from Microsoft Corporation.

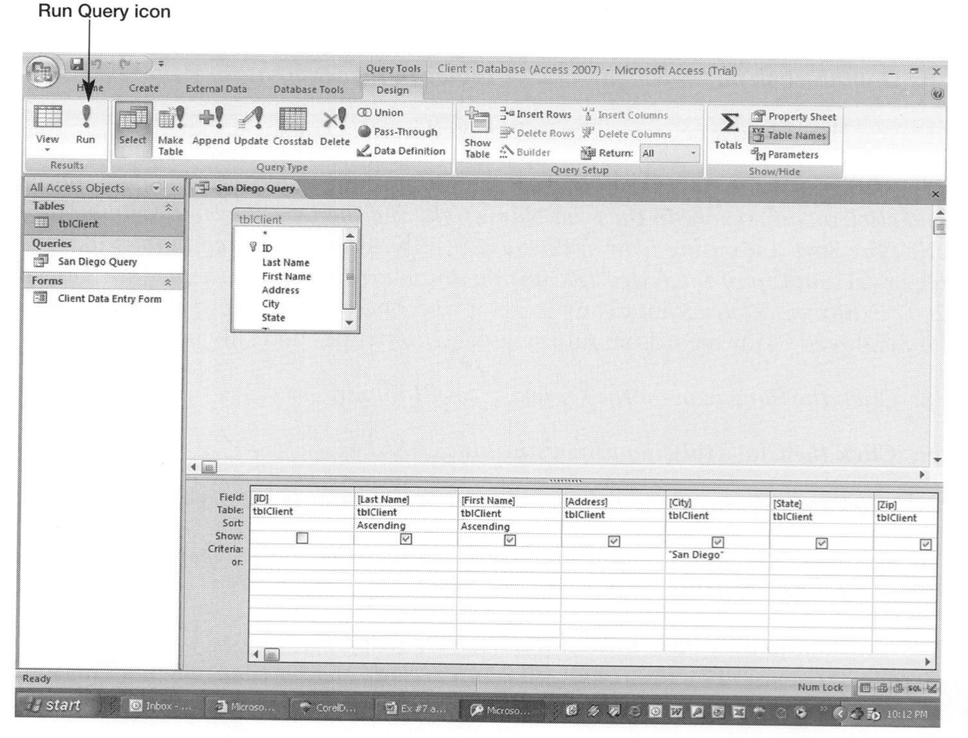

16. ***Point and click the Show row under the ID column (the first column).*** There should now be **an empty box (no check mark).** This is because we do not want this to show on our query (see Access 2007 Exhibit 8).

17. ***Point and click the Sort row under the Last Name column. Now, click the down arrow button and click Ascending*** (see Access 2007 Exhibit 8). This tells Access that the primary sort for the database will be on the Last Name field.

18. ***Point and click the Sort row under the First Name column. Now, click the down arrow button and click Ascending*** (see Access 2007 Exhibit 8). This tells Access that the secondary sort for the database will be on the First Name field. This is necessary because if we had two clients with the same last name, we would then want Access to sort the data based on the client's first name.

19. ***Point and click the Criteria row under City.*** Type **"San Diego"** (*Note: You must type the quotation marks*—see Access 2007 Exhibit 8).

20. This tells Access to select only those clients that have "San Diego" entered in the City field.

21. ***Click the Save icon on the Quick Access Toolbar.*** This will save the query.

22. ***Click the Run command on the toolbar (the icon that looks like a red exclamation mark).*** This will run the query.

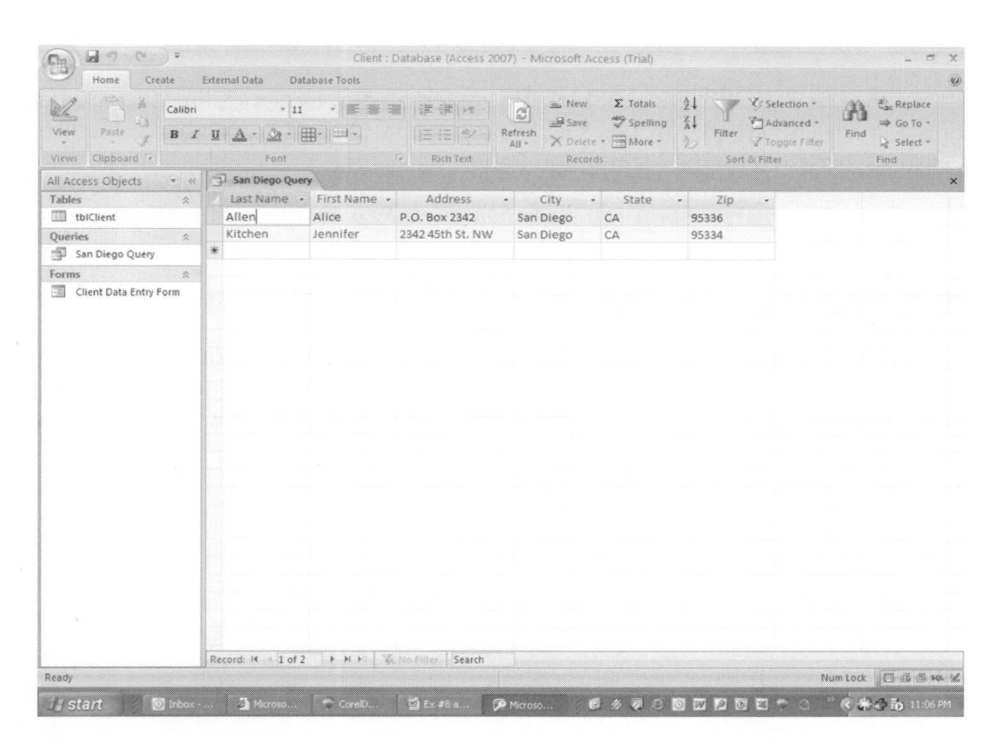

Access 2007 Exhibit 9
Results of the San Diego Query
Microsoft product screen shot reprinted with permission from Microsoft Corporation.

23. Two records should now be displayed on your screen, Alice Allen and Jennifer Kitchen (see Access 2007 Exhibit 9).

24. Click the Office Button, then Print, and then click OK to print the query results.

25. ***Click the Save icon on the Quick Access Toolbar.***

26. ***Click "Close San Diego Query" (the black "X").***

27. ***Click the Office Button and then click Exit Access to exit the program.***

This concludes Lesson 3.

Lesson 4: Creating a Report

In this lesson you will create and print a report using the database you created in Lessons 1–3.

1. Open Windows. Then, ***double-click the Microsoft Office Access 2007 icon on the desktop*** to open Access 2007 for Windows. Alternatively, ***click the Start button, point to Programs or All Programs, and then click the Microsoft Access 2007 icon (or point to Microsoft Office and then click Microsoft Office Access 2007).***

2. ***Point and click the Office Button (see Access 2007 Exhibit 1). Then, under Recent Documents, click on the name of the client file you created in Lessons 1 and 2 (Client.accdb).***

3. If a security warning (for example, "Security Warning: Certain content in the database has been disabled") is displayed just under the ribbon, ***click Options next to the security warning. Then, in the Microsoft Office Security Options window, click Enable this content and then click OK.*** There is no security problem, because you know the content came from a trustworthy source, as you are the one who created the file.

4. Notice that the "tblClient:Table" file you created in Lesson 1, the Client Data Entry Form you created in Lesson 2, and the San Diego Query you created in Lesson 3 are listed on the Navigation Pane.

5. ***Click the Create ribbon tab and then click Report Wizard in the Reports group.***

6. You should now have the Report Wizard window on your screen.

7. Under Tables/Queries in the Report Wizard window, ***click the down arrow icon and make sure that "Table:tbl Client" is selected.*** (*Note*: If "Query: San Diego Sort" is selected, your report will run, but it will only pull the records for clients

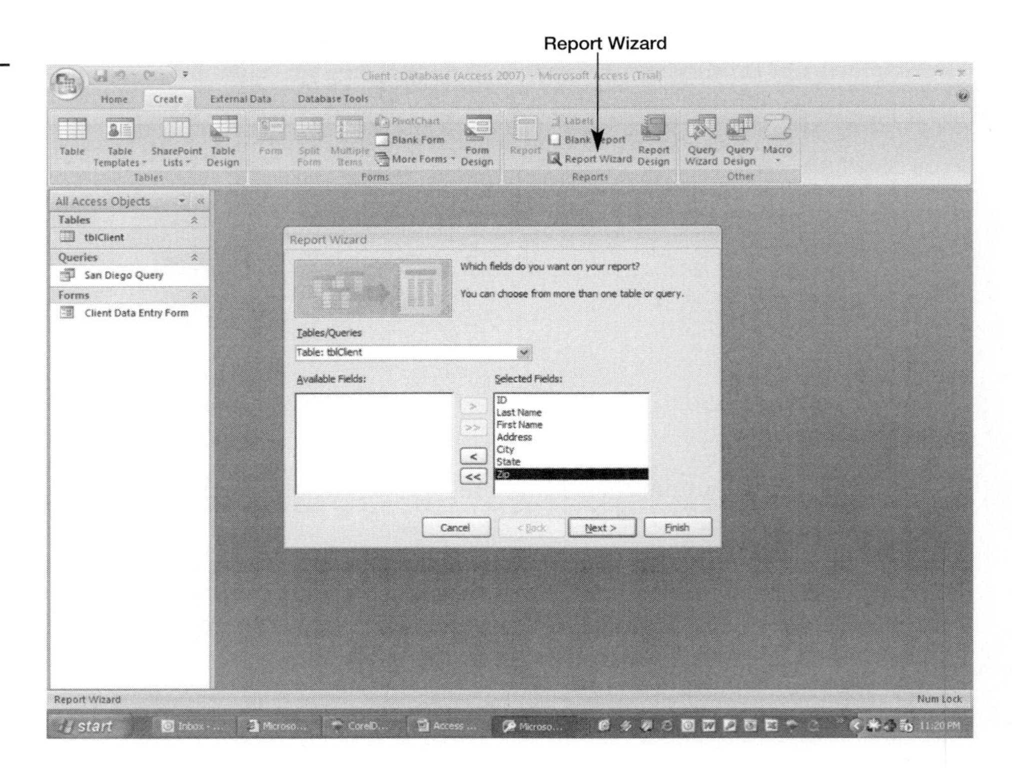

Access 2007 Exhibit 10
Creating a Report with the Report Wizard
Microsoft product screen shot reprinted with permission from Microsoft Corporation.

living in San Diego. This is how users can combine queries and reports. Because we want a list of all clients, make sure the "Table:tbl Client" file is selected).

8. ***Click the ">>" icon (two "greater than" signs).*** This will select all of the fields for our report (see Access 2007 Exhibit 10). ***Then, click Next.***

9. You will then be asked "Do you want to add any grouping levels?" You do not, so ***click Next.***

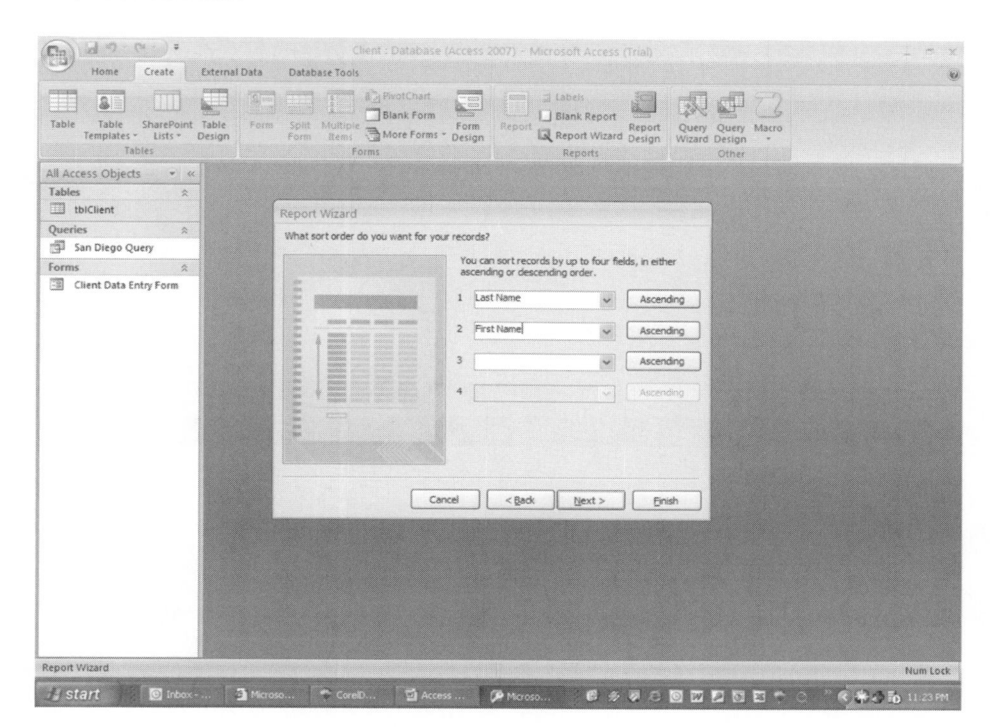

Access 2007 Exhibit 11
Sorting a Report in the Report Wizard
Microsoft product screen shot reprinted with permission from Microsoft Corporation.

10. You will then be asked "What sort order do you want for your report?" ***Click on the down arrow button on the "1" field and then select Last Name*** (see Access 2007 Exhibit 11). Notice that it defaults to an ascending sort.

11. ***Click the down arrow button next to the "2" field, and then select First Name*** (see Access 2007 Exhibit 11).

12. ***Then, select Next.***

13. You will then be asked how you would like to lay out the report. ***Click Tabular and then select Next.***

14. You will then be asked "What style would you like?" ***Click Trek and then select Next.***

15. You are then asked "What title would you like for the report?" Type **Client Report.** You want to preview the report, so ***click Finish.***

16. The report with the five clients is then displayed on your screen (see Access 2007 Exhibit 12).

17. ***Click the Office Button, then click Print, and then click OK to print the document.***

18. ***Click the Save icon on the Quick Access Toolbar.***

Access 2007 Exhibit 12
Print Preview of Client Report

Microsoft product screen shot reprinted with permission from Microsoft Corporation.

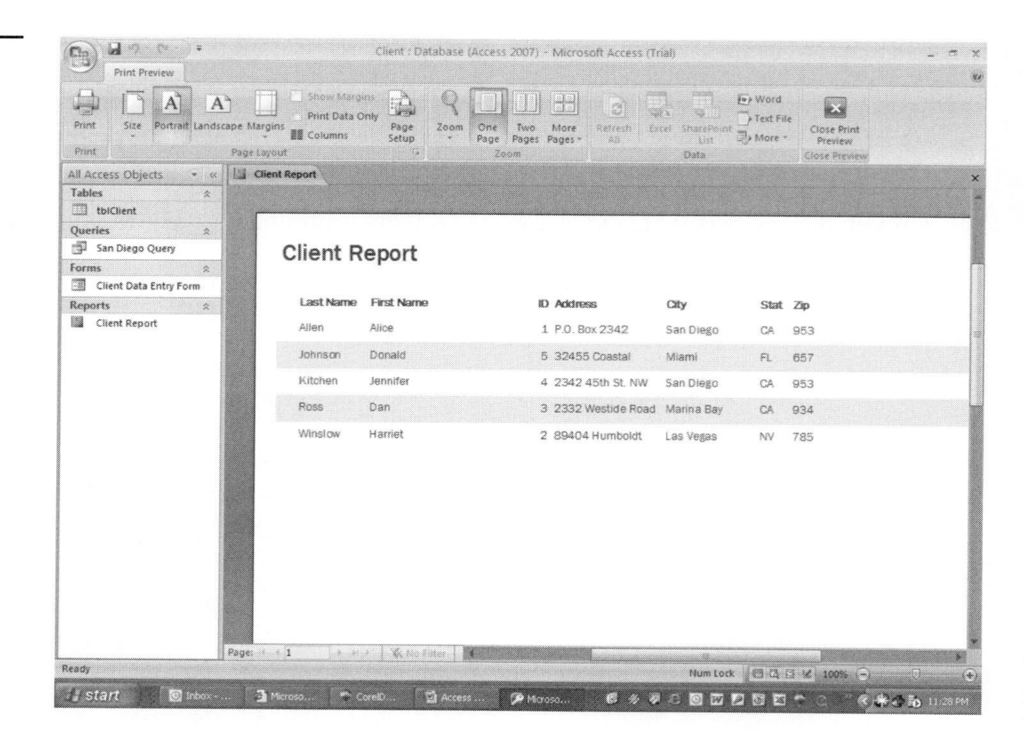

19. *Click the Close icon (the black "X").*

20. *Click the Office Button and then click Exit Access to exit the program.*

This concludes Lesson 4.

Lesson 5: Creating a Litigation Support Database

This lesson shows you how to build a new litigation support database from scratch, including creating a table, entering fields, creating a form, entering data, sorting the database, building a query, and producing a report.

1. Open Windows. Then, ***double-click the Microsoft Office Access 2007 icon on the desktop*** to open Access 2007 for Windows. Alternatively, ***click the Start button, point to Programs or All Programs, and then click the Microsoft Access 2007 icon (or point to Microsoft Office and then click Microsoft Office Access 2007).***

2. ***Click on "Blank Database. . ." just under the New Blank Database section.***

3. Notice that the right side of the screen now says "Blank Database." ***Click under "File Name,"*** use the **[DEL]** key to delete the current title, and type **Litigation Support**. *To save the new database in the default directory, click "Create." To browse to where you would like to save the new database, click the Browse icon (it looks like an open file folder with an arrow) just to the right of the file name. Then, select the directory or folder you would like to save the file to,* type **Litigation support** next to "File name," ***and then click OK. Finally, click Create.***

4. You should now have a blank table on the screen.

5. ***The Table Tools – Datasheet ribbon tab should already be displayed. Click View in the Views group to go to Design view.***

6. The Save As window should now be displayed. Under Table Name, type **Documents** and then *click OK.*

7. Notice that Access has created a field named "ID" and designated it as an AutoNumber data type. Press the **[TAB] key three times** to accept this and move to the second row.

8. Enter the following fields/information into the table:

Field Name	Data Type	Description	Field Size	Required
Doc Name	Text	Name of document	50	Yes
Doc Type	Text	Type of document	50	Yes
Doc Date	Date/Time	Date of document	-	Yes
Doc Author	Text	Author of document	50	Yes
Doc Number	Number	Internal document ID number	-	Yes
Primary Recipient	Text	Who the document was to	50	Yes
Subject Matter	Text	Subject of document	75	Yes
Issue Code	Number	Internal code	-	No
Notes	Memo	Coder's notes about document	-	No
Key Evidence	Yes/No	Is this a key piece of evidence in the case?	-	

8. ***Click Doc Type again in the Field Name column. Then, click the Lookup tab (just to the right of the General tab). Access 2007 Exhibit 13 shows the changes you will be making to the Lookup tab for the Doc Type field.***

9. ***Under the Lookup tab to the right of Display Control, click Text Box. Click the down arrow to the right of Text Box. Click Combo Box.*** Notice that a number of other options are now available on the "Lookup" tab (see Access 2007 Exhibit 13).

10. ***To the right of Row Source Type point and click Table/Query. Click the down arrow to the right of Table/Query. Click Value List.***

11. ***Click the blank box to the right of Row Source*** and type **"Contract," "Invoice," "Report," "Notes," "Bid," "Photo."** *Note: You must type the quotation mark* (see Access 2007 Exhibit 13). When you enter data into the table (either directly or with a form), these choices will appear in a drop-down box for you to select; this is a good way of creating data uniformity and consistency.

12. ***Click in the blank box to the right of Column Widths*** then type **1"** (you must include the quotation mark).

13. ***Click Auto next to List Width*** and use the **[DEL]** key to delete "Auto," and then type **1"** (you must include the quotation mark).

14. ***Click the Save icon on the Quick Access Toolbar.***

15. You are currently in Table Design View. ***The Table Tools – Design ribbon tab should already be displayed. Click View in the Views group to go to Datasheet view.***

Access 2007 Exhibit 13
Creating fields for a Litigation Support Database
Microsoft product screen shot reprinted with permission from Microsoft Corporation.

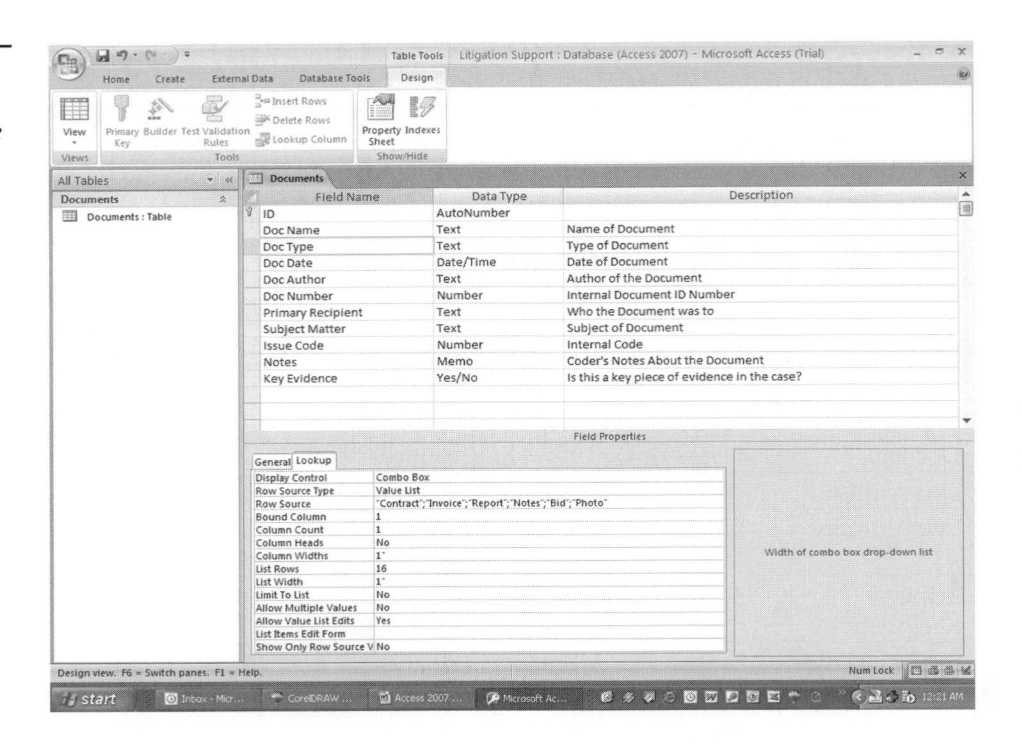

16. ***Click on the Close icon ("X") in the Field List task pane on the right side of the screen.***

17. You should now see the fields you just created displayed horizontally across the screen. To see all of your fields, you will need to use the scroll bar at the bottom of the screen or your cursor keys. You can toggle back and forth between Design view and Datasheet view by clicking on the View icon on the Home ribbon tab.

18. ***Click the Save icon on the Quick Access Toolbar.***

19. ***Click the Close Documents icon (e.g., the black "X").***

20. You are now ready to create a data entry form for entering data into the table. You must first ***click Documents:Table under All Tables and under Documents so that Access knows the table with which the new form will be associated.***

21. ***Click the Create ribbon tab, and then click Form in the Forms group.***

22. The form should now be displayed on your screen. Your screen should look similar to Access 2007 Exhibit 14. The default form is fine, and no modifications are necessary. If you would like to change the colors of the form, do so by selecting one of the AutoFormats on the ribbon.

23. ***Click the Save icon on the Quick Access Toolbar.*** The Save As window should now be displayed. Under Form Name, type **Doc Data Entry Form Smith vs EZ Pest Control** and then ***click OK.*** You are currently in Layout view. To switch to Form view so you can enter data into the table/form, ***click down arrow under the View icon on the ribbon (the Form Layout Tools – Format ribbon tab should already be selected), and then click Form View.***

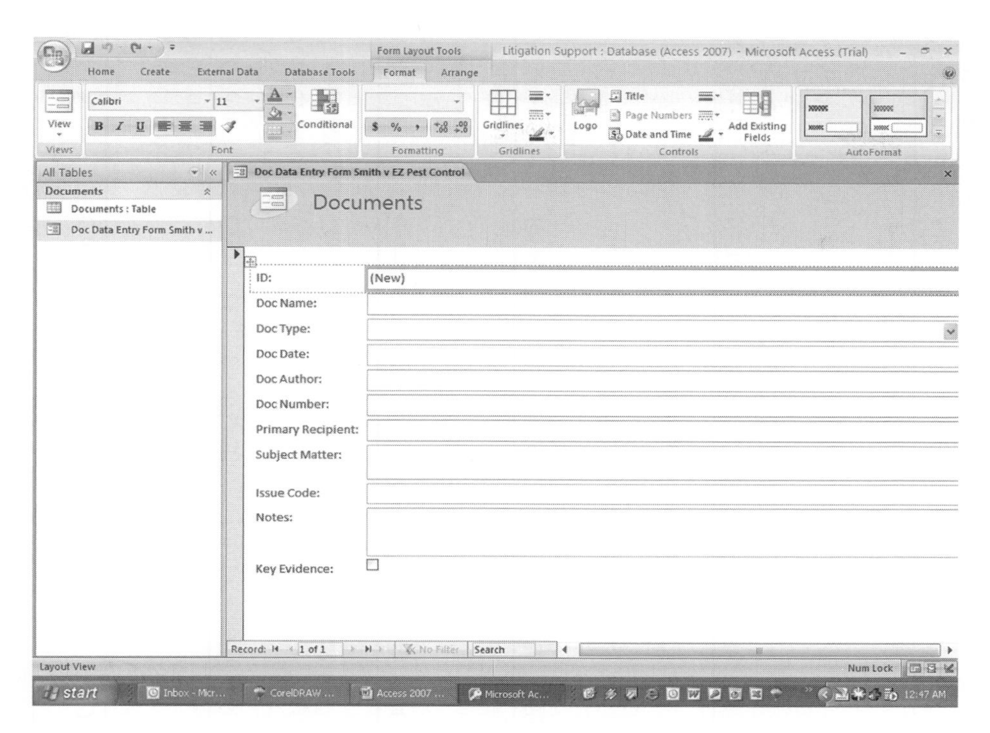

Access 2007 Exhibit 14
Litigation Support Data Entry Form

Microsoft product screen shot reprinted with permission from Microsoft Corporation.

24. Enter the records from the table into the database. You can go between fields by pressing the **[TAB]** or **[SHIFT]+[TAB]** keys, or by pointing and clicking with the mouse. Notice in the Doc Type field that there is a drop-down menu with choices you can select. Because it is a "combo box," you can also enter text into the field, but for this exercise, we will just select entries from the drop-down menu. Notice also in the Key Evidence field that if the document is a key piece of evidence, you just need to click in the box and a check mark will appear. When you are at the last field you can go to the next record by pressing **[TAB]**. You can also go between records by pressing the **[PAGE UP]** or **[PAGE DOWN]** keys or by pointing and clicking on the "greater than" and "less than" symbols at the bottom of the page.

25. When you have finished entering all of the data, ***click the Save icon on the Quick Access Toolbar.***

26. ***Click the "Close Doc Data Entry Form Smith v EZ Pest Control" (the black "X").***

27. ***Click All Tables on the Navigation Pane and click Object Type.*** You can now see the "Documents" table under Tables and "Doc Data Entry Form Smith v . . ." ***under Forms.***

28. ***Double-click Documents under Tables in the Navigation Pane.***

29. You should now see your fields displayed horizontally across the screen (although, due to the length of the entries, you may not be able to see all of the data). Use the scroll bar at the bottom of the screen to scroll left and right to see all of the fields (see Access 2007 Exhibit 15).

30. ***Click on the Save icon on the Quick Access Toolbar.***

Doc Name	Doc Type	Doc Date	Doc Author	Doc No	Primary Recipient	Subject Matter	Issue Code	Notes	Key Evidence
HUD Settlement Statement	Contract	06/01/2007	Judy Smith, Bill Lee	501	Judy Smith	Sale of house	1	Includes pest inspection cost of $300	Yes
EZ Pest Agreement for Termite Inspection	Contract	05/01/2007	John Lincoln, EZ Pest	502	Judy Smith	Agreement to inspect the house for termites	1	The contract states that EZ Pest will conduct a thorough examination of the property.	Yes
EZ Pest Invoice for Pest Inspection	Invoice	05/15/2007	John Lincoln, EZ Pest	503	Judy Smith	Invoice for pest inspection	1	Shows total due $300 and that it was paid on 5/20/2007	No
EZ Pest Inspection Report	Report	05/15/2007	John Lincoln, EZ Pest	504	Judy Smith	Inspection Report	2	The report states "No visible evidence of infestation from wood destroying insects was observed." Signed by John Lincoln.	Yes
EZ Pest Inspection Report Notes	Notes	05/07/2007	John Lincoln, EZ Pest	505	John Lincoln	Notes of John Lincoln taken to assist in preparation of Inspection Report	2	John Lincoln's notes do not show that he actually checked the east side of the house where termites were later found.	Yes
Bid from Stewart Construction	Bid	11/01/2007	Tim Stewart	506	Judy Smith	Bid to rebuild the east side where the termites destroyed house	3	Bid of $50,000 to repair the termite damage on the east side.	Yes
Photograph of east side of house	Photo	10/01/2007	Judy Smith	507	Judy Smith	Photograph of house	3	Photograph showing east side of house behind vinyl siding showing frame of house nearly eaten through.	Yes

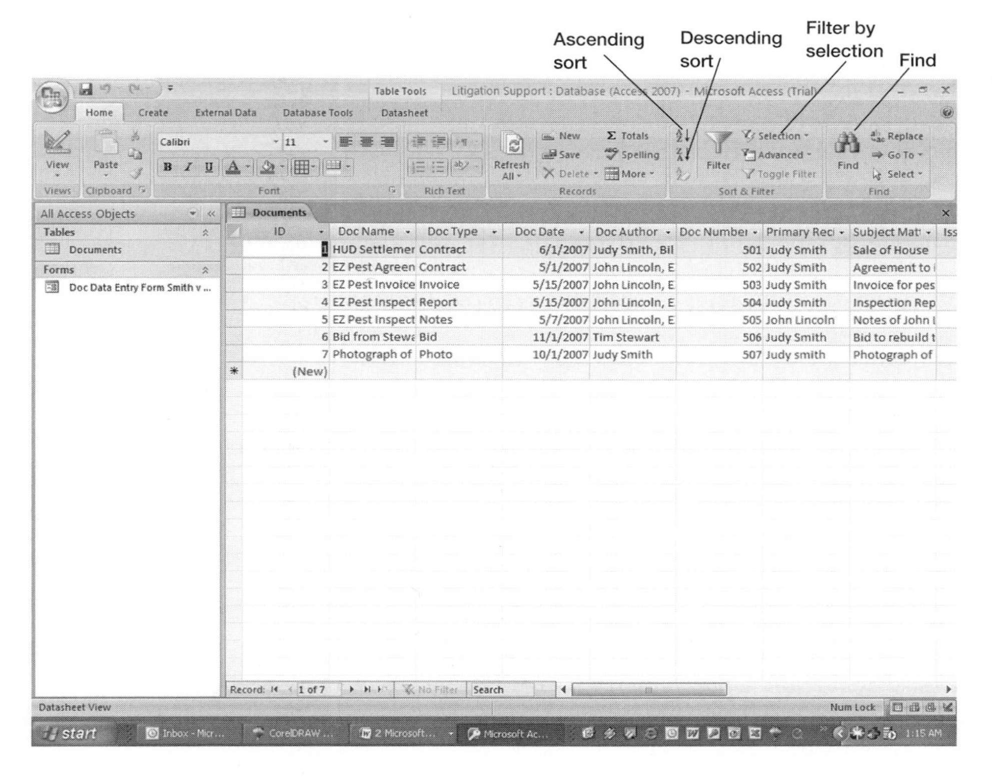

Access 2007 Exhibit 15
Datasheet View of Data in the Documents Table

Microsoft product screen shot reprinted with permission from Microsoft Corporation.

31. You will next see some different views of the data (without damaging the integrity of the data).

32. ***Click any record in the Doc Name field. Then, on the Home ribbon tab, click the Sort Ascending icon in the Sort & Filter group (it looks like the letter "A" on top of the letter "Z" with a down arrow next to them).*** (*Note:* Point to any icon on the toolbar for a second and the name of the icon will be displayed.) Your records should now be sorted alphabetically by document name.

33. ***Click any record in the Doc Date field and then click the Sort Descending icon on the toolbar.*** The documents are now sorted in date order, with the most recent first.

34. ***Click any record in the Subject Matter field, and then click the Find icon in the Find group on the Home ribbon tab (it looks like binoculars).*** The Find and Replace window should be displayed. Next to "Find What," type **vinyl siding** and then, next to "Look In," ***click the down arrow and select Documents.*** (This will allow you to search all fields in the Document table, not just the Subject Matter field.) ***Then, next to Match, click the down arrow, click Any Part of Field, and then click Find Next.*** Notice that the pointer went to document 507 and found where "vinyl siding" was entered. ***Click Cancel to make the Find and Replace window disappear.***

35. ***Click Document 502 and click in the Primary Recipient field.*** Notice that "Judy Smith" is in the field. ***Click the Filter by Selection icon in the Sort & Filter group in the Home ribbon tab (it looks like a silver funnel with a lightning bolt***—see Access 2007 Exhibit 15), ***then click Equals "Judy Smith."*** Notice that only documents with Judy Smith as the primary recipient are left. (The other documents are still in the database; Access just temporarily removed them from the current view.)

36. To bring back all of the documents, remove the filter by ***clicking the Toggle Filter icon in the Sort & Filter group on the Home ribbon tab.*** Notice that all of the documents are back.

37. To put the documents back in the order in which you entered them, simply ***click in the Doc Number field and click the Sort Ascending icon.***

38. ***Click the Save icon on the Quick Access Toolbar.***

39. ***Click the Close Documents icon (the black "X").***

40. You will now run a query to select only documents that have Issue Code 2 in them, and where Judy Smith was the recipient. The Documents table under Tables on the Navigation Pane should still be selected. ***Click the Create ribbon tab, then click Query Wizard in the Other group.***

41. You should now have the New Query window displayed on your screen. Simple Query Wizard should be selected ***so click OK.***

42. You should now have the Simple Query Wizard window on your screen. ***Click ">>" (two "greater than" signs).*** This will select all of the fields for your query.

43. ***Click Next.***

44. You will then be asked "Would you like a detail or a summary query?" ***Click Detail (shows every field of every record). Click Next.***

45. You will then be asked "What title do you want for your query?" Type **qry Smith Issue Code 2**. ***Then, click Modify the query design and click Finish.***

46. The query is displayed on your screen. Notice that each column shows one of the fields in the table.

47. ***Click in the Show row in the ID column (the first column).*** There should now be an empty box (no check mark). This is because we do not want this to show on our query.

48. ***Click in the Sort row under "Doc Number." Now, click the down arrow and click Ascending.*** This tells Access that the primary sort for the database will be on this field.

49. ***Click in the Criteria row under "Issue Code"*** then type **2.** (*Note*: *Do not* type anything else in the criteria for this field—just type the number 2.)

50. ***Then, click in the Criteria row under Primary Recipient*** and type "**Judy Smith.**" (*Note:* You *must* type the quotes for this field.) This tells Access to select only those records that meet both of these selection/search criteria.

51. ***Click the Run icon in the Results group on the Query Tools – Design ribbon tab (the icon that looks like a red exclamation mark).*** This will run the query. Document 504 should be displayed.

52. ***Click the Save icon on the Quick Access Toolbar.***

53. ***Click the down arrow just under the View icon in the Views group on the Home ribbon tab and then select Design view. Click back and forth between***

Design view and Datasheet view. Notice that you can make changes to the query in Design view, and then run the query and correct any problems that you may have had in your query.

54. In Datasheet view, ***click the Office Button, and then click Print and OK.*** Notice that the whole record did not print.

55. ***Click the Save icon on the Quick Access Toolbar.***

56. ***Click the "Close Smith Issue Code 2 Query" icon (the black "X").***

57. ***Click the Create ribbon tab, and then click Report Wizard.*** You should now have the Report Wizard window on your screen.

58. ***Click under Tables/Queries on the down arrow button and select "Query: Smith Issue Code 2 Query."***

59. ***Click the ">>" icon (two "greater than" signs).*** This will select all of the fields for our report. ***Then, click "Next."***

60. You will then be asked "Do you want to add any grouping levels?" ***Click "Next."***

61. You will then be asked "What sort order do you want for your report?" ***Click "Next."***

62. You will then be asked "How would you like to lay out your report?" ***Click Justified, then click Landscape, and then select Next.***

63. You will then be asked "What style would you like?" ***Click "Civic" and then select Next.***

64. You are then asked "What title would you like for the report?" Type **Judy Smith Primary Recipient—Issue Code 2 Report.**

65. ***Then, click Finish.***

66. The report should now be displayed on your screen.

67. ***Click the Office Button, then click Print, and then click OK to print the document.***

68. ***Click the Save icon on the Quick Access Toolbar.***

69. ***Click the "Close Judy Smith Primary Recipient—Issue Code 2 Report" icon (the black "X").***

70. ***Click the Office Button and then click Exit Access to exit the program.***

This concludes Lesson 5.

Lesson 6: Working With a Comprehensive Law Office Relational Database

In this lesson, you will work with a true relational database, including working with multiple tables, assigning relationships among tables, and writing queries and reports that access data from multiple tables. This lesson assumes that you have read Chapter 5 – Database Management Systems, and that you have completed Lessons 1–5. To begin, you will open the Access Lesson 6 Law Firm Database from Disk1, and work with a database with four related tables in it.

1. Open Windows. Then, ***double-click the Microsoft Office Access 2007 icon on the desktop*** to open Access 2007 for Windows. Alternatively, ***click the Start button, point to Programs or All Programs, and then click the Microsoft Access 2007 icon (or point to Microsoft Office and then click Microsoft Office Access 2007).***

2. The first thing you will do is to open the "Lesson 6 Law Firm Database" file from Disk 1 supplied with this text. Ensure that the disk is inserted in the disk drive, point and click on File on the Menu Bar, and then point and click on Open. The "Open" window should now be displayed. Point and click on the down arrow to the right of the white box next to "Look in:" and select the drive where Disk 1 is located. Point and double-click on the Database Files folder. Double-click on the "Lesson 6 Law Firm Database" file.

3. At the security warning ("Security Warning: Certain content in the database has been disabled") just under the ribbon, ***click Options next to the security warning. Then, in the Microsoft Office Security Options window, click "Enable this Content" and then click OK.*** There is no security problem, because you know the content comes from a trustworthy source.

4. ***Click "Tables" on the Navigation Pane. Click All Access Objects.*** This will allow you to see all of the objects in the database that have already been created.

5. In this lesson you are working with a true relational law office database. In the previous lessons, you have only worked with databases with one table. Notice that four tables are listed: Case Evidence, Case File, Client, and Opposing Attorney. You will now get an overview of the tables and create a relationship between two tables.

6. ***Click the Database Tools ribbon tab, then click Relationships in the Show/Hide group.***

7. Your screen should now be similar to Access 2007 Exhibit 16, except that there is no relationship between the Case File table and the Case Evidence table.

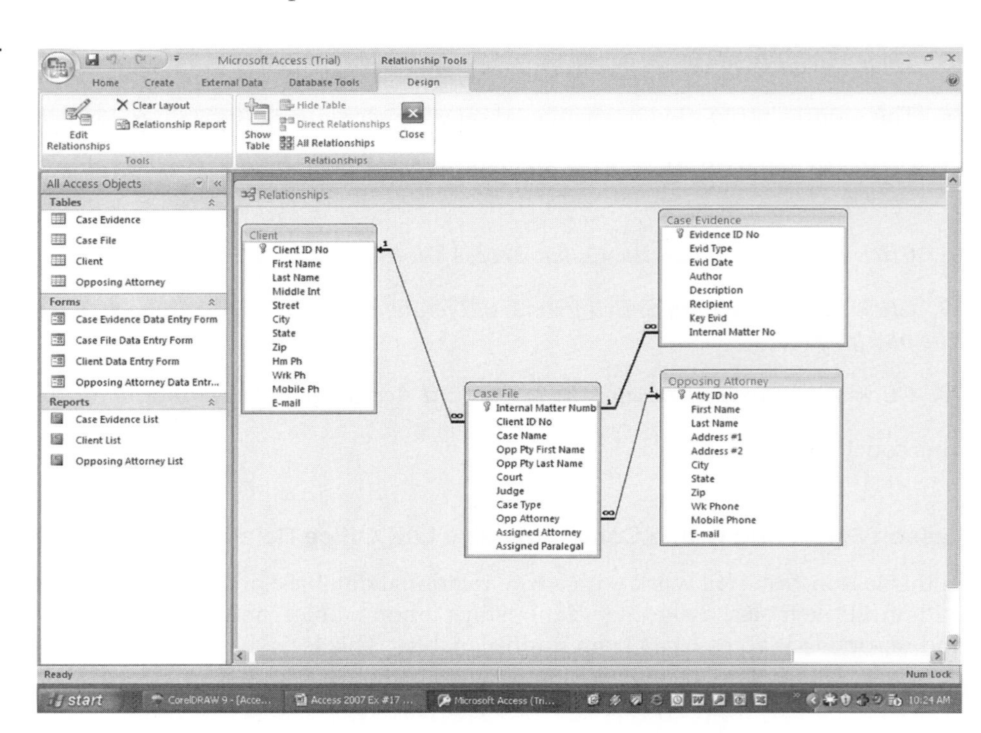

Access 2007 Exhibit 16
Completed Relationships for Access Lesson 6 Law Firm
Microsoft product screen shot reprinted with permission from Microsoft Corporation.

8. Look carefully at the four tables. The subject matter of the Client table is just the client. It includes a client ID number and client contact information only. The Case File table includes broad data about the legal subject matter of the case, including an internal matter number, the case name, court, judge, case type, and assigned attorney and paralegal. The Opposing Attorney table just tracks contact information for opposing counsel on cases. The Case Evidence table tracks specific pieces of evidence in each case. This type of structure, including multiple tables that hold a variety of client- and case-related information, can be found in legal organizations just about anywhere.

9. Each table in a relational database must be connected to another table or the tables will not be able to share information. For example, the Case Evidence table is not connected to any other table. The table can reside in the database and the user can enter information into it, but it will be a stand-alone table. For example, if you wanted to print a report that had the contact information for each client and a listing of all of the case evidence for the client, you would not be able to do so without creating a relationship between the tables. You will now create a one-to-many relationship between the Case File table and the Case Evidence table using the Internal Matter Number field as the conduit.

10. ***Click in the Internal Matter Number field in the Case File table, then drag it to the Internal Matter No field in the Case Evidence table and let go.*** The Edit Relationships window should now be displayed (see Access 2007 Exhibit 17).

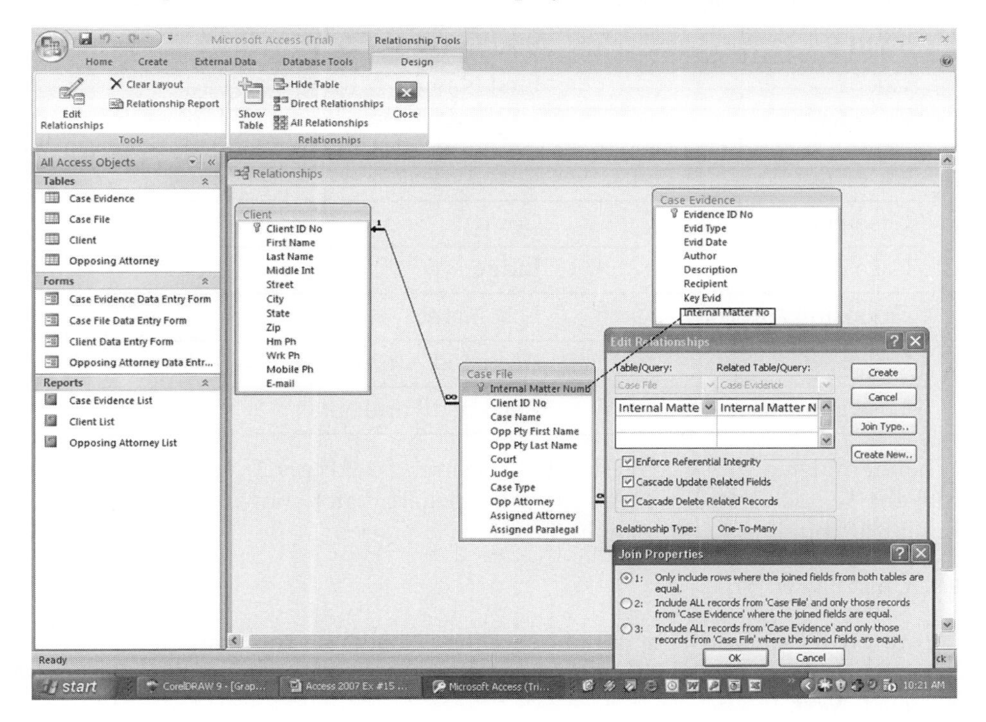

Access 2007 Exhibit 17
The Edit Relationships Window
Microsoft product screen shot reprinted with permission from Microsoft Corporation.

11. In the Edit Relationships window, ***click Enforce Referential Integrity, click Cascade Update Related Fields, then click Cascade Delete Related Records*** (see Access 2007 Exhibit 17). At the bottom of the Edit Relationships window, it should now say "Relationship Type: One-to-Many." That is because each case file can have many pieces of evidence that should be tracked in the Case Evidence table.

12. In the Edit Relationships window, ***click "Join Type..."*** (see Access 2007 Exhibit 17). In the Join Properties window, make sure that option 1, "Only

include rows where the joined fields from both tables are equal," is selected. *Then, click OK in the Join Properties window.*

13. *In the Edit Relationships window, click Create.* Your Relationships window should now look like Access 2007 Exhibit 16.

14. *Click Close on the Relationship Tools—Design ribbon tab (in the Relationships group.)*

15. You will now build a query that pulls information from three of the tables.

16. *Click the Create ribbon tab, and then click Query Wizard in the Other group.*

17. The New Query window should now be displayed. "Simple Query Wizard" should be highlighted, so just *click OK.*

18. The screen should now say "Which fields do you want in your query?" Under Tables/Queries *click the down arrow and select Table: Client.* Notice that now the fields for the Client table are shown under Available Fields. *Click Last Name and then click ">" to add the field under Selected Fields.* You will now build the query by selecting the tables and fields exactly as shown below. This should be done carefully, since you must skip around among the different tables to build the query correctly.

In addition to the Last Name field you have already selected, enter the following:

TABLE	FIELD TO SELECT
Client	First Name
Case File	Case Name
Case File	Case Type
Case File	Court
Case File	Judge
Opposing Attorney	Last Name
Case File	Assigned Attorney
Case File	Assigned Paralegal

When completed, your screen should look similar to Access 2007 Exhibit 18. Note that the last selected field (Assigned Paralegal) is not shown on Access 2007 Exhibit 18, but it is still present in the query.

19. *Click "Next."*

20. You will then be asked "Would you like a detail or a summary query?" The "Detail (Shows every field of every record)" option should already be selected so just *click Next.*

21. You will then be asked "What title do you want for your query?" Type **Case List Query**. *Then, click "Modify the query design" and click Finish.*

22. The query is displayed on your screen in Design view. Notice that each column shows one of the fields and that the table that it is drawn from is shown in the "Table" row (see Access 2007 Exhibit 19).

23. *Click on the Sort row in the first column (Client_Last Name:Las) and then click the down arrow and click Ascending* (see Access 2007 Exhibit 19). This tells Access that the primary sort for the database will be on this field.

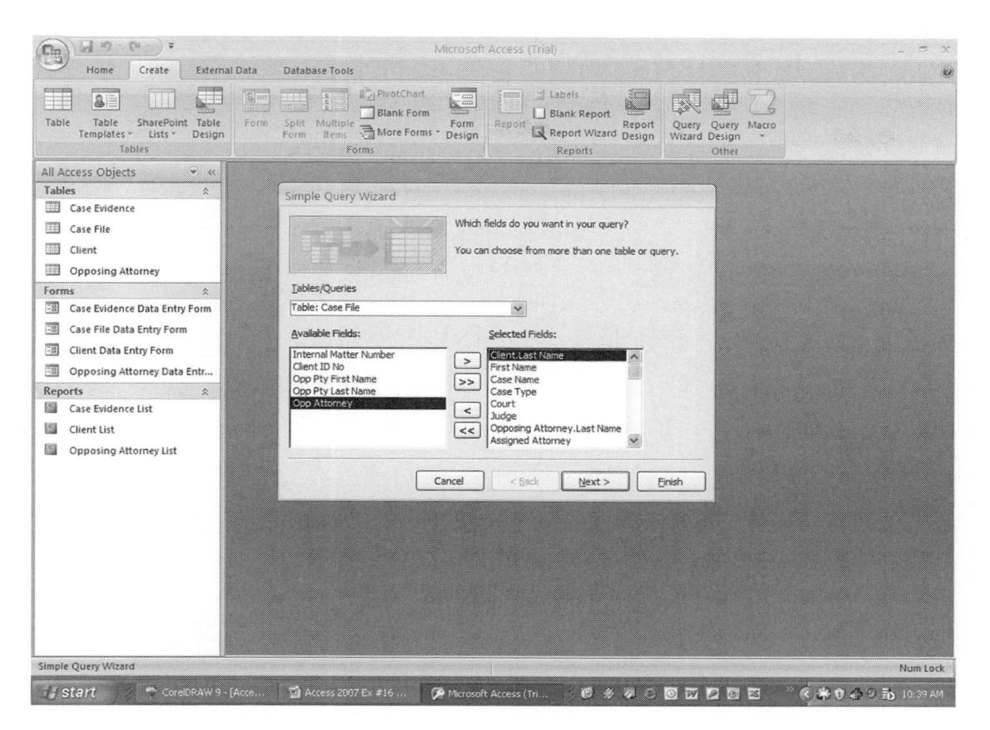

Access 2007 Exhibit 18

Building a Query With Multiple Tables in Query Wizard

Microsoft product screen shot reprinted with permission from Microsoft Corporation.

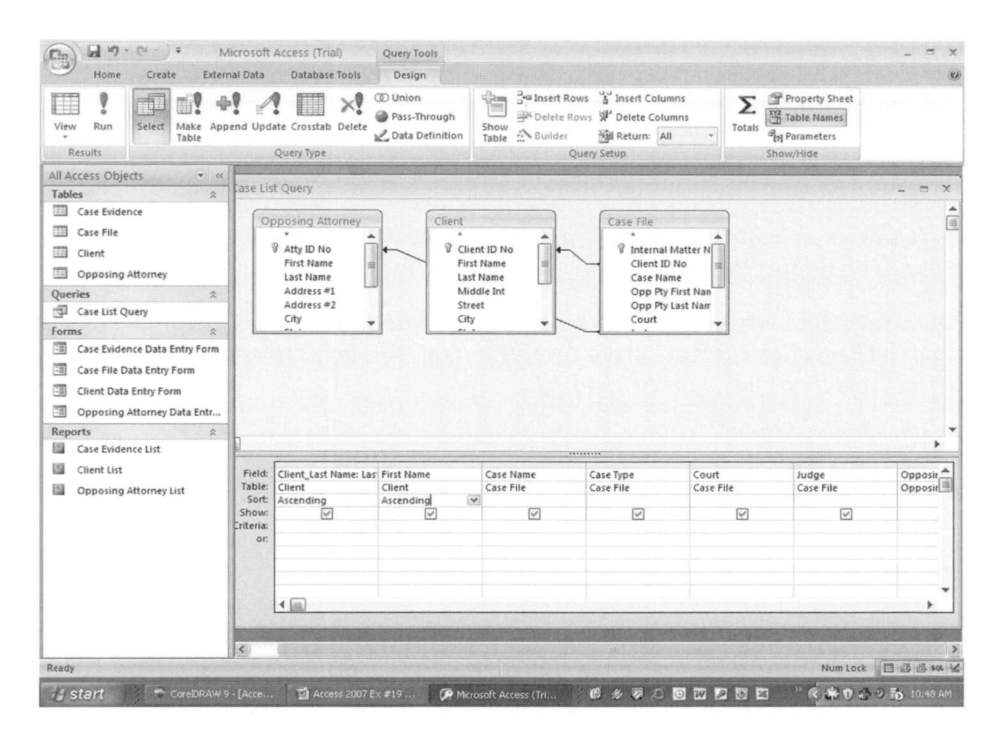

Access 2007 Exhibit 19

Modifying the Case List Query in Query Design View

Microsoft product screen shot reprinted with permission from Microsoft Corporation.

24. ***Click the Sort row in the second column (First Name), and then click the down arrow button and click Ascending*** (see Access 2007 Exhibit 19). This tells Access that the secondary sort for the database will be on this field.

25. ***Click the !Run icon (it looks like a bright red exclamation mark) in the Results group on the Query Tools – Design ribbon tab.*** Your query should look similar to Access 2007 Exhibit 20.

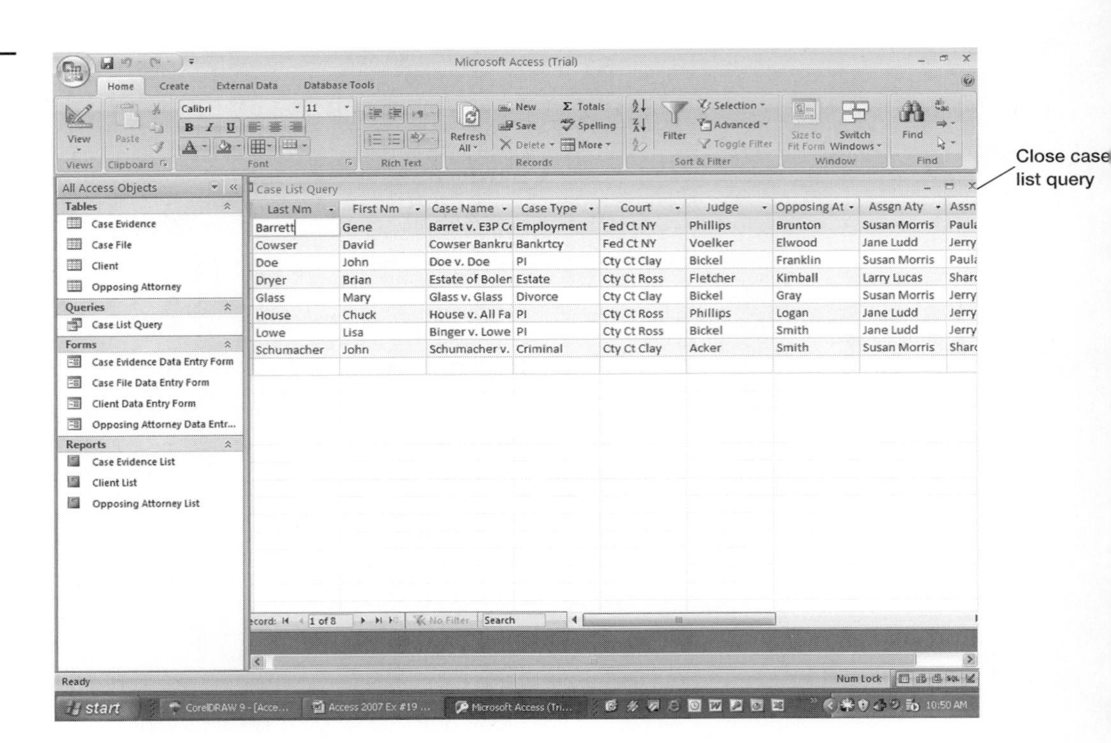

Access 2007 Exhibit 20
Completed Case List Query in Datasheet View
Microsoft product screen shot reprinted with permission from Microsoft Corporation.

26. ***Click the Save icon (it look like a floppy disk) on the Quick Access Toolbar.***

27. ***Click the Close icon for the Case List query*** (see Access 2007 Exhibit 20).

28. You will now build a report that uses the Case List query you just created.

29. ***Click the Create ribbon tab, and then click Report Wizard in the Reports group.*** The Report Wizard window should now be displayed.

30. Under Tables/Queries ***click the down arrow and select Query: Case List Query. Then, click the ">>" (two "greater than" symbols) to add all of the fields in the Case List Query to the report.***

31. ***Click Next.***

32. You will then be asked "How do you want to view your data?" ***Click Next.***

33. You will then be asked "Do you want to add any grouping levels?" ***Click Next.***

34. You will then be asked "What sort order do you want for detail records?" Because the query is already sorting the data, ***click Next.***

35. You are now asked "How would you like to lay out your report?" ***Click Block and then click Landscape under Orientation. Leave the check mark in the "Adjust the field width so all fields fit on a page" option. Then, select Next.***

36. You will then be asked "What style would you like?" ***Click Flow. Then, click Next.***

37. You are then asked "What title would you like for the report?" Type **Case List Report,** leave the "Preview the report" option selected, and ***click Finish.***

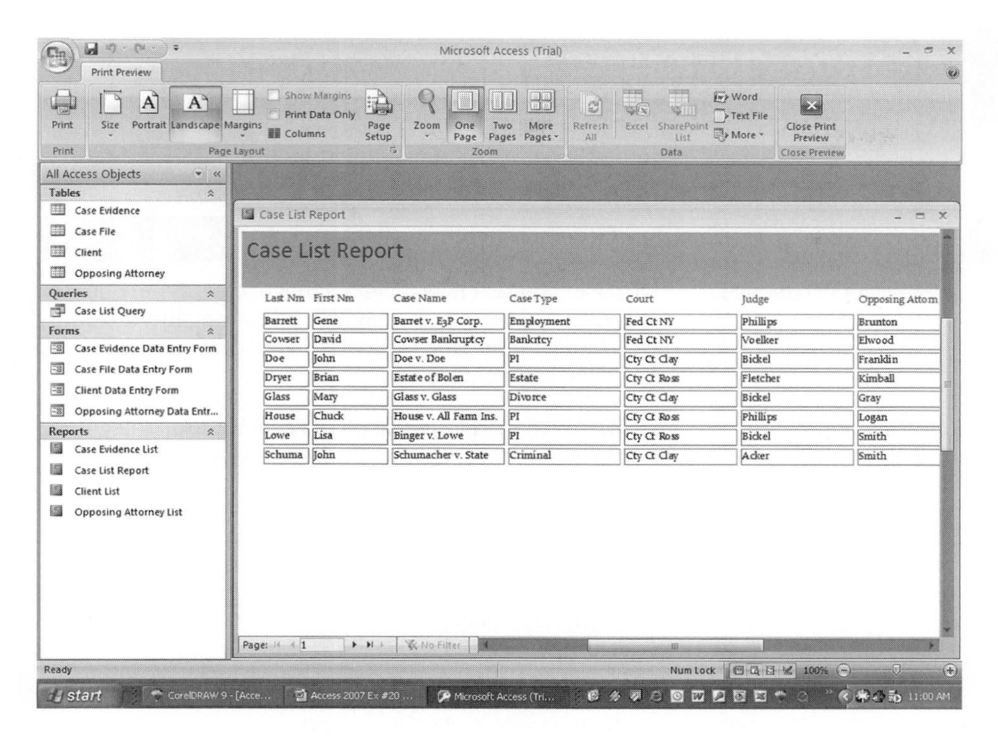

Access 2007 Exhibit 21
Finalized Case List Report
Microsoft product screen shot reprinted with permission from Microsoft Corporation.

38. The report should now be displayed on your screen. It should look similar to Access 2007 Exhibit 21.

39. ***Click the Print icon on the ribbon tab in the Print group. Then, click OK to print the document.***

40. ***Click Close Print Preview on the ribbon tab in the Close Preview group.***

41. ***Click the Save icon on the Quick Access Toolbar.***

42. ***Click the Close icon for the Case List Report (e.g., the black "X").***

43. ***Click the Office Button and then click Exit Access to exit the program.***

This concludes the Access 2007 Hands-On Exercises.

HANDS-ON EXERCISES

MICROSOFT ACCESS 2003 FOR WINDOWS

Basic Lessons

Number	Lesson Title	Concepts Covered
Lesson 1	Creating a Table—Client Database	How to create a new table/database, create and design fields, create a primary key, move between the Table Design view and the Datasheet view, enter a record, and save the database.
Lesson 2	Creating a Form/Entering Data—Client Database	How to create a form using the Form Wizard, enter data in the form, view the Datasheet view of the form, and close a form.
Lesson 3	Querying a Database—Client Database	How to use the Ascending Sort icon on the toolbar, create a query that searches and sorts the database, modify a query, use a primary and secondary sort option, run a query, and print a query.
Intermediate Lessons		
Lesson 4	Creating a Report—Client Database	How to create and print a report.
Lesson 5	Litigation Support Database	How to build a litigation support database that tracks documents in a case, create the fields, enter the data, run helpful sorts and filters to search the data, run a query, run a report, and print a report.
Advanced Lesson		
Lesson 6	Working with a Law Office Relational Database Access Lesson 6 Law Firm Database from Disk1 included with the text	Working with a true relational database, including working with multiple tables, assigning relationships among tables, and writing queries and reports that access data from multiple tables.

GETTING STARTED

Introduction

Throughout these lessons and exercises, information you need to type into the program will be designated in several different ways:

- Keys to be pressed on the keyboard will be designated in brackets, in all caps, and in bold (i.e., press the **[ENTER]** key).
- Movements will be designated in bold and italics (i.e., ***point to File on the menu bar and click the mouse***).
- Words or letters that should be typed will be designated in bold (i.e., type **Training Program**).
- Information that should be displayed on your computer screen is shown in the following style: ***Press ENTER to continue.***

OVERVIEW OF ACCESS 2003

Access 2003 is a relational database management application. Access 2003 Exhibit 1 shows the Access database window. Notice to the left of the database window that a number of icons and names are shown on the Objects bar. These objects are the main database tools used in Access 2003. Using the Tables object, the user creates

the structure of the database, including creating new tables and designing fields, among other things. With the Queries object, the user can create searches and extract data from the tables. Using the Forms object, the user can create forms for easy data entry, and other forms to enter, view, and modify data. Using the Reports object, the user can create finalized reports. Notice in Access 2003 Exhibit 1 that in addition to the database window there is also a menu bar and toolbar. The menu bar and toolbar also provide a number of options and tools for the user. Additional information about Access 2003 will be provided as you complete the exercises. By the end of the exercises, you should have a good understanding of the basics of Access 2003.

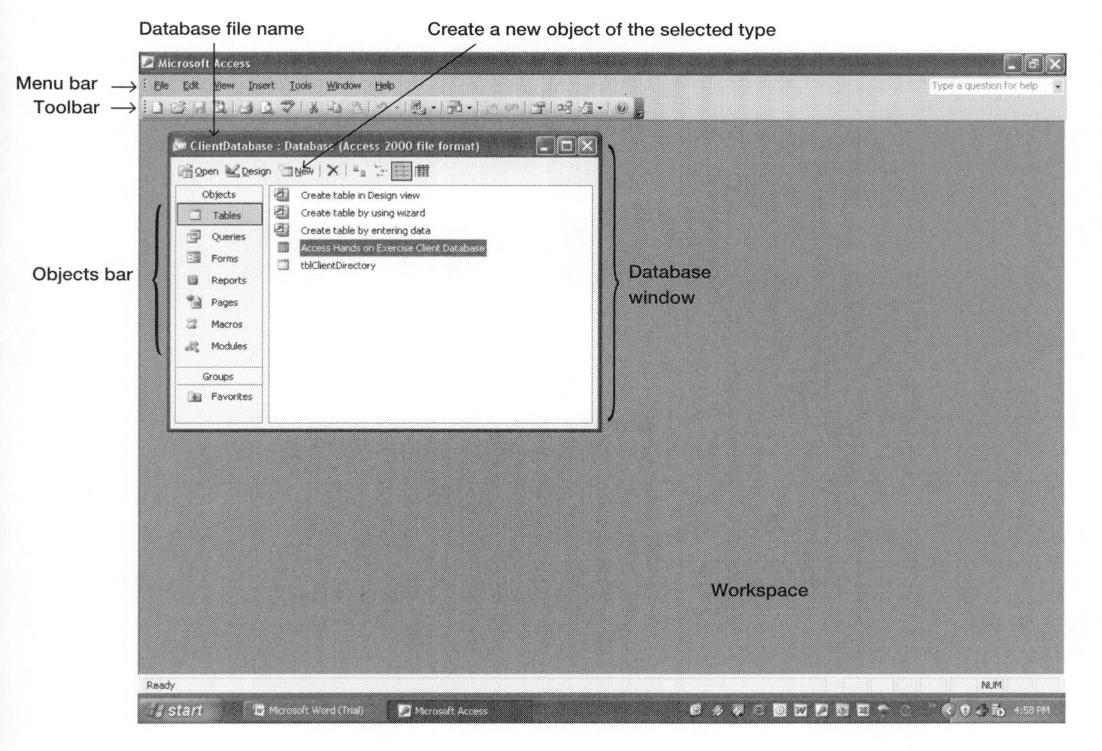

Access 2003 Exhibit 1
Access 2003 Database Window
Microsoft product screen shot reprinted with permission from Microsoft Corporation.

Basic Lessons

LESSON 1: CREATING A TABLE

This lesson shows you how to build the table shown in Access 2003 Exhibit 2. It explains how to create a new table/database, create new fields, create a primary key, move between the Table Design view and the Datasheet view, and save the database. Keep in mind that if you make a mistake in this lesson you may press **[CTRL]+[Z]** to undo what you have done, but note that in some cases this command will not work (e.g., when you delete a record, it is permanently deleted).

1. Open Windows. Then, ***double-click the Access 2003 icon on the desktop*** to open Access 2003 for Windows. Alternatively, ***click the Start button, point to Programs or All Programs, and then click the Microsoft Office Access icon (or point to Microsoft Office, and then click Microsoft Office Access 2003.)***

2. When Access 2003 opens, the Getting Started task pane is displayed on the right side. ***Click "Create a new file. . ." under Open in the Getting Started task pane.*** The New File task pane should now be displayed.

3. ***Click on "Blank database . . ." under New in the New File task pane.***

4. At the File New Database window, next to File Name, type **Client** and then ***click Create*** to save the new database in the default directory.

5. The Client: Database window (similar to Access 2003 Exhibit 1) should now be displayed on your screen. Notice on the left side of the window a list of Objects including Tables, Queries, Forms, Reports, Pages, Macros, and Modules. These Objects are the major tools used to create and manage a database. Notice that Tables is currently selected.

6. ***Double-click Create Table in Design view.***

7. The "Table1 : Table" window should now be displayed (see Access 2003 Exhibit 2) except that the table on your screen is blank. You will now begin to enter the fields shown in Access 2003 Exhibit 2.

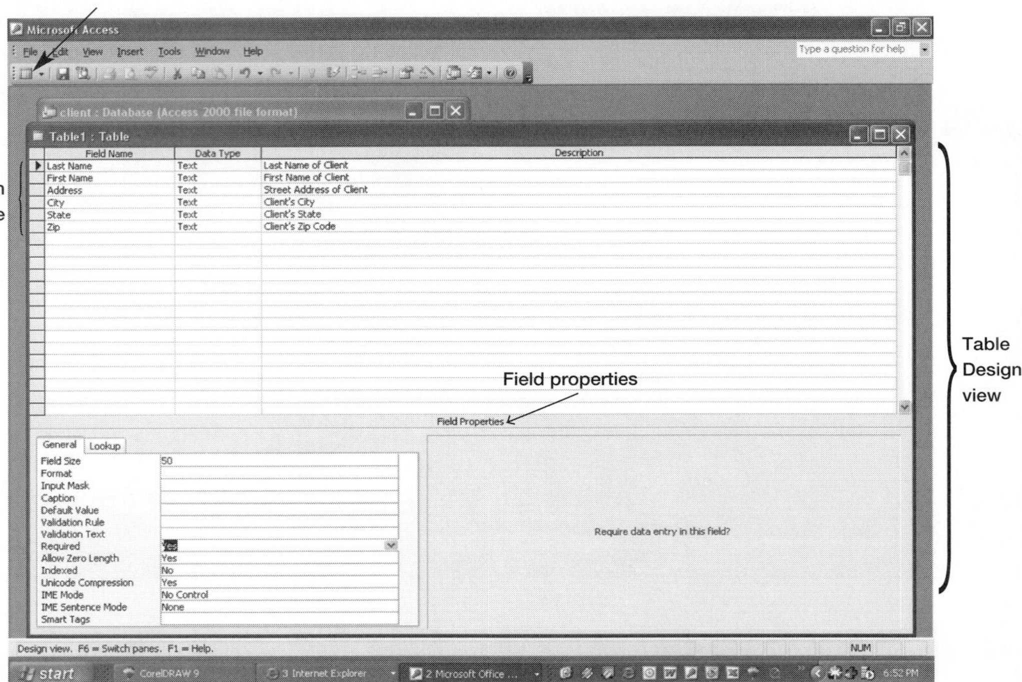

Access 2003 Exhibit 2
Creating Fields in a Table
Microsoft product screen shot reprinted with permission from Microsoft Corporation.

8. With your cursor in the first Field Name row, type **Last Name** and then press the **[TAB]** key on the keyboard.

9. Your cursor should now be in the Data Type column, and Text should be displayed in the field. If you click on the down arrow next to Text, you can see the different data types that Access has. By selecting the Data Type you tell Access what kind of information will be stored in the field. Since text will be stored in the Last Name field, press the **[TAB]** key to go to the Description column.

10. In the Description column type **Last Name of Client.**

11. Notice at the bottom of the screen under Field Properties that there are two tabs, General and Look up. The General tab should be displayed. It allows you to change the field size or number of characters in the field, and other items as well.

12. Next to the Required field under the General tab ***click "No." Click the down arrow next to "No" in the Required field, and then click "Yes."*** This will require

the user to enter this field when entering new data. The default field size and the other options are fine so you do not have to change them.

13. The Last Name field is now complete. ***Click in the second row directly under Last Name.***

14. Type the following information into the table:

Field Name	Data Type	Description	Field Size	Required
First Name	Text	First Name of Client	50	Yes
Address	Text	Street Address of Client	50	Yes
City	Text	Client's City	25	Yes
State	Text	Client's State	2	Yes
Zip	Text	Client's Zip Code	9	Yes

15. ***Click back to the General tab under Field Properties.***

16. Once all of the information has been entered, ***click File on the menu bar and then click Save.*** The Save As window should now be displayed. Under Table Name, type **tblClient** and then ***click OK.*** "Tbl" designates this as a table.

17. A Microsoft Office Access window is then displayed stating "There is no primary key defined." The window also asks "Do you want to create a primary key now?" ***Click Yes.*** Notice that Access created a new field called "ID" and gave it AutoNumber as the Data Type. The primary key is a field that uniquely identifies each record. In this instance, Access will automatically generate a unique ID number for each new client entered into the table.

18. You are currently in the Table Design view. Design view means that you are looking at the *design* of the table, and not the data in the table itself. You will now change your view to see the Datasheet view. Once data has been entered into the table, you can see the data in Datasheet view. ***Click the down arrow just to the right of the view icon (the first icon) on the toolbar*** (see Access 2003 Exhibit 2), ***and then select Datasheet View.*** *Note:* To see the name of any icon, just hover the mouse pointer over the icon for a second and the name of the icon will appear.

19. You should now see all of your fields displayed horizontally across the screen (see Access 2003 Exhibit 3). You can toggle back and forth between Design view and Datasheet view by clicking on the View icon.

20. Press the **[TAB]** key to go to the Last Name field.

21. Enter the following information (to go to the next field press the **[TAB]** key).

ID	Last Name	First Name	Address	City	State	Zip
	Allen	Alice	P.O. Box 2342	San Diego	CA	95336

22. While you can use Table Datasheet view to enter new records, it is not always the best way to enter data. In the next lesson, we will create a form to enter new records.

23. ***Click File on the menu bar and then click Save.***

24. ***Click the Close icon*** (the "X" in the upper right-hand corner) *of the tblClient: Table window only* (do not close the window for the whole Access program—see Access 2003 Exhibit 3).

Access 2003 Exhibit 3
Table Datasheet View
Microsoft product screen shot reprinted with permission from Microsoft Corporation.

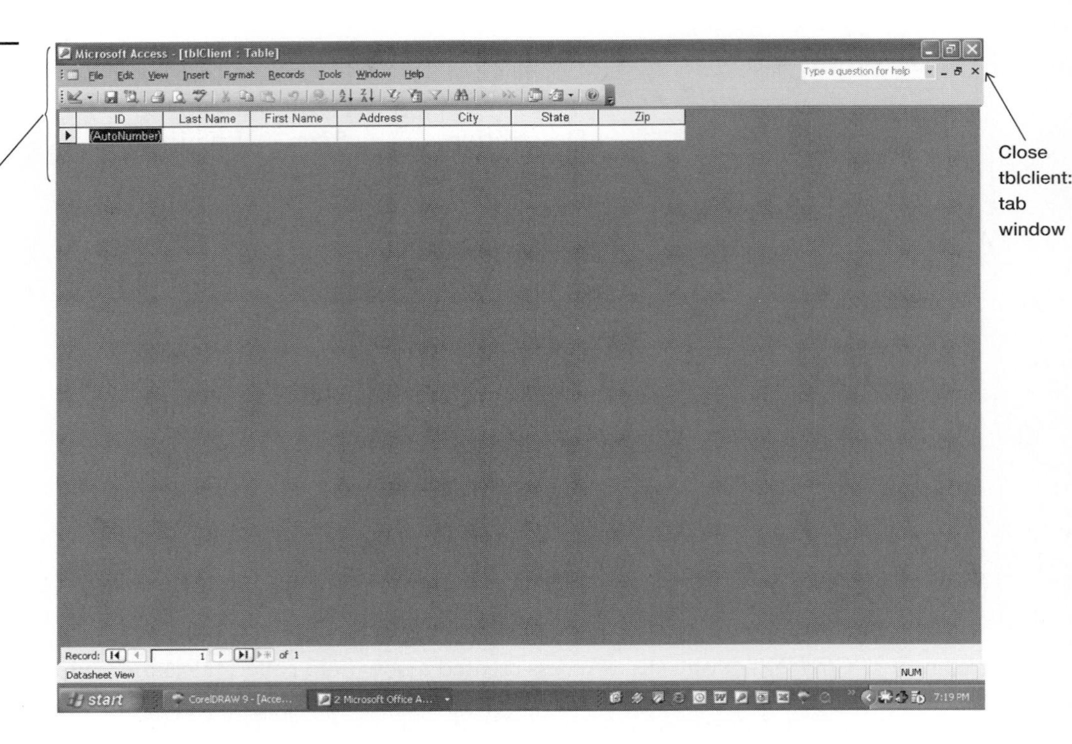

25. You should now be at the Client: Database window. Notice that the "tblClient" table you just created is now shown in the window.

26. ***Click File on the menu bar and then click Exit.***

This concludes Lesson 1.

LESSON 2: CREATING A FORM AND ENTERING DATA

In this lesson, you will create a form from which you can enter data into the database. You will then enter the rest of the data into the Client database using the form you created.

1. Open Windows. Then, ***double-click the Access 2003 icon on the desktop*** to open Access 2003 for Windows. Alternatively, ***click the Start button, point to Programs or All Programs, and then click the Microsoft Office Access icon (or point to Microsoft Office, and then click on Microsoft Office Access 2003.)***

2. At the Getting Started task pane, under Open, ***click "Client.mdb."*** If a Security Warning window is displayed, ***click Open***; there is no security problem because you are the one who created the file.

3. You should now be at the Client: Database window. ***Click Forms on the Objects bar.***

4. ***Double-click on the "Create form by using wizard" option in the Client: Database window.***

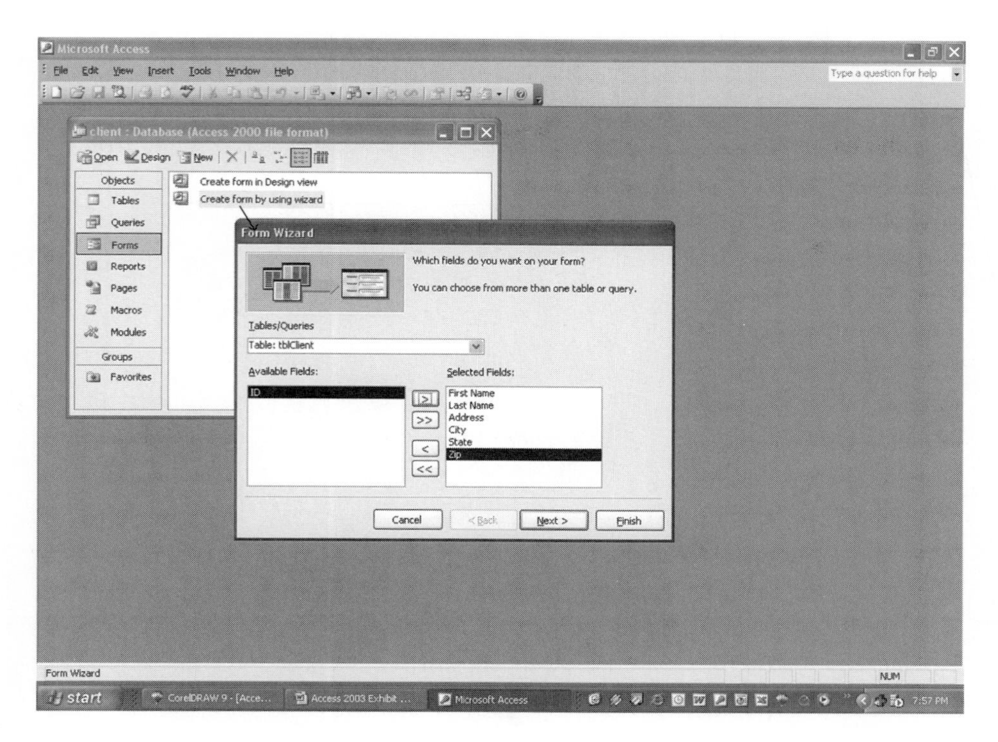

Access 2003 Exhibit 4

Form Wizard—First Screen

Microsoft product screen shot reprinted with permission from Microsoft Corporation.

5. The Form Wizard window should now be displayed. You will now complete this screen so it is similar to Access 2003 Exhibit 4.

6. Under Available Fields, ***click the First Name field and then click the ">" ("greater than") icon under Selected Fields.*** You are selecting the fields to be included in your form. You are also selecting them in the order they will appear in your form and in which you will enter them into the table.

7. ***Click the "Last Name" field and then point and click on the ">" icon under.***

8. ***Click "Address" and then click the ">" icon.***

9. ***Click "City" and then click the ">" icon.***

10. ***Click "State" and then click the ">" icon.***

11. ***Click "Zip" and then click on the ">" icon.***

12. *Note:* You do not need to include the ID field in the form because it is an automatic number that Access will be generating.

13. ***Click Next in the Form Wizard window.***

14. You will then be asked "What layout would you like your form?" ***Click Justified and then click Next.***

15. You will then be asked "What style would you like?" ***Click Standard and then click Next.***

16. You are then asked "What title do you want for your form?" Type **Client Data Entry Form.**

17. Under "Do you want to open the form or modify the form's design?" the selection "Open the form to view or enter information" should already be selected, so ***click Finish.***

18. The Client Data Entry Form window should now be displayed on your screen. ***Click the Maximize icon in the upper right of the Client Data Entry Form***

Access 2003 Exhibit 5
Form Wizard—Completed Form
Microsoft product screen shot reprinted with permission from Microsoft Corporation.

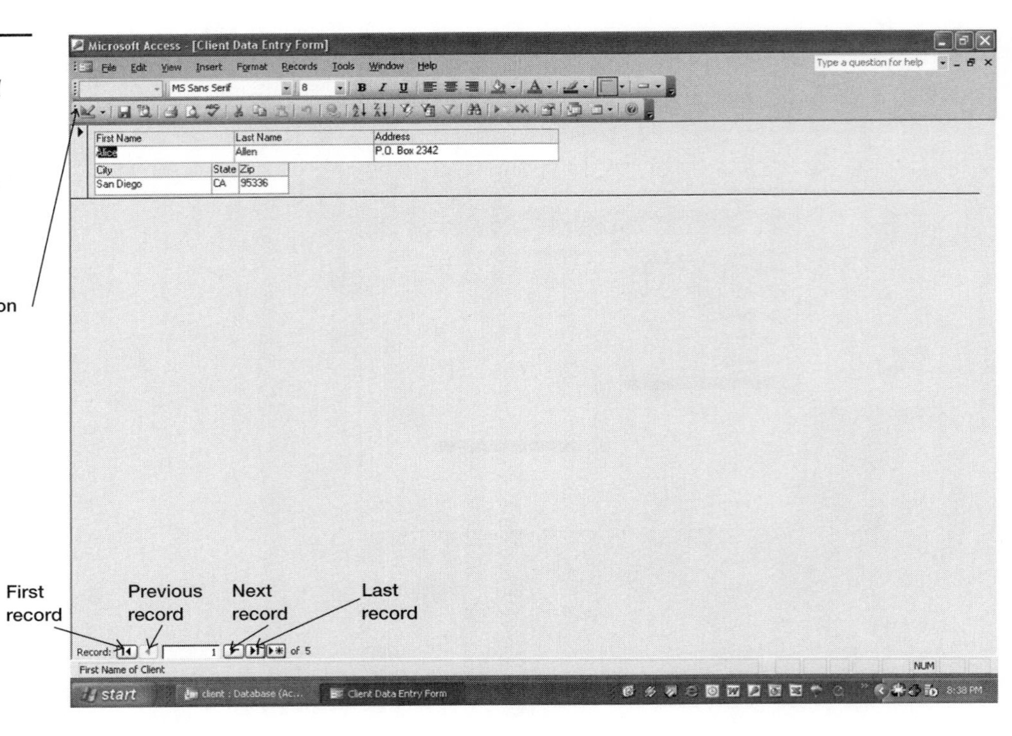

window (it is a rectangle just to the left of the Close icon). Your screen should look similar to Access 2003 Exhibit 5.

19. Notice that the first record you entered is now displayed (Alice Allen). Press the **[PAGE DOWN]** key on the keyboard to go to an empty record. You can go to the next record or the previous record by clicking on the "greater than" and "less than" icons at the bottom of the page or by pressing the **[PAGE-UP]** or **[PAGE-DOWN]** keys on the keyboard.

20. Enter the following records into the database. You can go between fields by pressing the **[TAB]** or **[SHIFT]+[TAB]** keys, or by pointing and clicking with the mouse. When you are on the last field, you can go to the next record by pressing **[TAB].**

Record 2	
First Name	**Harriet**
Last Name	**Winslow**
Address	**89404 Humboldt**
City	**Las Vegas**
State	**NV**
Zip	**78524**

Record 3	
First Name	**Dan**
Last Name	**Ross**
Address	**23332 Westide Road**
City	**Marina Bay**
State	**CA**
Zip	**93442**

Record 4	
First Name	Jennifer
Last Name	Kitchen
Address	2342 45th St. NW
City	San Diego
State	CA
Zip	95334

Record 5	
First Name	Donald
Last Name	Johnson
Address	32455 Coastal
City	Miami
State	FL
Zip	65773

21. When you have finished entering all of the data, ***click the down arrow next to the View icon on the toolbar.*** You are currently in Form view. ***Click Datasheet View.***

22. The Datasheet view is now displayed. ***Click the Maximize icon in the upper right of the Client Data Entry Form*** window. You should now see all of your fields displayed horizontally across the screen. *Note:* If you cannot see all of the data in a field, just click in the column heading on the vertical line that separates each field and drag it to the right to make the field larger (see Access 2003 Exhibit 6).

23. ***Click File on the menu bar and then click Save.***

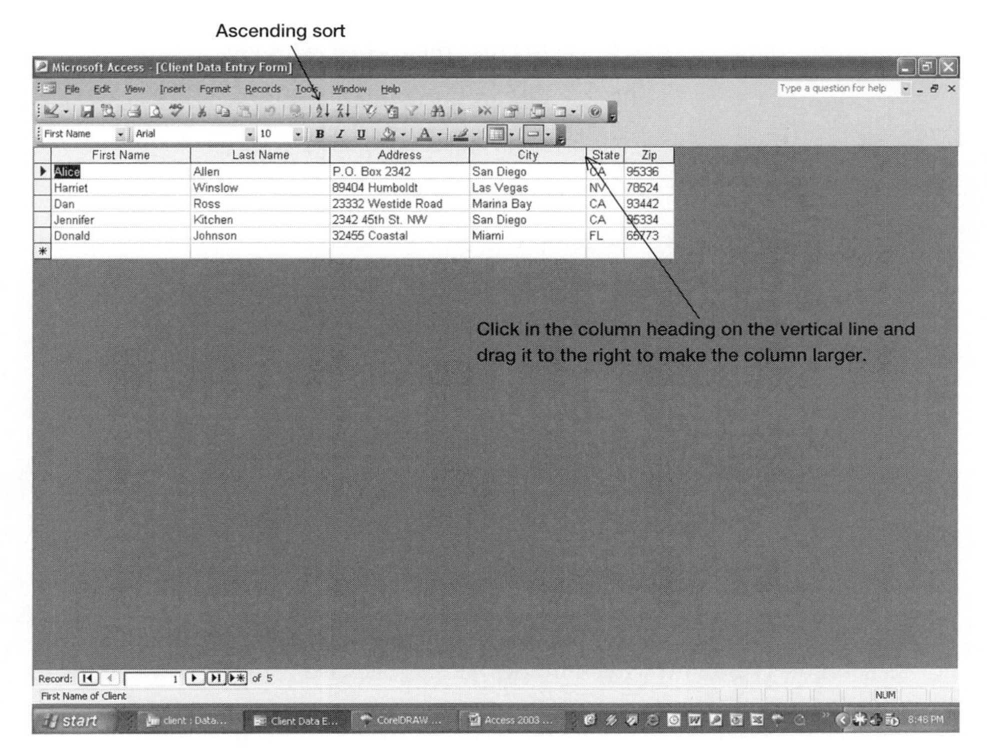

Access 2003 Exhibit 6
Datasheet View of the Client Data Entry Form
Microsoft product screen shot reprinted with permission from Microsoft Corporation.

24. *Click File on the menu bar and then click Close to close the Form view.*

25. You should now be at the Client: Database window.

26. *Click File on the menu bar and then click Exit.*

This concludes Lesson 2.

LESSON 3: QUERYING THE DATABASE

In this lesson, you will learn how to use the Ascending Sort icon on the toolbar, create a query that searches and sorts the database, modify a query, use a primary and secondary sort option, run a query, and print a query using the database you created in Lessons 1 and 2.

1. Open Windows. Then, *double-click the Access 2003 icon on the desktop* to open Access 2003 for Windows. Alternatively, *click the Start button, point to Programs or All Programs, and then click the Microsoft Office Access icon (or point to Microsoft Office, and then click Microsoft Office Access 2003.)*

2. At the Getting Started task pane, under Open, *point and click on Client.mdb.* If a Security Warning window is displayed, *click Open;* there is no security problem because you are the one who created the file. You should now be at the Client: Database window. *Click Tables on the Objects bar. Then, double-click "tblClient."*

3. You should now see your data displayed horizontally across the screen.

4. Notice that the data is not sorted. To quickly and easily sort the data, *click any record in the Last Name field, and then click the Sort Ascending icon on the toolbar (it looks like the letter "A" on top of the letter "Z" with a down arrow next to them—see Access 2003 Exhibit 6). Note:* Point with your mouse on any icon on the toolbar for a second and the name of the icon will be displayed. Your records should now be sorted alphabetically by last name.

5. *Click File on the menu bar and then click Save.*

6. *Click File and then click Close to close the Datasheet view.*

7. You should now be at the Client: Database window. *Click Queries on the Objects bar.*

8. *Double-click "Create query by using wizard."*

9. You should now have the Simple Query Wizard window on your screen. *Click ">>" (two "greater than" signs—see Access 2003 Exhibit 7).* This will select all of the fields for the query.

10. *Click "Next."*

11. You will then be asked "What title do you want for your query?" Type **San Diego Sort**. *Next, click "Modify the query design" and then click Finish.*

12. The query is displayed on your screen. You will now make the modifications shown in Access 2003 Exhibit 8. You will use the Query Design View mode (the view you are currently in) to make the revisions. Notice that each column shows one of the fields in the table.

13. *Click the Show row under the ID column (the first column).* There should now be **an empty box (no check mark)**. This is because we do not want this to show on our query.

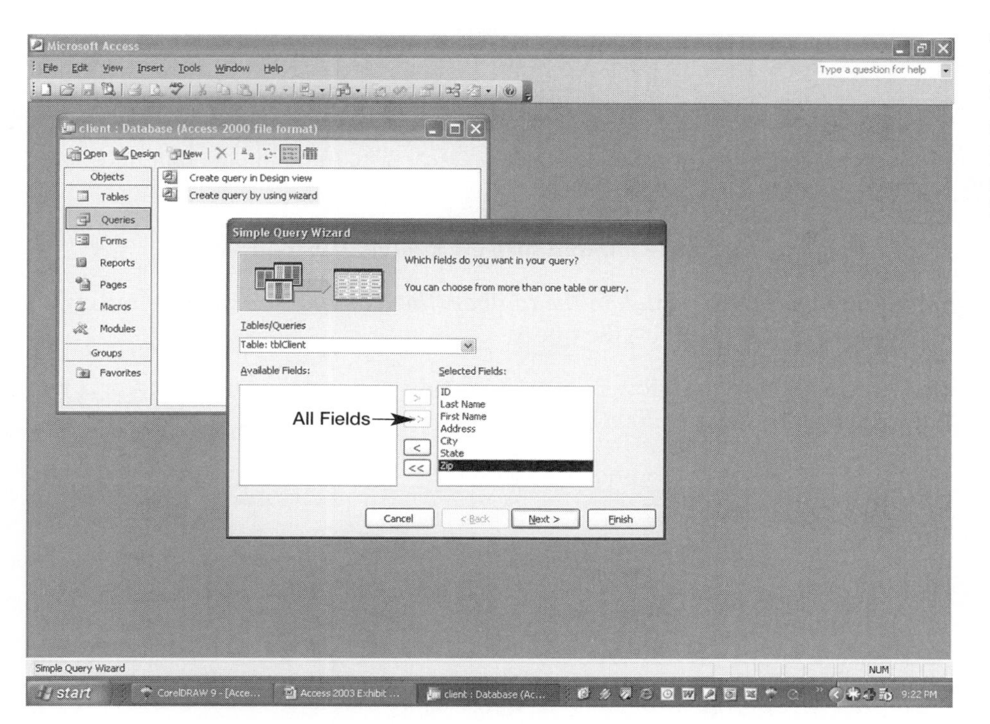

Access 2003 Exhibit 7
Creating a Query with the Query Wizard
Microsoft product screen shot reprinted with permission from Microsoft Corporation.

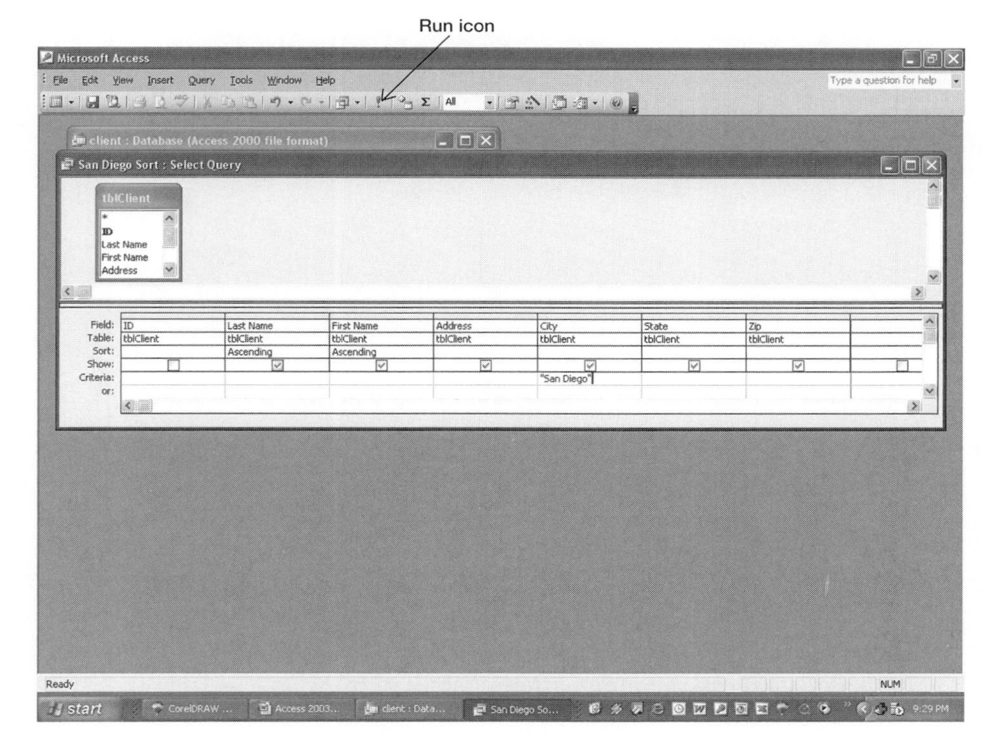

Access 2003 Exhibit 8
Modifying a Query in Design View
Microsoft product screen shot reprinted with permission from Microsoft Corporation.

14. ***Click the Sort row under the Last Name column. Now, click the down arrow and click Ascending.*** This tells Access that the primary sort for the database will be on the Last Name field.

15. ***Click the Sort row under the First Name column. Now, click on the down arrow and click on Ascending.*** This tells Access that the secondary sort for the database will be on the First Name field. This is necessary, because if we had two

clients with the same last name, we would then want Access to sort the data based on the client's first name.

16. ***Click the Criteria row under "City."*** Type **"San Diego."** (***Note:*** **You must type the quotation marks.)** This tells Access to select only those clients that have "San Diego" entered in the City field.

17. ***Click File on the menu bar and then click Save.*** This will save the query.

18. ***Click the Run command on the toolbar (the icon that looks like a red exclamation mark).*** This will run the query.

19. Two records should now be displayed on your screen, Alice Allen and Jennifer Kitchen (see Access 2003 Exhibit 9).

Access 2003 Exhibit 9
A Completed Query
Microsoft product screen shot reprinted with permission from Microsoft Corporation.

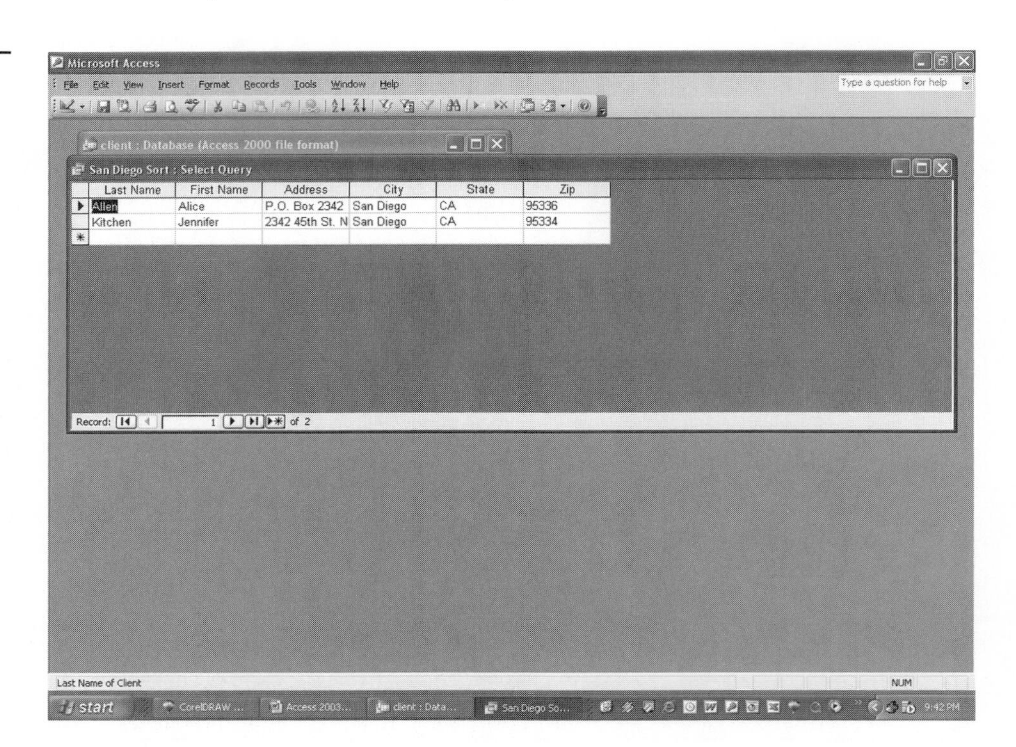

20. ***Click the printer icon on the toolbar to print your results.***

21. ***Click the Close icon (the X in a red square) in the "San Diego Sort : Select Query" window to close the Query view.***

22. You should now be at the Client: Database window.

23. ***Click File on the menu bar and then click Exit.***

This concludes Lesson 3.

LESSON 4: CREATING A REPORT

In this lesson, you will create and print a report using the database you created in Lessons 1–3.

1. Open Windows. Then, ***double-click the Access 2003 icon on the desktop*** to open Access 2003 for Windows. Alternatively, ***click the Start button, point to***

Programs or All Programs, and then click the Microsoft Office Access icon (or point to Microsoft Office, and then click Microsoft Office Access 2003.)

2. At the Getting Started task pane, under Open, ***click "Client.mdb."*** If a Security Warning window is displayed, ***click Open;*** there is no security problem, because you are the one who created the file.

3. You should now be at the Client: Database window. ***click Reports on the Objects bar.***

4. ***Next, double-click on "Create report by using wizard."***

5. You should now have the Report Wizard window on your screen.

6. Under Tables/Queries in the Report Wizard window, ***click the down arrow and make sure that "Table:tbl Client" is selected.*** (*Note:* If "Query: San Diego Sort" is selected, your report will run, but it will only pull the records for clients living in San Diego. This is how users can combine queries and reports. Because we want a list of all clients, make sure the "Table:tbl Client" file is selected.)

7. ***Click the ">>" icon (two "greater than" signs).*** This will select all of the fields for our report (see Access 2003 Exhibit 10). ***Then, Click Next.***

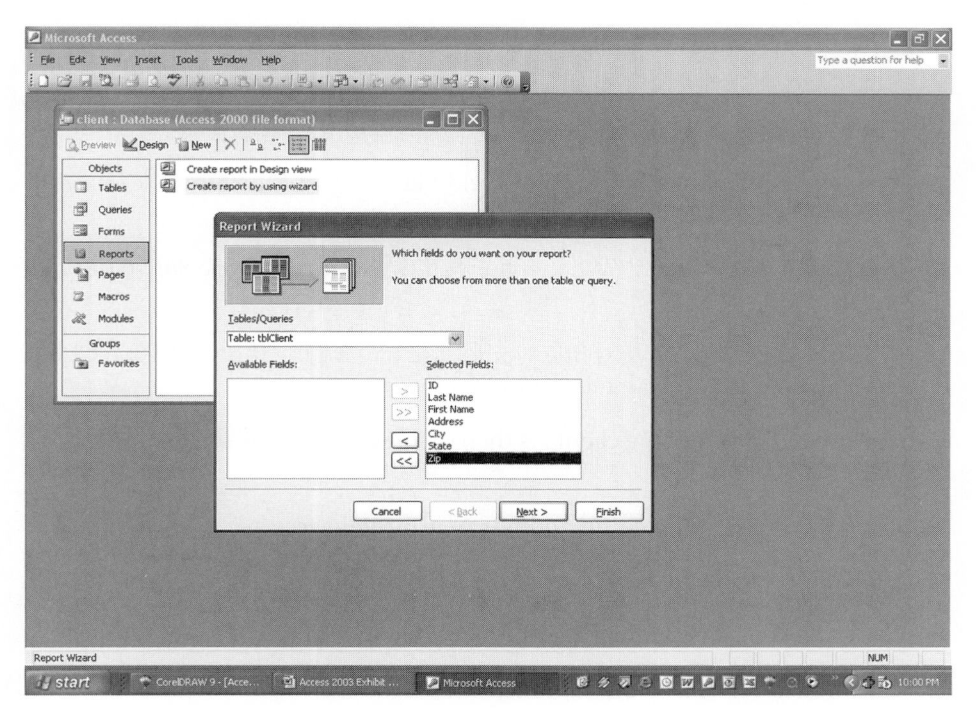

Access 2003 Exhibit 10
Creating a Report in the Report Wizard
Microsoft product screen shot reprinted with permission from Microsoft Corporation.

8. You will then be asked "Do you want to add any grouping levels?" You do not, so ***click Next.***

9. You will then be asked "What sort order do you want for your report?" ***Click the down arrow next to the "1" field, and then select Last Name*** (see Access 2003 Exhibit 11). Notice that it defaults to an ascending sort.

10. ***Click the down arrow next to the "2" field, and then select First Name*** (see Access 2003 Exhibit 11).

Access 2003 Exhibit 11
Sorting a Report in the Report Wizard
Microsoft product screen shot reprinted with permission from Microsoft Corporation.

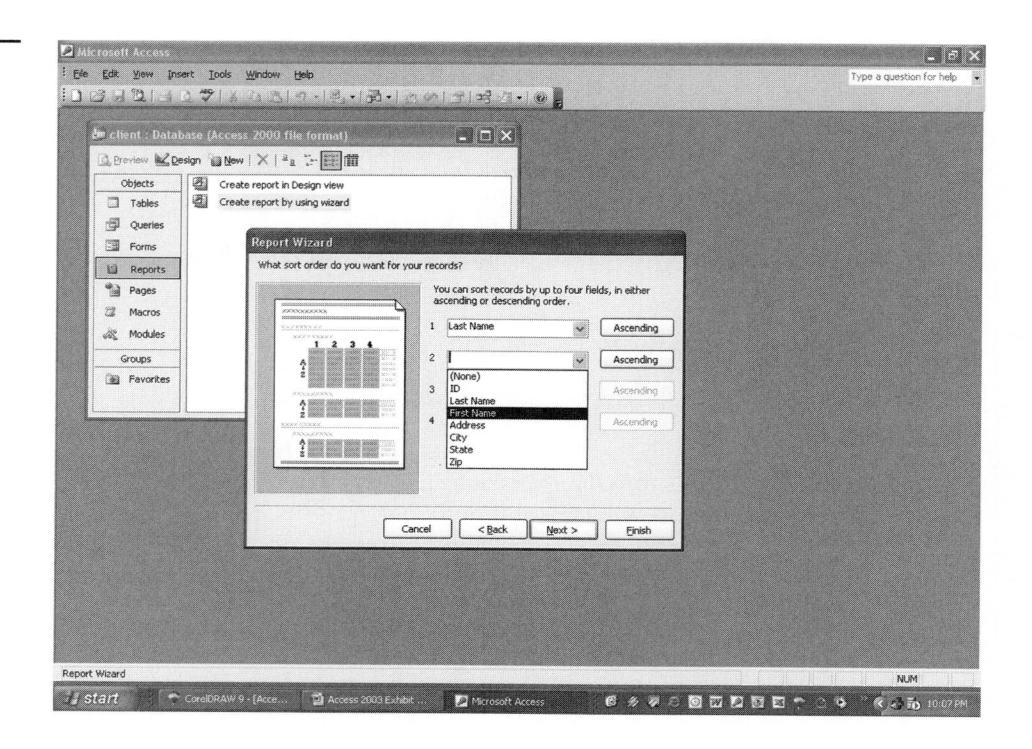

11. ***Then, select Next.***

12. You will then be asked how you would like to lay out the report. ***Click Tabular and then select Next.***

13. You will then be asked "What style would you like?" ***Click Soft Gray and then select Next.***

14. You are then asked "What title would you like for the report?" Type **Client Report.** We want to preview the report, so ***click Finish.***

15. The report with the five clients is then displayed on your screen (see Access 2003 Exhibit 12).

16. ***Click the printer icon on the toolbar to print your results.***

17. ***Click File and then Close to close the print preview.***

18. You should now be at the Client: Database window.

19. ***Click File on the menu bar and then click Exit.***

This concludes Lesson 4.

LESSON 5: CREATING A LITIGATION SUPPORT DATABASE

This lesson shows you how to build a litigation support database, including creating a table, entering fields, creating a form, entering data, sorting the database, building a query, and producing a report.

1. Open Windows. Then, ***double-click the Access 2003 icon on the desktop*** to open Access 2003 for Windows. Alternatively, ***click the Start button, point to***

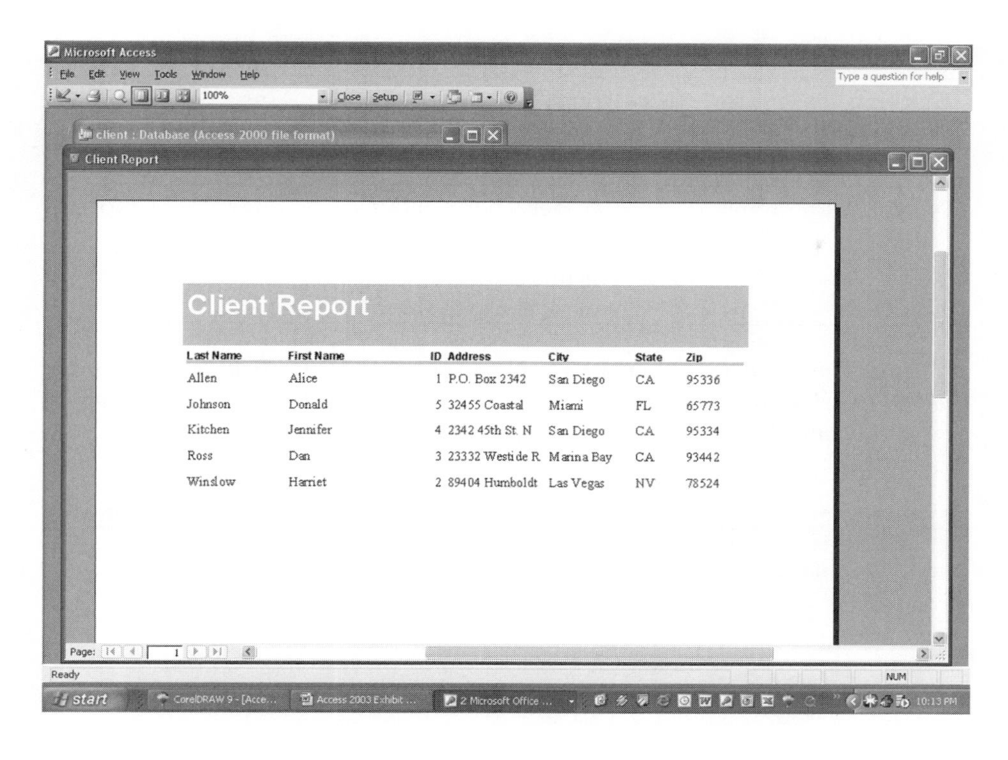

Access 2003 Exhibit 12
Preview of Client Report
Microsoft product screen shot reprinted with permission from Microsoft Corporation.

Programs or All Programs, and then click the Microsoft Office Access icon (or point to Microsoft Office and then click Microsoft Office Access 2003.)

2. When Access loads, the Getting Started task pane is displayed on the right side. ***Point and click on "Create a new file. . ." under Open in the Getting Started task pane.***

3. The New File task pane should now be displayed. ***Click on "Blank database . . ." under New in the New File task pane.***

4. At the File New Database window, next to File Name, type **Litigation Support** and then ***click Create.***

5. ***Click Tables on the Objects bar.***

6. ***Double-click on "Create table in Design view."***

7. You should now have a window open on your screen that says "Table1 : Table." This is where you will enter the field names and basic structure for the table.

8. Enter the following fields/information into the table:

Field Name	Data Type	Description	Field Size	Required
Doc Name	Text	Name of document	50	Yes
Doc Type	Text	Type of document	50	Yes
Doc Date	Date/Time	Date of document	-	Yes
Doc Author	Text	Author of document	50	Yes
Doc Number	Number	Internal document ID number	-	Yes
Primary Recipient	Text	Who the document was to	50	Yes

continued

Field Name	Data Type	Description	Field Size	Required
Subject Matter	Text	Subject of document	75	Yes
Issue Code	Number	Internal code	-	No
Notes	Memo	Coder's notes about the document	-	No
Key Evidence	Yes/No	Is this a key piece of evidence to the case?	-	Yes

8. *Click Doc Type again in the Field Name column. Then, click the Lookup tab (just to the right of the General tab). Access 2003 Exhibit 13 shows the changes you will be making to the Lookup tab for the Doc Type field.*

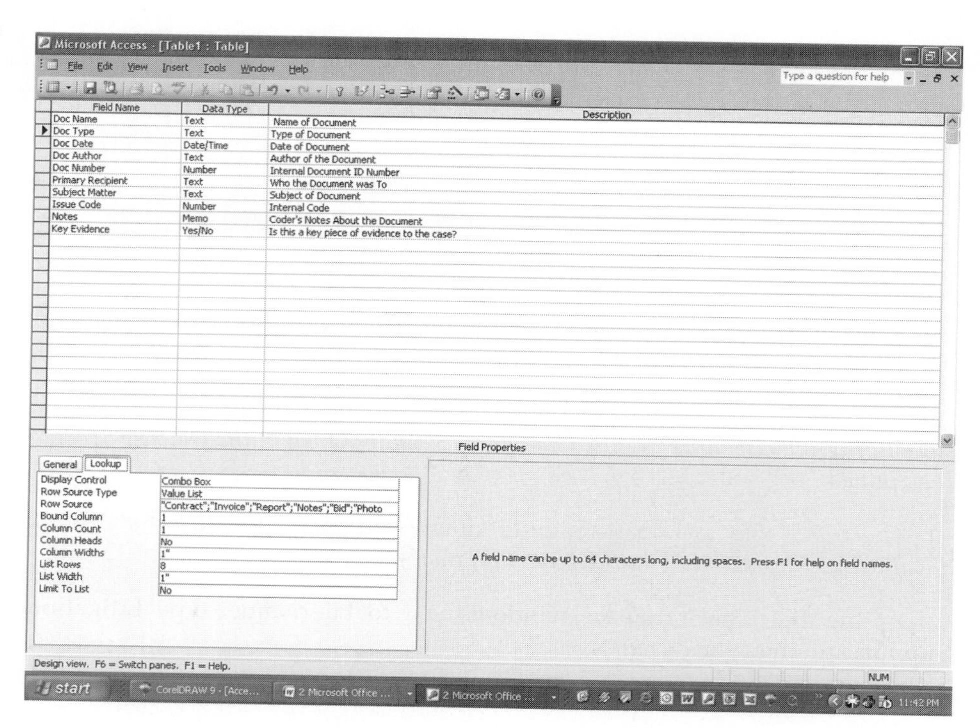

Access 2003 Exhibit 13
Creating Fields for Litigation Support Database
Microsoft product screen shot reprinted with permission from Microsoft Corporation.

9. *In the Lookup tab, to the right of Display Control, click Text Box. Click the down arrow to the right of Text Box. Click on Combo Box.* Notice that a number of other options are now available under the Lookup tab (see Access 2003 Exhibit 13).

10. *To the right of Row Source Type, point and click Table/Query. Click the down arrow to the right of Table/Query. Click Value List.*

11. *Click in the blank box to the right of Row Source* and type **"Contract" "Invoice" "Report" "Notes" "Bid" "Photo."** *Note:* **You must type the quotes** (see Access 2003 Exhibit 13). These choices will appear in a drop-down box for you to select; this is a good way of creating data uniformity and consistency for this field.

12. *Click in the box to the right of Bound Column,* then type 1.

13. *Click in the box to the right of Column Widths,* then type **1"**.

14. *Click in the box to the right of List Width,* then type **1"**.

15. Now, ***click File on the menu bar and then click Save.***

16. You will then be asked to enter the name of the table. Type **tblDocuments** ***and then click OK.***

17. You will be asked if you want to define a Primary Key. ***Click "Yes."*** Notice that Access created a new field called ID and gave it AutoNumber as the Data Type.

18. You are currently in the Table Design view. ***Click on the down arrow icon just to the right of the View icon on the toolbar, and then select Datasheet view.***

19. You should now see all of your fields displayed horizontally across the screen. You can toggle back and forth between Design view and Datasheet view by clicking the View icon on the toolbar.

20. ***Click File on the menu bar and then click Close.*** You should now be at the Litigation Support: Database window.

21. You are now ready to create a data entry form for entering data into the table.

22. ***Click Forms on the Objects bar.***

23. ***Double-click "Create form by using wizard."***

24. The Form Wizard should now be displayed. ***Click the ">>" icon (two "greater than" signs).*** This will select all of the fields in their current order, which is fine. ***Then click Next.***

25. You will then be asked "What layout would you like for your form?" ***Click Justified. Then, click Next.***

26. You will then be asked "What style would you like?" ***Click Sandstone and then click Next.***

27. You are then asked "What title do you want for your form?" Type **Document Data Entry Form Smith vs EZ Pest Control** and then ***click Finish.***

28. The form should now be displayed on your screen. If the form is not running in maximized mode (full screen), click the Maximize button for the "Document Data Entry Form Smith vs EZ Pest Control" window (The Maximize button is the middle icon in the upper right corner of the "Document Data Entry Form Smith vs. EZ Pest Control" window. It looks like a rectangle with a thick top border.) Your screen should look similar to Access 2003 Exhibit 14.

29. Enter the records from the table into the database. You can go between fields by pressing the **[TAB]** or **[SHIFT]+[TAB]** keys, or by clicking with the mouse. Notice that in the Doc Type field there is a drop-down menu with choices you can select. Because it is a combo box, you can also enter text into the field, but for this exercise you can just select entries from the drop-down menu. Notice also in the Key Evidence field that if the document is a key piece of evidence, you just need to click in the box and a check mark will appear. When you are at the last field you can go to the next record by pressing **[TAB]**. You can also go between records by pressing the **[PAGE UP]** or **[PAGE DOWN]** keys or by clicking the "greater than" and "less than" symbols at the bottom of the page.

30. When you have finished entering all of the data, ***click the down arrow key just to the right of the View icon on the toolbar and then select Datasheet view.***

31. You should now see your fields displayed horizontally across the screen (although due to the length of the entries you may not be able to see all of the data). Use the scroll bar at the bottom of the screen to scroll left and right to see all of the fields (see Access 2003 Exhibit 15).

Doc Name	Doc Type	Doc Date	Doc Author	Doc No	Primary Recipient	Subject Matter	Issue Code	Notes	Key Evidence
HUD Settlement Statement	Contract	06/01/2007	Judy Smith, Bill Lee	501	Judy Smith	Sale of house	1	Includes pest inspection cost of $300	Yes
EZ Pest Agreement for Termite Inspection	Contract	05/01/2007	John Lincoln, EZ Pest	502	Judy Smith	Agreement to inspect the house for termites	1	The contract states that EZ Pest will conduct a thorough examination of the property.	Yes
EZ Pest Invoice for Pest Inspection	Invoice	05/15/2007	John Lincoln, EZ Pest	503	Judy Smith	Invoice for pest inspection	1	Shows total due $300 and that it was paid on 5/20/2007	No
EZ Pest Inspection Report	Report	05/15/2007	John Lincoln, EZ Pest	504	Judy Smith	Inspection Report	2	The report states "No visible evidence of infestation from wood destroying insects was observed." Signed by John Lincoln.	Yes
EZ Pest Inspection Report Notes	Notes	05/07/2007	John Lincoln, EZ Pest	505	John Lincoln	Notes of John Lincoln taken to assist in preparation of Inspection Report	2	John Lincoln's notes do not show that he actually checked the east side of the house where termites were later found.	Yes
Bid from Stewart Construction	Bid	11/01/2007	Tim Stewart	506	Judy Smith	Bid to rebuild the east side where the termites destroyed house	3	Bid of $50,000 to repair the termite damage on the east side.	Yes
Photograph of east side of house	Photo	10/01/2007	Judy Smith	507	Judy Smith	Photograph of house	3	Photograph showing east side of house behind vinyl siding showing frame of house nearly eaten through.	Yes

Access 2003 Exhibit 14

Litigation Support Database Data Entry Form

Microsoft product screen shot reprinted with permission from Microsoft Corporation.

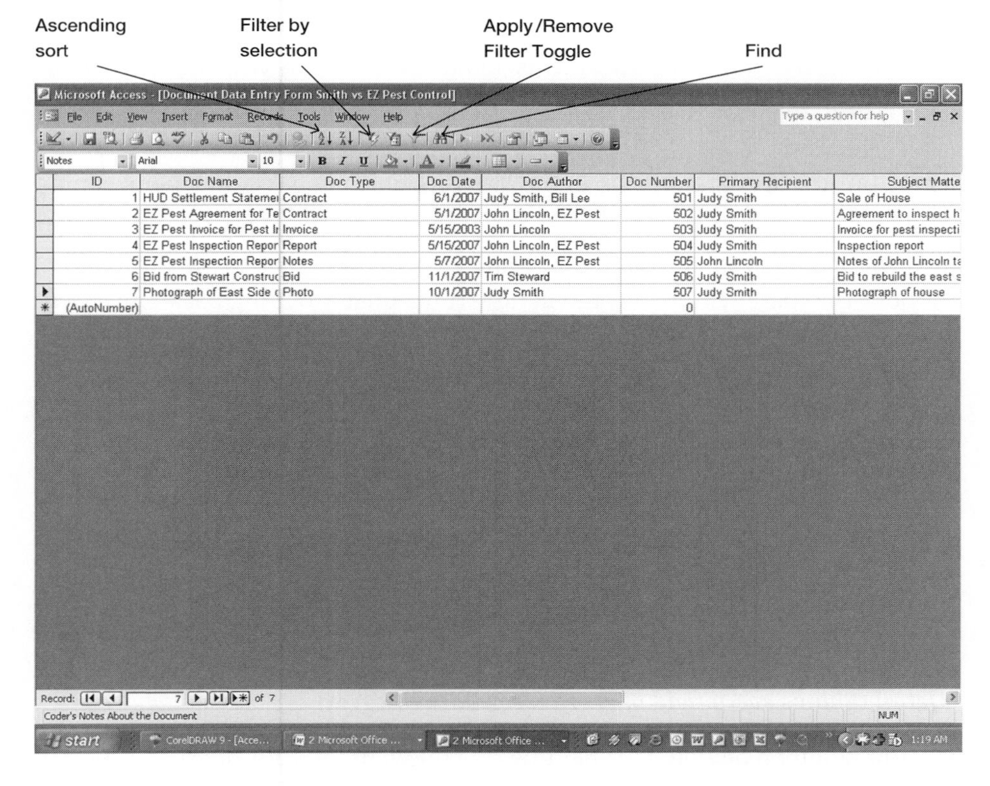

ID	Doc Name	Doc Type	Doc Date	Doc Author	Doc Number	Primary Recipient	Subject Matte
1	HUD Settlement Stateme	Contract	6/1/2007	Judy Smith, Bill Lee	501	Judy Smith	Sale of House
2	EZ Pest Agreement for Te	Contract	5/1/2007	John Lincoln, EZ Pest	502	Judy Smith	Agreement to inspect h
3	EZ Pest Invoice for Pest In	Invoice	5/15/2003	John Lincoln	503	Judy Smith	Invoice for pest inspecti
4	EZ Pest Inspection Repor	Report	5/15/2007	John Lincoln, EZ Pest	504	Judy Smith	Inspection report
5	EZ Pest Inspection Repor	Notes	5/7/2007	John Lincoln, EZ Pest	505	John Lincoln	Notes of John Lincoln ta
6	Bid from Stewart Construc	Bid	11/1/2007	Tim Steward	506	Judy Smith	Bid to rebuild the east s
7	Photograph of East Side c	Photo	10/1/2007	Judy Smith	507	Judy Smith	Photograph of house
(AutoNumber)					0		

Access 2003 Exhibit 15

Datasheet View of Data in Litigation Support Database

Microsoft product screen shot reprinted with permission from Microsoft Corporation.

32. *Click the Save icon on the toolbar to save the data you just entered.*

33. You will next see some different views of the data (without damaging the integrity of the data).

34. *Click any record in the Doc Name field and then click the Sort Ascending icon on the toolbar (it looks like the letter "A" on top of the letter "Z" with a*

down arrow next to them). (*Note:* Point with your mouse on any icon on the toolbar for a second and the name of the icon will be displayed.) Your records should now be sorted alphabetically by document name.

35. ***Click any record on the Doc Date field, and then click the Sort Descending icon on the toolbar.*** The documents are now sorted in date order with the most recent first.

36. ***Click any record in the Subject Matter field and then click the Find icon on the toolbar (it looks like binoculars).*** The Find and Replace window should be displayed. Next to "Find What," type **vinyl siding** and then, ***next to "Look In," click the down arrow and select "Document Data Entry Form Smith vs EZ Pest Control"*** (This will allow you to search all fields in the Data Entry form, not just Subject Matter.) ***Then, next to Match, click the down arrow and click Any Part of Field and then click Find Next.*** Notice that the pointer went to document 507 and found where "vinyl siding" was entered. ***Click Cancel to make the Find and Replace window disappear.***

37. ***Click Document 502 and click the Primary Recipient field.*** Notice that "Judy Smith" is in the field. ***Then, click the Filter by Selection icon on the toolbar (it looks like a silver funnel with a lightning bolt***—see Access 2003 Exhibit 15***).*** Notice that only documents with Judy Smith as the primary recipient are left. (The other documents are still in the database; Access just temporarily removed them from the current view.)

38. To bring back all of the documents, remove the filter by ***clicking the Remove Filter icon on the toolbar (it looks like a plain silver funnel).*** Notice that all of the documents are back.

39. To put the documents back in the order in which you entered them, simply ***click the Doc Number field and press the Sort Ascending icon.***

40. ***Click File and then click Close.*** You should now be back at the Litigation Support: Database window. You will now run a query to bring back only documents that have Issue Code 2 in them and where Judy Smith was the recipient.

41. ***Click Queries on the Objects bar.***

42. ***Double-click "Create query by using wizard."***

43. You should now have the Simple Query Wizard window on your screen. ***Click the ">>" icon (two "greater than" signs).*** This will select all of the fields for your query.

44. ***Click Next.***

45. You will then be asked "Would you like a detail or a summary query?" ***Click "Detail (Shows every field of every record)." Click Next.***

46. You will then be asked "What title do you want for your query?" Type **qry Smith Issue Code 2**. ***Then, click "Modify the query design," and click Finish.***

47. The query is displayed on your screen. Notice that each column shows one of the fields in the table.

48. ***Click the Show row under the ID column (the first column).*** There should now be an empty box (no check mark). This is because we do not want this to show on our query.

49. ***Click the Sort row under the Doc Number. Now, click the down arrow and click Ascending.*** This tells Access that the primary sort for the database will be on this field.

50. ***Click the Criteria row under the Issue Code field*** and type **2.** (*Note: Do not* type anything else in the criteria for this field—just type the number 2.)

51. ***Then, click the Criteria row under Primary Recipient*** and type **"Judy Smith"** (*Note:* You *must* type the quotes for this field.) This tells Access to select only those records that meet both of these selection/search criteria.

52. ***Click the Run command on the toolbar (the icon that looks like a red exclamation mark "!"). This will run the query.*** Document 504 should be displayed.

53. ***Click File on the menu bar and then click Save.***

54. ***Click the down arrow just to the right of the View icon on the toolbar and then select Design view. Click back and forth between Design view and Datasheet view. Notice that you can make changes to the query in Design view, and then run the query and correct any problems that you may have had in your query.***

55. ***In Datasheet view, click the printer icon on the toolbar to print the query.*** Notice that the whole record did not print.

56. ***Click File on the menu bar and then click Save.***

57. ***Click File and then Close to close the query view.***

58. You should now be at the Litigation Support: Database window. You will now print the query you just saved as a report.

59. ***Click Reports on the Objects bar and then*** **double-*click "Create report by using wizard."***

60. You should now have the Report Wizard window on your screen.

61. ***Click under Tables/Queries on the down arrow button and select "Query: qry Smith Issue Code 2."***

62. ***Click the icon ">>" icon (two "greater than" signs).*** This will select all of the fields for our report. ***Then, click Next.***

63. You will then be asked "Do you want to add any grouping levels?" ***Click Next.***

64. You will then be asked "What sort order do you want for your report?" ***Click Next.***

65. ***Click Justified and then select Next.***

66. You will then be asked "What style would you like?" ***Click Corporate and then select Next.***

67. You are then asked "What title would you like for the report?" Type **rpt – Judy Smith Primary Recipient—Issue Code 2**

68. ***Then, click Finish.***

69. The report is then displayed on your screen.

70. ***Click the printer icon on the toolbar to print your results.***

71. ***Click File on the menu bar and then click Close to close the report view.***

72. ***Click File on the menu bar and then click Exit to close Access.***

This concludes Lesson 5.

LESSON 6: WORKING WITH A COMPREHENSIVE LAW OFFICE RELATIONAL DATABASE

In this lesson, you will work with a true relational database, including working with multiple tables, assigning relationships among tables, and writing queries and reports that access data from multiple tables. This lesson assumes that you have read Chapter 5 – Database Management Systems and that you have completed Lessons 1–5.

1. Open Windows. Then, ***double-click the Access 2003 icon on the desktop*** to open Access 2003 for Windows. Alternatively, ***click the Start button, point to Programs or All Programs, and then click the Microsoft Office Access icon (or point to Microsoft Office and then click Microsoft Office Access 2003.)***

2. The first thing you will do is open the "Lesson 6 Law Firm Database" file from Disk 1 supplied with this text. Ensure that the disk is inserted in the disk drive, point and click on File on the Office Button, and then point and click on Open. The "Open" window should now be displayed. Point and click on the down arrow to the right of the white box next to "Look in:" and select the drive where Disk 1 is located. Point and double-click on the Database Files folder. Double-click on the "Lesson 6 Law Firm Database" file.

3. If a security warning window is displayed, ***just click Open,*** as there is no security problem with this file.

4. In this lesson, you are working with a true relational law office database. In the previous lessons, you have only worked with databases with one table. This database has four tables. You will now get an overview of the tables and create a relationship between two tables.

5. ***Click Tables on the Objects bar.*** Notice that four tables are listed: Case Evidence, Case File, Client, and Opposing Attorney.

6. ***Click Tools on the menu bar and then click Relationships.*** Your screen should now be similar to Access 2003 Exhibit 16, except that there is no relationship between the Case File table and the Case Evidence table.

7. Look carefully at the four tables. The subject matter of the Client table is just the client. It includes a client ID number and client contact information only. The Case File table includes broad data about the legal subject matter of the case including an internal matter number, the case name, court, judge, case type and assigned attorney and paralegal. The Opposing Attorney table just tracks contact information for opposing counsel on cases. The Case Evidence table tracks specific pieces of evidence in each case. This type of structure, including multiple tables that hold a variety of client- and case-related information, can be found in legal organizations just about anywhere.

8. Each table in a relational database must be connected or the tables will not be able to share information. For example, the Case Evidence table is not connected to any other table. The table can reside in the database and the user can enter information into it, but it will be a stand-alone table. For example, if you wanted to print a report that had the contact information for each client and a

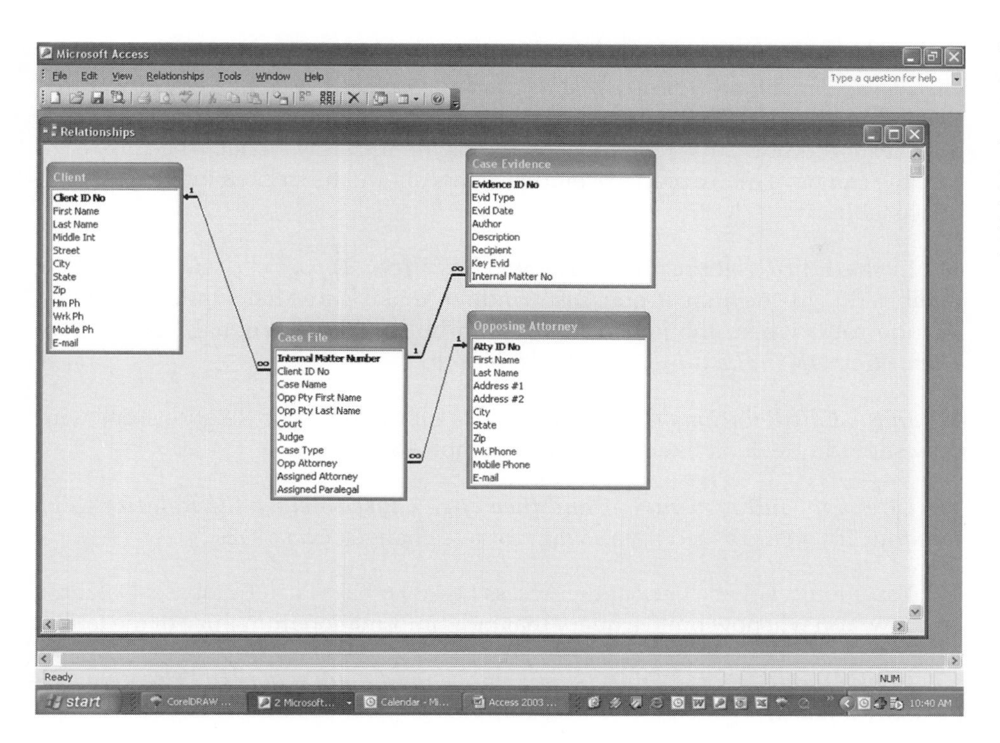

Access 2003 Exhibit 16

Completed Relationships for Access Lesson 6 Law Firm Database

Microsoft product screen shot reprinted with permission from Microsoft Corporation.

listing of all of the case evidence for the client, you would not be able to do so without creating a relationship between the tables. You will now create a one-to-many relationship between the Case File table and the Case Evidence table using the Internal Matter Number field as the conduit.

9. ***Click the Internal Matter Number field in the Case File table, then drag it to the Internal Matter No field in the Case Evidence table, and then let go.*** The Edit Relationships window should now be displayed (see Access 2003 Exhibit 17).

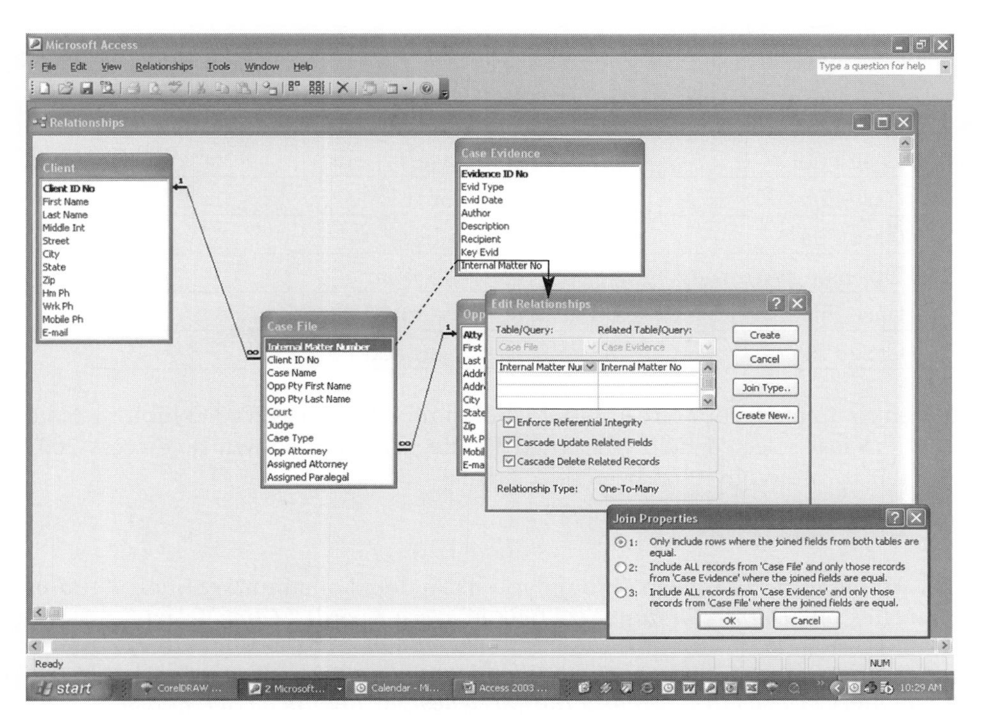

Access 2003 Exhibit 17

The Edit Relationships Window

Microsoft product screen shot reprinted with permission from Microsoft Corporation.

10. In the Edit Relationships window, ***click Enforce Referential Integrity, then click Cascade Update Related Fields, and then click Cascade Deleted Related Records*** (see Access 2003 Exhibit 17). At the bottom of the Edit Relationships window, it should now say "Relationship Type: One-to-Many." That is because each case file can have many pieces of evidence that should be tracked in the Case Evidence table.

11. In the Edit Relationships window, ***click "Join Type. . ."*** (see Access 2003 Exhibit 17). In the Join Properties window, make sure that Option 1, "Only include rows where the joined fields from both tables are equal," is selected. ***Then, click OK in the Join Properties window.***

12. ***In the Edit Relationships window, click on Create.*** Your Relationships window should now look like Access 2003 Exhibit 16.

13. ***Click File on the menu bar and then click Close to close the Relationships window.*** If you are asked if you want to save changes, ***click "Yes."***

14. You should now be back at the Access Lesson 6 Law Firm Database: Database window. You will now build a query that pulls information from three of the tables.

15. ***Click Queries on the Objects bar. Point and double-click on "Create query by using wizard."***

16. The Simple Query Wizard should now be displayed. Under Tables/Queries, ***click the down arrow and select Table: Client.*** Notice that now the fields for the Client table are shown under Available Fields. ***Click Last Name and then click ">" to add the field under Selected Fields.*** You will now build the query by selecting the tables and fields exactly as shown below. It is recommended that you do this carefully, since you must skip around among the different tables to build the query correctly.

In addition to the Last Name field you already selected, enter the following:

TABLE	FIELD TO SELECT
Client	First Name
Case File	Case Name
Case File	Case Type
Case File	Court
Case File	Judge
Opposing Attorney	Last Name
Case File	Assigned Attorney
Case File	Assigned Paralegal

When completed, your screen should look similar to Access 2003 Exhibit 18. Note that the last selected field (Assigned Paralegal) is not shown on Access 2003 Exhibit 18, although it has been selected.

17. ***Click Next.***

18. You will then be asked "Would you like a detail or summary query?" ***Point and click on "Detail (Shows every field of every record)." Click "Next."***

19. You will then be asked "What title do you want for your query?" Type **Case List Query**. ***Then, click "Modify the query design" and then click Finish.***

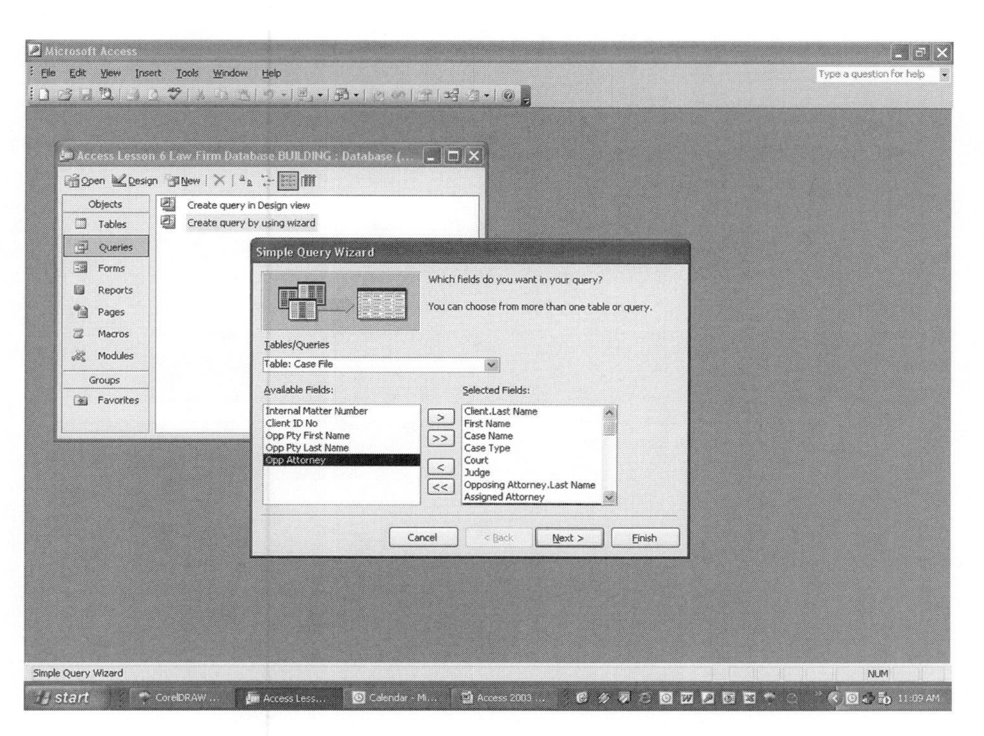

Access 2003 Exhibit 18
Building a Query With Multiple Tables in Query Wizard
Microsoft product screen shot reprinted with permission from Microsoft Corporation.

20. The query is displayed on your screen in Design view. Notice that each column shows one of the fields and that the table that it is drawn from is shown in the Table row (see Access 2003 Exhibit 19).

21. ***Click the Sort row in the first column, Client_Last Name:L, and then click the down arrow and click Ascending*** (see Access 2003 Exhibit 19). This tells Access that the primary sort for the database will be on this field.

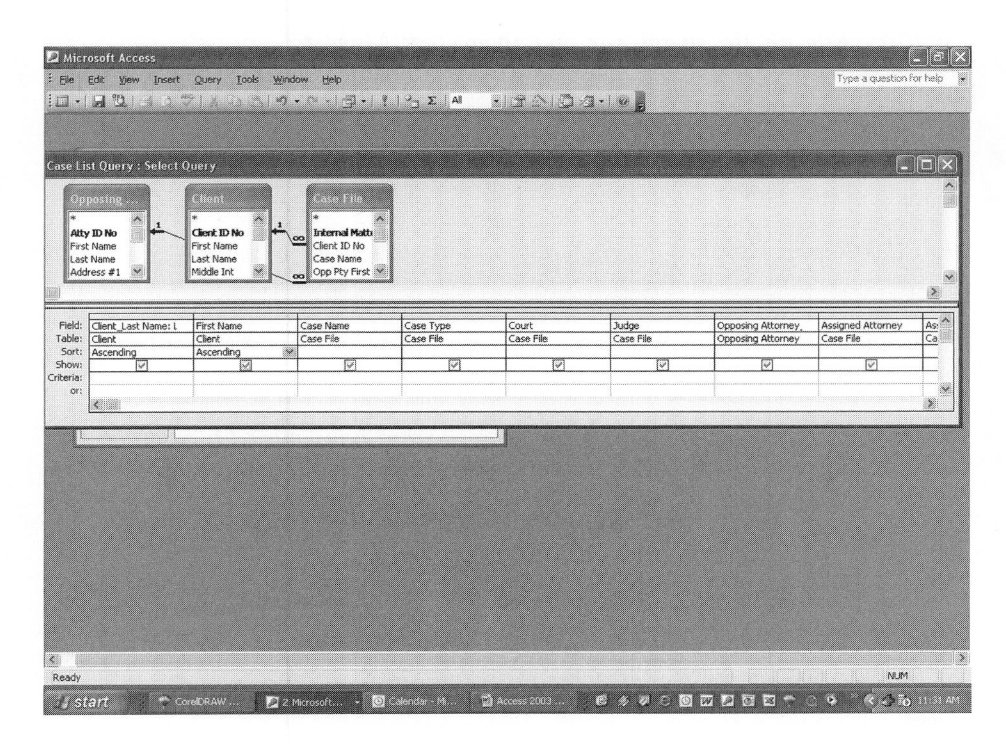

Access 2003 Exhibit 19
Modifying the Case List Query in Design View
Microsoft product screen shot reprinted with permission from Microsoft Corporation.

Access 2003 Exhibit 20
Completed Case List Query in Datasheet View
Microsoft product screen shot reprinted with permission from Microsoft Corporation.

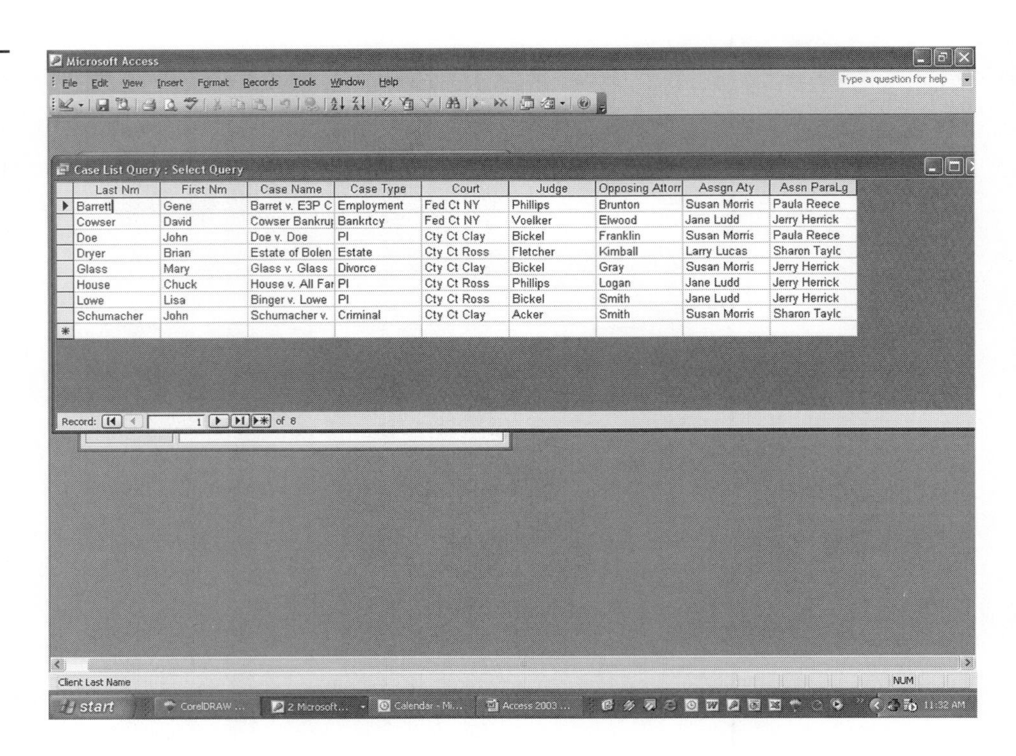

22. ***Click the Sort row in the second column, First Name, and then click the down arrow and click Ascending*** (see Access 2003 Exhibit 19). This tells Access that the secondary sort for the database will be on this field.

23. ***Click the Run icon on the toolbar (it looks like a bright red exclamation mark).*** Your query should look similar to Access 2003 Exhibit 20.

24. ***Click the Save icon on the toolbar (it looks like a floppy disk).***

25. ***Click File on the menu bar and then click Close to close the Case List Query.***

26. You should now be back at the Access Lesson 6 Law Firm Database : Database window. You will now build a report that uses the Case List Query you just created.

27. ***Click Reports on the Objects bar.*** Notice that there are already a few reports made. You will make another.

28. ***Double-click "Create report by using wizard."*** The Report Wizard window should now be displayed.

29. Under Tables/Queries, ***click the down arrow and select Query:Case List Query. Then, click the ">>" icon (two "greater than" symbols) to add all of the fields in the Case List Query to the report.***

30. ***Now, click Next.***

31. You will then be asked "How do you want to view your data?" ***Click "Next".***

32. You will then be asked "Do you want to add any grouping levels?" ***Click "Next".***

33. You will then be asked "What sort order do you want for your report?" Because the query is already sorting the data, ***click Next.***

34. You are now asked "How would you like to lay out the report?" ***Click "Block" and then click Landscape under Orientation. Leave the check mark in the "Adjust the field width so all fields fit on a page" option. Then, select Next.***

35. You will then be asked "What style would you like?" ***Click "Formal". Then, click Next.***

36. You are then asked "What title would you like for the report?" Type **Case List Report**, leave the "Preview the report" option selected, and ***click Finish.***

37. The report is then displayed on your screen. It should look similar to Access 2003 Exhibit 21.

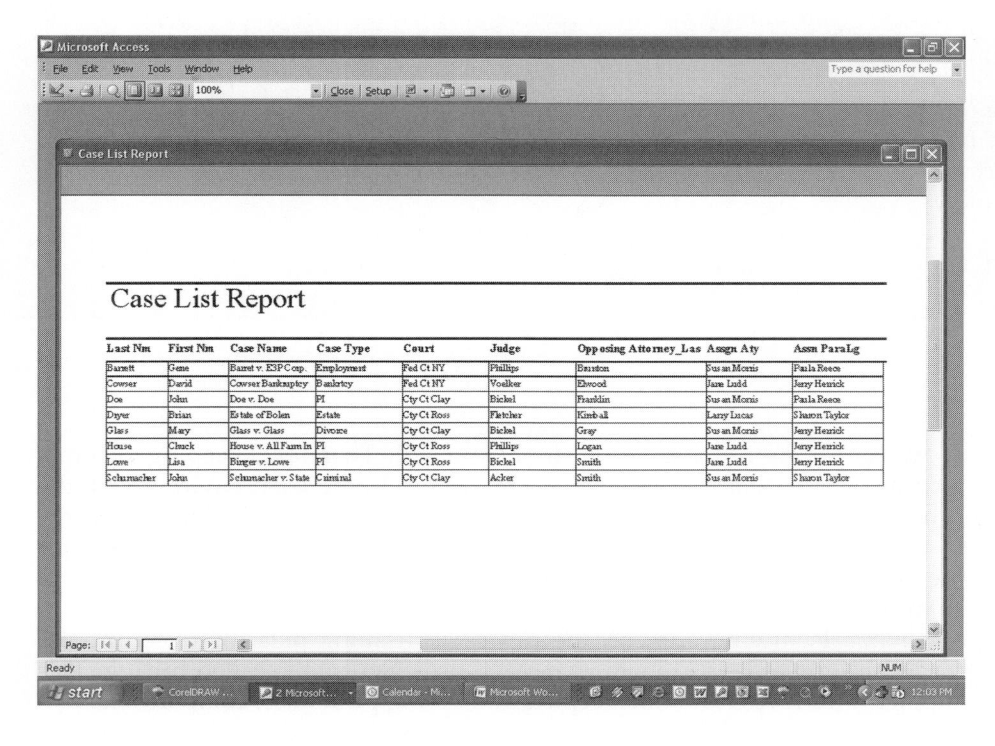

Case List Report

Last Nm	First Nm	Case Name	Case Type	Court	Judge	Opposing Attorney_Las	Assgn Aty	Assn ParaLg
Barrett	Gene	Barret v. E3P Corp.	Employment	Fed Ct NY	Phillips	Burton	Susan Morris	Paula Reece
Cowser	David	Cowser Bankruptcy	Bankrtcy	Fed Ct NY	Voelker	Elwood	Jane Ludd	Jerry Henrick
Doe	John	Doe v. Doe	PI	Cty Ct Clay	Bickel	Franklin	Susan Morris	Paula Reece
Dryer	Brian	Estate of Bolen	Estate	Cty Ct Ross	Fletcher	Kimball	Larry Lucas	Sharon Taylor
Glass	Mary	Glass v. Glass	Divorce	Cty Ct Clay	Bickel	Gray	Susan Morris	Jerry Henrick
House	Chuck	House v. All Farm In	PI	Cty Ct Ross	Phillips	Logan	Jane Ludd	Jerry Henrick
Lowe	Lisa	Binger v. Lowe	PI	Cty Ct Ross	Bickel	Smith	Jane Ludd	Jerry Henrick
Schumacher	John	Schumacher v. State	Criminal	Cty Ct Clay	Acker	Smith	Susan Morris	Sharon Taylor

Access 2003 Exhibit 21
Finalized Case List Report
Microsoft product screen shot reprinted with permission from Microsoft Corporation.

38. ***Click the printer icon on the toolbar to print your results.***

39. ***Click File on the menu bar and then click Close to close the report view.***

40. ***Click File on the menu bar and then click Exit to close Access.***

This concludes the Access 2003 Hands-On Exercises.

CHAPTER

LEGAL TIMEKEEPING AND BILLING SOFTWARE

CHAPTER OBJECTIVES

After completing chapter 6, you should be able to do the following:

1. Explain what timekeeping and billing are.
2. Identify why accurate billings are important to law firms.
3. Explain the computerized timekeeping and billing process.
4. Describe the different types of legal fee agreements.
5. Explain how management reports generated from a timekeeping and billing system can help a firm.
6. Describe how timeslips are entered into a timekeeping and billing system.
7. Describe the factors to determine whether a fee is reasonable.
8. Explain what electronic billing is.

timekeeping
Tracking time for the purpose of billing clients.

billing
The process of issuing bills to collect monies for legal services performed and for expenses incurred.

A lawyer's time is what he or she has to sell. Therefore, keeping accurate records of how that time is spent is important. In the legal environment, the process of tracking time for the purpose of billing clients is called **timekeeping.** In addition to being paid for their time, attorneys must also be reimbursed for the expenses that they incur on each case (such as those for postage, copies, and so forth).

In the legal environment, the process of issuing bills to collect monies for legal services performed and for expenses incurred is called **billing.** This chapter introduces legal timekeeping and billing principles, compares manual and computerized billing systems, introduces the kinds of fee agreements attorneys and clients enter into, indicates what a good billing system accomplishes, shows examples of management reports, shows how computerized timekeeping and billing software can greatly automate this process, and discusses timekeeping and billing ethical issues.

INTRODUCTION TO TIMEKEEPING AND BILLING

Law firms, like all businesses, must generate income. All that lawyers have to sell is their time. As with other businesses, the running of law firms has a management side. One important management duty law offices perform is to track the time and expenses of their staff and then generate accurate billings to their clients so that they can be paid. Attorneys spend their time advising clients, talking to witnesses, drafting documents, taking depositions (oral testimonies),

appearing in court, and so forth on behalf of their clients. These activities must be tracked so that clients can be accurately billed for the work that attorneys do. In addition, the expenses attorneys incur on behalf of clients must be tracked so that the attorneys can be reimbursed. Expenses incurred on behalf of clients include the cost of making photocopies of documents for a client's file, the cost of mailing letters and other documents, travel expenses incurred while working on a client's case, court filing fees, deposition transcription costs, and more.

Without tracking time and expenses, firms could not generate bills, get paid, and adequately run a business. Although timekeeping and billing are not glamorous, they are necessary to the survival of nearly all law firms. Firms that do not put a priority on billing clients on a regular and accurate basis will most likely not be around long. It is simply bad business practice to work 70 hours a week, bill 50 hours, and be paid for 30 hours.

The timekeeping and billing problem becomes even worse when large law firms have to track the time and expenses of hundreds of attorneys and hundreds of legal assistants. A good timekeeping and billing system is an absolute necessity.

Why Do Legal Assistants Need to Know Timekeeping and Billing?

There are several reasons why legal assistants need to know about timekeeping and billing. In many private law practices, legal assistants are required to track their time so it can be charged to the case(s) they are working on. According to a recent survey, a little more than 50 percent of all legal assistants are required to bill for their time. Many law practices that follow this system require legal assistants to bill a minimum number of hours a year. It is important to remember that private law firms are fundamentally businesses, and like any business, their function is to make money, operate at a profit, and earn money for their owners. Therefore, the billing of time to a firm's clients is crucial to its operations and success as a business. A recent survey of legal assistants found that legal assistants were most often expected to bill between 26 and 35 hours a week (1,352 and 1,820 annually). Thus, it is necessary for legal assistants to understand how timekeeping and billing works. **Legal assistants are sometimes discharged from their jobs because they fail to bill the required number of hours**. The issue of tracking time and billing to a minimum number of hours is very important in many offices.

In addition, legal assistants are sometimes put in charge of actually running the timekeeping and billing system, including managing the timekeeping process and generating bills. This usually occurs in smaller law offices. In those cases, it is important for them not only to know the process but also to know how to actually run and operate the system. Timekeeping and billing are important issues because the survival of law offices depends on their ability to track and bill time.

MANUAL VERSUS COMPUTERIZED BILLING SYSTEMS

Before legal billing software, billings were generated manually, using typewriters or word processors. The manual method was cumbersome and slow, commonly produced billings that had mathematical errors, and often produced billings that were outdated or inaccurate. This was especially true for large firms with hundreds and hundreds of clients.

Long ago, it was common for law firms to send out billings only when they needed to pay their bills (rent, staff salaries, etc.). Attorneys often sat down with a client's file months after work had been performed and tried to remember what they had done on the case and how much time it took them to do it. These billings were of course very inaccurate, since it is extremely hard to remember this type of information after the fact. In addition, the billings took hours and hours to prepare using manual methods, especially if a large number of them were being done.

timeslip
A slip of paper or computer slip where legal professionals record information about the legal services they provide to each client.

The more traditional way of handling manual billings is to send out billings based on timeslips that an attorney or legal assistant fills out every day. A **timeslip** is a slip of paper or computer slip where legal professionals record information about the legal services they provide to each client. Most timeslips contain information such as the name of the case worked on, the date a service was provided, a description of the service, and so on (see Exhibit 6–1). In addition to tracking time,

Exhibit 6–1
Typical Manual Timeslip/Time Record Form

		Time Conversion	
PC—Phone Conference	R—Review	6 Minutes 5.1 Hour	36 Minutes 5.6 Hour
LR—Legal Research	OC—Office Conference	12 Minutes 5.2 Hour	42 Minutes 5.7 Hour
L—Letter	T—Travel	15 Minutes 5.25 Hour	45 Minutes 5.75 Hour
D—Dictation	CT—Court Hearing	18 Minutes 5.3 Hour	48 Minutes 5.8 Hour
		24 Minutes 5.4 Hour	54 Minutes 5.9 Hour
		30 Minutes 5.5 Hour	60 Minutes 51.0 Hour

Date	Client/Case	File No.	Services Performed	Attorney	Time Hours & Tenths	
5-7	Smith v. United Sales	118294	Summarized 6 depositions; Client; Δ (Defendant) Helen; Δ Barney, Δ Rose; Witness Forrest & Johnson	BJP	6.	5
5-8	Marcel v. True Oil	118003	PC w/Client Re: Settlement offer; Discussions w/Attorney; Memo to file Re: offer	BJP	.	3
5-8	Johnson v. State	118118	PC w/Client's Mother, PC w/Client; LR Re: Bail; Memo to file; R correspondence	BJP	.	75
5-8	Potential claim of Watkins v. Leslie Grocery	Not Assigned Yet	OC w/Client; (New client); Reviewed facts; Received medical records Re; accident; Conf. w/atty	BJP	1.	50
5-8	Smith v. United Sales	118294	Computerized searches on depositions for attorney	BJP	.	75
5-8	Jay Tiller Bankruptcy	118319	PC w/Creditor, Bank One; Memo to file; Client; LJ to Client	BJP	.	3
5-8	Potential Claim of Watkins v. Leslie Grocery	—	LR Slip & Fall cases generally; Standard of care	BJP	1.	00
5-8	Marcel v. True Oil	118003	Conf. w/atty. & Client Re: Settlement; Drafted & prepared LJ to Δs Re: Settlement offer	BJP	1.	10
5-8	Jay Tiller Bankruptcy	118319	Drafted Bankruptcy petition; OC w/Client; List of Debts; Fin. Stmt; Conf. w/atty	BJP	1.	00
5-8	Smith v. United Sales	118294	Drafted and prepared depo notice to Witness Spring	BJP	.	25
5-9	Seeley Real Estate Matter	118300	Ran amortization schedule to attach to 'Contract for Deed'	BJP	.	25

all law firms must also track expenses. An **expense slip** is a record of each expense item a firm incurs on behalf of a client (see Exhibit 6–2). When a member of a firm incurs an expense for a client, such as by making copies of documents, using postage to send out material, or making long-distance phone calls, an expense slip is filled out (see Exhibit 6–3 for a list of the kinds of items billed to clients). Then, usually on a monthly basis, manual billings are sent out, based on the timeslips and expense slips that have been kept. Although the billings based on timeslips are more accurate than those based on memory, the billing process itself is still quite tedious and slow.

expense slip
A record of each expense item a firm incurs on behalf of the client.

Because manual billing systems are slow and cumbersome and take a great deal of time, many law firms using them experience cash flow problems. Billings are sent out infrequently, and it is only when they are sent that a firm receives the money it needs. During the time (months in some cases) that it takes to generate the billings, firms will not have enough money on hand to pay their current bills.

Johnson, Beck & Taylor
Expense Slip

Expense Type & Code

1 Photocopies	4 Filing Fees	7 Facsimile	10 Travel
2 Postage	5 Witness Fees	8 Lodging	11 Overnight Delivery
3 Long Distance	6 WESTLAW/LEXIS	9 Meals	12 Other ________

Date 4-5-08	Case Name: Smith v. United		File No. 118294
Expense Code: 1	Quantity 20 pages	Amount File rate	(Billable) Non-Billable
Expense Code: 2	Quantity 4 packages	Amount $4.66	(Billable) Non-Billable
Expense Code:	Quantity sent	Amount	Billable Non-Billable

Name of Person Making Expense Slip: JBP

Description of Expense(s) Incurred:
Copies and postage re: Motion to compel 4/5

Exhibit 6–2
Expense Slip

Expense Items Billed to Clients
Conference Call Costs
Copying Costs
Court Reporter Fees
Electronic Legal Research (Westlaw/Lexis)*
Expert Witness Fees
Fax Costs
Filing Fees
Overnight Delivery Charges (FedEx, etc.)
Postage
Travel Expenses
Witness Fees

*Some offices charge clients for this and some do not

Exhibit 6–3
Expenses Typically Billed to Clients

Computerized billing systems solve many of these problems. Exactly how much time a computerized time and billing program saves over a manual system is somewhat debatable, but a study by one attorney found that manual billing systems can take up to three times longer to produce bills *every billing cycle* (i.e., every time billings are sent, whether it be biweekly, monthly, or according to some other schedule) than computerized methods. Generally, timekeepers still must record what they do with their time on a timeslip, whether it be paper or computerized. A **timekeeper** is anyone, including partners, associates, and legal assistants, who bills out his or her time. Usually, paper timeslips are entered into the legal billing software on a daily basis. There is a growing trend for attorneys and legal assistants to enter their time directly into the computerized timekeeping and billing system without using a timeslip at all. This is particularly true in law offices where all timekeepers are connected to a local area network. It is common for firms using computerized billing systems to produce monthly or even weekly bills according to the wishes of the client. In addition to alleviating cash flow problems, most legal billing software produces reports that management can use to help operate the law firm business (this is covered in more detail later in the chapter). Computerized timekeeping and billing systems also produce billings that are more accurate than those produced by manual methods, since all mathematical computations are performed automatically by a computer.

timekeeper
Anyone, including partners, associates, and legal assistants, who bills out time.

THE COMPUTERIZED TIMEKEEPING AND BILLING PROCESS

Timekeeping and billing software packages differ greatly from one another. However, the computerized timekeeping and billing process for most billing packages is as shown in Exhibit 6–4.

Exhibit 6–4
Computerized Timekeeping and Billing Cycle

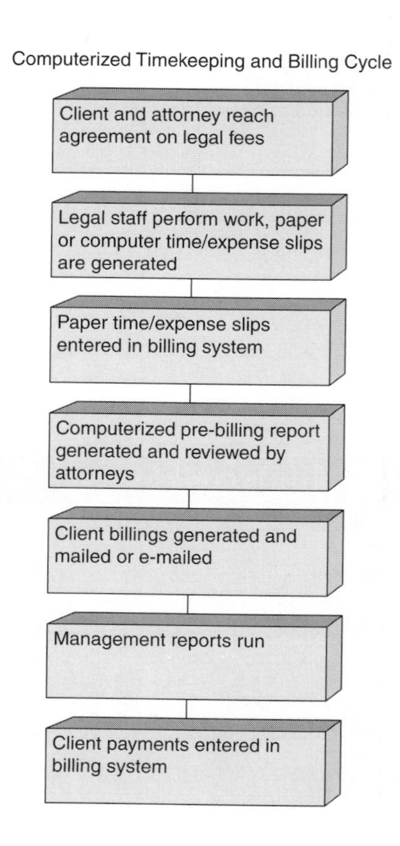
Computerized Timekeeping and Billing Cycle
Client and attorney reach agreement on legal fees
Legal staff perform work, paper or computer time/expense slips are generated
Paper time/expense slips entered in billing system
Computerized pre-billing report generated and reviewed by attorneys
Client billings generated and mailed or e-mailed
Management reports run
Client payments entered in billing system

1. The Client and the Attorney Reach an Agreement on Legal Fees

An attorney can bill for services in many different ways. At the outset of most cases, the client and the attorney reach an agreement regarding how much the attorney will charge for her or his services. Preferably, the agreement is in writing in the form of a contract. After the legal fee has been agreed on, the new matter is set up in the computerized billing package by entering information including the client's name and address, the type of case it is, and the type of legal fee that has been agreed on.

2. Legal Staff Perform Legal Services and Prepare Timeslips

When attorneys or legal assistants perform work on a legal matter for a client, they fill out a timeslip to track the exact services (either using a manual timeslip form or entering the information directly into the computer). Many timekeeping and billing programs also support data entry from a handheld PDA (Personal Digital Assistant). Expense slips are also generated.

3. Timeslips and Expense Slips Are Entered into the Billing System

If manual timeslips are used, they must be entered into the billing system. The information is typed into the computer in roughly the same format as it appears on the timeslip. It is essential that the information be accurately entered into the computer. In addition, expense slips are entered into the computer to track the expenses a firm incurs on behalf of a client.

4. A Pre-Billing Report Is Generated and Reviewed

After legal services have been performed and recorded in the time and billing software, the next step is for a **pre-billing report** to be generated. This is done before the final client bills are generated. A pre-billing report is a rough draft of billings that eventually will be sent to clients (see Exhibit 6–5). The pre-billing report is given to the attorney in charge of the case for review or to a billing committee to make sure the billing is accurate.

pre-billing report
A rough draft version of billings.

Attorneys may choose to discount bills for a variety of reasons, including thinking the task should have taken less time than it actually did. Discounts also are used for good customers, because of the client's hardship, for professional courtesy or for friends, or because the billing looks unreasonable. This can, however, be very frustrating to a legal assistant who has his or her time cut back. Typically, only the amount that is actually billed is counted against the target or minimum billable number of hours.

5. Client Billings Are Generated and Mailed or Emailed

Formal client billings are generated by the billing system (see Exhibit 6–6). Most timekeeping and billing software can produce many different billing formats. The computer automatically prints the bills, and they are subsequently mailed or emailed to the clients. Most computerized billing systems can now produce some form of electronic billing or can produce PDF files that can be emailed.

6. Management Reports Are Generated

Most computerized timekeeping and billing programs have a wide variety of management reports available. Management reports are not used for billing

Exhibit 6–5
Pre-billing Report

JOHNSON, BECK & TAYLOR

8/01	Pre-billing Report	Page 1

Refrigeration, Inc.	Corporate Matters
Miscellaneous Corporate Matters	Monthly
Case Number: Refrig-002	Trust Balance: $2,825
P.O. Box 10083	Case Rate: $125
500 East Fifth Street	Case Attorney: MJB
Los Angeles, CA 90014	
Phone: (213) 553-9342	

Previous Bill Owed $470.20

—Legal Fees—

7/6	MJB	Telephone conference with Stevenson re: June minutes	.50 hr	$62.50
7/7	MJB	Preparation of June minutes; prepared for review at next meeting of the board of directors	1.00 ~~1.50~~ hr	$125.00 MJB ~~$187.50~~
7/9	MJB	Conference with Stevenson at home	.25 hr	none
		Total Legal Fees	1.75 **~~2.25~~ hr**	$187.50 MJB **~~$250.00~~**

—Costs Advanced—

7/7	MJB	Photocopy documents; June 2005 minutes (for board meeting)	$.25 ea	
			100 items	$25.00
		Total Costs Advanced		**$25.00**

Continued on Page Two

clients; they are used to evaluate the effectiveness of a firm. For example, most programs generate a report that shows how much time is nonbillable (i.e., not chargeable to clients). If a firm has a lot of nonbillable time, it might indicate that the firm is not productive and is losing valuable time from its timekeepers.

Management reports can also be used to make management decisions, such as that particular types of cases are no longer profitable, the firm needs to raise hourly rates, or other types of decisions.

7. Client Payments Are Entered into the Billing System

Finally, payments made as a result of billings must be recorded or entered into the billing system, giving clients proper credit for the payments.

The timekeeping and billing process is a recurring cycle. Once billings are produced and payments are made for a period, the process starts over if more work is performed on a case. The timeslips for the new period must be entered, billings must be generated, and so forth. Once a year or so, old timeslips should be purged or deleted from the computer. This allows the computer to operate faster without the outdated information.

In essence, the manual systems have the same process or cycle as the computerized versions, except that the pre-billing report, final billings, and payments are all recorded by hand. In addition, most manual systems do not have the capability to produce management reports.

Exhibit 6–6
Final Client Billing

JOHNSON, BECK & TAYLOR
555 Flowers Street, Suite 200
Los Angeles, California 90038
(212) 585-2342

Mary Smith
Refrigeration, Inc.
P.O. Box 10083
500 East Fifth Street

Los Angeles, CA 90014

Billing Date: 8/02

Acct. Number: 4345AS3234
Previous Bal. in Trust
$2,825.00

RE: Refrigeration Miscellaneous Corporate Matters

DATE	PROFESSIONAL SERVICES	INDIV.	TIME	
7/6	Telephone conference with Stevenson re: June minutes	MJB	.50	$62.50
7/7	Preparation of June minutes: prepared for review at next meeting of the board of directors	MJB	1.00	$125.00
7/9	Conference with Stevenson at home	MJB	.25	$-0-
TOTAL FOR THE ABOVE SERVICES			**1.75**	**$187.50**

DATE	EXPENSES	
7/7	Photocopy documents; June minutes (for board meeting)	$25.00
TOTAL FOR ABOVE EXPENSES		**$25.00**
TOTAL BILLING		**$212.50**
CURRENT BALANCE IN TRUST		**$2,612.50**

KINDS OF LEGAL FEE AGREEMENTS

Legal fees can be structured in many different ways. The kind of legal fee depends on the type of case or client matter, the specific circumstances of each particular client, and the law practice's preference toward certain types of fee agreements. Fee agreements can be hourly rate fees, contingency fees, flat fees, and retainer fees.

Hourly Rate Fees

An **hourly rate fee** is a fee for legal services that is billed to the client by the hour at an agreed-upon rate. For example, suppose a client hires an attorney to draft a business contract. The client agrees to pay $250 for every hour the attorney spends drafting the contract and advising the client. If the attorney spent four hours working on the contract, the client would owe the attorney $1,000 ($250 times 4 hours equals $1,000).

hourly rate fee
A fee for legal services that is billed to the client by the hour at an agreed-upon rate.

Hourly rate agreements can be complicated. Law offices have several specific types of hourly rate contracts, including the following:

- attorney or legal assistant hourly rate
- client hourly rate
- blended hourly rate fee
- activity hourly rate

Some law practices use a combination of these to bill clients.

attorney or legal assistant hourly rate
A fee based on the attorney's or legal assistant's level of expertise and experience in a particular area.

Attorney or Legal Assistant Hourly Rate The attorney's or legal assistant's level of expertise and experience in a particular area determines the **attorney or legal assistant hourly rate.** Exhibit 6–7 is an example of this type of contract. If a partner or shareholder worked on a case, his or her hourly rate charge might be considerably more than an associate or legal assistant's hourly rate charge. Partners typically can bill from $300 to $600 or more an hour, compared with associates, who might bill $200 to $350 an hour. Legal assistants typically charge from $65 to $135 and above an hour. Exhibit 6–8 shows legal assistant billing rates. The difference in

Exhibit 6–7
Attorney/Legal Assistant Hourly Rate Contract

Hourly Rate Contract for Legal Services

This contract for legal services is entered into by and between H. Thomas Weber (hereinafter "Client") and Johnson, Beck & Taylor (hereinafter "Attorneys") on this _____ day of December, 200__. The following terms and conditions constitute the entirety of the agreement between Attorneys and Client and said agreement supersedes and is wholly separate and apart from any previous written or oral agreements.

1. Client hereby agrees to employ Attorneys and Attorneys hereby agree to represent Client in connection with a contract dispute in Jefferson County District Court of Client's claim against Westbridge Manufacturing.
2. Client agrees to pay a retainer fee of $5,000.00, which will be held in Attorney's trust account until earned.
3. Client agrees to pay associate attorneys at $250.00 per hour, partners at $350.00 per hour, legal assistants at $100.00 per hour and senior legal assistants at $115.00 per hour for legal services rendered regarding the matter in paragraph (1). Attorneys are not hereby obligated to take an appeal from any judgment at the trial court level; if an occasion for an appeal arises, Attorneys and Client hereby expressly agree that employment for such an appeal must be arranged by a separate contract between Attorneys and Client.
4. Client agrees to reimburse Attorneys for all expenses incurred in connection with said matter: and Client agrees to advance all expenses requested by Attorneys during the duration of this contract. Client understands that he is ultimately responsible for the payment of all expenses incurred in connection with this matter.
5. Client understands that Attorneys will bill Client periodically (usually on a monthly or quarterly basis, depending on how quickly the case moves through the system) for copying costs at the rate of $.25 per copy, postage and handling costs, long-distance telephone costs, travel costs, and other costs, and that Client is obligated to make payments upon said billing for said fees and expenses described at paragraphs (2), (3) and (4) above, or otherwise satisfy said fees and expenses. Attorneys will also bill Client for all deposition costs incurred and Client is solely responsible for said deposition costs and Client will be required to advance the sum of **$10,000.00** (or more as necessary) or trial costs (including subpoenas, travel costs, and preparation costs) once the case is set for trial.
6. Client understands and agrees that this litigation may take two to five years or longer to complete and that he will make himself available for Attorneys to confer with and generally to assist Attorneys in said matter. Client agrees he will not discuss the matter of his litigation with any unauthorized person at any time or in any way. Client understands and agrees that Attorneys may withdraw from representation of Client upon proper notice. Client further understands that he can apply for judicial review and approval of this fee agreement if he so desires.
7. Client agrees that associate counsel may be employed at the discretion of Attorneys and that any attorney so employed may be designated to appear on Client's behalf and undertake Client's representation in this matter and such representation shall be upon the same terms as set out herein. **Client understands that Attorneys cannot and do not guarantee any particular or certain relief and expressly state that they cannot promise or guarantee Client will receive any money damages or money settlement.**

Hourly rate language (paragraph 3)

The undersigned hereby voluntarily executes this agreement with a full understanding of same and without coercion or duress. All agreements contained herein are severable and in the event any of them shall be deemed to be invalid by any competent court, this contract shall be interpreted as if such invalid agreements or covenants were not contained herein. Client acknowledges receiving a fully executed copy of this contract.

Date ________ ____________________

Date ________ Johnson, Beck & Taylor

NOTE: THIS IS ONLY AN EXAMPLE AND IS NOT INTENDED TO BE A FORM. CHECK WITH YOUR STATE BAR FOR A PROPER FORM.

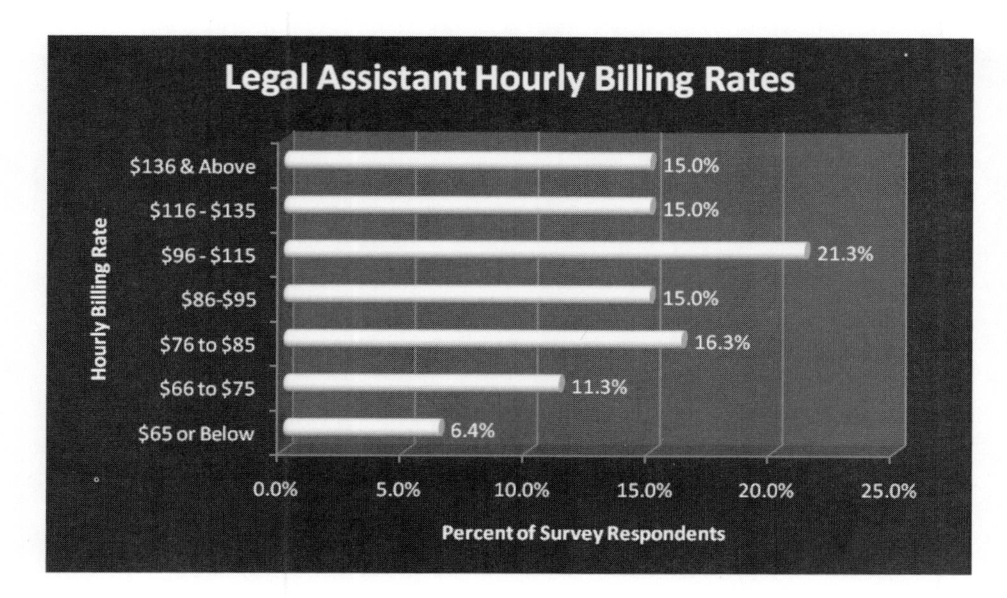

Exhibit 6–8
Legal Assistant Hourly Billing Rates
As seen in the March/April 2006 issue of *Legal Assistant Today*, Copyright 2006 James Publishing Inc. Reprinted courtesy of LEGAL ASSISTANT TODAY magazine. For subscription information call (800) 394-2626, or visit www.legalassistanttoday.com.

price is based on the expertise and experience of the individual working on the case and on locally acceptable rates. In this type of fee agreement, it is possible for a client to be billed at several different rates in a given period if several attorneys or legal assistants work on a matter, since they all may have different rates.

Client Hourly Rate The **client hourly rate** method is based on only one hourly charge for the client, regardless of which attorney works on the case and what is done on the case. For example, if an insurance company hired a law practice to represent it, the insurance company and the law practice might negotiate a client charge of $200 per hour for attorneys and $85 an hour for legal assistants. This means that no matter which attorney or legal assistant works on the case, whether the attorney or legal assistant has one year's or 20 years' experience, and regardless of what the attorney or legal assistant does (e.g., making routine phone calls or appearing in court), the insurance company would be charged $200 an hour for attorney time or $85 an hour for legal assistant time.

client hourly rate
A fee based on one hourly charge for the client, regardless of which attorney works on the case and what she or he does on the case.

Blended Hourly Rate Fee An hourly rate that is set taking into account the blend or mix of law office staff working on a matter is a **blended hourly rate fee.** The "mix" includes the mix among associates, partners, and sometimes legal assistants working on the matter. Some states allow the "blend" to include only associates and partners, while other states allow legal assistants to be included. The advantage to this is that billing is simpler, since there is one rate for all legal assistant and attorney time spent on the case. The bill is easier for the law office to produce and easier for the client to read. Some states will allow legal assistants to have their own "blend" and have one rate for all legal assistants whether experienced or inexperienced.

blended hourly rate fee
One hourly rate that is set taking into account the blend or mix of attorneys working on the matter.

Activity Hourly Rate An **activity hourly rate** is based on the different hourly rates depending on what type of service or activity is actually performed. For example, offices using this approach might bill legal staff time to clients as follows:

Court appearances	$350 per hour
Legal research by attorneys	$225 per hour

activity hourly rate
A fee based on different hourly rates depending on the type of service or activity performed and the degree of difficulty of the activity.

Drafting by attorneys	$175 per hour
Telephone calls by attorneys	$150 per hour
Legal research by legal assistants	$80 per hour
Drafting by legal assistants	$70 per hour

This is a sliding-scale hourly fee based on the difficulty of an activity. Hourly rate agreements, no matter what the type, are the most common kind of fee agreement.

Exhibit 6–9
Fee Projection Worksheet

Johnson, Beck & Taylor Law Firm
Fee Projection Worksheet (Litigation)

Case: *Redcliff Ski Technologies v. Powell Ski & Surf Industries Litigation*
Date: 12/1/xx

	Partner	Associate	Paralegal
Billing Rate	$325	$225	$85

No.	Description	Partner Hours	Associate Hours	Paralegal Others
I.	Preliminary Work	3	2	2
II.	Factual Investigation		2	4
III.	Strategy Conference	2	2	2
IV.	Initial Legal Research			
	Issue 1 - Mutuality of Contract	2	8	1
	Issue 2 - Agreement of Parties	2	8	1
V.	Complaint/Answer/Counterclaim	2	4	1
VI.	Motions (nondiscovery)			
	A. Motion to Dismiss	3	8	3
VII.	Witness Interviews	2	10	10
VIII.	Discovery			
	A. Drafting Interrogatories	1	2	14
	B. Answering Interrogatories	2	8	20
	C. Drafting Discovery Requests	5	8	30
	D. Reviewing Produced Documents & E-Discovery	10	8	50
	E. Responding to Doc. Requests	8	15	20
	F. Opposing Party Depos			
	Party 1: Jack Radcliff	18	18	
	Witnesses:		20	
	G. Our Depos			
	Our Client:	14	14	
	Witnesses	12	12	
IX.	Discovery Motions	2	8	8
X.	Additional Legal Research	2	14	5
XI.	Motions (Substantive)			
	Motion 1: Summary Judgment	12	20	4
	Motions: Other	10	20	3
XII.	Pretrial Memoranda/Conf	4	10	
XIII.	Settlement Conference	5	5	
XIV.	Trial			
	Preparation Hours	40	40	14
	Trial Hours	40	40	20
XV.	Miscellaneous phone calls/strategy	10	10	10
	Total Hours	211	316	222
	TOTAL PROJECTED FEES	$68,575	$71,100	$18,870
	GRAND TOTAL			$158,545

One of the frustrations for clients regarding legal professionals billing by the hour is that a client has no idea what the total cost of the matter will be. One of the things that can help in this regard is a fee projection worksheet. These are particularly helpful for clients in litigation because the costs can go on for a number of years. Using a tool like this at the beginning of a matter, legal staff can set the expectation regarding what the total costs will be.

Contingency Fees

A **contingency fee** is a fee that is collected if the attorney successfully represents the client. The attorney is entitled to a certain percentage of the total amount of money awarded to the client. If the client's case is not won and no money is recovered, the attorney collects no legal fees, but is still entitled to be reimbursed for all expenses incurred (see Exhibit 6–10). Contingency fees are typically used in representing plaintiffs in personal injury, workers' compensation, civil rights, medical malpractice, and other types of cases in which monetary damages are generated. The individual who would like to bring the lawsuit usually has little or no money to pay legal fees up front. Contingency fees typically range from 20 percent to 50 percent.

contingency fee
A fee collected if the attorney successfully represents the client, typically a precentage of the total recovery.

For example, suppose a client hires an attorney to file a personal injury claim regarding an automobile accident the client was involved in. The client has no money, but agrees to pay the attorney 20 percent of any money that is recovered (plus legal expenses) before the case is filed, 25 percent of any money recovered after the case is filed but before trial, and 33 percent of any money recovered during trial or after appeal. Suppose the claim is settled for $10,800 after the case is filed, but before trial. Suppose the legal expenses the attorney incurred are $800. Under most state laws, legal expenses are paid first, and then the contingency fee

Written Contingency Fee Agreement Provisions

Attorneys receive

- 20% of any money recovered (plus legal expenses) before case is filed;
- 25% of any money recovered (plus legal expenses) after case is filed, but before trial;
- 33% of any money recovered (plus legal expenses) during trial or after appeal.

Settlement

Case is settled for $10,800 after case is filed, but before trial.

Attorney has $800 worth of legal expenses.

Calculation of Contingency Fee

1. Legal expenses are paid first.		
Settlement of		$10,800
Minus legal expenses		– 800
Balance		$10,000
2. Contingency fee is calculated as follows:		
Total recovery minus legal expenses		$10,000
Attorney's 25% Contingency Fee		
($10,000 X 25% = $2,500)		–2,500
	TOTAL TO CLIENT	$ 7,500
3. Total fees and expenses to attorney		
Reimbursement of legal expense		$ 800
Contingency fee		$ 2,500
	TOTAL TO ATTORNEY	$ 3,300

Exhibit 6–10
Contingency Fee Example

is calculated. The attorney would deduct the expenses off the top, and the remaining $10,000 would be divided according to the contingency fee agreement. Because the suit was settled after the case was filed but before the trial, the attorney would be entitled to receive 25 percent of any recovery. The attorney would be entitled to $2,500, and the client would be entitled to 75 percent, or $7,500 (see Exhibit 6–10).

Contingency fee agreements must be in writing. Exhibit 6–11 contains a sample contingency fee contract. Some states put a cap or a maximum percent-

Exhibit 6–11
Contingency Fee Contract

Contingency Fee Contract for Legal Services

Date:
Name: D.O.B.
Address: Phone:

1. I hereby employ **Johnson, Beck & Taylor** (hereinafter "attorneys") to perform legal services in connection with the following matter as described below:
   Personal injury claims arising out of an automobile accident which occurred January 12, 2007, on Interstate I-70.
2. I agree to pay a nonrefundable retainer fee of $2,500; plus,
3. I agree attorneys will receive 20% of any recovery, if prior to filing suit;
   I agree attorneys will receive 25% of any recovery, if prior to pretrial conference;
   I agree attorneys will receive 33% of any recovery, if after first trial begins;
   I agree attorneys will receive 33% of any recovery, if after appeal or second trial begins.
   Attorneys are not hereby obligated to take an appeal from any judgment at the trial court level; if an occasion for an appeal arises, attorneys and client hereby expressly agree that employment for such an appeal will be arranged by a separate contract between these parties. Further, I agree that attorneys will be entitled to the applicable above-mentioned percentage of recovery minus whatever a court may award, if I am a prevailing party and the court awards fees following my request therefor.

Contingency fee language

4. As to the expenses of litigation: I agree to reimburse attorneys for all expenses incurred in connection with said matter, and any expenses not fully paid as incurred may be deducted from my portion of any recovery. I agree to advance any and all expenses requested by attorneys during the duration of this contract. I agree to make an advance of expenses upon execution of this contract in the amount of $1500.00. I understand that these litigation expenses do not pertain to the retainer fee or percentage of any recovery, and I am ultimately responsible for the payment of all litigation expenses.
5. I understand that attorneys will bill client periodically, and that client is obligated to make payments upon said billing for said fees and expenses described at paragraphs (2), and (4), or otherwise satisfy said fees and expenses.
6. I understand and agree that this litigation may take 2 to 5 years, or longer to complete, and that I will make myself available to attorneys to confer with, and generally to assist attorneys in said matter. I will not discuss the matter of my litigation with any unauthorized person at any time in any way. I understand and agree that attorneys may withdraw from representation of client at any time upon proper notice.
7. I agree that associate counsel may be employed at the discretion of Johnson, Beck & Taylor, and that any attorney so employed may be designated to appear on my behalf and undertake my representation in this matter and such representation shall be upon the same terms as set out herein. Attorneys have **not** guaranteed, nor can they guarantee, any particular or certain relief.
   The undersigned herewith executes this agreement with a full understanding of same, without coercion or duress, and understands the same to be the only agreement between the parties with regard to the above matter, and that if any other terms are to be added to this contract, the same will not be binding, unless and until they are reduced to writing and signed by all parties to this contract. I acknowledge receiving a fully executed copy of this contract. Further, the undersigned Client understands that said Client is entitled to apply for judicial review and approval of this fee agreement, if Client so desires.

Date

Date Johnson, Beck & Taylor

NOTE: THIS IS ONLY AN EXAMPLE AND IS NOT INTENDED TO BE A FORM. CHECK WITH YOUR STATE BAR FOR A PROPER FORM.

age on what an attorney can collect in areas such as workers' compensation and medical malpractice claims. For example, some states prevent attorneys from receiving more than a 25 percent contingency in a workers' compensation case. Contingency fees by their nature are risky because if no money is recovered, the attorney receives no fee. However, even if no money is recovered, the client must still pay legal expenses such as filing fees and photocopying. Contingency fees and hourly fees also may be used together. Some offices reduce their hourly fee and charge a contingency fee.

Flat Fees

A **flat fee** is a fee for legal services that is billed as a flat or fixed amount. Some offices have a set fee for handling certain types of matters, such as preparing a will or handling an uncontested divorce, a name change, or a bankruptcy (see Exhibit 6–12). For example, suppose a client agreed to pay an attorney a flat fee of $500 to prepare a will. No matter how many hours the attorney spends preparing the will, the fee is still $500. Flat fee agreements are usually used when a legal matter is simple, is straightforward, and involves few risks.

flat fee
A fee for legal services that is billed as a flat or fixed amount.

Retainer Fees

The word *retainer* has several meanings in the legal environment. Generally, retainer fees are monies paid by the client at the beginning of a case or matter. However, there are many types of retainers. When an attorney or legal assistant uses the term *retainer*, it could mean a retainer for general representation, a case retainer, a pure retainer, or a cash advance. In addition, all retainer fees are either earned or unearned.

Exhibit 6–12
Flat Fee Price List

PRICE LIST

Initial Consultation with Branch Lawyer	$100.00
REAL ESTATE	
Divorce—Uncontested	1,000.00
Domestic contracts and family litigation vary according to time involved.	
REAL ESTATE	
Purchase or Sale of House	750.00
Each Mortgage—Additional	199.00
Each Discharge of Mortgage—Additional	150.00
Refinancing	399.00
WILLS & ESTATES	
Basic Will	500.00
Estates, administrations, and estate litigation may vary according to time involved.	
BUSINESS	
Consultation	150.00–300.00
Incorporation	2,000.00

We provide many other business services, including
- *Commercial Leases*
- *Purchase and Sale of Businesses*
- *Trademarks & Copyright*

ADDITIONAL SERVICES

Collection—Demand Letter	200.00
Power of Attorney/ Promissory Note	100.00

PAYMENT POLICY

We require a retainer before commencing work on your behalf, which amount is paid into trust. We then draw checks on the retainer to pay out-of-pocket expenses made on your behalf and our fees.

Cash advance retainer language

We will advise you of completion of our services to you and ask you to come in and pick up the documentation involved and pay any balance owing at the same time.

In real estate transactions the balance must be paid prior to closing. In litigation and criminal matters, any outstanding account and the estimated fee for the appearance must be paid prior to the court appearance.

earned retainer
The money the law office or attorney has earned and is entitled to deposit in the office's or attorney's own bank account.

unearned retainer
Money that is paid up front by the client as an advance against the attorney's future fees and expenses. Until the money is actually earned by the attorney or law office, it actually belongs to the client.

trust or escrow account
A separate bank account, apart from a law office's or attorney's operating checking account, where unearned client funds are deposited.

Earned versus Unearned Retainers There is a *very* important difference between an earned retainer and an unearned retainer. An **earned retainer** means that the law office or attorney has earned the money and is entitled to deposit the money in the office's or attorney's own bank account and can use it to pay the attorney's or law office's operating expenses, such as salaries.

An **unearned retainer** is money that is paid up front by the client as an advance against the attorney's future fees and expenses as a kind of down payment. Until the money is actually earned by the attorney or law office, it belongs to the client. According to ethical rules, unearned retainers may *not* be deposited in the attorney's or law office's normal operating checking account. Unearned retainers must be deposited into a *separate* trust account and can be transferred into the firm's operating account as they are earned.

A **trust or escrow account** is a separate bank account, apart from a law office's or attorney's operating checking account, where unearned client funds are deposited. As an attorney or law office begins to earn an unearned retainer by providing legal services to the client, the attorney can bill the client and move the earned portion from the trust account to his or her own law office operating account.

The written contract should set out whether the retainer is earned or unearned. However, in some instances the contract may be vague on this point. Typically, when a contract refers to a nonrefundable retainer, this means an earned retainer.

Additionally, in many contracts, flat fee rates, as discussed earlier, are said to be nonrefundable and thus have been treated as earned. However, some state ethical rules regulate this area heavily, so it depends on the state. Some hold that all flat fees are a retainer, have been unearned, and must be placed in trust until they are earned. Whether a retainer is earned or unearned will depend on your state's ethical rules and on the written contract.

cash advance
Unearned monies that are an advance against the attorney's future fees and expenses.

Cash Advance Retainer One type of retainer is a cash advance. A **cash advance** is unearned monies and is an advance against the attorney's future fees and expenses. Until the cash advance is earned by the attorney, it actually belongs to the client. The cash advance is a typical type of unearned retainer.

For example, suppose a client wishes to hire an attorney to litigate a contract dispute. The attorney agrees to represent the client only if the client agrees to pay $200 an hour with a $10,000 cash advance against fees and expenses. The attorney must deposit the $10,000 in a trust account. If the attorney deposits the cash advance in his own account (whether it is the firm's account or the attorney's own personal account), the attorney has violated several ethical rules. As the attorney works on the case and bills the client for fees and expenses, the attorney will write a check out of the trust account for the amount of the billing. The attorney must tell the client that money is being withdrawn and keep an accurate balance of how much the client has left in trust. So, if after a month, the attorney billed the client for $500, the attorney would write a check for $500 from the trust account, deposit the $500 in the attorney's or the firm's own bank account, and inform the client that there was a remaining balance of $9,500 in trust. Look closely at the payment policy in Exhibit 6–12. The firm in Exhibit 6–12 requires a cash advance before it will take any case. Also, recognize that if the case ended at this point, the client would be entitled to a refund of the remaining $9,500 in trust.

retainer for general representation
A retainer typically used when a client such as a corporation or school board requires continuing legal services throughout the year.

Retainer for General Representation Another type of retainer is a **retainer for general representation**. This type of retainer is typically used when a client such as a corporation or entity requires continuing legal services throughout the year.

The client pays an amount, typically up front or on a prearranged schedule, to receive these ongoing services. For example, suppose a small school board would like to be able to contact an attorney at any time with general legal questions. The attorney and the school board could enter into this type of agreement for a fee of $7,500 every six months. The school board could contact the attorney at any time and ask general questions, and the attorney would never receive more than the $7,500 for the six-month period. Retainers for general representation allow the client to negotiate and anticipate what the fee will be for the year. This type of agreement usually covers only general legal advice and does not include matters such as litigation. Depending on the specific arrangements between the client and the attorney, and on the specific state's ethics rules, many retainers for general representation are viewed as being earned, since the client can call at any time and get legal advice. Retainers for general representation resemble a flat-fee agreement. The difference is that in a flat-fee agreement, the attorney or law office is contracting to do a specific thing for a client, such as prepare a will or file a bankruptcy. In the case of a retainer for general representation, the attorney is agreeing to make himself available to the client for all nonlitigation needs.

Case Retainer Another type of retainer is a **case retainer**, which is a fee that is billed at the beginning of a matter, is not refundable to the client, and is usually paid to the office at the beginning of the case as an incentive for the office to take the case. For example, a client comes to an attorney with a criminal matter. The attorney agrees to take on the case only if the client agrees to pay a case retainer of $1,000 up front plus $200 an hour for every hour worked on the case. The $1,000 is paid to the attorney as an incentive to take the case and thus is earned. The $200 an hour is a client hourly basis charge. Because the case retainer is earned, the attorney can immediately deposit it in the office's own bank account.

case retainer
A fee that is billed at the beginning of a matter, is not refundable to the client, and is usually paid at the beginning of the case as an incentive for the office to take the case.

Another example of a case retainer is a case involving a contingency fee. Suppose a client comes to an attorney to file an employment discrimination case. The attorney agrees to accept the case only if the client agrees to a 30 percent contingency fee and a nonrefundable or case retainer of $1,000. Again, the earned retainer is an incentive for the attorney to take the case and can be deposited in the attorney's or the office's own bank account.

Pure Retainer A rather rare type of retainer is a **pure retainer.** A pure retainer obligates the law office to be available to represent the client throughout the time period agreed upon. The part that distinguishes a pure retainer from a retainer for general representation is that the office typically must agree to not represent any of the client's competitors or to not undertake any type of representation adverse to the client. Some clients, typically major corporations, think that listing the name of a prestigious law firm as counsel has a business value that they are willing to pay for.

pure retainer
A fee that obligates the office to be available to represent the client throughout the time period agreed upon.

Retainers for general representation, case retainers, and pure retainers are *usually* earned retainers, and a cash advance is an unearned retainer. However, *the language of the contract will determine whether amounts paid to attorneys up front are earned or unearned.* The earned/unearned distinction is extremely important and is one reason all fee agreements should be in writing.

Value Billing

Recently, much has been written in the legal press about why private law practices should stop billing by the hour and use a different billing method. The reasons for the change from hourly billing include the following:

- The client never knows during any stage of the work how much the total legal fee will be.

- Clients sometimes avoid calling legal assistants and attorneys because they know they will be charged for the time, even if it is a simple phone call.
- Clients have trouble seeing the relationship between what is performed by the legal assistant or attorney and the enormous fees that can be generated.
- Hourly billing encourages lawyers and legal assistants to be inefficient. (i.e., the longer it takes to perform a job, the more revenue they earn).
- Many law offices force attorneys and legal assistants to bill a quota number of hours a year, which puts a tremendous amount of pressure on the individual legal assistant and attorney.

value billing
A type of fee agreement that is based not on the time to perform the work but on the basis of the perceived value of the services to the client.

So what is value billing? The **value billing** concept represents a type of fee agreement that is based not on the time required to perform the work but on the basis of the perceived value of the services to the client. Value billing typically provides that the attorney and client reach a consensus on the amount of fees to be charged. Because of increased competition in the legal environment and because of the power of the client as a buyer, clients are demanding that they have a say in how much they are going to pay for legal services, what type of service will be provided, and what the quality of the legal services will be for the price.

> *Value-billing works like the pricing method of your local mechanic. When a car needs work, you take it to a mechanic for an estimate. That estimate is a binding contract unless unforeseeable complications arise. To develop estimates, mechanics consult a shop manual that lists the approximate number of hours it takes to perform a given task. . . . In an industry as client-driven as the legal profession, it's only a matter of time (no pun intended) before time-billing gives way to value-billing.*[1]

LEGAL EXPENSES

Under most ethical canons, attorneys must charge for the expenses they incur on behalf of a client. Expenses include the costs of photocopies of documents, postage for mailing letters and documents regarding a case, long-distance telephone calls regarding the case, and so forth. Legal expenses for cases that are litigated or filed in court can sometimes be very high. They include court reporter fees (fees charged by a court reporter to transcribe hearings, oral statements, etc.), and expert witness fees (fees charged by experts on a particular subject, usually by the hour, to give testimony), just to name two.

TIMEKEEPING AND BILLING FOR LEGAL ASSISTANTS

Many law offices have a preoccupation with the billable hour concept and set billable hour quotas that legal assistants must meet. As indicated previously, an average number of billable hours for legal assistants ranges from 1,400 to 1,800 hours annually. Historically, this was not the case. In the late 1950s, 1,300 billable hours was thought to be realistic. The minimum number of billable hours depends greatly on the location and size of the law office and on the types of cases it handles.

> *—Then—*
> *There are only approximately 1,300 fee-earning hours per year unless the lawyer works overtime. Many of the eight hours per day available for office work are consumed in personal, civic, bar, religious, and political activities, general office administration, and other. . . matters. Either five or six hours per day would be realistic, depending upon the habits of the individual lawyer. ABA-1959*[2]

> *—Now—*
> *The overwhelming majority of law firms today have a minimum billable hour or target that they like for their legal assistants to achieve. [It's] anywhere from 1,400 to 1,800 billable hours a year depending on the law firm. In the last couple of years, more and more firms have realized they have got to be more strict about billable minimums.*[3]

Recording Time

There are several different ways to actually record and/or track your time. One method is to bill time in tenths of an hour, with .5 being a half-hour and 1.0 being an hour. Every six minutes is a tenth of the hour, so you would be billing on six-minute intervals. Billing in tenths works out as follows:

0–6 minutes = .1 hour	31–36 minutes = .6 hour
7–12 minutes = .2 hour	37–42 minutes = .7 hour
13–15 minutes = .25 hour	43–45 minutes = .75 hour
16–18 minutes = .3 hour	46–48 minutes = .8 hour
19–24 minutes = .4 hour	49–54 minutes = .9 hour
25–30 minutes= .5 hour	55–60 minutes = 1.0 hour

As an alternative, some offices will bill using a quarter of an hour as the basis, as follows:

0–15 minutes = .25 hour
16–30 minutes = .50 hour
31–45 minutes = .75 hour
46–60 minutes = 1.0 hour

> *PARALEGAL TRAPPED*
> *A paralegal, on his way to an assignment on another floor, became trapped in an elevator just after getting on. Fellow employees gathered around the elevator door. The time-conscious paralegal called out from inside the elevator, "Is this billable or nonbillable time?"*[4]

Although the quarterly basis is easier to use, it is not as accurate as the tenth of an hour system. Suppose you took a five-minute phone call from a client and your average billing rate was $70 an hour. Using the tenth of an hour system, the fee for the phone call would be $7 (.1 hour times $70 equals $7). However, using the quarterly system, the fee for the phone call would be $17.50, since .25 is the smallest interval (.25 times $70 equals $17.50), or more than twice as much.

It is important that you include as much detail as possible when completing your time records, that the language be clear and easily understood, and that the time record itself be legibly written. Clients are usually more willing to pay a bill when they know exactly what service was performed for them. For example, compare these bill excerpts:

1. Telephone conference—.50 hr. $35.00;
2. Telephone conference with client on Plaintiff's Request for Production of Documents regarding whether or not client has copies of the draft contracts at issue—.50 hr. $35.00.

Which of these bills would you rather receive?

Many clients would prefer the latter, since they are able to see, and hopefully remember, exactly what specific services they received.

Timekeeping Practices

If the average legal assistant is required to bill between 1,400 and 1,800 hours a year, it is very important that he or she take the timekeeping function extremely seriously. The following are some suggestions to consider regarding keeping track of time.

> *Be very careful with your billing. Billing extra hours just to look good is foolish. Consider how much time it should take you to complete a task and try to work within that time frame. If you are consistently a high biller because you spend an inordinate amount of time on projects, people will assume one of two things: (1) you don't know what you are doing, or (2) you are doing more than needed to accomplish the task. Remember that your client pays the bills. The most important consideration in being competitive is to provide the best service at the best price.*[5]

- *Find out how many hours you must bill annually, monthly, and weekly up front, and track where you are in relationship to the quota*—One of the first things you should do when you start a new legal assistant job is to find out how many billable hours you must have. If the office requires that you bill 1,400 hours a year, budget this on a monthly and weekly basis, and keep track of where you are so that you will not have to try to make it all up at the end of the year.
- *Find out when timesheets are due*—Another thing you should do when starting a new position is to find out exactly what day timesheets are due so that you can submit them on time.
- *Keep copies of your timesheets*—Always keep a copy of your timesheet for your own file in case the original is either lost or misplaced. Having a copy also allows you to go back and calculate your number of billable hours.

> *Just starting out as a new legal assistant I had a very hard time remembering to complete timesheets. At the end of the day. . . or week. . . I would try to recall what I had done and then put it on the timesheet. I just couldn't remember. Things happen so fast in a law office that I didn't record half of what I actually did. It didn't take long before I was getting attention—all bad. The firm assumed I wasn't doing anything, even though I was. I learned right then, record your time as you go along in a day and as you move from one task to another. That is the only way to be accurate and the only way I stayed employed.*
>
> *—Brent Roper*

- *Record your time contemporaneously on a daily basis*—One of the biggest mistakes you can make is to not record your time as you go along during the day. If you wait until the end of the day to try to remember all the things you did, there is absolutely no way you will be able to accurately reconstruct everything. In the end, you will be the one suffering, doing work you did not get credit for. So be sure to keep a timesheet handy and fill it out as you go along.
- *Record your actual time spent; do not discount your time*—Do not discount your time because you think you should have been able to perform a job faster. If it took you four hours to finish an assignment and you worked the whole four hours, there is no reason to discount the time. *If the supervising attorneys think a discount is warranted, they can decide that, but it is not up to you to do that.* However, if you made a mistake or had a problem that you do not think the client should be billed for, tell your supervising attorney, and let him or her help you make the decision.

- *Be aware if billable hours are related to bonuses or merit increases*—Be aware of how billable hours are used. In some law offices, billable hours are used in distributing bonuses and merit increases and can be used in performance evaluations, so know up front how they will be used.

> *I worked closely with a paralegal who consistently had two or three more [billable] hours a day than I did, although we arrived around the same time and did similar work all day. We usually walked each other out at night (for safety reasons). I'd look at my time for a day: 10.5 hours; and she had 13. She didn't subtract for lunch or breaks. . . . An attorney called me in to ask about the discrepancy between her time and mine. . . . The lawyer talked to her. . . . Her timesheet was accurate after that.*[6]

- *Be ethical*—Always be honest and ethical in the way you fill out your timesheets. Padding your timesheets is unethical and simply wrong. Eventually, wrongdoing regarding timekeeping, billing, or handling client funds will become apparent.
- *Be aware of things that keep you from billing time*—Be aware of things that keep you from having a productive day, such as:
  - People who lay their troubles at your feet or who are constantly taking your attention away from your work. An appropriate approach is to say, "I would really like to hear about it at lunch, but right now I am really busy."
  - Wasted time spent trying to track down other people or trying to find information you need.
  - Constant interruptions, including phone calls. If you really need to get something done, go someplace where you can get the work done, and tell others to hold your calls. However, check in every once in a while to return client phone calls. Clients should have their phone calls returned as soon as possible.

Billing for Legal Assistant Time—Legal Assistant Profitability

Many law offices bill for legal assistant time as well as for attorney time. Many clients prefer this, since the legal assistant hourly rates are much lower than attorney hourly rates. The average actual billing rate for legal assistants ranges from $65 to $135 per hour.

For example, assume an associate attorney and a legal assistant can both prepare discovery documents in a case and that the task will take seven hours. Assuming the legal assistant bills at $75 an hour and the associate bills at $150 an hour, the cost to the client if the legal assistant does the job is $525, and the cost if the associate drafts the discovery is $1,050. Thus, the client will have saved $525 by simply allowing the legal assistant to do the job. The client would still have to pay for the attorney's time to review the legal assistant's discovery, but the cost would be minimal. This represents substantial savings to clients.

The question of whether law offices can bill for legal assistant time was considered by the U.S. Supreme Court in *Missouri v. Jenkins,* 491 U.S. 274 (1989). In that case, the plaintiff was successful on several counts in a civil rights lawsuit and was attempting to recover attorney's fees from the defendant under a federal statute. The statutory language provided that the prevailing party could recover "reasonable attorney's fees" from the other party. The plaintiff argued for recovery for the time that legal assistants spent working on the case as well as for the time attorneys spent. The defendant argued that legal assistant time was not "attorney's fees." Alternatively, the defendants argued that if they did have to

pay something for legal assistant time, they should have to pay only about $15 an hour, which represents the overhead costs to the office for a legal assistant.

The Court found that legal assistants carry out many useful tasks under the direction of attorneys and that "reasonable attorney's fees" referred to the reasonable fee for work produced whether it be by attorneys or legal assistants. The Court also found that under the federal statute, legal assistant time should not be compensated for at the overhead costs to the office, but should be paid at the prevailing market rates in the area for legal assistant time. The Court noted that the prevailing rate for legal assistants in that part of the country at that time was about $40 an hour and held that the office was entitled to receive that amount for legal assistant hours worked on the case. Thus, it is clear that offices can bill for legal assistant time if they choose to do so. The case also reminds us that purely clerical tasks or secretarial tasks cannot be billed at the legal assistant rate, or any other rate.

Although the *Missouri v. Jenkins* case was a landmark decision for legal assistants, the opinion involved the interpretation of a specific statute, the Civil Rights Act. Fee questions occur in many different situations, and if another court is deciding a fee question other than in the context of the Civil Rights Act, it may reach a different decision. Since *Missouri v. Jenkins*, many courts in many different jurisdictions have allowed for the recovery of legal assistant time at the local prevailing rate. In addition, courts have also found that an attorney's time spent on a matter is not reasonable (for court-awarded fees) if the tasks performed "are normally performed by paralegals." Thus, many courts have recognized the unique niche that paralegals serve in the legal field.

FUNCTIONS OF A SUCCESSFUL BILLING SYSTEM

An often forgotten aspect of any billing system is that the system must please the firm's customers or clients. A good billing system is determined by whether or not the firm's clients are satisfied with the billings and whether or not they are paying the bills that are sent to them. One quick way a firm can lose a good client is by mishandling the client's money in some way, by overbilling the client, or by giving the client the impression that her or his money is being used unjustly or unfairly. In addition, mishandling a client's money is a top reason that attorneys are disciplined. A good billing system, whether it is computerized or not, must do several things, including accurately tracking the client's account, providing regular billings, and providing clients with an itemization of the services performed.

Accurately Track How Much a Client Has Paid the Firm

A successful billing system must be able to accurately track how much clients have paid the firm and whether the payments are made in cash, through a trust account, or otherwise. Although this may seem easy, it often is not. Consider how you feel when a creditor has either lost one of your payments or misapplied it in some manner. This is especially important for a law firm because in many instances large sums of money are involved. Payments can be lost, not entered into the system, or even applied to the wrong client. It is important that the firm take great care in what goes in and out of the billing system and that the information be accurate.

Send Regular Billings

Nearly all clients like to receive timely billings. We all expect to receive regular billings for routine things, such as credit card bills, utility bills, and so forth.

Likewise, most clients like to receive billings that are at least monthly. Imagine the frustration of a client who receives a quarterly billing that is four or five times more expensive than expected. Regular billings will alert the client to how he is being billed and how much needs to be budgeted. In addition, if a client sees timely bills that are more expensive than were planned for, he can tell the firm how to proceed so as to limit future bills before costs are incurred. This at least gives the client the option of cutting back on legal services instead of getting angry at the firm for not communicating the charges on a timely basis.

Provide Client Billings That Are Fair and Respectful

Billings that are fair and courteous are essential to a good billing system. If a client believes that the firm is overcharging for services or that the billings are curt and unprofessional, the client may simply not pay a bill or may hold payment. If you ever must speak to a client regarding a bill, always be courteous and respectful, and try to understand the situation from the client's point of view. If a dispute arises, simply take down the client's side of the story, relay the information to the attorney in charge of the matter, and let the attorney resolve the situation.

Provide Client Billings That Identify What Services Have Been Provided

When a client receives a billing, it is important that the client knows what services were received. Bills that just say "For Services Rendered" are for the most part a thing of the past. Although the format of bills will depend on the client, it is recommended that you indicate exactly what service was performed, by whom, on what date, for how long, and for what charge. If a client can see exactly what the firm is doing and how hard they are working, the client may be more willing to pay the bill.

Provide Client Billings That Are Clear

Finally, billings should be clear and without legalese. They should be easy to read and should provide the information that a client wants to see. Payments on billings that are complicated and hard to read are often held up while a client tries to decipher a bill.

In short, a billing system should satisfy your customers so that they are willing to make payments timely.

COMPUTERIZED TIMEKEEPING AND BILLING

> *Time and billing software has advanced dramatically in the past few years. There is a perfect solution out there for every size and type of law firm, and the features and functions are endless – accounts receivable and payable, timer, integration with case management systems, general ledger, invoices, and so much more.*[7]

Many different billing and timekeeping software programs are available. As with most of software applications, a wide diversity of features, structures, and prices exists among competing programs. Some programs cover just timekeeping and billing while others cover a variety of related areas such as general ledger, accounts payable, accounts receivable, payroll, trust accounting, docket control and calendaring, and case management. Programs are available for all sizes and types of law

firms. Some timekeeping and billing software packages are designed for particular sizes of law firms such as large (several hundred to 1,000 attorneys), medium (twenty-five to one hundred attorneys), and small (one to twenty-five attorneys).

Exhibit 6–13 shows a recent survey of legal assistants regarding the legal timekeeping and billing/accounting packages that they or their firm use. Currently, the legal timekeeping and billing market is so competitive that no one product enjoys a clear dominance in the market.

Exhibit 6–13
Computerized Timekeeping and Billing Program Market Share
As reported in a survey of practicing legal assistants
Source: Sarah K. Cron, "Technology to Go," *Legal Assistant Today*, May/June 2006, p. 59.

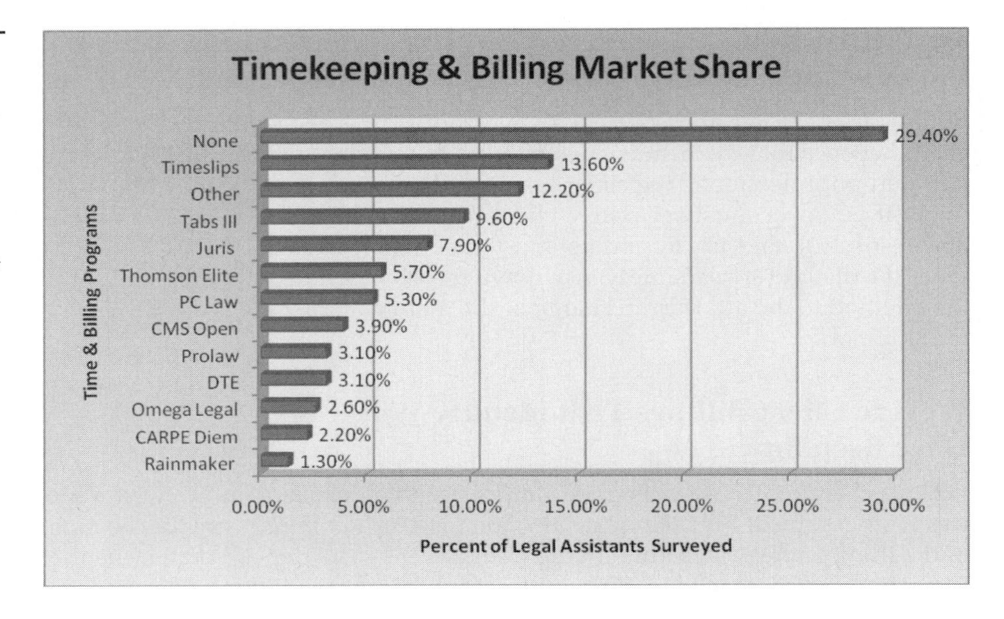

This text covers the basics of timekeeping and billing software; the manner in which any particular package handles these subjects will depend on the package. The fundamentals of computerized timekeeping and billing presented herein include learning about the main menu and the fundamental tasks that most timekeeping and billing programs perform; understanding the client information screen and how clients are set up in timekeeping and billing programs; learning how time and expense slips are entered into the billing system; how client bills are produced; and what management reports can be run by most systems.

Main Menu/Fundamental Tasks of Timekeeping and Billing Programs

Exhibit 6–14 shows the main menu of a popular timekeeping and billing program. Exhibit 6–14 is a good example of the functions found in most timekeeping and billing programs. These include entering and maintaining client accounts and preferences, entering time records, tracking attorneys' fees, entering and tracking expenses, recording client payments, managing client trust funds (some programs do this and others do not), managing and tracking client accounts, generating and managing pre-bills and final bills/statements, tracking accounts receivable, and producing management reports. Some of these tasks and activities will be discussed in more detail, but these are the general functions that most timekeeping and billing programs provide.

Entering Client-Related Information

Before timekeeping data can be entered into the computer or a bill can be generated for a client, certain information regarding the client must be entered into the

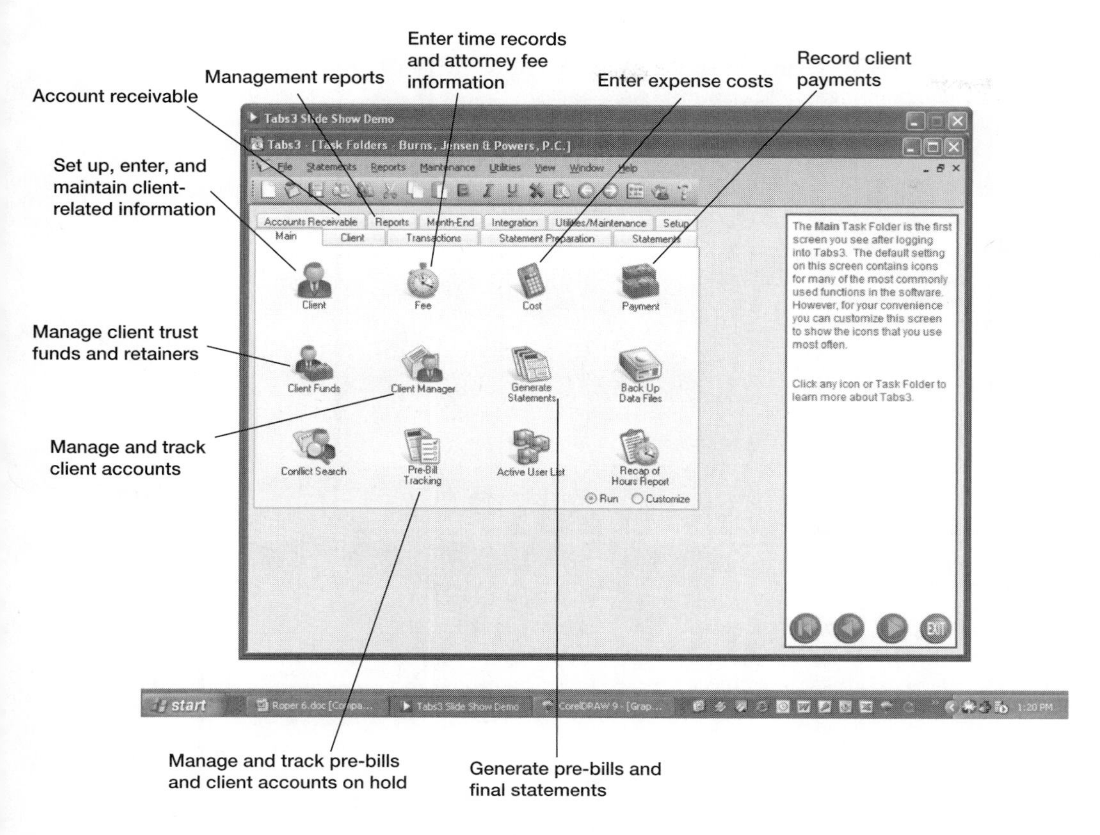

Exhibit 6–14
Timekeeping and Billing Program Main Menu

billing and timekeeping software. Exhibit 6–15 shows two client information screens in a timekeeping and billing system. Information such as a client's name and address and client identification number must be entered. Fee-related information must also be entered, such as how the case will be billed and whether the fee is an hourly rate, a flat fee, or another type of fee and who is the primary timekeeper for the file (see Exhibit 6–15). Most legal billing programs are very flexible regarding how cases are to be billed. Notice in the second screen of Exhibit 6–15 that the billing frequency for this particular client is monthly. This can be changed depending on how often the client would like to be billed. The billing preferences option allows a firm to set up different billing formats for each client. Some clients may want complete details and a description of every action that was performed on their behalf—who performed it, how long it took, and so forth. Other clients may want only a very brief description of what services were performed. Bill preference options allow the user to control this type of information.

Exhibit 6–16 shows the accounts receivable and fund balances screen for a client. This client information screen gives an overall view of the client's account and billing status as well as information related to any funds the client may have in trust.

Time Record Data Entry

Once the basic information about a firm's clients has been entered into the timekeeping and billing software, specific timekeeping information can be entered into the computer. Many timekeepers now enter their own timeslips directly into the computer. Time records can also be entered remotely using a handheld computer or PDA (personal digital assistant). The timekeeper enters the information into the PDA offsite, such as at a courthouse or deposition, and then, when she gets back to the office she synchronizes the PDA with the billing computer. Alternatively, a timekeeper may complete a manual timeslip and a clerk will enter it into the computer.

Exhibit 6–15

Client Information Screens

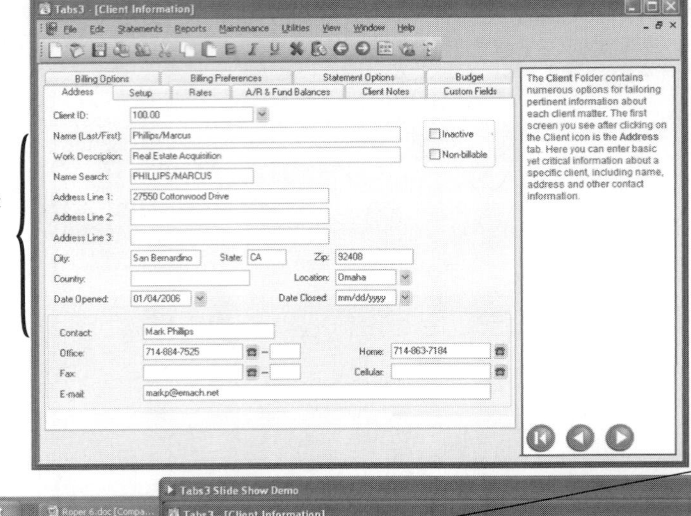

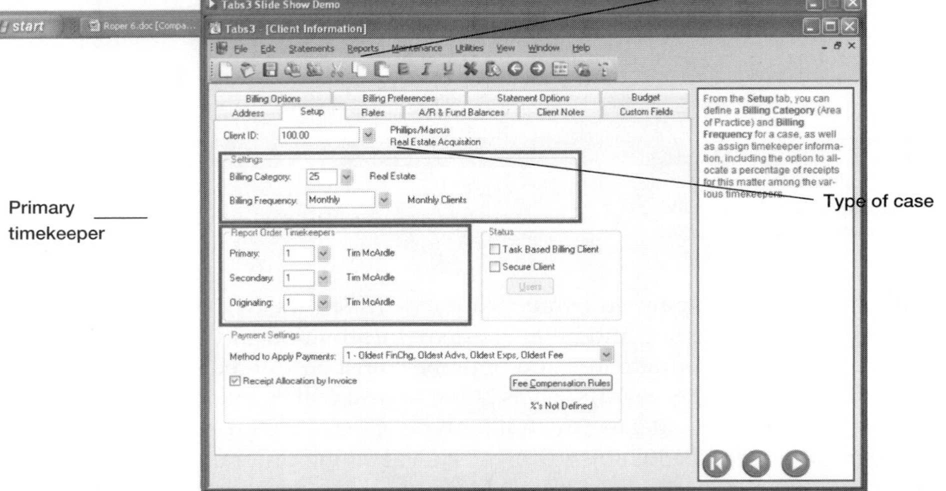

Exhibit 6–16

Client Information—Accounts Receivable and Fund Balances Screen

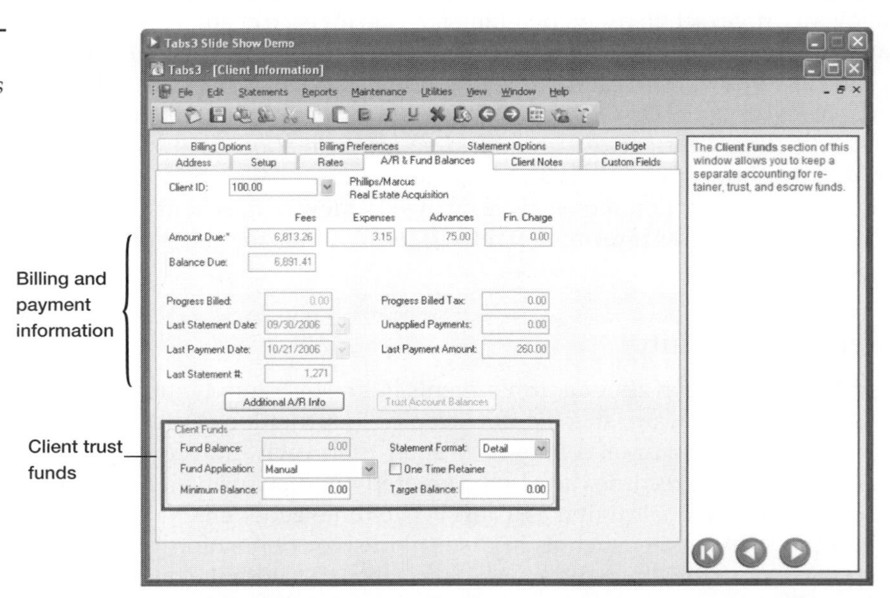

> *Several law firms recently asked me what would be involved in having their lawyers [and legal assistants] enter their time directly into the computer rather than write it on time sheets. For years, it has baffled me why so many lawyers [and legal assistants] resist one of the best ways to recoup some of the investment in computers and software.*[8]

Exhibit 6–17 shows a typical time record entry screen. A timekeeper is anyone (including attorneys and legal assistants) who bills for his or her time. In the Timekeeper field, the timekeeper's initials (or name) are entered. In Exhibit 6–17, the timekeeper's name is Michael Jensen. Many programs allow the user to "pop up" a list of all the possible timekeepers for a firm. Notice in Exhibit 6–17 the clock/timer feature. It shows that the timekeeper has been performing a task for the client for 12 minutes and 40 seconds. Many timekeeping and billing programs allow users to interactively turn on a clock or meter as they are providing legal services to clients so they know exactly how much time they have spent on a matter. Exhibit 6–17 also shows the current hours worked on the project (three-tenths of an hour), the rate at which the client is being billed, ($220 an hour), and the current amount that is being charged to the client for the task. The "Tcode" field in Exhibit 6–17 is a transaction code, 1, which in this system represents an office conference. Other examples of standard transaction codes would be legal research, court appearances, depositions, drafting, and so forth.

The Client ID code indicates which client the time record is to be billed to. In Exhibit 6–17, the client is Marcus Phillips and the matter is a real estate acquisition. Most programs allow the user to select a client's account from a list of active clients. The Description field contains a listing of what services were performed. This can be detailed or brief, depending on the needs of the client. The Date field obviously shows when the services were provided. The bill code in Exhibit 6–17 shows that the service is billable, as opposed to nonbillable. The time record screen in Exhibit 6–17 even shows a history of past time records that have been entered for the client.

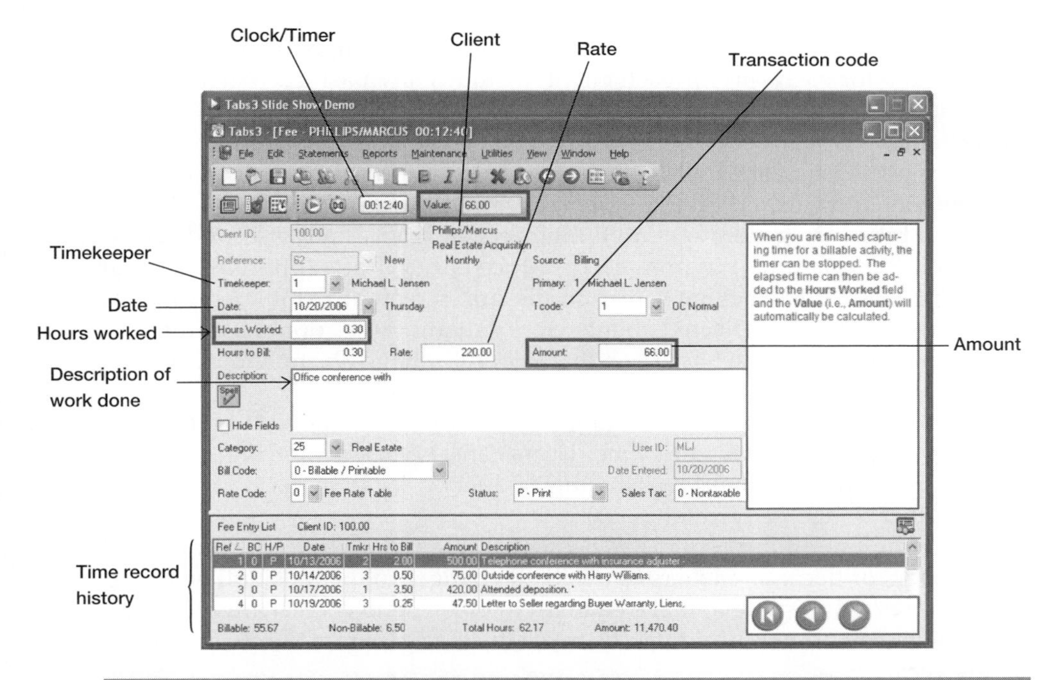

Exhibit 6–17
Entering a Time Record
Copyright 2007 Software Technology, Inc. www.Tabs3.com

Expense/Cost Record Data Entry

The data entry screen for entering expense or cost records is nearly the same as the time record data entry screen in most programs (see Exhibit 6–18). This includes entering a client ID, date, transaction code (fax costs in Exhibit 6–18), and units (here the number of pages faxed). Notice the expense history shown at the bottom of Exhibit 6–18.

Exhibit 6–18
Entering an Expense/Cost Record

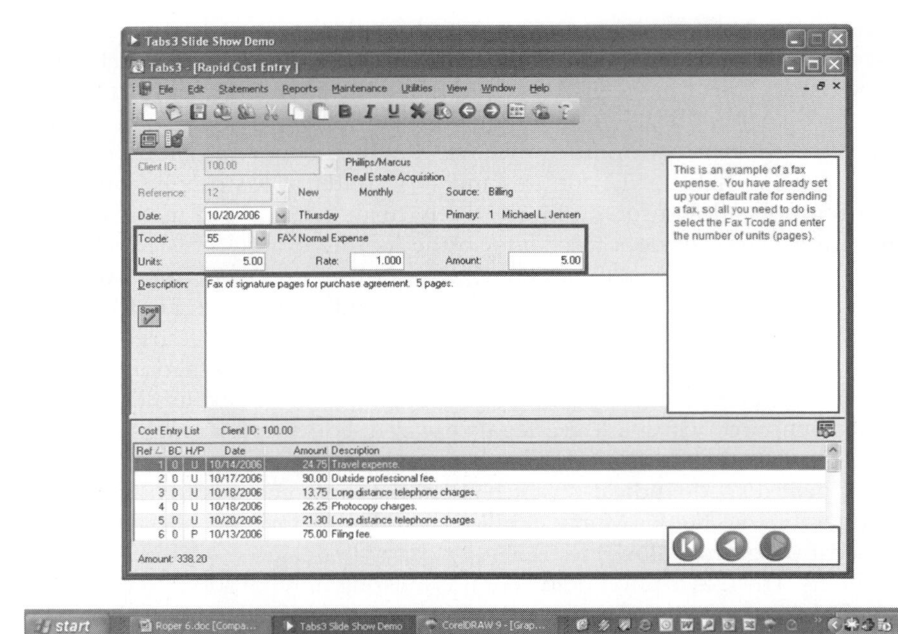

Pre-billing and Final Statements

Generating bills is the most important aspect of any timekeeping and billing program. In general, the timekeeping and billing program takes all the time and expense slips for a period, assembles them by client, and calculates the amount due for each slip for each client, includes any past due balances and payments by client, and then calculates a total amount due for that period for each client.

Once all the timeslips and expense slips for a period have been entered into the timekeeping and billing system, usually the next step toward preparing client bills is to generate a pre-billing report. Notice in the second screen of Exhibit 6–19 that the program can produce either drafts (pre-bills) or final bills. The pre-billing tracking screen in the first screen of Exhibit 6–19 shows when pre-bills for the selected clients were run and gives options at the bottom of the screen to put a "hold" on the account or to go ahead and issue final statements.

One of the first steps in generating pre-bills or bills is to select which time records and expense slips to include. Users can also select time and expenses records by client ID, timekeeper, billing frequency, location, or status of files among other things (see Exhibit 6–20).

Once the pre-billing report has been generated, it is up to the individual timekeepers or decision makers to decide if changes to the bills will be made. It is usually fairly simple to make changes in bills and to correct any mistakes. Once the information is accurate, the final step is to generate the client billings themselves.

In many programs, the format of a bill is set up in the client information screen. Law firms use many different formats to bill clients. For example, some

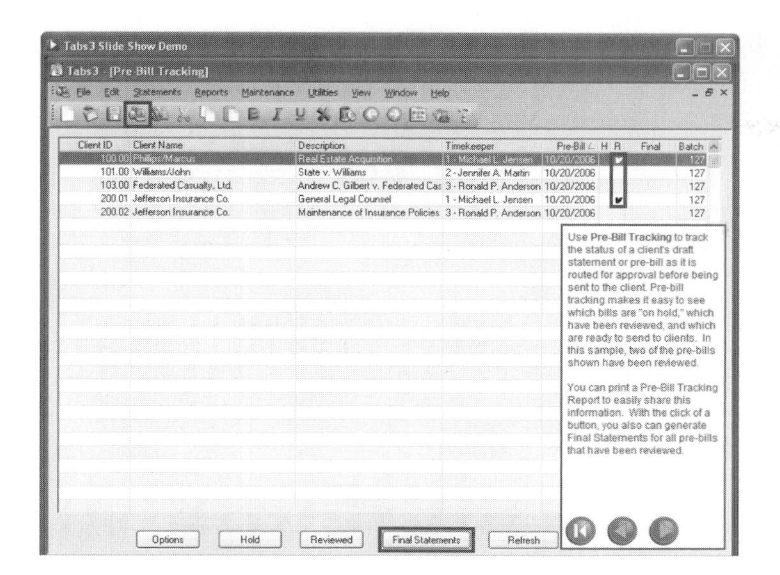

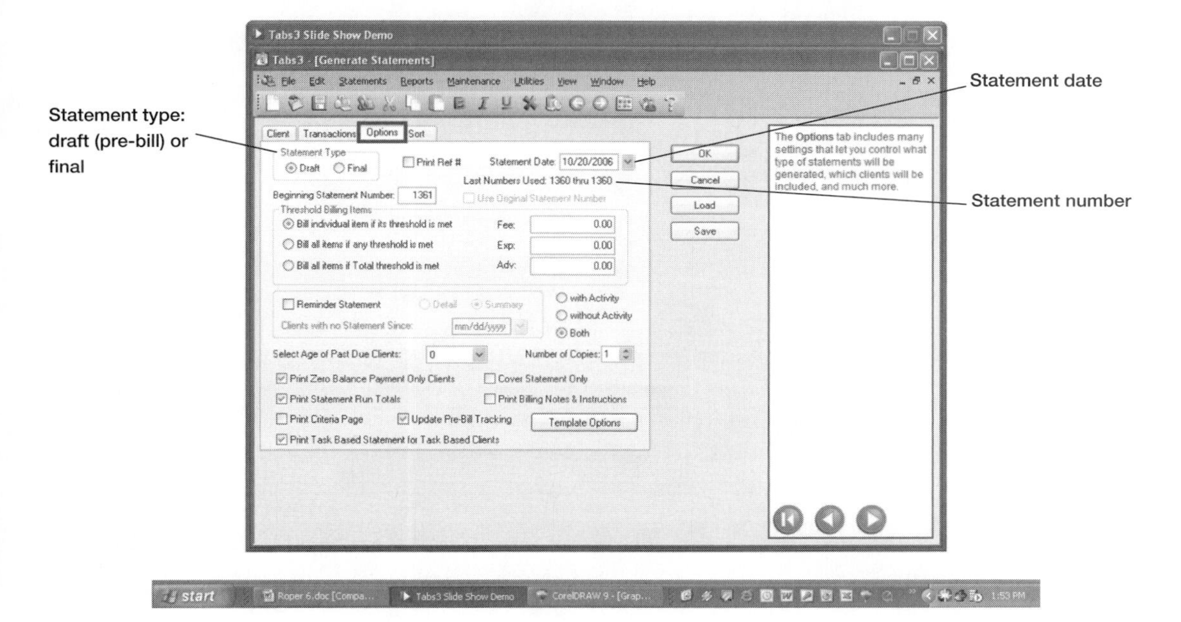

Exhibit 6–19
Pre-Bill and Final Statements
Copyright 2007 Software Technology, Inc. www.Tabs3.com

bill formats contain only general information about the services provided, whereas other bill formats show greater detail. The look and format of billings depend on the law firm, its clients, the type of law it practices, and so forth. Thus, it is important that any timekeeping and billing package be flexible in the number of client billing formats that are available.

Producing detailed bills takes work. It requires timekeepers to prepare accurate, current timeslips of what work they have provided. This seems easy enough, but it is not. It is sometimes difficult to convince timekeepers to write down each service they perform for each client. However, most clients simply prefer detailed billings. So, while itemized billings are sometimes inconvenient for the timekeeper and take longer to produce, if a bill is paid in the end, the extra work has paid off.

management reports
Reports used to help management analyze whether the office is operating in an efficient and effective manner.

Management Reports

Almost all timekeeping and billing software packages produce a wide variety of management reports (see Exhibit 6–21). **Management reports** are used to help

Exhibit 6–20
Generating Final Bills

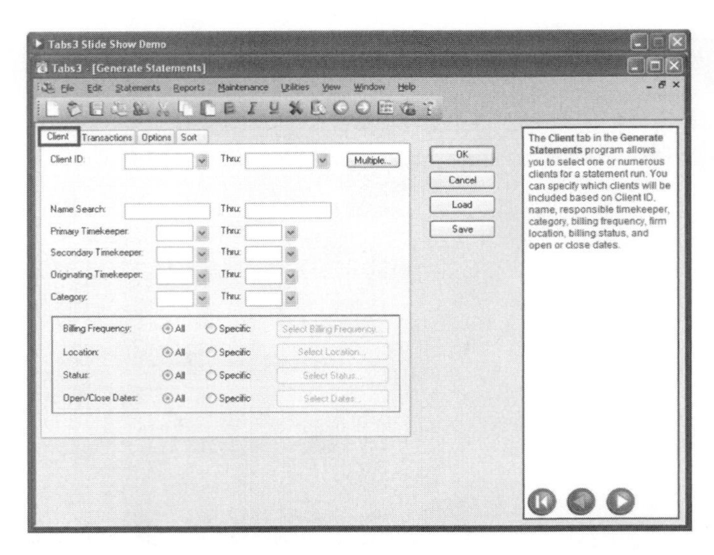

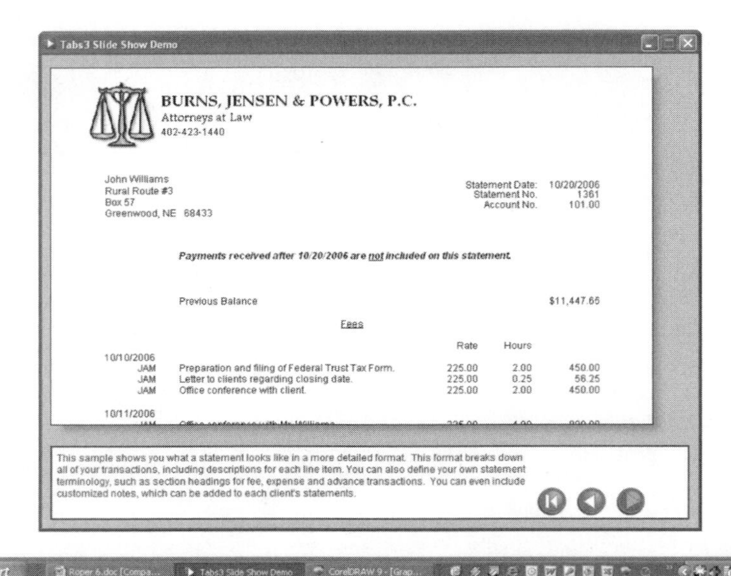

management analyze whether the office is operating in an efficient and effective manner. Management reports can be used to track problems an office may be experiencing and to help devise ways to correct the problems. The following are explanations of some common management reports and how they are used by offices.

Case/Client List Most billing packages allow the user to produce a case or client list. A list of all active cases is very important in trying to effectively manage a large caseload. Most reports list clients not only by name, but also by the appropriate account number (also called the client identification number by some programs). This cross-listing is useful when trying to locate a client's identification number.

aged accounts receivable report
A report showing all cases that have outstanding balances due and how long these balances are past due.

Aged Accounts Receivable Report The **aged accounts receivable report** shows all cases that have outstanding balances owed to the office and how long these balances are past due (see Exhibit 6–22). The report breaks down the current balances due and the balances that are thirty, sixty, and more than ninety

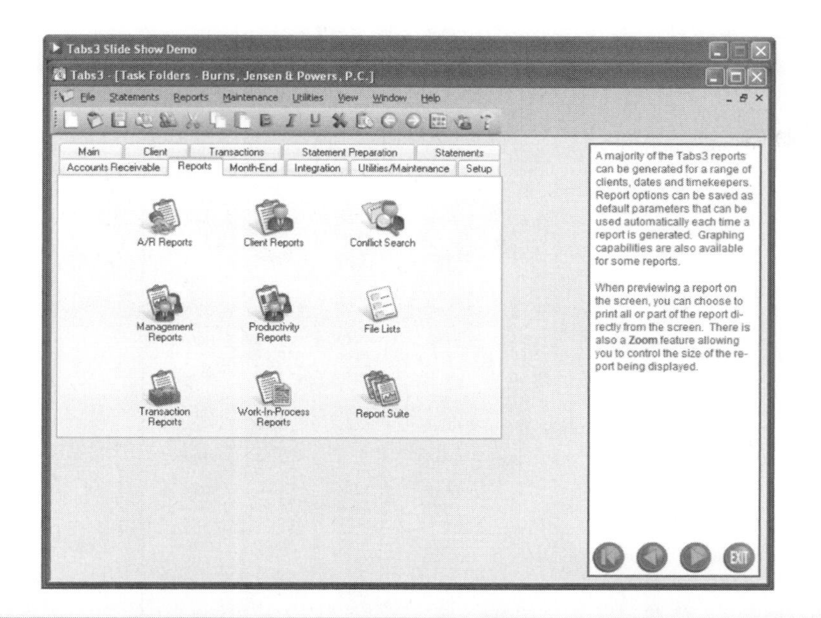

Exhibit 6–21
Management Reports
Copyright 2007 Software Technology, Inc. www.Tabs3.com

days past due. Using this report, management can clearly see which clients are not paying and how old the balances are. This report also is helpful for following up on clients who are slow in paying their bills. Most programs allow the report to be run according to the type of case. Thus, management can see what type of cases (criminal, divorce, tax, etc.) have the most aged accounts. If one particular type of case has more than its share of aged accounts, it might be more profitable to stop taking that type. So, from a management perspective, this can be a very important report. It should be noted that aged account information should not appear on bills sent to clients. Bills that are more than thirty days old should simply say "past due."

Timekeeper Productivity Report The amount of billable and nonbillable time being spent by each timekeeper is shown in the **timekeeper productivity report** (see Exhibit 6–22). This report can be used to identify which timekeepers are the most diligent in their work. For example, notice in Exhibit 6–22 that Arthur A. Alexander billed a total of only 77.75 hours for the month while the other staff billed more than 100 hours each. Also, notice that Byron B. Brown produced the most billable hours and payments received by the office.

timekeeper productivity report
A report showing how much billable and nonbillable time is being spent by each timekeeper.

Finally, note the totals section, which shows that although the office billed 280.25 hours for a total of $31,130.25, the office has received to date only $27,778.00. Although the report in Exhibit 6–22 shows the results for only one month, most packages allow the productivity report to be run for a quarter or even for a year.

Case Type Productivity Report The **case type productivity report** shows which types of cases (criminal, personal injury, bankruptcies, etc.) are the most profitable (see Exhibit 6–23). For example, in Exhibit 6–23 note that the bankruptcy and litigation areas of the law office brought in $17,500.50 and $44,550.75, respectively, for the month of July, or 11.73 percent and 29.87 percent of the income earned. This report obviously shows which types of cases are the most profitable and which types are the least profitable. Management will use this type of report to decide which areas to concentrate on to become more profitable.

case type productivity report
A report showing which types of cases (i.e., criminal, personal injury, bankruptcy, etc.) are the most profitable.

Exhibit 6–22
Aged Accounts Receivable Report and Timekeeper Productivity Report
Courtesy of CompuLaw, Inc.

LAW OFFICES OF SMITH, SMITH AND JONES

5/ 1 Aged Accounts Receivable PAGE 1

Entire Alphabet — All Bill Types
All Attorneys — All Case Types
Cycle: All Cycles (All Months) — Ignore Cycle Due Date

Client/Matter	Balance	Current	30 Days	60 Days	Over 90
All Right Manufacturing C					
General Corporate Matt	127.50	None	127.50	None	None
Hinge Division - Paten	975.00	975.00	None	None	None
	1,102.50	975.00	127.50	None	None
Alta Loma Bookkeeping					
Purchase of Johnson Ch	800.00	175.00	175.00	450.00	None
Burton, Sarah					
Divorce	147.50	None	147.50	None	None
Protective order	440.00	None	None	440.00	None
	587.50	None	147.50	440.00	None
Carla's Hard to Fit					
Incorporation	1,500.00	1,500.00	None	None	None
Chuck's Artist Supplies					
Liquidation	607.50	None	505.00	102.50	None
Drummond, Lester B.					
I.R.S. Matter	427.75	427.75	None	None	None
Long Beach Property	1,775.00	None	None	1,775.00	None
Possession	500.00	None	None	500.00	None
	2,702.75	427.75	None	2,275.00	None
Servi					
	175.00	175.00	None	None	None
iness					
	725.00	None	None	None	725.00
	112.50	None	None	None	112.50
	75.00	None	None	75.00	None
	912.50	None	None	75.00	837.50
Abe					
	632.75	None	632.75	None	None
napt	7,500.00	7,500.00	None	None	None
Inc.					
	4,410.00	None	1,410.00	3,000.00	None
ncy					
aud	475.00	475.00	None	None	None
ive	12,559.99	550.00	9,405.00	2,425.00	170.00
	330.00	330.00	None	None	None
	485.00	None	None	485.00	None
ted)	34,770.50	12,107.75	12,402.75	9,252.50	1,007.50

LAW OFFICES OF SMITH, SMITH AND JONES

5/ 1 Time/Productivity Analysis PAGE 1

April

			Fees	Hours
Arthur A. Alexander		Billed:	$8,852.50	77.75
		On Hold:	$100.00	1.00
Payments Rec'd	$7,277.50	Non Chargeable:	$100.00	.75
Standard Rate:	$75.00	Written Off:	$125.00	2.00
Realized Rate:	$112.00	Administrative:	$125.00	1.00

. . . .

			Fees	Hours
Byron B. Brown		Billed:	$10,527.75	101.50
		On Hold:	None	None
Payments Rec'd	$10,950.50	Non Chargeable:	None	None
Standard Rate:	$95.00	Written Off:	None	None
Realized Rate:	$93.00	Administrative:	None	None

. . . .

			Fees	Hours
Andrew B. Cabellero		Billed:	$12,750.00	101.00
		On Hold:	$1,250.00	10.00
Payments Rec'd	$9,550.50	Non Chargeable:	$100.00	1.00
Standard Rate:	$125.00	Written Off:	$250.00	2.20
Realized Rate:	$125.00	Administrative:	$125.00	1.00

. . . .

Monthly Summary - All Attorneys Listed

			Fees	Hours
		Billed:	$31,130.25	280.25
Payments Rec'd		On Hold:	$1,350.00	11.00
This Month:	$27,778.00	Non Chargeable:	$200.00	1.75
		Written Off:	$375.00	4.20
Realized Rate:	$110.00	Administrative:	$250.00	2.00

FENWICK, QUINT GERSON AND PECK
Case Type Productivity

7/31 PAGE 1

Case Type	Hours Billable	Fees Billed	Fees Income	% Total Fee Inc	% Total Hours
		July			
Bankruptcies	252.75	$26,450.00	$17,500.50	11.73	17.48
Civil Matters	32.50	$4,142.75	$3,655.75	2.45	2.24
Corporate Matters	125.75	$19,855.50	$12,500.25	8.38	8.70
Criminal Matters	22.00	$1,875.00	$2,250.00	1.51	1.52
Estate Planning	87.75	$9,475.00	$8,875.00	5.95	6.07
Family Law	52.25	$6,175.75	$5,495.75	3.68	3.61
General Business	108.70	$9,775.50	$8,975.50	5.95	7.52
General Practice	61.00	$6,552.75	$7,275.50	4.88	4.22
Litigation	225.00	$37,750.00	$44,550.75	29.87	15.56
Personal Injury	35.00	$4,500.00	$4,125.25	2.76	2.42
Probate Matters	0.00	0.00	0.00	0.00	0.00
Real Estate Matters	18.00	$2,150.00	$2,100.00	1.40	1.24
Taxation Matters	24.75	$2,650.00	$2,655.00	1.78	1.71
Other	9.00	$1,253.00	$1,253.50	.84	.62
Patents & Trademarks	36.50	$4,141.75	$4,155.50	2.78	2.52
International Law	44.00	$8,645.25	$3,440.00	2.31	3.04
Immigration Law	27.00	$3,150.00	$750.00	.50	1.86
Insurance Defense	111.50	$10,950.75	$7,555.25	5.06	7.71
Insurance Plaintiff	88.00	$8,125.00	$6,550.75	4.39	6.08
Consumer Law	6.75	$595.00	$500.00	.33	.46
Labor Unions	77.00	$5,845.00	$4,995.50	3.35	5.32
July Totals	1,445.20	$174,058.00	$149.161.00		

Exhibit 6–23
Case Type Productivity Report
Courtesy of CompuLaw, Inc.

Electronic Billing

Instead of [a client] writing comments on paper bills, checking math manually, organizing comments into categories and drafting a comment letter. . .a client can automate the process of bill review so that it can be done online by commenting electronically.

A client can use e-billing software to flag potential problems, including checking the math, and format the billing data for easier review. One client noted "I'm spending 25 to 50 percent less time [using/viewing e-bills] on the review process, and doing a more complete review.[9]

Electronic billing is when law firms bill clients in a fashion that conforms to standard billing codes and uses a standard electronic format, using such means as the Internet. Many large clients, such as Fortune 1000 corporations and other businesses, are demanding that law firms bill them using electronic means. Electronic billing is a term of art and does not mean, for example, just sending a bill as a PDF (Portable Data Format) or Microsoft Word attachment to an email to the client. Electronic billing means sending bills that conform to the Uniform Task-Based Management System (UTBMS, a standard way of referring to timekeeper tasks) and comply with the Legal Electronic Data Exchange Standard (LEDES), which specifies a uniform format for law firm time and billing systems to export to e-billing systems (see Exhibit 6–23A).

electronic billing
Billing clients in a fashion that conforms to standard billing codes and uses a standard electronic format, using such means as the Internet.

LEDES provides a standardized billing format to output billing data to clients regardless of the timekeeping and billing system that produced the bill. Some timekeepers do not like e-billing because it mandates that they keep track of their time according to rigid, inflexible UTBMS codes. Many of the e-billing vendors are application service providers (ASPs), third-party vendors that set up the e-billing part of the system, receive data from law firms, and operate the software over the Internet. Clients are able to see bills (from any law firm they use) in a standard format and then customize the reports they output to meet

Exhibit 6–23A
Example of Electronic Billing
Source: CT TyMetrix E-Billing (cttymetrix.com)

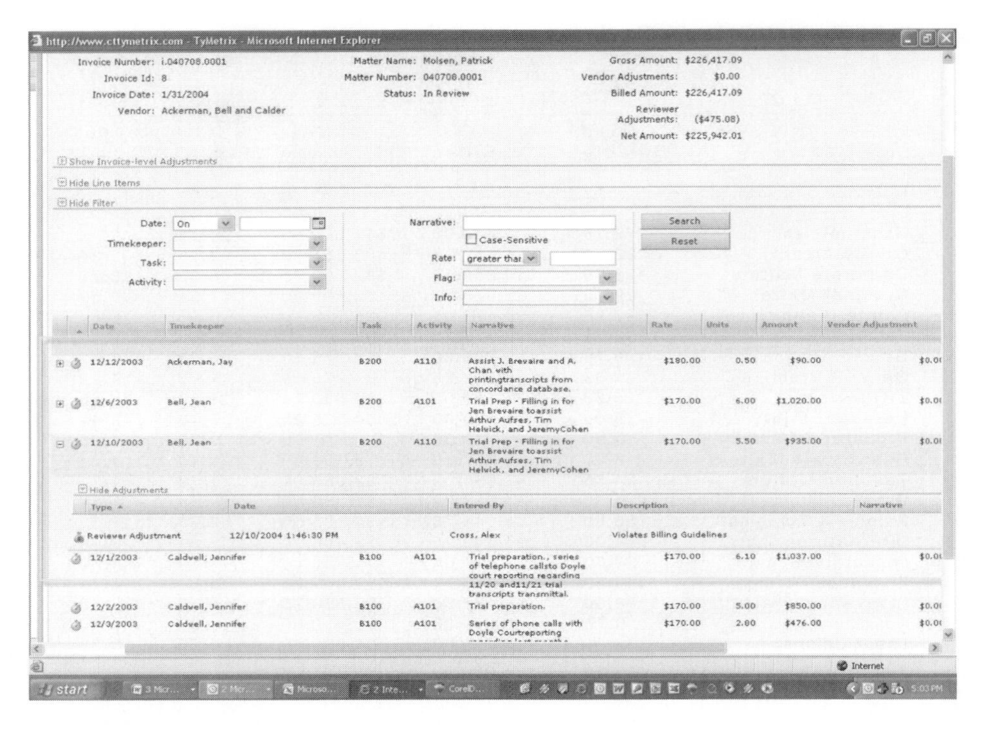

their particular needs. For large clients, electronic billing is a big improvement over traditional paper billing, but produces a certain amount of rigidity and burden on the law firms. Some clients are even taking e-billing to the next level by contracting with their own ASP clearinghouse to audit bills to ensure that their bills are in strict compliance with their internal requirements. If the law firm's bill does not meet the client's requirements, the ASP rejects the bill and the client does not even get the electronic data. For example, if a client's requirement is that each task must be billed for separately, the client's clearinghouse would reject bills that include block entries where one entry may cover three or four separate activities (i.e., "drafting letter to client; legal research for discovery motion, drafting discovery motion and telephone call with witness, 5 hours").

Just as email has become an electronic replacement for a pen and paper note, electronic billing, the paperless automation of sending the bill to a client, is becoming an alternative for generating a detailed paper invoice. Most of the time, however, no real bill actually is sent. E-billing is more of a process for sharing data between a law firm and a client.[10]

INTEGRATING TIMEKEEPING AND BILLING, ACCOUNTING, AND CASE MANAGEMENT

In a fully automated legal organization there will be at least three main components to a "back-office" computer system. These components include (1) timekeeping and billing software, (2) accounting software, and (3) case management software. Timekeeping and billing has already been discussed in this chapter. *Accounting* software handles the financial side of the legal organization: receiving and applying money, making deposits, issuing checks, paying taxes, aging accounts receivable, writing payroll checks, and the like. *Case management* software helps a legal organization provide services to clients by tracking client cases; tracking schedules, appointments, deadlines and things to be done in cases; and tracking case-related information such as opposing parties and opposing counsel. For example, when a new client comes to a legal organization with a

matter to be handled, case management software would be used to set up the new case, including client name, client address, client matter/case name, type of case, things to be done, and so forth. The same client will need to be set up in the time and billing system (to receive bills, have monies applied correctly, etc.), by entry of such data as client name, client matter, and when payments are made and recorded in the time and billing system. The legal organization's accounting software will need to know this so that deposits can be made, accounts receivable balances adjusted, and so on. The point is that all of these back-office systems need to be able to talk to each other; otherwise there will be much duplication of effort.

> *When I first became the executive director [of a law firm] it took me only 15 minutes to realize we needed to make a change – a big change. Our financial system, which consisted of separate billing and accounting programs, was a mess. The problem was not with the program we were using. . ., but the fact that the data was often only entered into one program, so the two were never balanced. This caused enormous inconsistencies. Billing also was sorely neglected. . .To solve our problems, the change needed to be two-fold. First, we needed an integrated system that would allow us to enter time once and run the reports needed to run the firm effectively. Second, we needed to change the entrenched habits of all our attorneys and other timekeepers by helping them understand the benefits of entering their time.*[11]

Software manufacturers typically handle integration in one of three ways: either (1) separate software programs (from different manufacturers) exchange information among themselves (this is becoming much more common, but does not always work as promised); (2) one manufacturer makes a product that handles all of the back-office needs of the legal organization (this is also fairly common); or (3) integration is ignored and the legal organization must duplicate its effort. In any case, there is much to be said for designing legal organization computer systems that are integrated and share information.

WHAT TO LOOK FOR IN TIMEKEEPING AND BILLING SOFTWARE

As with most software, no one timekeeping and billing program is best for all attorneys and all firms. Attorneys bill clients in very different formats and ways. The size of the firm also plays a role in choosing the right package. A timekeeping and billing package that works for a five-member law firm may not work well for a fifty-member firm.

Although legal assistants do not always play a part in deciding which timekeeping and billing package to purchase, often they are consulted. When considering purchasing timekeeping and billing software, keep in mind that the billing program should do the following:

1. Be flexible, allowing the firm to charge different hourly rates, mix different fee arrangements, and the like.
2. Provide a wide variety of billing formats for different types of clients. Purchasing a program that is inflexible and allows for only one or two types of billing formats is usually not a good idea.
3. Be easy to use. Programs that allow the user to look up information instead of memorizing keystrokes are almost always easier and more convenient to use.
4. Give the user the flexibility to bill each client whenever the user wishes, instead of having to bill all clients at one time.
5. Allow the user to define a list of timekeepers and activities. Such programs are almost always easier and faster to use than programs that have predefined lists.
6. Include plenty of room for a description of the legal service provided. Some programs allow only one or two lines. Sometimes this is inadequate to record a complicated entry.

7. Permit users to edit timeslips or expense slips instead of reentering slips that have mistakes in them.
8. Offer plenty of management reports formats to help management operate the firm.
9. Utilize a robust security system, such as passwords, to keep unwanted users from accessing the system. Some programs have different levels of security; for example, a secretary might have access to the password that allows him to enter data, but not to the password to run bills or management reports. Security is an important aspect of any system.
10. Have the ability to integrate with accounting and case management software.
11. Include the ability to comply with the Uniform Task-Based Management System and Legal Electronic Data Exchange Standard (LEDES) protocols.

Exhibit 6–24 lists a number of problems related to selecting and implementing timekeeping and billing systems.

BILLING FROM THE CORPORATE AND GOVERNMENT PERSPECTIVE

Corporate and governmental law practices sometimes hire outside counsel. **Outside counsel** refers to when corporate and government law practices contract with private law offices (i.e., outside of the corporation or government entity) to help them with legal matters, such as litigation, specialized contracts, stock/bond offerings, and so on. Thus, corporate and government law practices are purchasers of legal services and tend to look at billing from a different perspective.

outside counsel
Term referring to when corporate and government law practices contract with law offices (i.e., outside of the corporation or government entity) to help them with legal matters, such as litigation, specialized contracts, stock/bond offerings, etc.

Corporate and government law practices are concerned with limiting the costs of legal fees. Many corporate clients will state that they will not pay more than a certain amount, perhaps $225 an hour, for any attorney regardless of experience. If the office wants to maintain the particular client, it will agree to the terms. Because corporations and governments have access to large sums of money and typically are well-paying clients, many offices will reduce the price to get and keep the business.

Corporate and government clients usually require very detailed bills to monitor what is being done on the case and to control costs. In some cases, corporations and governments use a competitive bidding process to select outside counsel. Thus, summary billings are usually not accepted. They also typically will limit the type and cost of expenses that are billed to them. For instance, some corporations require that computerized legal research (WESTLAW, Lexis, etc.), postage, fax costs, and similar expenses be borne by the office.

It is not uncommon for a corporate law practice to publish policies and guidelines covering exactly what outside counsel will charge, when it will charge, how payments will be made, how much and what type of legal expenses will be reimbursed, and so on. Exhibit 6–25 shows the top ten reasons corporate law departments fail to pay private law offices.

THE ETHICS OF TIMEKEEPING AND BILLING

More ethical complaints related to timekeeping and billing are filed against attorneys and law offices than all other types of complaints. It is important that legal assistants completely understand the ethics of timekeeping and billing. In years past, timekeeping and billing complaints were viewed as simply "misunderstandings" between the client and the law office. Recently, state bars have viewed timekeeping and billing disputes as having major ethical implications for attorneys. That is, such disputes were not simply misunderstandings; law offices were sometimes flagrantly violating ethical rules regarding money issues.

Exhibit 6–24
Problems to Avoid When Selecting and Implementing Timekeeping and Billing Systems
Source: John "Tim" L. Mellitz and Patricia D. Namish, "14 Common Mistakes Firms Make," *Law Office Computing*, April/May 2006, p. 63.

1. *"I took the advice of a colleague and purchased a time and billing system that was overkill for my small practice. I ended up spending thousands of dollars on a program I hardly use... [and] I didn't allocate enough money for training."*

2. *"We purchased a billing program after seeing a demo. I thought at the time my staff would be excited... My secretary of 25 years was intimidated by it and still continues to use WordPerfect 5.1 for everything from calendar functions to billing...I should have involved my staff in the decision of selecting the software before I spent so much time, energy, and effort."*

3. *"A salesman demonstrated a practice management system and assured it was so easy to learn that we could teach ourselves how to use it. Big mistake."*

4. *"I was on a tight budget and at the time could not afford to pay for consulting and training services when I purchased my time and billing system. Because I had some experience in installing software, I did the installation myself and slogged through the manual to figure out how to configure it. For the next couple of weeks we had nothing but problems - computers crashing, lockups, and utter frustration. We lost days of productivity, and my staff was upset because they could not meet routine deadlines. We all were pretty miserable. I finally called in an expert, and in just a few hours things were working fine. My ego got in the way of good business sense."*

5. *"I saw my secretary typing bills in her word processor and asked her why she was spending so much time doing this. We use a time and billing system. She said that several clients objected to their bill and asked for revised copies. The original bills had been finalized and she didn't know how to undo them, so she decided to retype them. The court also requested a detailed bill for the case's extraordinary expenses, payments and credits. Not having had any training, she retyped the bills in her word processor. Meanwhile, other things in the office were not getting done and she got behind on her work. We found out later that she could have printed a history report from the billing system. In retrospect, I should have invested in adequate training and learned the functions when we first purchased the software - a costly mistake."*

Timekeeping and billing complaints by clients do not just lead to ethical complaints against attorneys but may also turn into criminal fraud charges filed against attorneys and legal assistants.

Ethical Considerations Regarding Legal Fee Agreements

There are several important ethical considerations that need to be stressed about fee agreements. The first is that *all fee agreements should be in writing*, especially when a contingency fee is involved. Second, contingency fees should not be used in criminal or domestic relations matters. Third, only a reasonable fee can be collected. Disputes regarding attorney handling of fees are taken seriously and can lead to adverse ethical findings or worse.

Exhibit 6–25
Reasons Corporate and Government Legal Departments Refuse to Negotiate Legal Bills

Reason	Explanation
Legal services are below standard	The legal services provided were below standard or didnít meet the needs of the corporate client. Corporate law departments will typically attempt to negotiate down the fees. In these instances, the corporate law department staff must take the time to correct the problems even though they paid to have it done correctly.
Too many attorneys and legal assistants working the case	When multiple timekeepers attend the same deposition, or bill for the same work provided the costs rise quickly. Many corporate law departments will try to set limits on the number of timekeepers working a case at one time. Also, if the attorneys or legal assistants that are working the case change, then the client must pay for the new attorneys or legal assistants to get up to speed.
Billing lacks detail	Most law departments want to see detailed reports of how timekeepers spent their time and not "for legal services provided."
Billing is incomplete	A bill doesn't include previous payments made or is otherwise incomplete.
Billing has numerical errors	The bill doesn't add up or wrong billing rates are used.
Sticker-shock	The corporate law department expects a bill for $5,000 and receives a bill for $25,000.
Attorneys and legal assistants conferencing with each other frequently	It is frustrating for a client to receive a bill where attorneys and legal assistants are frequently meeting to discuss strategy or otherwise because this greatly increases the client's bill. This is particularly frustrating for the client when the bill does not say why the staff working on the case were meeting.
Billing sent to the wrong person	Sending the bill to the wrong person can be frustrating in a large corporation. The bill can literally get lost inside the corporation unless the bill is sent to the correct person.
Billing every little thing	Clients strongly dislike being billed for every five-minute phone call, being billed for the time it takes to prepare the bill itself, or other items that in the big picture do not amount to much.
Being billed for another case	Occasionally, a client will be billed for time spent on another case. This undermines the whole billing process.
Billing is received late	Corporate clients become frustrated when they receive a bill for services that were delivered five months ago. Not only is the billing late, but it is difficult to remember that far back as to the details of the service.

Fee Agreements Should Be in Writing

It is highly recommended that as a matter of course all fee arrangements be in writing. The days of a handshake cementing an agreement between an attorney and a client are long over. There is no substitute for reducing all fee agreements

to writing. If the firm and the client have a dispute over fees, the document will clarify the understanding between the parties.

> *A fee agreement allows a lawyer and client to make clear from the inception of the legal representation the scope of that representation and the basis for the lawyer's compensation. A clearly drafted agreement, which is fully explained to the client at the time the representation begins, will minimize disagreement as the representation proceeds and assist in resolving any disputes that may arise when the representation ends.*[12]

The ABA *Model Rules of Professional Conduct* at 1.5(b) state that fee agreements should "preferably" be in writing. However, nearly every authority on the subject, as well as most attorneys who have been in business long, say that fee agreements absolutely must be in writing to protect both the attorney and the client. The reasons legal fee agreements should be in writing include:

1. Clients file more ethical complaints against attorneys and law offices for fee disputes than for any other type of complaint.
2. The client and the attorney may (will) forget what the exact fee agreement was unless it is reduced to writing.
3. In a factual dispute regarding a fee between a client and an attorney, the evidence is typically construed in the light most favorable to the client.

Contingency Fee Agreements Must Be in Writing When a contingency fee is involved, most jurisdictions state that the agreement *must* be in writing for the office to collect the fees. According to Rule 1.5(c) of the *Model Rules of Professional Conduct*.

Even the *Model Rules* make a distinction between contingency agreements and other types of fee agreements and require that contingency agreements be in writing. The reason that a contingency fee agreement must be in writing is that in many cases, large sums of money are recovered and the difference between 20 percent and 30 percent may mean tens of thousands of dollars. Contingency agreements are risky for the attorney, and they simply must be reduced to writing so that the client and the attorney know what the proper percentage of fees should be. It also is important that the contingency agreement state and the client understand that even if there is no recovery in the case, the client must still pay for expenses.

Contingency Fees Are Not Allowed in Criminal and Domestic Relations Proceedings in Some Jurisdictions Many jurisdictions, as well as Rule 1.5(d) of the *Model Rules of Professional Conduct*, prohibit contingency fees in criminal and domestic relations proceedings as a matter of public policy.

For example, assume an attorney agrees to represent a client in a criminal matter. The client agrees to pay the attorney $10,000 if the client is found innocent, but the attorney will receive nothing if the client is found guilty. This is an unethical contingency fee agreement. The thinking is that contingency fees in these types of cases are against public policy and should be prohibited.

Only a "Reasonable" Fee Can Be Collected

> *Billing a senior partner's rate for a lawyer to research discovery documents for several hours is a sure way to drive away clients. The work is essential, requiring someone with knowledge and savvy, but is more suited to a legal assistant who can ensure proficient performance while freeing the senior partner to address those tasks that only a senior partner can do—at a greater billing rate.*[13]

> *Today's clients are discriminating purchasers of legal services. Hourly rates and billing invoices are often challenged by long-standing clients.*[14]

It is important to keep in mind that no matter what the contract or legal fee agreement is with a client, attorneys and legal assistants can receive only a "reasonable" fee. Unfortunately, there is no absolute standard for determining reasonableness, except that reasonableness will be determined on a case-by-case basis. However, Rule 1.5 of the *Model Rules of Professional Conduct* gives a number of factors to be considered in determining reasonableness. These factors include the following:

1. The time and labor required, including the novelty and difficulty of the questions involved, and the skill required to perform the legal services.
2. The likelihood that the acceptance of the legal matter will preclude the lawyer from accepting other cases.
3. The customary fee in the area for such legal services.
4. The outcome of the matter, including the amount involved.
5. Any time limitations imposed by the client or by the circumstances.
6. The type, nature, and length of the professional relationship with the client.
7. The ability of the lawyer involved, including experience, reputation, and ability.
8. Whether the type of fee was fixed or contingent.

For example, in one case, a court found that a fee of $22,500 pursuant to a written agreement for a real estate matter that involved little time for the attorney and that was not unduly complex was unreasonable. Exhibit 6–26 shows some additional examples of unreasonable fees.

For many years, it was thought that overbilling and stealing from clients by attorneys was done only by sole practitioners and attorneys in small firms. Exhibit 6–26 shows that this is probably not true and that these practices happen at all levels.

> *. . .A lawyer may not bill more than one client for the same hours worked by charging a client for the time it took to produce a document that the lawyer had already created for another client. The lawyer also is prohibited from charging clients for the same hours when the lawyer works on one client's matter while traveling for the benefit of the other client on a different matter.*[15]

Many State Bars' Rules Provide for Oversight/Arbitration on Fee Issues

One of the ways that state bar associations and courts have dealt with the abundance of fee disputes is to provide for immediate and informal review and/or arbitration of fee disputes. Many state ethical rules and court rules provide that clients have the right at any time to request that the judge in the case or an attorney representing the state bar review the reasonableness of the attorney's fees. In many states, the attorney is required to inform the client of this right. In those states, the judge or attorney hearing the matter has the right to set the fee and determine what is reasonable under the particular facts and circumstances of the case.

Fraud and Criminal Charges

> *Intentionally overbilling clients for work not done is called fraud. You can be criminally prosecuted by government officials and civilly prosecuted by your clients.*

Charging an unreasonable fee is no longer simply a matter of ethics. Recently, attorneys and legal assistants have been criminally charged with fraud for intentionally recording time and sending bills for legal services that were

Exhibit 6–26
Unethical, Highly Questionable, and/or Fraudulent Billing Practices
Reprinted with permission of the publisher, *Georgetown Journal of Legal Ethics* © 1999.

- **Audit Questions Legal Assistant's 12-Hour Work Days**
  An audit of a paralegal's time found that for nearly a two-year period the legal assistant worked (ie., billed) an average of 12.45 hours each day, including Saturdays, Sundays, and holidays, without providing details to support the hours. During the nearly two-year period the legal assistant took only one day off (one Christmas day). The audit estimated that the paralegal overbilled by 2,220 hours at a cost of $39,960.
- **Client Charged for Individual Attorneys BIlling More than the 24-hour Day**
  A corporation recently received a monthly legal bill in excess of $300,000. The head of the corporate legal department was concerned. After hiring an outside audit firm to audit the billings he discovered that:
  - Individual attorneys were billing in excess of the 24-hour day;
  - Attorneys were assigned to tasks that could have been provided by legal assistants at greatly reduced costs;
  - The client was billed by the firm for duplicate items;
  - Conferences were often attended by many attorneys who were not needed and their time was charged to the client;
  - The client was billed for the same expert witness fees multiple times; and,
  - The firm charged the client for the time the firm spent working with an auditor to show them their overcharges.
- **Overbilling and Fraud by Elite Partners and Firms**
  In the winter of 1999, the *Georgetown Journal of Legal Ethics* published an exhaustive article on overbilling and fraud by sixteen elite attorneys and/or law firms. Below are some quotes from the article.
  "In recent years, a disturbing number of well-respected lawyers in large established firms have been caught stealing large amounts of money from their clients and their partners by padding, manipulating and fabricating time sheets and expense vouchers. Some have gone to prison, been disbarred, and/or fired. . ."
  Billing fraud takes many different forms. Here are some examples:
- Some lawyers are just sloppy about keeping time records.
- Some systematically "pad" timesheets, or bill one client for work done for another.
- Some create entirely fictitious timesheets.
- Some record hours based on work done by other lawyers, paralegals, or secretaries, representing that they did the work. This may result in nonbillable time being billed, or in work being billed at a rate higher than that of the person who actually did the work.
- Some lawyers bill for time that their clients might not regard as legitimately billable—for schmoozing with other lawyers, chatting with clients about sports or families, for doing administrative work that could be done by a non-lawyer, or for thinking about a case while mowing the lawn or watching television.

The methods of expense fraud are equally diverse; the lawyers who engage in expense fraud may be stealing from their clients or their partners or both . . .

Billing fraud is far more difficult to detect than expense fraud, unless the lawyer is reckless enough to bill more than twenty-four hours per day. But regulation of this type of conduct is very difficult because no one except the lawyer really knows how much time was spent and how much was billed . . .

I undertook the research for this article because in recent years, I periodically noticed reports of cases of elite lawyers who had gone to jail, been disbarred, or been investigated for stealing by billing and expense fraud . . . These sixteen cases involve lawyers who came from privileged backgrounds, attended elite schools, and have:

(a) been a managing partner, a member of the executive committee or a rainmaker at a large, respected law firm or a spin-off from such a firm;
(b) been publicly accused of stealing over $100,000 from clients or from his or her law firm by fraudulent representations as to hours worked or expenses incurred;
(c) been jailed and/or disbarred for billing or expense fraud.

These lawyers engaged in patterns of fraud that went on for an average of five years. Their collective total proven or admitted theft is about $16 million. These highly educated successful lawyers were at the pinnacle of the profession.

continued

Exhibit 6–26
Continued

[Here are some specific examples]:

Attorney
$3.1 Million over 5-year period

- Attorney wrote fake time sheets, engaged in expense fraud, inflated hours, billed for work not done, billed for time of persons who did no work on matters billed on, engaged in "ad hoc value billing." One judge who reviewed the case described the methods as "almost fictional," and offered these examples: $98,700 billed for services never performed by David Levin; almost $500,000 for time attributed to legal assistants, medical experts and law clerks, when the work billed for was in fact done by the firm's receptionist and secretaries, and $66,127.29 for legal and medical research that cost only $394.98.
- Attorney wrote over 100 checks on firm accounts for personal expenses, claiming they were payments to "expert witnesses" or other law-related work.

Attorney
$1.4 Million over 5-year period

- Attorney intentionally overbilled the federal government and destroyed and concealed records to conceal his activities. As managing partner, he reviewed the time records of associates and partners in the firm. He forwarded them to the bookkeeper with written instructions directing the bookkeeper to increase the number of hours billed above the numbers recorded by the lawyers. When audited by FDIC, the attorney gathered the original time records and either concealed them or destroyed them, and directed the firm office manager to provide false information to the government.

Attorney
$1.1 Million over 5-year period

- Attorney billed five firm clients (four corporations and one trade union) directly without firm authorization. He claimed to be taking vacation or doing client development during some periods when he was billing these clients. Attorney "had most of the payments mailed directly to his home, so that his secretary would not see them; he also forbade his secretary to open any of his mail . . . [He] spent many hours typing up facsimile legal bills to present to clients, himself, rather than having his secretary do them. And, of course, he kept all the records for the bills at his home." He "often shifted fees to expenses and vice-versa, to make the bottom line agree with the billing totals he was submitting to his firm's accounting department." Attorney deceived his firm, sometimes with the knowledge and cooperation of clients. He also deceived clients, sometimes billing over 24 hours per day, or billing one expense to two clients. He billed $16,000 of personal expenses to one client.

Attorney
$500,000 over 5-year period

- While at the firm, attorney persuaded a French pharmaceutical client to hire a dummy consulting firm he had set up (which had no clients or employees) to arrange drug testing needed for FDA approval. The client paid nearly $1 million to the consulting firm; Morrell paid about half this amount into his checking account, his profit-sharing plan, or took it in cash.

Attorney
$225,000 over 4 years

- Attorney charged personal expenses to the firm and to clients, including $27,000 for flowers for his children's weddings, and the cost of meals, floral displays for the office, plane tickets and hotel accommodations for non-business-related family vacations. . . Attorney denied most of the charges, but admitted billing clients for airfare and hotel accommodations if he was working on a client's case during a particular vacation. He said his "clients have approved and ratified the specific expenses in question. Attorney also arranged for legal fees to be paid directly to him without firm approval.

Attorney
over 4 years (1991-1995) .

- Attorney allegedly billed clients for hundreds of hours of work that he did not do; he continued to bill for legal work after he began to spend most of his time on investing that involved a $100 million Ponzi scheme.[17]

never provided. **Criminal fraud** is a false representation of a present or past fact made by the defendant, upon which the victim relies, resulting in the victim suffering damages.

criminal fraud
A false representation of a present or past fact made by a defendant.

Criminal charges for fraud are not filed against attorneys and legal assistants when there is simply a disagreement over what a reasonable fee is. Criminal charges are filed when an attorney or legal assistant acts intentionally to defraud clients. This usually happens when the attorney or legal assistant bills for time when he or she did not really work on the case, or in instances in which the office intentionally billed a grossly overstated hourly rate far above the market rate.

One of the most common temptations that can corrupt a paralegal's ethics is to inflate billable hours, since there is often immense pressure in law offices to bill high hours for job security and upward mobility. Such "creative billing" [or "padding"] is not humorous; it's both morally wrong and illegal.[16]

In John Grisham's modern classic, The Firm, *Avery Tolar advises the young lawyer Mitchell McDeere on how to charge clients. He explains that the client should be charged for "every minute you spend even thinking about a case." It was this philosophy that got the Mafia's legal team into trouble. Unethical billing practices do not only exist in legal novels like* The Firm *but have been a pervasive problem in law firms across the country.*

Interestingly, many of the most recent criminal cases being brought are against well-respected large and small offices specializing in insurance defense and corporate work. Some insurance companies and corporations, as a matter of course when a case has been concluded, hire an audit firm or independent attorney to go back and audit the firm's billing and files to be sure they were billed accurately. In some instances, these audits have concluded that intentional criminal fraud has occurred and the cases were referred to prosecutors where criminal charges have been filed. No matter what type of firm is involved, intentionally overstating bills can lead to very big problems. Most, if not all, of the examples in Exhibit 6–26 (excerpted from the *Georgetown Journal of Legal Ethics*) led to criminal prosecutions of the attorneys.

Ethical Problems

Several difficult ethical problems regarding timekeeping and billing need to be explored, although they have no definite solutions. The rule in answering ethical questions such as these is to use your common sense and notions of fairness and honesty.

Can You Bill More than One Client for the Same Time? From time to time a legal assistant or attorney has the opportunity to bill more than one client for the same time period. This is known as *double billing*. For instance, while you are monitoring the opposing side's inspection of your client's documents in case A, you are drafting discovery for case B. Another example: while traveling to attend an interview with a witness in case A, you work on case B.

If you were the client, would you think it is fair for the attorney to charge full price for travel time related to your case while billing another case? A reasonable approach is to bill only the case you are actively working on, to split the time between the cases, or to bill the case you are actively working on at the regular hourly rate and bill the case you are inactively working on at a greatly reduced rate. Be fair and honest; your clients as well as judges and others looking at the time will respect you for it.

When Billing by the Hour, Is There an Ethical Obligation to Be Efficient? Does the firm have to have a form file in lieu of researching each document each time? Must an office use a computer to save time? These types of ethical questions are decided on a case-by-case basis. The point is that billing by the hour rewards people to work slowly, since the more slowly they work, the more they are paid.

Common sense tells you that if you were the client, you would want your legal staff to be efficient and not to "milk" you for money. The real issue is whether the attorney or legal assistant acted so inefficiently and charged so much, when compared with what a similar attorney or legal assistant with similar qualifications would charge in the same community, that the fee is clearly unreasonable. When a judge rules on the reasonableness of fees, there is no doubt that he or she will consider what a reasonably efficient attorney or legal assistant in the same circumstances would have charged. Use your common sense and be honest and efficient because someone in your office might have to justify your time and charges someday.

Should You Bill for Clerical or Secretarial Duties? Law offices cannot bill clients for clerical or secretarial tasks. The reason is that these tasks are viewed as overhead costs or are a normal part of doing business. An easy, but unethical, way to bill more hours is for a legal assistant to bill time to clients for clerical functions such as copying documents or filing material. Legal assistants clearly should not bill for theses types of clerical tasks. Legal assistants bill time for professional services, not for clerical functions. If you are unsure about whether a task is clerical, ask your supervising attorney, or record the time initially and point it out to the supervising attorney and let him or her decide.

Should you Bill for the Mistakes of the Law Office? This is another tough problem. People make mistakes all the time. Clients generally feel that they should not have to pay for mistakes, since the reason they went to an attorney was to get an expert to handle their situation. This is a decision that should be left for every law office to decide, but generally the practice of billing for mistakes should be discouraged.

Must a Task Be Assigned to Less Expensive Support Staff When Possible? Common sense and efficiency will tell you that tasks should be delegated as low as possible. Clients should not have to pay for attorney time when the task could be completed by an experienced legal assistant. In addition, this practice is more profitable to the law office because higher-paid persons are free to do tasks for which they can bill clients at their normal rates.

> *Billing is important to the legal assistant because raises and bonuses may be reflected in the amount of time billed. Correctly bill no matter how much pressure there is about maintaining those high billable hours because at the end of the day, you will have to live with your conscience. Fortunately, I have never been placed in a position that I was asked to record time which I did not think was right. If I had that situation, I would obtain clarification for the reasoning because there could be a misunderstanding.*
>
> *Linda Rushton, CLA*

The general subject of timekeeping and billing brings up a wide variety of ethical considerations, only a few of which are raised here. It is important that, no matter what kind of timekeeping and billing is used, whether it be manual or computerized, the underlying agreement between the law office and the client should be in writing. Second, ethical rules state that only a "reasonable fee" can be collected from clients. It is very important that bills be accurately produced the

first time and that no errors occur, so only a "reasonable fee" is collected. Data entry is absolutely crucial to timekeeping and billing. If a timeslip is entered twice so a client is billed twice for the same service, if a payment is not recorded to a client's account, or if a client is overcharged for legal services, the firm could lose that client or be faced with an ethical complaint. Thousands of ethical complaints are filed every year against attorneys regarding timekeeping and billing practices, so it is very important that this function be handled properly.

SUMMARY

In the legal environment, the process of tracking time for the purpose of billing clients is called timekeeping. The process of issuing bills for the purpose of collecting monies for legal services performed and for expenses is called billing. Timekeeping and billing software is the second most popular kind of software for law offices, behind word processing.

The computerized timekeeping and billing process or cycle includes these steps: the client and the attorney reach an agreement with regard to how fees will be calculated, the attorney performs legal services and prepares manual or computer timeslips, paper timeslips and expense slips are entered into the timekeeping and billing software, a pre-billing report is generated, client billings are generated, management reports are generated, and client payments are entered into the computer.

Many types of fee arrangements are available, including hourly rate fees, contingency fees, flat fees, and retainers.

Every timekeeping and billing program has a screen, sometimes called the client information screen, where relevant information about each client is entered. The client information screen usually contains information about a client, such as name, address, identification number, fee arrangements, bill formatting options, and so forth.

The data entry screen is where timeslips and expense slips are entered into the computer. Each computerized timeslip looks similar to the manual timeslip.

Generating client bills is an important aspect of a timekeeping and billing program. Many timekeeping and billing programs have several different billing formats that can be used.

Management reports are used to help management analyze whether a law firm is operating in an efficient and effective manner. Some of the management reports included in most programs are the case or client list, aged accounts receivable report, timekeeping productivity report, attorney time per case report, case type productivity report, and more.

Many ethical complaints are filed against attorneys due to timekeeping and billing issues. It is important to have written fee agreements and bill only for reasonable fees.

KEY TERMS

timekeeping
billing
timeslip
expense slip
timekeeper
pre-billing report
hourly rate fee
attorney or legal assistant hourly rate
client hourly rate
blended hourly rate fee
activity hourly rate
contingency fee
flat fee
earned retainer
unearned retainer
trust or escrow account
cash advance
retainer for general representation
case retainer
pure retainer
value billing
management reports
aged accounts receivable report
timekeeper productivity report
case type productivity report
electronic billing
outside counsel
criminal fraud

INTERNET SITES

Organization	Product/Service	World Wide Web Address
Abacus Data Sytems, Inc.	Abacus Silver, timekeeping, billing, accounting and case management	<http://www.abacuslaw.com>
ADC Legal Systems, Inc.	Perfect Practice Billing & Accounting	<http://www.adclegal.com>
Aderamt	CMS Open Billing (for large law firms)	<http://www.cmsopen.com>
DDI, Inc.	DDI Time & Billing	<http://www.ddisoft.com>
Journyx, Inc.	Journyx Timesheet – E-billing	<http://www.journyx.com>
Juris	Juris legal timekeeping and billing software	<http://www.juris.com>
LexisNexis	PC LAW legal timekeeping and billing software	<http://www.pclaw.com>
Micro Craft, Inc.	Verdict Time & Billing	<http://www.micro-craft.net>
Omega Legal Systems	Omega Billing & Accounting	<http://www.omegalegal.com>
OpenAir, Inc.	OpenAir – E-billing	<http://www.openair.com>
Orion Law Manage ment Systems	Timekeeping and billing software	<http://www.Orionlaw.com>
Perfect Law Software	Timekeeping and billing software and comprehensive back-office systems	<http://www.perfectlaw.com>
ProVantage Software, Inc.	Timekeeping and billing software and comprehensive back-office systems	<http://www.provantagesoftware.com>
Rainmaker Software, Inc.	Rainmaker Gold timekeeping and billing	<http://www.rainmakerlegal.com>
Sage Software	Timeslips legal timekeeping and billing software	<http://www.timeslips.com>
Software Technology, Inc.	Tabs3 legal timekeeping and billing software	<//http://Tabs3.com>
Thomson	Elite Enterprise timekeeping and billing software	<http://www.elite.com>
Thomson	Prolaw legal timekeeping and billing software	<http://www.prolaw.com>

TEST YOUR KNOWLEDGE

Test your knowledge of the chapter by answering these questions.

1. What is the difference between timekeeping and billing?
2. Name four types of hourly rates: ________, ________, ________, ________.
3. When a lawyer takes a percentage of the recovery in the case it is called a ____________ fee.
4. True or False: It is strongly recommended that all fee arrangements be in writing.
5. True or False: A flat-fee agreement must be in writing.
6. A retainer that can be deposited in the firm's or attorney's operating checking account is called a(n) ________ retainer.

7. True or False: An account where unearned client monies are deposited is called a trust fund.
8. A retainer for general representation is a(n) ________ retainer.
9. A case retainer is a(n) ________ retainer.
10. A cash advance retainer is a(n) ________ retainer.
11. A legal billing arrangement that is similar to the type used when you get your car fixed is called ________ billing.
12. For what activity do clients file the most ethical complaints against lawyers?
13. True or False: A contingency agreement can be used in all kinds of cases.
14. True or False: If a client signs a contract with an attorney and the fee turns out to be clearly excessive, it doesn't matter, because a contract was signed and the contract prevails.
15. Name four of the eight factors that courts use to determine if a fee is unreasonable.
16. True or False: Legal assistants can bill for time spent copying and other clerical duties.
17. Define electronic billing.
18. True or False: Integrated programs that include timekeeping and billing, accounting, and other features do not really offer the modern law office much advantage.

ON THE WEB EXERCISES

1. Using a general Internet search engine such as google.com or yahoo.com, or the Internet sites listed in this chapter, research three timekeeping and billing programs. Compare the features, price, training options, and other information about the products and write a three-page paper on your findings, including which program you liked the best and why.
2. Using a general Internet search engine such as google.com or yahoo.com, or the Internet sites listed in this chapter, research legal electronic billing. Write a three-page paper on the results of your research. Include what it is, how it works, what if any problems there are regarding implementing electronic billing and what benefits clients and legal organizations receive by implementing electronic billing.
3. Go to the ABA Center for Professional Responsibility at http://www.abanet.org/, find the *ABA Model Rules of Professional Conduct*, and read and print out Rule 1.5 (Fees) and the Comment thereto. Write a two-page summary of what the rule and comment say and why they are important.
4. Using a general Internet search engine such as google.com or yahoo.com, or the Internet sites listed in this chapter, find a minimum of three articles on legal timekeeping and billing. Write a one-page summary of each article.
5. Visit five state bar associations' websites and find three articles on either legal timekeeping, billing, or legal fees.
6. Go to the Georgia Bar Association's website at http://www.gabar.org/ and find a sample contingency fee agreement. Go to several other state bar association websites and try to find another sample contingency fee or hourly rate contract agreements.
7. Go to http://www.findlaw.com and print out and read the United States Supreme Court case of *Missouri v. Jenkins*, 491 U.S. 274 (1989). Try selecting "For Legal Professionals," scroll until you see "Cases & Codes," and then click "Supreme Court" and "Supreme Court Opinions." You should then be able to enter the citation of the case—491 U.S. 274.
8. Visit the National Association of Legal Assistants website at www.nala.org and review the latest NALA National Utilization and Compensation Survey Report. Read and print out the section related to legal assistant billing rates. If you have difficulty finding it, try using the "Search" feature on the website. If you still have trouble finding it, use www.google.com and search for the full title.
9. Go to the ABA Law Practice Management Section home page at www.abanet.org and find two articles on timekeeping, billing, fees, and financially related matters and summarize them in a two-page paper.

QUESTIONS AND EXERCISES

1. You are a new legal assistant and have worked for a medium-sized law office for three months. It has been a tremendous learning experience for you. It has taken time to learn how the office does business; its policies and procedures; what type of service you are expected to give to clients; where resources are; and how to use them, such as the office's computer systems, law library, copy

machines, and form files. Although it has taken time for you to learn these things, you also have been productive and have received several compliments on the quality of your work.

One day, you read in the office's staff manual that all legal assistants are required to bill 1,500 hours annually or face possible discipline. You immediately contact your supervisor and ask whether, as a new legal assistant, you will be expected to bill this amount. Your supervisor responds, "Of course. You were told that when you were hired." You immediately begin gathering copies of your timesheets to compile your total. You also request that the billing department send you the total numbers of hours you have billed to date. When you get the report from billing, you panic; you have billed only 300 hours. What do you do now, and how could you have avoided this unfortunate situation?

2. On June 30, a billing goes out to Susan Simon, one of the clients whose cases you have been working on. Ms. Simon calls you a few days later and complains about the amount of time shown on the bill. She is extremely rude and discourteous. Ms. Simon flatly states that she thinks she is being overbilled. How do you handle the phone call?
3. You are interviewing a new client. The client wants to hire your office to help negotiate the purchase of a small business. The seller has proposed $20,000. The new client would be willing to pay this amount, although she thinks it is a bit high, but she does not feel comfortable negotiating with the seller and would rather have an attorney involved in the deal for her protection. However, she is suspicious of legal assistants and attorneys and is especially concerned about how much her case will cost. You inform the client that the attorney will be the one who actually talks to her about the fee issue, but that typically this type of case is taken on an hourly basis and that the attorney will be able to give her only a very broad estimate of what the total matter will cost. The client states that this would be unacceptable to her because does not have a lot of money to pay overpriced attorneys. The client also states that she would like this matter settled as soon as possible. You must prepare a memorandum to the attorney outlining the issue and possible solutions. What type of fee arrangement would you suggest to the attorney? Please keep in mind the client's anxieties and her particular needs.
4. Recently, your office has found a niche in representing spouses collecting on past-due child support. In most cases, your clients have little money to pay you with and are financially strapped because they no longer have the income of their former spouses to support their children and have not been receiving the child support. In some cases, large amounts of money are owed, but finding the former spouses has proved difficult. Your supervising attorney decides that the best way to handle these types of cases is on a one-third contingency basis. Your supervising attorney asks for your comments. How do you respond?
5. Yesterday was a hectic day. Although you wanted to record your time earlier, you just could not get to it. Please record your time in a spreadsheet. Build the spreadsheet so it has columns set up for the date, client/case name, timekeeper, services rendered, billable time, and nonbillable time. For each activity listed, decide whether it is billable or not billable. Record your time, first using tenths of hours. Also, you should fill out expense slips for items that should be charged back to clients. Build the spreadsheet to include date, client/case name, type of expense, and cost. The firm charges 25 cents each for copies and 50 cents per page to send a fax. Assume long-distance phone calls cost 25 cents a minute. Please total the cost of each expense slip.

As best you can recall, this is how your day went:

8:00 A.M.–8:12 A.M. Got a cup of coffee, talked to other law office staff members, reviewed your schedule/things to do sheet for the day, and reviewed the email in your inbox.

8:13 A.M.–8:25 A.M. Talked to your supervising attorney (Lisa Mitchell) about some research she needs done on the grounds to support a motion to dismiss *Johnson v. Cuttingham Steel*. Ms. Mitchell also asked you to find a bankruptcy statute she needs for *Halvert v. Shawnee Saving & Loan*.

8:26 A.M.–8:37 A.M. A legal assistant from another office calls to remind you that the legal assistant association you belong to is having a meeting at noon and that you are running the meeting.

8:38 A.M.–8:40 A.M. One of your least favorite clients, John Hamilton, calls to ask you when he is supposed to be at your office to prepare for his deposition tomorrow. You access the weekly schedule electronically and read him the information he needs.

8:40 A.M.–8:50 A.M. You find the information you need for the motion to dismiss in *Johnson v. Cuttingham Steel* in a motion in another case you helped to prepare last month. The research is still current, and

Ms. Mitchell is pleased you found it so fast. You note that it took you two hours to research this issue when you did it the first time. You copy the material Ms. Mitchell needs (five-pages), and put it on her desk, and also send it to her electronically.

8:55 A.M.–9:30 A.M. You speak with a witness you have been trying to contact in *Menly v. Menly*. The call is long-distance. The call lasts fifteen minutes and writing the memo to the file documenting the call takes fifteen minutes.

9:30 A.M.–9:54 A.M. Ms. Mitchell asks you to contact the attorney in *Glass v. Huron* regarding a discovery question. You spend ten minutes on hold. The call is long-distance but you get an answer to Ms. Mitchell's question.

10:00 A.M.–10:45 A.M. One of the secretaries informs you that you must interview a new client, Richard Sherman. The person who was supposed to see Mr. Sherman got delayed. Mr. Sherman comes to your office regarding a simple adoption. However, in talking to Mr. Sherman you find out that he also needs someone to incorporate a small business that he is getting ready to open. You gladly note that your office has a department that handles this type of matter. You take the basic information down regarding both matters. You tell the client that you will prepare a memo regarding these matters to the appropriate attorney and one of the office's attorneys will contact him within two days to further discuss the matter. You also copy ten pages of information that Mr. Sherman brought.

10:45 A.M.–10:54 A.M. One of the secretaries asks you to cover her phone for her while she takes a quick break. Because the secretary always helps you when you ask for it, you gladly cover the phone for a few minutes. Ms. Mitchell asks you to send a fax in *Stewart v. Layhorn Glass*, so you use this time to send the six-page fax.

10:55 A.M.– Yesterday Ms. Mitchell asked you to organize some exhibits in *Ranking v. Siefkin*. The deadline was noon today. You finally have some free time to organize the exhibits.

12:00 noon–1:00 P.M.You attend the legal assistant association lunch.

1:00 P.M.–2:00 P.M. You work on a pro bono criminal case that Ms. Mitchell is representing on appeal. In an effort to become familiar with the case, you read some of the transcripts from the trial.

2:00 P.M.–5:30 P.M. Ms. Mitchell hands you a new case. Ms. Mitchell says that your firm will be representing the defendant. She asks you to read the petition and client file, analyze the case, and draft interrogatories to send the plaintiff. You spend the rest of the day working on this case.

END NOTES

[1] Timothy L. Takacs and Gill E. Wagner, "The Time Has Come," *Law Office Computing*, February/March 2001, 8.
[2] Special Committee on Economics of Law Practice of the American Bar Association, 1959. Reprinted by permission.
[3] John P. Mello, Jr., "Paralegal Billing Trends," *Legal Assistant Today*, September/October 1993, 127. Copyright 1993. James Publishing, Inc. Reprinted with permission from *Legal Assistant Today* magazine. For subscription information call 800-394-2626, or visit <http://www.legalassistanttoday.com>.
[4] William Statsky, *Introduction to Paralegalism*, (St. Paul, Minn.: West Publishing Co., 1992) at 826, citing A Lighter Note, NALA Advance 15, Summer 1989.
[5] Terrie I. Murray, "The Unwritten Rules: Survival in a Law Firm," *Legal Assistant Today*, May/June 1998, 13. Copyright 1998. James Publishing, Inc. Reprinted with permission from *Legal Assistant Today* magazine. For subscription information call 800-394-2626, or visit <http://www.legalassistant-today.com>.
[6] Carol Milano, "Hard Choices: Dealing with Ethical Dilemmas on the Job," *Legal Assistant Today*, March/April 1992, 79. Copyright 1992. James Publishing, Inc. Reprinted with permission from *Legal Assistant Today* magazine. For subscription information call 800- 394-2626, or visit <http://www.legalassistanttoday.com>.
[7] Amanda Flatten, "The Time & Billing Jackpot," *Law Office Computing*, April/May 2005, 62.
[8] Carol Schlein, "Maximize Your Billing: Good Timekeeping Habits Can Save You Megabucks," *Lawyer's PC*, August 1, 2001, 1.
[9] Robert J. Thomas, "Electronic Billing: What Happens When You Ditch the Paper Invoices?," *Law Practice Management*, April 2001, 40.
[10] Brett Burney, "E-Billing Friend or Foe?," *Legal Assistant Today*, September/October 2005, 68.
[11] Mimi Shore, "A Time for Change," *Law Office Computing*, June/July 2006, 14.
[12] *The Legal Assistant's Practical Guide to Professional Responsibility*, 2nd ed. (American Bar Association, 2004), 120. Reprinted by permission.
[13] Kenny C. Bailey, "All I Really Need to Know I Learned from a Paralegal," *Facts and Findings*, August 2000, 29. Reprinted with the permission of the National Association of Legal Assistants, 1516 S. Boston, #200 Tulsa OK. <http://www.nala.org>.
[14] Terry Conner, "The Challenges Facing Law Firms," *Texas Bar Journal*, January 2000, 22.
[15] *The Legal Assistant's Practical Guide to Professional Responsibility*, 2nd ed. (American Bar Association, 2004) 122. Reprinted by permission.
[16] Smith, "AAFPE National Conference Highlights," *Legal Assistant Today*, January/February 1991, 103. Copyright 1991. James Publishing, Inc. Reprinted with permission from *Legal Assistant Today* magazine. For subscription information call 800-394-2626, or visit <http://www.legalassistanttoday.com>.
[17] Lisa Lerman, "Blue Chip Billing: Regulation of Billing and Expense Fraud by Lawyers," *Georgetown Journal of Legal Ethics* 12 (2), 1999, 205. Reprinted with permission of the publisher, Georgetown University and *Georgetown Journal of Legal Ethics*, copyright 1999.

HANDS-ON EXERCISES

TABS3 TIMEKEEPING AND BILLING

READ THIS FIRST!

I. Introduction–Read This!

The Tabs3 timekeeping and billing program demonstration version is a full working version of the program with a few limitations. The main limitation is that only a limited number of clients can be entered into the program. The demonstration version does *not* time out (quit working after a set number of days).

II. Using the Tabs3 Hands-on Exercises

The Tabs3 Hands-on Exercises are easy to use and contain step-by-step instructions. Each lesson builds on the previous exercise, so please complete the Hands-on-Exercises in order. Tabs3 is a user-friendly program, so using the program should be intuitive. Tabs3 also comes with sample data, so you should be able to try many features of the program.

III. Installation Instructions

Below are step-by-step instructions for loading the Tabs3 timekeeping and billing demonstration version on your computer.

1. ***Insert Disk 2 supplied with this text into your computer.***

2. When prompted with "What do you want Windows to do?" select "Open folder to view files using Windows Explorer," then click OK. If your computer does not automatically recognize that you have inserted a CD, double-click the My Computer icon, then double-click the drive where Disk 2 is.

3. Double-click the Tabs3 folder. Then double-click the launch.exe file. This will start the Tabs3 installation wizard.

Tabs3 Installation Exhibit 1

Copyright 2007 Software Technology, Inc. www.Tabs3.com

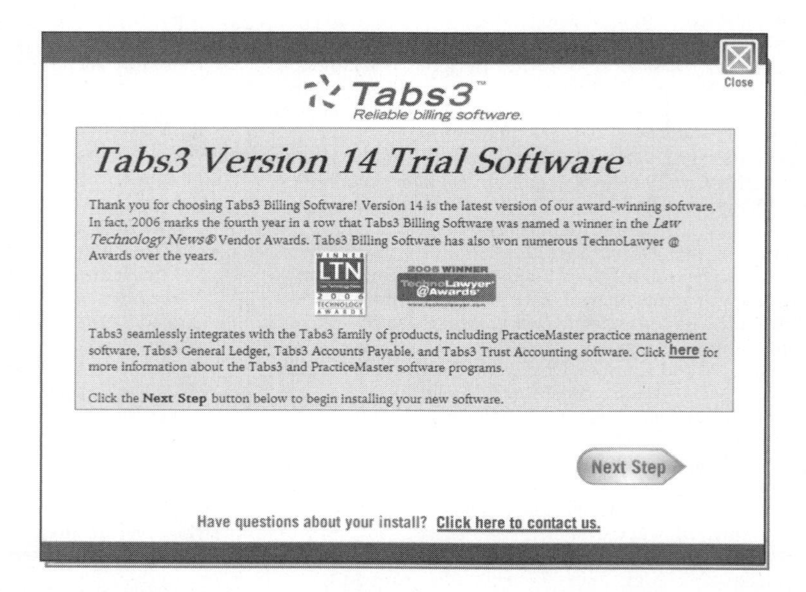

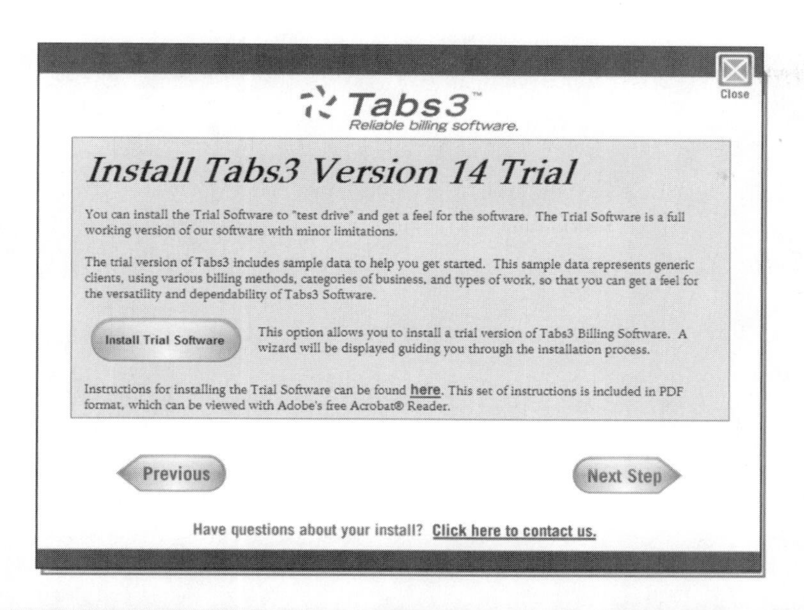

Tabs3 Installation Exhibit 2

Copyright 2007 Software Technology, Inc. www.Tabs3.com

4. The screen in Tabs3 Installation Exhibit 2 should now be displayed.

5. *Click "Next Step".*

6. The screen in Tabs3 Installation Exhibit 2 should now be displayed. *Click "Install Trial Software".*

7. The Trial Software Installation Setup window should now be displayed (see Tabs3 Installation Exhibit 4). *Click "Next".*

8. The screen in Tabs3 Installation Exhibit 4 should now be displayed. This screen refers to a License Agreement. *Click Yes to accept the license agreement.*

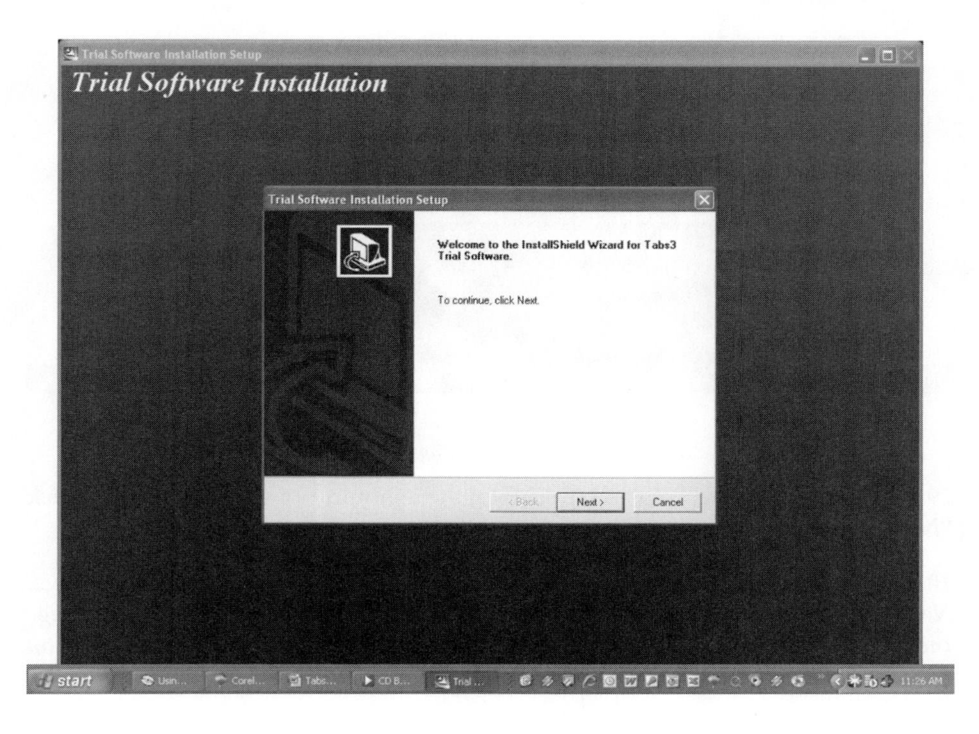

Tabs3 Installation Exhibit 3

Copyright 2007 Software Technology, Inc. www.Tabs3.com

Tabs3 Installation Exhibit 4

Copyright 2007 Software Technology, Inc. www.Tabs3.com

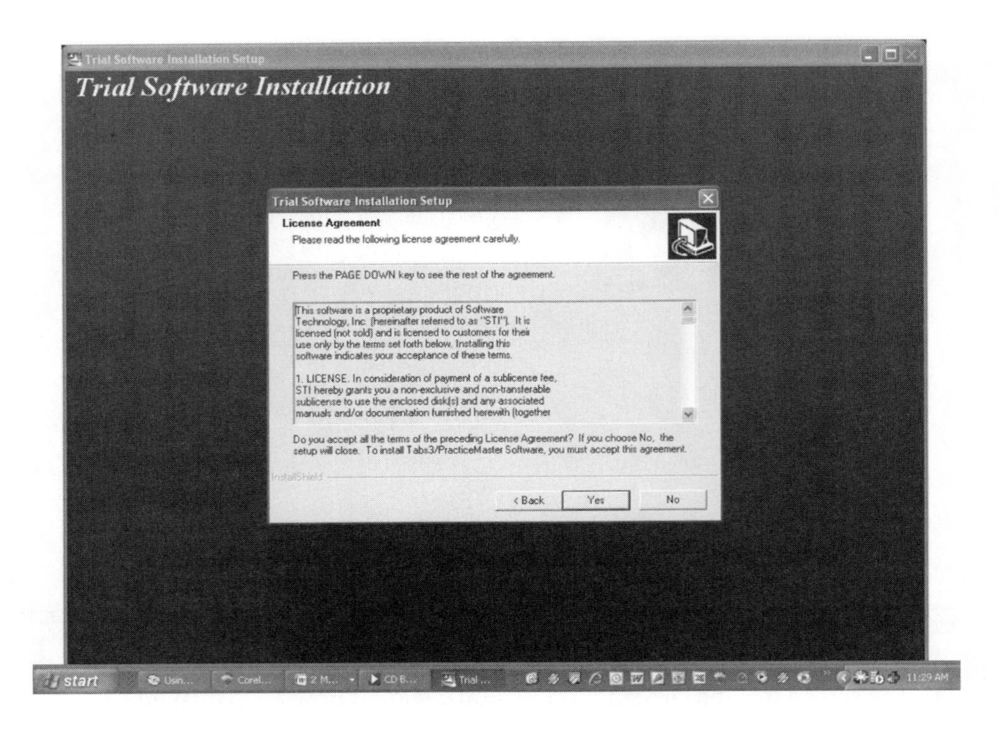

Tabs3 Installation Exhibit 5

Copyright 2007 Software Technology, Inc. www.Tabs3.com

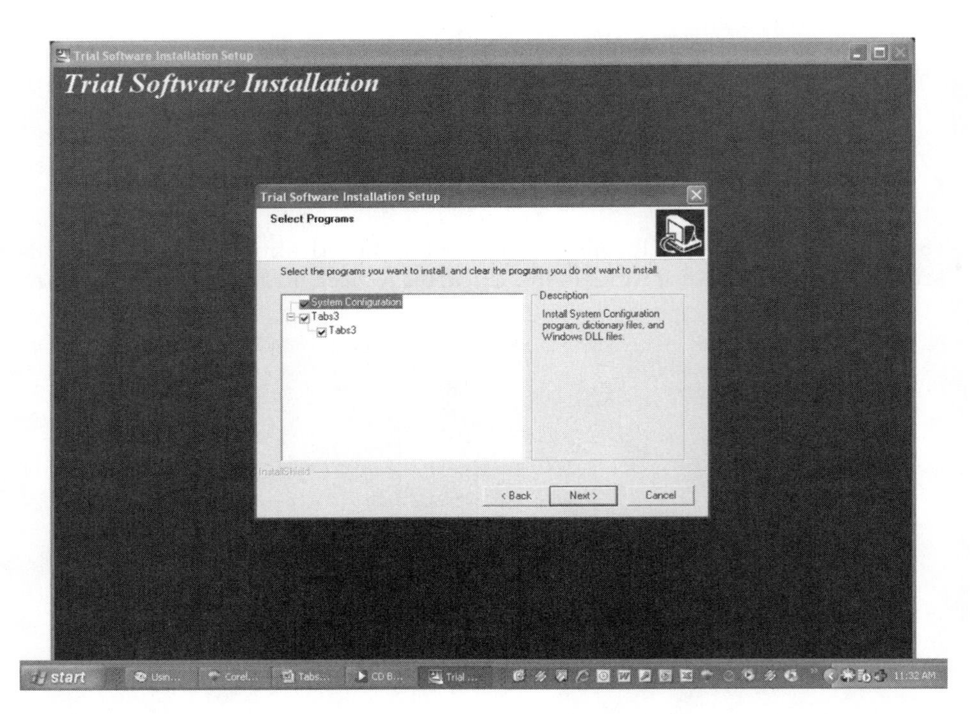

9. The screen in Tabs3 Installation Exhibit 5 should now be displayed. ***Click "Next".***

10. The screen in Tabs3 Installation Exhibit 6 should now be displayed. ***Click Next to install the software in the default directory (or select Browse to change the directory). Note: if a "Confirm New Folder" message is displayed click on "Yes." If a "Install Starter Data" message is displayed click on "Yes."***

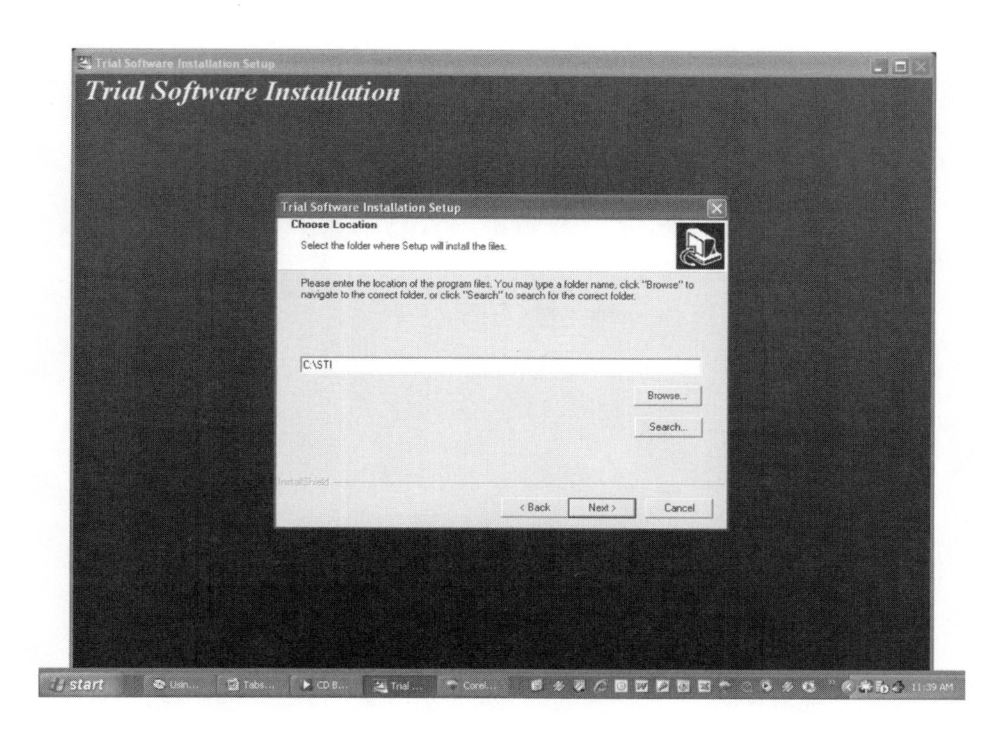

Tabs3 Installation Exhibit 6

Copyright 2007 Software Technology, Inc. www.Tabs3.com

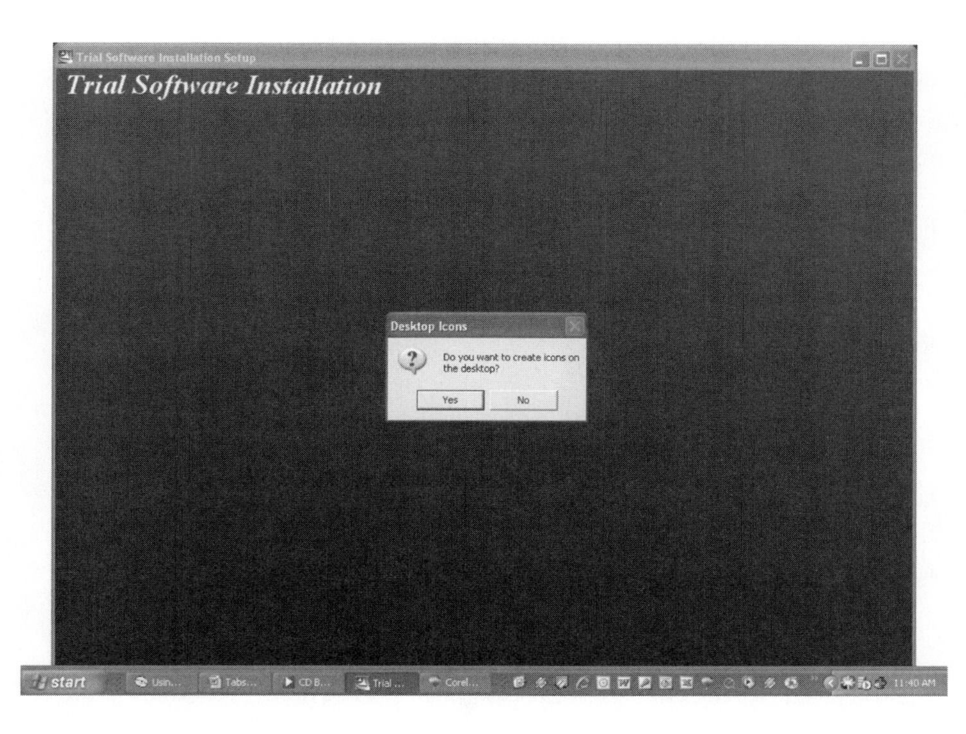

Tabs3 Installation Exhibit 7

Copyright 2007 Software Technology, Inc. www.Tabs3.com

11. The screen in Tabs3 Installation Exhibit 7 should now be displayed.

12. ***Click Yes to install icons on your desktop.***

13. The screen in Tabs3 Installation Exhibit 9 should now be displayed. The files should now be copied on to your computer.

14. The screen in Tabs3 Installation Exhibit 9 should now be displayed. The installation of the program should now be complete. ***Click "Finish".***

Tabs3 Installation Exhibit 8

Copyright 2007 Software Technology, Inc. www.Tabs3.com

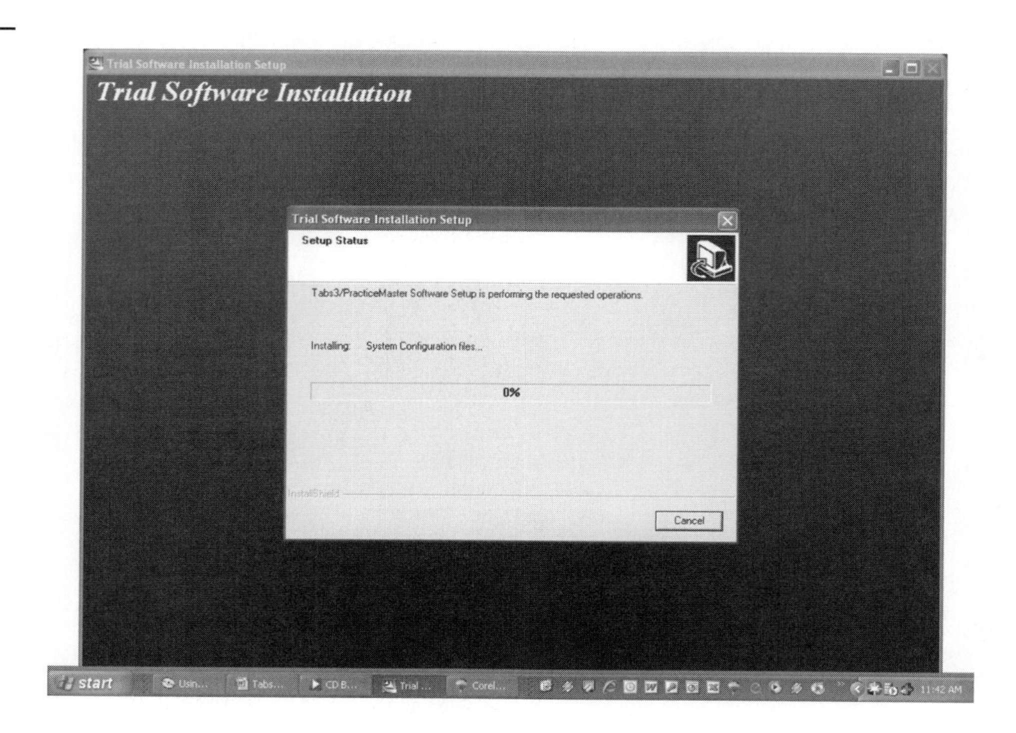

Tabs3 Installation Exhibit 9

Copyright 2007 Software Technology, Inc. www.Tabs3.com

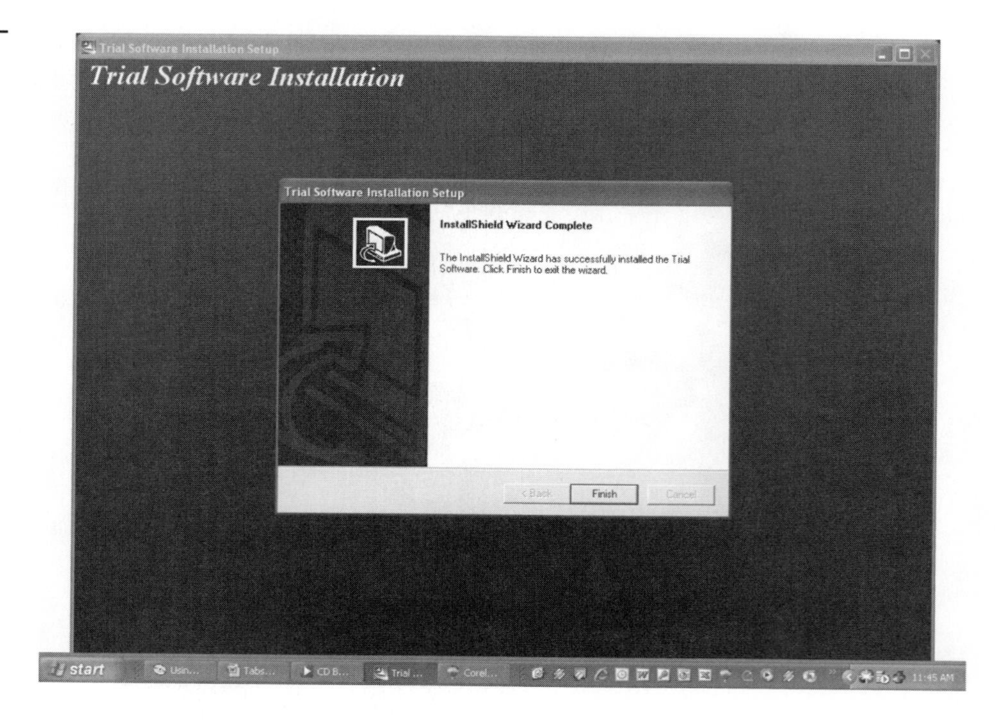

15. The screen in Tabs3 Installation Exhibit 10 should now be displayed. You may install the Tabs3 manual and other information by clicking Next Step, but this is not necessary for completion of the exercises here. ***Click the Close icon (a red square with a white "X") in the upper right of the window.***

IV. Installation Technical Support

If you have problems installing the demonstration version of Tabs3 from the Disk2 included with this text, please contact Thomson Delmar Learning

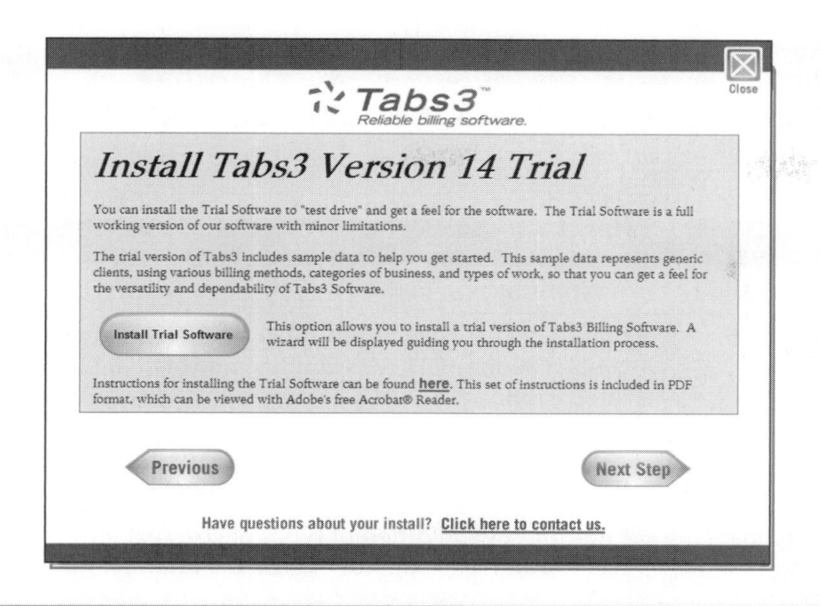

Tabs3 Installation Exhibit 10

Copyright 2007 Software Technology, Inc. www.Tabs3.com

Technical Support first at (800) 477-3692. Please note that Tabs3 is a licensed product of Software Technology, Inc. If Thomson Delmar Learning Technical Support is unable to resolve your installation question, or if you have a non-installation–related question, you will need to contact Software Technology, Inc. directly at (402) 423-1440.

HANDS-ON EXERCISES

TABS3 TIMEKEEPING AND BILLING SOFTWARE

Basic

Number	Lesson Title	Concepts Covered
Lesson 1	Introduction to Tabs3	An introduction to the Tabs3 interface
Lesson 2	Entering a New Client	Entering a new client into Tabs3, including entering contact data, setup, rates, billing, and statement information
Intermediate		
Lesson 3	Entering Fee/Time Records	Entering several different types of fee/time record entries
Lesson 4	Entering Cost/Expense Records and Using The Timer Feature	Entering several different types of cost/expense records and learning how to use the timer feature
Lesson 5	Producing And Printing Draft and Final Statements	Producing and printing draft statements and final statements and updating statements
Lesson 6	Processing a Payment	Processing and applying a payment
Advanced		
Lesson 7	Processing and Printing Reports	Processing and producing a number of management, productivity, and client reports

GETTING STARTED

Introduction

Throughout these lessons and exercises, information you need to type into the program will be designated in several different ways:

- Keys to be pressed on the keyboard will be designated in brackets, in all caps, and in bold (press the [ENTER] key).
- Movements will be designated in bold and italics (***point to File on the menu bar and click the mouse***).
- Words or letters that should be typed will be designated in bold (type **Training Program**).
- Information that should be displayed on your computer screen is shown in the following style: ***Press ENTER to continue.***

OVERVIEW OF TABS3

Tabs3 is a full-featured timekeeping and billing program. There are also many additional modules available that integrate with the timekeeping and billing program, including general ledger, accounts payable, trust accounting, a report writer, and case management. In this tutorial, only the timekeeping and billing functions will be covered. Tabs3 Exhibit 1 shows the Tabs3 window with task folders displayed. With Tabs3, users can enter new clients, enter fee/time entries, make expense entries, make and apply payments, run billing reports, run management

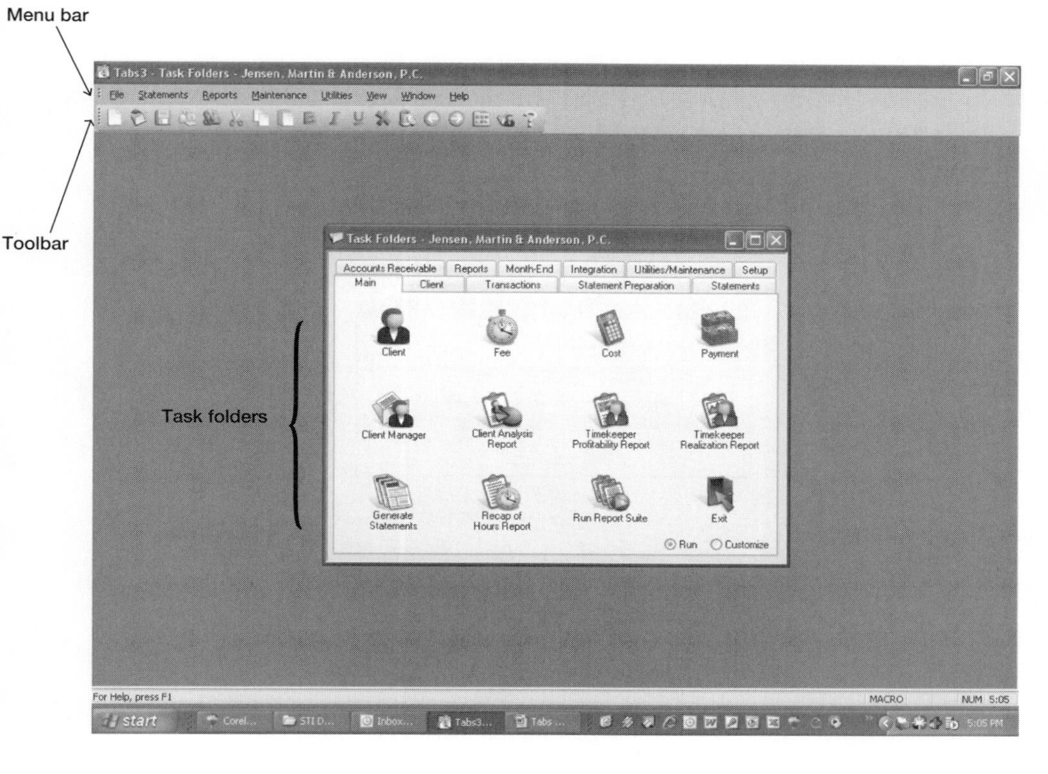

Tabs3 Exhibit 1
Tabs3 Window with Task Folders

reports, and control a firm's overall timekeeping and billing function. While Tabs3 is robust and offers many advanced timekeeping and billing functions, it is also easy to use. By the end of the exercises, you should have a good understanding of the basics of legal timekeeping and billing with Tabs3.

Basic Lessons

LESSON 1: INTRODUCTION TO TABS3

This lesson introduces you to Tabs3. It explains basic information about the Tabs3 interface, including an overview of clients, fees, costs, payments, generating bills and statements, and running reports.

Before you start, install the Tabs3 demonstration version on your computer by following the instructions at the end of Chapter 6 entitled "Tabs3 Hands-On Exercises – Read This First!" *Note:* The Tabs3 Law demonstration version does *not* time out (quit working after a set number of days). The only major limitation the demonstration version has is that only a limited number of clients can be entered in the system.

1. Open Windows. Then, ***double-click Tabs3 Trial on the desktop or click the Start button on the Windows desktop, point to Programs or All Programs, point to the Software Technology group, point to Trial Software with Sample Data, and then click Tabs3 with Sample Data.*** Tabs3 will then be open with some sample data already entered into the program.

2. The Tip of the Day window should now be displayed. ***Click "Close" in the Tip of the Day window.***

3. The screen in Tabs3 Exhibit 2 should now be displayed. The Tabs3 window states that sample data is being used and that the system date in use with the sample data is set to 11/14/2006. This date will not affect any other software on your computer.

Tabs3 Exhibit 2
Sample Data/Date Notice
Copyright 2007 Software Technology, Inc. www.Tabs3.com

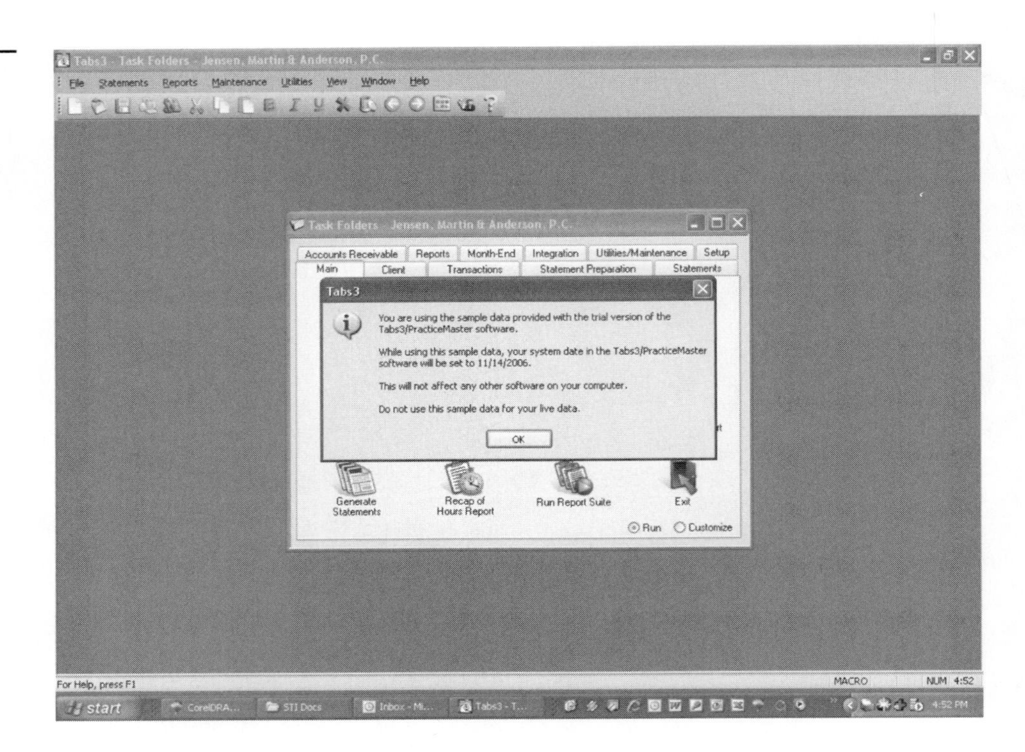

4. ***Click OK in the Tabs3 window.*** The screen in Tabs3 Exhibit 1 should now be displayed. Notice the Task Folders—Jensen, Martin & Anderson, P.C. (hereinafter Task Folders) window in the middle of the screen in Tabs3 Exhibit 1. *Note:* Sample data for the fictitious law firm of Jensen, Martin & Anderson, P.C. is being used throughout this tutorial.

5. Notice in Tabs3 Exhibit 1 that the Main tab in the Task Folders window is currently displayed (other tabs include Client, Transactions, Statements and Reports). The icons change depending on which tab is selected.

6. ***Click the Client icon in the Task Folders window.***

7. A blank Client Information window should now be displayed. *Note:* if a message about the configuration of Tabs3 is displayed, click "OK." This is where information about a client is entered, including name, contact information, billing options, setup options, statement options, and the like. In Lesson 2 you will set up a new client using this window.

8. ***Click the Close icon (the red square with a white "X") at the upper right of the Client Information window.*** Remember, to display the name of an icon, just hover the mouse pointer over the icon for a second and the name will be displayed.

9. ***Click Fee in the Task Folders window.***

10. The Rapid Fee – Admin window should now be displayed. This is where client time/fee entries (time records) are entered into Tabs3. In this screen, the user uses the Client ID field to designate the client to be billed, the timekeeper, the date of the time record, the transaction code (the activity), the number of hours worked, a description of the activity, and other data. In Lesson 3, you will enter a number of time records into Tabs3.

11. ***Click the Close icon in the upper right of the Rapid Fee – Admin window.***

12. ***Click "Cost" in the Task Folders window.***

13. The Rapid Cost Entry window should now be displayed. This is where client cost entries (cost records) are entered into Tabs3. These include costs such as photocopying, courier fees, transcription fees, and travel expenses. In this screen the user designates the client to be billed, the date the cost was incurred, a description of the cost, and related information. In Lesson 4, you will enter a number of cost records into Tabs3.

14. ***Click the Close icon in the upper right of the Rapid Cost Entry window.***

15. ***Click "Generate Statements" in the Task Folders window.***

16. The Generate Statements window should now be displayed. This is where users designate which clients to bill.

17. ***Click the Transactions tab in the Generate Statements window.*** This is where users control what type of fees, expenses, advances, and payments are billed/credited to a client for billing puposes.

18. ***Click the Options tab in the Generate Statements window.*** This is where users select whether to produce draft (pre-billing) statements, final statements, beginning statement numbers, individual billing thresholds (e.g., only producing statements that are more than $100), and related options.

19. ***Click the Close icon at the upper right of the Generate Statements window.***

20. ***Click "Payment" in the Task Folders window.***

21. The Rapid Payment Entry window should now be displayed. This is where users can enter and apply payments to client invoices and accounts.

22. ***Click the Close icon at the upper right of the Rapid Payment Entry window.***

23. ***Click the Client tab in the Task Folders window.*** Notice that the icons have now changed.

24. ***Click each of the tabs in the Task Folders window to see all of the icons listed.***

25. ***Click back to the Main tab in the Task Folders window.***

26. ***Click "File" on the menu bar and then click Exit.***

This concludes Lesson 1.

LESSON 2: ENTERING A NEW CLIENT

In this lesson you will learn how to enter a new client into Tabs3, including exploring the many options users have to set up a client with respect to billing and payments.

1. Open Windows. Then, ***double-click Tabs3 Trial on the desktop or click the Start button on the Windows desktop, point to Programs or All Programs, point to the Software Technology group, point to Trial Software with Sample Data, and then click Tabs3 with Sample Data.*** Tabs3 will then open with some sample data already entered into the program.

2. The Tip of the Day window should now be displayed. ***Click "Close" in the Tip of the Day window.***

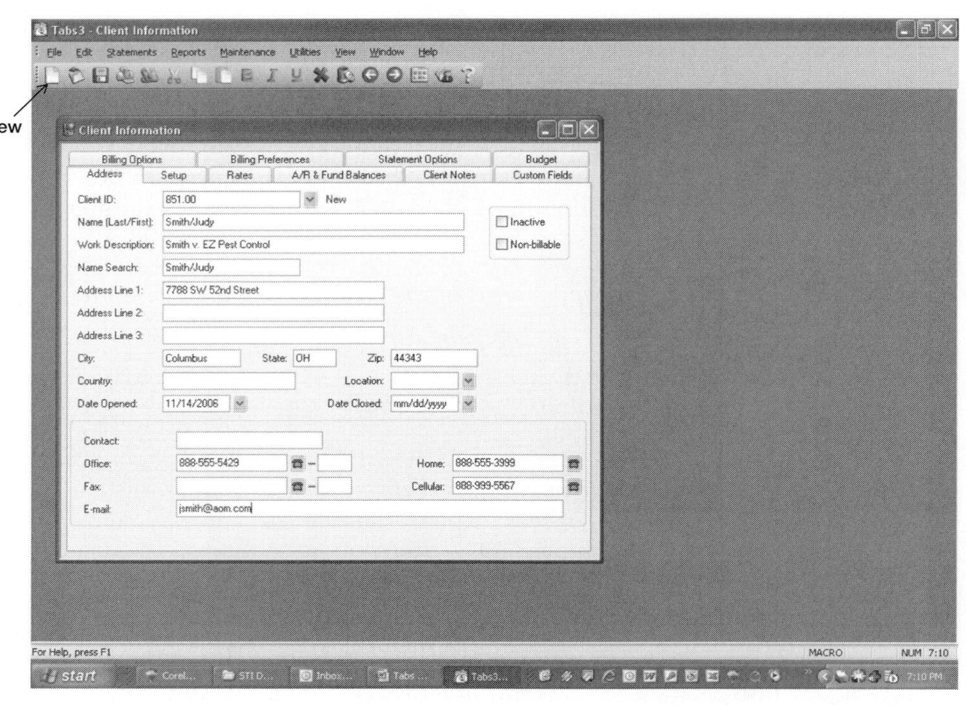

Tabs3 Exhibit 3
Entering a New Client in the Address Tab of the Client Information Window.

3. ***Click "OK" in the Tabs3 window to accept the date 11/14/2006.***

4. ***Click "Client" in the Task Folders window.*** The Client Information window should now be displayed (see Tabs3 Exhibit 3). Notice that the Address tab is selected.

5. Your pointer should be in the Client ID field. ***Click the New icon on the toolbar (see Tabs3 Exhibit 3).*** Tabs3 responds by automatically generating the next Client ID number, which is 851.00. Notice also that New is displayed to the right of the Client ID field, indicating that this is a new client.

6. Enter the following information in the Address tab of the Client Information window (see Tabs3 Exhibit 3). *Note:* You can press the [TAB] key to move forward through the fields, or press [SHIFT]+[TAB] to move backwards through the field. If a field is left blank below, just skip it.

Field	**Information to be Entered**
Name (Last/First):	Smith/Judy
Work Description:	Smith v. EZ Pest Control
Name Search:	Smith/Judy
Address Line 1:	7788 SW 52nd Street
Address Line 2:	
Address Line 3:	
City:	Columbus
State:	OH
Zip:	44343
Country:	
Location:	
Date Opened:	11/14/2006

continued

Field	Information to be Entered
Date Closed:	mm/dd/yyyy
Contact:	
Office:	888-555-5429
Home:	888-555-3999
Fax:	
Cellular:	888-999-5567
Email	jsmith@aom.com

7. *Click the Setup tab in the Client Information window (see Tabs3 Exhibit 4).*

8. *Click the down arrow to the right of the Billing Category field.* The Category Lookup window should now be displayed (see Tabs3 Exhibit 4). *Scroll down, click "60 General Litigation," and then click OK in the Category Lookup window.*

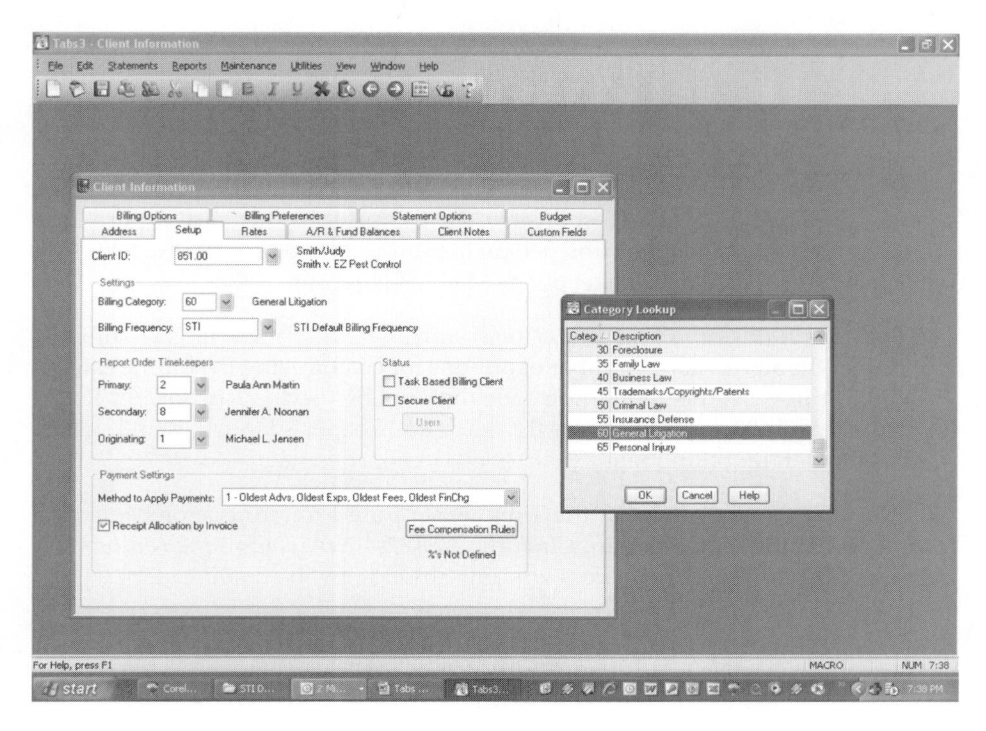

Tabs3 Exhibit 4
Entering a New Client—Setup Options

9. *Click the down arrow to the right of Billing Frequency.* The Billing Frequency Lookup window should now be displayed. Notice that you can select Bill on Demand, Monthly, Quarterly, etc. We will use the default setting of STI so just *click Cancel in the Billing Frequency Lookup window.*

10. *Under Report Order Timekeepers, click the down arrow next to Primary.* The Timekeeper Lookup window should now be displayed.

11. *Double-click "Paula Ann Martin."* The primary timekeeper is the attorney that is responsible for the case, in this case a partner.

12. *Under Report Order Timekeepers, click the down arrow next to Secondary.* The Timekeeper Lookup window should again be displayed.

Tabs3 Exhibit 5
Entering a New Client—Billing Rate Options

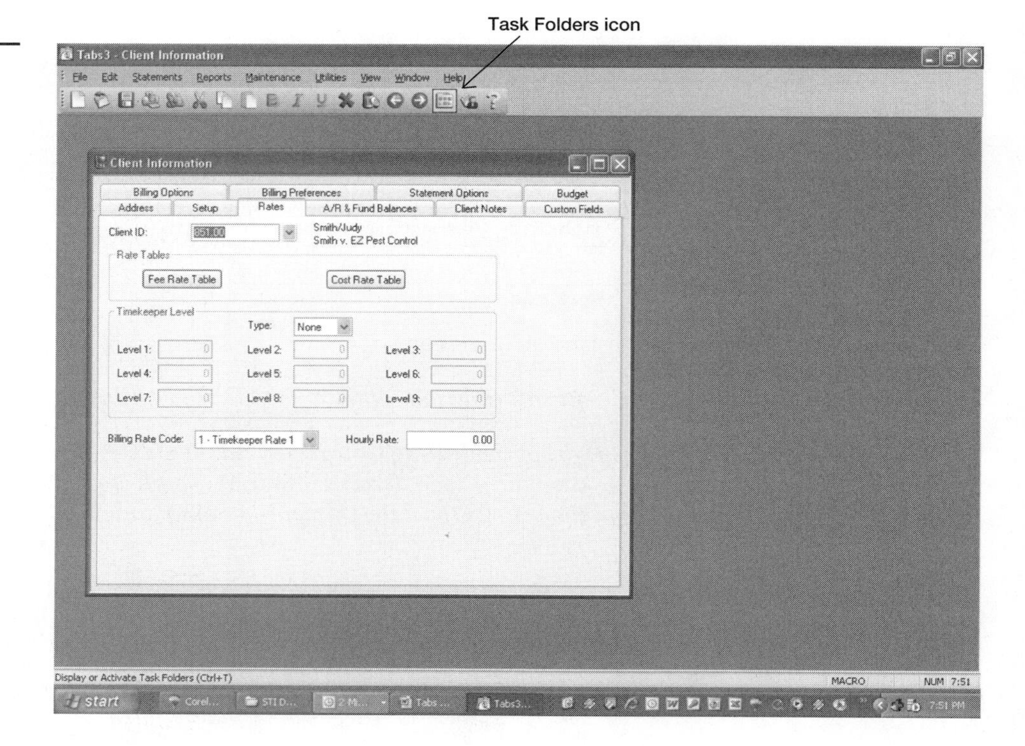

13. ***Double-click on "Jennifer A. Noonan."*** The secondary timekeeper is the support staff person that is responsible for the case, in this case a paralegal. (The originating timekeeper is the person that brought the client to the firm.) We will leave the originating timekeeper as Michael L. Jensen.

14. ***Click the Rates tab in the Client Information window*** (see Tabs3 Exhibit 5). Notice that the screen has a number of options for customizing the billing rate for a client. In this case, the billing rate code that will be used is Timekeeper Rate 1 (see Tabs3 Exhibit 5). This indicates that each timekeeper's Hourly Rate 1 will be used as the default billing rate.

15. You will now look at what the Timekeeper Rate 1 amount is for Paula Ann Martin and Jennifer A. Noonan. ***Click the Task Folders icon on the toolbar (see Tabs3 Exhibit 5).*** The Task Folders window should now be displayed.

16. ***Click the Setup tab in the Task Folders window.***

17. ***Click Timekeeper on the Setup tab.***

18. ***In the Miscellaneous window, click the down arrow next to Timekeeper*** (see Tabs3 Exhibit 6).

19. ***Double-click "Paula Ann Martin."*** Notice that her Hourly Rate 1: amount is $225.00.

20. ***In the Miscellaneous window, click the down arrow next to Timekeeper.***

21. ***Double-click "Jennifer A. Noonan."*** Notice that her Hourly Rate 1: as a paralegal is $100.00.

22. ***Click the Close icon at the upper right of the Miscellaneous window.***

23. ***Click anywhere in the Client Information window. (Note: To move a window, just click and drag the blue bar at the top of the window).***

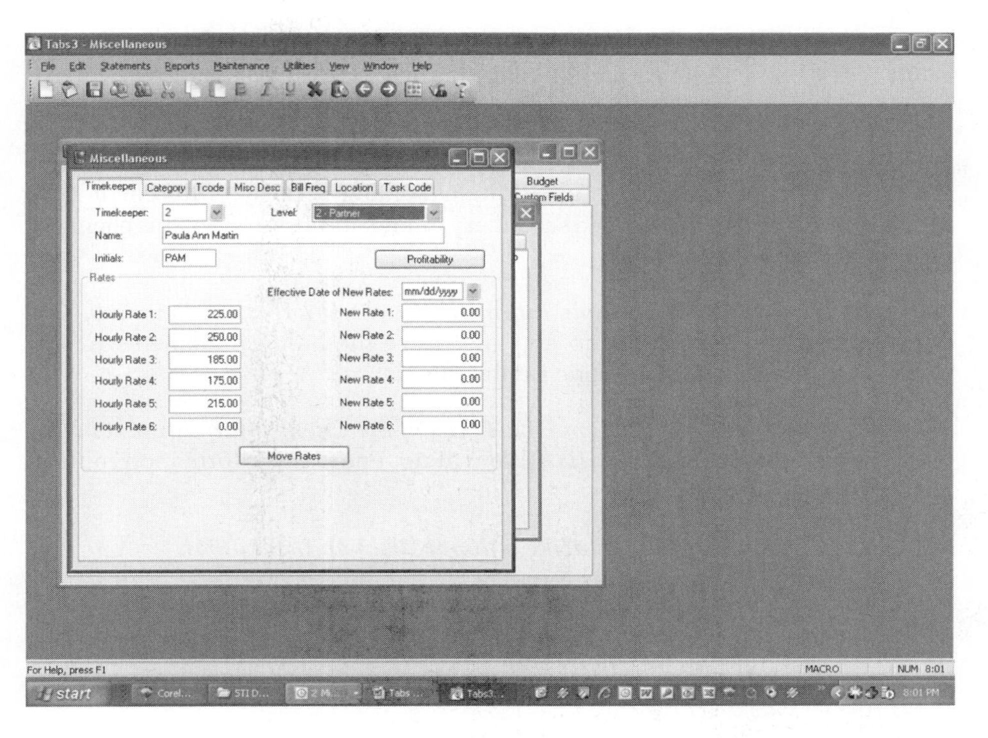

Tabs3 Exhibit 6
Hourly Rates for Paula Ann Martin

24. ***Click the A/R & Fund Balances tab in the Client Information window.*** Once fees, expenses, and billings take place, this screen will contain current balances for the client.

25. ***Click the Client Notes tab in the Client Information window.***

26. ***Your pointer should be in the Client Notes field.*** Type **The client says that she wants to be billed monthly but will typically pay off the balance every 60 days** (see Tabs3 Exhibit 7).

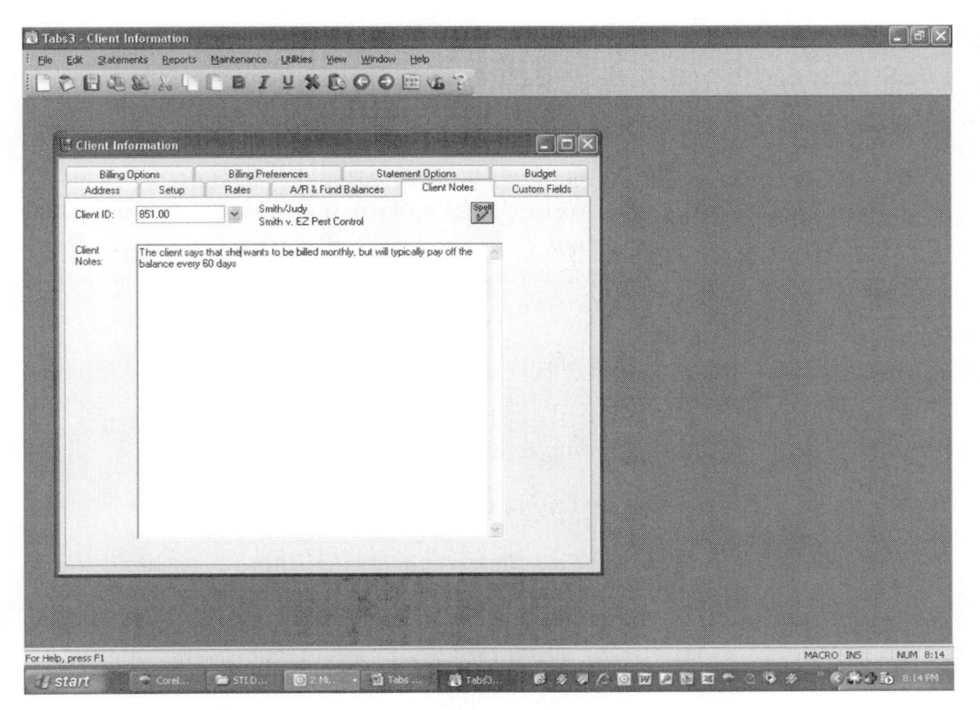

Tabs3 Exhibit 7
Entering a New Client–Client Notes

27. *Click the Billing Options tab in the Client Information window.* This screen is where the user can set up a billing threshold, a courtesy discount, sales tax, or a finance charge. This client does not have or need any special billing options.

28. *Click the Billing Preferences tab in the Client Information window.* This screen is where the user can set up additional billing options for the client, such as special billing instructions or a secondary billing address. Again, this client has no special needs.

29. *Click the Statement Options tab in the Client Information window.* This screen allows the user to set up and customize the billing statements for the client. The default options are fine for this client.

30. *Click the Budget and Custom Fields tabs in the Client Information window to see what these screens look like.* We will not enter any information in these screens.

31. *Click the Save icon (it looks like a floppy disk) on the toolbar.*

32. *Click the Close icon at the upper right of the Client Information window.*

33. To make sure the client has been entered into Tabs3, *click the Main tab in the Task Folders window. Then, click the Client icon.*

34. *In the Client Information window, click the down arrow next to the Client ID: field.* The Client Lookup screen should now be displayed.

35. *Double-click on "851.00 smith/judy."* The information for Judy Smith and *Smith v. EZ Pest Control* should now be displayed.

36. *Click the Close icon at the upper right of the Client Information window.*

37. *Click File on the menu bar and then click Exit.*

This concludes Lesson 2.

LESSON 3: ENTERING FEE/TIME RECORDS

In this lesson, you will learn how to enter time records into Tabs3.

1. Open Windows. Then, *double-click Tabs3 Trial on the desktop or, click the Start button on the Windows desktop, point to Programs or All Programs, point to the Software Technology group, point to Trial Software with Sample Data, and then click Tabs3 with Sample Data.* Tabs3 will then open with some sample data already entered into the program.

2. The Tip of the Day window should now be displayed. *Click Close in the Tip of the Day window.*

3. *Click OK in the Tabs3 window to accept the date 11/14/2006.*

4. *Click Fee in the Task Folders window.*

5. *Click the Detail/Rapid icon on the toolbar in the Rapid Fee – Smith/Judy window* (*not* the main toolbar – see Tabs3 Exhibit 8). Notice that additional fields are now displayed; the Detail/Rapid icon toggles between a detail data entry screen, which has several fields, and a rapid data entry screen, which has fewer fields.

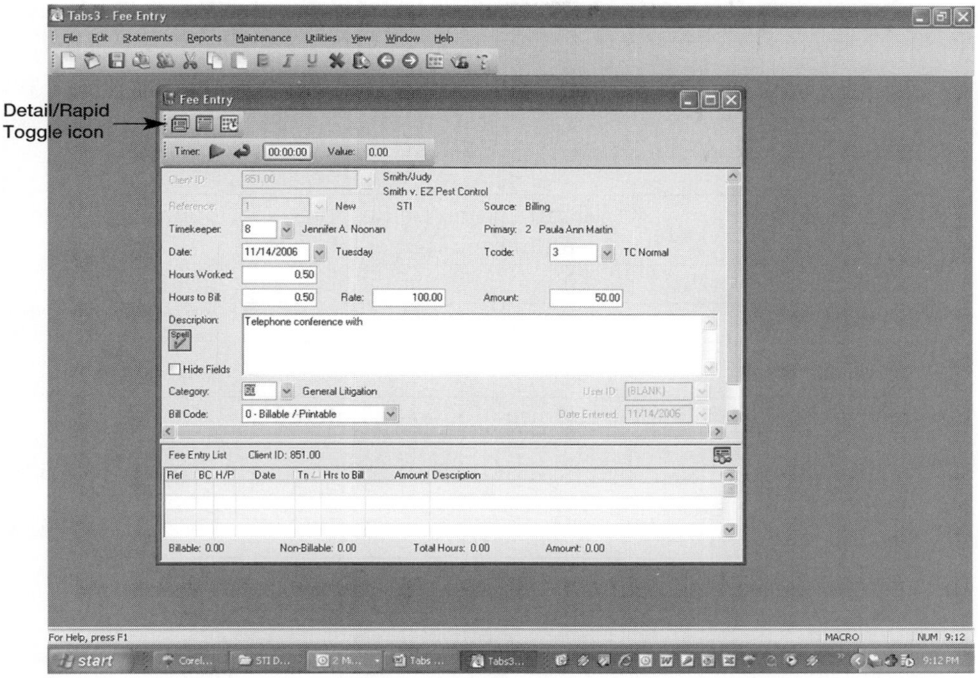

Detail/Rapid Toggle icon

Tabs3 Exhibit 8
Entering a Fee/Time Record

6. Your points should already be in the Client ID field, with the last Client ID number, 851.00, listed. Press the **[TAB]** key to go to the Reference field.

7. Press the **[TAB]** key to go to the Timekeeper field.

8. ***Click the down arrow next to the Timekeeper field. Double-click on Jennifer A. Noonan.***

9. At the Date field, press the **[TAB]** key to accept the default date of 11/14/2006.

10. ***Click the down arrow next to the Tcode (transaction code) field.*** The Tcode Lookup window should now be displayed. ***Point and double-click on "3 TC Telephone conference with."***

11. In the Hours Worked field type **.50** and then press the **[TAB]** key.

12. The pointer should now be in the Amount field and 50.00 should be entered. Press the **[TAB]** key.

13. The pointer should now be in the Description: field at the end of "Telephone conference with." Type **client** and then press the **[TAB]** key.

14. ***Click the Save icon on the main toolbar.*** A blank fee/time record slip is now displayed.

15. Enter and save each of the following fee/time records:

Field	Information to be Entered
Client ID:	851.00
Reference:	
Timekeeper:	2
Date:	11/14/2006

continued

Tcode:	8
Hours Worked:	6.00
Hours to Bill:	6.00
Rate:	225.00
Amount:	1,350
Description:	Draft and revise Response to Motion for Summary Judgment
Category:	60
Bill Code:	0 – Billable / Printable

Field	**Information to be Entered**
Client ID:	851.00
Reference:	
Timekeeper:	8
Date:	11/14/2006
Tcode:	10
Hours Worked:	3.00
Hours to Bill:	3.00
Rate:	100.00
Amount:	300.00
Description:	Legal research—Response to Motion for Summary Judgment
Category:	60
Bill Code:	0 – Billable / Printable

Field	**Information to be Entered**
Client ID:	851.00
Reference:	
Timekeeper:	2
Date:	11/14/2006
Tcode:	3
Hours Worked:	1.00
Hours to Bill:	1.00
Rate:	225.00
Amount:	225.00
Description:	Telephone conference with expert witness
Category:	60
Bill Code:	0 – Billable / Printable

Field	**Information to be Entered**
Client ID:	851.00
Reference:	
Timekeeper:	8

continued

Field	Information to be Entered
Date:	11/15/2006
Tcode:	3
Hours Worked:	1.00
Hours to Bill:	1.00
Rate:	100.00
Amount:	100.00
Description:	Telephone conference with client regarding Response to Motion for Summary Judgment
Category:	60
Bill Code:	0 – Billable / Printable

16. ***Click the Save icon on the main toolbar.***

17. Notice in the bottom of the Fee window that you can see the prior fee/time records you have entered. ***Click the Close icon at the upper right of the Fee – Smith/Judy window.***

18. The Fee Verification List window should now be displayed. This feature can print a report summarizing all of the entries you just made. This is not necessary for the small number of time records we just entered, so ***click the Close icon the Fee Verification List window.***

19. ***Click File on the menu bar and then click Exit.***

This concludes Lesson 3.

LESSON 4: ENTERING COST/EXPENSE RECORDS AND USING THE TIMER FEATURE

In this lesson, you will learn how to enter cost/expense records into Tabs3 and how to use the timer feature.

1. Open Windows. Then, ***double-click Tabs3 Trial on the desktop or click the Start button on the Windows desktop, point to Programs or All Programs, point to the Software Technology group, point to Trial Software with Sample Data, and then click Tabs3 with Sample Data.*** Tabs3 will then open with some sample data already entered into the program.

2. The Tip of the Day window should now be displayed. ***Click "Close" in the Tip of the Day window.***

3. Click OK in the Tabs3 window to accept the date 11/14/2006.

4. ***Click Cost in the Task Folders window.***

5. ***The Rapid Cost Entry window should now be displayed*** (see Tabs3 Exhibit 9).

6. Your pointer should be in the Client ID field with **851.00** filled in. Press the **[TAB]** key to accept the entry.

7. Press the **[TAB]** key again to go to the Date field.

8. Press the **[TAB]** key to accept the default date of 11/14/2006.

9. ***Click the down arrow next to the Tcode field. Scroll and double-click "251 COP Photocopy charges."***

Tabs3 Exhibit 9
Entering a Cost/Expense Record

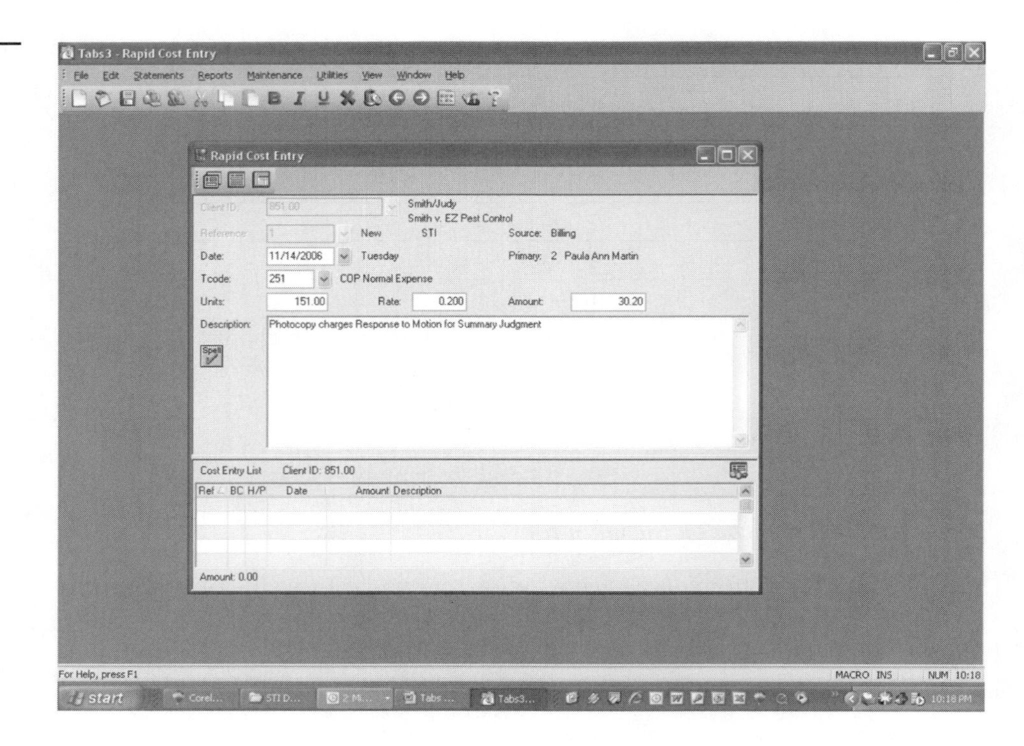

10. In the Units: field type **151** (151 copies at the firm default rate of 20 cents a copy). Press the **[TAB]** key.

11. The calculation in the Amount field is $30.20. Press the **[TAB]** key.

12. In the Description field enter **Photocopy charges—Response to Motion for Summary Judgment.**

13. ***Click the Save icon on the main toolbar.***

14. Enter and save each of the following cost/expense records:

Field	Information to be Entered
Client ID:	851.00
Reference:	
Date:	11/14/2006
Tcode:	102
Units:	1.00
Rate:	
Amount:	20.00
Description:	Courier fee—info related to Response to Motion for Summary Judgment

Field	Information to be Entered
Client ID:	851.00
Reference:	
Date:	11/14/2006
Tcode:	106

continued

Field	Information to be Entered
Units:	1.00
Rate:	
Amount:	50
Description:	Online legal research—Response to Motion for Summary Judgment

Field	Information to be Entered
Client ID:	851.00
Reference:	
Date:	11/14/2006
Tcode:	250
Units:	1.00
Rate:	
Amount:	7.90
Description:	Long distance telephone charges — call with client

15. *Click the Save icon on the main toolbar.*

16. *Click the Close icon (the red square with a white "X") at the upper right of the Rapid Cost Entry window.*

17. *Click on the Close icon at the upper right of the Cost Verification List window.*

18. You will now learn how to use the timer feature in Tabs3. *Click "Fee" in the "Task Folder" window.* The Fee Entry window should now be displayed.

19. *Click the green triangle just to the right of the word "Timer" in the Fee Entry window.* This is the Start Timer icon. Notice that the timer begins to count. The timer is now timing how long it takes you to complete a task such as making a phone call or drafting a letter.

20. Fill in the rest of the information below in the Fee – Smith/Judy window:

Field	Information to be Entered
Client ID:	851.00
Reference:	
Timekeeper:	2
Date:	11/15/2006
Tcode:	3
Hours Worked:	0.00
Hours to Bill:	0.00
Rate:	225
Amount:	0.00
Description:	Telephone conference with counsel
Category:	60
Bill Code:	0 – Billable / Printable

21. *Click the red square next to Timer: on the Fee – Smith/Judy toolbar to stop the timer.* (Assuming it took you less than a few minutes to enter the fee information, the value should be $22.50).

22. *Click the Save icon on the main toolbar.*

23. *A window should now be displayed asking you if you want to "Add timer to Hours?" Click "Yes".*

24. *At the window that says Add to Amount? click Yes.* Notice at the bottom of the screen that the entry has been added and a cost of $22.50 has been recorded.

25. *Click the Close icon at the upper right of the Fee – Smith/Judy window.*

26. *Click the Close icon at the upper right of the Fee Verification List window.*

27. *Click File on the menu bar and then click Exit.*

This concludes Lesson 4.

LESSON 5: PRODUCING AND PRINTING DRAFT AND FINAL STATEMENTS

In this lesson, you will learn how to produce and print draft and final statements in Tabs3.

1. Open Windows. Then, *double-click Tabs3 Trial on the desktop or click the Start button on the Windows desktop, point to Programs or All Programs, point to the Software Technology group, point to Trial Software with Sample Data, and then click Tabs3 with Sample Data.* Tabs3 will then open with some sample data already entered into the program.

2. The Tip of the Day window should now be displayed. *Click Close in the Tip of the Day window.*

3. *Click OK in the Tabs3 window to accept the date 11/14/2006.*

4. *Click Generate Statements in the Task Folders window.*

5. In the Client ID: field type **851** and then press the **[TAB]** key. At the Thru field, press the **[TAB]** key again.

6. *Click the Options tab in the Generate Statements window.* Notice that the default entry for Statement Type is "Draft." Since we want to print a draft statement for Judy Smith, we will leave it as is.

7. *Click the down arrow next to Statement Date and select November 15, 2006. (Note: Usually, statements are done at the end of the month, but this client has asked for a special mid-month report.) Then click OK.*

8. *Click OK in the Generate Statements window.*

9. *Click Print in the Generate Statements window, and then click the down arrow next to Print to select a printer.*

10. *Next, click OK in the Generate Statements window (Note: You can also save the statement as a PDF or text file, or print it to the DropBox for easy attachment to an email).*

11. The draft statement should look similar to Tabs3 Exhibit 10. Normally, the timekeeper responsible for the case reviews and approves the draft statement.

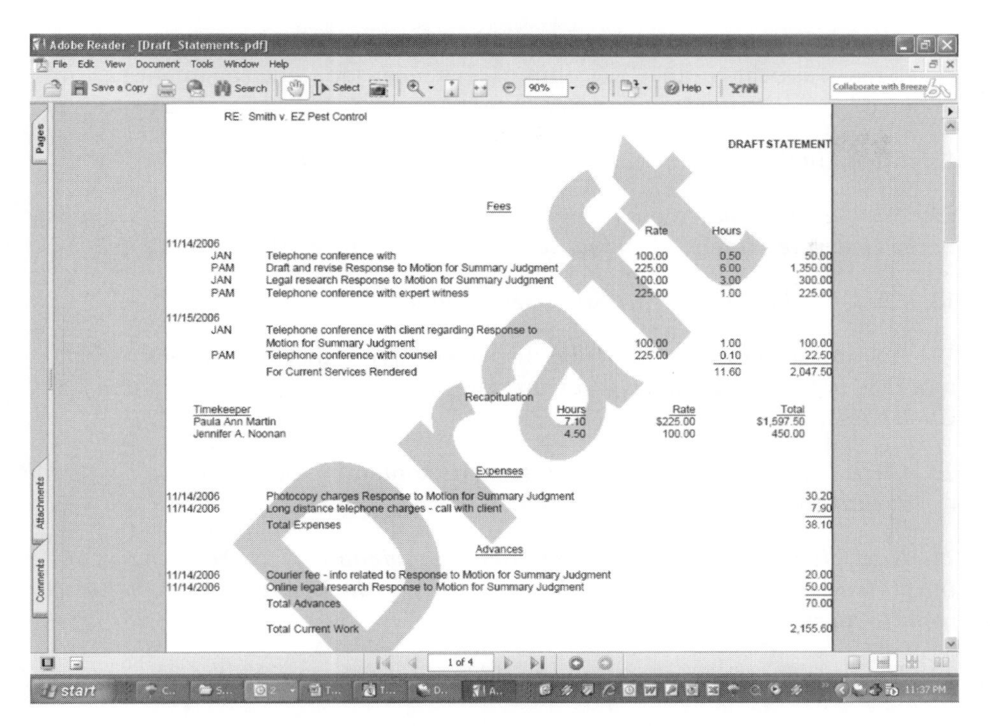

Tabs3 Exhibit 10

Draft Statement for Smith v. EZ Pest Control

Copyright 2007 Software Technology, Inc. www.Tabs3.com

The next steps will instruct you on how to mark a statement as having been reviewed, how to run the statement as final, and how to update it.

12. ***Click the Close icon at the upper right of the Generate Statements window.***

13. ***Click Statements on the menu bar*** (see Tabs3 Exhibit 11).

14. ***Click Pre-Bill Tracking.*** The Pre-Bill Tracking window should now be displayed (see Tabs3 Exhibit 11).

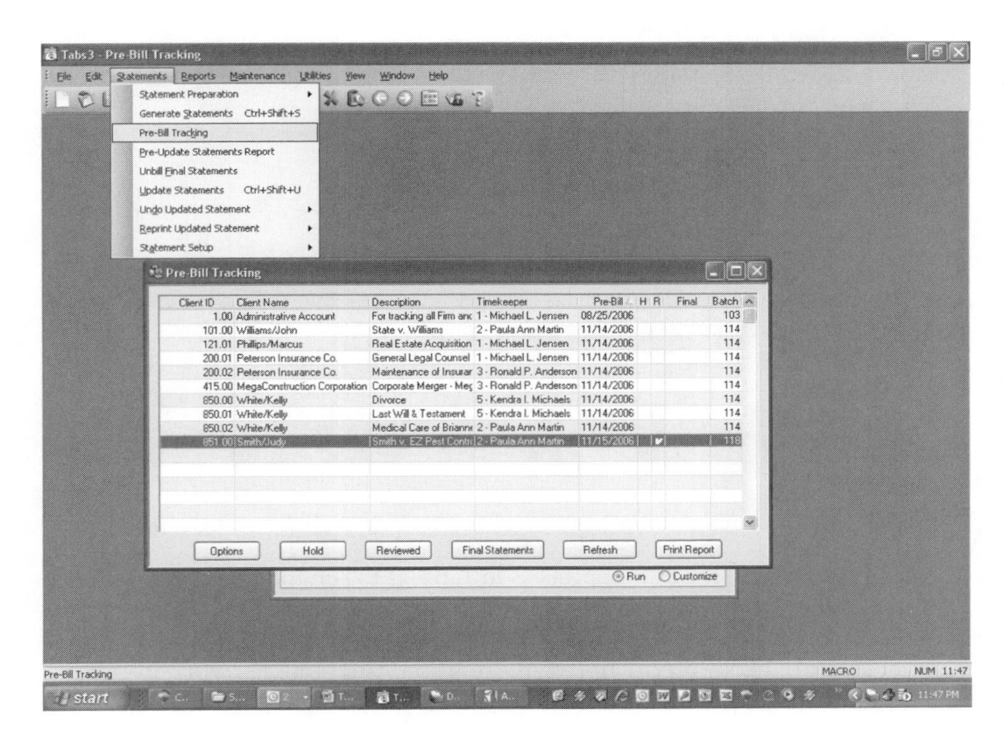

Tabs3 Exhibit 11

Pre-Billing Tracking

Copyright 2007 Software Technology, Inc. www.Tabs3.com

15. ***Double-click "851.00, Smith/Judy, Smith v. EZ Pest Control."*** Notice that a check mark appears in the "R" column. This means that the statement has been reviewed and is ready for a final statement.

16. ***Click Final Statements in the Pre-Billing Tracking window.***

17. The Generate Statements window is now displayed. ***Click the Options tab in the Generate Statements window. Change the statement date to 11/15/2006.***

18. ***Click OK in the Generate Statements window.***

19. A warning screen will now be displayed saying that the current reporting month is 10/2006 and asking if you are sure you want to use this Statement Date. ***Click "Yes".***

20. ***Click Print in the Generate Statements window and then click the down arrow next to Print to select a printer.***

21. ***Next, click OK in the Generate Statements window (Note: You can also save the statement as a PDF or text file, or print it to the DropBox for easy attachment to an email).***

22. The final statement produced should be similar to Tabs3 Exhibit 12.

23. ***Click the Close icon at the upper right of the Generate Statements window.***

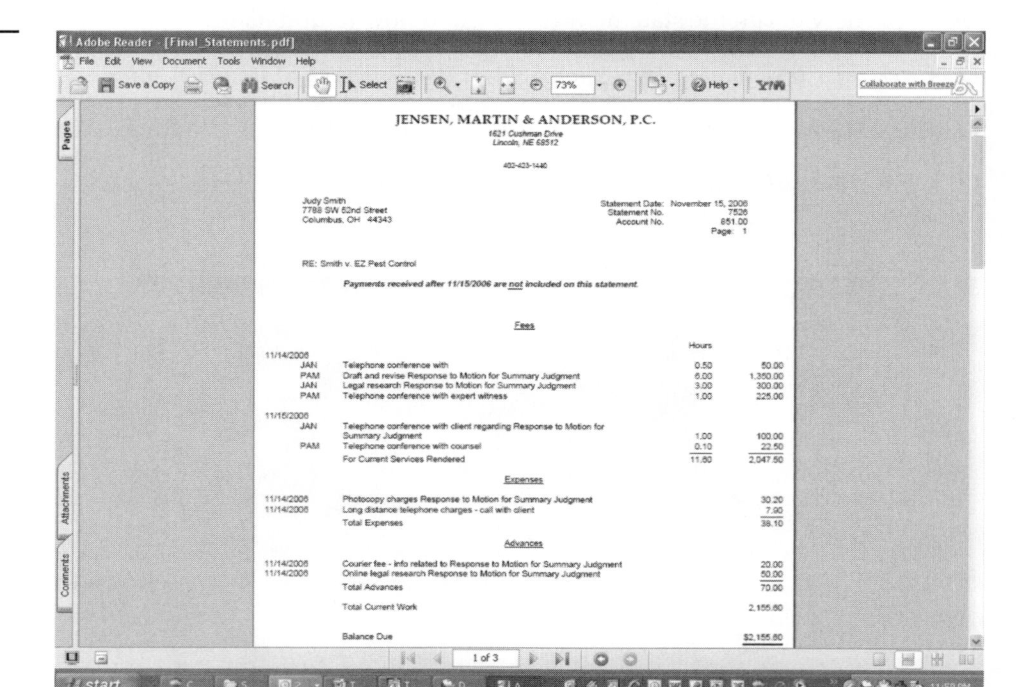

JENSEN, MARTIN & ANDERSON, P.C.
1621 Cushman Drive
Lincoln, NE 68512

402-423-1440

Judy Smith
7788 SW 52nd Street
Columbus, OH 44343

Statement Date: November 15, 2006
Statement No. 7526
Account No. 851.00
Page: 1

RE: Smith v. EZ Pest Control

Payments received after 11/15/2006 are not included on this statement.

Fees

			Hours	
11/14/2006				
	JAN	Telephone conference with	0.50	50.00
	PAM	Draft and revise Response to Motion for Summary Judgment	6.00	1,350.00
	JAN	Legal research Response to Motion for Summary Judgment	3.00	300.00
	PAM	Telephone conference with expert witness	1.00	225.00
11/15/2006				
	JAN	Telephone conference with client regarding Response to Motion for Summary Judgment	1.00	100.00
	PAM	Telephone conference with counsel	0.10	22.50
		For Current Services Rendered	11.60	2,047.50

Expenses

11/14/2006	Photocopy charges Response to Motion for Summary Judgment	30.20
11/14/2006	Long distance telephone charges - call with client	7.90
	Total Expenses	38.10

Advances

11/14/2006	Courier fee - info related to Response to Motion for Summary Judgment	20.00
11/14/2006	Online legal research Response to Motion for Summary Judgment	50.00
	Total Advances	70.00
	Total Current Work	2,155.60
	Balance Due	$2,155.60

Tabs3 Exhibit 12
Final Statement—Judy Smith

24. ***Click the Close icon at the upper right of the Pre-Bill Tracking window.***

25. The final stage in the billing process in Tabs3 is to run the Update Statements Process. In Tabs3, changes can be made to the final statements until the Update Statements process is run. The Update Statements process updates accounts receivable and billed productivity information, and moves work-in-process transactions into the archive.

26. *Click the Statements tab (not the Statement Preparation tab) in the Task Folders window. Click Update Statements.*

27. A warning window will be displayed asking if you would like to back up your data first. *Click "No".*

28. In the Update Statements window, in the Client ID: field, type **851 in the first box, and 851 in the second box. Then, click OK.**

29. When the Update Statements Status window indicates that "Statements are now updated," *click OK in the Update Statements window.*

30. *In the Update Statements Status window, click OK.*

31. *Next, click the Close icon at the upper right of the Update Statements window.*

32. *In the Update Statements Verification List window, click Cancel.*

33. *In the Task Folders window, click the Main tab, and then click Client.*

34. *In the Client Information window, click the A/R & Fund Balances tab.* Notice that you can see the total balance due and the amount due for fees, expenses and advances. The billing process has been successful.

35. *Click the Close icon at the upper right of the Client Information window.*

36. *Click File on the menu bar and then click Exit.*

This concludes Lesson 5.

LESSON 6: PROCESSING A PAYMENT

In this lesson, you will learn how to process a payment and apply it to a client's account.

1. Open Windows. Then, *double-click Tabs3 Trial on the desktop or click the Start button on the Windows desktop, point to Programs or All Programs, point to the Software Technology group, point to Trial Software with Sample Data, and then click Tabs3 with Sample Data.* Tabs3 will then open with some sample data already entered into the program.

2. The Tip of the Day window should now be displayed. *Click Close in the Tip of the Day window.*

3. *Click OK in the Tabs3 window to accept the date 11/14/2006.*

4. *Click Payment in the Task Folders window.* The Rapid Payment Entry window should now be displayed (see Tabs3 Exhibit 13).

5. The pointer should be in the Client ID field and **851.00** should be entered. Press the **[TAB]** key to go to the Reference field.

6. Press the **[TAB]** key to go to the Date field.

7. Enter **11/20/2006** in the Date field.

8. Press the **[TAB]** key to go to the Tcode field. A Tcode of **900** should be entered in the field.

9. Press the **[TAB]** key to go to the Statement field.

Tabs3 Exhibit 13
Making a Payment

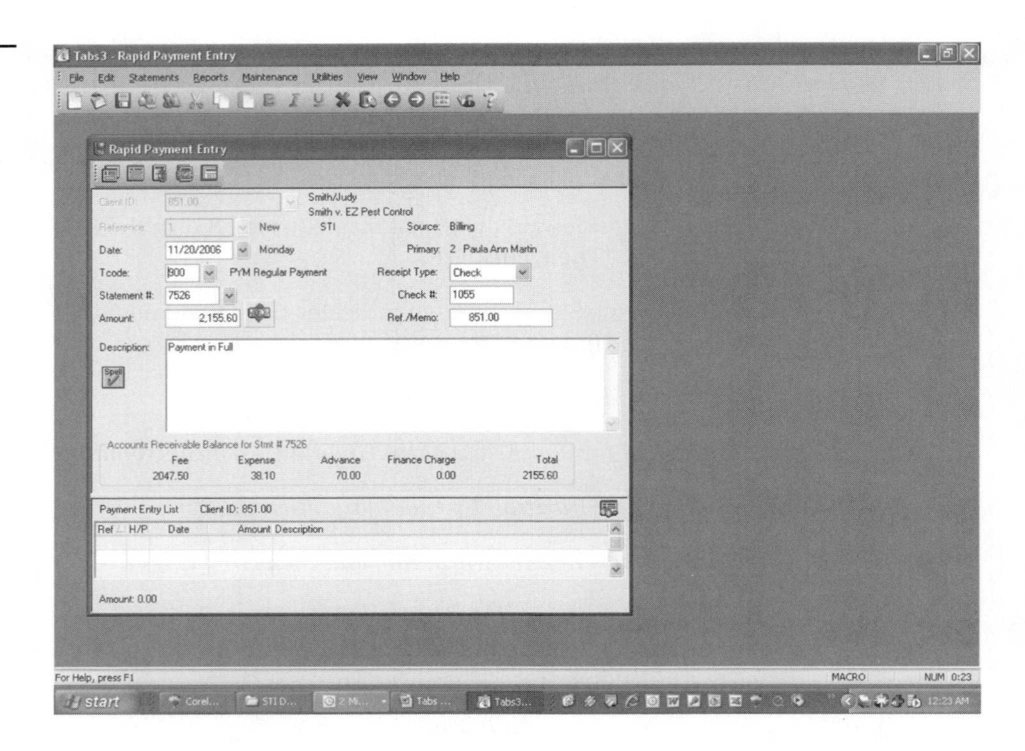

10. Press the **[TAB]** key to go to the Amount field. In the Amount field type **2155.60**

11. Press the **[TAB]** key to go to the Description field. In the Description field type **Payment in Full.**

12. Press the **[TAB]** key to go to the Receipt Type field.

13. Press the **[TAB]** key to accept the default value of Check.

14. Press the **[TAB]** key to go to the Check # field. Enter **1055** as the check number.

15. ***Click the Save icon on the main toolbar.***

16. ***Click the Close icon (the red square with a white "X") at the upper right of the Rapid Payment Entry window.***

17. ***Click the Close icon at the upper right of the Payment Verification List window.***

18. ***In the Task Folders window, click Client.***

19. ***The number 851 should be entered in the Client ID field. Click the A/R & Fund Balances tab in the Client Information window.*** Notice that the Amount Due is $0.00 and the Last Payment Amount is $2,155.60.

20. ***Click the Close icon at the upper right of the Client Information window.***

21. ***Click File on the menu bar and then click Exit.***

This concludes Lesson 6.

LESSON 7: PROCESSING AND PRINTING REPORTS

In this lesson, you will learn how to process and print several reports using Tabs3.

1. Open Windows. Then, ***double-click Tabs3 Trial on the desktop or click the Start button on the Windows desktop, point to Programs or All Programs, point to the Software Technology group, point to Trial Software with Sample Data, and then click Tabs3 with Sample Data.*** Tabs3 will then open (with some sample data already entered into the program).

2. The Tip of the Day window should now be displayed. ***Click Close in the Tip of the Day window.***

3. ***Click OK in the window that asks about the date being 11/14/2006.***

4. ***Click the Reports tab in the Task Folders window.***

5. ***Click "Productivity Reports."***

6. ***Click "Category Productivity."***

7. The default values for the report are all fine, so ***click OK in the Category Productivity Report window.***

8. ***Click Print in the Print Category Productivity Report window and then click the down arrow next to Print and select a printer.***

9. ***Next, click OK in the Print Category Productivity Report window. (Note: You can also save the statement as a PDF or text file, or print it to the DropBox for easy attachment to an email.)***

10. The report breaks out hours worked, billed hours, and other information by category (case type) for the reporting period of January to October 2006.

11. ***Click the Close icon (the red square with a white "X") at the upper right of the Category Productivity Report window.***

12. ***Click Productivity Reports in the Reports tab of the Task Folders window.***

13. ***Print the Timekeeper Productivity report.***

14. ***Print the Timekeeper Analysis Report.***

15. ***Print the Client Analysis Report.***

16. At the Reports tab of the Task Folders window, ***click Management Reports.***

17. ***Print the Client Realization Report.***

18. ***Print the Timekeeper Realization Report.***

19. ***Print the Timekeeper Profitability Report.***

20. At the Reports tab of the Task Folders window, ***click A/R Reports.***

21. ***Print the Collections Report.***

22. ***Print the A/R by Invoice Report.***

23. ***Close all of the open windows.***

24. ***Click File on the menu bar and then click Exit.***

This concludes the Tabs3 Hands-on Exercises.

CHAPTER 7

CASE MANAGEMENT AND DOCKET CONTROL SOFTWARE

CHAPTER OBJECTIVES

After completing chapter 7, you should be able to do the following:

1. Explain what a docket system is.
2. Describe how a computerized case management system can prevent cases from being "forgotten."
3. Describe the computerized docket cycle.
4. Explain what case management is.
5. Discuss why docket control and case management are important to a legal organization from an ethics perspective.

A client sued his former attorney (and the attorney's partners) for legal malpractice for failing to file a medical malpractice claim in a timely manner. Nearly two years before, the client had met with the Michigan attorney regarding a claim against a hospital for medical malpractice. After the initial meeting, the client made repeated telephone calls and sent letters to the attorney. However, the attorney never responded to the client's communications. Twenty months later, the attorney finally responded with the following letter.

> *My sincere apologies for the delay in responding to your earlier communications; however, we have been making a thorough inquiry into the facts of your alleged complaints. We have not been able to find an expert to make the appropriate causal relationship to support our theories of possible malpractice. Accordingly, we are not going to be proceeding on your claim and will close our file.*[1]

Within two weeks, the client sought the advice of another attorney and filed a legal malpractice claim against the first attorney. A jury awarded the client $150,000 in damages against the attorney for allowing the statute of limitations on the medical malpractice claim to lapse.[1]

CALENDARING, DOCKET CONTROL, AND CASE MANAGEMENT

The practice of law is filled with an array of appointments, deadlines, hearings, and many other commitments for every case that is handled. Considering that a single legal professional can have a case load of between 20 and 100 cases at

any one time, just staying organized and on top of all of the things to get done is a big job. It is extremely important that these dates, deadlines, and commitments be accurately tracked and that the legal work get done accurately and on time for ethical reasons, customer service reasons, general business/profitability reasons, and malpractice avoidance reasons. All legal organizations must track these deadlines, whether they are using manual systems or computers or both. Most legal organizations now use some type of computerized method to track these deadlines.

This chapter introduces computerized calendaring, docket control, and case management. These terms are somewhat confusing and are often used interchangeably.

> *Calendaring and docketing is a key to a paralegal's upward mobility including the importance of knowing what rules databases are and how to integrate them into any case management database.*[2]

Calendaring is a generic term used to describe the recording of appointments and other scheduling items. Many personal information managers (PIMs), such as Microsoft Outlook, fall into this category. These are programs that can be used by any business to manage appointments and scheduling. In addition, most include a host of other general productivity tools as well.

Docket control is a legal-specific term that refers to entering, organizing, and controlling the appointments and deadlines for a legal organization. Docket control is sometimes referred to as a "tickler" or a "tickler system" because it "tickles" the memory for upcoming events.

Case management (sometimes called practice management) is also a legal-specific term, but it always means more than just tracking appointments and schedules. The breadth of features in current case management programs seem to grow every day. Some of the features found in case management programs include docket control (scheduling/appointments), things to do, a contact information database (name, address, email, phone, etc.) organized by case (parties, co-counsel, opposing counsel, judges, etc.), case notes, document assembly, integrated billing, email, and more. In case management programs, all information is tied to cases. This is very helpful for legal organizations that view and organize most of their data according to what case it is tied to. This is a different approach than general calendaring/PIM applications.

calendaring
A generic term used to describe the function of recording appointments for any type of business. This includes personal information managers.

docket control
A legal specific term that refers to entering, organizing, tracking, and controlling all the appointments, deadlines, and due dates for a legal organization.

case management
A legal term that usually refers to functions like docket control, deadlines, things to do, contact information by case, case notes, document assembly, document tracking by case, integrated billing, and email.

As the legal software market has matured, more and more legal software manufacturers have entered this market. In addition, nearly all of the current legal products available in this market have gotten significantly more sophisticated at meeting the needs of attorneys, legal assistants, and legal organizations. The products today do far more than just docket control. The end result is that there are currently really only two kinds of products that are used in legal organizations to handle calendaring/docket control functions:

1. Generic calendaring/personal information management programs such as Microsoft Outlook. These are found in many legal organizations because they come as a part of office suite programs (bundled together with word-processing, spreadsheet, and database programs) and because they typically have an email component.
2. Full case management programs that have a wide array of features for handling client cases in addition to calendaring and docket control. The advantage to legal organizations of case management programs is that information is stored by case.

> *Case management software is different from PIM software in that it starts from the perspective that a lawyer's* [legal professional's] *life is oriented around files rather than contacts. Case management software builds on its* [case] *file orientation by integrating itself with other essential systems in a law office such as accounting* [timekeeping and billing], *document generation, knowledge management (case diaries/notes)... .As you can see, case management has come a long way since the days of PIM.*[3]

A recent survey found that only 20 percent of legal organizations use case management software, while the majority of legal organizations use generic calendaring/PIMs (notably Microsoft Outlook). This is beginning to change as case management programs add more and more features. Most PIMs and case management programs can now synchronize with handheld computers (PDAs); this adds another element to the ability of attorneys and legal assistants to control their appointments, scheduling, and things-to-do lists. Also, nearly all legal organizations operate in a computer network environment. Most PIMs and case management programs now have group scheduling capabilities over the network so users can share information related to scheduling/case management. All of these factors complicate the calendaring, docket control, and case management functions in legal organizations. How a particular legal organization decides to set up and structure these functions is entirely up to it. It is clear that most legal organizations have many options to choose from when deciding how to approach tracking schedules and appointments.

Throughout the rest of the chapter the terms docket control or case management will be used to describe the process of tracking appointments, deadlines, and schedules in legal organizations. Topics that will be covered include general information about docket control in legal organizations and an overview of features found in many legal case management programs.

INTRODUCTION TO DOCKET CONTROL/ CASE MANAGEMENT

Docket control/case management works differently depending on the specific legal organization, the type of cases handled, and differing philosophies on how the function should be managed. In many legal organizations, each attorney and legal assistant enters docket control information in a central office-wide system but manage their own docket. In others, secretaries enter and manage the docket. Some of the events that are regularly tracked include appointments, deadlines and reminders, and hearing and court dates.

Appointments

During the course of a case or legal matter, a legal professional will have many appointments: meetings with clients and co-counsel, witness interviews, interoffice meetings, and so forth. Keeping appointments is very important. Law offices that must constantly reschedule appointments with clients may find their clients going to other attorneys who provide better service.

statute of limitations
A statute or law that sets a limit on the length of time a party has to file a suit. If a case is filed after the statute of limitations, the claim is barred and is dismissed as a matter of law.

Deadlines and Reminders

The practice of law is filled with deadlines at practically every stage of a legal matter. One of the most important types of deadlines is a statute of limitations. A **statute of limitations** is a statute or law that sets a limit on the length of time a party has to file a suit. For instance, some states impose a five-year statute of

limitations on lawsuits alleging a breach of a written contract. That is, if a lawsuit is brought or filed more than five years after a contract is breached or broken, the lawsuit is barred by the statute, and a court will dismiss the action. The purpose of a statute of limitations is to force parties to bring lawsuits in a timely fashion so that evidence is not destroyed, witnesses have not left the area, and so forth. If an attorney allows a statute of limitations to run, or expire, without filing a case, he or she may be liable for legal malpractice.

There also are many deadlines that are set after a case has been filed. In some courts, the judge and the attorneys on both sides sit down and schedule a list of deadlines that the case must follow. The schedule may look something like the one shown in Exhibit 7–1. These deadlines must be tracked and adhered to. An attorney who does not adhere to the deadlines may cause the case to be dismissed or may be penalized. Some courts are very reluctant to extend deadlines once they have been set.

> *Docket control is not just a "secretarial" function. The importance of working closely with the secretarial staff in calendaring and docketing matters cannot be stressed enough. In litigation firms, one of the legal assistant's primary responsibilities is tracking deadlines relating to timeliness of pleadings, discovery requests, interrogatories and answers, mediation statements, pretrial requirements, timely notification and service regarding discovery and trial subpoenas. All deadlines, dates, and appointments should be maintained on one central calendar (preferably computerized) for each attorney. This calendar should be accessible by the attorney, the secretary, and the legal assistant. All three should be cognizant of all deadlines, depositions, appointments, meetings, and hearings. All three should review upcoming deadlines and docket (tickler) notes on a daily basis.*
>
> *—Lenette Pinchback, CLA*

Because attorneys and legal assistants are busy, usually working on many cases, a legal organization must have a system of tracking upcoming deadlines. This is done not only by calendaring the deadline itself, but also by creating reminder notices in the calendar so that a deadline does not catch a person by surprise. These reminders are also called warnings. For example, in Exhibit 7–1, regarding the January 30 motion to dismiss, the attorney or legal assistant may want to be reminded 30, 15, and 5 days before the deadline. Therefore, reminder notices would be made on January 1, January 15, and January 25, in addition to the deadline itself being recorded on January 30. It is common for an attorney or legal assistant to request from one to four reminders for each deadline. If reminders are not entered in the docket system, it may make it hard to meet the deadline. Thus, logging reminder notices of upcoming events is crucial to the effective practice of law.

Some deadlines are automatically set by the rules of procedure that are in effect in any given court. Rules of procedure are court rules that govern and tell parties what procedures they must follow when bringing and litigating cases.

DEADLINE ITEM	DEADLINE DATE
Motion to Dismiss must be filed by	Jan. 30
Response to Motion to Dismiss must be filed by	Mar. 1
Discovery (interrogatories, request for production/admissions, depositions) must be completed by	July 1
Summary Judgment Motion must be filed by	July 15
Response to Summary Judgment Motion must be filed by	Aug. 1
Pretrial Order must be filed by	Sept. 1
Settlement Conferences must be completed by	Sept. 15
Pretrial Motions must be completed and decided by	Oct. 15
Trial to start no later than	Dec. 1

Exhibit 7–1
A Typical Case Schedule

Exhibit 7–2
Common Docket Control Entries

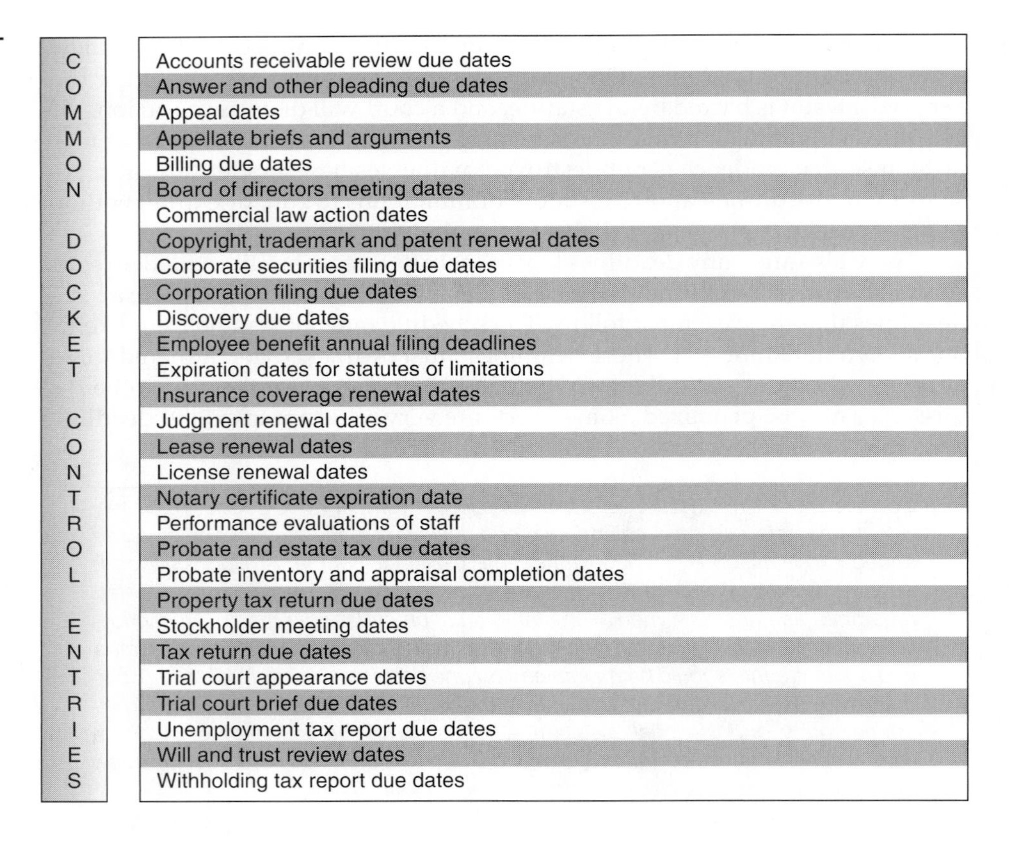

COMMON DOCKET CONTROL ENTRIES
Accounts receivable review due dates
Answer and other pleading due dates
Appeal dates
Appellate briefs and arguments
Billing due dates
Board of directors meeting dates
Commercial law action dates
Copyright, trademark and patent renewal dates
Corporate securities filing due dates
Corporation filing due dates
Discovery due dates
Employee benefit annual filing deadlines
Expiration dates for statutes of limitations
Insurance coverage renewal dates
Judgment renewal dates
Lease renewal dates
License renewal dates
Notary certificate expiration date
Performance evaluations of staff
Probate and estate tax due dates
Probate inventory and appraisal completion dates
Property tax return due dates
Stockholder meeting dates
Tax return due dates
Trial court appearance dates
Trial court brief due dates
Unemployment tax report due dates
Will and trust review dates
Withholding tax report due dates

For instance, in some courts the rules of procedure hold that after a final decision in a case has been rendered, all parties have 30 days after that to file an appeal.

For a law office that practices in the tax area, April 15, the date that federal income tax returns are due, is an example of an automatic or procedural deadline that must be tracked. Thus, this automatic or procedural deadline must be tracked by the office's docket system, and appropriate reminders must be made so that returns are not filed late and penalties assessed.

Hearings and Court Dates

Hearings and court dates are formal proceedings before a court. It is extremely important that these dates be carefully tracked. Most courts have little tolerance for attorneys who fail to show up for court. In some instances, the attorney can be fined or disciplined for missing court dates.

In larger cases, especially when the case is being litigated in court, there may be hundreds of entries into the docket system. Exhibit 7–2 illustrates a list of common docket entries, including both substantive and law office management related entries.

> *At one point in time, because we were so busy—we were in the process of bringing on another person for clerical support—we missed a deadline for filing [a] response to requests for admissions . . . . We did file a motion to approve an extension of time in order to file* [a response], *and we were granted that . . . but had that not been the case, the admission would have been deemed admissible or admitted and that could have really hindered the defense of the case. That was a horror story I about had a nervous breakdown over . . . . You never want that. Your heart drops to the floor.*[4]

MANUAL DOCKET CONTROL

Attorneys have used manual docket control methods for centuries. The most popular manual docket systems use a simple calendar.

Calendar

Small law offices sometimes use a simple page-a-day calendaring system. Many calendars provide a section to record "things to do" or reminders, in addition to providing a place to schedule appointments.

Before computerized systems, as cases were opened, deadlines and reminders (i.e., ticklers) would be entered into the calendar. Notices from courts, attorneys, and so forth that were received in the mail would also be entered into the calendar. In addition to the due date or appointment date, any reminders would also have to be manually entered into the calendar. This process could be time-consuming. For instance, if a deadline that had two reminders was entered, the whole entry would have to be manually entered a total of three times.

Although manual calendaring systems may minimally work for small offices that have few entries, they do not work well for large offices that have many attorneys and many appointments and deadlines. They simply do not have enough room to enter all the appointments, unless each attorney has his own calendar.

Many calendaring systems are decentralized. In a decentralized system, each attorney or timekeeper has her or his own calendar and staff to record appointments, things to do, reminders, and so forth. In addition, because the administrators of the firm do not have a centralized system at their disposal, they never know where an attorney or other person should be without tracking down that person's secretary and so on. The problem is compounded when a staff meeting for the entire office must be scheduled. Instead of going to a centralized calendar, checking what dates are available, and scheduling the meeting, the organizer must contact each attorney, take down a list of available dates for each attorney, find acceptable dates and times for all parties, and then notify each party of the date and time of the meeting.

Manual calendaring systems also lack the ability to track information by case. For example, if a client asked to see all the upcoming events for her case, a staff person would have to go through the calendar and manually put together a list. Depending on the case, there could be many entries. Again, this is a time-consuming process.

Another problem with a manual calendaring system is that successive calendars must be purchased every year (one for 2008, one for 2009, one for 2010, etc.). It is also difficult to schedule dates far in the future—five years down the road for a statute of limitations entry, for instance—because you will need the appropriate calendar.

Manual calendaring systems are prone to error and are tedious and time-consuming to administer. Because the process is slow and tedious, it encourages users to make as few docket entries as possible. Further, manual systems simply do not have the flexibility and reporting capabilities that computerized versions can deliver. Even in small law offices, manual docket control systems have nearly disappeared.

TYPES OF COMPUTERIZED DOCKET CONTROL SYSTEMS

There are a variety of computer programs that can be used to schedule and track events for a legal organization. These include generic calendaring/personal

information manager programs and case management programs. Most of these programs can be purchased for stand-alone computers or for local area networks. Networked systems, whether they are generic or legal-specific, have the principal advantage of allowing individual users throughout an organization to see and have access to the calendars of other users in the office.

Generic Calendaring and Personal Information Manager Programs

Generic calendaring programs computerize the functions of a paper desk calendar. Since they are generic and can be used by any type of business, they lack many features that are helpful to a legal organization. These types of programs are usually very inexpensive and typically manage only calendaring, things to do, contacts, and email functions.

personal information manager (PIM)
Consolidates a number of different tasks into one computer program. Most PIMs include calendaring, things to do, a contact database that tracks names and addresses of people, note taking, email, and other tasks as well.

A generic **personal information manager (PIM)** program consolidates a number of different tasks into one computer program. Most PIMs include calendaring, things to do, a contact database that tracks names and addresses of people, note taking, email, and other tasks. Exhibit 7–3 shows Microsoft Outlook, which is a PIM that can come bundled with Microsoft's Office suite of programs.

As the generic calendaring and scheduling software market has matured, most new programs are PIMs. PIMs are very popular and convenient to use since they allow a user to organize a number of related tasks into one easy-to-use interface. Generic PIMs, such as the one shown in Exhibit 7–3, are not specifically suited to the needs of legal professionals but still have useful features and some legal organizations use these programs. For example, for consistency purposes a corporate law department might use a product like Microsoft Outlook, which can be implemented throughout the corporation, instead of a legal-specific program that only the legal department can use. As good as some PIMs are, they fundamentally lack the ability to track information by case and lack the power and resources of true case management programs.

Exhibit 7–3
Calendaring/PIM Program—Microsoft Outlook
Microsoft product screen shot(s) reprinted with permission from Microsoft Corporation.

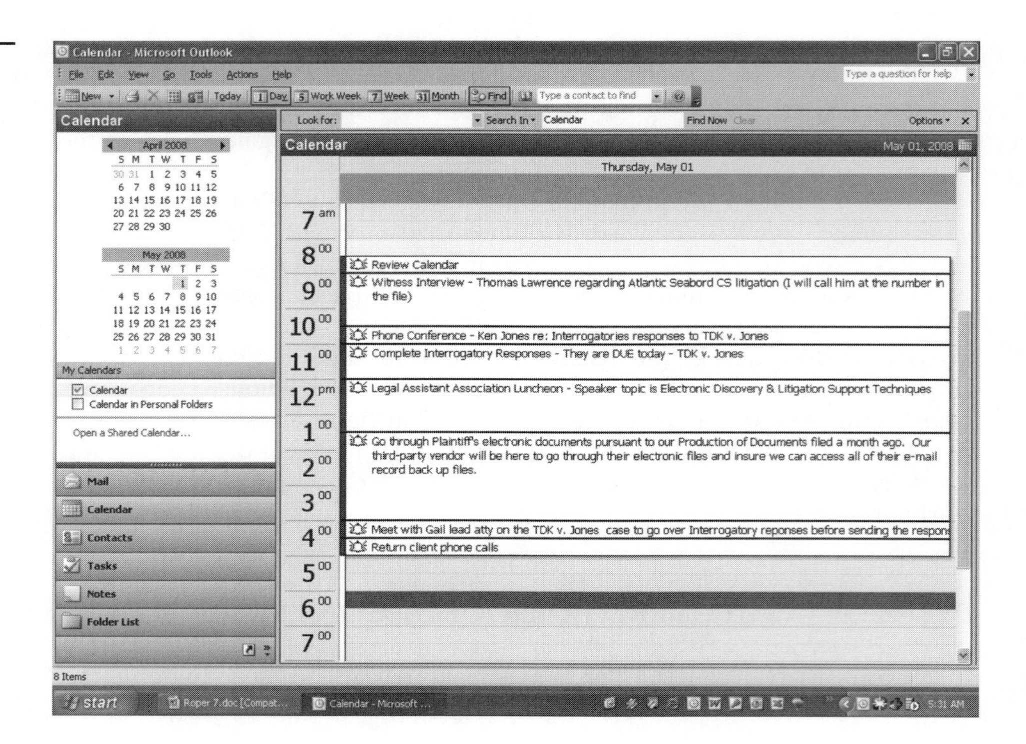

OVERVIEW OF COMPUTERIZED LEGAL CASE MANAGEMENT AND DOCKET CONTROL

The case management (sometimes called practice management) niche of the legal software market is mature and competitive, and the available programs are rich with features. Some case/practice management programs are designed for specific specialties of the law such as real estate, tax, collections, criminal defense, and so forth. Most case management programs, however, are designed for a broad spectrum of legal organizations no matter what type of law they practice.

> *Products like Outlook are not designed from a "file" or "matter" focused perspective (i.e., they do not allow you to work from a matter rather than a contact.) What the legal packages allow you to do is to gather in one place all the information regarding a specific file or matter.*
>
> *I do the following with* [my case management] *program:*
>
> - *Track every case in my office*
> - *Manage all my contacts*
> - *Schedule everything*
> - *Set up new cases and, with about two clicks, schedule every statute [of limitations], every deadline, and every other important date*
> - *Write letters by importing data in WordPerfect*
> - *Archive my old cases so I still have them around*
> - *Check for conflicts quickly*
> - *Keep notes on files.*[5]

Exhibit 7–4 shows a recent survey of legal assistants regarding the case/practice management packages that they or their firm use. Currently, the case management market is so competitive that no one product enjoys a clear dominance in this area. In fact, interestingly, 55 percent of the practicing legal assistants surveyed in Exhibit 7–4 indicated that they did not use a case management program. Prior surveys have indicated that in lieu of a case management program many law offices use a PIM, most commonly Microsoft Outlook. The basics of case management software are covered in this section; the manner in which any particular package handles these subjects will depend on the package.

Main Menu/Fundamental Tasks of Case Management Programs

Exhibit 7–5 shows the daily calendar and menu for a popular case management program. Exhibit 7–5 is a good example of the functions found in most case management programs. These functions include viewing calendars in a variety of different views, capturing complete contact information for clients and others, tracking and managing events (e.g., appointments, reminders, things to do, and calls to make), recording information about matters and case files, including links to documents and case notes, conflict checking, managing phone calls, and dates calculating, among others. Some of these tasks and activities will be discussed in more detail, but these are the general areas that most case management programs provide.

Contacts/Name Tracking

Before events such as appointments and reminders can be calendared for a case or matter in a case management system, the user must first create basic contact information for the client. Exhibit 7–6 shows a contact/name entry for a new

Exhibit 7–4
Case Management Programs Market Share According to Practicing Legal Assistants
As seen in the May/June 2006 issue of Legal Assistant Today, Copyright 2007 James Publishing, Inc. Reprinted courtesy of LEGAL ASSISTANT TODAY magazine. For subscription information call (800) 394-2626, or visit www.legalassistanttoday.com

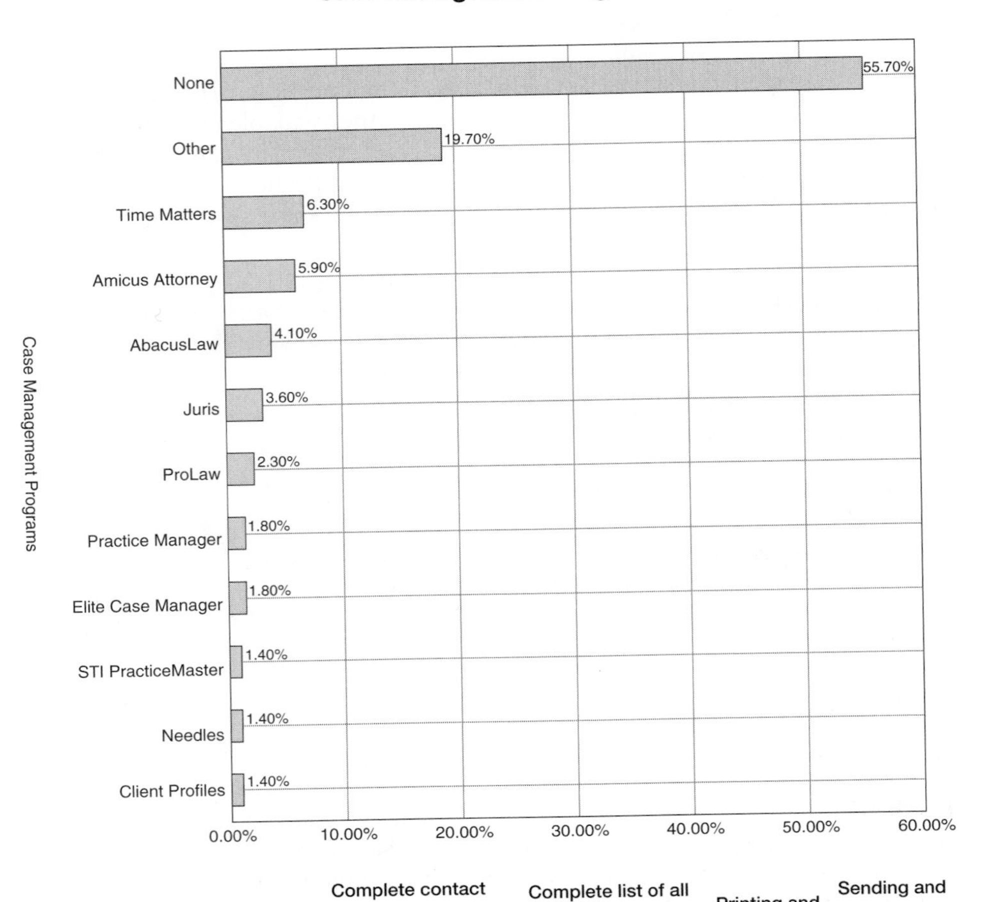

Exhibit 7–5
Daily Calendar and Menu Bar/Toolbar in a Case Management Program
Copyright 2007 Abacus Data Systems, Inc.

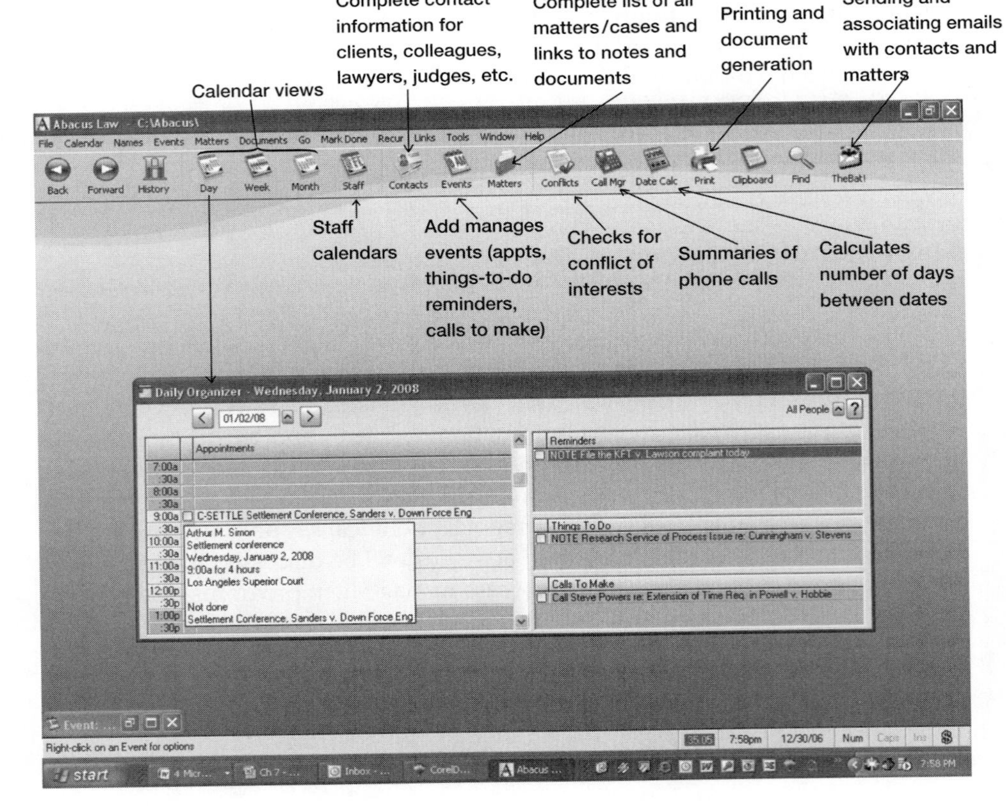

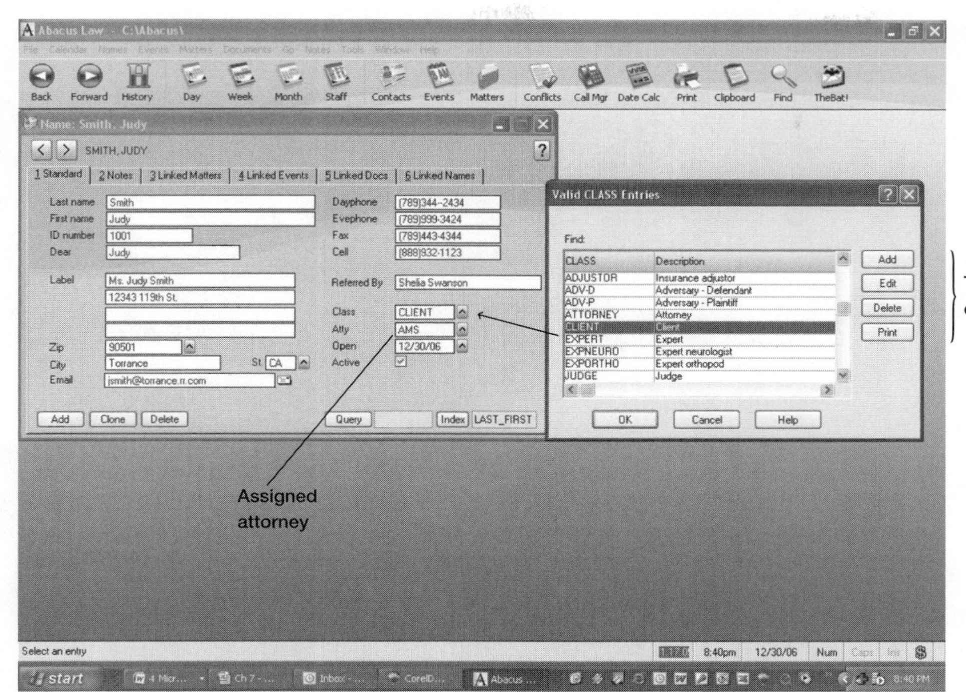

Exhibit 7–6

Entering a New Contact Name—Judy Smith, Client

client, Judy Smith. Contact information that the user can enter including address, phone, and email. In addition, the type or class of name entry is entered from a list; in this instance the contact is a client. Judges, vendors, colleagues, attorneys, and anyone the user comes in contact with can be entered as a contact/name. Notice in Exhibit 7–6 that the client can be assigned to "linked matters" such as cases or legal matters, "linked events" such as calendar entries, "linked documents" such as legal documents, and "linked names" such as opposing counsel or other people associated with the client. The ability to link contacts/names with cases and other case-related information is what separates case management systems from PIMs. Also, notice in Exhibit 7–6 that initials indicate which attorney has been assigned to the client (here AMS). This allows the case management system to track and produce reports regarding which attorneys are assigned to which cases.

Matters/Cases

Notice in Exhibit 7–7 that a new matter has been created, *Smith v. EZ Pest Control*, and that the matter has been linked to Judy Smith's contact/name record. In addition, the new matter shows the attorney assigned to the case, the case code (here a contract case), and the court, among other things. If Judy Smith had additional legal matters, the user would simply create the new matters in the matters window and link that case to her contact/name record. Notice in Exhibit 7–8 that the user opened the Matters window for *Smith v. EZ Pest Control, Inc.* The user can immediately see the linked names for the case, which now include not only the client but also Steve Roberts, the defendant's attorney. In the Matter window in Exhibit 7–8 the user can also find case notes, all events associated with the case, and all linked documents that are related to the case. This allows users to have a tremendous amount of information at their fingertips.

Events

Once client contact and case matter information has been entered in the case management system, events can be entered and associated with the client or case.

Exhibit 7–7
Creating a Case/Matter and Assigning it to Judy Smith, Client

Matters associated with Judy Smith

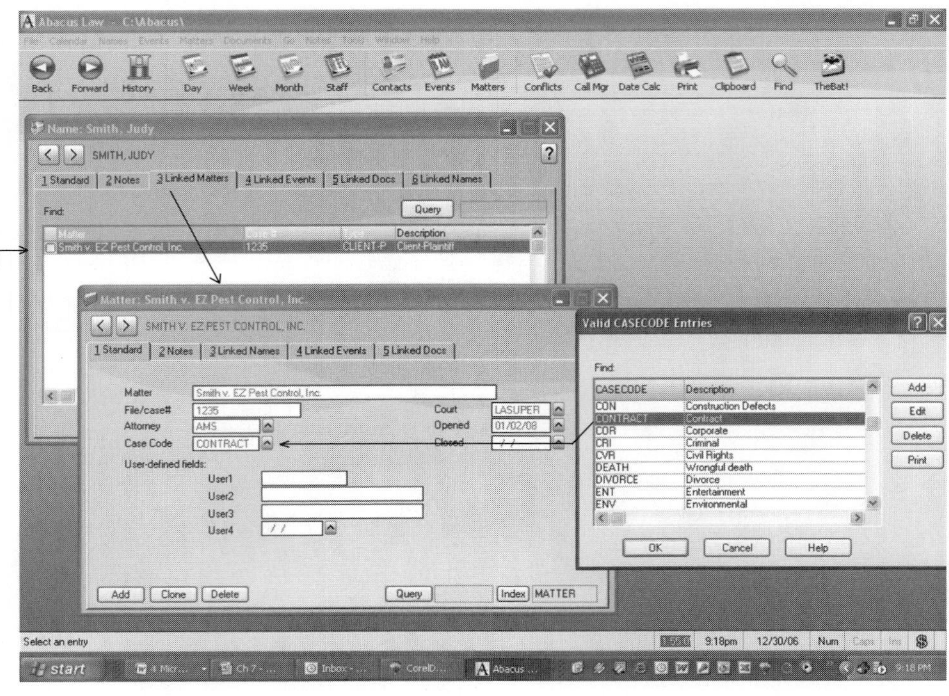

Exhibit 7–8
Accessing Case Information from the Matter Window

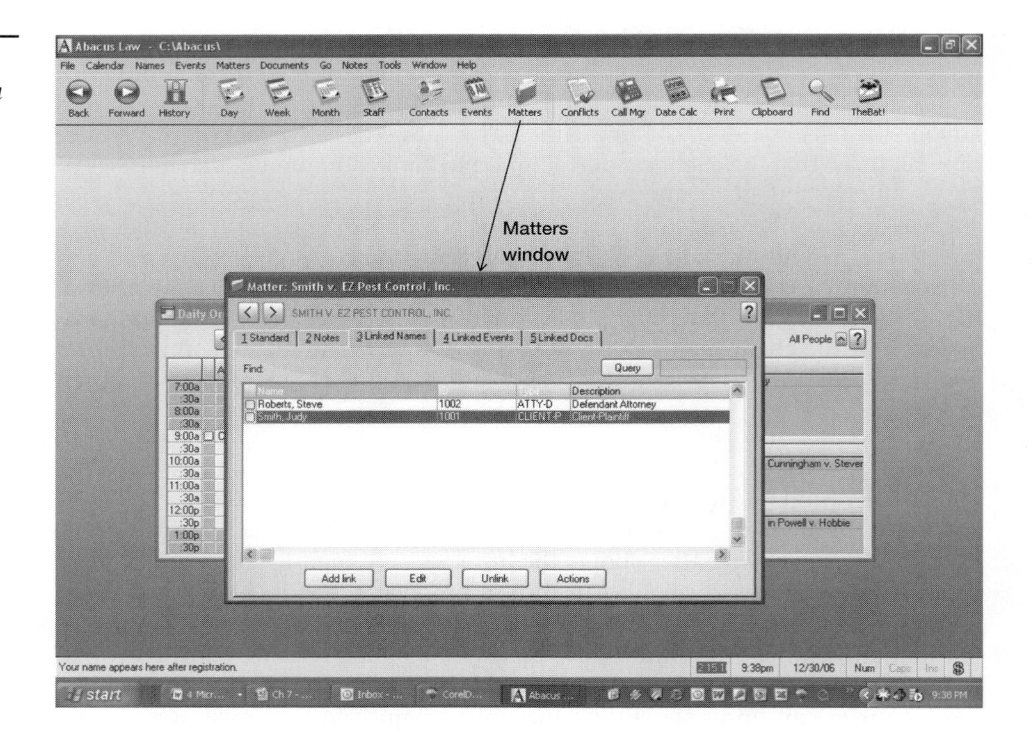

Notice in Exhibit 7–9 that an appointment has been entered and associated with Judy Smith and with the matter *Smith v. EZ Pest Control.* The event window in Exhibit 7–9 allows the user to select who the event is for (Arthur M. Simon) and what kind of event it is (an appointment). Notice in Exhibit 7–9 that valid "what" entries include appointments, client conferences, and many other standard event types. Events can also include reminders, things to be done, calls to be made, trials, hearings and many other items. Also, notice in Exhibit 7–9 that there are two numerals next to "Reminders": a *1* and a *3*. This means that one and three days before the actual event a notice will appear in the Reminders section of the daily

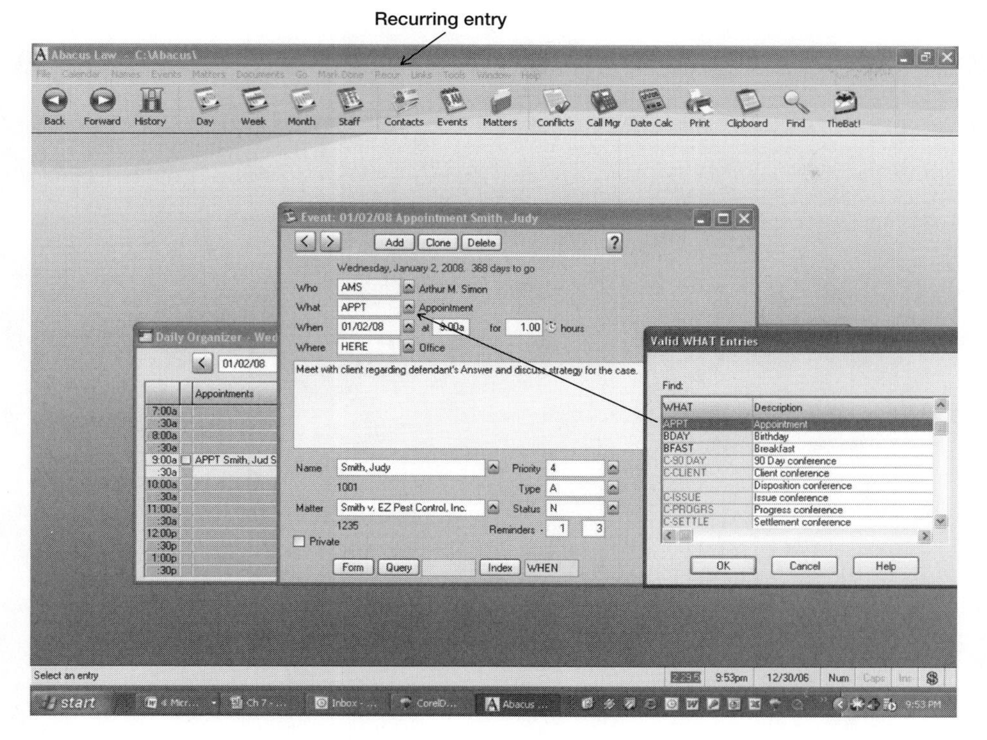

Exhibit 7–9
Creating a New Event
Copyright 2007 Abacus Data Systems, Inc.

calendar that this event is coming up. In Exhibit 7–9 there is also a priority field, which allows a user to assign different priorities such as "high" or "low" to events. There is also a field for Status; in this instance the *N* in Exhibit 7–9 stands for "not done". This allows the user to track events that did not get completed.

Users can also create recurring entries in most case management systems. A **recurring entry** is a calendar entry that happens repeatedly, typically daily, weekly, monthly, or annually. For instance, if an office has a staff meeting every Monday morning, the entry could be entered once as a weekly recurring appointment. Notice the "Recur" menu item on the menu bar in Exhibit 7–9. This is where a recurring entry would be designated in the case management program shown in Exhibit 7–9.

recurring entry
A calendar entry that recurs.

Exhibit 7–10 shows the Matter screen for *Smith v. EZ Pest Control*, except that now the Linked Events tab is selected. Notice that the user gets a quick snapshot of exactly what deadlines are coming up in the case. They include the two reminders and the appointment mentioned above, and a new discovery conference that was added a few days later. By linking events to the matter and the name/contact the user has a powerful tool with which to manage a case.

Most case management programs allow a user to create rule-based entries. In a rule-based entry one event automatically triggers a list of subsequent calendaring events based on a rule that was programmed into the application. For example, in Exhibit 7–11, notice that a rule entitled "New Case" has been created. This rule says that on the day it is executed, staff will meet with the client; that one day after the initial meeting, a conflict check entry/event will automatically be generated; and that an entry/event will be entered for client file to be opened. Seven days after the initial meeting, the case management program will automatically create an event for a confirmation letter to the client, and fourteen days after the initial conference an entry/event will be created to draft a fee contract. All of this will take place automatically after the New Case rule is executed. Most case management programs allow the user to program his or her own rules (such as in Exhibit 7–11). Additionally, most case management programs have court-based rules that users can purchase. Using court-based rules that automatically generate many events is a large timesaver when users have many cases to handle.

Exhibit 7–10
List of Linked Events by Matter/Case
Copyright 2007 Abacus Data Systems, Inc.

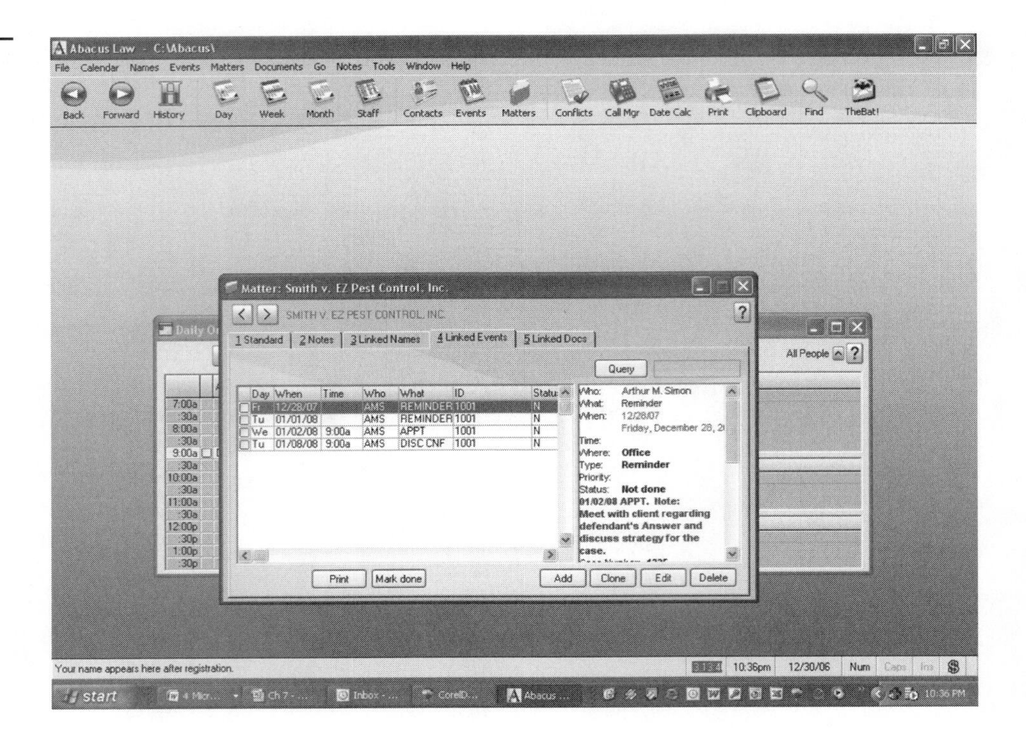

Exhibit 7–11
Entering Rule-Based Events
Copyright 2007 Abacus Data Systems, Inc.

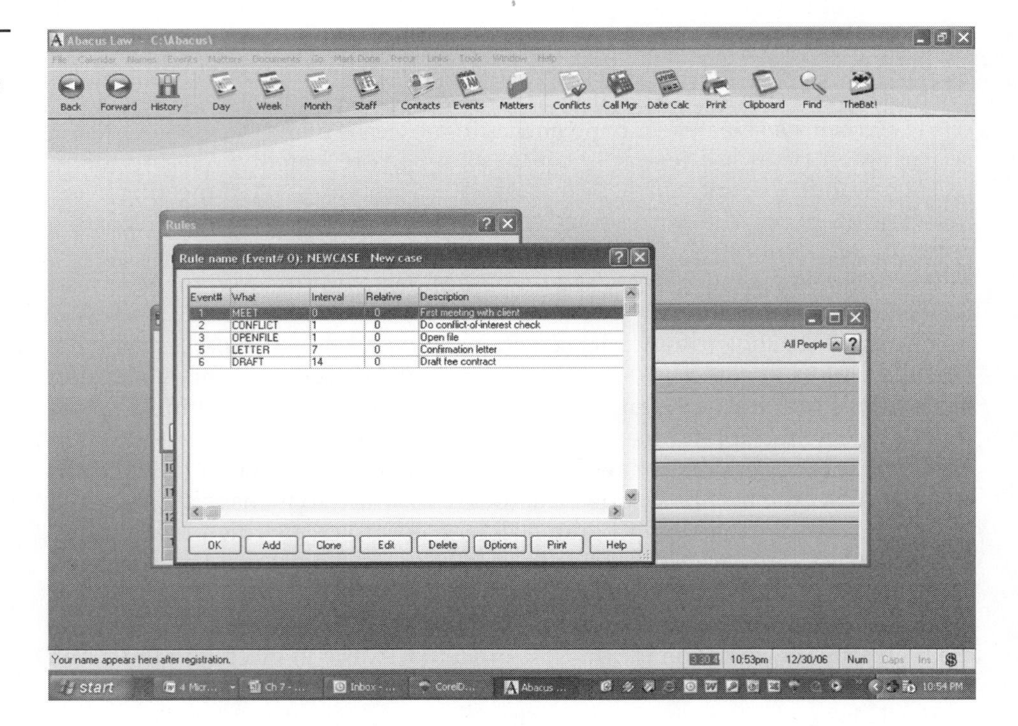

Calendar Views

All case management programs come with a number of calendar views in which users can view their calendar. A daily calendar view is shown in Exhibit 7–5, but there are several additional views as well. Exhibit 7–12 shows a weekly view, a monthly view, and a staff calendar view. The staff calendars view shows the calendars for one day for different staff side by side.

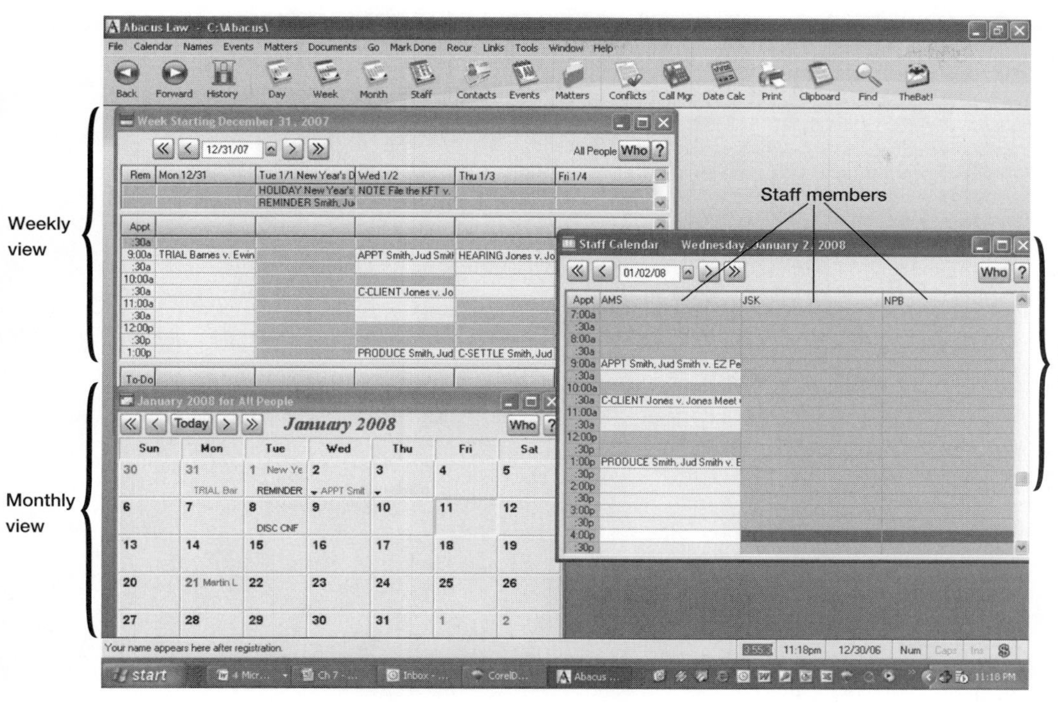

Exhibit 7–12
Weekly, Staff, and Monthly Calendar Views
Copyright 2007 Abacus Data Systems, Inc.

Date Calculator

Some case management systems have a date calculator that automatically calculates the number of days between dates. For instance, suppose a user automatically gets a hearing on a motion ten court days after the motion is filed. If the motion is filed on January 2, 2008, for what day should the hearing be set? The Date Calculator window in Exhibit 7–13 shows that the hearing should be set for January 16, 2008. Date calculators are handy features, particularly when users need to calculate precise deadlines.

Notes/Case Diary

Most case management systems provide a place in which to maintain a case diary or notes for the file. This gives legal professionals a central place to place their notes, and record summaries of phone calls and other information. Notice in Exhibit 7–14 that in the *Smith v. EZ Pest Control* matter file, the Notes tab is selected. A new note is being added regarding a call from an expert witness. The notes section allows the user to create a running diary of what is happening in a case as it progresses. This is particularly helpful when multiple people are working on a case. If anyone wants an update of the case, all that person has to do is read the notes.

> *The case diary is a key component in a case management system. The attorney and paralegal will use this function more than any other feature because it becomes the center for case information and communications. Your attorney no longer has to search a file for details about the last conversation you had with the client. No more searching through endless computer directories for the last letter sent to opposing counsel. It's all tied together in the case management system.*[6]

Document Assembly and Generation

Case management programs can store extensive information about a case, including items such as parties, attorneys, case-related information, and case numbers. Most case management programs can assemble this information into a merged document (see Exhibits 7–15 and 7–15A). A legal professional can therefore automatically

Exhibit 7–13
Date Calculator
Copyright 2007 Abacus Data Systems, Inc.

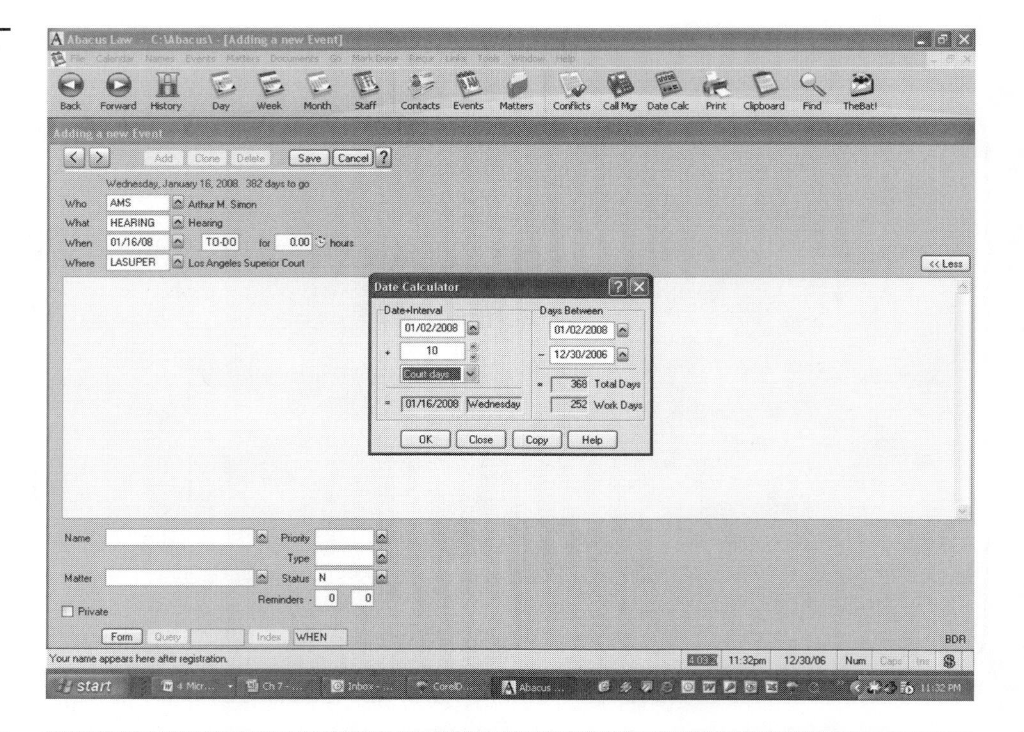

Exhibit 7–14
Adding Notes/Case Diary
Copyright 2007 Abacus Data Systems, Inc.

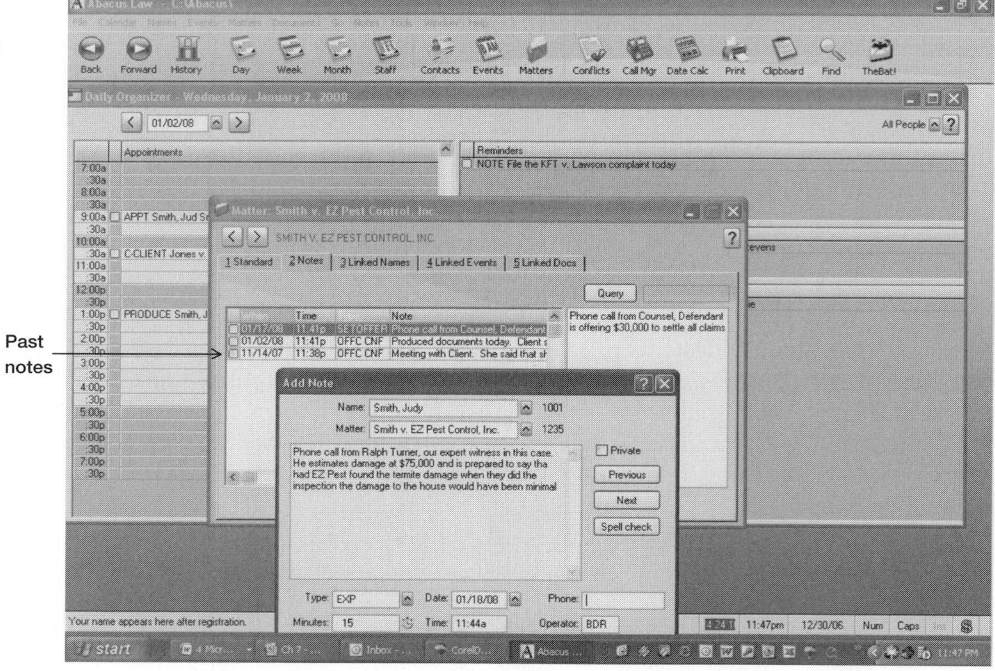

generate standard letters, forms, pleadings, and reports either from the case management program itself or in combination with a word processor such as Word or WordPerfect. Also, in some programs, when a user creates a document using document generation, the case management system automatically note this, including the date, in the case diary/notes. The ability to automatically generate standard letters and forms from a case management program is a tremendous time saver.

> *The data entered into the case management system is merged automatically into the documents, printed and is ready for the review and signature of the supervising attorney.*[7]

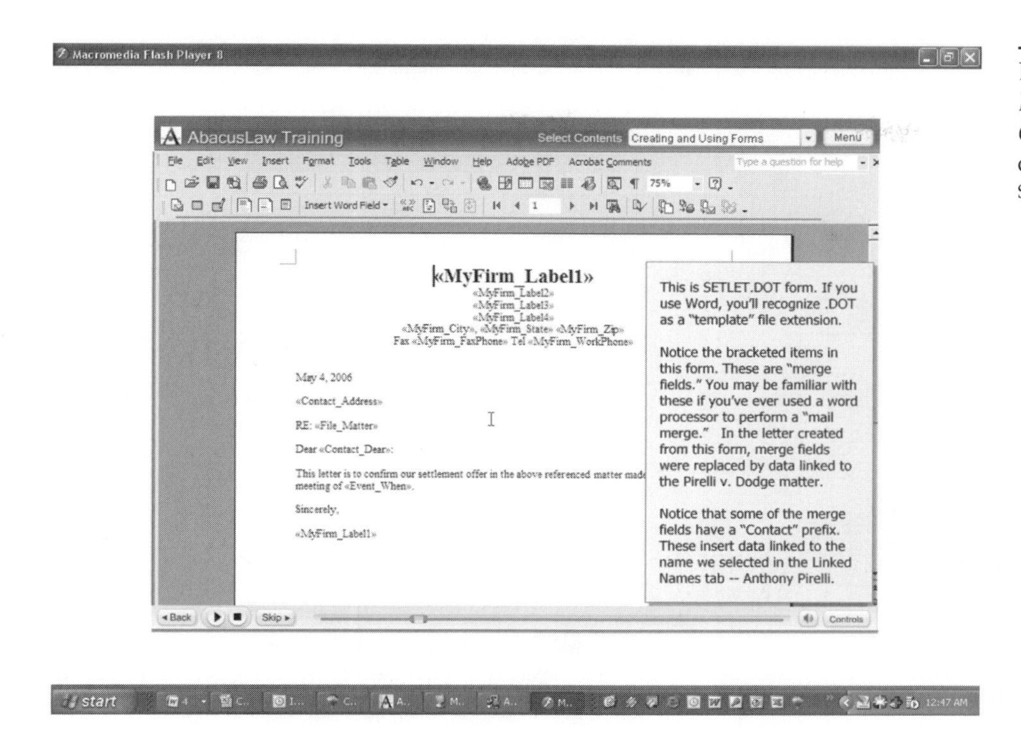

Exhibit 7–15
Document Generation in a Case Management Program
Copyright 2007 Abacus Data Systems, Inc.

Synchronizing with PIMs / PDAs

Most case management systems will synchronize calendars with PIMs such as Outlook and devices such as PDAs (personal digital assistants). Thus, if a corporate law department wanted to use a case management system, but the rest of the corporation was using Outlook, the two could be set up to share and/or synchronize information so that all of the entries in the case management program would not have to be entered by hand in Outlook.

Conflict of Interest Searches

Most case management programs allow the user to do conflict of interest searches. Since the database tracks clients, parties, counsel, and much other case-related information, the conflict search can be very comprehensive. In Exhibit 7–16, the user executed a conflict of interest search on "Smith." The case management program returned with two possible hits, a matter/case (*Smith v. EZ Pest Control*), and a contact name-client (*Judy Smith*).

Email Interface

> *For me, an email...[interface] is an essential part of a case management package. The less places I have to look for something, the better. I use... [my case management program] to track incoming and outgoing e-mail and associate it with particular projects [cases] and clients. The process is extremely easy: open the email message, select your project or client from a pull-down menu and save.*[8]

Most case management programs include an email interface that allows users to send emails in conjunction with the program and to link emails with cases. This is extremely important given the heavy use of emails in communicating with clients and in handling client matters.

Document Tracking

Most case management programs can now associate documents with cases. A link can be made between a document or file and a matter or contact in a case

Exhibit 7–15A
Case Management Program
Document Asssembly/Generation

CASE MANAGEMENT DATABASE

Client Name:	First National Bank
Contact Person–First Name:	Sam
Contact Person–Last Name:	Johnson
Client Address:	P.O. Box 1000
Client City:	Philadelphia
Client State:	Pennsylvania
Client Zip:	98934
Client Phone:	943/233-9983
Case Number:	2001-9353
Court:	Philadelphia Superior Court—District 13, Philadelphia, Pennsylvania
Debtor Name:	Philip Jones
Debtor Address:	3242 Wilson Ave. SW
Debtor City:	Philadelphia
Debtor State:	Pennsylvania
Debtor Zip:	98984
Amount Owed to Client:	$25,234
Type of Debt:	Mortgage
Type of Asset:	House at 3242 Wilson Ave SW, Philadelphia, Pennsylvania

DOCUMENT TEMPLATE 1—Complaint

In the {Court}
{Client Name}
Plaintiff
Case No. {Case Number}

{Debtor Name}
{Debtor Address}
{Debtor City} {Debtor State} {Debtor Zip}

Defendant.

COMPLAINT

Comes now the plaintiff, {Client Name}, and states that the defendant, {Debtor Name}, is indebted to the plaintiff in the amount of {Amount Owed to Client} on a {Type of Debt} regarding a {Type of Asset}. Attached to this complaint as Appendix "A" is a fully executed copy of the mortgage above referenced.

Merge function

MERGED DOCUMENT—Complaint

In the Philadelphia Superior Court – District 13, Philadelphia, Pennsylvania

First National Bank
Plaintiff
Case No. 2001-9353

Philip Jones
3242 Wilson Ave. SW
Philadelphia, Pennsylvania 98984

Defendant.

COMPLAINT

Comes now the plaintiff, First National Bank, and states that the defendant, Philip Jones, is indebted to the plaintiff in the amount of $25,234 on a mortgage regarding a house at 3242 Wilson Ave SW, Philadelphia, Pennsylvania. Attached to this complaint as Appendix "A" is a fully executed copy of the mortgage above referenced.

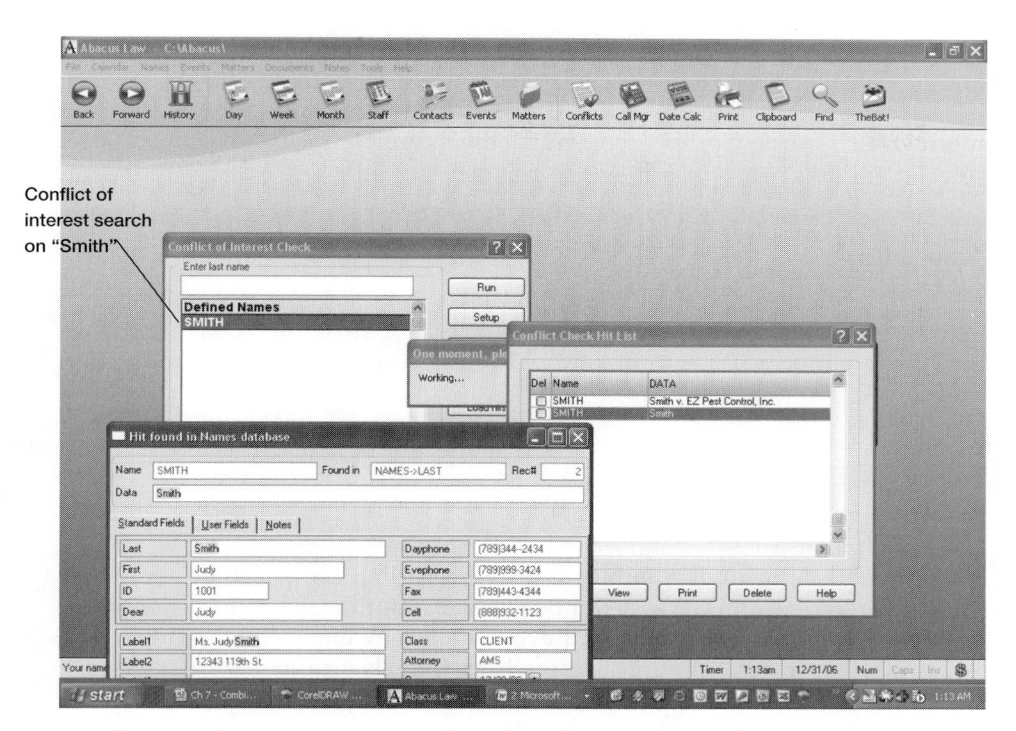

Exhibit 7–16
Conflict of Interest Checking in a Case Management Program
Copyright 2007 Abacus Data Systems, Inc.

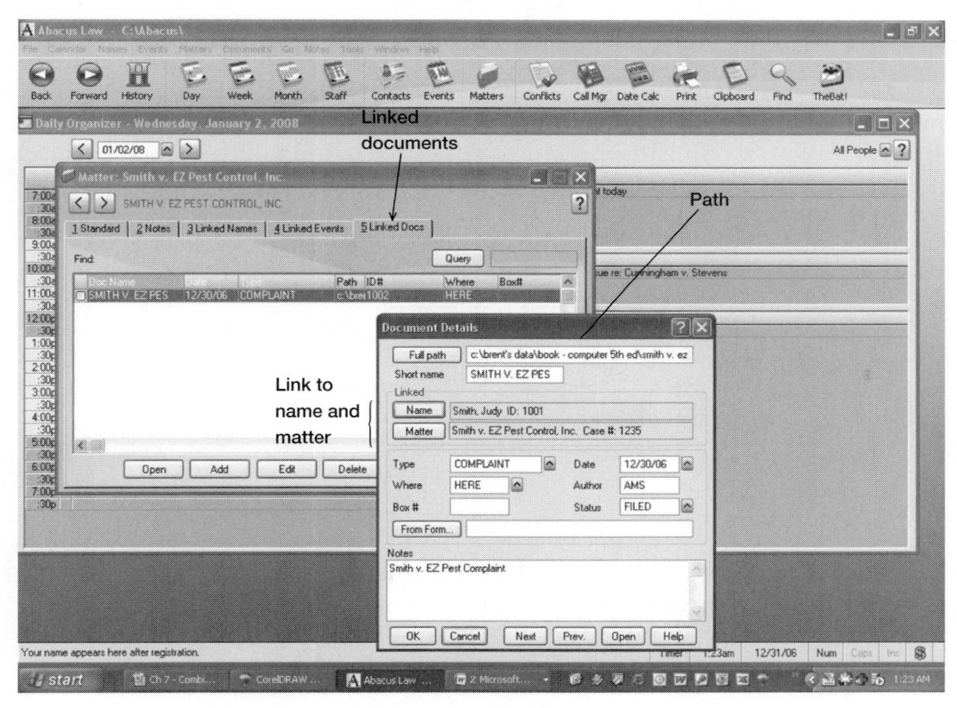

Exhibit 7–17
Linking Documents to Matters/Cases and Contacts
Copyright 2007 Abacus Data Systems, Inc.

management program. This can allow legal professionals to index and manage case documents directly from the case management program. In Exhibit 7–17 the user has linked the electronic "Complaint" word-processing file with the matter and name of the client. Thus, when the user pulls up the matter window, he or she can click the Linked Documents tab and see a list of all of the electronic documents in the case.

Time and Billing/Accounting Interface

Many case management programs share information with timekeeping and billing programs and in some instances with accounting programs as well.

Thus, when a user creates a case event (such as an appointment) he or she can automatically generate a time record for the event without having to retype all of the information. Some case management programs have time and billing modules that must be purchased, while others can interface with popular legal time and billing programs.

Reporting

Most computerized systems allow the user to generate a vast number of standard reports covering every aspect of case management. Most systems also come with a report writer so the user can write customized reports and queries.

IMPLEMENTING CASE MANAGEMENT SYSTEMS—WHY THEY FAIL

Much has been written in the legal press regarding the fact that while case management programs have never been better, many legal organizations have been slow to implement them, and even when they have been implemented, it appears that many legal professionals are not using them. For example, a recent survey by the American Bar Association revealed that while about 40 percent of the respondents indicated their firm had a case management program, only 18 percent indicated that they actually used it. A commonly mentioned reason for why legal professionals fail to use case management systems is the lack of training. This problem has two facets. The first facet is that because a case management system can be somewhat expensive, a firm may stop short of purchasing the training tools needed to train staff. The second facet is that legal professionals may not attend the training that is offered because they are too busy. Exhibit 7–18 lists the top ten reasons case management systems fail.

> *Training is the No. 1 reason for successful case management system implementations. Lack of training is the No. 1 reason for failed implementations. If I had a nickel for every excuse I have heard about why attorneys and staff don't attend training, I would be able to retire.*[9]

THE DOCKET CYCLE

The docket cycle refers to how information is entered into a case management program. There are three primary ways that information can flow into and out of such a program. These are centralized, decentralized, and combined cycles.

Centralized Docket Control Cycle

In a centralized docket control cycle, one person typically is responsible for entering all docket entries into the case management program. This is usually a secretary or in some cases a legal assistant. In this type of system, step one would be for a user to manually complete a docket slip (see Exhibit 7–19). The second step would be for the secretary to enter the event into the docket control program. The third step would be for reports to be generated, and the last step would be for entries to be marked "done."

No.	Reason
1.	Lack of comprehensive training.
2.	Failure to achieve buy-in from staff early on.
3.	Failing to keep the needs of the end users in mind when making a final selection on which program to purchase.
4.	Failing to spend the money on an expert consultant that can fully and completely install and setup the system and train users on its basic and advanced uses.
5.	Failing to make necessary customizations in the program to make it truly usable for the specific needs of the legal organization.
6.	Failing to document how the system works so that when key staff leave, the system can continue to be used effectively.
7.	Failing to implement the case management system over time, in planned stages, but instead forcing it on everyone at once.
8.	Failing to have support for the project from the top.
9.	Failing to truly understand how the case management system will fully integrate with other office systems such as time and billing, accounting, electronic mail, and word processing.
10.	Trying to implement too many new computer applications or process changes at one time.

Exhibit 7–18
Top Ten Reasons Case Management Systems Fail

Exhibit 7–19
Sample Docket Slip

JOHNSON, BECK & TAYLOR **DOCKET SLIP**

Client/Case Matter: *Smith v. United States* **File No:.** *118294*

Event: *Pre-Trial Hearing*

Date of Event: *10/1* **Time of Event:** *10:00 am—1:00 pm*

Place of Event: *U.S. Ct. House, Div. 8*

To Be Handed By: *MJB* **Reminder Dates:** *9/15*

Priority: ①**2 3 4 5 (Circle one, Top Priority is 1).**

Slip Completed by: *BRR* **Date Slip Completed:** *8/15*

Notes: *Meet Client at 9:45 at Ct. House*

Docket Clerk Use Only

Date Entered in Docket: *8/17*

Entered by: *JCC*

Decentralized Docket Control Cycle

In a decentralized docket control cycle, the user enters docket information directly into the computer, controlling her or his own docket. In this type of system, the first step would be for the user to enter a docket entry into the case management program. Second, the user would view or print reports as necessary, and third, the user would mark entries "done." The advantage of this system is that the user has ultimate control over his or her own docket. The disadvantage is that the user instead of a clerk or secretary is doing the data entry.

Combined Docket Control Cycle

In a combined docket control cycle, a user can decide whether to enter information into the program or have a clerk or secretary do it. Some docket control

programs allow multiple people to enter data into a user's schedule. For example, some networked docket programs allow both an attorney and his or her secretary to enter information into the attorney's schedule. Both have full access to the attorney's calendar.

In this type of system, the first step would be for either the user or a third party to enter a docket entry into the case management program. Second, either the user or the third party views or prints reports as necessary, and third, either the user or third party marks entries "done." In some ways, this is the best of both worlds, since the user still has control over his or her calendar but can delegate the data entry to someone else.

ETHICAL AND MALPRACTICE CONSIDERATIONS

The ramifications of missing deadlines and otherwise failing to track the progress of cases can be severe. In fact, there are two types of negative outcomes that can result from case neglect: an ethics board proceeding against the attorney and a legal malpractice claim filed against the attorney or firm. An attorney who neglects a case can be disciplined by a state ethics board. Such discipline in an ethics case may include reprimand, suspension, or even disbarment. In a legal malpractice case, the attorney involved is sued for damages for providing substandard legal work. These types of cases are not remote or obscure. There are thousands of legal ethics and malpractice proceedings filed throughout the country every year alleging case neglect.

Ethical Considerations

A recent nationwide statistical study of attorney disciplinary opinions found that the number one and two reasons that clients file disciplinary proceedings against attorneys, and that courts discipline attorneys, are (1) attorneys failing to communicate with their clients and (2) attorneys neglecting or not pursuing client cases diligently. This confirms what studies have shown since the early 1980s. Both of these problems are easily preventable when attorneys and legal assistants use good docket control systems and effective time management.

The *ABA Model Rules of Professional Conduct* give direct guidance on these issues. The *Model Rules* state that attorneys should be competent in the area they are practicing in and that they should be reasonably prepared to represent the client. The *Model Rules* state that the attorney must act with reasonable diligence and promptness when representing a client, and, finally, the *Model Rules* state that an attorney must keep the client reasonably informed about what is going on in the representation of the client. Each of these areas is explored in detail.

Competence and Adequate Preparation The *Model Rules* hold that an attorney must be competent to represent the client. That is, she or he must reasonably know the area of law that the client needs representation in, and, assuming the attorney does not know the area of law, must take the preparation time to become familiar with the case to represent the client adequately. (See Model Rule 1.1)

The purpose of this rule is to ensure that an attorney does not undertake a matter that he or she is not competent in and to ensure that the attorney has had adequate preparation. The amount of "adequate preparation" depends on what type of legal matter the client has. Major litigation, for example, will require far more preparation time than the amount of time it takes to prepare a simple will. The point is that attorneys should not undertake to represent a client if for some reason they cannot do it with the skill and preparation time necessary.

Diligence The *Model Rules* require that an attorney act with a reasonable degree of diligence in pursuing the client's case. (See Model Rule 1.3.)

Rule 1.3 specifically requires an attorney to act with commitment and dedication when representing a client and to avoid procrastination.

The comment to Rule 1.3 also notes that the attorney should carry through to conclusion all legal matters undertaken for a client unless the relationship is properly and clearly terminated. If doubt exists about whether an attorney-client relationship exists, the attorney should clarify the situation "in writing so that the client will not mistakenly suppose the attorney is looking after the client's affairs when the lawyer has ceased to do so." The purpose of this rule is to ensure that attorneys put forth reasonable effort and diligence to represent a client. Attorneys cannot adequately represent the interests of clients if they ignore the case, if they are lazy and do not work on the case, and so forth.

Communication with Clients An attorney also must communicate regularly with a client. (See Model Rule 1.4.)

The rule specifically requires the attorney to keep in reasonable contact with the client, to explain general strategy, and to keep the client reasonably informed regarding the status of the client's legal matter. The "reasonableness" of the situation will depend on the facts and circumstances of the particular case.

Clients become extremely frustrated when they pay for legal services and then the attorney refuses to take their calls, answer their letters, or otherwise communicate with them in any way. The purpose of this rule is to ensure that attorneys talk to their clients, keep them informed about what is happening with their cases, and keep them involved in their cases. Often, legal assistants are more accessible to clients than attorneys are and can play an important role in communicating with clients. Exhibit 7–20 shows some examples of actual ethical and malpractice cases.

Legal Malpractice Considerations

[A] client sued his former attorney(s) alleging that they neglected his case by among other things: not taking the depositions of the defendants, not taking depositions of related witnesses, and failing to secure expert witness testimony which all led to the dismissal of the client's case. The client also testified that when he questioned the attorney about when the depositions would be taken, the attorney responded "all in due time." The client was awarded a judgment of $700,000.00 against his former attorneys.
Mayol v. Summers, 223 Ill. App. 3d 794, 585 N.E.2d 1176 (1992).

In addition to the ethical considerations of neglecting a client's legal matter, the client may have a legal malpractice claim against the attorney for negligence. The general theory in a **legal malpractice** claim is that the attorney breached an ordinary standard of care applicable to a reasonable attorney under those circumstances. In a legal malpractice case, both the plaintiff and the defendant must rely on attorneys who are expert witnesses to testify that the defendant either did or did not act as a reasonable attorney would in the same situation. A recent study by the American Bar Association of malpractice claims over a five-year period found that approximately 23 percent of all malpractice claims were filed because the attorney failed to calendar an item or failed to follow up on a matter.

legal malpractice
An attorney's breach of an ordinary standard of care that a reasonable attorney would have adhered to in that same circumstance.

Exhibit 7–21 shows some common deadlines that when missed may lead to malpractice claims. In fact, many malpractice insurers will refuse to write malpractice insurance for a law office that does not have an effective docket control system.

Exhibit 7–20
Ethical Cases Regarding Lack of Diligence

Attorney Files Case, Then Loses Interest
An attorney filed suit on behalf of a mother and her daughter (a special education student) so that the daughter could be placed in a public school. The attorney then took no action in the case, never sent the client a detailed accounting, and refused to communicate with the client. Three and a half years later the client received a letter from the attorney stating that in light of his "other business projects," he did not anticipate practicing law any more. When the client requested her $4,000 in legal fees back and her file the attorney denied both requests. The attorney received a one-year suspension followed by a six-month period of supervised probation. In Re Dunn, 2002 WL 31488272 (L.A.).

Attorney Receives One-Year Suspension for Neglecting Legal Matters
A New York attorney of 25 years received a one-year suspension for misconduct in neglecting legal matters which caused harm to his clients. This came after the attorney previously received a letter of caution and letter of admonition as a result of his neglect of other legal matters from the court. Matter of Aiello, 246 A.D.2d 55, 676 N.Y.S.2d 385 (1998).

Attorney of 37 Years Receives a Public Censure for Neglecting a Client's Case and Lying About It
An attorney of 37 years was publicly censured after he neglected a personal injury action he had commenced on behalf of a client. The client's case was eventually dismissed with prejudice due to the attorney's neglect of the case. In addition, after the case was dismissed the attorney repeatedly and falsely advised his client that the matter was still pending and after the client discharged him the attorney failed to forward the file to the new attorney. Matter of Welt, 1999 WL 130600 (N.Y.A.D. 31 Dept.).

Oregon Attorney Suspended for One Year for Failing to File Documents His Client Executed and for Failing to Respond to a Show Cause Order
An Oregon attorney failed to file a Uniform Support Affidavit that his client had executed in a divorce action and he failed to respond to a show cause order. The attorney also failed to respond to numerous telephone calls from his client and several letters from counsel. The court suspended the attorney for one year. Conduct of Meyer, 970 P.2d 647 (1999).

Minnesota Attorney Appeals a Client's Case, Neglects to File a Brief to the Court, and Writes a Bad Check
A Minnesota attorney filed a lawsuit for a client. The lawsuit was dismissed and the client paid $250 to file an appeal. The attorney wrote a $250 check out of his law office account to pay the filing fee for the appeal. The attorney failed to file a brief to the court and the attorney's check was returned for insufficient funds. After numerous requests for repayment of the fee and submission of the brief the court of appeals dismissed the appeal and issued an order directing entry of a $250 judgment against the attorney personally. The attorney did not satisfy the judgment. The attorney also neglected other cases as well. The attorney was disbarred. Disciplinary Action Against Grzybek, 567 N.W.2d 259 (1997).

Attorney Fails to Tell Convicted Client About Five Extensions of Time and Fails to Communicate With Client about His Appeal
Attorney filed an appeal of a criminal conviction for first degree theft for a client. The attorney filed the brief but only after the court granted him five extensions of time. The attorney never communicated with the client, never advised the client of the five extensions, never discussed or reviewed the brief with the client, never told the client that the brief was filed or gave him a copy, never told the client about the oral arguments, never told the client about the court's decision to affirm the conviction, and never gave the client a copy of the decision. The attorney was disbarred. Conduct of Bourcier, 325 Or. 429, 939 P.2d 604 (1997).

1. Expiration of the statute of limitations.
2. Failure to appear or plead, resulting in a default judgment.
3. Dismissal of a lawsuit for lack of prosecution.
4. Failure to file tax returns or other documents within the time required.
5. Failure to file pleadings or to comply with an order within the time required.
6. Failure to answer interrogatories within the time required.
7. Failure to give timely notice when such notice is a precondition to a recovery of damages.
8. Failure to communicate with clients.
9. Not knowing what to do next (i.e., not being competent in an area of law).

Exhibit 7–21
Common Reasons for Malpractice Claims
Lenette Pinchback, CLA

We [legal malpractice insurance carriers] believe that a majority of our claims come from poorly managed time and docket systems. . . . If we see evidence of a superior docket control system, we can reduce premiums up to five percent annually.

Martin L. Dean, "Software Guaranteed to Save Money," California Lawyer, November 1989, 77.

A computerized case management system that is used correctly and effectively will greatly decrease an attorney's or a law office's chances of being the subject of ethical complaints or malpractice suits. However, ultimately the responsibility lies with the individuals working at the law office. Even the most technologically advanced software cannot prevent an attorney or a legal assistant from forgetting to enter a deadline in the case management system or putting in a wrong date when entering a docketing deadline.

SUMMARY

The practice of law is filled with appointments, deadlines, hearings, and other commitments that must be carefully tracked. Docketing means entering, organizing, and controlling appointments and deadlines for a legal organization. Case or practice management computer systems offer legal organizations a wide variety of features such as docket control, contact information, case notes, document assembly, document tracking, integrated billing, email, and conflict checking. Personal information managers (PIMs) such as Outlook are contact/ and calendar-based programs, as opposed to case management systems, which are matter-or case-based systems.

Case management systems have the ability to link and create relationships among contact information, matters/cases, events, and documents and to combine them into one integrated system. Other features include various calendar views, date calculators, notes/case diaries, synchronization with PIMs and personal digital assistants, time and billing interfaces, and reporting capabilities.

The docket control cycle of tracking legal/case events differs depending on whether a legal organization has a centralized, decentralized, or combined procedure for entering docket entries into a docket system.

Ethical considerations related to case management and docket control include an attorney's duties to perform work competently and diligently and to communicate regularly with clients. Failure of attorneys to complete work in a timely manner is a common reason for ethical and malpractice claims.

INTERNET SITES

Organization	Product/Service	World Wide Web Address
Abacus Data Systems	AbacusLaw (legal PIM/case management)	<http://www.abacuslaw.com>
Bridgeway Software	Law Quest (case management for corporate law departments)	<http://www.bridge-way.com>
Compulaw	Compulaw (case management)	<http://www.compulaw.com>
Data.txt Corp.	Time Matters (legal PIM/case management)	<http://www.timematters.com>
De Novo Systems Inc.	Trial De Novo (legal PIM/case management)	<http://www.denovosys.com>
Thomson Elite	Legal practice management system	<http://www.elite.com>
Thomson Elite	Pro Law practice management system	<http://www.elite.com>
Gavel & Gown Software	Amicus Attorney legal case management	<http://www.amicusattorney.com>
Lawex Corp.	Legal case management	<http://www.trialworks.com>
Legal Files Software	Legal Files (legal PIM/case management)	<http://www.legalfiles.com>
LegalEdge Software	Case management for criminal defense attorneys, prosecutors, and general law offices	<http://www.legaledge.com>
Software Technology	PracticeMaster (legal PIM/case management)	<http://www.stilegal.com>
ADC Legal Systems	Practice management system	<http://www.perfectpractice.com>
Client Profiles	Practice management system	<http://www.clientprofiles.com>
Orion Law Management Systems	Practice management system	<http://www.orionlaw.com>
Perfect Law Software	Practice management system	<http://www.perfectlaw.com>
RainMaker Software	Practice management system	<http://www.rainmakerlegal.com>
Corporate Legal Solutions, Inc.	Practice management system for corporate legal departments	<http://www.caseandpoint.com>
Solutions in Software, Inc.	Practice management system	<http://www.casemanagerpro.com>
Corprasoft, Inc.	Practice management system for corporate legal departments	<http://www.corprasoft.com>
Chesapeake Interlink, Ltd.	Practice management system specializing in personal injury practices	<http://www.needleslaw.com>

Manual docket systems are prone to mistakes, are slow and cumbersome to administer, are generally inflexible, and fail to provide the amount of quality information that a computerized case management system can.

Two types of computer programs that can be used by a legal organization for docket control are generic calendaring programs and case management software.

Computerized case management systems can perform functions such as maintaining perpetual calendars, making recurring entries, alerting the user to possible scheduling conflicts, providing for centralized or decentralized case management, generating past due reports, performing document assembly, and tracking case information.

Most case management programs can generate many types of reports, such as daily calendar reports for an individual or a firm, per case docket reports, and free time reports.

Attorneys and law firms that fail to operate an accurate docket may be subject to malpractice lawsuits, and sanctions such as disbarment or suspension from the practice of law.

KEY TERMS

calendaring	case management	personal information manager (PIM)	recurring entry
docket control	statute of limitations		legal malpractice

TEST YOUR KNOWLEDGE

Test your knowledge of the chapter by answering these questions.

1. True or False: Calendaring and docket control are purely secretarial functions with little relationship to the practice of law.
2. _____________ is a legal specific term that always means more than just tracking appointments and schedules.
3. What is the difference between PIMs and case management programs?
4. True or False: The legal case management software market is very competitive and there is no clearly dominant program in the marketplace.
5. Case management systems allow the user to link or create relationships among which types of information? Name three.
6. What is a rule-based case management event entry?
7. What benefits do document assembly features offer to case management users?
8. True or False: Case management systems are universally accepted in most law offices and have a high success rate when they are implemented.
9. True or False: There is virtually no connection among ethical claims, legal malpractice, case management, and docket control.

ON THE WEB EXERCISES

1. Research and write a paper on computerized case management and docket control systems. Go to the Docket Control and Case Management Web sites in the Internet Sites section of this chapter. Obtain demonstration copies of the programs if you can. Compare and contrast at least two of the different products that are available. Which one were you most impressed with, and why?
2. Go to the ABA Center for Professional Responsibility at http://www.abanet.org, find the *ABA Model Rules of Professional Conduct,* and read and print out the Comments to Rules 1.1, 1.3, 1.4, and 1.7. Summarize what you found in a two-page paper.
3. Visit several bar association Web sites (including that of the Georgia Bar Association http://www.gabar.org) and find three articles on case management, docket control, or a related subject. Write a short paper summarizing the articles you found.
4. Visit the American Bar Association Technology Resource Center at http://www.abanet.org, and review any materials it provides on case management software programs. Write a short paper summarizing the article(s) you found.
5. Using a law library, state bar journal legal research database, or the Internet, write a paper that summarizes a minimum of three attorney discipline cases regarding the failure to complete work on time. Be sure to include an analysis of the case, the court's or tribunal's findings, the ethical rules that were at issue, the rules that were violated, and what discipline was imposed.

QUESTIONS AND EXERCISES

1. A legal organization is considering moving to a computerized case management system even though its manual system has worked adequately. Identify reasons why a computerized case management system is still a good idea to consider.
2. A medium-sized law firm handles most of its cases by appointing an attorney and a legal assistant for every case. How can a computerized case management system help in this situation?
3. Several of your firm's clients have complained because they never get notice of what is going on in their cases, what deadlines have been set, or even when to call after a major event has taken place in their cases. How could a case management system help?
4. Research your state's disciplinary proceedings regarding attorneys who have been disciplined for client neglect. Write a short paper on one of the cases.
5. Contact three legal organizations in your area, find out how they control or manage their docket (manual or computer method), explain their procedures in detail, and then compare and contrast the three.
6. Set up and maintain a docket of class assignments for a semester using a PIM such as Outlook or a word processor. For quizzes and assignments give yourself one three-day reminder before the assignment or quiz is due, in addition to recording the quiz or assignment itself. For exams or lengthy papers, give yourself three reminders: a ten-day reminder, a five-day reminder, and a three-day reminder, in addition to docketing the deadline itself.

END NOTES

[1] *Gore v. Rains and Block*, 189 Mich. App. 729, 473 N.W. 2d 813 (1991).

[2] John Caldwell, "Climbing the Technology Ladder," *Legal Assistant Today*, May/June 2001, 52.

[3] David Bilinsky, "Evolution to Practice Management," *Law Office Computing*, December/January 2003, 61.

[4] Kathy Ruff, "Time Out—Incorporation of a Tickler System Will Help You Best Utilize Your Time, Energy, and Resources," *Legal Assistant Today*, September/October, 1999, 70.

[5] David J. Bilinsky, "Having the Genie on Your Side: All You Have to Do Is Rub that Lamp...," *Law Practice*, July 2005.

[6] Andrew A. Adkins, III, "Case Management Might be Exactly What Your Firm Needs," *Legal Assistant Today*, May/June 2002, 49.

[7] Andrew A. Adkins, III, "Case Management Might be Exactly What Your Firm Needs," *Legal Assistant Today*, May/June 2002, 49.

[8] Kevin Grierson, "The Verdict Is Unanimous," *Law Office Computing*, August/September 2001, 12.

[9] Andrew Z. Adkins III, "Catching the Right Case Management System," *Law Office Computing*, December/January 2006, 64.

HANDS-ON EXERCISES

ABACUS LAW CASE MANAGEMENT AND DOCKET CONTROL

READ THIS FIRST!

I. Introduction – Read This!

AbacusLaw is a case management and docket control program. The AbacusLaw demonstration version is a full working version of the program (with a few limitations). **The program demonstration version times out 90 days after installation. This means that the program will only work for 90 days from when you install it. So, it is highly recommended that you do not install the program on your computer until you are actually ready to go through the Hands-on Exercises and learn the program.** When you are ready to install the program, follow the instructions below.

II. Using the AbacusLaw Hands-On Exercises

The AbacusLaw Hands-on Exercises are easy to use and contain step-by-step instructions. Each lesson builds on the previous exercise so please complete the Hands-on Exercises in order. AbacusLaw comes with sample data so you should be able to utilize many features of the program.

III. Installation Instructions

Below are step-by-step instructions for installing the AbacusLaw demonstration version on your computer.

1. ***Insert Disk1 supplied with this text into your computer.***

2. When prompted with "What do you want Windows to do?" select "Open folder to view files using Windows Explorer," then click OK. If your computer does not automatically recognize that you have inserted a CD, double-click the My Computer or in Windows Vista the Computer icon, then double-click the drive where Disk 1 is.

3. Double-click the AbacusLaw folder. Then, double-click the Setup.exe file. This will start the AbacusLaw installation wizard.

4. The screen in AbacusLaw Installation Exhibit 1 should now be displayed. ***Click Install AbacusLaw Programs.***

5. The AbacusLaw Installation window with the words "Welcome to AbacusLaw!" (see AbacusLaw Installation Exhibit 2) should now be displayed. ***Click "Next".***

6. The AbacusLaw License agreement window should now be displayed (see AbacusLaw Installation Exhibit 3). ***Click "Accept".***

7. The Select Components window should now be displayed (see AbacusLaw Installation Exhibit 4). ***Make sure all options other than "AbacusLaw"*** are deselected (see AbacusLaw Installation Exhibit 4). When you are done only "AbacusLaw" should have a check mark next to it. ***Click "Next".***

HANDS-ON EXERCISES

AbacusLaw Installation Exhibit 1

Copyright 2007 Abacus Data Systems, Inc.

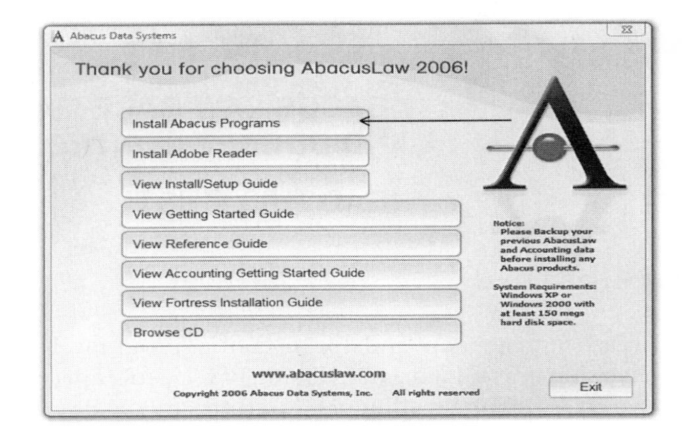

AbacusLaw Installation Exhibit 2

Copyright 2007 Abacus Data Systems, Inc.

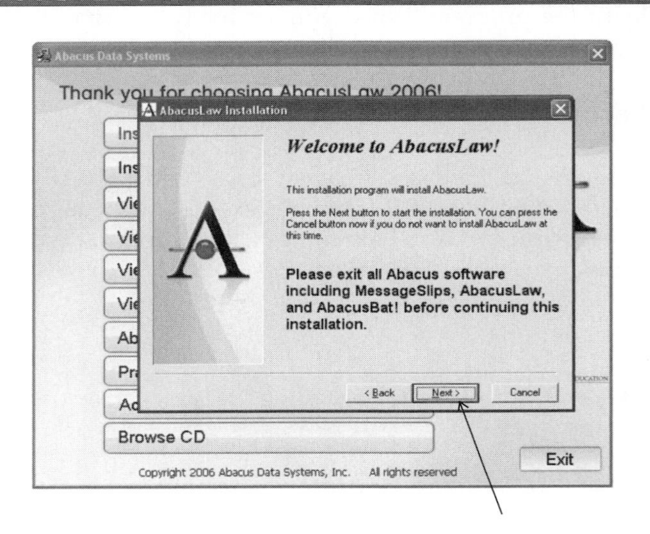

AbacusLaw Installation Exhibit 3

Copyright 2007 Abacus Data Systems, Inc.

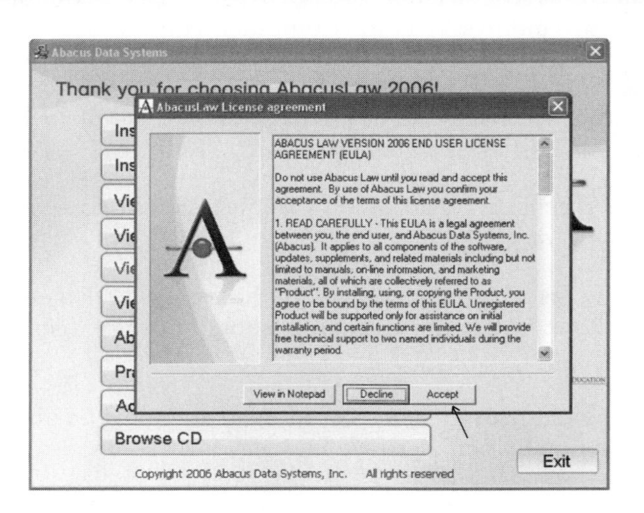

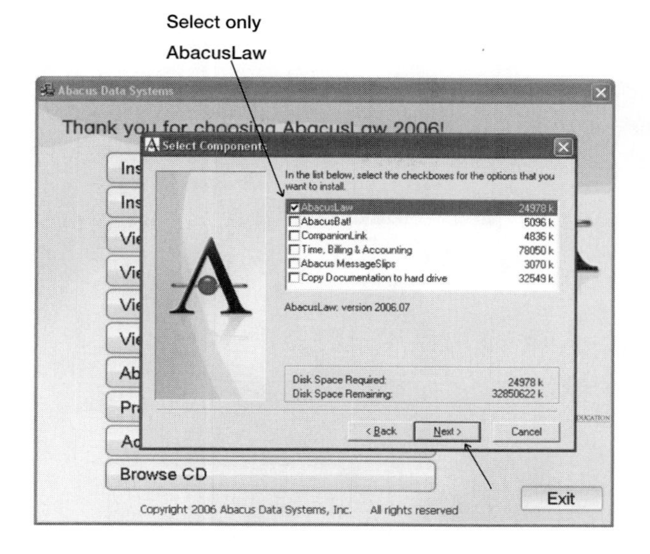

AbacusLaw Installation Exhibit 4

Copyright 2007 Abacus Data Systems, Inc.

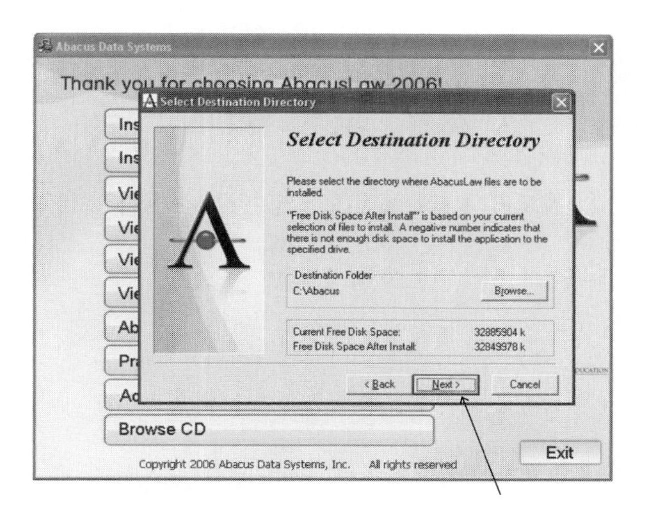

AbacusLaw Installation Exhibit 5

Copyright 2007 Abacus Data Systems, Inc.

8. The Select Destination Directory window should now be displayed (see AbacusLaw Installation Exhibit 5). While you could click Browse to change where AbacusLaw will be saved on your computer, it is not recommended that you change this setting. ***Click Next.***

9. The Installing to a Local Drive window should now be displayed (see AbacusLaw Installation Exhibit 6). It is recommended that you install the program on a local hard drive and not reset the destination directory, so ***Click No.***

10. The Start Installation window (see AbacusLaw Installation Exhibit 7) should now be displayed and the screen should say Ready to Install. ***Click Next.***

11. The Installing window should now be displayed and the program should start installing (see AbacusLaw Installation Exhibit 8).

AbacusLaw Installation Exhibit 6

Copyright 2007 Abacus Data Systems, Inc.

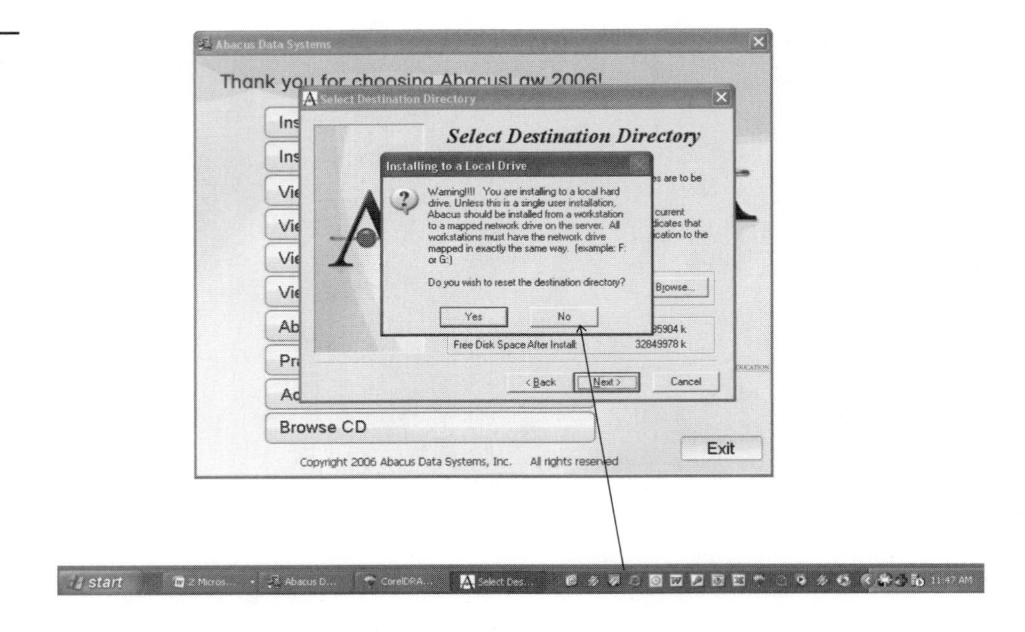

AbacusLaw Installation Exhibit 7

Copyright 2007 Abacus Data Systems, Inc.

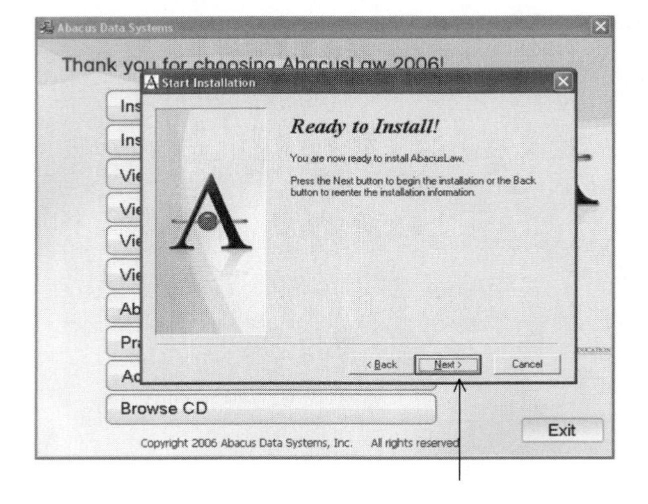

12. When the program installation is complete, the Run AbacusLaw window should be displayed. ***Click OK to open AbacusLaw.***

13. If the User Log on window is now displayed then the program has installed correctly. ***Click the red "X" in the upper right of the User Log on window, and when it asks you if you are sure that you want to exit AbacusLaw, click Yes. Note: If any further messages are displayed requesting that you setup a user account, click the red "X" in the corner of the message dialog box to close it. If you see a screen that says the installation is completed, just click OK.***

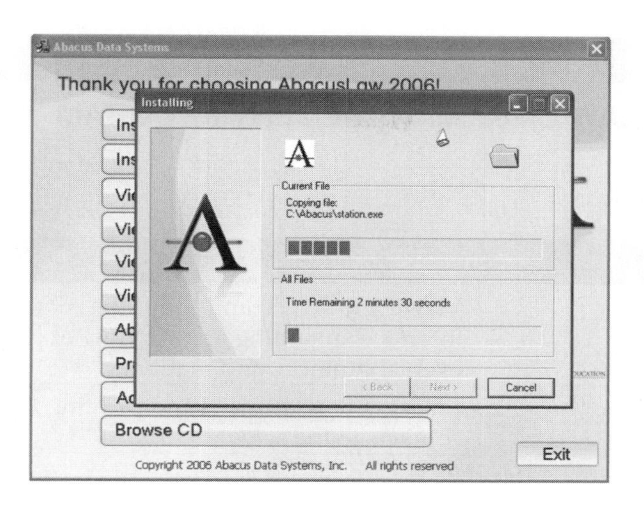

AbacusLaw Installation Exhibit 8

Copyright 2007 Abacus Data Systems, Inc.

14. This concludes the installation instructions for AbacusLaw.

15. You are now ready to start the AbacusLaw Hands-on Exercises on the next page.

IV. Installation Technical Support

AbacusLaw is a licensed product of Abacus Data Systems: However, if you have problems installing the demonstration version of AbacusLaw from the CD-ROM included with this text, please contact Thomson Delmar Learning Technical Support first at (800) 477–3692.

HANDS-ON EXERCISES

ABACUSLAW CASE MANAGEMENT PROGRAM

Basic

Number	Lesson Title	Concepts Covered
Lesson 1	Introduction to AbacusLaw	Viewing and learning about the AbacusLaw interface, including an overview of calendars, events, contacts, and matters.
Lesson 2	Entering New Contacts	Entering new contacts and printing a list of contacts to the screen

Intermediate

Number	Lesson Title	Concepts Covered
Lesson 3	Entering New Matters/Cases	Entering new matters/cases and associating them with clients
Lesson 4	Creating Events – Part I	Adding a staff person who can perform events; creating events, including appointments, reminders, things to do, and calls to be made
Lesson 5	Creating Events – Part II	Entering a recurring event, making a rule-based entry, and working with the date calculator
Lesson 6	Creating Linked Names, Linked Notes, and Checking for Conflicts	Associating a non-client linked name with a case, creating notes that are linked to contacts and matters, and checking for conflicts of interest

Advanced

Number	Lesson Title	Concepts Covered
Lesson 7	Linking Documents, Using the Call Manager, and Using the Form Generation feature	Linking documents, using the call manager feature, and using the form generation feature
Lesson 8	Reports	Running a number of event and matter reports

GETTING STARTED

Introduction

Throughout these lessons and exercises, information you need to type into the program will be designated in several different ways:

- Keys to be pressed on the keyboard will be designated in brackets, in all caps, and in bold (i.e. press the **[ENTER]** key).
- Movements will be designated in bold and italics (i.e. ***point to File on the menu bar and click the mouse***).
- Words or letters that should be typed will be designated in bold (i.e. type **Training Program**).
- Information that should be displayed on your computer screen is shown in the following style: ***Press ENTER to continue.***

OVERVIEW OF ABACUSLAW

AbacusLaw is a full-featured legal case management program. AbacusLaw Exhibit 1 shows the daily organizer calendar and the program's menu bar and toolbar. With AbacusLaw, users can track case information; create and manage contract information for clients and others; make case notes and diaries; create calendar events that are tied to a case; and create a myriad of reminders, things-to-do, and calls-to-make entries. Users can also link electronic documents to cases, create forms and routine letters using its document assembly capabilities, make recurring calendar entries, create rule-based entries, search and query the database for information, and print reports. Additional information about AbacusLaw will be provided as you complete the exercises. By the end of the exercises you should have a good understanding of the basics of legal case management and AbacusLaw.

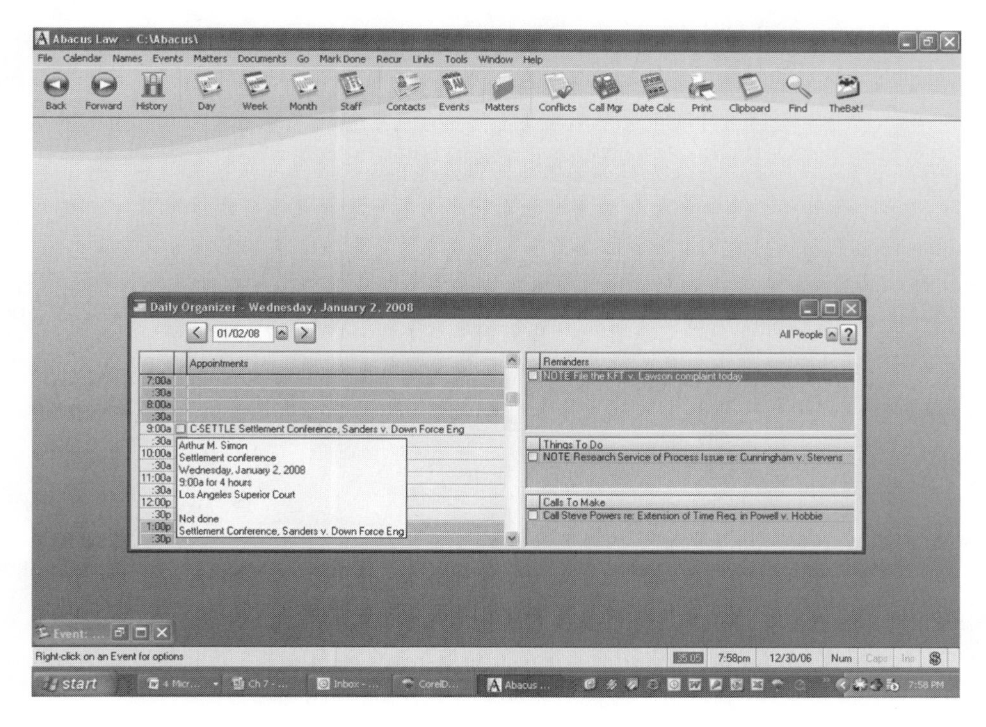

AbacusLaw Exhibit 1
AbacusLaw Daily Organizer, Menu Bar and Toolbar

LESSON 1: INTRODUCTION TO ABACUSLAW

This lesson introduces you to AbacusLaw. It explains basic information about the AbacusLaw interface, including an overview of Calendars, Contacts, Matters, and Events.

Install the AbacusLaw demonstration version on your computer, following the instructions at the end of Chapter 7. Note that the AbacusLaw demonstration version will time out (cease to work) 90 days after installation. Therefore, it is highly recommended that you do not install the program on your computer until you are ready to complete these Hands-on Exercises.

1. The first thing you will do in this lesson is to populate AbacusLaw with sample data. *If you start AbacusLaw from the icon on the desktop the sample data will not be loaded, so please follow these directions.*

2. Start Windows. ***Click the Start button on the Windows desktop point to Programs or All Programs, then point to the AbacusLaw group, and then click Sample Data.*** This will load Abacus with some sample data.

3. The User Log on window should now be displayed (see AbacusLaw Exhibit 2). Note that if you get a message requesting to you set yourself up as the first user, click OK and the AbacusLaw desktop (see AbacusLaw Exhibit 2) should say Sample Data.

4. In the User ID field of the User Log on window, **type your initials** (see AbacusLaw Exhibit 2). It is important that you enter the same initials each time you load Abacus. Do not type anything in the Password field. ***Click OK in the User Log on window.*** Abacus will notify you that only these initials will be valid to open the demonstration version of Abacus.

AbacusLaw Exhibit 2
User Log on Window in AbacusLaw
Copyright 2007 Abacus Data Systems, Inc.

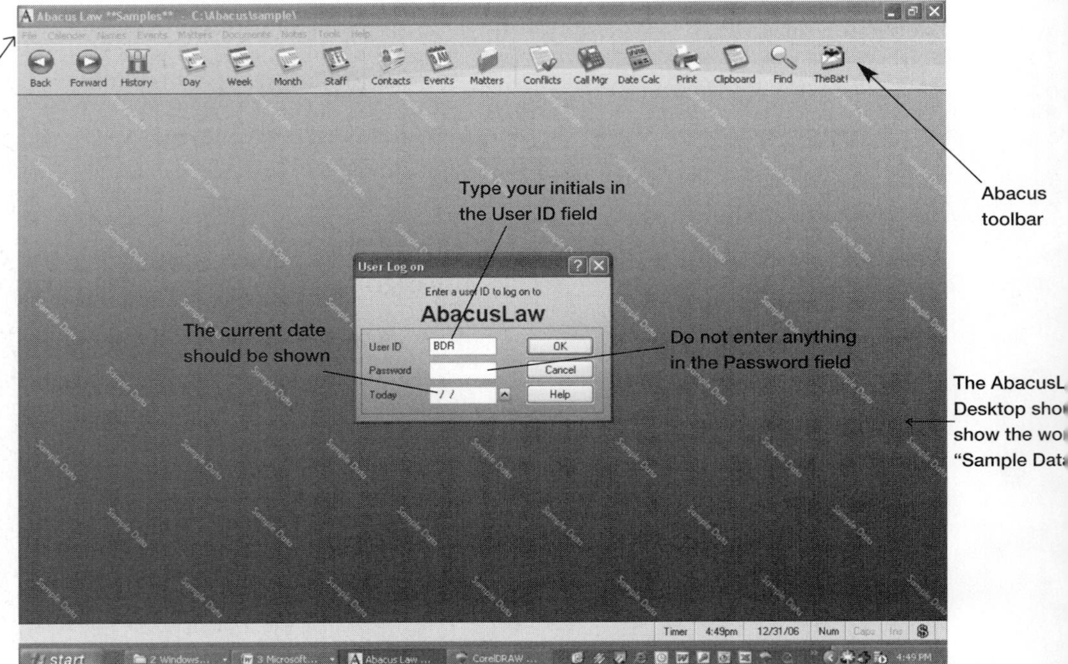

5. The Tip of the Day window should now be displayed on your screen. ***Click OK in the Tip of the Day window.*** You should now be at the Abacus desktop with the name plate "Your name appears here after registration."

6. ***Click the icon that says Day on the toolbar.*** AbacusLaw refers to this as the Daily Organizer. (To see the name of any icon, just hover the mouse pointer on the icon for a second and its name will appear.)

7. The Daily Organizer window should now be displayed for the current day. The Daily Organizer is where the user manages his or her daily calendar. The current date should be displayed at the top of the Daily Organizer window. ***Click the current date in the Daily Organizer,*** type **070207,** and then press the **[ENTER]** key.

8. Your screen should now look similar to AbacusLaw Exhibit 3, except that the Who setting for the Calendars window is not yet open. This is sample data that was already loaded in the program. ***Click the less-than sign (<) which is the Previous Day icon next to the date 07/02/07 in the Daily Organizer window (see AbacusLaw Exhibit 3).*** The date field should now show 07/01/07.

9. ***Click the greater-than sign (>) which is the Next Day icon next to the date 07/01/07 in the Daily Organizer window (see AbacusLaw Exhibit 3).*** The date should once again be 07/02/07.

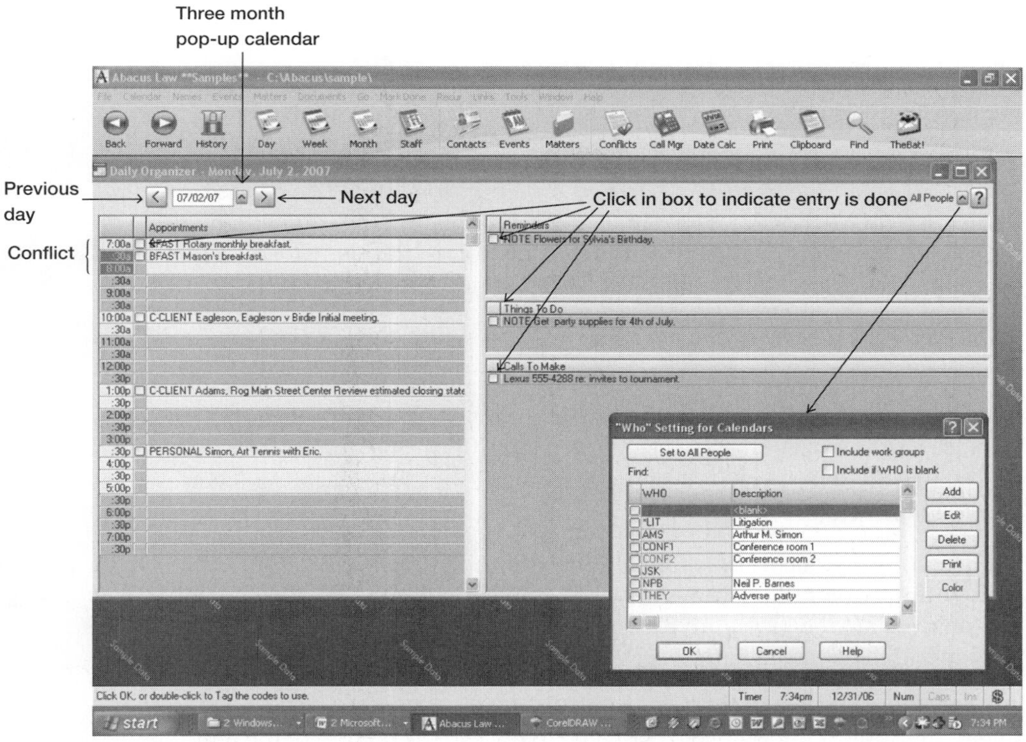

AbacusLaw Exhibit 3
Daily Organizer View for July 2, 2007

10. ***Click the up arrow just to the right of the date 07/02/07.*** This is the three-month pop-up calendar. By clicking on the left and right arrows in the three-month calendar, you can go backward or forward three months at a time. ***Click the Close icon (a red square with a white "X" in it) in the upper right corner of the three-month calendar window to close the window.***

11. Notice in the Daily Organizer at 7:30 a. and 8:00 a. that these appointments are in red. This indicates a scheduling conflict. However, notice also the up arrow next to All People in the upper right of the Daily Organizer window. "All People" means that you are looking at the Daily Organizer for everyone in the office. Because everyone's calendar is being shown at the same time in the Daily Organizer, there may or may not be an actual scheduling conflict, since one person could be going to one breakfast, and another person going to the other breakfast.

12. ***Point and click on the up arrow next to All People (see AbacusLaw Exhibit 3).*** Notice that the 'Who' Setting for Calendars window is displayed ***(see AbacusLaw Exhibit 3).*** Notice that several people as well as several conference rooms are listed.

13. ***Click the box to the left of AMS (Arthur M. Simon) in the 'Who' Setting for Calendars window. Then, click OK at the bottom of the 'Who' Setting for Calendars window.*** The upper right of the Daily Organizer window now shows the name "Arthur Simon," so you are just looking at his schedule now. Notice that one of the breakfast entries for the morning is now gone, so there is no actual scheduling conflict.

14. ***Double-click NOTE Flowers for Sylvia's Birthday in the Reminder section of the Daily Organizer window.*** The Event window for this note is now displayed. Notice at the bottom of the Event window that the field is blank next to Name and Matter. This means that the event is not related or associated with a

contact name or matter. *Note:* If you do not see the Name and Matter fields, click the More button in the Event window.

15. Notice also that there is an "N" displayed at the bottom of the window next to the Status field. ***Click the up arrow to the right of the "N" on the Status line.*** The Valid STATUS Entries window is now displayed. This is where the user can indicate if the item has been completed or not. ***Click the Close icon (the red square with a white "X") in the Valid STATUS Entries window.***

16. ***Click the Close icon (the red square with a white "X") in the Event window.***

17. Look again at the "Flowers for Sylvia's Birthday" reminder and notice that to the left of it there is a an empty white box (***see AbacusLaw Exhibit 3).*** When a user clicks the box a check mark appears and indicates the item is completed. Notice that all of the event entries have the white box for indicating when an item has been completed.

18. ***Point to the 7:00 a entry for "Rotary Monthly breakfast".*** Notice that a light yellow drop-down box shows additional information regarding the entry. You can point at any entry on any calendar and see the expanded information without having to open the item.

19. ***Double-click the 10:00 a entry for "*****Eagleson v. Birdie** ***Initial Meeting."*** The Event window should now be displayed. Notice at the bottom of the window that next to the Name field that Eagleson, George is shown (see AbacusLaw Exhibit 4). Also, notice that next to the Matter field the case of *Eagleson v. Birdie* is shown. This indicates that this event – a client conference – is linked to "Eagleson, Geroge" in the Contacts list, and is also linked to the matter (case) of *Eagleson v. Birdie.*

20. ***Click the Close icon (the red square with a white "X") in the Event window to close it.***

21. ***Click the Close icon (the red square with a white "X") in the Daily Organizer window to close it.***

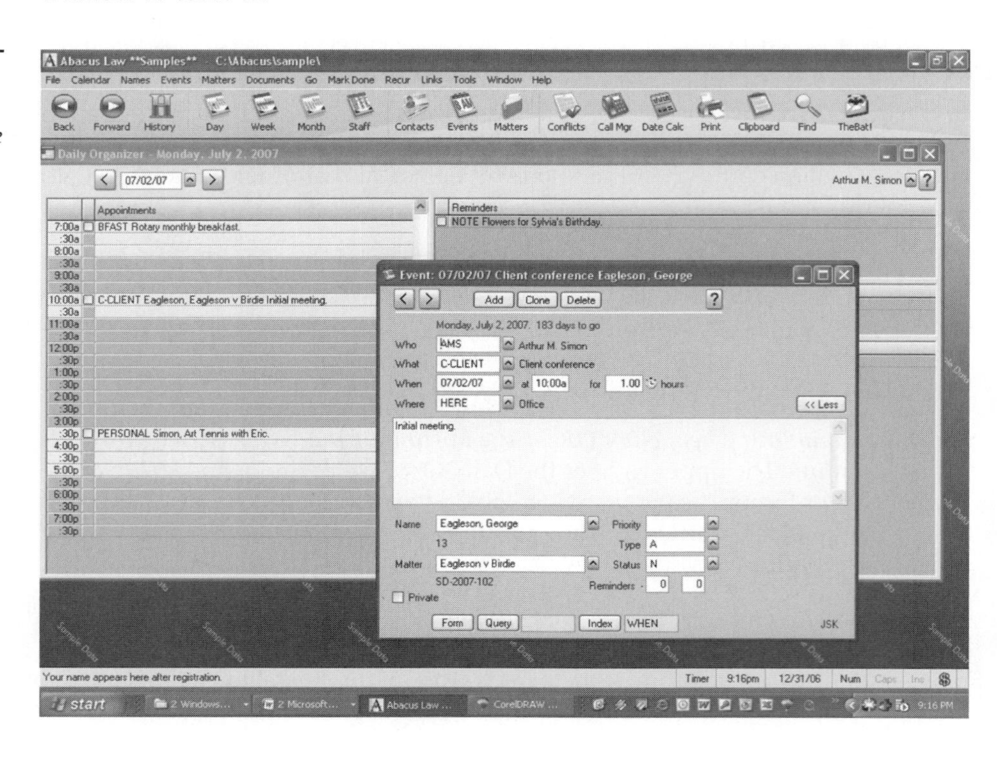

AbacusLaw Exhibit 4
Event Window for a Client Conference Linked to a Name and a Matter

22. ***Click the Contacts icon on the toolbar.*** The Names Browse window should now be displayed ***(see AbacusLaw Exhibit 5).*** Press the **[HOME]** key if the first entry, "A T & T," is not selected. Notice that in the Names Browse window there are three columns: Name, ID, and Class. You can easily see the different types of contacts by looking at the Class field. For each name you can see the class of the entry. For example, "Adams, Roger" has a class of Client. Notice also that the contact information for each name is displayed on the right side of the Names Browse window when a client is selected.

23. ***Click the right arrow in the horizontal scroll bar (see AbacusLaw Exhibit 5) to scroll to the right and see the additional fields in the window.***

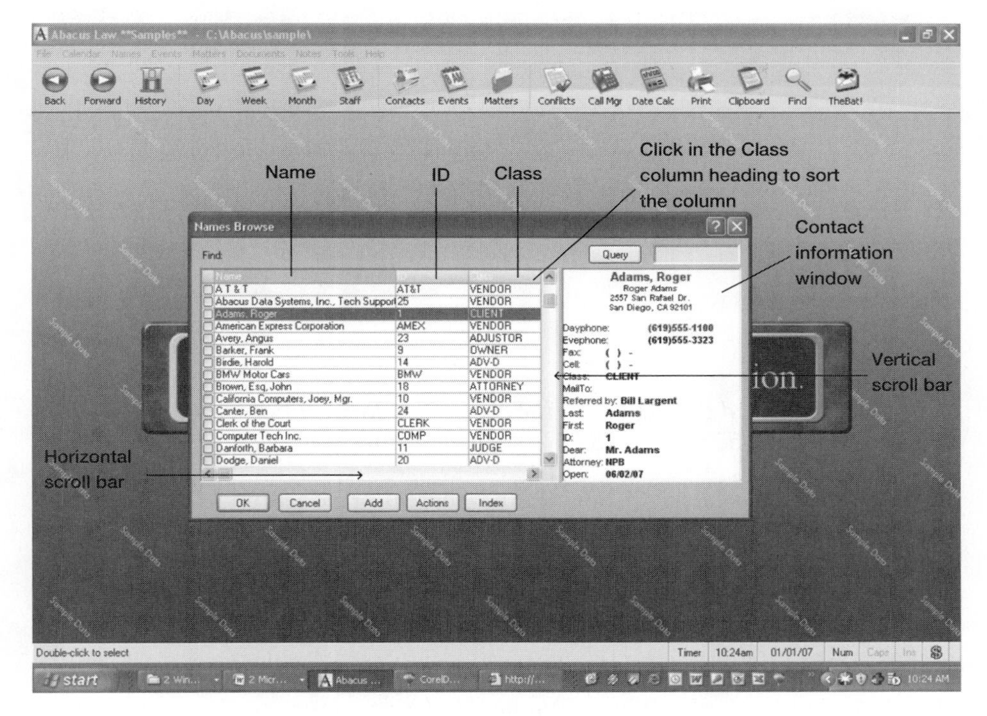

AbacusLaw Exhibit 5
Contacts—Names Browse Window
Copyright 2007 Abacus Data Systems, Inc.

24. ***Click the left arrow in the horizontal scroll bar to once again display the Name, ID, and Class fields.***

25. ***Click the Adams, Roger name. Then, click the column heading Class.*** This will sort the name entries by class. Notice all of the client entries.

26. ***Click the Names column heading*** to display the contacts sorted by name.

27. ***Double-click on the Adams, Roger entry.***

28. The Name: Adams, Roger window should now be displayed ***(see Abacus-Law Exhibit 6).*** Notice that a picture of the person can be attached to the name entry. This window is where users enter information about each contact.

29. ***Click the Notes tab in the Name window.*** Notice that the first note is a phone entry; the full text of the phone entry is displayed in the right portion of the Name window.

30. ***Click the Linked Matters tab in the Name window.*** Notice that one matter is shown, "Main Street Center" (a real estate matter).

AbacusLaw Exhibit 6
Name Window
Copyright 2007 Abacus Data Systems, Inc.

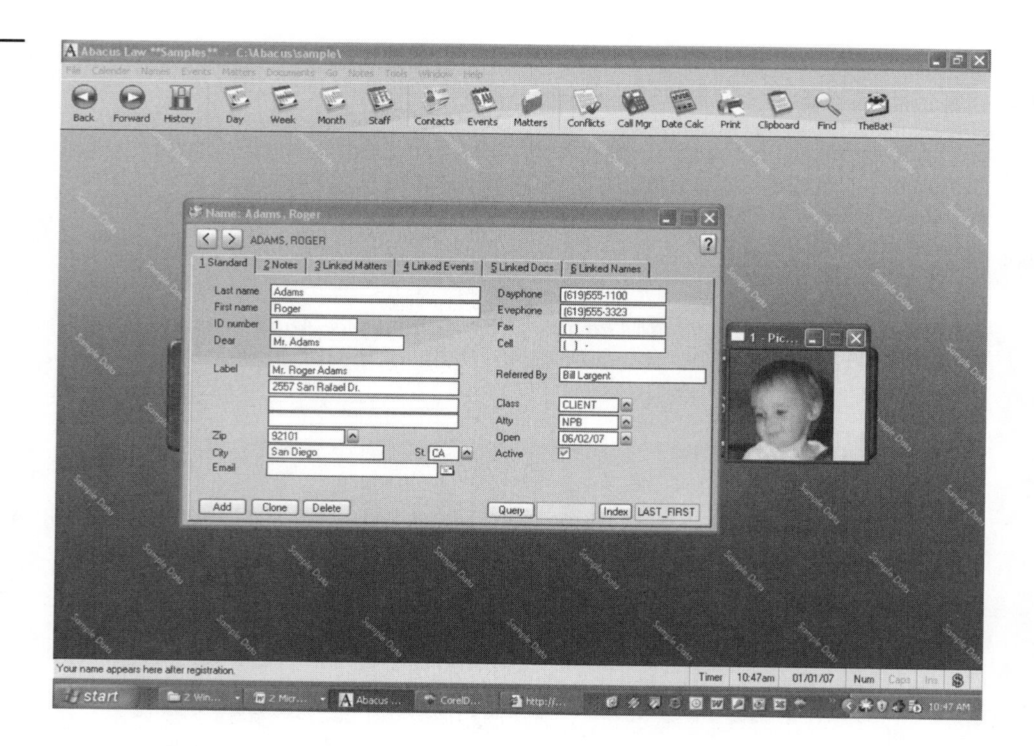

31. ***Click the Linked Events tab in the Name window.*** Notice that you can scroll to the right to see the other fields in the event entries.

32. ***Click the Linked Docs tab.*** Notice that there is one document listed. This is a welcome document that was sent to the client.

33. ***Click the Linked Names tab.*** Notice that one name, "Barker, Frank," is listed. Mr. Barker is the owner of the Main Street Center building that Roger Adams is purchasing.

34. ***Click the Standard tab in the Name window to return to the contact information for Roger Adams.***

35. ***Click the Close icon (the red square with a white "X") in the Name window to close it.***

36. ***Click Matters on the toolbar.*** The Matters Browse window should now be displayed (see AbacusLaw Exhibit 7). ***Select the Main Street Center case*** and notice that information about the case is shown on the right side of the Matters Browse window. Notice also that the third column header says "Casecode." This column lists the type of case for each matter.

37. ***Click the column heading Casecode.*** Press the **[HOME]** key to go to the beginning of the list. Notice that several types of cases are listed.

38. ***Double-click on the Main Street Center matter in the Matters Browse window.*** The Matter: Main Street Center window should now be displayed (see AbacusLaw Exhibit 8).

39. ***Click each of the tabs in the Matter window.*** Notice that they are similar to the tabs you accessed in the Name window.

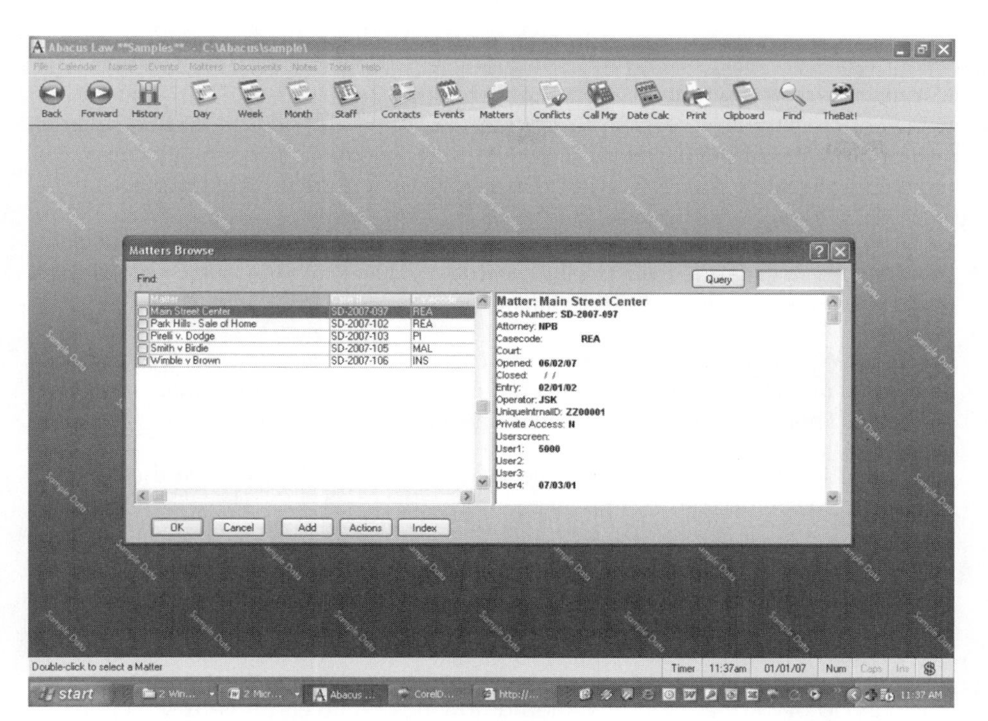

AbacusLaw Exhibit 7
Browse Matters Window
Copyright 2007 Abacus Data Systems, Inc.

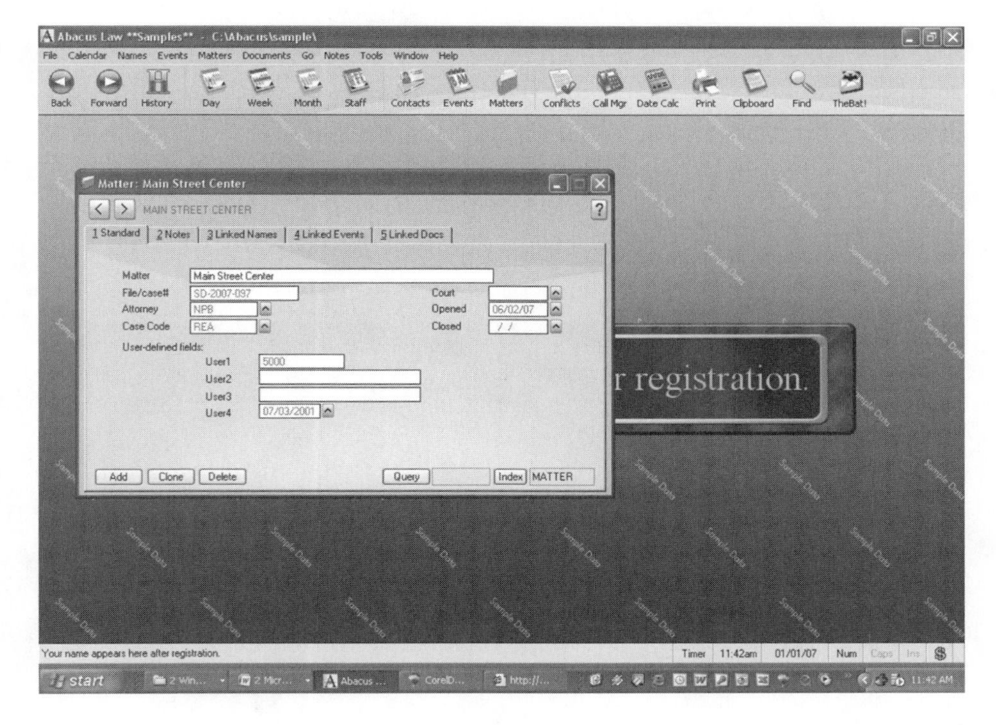

AbacusLaw Exhibit 8
Matter Window—Main Street Center Real Estate Transaction
Copyright 2007 Abacus Data Systems, Inc.

40. ***Click the Close icon (the red square with a white "X") in the Matter: Main Street Center window to close it.***

41. ***Click File on the menu bar and then click Exit (the very last entry under the Recent Files Accessed list).***

42. At the "Please register now!" window ***click OK.***

This concludes Lesson 1.

LESSON 2: ENTERING NEW CONTACTS

In this lesson, you will learn to enter new contacts into AbacusLaw and print a list of contacts to the screen. In subsequent lessons you will link matters, events, and documents to the names you create in this lesson. This lesson assumes you have completed Lesson 1 and are familiar with the AbacusLaw interface.

1. The first thing you will do in this lesson is to populate AbacusLaw with sample data. *If you start AbacusLaw from the icon on the desktop the sample data will not be loaded, so please follow these directions.*

2. Start Windows. ***Click the Start button on the Windows desktop, point to Programs or All Programs, point to the AbacusLaw group, and then click Sample Data.*** This will populate Abacus with some sample data.

3. The User Log on window should now be displayed. Note that the AbacusLaw desktop should say Sample Data.

4. **In the User ID field of the User Log on window, type the same initials you entered in Lesson 1.** It is important that you enter the same initials each time you start Abacus. Do not type anything in the Password field. ***Click OK in the User Log on window.***

5. The Tip of the Day window should now be displayed on your screen. ***Click OK in the Tip of the Day window.*** You should now be at the Abacus desktop with the name plate that says "Your name appears here after registration."

6. ***Click Contacts on the toolbar.*** The Names Browse window will be displayed. ***Then, click Add.***

7. The Adding a new Name window should be displayed (see AbacusLaw Exhibit 9). Enter the following contact information into the "Adding a new Name" window. You can use the **[TAB]** key to go the next field or **[SHIFT]+[TAB]** to go

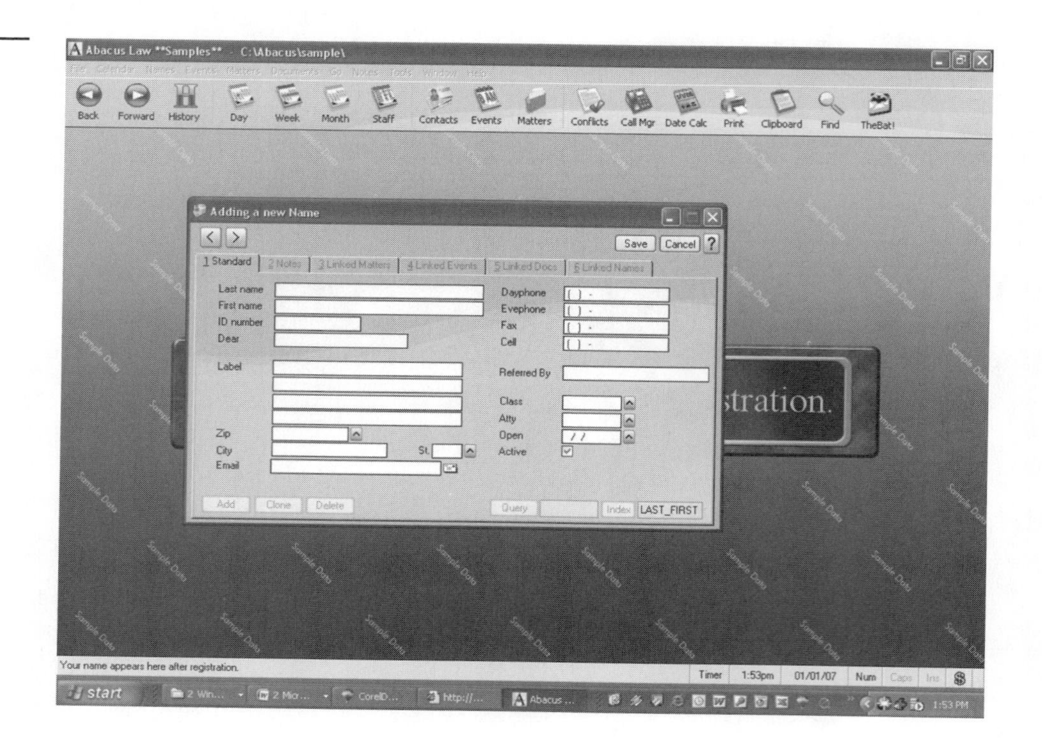

AbacusLaw Exhibit 9
"Adding a new Name" Window

to the previous field. You can also use the mouse to point and click in a field. When you come to a field below that is blank, just skip over it.

Field Name	Data to Enter
Last name	Lewis
First name	Debra
ID number	1001
Dear	Debra
Label	Debra Lewis
	34323 Creekview Ln
Zip	90014
City	Los Angeles
St.	CA
Email	dlewis@rr.la.com
Dayphone	323 555 2343
Evenphone	
Fax	
Cell	
Referred By	
Class	CLIENT
Atty	AMS
Open	06/01/08

8. When you have entered all of the information (your screen should look similar to AbacusLaw Exhibit 10), ***click Save in the Name window.***

9. You will now make three additional contact entries, including one additional client, one attorney, and one vendor.

10. In the Name: Lewis, Debra window, ***click Add to add another name***. Enter the data from the adjacent tables into AbacusLaw. *Note:* When you have completed an entry, click Save to save the record. Then, click Add to add the next record. Once the records are entered you can use the Previous Record (<) and Next Record (>) icons (see AbacusLaw Exhibit 10) to go between records if you need to.

Field Name	Data to Enter
Last name	Price
First name	Jerry
ID number	1002
Dear	Jerry
Label	Jerry Price
	1801 Campbell Ave
Zip	92037
City	La Jolla

continued

Field Name	Data to Enter
St.	CA
Email	jpprice@aom.com
Dayphone	858 777 8933
Evenphone	
Fax	
Cell	
Referred By	
Class	CLIENT
Atty	AMS
Open	06/01/08

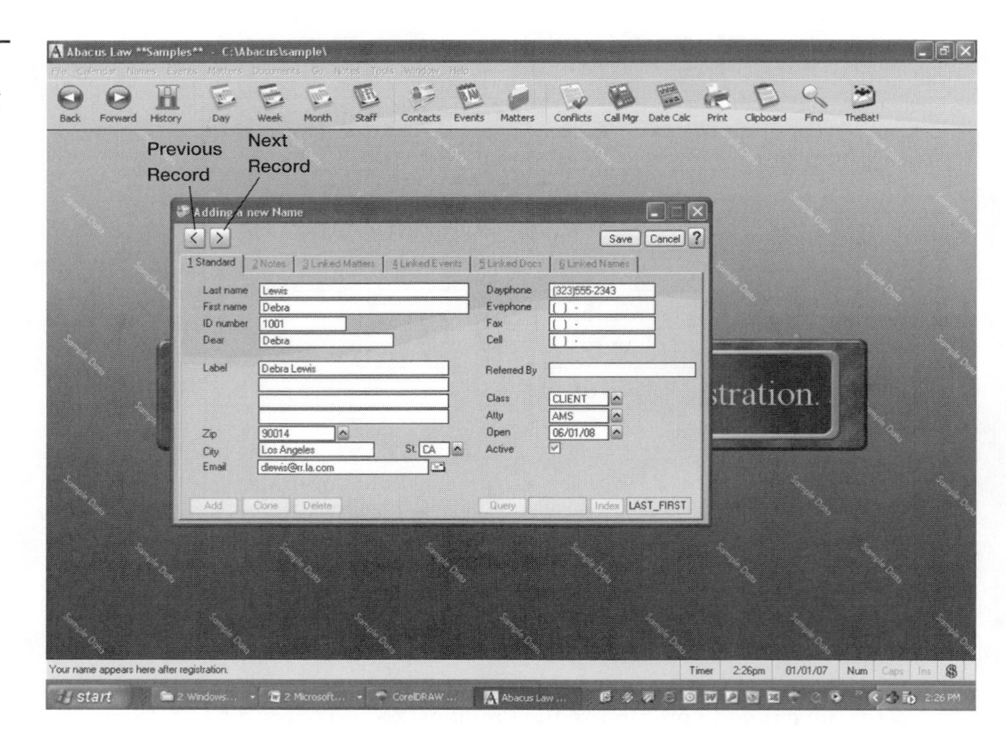

AbacusLaw Exhibit 10
Completed Entry—"Adding a new Name" Window
Copyright 2007 Abacus Data Systems, Inc.

Field Name	Data to Enter
Last name	Schneider
First name	Paula
ID number	1003
Dear	Ms. Schneider
Label	Paula Schneider
	Schneider, Kelley & Beal
	42001 Flowers
Zip	90014
City	Los Angeles

St.	CA
Email	pschneider@la.rr.com
Dayphone	323 989 8001
Evenphone	
Fax	
Cell	
Referred By	
Class	ATTORNEY
Atty	
Open	06/01/08

Field Name	Data to Enter
Last name	Rayburn
First name	Cindy
ID number	1004
Dear	Ms. Rayburn
Label	Cindy Rayburn
	Digital Media Equipment, Inc.
	9834 Overbrook Ave
Zip	92101
City	San Diego
St.	CA
Email	crayburn@digitalm.com
Dayphone	858 999 0003
Evenphone	
Fax	
Cell	
Referred By	
Class	VENDOR
Atty	
Open	06/01/08

11. Once you have saved the last record, ***click the Close icon (the red square with a white "X") in the Name window to close it.***

12. ***Click Contacts on the toolbar.*** The Names Browse window should now be displayed.

13. ***Click Query in the upper right of the Names Browse window. Click Quick Query in the drop-down menu.***

14. ***Click in the Last name field*** and type **Price,** then ***click OK.***

15. The entry for "Price, Jerry" should be displayed in the Names Browse window.

16. ***Click "Query."*** Then, ***click "Clear current query."*** The Names Browse window should now be displayed. Press the **[HOME]** key to go to the beginning of the list.

17. ***Click Actions in the Name Browse window. Then, point to Reports and click "All (in query)."*** The Names Report Control window should now be displayed. Notice next to "Output to" that "Screen" is selected. (*Note:* If "Screen" is not selected, ***click "Output to," then click Screen, then click OK.)*** You will be printing a Names report to the screen. ***Point and click on Print.*** If a printer window opens, just ***click Print.*** (*Note:* The program will not actually print the report to the printer at this time; it will only print to the screen). The "Names List" report should now be displayed.

18. ***Click the Exit icon (a red "X") on the toolbar. At the Names Report Control window, click Close.***

19. ***Click the Close icon (the red square with a white "X") in the Names Browse window to close it.***

20. ***Click File on the menu bar and then click Exit (the very last entry under the Recent Files Accessed list).***

21. At the "Please register now!" window, ***click OK.***

This concludes Lesson 2.

LESSON 3: ENTERING NEW MATTERS

In this lesson, you will enter new matters/cases and associate them with existing clients. This lesson assumes you have completed Lessons 1 and 2 and that you are familiar with the AbacusLaw interface.

1. The first thing you will do in this lesson is to populate AbacusLaw with sample data. *If you start AbacusLaw from the icon on the desktop, the sample data will not be loaded, so please follow these directions.*

2. Start Windows. ***Click the Start button on the Windows desktop, point to Programs or All Programs, point to the AbacusLaw group, and then click Sample Data.*** This will populate Abacus with some sample data.

3. The User Log on window should now be displayed. Note that the AbacusLaw desktop should say Sample Data.

4. In the User ID field of the User Log on window, type the same initials you entered in Lesson 1. It is important that you enter the same initials each time you start Abacus. Do not type anything in the Password field. ***Click OK in the User Log on window.***

5. The Tip of the Day window should now be displayed on your screen. ***Click OK in the Tip of the Day window.*** You should now be at the Abacus desktop with the name plate "Your name appears here after registration."

6. ***Click Matters on the toolbar. Then, click Add in the Matters Browse window.*** The Adding a new Matter window should be displayed (see AbacusLaw Exhibit 11).

7. Enter the matter information from the adjacent table in the Adding a new Matter window. You can use the **[TAB]** key to go the next field or **[SHIFT]+[TAB]** to go to the previous field. You can also use the mouse to click in a field. When you come to a field that is blank, just skip over it.

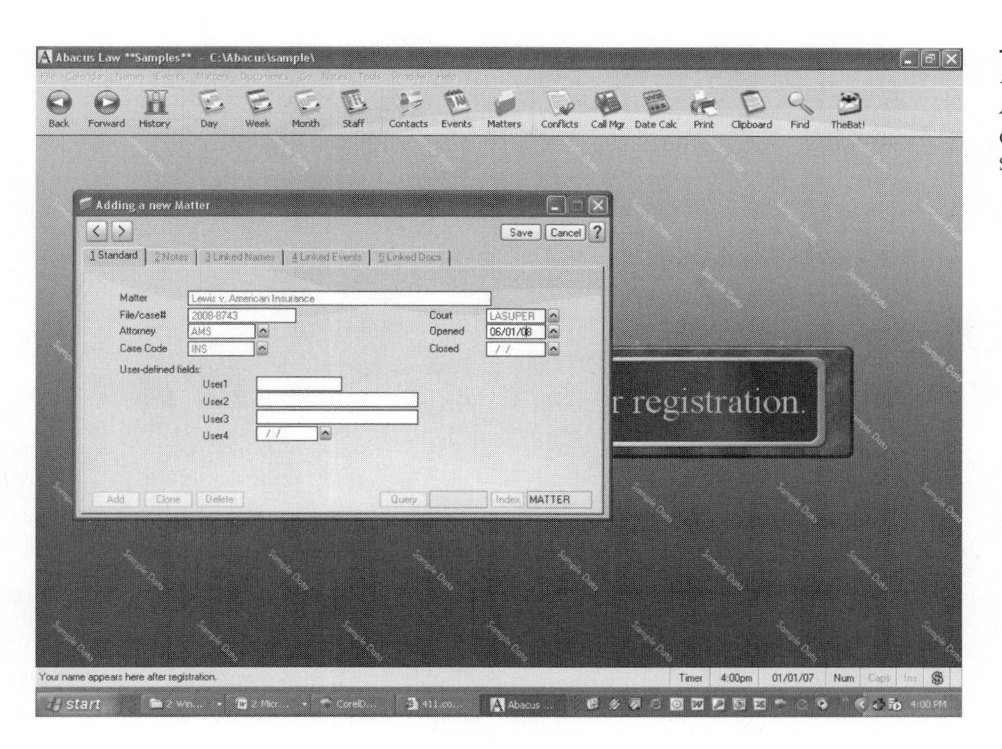

AbacusLaw Exhibit 11
Adding a New Matter
Copyright 2007 Abacus Data Systems, Inc.

Field Name	Data to Enter
Matter	Lewis v. American Insurance
File/case#	2008–8743
Attorney	AMS
Case Code	INS
Court	LASUPER
Opened	06 01 08
Closed	
User1	
User2	
User3	
User4	

8. When you have finished entering the information, ***click Save in the Adding a new Matter window.***

9. You will now create a link (or relationship) between Debra Lewis in the Contact portion of the program and *Lewis v. American Insurance* in the Matter portion of the program. ***In the Matter: Lewis v. American Insurance window, click the Linked Names tab. Click "Add link."*** The Names Browse window should now be displayed.

10. ***In the Names Browse window, scroll down until you see the entry for Debra Lewis and then click it. Then, in the Names Browse window, click OK.***

11. The Name-to-Matter Link window should now be displayed (see AbacusLaw Exhibit 12). ***Click the up arrow next to Link Type in the Name-to-Matter Link window.*** The Valid Link Types Entries window will now be displayed.

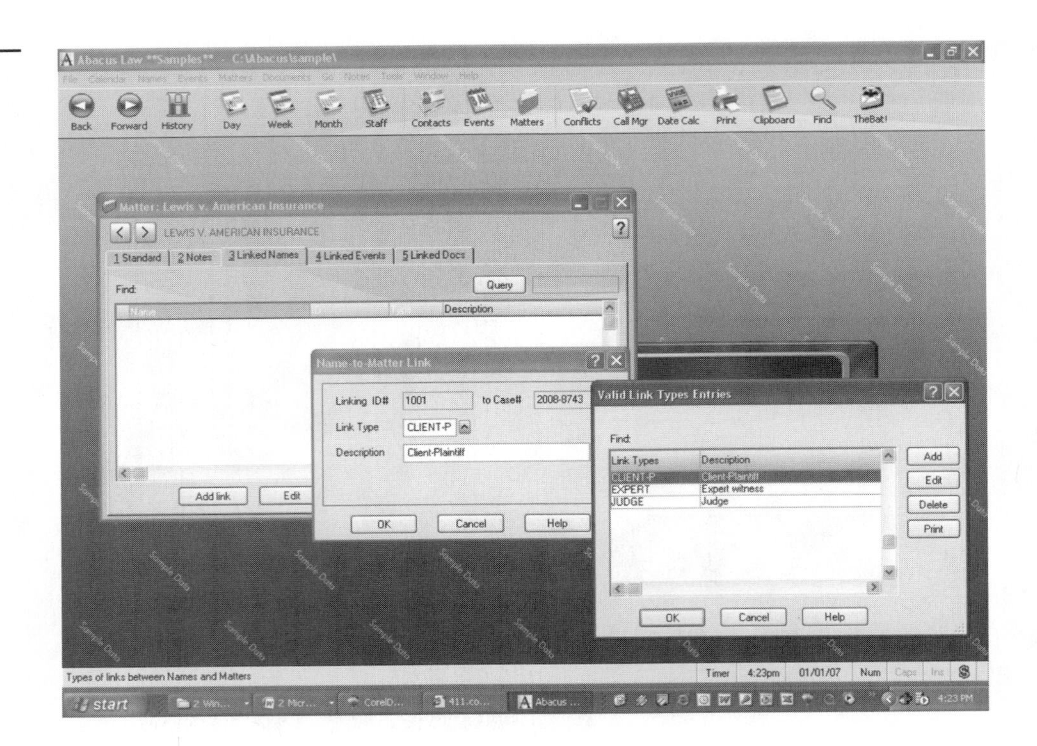

AbacusLaw Exhibit 12
Linking a Matter with a Name

In this window, scroll until you come to Client-P Client-Plaintiff (see AbacusLaw Exhibit 12) and then click OK.

12. ***In the Name-to-Matter Link window, click OK.*** Notice in the Matter: *Lewis v. American Insurance* window that the name "Lewis, Debra" now shows up in the Linked Names tab.

13. ***Click the Close icon (the red square with a white "X") in the Matter: Lewis v. American Insurance window to close it.***

14. Now, you will check to see if the "Lewis, Debra" entry in the Contact-section of the program is linked to the matter *Lewis v. American Insurance*. ***Click Contacts on the toolbar, and scroll until you find "Debra Lewis." Click "Debra Lewis" and then click OK. In the Name: Lewis, Debra window, click the Linked Matters tab.*** The *Lewis v. American Insurance* matter should be shown (see Abacuslaw Exhibit 13).

15. ***Double-click Lewis v. American Insurance in the Name: Lewis, Debra window.*** The Matter: Lewis v. American Insurance window is now displayed. The name and matter are linked.

16. ***Click the Close icon (the red square with a white "X") in the Matter: Lewis v. American Insurance window to close it.***

17. ***Click the Close icon in the Name: Lewis, Debra window to close it.***

18. You will now create one more matter and link it to another client. ***Click Matters on the toolbar. Then, click Add in the Matters Browse window.*** The Adding a new Matter window should be displayed.

19. Enter the matter information from the adjacent table in the Adding a new Matter window. *Note:* When you get to Case code, you will not see an existing

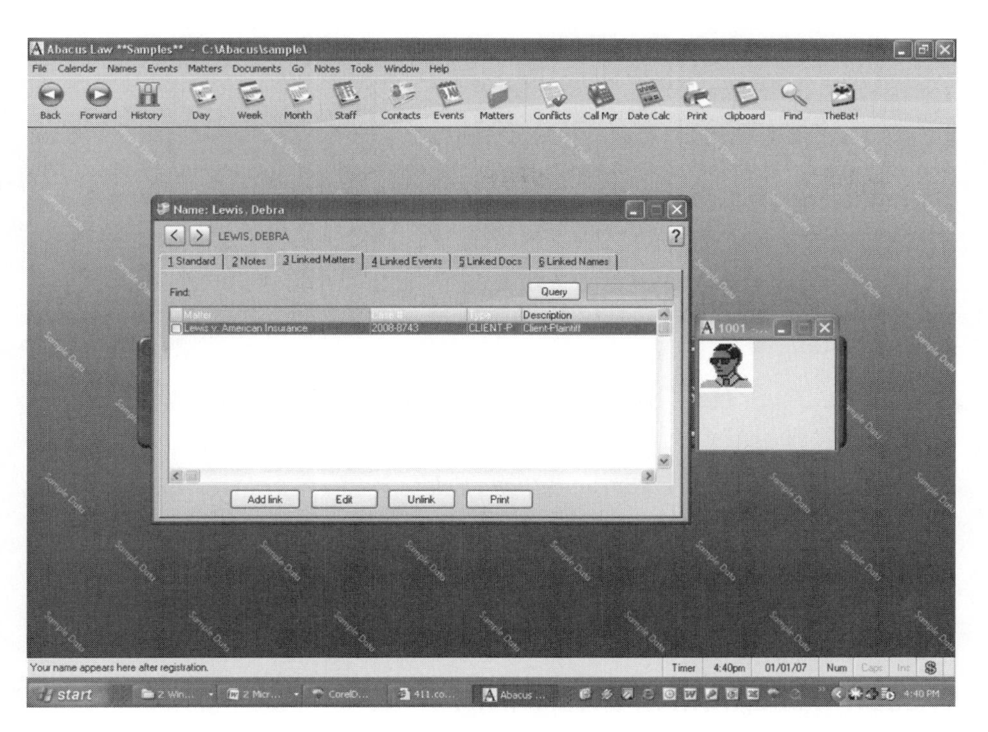

AbacusLaw Exhibit 13
A Contact Name Linked with a Matter
Copyright 2007 Abacus Data Systems, Inc.

entry for Adoption, so you will need to add it. In the "Valid CASECODE Entries" window, click Add. In the New 'CASECODE' Code window, type **Adoption** and then ***click OK.*** In the "CASECODE Code Description" window, type **Adoption in Family Court** and then ***click OK.*** Now, ***click Adoption in the Valid CASECODE Entries window and then click OK.*** A nice feature in Abacus is that you can create new items on the fly without having to get out of where you are and go to a special screen.

Field Name	Data to Enter
Matter	Price Adoption
File/case#	2008-A-203
Attorney	AMS
Case Code	ADOPTION
Court	SDSUPER
Opened	06 01 08
Closed	
User1	
User2	
User3	
User4	

20. When you have finished entering the information, ***click Save in the Adding a new Matter window.***

21. You will now create a link (or relationship) between Jerry Price in the Contact portion of the program and Price Adoption in the Matter portion of the program. ***In the Matter: Price Adoption window, click the Linked Names tab. Click Add link.*** The Names Browse window should now be displayed.

22. ***In the Names Browse window, scroll down until you see the entry for Jerry Price and click it. Then, in the Names Browse window, click OK.***

23. The Name-to-Matter Link window should now be displayed. ***Click the up arrow next to Link Type in the Name-to-Matter Link window.*** The Valid Link Types Entries window will now be displayed. ***In the window, scroll until you come to Client-P Client-Plaintiff and then click OK.***

24. ***In the Name-to-Matter Link window, click OK.*** Notice in the Matter: Price Adoption window that the name "Price, Jerry" now shows up in the Linked Names tab.

25. ***Click the Close icon (the red square with a white "X") in the Matter: Price Adoption window to close it.***

26. ***Click File on the menu bar and then click Exit (the very last entry under the Recent Files Accessed list).***

27. In the "Please register now!" window, ***click OK.***

This concludes Lesson 3.

LESSON 4: CREATING EVENTS, PART 1

In this lesson, you will add a staff person to the list of available people that perform work for clients. You will also create events, including appointments, reminders, and things to do, that are either related and unrelated to cases. This lesson assumes you have completed Lessons 1 to 3, and that you are familiar with the AbacusLaw interface.

1. The first thing you will do in this lesson is to populate AbacusLaw with sample data. *If you start AbacusLaw from the icon on the desktop the sample data will not be loaded, so please follow these directions*.

2. Start Windows. Then, ***click the Start button on the Windows desktop, point to Programs or All Programs, point to the AbacusLaw group, and then click populate Sample Data.*** This will populate Abacus with some sample data.

3. The User Log on window should now be displayed and the AbacusLaw desktop should say Sample Data.

4. **In the User Log on window, in the User ID field, type the same initials you entered in Lesson 1.** It is important that you enter the same initials each time you start Abacus. Do not type anything in the Password field. ***Click OK in the User Log on window.***

5. The Tip of the Day window should now be displayed on your screen. ***Click OK in the Tip of the Day window.*** You should now be at the Abacus desktop with the name plate "Your name appears here after registration."

6. The first thing you will do in this lesson is to add a legal assistant staff member to AbacusLaw. ***Click File on the menu bar, then point to Setup and click Codes….*** The Code Types window should now be displayed (see AbacusLaw Exhibit 14).

7. ***In the Code Types window, scroll down and click the "Who" code type and then click Edit codes*** (see AbacusLaw Exhibit 14). The Valid WHO Entries window should now be displayed.

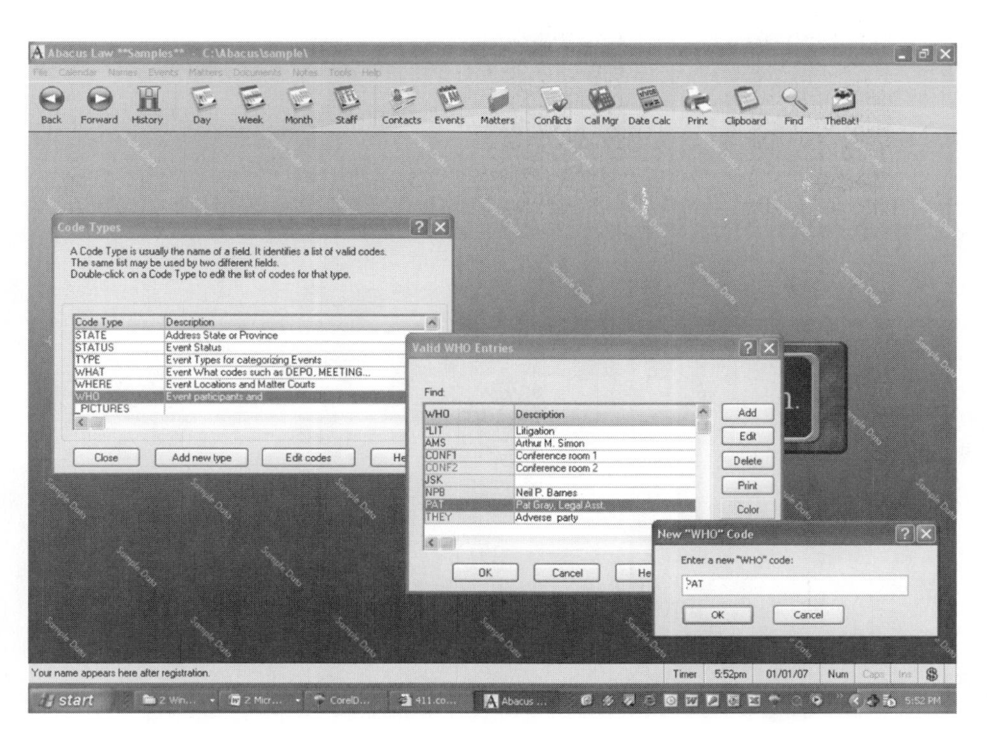

AbacusLaw Exhibit 14
Entering a New Staff Member in the "WHO" Code

8. *Click "Add."* The New "WHO" Code window should now be displayed (see AbacusLaw Exhibit 14). Under "Enter a new "WHO" code:" type **PAT** and then *click OK.*

9. The WHO Code Description window should now be displayed. Under "Description for PAT:" type **Pat Gray, Legal Asst.** ***and then click OK.*** The entry should now be entered in the Valid WHO Entries window. ***Click OK in the Valid WHO Entries window.***

10. ***Click Close in the Code Types window.***

11. You will now be entering a number of appointments, reminders, things to do, and calls to be made into Pat Gray's calendar. ***Click Day on the toolbar to load the Daily Organizer.***

12. ***Change the date in the Daily Organizer to 06 09 08*** and then press **[ENTER].**

13. ***Click the up arrow next to "All People" in the upper right corner of the Daily Organizer – Monday, June 9, 2008 window.***

14. ***Click Pat—Pat Gray, Legal Asst. and then click OK.*** Notice that the Daily Organizer is now set for Pat Gray, Legal Asst.

15. The first event entry you will make will not be linked to a case. ***In the Daily Organizer—Monday, June 9, 2008 window, double-click on 12:00p.***

16. The Adding a new Event window should now be displayed (see AbacusLaw Exhibit 15). *Note:* The Adding a new Event window can either be expanded (More) or contracted (Less). In AbacusLaw Exhibit 15, the screen is contracted, so to see additional options (such as name and matter) the user would just click More. The contracted screen is fine for this entry.

17. Pat should already be in the Who field. ***In the What field, click the up arrow.*** The Valid WHAT Entries window should now be displayed. There are many

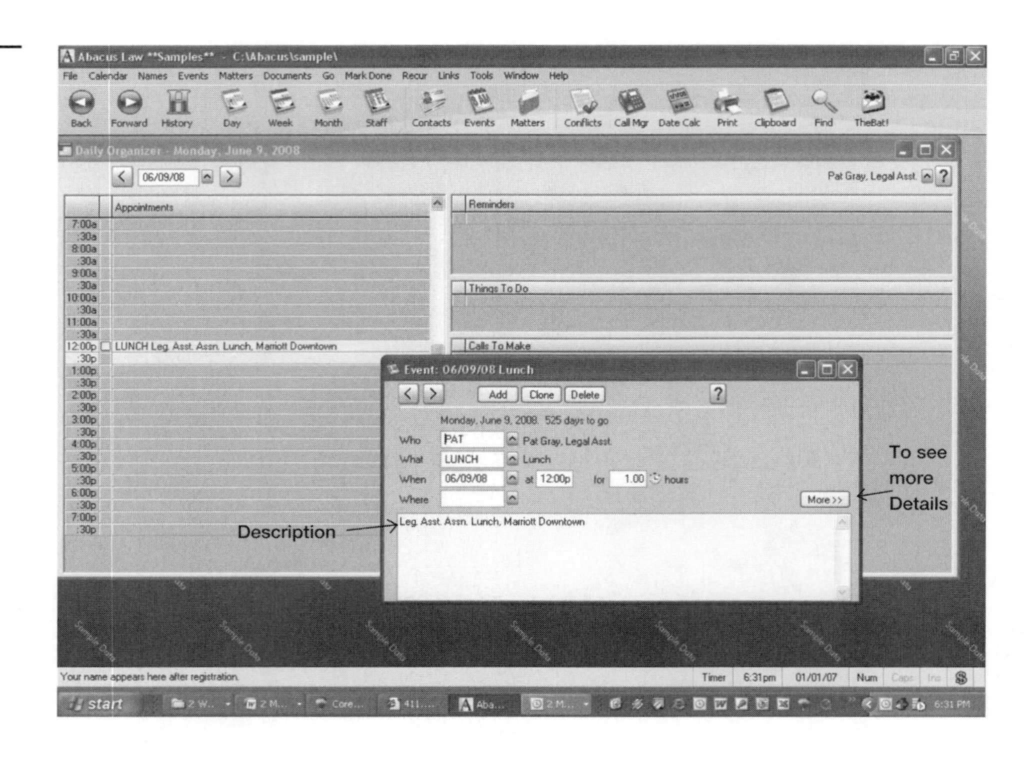

AbacusLaw Exhibit 15
Entering a New Event Not Associated with a Matter

entries in the screen, so type **L** to bring you to the WHAT entries that begin with L, ***click LUNCH, and then click OK.***

18. The date of 06/09/08 at 12:00p should already be entered. ***Click .50 next to "hours" and change it to 1.00.***

19. ***In the Description field*** (see AbacusLaw Exhibit 15) type **Leg. Asst. Assn. Lunch, Marriott Downtown.**

20. ***Click Save.*** The entry should now be made in your calendar (see AbacusLaw Exhibit 15).

21. You will now enter an event linked with a case. ***In the Daily Organizer—Monday, June 9, 2008 window, double-click on 1:30p.*** Because you will be linking the event to a contact and a matter, you need the expanded (More) version of the Adding a new Event screen. ***If you do not see the Name and Matter fields on your screen click More >> in the Adding a new Event window*** (see AbacusLaw Exhibit 15).

22. Enter the matter information from the adjacent table in the Adding a new Event window. You can use the **[TAB]** key to go the next field or **[SHIFT]+ [TAB]** to go the previous field. You can also use the mouse to click in a field. When you come to a field below that is blank, just skip over it. ***When you get to the Name field, just point on the up arrow, scroll to "Lewis, Debra" in the Names Browse window, and click OK.*** Because the "Lewis, Debra" entry is linked to *Lewis v. American Insurance,* the case should automatically appear in the Matter field.

Field Name	Data to Enter
Who	PAT
What	C-CLIENT
When	06/09/08 at 1:30 p for 3.00 hours

Where	HERE
Description (open light yellow box)	Discuss electronic discovery production issues with client
Name	Lewis, Debra
Matter	Lewis v. American Insurance
Priority	
Type	A
Status	N
Reminders -	3 5

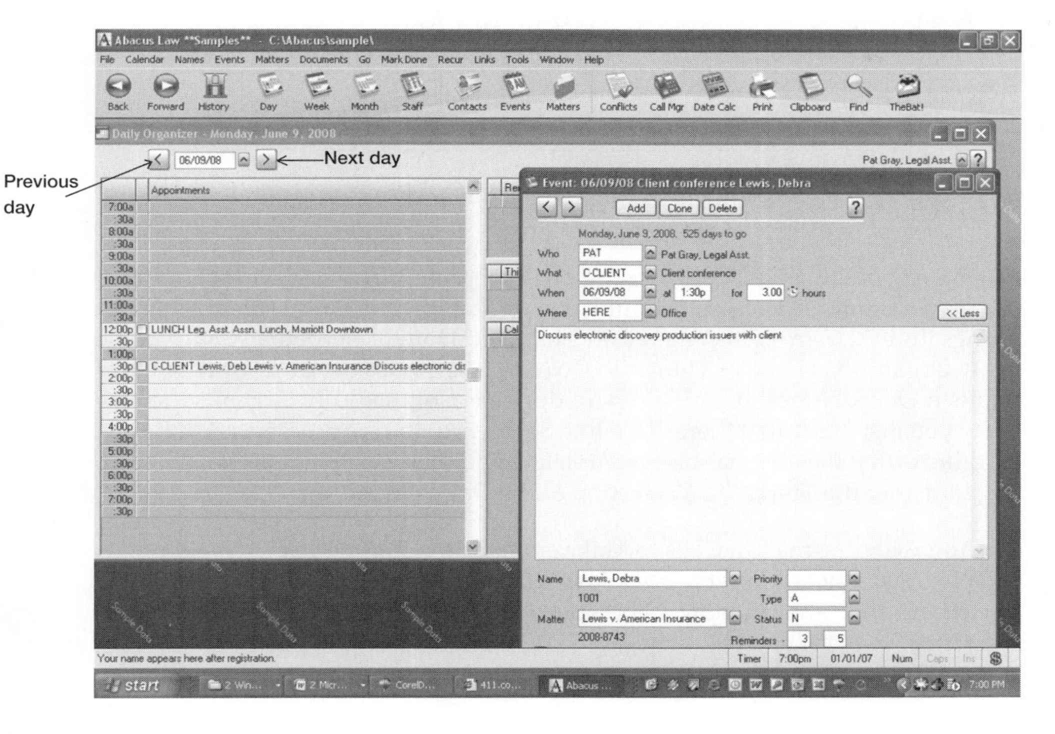

AbacusLaw Exhibit 16
Entering a New Event Not Associated with a Name/ Matter

23. When you have finished entering all of the data, ***click Save in the Adding a new Event window.*** The entry should now appear in your Daily Organizer.

24. You entered three- and five-day reminders for the entry you just made. Let's see if the reminders appear correctly in the calendar. ***Click on the Previous Day icon (<) just to the left of the date in the Daily Organizer*** (see AbacusLaw Exhibit 16) ***three times so the date 06/06/08 is shown in the Daily Organizer.*** The reminder for the client conference on 6/9/08 regarding electronic discovery should be shown in the Reminders section of the Daily Organizer.

25. ***Click the Next Day icon (>) just to the right of the date in the Daily Organizer*** (see AbacusLaw Exhibit 16) ***four times so the date 06/10/08 is displayed in the Daily Organizer.***

26. You will now make a Things To Do entry. ***In the Daily Organizer – Tuesday, June 10, 2008 window, double-click just below Things to Do.*** The Adding a new Event window should now be displayed. Notice that AbacusLaw entered "NOTE" in the What field. Also, in the When field next to the date of 06/10/08, it says "TO-DO" for this entry.

27. Enter the matter information from the adjacent table in the Adding a new Event window.

Field Name	Data to Enter
Who	PAT
What	NOTE
When	06/10/08 TO-DO
Where	HERE
Description (open light yellow box)	Send Digital Media Equipment, Inc. an email electronic discovery in Lewis case.
Name	Lewis, Debra
Matter	Lewis v. American Insurance
Priority	
Type	T
Status	N
Reminders -	0 0

28. When you have finished entering all of the data, ***click Save in the Adding a new Event window.*** The entry should now appear in your Daily Organizer under Things To Do. *Note:* Items entered in Things to Do will perpetually stay in the Daily Organizer section of Things To Do (once the data is overdue) until the user marks it Done. Notice in the Things To do section of the Daily Organizer for the entry you just made that there is a white box next to the entry. Users click the box to indicate that the item has been completed, and then the item does not show up any longer in the Things To Do section of the Daily Organizer.

29. You will now make a Calls to Make entry. ***In the Daily Organizer—Tuesday, June 10, 2008 window, double-click just below Calls to Make.*** The Adding a new Event window should now be displayed. Notice that AbacusLaw entered "PHONE" in the What field. Also, in the When field next to the date of 06/10/08, it says "TO-DO" for this entry.

30. Enter the matter information from the adjacent table in the Adding a new Event window.

Field Name	Data to Enter
Who	PAT
What	PHONE
When	06/10/08 TO-DO
Where	HERE
Description (open light yellow box)	Call Jerry Price to see if he and Linda returned from Russia with child.
Name	Price, Jerry
Matter	Price Adoption
Priority	
Type	P
Status	N
Reminders -	0 0

31. When you have finished entering all of the data, ***click Save in the Adding a new Event window.*** The entry should now appear in your Daily Organizer under Calls to Make. Notice that Abacus automatically entered the client's phone number in the entry. *Note:* You can also make entries in the Reminders section of the Daily Organizer by double-clicking just below "Reminders." Reminders just show up on the day they are scheduled for and do not carry forward from day to day, even if they are not marked as completed.

32. Create the following events.

Date: 6/10/2008 Appointment	
Who	PAT
What	DRAFT
When	06/10/08 at 9:00a for 8.00 hours
Where	HERE
Description (open light yellow box)	Draft Discovery Documents (IGs, RPDs, RAs)
Name	Lewis, Debra
Matter	Lewis v. American Insurance
Priority	1
Type	A
Status	N
Reminders -	1 0

Date: 6/11/2008 Things to Do	
Who	PAT
What	NOTE
When	06/11/08 TO-DO for 0.00 hours
Where	HERE
Description (open light yellow box)	Work on Depo. Summary of Plaintiff
Name	Lewis, Debra
Matter	Lewis v. American Insurance
Priority	
Type	T
Status	N
Reminders -	0 0

Date: 6/12/2008 Appointment	
Who	PAT
What	APPT
When	06/12/08 at 9:30a for 2.00 hours
Where	HERE
Description (open light yellow box)	Call immigration agency as scheduled re:adoption papers
Name	Price, Jerry
Matter	Price Adoption
Priority	1

Type	A
Status	N
Reminders -	1 3

Date: 6/11/2008 Appointment	
Who	PAT
What	APPT
When	06/11/08 at 9:00a for 3.00 hours
Where	HERE
Description (open light yellow box)	Draft responses to Defendant's IGs and RPDs
Name	Lewis, Debra
Matter	Lewis v. American Insurance
Priority	1
Type	T
Status	N
Reminders -	1 3

Date: 6/9/2008 Appointment	
Who	PAT
What	APPT
When	06/09/08 at 9:00a for 2.50 hours
Where	HERE
Description (open light yellow box)	Draft Amended Adoption Papers
Name	Price, Jerry
Matter	Price Adoption
Priority	
Type	T
Status	N
Reminders -	0 0

Date: 6/11/2008 Appointment	
Who	PAT
What	APPT
When	06/11/08 at 2:00p for 2.00 hours
Where	HERE
Description (open light yellow box)	Meet with Arthur to discuss electronic discovery issues and discovery responses
Name	Lewis, Debra
Matter	Lewis v. American Insurance
Priority	
Type	T
Status	N
Reminders -	1 0

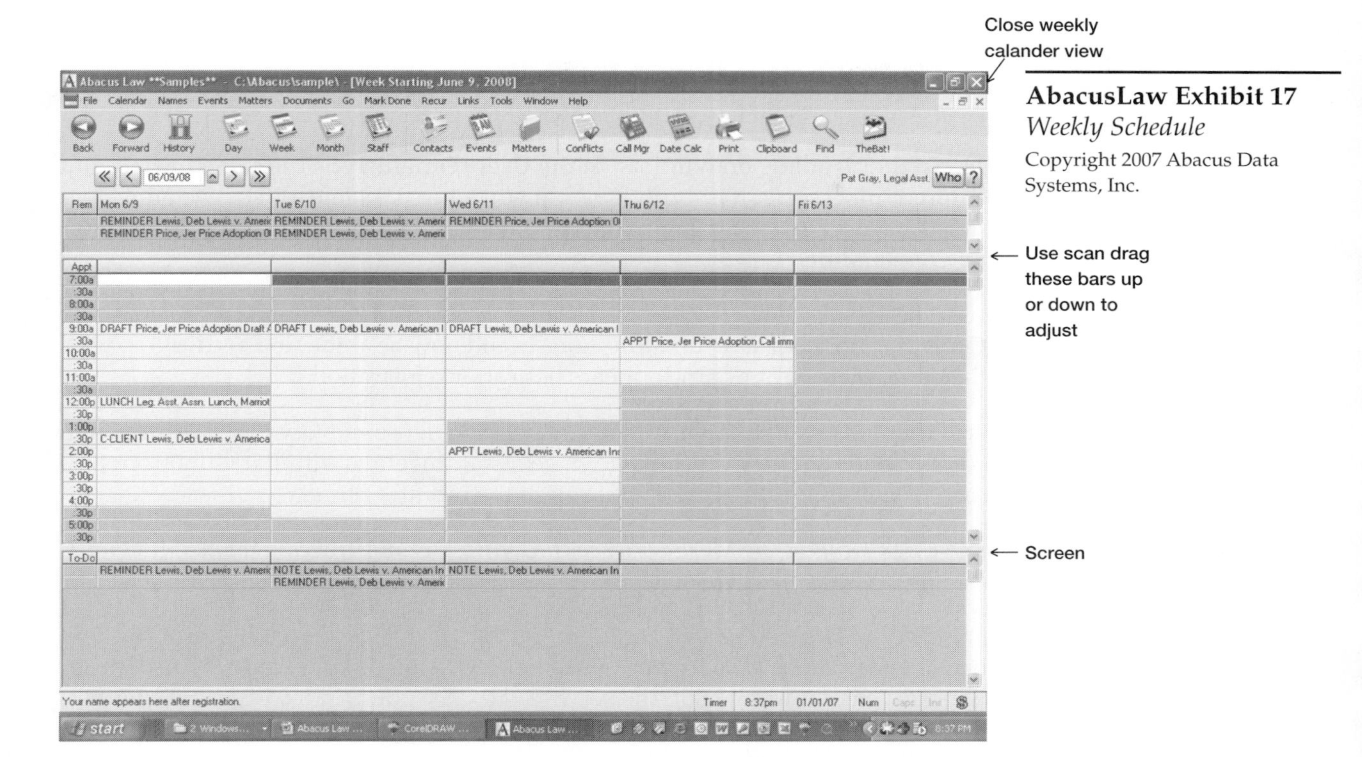
Close weekly
calander view
Use scan drag
these bars up
or down to
adjust
Screen

AbacusLaw Exhibit 17
Weekly Schedule
Copyright 2007 Abacus Data Systems, Inc.

33. After you have made all of the entries, ***click Week on the toolbar.*** Your weekly calendar for the week of June 9, 2008 should look similar to AbacusLaw Exhibit 17. *Note:* The gray bars that separate the reminders, appointment, and things to do sections can be dragged up or down to adjust how the information is viewed on the screen (see AbacusLaw Exhibit 17).

34. ***Click the Close (X) icon for the Weekly calendar view*** (see AbacusLaw Exhibit 17).

35. ***Click the Close (X) icon for the Daily Organizer.***

36. ***Click File on the menu bar and then click Exit (the very last entry under the Recent Files Accessed list).***

37. At the "Please register now!" window ***click OK.***

This concludes Lesson 4.

LESSON 5: CREATING EVENTS, PART 2

Rule-based entries are extremely efficient and can greatly enhance data entry. In this lesson, you will create a recurring event, make a rule-based entry, and work with the date calculator. This lesson assumes you have completed Lessons 1 to 4 and that you are familiar with the AbacusLaw interface.

1. The first thing you will do in this lesson is to populate AbacusLaw with Sample Data. *If you start AbacusLaw from the icon on the desktop, the sample data will not be loaded, so please follow these directions.*

2. Start Windows. ***Click the Start button on the Windows desktop, point to Programs or All Programs, point to the AbacusLaw group, and then click Sample Data.*** This will populate Abacus with some sample data.

3. The User Log on window should now be displayed. Note that the Abacus-Law desktop should say Sample Data.

4. In the User Log on window, in the User ID field, type the same initials you entered in Lesson 1. It is important that you enter the same initials each time you start Abacus. Do not type anything in the Password field. ***Click OK in the User Log on window.***

5. The Tip of the Day window should now be displayed on your screen. ***Click OK in the Tip of the Day window.*** You should now be at the Abacus desktop with the name plate "Your name appears here after registration."

6. You will next make a recurring entry that will occur every day. Arthur Simon has decided that he would like to have a staff meeting with Pat Gray from 8:30 a.m. to 9:00 a.m. every morning through the month of June.

7. *Click Day on the toolbar to see the Daily Organizer. Change the date on the Daily Organizer to 06/09/2008.*

8. *Double-click on 8:30a.* Create the events listed in the table. *Note:* You will need to add a new WHAT entry for the staff meeting. In the Valid WHAT Entries window, click Add; then, in the New "WHAT" Code window, type **STAFF MT**; then, in the WHAT Code Description window, type **Staff Meeting**. Finally, click on Staff Meeting and click OK.

Who	PAT
What	STAFF MT
When	06/10/08 at 8:30a for .50 hours
Where	HERE
Description (open light yellow box)	
Name	
Matter	
Priority	
Type	A
Status	N
Reminders -	0 0

9. Once you have finished creating the entry, ***click Save in the Event window.***

10. In the Daily Organizer, the STAFF MT entry you just created should be selected. ***Click Recur on the menu bar*** (see AbacusLaw Exhibit 18.) The Recur Event: Staff MT… window should now be displayed. ***Click Daily under Interval, change the End entry to 06/30/08, click the box to the left of "Omit weekend events," and then click OK.***

11. The "Select an option" window should appear and ask "Ready to schedule up to 21 events through 06/30/08. Are you sure?" ***Click "Yes."*** The Linked Events Browse window is then displayed (see AbacusLaw Exhibit 19). You can see all of the entries that the program is about to make. ***Click "OK."***

12. *In the Daily Organizer, next to the date, click Next day > several times and notice that the Staff Meeting has been added.*

13. You will next enter a new matter and learn how to make a rule-based entry for the new matter. Arthur Simon has told you that the firm will be handling a

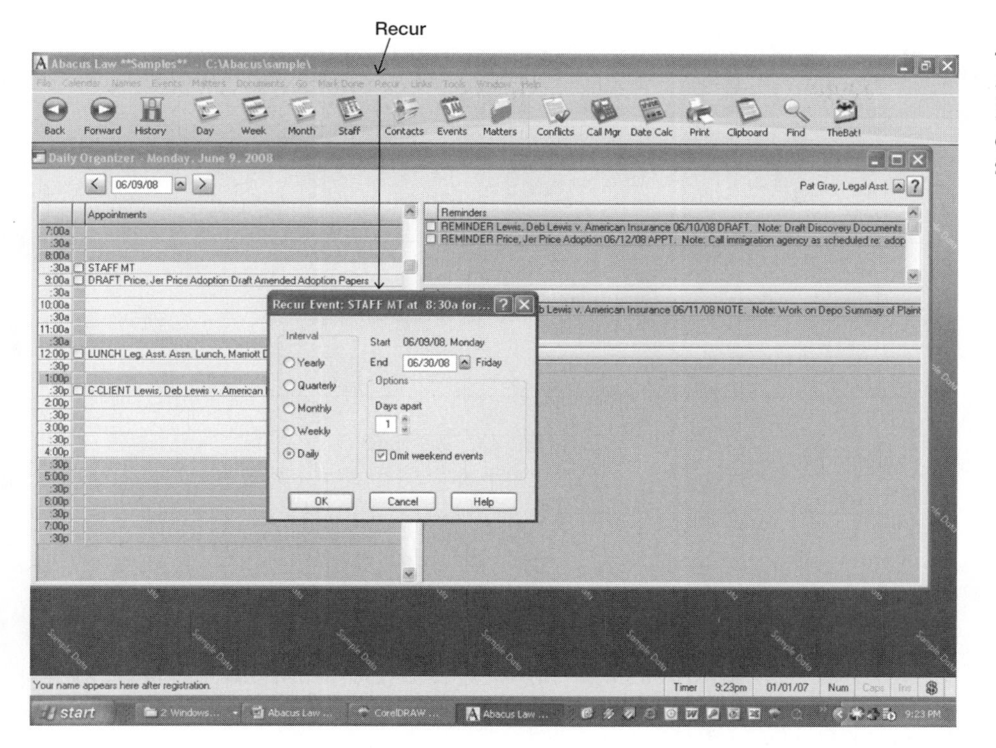

AbacusLaw Exhibit 18
Entering a Recurring Event
Copyright 2007 Abacus Data Systems, Inc.

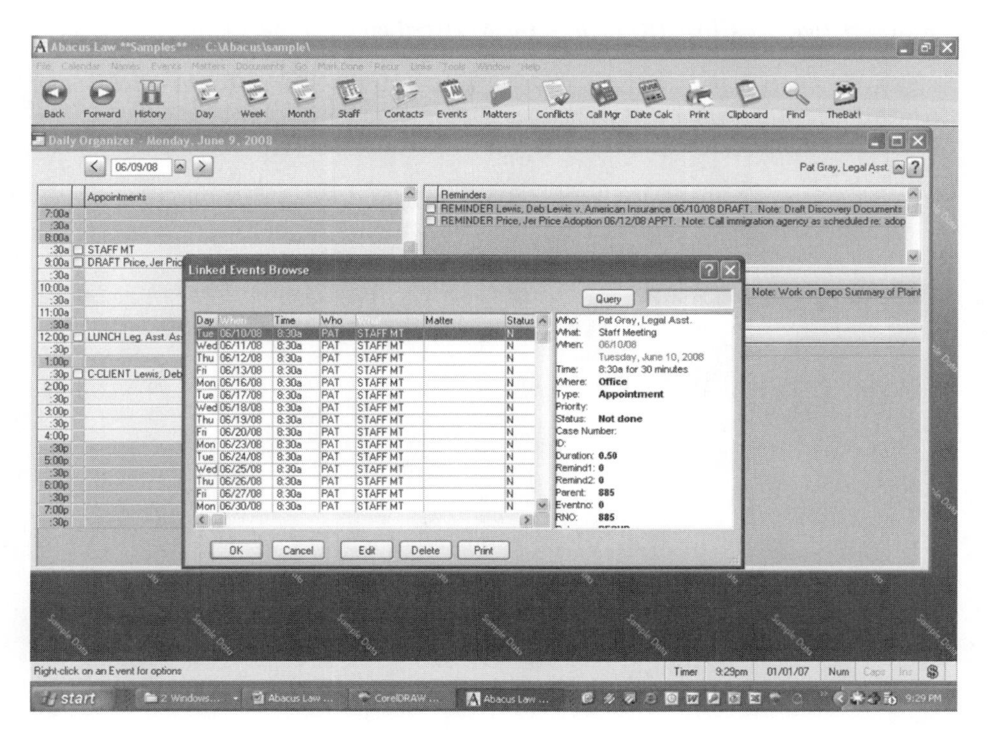

AbacusLaw Exhibit 19
Recurring Entry—Linked Events Browse Window
Copyright 2007 Abacus Data Systems, Inc.

new matter for Debra Lewis regarding the sale of a piece of property and that he would like you to schedule the normal New Matter deadlines. The initial client meeting for the matter will be on 6/12/08.

14. ***Click Matters on the toolbar. Then, point and click on Add.***

15. In the "Adding a new Matter" window, enter the data from the table:

Field Name	Data to Enter
Matter	Lewis Property Sale, 1001 Main
File/case#	1005
Attorney	AMS
Case Code	REA
Court	
Opened	06 09 08
Closed	
User1	
User2	
User3	
User4	

16. When you are finished, ***click Save in the Adding a new Matter window. From the Matter: Lewis Property Sale window, click the Linked Names tab, click "Add link," click "Lewis, Debra," and click OK in the Names Browse window.***

17. ***Click the up arrow next to Link Type. In the Valid Link Types Entries window, click CLIENT-P Client-Plaintiff and then click OK. Click OK in the Name-to-Matter Link window.***

18. An entry for "Lewis, Debra," now appears in the Matter:Lewis Property Sale window. ***Click the Close (X) icon in the Matter:Lewis Property Sale window.***

19. You should be back at the Daily Organizer for 06/12/08. ***Right-click 1:00p. Click Add Events from a Rule.*** The Rules window should now be displayed (see AbacusLaw Exhibit 20).

20. ***In the Rules window, click NEWCASE. Then, in the Rules window, click Edit.***

AbacusLaw Exhibit 20
Making a Rules Based Entry
Copyright 2007 Abacus Data Systems, Inc.

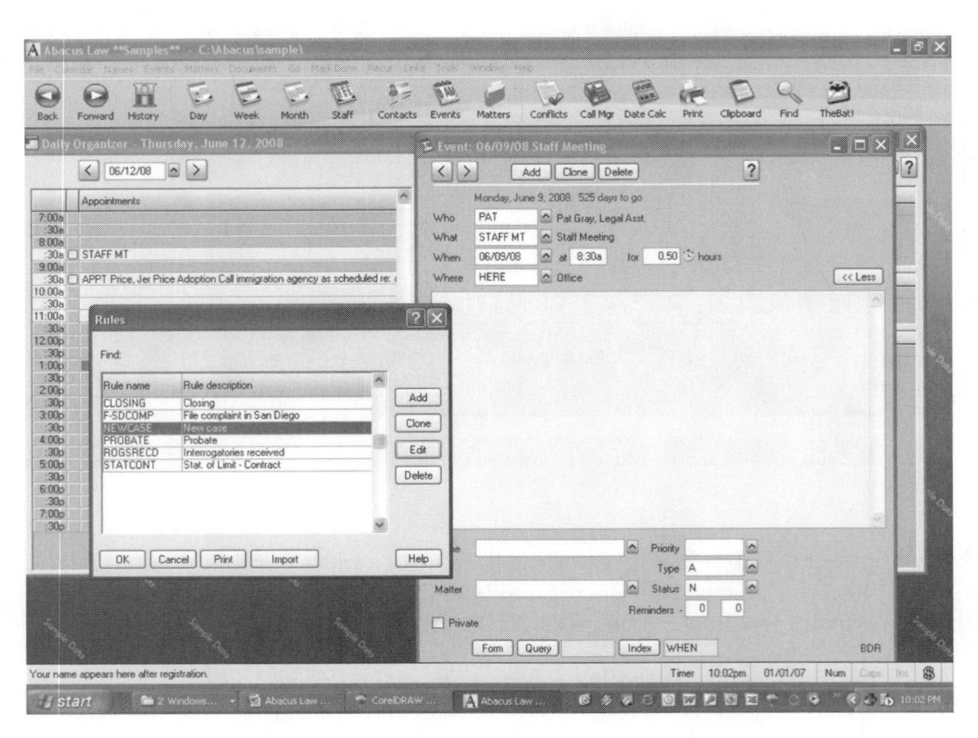

21. The Rule name (Event #0): NEWCASE New Case window should be displayed (see AbacusLaw Exhibit 21). This screen shows the entries that will automatically be made. The Interval column refers to the number of days from the initial event (e.g., 0 days, 1 day, 1 day, 0 days, 7 days or 14 days).

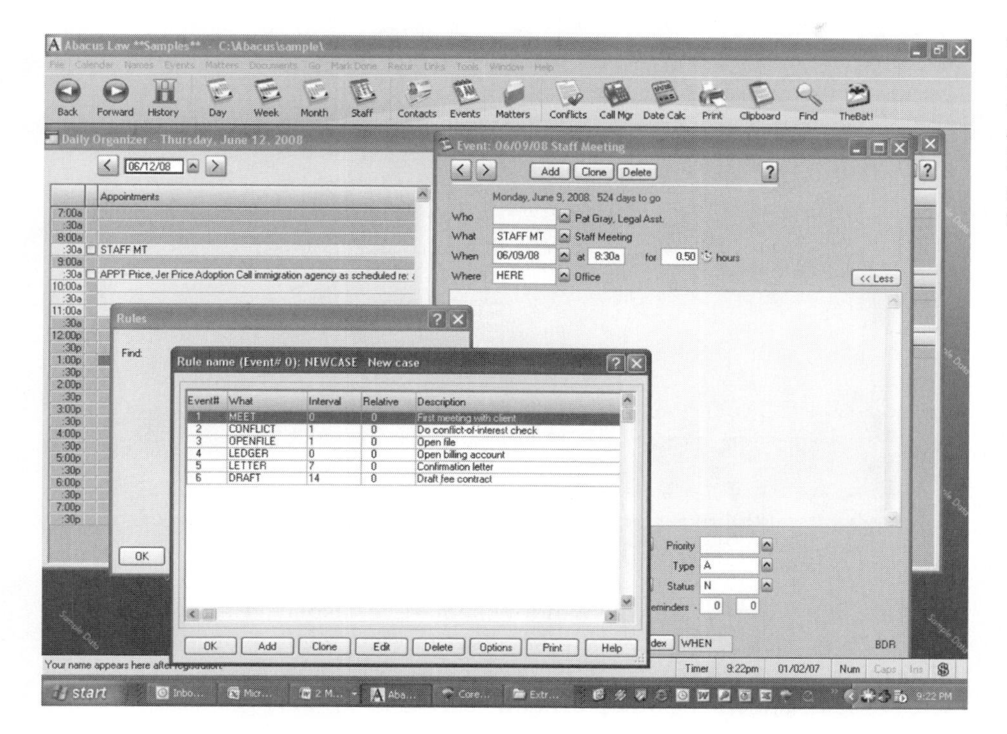

AbacusLaw Exhibit 21
Rule Based Entry—Automatic Entries to Be Made

22. *Click OK in the Rule name (Event #0): NEWCASE New Case window.*

23. *In the Rules window, click OK.* Notice that NEWCASE has now been added to the open Event on the screen. Enter the following information in the Event window. Note that in the Matter field you will need to click the Lewis Property Sale matter in the Matters for Lewis, Debra window, then click OK.

Who	PAT
What	NEWCASE
When	06/12/08 at 1:00p for 1.00 hours
Where	HERE
Description (open light yellow box)	
Name	Lewis, Debra
Matter	Lewis Property Sale
Priority	
Type	A
Status	N
Reminders -	0 0

24. When you are finished creating the entry, *click Save in the Adding a new Event window.*

25. The Creating Events from Rule: NEW CASE window is displayed. You are asked if you want the related events scheduled. *Click "Yes."*

AbacusLaw Exhibit 22
Rule Based Entry—Linked Events Browse Window

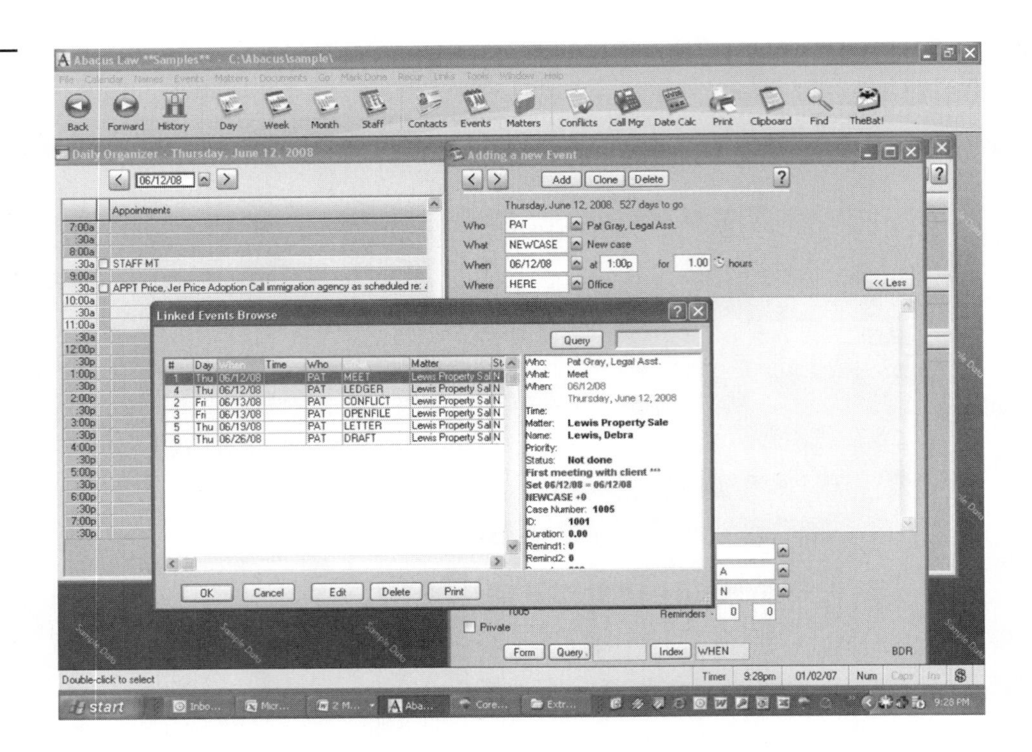

26. The Linked Events Browse window should be displayed (see AbacusLaw Exhibit 22). ***Click OK in the Linked Events Browse window.*** Notice that the initial meeting is set at 1:00 and that in the reminders section of the Daily Organizer there are some entries regarding the new case.

27. ***Click the Next Day icon (>) in the Daily Organizer until you come to 06/19/08.*** Notice that there is a reminder to do the Confirmation Letter.

28. ***Click the Next Day icon (>) in the Daily Organizer until you come to 06/26/08.*** Notice that there is a reminder to do the fee contract.

29. In the date field in the Daily Organizer, type **06/09/08** and press **[ENTER].**

30. You will now use the Date Calculator feature. On 06/09/08 the office received a Motion to Quash that needs to be responded to. The motion must be responded to in fifteen court days. Arthur Simon asks you to let him know exactly what date the response it is due using the AbacusLaw Date Calculator.

31. ***Click Date Calc on the toolbar. The Date Calculator window should now be displayed*** (see AbacusLaw Exhibit 23).

32. Under Date+Interval type **06/09/08,** then enter **10** next to the plus sign (+). Next to "days," ***click the down arrow and select "Court days."*** The Date Calculator should return a date of 6/23/2008 (Monday).

33. ***Click OK to close the Date Calculator.***

34. ***Click the Close (X) icon for the Daily Organizer.***

35. ***Click File on the menu bar and then click on Exit (the very last entry under the Recent Files Accessed list).***

36. At the "Please register now!" window ***click OK.***

This concludes Lesson 5.

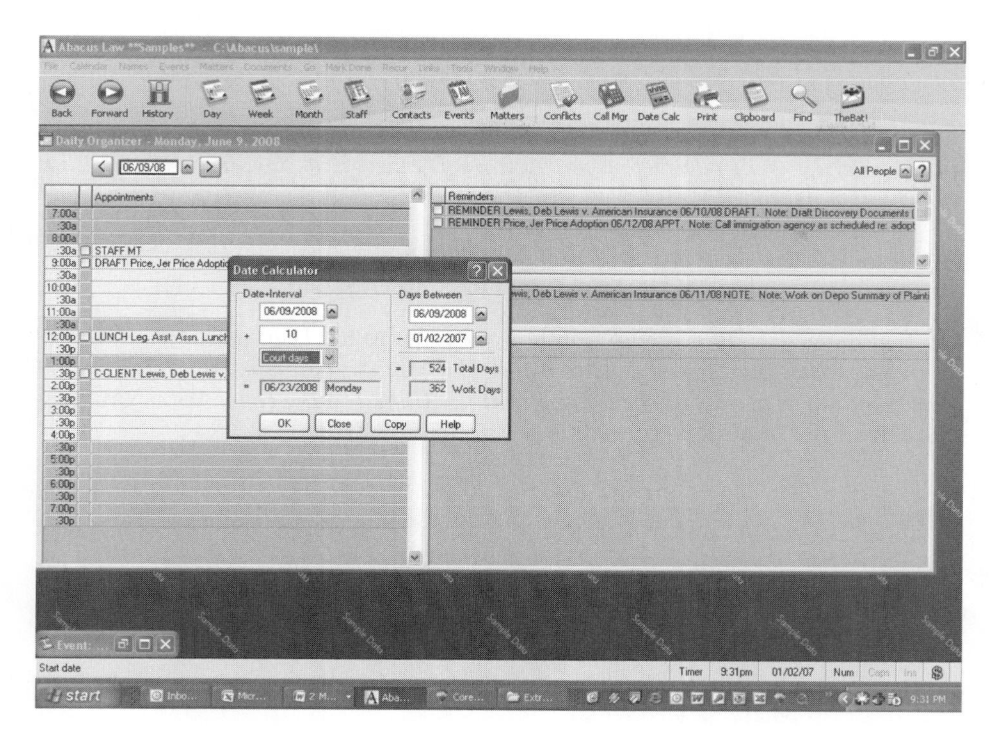

AbacusLaw Exhibit 23
Date Calculator

LESSON 6: CREATING LINKED NAMES AND LINKED NOTES, AND CHECKING FOR CONFLICTS

In this lesson, you will link a non-client to a case, create notes that are linked to contacts and matters, and run a conflict of interest search. This lesson assumes you have completed Lessons 1 to 5 and that you are familiar with the AbacusLaw interface.

1. The first thing you will do in this lesson is to populate AbacusLaw with Sample Data. *If you start AbacusLaw from the icon on the desktop, the sample data will not be loaded, so please follow these directions.*

2. Start Windows. Then, ***click the Start button on the Windows desktop, point to Programs or All Programs, point to the AbacusLaw group, and click Sample Data.*** This will populate Abacus with some sample data.

3. The User Log on window should now be displayed. Note that the AbacusLaw desktop should say Sample Data.

4. **In the User Log on window, in the User ID field, type the same initials you entered in Lesson 1.** It is important that you enter the same initials each time you load Abacus. Do not type anything in the Password field. ***Click OK in the User Log on window.***

5. The Tip of the Day window should now be displayed on your screen. ***Click OK in the Tip of the Day window.*** You should now be at the Abacus desktop with the name plate "Your name appears here after registration."

6. The first thing you will do is to link an opposing attorney to a case. Just like you can link clients to matters, you can link people who are not clients to other people and to matters.

7. ***Click Matters on the toolbar. Double-click Lewis v. American Insurance.***

8. ***Click the Linked Names tab. Click Add link. Click "Schneider, Paula" and then click OK.***

9. ***In the Name-to-Matter Link window, Click the up arrow next to Link Type and then click "ATTY-D Defendant Attorney." Next click OK in the Valid Link Types Entries window.***

10. ***Click OK in the Name-to-Matter Link window.*** Notice that Paula Schneider, the defendant's attorney, has now been linked to the case.

11. You have already added a number of events to the *Lewis v. American Insurance* case. ***Click the Linked Events tab in the Matter: Lewis v. American Insurance window to see all of the entries that are linked to the case.*** Approximately thirteen entries should be present (see AbacusLaw Exhibit 24).

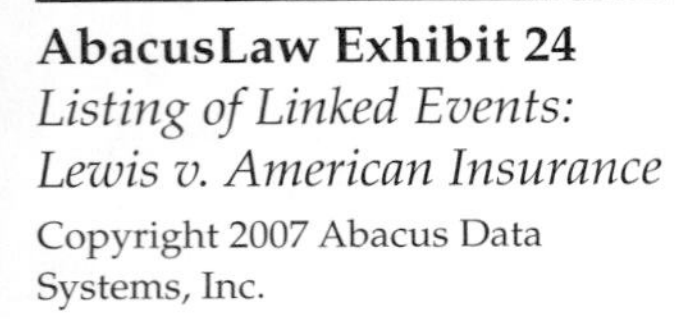

AbacusLaw Exhibit 24
Listing of Linked Events: Lewis v. American Insurance

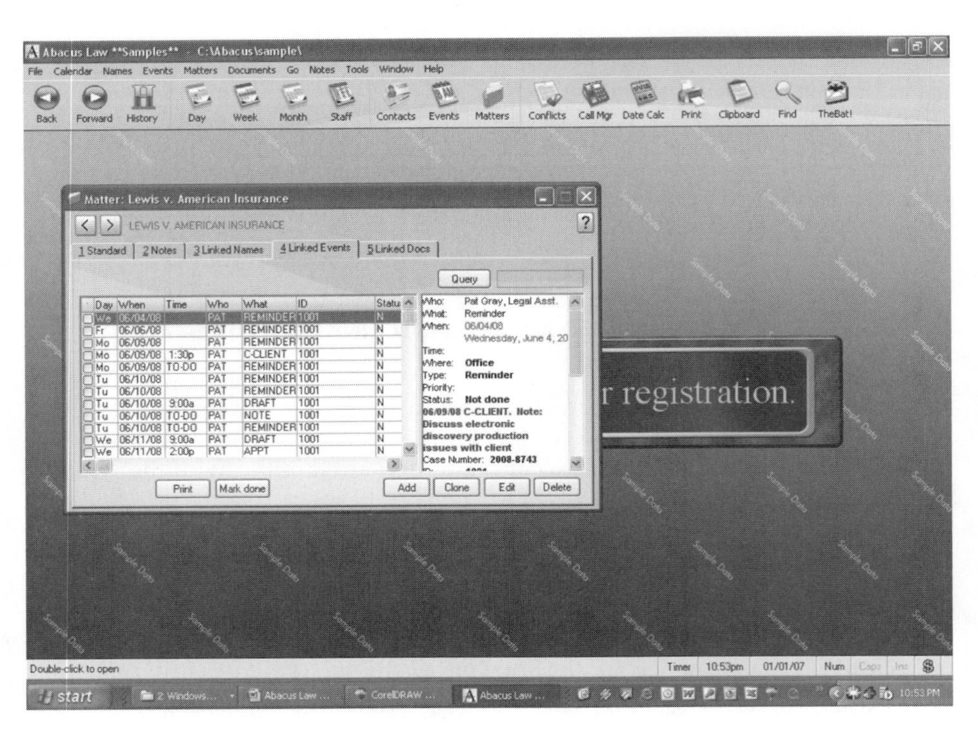

12. You will now create two notes that will be linked to the case.

13. ***Click the Notes tab in the Matter: Lewis v. American Insurance window. click Add.***

14. The Add Note window should now be displayed (see AbacusLaw Exhibit 25). Notice that "Lewis, Debra" has already been entered and linked to the Name Field and *Lewis v. American Insurance* has already been linked as the matter concerning the note.

15. ***Click in the note description*** field and type **Paula Schneider called today and left a message for Arthur that she had authority to settle the Lewis case for $50,000. She said that she needs to hear back from Arthur by 6/12/08.** (See AbacusLaw Exhibit 25)

16. ***Click the up arrow next to Type, click SETOFFER Settlement Offer, and then click OK in the Valid NOTETYPE Entries window*** (see AbacusLaw Exhibit 25).

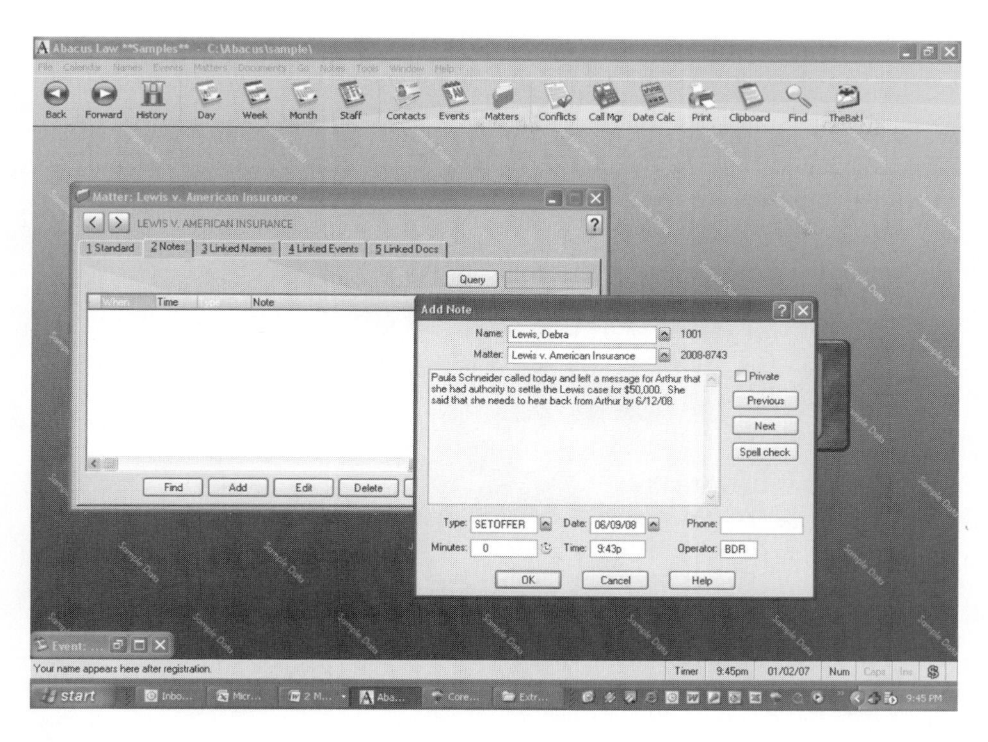

AbacusLaw Exhibit 25
Adding a Note

17. In the Date field of the Add Note window, type **06/09/08**.

18. In the Operator field of the Add Note window, type **PAT** and then ***click OK.***

19. Notice that the note has now been added.

20. ***Click Add to add one more note.*** Create the note using the data in the table.

Name	**Lewis, Debra**
Matter	Lewis v. American Insurance
Description	Debra Lewis called and left a message for Arthur stating that she would be accepting the defendant's offer to settle the case for $50,000.
Type:	SETOFFER
Date:	06/10/08
Operator:	PAT

21. When you have finished creating the note, ***click in the Add Note window.***

22. ***Click the Close (X) icon in the Matter: Lewis v. American Insurance window.***

23. You will now run a conflict of interest search. Arthur Simon called and asked you to run the name of Cindy Rayburn for conflicts of interest. A possible new client named John Rayburn has asked the firm to handle a custody dispute with his former wife, Cindy. Arthur said that the name sounded familiar, but he did not know why.

24. ***Click Conflicts on the toolbar.*** The Conflict of Interest Check window is then displayed (see AbacusLaw Exhibit 26). Under "Enter last name" type **Rayburn** and then press **[ENTER].**

25. *Click Run in the Conflict of Interest Check window* (see AbacusLaw Exhibit 26). The Conflict Check Hit List window is then displayed.

26. *Double-click RAYBURN in the Conflict Check Hit List window.* The "Hit found in Names database" window is then displayed (see AbacusLaw Exhibit 26). She is a vendor that the firm works with.

AbacusLaw Exhibit 26
Running a Conflict of Interest Search

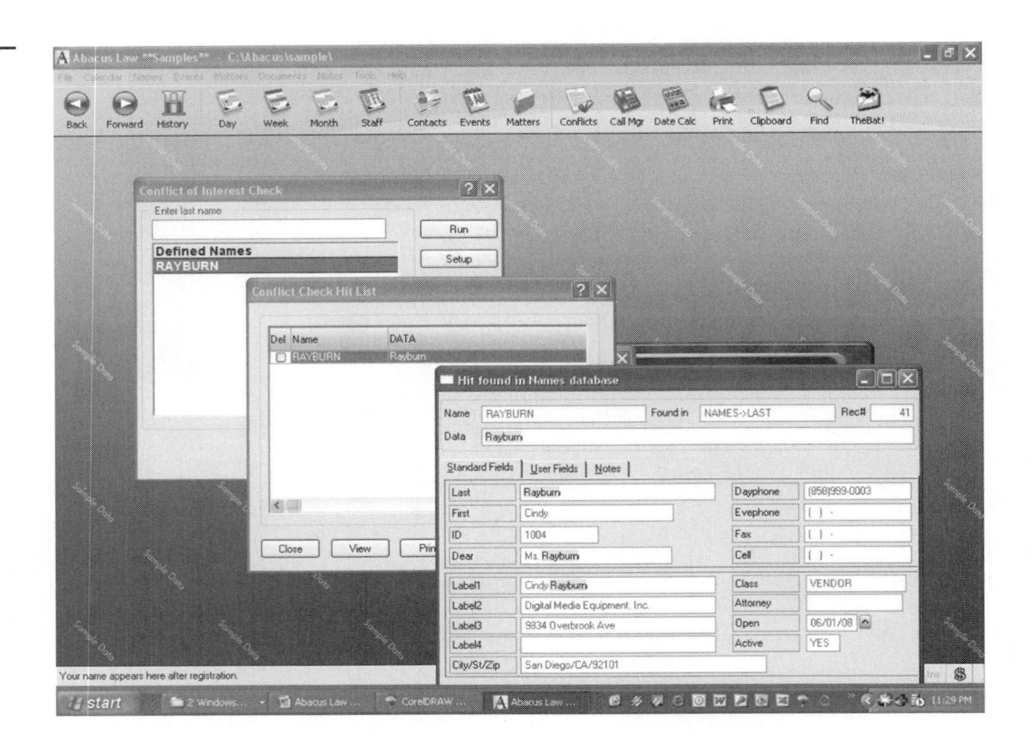

27. *Click Close in the Conflict Check Hit List window and then click the Close (X) icons for the other open windows.*

28. *Click File on the menu bar and then click Exit (the very last entry under the Recent Files Accessed list).*

29. At the "Please register now!" window, *click OK.*

This concludes Lesson 6.

LESSON 7: LINKING DOCUMENTS, USING THE CALL MANAGER, AND USING THE FORM GENERATION FEATURE

In this lesson, you will link documents, use the call manager feature, use the form generation feature, and work with the Events Browse tool. This lesson assumes you have completed Lessons 1 to 6 and that you are familiar with the AbacusLaw interface.

1. The first thing you will do in this lesson is to populate AbacusLaw with sample data. *If you start AbacusLaw from the icon on the desktop the sample data will not be loaded, so please follow these directions.*

2. Start Windows. ***Then, Click the Start button on the Windows desktop, point to Programs or All Programs, point to the AbacusLaw group, and then click Sample Data.*** This will populate Abacus with some sample data.

3. The User Log on window should now be displayed. Note that the Abacus-Law desktop should say Sample Data.

4. In the User Log on window, in the User ID field, type the same initials you entered in Lesson 1. It is important that you enter the same initials each time you load Abacus. Do not type anything in the Password field. ***Click OK in the User Log on window.***

5. The Tip of the Day window should now be displayed on your screen. ***Click OK in the Tip of the Day window.*** You should now be at the Abacus desktop with the name plate "Your name appears here after registration."

6. You will now learn how to link an electronic document to a matter. ***Click Matters on the toolbar.*** Press the **[HOME]** key to go to the beginning of the matters in the Matters Browse window.

7. ***Double-click*** **Cal. Computers v. Multimedia.** ***In the Matter: Cal. Computers v. Multimedia window, click the Linked Docs tab*** (see AbacusLaw Exhibit 27).

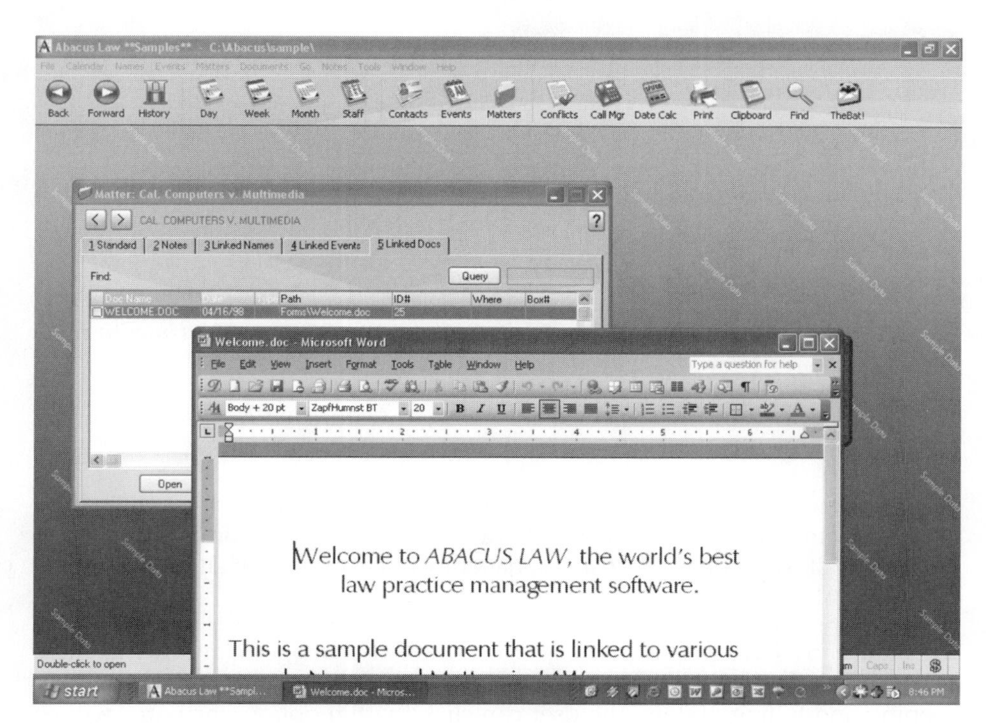

AbacusLaw Exhibit 27
A Linked Document in AbacusLaw
Copyright 2007 Abacus Data Systems, Inc.

8. ***Double-click WELCOME.DOC.*** If your computer has Microsoft Word installed, the Welcome.doc file should be displayed in a Microsoft Word window (see AbacusLaw Exhibit 27). This is a welcome message but Abacus can open any type of electronic legal file. Using this feature you can link electronic documents to matters and be able to quickly access them.

9. ***In the Microsoft Word window, click File on the menu bar and then click Exit to leave Microsoft Word.***

10. You should once again be at the Matter: Cal. Computers v. Multimedia window. ***Click Edit*** to see the screen that is used to add/edit a link (see AbacusLaw Exhibit 28). The process is extremely easy: the user types the path of the document,

AbacusLaw Exhibit 28
Adding and Editing a Link to a Document
Copyright 2007 Abacus Data Systems, Inc.

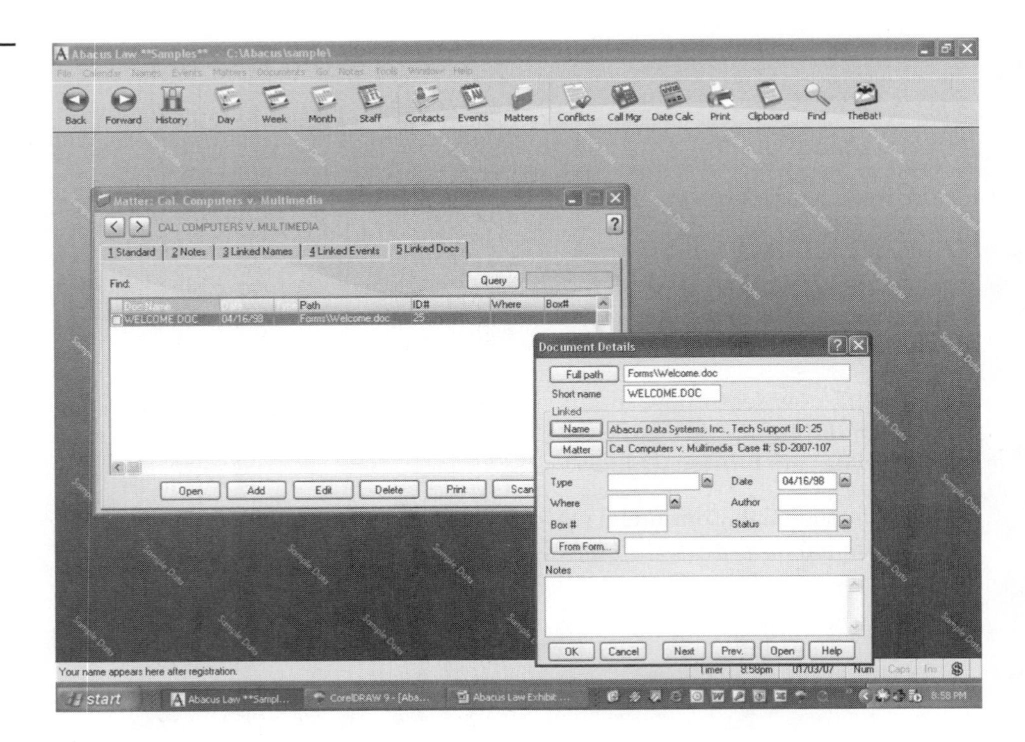

links the document to a name and/or matter, and then completes the rest of the options in the screen, if desired (see AbacusLaw Exhibit 28).

11. ***In the "Document Details" window, click OK.***

12. ***Click the Close (X) icon in the Matter: Cal. Computers v. Multimedia window. In the Save window, click No.***

13. You will now learn to use the Call Manager feature. ***Click Call Mgr on the toolbar.***

14. Enter the call in the Call Manager window as shown in AbacusLaw Exhibit 29. Notice that you can indicate whether the call is an incoming call or an outgoing call. You can use the Call Manager to make a record of all incoming and outgoing calls.

15. Notice in AbacusLaw Exhibit 29 that in the Call Manager window that there is an option called "Bill." If Abacus is set up to exchange information with a timekeeping and billing system, the user can click the Bill option, the entry will be sent to timekeeping and billing, and the client would be billed for the time.

16. When you have entered the call, ***click Save and then click Close in the Call Manager window.***

17. You can see all calls entered in the Call Manager in either the Matters or Contacts Notes tab. ***Click Matters on the toolbar, double-click Price Adoption, and click the Notes tab.*** You should now see the entry for the phone call.

18. ***Click the Close (X) icon in the Matter: Price Adoption window.***

19. You will now learn how to use the Form Generation feature in AbacusLaw. (*Note:* This part of the lesson requires Microsoft Word). ***Click Contacts on the toolbar, then scroll to and double-click Lewis, Debra.***

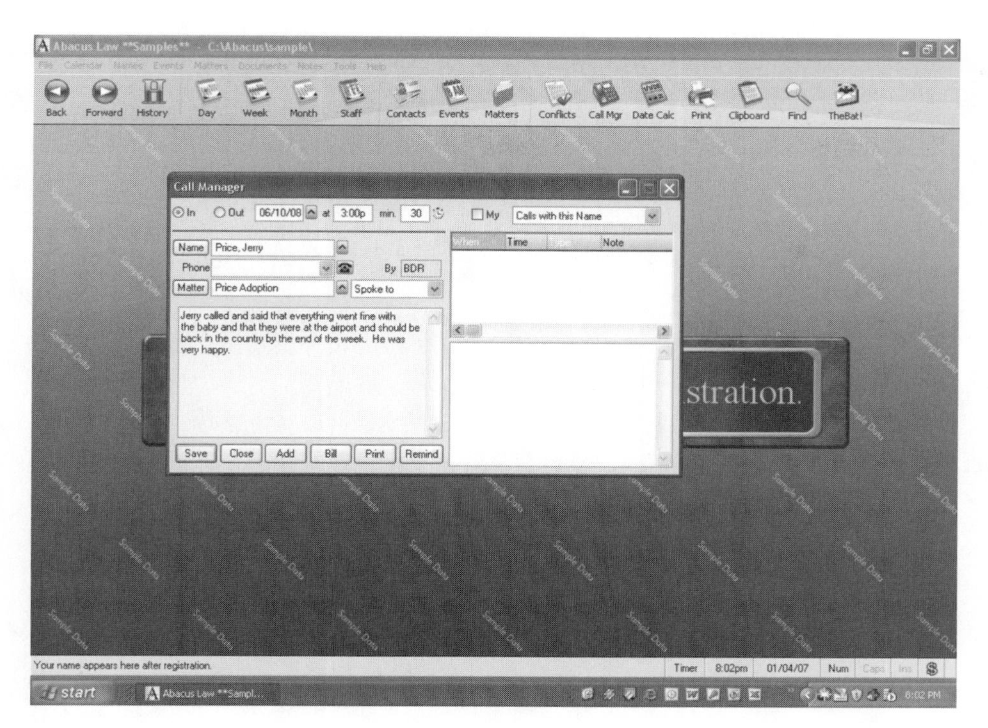

AbacusLaw Exhibit 29
Entering a Call in Call Manager

20. ***Click the Linked Events tab, click the 06/09/08 1:30 p C-CLIENT entry.*** The data from this entry will be referenced in the form letter you will generate.

21. ***Click Print on the toolbar, click Form Generation, then click MS Word.***

22. ***The Select an MSWord Form/Template window should now be displayed*** (see AbacusLaw Exhibit 30). ***Double-click the folder called "forms"*** (see AbacusLaw Exhibit 30). ***Then, double-click Setlet.dot.*** If you get an error message, click OK or End.

23. You should now be in Microsoft Word with the settlement template filled in (see AbacusLaw Exhibit 31, first screen). Notice that Abacus automatically inserted the client's address, case name, and date of the event in the form. ***Close the file in Word.***

24. ***Click once more on the AbacusLaw window if it is not already shown. Close the Name window.***

25. ***Click Events on the toolbar.*** This feature shows you all of the events that have been entered into AbacusLaw (see AbacusLaw Exhibit 32). The default setting sorts events on the When (date) field. You can also sort the events by What by clicking in the What column heading. You can also use the Query feature in the Events Browse window to select fewer than all events. The Events Browse window allows you to manage all events in a quick and easy interface.

26. ***Click File on the menu bar and then click Exit (the very last entry on the Recent Files Accessed list).***

27. At the "Please register now!" window, ***click OK.***

This concludes Lesson 7.

AbacusLaw Exhibit 30
Selecting a Template to Run with the Form Generation Feature

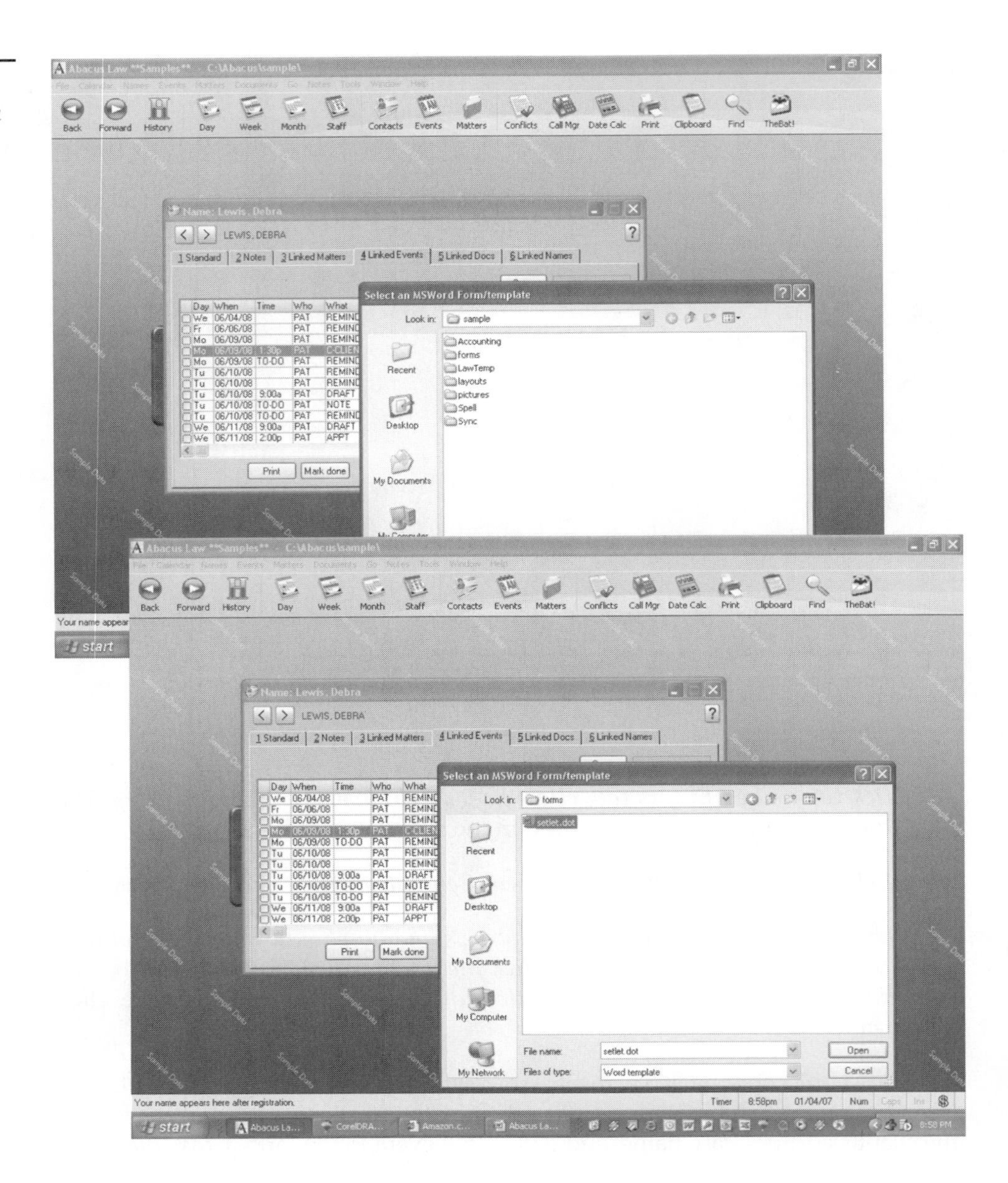

LESSON 8: REPORTS

In this lesson, you will run a number of reports in AbacusLaw. This lesson assumes you have completed Lessons 1 to 7 and that you are familiar with the AbacusLaw interface.

1. The first thing you will do in this lesson is to populate AbacusLaw with sample data. *If you start AbacusLaw from the icon on the desktop the sample data will not be loaded, so please follow these directions.*

2. Start Windows. ***Click the Start button on the Windows desktop, point mouse to Programs or All Programs, point to the AbacusLaw group, and then click Sample Data.*** This will populate Abacus with some sample data.

3. The User Log on window should now be displayed. Note that the Abacus-Law desktop should say Sample Data.

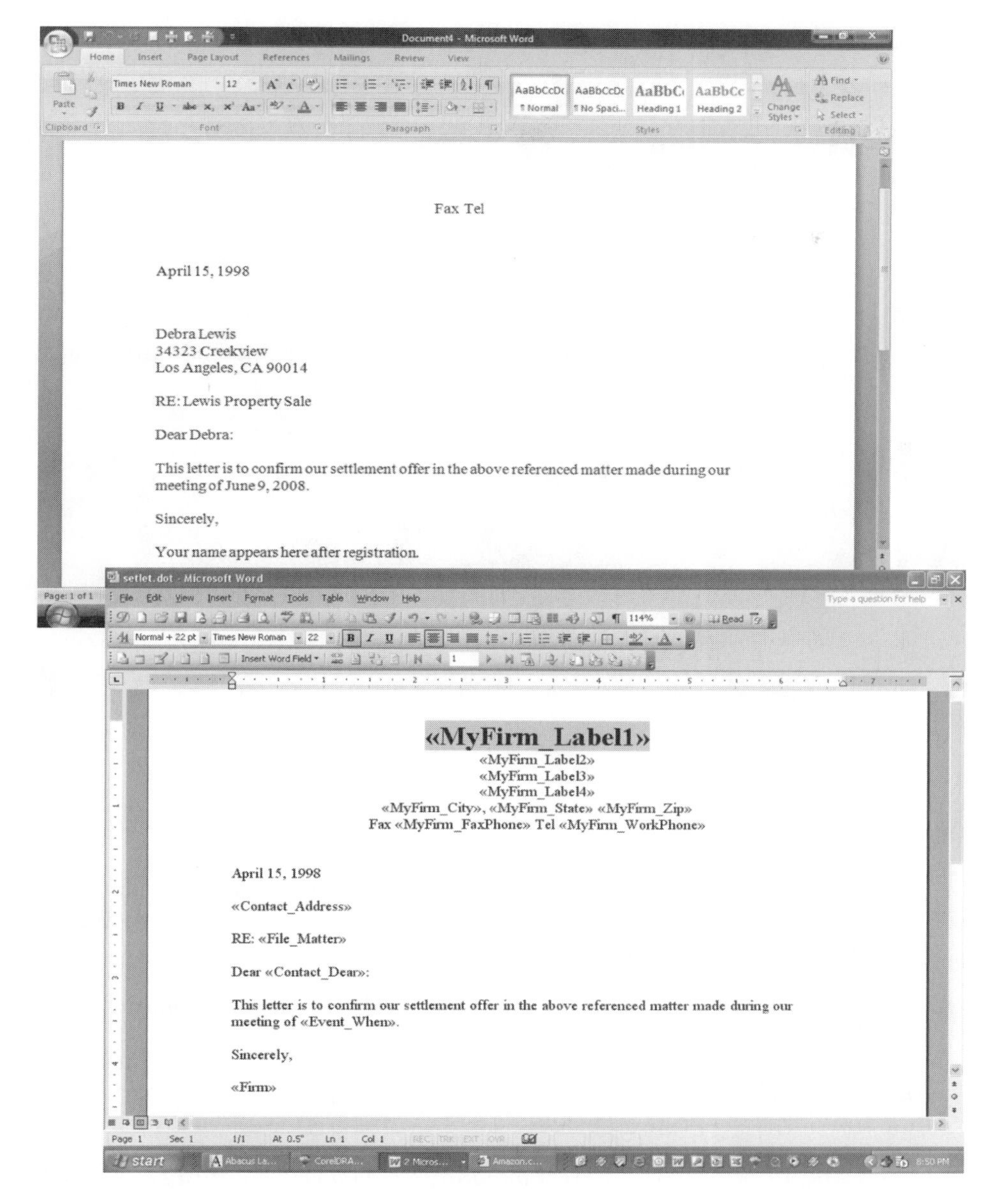

AbacusLaw Exhibit 31
Document Generation—Completed Form and Templete

4. In the User Log on window, in the User ID field, type the same initials you entered in Lesson 1. It is important that you enter the same initials each time you load Abacus. Do not type anything in the Password field. ***Click OK in the User Log on window.***

5. The Tip of the Day window should now be displayed on your screen. ***Click OK in the Tip of the Day window.*** You should now be at the Abacus desktop with the name plate "Your name appears here after registration."

6. AbacusLaw comes with more than one hundred standard reports. You will run just a few of them. ***Click File on the menu bar, point to Reports, then click All Reports.***

7. ***Click Matters List (Landscape) and click OK. The Report Control window should now be displayed.*** This report will run a matters or case list for the whole office. The default setting will print the reports to the screen. If you want to

AbacusLaw Exhibit 32
Events Browse Window
Copyright 2007 Abacus Data Systems, Inc.

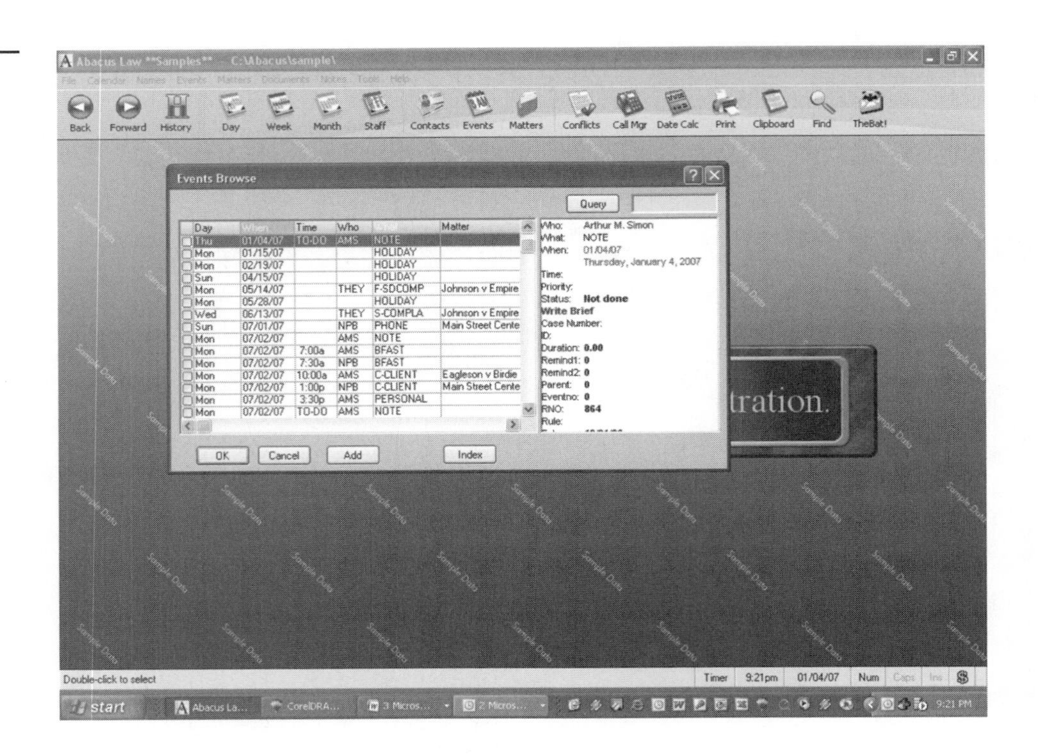

change that, you can click "Output to" and select a printer, but Screen is fine for this exercise.

8. ***Click Print in the Report Control window and then click Print in the Print window.*** A listing of all of the clients and names linked to the cases should be displayed.

9. ***Click the red "X" (Exit) on the toolbar in the Abacus Report window.***

10. The Report Control window is again displayed. ***Click Report and then click Matter List (Landscape).*** This time you will run a report just of the cases that Arthur Simon is the lead attorney on.

11. ***Click OK. In the Report Control window, click Query and then click Quick query. The Quick Query for Matters window is displayed.***

12. ***Click the up arrow key next to Attorney and double-click AMS Arthur M. Simon. Then, click OK in the Quick Query for Matters window.***

13. ***In the Report Control window, click Print and then click Print in the Print window.*** If you would like to magnify the print on the screen, ***double-click the mouse. Scroll through the document and look at only the matters that Arthur Simon is managing. When you are done viewing the report, click the red "X" (Exit) on the toolbar in the Abacus Report window.***

14. The "Report Control" window should again be displayed. ***Click "Query" and then click Clear current query.***

15. The "Report Control" window should again be displayed. ***Click Report and then click Matter Format Calendar.*** This will produce a list of calendar events for cases. Because this could be long, we will just run this report for the *Lewis v. American Insurance* case.

16. *Click OK. In the Report Control window, click Query and then click Quick query. The Quick Query for Events window should be displayed.*

17. *Click the up arrow key next to Matter and double-click Lewis v. American Insurance. Then, click OK in the Quick Query for Events window.*

18. *In the Report Control window, click Print and then click Print in the Print window.* If you would like to magnify the print on the screen, ***double-click the mouse. Scroll through the document and look at all of the events for the*** *Lewis v. American Insurance* ***case.***

19. *When you are done viewing the report, click the red "X" (Exit) on the toolbar in the Abacus Report window.*

20. The Report Control window is again displayed. ***Click Query and then click Clear current query.***

21. The Report Control window should again be displayed. ***Click Close in the Report Control window.***

22. You will now print a report for a date range. ***Click File on the menu bar, point to Reports, then click Events (Calendar).*** In the Events Report Control window under All, type **06/09/2008—06/13/2008** ***and then click Print. In the "Print" window, click Print.***

23. *When you are done viewing the report, point and click on the red "X" (Exit) on the toolbar in the AbacusReport window.*

24. *Click Close in the Events Report Control window.*

25. *Click File in the Menu Bar and then click Exit (the very last entry on the Recent Files Accessed list).*

30. At the "Please register now!" window, ***click OK.***

This concludes the AbacusLaw Hands-on Exercises. AbacusLaw gives users a myriad of tools and features for managing just about any aspect of a case, including managing contacts, events, documents, form generation, phone calls, and notes/diary.

CHAPTER 8

ELECTRONIC DISCOVERY

CHAPTER OBJECTIVES

After completing Chapter 8, you should be able to do the following:

1. Explain why electronic discovery is an important aspect of litigation.
2. Identify the name that the Federal Rules of Civil Procedure gives to all electronic data.
3. Explain the purpose of the "meet and confer" pretrial conference parties must have pursuant to the Federal Rules of Civil Procedure.
4. Discuss the duty of parties to preserve electronic information.
5. Explain what native and image formats are.

ELECTRONIC DISCOVERY OVERVIEW

> *The first and foremost thing to get through your brain is that electronic evidence is now center stage. You must address it — and early on. You may not like it, but you're going to have to deal with it.*[1]

electronic discovery
The process of producing and receiving litigation documents in electronic format.

discovery
The pre-trial stage of litigation where parties disclose to each other information about their case.

Electronic discovery refers to the process of producing and receiving litigation documents in electronic format. The **discovery** stage of litigation takes place before trial and is when parties disclose information about their case to each other. For decades discovery has revolved around (1) taking pretrial verbal testimony from parties and witnesses in the form of depositions; (2) the exchange of written questions and answers in the forms of interrogatories; (3) the exchange of statements of fact, called requests for admissions, which each party must admit or deny and; (4) the production of hard-copy documents in response to either of a subpoena duces tecum (a command for a witness to appear at a certain time and place and bring documents or records) or a request for the production of documents. Document production is a crucial aspect of discovery because documents sometimes tell a different story than witnesses. Documents can establish the facts, time lines, conclusions, complex ideas, and inferences that are vital to any litigation.

> *The increasing trends of storing electronic data and using software applications that maintain potentially discoverable information have rendered the process of obtaining and producing discovery a monumental task.*[2]

For decades documents have been produced in hard-copy format. In large litigation each party would send a request for the production of documents and the other party would have boxes and boxes of documents copied (sometimes hundreds and hundreds of boxes) and give them to the opposing party. The opposing party would then have to sort through the boxes by hand and learn what they could about each document.

The use of computers in all sizes of businesses and in every aspect of life has fundamentally altered how information is exchanged. Now, information is exchanged to a large degree in electronic format. Recent studies have shown that more than 95 percent of all documents are now electronic. Web pages, databases, emails, word-processing files, spreadsheet files, accounting information, billings, payroll, corporate records, personal digital assistant (PDA) files, and other documents are all stored electronically. North Americans alone send approximately four trillion emails each day.

A Fortune 50 company recently stated that its employees generate five million emails a day; they have 65,000 desktop computers and 30,000 laptops; and their disaster recovery system generates more than 100,000 backup tapes a month, or more than one million tapes a year. Practically everything produced in most organizations, large or small, is done in electronic format.

Many courts have held that the production of hard-copy documents when electronic versions are available is unacceptable. These courts have been on the forefront of mandating the production of electronic documents. The federal courts, for example, have adopted rules regarding the discovery of electronic documents.

Unlike hard-copy documents, which can be read by anyone, which have physical dimensions, and which can be observed and examined, electronic documents are not as tangible and have many more complexities and problems when it comes to producing them in litigation.

Electronic information is said to be "distributed," meaning that it is not held in just one place. Electronic information in large organizations can be disposed among hundreds of servers, thousands of desktop computers, thousands of laptops, and hundreds or thousands of personal digital assistants (PDAs), thumb drives, CD-ROMs, DVDs and even home computers when employees take documents home to work on them. Controlling, discovering, and copying information in a distributed electronic environment is not easy. Also, many companies outsource goods, services, information, administration, operations, production, technology, and other functions. Controlling and discovering information in an outsourced environment is not easy.

Electronic documents exist in countless formats, which increases the complexity of producing and reading documents. Some documents and systems have standard formats, while many others come from completely proprietary systems owned, licensed, and controlled by vendors. Just accessing data in a format accessible to these millions of computer systems and thousands of file formats is daunting. Computer systems can come from a large variety of manufacturers, many of which are not necessarily standard. Computers run in a variety of operating systems, and come in different sizes, with memory, components, and other hardware and software that further increase the complexity of producing electronic documents in litigation.

Electronic data is inherently different from hard-copy data because the content of tens of thousands of feet of books on a library shelf can be stored electronically in a couple of feet.

All of these issues and many more make the exchange of electronic data inherently complex. Why is this an important issue for legal assistants? Because legal assistants have historically been the people on the ground handling, tracking, and managing document production. In many legal organizations legal

assistants will be the ones working with clients and vendors regarding electronic document requests. More than ever before, legal assistants must have outstanding technological skills to be effective.

> *Why should [you] ... care about electronic evidence and discovery? It's often the paralegal and other members of the legal team who end up sifting through the evidence and doing much of the work in selecting an expert to help when it comes to e-discovery.*[3]

In Chapter 9, litigation support software, which is closely associated with electronic discovery, will be discussed. While electronic discovery and litigation support are pieces of the same puzzle and closely aligned, they are different. Litigation support software organizes, stores, retrieves, and summarizes information used in litigation. Once information has been obtained during the discovery process, litigation support software helps to craft and manipulate the information to assist attorneys. Electronic discovery, on the other hand, is the process of receiving or providing electronic information during the discovery process.

THE FEDERAL RULES OF CIVIL PROCEDURE AND ELECTRONICALLY STORED INFORMATION

electronically stored information (ESI)
The term used by the Federal Rules of Civil Procedure to refer to all electronic data including writings, drawings, graphs, charts, photographs, sound recordings, images, and other data compilations stored in any medium from which information can be obtained.

The Federal Rules of Civil Procedure (FRCP) were amended in December 2006 to specifically address the issue of electronic discovery. It is believed that many state courts will follow the lead of the federal courts and adopt similar rules. The FRCP now refers to any electronic data as **electronically stored information** (ESI). FRCP 34 (a) states that ESI includes "writings, drawings, graphs, charts, photographs, sound recordings, images, and other data compilations stored in any medium from which information can be obtained or translated." ESI is a term of art and it is intentionally referred to extremely broadly by the FRCP so that any new form of electronic information will be covered by the rules.

> *The wide variety of computer systems currently in use, and the rapidity of technological change, counsel against a limiting or precise definition of electronically stored information. Rule 34(a)(1) is expansive and includes any type of information that is stored electronically. A common example often sought in discovery is electronic communications, such as email. The rule covers—either as documents or as electronically stored information—information "stored in any medium," to encompass future developments in computer technology. Rule 34(a)(1) is intended to be broad enough to cover all current types of computer-based information, and flexible enough to encompass future changes and developments. References elsewhere in the rules to "electronically stored information" should be understood to invoke this expansive approach.*
>
> FRCP, Rule 34, Comment from 2006 Amendment

Mandatory Meet and Confer Sessions

> *At every avenue, you are encouraged to think about [e-discovery] issues, do your homework, involve the technical people, get to know your client, get to know your client's information systems and then go to the other side and exchange information.*[4]
>
> *Lawyers had better make a quick call to their computer forensics or e-discovery expert and make sure that the expert attends this [meet and confer] conference. Moreover, a senior representative from the IT department of both parties is going to be needed.*[5]

The FRCP at Rule 26 (f) clearly states that as soon as practicable ESI must be discussed between the parties, including the preservation of discoverable information and any issues relating to disclosure or discovery of ESI, such as the format(s) in which ESI should be produced.

The rules create an expectation that the attorneys involved will work collaboratively regarding the exchange of ESI, that games of "hide the ball" should not take place, and that any matters related to the production of ESI will be openly discussed early in the case. The Judicial Conference Rules Advisory Committee noted that "the parties' discussion should pay particular attention to the balance between the competing needs to preserve relevant evidence and to continue routine operations critical to ongoing activities." Another aspect of the meet and confer session is for the parties to understand the volume of the materials that may need to be reviewed, sampled, and possibly produced. Businesses, particularly large ones, have an enormous volume of data (terabytes of information representing tens of millions of pages of hard-copy data), and the parties need to come to terms with what is discoverable.

> *[The] obligation to preserve data in electronic form is no different than in paper discovery. However, the swiftness with which electronic documents may be destroyed makes the process more challenging and demands immediate attention from attorneys as soon as litigation is anticipated.*[6]

Duty to Exchange and Preserve Electronically Stored Information

The FRCP in no uncertain terms specifically requires that the parties preserve and exchange ESI. No longer can there be any argument that electronic data is not a discoverable "document" under the FRCP. FRCP Rule 26(a)(1)(B) provides that "without awaiting a discovery request" a party *must* provide to the other party "a copy of, or a description by category and location of, all documents, electronically stored information, and tangible things..." that are in their possession or control. The FRCP therefore makes it mandatory for the parties to disclose ESI even before they receive a discovery request. In addition, the FRCP at Rule 34(a) specifically requires that the producing party allow the requesting party to copy, test, and sample discoverable information, including ESI. This is particularly important where large amounts of data might need to be produced. This allows the requesting party to look at and inspect data, including the format of the data, before it is actually produced. **Sampling data** also refers to the process of testing a database to see if it contains relevant information to the subject matter of the case. The FRCP contemplate a very open environment regarding the preservation and exchange of ESI.

sampling data
The process of testing data to determine if it is appropriate for production.

> *Hard drives are a pervasive problem. Most IT staff routinely wipe a drive clean soon after an employee leaves, reformat it and give it to a new worker, destroying potentially important hidden digital data.*[7]

In addition, as soon as a potential party reasonably anticipates litigation there is an obligation to preserve electronic data. When this occurs parties must stop their normal practice of document destruction and put a "litigation hold" in place. A **litigation hold** for ESI would include stopping all destruction of possible data regarding the subject matter of the litigation no matter the form, including email, voicemail, calendars, information in handheld devices, word-processing files, spreadsheets, databases, hard disk drives, and all other forms of ESI.

litigation hold
When a party reasonably anticipates litigation, the party must invoke a litigation hold on all relevant hard-copy and electronically stored information so that such information is not destroyed.

In one recent case an employee was terminated according to the organization for viewing sexually explicit material on the Internet. The employee sued, alleging racial discrimination and arguing that someone either stole his password and used the computer to view the material or a previous user of the hard drive had viewed the material. The employee argued that the hard drive would prove his innocence. Unfortunately, IT staff wiped the drive clean, reformatted the drive and gave it to another employee. The court stopped short of actually fining the organization but in its ruling it strongly reprimanded the organization for destroying the central piece of evidence in the case.

In Zubulake v. UBS Warburg (No. 02 Civ. 1243 (SAS) (S.D.N.Y. 2004)), *Laura Zubulake, a former trader at UBS Warburg, filed an EEOC claim against UBS after she was passed over for a promotion. The court ruled that UBS should have discontinued its email deletion policy several months before Zubulake filed her complaint. The judge said it should have been clear when other employees began talking about her situation that a suit was likely, and that should have triggered a "litigation hold" to preserve the emails. A litigation hold has long been an important concept in discovery. In blunt terms: Once sued, you have to stop shredding documents. In Zubulake... many emails had been destroyed, the judge took the rare position of ruling "adverse inference" telling the jury to assume that the defendant had purged the missing evidence because it would have hurt its case. The judge also levied expensive sanctions. UBS Warburg shelled out $29 million in penalties and damages.*[8]

An important thing to note about the FRCP at Rule 34(b)(iii) is that a producing party only has to produce information in one form, so if a producing party produces ESI it does not have to also produce hard copies.

Now electronically stored information is fair game of discovery in every federal case and is probably going to be in the state cases too. Before, ESI was sort a second-class citizen. You could ask for it, but there was not necessarily a full concrete right to get it. Now, you have an absolute duty to produce it.[9]

The Electronic Format of ESI

The electronic format in which ESI is produced is extremely important. FRCP at 34(b) allows the requester to at least initially specify the form in which the ESI is to be produced. The producing party can object to the form requested but they must specifically state the reason for objecting to the form and what format they propose to transfer the ESI in. FRCP Rule 34(b)(i) says that a party who produces ESI shall produce it as it is kept in the usual course of business and goes on to say in 34(b)(ii) that if the requesting party does not specify a format, the responding party is required to produce the ESI in the format in which it is ordinarily maintained or in reasonably usable format (see FRCP Rule 34(b)). For example, suppose a Microsoft Word 2003 file is being produced. In Microsoft Word 2003 the native format of a word file is ".doc." That is, Microsoft Word 2003 files all have the file extension of ".doc" (e.g., "letter.doc"). Would it be acceptable for the producer to produce the ".doc" file in a PDF format instead of its native format of ".doc?" If the request for production did not state a format, then the production in PDF would be a reasonably usable format and would most likely be allowed. Native formats are discussed later in the chapter, but they generally refer to the file structure/program that originally created the file. If the requesting party wanted a Microsoft Word 2003 file to be produced as a ".doc" file, then the request should have specifically stated it.

No Duty to Produce Inaccessible Data if There is Undue Burden or Undue Cost

The FRCP creates two classes of ESI: accessible and inaccessible data. The FRCP at Rule 26(b)(2)(B) says that ESI does not need to be produced if the source is not reasonably accessible because of undue burden or undue cost. If the producing party takes this position, it must be ready to give specific factual reasons to backup their claims. In addition, some courts have allowed the requesting party's expert to examine the system in question to determine whether the ESI is in fact inaccessible. ESI that might fall into this category includes electronic data that has been erased, fragmented, or stored on out-of-date storage systems that are no longer supported by the organization. In any case, the producing party may still be required to produce the ESI if the requesting party can show that the information is important, relevant, and unavailable anywhere else.

Claims of Privilege Can be Asserted After Inadvertent Production

Federal Rule of Civil Procedure Rule 26(b)(5)(B) provides a process for a producing party to recover information that was inadvertently produced when it was in fact privileged. This is sometimes referred to as the "claw-back" provision. The reason for the rule is to level the playing field. When producing parties are requested to produce millions of pages of ESI, it is probable if not highly likely that from time to time privileged information will be inadvertently produced. If this happens, the rule states that the party receiving the information "must promptly return, sequester or destroy the specified information and any copies it has and may not use or disclose the information until the claim is resolved." The receiving party may also bring the matter to the court to decide if the ESI is in fact privileged.

> *The sheer volume of electronic document production makes inadvertent disclosure of a privileged document a serious concern for in-house counsel and litigators alike. More and more lawyers are being compelled to produce millions of documents that at some point earlier in time were disorganized, existed only on computer hard drives or backup tapes, or had never before been put in physical form.*[10]

Safe Harbor Regarding Electronic Information that Is Lost as a Result of Routine, Good-Faith Operation of an Electronic Information System

According to the FRCP, parties that act in good faith but inadvertently destroy ESI as a routine part of their information systems are not subject to sanctions. This is often referred to as the "safe harbor" provision. This includes inadvertent routine deletion of information such as emails to create additional space or backup tapes being recycled. Rule 37(f) of the FRCP says that "a court may not impose sanctions under these rules on a party for failing to provide electronically stored information lost as a result of the routine, good-faith operation of an electronic information system." This rule assumes, however, that the party in question has acted in good faith, including discussing the issue of preservation of ESI with the other party, putting a litigation hold in place, and making some effort to not intentionally destroy ESI.

PRODUCING AND RECEIVING ESI

When it comes to ESI, legal professionals must be prepared to both request ESI from the other party and assist the client in producing their own ESI for the other party.

Clients Must Preserve ESI—Preservation Letter to Client

Attorneys and legal assistants must inform clients early on in the process (even before an actual case is filed) that they must not destroy ESI. This includes not deleting emails, reformatting hard drives, destroying backup tapes, or otherwise erasing data that might be discoverable in litigation. Legal staff should also document the process in a preservation letter to the client so it can be proven at a later time that there was no intentional destruction of ESI.

> *[In]* Coleman v. Morgan Stanley *(Florida Circuit Court, May 2005), [the case concerned] an accounting fraud action arising out of a corporate merger. Morgan Stanley became a textbook example of what can go wrong in electronic data preservation and collection. In the course of the matter the defendant and, at times, their attorneys failed to preserve email messages pursuant to applicable SEC rules, they failed to adopt an immediate litigation hold; they failed to identify and gather all potentially relevant files; they failed to search all parts of recovered files (e.g., email attachments); they failed to produce documents timely; they made false statements to the court; and they failed to supplement responses/correct prior misstatements in a timely fashion. The court eventually took the drastic step of instructing the jury to assume that the defendant defrauded the plaintiff. The jury awarded plaintiff $1.45 billion in damages, of which $850 million were punitive damages.*[11]

Sending a Preservation Letter to the Opposing Party

If the opposing party has ESI, it is recommended that a letter be sent as soon as possible, even before litigation is commenced, to the party or their counsel stating that ESI should not be destroyed. It is recommended to be as specific as possible in the letter, since normal business operations must still continue and too broad of a letter will make it difficult and burdensome to comply. A specific preservation letter puts the other side on notice regarding what type of information they should be preserving. A specific request made early in the matter makes it difficult for the other side to argue that ESI was accidentally deleted. If specific hard drives are at issue in a case, the preservation letter should also state that new software, encryption, defragmenting, data compression, and other processes that change the file structure of the hard disk should not be implemented until a copy of the hard drive is secured.

Items to be Negotiated Between the Attorneys/Parties at the Meet and Confer Session

Items that should be negotiated during the meet and confer session between the parties include:

- Exchange of basic system data
- Exchange of listing of electronic collections of data
- Exchange of information related to backup and archival data and its preservation, including standard dates, times, and reuse of storage devices
- Discussion of how the principal actors store data (laptop, PDA, voicemail, email, calendar, word-processing, etc.)

- Agreement to a common document production format, including methods of dealing with native format documents
- Whether metadata is being produced in whatever file formats are agreed to
- Any privelege related to ESI
- Disclosure of databases
- Any "inaccessible" data

Catalog All Client ESI

It is recommended that before the meet and confer session takes place, the attorney and/or legal assistant meet with the client to specifically catalog and understand all sources of the client's ESI. The catalog is crucial in preparing for the meet and confer session to document exactly what the client has. In addition, it is important to document this process, because if opposing counsel later makes spoliation claims, the attorneys will have documentation to support the fact that reasonable measures were taken to prevent this. **Spoliation** refers to the destruction of relevant documents in litigation. Exhibit 8–1 contains a sample checklist that can be used with clients to catalog their systems and ESI issues. Exhibit 8–1 can also be used as a tool to request ESI from the opposing party.

spoliation
The destruction of relevant documents in litigation.

Assisting Clients in Producing ESI

Attorneys and legal assistants should begin thinking about helping a client to produce ESI as soon as the client walks in the door. Putting off planning for ESI production until the actual request for production of documents is received can have disastrous consequences. There are three primary ways for clients to produce ESI. The first is to hire a professional third-party vendor to go on site and to assist the client's information technology staff in collecting the ESI. This has the advantage of having a third party involved, so if the opposing party claims that not all of the data was produced, the vendor can speak to the authenticity and completeness of their review. This is the easiest method for the law firm, but the most expensive one for the client. Second, the client gathers all of the data and sends it to you. The success of this option depends on the expertise of the client's information technology staff and still leaves the client open to arguments from the opposing side that not all of the information was produced. A third option is for the ESI to be remotely collected by a third-party vendor. Each of the options has advantages and disadvantages. The decision should be made on a case-by-case basis depending on the unique circumstances in each instance.

Document Formats

There are thousands of formats and structures in which electronic documents can be saved. **Native format** refers to an associated file structure as defined by the original creating application. As noted earlier in the chapter, the native format for a Microsoft Word 2003 document is ".doc." Native formats cause problems because often the native format requires the original application to view or search a document. (For example, a copy of Microsoft Word 2003 may be needed to read and access a ".doc" file). However, some large third-party vendors have developed proprietary software solutions that allow users to see ESI in native format without having the original program.

native format
A file structure as defined by the original creating application.

> *In a perfect world, you'd want everything in native electronic format. But in the real world, you may lack the systems, software or expertise to access native data and preserve its evidentiary integrity.*[12]

Many electronic documents can be converted to vendor-neutral file structures such as PDF (Portable Document Format) or TIFF (Tagged Image

Exhibit 8–1
Checklist of Items to Review Regarding Electronically Stored Information Relevant to the Litigation

Item	Date Range (x/xx/xx to xx/xx/xx)	Program Created In	Format of Data	Physical Location of Data	Estimated File Size/Volume
Email files and attachments					
Calendar files					
Contact/task list files					
Word-processing files					
Spreadsheet files					
Database files					
Graphic/sound files					
Accounting/billing/budgeting files					
Sales files					
Marketing files					
Internal/operations report files					
Payroll files					
PDF files					
Presentation files					
Files stored in file management systems					
Voicemail (and voicemail files in email)					
Network logs, audit trails, and monitoring software					
Data that is hosted by application service providers					
Internet-related files					
Intranet/Extranet					
Backup/archive data					
Personal digital assistants (PDAs) and smart phones					
Telephone logs					
Laptops					
Servers					
Portable storage devices (thumb drives, CD-ROMS, DVDs, zip disks, memory sticks, etc.)					
Disaster recovery storage and storage in co-location sites					
Home computers					

Listing of basic information system data, including

- Network type/configuration/structure
- Operating system
- Class/type of computers used
- All application programs (custom and off-the-shelf)
- Backup/archival systems and backup protocols
- Name of the system administrator
- Encryption systems (ask for keys)
- Email client/server
- Janitorial (email deletion) programs

File Format). They are sometimes called **image format** or "static format" file structures because the image of the document is displayed as it would be in the original application without the need to have the original application. A downside of some image formats, such as TIFF, is that the metadata associated with the file is no longer present. In addition, what some litigants have done is to purposefully convert documents from a native format that the requesting party could process (such as Microsoft Word) to an image format to delete the metadata and make it more expensive and difficult for the requesting party to work with the document. PDF is an image format that can associate metadata, so it offers an advantage over TIFF.

image format
A file structure that shows an image of a document as if it was viewed in the original application without having the original application.

[In employment litigation] each time your employees edit a Word document or create an Excel spreadsheet, they unknowingly leave behind vital hidden electronic data. [This] data can include, for example, text that a manager added or deleted to a performance review, formulas employees used for making spreadsheet calculations, and information regarding which individuals accessed a file, when they accessed it and how they changed it. These records can be so important in legal proceedings that courts increasing are requiring employers to maintain and track such hidden data, which do not exist in paper records.[13]

Metadata

Metadata is information stored electronically in files that may identify the origin, date, author, usage, comments, or other information about a file. Metadata is often described as "data about data." Some courts have found that parties are entitled to the metadata that goes with ESI when it is produced. Parties often use metadata to prove their theory of a case. In a recent case a woman brought a class action against an employer arguing that age was a determining factor in the employer's decision to lay off workers. The employee requested the spreadsheets that were used to analyze layoff options in the native format so the hidden formulas could be analyzed. The employer provided the spreadsheets with the cells locked so the formulas and other metadata could not be viewed. The court ruled that the employer had to produce the documents in their native format, which included being able to access the metadata.

metadata
Information stored electronically in files that may identify the origin, date, author, usage, comments, or other information about a file. Metadata is often described as "data about data."

Using In-House Staff or Hiring Third-Party Vendors

[Third-party vendors and] technologists know where to look for the information you need, and can help you tailor your discovery requests if you need to narrow discovery while procuring as much useful information as possible. A technologist is prepared with huge amounts of drive space and can recreate all sorts of native environments to analyze evidence. Having an expert helps preserve the chain of custody and prove authenticity of the evidence—an expert is far better qualified than an attorney or an information technology staff member to explain the technical side of computer forensics and defend against common charges that the evidence is unreliable or might have been tampered with.[14]

When a party is producing documents pursuant to a production request, it is necessary to decide whether the party wants their own information technology department to prepare the ESI or whether a third-party vendor will be hired to coordinate the production. A number of factors must be weighed regarding this decision. Three key factors include the amount of data needing to be produced, the amount of time the organization has to produce it, and the complexity of transferring the data itself. Exhibit 8–2 shows the process whereby a client and their legal team might produce documents in a case.

Exhibit 8–2
Steps in the E-Discovery Production Process

No.	E-Discovery Production Steps
1.	Legal team issues letter to client advising them to preserve data related to litigation.
2.	Legal team meets with client to discuss strategies and problems related to ESI early on in case, including cataloging the ESI and discussing any special problems (unique or uncommon file formats, location of files/access, dates of files that may be requested, and any problems such as backup issues, etc.)
3.	If litigation is imminent, client and legal team decide whether production will be handled by a third-party vendor or the client's internal information technology (IT) team.
4.	If a third party will be used, a request for proposal may be issued, bids received, and a vendor selected.
5.	Parties to the lawsuit have a meet and confer conference to disclose ESI information and try to reach an understanding/resolution on ESI issues, including format of requested ESI.
6.	Document request is received. Legal team analyzes the request and decides if a protective order should be sought.
7.	Legal team meets with client and third-party vendor/client's IT team regarding production strategy, timelines, and any problems.
8.	Third-party vendor/client's IT team harvests ESI, processes the data into a common file format, and creates a database.
9.	Legal team reviews the ESI gathered. Sufficient time is allowed so that relevance and privilege issues are considered. If a third-party vendor is used it is usually done at their site or remotely using the Internet and proprietary custom software. Such review includes the ability to search the database.
10.	ESI is produced and delivered to the opposing party.

In a recent Fortune 500 business merger, the U.S. Department of Justice requested a large amount of documents in a number of categories in conjunction with the merger. The organizations and their attorneys decided that the document production was too large for the organizations' own IT departments. Instead, they issued a request for proposals and hired a third-party vendor. The vendor assisted the businesses in producing more than thirty million pages of documents (2 gigabytes of files) in less than 60 days. To make matters worse, the Department of Justice required some files to be in their native format, while other files were to be produced as TIFF files. The vendor had special proprietary software that allowed the attorneys to review the ESI in a single database/platform while still being able to deliver the documents to the Department of Justice in multiple formats and meet its deadlines and requirements.

> *When choosing a vendor [for e-discovery] save a couple of hundred public documents of all different file types on a CD-ROM, then ask the vendors to load the documents into their system, create a dummy database and allow the legal team at the firm to log into the vendor's system and test the software before committing to the vendor for the duration of a large document discovery project.*[15]

In another large case regarding potential fraud and conspiracy allegations arising out of a complex multiparty transaction a law firm representing the plaintiff reviewed more than 30 gigabytes of restored email from the defendants. The attorneys hired a consulting firm to assist them with reviewing of the production. The attorneys and consultants used specialized software to assist

them in narrowing the millions of documents to a little more than ten thousand documents and a database to store, search, and retrieve them. In the end, the review was a success and led to a stronger case. The strategy allowed them to focus on slightly more than ten thousand documents rather than millions. They were able to find what they needed without wading through every single document, which would have taken more than a year. They accomplished the review of the records in a few months.

Thus, third-party vendors that specialize in e-discovery can help both when producing documents and when receiving them. The downside of third-party vendors is the cost. Hourly costs for large third-party vendors can be between $300–$500 a vendor, and this is just the hourly cost of the professionals that consult and work with the data. There can also be conversion costs and other expenses related to working with the data that can run in the tens of thousands of dollars, depending on the needs of the attorneys and clients. On the other hand, the cost is well worth it if the ESI is usable, meets the needs of the attorneys and users, and prevents the client from being sanctioned in court for failure to comply with ESI rules.

What Services Do Third-Party Vendors Provide and How Do They Work?

Whether a client must produce or receive ESI, third-party vendors can be helpful. Exhibit 8–3 shows a list of services that most high quality e-discovery vendors can provide. Exhibit 8–4 shows the results of a recent survey of legal assistants regarding third-party e-discovery vendors. This is a developing market and as legal organizations become more involved in ESI, the use of e-discovery vendors will rise.

Below is a more detailed explanation of the services that third-party vendors provide.

Harvesting Data As mentioned previously, third-party vendors can assist clients in **harvesting data,** meaning collecting data that needs to be produced from the client's information systems. Depending on the size of the production, the age of the data (for example, if it includes data from out-of-date systems), its

harvesting data
The process of collecting ESI from the client's information systems.

Exhibit 8–3
High-Quality Third-Party E-Discovery Vendor Services

- Analyze IT infrastructure and make recommendations on producing/receiving ESI
- Authenticate and provide testimony regarding ESI, including providing workflow certification affidavits regarding software processes, accuracy test results, and anything that shows the validity of the processing, searching, and filtering methods
- Ability to harvest, restore, and read a large variety of standard and unique file formats, databases, and structures, including ability to restore backups and harvest restored data
- Harvest, de-dupe, and filter data set as needed
- Process and produce data set in an electronically searchable format
- Present data in an easy-to-use viewable interface, no matter the format of the original data, and include options such as Bates numbering, redaction, document tagging, and notes
- Preserve metadata
- Integrate paper documents and ESI into one database
- Provide data recovery and forensic services
- Deliver native format and image files to opposing party

Exhibit 8–4
Electronic Discovery Vendors Used by Legal Assistants
Source: As seen in the May/June 2006 issue of Legal Assistant Today, Copyright 2006 James Publishing, Inc. Reprinted courtesy of LEGAL ASSISTANT TODAY magazine. For subscription information call (800) 394-2626, or visit http://www.legalassistanttoday.com.

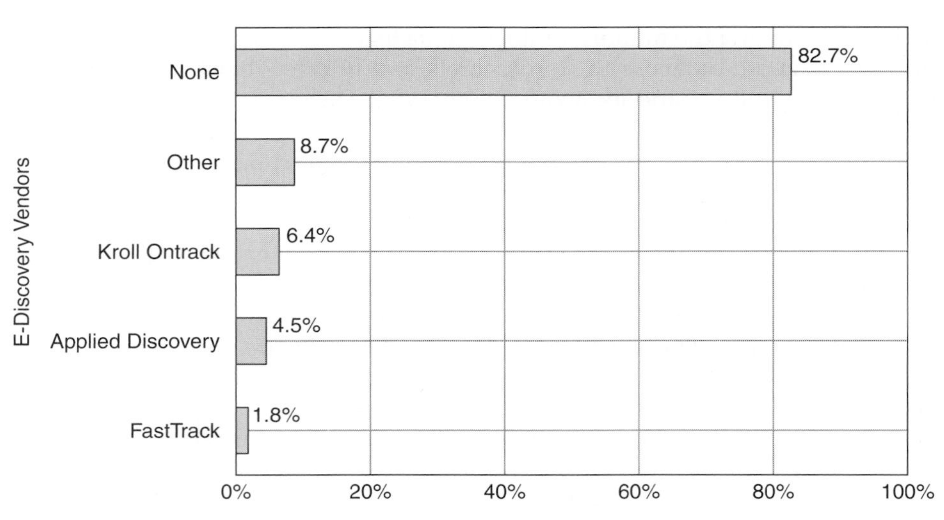

location, the amount of the data, and its native format, the harvesting of the data can either be routine or extremely complex. Because most production requests are time sensitive, it is important to have a plan for how the data will be harvested in advance of the actual production request and to know in what format the data will need to be processed.

de-duplication or "de-duping"
The process of marking or deleting records that are duplicates.

De-duplication **Deduplication or "de-duping"** is the process of marking or deleting records that are duplicates. For example, think of the number of duplicate records that are generated when a group of people exchange a series of emails. De-duping reduces the data set, which makes searching the data more efficient. It is also less expensive to produce and process the data, because de-duping can significantly cut down on the amount of data to produce.

data filtering
The process of searching and culling the data to find relevant information and reduce the overall size of the data set.

Data Filtering **Data filtering** is the process of searching and culling the data to find relevant information and reduce the overall size of the data set. Many third-party vendors claim that by using advanced filtering software they can reduce the size of a data set by 75 percent. When millions of documents are at issue, the ability to reduce the data set by 75 percent to even several hundred thousand relevant documents can represent an enormous savings in terms of time and money. Filtering can be used by the producer of the documents to help narrow the universe of potentially relevant and responsive documents so that document production requests can be met timely, cost effectively, and efficiently. Filtering can also be used by the requestor when the requestor receives a large amount of data and needs to reduce that data set to a more manageable size.

Processing Data If the third-party vendor is producing the ESI, they can harvest it and then produce it on CDs, DVDs, hard disks, or whatever media and format have been agreed to. If the third-party vendor has been hired to receive the data that has been produced, some vendors can convert the data to a common file format and create a unified database, which can then be filtered and viewed.

Viewing Data Whether a vendor is producing documents for the client to review prior to their being sent to the requesting party, or is filtering the data that has been produced by the other party, the vendor may provide the client with proprietary viewing software. This allows the attorney, legal assistant, or client to view documents in one central window no matter what format the files are in.

The viewing software provided by many vendors allows the user to see, magnify, print, add Bates numbers, redact information, add bookmarks/tags/notes, and in some cases view the metadata associated with the ESI.

Computer Forensics

Computer forensics is used to recover, authenticate, or analyze electronic data. Computer forensics can be used in a number of ways, including instances where it is suspected that electronic data has been deleted or modified, or where advanced computer expertise is necessary concerning extremely complex computer issues. Using advanced computer forensic techniques, experts can in some cases reconstruct or recover previously deleted or destroyed information. Computer forensics is sometimes used in lawsuits to recover data that has been destroyed or to prove that electronic data was intentionally deleted or destroyed. "Deleted data" is data that at one time was live on a computer, but which is now deleted. "Deleted data" may stay on storage media either completely or partially until it is overwritten. Even after data has been overwritten, some information may still remain, such as directory entries. **Soft deletions** refers to information that has been deleted and is not available to the user, but which nonetheless has not been overwritten. Soft deletions can often be fully restored with complete integrity. Computer forensics experts can also be used to locate and find data and operate as computer consultants to organizations.

Soft deletions
Information that has been deleted and is not available to the user, but which nonetheless has not been overwritten. Soft deletions can often be fully restored with complete integrity by forensic experts.

> *Consider a recent case where I was asked to assess whether a departing associate [at a law firm] stole files and diverted cases. The firm used Microsoft Exchange email server, so I could have [only] collected or searched the associate's email there. Had I looked only at the server, I would've missed the Hotmail traffic in the temporary Internet files folder and the short message service (SMS) exchanges in the PDA synchronization files. Or the Microsoft Outlook archive file (.pst) and offline synchronization file (.ost), both stored on a laptop hard drive, and holding thousands more emails. Just looking at the server wouldn't have revealed the stolen data or the diverted business—searching elsewhere uncovered a treasure trove of damning evidence.*[16]

Chain of Custody

It is important when dealing with ESI that the chain of custody be preserved. ESI must be able to be systematically traced back to anyone that has had access to it, and it must be proved that such access was never improper or contaminated the ESI from the time it left the hands of the opposing party to its introduction in court. It is imperative to be able to prove that no information was added, deleted, or altered. Experts can make a forensic copy of the data with matching marks to that prove the copy is complete. Exhibit 8–5 shows a sample chain of custody log. Without establishing a proper chain of custody and authentication, ESI data will never make into evidence in a case.

> *As silly as it sounds, the failure to maintain a proper chain of custody frequently comes into play. The smartest move, once you know electronic evidence is involved, is to get it into the hands of your expert, sign a chain of custody form, have the evidence forensically imaged, and then return the original evidence, again with the chain of custody form... The expert will carefully keep the imaged evidence under lock and key. Returning the original also helps defuse the business impact argument.*[17]

Exhibit 8–5
Chain of Custody Log

CHAIN OF CUSTODY LOG

Specific Description of Item	*Lomax 40 Gb. Hard Drive*
Evidence ID #	*1001*
Evidence Serial Number	*2934809234*
Evidence Custodian	*Steven Keys, IT Director, Chase Limited Co.*
Case/Matter	*Chase Limited v. Wax, Layman Mortgage Bankers*
Case No.	*2008-23434*

Name of Person Receiving Evidence	Date	Time	Place of Collection or Receipt	Purpose of Transfer	Signature of Person Receiving Item
Lisa Jenkins, Alpha Data Collection & Forensic Scientists, Inc.	*1/3/08*	*9:50 a.m.*	*Chase Limited Co, Exec. Headquarters, 64 Wall St. NY, NY*	*Copy and Review of Hard Drive to Determine if Confidential Trademark Secrets Were Released*	*Lisa Jenkins*
Steven Keys, IT Director, Chase Limited Co.	*1/17/08*	*4:00 p.m.*	*Chase Limited Co, Exec. Headquarters, 64 Wall St. NY, NY*	*Return of Hard Drive - Hard Drive Appears in Same Condition as it Left*	*Steven Keys*

Relying Too Much on Third-Party Vendors

> *If you engage in e-discovery, chances are you depend on vendors to help you harvest, process, search, and filter digital evidence. But is that a dependency that blurs the line between lawyer and service provider? Selecting responsible information, planning search strategies, and deciding forms of production are responsibilities traditionally reserved to counsel... Lawyers now share, and sometimes surrender, aspects of that role to vendors and experts. When all goes well, delegation seems sensible. But what happens when a vendor error exposes lawyers to malpractice allegations, or clients to needless expenses, sanctions, or even an adverse judgment?... An attorney has a duty to manage a vendor's processing, even if the systems are proprietary and complex, and even if the attorney must do so through an expert. In the ESI context, attorneys must assign appropriately trained litigation support professionals, technology paralegals, or associates to oversee evidence management.*[18]

Legal professionals must be careful when delegating work, including ESI related work, to third-party vendors. They must ensure that they are closely watching and scrutinizing the vendors. In several recent high-profile cases, attorneys have delegated too much of the responsibility for ESI related matters to vendors and been reprimanded by judges and sued by clients for malpractice when the third-party vendor/expert's advice was wrong.

SUMMARY

Electronic discovery refers to the process of producing and receiving litigation documents in electronic format. The Federal Rules of Civil Procedure (FRCP) refers to any electronic data as "electronically stored information" (ESI). In the FRCP ESI includes "writings, drawings, graphs, charts, photographs, sound recordings, images and other data compilations stored in any medium from which information can be obtained or translated."

The FRCP has many rules regarding ESI, including the duty of the parties to meet and confer early in the case to discuss ESI. There is also a duty for each side to preserve evidence in a case, including having the client put a litigation hold in place and to willingly and cooperatively exchanging ESI. The FRCP provides that data that is inaccessible may or may not have to be produced depending on the circumstances, and that even after a document has been produced, if it is privileged the receiving party may be required to return or otherwise destroy the document and may not disclose it. The FRCP also has for a safe harbor provision that states that if a party acts in good faith but inadvertently destroys ESI as a part of a routine aspect of their information system, a court may not sanction them.

When producing documents "native format" refers to an associated file structure as defined by the original creating application. When producing documents, some are produced in image formats or a "static format." This is an image of the document as it would appear in the original application without the need to have the original application. Metadata is information that is stored electronically in files that may identify the origin, date, author, usage, comments, or other information about a file. Some courts have found that parties are entitled to the metadata that goes with ESI when they are produced. Third-party vendors may be used in producing or receiving litigation documents. Third-party vendors may provide a number of services, including harvesting data, which is the process of collecting ESI from the client's information system, and data filtering, which is the process of searching and culling the data to find relevant information and reduce the overall size of the data set.

INTERNET SITES

Organization	Product/Service	World Wide Web Address
Alpha Systems	Electronic discovery services	<http://www.alpha-sys.com>
Altep, Inc.	Electronic discovery services	<http://www.altep.com>
Attenex Corp	Electronic discovery services	<http://www.attenex.com>
Capital Legal Solutions	Electronic discovery services	<http://www.capitallegals.com>
Capitol Digital Document Solutions	Electronic discovery services	<http://www.capitolllc.com>
CaseCentral	Electronic discovery services	<http://www.casecentral.com>
Compulit	Electronic discovery services	<http://www.compulit.com>
Cricket Technologies	Electronic discovery services	<http://www.crickettechnologies.com>
Daticon, Inc.	Electronic discovery services	<http://www.daticon.com>
Discover-e Legal	Electronic discovery services	<http://www.discover-e-legal.com>
Docuity, Inc.	Electronic discovery services	<http://www.docuity.com>
DocuLex, Inc.	Electronic discovery services	<http://www.doculex.com>
DocuServe Group	Electronic discovery services	<http://www.edocuserve.com>
Electronic Evidence Discovery Inc.	Electronic discovery services	<http://www.eedinc.com>
Fios Inc.	Electronic discovery services	<http://www.fiosinc.com>
Forensics Consulting Solutions	Electronic discovery services	<http://www.forensicsconsulting.com>
IE Discovery Inc.	Electronic discovery services	<http://www.iediscovery.com>
Image Capturing Engineering	Electronic discovery services	<http://www.imagecap.com>
Kroll OnTrack	Electronic discovery services	<http://www.krollontrack.com>
Lexis Nexis	Electronic discovery services	<http://www.applieddiscovery.com>
Planet Data Solutions	Electronic discovery services	<http://www.planetds.com>
Xact	Electronic discovery services	<http://www.xactids.com>

KEY TERMS

electronic discovery
discovery
electronically stored information
litigation hold
spoliation
native format
image format
metadata
harvesting data
de-duplication
data filtering
soft deletions

TEST YOUR KNOWLEDGE

Test your knowledge of the chapter by answering these questions.

1. Define the term "electronic discovery."
2. What do the Federal Rules of Civil Procedure refer to electronic data as?
3. True or False: Under the FRCP, parties are required to disclose information about ESI even before they receive a discovery request.
4. What is a litigation hold?
5. True or False: Under the FRCP, if a party produces a document in ESI format they still may have to produce a hard-copy of the document.
6. What does the "claw-back" provision in the FRCP refer to?

7. According to the FRCP, when might a party be required to produce inaccessible data?
8. What is the safe harbor provision of the FRCP?
9. When a party destroys relevant documents in litigation it is called _______.
10. An associated file structure that is defined by the original creating application is called _______.
11. True or False: Data harvesting is searching and culling data.

ON THE WEB EXERCISES

1. Go to three e-discovery Web sites in the Internet Sites section of this chapter and compare and contrast the services of the vendors. Which one were you most impressed with, and why? Write a one-page summary regarding your research.
2. Using a general search engine such as google.com or yahoo.com, find the 2006 amended Federal Rules of Civil Procedure and read Rules 26 and 34. Summarize what you find regarding ESI in a two-page paper.
3. Using a general search engine such as google.com or yahoo.com, find three articles on e-discovery. Write a short paper summarizing the articles you found.
4. Using a general search engine such as google.com or yahoo.com, or a legal search engine such as findlaw.com, find one case related to e-discovery, either cited in an article or reproduced in full. Write a one-page summary of the case.
5. Using a general search engine such as google.com or yahoo.com, find a sample of a request for proposal that a law firm might send to an e-discovery vendor for document production services related to a large case.
6. Using a general search engine such as google.com or yahoo.com, find a draft preservation letter for a client and an opposing party.

QUESTIONS AND EXERCISES

1. A legal organization is trying to decide whether to recommend to a client the use of a third-party e-discovery vendor for document production in a case. What factors should the firm consider in making this recommendation?
2. You are a new legal assistant in a law firm and a client you are working with cannot understand why they should preserve evidence in a case that is not favorable to them. Write a one-page memo explaining how you would try to convince the client to preserve evidence.
3. You are a new legal assistant in a law firm and you are trying to convince a client to spend $300 an hour for data filtering services from a third-party vendor in a case where twenty thousand documents will be produced. Write a one-page summary of how you would handle the matter.

END NOTES

[1] Sharon Nelson and John Simek, "The New Federal Rules of Civil Procedure: An ESI Primer," *Law Practice*, December 2006, 23.
[2] Elissa A. Santa, "E-Discovery Explosion," *Legal Assistant Today*, July/August 2006, 57.
[3] Sharon D. Nelson and John W. Simek, "E-Discovery: Don't Let Electronic Evidence Bury Your Firm," *Legal Assistant Today*, May/June, 2004, 63.
[4] Elissa A. Santa, "E-Discovery Explosion," *Legal Assistant Today*, July/August 2006, 59.
[5] Sharon Nelson and John Simek, "The New Federal Rules of Civil Procedure: An ESI Primer," *Law Practice*, December 2006, 25.
[6] Maureen Mulligan, "Preserving Electronic Materials – A Practical Guide," *Tort Source*, Vol 9, No. 1 Fall 2006, 1.
[7] Bill Roberts, "Avoiding the Perils of Electronic Data," *HR Magazine*, January 2007, 75.
[8] Bill Roberts, "Avoiding the Perils of Electronic Data," *HR Magazine*, January 2007, 77.
[9] Elissa A. Santa, "E-Discovery Explosion," *Legal Assistant Today*, July/August 2006, 60.
[10] "Top 10 Tips to Prepare for FRCP Changes," *Lexis Nexis Applied Discovery*, www.lexisnexis.com/applieddiscovery, 4.
[11] *Litigation Support Tools and Techniques*, International Legal Technology Association, March 2006, 4.
[12] Craig Ball, "The Train's About to Depart," *Law Technology News*, June 2006, 44.
[13] Bill Roberts, "Avoiding the Perils of Electronic Data," *HR Magazine*, January 2007, 72.
[14] Sharon D. Nelson and John W. Simek, "E-Discovery: Don't Let Electronic Evidence Bury Your Firm," *Legal Assistant Today*, May/June, 2004, 63.
[15] Janet Roberts, "Spotlight on the Discovery Process," *Law Office Computing*, June/July 2005, 61.
[16] Craig Ball, "The Path to E-mail Production," *Legal Technology News*, October 2005, 18.
[17] Sharon D. Nelson and John W. Simek, "E-Discovery: Don't Let Electronic Evidence Bury Your Firm," *Legal Assistant Today*, May/June, 2004, 66.
[18] Craig Ball, "Worst Case Scenario," Legal Technology News, October 2006, 1, 35.

CHAPTER 9

LITIGATION SUPPORT SOFTWARE

CHAPTER OBJECTIVES

After completing Chapter 9, you should be able to do the following:

1. Explain what litigation support is.
2. Explain why computerized litigation support methods are more successful than manual methods.
3. Explain why legal organizations might use a litigation support service provider.
4. Identify the three major types of litigation support systems.
5. Describe the litigation support process.

litigation support software
Software that assists attorneys and legal assistants in organizing, storing, retrieving, and summarizing information that is gathered in the litigation of a lawsuit.

Litigation support software assists attorneys and legal assistants in organizing, storing, retrieving, and summarizing information that is gathered in the litigation of a lawsuit. During the course of a lawsuit, large quantities of information are acquired. Litigation support software helps to manage and control this information so that it is presented in a usable format to the attorney working on the case. This chapter introduces the fundamentals of computerized litigation support and describes how it can be used effectively in the practice of law, including information and documents to be tracked in litigation, manual litigation support methods, types of computer litigation support systems, the litigation support process, the purchase of litigation support systems, and questions and fears about using computerized litigation support.

INFORMATION AND DOCUMENTS TO BE TRACKED IN LITIGATION

> *Case and litigation management is a constantly changing interactive process. Legal issues change, witness testimony can take on added importance, pleadings can impact pretrial motions, trial exhibits are affected by information in interrogatories, calendaring and trial dates affect settlement positioning, and changes in the law can overturn the best laid plans.*[1]

During litigation, the legal team (including attorneys, legal assistants, etc.) must organize, summarize, control, and understand a great deal of information so that it can be presented to a fact finder such as a judge, jury, or administrative hearing officer in a way that defeats the opposition's case and promotes the

client's interests the most. This is not an easy task since legal issues, factual issues, and legal theories are constantly changing both during the course of the litigation and at trial. The more parties there are, the more complex the issues are, the more documents there are, the more attorneys/legal assistants there are, and the larger the stakes, the harder it is to succeed at organizing and controlling the information.

> *From simple to complex cases, attorneys [and legal assistants] are struggling to handle and control paper and electronic information...*[2]

Information and documents that need to be tracked in litigation vary according to the type of case that is being litigated. However, the following are some of the more common documents that need to be tracked:

- *Litigation documents*—These are documents prepared during the course of the lawsuit. They include correspondence and email between the attorneys and the court, discovery documents, pleadings, depositions and transcripts (including summaries), expert witness reports, and other information that is filed in the case.
- *Factual documents*—These are documents that arise out of the subject matter of the litigation. They might include contracts, correspondence, emails, business/financial records, photographs, diagrams, and other information between the parties or relevant to the lawsuit. These also include anything that might be presented as evidence in the case to prove or disprove the claim.
- *Knowledge management documents*—This refers to information that is used to help strategize, analyze, and administratively prepare the litigation. The focus of knowledge management is not on documents but on information. These might include chronologies and timelines of the case, analysis of the issues, legal precedent, case law, management/tracking of the case docket, lists of witnesses and exhibits, internal reports or analysis of the facts of the case, and other information.

The following section explores each of these areas in more detail.

Litigation Documents

These are documents that are prepared during the course of the lawsuit. They are extremely important, both because they are filed with a court, typically under deadlines, and because they contain the basic theories and strategies for winning the case. It is important that the legal team involved has control over these documents. Types of litigation documents include miscellaneous documents, discovery documents, and pleadings.

Miscellaneous Documents Miscellaneous documents in litigation include notes, internal memorandums, and correspondence, including emails.

Notes Written records of conversations and events are made from the first time a client steps in the door until the conclusion of a lawsuit.

Internal Memorandums Interoffice memorandums and e-mails are documents that are more formal than handwritten notes and are usually circulated within a legal organization. They may be notes to a client's file, requests to other members of the firm to do things, or an exchange of information between individuals on a legal team.

External Correspondence Letters, email, and written communications that are exchanged between attorneys and their clients, between opposing attorneys, between attorneys and potential witnesses, and between attorneys and the court are external correspondence.

discovery
The stage of a lawsuit in which the parties share and discover information about a case.

interrogatories
A series of written questions that are directed to an opposing party in a lawsuit.

request for admissions
A series of questions directed to an opposing party in a lawsuit that must be either admitted or denied.

request for production of documents
A series of requests that direct an opposing party in a lawsuit to produce documents and ESI that are in its possession or control so that the documents or evidence can be given to or examined by the requesting party.

deposition
Oral testimony taken before a court reporter who transcribes the testimony word for word.

expert witness report
A report produced by an expert witness that states the factual basis for the expert's opinion on the matter.

pleadings
Formal documents filed with a court that usually state a party's contentions regarding specific issues.

motions and briefs
Filed in cases during the litigation to argue whatever position the party is taking on how the case should proceed in court.

Discovery Documents In most lawsuits, all parties (plaintiffs and defendants) are entitled to discover the facts and documents that the other party has. That is, each party is given the opportunity to ask the other party questions about the case and to obtain documents and evidence that the other party may have. The process whereby the parties share and discover information about a case is called the **discovery** stage of a lawsuit. Discovery documents include interrogatories, requests for admissions, requests for production of documents, depositions, expert witness reports, and so forth.

Interrogatories Comprising a series of written questions that are directed to an opposing party in a lawsuit (see Exhibit 9–1), **interrogatories** must be answered under oath and returned to the issuing party.

Requests for Admissions A series of questions directed to an opposing party in a lawsuit, a **request for admissions** must be either admitted or denied (see Exhibit 9–2).

Requests for Production of Documents A **request for production of documents** is a series of requests that direct an opposing party in a lawsuit to produce documents and electronically stored information ESI that are in its possession or control so that the documents and ESI or evidence can be given to or examined by the requesting party (see Exhibit 9–3). In some cases, especially those that are complex or span a number of years, anywhere from one thousand to one million documents or more can be produced. The documents that are actually produced are discussed in the next section on factual documents.

Depositions A **deposition** is oral testimony that is taken before a court reporter who transcribes the testimony word for word. Exhibit 9–4 shows a deposition transcript. Depositions can be taken of parties or witnesses.

Expert Witness Reports A report that is produced by an expert witness and states the factual basis for the expert's opinion on a matter is called an **expert witness report.**

Pleadings Formal documents filed with a court that usually state a party's contentions regarding specific issues are **pleadings.** The complaint, answer (and any amendments to these documents), and pretrial questionnaires are examples of pleadings.

Motions and Briefs During the litigation **motions and briefs** are filed to argue the position a party is taking on how the case should proceed in court. These can be voluminous, especially if the issues are complex. Motions and briefs are critical to a case because they set forth the legal/factual theories of each party to the case. Some of the more important motions typically filed in cases include motions to dismiss and motions for summary judgment, among others, because both of these motions seek to dismiss the lawsuit before it ever reaches the fact finder.

Factual Documents and Electronically Stored Information

Factual documents and electronically stored information arise out of the subject matter of the litigation. Depending on the case, these can range from a couple of documents to a million documents. For example, suppose a jet airliner crash is being litigated. Factual documents that might be produced in the case include

Exhibit 9–1
Interrogatories

IN THE UNITED STATES DISTRICT COURT
FOR THE WESTERN DISTRICT OF MISSOURI

JACK C. CAMPBELL,	)	
PLAINTIFF,	)	
	)	
-vs-	)	CASE NO. 592-2344
	)	
RANDY C. JACOBS	)	
	)	
DEFENDANT,	)	
	)	

INTERROGATORIES DIRECTED TO DEFENDANT
RANDY C. JACOBS

COMES NOW the plaintiff, Jack C. Campbell, and moves that the defendant in this automobile negligence action, Randy C. Jacobs, answers the following written interrogatories in writing, under oath, to wit:

1. HOW MANY NIGHTCLUBS DID YOU VISIT THE NIGHT OF THE ACCIDENT, JANUARY 21, AND WHAT WERE THEIR NAMES?

Answer: I visited one nightclub, the Casablanca.

2. HOW MANY MIXED DRINKS DID YOU HAVE THE NIGHT OF THE ACCIDENT, JANUARY 21?

Answer: I had 12 mixed drinks the night of January 21.

3. HOW MANY CONVICTIONS HAVE YOU RECEIVED FOR DRIVING UNDER THE INFLUENCE OF ALCOHOL?

Answer: I have received four convictions for driving under the influence.

years' worth of maintenance records, Federal Aviation Administration (FAA) registration and other documents, passenger lists, technical design schematics possibly on many areas of the plane, computer models, memorandums and email from aeronautical engineers regarding the actual manufacturing of the aircraft, and so on. Again, the kinds of documents and ESI that will be important in the case depend on the specific facts of the case and the complexity of the case. Factual documents and ESI include any information that might be presented to the fact finder as evidence to prove or disprove a claim.

While many factual documents and ESI are discoverable, some are not. Some documents that might be attorney work product are privileged and are not discoverable.

Exhibit 9–2
Requests for Admissions

IN THE UNITED STATES DISTRICT COURT
FOR THE WESTERN DISTRICT OF MISSOURI

JACK C. CAMPBELL,)
)
PLAINTIFF,)
)
-vs-) CASE NO. 592-2344
)
RANDY C. JACOBS)
)
DEFENDANT,)
)

REQUEST FOR ADMISSIONS

DIRECTED TO DEFENDANT RANDY C. JACOBS

COMES NOW the plaintiff, Jack C. Campbell, and moves that the defendant in this automobile negligence action, Randy C. Jacobs, either admit or deny the following admissions in writing, under oath, to wit:

1. ON THE NIGHT OF THE ACCIDENT, JANUARY 12, YOU CONSUMED MORE THAN ONE QUART OF VODKA.

Admitted—or Denied: ADMITTED.

2. ON THE NIGHT OF THE ACCIDENT, JANUARY 21, YOUR BLOOD ALCOHOL LEVEL WAS TESTED BY A MISSOURI POLICE OFFICER AT .80 (WHICH IS LEGALLY DRUNK IN THIS STATE).

Admitted—or Denied: ADMITTED.

3. YOU HAVE HAD SIX PREVIOUS CONVICTIONS FOR DRIVING UNDER THE INFLUENCE OF ALCOHOL.

Admitted—or Denied: DENIED.

Knowledge Management

In addition to tracking litigation documents and factual documents in a case, legal professionals must also track and organize internal organizational knowledge or knowledge management about a case. This class of information is usually prepared internally by legal professionals and can include a wide variety of miscellaneous information that can be helpful when litigating a case, such as the following:

- chronologies or timelines of the facts of a case, which are often critical for presenting theories on a case including what, when, how, and why things happened in a case

Exhibit 9–3
Requests for Production of Documents

IN THE UNITED STATES DISTRICT COURT
FOR THE WESTERN DISTRICT OF MISSOURI

JACK C. CAMPBELL,	)	
	)	
PLAINTIFF,	)	
	)	
-vs-	)	CASE NO. 592-2344
	)	
RANDY C. JACOBS	)	
	)	
DEFENDANT,	)	
______________________	)	

REQUEST FOR PRODUCTION OF DOCUMENTS
DIRECTED TO DEFENDANT RANDY C. JACOBS

COMES NOW the plaintiff, Jack C. Campbell, and moves that the defendant in this automobile negligence action, Randy C. Jacobs, answer and/or produce the following requests for production of documents in writing, under oath, to wit:

1. Produce all maintenance and repair bills regarding your automobile, a Ford Thunderbird, that was involved in the accident on January 21.

Answer: Enclosed are 3 repair bills for the Ford Thunderbird.

2. Produce all documents in your possession regarding your treatment of alcoholism.

Answer: None.

- analysis and strategies regarding factual issues, legal issues, evidentiary issues, and other problems that need to be addressed at trial or at other stages of the litigation
- analysis of current case law and how it will impact the case at various stages of the litigation
- scheduling and docket control reports that can be important in litigation because they give a factual summary of the litigation process, including how and when things were accomplished in the case. This can be particularly important in large cases that are litigated for many years. In many cases, attorneys and clients strategize the timing of the litigation, including stalling techniques or trying to "push" cases through to trial.
- case diaries and notes made during litigation
- other internal reports such as queries and searches that show cause and effect in evidence, reports about witnesses (such as a report that shows every time the witnesses' names were brought up in the lawsuit), and anything else that provides information or knowledge to a case that is not a litigation or factual document but may be important to the case

Exhibit 9–4
Deposition Transcript

<u>Deposition of Jack Campbell</u>

Deposition of Jack Campbell, taken October 12.

QUESTIONING BY JIM SMITH ATTORNEY FOR THE DEFENDANT

Q. PLEASE STATE YOUR NAME FOR THE RECORD.
A. JACK CAMPBELL.

Q. PLEASE STATE YOUR ADDRESS.
A. 3600 HOLLY LANE, BRANSON, MISSOURI.

Q. ARE YOU THE PLAINTIFF IN THIS ACTION?
A. YES, I AM.

Q. PLEASE STATE WHERE YOU ARE CURRENTLY EMPLOYED.
A. I AM EMPLOYED AT THE BRANSON AIRPORT.

Q. WHAT IS YOUR SUPERVISOR'S NAME?
MR. EDWARD (ATTORNEY FOR PLAINTIFF): JIM, THAT SIMPLY IS NOT RELEVANT TO THE SCOPE OF THIS ACTION AND I OBJECT ON THE GROUNDS OF RELEVANCE—I'LL LET HER ANSWER BUT LET'S GET ON TO SOMETHING RELEVANT TO THIS ACTION.

WHY LITIGATION SUPPORT?

In a typical case that is being litigated, it is possible to have hundreds of documents and extensive ESI in a file. When complex litigation is considered, the mountains of documents and ESI that are generated can be astounding. Some complex cases may have a million factual documents and pieces of ESI and years' worth of litigation documents. Can you imagine trying to remember all of that information in your head?

The purpose of litigation support, whether through manual or computerized methods, is to organize the litigation/factual documents and knowledge in a case so that they are useful to the attorney. For example, suppose an attorney is questioning a witness in open court and knows the witness is perjuring himself and changing his testimony from what he gave at a prior deposition. *If* the attorney can show this, she can prove a point and create doubt as to the witness's credibility and believability. Unfortunately, the attorney is unable to find the place in the volumes of depositions where the prior answer was given to the same question. She is unable to discredit the witness because of poor litigation support. This is how litigation support wins or loses cases.

The goal of litigation support is to make sure this scenario does not happen. At trial, and throughout litigation, attorneys are engaged in cross-examining hostile witnesses, preparing their own witnesses, and making objections and other legal arguments. This is a full-time job. Thus, attorneys must be backed up by a support system that can help them quickly find information they need to effectively handle a case.

Since attorneys never know what to expect or what may transpire during litigation (depending on the case), many of the documents generated or collected by a firm during the litigation process may need to be tracked and organized. Litigation support can make the difference between winning and losing cases. It therefore plays a vital role in how lawsuits are litigated.

> *Documents have always presented accessibility and retrieval problems. Many three-ring notebooks are put together to assist in the location and indexing of case information. They are routinely pulled apart to copy a document, prepare for summary judgment, or as an exhibit for a deposition or trial. Oftentimes, the original is lost...or a 4th or 5th generation copy becomes illegible. If more than one legal professional is working on the case, the document we need always seems to be checked out. . . .Manually controlling paper is also drudgery, and it is not what the practice of law is about. The goal should be to spend more time using information and less time looking for it.*[3]

MANUAL LITIGATION SUPPORT METHODS

One type of manual litigation support system is a simple index produced on a word processor that lists key issues, facts, or other items to remember. This index is usually kept in a notebook that is used at trial. The major limitations of this manual system are that it is impossible to cover all topics that might be brought up during the course of a trial and the index must be continually updated as new issues arise.

Another type of manual litigation support system used to organize a case is an index card system, usually based on key issues. For every essential document in the case, one or more index cards are prepared. If a document is related to two different key issues, then two index cards must be prepared, summarizing the document's contents on those issues. Then each card is filed behind the appropriate issue divider.

Although the index card system is more sophisticated than the simple index, its use also has several disadvantages:

1. This type of manual system is time-consuming and tedious to set up, since the cards must usually be prepared by hand or typed. In addition, the process is slow, since a single document might have many issues that must be indexed.
2. Because this type of system is tedious, it facilitates entering the least number of documents instead of being thorough and entering all relevant documents.
3. This type of system is useful only for simple searches. Because it is slow and tedious, other types of indexes, such as author and chronological indexes, usually cannot be created.
4. The system is vulnerable to human errors, such as the misfiling of cards.
5. If cards are not put back, are lost, or if the system should be knocked off a desk and the cards scattered, it could be a major disaster.

Manual litigation support systems, whether they use an index card system or other manual methods, do not suit the legal environment well, since they are inherently inflexible and unable to meet changing needs. A lawsuit is an ever-changing environment, where key issues can change in an instant. What was important one minute can be unimportant the next. Especially at trial, the litigation support system must be flexible and adaptable as a case progresses.

OVERVIEW OF COMPUTERIZED LITIGATION SUPPORT

Computerized litigation support solves many of the problems associated with manual methods and has many benefits. In addition, there are many different kinds of computerized litigation support software available and litigation support can either be provided in-house by using existing staff or outsourced to a litigation support service provider.

Manual v. Computerized Litigation Support

A comparison of the time- and cost-saving features of computerized methods over manual methods shows why computerized litigation support is popular. A study by the American Bar Association's Law Practice Management Section showed that a manual search of 10,000 documents took 67 paralegal hours and produced 15 relevant documents, compared with a computerized litigation support system that made the same search in a few seconds and produced 20 relevant documents. The time it took to input the data into the computerized system was not included, but even considering that, the computerized system will still be much more efficient in most cases. The productivity and cost-saving features of computerized litigation support are substantial. Computerized litigation support can also be viewed as a service to the legal organization's clients, since legal organizations with computerized litigation support can provide better-quality service.

The litigation support market is competitive and mature and there are many specialized computer programs on the market (see Exhibit 9–5) that use a variety of techniques and approaches. Some legal organizations also use general spreadsheet and database software for litigation support (see Exhibit 9–6).

General Benefits of Computerized Litigation Support

General benefits of computerized litigation support include:

Electronic Storage and Immediate Retrieval Using electronic technologies, computers can store a vast amount of data in a fraction of the space required by hard-copy documents. One CD-ROM (600 MB) can hold 300,000 pages of text or 15,000 document images. A DVD (4.2 GB) can hold over 4,000,000 pages of text or 100,000 document images. External hard drives and removable disk cartridges can hold 200 GB or 5,000,000 document images or 200,000,000 pages of text. In addition, a document's images can be retrieved almost immediately without the hard copy of the document being lost or affected in any way.

Searches/Queries Using database technology, electronic documents—even hundreds of thousands of them—can be searched in seconds and the document you are looking for immediately retrieved.

Organization/Control Electronic documents can be numbered, have links associated to other electronic documents with them, be annotated and have electronic "notes" attached to them, and be organized in many different ways without affecting the documents themselves.

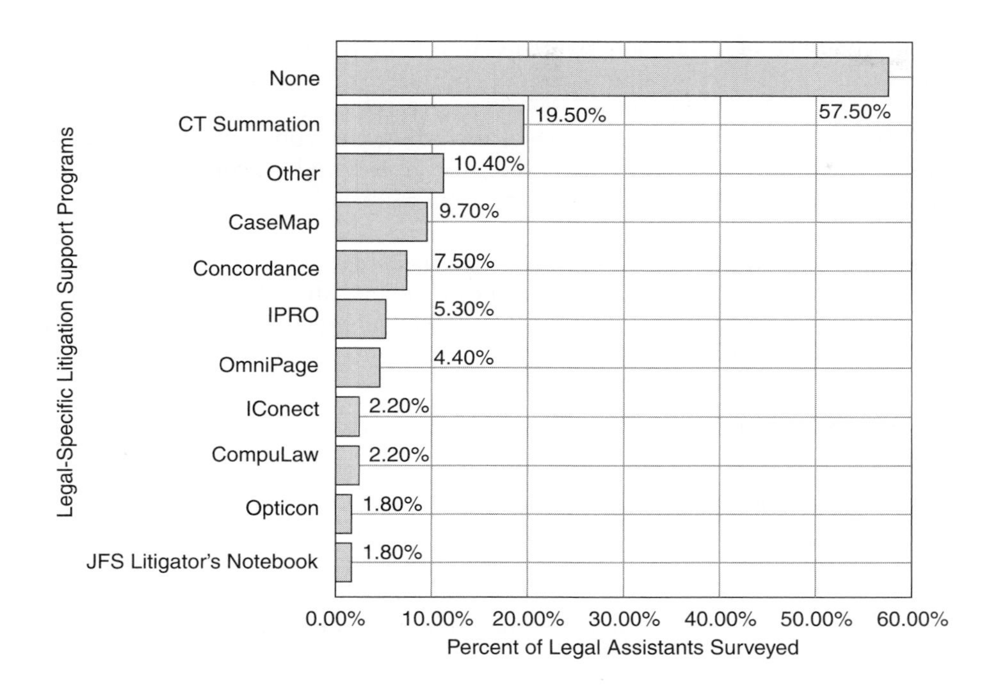

Exhibit 9–5
Litigation Support Market Share
As seen in the May/June 2006 issue of *Legal Assistant Today,* Copyright 2006 James Publishing, Inc. Reprinted courtesy of LEGAL ASSISTANT TODAY magazine. For subscription information call (800) 394–2626, or visit www.legalassistanttoday.com

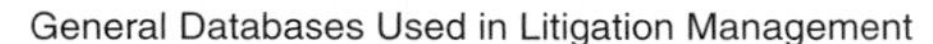

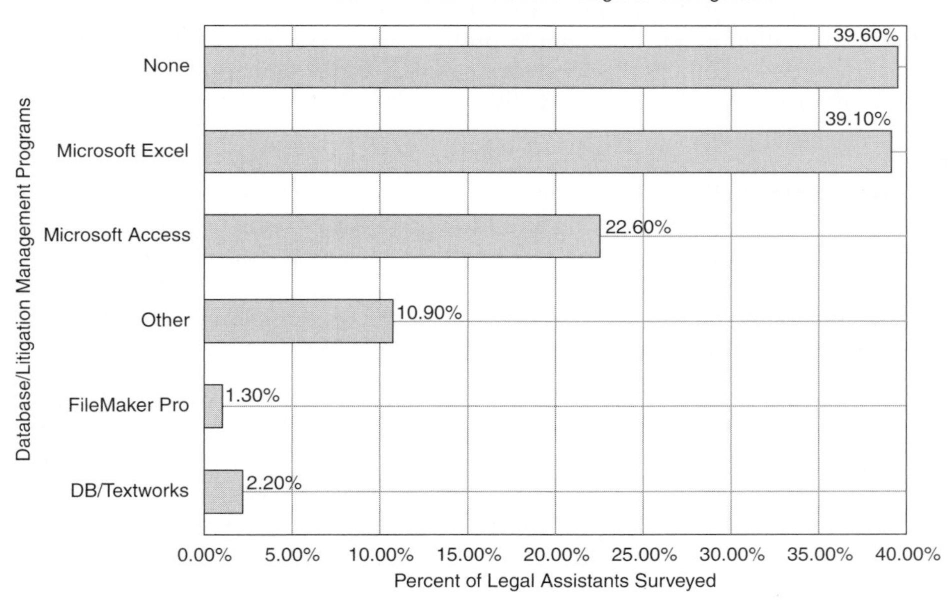

Exhibit 9–6
General Databases Used for Litigation Management Program
As seen in the May/June 2006 issue of *Legal Assistant Today,* Copyright 2006 James Publishing, Inc. Reprinted courtesy of LEGAL ASSISTANT TODAY magazine. For subscription information call (800) 394–2626, or visit www.legalassistanttoday.com.

Analytical Reports Analytical reports can be assembled from queries and searches on documents, and information can be gathered that would be impossible using manual methods.

Flexibility Computerized litigation support is inherently flexible and can be changed and adapted according to the needs of different cases. The information can also be presented with a number of different "looks" and formats and can be exported to many different computer programs, including word processing, spreadsheet, presentation graphics, or trial presentation software.

Sharing of Information A benefit of computerized litigation support is that information can be shared with others over a local area network or the Internet,

giving a variety of users access to the information 24 hours a day, 7 days a week.

Mobility Litigation support databases including electronic images and transcripts can be downloaded to a CD-ROM or laptop and be completely transportable, unlike boxes and boxes of hard-copy records.

Preservation of Information and Theories Because litigation support creates a record of factual documents, litigation documents, and case knowledge, the information can be preserved and quickly passed along to others if attorneys or legal assistants in a case change.

Types of Computerized Litigation Support

Many computerized litigation support programs and options are currently available. The legal market for computerized litigation support programs is continually growing, offering new and exciting ways to organize, control, and present information.

All of them have their own strengths and weaknesses. A brief summary of them follows (in-depth coverage is included later in the chapter).

Document Abstracts Using a litigation support program or database management program, abstracts of documents can be entered into the computer. The "abstracts" are basically a short summary of each document. The fields in the database usually include document number, document type, author, date, subject, summary, and others. The abstracts can then be used to organize, track, sort, and summarize the documents in the case. In addition, the abstracts can be searched and queried.

Full-Text Retrieval In this system the full text of documents is available to the user for searching and querying the text. Unlike a document abstract, which contains only summary information, a full text system includes all of the text of the document. The full text of the documents can then be searched and/or queried on. Two types of documents that full-text systems can search on include real-time transcription and electronic discovery or ESI.

Real-time Transcription With real-time transcription, an attorney or legal assistant is able to connect his or her computer to a court reporter's transcription machine and, using transcription software, get an electronic rough draft version of the transcript within seconds of the testimony being spoken. The transcription, which is full-text, can be searched or queried using a full-text retrieval system.

Electronic Discovery Most litigation support programs now support the ability to store electronic documents such as emails, word processing files, spreadsheets, and other ESI data that is produced during discovery. With a full-text retrieval system the electronic discovery database may be searched and queried.

Imaging Documents can be imaged so that an electronic "photograph" of the document can be maintained electronically. The image cannot be searched like full text, and there is no summary (as found in an abstract system), but the document can be viewed in its entirety electronically.

Case Management Software Case management software can be used in a litigation support capacity to electronically track and manage the scheduling and

docket control of a case in addition to creating case diaries/notes, tracking legal research for the case, generating documents, and much more.

Analytical Software Analytical litigation support software can be used to create case outlines, chronologies, timelines, analyses of the issues and witnesses in a case (including linking documents and facts to issues or witnesses), and much more.

Trial Presentation Software Once litigation support information is in an electronic format it can be put into trial presentation software and presented to fact finders in a visually compelling manner (this topic is covered in Chapter 12).

External or Internal Litigation Support

Legal organizations have two main options when deciding how to go about providing litigation support for a case. They can either use an external litigation support service provider or handle the project in-house. Alternatively, they can use a combination of both. All of the options have their strengths and weaknesses.

Litigation Support Service Providers

A **litigation support service provider** is a company that for a fee sets up a litigation support system and enters all necessary documents for a case. The advantage of using a litigation support service provider is that the work is essentially done by someone else. The service provider consults with the law firm or attorney on how the system is to be set up. Once the structure of the system is set up, the law firm delivers the documents and/or ESI to be entered to the service provider. The service provider then enters the documents into its computer or downloads /converts the ESI so it can be used by their system. When an attorney wants to search or retrieve information, he connects to the service provider's computer using the Internet to access the data. Alternatively, the service provider can save the information to CD-ROM or DVD. Even if the content is constantly being changed or multiple people need access to the information, users can easily access the data using the Internet because the data can be centrally located on the service provider's computer. Some vendors can provide electronic discovery services as well as litigation support services.

litigation support service provider
A company that, for a fee, sets up a litigation support system and enters all necessary documents for a case.

The main advantage of a service provider is that the labor-intensive task of entering data into the computer is performed by the service provider, not the law firm's staff. In addition, the law office does not have to hire, train, pay, manage, and then let go extra employees. Also, by virtue of specializing in this area, a service provider can bring a great deal of experience, technological power, and knowledge to bear on the project.

The main disadvantage of using a litigation support service provider is that it can be expensive. Most service providers charge a consulting fee, a fee for entering information into the computer, a fee for each time an attorney or a firm connects to the computer, a fee for each search of information in the computer, and a storage fee. Nevertheless, using a service provider becomes economical when a case involves tens of thousands of documents.

In-House Computerized Litigation Support Systems An in-house computerized litigation support system uses a firm's or an attorney's own staff and computer to perform litigation support. Many litigation support programs are available for in-house use.

in-house computerized litigation support system
A litigation support system set up by the firm's or attorney's own staff and computer.

The advantage of in-house litigation support systems is that they are significantly less expensive than hiring a service provider. They also allow a legal

organization or attorney to have more control over a project. This is important, since the attorney is ultimately responsible for the litigation process and the success or failure of a suit. In-house systems also allow a legal organization or an attorney to use litigation support for even small cases for which it would not be cost-effective to hire a service provider.

The disadvantage of an in-house computerized litigation support system is that a significant amount of front-end work is associated with setting up and entering information into the system. The setting up and entering of documents take staff time away from other duties. However, this problem can be somewhat alleviated by hiring temporary employees to enter, or code, documents into the system. The problem with temporary employees is that they often have no experience in litigation support. Whether to use a service provider or an in-house system will depend on the circumstances of a case.

An alternative to using one or the other is to use a combination. For example, a service provider might be hired to consult with a law firm regarding ESI and to assist with converting the ESI to a format compatible with the firm's own litigation support program. Given the complexity of ESI and all of the technical issues involved, this sometimes provides an alternative to a firm doing all of the work themselves.

Litigation Support in Legal Organizations

The use of litigation support has grown in recent years as software has become easier to use and the variety of litigation support programs has risen. According to a recent survey, approximately 34 percent of legal organizations use litigation support software. Interestingly, according to the survey, of the legal organizations that had litigation support software, legal assistants actually used the software the most—more than associates, partners, or anyone else. The two most popular litigation support programs used, according to the survey, were Summation and CaseMap (see Exhibit 9–5).

> *In the field of legal software, there is no area more misunderstood, and therefore more underutilized, than litigation support. Part of the reason is that litigation support programs were previously synonymous with full-text searchable databases. This software was traditionally difficult to learn and often required a technician to operate... . Today's generation of litigation support programs not only perform many more functions but also are much simpler to use. The new software helps litigators make the most of case information yet does not require a huge investment of time in the technology.*[4]

TYPES OF COMPUTERIZED LITIGATION SUPPORT SYSTEMS

As indicated earlier, there are primarily five major types/functions of litigation support software. They include document abstracts, full-text retrieval, imaging, case management, and analytical software. Many litigation support programs can perform one or more of these functions. The lines between these different programs/functions are somewhat blurred. Exhibit 9–7 shows an overview of the programs. The following section describes each of the different types of litigation support programs.

document abstract litigation support system
A litigation support system that allows users to enter document abstracts or summaries into a computer and then search and retrieve information contained in those abstracts or summaries.

Document Abstract Litigation Support Systems

A **document abstract litigation support system,** also called an indexing system, allows users to enter document abstracts or document summaries into a

Exhibit 9–7
Different Types/Functions of Litigation Support Programs

Type of Program/Function	Description	Strengths	Weaknesses/Limitations
Document Abstract	A database where abstracts or summaries of documents are entered. Each document is a record and each record contains fields such as doc. number, name, date, type, author, subject, legal issue, etc. The database can either be setup to be objective/biographical data or can be subjective and include why the document is significant to the case	• Provides a short summary of each document that can usually be read quickly • Excellent for drafting exhibit lists • Can produce a chronology of documents • Can produce reports based on any of the field names, documents sorted by author, subject, type, legal issue, etc. • Can be linked to file with full text, images or photos • Document reports can be sorted as needed • Documents can be searched on • Can be used to identify relationships between documents, people, etc.	• The full text of a document cannot be searched • The document must be coded and the abstract entered into the database
Full-Text Retrieval	The full text of documents is available for searches. Hard-copy documents are scanned and run through optical character recognition software or electronic files are used (such as electronic deposition transcripts or electronic discovery)	• The entire text of a document can be searched for individual words and phrases • Can be used for searching for words in depositions, trial transcripts, documents obtained from electronic discovery, and word processing documents • Can be used to impeach witnesses when testimony does not match • Annotations and notes can be attached to an electronic document without it affecting the underlying document itself • Electronic documents can have electronic Bates numbers added	• Uniform words are not always used (Jim, James, Jimmy, Mr. Smith) • Cannot produce indexes and reports like an abstract system
Imaging	Produces a "photograph" of the document	• Produces an exact electronic duplicate of the hard copy that can be instantly viewed • Can be included in electronic presentation graphic programs • Thousands of documents can be stored on CD-ROM and easily transported almost anywhere	• Cannot be searched on • Cannot produce indexes and reports like an abstract system
Case Management	Organizes docket control, scheduling, case diaries, document assembly/generation, legal research, and some document tracking capabilities and makes date available over a network to the whole legal team	• Captures information such as case diaries/notes, docket control, legal research, timekeeping, phone log, etc. that is not typically maintained by other litigation support programs/functions	• Is not a substitute for abstract, full-text retrieval, or imaging
Analytical Software	Creates chronologies, timelines, and tools for analyzing, issues, facts, witnesses, and other aspects of a case	• Creates documents for analyzing important aspects of a case	• Is typically not a substitute for abstract, full-text retrieval, or imaging

Exhibit 9–8
Document Abstract
Litigation Support

Reprinted with permission of CT Summation, Inc., All Rights Reserved, For more information, call 1/800-735-7866 or visit http://www.summation.com.

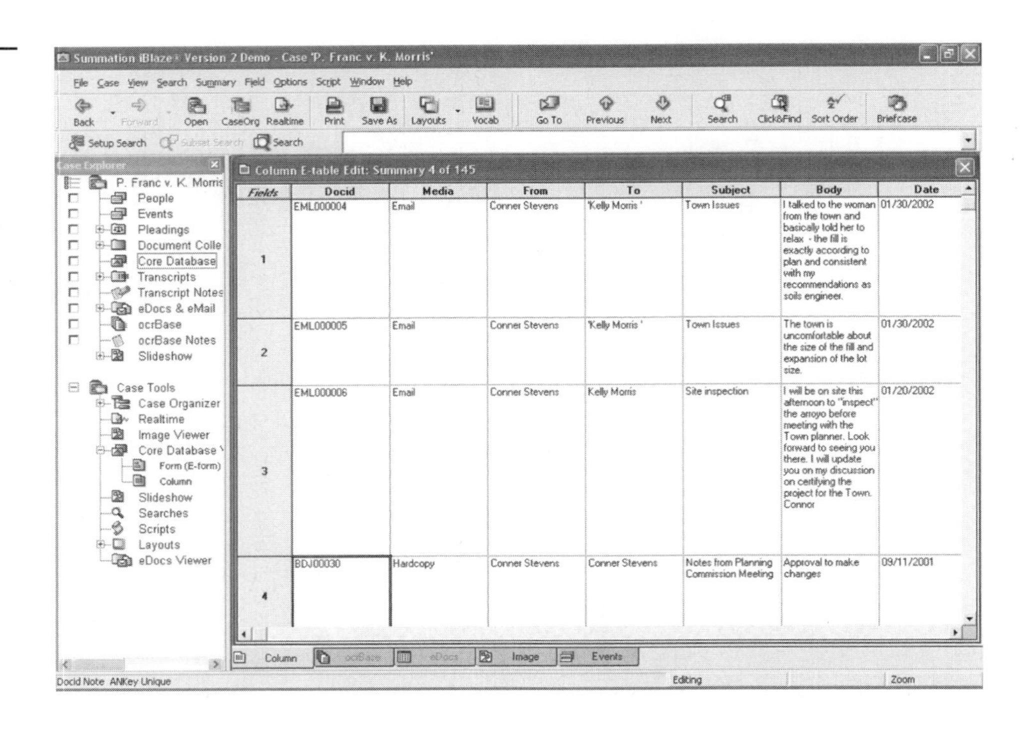

computer and to subsequently search and retrieve information contained in the abstract or summary. Exhibit 9–8 is an example of a document abstract. Notice in Exhibit 9–8 that an abstract of four documents is shown. The fields that are shown include document ID, media, from, to, subject, body, and date. A short description for each document for each of these fields is shown. For example, in Exhibit 9–8 document ID number EML000004 is an email from Conner Stevens to Kelly Morris about "town issues," dated 1/30/2002. This is exactly how a document abstract database/litigation support program is designed. The system is in essence a database and, in fact, many legal organizations use generic database programs to create their document abstract litigation support systems. There are, however, many prepackaged litigation support systems that include an abstracting module. One main difference between a generic database program and a litigation support program with an abstract function is that a prepackaged program designed specifically for litigation support will already have fields that are designed and set up for abstracting. For example, Exhibit 9–9 shows the standard fields for the document abstracting feature in a popular litigation support program. The user can customize the fields or the form, but it is convenient to have a predesigned form to work from.

> *Unlike full-text searching (which is limited to searching testimony or the words on the document), [document abstract] databases allow litigators to catalog and organize all crucial information for each piece of evidence.*[5]

objective/bibliographical coding
Recording only basic information about documents (document number, document name, date, author, recipient, and so forth) into a document abstract database. The coder makes no subjective characterizations about the document.

There are two ways to construct a document abstract database: objective/bibliographical coding and subjective coding. **Objective/bibliographical coding** records only basic information about the documents, including document number, document name, date, author, recipient, and so forth. Whoever is coding the document does not need to know anything about the case because he or she is only entering information that comes from the face of the document. The coder makes no subjective characterizations about the document. Objective coding is fairly fast and straightforward. It might be used in very large cases where there

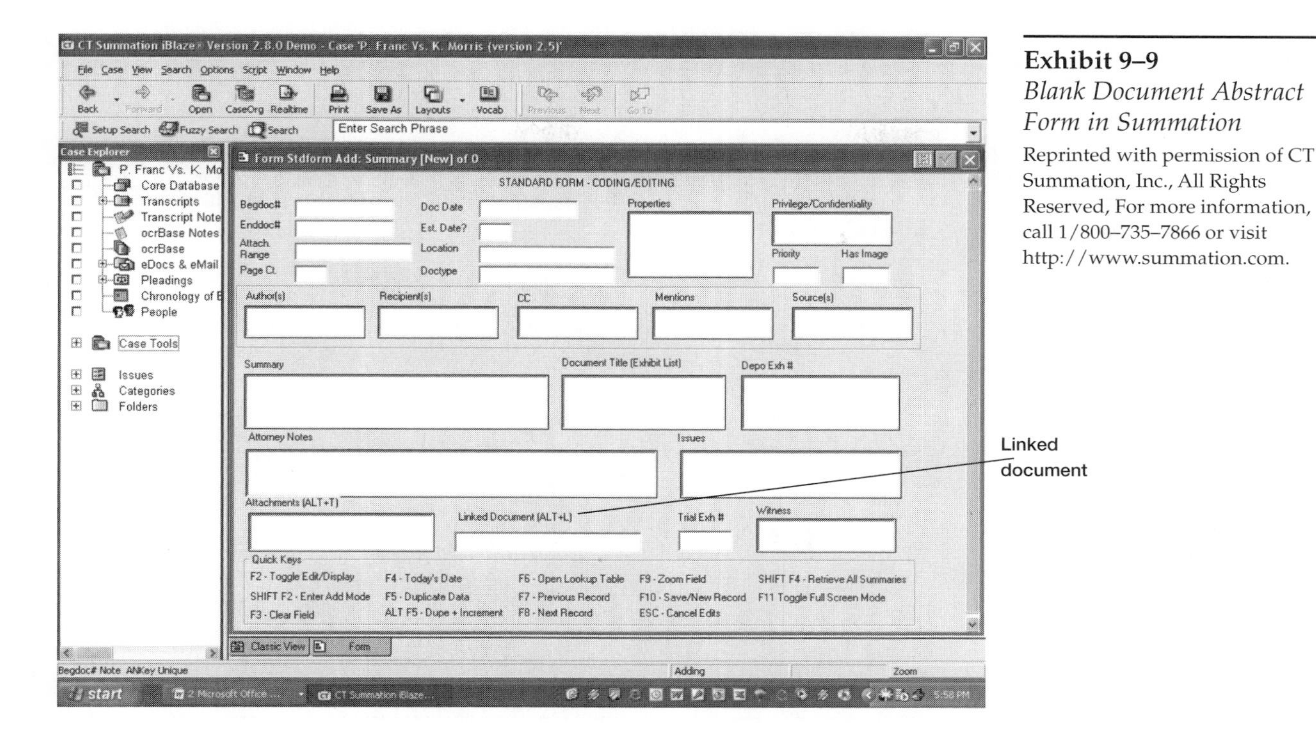

Exhibit 9–9

Blank Document Abstract Form in Summation

Reprinted with permission of CT Summation, Inc., All Rights Reserved, For more information, call 1/800–735–7866 or visit http://www.summation.com.

are hundreds of thousands of documents. Objective coding is many times outsourced to a litigation support service provider because the coders do not need to know anything about the case.

subjective coding
Entering information in the document abstract program about what the document means, including what case issues are relevant in the document or notes about the document.

Subjective coding is where coders enter information into the document abstract program about what the document means, including what case issues are relevant in the document or notes about the document. Subjective coding takes longer than objective coding since much more thought must go into the abstract. Exhibit 9–9 is an example of a subjective document abstract, since "summary," "attorney notes," "issues," and others are included in the design. To subjectively code documents the coder needs to have a good understanding of the facts and legal issues involved in the case. There are pros and cons involved with both objective and subjective coding, so the particular circumstances of the case should determine which is used.

Notice at the bottom of Exhibit 9–9 that there is a field that says "Linked Document." The litigation support program in Exhibit 9–9 is able to link a file such as an image file, an electronic discovery file (like an email), or the full text of a file to the document abstract. Exhibit 9–10 shows an example of a linked file.

Exhibit 9–11 shows a completed record in a document abstract system. Compare Exhibits 9–11 and 9–9. Notice that the forms are somewhat different but many of the field names are similar. The following explains the fields in Exhibit 9–11.

Document Reference Number Before document abstracts or summaries are entered into a computer, each physical document must be given a reference number or bar code. If each document is not given a reference number and stored in order, it has an excellent chance of being lost. Throughout litigation, the documents are moved, handled, and used so frequently that a reference number is the only way to keep a document from being misfiled (unless electronic document imaging is used). In addition, the only link between the information contained in the litigation support system and the hard copy of a document is this number.

Figure 9–10
Linking an Email/Full-Text Document to a Document Abstract
Reprinted with permission of CT Summation, Inc., All Rights Reserved, For more information, call 1/800-735-7866 or visit http://www.summation.com.

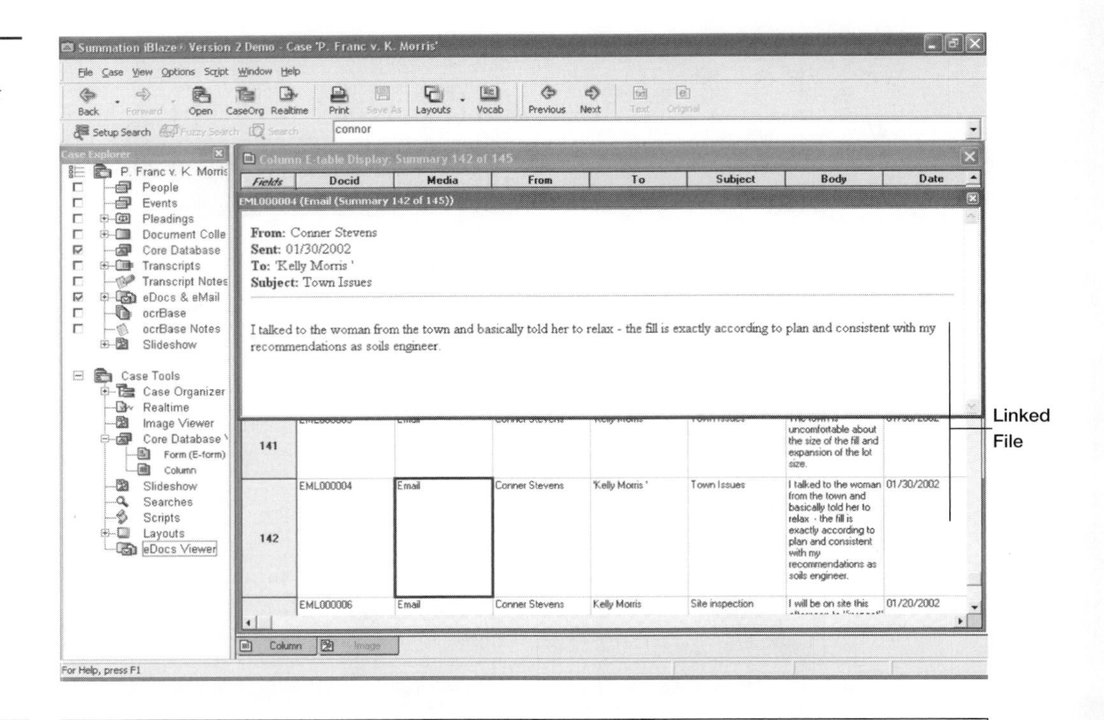

Exhibit 9–11
Completed Record in a Document Abstract System

Document Reference No.:	2342
Document Title:	Employment Contract
Type of Document:	Contract
Date of Document:	February 22, 2002
Author of Document:	Jim Hill
Recipient of Document:	Mary Rhodes
Subject of Document:	Employment
Physical Location of Doc.:	Box 211
Importance (1-10):	8
Names Mentioned:	Jim Hill; Mary Rhodes; RXY Corp.
Issues:	Liquidated damages; material breach; noncompete
Description 1:	This employment contract sets out the terms and conditions of Mary Rhodes's employment.
Description 2:	There is a provision in the contract requiring each party to act in good faith to the other.
Keywords:	Employment, contract, damages, noncompete
Notes:	
Source of Document:	Plaintiff
Production History:	Plaintiff's Deposition Exhib. 1
Plaintiff's Exhibit No.:	62
Defendant's Exhibit No.:	27
Beginning Bates No.:	734
Ending Bates No.:	744
Attorney Comments:	Was signed without attorney's advice
Authenticated:	Y/N
Stipulated:	Y/N
Offered during what witness:	Jim Hill
Admitted:	Y/N
Privileged/Confidential:	NO

Document Title If a document that is being entered has a title, it can be entered in the Document Title field. Coding rules (discussed later) provide guidelines so that documents are given uniform, informative titles. Also, your coding rules should include directions for how to assign titles to untitled documents like memos and letters so that you can retrieve such documents if necessary.

Type of Document The Type of Document field indicates whether a document is a letter, contract, memorandum, pleading, or other type. Again, coding rules are made so that similar documents are given the same name (sometimes referred to as vocabulary control). For instance, a user would not want one letter entered into this field as a "letter" and another similar type of letter entered as "correspondence." It is important that there be strict uniformity. Many litigation support programs use drop-down menus with set options for fields like this to ensure uniformity.

Date of Document The date of a document is entered in the Date of Document field. Undated documents are also captured in this field. The date of a document is a critical feature in a litigation support system. Providing chronologies of events and comparing documents by date are functions used throughout the litigation of a case.

Author of Document and Recipient of Document These fields record the personal and organizational author and recipient or recipients of each document.

Subject of Document This field records what the subject or topic of a document is.

Physical Location of Document This refers to the place the document is stored, whether it is in a numbered box, a file drawer, a CD-ROM, or some other place.

Importance This field records the relative importance of each document entered. This is usually accomplished using a numbering system such as one establishing a range between 1 and 10, with relatively unimportant documents having a 1 and critical documents having a 10. This allows users to sort documents based on their relative importance. This is useful at trial, since it is possible to forget or simply overlook important documents that have not been admitted or entered into evidence. Since this is a subjective field, the rating is usually decided by either an attorney or a legal assistant.

Names Mentioned This field is where a user enters the relevant names of people and organizations mentioned in a document. This allows users to search for people's names and obtain a list of all documents that concern them. It is useful at trial or in preparing for the deposition of a particular witness or party. It is sometimes useful to separate these names into two fields: a Persons Mentioned field and an Organizations Mentioned field.

Issues The Issues field allows a user to note when a document concerns a key issue in a case. The user can then search the document database for documents that pertain to a specific issue. This is helpful throughout the litigation of a case and helps an attorney get a handle on specific issues.

Description, Keywords, and Notes These fields are where a user enters notes or a summary of the documents.

Source of Document This field allows a user to track where a document came from, whether it was produced in discovery by the opposing side, whether it was given to the attorney by her own client, and so forth. It is always important to keep the history of a document straight. This can be as simple as indicating whether the document came from plaintiff or defendant or as specific as giving a person's name.

Production History This field allows a user to track how a document has been used in litigation. For instance, if a document was used as an exhibit in a particular deposition, this could be tracked in this field.

Plaintiff's and Defendant's Exhibit Number Both parties to the lawsuit prepare their own list of potential documents and give them numbers. This allows each party to know how the other party numbered the document for tracking purposes.

Beginning and Ending Bates Number Every page of every document is usually given a reference number using a Bates stamp, or a computer-generated label or number. A **Bates stamp** stamps a page with a sequential number and then automatically advances to the next number. When all the pages have been numbered, they are maintained in numerical-order files. This makes documents easier to locate. The Bates numbers (beginning and ending for each document) are then entered in the computer. Depending on the case, a document may have either a document reference number, Bates numbers, or both depending on how the document needs to be tracked.

Bates stamp
Stamps a page with a sequential number and then automatically advances to the next number.

Attorney Comments These are simply personal notes about the document that an attorney wants to remember.

Authenticated This means that the document is "authenticated" for evidence purposes. Some documents are self-authenticating, which means that by statute they are admissible into evidence without further proof.

Stipulated This refers to whether the parties have stipulated or agreed to the admissibility of the document.

Offered During What Witness At trial, documents are offered into evidence during witness testimony. This field records what witness the document was offered during testimony.

Admitted This tracks whether the judge admitted the document into evidence.

Privileged/Confidential This refers to whether the document is privileged or confidential and thus should not be produced in discovery.

The Use of Document Abstract Systems

Document abstracts can be helpful when attorneys are litigating cases. For example, suppose an attorney is representing Mary Rhodes in a breach of employment contract case against her former employer. The attorney's task is to cross-examine Jim Hill, Rhodes's former supervisor, at trial. To prepare for the cross-examination, the attorney would like to see every time Hill's name was mentioned in any of the documents that the plaintiff has been able to obtain in discovery. This is a simple task using a computerized document abstract litigation support system. The user simply instructs the system to search for every

SEARCH REQUEST:	"Jim Hill"		
Document Ref. No.	Type of Document	Recipient of Document	Date of Document
2342	Contract	Mary Rhodes	2/22/08
2346	Letter	Mary Rhodes	2/27/08
2359	Letter	John Hays	3/30/08
2365	Memo	John Hays	4/10/08
2377	Memo	John Hays	5/06/08
2390	Letter	Mary Rhodes	6/01/08
2400	Letter	Bill Green	6/30/08

Exhibit 9–12
Document Abstract Search Report on the Name "Jim Hill"

document abstract that mentions Hill's name. The user then instructs the system to print a list of all the documents where the search request was found (see Exhibit 9–12). The user can then use the document reference number to pull the original of a document for the attorney's inspection.

Document abstracts can also be used to give the attorney a chronological list of all or a subset of the documents by sorting the dates of the documents in chronological order. This type of list is important in trying to put together time frames and sequences of events in cases. Document abstract systems are sometimes called document indexing systems, since the printouts they produce are nothing more than an index (see Exhibit 9–12).

Document abstracts can be used as a quick reference for a legal professional to refresh himself about the documents of a case (see Exhibit 9–8). Notice in Exhibit 9–8 that a document abstract can be used to prepare a list of exhibits for trial. Document abstract systems can also be used to search for and sort reports based on any of the field names in the database. Thus, in Exhibit 9–11 a report could be run for all documents that were authored by "Jim Hill," or every document that concerned the issue of "liquidated damages," or was produced by the plaintiff. Document abstract databases allow the user to produce an infinite number of reports, searches, and queries depending on the user's particular needs at the time.

Disadvantages of Document Abstracts

There are several disadvantages of using document abstracts. The first is that if a subjective abstract is going to be used, the abstractors preparing the document abstracts must be trained in *exactly* what the issues of the case are. That is, nonlawyers have to make decisions about evidence and relevance, so the lawyer is in essence delegating legal judgments to nonlawyers. The potential exists for irrelevant information that has no real bearing on the case to be entered in the abstracts, while relevant and important information can be left out. As long as experienced, highly skilled legal assistants are used, there is little reason to worry, but if data entry clerks or untrained temporary staff are used, this could present a real problem. Also, abstractors must be careful to use a controlled vocabulary so that information is entered uniformly into the abstracts. If information is not entered uniformly, searches of the document abstracts will be inconclusive. For example, if one abstractor referred to an important incident as a "collision," another abstractor referred to the same thing as an "accident," and another referred to the incident as a "wreck," this would pose a significant problem for anyone searching the document abstract database, since three different word searches would need to be done to get information about the same incident. Another disadvantage of using document abstracts is that the issues in a lawsuit are constantly changing. This is particularly true in complicated cases

where litigation support can be invaluable. When issues are added or modified, then documents must be rereviewed and abstracts updated.

Finally, the facts that the document abstract database itself does not contain the full text of a document and that the documents have to be coded and entered into the system may also be viewed as disadvantages.

Full-Text Retrieval Litigation Support Systems

full-text retrieval litigation support system
A litigation support system that enables a user to search and retrieve information contained in the full text of documents stored in the system.

A **full-text retrieval litigation support system** enables a user to search and retrieve information contained in the full text of documents stored in the system. Unlike document abstract systems, they are not set up like a database. They do not have fields or a file structure. In full-text retrieval systems, a whole document, not just an abstract or a summary, is entered and stored.

The full text of a document can be entered into a computer in several ways: through scanners, keyboards and word processing, computer-aided transcription, real-time transcription, service providers, or electronic discovery.

Scanners Optical character recognition (OCR) scanners allow a user to translate hard copy documents into a computer-readable format almost instantly. Once a document is scanned into a computer, the document file is saved to a disk for later retrieval by the full-text retrieval litigation support system. OCR is not 100 percent accurate. Most OCR systems have accuracy rates around 99 percent, so documents must be thoroughly reviewed for accuracy.

Keyboards and Word Processing A word processor can be used to type the content of a document into a computer. Once the complete document is typed into the computer, the file is then saved to a disk for later retrieval by the full-text retrieval litigation support system.

computer-aided transcription (CAT)
A process that automatically deciphers a court reporter's notes and converts them into a computer-readable format.

Computer-Aided and Real-Time Transcription According to most court rules, deposition testimony, court hearings, trials, and other types of formal proceedings are recorded by a court reporter. **Computer-aided transcription (CAT)** is a process that automatically deciphers a court reporter's notes and converts them into a computer-readable format. Before CAT, a court reporter, using a shorthand reporting machine to abbreviate common words and phrases by certain keystrokes, recorded the testimony that was given. The court reporter then deciphered the notes and prepared a full transcript of the testimony, using either a typewriter or a word processor.

Most CAT systems automatically prepare a transcript in computer-readable format. The court reporter, using a word processor, then makes any corrections that are necessary and saves the file. Since the file is saved in a machine-readable format, the court reporter can, in addition to selling attorneys hard copies of transcripts, provide transcripts on disk. Most full-text retrieval systems can then use the disk or file of a transcript automatically. Thus, using CAT, it is easy and fairly inexpensive to get the full text of depositions and other formal documents into a full-text retrieval system.

real-time transcription
An attorney or legal assistant connects a computer (typically a laptop) with realtime software to the court reporter's transcription machine; within seconds of the testimony being spoken the attorney has a rough-draft version of the transcript.

In addition, many court reporters now have **real-time transcription.** This means that a cable can be attached from the court reporters' equipment to the attorney's computer (with appropriate software) and as the court reporter types, the attorney has access to the testimony within seconds. Most court reporters go back and edit the document, but it is possible for an attorney to have a draft of the transcript within seconds.

Service Providers Some service providers allow a user to rent their trained personnel to scan the data and design the system.

> *Electronic data is playing a larger role in the legal discovery process. Traditionally, the primary discovery method was for lawyers to request paper documents. Now, discovery requests ask for the actual electronic data that initially created the printed version of the document.... Requests for electronic data have increased because there is more information available from electronic files versus printed documents.*[6]
>
> *The current definition of "document" includes paper documents, e-mail messages with attachments and other electronic files. Electronic files subject to discovery include word processor files, spreadsheets, presentation graphics, databases, point-of-sale data, human resource system records, payroll data... and other digital records.*[7]

Electronic Discovery **Electronic discovery** is where discovery "documents" (emails, word processing documents, spreadsheets, databases, etc. (see Chapter 8) are produced electronically. Many times attorneys want documents produced electronically since it is more difficult to destroy electronic documents. Backup tapes can be requested before documents are destroyed or possibly altered, and additional information can sometimes be learned from electronic documents over hard-copy documents (such as date and author's name). Electronic documents can contain other documents, such as attachments, that may or may not show up on hard copies or automatically print out. Having documents produced electronically allows the user to use full-text retrieval on the items produced without having to use OCR.

electronic discovery
Discovery "documents," such as emails, word processing documents, spreadsheets, and databases that are produced in a lawsuit electronically.

The Use of Full-Text Retrieval Systems Full-text retrieval systems allow a user to conduct searches on the full text of a document. In the breach of employment contract example used earlier, the attorney representing Mary Rhodes has a listing of all the documents that have Jim Hill's name in them. However, the attorney also would like to see a listing of every time Hill's name is mentioned in the fifteen depositions that were taken in this case. This will save the attorney from having to reread all fifteen depositions and will allow the attorney to read only the parts relating to Hill. This cannot be done using a document abstract system, but it is quite easy using a full-text retrieval system. The user simply tells the system to search the fifteen deposition files for the name *Jim Hill* or to search each file separately for the name *Jim Hill* (depending on the litigation support system). Most systems respond by either producing a list of the found occurrences (see Exhibit 9–13), which includes the deposition name and page number of each occurrence, or displaying each found occurrence on the computer screen. Some full-text systems have the capability to search across many different files (such as different depositions, etc.) at the same time.

> *Paralegals should know how to annotate transcripts in full-text systems with notes and how to scan, load, organize, and retrieve documents, and be able to do quick searches for names and information in a database.*[8]

SEARCH REQUEST: "Jim Hill"

Found Occurrences: 19

Deposition Name	Deposition Page
Depo of Mary Rhodes	Page 24, 34, 56, 67, 89, 94
Depo of Bill Green	Page 11, 23, 44
Depo of John Hays	Page 10, 15, 16, 19, 20
Depo of Alice Hall	Page 15, 16, 17, 45, 46

Exhibit 9–13
Full-Text Retrieval Search Report on the Name "Jim Hill"

Exhibit 9–14

Full-Text Transcript Search and Electronic Annotations of Full-Text Documents

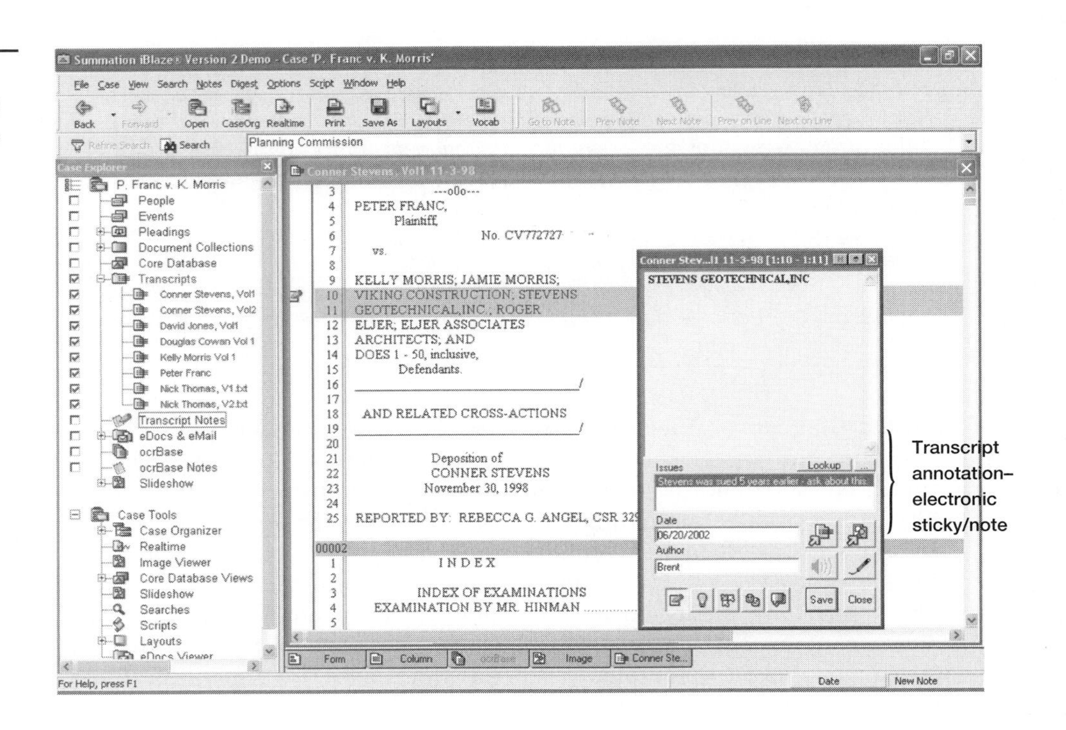

Notice in Exhibit 9–14 just to the right of the word "Search" (just underneath the Tool Bar) that the user has entered the search term "Planning Commission." Also notice to the left of the screen under "Case Explorer" that check marks have been placed next to all of the transcripts for the case. The check marks mean that when the search "Planning Commission" is made, all of the transcripts will be included in the search at one time. Notice in Exhibit 9–14 that the full text of the Conner Stevens deposition is displayed. In addition, one powerful feature found in many full-text retrieval systems is that users can add annotations (electronic sticky notes) to the file without affecting the transcript itself. Notice in Exhibit 9–14 that the lines with "Stevens Geotechnical, Inc." have been highlighted and that a note has been created reminding the user to ask Stevens (at trial) about a lawsuit that was filed five years ago. Also, notice in Exhibit 9–14 to the left under "Case Explorer" that "Pleadings" are listed. The full text of the pleadings in the case, including the complaint, answer, and other documents, is included.

In addition to being able to conduct searches on the full text of a document, some full-text systems can produce a summary or digested version of a transcript or document. Full-text systems are also convenient if a document or transcript is lost, since the full text can be retrieved and printed. In addition, full-text retrieval avoids the potential of important issues or aspects of a case being missed. Finally, most full-text retrieval systems can even be used to search a firm's own word-processing documents, such as correspondence, memorandums, and other documents prepared in-house.

Disadvantages of Full-Text Retrieval Several disadvantages are associated with full-text retrieval systems. One disadvantage is that they tend to take up a large amount of hard disk space. This may strain the physical limits of storage space on a computer system, although optical storage devices and large internal and external storage devices now make this less of a problem. Another disadvantage is the substantial amount of time and expense that can be expended in entering the full text of documents. In some cases only the most important documents are in full text format, while in others all of the depositions, pleadings, and transcripts are in full text. This will depend on how much of the information can be

obtained in a computer-recognized format or how much of the data can be scanned into the computer. Another disadvantage is that it is difficult to create chronologies. Still another is that because the vocabulary entered into the system is not controlled, it may be impossible to find all occurrences of a subject. In some cases, subjects are referred to as concepts, and it is difficult to enter concepts. For example, the person Jim Hill in the preceding example may be referred to in documents as "Mr. Jim Hill," "Mr. Hill," "Jim," "the boss," "supervisor," and so on. A final disadvantage is that a user cannot manipulate data and report formats as with an abstract system, since a full-text system has no fields to work with.

> *We implemented document imaging technology. . . .Once documents were organized using any combination of imaging, coding, and optical character recognition (OCR), our legal assistants experience increased efficiency in the preparation of lawyers' document sets for production, depositions and trial. This increase in efficiency allows our lawyers more time to review relevant documents.*[9]

document imaging
A litigation support system in which documents are scanned into a computer and the documents' actual images (similar to photographs) are retained in the computer.

Document Imaging Litigation Support Systems

Document imaging is a litigation support method in which documents are scanned into a computer and the documents' actual images (similar to photographs) are retained in the computer, either on a hard disk, CD-ROM, or another device (see Exhibit 9–15). Document images offer several advantages over paper. With document imaging, paper is handled only once, when it enters the legal organization. It is then scanned into the computer, and reviewing, copying, and filing can be done electronically. Unlike paper documents, imaging allows multiple people on a network to access and view the same document at the same time without moving from their computers and without requiring staff to pull the document. Document imaging also reduces physical storage space, since a file cabinet of documents can be stored on one CD-ROM. Anyone who has worked with paper documents in a legal office can testify that there is always a risk of losing files or losing documents, especially when preparing for

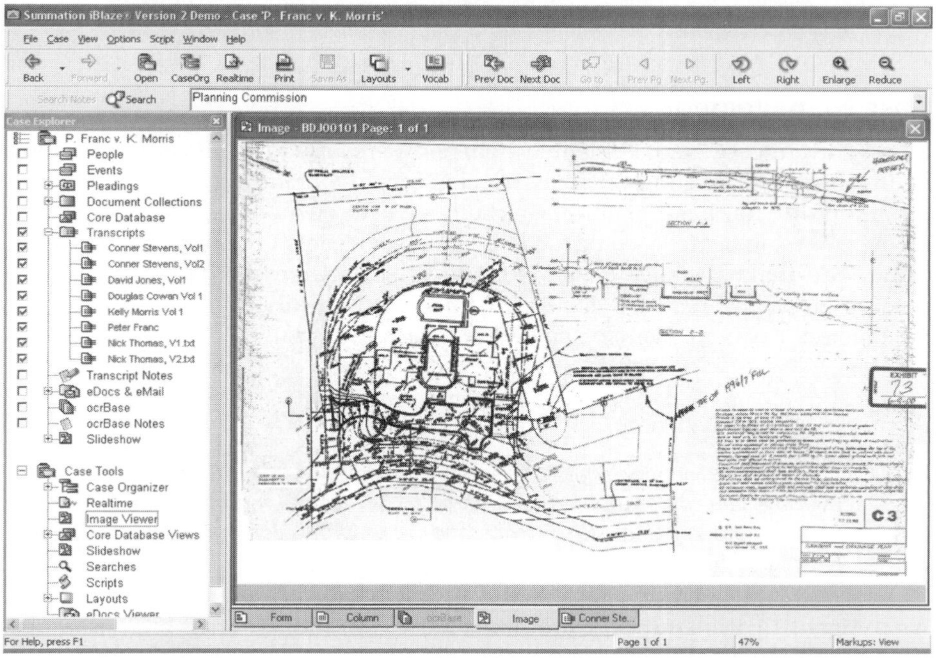

Exhibit 9–15
Document Imaging
Reprinted with permission of CT Summation, Inc., All Rights Reserved, For more information, call 1/800-735-7866 or visit http://www.summation.com.

and at trial, where documents are constantly being used and moved by many different people. Document images solve this problem, because the document is always available for review.

A disadvantage of document imaging is that the documents can take up a lot of electronic storage space and must be scanned into the computer, which requires obtaining a certain amount of computer hardware or hiring a firm to scan the documents. There is also a risk of inaccuracy with scanned images. Document images typically cannot be sorted or searched by themselves, unlike the information in a document abstract or full-text retrieval system. However, scanned images can be turned into searchable text using optical character recognition (OCR) software. Also, some systems allow scanned images to be linked to the document abstract of the document. Scanners, including those with OCR, are readily available and inexpensive. This is becoming a popular option in litigation support. In addition, software is available that will electronically enter Bates numbers and allow legal team members to manipulate the images.

Another aspect of document imaging is that electronic discovery service providers can now take just about any kind of ESI and convert it to TIFF or PDF image files and then electronically convert the information to text as well. In this way, the service provider can provide to the party both an image of a document and the full text of it. Document imaging, whether it is hard copy or electronic, can be a very powerful and important tool in providing support to litigators.

> *Another time and cost savings can be found in the imaging of documents...the reality is that imaging saves clients copy charges and keeps legal professionals in their chairs instead of hunting through file cabinets and boxes.*[10]

Case Management

Many current case management systems now include features that are helpful to litigators, such as comprehensive docket control (including a historical representation of what has transpired in the case in the way of deadlines, appointments, hearings, etc.), comprehensive case diaries/notes about the case, documents that have been generated in the case, legal research prepared for the case, timekeeping records, document tracking, and other such features. Case management systems were discussed at length in Chapter 7.

Analytical Software

> *This category of litigation support programs [analytical software] helps litigators uncover the fact and evidence patterns of a case. They work by having attorneys evaluate each piece of evidence and link it to the elements that must be established at trial.*[11]

analytical litigation support programs
A type of litigation support program that helps legal professionals analyze a case from a number of different perspectives and create cause and effect relationships between facts and evidence in a case.

Analytical litigation support programs help legal professionals analyze a case from a number of different perspectives and create cause-and-effect relationships between facts and evidence in a case. Analytical litigation support programs help legal professionals conceptualize and think about facts, documents, people, and related matters and the relationships among them. For example, the first computer screen in Exhibit 9–16 is a chronology of facts in a case. Notice in Exhibit 9–16 that not only are the dates and facts listed but a source for each fact also is listed, with a note of whether it is key to the case, whether the "fact" is disputed or undisputed, and what factual or legal issue it is linked to. Notice in the bottom screen of Exhibit 9–16 that an analysis of the legal issues has been conducted. Each factual/legal issue in the case has been broken down and facts, documents, and people have been linked to each issue. Notice further in the

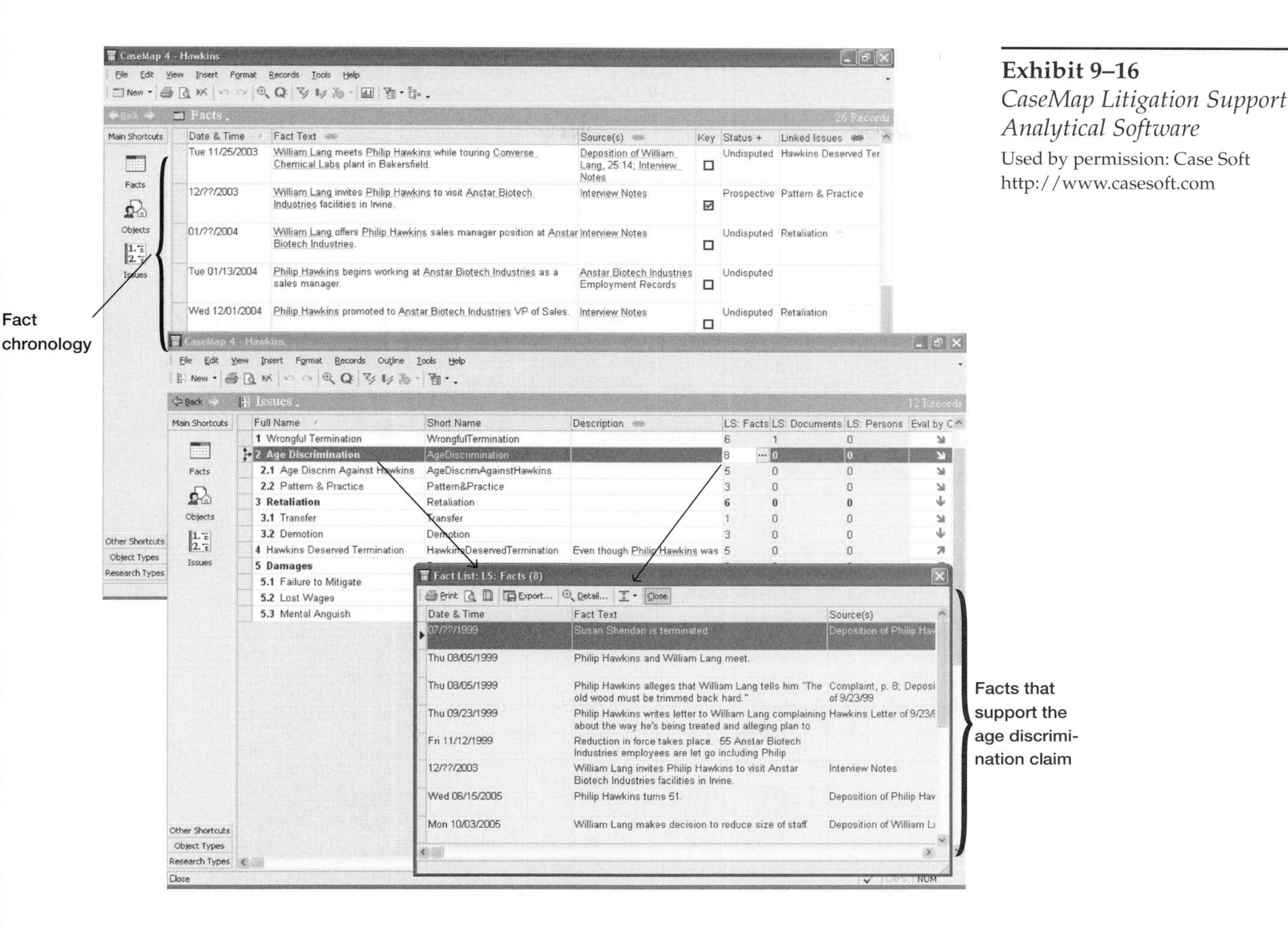

Exhibit 9–16
CaseMap Litigation Support Analytical Software
Used by permission: Case Soft http://www.casesoft.com

bottom screen of Exhibit 9–16 that the issue of "Age Discrimination" has been highlighted and a list of the facts that support the claim has been opened. This allows litigators to see with specificity what evidence goes with what issues that need to be proved or disproved.

> *In litigation, it's vitally important to discover facts involving time. The sequence of how events happen often is crucial to establish alibis, show patterns, corroborate or refute witness testimonies and even organize the case. A timeline is a visual aid to keep the attention of jurors focused on the area you want to emphasize and helps build the story of the case. As a legal assistant, you are aware of the key dates and facts in your attorney's cases...With an effective timeline diagram, you can project a clear understanding of the facts and dates associated with your case, helping the jury along with your theory of the case instead of depending on their personal memory or note-taking skills during testimony.*[12]

Exhibit 9–17 is an example of an analytical tool that builds a timeline of the facts in a case. Notice in Exhibit 9–17 that the top of the timeline represents one account of the facts of the case and the bottom of the timeline represents the other.

Another kind of analytical litigation support program is called an "outliner". An outliner helps the legal professional create outlines for opening and closing arguments, questioning witnesses, and other uses. While an outline can be created in a word processor, outlining programs offer special features that can assist in drafting the outline. In summary, analytical litigation support programs are a powerful tool in terms of a legal professional understanding his or her own case,

Exhibit 9–17
TimeMap Litigation Support Analytical Software
Used by permission: Case Soft http://www.casesoft.com

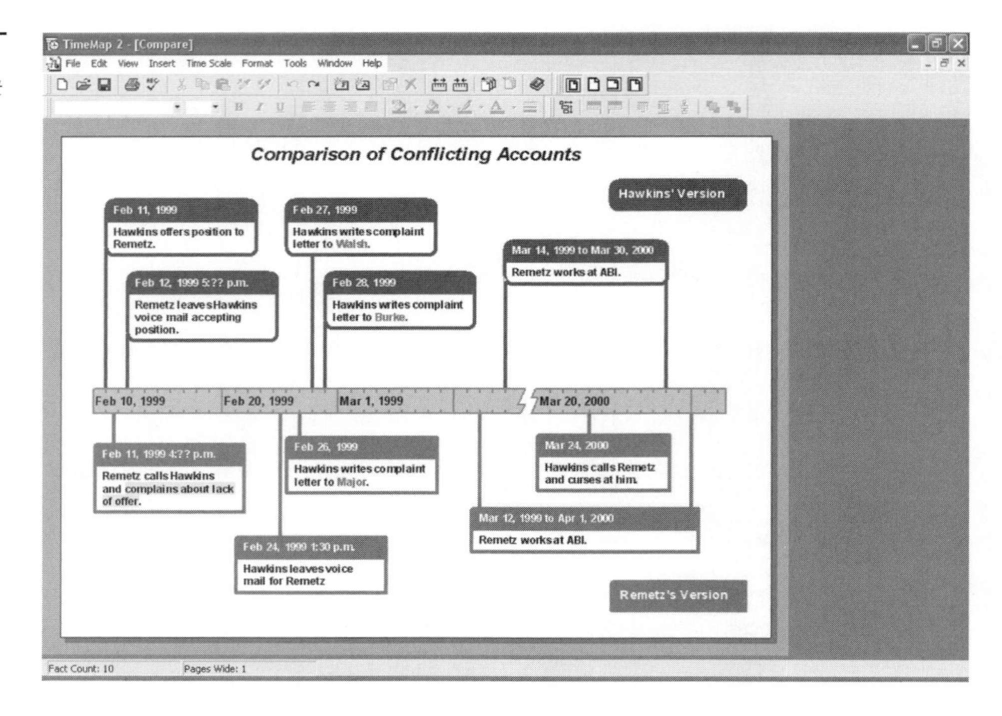

understanding the strengths and weaknesses of the case, and being able to persuade a fact finder about the evidence in a case and what it means.

Integrated Litigation Support Systems

Document abstract systems are beneficial when a user needs an index of documents, such as a chronological listing. Indexes cannot be made effectively using a full-text retrieval system. However, full-text retrieval systems are useful for searching the full text of depositions, transcripts, and so forth where completeness is needed. Imaging is useful when a user needs immediate access to the documents themselves. And analytical software is helpful to analyze a case.

Integrated litigation support systems are programs that offer the best of all worlds, providing essentially a database program for entering document abstracts, a full-text retrieval system for searching the full text of documents, imaging management software, real-time transcription, and even analytical tools.

As mentioned earlier, there are many litigation support programs on the market. Several of them offer all of these capabilities in a single program. The main downside to a fully integrated litigation support package that offers all of these features is that such programs, which are so powerful and do so many things, are fairly complex.

THE LITIGATION SUPPORT PROCESS

Many questions and problems need to be resolved when setting up a litigation support system for a particular case. Every case has different facts and issues. Therefore, each case has different needs and requirements that must be taken into account. Five steps should be considered when setting up a litigation support system for a particular case (see Exhibit 9–18).

1. Determine Whether the Case Justifies Litigation Support

The first step in the litigation support process is to determine whether the case is worth the time and expense it takes to design and set up the system and enter

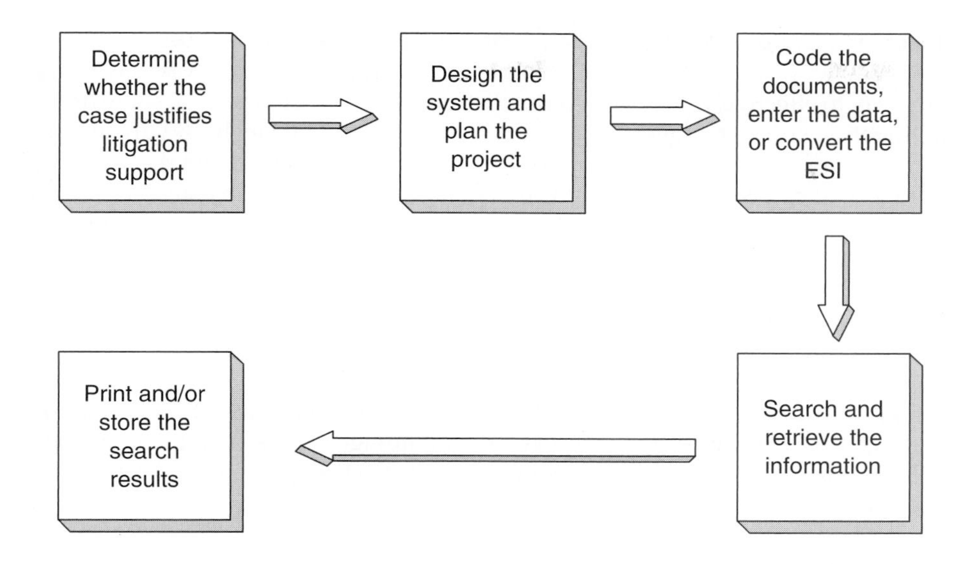

Exhibit 9–18
Litigation Support Process

the data to use it. Before litigation support was available on microcomputers, the thinking was that only large or complex cases justified the expense of litigation support. Now, however, even attorneys with routine cases are using litigation support to organize documents and evidence.

Several issues must be considered when determining whether a case should be entered into a litigation support system.

How Many Parties and Witnesses Are Involved? If only a few parties and witnesses are involved, a case might not justify the expense of litigation support. If, on the other hand, numerous parties and witnesses are involved, it might be wise to use a litigation support system in order to best organize the parties, witnesses, and documents.

How Many Issues Are Involved? If only a few issues are involved, again it might not be worth the expense of litigation support. However, if a large number of issues are involved in a case, it might be prudent to use a litigation support program to keep the issues clear and separate.

How Complex or Difficult to Grasp Are the Issues? If the issues in a case are easy to understand, again it might not be worth the effort and expense to set up a litigation support system.

How Long Is the Litigation Expected to Last? Litigation that is expected to last a long time has its own inherent problems. A turnover in the attorneys and legal assistants working the case is very possible. If the information they acquire is never entered into a database for later retrieval or is lost, this is a problem.

How Large Are the Damages? If a case involves the possibility of large damages, it is worth the time and expense to use a litigation support system.

Is the Case Expected to Settle Out of Court? It is obviously a waste to have hundreds of documents entered into a computer only to have the case settled and dismissed, unless the presence of litigation support raises the settlement value of the case. Usually, only cases that will most likely go to trial should be entered.

How Many Documents Have Been Produced and Must Be Tracked? If thousands of documents are to be tracked, computerized litigation support may be the only way to effectively manage this number of documents. In the past, some books on litigation support suggested that a case must have 1,000 to 10,000 documents before computerized litigation support pays off. This is probably not the case anymore. Whether a case can benefit from litigation support depends on many issues other than just how many documents have been produced. Computerized litigation support can be used effectively in small cases as well as large ones.

Does the Client Request Automation? In some cases, a client may request that computerized litigation support be used.

Is Opposing Counsel Automating? If one party to a lawsuit has litigation support, this puts all other parties at a disadvantage. Therefore, in some cases, if the opposing counsel begins using computerized litigation support, it will force you to do so as well.

> *While litigation support technology has proven to add tremendous value to the cost-effective management of cases, poor management of litigation support projects can quickly erase any anticipated savings. This dissatisfaction frequently stems from two things: poor planning and poor communication. . ..You should thoroughly understand the goals of imaging and coding of your document as well as manage the project to its ultimate conclusion.*[13]

2. Design the System and Plan the Project

Once the decision has been made to put case information on a litigation support system, the next question is which type of design the system will have. System design includes planning what level of detail the fields of the database will have (when using abstracts), what information will be tracked, how many fields the database will have (when using abstracts), what documents will or will not be included, what will be done with duplicates, what information will be needed during the litigation, and how the database will be used at trial.

The user must also decide whether a brief summary of a document's characteristics will be sufficient or whether the full text of each document will be needed. If the system design is poorly thought out, the litigation system will surely fail. It is important that the user think the system through clearly and take all options into account when approaching system design. The responsible attorney and legal assistant should help design the system, since they will most likely have the clearest understanding of the facts and issues in the case.

In some cases, a budget is necessary so that the firm can decide how many resources should be devoted to a project. This will also affect whether a service provider will be used or whether the system will be developed in-house.

When developing the system design, the user should consider two questions.

> *At the outset, it is important for you to determine which documents will be key, marginal, or irrelevant to your case. Obviously, you do not want to abstract or input into your computer irrelevant documents, since it would be a waste of time and your client's money.... Documents which are highly relevant should be abstracted... documents which have marginal value may develop a higher priority as a case progresses. Though you may decide initially not to enter data from these records... you may want to enter a record that summarizes all of these marginal documents so that you know that they're available at a later time.*[14]

Which Type of System Will Be Used? In designing a litigation support system for a case, it is first necessary to decide which type of system will be used:

document abstract, full-text retrieval, document imaging, or a combination. Each case is different, but many firms use a combination. For example, it might be beneficial to use a full-text system to track all depositions and testimony and to use an abstract system and document imaging to track documents. It is important to understand what you want to get out of the litigation support system in the beginning so that the system can be designed to accomplish those goals.

What Kinds of Information Should Be Entered? The next step is to decide what kinds of information will be entered into the system. For example, when using a full-text retrieval system, the user must determine what documents need to be scanned in: all documents or just those that are relatively important.

One way to go about solving this problem is to identify all the relevant issues of fact and law in the case, the relevant parties, and the documents that will affect the fact-finding. All the information concerning these questions should be tracked.

Once the design is complete, the user should enter test data into the system to see if the design is accomplishing what it is intended to.

3. Code the Documents and Enter the Data (Using a Controlled Vocabulary) or Convert the ESI

The information must then be entered into the litigation support system. The coding of documents refers to the process of deciding what information will be entered into the system and what form it will take.

In many cases, clerical staff enter objective data into the litigation support database (in an objective/biographical document abstract design). Since all the information must be entered into the database in the same format (so that searches retrieve all the requested information), coding rules must be developed. Coding rules limit the vocabulary that goes into a litigation support system. It is important to understand that what you put into the system is what you get out of it. For instance, if a user is entering a piece of correspondence into a document abstract litigation support database, the user can enter many different abbreviations and synonyms for this into the Document Type field, including *letter, lt, ltr,* and *correspondence.* The coding rules tell the data entry operator exactly what vocabulary choices to enter (e.g., they might say, "The following types of documents should be entered into the Document Type field: letters, pleadings, memos, notes."). A description of exactly what is meant by each title should also be listed. The format for entering a date might be "MM, DD, YY", or the formula for entering a name in a name field might be "LAST, FIRST", and so on.

It is important that all information entered into the database be uniform and as objective as possible. The use of coding rules will keep the clerical staff from guessing when entering information. Coding rules should be drafted for all fields in the litigation support database. Note that some firms decide to use codes or abbreviations instead of words. For example, a firm could code a statute of limitations issue in the Subject of Document field as the number 1 instead of using the words *statute of limitations.* Firms sometimes do this to reduce the number of errors incurred, since far less typing is involved in numbering items.

Fields that require subjective determinations (such as the Importance field) must be entered by trained legal assistants or attorneys, not clerical staff.

Some litigation support programs allow a user to set up exactly what information can and cannot be entered into the system. For example, in the Date field, the user can instruct the system to accept only dates between January 2008 and January 2009. If a clerical staff person tries to enter a date before January 2008, the program will not allow the document to be entered. In this way, data can be verified right on the spot, as it is entered.

It is sometimes hard to determine how long it will take to enter case information into a litigation support system. This will depend on what level of detail is being entered into the system, how many people are entering data, how many documents are being entered, and so on. However, once a staff member has coded documents or entered information into a computer, the next time she does it, it is considerably easier. Experienced coders will make a big difference in how fast the data is entered into the system.

It is also important to take into account the use of ESI in the case. Using service providers or other tools, a user may be able to quickly convert ESI into a litigation support program. This will often include images and the full text of documents.

4. Search and Retrieve the Information

Using the proper search and retrieval techniques helps a user obtain the information needed. An in-depth discussion of the different searching and retrieving techniques and strategies is presented later in this chapter under the "Searching and Retrieving Litigation Support Data" section.

5. Print and/or Store the Search Results

It is sometimes necessary to produce a hard copy of search results or to save the search results.

SEARCHING AND RETRIEVING LITIGATION SUPPORT DATA

The accurate searching and retrieving of documents is very important and takes some practice at first. In some cases, it may take four or five changes to the search request to get a litigation support system to retrieve the information you want it to. Litigation support programs, whether they are document abstract or full-text retrieval systems, generally provide the same type of search features. Nevertheless, the syntax for entering the search requests varies from one program to another.

When a search request (sometimes called search criteria) is entered, a litigation support program searches through every word in the documents or abstracts associated with that case, looking for matches. If a match is found, the program will show a list of the occurrences and where they were found. In most programs, a user has the option of pulling up and viewing on the screen the text surrounding a match.

Most programs allow a user to enter several different kinds of searches, including single-word searches, wildcard searches, Boolean logic searches, and proximity searches (see Exhibit 9–19).

Single-Word Searches

single-word search
A computer search that scans a database for matches to a single word.

A **single-word search** searches a database for matches to a single word. For example, in Exhibit 9–19, the user requested that the program find any match to the single word *approve.* The system responded by retrieving a list of only the occurrences where the word *approve* was found. The potential problem of single word searches is that derivatives or synonyms of words will not be found. For example, the single word search for *approve* would not find derivatives or forms of the word such as *approval* or synonyms such as *accept, affirm,* and *ratify.*

Single-word searches are useful when a user knows exactly what he or she is looking for, or when the coding of the documents has controlled the vocabulary used in entering the information.

Exhibit 9–19
Search Types and Examples

Search Type	Search Request	Words Found
Single word	approve	*approve*
Wildcard	approv*	*approve, approved, approval, approving*
Super wildcard	*approv*	*disapprove, disapproved, disapproval, disapproving, approve, approved, approval, approving*
Boolean OR	approval OR consent	*approval, consent*
Boolean AND	approval AND rate	*approval rate*
Boolean NOT	approval NOT rate	*approval but not approval rate*
Proximity—word	approval w/4 w rate	*approval* and *rate* where they are within four words of one another (the four words are retrieved each time)
Proximity—line	approval w/4 l rate	*approval* and *rate* where they are within four lines of one another (the four lines are retrieved each time)
Proximity—paragraph	approval w/4 p rate	*approval* and *rate* where they are within four paragraphs of one another (the four paragraphs are retrieved each time)
Proximity—page	approval w/4 pp rate	*approval* and *rate* where they are within four pages of one another (the four pages are retrieved each time)

Wildcard Searches

Searching a database for derivatives of a word is called a **wildcard search**. Most litigation support programs, as well as most database programs, use an asterisk (*) to represent wildcard searches. For example, if a user wanted to retrieve all the derivatives of the word *international,* the user would enter the search request as follows: "internation*". The system would respond by showing all matches to the words *international, internationally,* and so forth.

wildcard search
A computer search that scans a database for derivatives of a word.

Some litigation support systems can also perform what one program calls a super wildcard search. A **super wildcard search** searches a database for derivatives of a word both in front of and in back of the root word. For example, the search request "*approv*" would find all occurrences of the words *disapprove, disapproved, disapproval, disapproving, approve, approved, approval,* and *approving.*

super wildcard search
A computer search that scans a database for derivatives of a word both in front of and in back of the root word.

Wild card searches are beneficial when a user is not sure what derivatives the word or words being searched for might take.

Boolean Logic Searches

A **Boolean logic search** allows a search request to include or exclude words or other search criteria so that the search is either refined or broadened. Boolean searches are sometimes called logic searches or OR, AND, NOT searches.

Boolean logic search
A computer search that allows a search request to include or exclude words or other search criteria so that the search is either refined or broadened.

OR The Boolean search operator OR is used to include synonyms of words in a search request. For example, if a user wanted to search for the word *approval* and also wanted to include all synonyms of the word so that he would not miss any occurrences of like words such as *consent* and *permission,* the user would enter the

search request as follows: "approval OR consent OR permission." This request would find all occurrences of *any* of these three words throughout the database.

AND The Boolean search operator AND is used to include two or more words in a search request. For example, a user might want to find the occurrences of the words *approval rate.* Using a Boolean search, the request would be as follows: "approval AND rate." This request would find all occurrences where the words *approval* and *rate* were located.

NOT The Boolean search operator NOT excludes words from a search request. For example, if a user wanted to find the word *approval* but did not want to find the words *approval rate,* the user would enter the search request as follows: "approval NOT rate." This search would find all the occurrences of the word *approval* in the database but would not find occurrences of *approval rate.*

Proximity Searches

proximity search
A computer search that scans a database for words that are in a given proximity to one another.

Searching a database for words that are in a given proximity to one another is called a proximity search. For example, a **proximity search** could be employed if a user wanted to find the name Cindy within two words of the name John. The syntax of a proximity search will depend on the program, but a typical proximity search might look like this: "Cindy w/2 John".

Proximity searches can usually be performed based on the number of words, lines, paragraphs, or pages between two or more words. They are usually available only for full-text retrieval systems.

LITIGATION SUPPORT TIPS

There are advantages and disadvantages to using abstracts, full-text retrieval, imaging case management, and analytical litigation support systems. To obtain the advantages of each, the user will need to use all of them. A mistake beginners sometimes make is to throw every possible document into the database. Generally, "big is bad" no matter if it is a big document abstract database, full-text database, or image database. Basically, this follows the "garbage in garbage out" rule. The database should be only as big as you absolutely have to have it to get the information you need. Include only relevant documents if you can. Bigger databases slow down performance. Bigger databases also will retrieve more "hits" or documents than smaller ones. For example, if you search 1,500 documents and you get 40 documents back, this is manageable. You can just work your way through the 40 documents until you find what you need. However, if your database has 90,000 documents and you get 4,000 documents back, the database is basically useless. If you have a really big document collection, try to break it up into smaller document collections if you can. Finally, follow the rules in Exhibit 9–20.

QUESTIONS AND FEARS ABOUT COMPUTERIZED LITIGATION SUPPORT

People have several fears and questions about converting their manual litigation support system to a computerized version, including these: How long will it take to enter data? Is training hard? Can you convert a case to a computerized system in the middle of the case or only at the beginning? What are the most popular programs? Can computerized litigation support be used in the courtroom?

Exhibit 9–20
Litigation Support Tips

1. **Efficient and clean databases work best.** When you design and populate a litigation support database, keep it simple and straightforward, and enter only *relevant* information. Do not clutter your database with irrelevant information that will slow down the speed of the system or may retrieve unnecessary information during searches.
2. **Be an expert on the facts and legal issues in the case.** Before you can truly design a litigation support database that will meet your needs, you must fully understand the facts and legal issues of the case and understand the significance of the documents or information that you will be tracking.
3. **Legal documents are easier to search on than discovery documents.** You can search legal documents (depositions, pleadings, hearings, transcripts) more easily than discovery documents produced by parties.
4. **It is easier to search on documents that you produce rather than on documents the other party produces.** You can search your own documents more easily than documents you have never seen before.
5. **Searching on concepts is more difficult than searching on proper names or dates.** You can search for names and dates more easily than concepts. Concepts can be ambiguous and require you to be creative regarding what words might be used to describe them, whereas dates and names are usually straightforward and standard.
6. **Complex Boolean searches can be difficult to master.** It is sometimes difficult to construct complex Boolean searches that retrieve everything you need. It is sometimes easier to break down complex searches into smaller chunks.
7. **A quality team of legal staff who are educated on the specifics of the case and are using a well-thought-out database are more valuable than armies of untrained temporaries.** Computers cannot take the place of a good legal team. Armies of untrained office staff notwithstanding, often only an attorney or a legal assistant is going to recognize the implications of a piece of evidence. Quality is more important than quantity.
8. **One piece of the pie is not enough.** Litigation support users truly need document abstract, full-text, and imaging capability for documents. The best approach is usually to standardize with one software package that can handle it all and search all of the modules at one time. And don't forget case mangement and analytical applications, they also add great value to litigation support.
9. **Don't build an inflexible litigation support database.** Design your database from the beginning for multiple purposes and multiple users. This way, if the players or the issues change you will be prepared.
10. **Carefully number every page of every document.** Assign every document/page a Bates number, or use alternative technologies such as bar coding. To admit a document into evidence, you typically need a hard copy of the document. Thus, you must be able to lay your hands on the document. The only way this is possible is for your documents to be carefully numbered so that the needle can be found in the haystack under pressure and when it counts. If you will use imaging, you will need electronic Bates numbering as well.
11. **Make standardized rules.** Establish rules to govern the inputting of information and stick to them. Create and distribute a list of standardized rules for inputting data, and train all staff that are entering data on them. Data in the database must be consistent or problems will arise.
12. **Use the fewest amount of people possible to enter data.** The more people that are involved in entering information into the database, the more you have to train, the more you have to audit, and the harder it is to manage.
13. **Do quality audits and test as you go along.** Again, quality is more important than quantity. Don't wait until the end of the project to find out half the data was entered wrong. Do periodic quality audit checks as you go along, and test the data regularly to make sure the database is working properly. "Garbage in—garbage out" applies to databases.
14. **Input trial exhibit numbers for your opponents.** Input the opposing party's trial exhibit numbers into the database so that you will be able to quickly find your copy in the corresponding database folder when the opposing party offers the exhibit into evidence.

Exhibit 9–20
(Continued)

15. **Don't wait until trial to enter your documents.** Enter all documents in the database as they come into the case if possible. Preparing for trial is hard enough without trying to do a big project like creating a litigation support database at the last minute.
16. **Update the database every day at trial.** Update the database after each day of trial with all exhibits, so at the end of trial you will have an up-to-date list of what was offered and admitted.
17. **Print hard copies of documents and make backups.** Print a paper copy of anything you could not live without at trial and make *regular* backup copies of your databases. Computer systems sometimes fail and usually at the worst possible moment.

How Long Will It Take to Enter Data?

The question of how long it takes to enter data into a litigation support system is hard to answer, since many variables are involved. Three major variables must be considered:

1. How big is the litigation? (In other words, how many documents will need to be entered? How many witnesses are involved?) Small- to medium-sized cases with a few hundred documents and twenty to thirty witnesses can be entered in a week or two using a document abstract program, depending on some of the other variables listed here. Large cases with thousands of documents may take three to four months or more to complete. A lot depends on what information is contained in the support system and the complexity of the issues.
2. Are you using a full-text retrieval or a document abstract system? If you are using a full-text retrieval system, how will the full text be entered? If documents can be scanned into the computer or are available on disk through electronic discovery as opposed to being typed into the computer, the process will be much faster.
3. How many people experienced with litigation support will be entering the data? Experienced people can input data much faster than nonexperienced people. In addition, many firms believe that it is smarter to have their experienced people do only the coding of the forms and to hire typists to actually enter the data into the computer. Another thing to consider is that if you begin the process of inputting data and find that you are running short of time or are shorthanded, many good litigation support service bureaus can come in and finish the inputting job for you.

How Long Will It Take to Learn a Litigation Support Program?

Generally speaking, most litigation support programs are not difficult to learn. The real "trick" is learning not the program itself, but learning how to set up and design the system so that you are able to retrieve the information you want to get at when it comes to trial. This is something that you will quickly pick up with each new case you work on. As you gain experience, the process will get much smoother.

Do You Have to Computerize a Case from the Beginning?

Cases can be switched over to a litigation support program even after they have started. In fact, it might be a good idea to wait a few weeks to begin designing a system until after the adversary answers some of your more important arguments. This will allow you to see where the crux of the litigation will be. If you design a litigation support system without knowing even the basics of how the adversary will argue the case, you may not end up with a very good system that can adapt to the adversary's arguments.

It is best not to wait until a case is almost ready to go to trial, however, because in many instances you will not be able to get all the information you need into the system. Further, a litigation support system can be quite helpful in the middle of a litigation process for tasks such as preparing to take depositions of key witnesses and framing your arguments for motions and memorandums.

Can Computerized Litigation Support Be Used in the Courtroom?

Computerized litigation support systems are welcome in most courtrooms. Laptop computers are commonplace, not only for the litigators but also for the judges, court reporters, and other judicial staff. It is not uncommon to see separate tables for computers and litigation support staff in the courtroom. This is a real benefit for litigators, because searches in the litigation support system can be performed in the courtroom whenever information is needed.

ETHICAL CONSIDERATIONS

In many cases, litigation support means the difference between winning and losing. This is particularly true in large cases where the litigants have much at stake. In some cases, the stakes are even as much as hundreds of millions of dollars. No matter if the case is large or small, the law office has the ethical duty to present the client's case as well as it possibly can. This includes being competent and acting diligently. If a litigation support system is set up poorly, if the litigation support system is not used competently, or if the litigation support system fails entirely, then the client's case suffers. In addition, in most cases the client is actually paying for staff time and expenses to set up and use the litigation support system. If the litigation support system fails, then not only does the client's case suffer, but the client has been billed and has paid for a service that he did not get any benefit from. Litigation support definitely includes ethical responsibilities in that it is an extremely important aspect of any client's case and often determines whether the client wins or loses.

SUMMARY

Litigation support software is designed to assist attorneys in organizing information that has been gathered during litigation. The purpose of these programs is to help an attorney find the information she or he needs to adequately work and try a case.

Manual litigation support methods do not work well in the legal environment, because they are not flexible enough for the ever-changing pace of a lawsuit. Computerized litigation support methods can adapt to the changing environment, because they allow users to search an unlimited amount of data.

Computerized litigation support can be either performed by a litigation support service provider or done in-house. Service providers offer a number of benefits including being able to draw on their knowledge and experience, having someone other than the legal team be fully responsible for the litigation support system, being able to tie electronic discovery duties and litigation support together, and being able to handle and work with tens or even hundreds of thousands of documents or more.

No matter whether litigation support is performed by a service provider or in-house, a legal organization must decide whether a document abstract or document summary system will be used and whether full text, imaging, case management, or analytical programs, or a combination of all of them, will be used.

A document abstract litigation support system allows users to enter document abstracts or document summaries into a computer and to subsequently search and retrieve information contained in the abstract or summaries. Full-text retrieval systems, on the other hand, enable users to search and retrieve information contained in the full text of documents entered into the system. In some instances, a document abstract system will be used to track documents, and a full-text retrieval system will be used to track depositions and other types of testimony in the same case.

Document imaging allows a legal professional to see the actual image of a document as opposed to seeing its full text or an abstract of the document. Document imaging can be accomplished by scanning hard-copy images into a computer or converting electronic documents into an image file format such as TIFF or PDF.

Analytical litigation support software helps legal professionals analyze a case from a number of perspectives and helps them conceptualize and think about facts, documents, people, and the relationships among them. This type of software includes programs that create timelines or outlines of cases or itemize facts, documents, issues, and people.

Some litigation support systems now offer document abstract, full-text retrieval, imaging, and analytical tools in one program. They offer the advantages of all these types of systems, but are typically complex due to the large amount of power they have. No matter what type of litigation support system is used, it is necessary that a user carefully plan the design of the system, taking into account what type of information is most relevant to the case and how it will be used during litigation and at trial. A litigation support system that is poorly planned will surely fail and perhaps cause the case to be lost.

KEY TERMS

litigation support software
discovery
interrogatories
request for admissions
request for production of documents
deposition
expert witness report
pleadings
motions and briefs
litigation support service bureau
in-house computerized litigation support system
document abstract litigation support system
objective/biographical coding
subjective coding
Bates stamp
full-text retrieval litigation support system
computer-aided transcription (CAT)
real-time transcription
electronic discovery
document imaging
analytical litigation support programs
single word search
wildcard search
super wildcard search
Boolean logic search
proximity search

TEST YOUR KNOWLEDGE

1. True or False: Litigation support software primarily assists legal professionals in responding to electronic discovery requests.
2. True or False: Litigation support is an easy task because for the most part legal issues, factual issues, and legal theories are static during the litigation of a case.
3. Distinguish between litigation documents and factual documents.
4. What is knowledge management?
5. Name three benefits of computerized litigation support.
6. Distinguish document abstract, full-text retrieval, and imaging.
7. What advantages does using a litigation support service provider offer?
8. Differentiate between objective and subjective coding as they relate to creating document abstracts.
9. What is a controlled vocabulary and what litigation support system is this important to?
10. What type of search uses "and," "or," and "not?"

INTERNET SITES

Organization	Description	World Wide Web Address
1360 Studios, Inc.	Litigation support and transcript management	<http://www.1360studios.com>
Bowne & Co.	JFS Litigator litigation support	<http://www.bowne.com>
C2 Legal	E-discovery and litigation support services	<http://www.c2legal.com>
Case Logistix, Inc.	Case Logistix litigation support program	<http://www.caselogistix.com>
CaseCentral	E-discovery and litigation support services	<http://www.casecentral.com>
Cricket Technologies	E-discovery and litigation support services	<http://www.crickettechnologies.com>
CT Summation, Inc.	Summation litigation support products	<http://www.summation.com>
DT Software Inc.	Data searching and litigation support	<http://www.dtsearch.com>
Encore Legal Solutions	E-discovery and litigation support services	<http://www.lexsolutio.com>
Gigatron Software	Transcription software	<http://<http://www.gsclion.com>
I Connect Development	Litigation support and e-discovery products and services	<http://www.iconect.com>
Inmagic	Litigation support products	<http://www.inmagic.com>
ISYS/Odyssey Development	Litigation support products	<http://www.isysdev.com>
Kroll Ontrack	Litigation support and e-discovery services	<http://www.krollontrack.com>
LexisNexis	Case Map and Time Map litigation support	<http://www.casesoft.com>
LexisNexis	Concordance litigation support	<http://www.dataflight.com>
Nuance Communication	Omnipage optical character recognition software	<http://www.nuance.com>
Pitney Bowes	Caselit litigation support services	<http://www.compulit.com>
Real Legal	Litigation support and transcript management products	<http://www.reallegal.com>
Rosen Technology Resources	Litigation support and e-discovery services	<http://http://www.rosentech.net>
Zylab	Searching and litigation support products	<http://www.zylab.com>

ON THE WEB EXERCISES

1. Using the addresses listed in the Internet Sites section of this chapter, visit the websites of the following three vendors: Case Logistix, CT Summation (iBlaze), and LexisNexis (Concordance litigation support software, at www .dataflight.com), and then write a two-page paper that summaries the features of each product.
2. Visit the American Bar Association's website and search for articles on litigation support. Try to find three articles on the topic. Write a one-page summary of each article.
3. Using a general search engine such as google.com or yahoo.com, research computer-aided transcription and write a two-page article on what it is, how it works, and why it is helpful to practicing legal professionals like attorneys and legal assistants.

QUESTIONS AND EXERCISES

1. As the chief litigation legal assistant, you are preparing to have clerical staff enter approximately one thousand documents into a computerized litigation support system. You are concerned that the information may not be entered uniformly, since ten different people will be entering the data. What should you do to solve the problem? Describe your answer in detail.
2. An attorney in your firm is having trouble deciding whether she should switch her staff from their manual litigation support system to a computerized system. Tell the attorney what you think about the situation.
3. You have been asked to give your opinion regarding whether a litigation support database should be created for a particular case. The case has approximately two hundred documents. The documents average one hundred fifty pages each. The issues are complex and will require four attorneys five months to try the case. Damages asked for are minimal, but the public relations damage to your client could be devastating should your client lose. The opposing counsel may or may not use a litigation support database; your firm does not know. Should the case be entered into a litigation support database?
4. Using this chapter as a guide, and specifically the tips in Exhibit 9–20, design a litigation support system for one of the following types of lawsuits:
   - high-speed auto accident involving multiple cars, multiple witnesses, and no evidence of design defects
   - wrongful termination claim based on age discrimination involving multiple witnesses
   - securities fraud case where investors claim they invested in a company that withheld information about its true financial situation
   - medical malpractice claim involving a wrongful death case of a patient undergoing a medical procedure
   - product liability class action against a manufacturer alleging design defects in a tractor

   Your design should consider what type of litigation support method you will use, who will enter the data and how, what type of information will be entered, when it will be entered, what issues will be disputed at trial, and other such information. Prepare a minimum three-page summary of your design including specifics of how you arrived at your design.

END NOTES

[1] Michael R. Arkfeld, *The Digital Practice of Law*, 5th ed., Law Partner Publishing, 2001, 7–7.
[2] Michael R. Arkfeld, *The Digital Practice of Law*, 5th ed., Law Partner Publishing, 2001, 7–3.
[3] Michael R. Arkfeld, *The Digital Practice of Law*, 5th ed., Law Partner Publishing, 2001, 7–4.
[4] Daryl Teshima and Rebecca Thompson Nagle, "Litigation Support Software Comes of Age," *Los Angeles Lawyer*, July 1999.
[5] Daryl Teshima and Rebecca Thompson Nagle, "Litigation Support Software Comes of Age," *Los Angeles Lawyer*, July, 1999.
[6] Dwayne E. Krager and Rick R. Thompson, "Tech Trends for 2002," *Legal Assistant Today*, May/June 2002, 41.
[7] Khrhysna McKinney, "Creating a Virtual Litigation Support Environment to Aid in Discovery," *Legal Tech Newsletter*, January 2002, 6.
[8] John Caldwell, "Climbing the Technology Ladder," *Legal Assistant Today*, May/June 2001, 52.
[9] Khrhysna McKinney, "Creating a Virtual Litigation Support Environment to Aid in Discovery," *Legal Tech Newsletter*, January 2002, 6.
[10] Cindy Langan, "Technology for All Occasions," *Facts and Findings*, August 2001, 39.
[11] Daryl Teshima and Rebecca Thompson Nagle, "Litigation Support Software Comes of Age," *Los Angeles Lawyer*, July, 1999.
[12] Milton Hooper, "Do You Have the Timeline?," *Legal Assistant Today*, July/August 2006, 63.
[13] Dawn R. Acker, "A Picture is Worth a Thousand Pages," *Legal Assistant Today*, July/August 2001, 70.
[14] Michael R. Arkfeld, *The Digital Practice of Law*, 5th ed., Law Partner Publishing, 2001, 7–27.

HANDS-ON EXERCISES

READ THIS FIRST!

I. Introduction – Read this!

CT Summation iBLAZE is a powerful litigation support program. The CT Summation iBLAZE demonstration version is a full working version of the program (with a few limitations). The program demonstration version times out after February 1, 2010. This means that the program will not work after February 1, 2010. When you are ready to install the program, follow the instructions below.

II. Using the CT Summation iBLAZE Hands-on Exercises

The CT Summation iBLAZE Hands-on Exercises are easy to use and contain step-by-step instructions. Each exercise builds on the previous one, so please complete the Hands-on Exercises in order. CT Summation iBLAZE comes with sample data, so you should be able to utilize many features of the program.

III. Installation Instructions

Below are step-by-step instructions for installing the CT Summation iBLAZE demonstration version on your computer.

1. *Insert Disk 2 from the inside back cover of the text into your computer.*

2. When prompted with "What do you want Windows to do?" *select "Open folder to view files using Windows Explorer."* If your computer does not automatically recognize that you have inserted a CD, double-click the My Computer icon, then double-click the drive where Disk 2 is.

3. *Double-click the Summation iBlaze folder. Then, double-click the setup.exe file.* This will start the Summation iBlaze installation wizard.

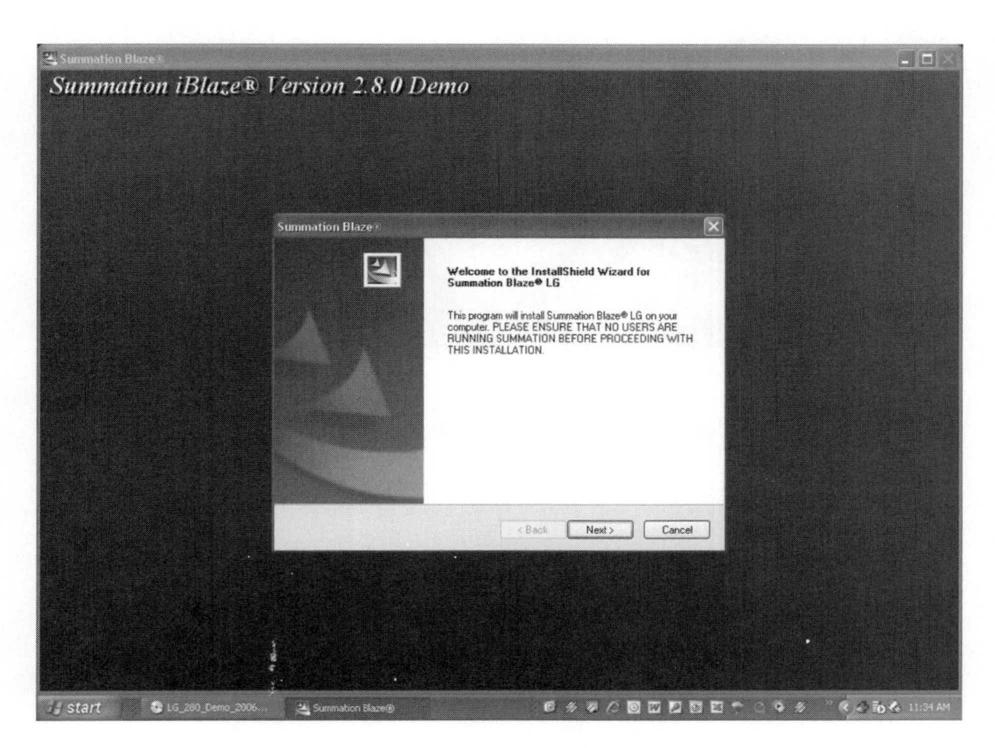

Summation Installation Exhibit 1

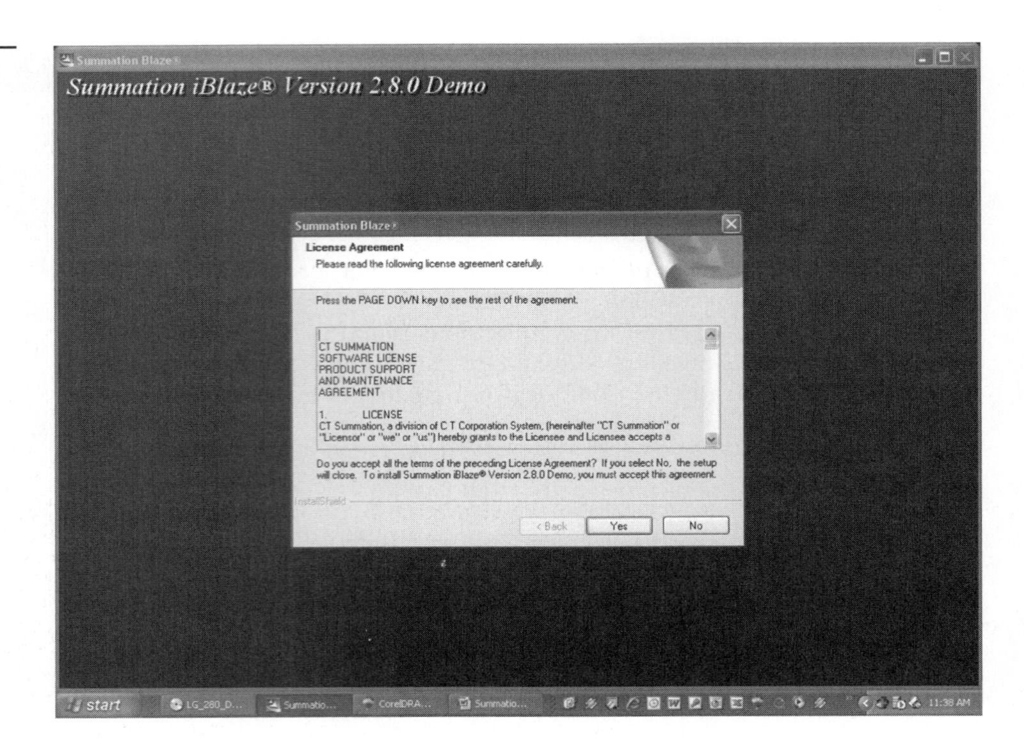

Summation Installation Exhibit 2

Reprinted with permission of CT Summation, Inc. All Rights Reserved. For more information, call 1/800–735–7866 or visit http://www.summation.com.

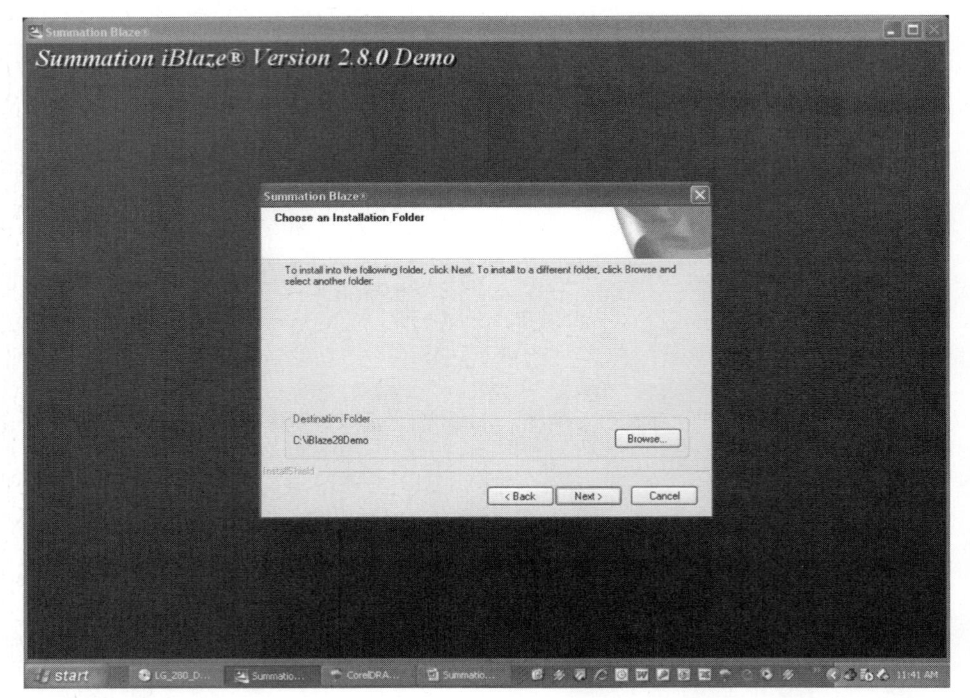

Summation Installation Exhibit 3

Reprinted with permission of CT Summation, Inc. All Rights Reserved. For more information, call 1/800–735–7866 or visit http://www.summation.com.

4. A screen that looks like Summation Installation Exhibit 1 should now be displayed. ***Click "Next."***

5. The screen regarding the License Agreement (see Summation Installation Exhibit 2) should now be displayed. ***Click "Yes."***

6. The Choose an Installation Folder screen should now be displayed (see Summation Installation Exhibit 3). ***Click Next to install the program in the default directory.***

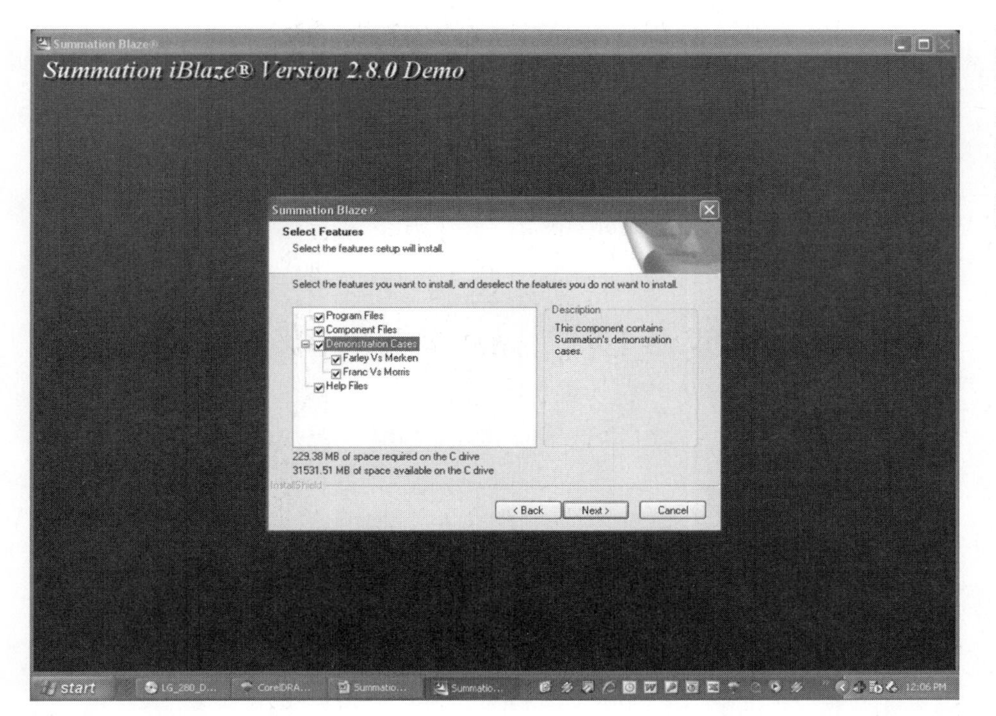

Summation Installation Exhibit 4

Reprinted with permission of CT Summation, Inc. All Rights Reserved. For more information, call 1/800–735–7866 or visit http://www.summation.com.

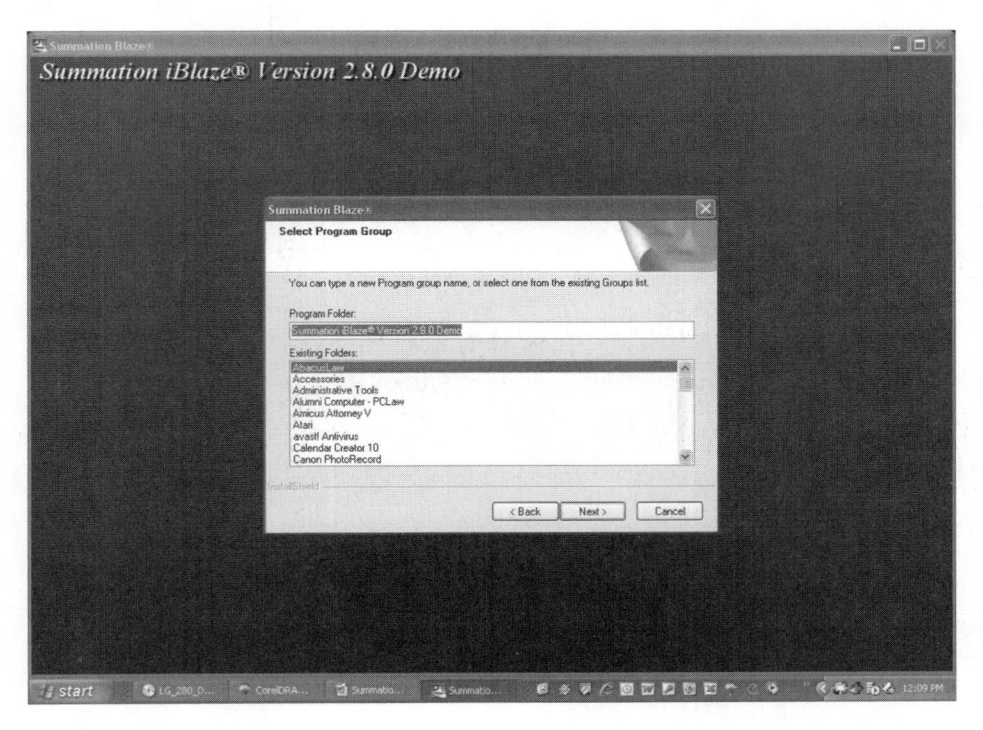

Summation Installation Exhibit 5

Reprinted with permission of CT Summation, Inc. All Rights Reserved. For more information, call 1/800–735–7866 or visit http://www.summation.com.

7. The Select Features screen should now be displayed (see Summation Installation Exhibit 4). ***Click the box next to Demonstration Cases*** (see Summation Installation Exhibit 4). Before proceeding, verify that the cases of *Farley vs Merken* and *Franc vs Morris* have check marks next to them.

8. ***Click "Next."***

9. The Select Program Group screen should now be displayed (see Summation Installation Exhibit 5).***Click Next to accept the default program group where the program will be located.***

10. The program will begin installing (see Summation Installation Exhibit 6).

11. The Summation iBlaze Version 2.8.0 Demo screen that says that the setup is now complete should now be displayed (see Summation Installation Exhibit 7).

12. The installation is now complete. ***Click "Finish."*** You are now ready to start the Summation Hands-on Exercises.

Summation Installation Exhibit 6

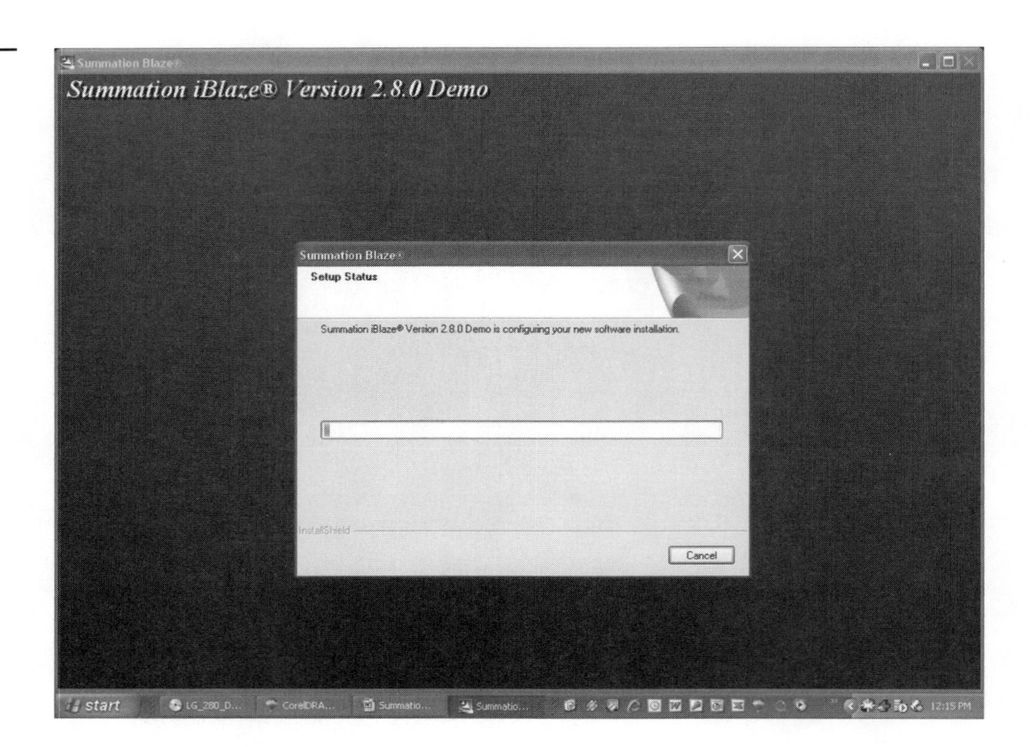

Summation Installation Exhibit 7

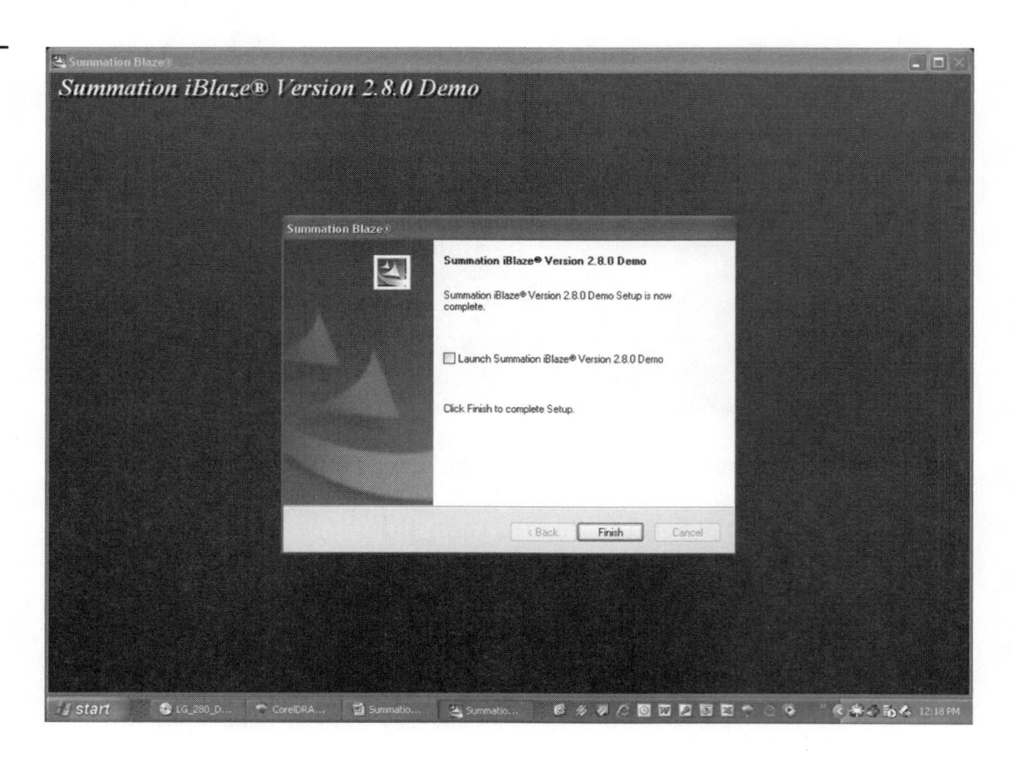

IV. Installation Technical Support

If you have problems installing the demonstration version of CT Summation from the CD-ROM included with this text, please contact Thomson Delmar Learning Technical Support first at (800)477–3692. Please note that CT Summation is a licensed product of CT Summation, Inc. If Thomson Delmar Learning Technical Support is unable to resolve your installation question or if you have a non-installation related question, you will need to contact CT Summation, Inc. directly at (800–786–2778).

HANDS-ON EXERCISES

CT SUMMATION IBLAZE

Basic

Number	Lesson Title	Concepts Covered
Lesson 1	Introduction to CT Summation iBLAZE	Explanation and introduction to the Summation interface.
Lesson 2	Exploring the Summation Databases	Introduction to the separate databases in Summation including People, Events, Pleadings, Core Database (document abstracts), Transcripts, and e-docs/email. Introduction to column view, form views, and imaging.
Lesson 3	Searching Summation Databases	Introduction to conducting searches in Summation across multiple databases simultaneously.
Intermediate		
Lesson 4	Marking up a Document	Marking up and emphasizing documents electronically.
Lesson 5	Working with Transcripts	Earmarking key testimony, assigning issue codes to key testimony, creating rapid-fire deposition summaries, and printing deposition summaries.
Lesson 6	Working with the Case Organizer	Creating outlines and lists for case blueprints, chronologies of case events, exhibit lists, and to-do lists in Case Organizer. Creating automatic links to documents referenced in outlines and creating new sections/tabs in Case Organizer.
Lesson 7	Customizing the Column Core Database View	Customizing and changing the fields displayed in the Column Database view and Core Database view, including adding and deleting information displayed and changing how information is sorted.
Advanced		
Lesson 8	Additional Search Techniques	Additional search techniques in Summation including Boolean searching, issue searching, using the vocabulary option, and other search techniques.
Lesson 9	Load a Transcript, Load a Pleading, and Enter a Document Abstract	Loading transcripts, loading pleadings, entering documents, and entering document abstracts into Summation.
Lesson 10	Creating a New Case	Entering and setting up a new case in Summation, including entering issues, names, a blueprint for the case, and other information.

GETTING STARTED

Introduction

Throughout these exercises, information you need to enter into the program will be designated in several different ways.

- Keys to be pressed on the keyboard will be designated in brackets, in all caps, bold, and enlarged type (i.e., press the **[ENTER]** key).
- Movements with the mouse will be designated in bold and italics (i.e., ***point to File on the menu bar and click the mouse*)**.
- Words or letters that should be typed will be designated in bold (i.e., type **Training Program**).
- Information that is or should be displayed on your computer screen is shown in the following style: **Press ENTER to continue.**

OVERVIEW OF CT SUMMATION iBLAZE

CT Summation iBLAZE is a powerful litigation support program. Summation includes a number of features, including the ability to enter, organize, track, and search on document abstracts, transcripts (full-text retrieval), pleadings (full-text retrieval), e-discovery, email and attachments (full-text retrieval), and other electronic documents. In addition, Summation can store document images, create and attach electronic notes to transcripts and other electronic documents, track the production history of documents, organize and track information about cases using a case organizer function, and create chronologies.

The purpose of these exercises is to give you a general introduction to Summation and how it is used in litigation. A fully functioning demonstration version of Summation is used. The demonstration version of Summation includes two sample cases (only one of which is used in these exercises—*P. Franc v. K. Morris*). The hypothetical case of *P. Franc v. K. Morris* is ready for trial and includes documents and information that you will use to learn about Summation. (For more about the *P. Franc v. K. Morris* case, see below.)

In addition, this tutorial provides an exercise that allows the user to create a file in Summation for the sample case of *Smith v. EZ Pest Control*. The *Smith v. EZ Pest Control* case will allow you to create a new database from scratch.

The *P. Franc V. K. Morris* Case

The facts of the *P. Franc v. K. Morris* case are that a mudslide significantly damaged the plaintiff's (P. Franc's) house. The plaintiff alleges that the defendant (K. Morris) negligently built a structure on a slope above the plaintiff's house, and that in a heavy rainstorm the slope gave way and subsequently flooded and otherwise damaged plaintiff's property. The plaintiff also alleges that the municipal planning authority only approved the defendant for a slope of twenty (20) vertical feet, that the defendant instead built a slope that exceeded sixty (60) vertical feet, and that the slope was inherently unsafe.

Note: Summation is an extremely powerful program and the demonstration case that is used is quite extensive. It contains many documents, digital pictures, and images, and uses a great deal of RAM. If for any reason you have computer problems during the exercises, please exit the program, exit Windows, and reboot your computer. This should correct the problem. If the problem persists contact CT Summation technical support at 1/800/786-2778.

LESSON 1: INTRODUCTION TO CT SUMMATION iBLAZE

This lesson introduces you to CT Summation iBlaze litigation support programs. It explains basic information about the Summation interface.

1. Start Windows. Then, ***double-click on the Summation iBLAZE2.8.0 Demo icon on the desktop*** (it looks like a briefcase with the letter CT on it) or ***click the Start button, click Programs or All Programs, point to the Summation iBLAZE 2.8.0 Demo folder, and then click Summation iBLAZE 2.8.0 Demo.***

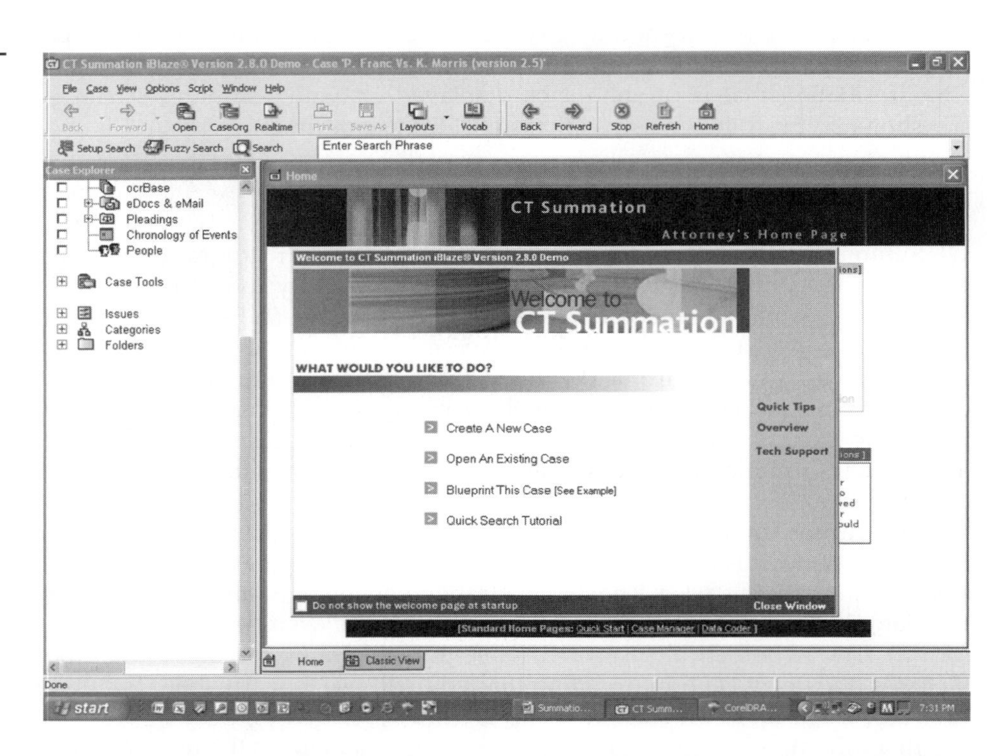

Summation Exhibit 1

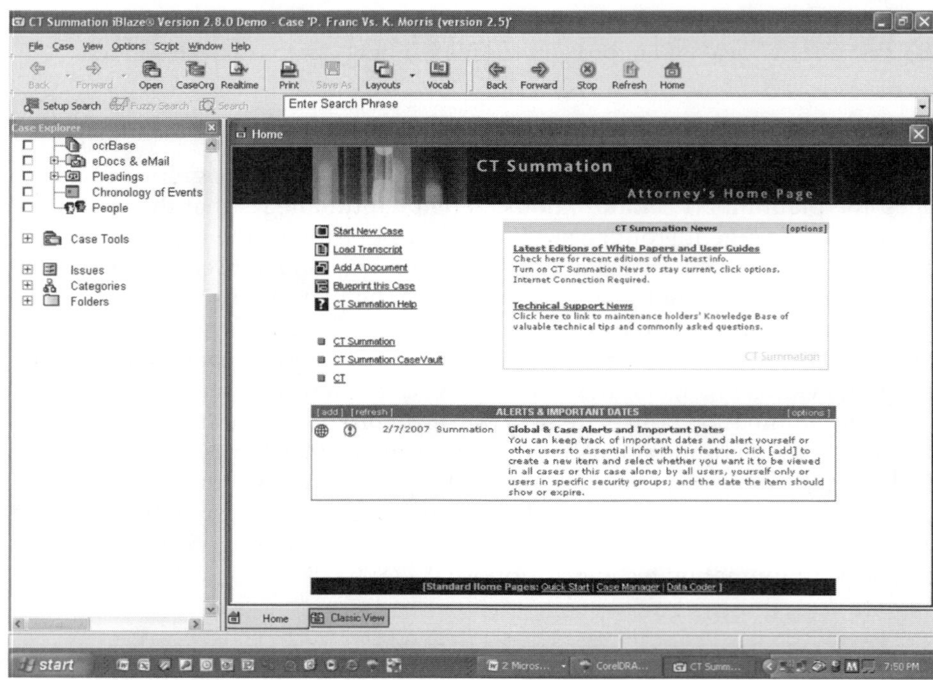

Summation Exhibit 2

2. When you start Summation for the first time you will see the Welcome to Summation iBlaze screen (see Summation Exhibit 1). From this screen you can create a new case, open an existing case, and access other options. When learning Summation for the first time, it is easiest to start with a case that already has all of the transcripts and documents entered into the program.

3. You will now load the *P. Franc v. K. Morris* case. ***Click Open an Existing Case on the Welcome to CT Summation screen. Then, double-click*** P. Franc v. K. Morris.

4. The title bar at the top of the screen should say "CT Summation iBlaze Version 2.8.0 Demo – P. Franc v. K. Morris (version 2.5)" (see Summation Exhibit 1).

5. The CT Summation Attorney's Home Page is now displayed (see Summation Exhibit 2).

6. Notice that the screen is split. On the left side of the screen is the Case Explorer. Case Explorer is the major interface for working in Summation. Case Explorer allows you to access most of Summation's different screens, views, and programs in one convenient place. In addition, the Case Explorer allows you to select exactly what type of data will be searched on when you enter searches. Case Explorer will be covered in depth later in the exercises.

7. On the right side of the screen is the Home screen. As you select different views from the Case Explorer, the right side of the screen will change. The left side of the screen stays in the Case Explorer. This split screen layout is called the Docked Explorer Layout.

8. Notice at the bottom of the page that there are additional standard home pages for Quick Start, Case Manager, and Data Coder. You are currently using the Attorney's Home Page, but it can be changed depending on your role. We will leave it as the Attorney's Home page for now. This will be covered in more detail later in this exercise.

9. Also, notice at the bottom of the screen there are two tabs, Home and Classic View.

10. ***Click the Classic View tab*** at the bottom of the screen.

11. Notice that a new window, Case Folder—Main Window (it looks like a file drawer with many files in it) is now displayed on the right side of the screen, and that the Case Explorer is still displayed on the left side. *Note:* The Classic View is the interface that older versions of Summation used. Some users still like this view.

12. ***Click the Home tab*** at the bottom of the screen.

13. As you open Summation windows, additional tabs at the bottom of the screen will be added. You can move in and out of these different views by clicking on these tabs.

14. Notice that there is a small "X" icon in the top right of the Case Explorer window (in the blue bar that says Case Explorer). This is the Close icon, which allows you to close the Case Explorer window. *Note:* If you place your mouse over the X icon for a second—or any icon in Windows, it will display the name of the icon. In this case it will say "Close." It is possible during these exercises to accidentally close the Case Explorer and the Home window. Since these are the major interfaces for working in Summation, you need to know how to bring them back in case this happens.

Summation Exhibit 3

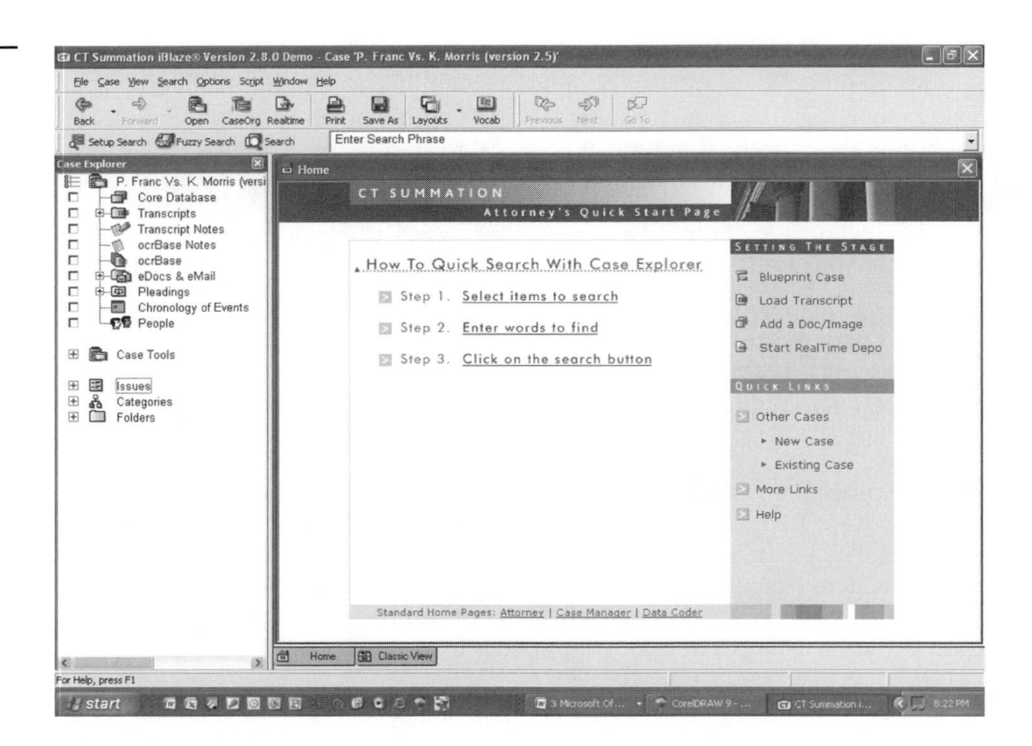

15. ***Click the "X" (Close) icon in the Case Explorer window.*** Be sure to click on the Close icon in the Case Explorer window and not on the Close icon in the Home window or the Summation iBlaze Version 2.8.0 Demo main window.

16. Notice that only the Attorney's Home Page window is now displayed.

17. To bring back the Case Explorer window, ***click View on the menu bar, point to Show, and then click on Docked Explorer Layout.*** Notice that the Case Explorer window is now back on the left side of the screen.

18. Now, ***click the "X" (Close) icon in the Home window.*** Notice that the Classic View Case Folder—Main window is now displayed.

19. To bring back the Home window, ***click View on the menu bar, point to Show, and then click on Show Home View.*** Notice that the Home window is now back on the right side of the screen.

20. Notice that in the Attorney's Home Page window there are options including Start New Case, Load Transcript, Add a Document, Blueprint This Case, and CT Summation Help. One of the most helpful features for new users is the CT Summation Help option. You will not access this option in these exercises, but it is helpful if you would like additional training on Summation.

21. As mentioned earlier, at the bottom of the Home page are the Standard Home Pages: Quick Start, Case Manager, and Data Coder.

22. ***Click Quick Start*** next to the Standard Home Pages at the bottom of the Home window.

23. Notice that the Attorney's Quick Start Page home is now displayed (see Summation Exhibit 3). The options here are slightly different and are designed to accommodate the needs of an attorney who is more familiar with Summation.

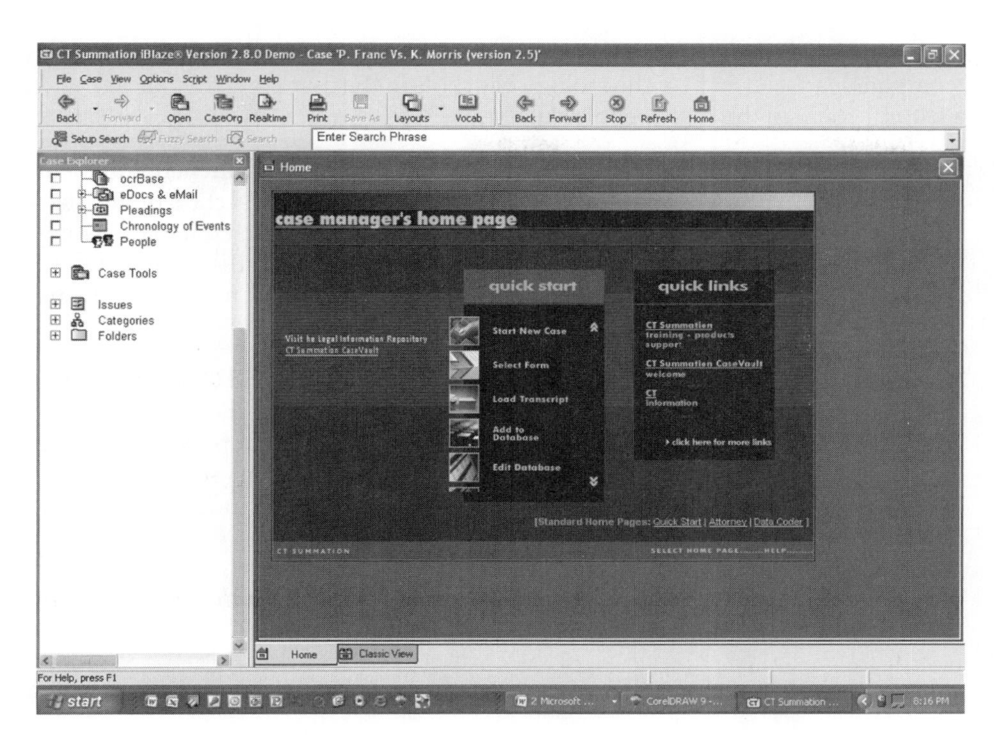

Summation Exhibit 4

Reprinted with permission of CT Summation, Inc. All Rights Reserved. For more information, call 1/800–735–7866 or visit http://www.summation.com.

Note: The How to Quick Search With Case Explorer mini-tutorial is extremely helpful when learning to search in Summation. If you have time later and would like to know more about Summation, this is an excellent feature.

24. To view the Case Manager home page, ***click Case Manager*** near the middle of the screen under Standard Home Pages.

25. Notice that the Case Manager home page is now displayed (see Summation Exhibit 4). A case manager would likely be a legal assistant or other legal professional that is in charge of the litigation support function for a case. Again, the menu and functions are slightly different to reflect the specific needs of a case manager.

26. To view the Data Coder's Home Page, ***click Data Coder*** next to Standard Home Pages at the bottom of the Home window.

27. The Data Coder's Home Page should now be displayed. A data coder may be a legal assistant or a clerk (depending on the type of data being entered). The data coder is the person that is actually entering the data into the database. Again, the screen is formatted to meet the needs of the data coder.

28. To go back to the Attorney's Quick Start Page home, ***click Quick Start*** next to Standard Home Pages at the bottom of the screen.

29. Notice that there are two main parts to the Case Explorer window (see Summation Exhibit 3). *Note:* You may need to scroll up in the Case Explorer window to see all of the options in Case Explorer that are shown in Summation Exhibit 3. The top portion of the Case Explorer window contains all of the databases of the case that you will be conducting searches on. This includes the Core Database (which contains the document abstracts database), document transcript database (depositions, trial transcriptions, etc.), transcript notes, the full text of other documents that have been entered (such as ocrBase database) and notes to those

documents, an electronic documents/email database, a pleadings database (complaint, answer, etc.), a chronology of events in the case (event database), and a list of people in the case (people database).

30. The important thing to remember is that anything to be searched will be in the top section of the Case Explorer window. Notice in the top section of the Case Explorer window that there are blank check boxes next to each database listing (Core Database, Transcripts, etc.). When conducting a search the user will click in these check boxes to indicate which database they want to include in the search. This is covered in more detail in later exercises.

31. The bottom portion of the Case Explorer window is entitled Case Tools. This section includes tools in Summation that you can use to view and organize your data and perform other tasks. Throughout these exercises the top section of Case Explorer will be called the Database section and the bottom section of Case Explorer will be referred to as Tools. The Tools section includes Case Tools, Issues, Categories, and Folders.

This concludes Lesson 1. To exit CT Summation, ***click File on the menu bar and then click Exit CT Summation*** or go to Lesson 2.

LESSON 2: EXPLORING THE SUMMATION DATABASES

This lesson introduces you to the different databases in Summation. As indicated in the previous chapter, Summation has databases, or collections of information, for people, events, pleadings, document, abstracts, transcripts, and electronic documents. This exercise will explore the different databases and database functions in Summation.

If you did not exit Summation after Lesson 1, then skip Steps 1 and 2 and go directly to Step 3.

1. Start Windows. Then, ***double-click on the Summation iBLAZE2.8.0 Demo icon on the desktop*** (it looks like a briefcase with the letter CT on it), or ***click the Start button, point to Programs or All Programs, point to the Summation iBLAZE 2.8.0 Demo folder, and then click Summation iBLAZE 2.8.0 Demo.***

2. The Welcome to Summation window should now be displayed. ***Click Close Window*** in the lower right of the Welcome to Summation window.

3. You should now be back at the Attorney's Quick Start Page home with *P. Franc v. K. Morris* in the Case Explorer window. Please note that in Summation you are automatically taken back to the case you were in when you exited the program last. You will now explore the databases in the top section of the Case Explorer window. Remember, if at any time you cannot see all of the options listed in the Case Explorer window, just use the scroll bar in the Case Explorer window to scroll up or down to see all of the options.

4. ***Double-click on the word "People"*** in the Case Explorer window.

5. The People database window should now be displayed (see Summation Exhibit 5). The People database allows a user to organize and understand all of the players in a case. Notice that an additional tab has been added at the bottom of the screen. There are now three active windows open in Summation: Home, Classic View, and People.

6. ***Click the Home tab*** at the bottom of the screen. Notice that you were taken back to the Attorney's Quick Start Page home.

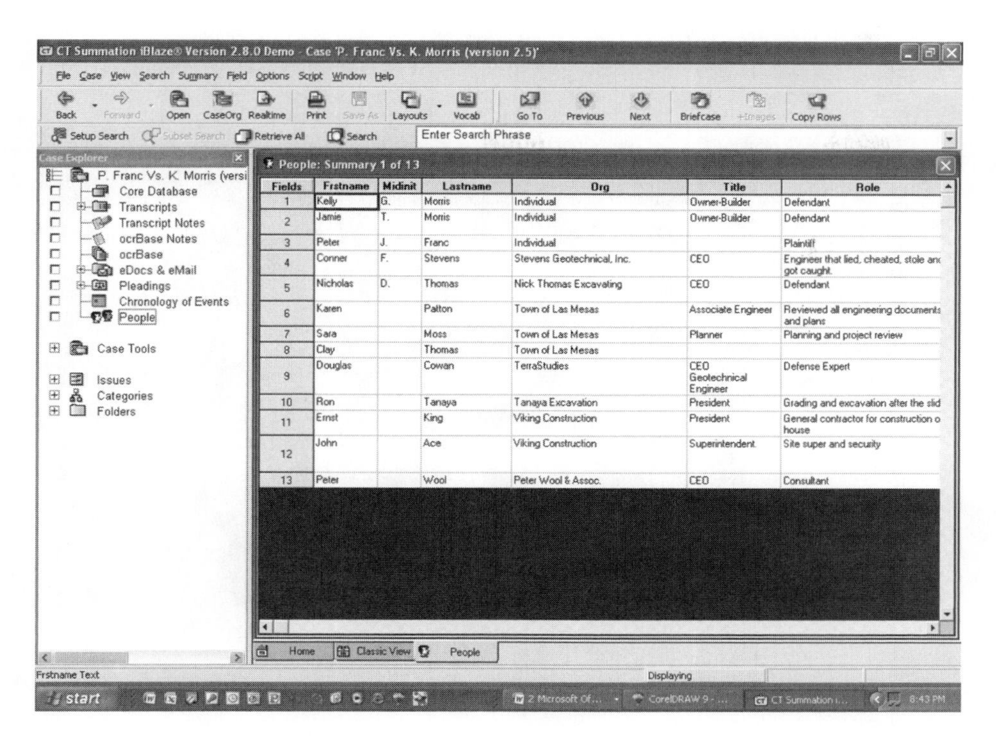

Summation Exhibit 5

7. ***Point and click on the People tab*** at the bottom of the screen to return back to the database. You can move between different open views, tools and databases by clicking the tabs at the bottom of the screen.

8. With the People database window open on your screen, ***use the right arrow on the keyboard or the scroll bar at the bottom of the window to scroll over to the right to see all of the columns in the People database.***

9. Notice that there is summary information listed in the database about each of the people in the case, including their first name, middle initial, last name, organization, title, role, and other information.

10. It is important to note that in the People database view, you can only see the data in the database. You cannot actually enter data.

11. Press **[CTRL]+[HOME]** to put your cursor on the first field/column in the People database.

12. ***Right-click and select Edit.***

13. Notice that a new window has been opened (the Edit: People window) to edit the data for Kelly G. Morris. Notice that at the top of the window it says Edit/Add Form (see Summation Exhibit 6). You can only enter or edit data in the Edit/Add Form mode. You could now edit the form if you needed to.

14. ***Click the Forward icon*** (it also has a right arrow next to it) ***on the toolbar***. This will take you to the second record in the database (Jamie T. Morris).

15. ***Click Close*** in the Edit: People window. You should now be back at the People window.

16. ***Click File on the menu bar and then click Print Preview. At the "Would you like to switch to landscape mode?" prompt, click Yes.***

Summation Exhibit 6

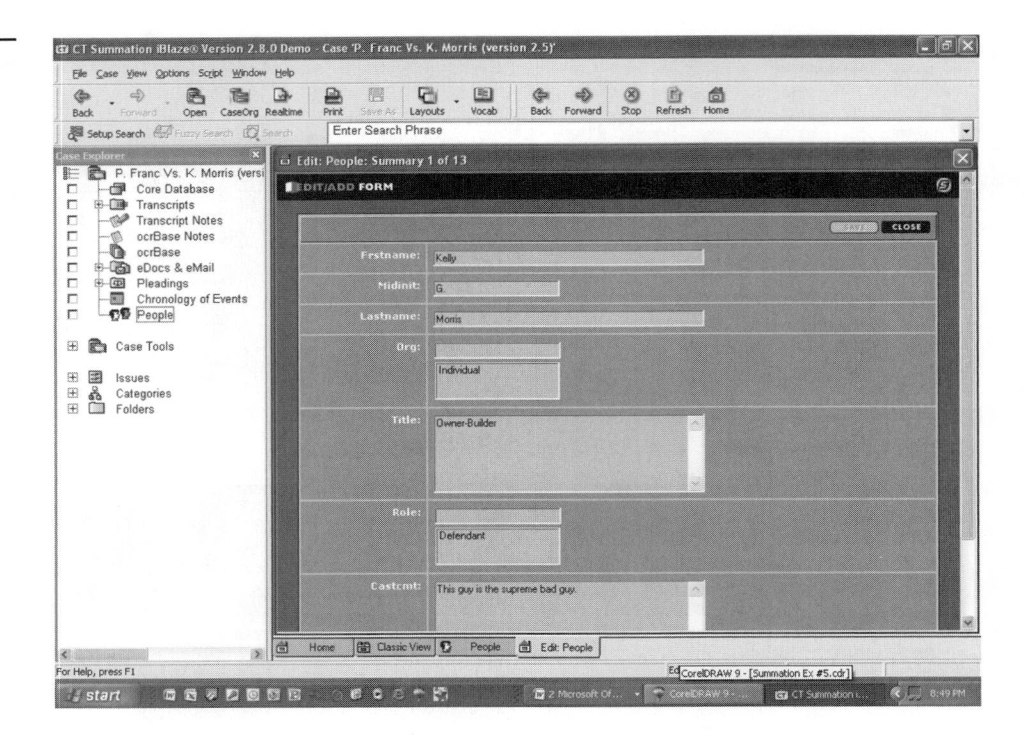

17. Notice that your cursor has now turned into a magnifying glass. The screen will be difficult to see, so click anywhere in the document and it will be magnified.

18. ***Click Close*** to close the print preview screen.

19. ***Double-click Chronology of Events*** in the Case Explorer window to see the events database.

20. Notice at the bottom of the screen that a fourth tab has now been added (for Events), showing that there are four windows now open in Summation. The ability to quickly switch in and out of a multitude of windows is a strength of Summation. During a trial, things move extremely quickly, so it is beneficial that legal professionals can move in and out of databases and views in Summation seamlessly.

21. The Events database allows a legal professional to get the big picture of key events in a case and to track and organize what those events are, who was involved, when they occurred, what legal issues they impact, and other important factors (see Summation Exhibit 7).

22. ***Use your right cursor key or the horizontal scroll bar at the bottom of the window to scroll over to the right to see all of the columns in the Events database.***

23. ***Use the down arrow key on the keyboard or the vertical scroll bar to scroll down to see all of the rows in the Events database.*** You can edit the Events database by double-clicking in a field.

24. We will now look at the Pleadings database. ***Click the + (plus sign)*** next to Pleadings in the Case Explorer.

25. ***Double-click Documents*** under Pleadings in the Case Explorer.

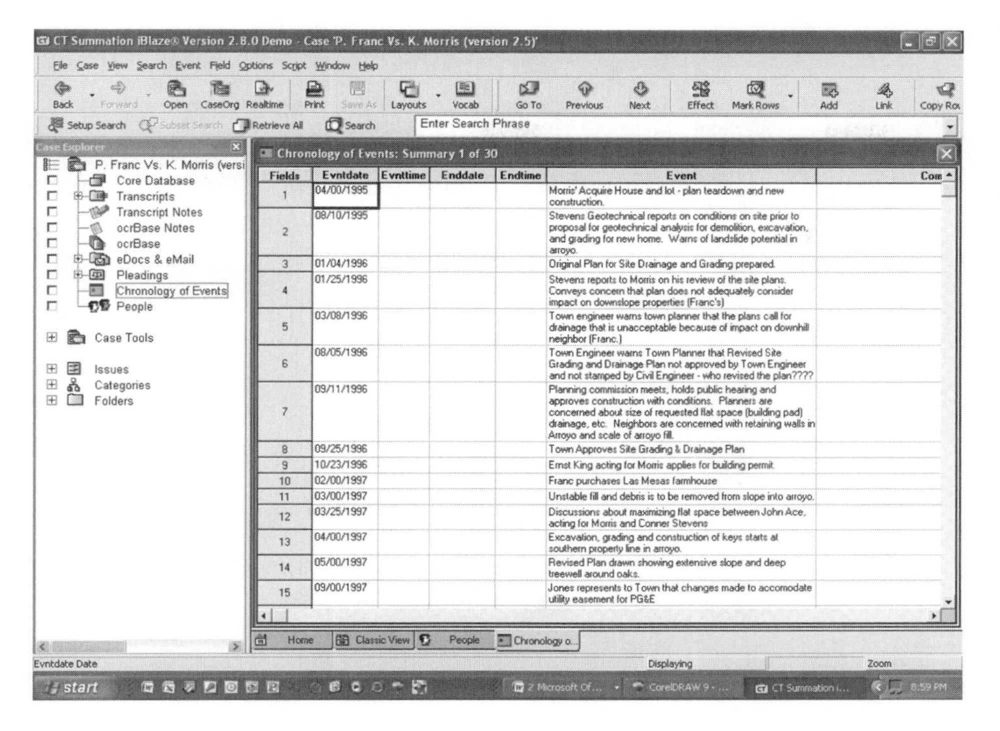

Summation Exhibit 7

26. Notice that a Windows Explorer screen is now displayed that shows a directory of pleading documents for the case. The documents are either Microsoft Word files or PDF files. You could now double-click any of these documents (assuming you have Microsoft Word or Adobe Acrobat, or a similar program that reads these file formats) to read the documents/pleadings. The Word documents can be searched on using Summation, but the PDF files cannot. However, in this way, the legal professional can at least have full access to all pleadings in a case to review them at any time from within the Summation program.

27. *Click the "X" (Close) icon* in the upper right of the Documents window to close it.

28. Since you will not be using the People window again in this exercise, *click on the People tab* at the bottom of the screen. Then *click the "X" (Close) icon* in the upper right of the People window to close it.

29. You will also not use the Chronology of Events window again in this exercise, so *click the Chronology of Events tab* at the bottom of the screen, and then *click the "X" (Close) icon* in the upper right of the Events window to close it.

30. *Right-click Core Database* in the Case Explorer window.

31. *Click Select Form.* The Choose New Form to Load window should now be displayed.

32. *Click Estdfrm—E-table, and then click Load Form.* The Choose New Form to Load window should now be gone.

33. Now, *double-click Core Database* in the Case Explorer window.

34. The Column E-table Display: Summary 1 of 143 window should now be displayed (see Summation Exhibit 8). Notice that the title Column is displayed in

Summation Exhibit 8

Reprinted with permission of CT Summation, Inc. All Rights Reserved. For more information, call 1/800–735–7866 or visit http://www.summation.com.

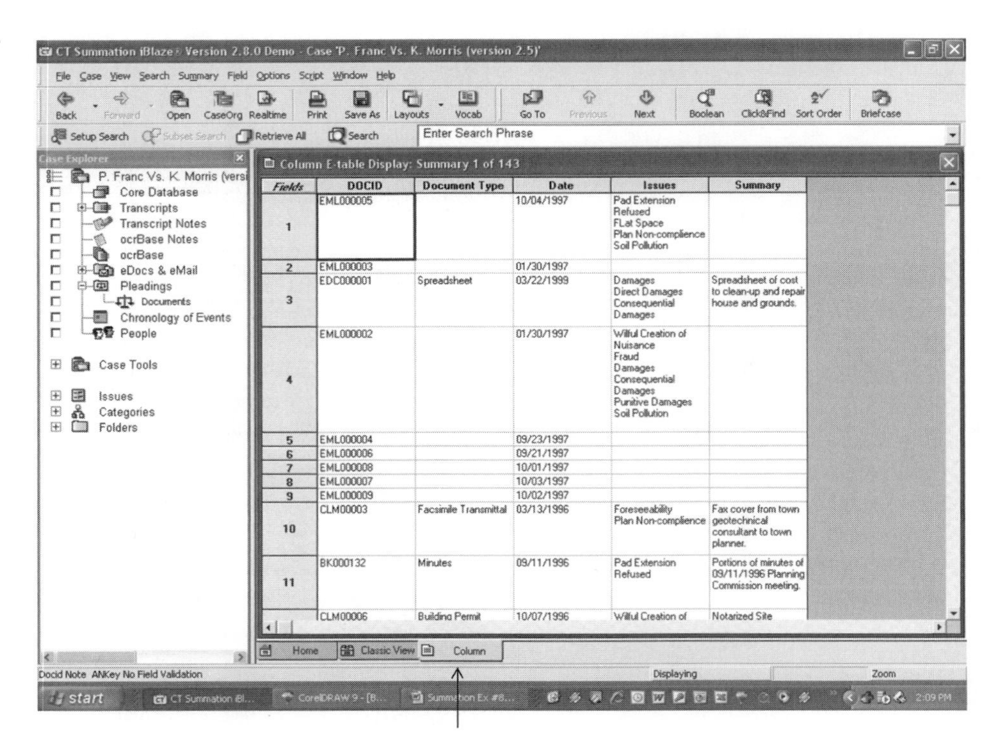

the tab at the bottom of the Column E-table Display: Summary 1 of 143 window (see Summation Exhibit 8).

35. This window shows part of the document summaries/abstracts of the 143 documents that have been entered for this case.

36. Notice that the fourteenth document that is listed is KMP00004, and is a photograph (see Summation Exhibit 9). Summation can link document abstracts to the actual image or file of a document.

37. ***Click KMP00004 in the fourteenth row, first column of the spreadsheet (DOCID).***

38. ***Click Case Tools in the Case Explorer.*** Notice that a number of new tools are displayed (see Summation Exhibit 9).

39. ***Next, double-click Image Viewer in the Case Tools section of the Case Explorer*** (see Summation Exhibit 9). Notice that the photograph for KMP00004 is displayed (one of the pictures is of a bulldozer). See Summation Exhibit 9. *Note:* When you load the photograph it will take up the whole right section of the screen.

40. ***Click the Close icon (the red square with a white "X") in the Image – KMP00004 Page: 1 of 1 window.***

41. ***Click the twelfth document, CLM00006, which is a Building Permit dated 10/07/1996.***

42. ***Double-click ImageViewer the Case Explorer in the Case Tools section.*** Notice that the image of the document is now displayed.

43. Press the **[PAGE DOWN]** key twice to go to page 3 of the document.

44. ***Click the Close icon (a red square with a white "X") in the Image–CLM00006 Page: 3 of 3 window.***

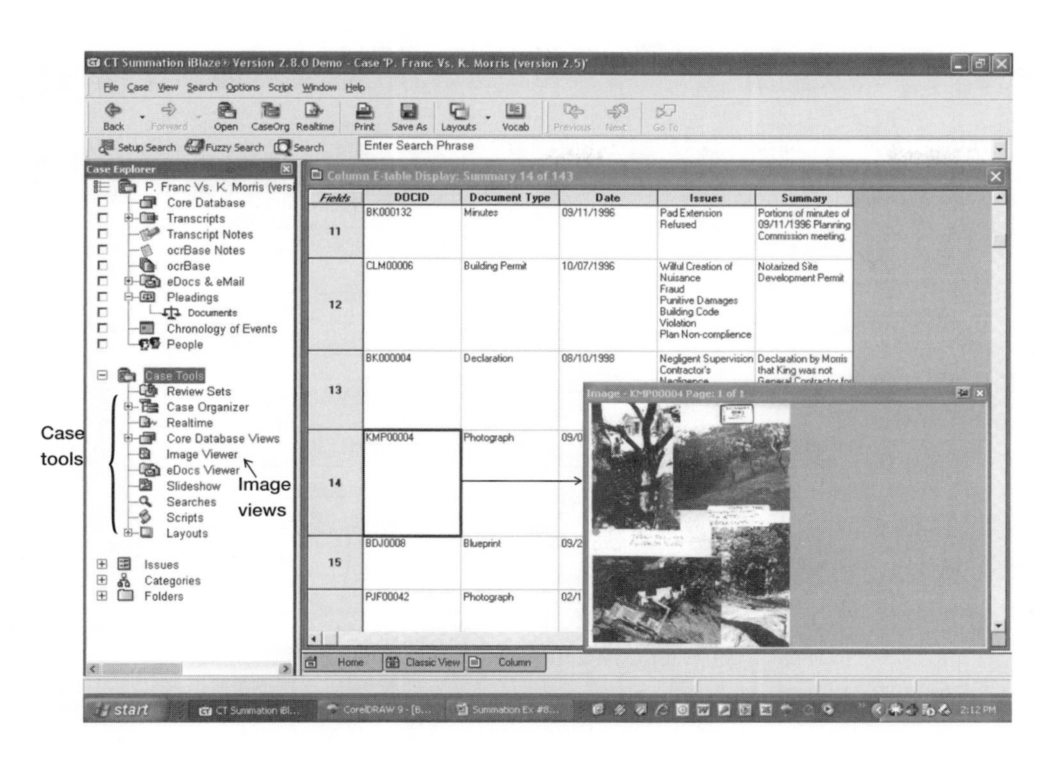

Summation Exhibit 9

Reprinted with permission of CT Summation, Inc. All Rights Reserved. For more information, call 1/800-735-7866 or visit http://www.summation.com.

45. Notice that the information in the Column E-Table Display window is shown in columns. Summation can show Core Database (document abstract) data two ways: in columns and in the form view (one document abstract at a time). The Column view shows information from all of the documents, but only some of the fields in the document abstract are shown. You will next switch from the Column view to the Form view so that you can see all of the data regarding any one document abstract.

46. ***In the Case Tools section, click the + (plus) sign next to Core Database Views.***

47. With document CLM00006 still selected, ***double-click Form (E-Stdfrm)*** under Core Database Views in the Case Explorer window.

48. The Form E-Stdfrm Display: Summary 12 of 143 window should now be displayed (see Summation Exhibit 10). Notice that "Form" is displayed in the tab at the bottom of the Form E-stdfrm Display Summary 12 of 143 window.

49. Notice that you can now see all of the document abstract data for document CML0006, although you can only use this view to examine one document at a time. It is important to be able to switch in and out of both of these views depending on what you are trying to accomplish.

50. Read the abstract/summary of the document. Notice the amount of information that can be summarized for the document.

51. ***In the Case Explorer, double-click Image under Core Database Views in the Case Tools section.*** The image of the document is once again displayed.

52. ***Click the Close icon (a red square with a white "X") in the Image–CLM00006 Page: 3 of 3 window.*** The Form view of the document should once again be displayed (see Summation Exhibit 10).

53. ***Click the Column tab at the bottom of the screen to go back to the column view.***

Summation Exhibit 10

Reprinted with permission of CT Summation, Inc. All Rights Reserved. For more information, call 1/800–735–7866 or visit http://www.summation.com.

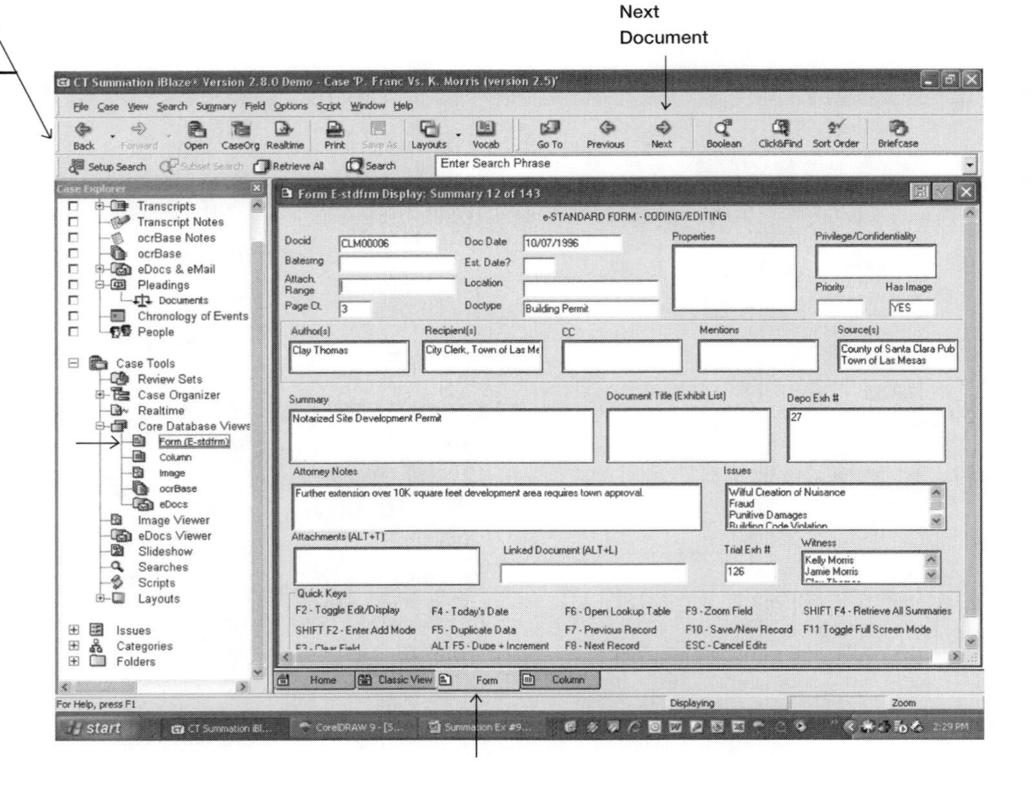

54. ***Click the Form tab at the bottom of the screen to go back to the Form view.***

55. ***Click the Next icon on the toolbar*** (it has a right arrow on it— see Summation Exhibit 10). The title of the window should now say Summary 13 of 143 and you should have document BK000004 displayed. The Next feature will take you to the next document in the list.

56. Using these tools you can see summaries and in-depth information about documents.

57. To close the Form Display window, ***click the Close icon*** (a red square with a white "X") in the upper right of the Form E-stdfrm Display: Summary 13 of 143 window.

58. To close the "Column E-table Display" window, ***click the Close icon*** (a red square with a white "X") in the upper right of the Column E-table Display window.

59. You should now have either the Home or Classic View window displayed.

60. ***Click the + (plus) sign*** next to Transcripts in the Case Explorer window. Notice that there are seven transcripts listed. Most court reporters can now provide transcripts in electronic format. They can then easily be imported into Summation.

61. ***Double-click on the second transcript listed, "Conner Stevens, Vol 1,"*** in the Case Explorer window under Transcripts (see Summation Exhibit 11).

62. Notice that the full text of the transcript is displayed. You can use the down arrow key on the keyboard, the Page Down key on the keyboard, or the vertical scroll bar to scroll down through the document.

63. To close the Conner Stevens, Vol 1 transcript, ***click the Close icon (a, red square with a white "X") in the upper right of the Conner Stevens, Vol 1 window.***

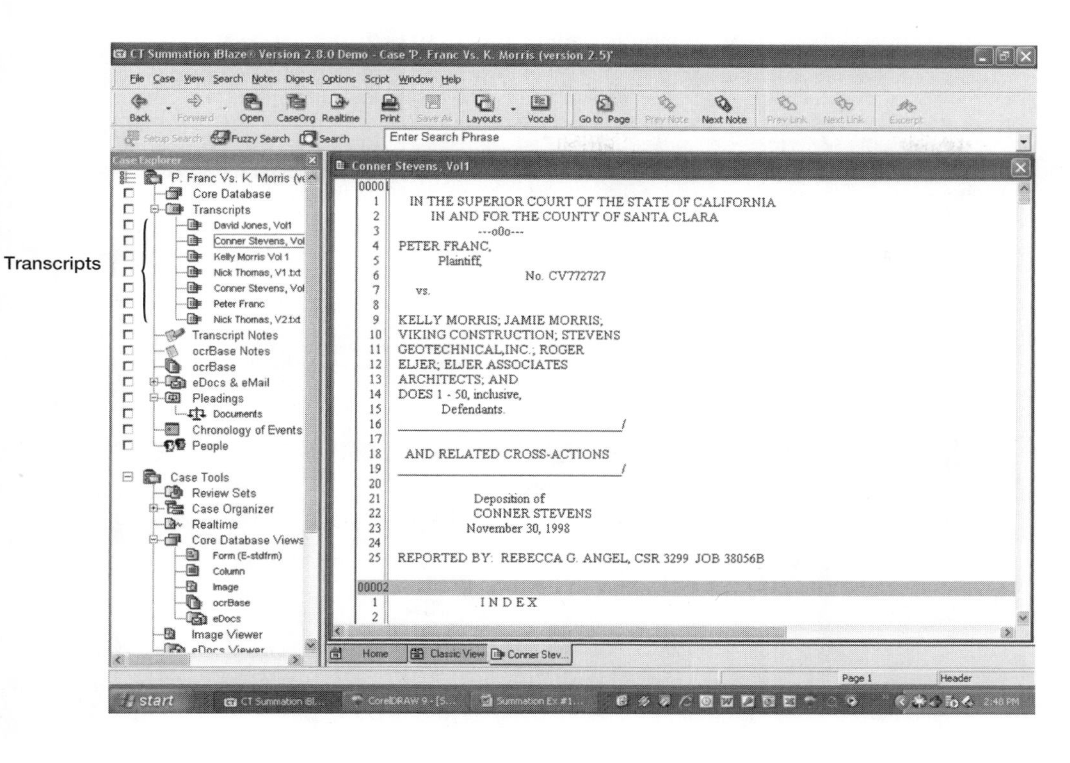

Summation Exhibit 11

64. ***Click the plus (+) sign next to eDocs & eMail in the Case Explorer window*** (see Summation Exhibit 12).

65. ***Double-click eMail under eDocs & eMail.*** Notice that a list of email is shown. (see Summation Exhibit 12). Notice that the tab at the bottom of the screen says "eDocs."

66. ***Click the third record, "EML000002."***

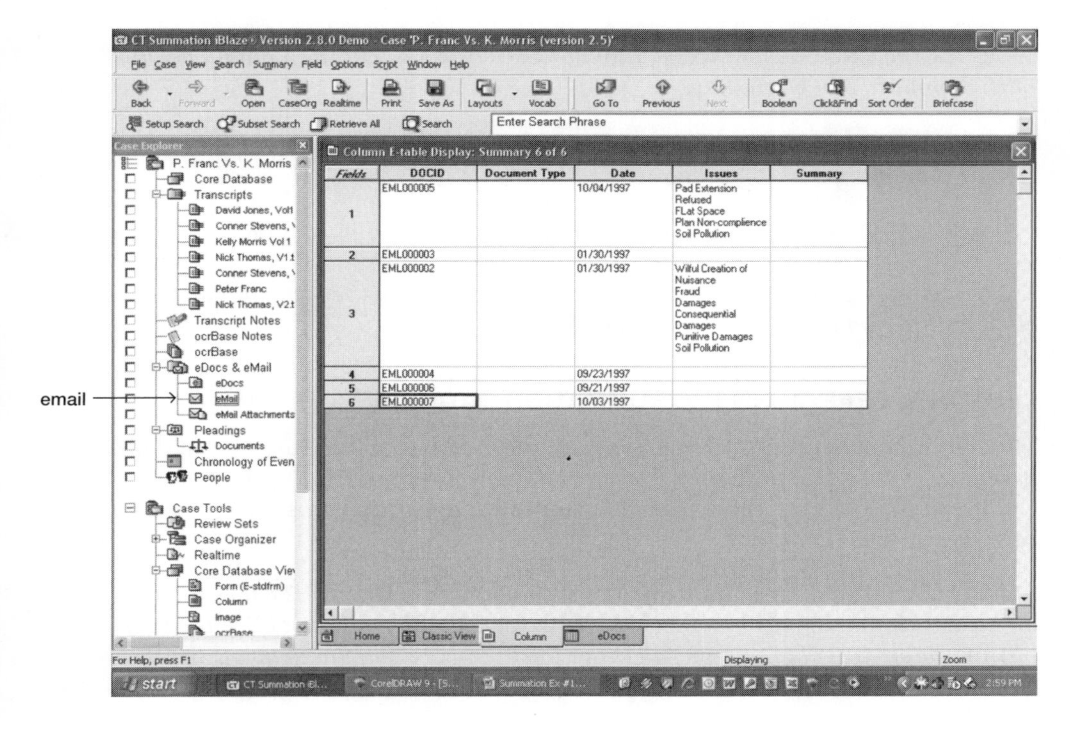

Summation Exhibit 12

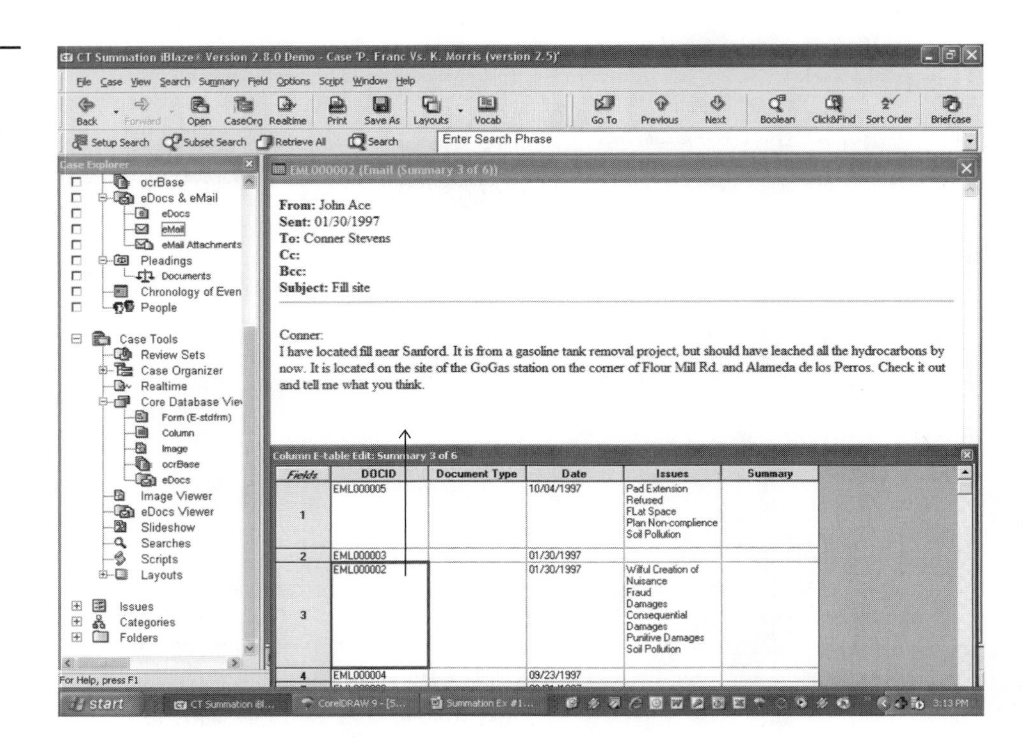

Summation Exhibit 13

67. ***Click in the blue window bar entitled Column E-table Edit: Summary 3 of 6 and drag the window about halfway down the screen*** **(see Summation Exhibit 13).** Notice that you can now see the email itself.

68. ***Click again in the blue window bar entitled Column E-table Edit: Summary 3 of 6 and drag the window back up to the top of the screen.*** Make sure that you drag the window high enough so that you can see the tabs at the bottom of the screen.

69. ***Click the Close icon (a red square with a white "X") in the Column e-table Edit: Summary 3 of 6 window.***

70. ***Click the Close icon (a red square with a white "X") in the EML000002 (Email (Summary 3 of 6)) window.***

71. You should now be back at the Attorney's Quick Start Page home.

This concludes Lesson 2. To exit Summation, ***click File on the menu bar and then click Exit Summation,*** or go to Lesson 3.

LESSON 3: SEARCHING THE SUMMATION DATABASES

This lesson shows you how to perform simple searches on the Summation databases.

If you did not exit Summation after Lesson 2, then skip Steps 1 and 2 and go directly to Step 3.

1. Start Windows. Then, ***double-click the Summation iBLAZE2.8.0 Demo icon on the desktop*** (it looks like a briefcase with the letter CT on it), or ***click the Start button, point to Programs or All Programs, point to the Summation iBLAZE 2.8.0 Demo folder, and then click Summation iBLAZE 2.8.0 Demo.***

2. The Welcome to Summation window should now be displayed. ***Click Close Window*** in the lower right of the Welcome to Summation window.

3. You should now be back at the Attorney's Quick Start Page home with *P. Franc v. K. Morris* in the Case Explorer window.

4. As you saw in Lesson 2, Summation includes a number of separate databases. One of Summation's most useful features is that you can search for information extremely easily, and can include all of the databases in the search or just some of them.

5. Suppose, for example, that the lead attorney in the *P. Franc v. K. Morris* case is going to take the deposition of John Ace. To prepare for the deposition, the lead attorney would like to see every point in the documents and the transcripts where John Ace was discussed or referenced. Using Summation, this is easy.

6. ***Click in the blank check box next to Core Database in the Case Explorer window.*** There should now be a blue check in the check box next to Core Database.

7. ***Click in the blank check box next to Transcripts in the Case Explorer window***. There should now be a blue check in this check box.

8. ***Click in the blank check box next to ocrBase in the Case Explorer window.*** There should now be a blue check in this check box.

9. You have now instructed Summation to search all of these databases at one time when you enter your search query.

10. ***Click in the white box that says "Enter Search Phrase" just under the toolbar near the top and middle of the screen*** (see Summation Exhibit 14). Then type **John OR Ace.**

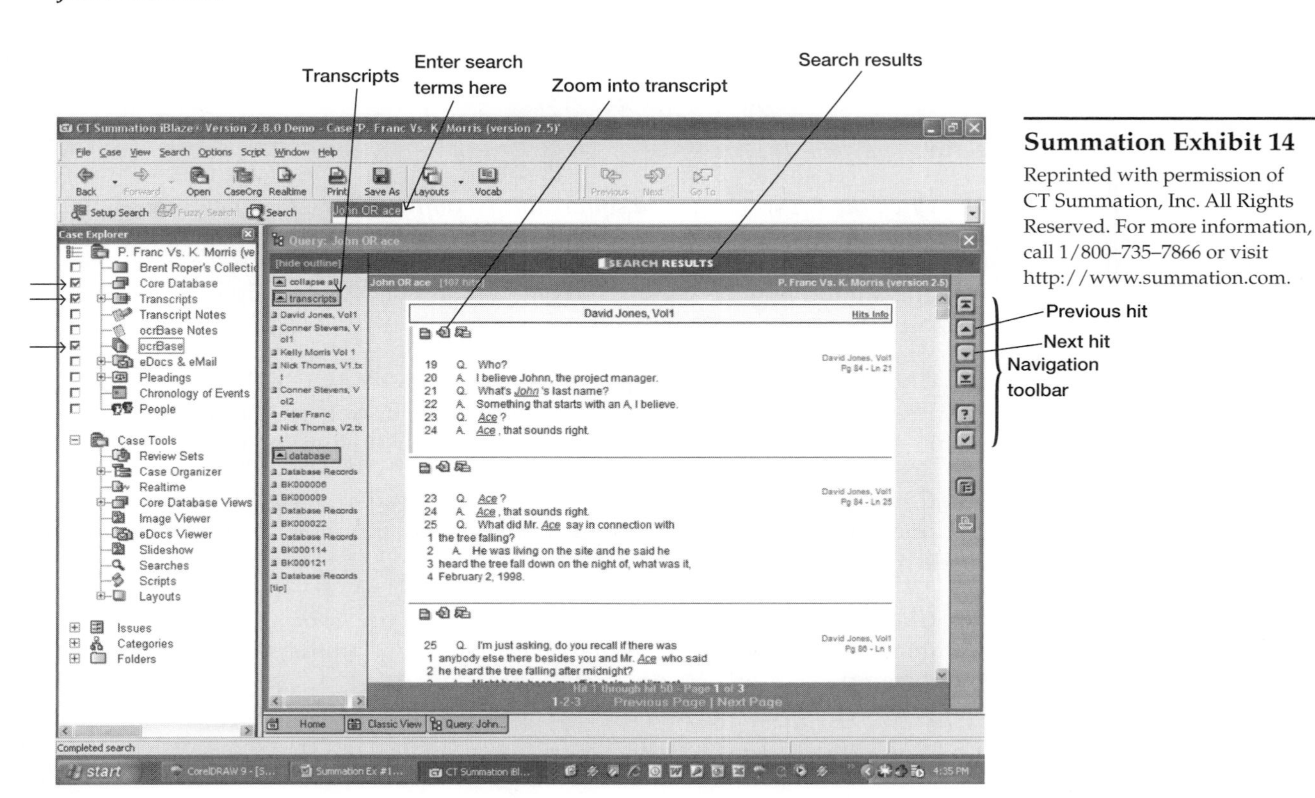

Summation Exhibit 14

11. ***Click the Search icon*** that is just to the left of the white box where you typed "John OR ace."

12. Notice that Summation opens a new window to display the Search Results and that 107 hits were found (see Summation Exhibit 14).

13. ***Point to the word "Transcripts" (see Summation Exhibit 14).*** Notice that Summation tells you that your search request was found in seven transcripts and that there was a total of eighty-two hits.

14. ***Point to the word "database" (see Summation Exhibit 14).*** Notice that twenty-five hits were found in the database documents.

15. Look at the first returned hit at the top of the screen (David Jones, Vol. 1 —Page 84—Ln 21). Notice that Summation includes a couple of lines before and after the returned search phrase so that you can see the context.

16. ***Scroll through some of the hits by using the down arrow key on the keyboard, the page down key on the keyboard, the vertical scroll bar, or the Navigational toolbar*** (see Summation Exhibit 14).

17. The Navigational toolbar (the orange icons at the far right) includes buttons that will take you to the first hit, the last hit, the next hit, and the previous hit. Remember that you can display the name of any icon in Summation ***by simply pointing to it for a second.***

18. Go back to the first hit (David Jones, Vol. 1 —Page 84—ln 21).

19. Suppose, for example, that you think you have found an important piece of information and you would like to go into the full transcript to read several pages worth of text around the search phrase.

20. ***Click the Zoom into Transcript icon.*** (It is to the left and looks like a right arrow superimposed over a piece of paper—see Summation Exhibit 14.)

21. Notice that a new window has opened and you can now see the full transcript.

22. ***Click the Close icon (a red square with a white "X")*** in the David Jones, Vol. 1 window to close it.

23. You should now be back at the Query: John OR Ace window (Summation Exhibit 14).

24. ***Click the different transcripts*** ("Conner Stevens, Vol1," "Kelly Morris, Vol1," etc.) under the orange Transcripts heading. By clicking on the different transcripts you do not have to look at all of the hits sequentially; you can skip around.

25. ***Click "database records" just under the orange database heading.*** The first document that is retrieved should be the document abstract of a declaration made by John Ace.

26. ***Click the second record under the orange database heading "BK000006"*** **(see Summation Exhibit 15).** This is the full text of the declaration document (not just the abstract).

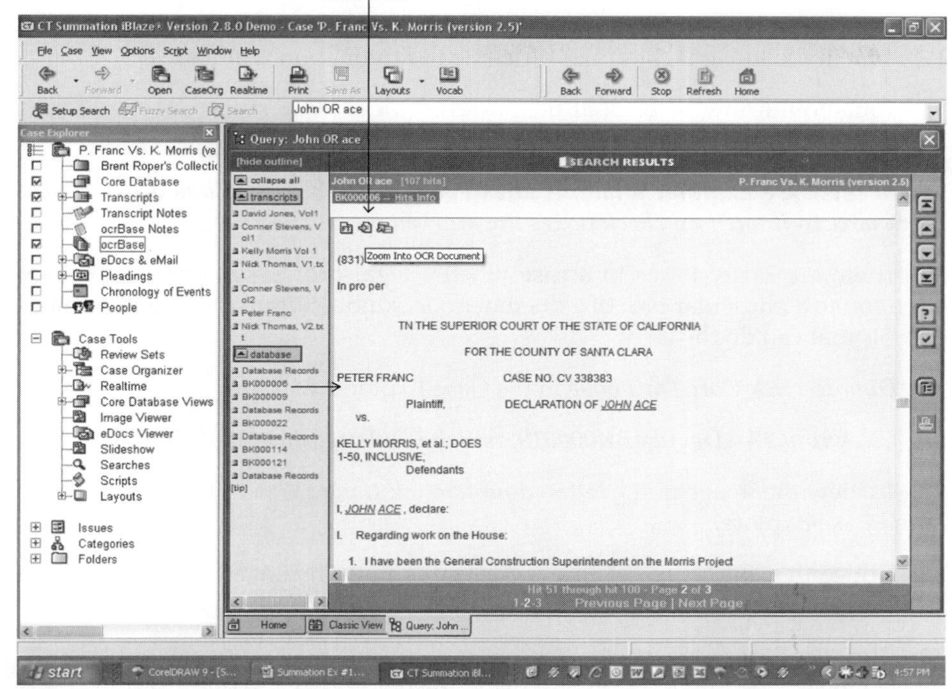

Summation Exhibit 15

27. To see the full text of the document, click the Zoom Into OCR Document icon (see Summation Exhibit 15). The "BK00006 (Document (Summary 1 of 14))" window should now be displayed. You can now see the full text of the Declaration.

28. ***Click the Close icon (a red square with a white "X") in the BK00006 (Document (Summary 1 of 14)) window.***

29. You should now be back at the Search Results screen (see Summation Exhibit 15).

30. ***Double-click on Core Database*** in the Case Explorer window. Notice that fourteen documents were returned. These are all documents that are associated with John Ace.

31. Close all of the open windows except for Home and Classic View.

This concludes Lesson 3. To exit Summation, ***click File on the menu bar and then click Exit Summation,*** or go to Lesson 4.

LESSON 4: MARKING UP A DOCUMENT

This lesson introduces you to how to mark up, or highlight particularly important aspects of, a document.

If you did not exit Summation after Lesson 3, then skip Steps 1 and 2 and go directly to Step 3.

1. Start Windows. Then, ***double-click on the Summation iBLAZE2.8.0 Demo icon on the desktop*** (it looks like a briefcase with the letter CT on it), or ***click the Start button, point to Programs or All Programs, point to the Summation iBLAZE 2.8.0 Demo folder, and then click Summation iBLAZE 2.8.0 Demo.***

2. The Welcome to Summation window should now be displayed. ***Click Close Window*** in the lower right of the Welcome to Summation window.

3. You should now be back at the Attorney's Quick Start Page home with *P. Franc v. K. Morris* in the Case Explorer window.

4. ***In the Case Explorer window, click every check box that has a blue check mark next to it until no check boxes are marked.***

5. There are many times in a case when a legal professional needs to draw attention to a particular part of a document or exhibit. Summation has a number of tools that can do this.

6. ***Double-click Core Database*** in the Case Explorer window.

7. ***Click row 97—Docid #BK000019, which is a letter dated 10/07/1996.***

8. To view the image of the letter, ***double-click Image Viewer under Case Tools*** in the Case Explorer.

9. Notice that the image of the document is now displayed (see Summation Exhibit 16). Unfortunately, it may be too small to read in its present form.

10. ***Click the Enlarge icon*** on the toolbar to make the image large enough to read. By clicking on the Enlarge icon and using the horizontal and vertical scroll bars, you should be able to read the entire image.

11. If you have a mouse with a wheel, you can roll the wheel forward to enlarge the image and backward to reduce it. You can also right-click anywhere in the image and access Enlarge, Reduce, and other tools (see Summation Exhibit 16).

12. ***Point to the Image—BK000019 window, right-click, and click Markup Bar.*** The Markup Bar allows you to highlight an image, draw on an image, and mark it up (see Summation Exhibit 16).

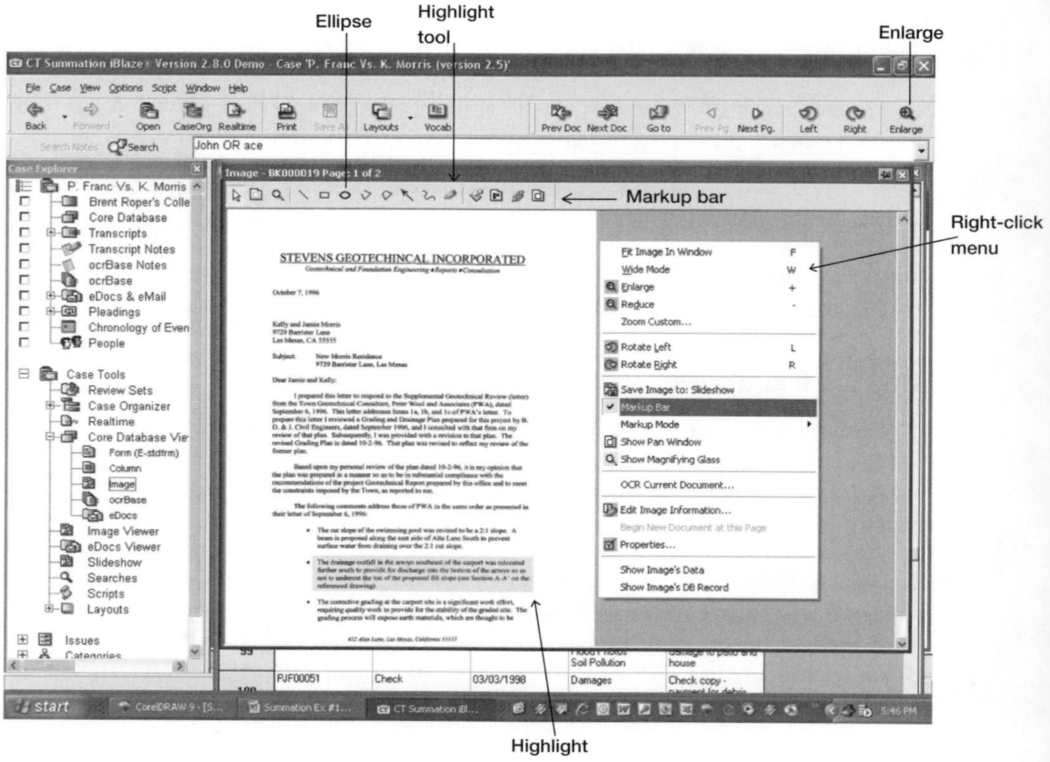

Summation Exhibit 16

Reprinted with permission of CT Summation, Inc. All Rights Reserved. For more information, call 1/800–735–7866 or visit http://www.summation.com.

13. ***Click the Highlight tool (the fifth icon from the right—it looks like a pencil with yellow highlighting behind it) on the Markup Bar in the Image—BK 000019 Page 1 of 2 window.***

14. ***Point to the upper left of the first paragraph and drag the mouse pointer down and to the right until the whole first paragraph is in the square frame and then let go of the mouse button.*** Notice that everywhere in the square frame is now highlighted yellow.

15. ***Click on the Ellipse icon (the sixth icon from the left—a black ellipse/circle) on the Markup bar.***

16. ***Point to the upper left of the date of the letter (October 7, 1996) and drag the mouse pointer to the right until the whole date is in the ellipse frame, then let go of the mouse button.*** Notice that the date is now inside a red ellipse.

17. ***Point and right-click anywhere in the Image—BK000019 window. Point to Markup Mode and then point to Hide Markups.*** Notice that all of the markups are now gone. Markup Mode allows you to create markups and then hide them if you need to, all without affecting the underlying document. The Markup bar can also be used with photographs and other images.

18. Close all of the open windows except for Home and Classic View.

This concludes Lesson 4. To exit Summation, ***click File on the menu bar and then click Exit Summation*** or go to Lesson 5.

LESSON 5: WORKING WITH TRANSCRIPTS

This lesson introduces you to working with transcripts, including earmarking testimony, assigning issue codes to key testimony, creating rapid-fire deposition summaries, and printing the summaries.

If you did not exit Summation after Lesson 4, then skip Steps 1 and 2 and go directly to Step 3.

1. Start Windows. Then, ***double-click the Summation iBLAZE2.8.0 Demo icon on the desktop*** (it looks like a briefcase with the letter CT on it) or, ***click the Start button, point to Programs or All Programs, point to the Summation iBLAZE 2.8.0 Demo folder, and then click on Summation iBLAZE 2.8.0 Demo.***

2. The Welcome to Summation window should now be displayed. ***Click Close Window*** in the lower right of the Welcome to Summation window.

3. You should now be back at the Attorney's Quick Start Page home with *P. Franc v. K. Morris* in the Case Explorer window.

4. ***Click the + (plus) sign*** to the left of Transcripts in the Case Explorer window.

5. ***Double-click the first transcript, David Jones, Vol. 1.***

6. Using the down arrow key on the keyboard, the Page Down key on the keyboard, or the vertical scroll bars, move the cursor to page 9, line 1 of the David Jones transcript.

7. Suppose, for example, that the testimony on page 9, lines 1–10 is important. In Summation you can create the electronic version of a sticky note that cannot be lost and that allows you to earmark and remember important testimony.

8. ***Point to Page 9, line 1 and drag the mouse pointer down until lines 1–10 are highlighted. Right-click and then click Copy Excerpt into New Note.***

Summation Exhibit 17

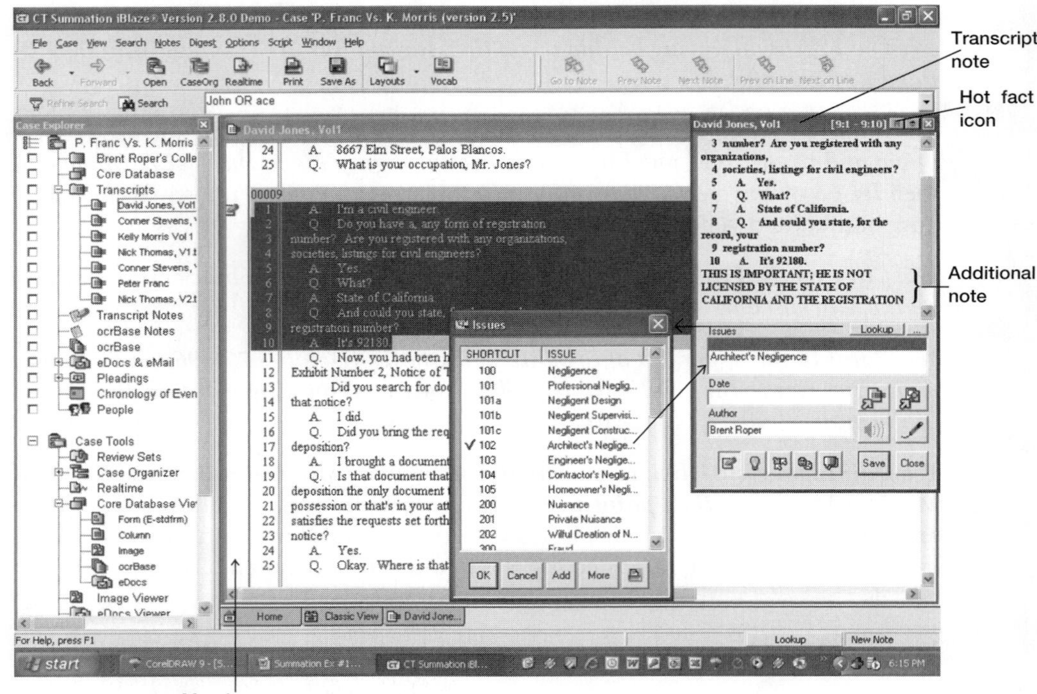

9. Notice that the highlighted text has been copied and placed into a transcript note window (see Summation Exhibit 17). Now you can make a note regarding the testimony (you will just type it after the copied testimony). If your cursor is not already in the transcript note window after line 10, ***click there.*** Then, type the following note: ***THIS IS IMPORTANT; HE IS NOT LICENSED BY THE STATE OF CALIFORNIA AND THIS REGISTRATION NUMBER DOES NOT EXIST*** (see Summation Exhibit 17). Summation gives you the option to print out all of your notes and search your notes, and also gives you other ways to organize them.

10. ***Click Lookup*** in the transcript note window. This allows you to link testimony to key issues in a case and then later go back and print it, retrieve it, or search on it.

11. The Issues window should now be displayed (see Summation Exhibit 10). ***Click 102 Architect's Negligence and then click OK.*** Notice that Architect's Negligence has now been entered in the Issues line of the transcript note (see Summation Exhibit 10). ***Click Save*** to save the transcript note.

12. Also, notice at the bottom of the transcript note window that there are five icons just under the name of the author in the transcript note window. The icons allow you to designate a note as standard notes, a thought, rebuttal, revised testimony (helpful when cross-examining witnesses that have changed the testimony), or follow-up questions (helpful when considering additional questions that need to be asked of the witness). Remember that you can ***place the mouse pointer over an icon*** for a second to see the name of the icon displayed.

13. ***Click on the Close icon (a red square with a white "X")*** in the Transcript note to close the Transcript Note window.

14. ***Click anywhere outside of the highlighting to make the highlighting disappear.***

15. Notice that next to page 9, line 1 in the transcript (the David Jones, Vol 1 window) there is now a transcript note icon (a note pad with a pencil) indicating that there is a note there.

16. You can also create a note that does not have any testimony in it, but instead just contains your thoughts. ***Point to Page 9, line 13 and drag the mouse down until lines 13 to 18 are highlighted. Then, double-click in the left margin of the transcript adjacent to the highlighted range*** (in the small blank margin between the left side of the window and where the line numbers are—see Summation Exhibit 17).

17. Notice that a blank transcript note has been opened. In the body of the transcript note type ***I AM SURE HE HAS MORE DOCUMENTS.***

18. ***Click Save*** to save the transcript note.

19. ***Click the Close icon (a red square with a white "X")*** in the transcript note to close the Transcript Note window.

20. Summation allows you to go back and edit your transcript notes at any time. For example, suppose you would like to add another thought to your previous note. ***Click PrevNote on the toolbar.***

21. ***Click the transcript note icon next to line 1 of page 9*** to display the transcript note.

22. Summation can create HotFact notes that are very important. They are typically used to show where a "smoking gun" or a very important fact is. To make the note at Page 9, line 1 a HotFact, ***click on the "H" icon*** in the title bar of the transcript note (see Summation Exhibit 17). Note that the "H" is now red.

23. ***Click the Close icon (a red square with a white "X") in the transcript note*** to close the Transcript Note window. *Note:* You can mark all kinds of evidence as HotFacts, typically ***by right-clicking the document and selecting HotFact.***

24. The significance of marking a transcript note as a HotFact is that you can search for and print all HotFacts in the case at any time. This allows you to separate really important notes from marginal ones.

25. ***Click the Close icon (a red square with a white "X") in the David Jones, Vol1 window.***

26. Another way to use transcript notes is to use them to summarize depositions. A common practice in legal organizations is for legal assistants to summarize a deposition. A summary of the deposition that contains just the salient portions without all of the objections and irrelevant information in them—is much easier and quicker to read right before trial than a whole deposition. The problem with deposition summaries is that they take quite a while to write because the user must type the summary into the computer. Using Summation, a legal professional can get a good deposition summary in half the time with virtually no typing by using what Summation calls rapid-fire digesting. Using this method, a legal professional can much more quickly summarize depositions than by retyping them.

27. Say, for example, that we need to create a summary of the deposition of Kelly Morris.

28. ***Double-click Kelly Morris, Vol 1*** under Transcripts in the Case Explorer window.

29. *Scroll down to page 3, line 16, and drag the mouse pointer down to line 21.*

30. *Click the Excerpt icon on the toolbar (it is all the way over to the right).*

31. Notice that a transcript window has opened (see Summation Exhibit 18).

32. *Click Save and then click Close.*

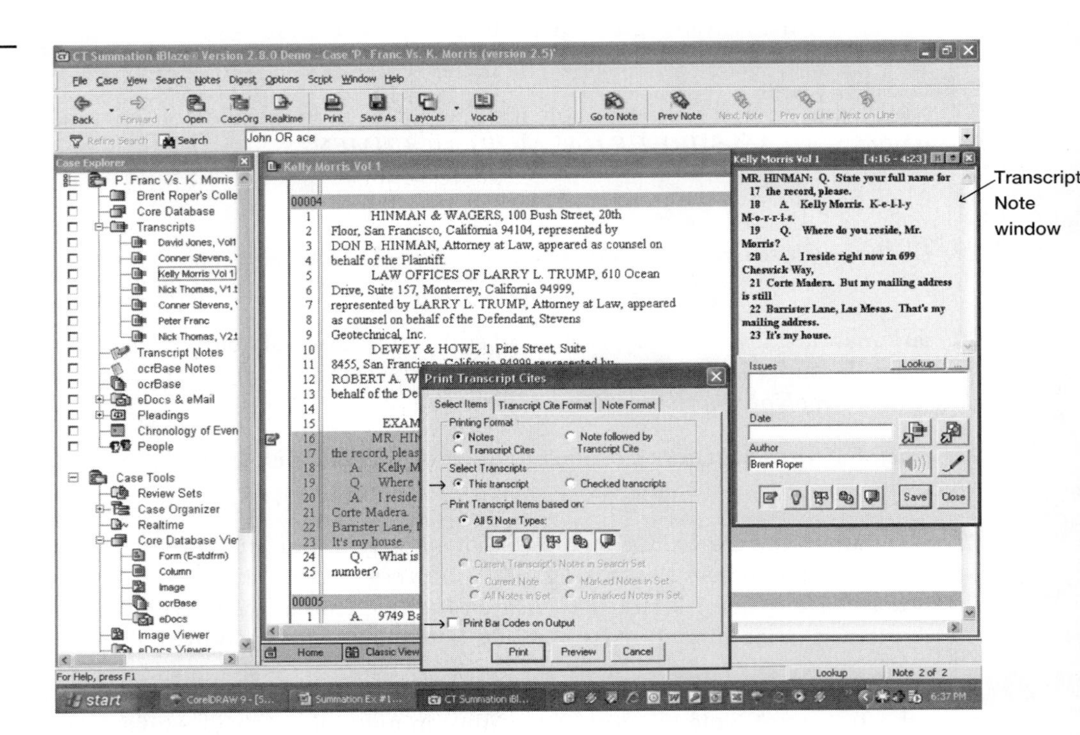

Summation Exhibit 18

33. *Scroll down to page 4, line 16, and drag the mouse pointer down to line 23.*

34. *Click with the mouse the Excerpt icon on the toolbar.*

35. *Click Save and then click Close in the Transcript Note window.*

36. *Click File on the menu bar and then click on Print Transcript Cites.* The Print Transcript Cites window should now be displayed.

37. In the Print Transcript Cites window, *click This Transcript under Select Transcript.*

38. *Click Print Bar Codes on Output* to uncheck this box.

39. *Click Print and then click OK* (assuming the proper printer is selected) to print the summary.

40. Close all of the open windows except for Home and Classic View.

This concludes Lesson 5. To exit Summation, *click File on the menu bar and then click Exit Summation* or go to Lesson 6.

LESSON 6: WORKING WITH THE CASE ORGANIZER

This lesson introduces you to the Case Organizer. The Case Organizer is a powerful tool for analyzing, understanding, and preparing a case for trial. The Case

Organizer allows the user to organize information using an outline format. The Case Organizer is completely customizable, but comes with predefined sections for a Case Blueprint (an overall look at the facts and legal issues of the case), a Chronology (a timeline of events), Witness/Depo Questions, Exhibits (for outlining exhibits for trial), and a To Do list.

If you did not exit Summation after Lesson 5, then skip Steps 1 and 2 and go directly to Step 3.

1. Start Windows. Then, ***double-click the Summation iBLAZE2.8.0 Demo icon on the desktop*** (it looks like a briefcase with the letter CT on it), or ***click the Start button, point to Programs or All Programs, point to the Summation iBLAZE 2.8.0 Demo folder, and then click Summation iBLAZE 2.8.0 Demo.***

2. The Welcome to Summation window should now be displayed. ***Click Close Window*** in the lower right of the Welcome to Summation window.

3. You should now be back at the Attorney's Quick Start Page home with *P. Franc v. K. Morris* in the Case Explorer window.

4. ***Double-click Case Organizer under Case Tools in the Case Explorer.*** There are five predefined sections of the Case Organizer, but you are free to create your own. (In fact, Summation says that you can have up to 100 sections/tabs in Case Organizer).

5. Case Organizer is an outline tool where you can keep track of lists and information about a case. The advantage of having the outlines in Summation as opposed to a word processor is that they are saved by case, so your case outlines are automatically loaded every time you load the case in Summation. More importantly, it gives you a central location where everything about the case is stored, instead of having information spread across multiple programs.

6. ***Click on the Case Blueprint tab*** in the Case Organizer window. Notice that the legal professional in this case has created an outline in the Case Blueprint that contains three main issues in the case: (1) contractor negligence, (2) private nuisance, and (3) willful creation of nuisance.

7. ***Click the + (plus) sign and the – (minus) sign next to Contractor Negligence*** to expand and contract the outline list for this cause of action.

8. ***Click the – (minus) sign next to "Case Blueprint for P. Franc vs. K. Morris" several times*** to expand and contract the entire outline list for the case.

9. ***Continue to the – (minus) sign until the list is contracted to the main issues*** (without all of the detail).

10. We will now add another main issue to the Case Blueprint.

11. ***Click Add Item from the toolbar.***

12. ***Click Insert it After, and then click OK*** when Summation tells you that the item will be placed after the current item.

13. ***Click after the last character*** in the PRIVATE NUISANCE line.

14. ***Click Add Item from the toolbar and then click Insert Heading.*** Alternatively, you can press the **[ENTER]** key.

15. Type **BATTERY** and then press the **[ENTER]** key.

16. Press the **[TAB]** key and then type **Unlawful application of force.**

17. The Case Organizer is a fairly straightforward outlining tool. You can add headings and subheadings using the **[ENTER]** and **[TAB]** keys, change text between headings, and add subheadings, color, and other formatting options using the Add Item and Format icons, as well as the Expand and Options icons on the toolbar. You can also use simple commands such as the **[DELETE]** key to delete text you no longer need.

18. ***Click the To Do tab*** in the Case Organizer window.

19. ***Double-click at the end of the line To Do for P. Franc v. K. Morris*** and then press **[ENTER].**

20. You can now create a list of To Dos for the case.

21. A very useful feature of the Case Organizer is that you can copy practically any text in Summation and automatically place it in the Case Organizer.

22. ***Double-click Nick Thomas, V2 transcript*** under Transcripts in the Case Explorer. *Note:* If the Transcripts list is contracted, click the + (plus) sign to expand it.

23. The transcript for Nick Thomas should now be displayed.

24. ***Click Line 11 of the first page (page 134) and drag the mouse pointer down to line 14.***

25. ***Right-click anywhere in the highlighted area and click Copy Excerpt to Outline: To Do.***

26. ***Double-click the Case Org tab*** at the bottom of the screen. Notice that the transcript site and the text have been copied to the To Do list.

27. ***Click just to the left of Nick Thomas, V2.txt*** in the To Do list and type **Schedule another day to continue his depo.**

28. Another useful tool in Summation is that you can create a hyperlink from one piece of information to another. Hyperlinks can be a very powerful tool for linking pieces of information together in a case.

29. For example, ***click the hyperlink icon*** that is just to the left of "Schedule another day…." (a gray circle with a left-handed arrow on it).

30. Notice that by clicking the hyperlink icon you were taken directly back to the deposition transcript where the note was copied from.

31. ***Click the Close icon (a red square with a white "X")*** in the Nick Thomas transcript. You should now be at the Case Organizer in the To Do list.

32. We will now add our own new section/tab to the Case Organizer. Adding information to any section of the Case Organizer is easy.

33. ***Click New Tab on the toolbar.***

34. At the Enter Name for New Outline's Tab window, type **Witness List** and then ***click OK.***

35. ***Click Add Item on the toolbar, and then click Insert Heading.***

36. Type **Linda Smith, Ex-City Inspector** and then press the **[ENTER]** key.

37. Type **John Jones, State Building Inspector**.

38. ***Click the Chronology tab*** in the Case Organizer window.

39. Notice that the legal professional in this case has created a chronology of events in the case. Nearly every case can benefit from a chronology of events, because it gives the lead attorney a basic understanding of timing and events that took place in a case. Notice that the user in this case has organized the timing of events into headings such as "Events Leading Up to the Slide," "The Slide Itself," and then "Franc's Slide Damages & Cleanup." In addition, the user has tied documents (including the actual document) to the chronology.

40. ***Click the + (plus) sign*** next to the first document, 08/10/1995 Proposal Letter, in the Events Leading up to the Slide section. Notice that you can see a brief abstract of the document.

41. ***Click the hyperlink icon*** (the gray circle with a left-handed arrow on it) that is to the left of the text. You should be then taken directly to the image of the document.

42. ***Click the Close icon (a red square with a white "X")*** in the Image—SGD00100 window. You should now be back at the Chronology tab in the Case Organizer window.

43. ***Click the Exhibits tab*** in the Case Organizer window. Notice that a list of exhibits that will be used at trial has been added, and that in addition to the list itself, links to the actual documents have also been included.

44. Close all of the open windows except for Home and Classic View.

This concludes Lesson 6. To exit Summation, ***click File on the menu bar and click Exit Summation,*** or go to Lesson 7.

LESSON 7: CUSTOMIZING THE COLUMN CORE DATABASE VIEW

This lesson shows you to how to customize and use the column core database view in more detail, including how to select and deselect fields in the database and how to change how information is sorted in the database view.

If you did not exit Summation after Lesson 6, then skip Steps 1 and 2 and go directly to Step 3.

1. Start Windows. Then, ***double-click the Summation iBLAZE2.8.0 Demo icon on the desktop*** (it looks like a briefcase with the letter CT on it) or ***click the Start button, point to Programs or All Programs, point to the Summation iBLAZE 2.8.0 Demo folder, and then click Summation iBLAZE 2.8.0 Demo.***

2. The Welcome to Summation window should now be displayed. ***Click Close Window*** in the lower right of the Welcome to Summation window.

3. You should now be back at the Attorney's Quick Start Page home with *P. Franc v. K. Morris* in the Case Explorer window.

4. ***Double-click Core Database*** in the Case Explorer.

5. ***Click the word "Fields"*** in the Column E-table Display: Summary 1 of 143 window.

Summation Exhibit 19

Reprinted with permission of CT Summation, Inc. All Rights Reserved. For more information, call 1/800–735–7866 or visit http://www.summation.com.

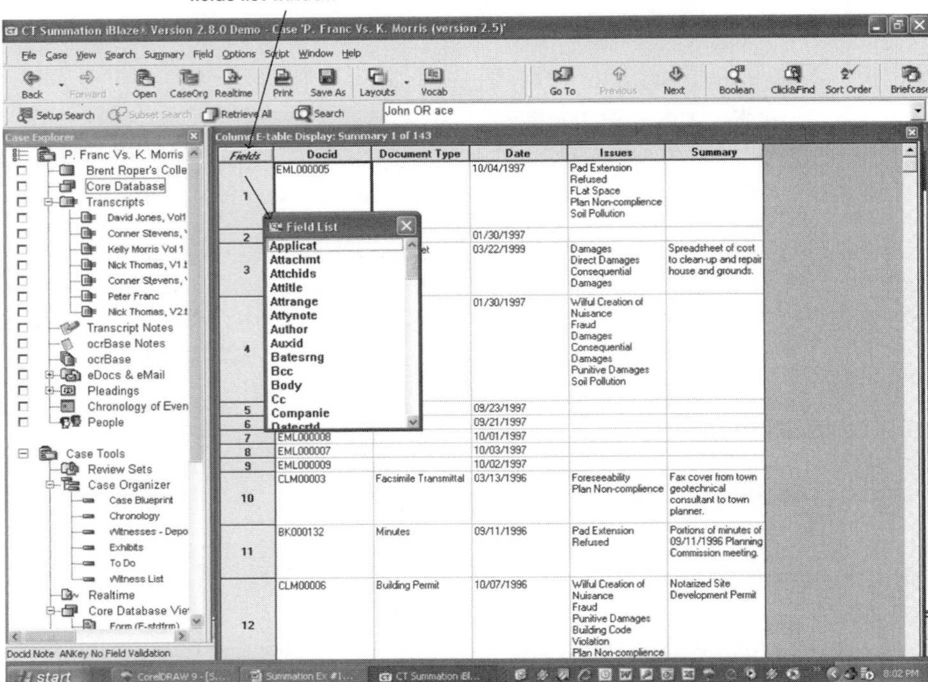

6. The "Fields List" window should now be displayed (see Summation Exhibit 19). The fields you see in the columns are completely customizable.

7. ***Double-click the Author field.*** Notice that the Author field has now been added.

8. ***Double-click the Issues field.*** It is already selected (shown in gray), so reselecting it deletes the field from the list. Notice that the Issues field has now been deleted from the view. Please note that the information is still in the database; it is just not being displayed on the screen currently.

9. ***Double-click the Privilege field.*** Notice that the Privileged field is now displayed. If you were responding to a Production of Documents request, you would want to exclude any documents that were privileged, so this is an important field. The ability of users to completely customize how you see information in Summation is one of the program's strengths.

10. ***Click the Close icon (a red square with a white "X") in the Field List window.***

11. ***Click anywhere in the Column E-table Display: Summary 10 of 143 window.***

12. Press the [LEFT CURSOR] key until the mouse pointer moves all the way over to the first column. You should now be able to see all of the columns.

13. You can also easily change how information is sorted. Suppose that you wanted to sort all of the documents in the core database by date.

14. ***Right-click the word Date*** at the top of the column in the Column E-table Display window.

15. ***Click Sort Docdate Newest to Oldest.*** The documents are now sorted by date with the most current at the top of the list.

16. Suppose that you want to see the list of documents sorted instead by author.

17. ***Right-click the word Author*** at the top of the column in the Column Stdtable Display window.

18. Then, ***click Sort by Author.***

19. Notice that all of the documents have now been sorted by author. Again, this is a powerful feature for viewing, understanding, and analyzing data in a case.

20. Close all of the open windows except for Home and Classic View.

This concludes Lesson 7. To exit Summation, ***click File on the menu bar and then click Exit Summation,*** or go to Lesson 8.

LESSON 8: ADDITIONAL SEARCH TECHNIQUES

This lesson introduces you to the use of additional search techniques in Summation, including Boolean searching, issue searching, using the vocabulary option, and other techniques.

If you did not exit Summation after Lesson 7, then skip Steps 1 and 2 and go directly to Step 3.

1. Start Windows. Then, ***double-click the Summation iBLAZE2.8.0 Demo icon on the desktop*** (it looks like a briefcase with the letter CT on it), or ***click the Start button, point to Programs or All Programs, point to the Summation iBLAZE 2.8.0 Demo folder, and then click Summation iBLAZE 2.8.0 Demo.***

2. The Welcome to Summation window should now be displayed. ***Click Close Window*** in the lower right of the Welcome to Summation window.

3. You should now be back at the Attorney's Quick Start home page with *P. Franc v. K. Morris* in the Case Explorer window.

4. Summation gives users a wide variety of options for conducting searches. Suppose, for example, that you must reply to a Production of Documents request for all photos.

5. ***Double-click Core Database*** in the Case Explorer. Notice that the window says Summary 1 of 143.

6. ***Right-click with the mouse in the Document Type field on any record that contains the word Photograph*** (such as field 42—Docid KMP00039).

7. ***Then, click Search with Doctype eq Photograph.***

8. Notice that the title of the window no longer says "Summary 1 of 143."

9. ***Scroll down the list of the documents*** and notice that there are now only sixty-eight records displayed. You can now print the list of the documents you needed to produce.

10. ***Click the Close icon (a red square with a white "X") in the Column E-table Display window.***

11. Assume now that you would like to enter another search of the core database (document abstracts).

12. ***Double-click Core Database*** in the Case Explorer. Notice that only sixty-eight records are retrieved. Any searches you would conduct now would be only on the sixty-eight photographs. You will need to right-click Core Database and reload the entire form/database.

13. ***Click the Close icon (a red square with a white "X") in the Column E-table Display window.***

14. ***Right-click Core Database in the Case Explorer, and click Select Form. Then, in the Choose New Form to Load" window, click "E-stdfrm E-table.***

15. ***Click Load Form.***

16. ***Double-click Core Database*** in the Case Explorer. Notice that the window now says Summary 1 of 143.

17. Instead of searching on terms that we believe may be in the database, we will now use Summation to tell us what words are used in the database so that we can search on them.

18. ***Click the Vocab icon*** on the toolbar.

19. The CT Summation Blaze LG window should then be displayed. It will ask "Blaze your current database table (E-table)?" ***click "Yes".***

20. ***Then, press any key*** to exit the BLAZE—Summation Windows Utility window.

21. ***Scroll through the list*** and look at all of the words used in the Core Database. You can now search for one or more of these terms.

22. ***Scroll to the word "Magnetically" and then double-click it.***

23. Notice that one document, Bases # NTP00007, is now displayed.

24. ***Double-click Form (E-stdfrm) under Core Database View in the Case Tools section of Case Explorer.***

25. ***Click the Close icon (a red square with a white "X") in the Column E-table Display: Summary 1 of 1 window.***

26. The Form E-stdfrm Display: Summary 1 of 1 window should now be displayed. If the "Database Vocabulary" window is still open, ***click the Close icon*** to close it.

27. Notice in the Attorney Notes field that the word "magnetically" is listed in blue.

28. ***Click the Close icon in the "Form E-stdfrm Display" window.***

29. ***Right-click Core Database in the Case Explorer, click Select Form, and then, in the Choose New Form to Load window, click E-stdfrm E-table.***

30. ***Click "Load Form."***

31. It is sometimes necessary to search for specific phrases. This is done in Summation by typing in the phrase.

32. ***Click the check box*** next to Transcripts in the Case Explorer so that you can execute a search for a phrase in the transcripts. Nothing else should be selected.

33. ***Click in the white box*** in the toolbar at the top middle of the screen just to the right of Search and type **concrete piers**. If anything else is in the field, delete it.

34. ***Click the Search icon*** on the toolbar.

35. Notice that one hit was found. ***Click the "X" (Close) icon*** in the "Query: concrete piers" window.

36. Summation can also use alternative words in a search. With "Transcripts" still checked in the Case Explorer, ***click the white box*** on the toolbar at the top middle

of the screen, just to the right of Search, and type **grates OR drainage.** *Note:* You could also have used the \ (backslash) character, since Summation treats this character the same as OR.

37. ***Click the Search icon*** on the toolbar. If Summation asks to continue the search from the top of the document, ***click Yes.*** Summation responds by finding all transcripts where either the word grates OR drainage or both are used.

38. ***Click the Close icon (a red square with a white "X") in the Query: grates OR drainage window.***

39. Summation can also search for a specific date or a date range. ***Click the Setup Search icon*** on the toolbar. Notice that Summation has specific search options for searching on dates or date ranges.

40. ***Click Issue (Field)*** in the Setup Search menu. ***Click 102 Architect's Negligence and then click OK.***

41. ***Click in the check box next to Transcripts*** in the Case Explorer to deselect transcripts.

42. ***Double-click Core Database*** in the Case Explorer.

43. ***Click the Search icon*** on the toolbar. Notice that Summation brings up a list of five documents in the Core Database where the issue Architect's Negligence is listed.

44. ***Click Field1, docid NTE00002.***

45. **Then,** ***double-click "Form (E-stdfrm)" under Core Database Views in the Case Tools section of Case Explorer.***

46. ***Click the Close icon (a red square with a white "X") in the Column E-table Display window so that you can see the form view.***

47. Notice in the Form E-stdfrm Display: Summary 1 of 5 window that Architect's Negligence is listed in the Issues field.

48. Close all of the open windows except for Home and Classic View.

This concludes Lesson 8. To exit Summation, ***click File on the menu bar and then click Exit Summation,*** or go to Lesson 9.

LESSON 9: LOAD A TRANSCRIPT, LOAD A PLEADING, AND ENTER A DOCUMENT ABSTRACT

This lesson gives an introduction to how to load transcripts, load pleadings, and enter document abstracts into Summation.

If you did not exit Summation after Lesson 9, then skip Steps 1 and 2 and go directly to Step 3.

1. Start Windows. Then, ***double-click the Summation iBLAZE2.8.0 Demo icon on the desktop*** (it looks like a briefcase with the letter CT on it) or, ***click the Start button, point to Programs or All Programs, point to the Summation iBLAZE 2.8.0 Demo folder, and then click on Summation iBLAZE 2.8.0 Demo.***

2. The Welcome to Summation window should now be displayed. ***Click Close Window*** in the lower right of the Welcome to Summation window. When prompted regarding the Help menu, *click OK.*

3. You should now be back at the Attorney's Quick Start home page with *P. Franc v. K. Morris* in the Case Explorer window.

4. ***Point to Load Transcript*** **in the Setting The Stage section of the Home—Attorney's Quick Start Page window.** Notice that when you point to it a message appears. The message states that all you have to do is to click the option and place the disk with the transcript on it (given to you from a court reporter) and the transcript will be loaded.

5. ***Click Load Transcript*** under the Setting The Stage section of the Attorney's Quick Start Page home window.

6. Notice that the Load Transcript window is displayed. Typically, you would click the drive the transcripts are on and select "Copy All" from the Copy Options section of the screen; the transcripts would then be copied.

7. All of the transcripts have already been loaded in our case, but the process is very simple and straightforward.

8. ***Click the Close icon (a red square with a white "X") in the Load Transcript window.***

9. Loading a pleading is likewise very straightforward. To load a pleading, the user creates a subdirectory on his or her hard disk or network drive where all of the pleading documents for a specific case will be saved. Once the user has moved or copied all of the PDF files there, he or she would right-click Pleadings in the Case Explorer window, point to Pleadings Utilities, and click Add Pleadings Directory. The user would designate what directory to save the pleadings in to complete and the process.

10. The process for loading pleadings in our case has already been accomplished, but we can still see where all of the documents are saved.

11. ***Click the + (plus) sign to the left of Pleadings in the Case Explorer.***

12. ***Next, double-click Documents under Pleadings in the Case Explorer.*** Notice that all of the pleading documents are saved in the directory iBlaze20Demo\CASEDATA\P.FRANC Vs. K. MORRIS\Pldings\documents.

13. ***Click the Close icon (a red square with a white "X") in the Documents window*** where the pleading documents were saved.

14. You are now ready to enter a document abstract into the Core Database.

15. ***Right-click Core Database.***

16. ***Then, click Select Form.***

17. ***Click E-stdfrm E-table, and then click Load Form.***

18. ***Point to Add a Doc/Image under the Setting The Stage section of the Attorney's Quick Start Page home window.*** Notice that when you point to it a message appears stating that you can use the option to enter a new document abstract and that if the document has an image associated with it that you can link the two together.

19. ***Click Add a Doc/Image*** under the Setting The Stage section of the Attorney's Quick Start Page home window.

20. If a blank image screen was loaded with the document, ***click the Close icon in the No Images for: window.***

21. The Form E-Stdfrm Add: Summary [New] of 0 window should now be displayed.

22. You are now ready to enter a new document abstract. You can use the **[TAB]** and **[SHIFT]+[TAB]** keys to go forward and backward in the form.

Enter the following information in the form:

Field Name	Special Instructions	Contents to Enter
Docid		**AAA000999**
Batesrng		**AAA000999**
Attach. Range	Leave this field blank	
Page Ct (Page Count)		**1**
Doc. Date		**01/01/07**
Est. Date?	Leave this field blank	
Location	Leave this field blank	
Doc Type	PRESS F6 (to review the list from the Look up Table), click Lt—Letter, and then click OK	**Letter**
Properties	Leave this field blank	
Privilege/ Confidentiality	Leave this field blank	
Priority	Leave this field blank	
Has Image		**No**
Author(s)	PRESS F6 (to review the list from the Look up Table), click EKI—Ernst King, and then click OK	**Ernst King**
Recipients	PRESS F6 to review the list from the Look up Table, click PFR—Peter Franc and then click OK	**Peter Franc**
CC	Leave this field blank	
Mentions	Leave this field blank	
Source(s)	Leave this field blank	
Summary		**Letter from the State condemning the plaintiff's property**
Document Title (Exhibit List)	Leave this field blank	
Depo Exh #	Leave this field blank	
Attorney Notes	Leave this field blank	
Issues	PRESS F6 to review the list from the Look up Table, click 900—Damages, and then click OK	**Damages**
Attachments	Leave this field blank	
Linked Document	Leave this field blank	
Trial Exh #		160

Witness	PRESS F6 to review the list from the Look up Table, click PFR—Peter Franc EKI—Ernst King, and then click OK	**Peter Franc** **Ernst King**

23. After you have entered all of the information, press the **[F10]** key to save the record.

24. Close all of the open windows except for Home and Classic View.

25. ***Right-click Core Database.***

26. ***Click Select Form, click E-stdfrm E-table, and then click Load Form.***

27. ***Double-click Core Database*** in the Case Explorer.

28. ***Scroll down to the last record (number 144—Bates AAA000999).*** The record that you just entered should be the last record.

29. Close all of the open windows except for Home and Classic View.

This concludes Lesson 9. To exit Summation, ***click File on the menu bar and then click Exit Summation,*** or go to Lesson 10.

LESSON 10: CREATING A NEW CASE

This lesson gives a general overview on how to enter a new case into Summation, including entering issues, entering names, creating a blueprint for the case, and generally setting up the case.

If you did not exit Summation after Lesson 9, then skip Steps 1 and 2 and go directly to Step 3.

1. Start Windows. Then, ***double-click the Summation iBLAZE2.8.0 Demo icon on the desktop*** (it looks like a briefcase with the letter CT on it), or ***click the Start button, point to Programs or All Programs, point to the Summation iBLAZE 2.8.0 Demo folder, and then click Summation iBLAZE 2.8.0 Demo.***

2. The Welcome to Summation window should now be displayed. ***Click Close Window*** in the lower right of the Welcome to Summation window. When prompted regarding the Help menu, ***click OK.***

3. You should now be back at the Attorney's Quick Start Page home with *P. Franc v. K. Morris* in the Case Explorer window.

4. ***Point to New Case*** under Other Cases in the Quick Links section of the Attorney's Quick Start Page home window. Read the message.

5. ***Click New Case under Other Cases in the Quick Links section of the Attorney's Quick Start Page home window.***

6. The Start A New Case window should now be displayed.

7. Type **Smith v. EZ Pest Control** and then ***click OK.***

8. At the "Would you like to password new case: Smith v. EZ Pest Control" prompt, and ***click No.***

9. The Getting Started with Your New Case—Working with Your New Case window should be displayed. Summation offers prompts and helps to assist you in properly setting up your new case.

10. ***Point to Structure Your Case.*** Notice the helpful hints.

11. ***Click Structure Your Case.***

12. ***Point to Add Issues To This Case*** and read the helpful hints.

13. ***Click Add Issues To This Case.***

14. The New Entry for Issues window should now be displayed. In the Shortcut box type **BRC** and then press **[TAB]**.

15. In the Issue box type **Breach of Contract.** Then, ***click Save.***

16. Another New Entry for Issues window should be displayed. In the Shortcut box type *NEG* and then press **[TAB]**.

17. At the Issue box type ***Negligence. Click Save and then click Cancel.***

18. ***Point to Add Names To This Case*** and read the helpful hints.

19. ***Click Add Names To This Case.***

20. The New Entry for Names window should be displayed. In the Shortcut box type **JS** and then press **[TAB]**.

21. In the Name box type **Judy Smith.** Then, ***click on Save.***

22. Another New Entry for Names window should be displayed. In the Shortcut box type **JL** and then press **[TAB]**.

23. In the Name box type **John Lincoln.** ***Click Save and then click Cancel.***

24. ***Point to Blue Print This Case*** and read the helpful hints.

25. ***Click Blue Print This Case.***

26. An example of a Case Blueprint should be displayed. At the bottom of the Example of a Case Blueprint window, ***click "Click here to proceed."***

27. The Case Organizer—Case Blueprint screen is now displayed.

28. Type **BREACH OF CONTRACT** and then press the **[ENTER]** key.

29. Then, type **NEGLIGENCE**.

30. ***Click the Close icon (a red square with a white "X") in the Case Organizer—Case Blueprint window.***

31. To go back to the New Case page, ***click Help on the menu bar and then click New Case Page.*** The Getting Started With Your New Case window should now be displayed.

32. ***Point to Load Evidentiary Info*** and read the helpful hints.

33. ***Click Load Evidentiary Info.*** In the last lesson, you learned how to load a transcript and add a document/image so you already know the basics of doing these tasks.

34. ***Point to Select Data Entry Form*** and read the helpful hints. This is where you can decide which standard entry form best meets the type of information that you want to abstract into Summation.

35. ***Click Select Data Entry Form.***

36. ***In the Forms Available list, click E-review, then click Exit at the bottom of the Forms Available list.***

37. ***Point to Add a Document/Image*** *and read the helpful hints.*

38. ***Click Add A Document/Image.*** A blank e-Review Form should now be loaded. This is where you could add documents and images to your new case.

39. ***Click the Close icon (a red square with a white "X") in the Form E-review Add: Summary [New] of 0 window.***

40. ***Click the Close icon in the No Images for: window.***

41. ***Click File on the menu bar and then click Exit CT Summation.***

This concludes the Summation hands-on exercises.

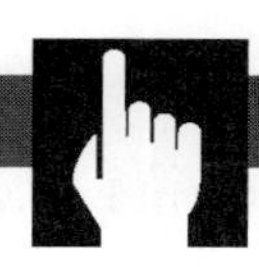

HANDS-ON EXERCISES

LEXISNEXIS CASEMAP

I. Introduction–Read This!

LexisNexis CaseMap is a litigation support analytical tool. The LexisNexis CaseMap demonstration version is a full working version of the program (with a few limitations). The program demonstration version times out 120 days after installation. This means that the program will only work for 120 days once you install it. So, it is highly recommended that you do not install the program on your computer until you are actually ready to go through the Hands-on Exercises and learn the program. When you are ready to install the program, follow the instructions below.

II. Using the LexisNexis CaseMap Hands-on Exercises

The LexisNexis CaseMap Hands-On Exercises are easy to use and contain step-by-step instructions. Each lesson builds on the previous exercise so please complete the Hands-on Exercises in order. CaseMap comes with sample data so you should be able to utilize many features of the program.

III. Installation Instructions

Below are step-by-step instructions for loading the LexisNexis CaseMap demonstration version on your computer.

1. *Insert Disk 1 supplied with this text into your computer.*

2. When prompted with "What do you want Windows to do?" select "Open folder to view files using Windows Explorer," then click OK. If your computer does not automatically recognize that you have inserted a CD, double-click the My Computer icon, then double-click the drive where Disk 1 is.

3. Double-click the CaseMap7.exe file. This will start the CaseMap installation wizard.

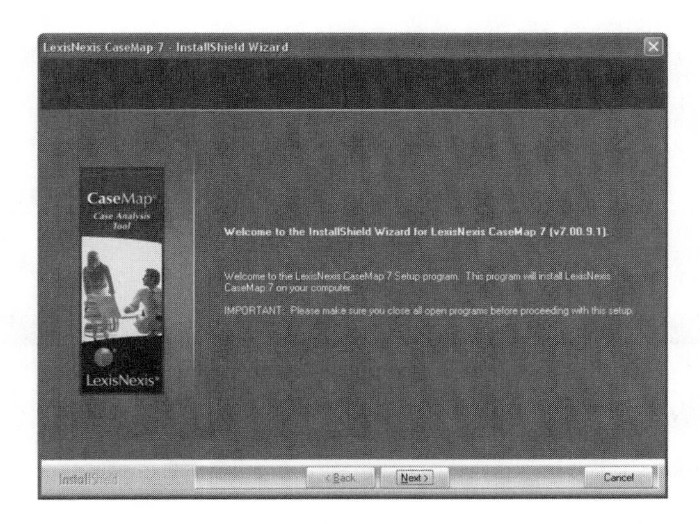

CaseMap Installation Exhibit 1

4. ***Click Next (see CaseMap Installation Exhibit 1).***
5. The screen in CaseMap Installation Exhibit 2 should now be displayed.
6. ***Click Yes to agree to the License Agreement.***
7. The screen in CaseMap Installation Exhibit 3 should now be displayed.

CaseMap Installation Exhibit 2

LexisNexis® CaseMap® screen shots used with the permission of LexisNexis, a division of Read Elsevier Inc. LexisNexis is a registered trademark of Reed Elsevier Properties Inc. CaseMap is a registered trademark of LexisNexis Courtlink, Inc.

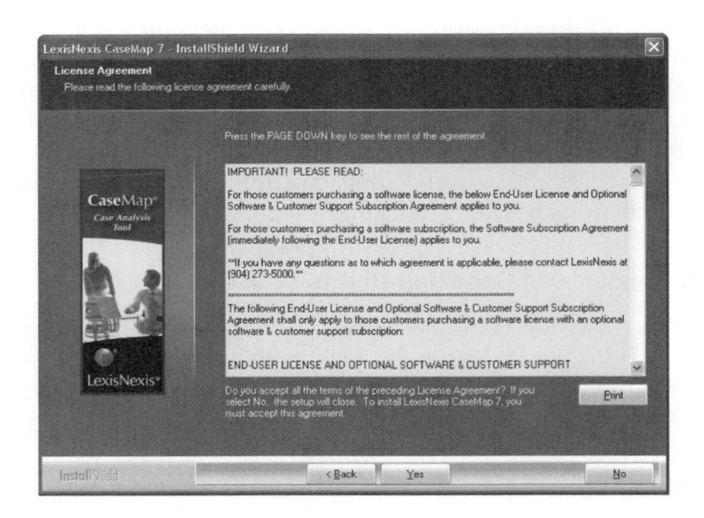

CaseMap Installation Exhibit 3

LexisNexis® CaseMap® screen shots used with the permission of LexisNexis, a division of Read Elsevier Inc. LexisNexis is a registered trademark of Reed Elsevier Properties Inc. CaseMap is a registered trademark of LexisNexis Courtlink, Inc.

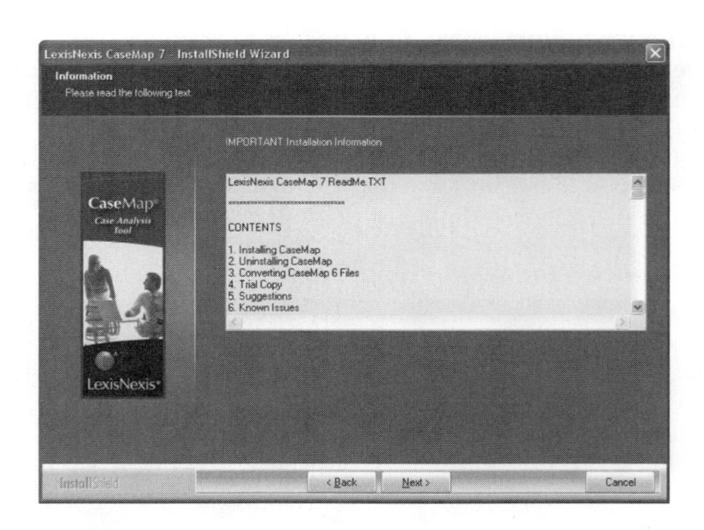

8. ***Click "Next."***
9. The screen shown in CaseMap Installation Exhibit 4 should now be displayed.
10. ***Click "Next" to install CaseMap in the default directory.***
11. The screen shown in CaseMap Installation Exhibit 5 should now be displayed.

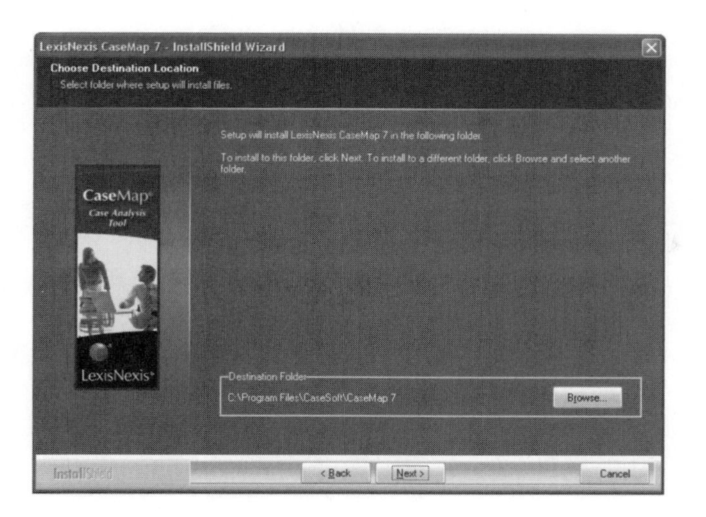

CaseMap Installation Exhibit 4

LexisNexis® CaseMap® screen shots used with the permission of LexisNexis, a division of Read Elsevier Inc. LexisNexis is a registered trademark of Reed Elsevier Properties Inc. CaseMap is a registered trademark of LexisNexis Courtlink, Inc.

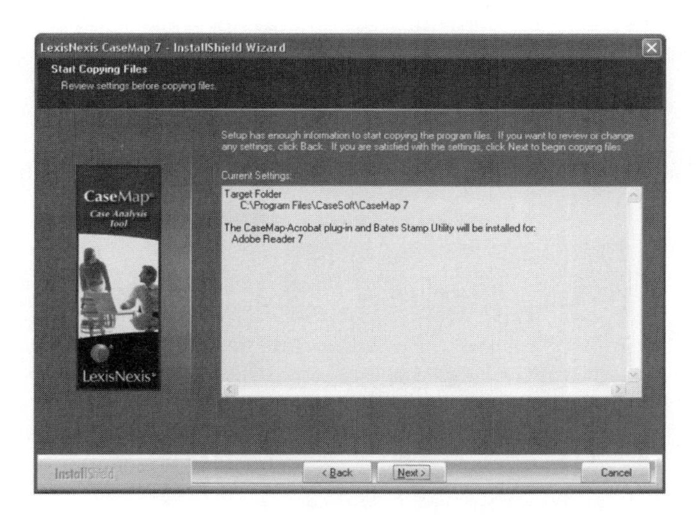

CaseMap Installation Exhibit 5

LexisNexis® CaseMap® screen shots used with the permission of LexisNexis, a division of Read Elsevier Inc. LexisNexis is a registered trademark of Reed Elsevier Properties Inc. CaseMap is a registered trademark of LexisNexis Courtlink, Inc.

12. *Click on "Next."*

13. The screen in CaseMap Installation Exhibit 6 should now be displayed.

14. When the program is through copying files, the screen in CaseMap Installation Exhibit 7 should be displayed.

15. *Click "Finish."*

16. The screen in CaseMap Installation Exhibit 8 should now be displayed.

17. *Click "Continue."*

18. The screen in CaseMap Installation Exhibit 9 should now be displayed.

CaseMap Installation Exhibit 6

LexisNexis® CaseMap® screen shots used with the permission of LexisNexis, a division of Read Elsevier Inc. LexisNexis is a registered trademark of Reed Elsevier Properties Inc. CaseMap is a registered trademark of LexisNexis Courtlink, Inc.

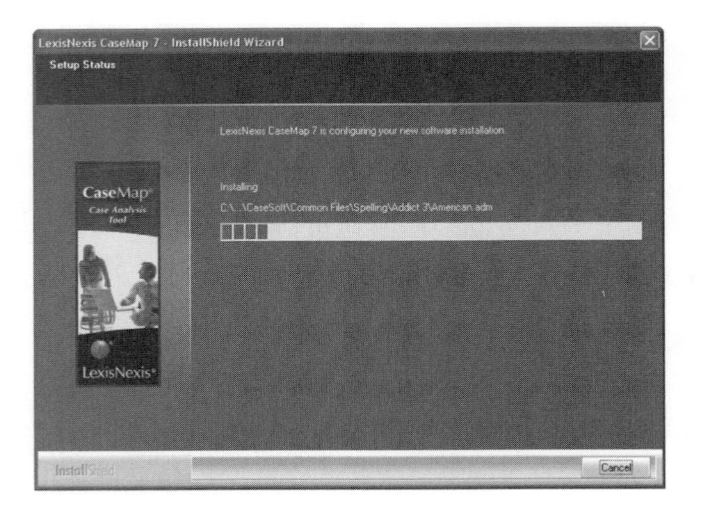

CaseMap Installation Exhibit 7

LexisNexis® CaseMap® screen shots used with the permission of LexisNexis, a division of Read Elsevier Inc. LexisNexis is a registered trademark of Reed Elsevier Properties Inc. CaseMap is a registered trademark of LexisNexis Courtlink, Inc.

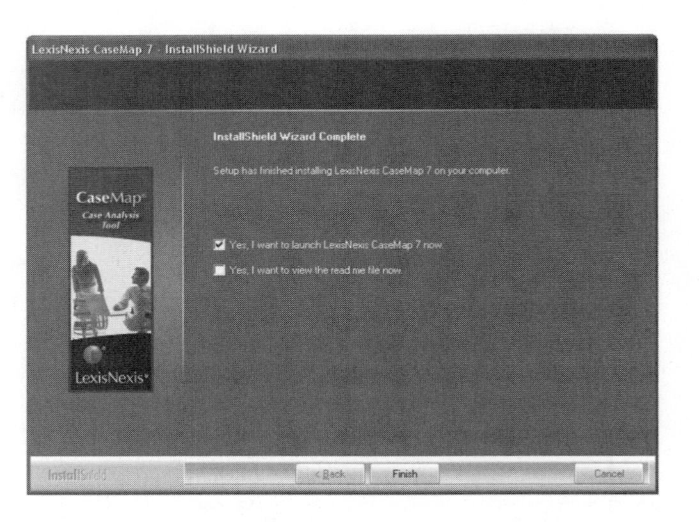

19. The installation of CaseMap is now complete. ***Click File on the menu bar and then click Exit.***

IV. Installation Technical Support

If you have problems installing the demonstration version of LexisNexis CaseMap from the CD-ROM included with this text, please contact Thomson Delmar Learning Technical Support first at (800)477–3692. Please note that LexisNexis CaseMap is a licensed product of LexisNexis. If Thomson Delmar Learning Technical Support is unable to resolve your installation question or if you have a non–installation–related question you will need to contact Lexis-Nexis CaseMap directly at (904)273–5000.

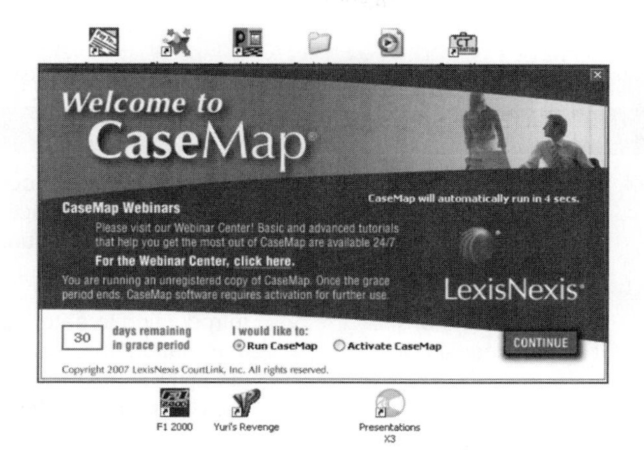

CaseMap Installation Exhibit 8

LexisNexis® CaseMap® screen shots used with the permission of LexisNexis, a division of Read Elsevier Inc. LexisNexis is a registered trademark of Reed Elsevier Properties Inc. CaseMap is a registered trademark of LexisNexis Courtlink, Inc.

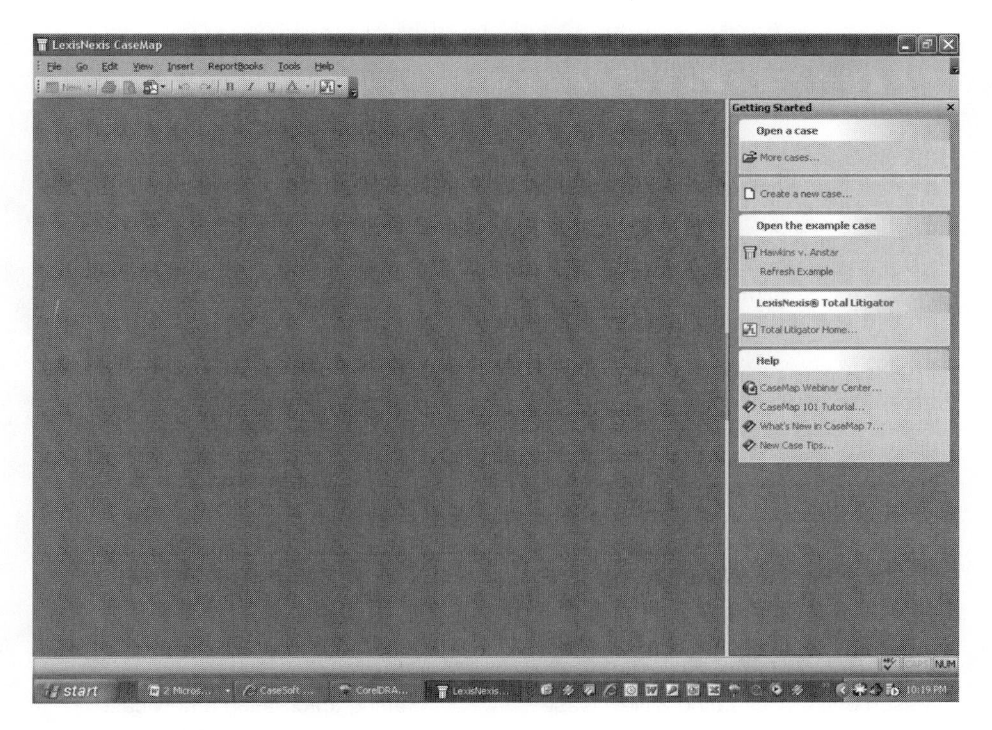

CaseMap Installation Exhibit 9

LexisNexis® CaseMap® screen shots used with the permission of LexisNexis, a division of Read Elsevier Inc. LexisNexis is a registered trademark of Reed Elsevier Properties Inc. CaseMap is a registered trademark of LexisNexis Courtlink, Inc.

HANDS-ON EXERCISES

LEXISNEXIS CASEMAP

Number	Lesson Title	Concepts Covered
Basic		
Lesson 1	Introduction to CaseMap	Explanation and introduction to the CaseMap interface, including the Fact, Object, Issue, Question, and Research spreadsheets.
Lesson 2	Working with the Facts Spreadsheet	Introduction to entering information, fuzzy dating, date stamping, data format options, auto-sizing cell widths, correcting spelling errors, linking files, short names, sorting, linking issues (Link Assistant), Filter by Selection, Filter Tagging, and evaluating facts.
Intermediate		
Lesson 3	Working with the Objects Spreadsheet	Entering objects, executing primary and secondary sorts, expanding and contracting column widths, the meaning of columns in the Objects spreadsheet, the different views in the Objects spreadsheet, and using the Objects spreadsheet in litigation.
Lesson 4	Working with the Issues Spreadsheet	Entering issues, promoting issues, demoting issues, and deleting issues.
Lesson 5	Working with Advanced Features	Using the Viewing CaseWide command, hiding columns, inserting columns, adjusting rows, moving columns, printing and viewing reports, adding objects on the fly, hiding shortcuts, and viewing the detail of a record.
Advanced		
Lesson 6	Creating a New Case	Setting up/creating a new case in CaseMap and entering new objects, including people, organizations, and documents.
Lesson 7	Entering Issues and Facts in a New Case	Entering new issues in a case, entering new facts in a case, and copying data automatically from one cell to another.

Number	Lesson Title	Concepts Covered
Lesson 8	Using CaseMap for a New Case	Using CaseMap for a new case, including printing reports, viewing case data in a variety of ways, exporting to a PDF file, exporting a summary judgment report to a word processor, using the CaseWide tool, and searching/filtering data.

GETTING STARTED

Introduction

Throughout these exercises, information you need to enter into the program will be designated in several different ways.

- Keys to be pressed on the keyboard will be designated in brackets, in all caps, bold, and enlarged type (press the **[ENTER]** key).
- Movements with the mouse will be designated in bold and italics (***point to File on the Menu Bar and click the mouse***).
- Words or letters that should be typed will be designated in bold (type **Training Program**).
- Information that is or should be displayed on your computer screen is shown in the following style: **Press ENTER to continue.**

OVERVIEW OF CASEMAP

CaseMap is a powerful knowledge management and litigation support tool. CaseMap helps legal professionals organize and understand facts, issues, people, documents, and other information about a case. Using CaseMap, a legal professional can prepare detailed chronologies of the facts and events in a case, a cast of characters (people) in a case, a list of important factual and legal issues in a case, a list of documents in a case, and much more. In addition, CaseMap can link all of this information together, is very flexible, and allows the user to change views and change how information is sorted "on the fly." CaseMap also allows the legal professional to evaluate the strength of his or her case, to track what data/information in the case is agreed on by the parties or disputed (and by whom), and allows the images or text of documents to be attached or linked to information stored in CaseMap.

CaseMap fills a unique niche in the litigation support market. It is not designed to be a full litigation support tool (like Summation, which can handle millions of document abstracts, transcripts, full-text documents, etc.). It is instead designed to be a strategy/knowledge management tool that helps legal professionals think, prepare, and strategize about their case. It is somewhat similar to, though still different from, the Case Organizer, People database and Event database in Summation. CaseMap is a database program, but looks more like a spreadsheet because it is based on storing data in columns and rows.

The purpose of these exercises is to give you a general introduction to CaseMap and how it is used in litigation. CaseMap, like Summation, is a very popular litigation support program that is used extensively in all types of legal organizations throughout the country. A fully functioning demonstration version of CaseMap is used. The demonstration version of CaseMap includes a sample case, *Philip Hawkins v. Anstar Biotech Industries*. This hypothetical case is ready for trial and most of the information about the case has

already been entered into CaseMap. In addition, this tutorial includes exercises that will allow you to create a new file in CaseMap for the sample case of *Smith v. EZ Pest Control.*

The Philip Hawkins v. Anstar Biotech Industries Case

An overview of the facts of the *Philip Hawkins v. Anstar Biotech Industries* case follows. Philip Hawkins (the plaintiff) was hired to be a sales manager by William Lang, the CEO of Anstar Biotech Industries (the defendant), in early 1997. In late 1997, Hawkins was promoted to Vice President of Sales. In January 1999, Hawkins turned age 51. In May 1999, Hawkins received an outstanding performance review from Lang. In June 1999, Lang made the decision to lay off some of the company's staff. In early July 1999, Anstar's second-quarter sales were announced. Sales had dropped by 8 percent. In late July, Hawkins was demoted to a sales manager. Hawkins alleges that in August 1999, Lang told him that "old wood must be trimmed back hard." Hawkins claims that this was a reference to him being over 40, and that he is "old wood" that must be "trimmed." Hawkins was transferred to another office a few weeks later. In September, Hawkins wrote Lang and complained about the way he was being treated and that the purpose of the layoffs was to eliminate older staff. In November, Anstar laid off fifty-five employees, including Hawkins. Ten days later Hawkins sued Anstar for age discrimination, wrongful termination, and retaliation. Anstar claims the layoffs were due to poor sales and were completely lawful. You are acting on behalf of the law firm representing the defendant, Anstar Biotech Industries.

The Judy Smith v. EZ Pest Control Case

The facts of the *Smith v. EZ Pest Control* case are that Judy Smith had a contract with EZ Pest Control to conduct periodic reviews of her house several times a year and to provide preventative pest control maintenance to keep termites out. John Lincoln of EZ Pest Control came out several times and inspected the house. Nonetheless, Judy Smith discovered that there were several colonies of termites in her house and that massive damage was being done. She called a contractor, Tim Stewart, to look at the house and he determined that there was damage to the house and that it needed to be repaired as soon as the termites were removed. Judy Smith is suing EZ Pest Control for breach of contract and negligence. You represent the plaintiff, Judy Smith.

Basic

LESSON 1: INTRODUCTION TO CASEMAP

This lesson introduces you to the CaseMap litigation support program. It explains basic information about the CaseMap interface, including information about the Fact, Object, Issue, Question, and Research spreadsheets.

Install the CaseMap demonstration version on your computer following the instructions at the end of Chapter 9 entitled. "CaseMap Hands-On Exercises–Read This First!" *Note*: The CaseMap demonstration version times out (stops working) **120 days after installation.** It is highly recommended that you do not install the program on your computer until you are ready to complete these Hands-on Exercises.

1. Start Windows. Then, ***double-click the LexisNexis CaseMap 7 icon on the desktop, or click the Start button on the Windows desktop, point to Programs or All Programs, point to the LexisNexis CaseMap Suite, and then click LexisNexis CaseMap 7.*** LexisNexis CaseMap 7 will then start.

2. When you start CaseMap, you will see a small window in the middle of the screen that says "CaseMap" with some additional information about a grace period. ***Click Continue in the CaseMap window.*** CaseMap will then start, with several options listed to the right of the screen.

3. Your screen should now look similar to CaseMap Exhibit 1. The Getting Started task pane should be displayed on the right side of the screen. Under "Open the example case," ***click*** **Hawkins v. Anstar.**

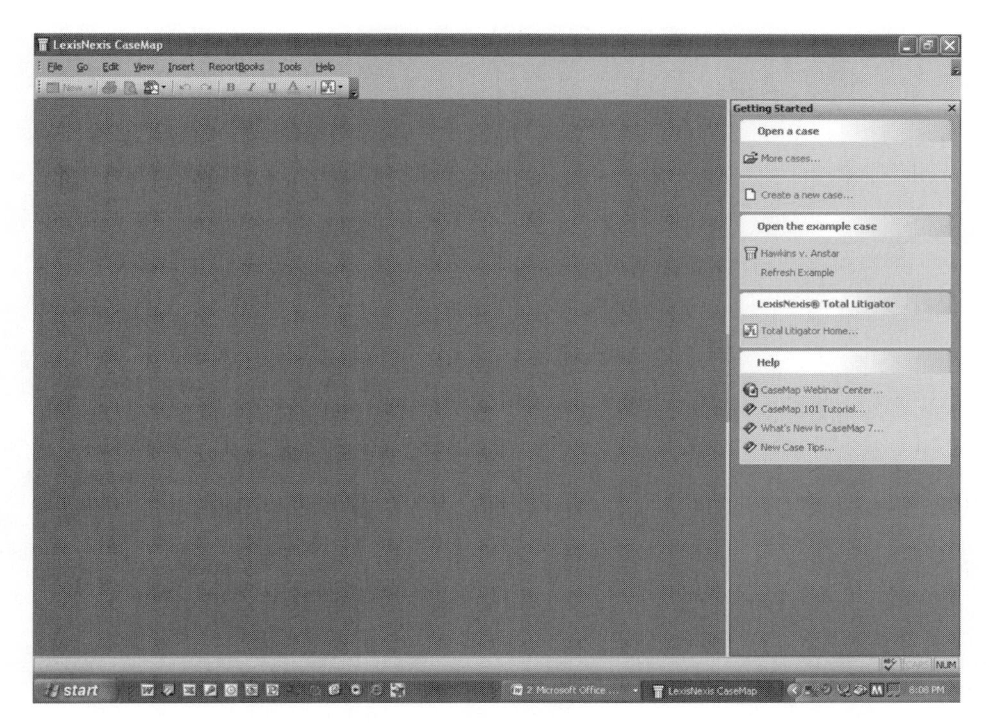

CaseMap Exhibit 1

LexisNexis® CaseMap® screen shots used with the permission of LexisNexis, a division of Reed Elsevier Inc. LexisNexis is a registered trademark of Reed Elsevier Properties Inc. CaseMap is a registered trademark of LexisNexis Courtlink, Inc.

4. The Case Log On window should now be displayed. ***Click the down arrow icon to the right of Staff Member: Chris Attorney.*** A dialog box should now be displayed with the name of several staff members. This is actually a very useful function in CaseMap. Using a network, many staff members can access a CaseMap case/database. In addition, because each staff member must log in with their own name, CaseMap can track the new information that has been entered since each staff member logged in. Using a feature called What's New, a staff member can get a summary of what new information has been entered into CaseMap since they last logged in.

5. ***Click Dave Paralegal, and then click OK.***

6. The CaseMap Fact spreadsheet for the Hawkins case should now be displayed (see CaseMap Exhibit 2). CaseMap, uses a series of spreadsheets to organize a case. The primary spreadsheets are Facts, All Objects, Documents, and Issues. CaseMap refers to these screens as spreadsheets because it uses an interface that has rows and columns, and thus looks like a spreadsheet.

7. Each of the four primary spreadsheets tracks different data about a case. The Fact spreadsheet allows the user to build a chronology of case facts. Notice that the first six records on your screen (and in CaseMap Exhibit 2) provide you, as a new user, with information about the program. After that, the Fact spreadsheet contains a separate fact about the *Hawkins v. Anstar Biotech Industries* case.

CaseMap Exhibit 2

LexisNexis® CaseMap® screen shots used with the permission of LexisNexis, a division of Reed Elsevier Inc. LexisNexis is a registered trademark of Reed Elsevier Properties Inc. CaseMap is a registered trademarks of LexisNexis Courtlink, Inc.

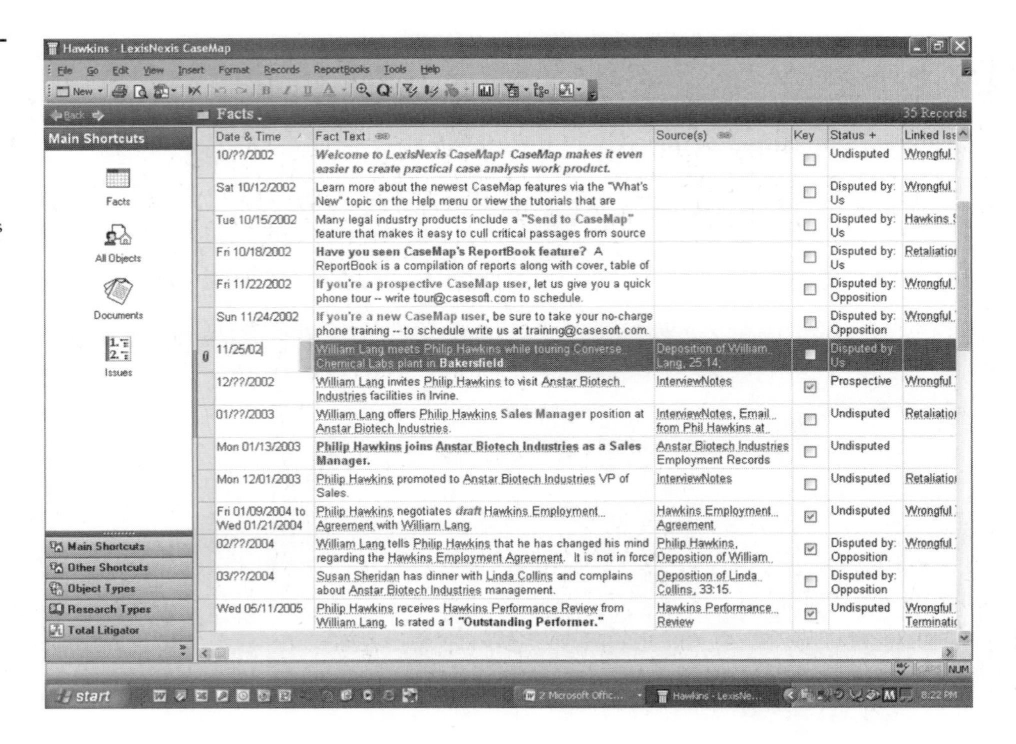

8. *Click the All Objects icon* to the left of the screen under the Main Shortcuts heading.

9. The Objects spreadsheet tracks a number of items including people (this allows you to create a cast of characters in a case), documents (this allows you to create a document abstract database and document index), organizations (to track the different organizations/parties in a case), pleadings (to track pleadings in a case), and other information as well (see CaseMap Exhibit 3). You can also attach document images to any information or record in the Objects spreadsheet.

CaseMap Exhibit 3

LexisNexis® CaseMap® screen shots used with the permission of LexisNexis, a division of Reed Elsevier Inc. LexisNexis is a registered trademark of Reed Elsevier Properties Inc. CaseMap is a registered trademarks of LexisNexis Courtlink, Inc.

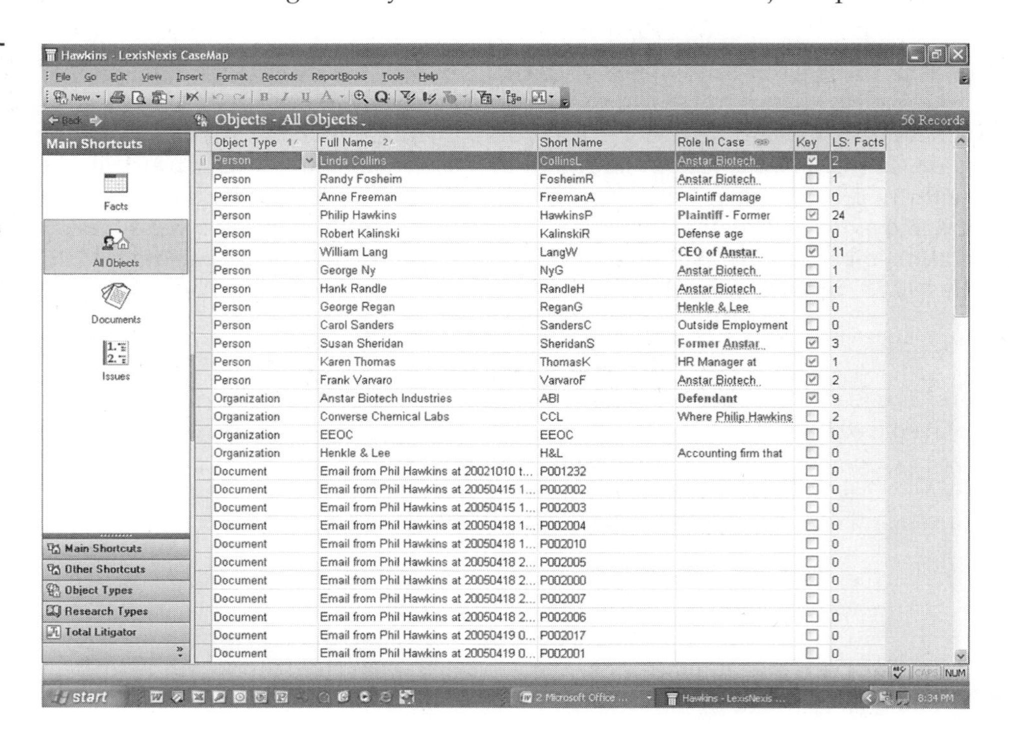

In the Objects spreadsheet, you can see all of the objects (notice in CaseMap Exhibit 3 that you can see Person, Organization, Document, Pleading, and others) or you can select another view and just see a specific type of object, such as all Persons or all Documents.

10. ***Click the Issues icon*** to the left of the screen under the Main Shortcuts heading.

11. The Issues spreadsheet tracks all of the different issues in a case (see CaseMap Exhibit 4). This usually includes all of the causes of action in a lawsuit and may include the specific elements of each cause of action. Notice in CaseMap Exhibit 4 that there are five main issues/causes of action or controversies in the case, including wrongful termination, age discrimination, retaliation, whether the plaintiff deserved to be terminated, and damages.

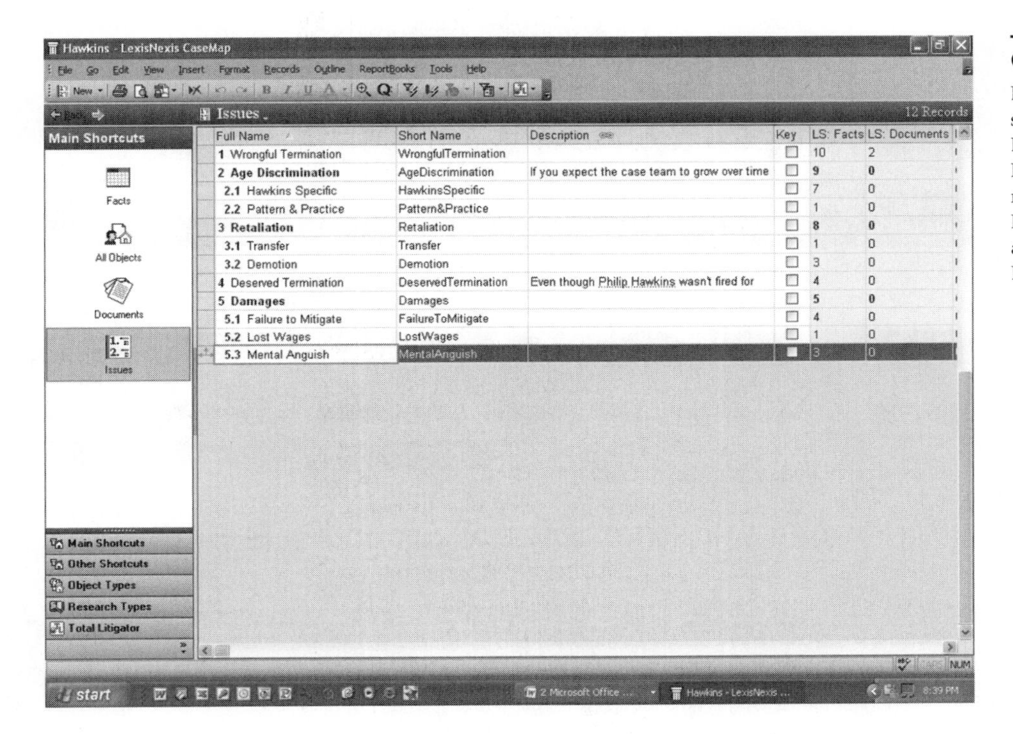

CaseMap Exhibit 4

LexisNexis® CaseMap® screen shots used with the permission of LexisNexis, a division of Reed Elsevier Inc. LexisNexis is a registered trademark of Reed Elsevier Properties Inc. CaseMap is a registered trademarks of LexisNexis Courtlink, Inc.

12. ***Click the Documents icon*** to the left of the screen under the Main Shortcuts heading.

13. Your screen should now look similar to CaseMap Exhibit 5. Notice that the heading in CaseMap Exhibit 5 says "Objects – Documents." These are the same documents listed previously in "All Objects," but in this screen the information is more complete and other objects (such as people and organizations) are not shown.

14. There are two other spreadsheets in CaseMap that are not listed in the Main Shortcuts.

15. ***Click Other Shortcuts in the lower left of the screen.***

16. Notice that two selections appeared in the upper left of the screen, Questions and Research.

17. ***Click Questions.*** The Questions spreadsheet should now be displayed (see CaseMap Exhibit 6).

CaseMap Exhibit 5

LexisNexis® CaseMap® screen shots used with the permission of LexisNexis, a division of Reed Elsevier Inc. LexisNexis is a registered trademark of Reed Elsevier Properties Inc. CaseMap is a registered trademark of LexisNexis Courtlink, Inc.

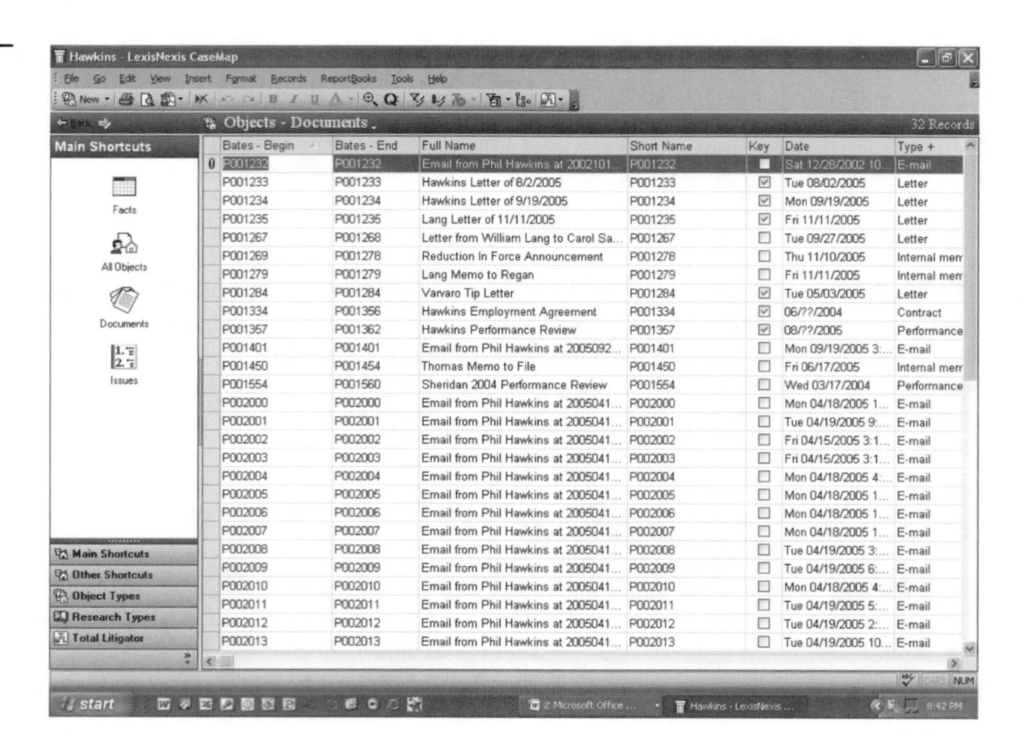

Bates - Begin	Bates - End	Full Name	Short Name	Key	Date	Type +
P001232	P001232	Email from Phil Hawkins at 2002101...	P001232		Sat 12/28/2002 10...	E-mail
P001233	P001233	Hawkins Letter of 8/2/2005	P001233	☑	Tue 08/02/2005	Letter
P001234	P001234	Hawkins Letter of 9/19/2005	P001234	☑	Mon 09/19/2005	Letter
P001235	P001235	Lang Letter of 11/11/2005	P001235	☑	Fri 11/11/2005	Letter
P001267	P001268	Letter from William Lang to Carol Sa...	P001267	☐	Tue 09/27/2005	Letter
P001269	P001278	Reduction In Force Announcement	P001278	☐	Thu 11/10/2005	Internal mem
P001279	P001279	Lang Memo to Regan	P001279	☐	Fri 11/11/2005	Internal mem
P001284	P001284	Varvaro Tip Letter	P001284	☑	Tue 05/03/2005	Letter
P001334	P001356	Hawkins Employment Agreement	P001334	☑	06/??/2004	Contract
P001357	P001362	Hawkins Performance Review	P001357	☑	08/??/2005	Performance
P001401	P001401	Email from Phil Hawkins at 2005092...	P001401	☐	Mon 09/19/2005 3:...	E-mail
P001450	P001454	Thomas Memo to File	P001450	☐	Fri 06/17/2005	Internal mem
P001554	P001560	Sheridan 2004 Performance Review	P001554	☐	Wed 03/17/2004	Performance
P002000	P002000	Email from Phil Hawkins at 2005041...	P002000	☐	Mon 04/18/2005 1...	E-mail
P002001	P002001	Email from Phil Hawkins at 2005041...	P002001	☐	Tue 04/19/2005 9:...	E-mail
P002002	P002002	Email from Phil Hawkins at 2005041...	P002002	☐	Fri 04/15/2005 3:1...	E-mail
P002003	P002003	Email from Phil Hawkins at 2005041...	P002003	☐	Fri 04/15/2005 3:1...	E-mail
P002004	P002004	Email from Phil Hawkins at 2005041...	P002004	☐	Mon 04/18/2005 4:...	E-mail
P002005	P002005	Email from Phil Hawkins at 2005041...	P002005	☐	Mon 04/18/2005 1...	E-mail
P002006	P002006	Email from Phil Hawkins at 2005041...	P002006	☐	Mon 04/18/2005 1...	E-mail
P002007	P002007	Email from Phil Hawkins at 2005041...	P002007	☐	Mon 04/18/2005 1...	E-mail
P002008	P002008	Email from Phil Hawkins at 2005041...	P002008	☐	Tue 04/19/2005 3:...	E-mail
P002009	P002009	Email from Phil Hawkins at 2005041...	P002009	☐	Tue 04/19/2005 6:...	E-mail
P002010	P002010	Email from Phil Hawkins at 2005041...	P002010	☐	Mon 04/18/2005 4:...	E-mail
P002011	P002011	Email from Phil Hawkins at 2005041...	P002011	☐	Tue 04/19/2005 5:...	E-mail
P002012	P002012	Email from Phil Hawkins at 2005041...	P002012	☐	Tue 04/19/2005 2:...	E-mail
P002013	P002013	Email from Phil Hawkins at 2005041...	P002013	☐	Tue 04/19/2005 10...	E-mail

CaseMap Exhibit 6

LexisNexis® CaseMap® screen shots used with the permission of LexisNexis, a division of Reed Elsevier Inc. LexisNexis is a registered trademark of Reed Elsevier Properties Inc. CaseMap is a registered trademark of LexisNexis Courtlink, Inc.

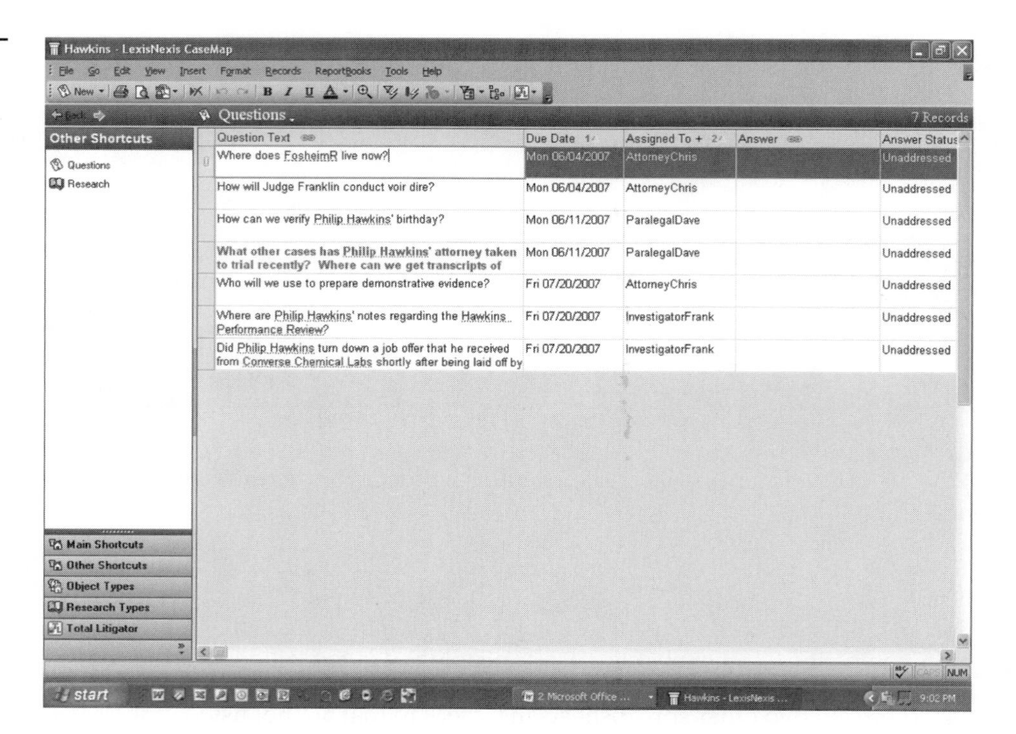

Question Text	Due Date	Assigned To +	Answer	Answer Status
Where does FosheimR live now?	Mon 06/04/2007	AttorneyChris		Unaddressed
How will Judge Franklin conduct voir dire?	Mon 06/04/2007	AttorneyChris		Unaddressed
How can we verify Philip Hawkins' birthday?	Mon 06/11/2007	ParalegalDave		Unaddressed
What other cases has Philip Hawkins' attorney taken to trial recently? Where can we get transcripts of	Mon 06/11/2007	ParalegalDave		Unaddressed
Who will we use to prepare demonstrative evidence?	Fri 07/20/2007	AttorneyChris		Unaddressed
Where are Philip Hawkins' notes regarding the Hawkins Performance Review?	Fri 07/20/2007	InvestigatorFrank		Unaddressed
Did Philip Hawkins turn down a job offer that he received from Converse Chemical Labs shortly after being laid off by	Fri 07/20/2007	InvestigatorFrank		Unaddressed

18. The Questions spreadsheet allows you to enter questions that you need to find out about the case, gives you the opportunity to assign someone in the office the responsibility for finding the answer to the question, allows you to assign a due date to the person, and provides for a place to put the answer to the question (see CaseMap Exhibit 6). The Questions spreadsheet is somewhat similar to a things-to-do list and helps to make sure that you learn and discover everything you need to know about a case.

19. ***Click the Research icon.*** The Research spreadsheet should now be displayed (see CaseMap Exhibit 7).

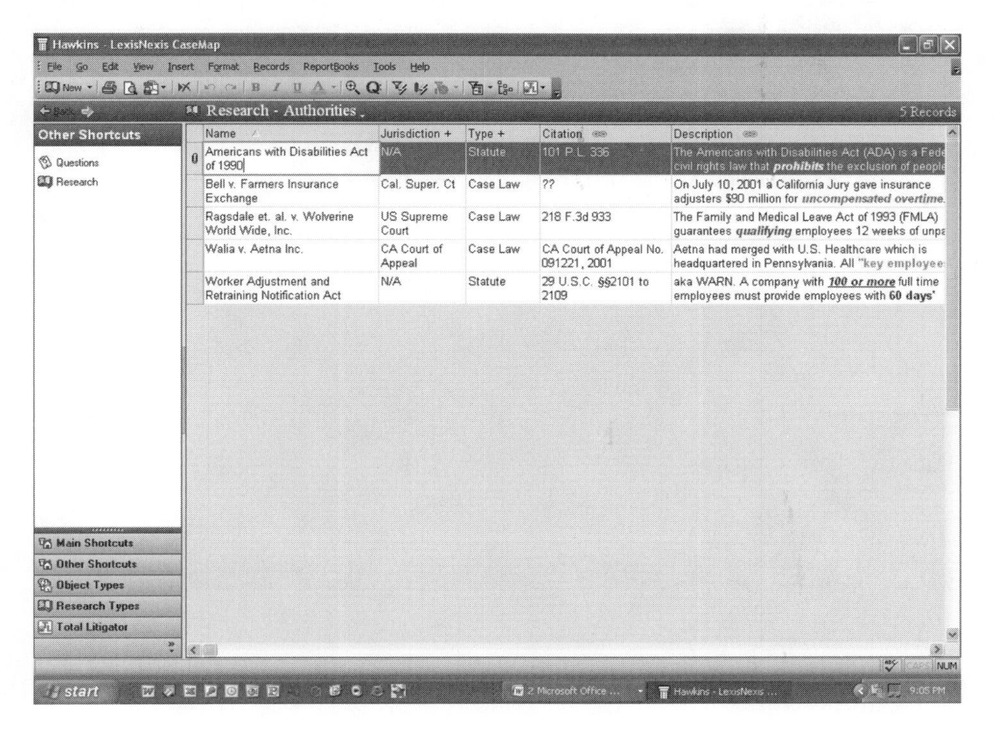

CaseMap Exhibit 7

LexisNexis® CaseMap® screen shots used with the permission of LexisNexis, a division of Reed Elsevier Inc. LexisNexis is a registered trademark of Reed Elsevier Properties Inc. CaseMap is a registered trademark of LexisNexis Courtlink, Inc.

20. The Research spreadsheet allows you to track legal citations and legal references about your case. CaseMap Exhibit 7 shows the Research—Authorities spreadsheet, which lists the major statutes and cases that concern the case.

21. ***Click Research Types in the lower left of the screen.*** Notice that three options appears in the upper left of the screen: Authorities, Extracts from Authorities, and Authorities and Extracts.

22. ***Click Extracts from Authorities in the upper left of the screen.***

23. ***Click in the second column of the first row.*** Your screen should now look similar to CaseMap Exhibit 8.

24. Notice that this is a long quote from Section 102, Part A of the Americans with Disabilities Act. The Extracts from Authorities option is where you can store long quotes from authorities. It is a sub-element of the Research spreadsheet that has the ability to display in-depth excerpts from cases, quotes, and other more detailed information. You can also link the research to the specific legal issues in the Issues spreadsheet.

25. ***Click Authorities in the upper left of the screen.*** Notice that the screen changes back to more summarized research information (see CaseMap Exhibit 7).

26. ***Click Main Shortcuts*** in the lower left of the screen. Notice that the Facts, All Objects, Documents and Issues icons appear on the left side of the screen (even though the Research spreadsheet is still shown).

27. ***Click the Facts icon*** to go back to the Facts spreadsheet.

This concludes Lesson 1. To exit CaseMap, ***click File on the menu bar, then click Exit,*** or go to Lesson 2.

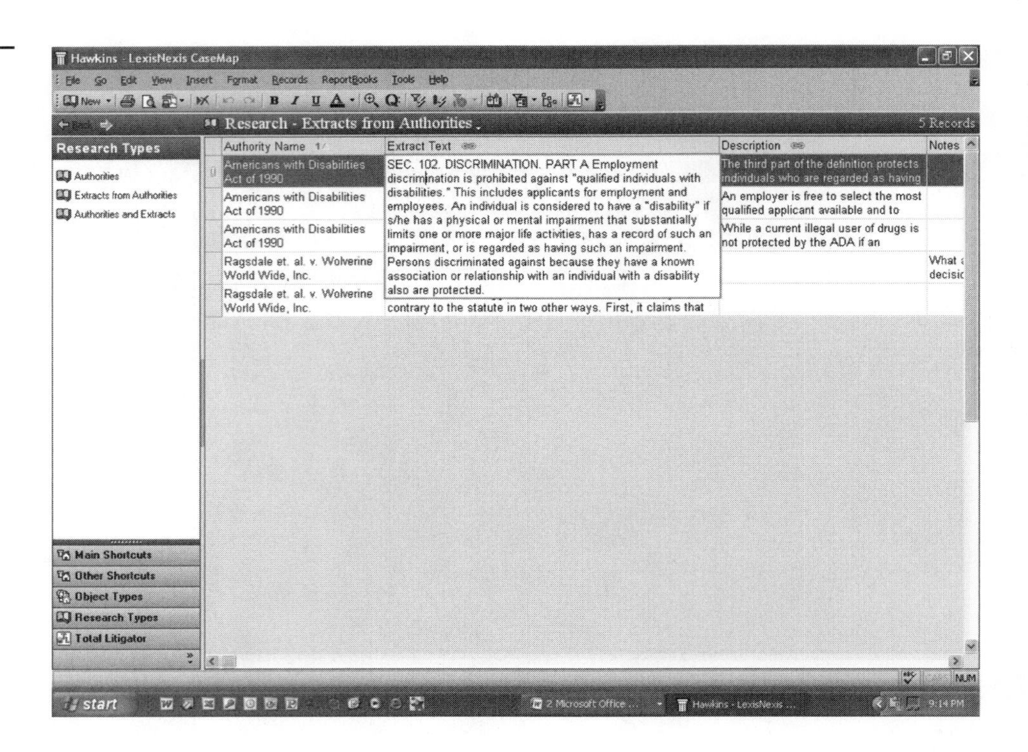

CaseMap Exhibit 8

LexisNexis® CaseMap® screen shots used with the permission of LexisNexis, a division of Reed Elsevier Inc. LexisNexis is a registered trademark of Reed Elsevier Inc. CaseMap is a registered trademark of LexisNexis Courtlink, Inc.

LESSON 2: WORKING WITH THE FACTS SPREADSHEET

This lesson introduces you to the CaseMap Facts spreadsheet, including how to enter information in CaseMap, and provides information about a variety of CaseMap features, including fuzzy dating, date stamping, data format options, auto-sizing cell widths, correcting spelling errors, linking files, short names, sorting, linking issues (Link Assistant), filtering by Selection, filter tagging, and evaluating facts.

If you did not exit CaseMap after Lesson 1, then skip Steps 1–5 and go directly to Step 6.

1. Start Windows. Then, ***double-click the LexisNexis CaseMap 7 icon on the desktop, click the Start button on the Windows desktop, point to Programs or All Programs, point to the LexisNexis CaseMap Suite, and then click LexisNexis CaseMap 7.*** LexisNexis CaseMap 7 will then start.

2. When you start CaseMap you will see a small window in the middle of the screen that says CaseMap with some additional information about a grace period. ***Click Continue in the CaseMap window.*** CaseMap will then start, with several options listed to the right of the screen.

3. Your screen should now look similar to CaseMap Exhibit 1. The Getting Started task pane should be displayed on the right side of the screen. Under "Open the example case," ***click*** Hawkins v. Anstar.

4. The Case Log On window should now be displayed. ***Click the down arrow icon to the right of Staff Member: Chris Attorney. Click Dave Paralegal and then click OK.***

5. CaseMap should put you back at the last spreadsheet you were at when you exited the program. Thus, the Facts spreadsheet for the Hawkins case should be displayed.

6. As indicated previously, the Facts spreadsheet gives you a chronology of a case. Chronologies are very useful when litigating a case. They are a great tool for refreshing the recollection of the legal professionals in a case (particularly if it has been a while since they worked on the case). They are useful for sharing knowledge with everyone on the legal team, working with clients, aiding in preparation of depositions, preparing summary judgment motions, and preparing for trial. The chronologies that CaseMap can produce are particularly helpful because they also help a legal professional evaluate the strength of the case and link facts to central issues in the case. Chronologies are also extremely helpful when attorneys or legal professionals on a case change, such as when an attorney leaves the firm and another attorney takes over the case.

7. Notice in the Facts spreadsheet that the first column is Date & Time. Also, notice in the first entry, 10/??/2002, (see CaseMap Exhibit 2) that there are question marks where the day should be.

8. CaseMap comes with a feature called "fuzzy dating." Many times, parties or witnesses to a lawsuit cannot remember exactly when something happened. When you do not know exactly when an event or fact happened, just put in question marks. When you see a fuzzy date, you immediately know that additional research needs to be done, that the date is not completely set, or that the party or witness cannot remember the date with certainty. The 10/??/2002 date means that the event occurred sometime during the month of October 2002. CaseMap reads the date as 10/01/02 for the purpose of sorting the date.

9. ***Click in the first record on the date 10/??/2002.*** Notice that there is a gray box to the right of the date in the Date and Time field (see CaseMap Exhibit 9). This is called the Date Stamper.

10. ***Click the gray Date Stamper box next to the date 10/??/2002 in the first record (see CaseMap Exhibit 9).***

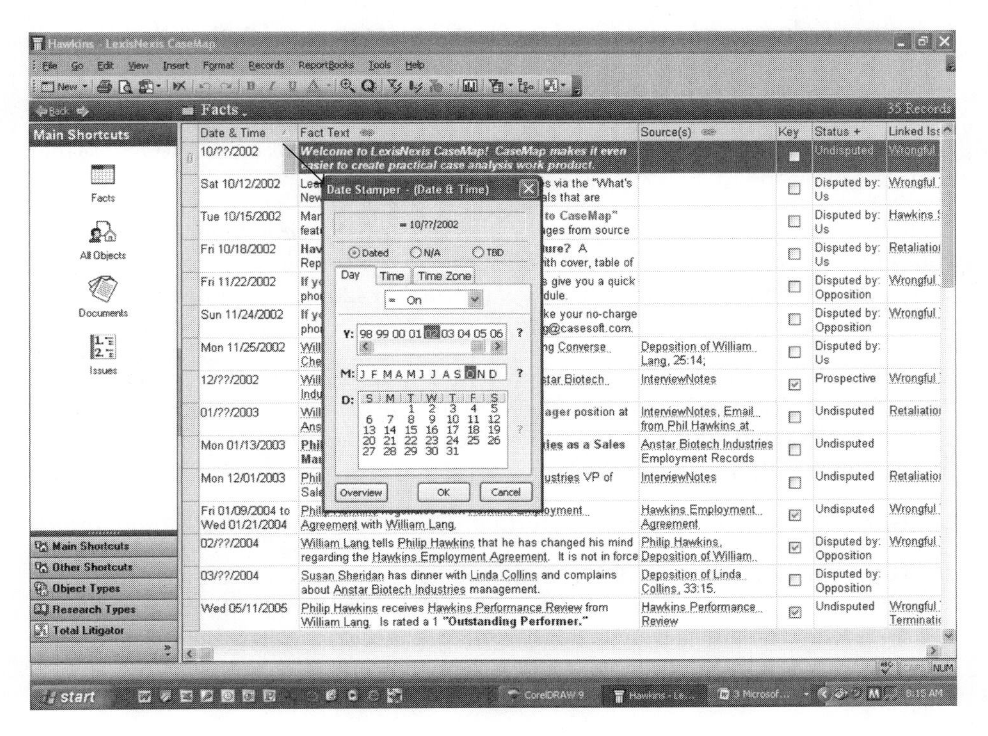

CaseMap Exhibit 9

LexisNexis® CaseMap® screen shots used with the permission of LexisNexis, a division of Reed Elsevier Inc. LexisNexis is a registered trademark of Reed Elsevier Properties Inc. CaseMap is a registered trademark of LexisNexis Courtlink, Inc.

11. You should now see the Date Stamper (Date & Time) window displayed (see CaseMap Exhibit 9). Notice that a calendar is displayed. Using the Date Stamper you can change the date interactively while you view the calendar. ***Click Cancel in the Date Stamper window.***

12. Notice in the second record from the top in the Date & Time column, Sat 10/12/2002, that the day of the week, "Sat," is entered. It is sometimes helpful in cases to know the day of the week that a particular event occurred. CaseMap does this automatically for you. When you enter a date (e.g., 10/12/2002) CaseMap automatically calculates and enters the day of the week for you if that is how the Date & Time column has been configured.

13. You can change how the Date & Time column is formatted. ***Click Tools on the menu bar, then click Options.*** The Options window should now be displayed. ***Click the Date tab.***

14. ***Click the down arrow just to the right of Style: MM/dd/yyyy.*** Notice that there are many different date formatting options available.

15. ***Click the first style, MM/dd/yyyy,*** to close the option list.

16. Notice under Style that there is a check mark in the box next to Show Day of Week. If you did not want CaseMap to show the day of the week in the Date & Time column, you could click in the check box to turn the feature off.

17. ***Click Cancel on the Options menu.***

18. Notice in the twelfth record down from the top that a date range is listed (Fri 01/09/2004 to Wed 01/21/2004). CaseMap is very flexible and can even handle date ranges. Date ranges are sorted by the first date in the range. This is a very useful feature because witnesses often do not remember exact dates or events that happened over a certain range of dates.

19. ***Click in the third record in the Fact Text column where it says "Many legal industry products include a 'Send to CaseMap' feature..."*** Notice that the cell expanded so that you could read the full text in the cell. This is CaseMap's auto-sizing feature.

20. ***Click anywhere outside of the cell.*** The cell will collapse back to its normal size.

21. ***Click the seventh record down from the top (William Lang meets Philip Hawkins while touring Converse Chemical Labs plant in Bakersfield).*** Notice that there is a paper clip just to the left of the date 11/25/02. The paper clip means that there is a file linked to this fact.

22. ***Click the paper clip icon just to the left of 11/25/02 in the seventh record down from the top. Then, point to the P001401 file (this is a PDF file).*** As long as you have Adobe Reader or some other PDF file reader, you should see an email from Philip Hawkins to William Lang.

23. ***Click the Close icon (a red box with a white "X") in the P001401 window.***

24. Notice in the seventh record from the top in the Fact Text column, where it says "William Lang meets Philip Hawkins," that "William Lang," "Philip Hawkins," and "Converse Chemical Labs" have small dotted lines under them. The dotted lines mean that they are in the database. Lang and Hawkins are listed as persons and Converse Chemical Labs is listed as an organization.

25. ***Click in the seventh record from the top in the Fact Text column where it says "William Lang meets Philip Hawkins."*** Notice that once you click on the cell it says "LangW meets HawkinsP while touring CCL plant." LangW, Hawkins P and CCL are short names for William Lang, Philip Hawkins and Converse Chemical Labs. The reason that short names are critical in a database is that there are many times in a case where someone is referred to by a nickname, a first name but no last name, initials, etc. If one person was referred to in all of these different ways it would make it difficult to search for anything. Short names standardize names (they actually can apply to any Object in CaseMap) so that all names that refer to the same person are entered exactly the same.

26. Notice that the third column in the Facts spreadsheet is Source(s). The Sources column allows you to enter where the information came from. Notice that in the seventh record down from the top in the Sources column it says Deposition of William Lang, 25:14; this is a reference to that deposition at page 25, line 14. This is very important because in a summary judgment motion, for example, you must include a citation for every fact in the motion. Also, during trial, when a witness contradicts what he or she previously said in a deposition, if the citation is shown for the page in the deposition where the prior testimony is recorded, the attorney can read the prior testimony from the deposition and impeach the witness.

27. The fourth column in the Facts spreadsheet is the Key column, which classifies facts as "key," or particularly important, to the case. This field allows a legal professional to quickly see whether a specific fact is particularly important to the case. You can also sort on key facts, and thus see all at once the facts in the case that are the most important. This keeps legal professionals from forgetting important evidence.

28. ***Right-click the word Key at the top of the fourth column.*** Then, ***click Sort Descending.***

29. Notice that all of the facts that have a check mark in the Key column have now been sorted and are at the top of the screen. This allows you to see all of the key facts in the case at one time. When you have hundreds of facts in a case this can be very helpful.

30. To sort the facts by date (the way it was before the sort on key facts), ***right-click the word Date & Time at the top of the first column. Then, click Sort Ascending.*** Notice that the Fact spreadsheet is now sorted the way it was previously.

31. Look carefully at the Date & Time header. Notice that there is a small, faint outline of a triangle pointing up. Whenever you see the triangle in a column header it means that column is what the spreadsheet is being sorted on. In addition, a triangle pointing up means that the sort is ascending (A to Z), and a triangle pointing down means the sort is descending (Z to A).

32. The fifth column in the Facts spreadsheet says Status +. ***Click the word Undisputed in the ninth record down from the top*** (01/??/03 – William Lang offers Philip Hawkins Sales Manager position...) ***in the Status + column. Then, click the down arrow next to Undisputed.*** A list of options is now displayed.

33. The list of options allows you to identify whether the fact is undisputed, disputed by opposition, disputed by us, unsure, or prospective. A prospective fact is one that you would like to be true, but that you need to develop a source for.

34. ***Click Undisputed*** to leave the status unchanged and to close the option list.

35. The sixth column in the Facts spreadsheet is the Linked Issues column. This is where you can connect or link a specific fact in a case to an issue. This is very helpful when you are making legal arguments about specific legal causes of action or legal issues because you can display only the facts that are related to the legal issue you are addressing.

36. ***Click the ninth record down from the top*** (01/??/2003 — William Lang offers Philip Hawkins Sales Manager position…) ***in the Linked Issues column.***

37. ***Then, right-click anywhere in the selected cell, and click Link Assistant.*** A list of legal issues, is now displayed; to delete the current issue, click on another issue. To add another issue, type a comma after the first issue, and then right-click and select another issue.

38. ***Click on Retaliation*** to keep the selection.

39. Suppose, for example, that you are writing a summary judgment motion and you would like to see all of the facts regarding the issue of retaliation.

40. ***Point to the word Retaliation in the ninth record down from the top.*** Then, ***click the Filter by Selection icon on the toolbar.*** (Remember that you can place your mouse pointer over any icon for a second and the name will be displayed). The Filter by Selection icon looks like a funnel with a lightning bolt next to it.

41. A small LexisNexis Case Map window should appear, stating that the issue you selected has sub-issues and asking whether you want to include the sub-issues in the search. ***Click No.*** Notice that only the facts with "retaliation" somewhere in the Linked Issues are listed.

42. To cancel the filter, ***click the Cancel Filter/Tag icon on the toolbar.*** (It looks like a funnel with a red circle and has a white "X" in the middle of the circle).

43. The screen should now return to what it looked like before the filter. Using the Filter by Selection tool you can click a cell and point to the Filter by Selection icon (or right-click the cell and select Filter by Selection), and CaseMap will then search and retrieve the item in the cell you selected.

44. Now, suppose you are writing a summary judgment motion and you want to see all of the facts in chronological order, but you would like the undisputed facts tagged or marked so you can easily identify them.

45. ***Click the word Undisputed in the ninth record down from the top*** (William Lang offers Philip Hawkins Sales Manager position……) ***in the fifth column*** (Status +).

46. Then, ***click the Tag by Selection icon on the toolbar.*** (It looks like a red vertical oval with a lightning bolt next to it and it is just to the right of the Filter by Selection icon). Alternatively, you could ***right-click the same cell and select Tag by Selection.*** Notice in the far left column that there are now red vertical ovals ("tags") next to every cell that has Undisputed in the Status + column.

47. To cancel the tag, ***click the Cancel Filter/Tag icon on the toolbar.***

48. The tags should now be gone.

This concludes Lesson 2. To exit CaseMap, ***click File on the menu bar, then click Exit, and then click OK*** to acknowledge the need to back up your files (if it asks), or go to Lesson 3.

INTERMEDIATE

LESSON 3: WORKING WITH THE OBJECTS SPREADSHEET

This lesson introduces you to the CaseMap Objects spreadsheet, including entering objects, executing primary and secondary sorts, expanding and contracting column widths, what the columns mean in the Objects spreadsheet, the different views in the Objects spreadsheet, and how to use the Objects spreadsheet to its full potential.

If you did not exit CaseMap after Lesson 2, then skip Steps 1–5 and go directly to Step 6.

1. Start Windows. Then, ***double-click on the LexisNexis CaseMap 7 icon on the desktop, or click the Start button on the Windows desktop, point to Programs or All Programs, point to the LexisNexis CaseMap Suite, and then point and click on LexisNexis CaseMap 7.*** LexisNexis CaseMap 7 will then start.

2. When you start CaseMap you will see a small window in the middle of the screen that says "CaseMap" with some additional information about a grace period. ***Click Continue in the CaseMap window.*** CaseMap will then start, with several options listed to the right of the screen.

3. Your screen should now look similar to CaseMap Exhibit 1. The Getting Started task pane should be displayed on the right side of the screen. Under "Open the example case," ***click*** **Hawkins v. Anstar**.

4. The Case Log On window should now be displayed. ***Click the down arrow icon to the right of Staff Member: Chris Attorney. Click Dave Paralegal and then click OK.***

5. CaseMap should put you back at the last spreadsheet you were at when you exited the program. Thus, the Facts spreadsheet for the Hawkins case should be displayed.

6. ***Click the All Objects icon*** on the left side of the screen under Main Shortcuts.

7. Notice in the header of the Object Type column that there is a "1" next to a triangle pointing up. Also notice that in the header of the Full Name column there is a "2" next to a triangle pointing up. As indicated previously, the triangle shows which columns the spreadsheet is being sorted on, and the triangle's direction (pointing up) means that it is an ascending sort. The "1" indicates the primary sort column and the "2" indicates the secondary sort column. CaseMap will first sort the spreadsheet by object (not alphabetically, however; CaseMap prioritizes objects based on Persons first, then Organizations, then Documents, etc.) and then will sort the spreadsheet by the full name field. By ***right-clicking in the header of any column,*** you can sort a spreadsheet by that column; however, if you want to do a primary and secondary sort you must use a menu option.

8. ***Click Records in the Menu Bar, and then click Advanced Sort.*** The Advanced Sort: Object window is now displayed. Notice that in the Sort By field it says "Object Type." Under that, it says "Then by," and "Full Name." Thus, using the Advanced Sort option you can create a primary, secondary, and even a third level sort. Notice that if you did not have a secondary sort, the Object Types would be sorted, but there would be no order beyond that.

9. ***Click Cancel in the Advanced Sort: Objects window.***

10. Notice the title "Objects – All Objects" just under the toolbar. Also, notice that in the first column (Object type) of the spreadsheet that there are several

different kinds of object types, including Person, Organization, Document, and others.

11. CaseMap is currently combining all of the objects into one view. This is the All Objects view. However, you can change this so that you only see Persons, or Organizations, or another object type. The reason you may want to do this is that additional fields are shown when you do this.

12. For example, notice on your screen that there is no "Type" field shown for the object type (e.g., whether the witness is a fact witness or an expert witness). When you view only the Persons object list, you will be able to see the Type column.

13. ***Click Object Types*** in the bottom left of the screen. A number of new icons are now displayed in the left portion of the screen.

14. ***Click Persons*** on the left side of the screen under Object Types.

15. The title directly under the Menu Bar should now read Objects—Persons (see CaseMap Exhibit 10). You should now only see People objects displayed on the screen. Notice that in the fourth column from the left (the "Type +" column) you can see whether the person is a fact witness or an expert witness. This column was not viewable in the All Objects view. Notice that there is a column for short name. Also, notice the Role in Case column, where you can see a short description about the role of each person in the case.

CaseMap Exhibit 10

LexisNexis® CaseMap® screen shots used with permission of LexisNexis, a division of Reed Elsevier Inc. LexisNexis is a registered trademark of Reed Elsevier Properties Inc. CaseMap is a registered trademark of LexisNexis Courtlink, Inc.

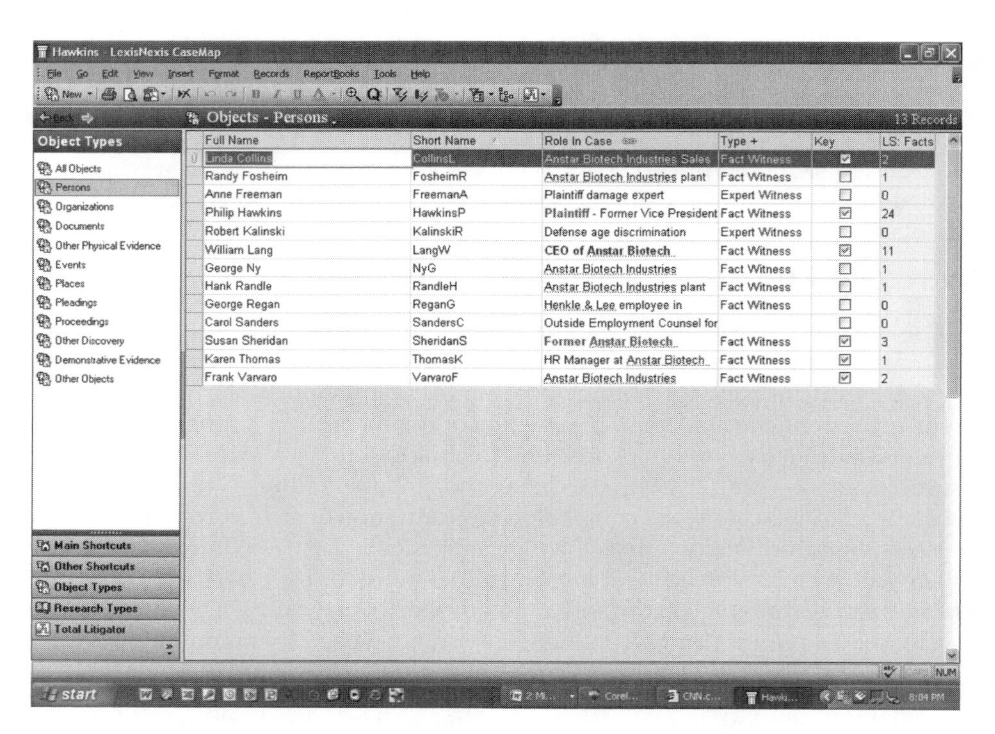

16. The Objects – Persons view also has a key column so you can identify whether a person is a key player in the case.

17. Notice that there is a column called LS: Facts. LS stands for Linked Summary. The fourth record down from the top is Philip Hawkins. Notice in the LS:Facts column that he was referenced in twenty-four separate Fact records. Any time LS is used in a column it is a calculation by CaseMap, so you cannot type information in it.

18. ***Click the Documents icon*** on the left side of the screen under Object Types. The Objects – Documents view should now be displayed. *Note:* You can also access the Objects – Documents view from the Main Shortcuts window.

19. Notice that the first and second columns are called "Bates—Begin" and "Bates—End." Bates numbers are important because they allow you to track and find documents numerically (assuming that every document in the case has a Bates number).

20. ***Click the second record from the top*** (Hawkins Letter of 8/2/2005) ***in the Type + column.*** Then, ***click the down arrow icon next to Letter.*** The box lists document types, including Contract, Deposition, E-mail, Internal memo, Letter, and Performance Review.

21. ***Click Letter*** to keep the current selection.

22. Scroll to the right using the right cursor key on the keyboard or ***use the horizontal scroll bar.*** There are columns for the document author(s) and recipients. Also, there is a Linked Issues column for linking the document to a specific legal issue, an LS: Sourced Facts – Linked Summary column for the number of times the document was mentioned in the Facts spreadsheet, and linked file so you can see the actual image, or full text, of the document and evaluation columns.

23. ***Click the Organizations icon*** on the left side of the screen under Object Types. The Objects – Organizations view should now be displayed. The Organization columns are similar to other object columns.

24. ***Click the All Objects icon*** to the left side of the screen to display all of the objects again.

25. ***Click Main Shortcuts, and then click Facts*** to return to the Fact spreadsheet.

This concludes Lesson 3. To exit CaseMap, ***click File on the menu bar, then click Exit, and then click OK*** to acknowledge the need to back up your files (if it asks), or go to Lesson 4.

LESSON 4: WORKING WITH THE ISSUES SPREADSHEET

This lesson introduces you to the CaseMap Issues spreadsheet, including how to enter new issues, promote and demote issues, and delete issues.

If you did not exit CaseMap after Lesson 3, then skip Steps 1–5 and go directly to Step 6.

1. Start Windows. Then, ***double-click the LexisNexis CaseMap 7 icon on the desktop, or click the Start button on the Windows desktop, point to Programs or All Programs, point to the LexisNexis CaseMap Suite, and then click LexisNexis CaseMap 7.*** LexisNexis CaseMap 7 will then be start.

2. When you start CaseMap you will see a small window in the middle of the screen that says "CaseMap" with some additional information about a grace period. ***Click Continue in the CaseMap window.*** CaseMap will then start, with several options listed to the right of the screen.

3. Your screen should now look similar to CaseMap Exhibit 1. The Getting Started task pane should be displayed on the right side of the screen. Under "Open the example case," ***click*** **Hawkins v. Anstar**.

4. The Case Log On window should now be displayed. ***Click the down arrow icon to the right of Staff Member: Chris Attorney. Click Dave Paralegal and then click OK.***

5. CaseMap should put you back at the last spreadsheet you were at when you exited the program. Thus, the Facts spreadsheet for the Hawkins case should be displayed.

6. ***Click the Issues icon*** on the left side of the screen under Main Shortcuts. The Issues spreadsheet should be displayed. The Issues spreadsheet is where you enter the legal issues that the case will revolve around.

7. Notice that in the Full Name column there are issues with whole numbers (e.g., 1, 2), and then there are sub-issues with decimals (e.g., 2.1, 2.2, etc.). CaseMap allows you to categorize whether an issue is a stand-alone issue, or is part of a more detailed issue.

8. ***Click the first record, 1 Wrongful Termination, in the Full Name column.***

9. On the toolbar there is an icon called "New." Directly next to this icon is a down arrow. ***Click the Down icon immediately to the right of the word "New" on the toolbar.*** When you click the down arrow, you can select the type of item you want to enter, such as New Fact, New Object, etc. *Note*: If you had clicked the word "New" instead of the Down icon next to New, CaseMap would have assumed you wanted to add a new issue and placed you directly in a New Issue row.

10. *Click "New Issue."*

11. A blank record with the number "2" has been created. Just to the left of the "2," notice that there is a line with an up arrow, right arrow, and down arrow. ***Point to the up arrow, and notice that it displays Move Up. Click the up arrow.*** The entry has now been moved up and is listed as 1.

12. Now, notice that the line next to the "1" only has a down arrow. ***Point to the down arrow, and notice that it displays Move Down. Click the down arrow.*** It is back to number 2.

13. ***Point to the right arrow next to 2,*** and notice that it displays Demote. ***Click the right arrow next to 2.*** It is now 1.1. Using these arrows, you can control where each issue in the Issues list is displayed.

14. ***Click Outline on the menu bar.*** A list of options is displayed, including the ability to promote, demote, move up, and move down an issue in the outline hierarchy.

15. Press the **[ESC]** key to make the menu list go away.

16. With the pointer still on 1.1, type **Against Public Policy** and press the **[TAB]** key. Notice that CaseMap has entered AgainstPublicPolicy in the Short Name Field. It is best to keep all Short Name entries as short as possible.

17. Press the **[DELETE]** key, type **AgPubPolicy,** and then press the **[ENTER]** key.

18. To delete the issue, ***click the Delete Record icon on the toolbar.*** (It looks like a red script "X" with a red left arrow next to it).

19. ***Click "Yes"*** when CaseMap asks if you are sure if you want to delete this issue. The issue is now deleted.

20. ***Click Main Shortcuts and then click Facts*** to return to the Fact spreadsheet.

This concludes Lesson 4. To exit CaseMap, ***click File on the menu bar, then click Exit, and then click OK*** to acknowledge the need to back up your files (if it asks), or go to Lesson 5.

LESSON 5: WORKING WITH ADVANCED FEATURES

This lesson introduces you to some advanced features in CaseMap, including using the View CaseWide command, hiding columns, inserting columns, adjusting rows, moving columns, printing and viewing reports, adding objects on the fly, hiding shortcuts, and viewing the detail of a record.

If you did not exit CaseMap after Lesson 4, then skip Steps 1–5 and go directly to Step 6.

1. Start Windows. Then, ***double-click the LexisNexis CaseMap 7 icon on the desktop, or click the Start button on the Windows desktop, point to Programs or All Programs, point to the LexisNexis CaseMap Suite, and then click LexisNexis CaseMap 7.*** LexisNexis CaseMap 7 will then start.

2. When you start CaseMap you will see a small window in the middle of the screen that says "CaseMap" with some additional information about a grace period. ***Click Run in the CaseMap window.*** CaseMap will then start, with several options listed to the right of the screen.

3. Your screen should now look similar to CaseMap Exhibit 1. The Getting Started task pane should be displayed on the right side of the screen. Under "Open the example case," *click* **Hawkins v. Anstar**.

4. The Case Log On window should now be displayed. ***Click the down arrow icon to the right of Staff Member: Chris Attorney. Click Dave Paralegal and then click OK.***

5. CaseMap should put you back at the last spreadsheet you were at when you exited the program. Thus, the Facts spreadsheet for the Hawkins case should be displayed.

6. ***Click the View CaseWide icon on the toolbar*** (it looks like a graph — see CaseMap Exhibit 11).

7. The CaseWide view allows you to see a timeline of when the facts of the case occurred. Notice in the right corner of the graph that the "Y" is selected (see CaseMap Exhibit 11). The current graph in the CaseWide view is by year. Notice that the largest number of events occurred in 2005 (see CaseMap Exhibit 11).

8. ***Click M to the right of the CaseWide graph.*** CaseMap responds by displaying the same data on a monthly basis.

9. ***Using the horizontal scroll bar under the CaseWide graph, scroll to the right.*** You can see that the largest number of events occurred in October 2002 and July and August 2005.

10. ***Click "D" to the right of the CaseWide graph.*** CaseMap responds by displaying the same data on a daily basis.

11. ***Use the horizontal scroll bar under the CaseWide graph to scroll to the right until you see some blue bars showing daily activity.***

CaseMap Exhibit 11

LexisNexis® CaseMap® screen shots used with the permission of LexisNexis, a division of Reed Elsevier Inc. LexisNexis is a registered trademark of Reed Elsevier Properties Inc. CaseMap is a registered trademark of LexisNexis Courtlink, Inc.

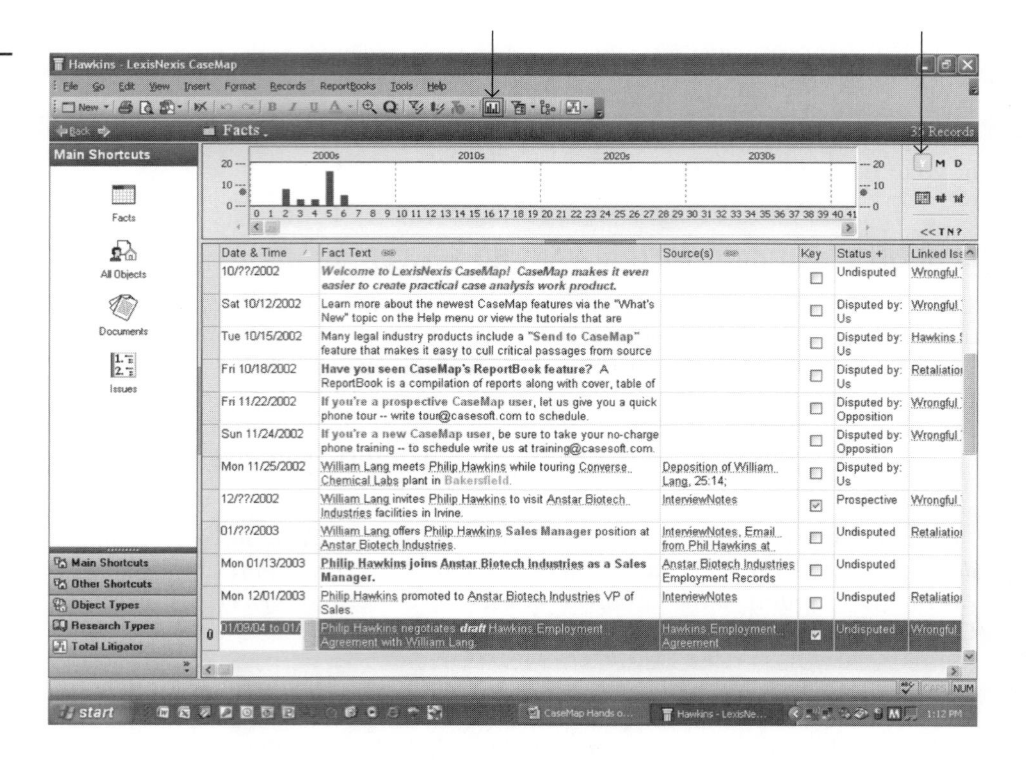

12. The CaseWide view gives you an overview of the general timing involved in a case.

13. ***Click the View CaseWide icon on the toolbar*** to close the CaseWide view.

14. ***Scroll to the right until you see the Linked Issues column.*** Suppose that this column is no longer important and is just taking up space in the spreadsheet view. ***Right-click the header of the Linked Issues column, then click Hide Field.***

15. ***Scroll back to the right and notice that the column can no longer be seen on the spreadsheet.*** *Note*: The data in the column/database has not been deleted; it has just been hidden and is no longer in the current view.

16. ***Right-click the header of the Status + column, then click Insert Field.***

17. The Selected Field(s) to Insert window should now be displayed. Notice that a number of fields are listed, including the field that was just deleted (Linked Issues). You can use the Insert Field command to customize the views of your spreadsheets and to add other columns that include additional data. ***Scroll down and click Linked Issues, then click OK.***

18. ***Scroll to the right to see the Linked Issues column. If the Linked Issues column is to left of the "Status +" column, click the "Linked Issues" column title and drag it to the right of the "Status +" column.*** The column has now been added back to the Facts spreadsheet view.

19. ***Scroll back to the left to see the first columns of the Facts spreadsheet.***

20. ***Click Format on the menu bar, click Row Height, and then click "6."*** You can now see more detail for each cell. Changing the row height only changes the height for a specific spreadsheet, so if you change the Facts spreadsheet row height, it does not change the Object spreadsheet.

21. ***Click Format on the menu bar, then click Row Height, and then click "2"*** to restore the height to two lines.

22. ***Click File and then click Print Preview*** to see how the Facts spreadsheet would look printed. ***Click Print*** if you would like to print the report ***or click Close*** to close the Print Preview window.

23. ***Click File and Page Setup, then click the Report Options tab.*** Sometimes the spreadsheets are too long to print on one page, but by changing the size of the type and other options, you can manipulate the reports to print on one page. You can also hide columns to get your reports to print on one page.

24. ***Click Cancel in the Print Setup window.***

25. Suppose that you are entering a new fact in the Facts spreadsheet and you need to reference a new person. You do not need to go to the Object spreadsheet to enter it.

26. ***Click New on the toolbar.*** A new record should now be displayed at the bottom of the Facts spreadsheet.

27. In the Date & Time column, type **10/1/05** and press the **[TAB]** key. Notice that CaseMap converted the date to Sat 10/01/2005.

28. The cursor should now be in the Fact Text column of the new record. Type **John Allen admitted HawkinsP to Laketown Hospital.**

29. ***Drag the mouse over the name John Allen until it is highlighted. Then, right-click in the highlighted area and click Add Object.*** The Add Object window is now displayed. Everything in the Add Object window is correct, but if it were not, it could be edited.

30. ***Click OK in the Add Object window.*** The name "AllenJ" should now have a dotted line underneath it showing that it has been listed as a Person in the Object spreadsheet, and that a Short Name has been made for the person.

31. ***Click the All Objects icon*** on the left side of the screen. Notice that John Allen has been added.

32. ***Click the Role in Case column in the row for John Allen.*** Type **Doctor for Philip Hawkins,** and then ***click any cell to enter the text.***

33. ***Click Linda Collins in the second record from the top of the Objects – All Objects spreadsheet in the Full Name column. Click Records on the menu bar and then click Record Detail.*** The Object Detail window has now been displayed. Notice that you can now collect and/or view a wide variety of other information about the person, including how to contact them and other information. This is extremely helpful at trial when it is necessary to schedule witness testimony.

34. ***Click Close in the Object Detail window.***

35. ***Scroll down and click the document Hawkins Performance Review (P001357) in the Objects – All Objects spreadsheet.***

36. ***Click Records on the menu bar and then click Record Detail.*** Notice that the Object Detail window, which shows a number of additional fields about the document is displayed. ***Scroll down in the Object Detail window to see all of***

them. Some of the additional fields include Privilege, Producing Party, Trial Ex(hibit) #, and others. *Note:* Any of these additional fields that are listed can be included in the spreadsheet view at any time by ***clicking in a header and selecting Insert Field.*** For Objects, you will need to go to the specific object spreadsheet (e.g., the Objects — Documents spreadsheet and not the Objects — All Objects spreadsheet).

37. ***Click Close in the Object Detail window.***

38. ***Click Main Shortcuts and then click on Facts*** to return to the Fact spreadsheet.

This concludes Lesson 5. To exit CaseMap, ***click File on the menu bar, then click Exit, and then click OK*** to acknowledge the need to back up your files (if it asks), or go to Lesson 6.

LESSON 6: CREATING A NEW CASE

This lesson introduces you to setting up/creating a new case in CaseMap and entering new Objects, including people, organizations, and documents.

If you did not exit CaseMap after Lesson 5, then skip Steps 1–5 and go directly to Step 6.

1. Start Windows. Then, ***double-click the LexisNexis CaseMap 7 icon on the desktop, or click the Start button on the Windows desktop, point with the mouse to Programs or All Programs, point to the LexisNexis CaseMap Suite, and then click LexisNexis CaseMap 7.*** LexisNexis CaseMap 7 will then start.

2. When you start CaseMap you will see a small window in the middle of the screen that says "CaseMap" with some additional information about a grace period. ***Click Run in the CaseMap window.*** CaseMap will then start, with several options listed to the right of the screen.

3. Your screen should now look similar to CaseMap Exhibit 1. The Getting Started task pane should be displayed on the right side of the screen. Under "Open the example case," ***click*** **Hawkins v. Anstar**.

4. The Case Log On window should now be displayed. ***Click the down arrow icon to the right of Staff Member: Chris Attorney. Click Dave Paralegal and then click OK.***

5. CaseMap should put you back at the last spreadsheet you were at when you exited the program. Thus, the Facts spreadsheet for the Hawkins case should be displayed.

6. You will now create a new case. ***Click File on the menu bar and then click New.***

7. The New Case window should now be displayed. Because we will use the CaseMap Default template, ***click OK.***

8. The "Select the name and location of the new case file" window should now be displayed.

9. In the File Name box, type **Smith** and then ***click Save.*** (This will save the file in the default directory.)

10. At the New Case Set Up window under Staff Member Name, type **Dave Paralegal** in the Org. Name field, type **Johnson Beck and Taylor**; in the Case Name field, type **Smith v. EZ Pest Control;** and then ***click OK.***

11. At the LexisNexis CaseMap window, ***click "Yes"*** to show that this is correct.

12. CaseMap will then tell you that the password has been set to <blank>. ***Click OK.***

13. Read the information in the New Case Tips window. Notice that CaseMap suggests that you begin by entering. Persons information in the Object spreadsheet to build a cast of characters in the case. (Only enter information such as name and role in cases now, and add detail later.) The application will suggest that you enter the core issues in the case next, and finally will suggest that you begin entering the facts in the case, even facts that are in dispute.

14. ***Click Close in the upper right of the New Case Tips window.***

15. You should now be at the Objects – All Objects spreadsheet and the pointer should be in a blank record.

16. ***Click the down arrow next to Other Object in the Object Type column*** (see CaseMap Exhibit 12). ***Click "Person."*** Then, press the **[TAB]** key to go to the Full Name field.

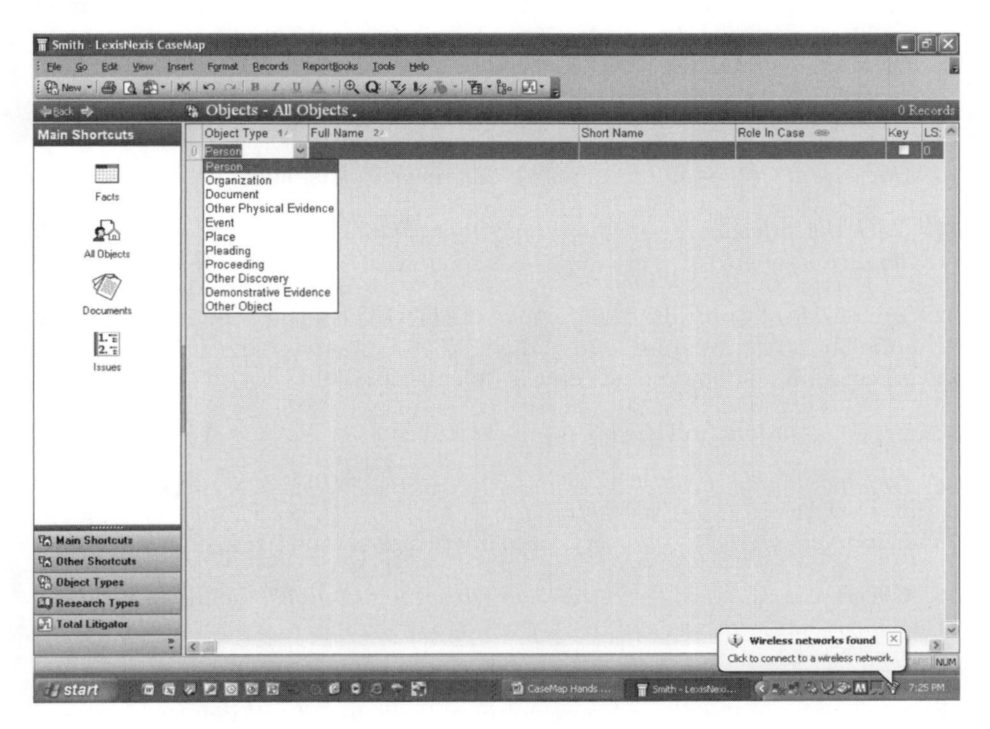

CaseMap Exhibit 12

LexisNexis® CaseMap® screen shots used with the permission of LexisNexis, a division of Reed Elsevier Inc. LexisNexis is a registered trademark of Reed Elsevier Properties Inc. CaseMap is a registered trademark of LexisNexis Courtlink, Inc.

17. Type **Judy Smith** and then press the **[TAB]** key. The pointer should now be in the Short Name column. Press the **[TAB]** key to accept the default entry of SmithJ. The cursor should now be in the Role in Case field.

18. Type **Plaintiff — homeowner at house on 7788 SW 52nd Street that is full of termites** and then press the **[TAB]** key.

19. ***Double-click in the check box under Key in the Judy Smith record.***

20. ***Click New on the toolbar.*** A new blank record is displayed.

21. ***Click the down arrow next to Other Object in the Object Type column. Click "Person."*** Then, press the **[TAB]** key to go to the Full Name field.

22. Type **John Lincoln** and then press the **[TAB]** key. The pointer should now be in the Short Name column. Press the **[TAB]** key to accept the default entry of LincolnJ. The pointer should now be in the Role in Case field.

23. Type **EZ Pest Control Branch Manager and Head Inspector who inspected the property multiple times, year in and year out, over a five-year period. At all times in his written reports he indicates the house has no visible evidence of infestation from wood-destroying insects.** Then press the **[TAB]** key.

24. ***Double-click in the check box under Key in the John Lincoln record.***

25. ***Click New on the toolbar.*** A new blank record should be displayed.

26. ***Click the down arrow next to Other Object in the Object Type column. Then, click Person*** and press the **[TAB]** key to go to the Full Name field.

27. Type **Tim Stewart** and then press the **[TAB]** key. The pointer should now be in the Short Name column. Press the **[TAB]** key to accept the default entry of StewartT. The pointer should now be in the Role in Case field.

28. Type **Contractor that was hired by SmithJ to repair the immense termite damage to the house. He will testify at length about the extensive damage to the house.** Then press the **[TAB]** key.

29. ***Double-click in the check box under Key in the Tim Stewart record.***

30. ***Click New on the toolbar.*** A new blank record is displayed.

31. ***Click the down arrow next to Other Object in the Object Type column. Click Organization.*** Then, press the **[TAB]** key to go to the Full Name field.

32. Type **EZ Pest Control** and then press the **[TAB]** key. The pointer should now be in the Short Name column. Press the **[TAB]** key to accept the default entry of EPC. The pointer should now be in the Role in Case field.

33. Type **Defendant** and then press the **[TAB]** key.

34. ***Double-click in the check box under Key in the EZ Pest Control record.***

35. ***Click New on the toolbar.*** A new blank record should be displayed.

36. ***Click the down arrow next to Other Object in the Object Type column. Click "Document"*** and press the **[TAB]** key to go to the Full Name field.

37. Type **Termite Agreement** and then press the **[TAB]** key. The pointer should now be in the Short Name column. Press the **[TAB]** key to accept the default entry of TermiteAgreement. The pointer should now be in the Role in Case field.

38. Type **Contract between SmithJ and EPC for termite inspections and preventative maintenance** and then press the **[TAB]** key. (*Note:* If you decide to type "Judy Smi…" instead of "SmithJ," that is fine, but after you get "Judy Smi" typed, CaseMap will display a bar that says "SmithJ." Press the **[ENTER]** key to accept the short name.

39. ***Double-click in the check box under Key in the Termite Agreement record.***

40. ***Click Main Shortcuts and then click Facts*** to return to the Fact spreadsheet, which is blank.

This concludes Lesson 6. To exit CaseMap, ***click File on the menu bar, then click Exit, and then click OK*** to acknowledge the need to back up your files (if it asks), or go to Lesson 7.

LESSON 7: ENTERING ISSUES AND FACTS IN A NEW CASE

This lesson introduces you to entering issues and facts in a new case and automatically copying data from one cell to another.

If you did not exit CaseMap after Lesson 1, then skip Steps 1–5 and go directly to Step 6.

1. Start Windows. Then, ***double-click on the LexisNexis CaseMap 7 icon on the desktop, or click the Start button on the Windows desktop, point to Programs or All Programs, point to the LexisNexis CaseMap Suite, and then click LexisNexis CaseMap 7.*** LexisNexis CaseMap 7 will then start.

2. When you start CaseMap you will see a small window in the middle of the screen that says "CaseMap" with some additional information about a grace period. ***Click Continue in the CaseMap window.*** CaseMap will then start, with several options listed to the right of the screen.

3. Your screen should now look similar to CaseMap Exhibit 1. The Getting Started task pane should be displayed on the right side of the screen. Under "Open a case," ***click Smith.cm7.***

4. The Case Log On window should now be displayed. ***Dave Paralegal should be the default selection, so click OK.***

5. CaseMap should put you back at the Facts spreadsheet.

6. ***Click the Issues icon*** on the left side of the screen. The Issues spreadsheet should now be displayed and the pointer should be in a blank record.

7. In the Full Name column, type **Breach of Contract** and then press the **[TAB]** key.

8. Press the **[TAB]** key to accept the default entry of BreachOfContract in the Short Name field. Press the **[TAB]** key until the pointer is in the Description field.

9. Type **Defendant had a maintenance contract to spray the house preventively for termites for five years prior to the discovery of extensive termite damage.**

10. ***Double-click in the check box under Key in the Breach of Contract record.***

11. Press the **[TAB]** key until you are in a new record. In the Full Name column type **Negligence** and then press the **[TAB]** key.

12. Press the **[TAB]** key to accept the default entry of Negligence in the Short Name field. Press the **[TAB]** key until the pointer is in the Description field. Type **Defendant negligently failed to discover an enormous termite colony that had done extensive damage to the house.**

13. ***Double-click in the check box under Key in the Negligence record.***

14. ***Click Facts*** on the left side of the screen. The Facts spreadsheet should now be displayed and the cursor should be in a blank record.

15. In the Date & Time column, type **01/02/2006** and then press the **[TAB]** key to go to the Fact Text field.

16. Type **SmithJ and EPC sign TermiteAgreement** and then press the **[TAB]** key to go to the Source(s) column.

17. Type **Ter** and then press the **[ENTER]** key to accept the "Termite Agreement" short name.

18. Press the **[TAB]** key. The pointer should now be in the Material+ field.

19. ***Click the down arrow in the Material+ field. Then, click Yes,*** and then press the **[TAB]** key.

20. ***Click in the Status + column in the record, click the down arrow icon, and then click Undisputed.***

21. Press the **[TAB]** key.

22. ***Right-click in the Linked Issues column in the record, click Link Assistant, then click BreachOfContract.***

23. Press the **[TAB]** key. You should now be in a blank Fact record.

24. In the Date & Time column, type **5/15/2006** and then press the **[TAB]** key to go to the Fact Text field.

25. Type **LincolnJ completes full termite inspection of house** and then press the **[TAB]** key to go to the Source(s) column.

26. Type **Deposition of SmithJ, 32:18 and Deposition of LincolnJ, 45:9** and then press the **[TAB]** key.

27. The pointer should now be in the Material+ column. ***Click the down arrow and click Yes.*** Then, press the **[TAB]** key.

28. The pointer should now be in the Status + column. ***Click the down arrow icon and then click Undisputed.***

29. Press the **[TAB]** key. The pointer should now be in the Linked Issues column.

30. ***Right-click in the Linked Issues column in the record, click Link Assistant, and then click Breach of Contract.***

31. Type **;** (a semi-colon).

32. ***Right-click again in the Linked Issues column in the record, click Link Assistant, and then, click Negligence.***

33. Press the **[TAB]** key. You should now be at a blank Fact record.

34. In the Date & Time column, type **8/??/2006** and then press the **[TAB]** key to go to the Fact Text field.

35. Type **SmithJ hears noise inside the walls at night, which she later learns is termites**, and then press the **[TAB]** key to go to the Source(s) column.

36. Type **Deposition of SmithJ, 45:6**, and then press the **[TAB]** key.

37. ***Click the down arrow in the Material+ column and click Yes.*** Then, press the **[TAB]** key.

38. ***Click the down arrow in the Status+ column and then click Undisputed.***

39. Press the **[TAB]** key.

40. Press the **[CTRL]+["]** (quotation mark) keys on the keyboard. [CTRL]+["] copies the value from the cell above. Notice that "Breach of Contract, Negligence" was copied from the cell above to the current cell. Using this command you can greatly decrease your data entry time if there are a number of duplicate entries.

41. Press the **[TAB]** key. You should now be at a blank Fact record.

42. In the Date & Time column, type **10/15/2006**, then press the **[TAB]** key to go to the Fact Text field.

43. Type **StewartT inspects the house to make a bid on some repairs to the house and finds massive termite damage to the house**, then press the **[TAB]** key to go to the Source(s) column.

44. Type **Deposition of StewartT, 14:12**, then press the **[TAB]** key.

45. ***Click the down arrow in the Material+ column and click Yes.*** Then, press the **[TAB]** key.

46. ***Click the down arrow in the Status+ column and then click Undisputed.***

47. Press the **[TAB]** key.

48. Press the **[CTRL]+["]** (quotation) keys on the keyboard to copy the cell above to the current cell.

49. Then, press the **[TAB]** key. You should now be at a blank Fact record.

50. In the Date & Time column, type **11/01/2006**, and then press the **[TAB]** key to go to the Fact Text field.

51. Type **SmithJ hires another pest control service to look at the property and the new pest control service confirms massive termite damage**, and then press the **[TAB]** key to go to the Source(s) column.

52. Type **Deposition of SmithJ, 22:7**, and then press the **[TAB]** key.

53. ***Click the down arrow in the Material+ column and click Yes.*** Then, press the **[TAB]** key.

54. ***Click the down arrow icon in the Status+ column, and then click Undisputed.***

55. Press the **[TAB]** key.

56. Press the **[CTRL]+["]** (quotation) keys on the keyboard to copy the cell above to the current cell.

57. Press the **[TAB]** key. You should now be at a blank Fact record.

58. In the Date & Time column, type **07/15/2006** and then press the **[TAB]** key to go to the Fact Text field.

59. Type **LincolnJ attempts to inspect property; sees SmithJ in the house, but SmithJ will not open the door. LincolnJ is not able to inspect the house.** Then press the **[TAB]** key to go to the Source(s) column.

60. Type **Deposition of LincolnJ, 52:20**, and then press the **[TAB]** key.

61. ***Click the down arrow in the Material+ column and click Yes.*** Then, press the **[TAB]** key.

62. ***Click the down arrow in the Status+ column and then click Disputed by Us.***

63. Press the **[TAB]** key.

64. Press the **[CTRL]+["]** (quotation) keys on the keyboard to copy the cell above to the current cell.

This concludes Lesson 7. To exit CaseMap, ***click File the menu bar, then click Exit, and then click OK*** to acknowledge the need to back up your files (if it asks), or go to Lesson 8.

LESSON 8: USING CASEMAP FOR A NEW CASE

This lesson introduces using CaseMap for a new case, including printing reports, viewing case data in a variety of ways, exporting to a PDF file, exporting a summary judgment report to a word processor, using the CaseWide tool, and searching/filtering data. This lesson assumes that you have completed all of the prior exercises, and therefore step-by-step directions are not necessary.

If you did not exit CaseMap after Lesson 7, then skip Steps 1–5 and go directly to Step 6.

1. Start Windows. Then, ***double-click the LexisNexis CaseMap 7 icon on the desktop, or click the Start button on the Windows desktop, point to Programs or All Programs, point to the LexisNexis CaseMap Suite, and then click LexisNexis CaseMap 7.*** LexisNexis CaseMap 7 will then start.

2. When you start CaseMap you will see a small window in the middle of the screen that says "CaseMap" with some additional information about a grace period. ***Click Run in the CaseMap window.*** CaseMap will then start, with several options listed to the right of the screen.

3. Your screen should now look similar to CaseMap Exhibit 1. The Getting Started task pane should be displayed on the right side of the screen. Under "Open a case," ***click Smith.cm7.***

4. The Case Log On window should now be displayed. ***Dave Paralegal should be the default selection, so click OK.***

5. CaseMap should put you back at the Facts spreadsheet.

6. ***Right-click in the header of the Date & Time field in the Facts spreadsheet, and sort the column in descending order.***

7. ***Print the Fact spreadsheet (click File on the menu bar, and then click Print) or view it on the screen (click File on the menu bar, and then click Print Preview).***

8. ***Click the record that has "Disputed by Us" in the Status + column, and filter the selection*** using the icon on the toolbar or by ***right-clicking on the entry.***

9. ***Cancel the filter using the Cancel Filter/Tag icon on the toolbar.***

10. In the Issues spreadsheet, move the LS: Facts column to the fourth column ***by clicking in the column header and dragging it to the new location.***

11. Print a report that contains only Persons in the Object spreadsheet. First, ***click Object Types in the lower left side of the screen; then click Persons on the upper left side of the screen; then, click File on the menu bar, and finally, click Print).***

12. Print a report of All Objects using the Objects — All Objects spreadsheet view.

13. ***Return to the Facts spreadsheet on the left side of the screen.***

14. Using CaseMap you can automatically print any CaseMap report to a PDF file that can then be emailed to a client. ***Click the Print to PDF icon on the toolbar (the fourth icon from the left). Then, click Print to PDF.***

15. At the Save to PDF window, ***click Save to save the document to the default directory with the default file name.***

16. There should now be a window displayed that says "The report has been saved as an Adobe PDF file. Do you want to open it now?" ***Click "Yes."***

17. If Adobe Reader is installed on your computer the Fact Chronology report should now be displayed.

18. ***Click the Close icon (a red box with a white "X") in the Adobe Reader window.***

19. You will now print the Case Summary Report. This is a report that prints out each of the key spreadsheets automatically. ***Click ReportBooks on the menu bar. Next, point to Case Summary and point to Preview.*** CaseMap will then display a window that states that some spreadsheets are empty. ***Click Yes to indicate that you want to continue.***

20. ***Page down through the report, and when you are done, click Close.***

21. CaseMap has a convenient feature specifically related to summary judgment motions. CaseMap can export a word-processing file directly to Word or Word-Perfect that will assist in creating a summary judgment motion or response. In the Facts spreadsheet, ***click File on the menu bar, point to Send to, then click Summary Judgment Report.***

22. ***In the Summary Judgment Report window, read the text and then click Next.***

23. ***In the Summary Judgment Report window regarding confirming the report settings, click either Word, WordPerfect, or HTML and then click Finish.***

24. Notice that a table has been created showing all of the facts that relate to each legal issue, including the citation for each factual reference.

25. ***After reading the document, close the word-processing file.***

26. ***Click the View CaseWide icon on the toolbar. (It looks like a chart.)***

27. ***Click "M" (for Month) in the upper right of the screen.***

28. ***Click the View CaseWide icon on the toolbar to make the CaseWide view disappear.***

29. Suppose that you are assisting your supervising attorney in preparing for the deposition of John Lincoln and that you would like to retrieve all of the Fact records that have his name.

30. ***Right-click any occurrence of John Lincoln's name in the Fact spreadsheet.*** Notice that the first option in the menu is Selection: LincolnJ. ***Click Filter by Selection just below Selection: LincolnJ.***

31. Notice that only the records for John Lincoln are shown. ***Click Cancel Filter/Tag on the toolbar. (It looks like a funnel next to a red ball.)***

32. If you would like additional training on CaseMap, ***click Help on the menu bar and then click CaseMap Webinar Center***. Several free "webinars" (web seminars) are available on the Internet that will further assist you in learning CaseMap.

33. This concludes Lesson 8. To exit CaseMap, ***click File on the menu bar, then click Exit, and then click OK*** to acknowledge the need to back up your files (if it asks).

This concludes the CaseMap exercises.

HANDS-ON EXERCISES

LEXIS NEXIS TIMEMAP

I. Introduction – Read This!

LexisNexis TimeMap is a litigation support analytical tool that creates time maps or timelines. The LexisNexis TimeMap demonstration version is a full working version of the program (with a few limitations). The program demonstration version times out 120 days after installation. This means that the program will only work for 120 days after you install it. So, it is highly recommended that you do not install the program on your computer until you are actually ready to go through the Hands-on Exercises and learn the program. When you are ready to install the program, follow the instructions below.

II. Using the LexisNexis TimeMap Hands-on Exercises

The LexisNexis TimeMap Hands-on Exercises are easy to use and contain step-by-step instructions. Each lesson builds on the previous exercise, so please complete the Hands-on Exercises in order. TimeMap comes with sample data, so you should be able to utilize many features of the program.

III. Installation Instructions

Below are step by step instructions for loading the LexisNexis TimeMap demonstration version on your computer.

1. *Insert Disk 1 supplied with this text into your computer.*

2. When prompted with "What do you want Windows to do?" select "Open folder to view files using Windows Explorer," then click OK. If your computer does not automatically recognize that you have inserted a CD, double-click the My Computer icon, then double-click the drive where Disk 1 is.

3. *Double-click the TimeMap4.exe file.* This will start the TimeMap installation wizard.

4. *Click Next (see TimeMap Installation Exhibit 1).*

5. The screen shown in TimeMap Installation Exhibit 2 should now be displayed.

6. *Click Yes to agree to the License Agreement.*

7. The screen shown in TimeMap Installation Exhibit 3 should now be displayed.

8. *Click Next.*

9. The screen shown in TimeMap Installation Exhibit 4 should now be displayed.

10. *Click Next to install TimeMap in the default directory.*

11. The screen shown in TimeMap Installation Exhibit 5 should now be displayed.

TimeMap Installation Exhibit 1

LexisNexis and the Knowledge Burst logo are registered trademarks of Reed Elsevier Properties Inc. HotDocs is a registered trademark of Matthew Bender & Company. TimeMap and CaseMap are registered trademarks of LexisNexis Courtlink, Inc. Used with the permission of LexisNexis.

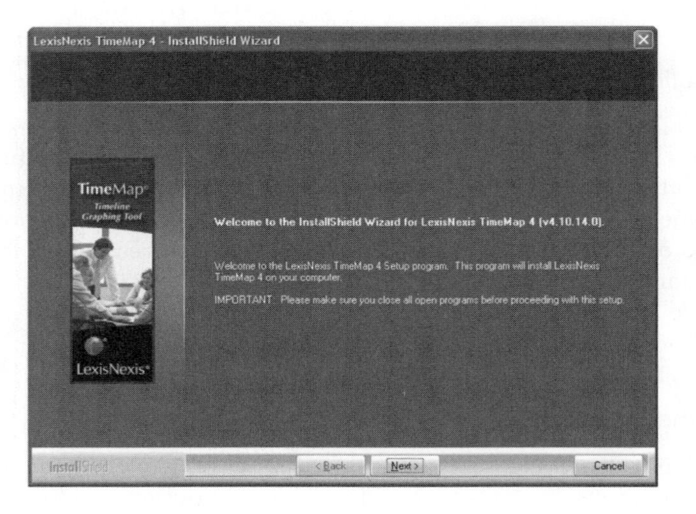

TimeMap Installation Exhibit 2

LexisNexis and the Knowledge Burst logo are registered trademarks of Reed Elsevier Properties Inc. HotDocs is a registered trademark of Matthew Bender & Company. TimeMap and CaseMap are registered trademarks of LexisNexis Courtlink, Inc. Used with the permission of LexisNexis.

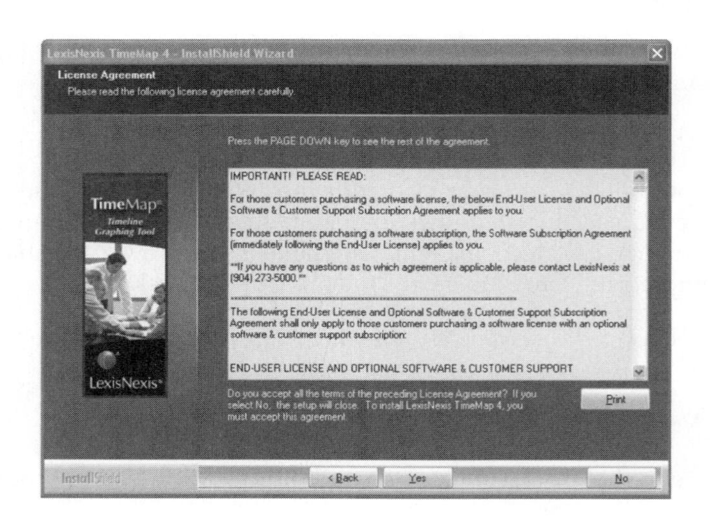

12. *Click Next.*

13. The screen shown in TimeMap Installation Exhibit 6 should now be displayed.

14. When the program is through copying files, the screen shown in TimeMap Installation Exhibit 7 should be displayed.

15. *Click Finish.*

16. The screen shown in TimeMap Installation Exhibit 8 should now be displayed.

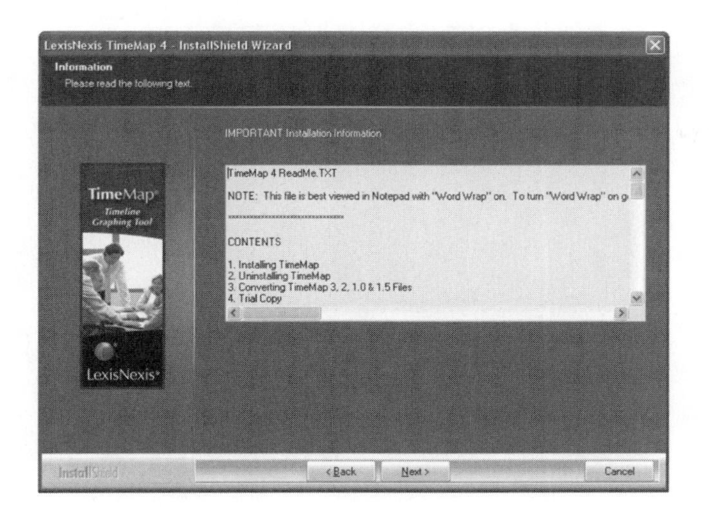

TimeMap Installation Exhibit 3

LexisNexis and the Knowledge Burst logo are registered trademarks of Reed Elsevier Properties Inc. HotDocs is a registered trademark of Matthew Bender & Company. TimeMap and CaseMap are registered trademarks of LexisNexis Courtlink, Inc. Used with the permission of LexisNexis.

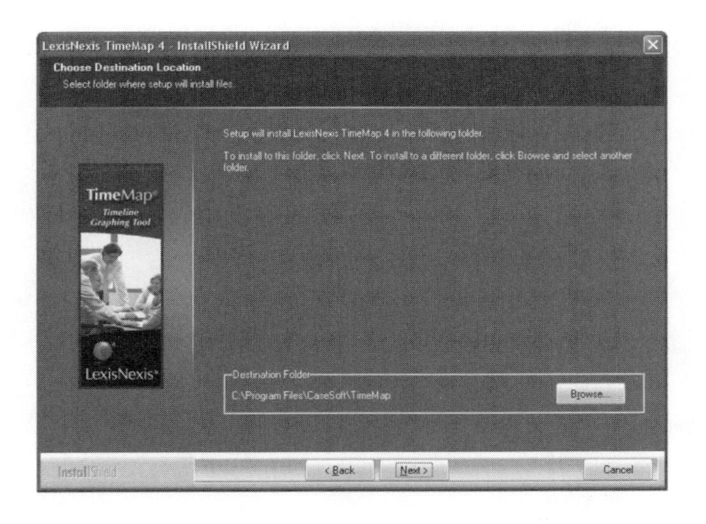

TimeMap Installation Exhibit 4

LexisNexis and the Knowledge Burst logo are registered trademarks of Reed Elsevier Properties Inc. HotDocs is a registered trademark of Matthew Bender & Company. TimeMap and CaseMap are registered trademarks of LexisNexis Courtlink, Inc. Used with the permission of LexisNexis.

17. *Click Continue.*

18. The screen shown in TimeMap Installation Exhibit 9 should now be displayed.

19. The installation of TimeMap is now complete. ***Click File on the Menu Bar and then click on Exit.***

IV. INSTALLATION TECHNICAL SUPPORT

LexisNexis TimeMap is a licensed product of LexisNexis. If you have problems installing the demonstration version of LexisNexis TimeMap from the CD-ROM included with this text, please contact Thomson Delmar Learning Technical Support at (800)477–3692.

TimeMap Installation Exhibit 5

LexisNexis and the Knowledge Burst logo are registered trademarks of Reed Elsevier Properties Inc. HotDocs is a registered trademark of Matthew Bender & Company. TimeMap and CaseMap are registered trademarks of LexisNexis Courtlink, Inc. Used with the permission of LexisNexis.

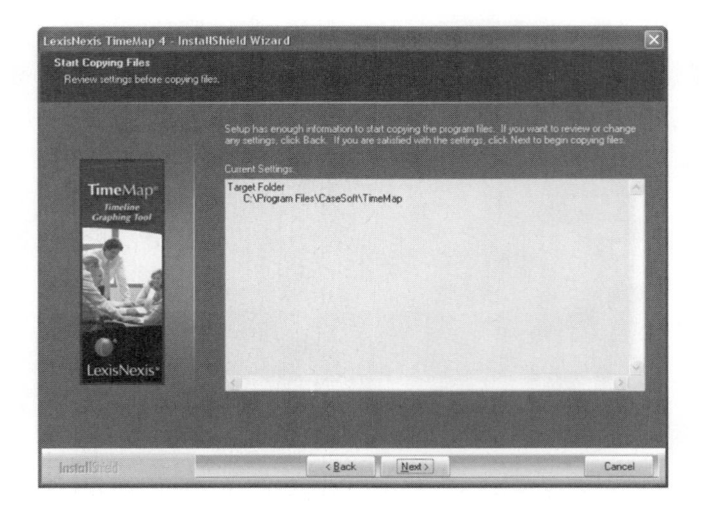

TimeMap Installation Exhibit 6

LexisNexis and the Knowledge Burst logo are registered trademarks of Reed Elsevier Properties Inc. HotDocs is a registered trademark of Matthew Bender & Company. TimeMap and CaseMap are registered trademarks of LexisNexis Courtlink, Inc. Used with the permission of LexisNexis.

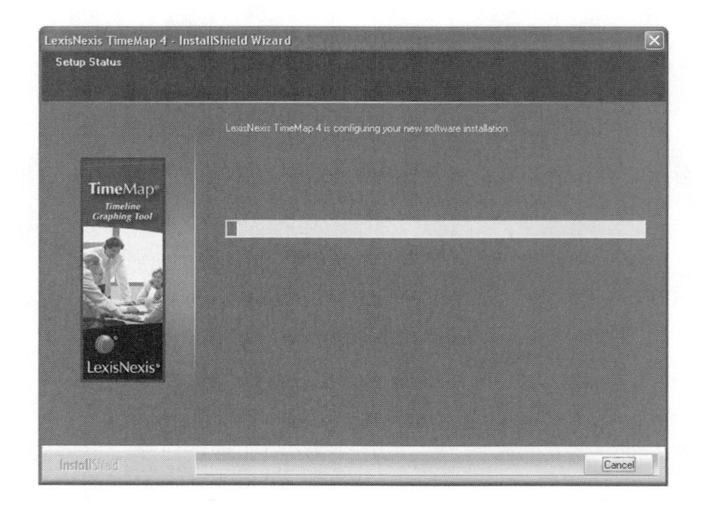

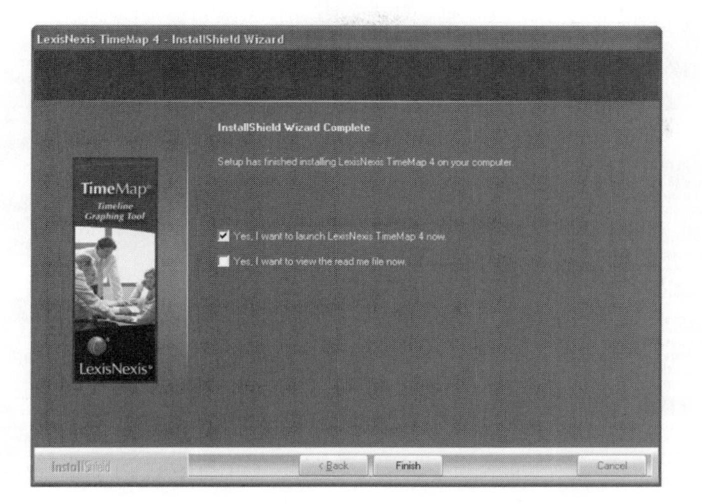

TimeMap Installation Exhibit 7

LexisNexis and the Knowledge Burst logo are registered trademarks of Reed Elsevier Properties Inc. HotDocs is a registered trademark of Matthew Bender & Company. TimeMap and CaseMap are registered trademarks of LexisNexis Courtlink, Inc. Used with the permission of LexisNexis.

TimeMap Installation Exhibit 8

LexisNexis and the Knowledge Burst logo are registered trademarks of Reed Elsevier Properties Inc. HotDocs is a registered trademark of Matthew Bender & Company. TimeMap and CaseMap are registered trademarks of LexisNexis Courtlink, Inc. Used with the permission of LexisNexis.

TimeMap Installation Exhibit 9

LexisNexis and the Knowledge Burst logo are registered trademarks of Reed Elsevier Properties Inc. HotDocs is a registered trademark of Matthew Bender & Company. TimeMap and CaseMap are registered trademarks of LexisNexis Courtlink, Inc. Used with the permission of LexisNexis.

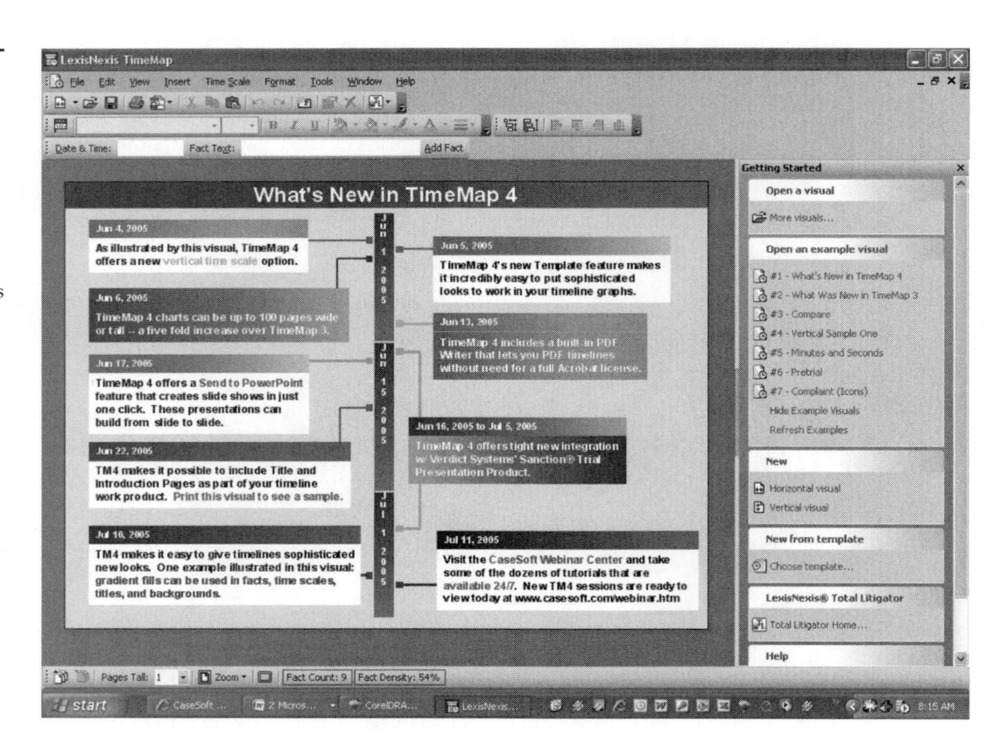

HANDS-ON EXERCISES
LEXISNEXIS TIMEMAP

Basic Lessons

Number	Lesson Title	Concepts Covered
Lesson 1	Introduction to TimeMap	Explanation and introduction to the TimeMap interface.

Intermediate

Number	Lesson Title	Concepts Covered
Lesson 2	Creating a new timeline in TimeMap	Entering new fact boxes and customizing the chronology.

Advanced

Number	Lesson Title	Concepts Covered
Lesson 3	Exporting Entries in CaseMap to TimeMap	Exporting entries from CaseMap into TimeMap.

GETTING STARTED

Introduction

Throughout these exercises, information you need to enter into the program will be designated in several different ways.

- Keys to be pressed on the keyboard will be designated in brackets, in all caps, bold, and enlarged type (press the **[ENTER]** key).
- Movements with the mouse will be designated in bold and italics (***point to File on the menu bar and click the mouse***).
- Words or letters that should be typed will be designated in bold (type **Training Program**).
- Information that is or should be displayed on your computer screen will be shown in the following style: **Press ENTER to continue.**

OVERVIEW OF TIMEMAP

TimeMap is a litigation support product that creates timelines or timemaps. A timeline or timemap is a visual representation of time, showing when events occurred and in what sequence. TimeMap computerizes this process. Timelines are extremely helpful in a litigation context because they allow a jury or other fact finder to visualize how the events in the case occurred. TimeMap is straightforward and easy to use. It can accept entries imported directly from a CaseMap chronology, so the user does not have to type the information into the computer a second time.

LESSON 1: INTRODUCTION TO TIMEMAP

This lesson introduces you to the TimeMap litigation support program. It explains basic information about the TimeMap interface.

1. Start Windows. Then, ***double-click on the LexisNexis TimeMap 4 icon on the desktop, or click the Start button on the Windows desktop, point with the mouse to Programs or All Programs, point to the LexisNexis CaseMap Suite, and***

then point and click on LexisNexis TimeMap4. LexisNexis TimeMap 4 will then be started.

2. Intermittently, when you start TimeMap you may see a small window in the middle of the screen that says "TimeMap" with some additional information about a grace period. If this occurs, ***click Continue.***

3. Your screen should now look similar to TimeMap Exhibit 1. On the right side of the screen is the Getting Started task pane.

TimeMap Exhibit 1

LexisNexis and the Knowledge Burst logo are registered trademarks of Reed Elsevier Properties Inc. Hot Docs is a registered trademark of Matthew Bender & Company. TimeMap and CaseMap are registered trademarks of LexisNexis Courtlink, Inc. Used with the permission of LexisNexis.

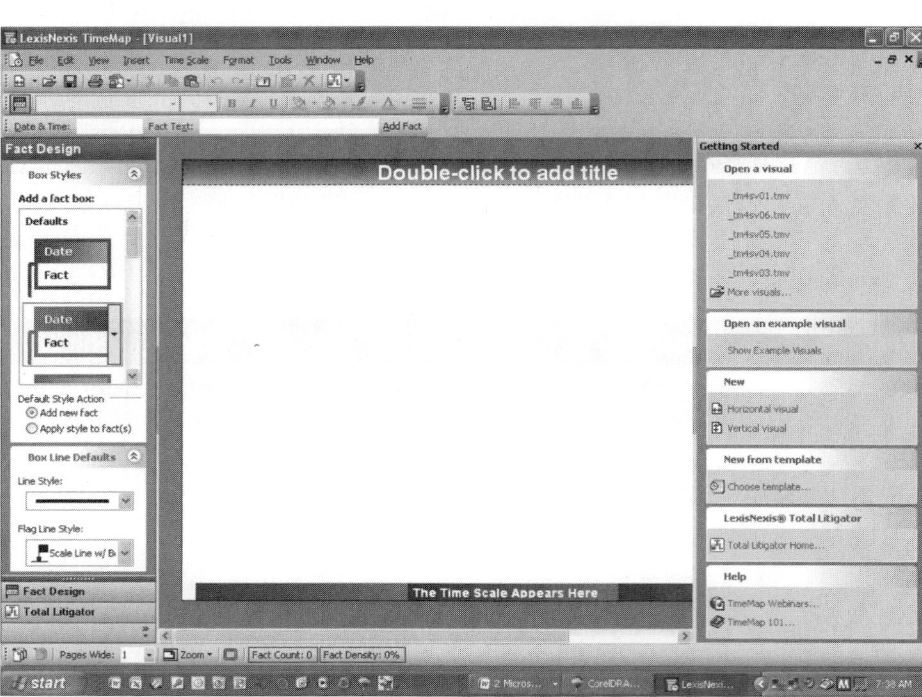

4. ***In the Getting Started task pane, under "Open an example visual," click "#6 – Pretrial."***

5. The Key Events Before Trial timemap should now be displayed (see TimeMap Exhibit 2).

6. In TimeMap, there are three types of visual elements: Fact Boxes, Text Boxes, and the Time Scale.

7. Notice in TimeMap Exhibit 2 that there are ten entries displayed in the timemap (ten rectangular boxes that contain dates and descriptive information). These are called Fact Boxes.

8. ***Double-click the March 2006—Crandall Deposition Fact Box*** (it is the second Fact Box down from the top on the left side of the screen).

9. Notice that a Fact Box Properties window is now displayed. ***Click the date and edit it so that it reads 03/15/2006.*** Then, change "Crandall Deposition" so that it reads **John Crandall Deposition**, and ***click OK in the Fact Box Properties window.***

10. You will now create a new Fact Box. ***Click the New Fact Box (Ins) icon on the toolbar.*** (It looks like a yellow file folder with an "F" on it and a star in the upper left corner – see TimeMap Exhibit 2.)

11. The New Fact Box window is displayed. ***Click in the white box to the right of the Date & Time field,*** and type **01/15/2006**.

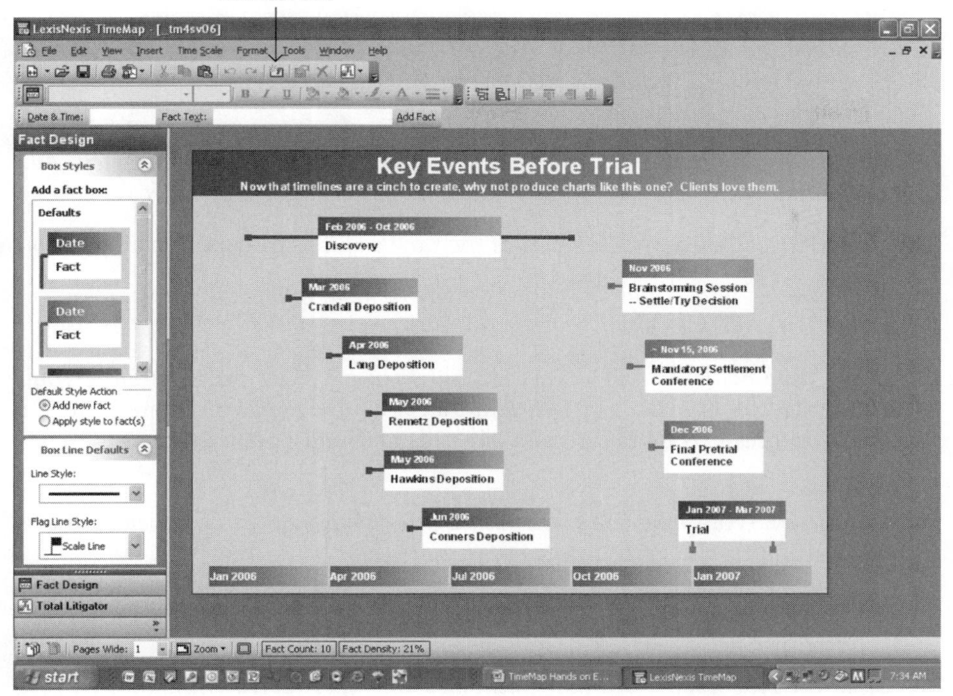

TimeMap Exhibit 2

LexisNexis and the Knowledge Burst logo are registered trademarks of Reed Elsevier Properties Inc. HotDocs is a registered trademark of Matthew Bender & Company. TimeMap and CaseMap are registered trademarks of LexisNexis Courtlink, Inc. Used with the permission of LexisNexis.

12. ***Click in the large white box in the New Fact Box window.*** Type **Client Discovery Meeting** and then ***click OK in the New Fact Box window.***

13. Notice that TimeMap has placed the Fact Box on the left side of the screen.

14. ***Double-click on the "January 15, 2006" Fact Box.***

15. ***Click the Colors and Lines tab in the Fact Box Properties window.***

16. ***Click the down arrow to the right of Date under the Fill section. Then, click Plum*** (medium purple). Notice that under the Fill section, next to Box, the color selected is white. This is the color for the lower part of the Fact Box where the text goes. You can control the font, color, lines and all other aspects of Fact Boxes. ***Click OK in the Fact Box Properties window.***

17. On the left side of the screen is the Fact Design pane (see TimeMap Exhibit 2). Notice in TimeMap Exhibit 2 under "Add a Fact Box" that there are several different styles of box. For example, if you want to add a blue box, ***click the blue style fact box under "Add a Fact Box."*** Notice that the New Fact Box window is now displayed. You can now enter a new fact box in the blue style quickly and easily.

18. ***Click Cancel in the Add a Fact Box window.***

19. In the Fact Design pane, just under "Add a Fact Box" and to the right, notice that there is a small scroll bar. ***Scroll down and notice that there is a plum style fact box (the one you previously created).*** You can now add fact boxes with this style by clicking on the style.

20. ***Double-click anywhere in the title Key Events Before Trial.*** This is a Text Box. Notice that the Text Box Properties window is now displayed. You can create a text box anywhere in a timemap.

21. Edit the Text Box Properties so that instead of saying Key Events Before Trial, it says **Key Dates—Crandall v. Conners**.

22. *Click the Colors and Lines tab of the Text Box Properties window.*

23. *Under Fill—Box, click the down arrow and select yellow.*

24. *Click the Text tab. Drag the mouse pointer so that "Key Dates – Crandall v. Conners" is highlighted. Click the Font Color icon. (It looks like the letter "A".) It should already be black.*

25. *Click "OK."* Notice that the title of the timemap has now been changed.

26. The time scale in TimeMap can be easily adjusted. *Click Time Scale on the menu bar. Then, click Expand.*

27. *Click Time Scale on the menu bar and then click Expand one more time.* Notice that the scale has expanded and that it is now on two screens. You can make the time scale as large as you wish. This is usually done to make room for more Fact Boxes.

28. You can also compress the scale width. *Click Time Scale on the menu bar and then click Compress. Do this a total of three times.*

29. *Click Time Scale on the menu bar and then click Expand* to put the scale back to where it started.

30. *Click the Nov 2006—Brainstorming Session—Settle/Try Decision fact box.* Notice that the entire box is now surrounded by small white squares. These are called handles. If you point to one of the handles that are in the middle, on either side, or on the bottom in the middle the cursor will change to a double-sided arrow and you can expand or contract the box.

31. *Point to the middle handle on the right side and then drag the mouse pointer to the left toward the center of the box about a quarter of an inch.* Notice that the box just got smaller.

32. You can also easily delete a Fact or Text box by *clicking to select it* and then pressing the **[DELETE]** key, or by *clicking the Delete icon on the toolbar.*

33. *Click Time Scale on the menu bar and then select Increase Pages Wide.* TimeMap responds by expanding the timemap out by a whole page. It is possible to expand the timemap out over many pages.

34. *Click Time Scale on the menu bar and then click Decrease Pages Wide* to restore the timemap to its original size.

35. *Click the Auto-Stack Fact Boxes icon on the toolbar.* (It looks like three stacked boxes with a single vertical line to the right.) TimeMap will condense the Fact Boxes so that they are arranged more tightly.

36. *Drag the timeline dates at the bottom of the screen* (the gray bar with the months on it) up. *Drag the timeline straight up to the top of the page.* Notice that you can change the position of the timeline by dragging it.

37. Press the **[CTRL]+[Z]** keys to undo the move. If you change something in TimeMap and then do not like how it looks, just press **Undo** or **[CTRL]+[Z]** and TimeMap will put it back to the way it was.

38. In TimeMap you do not have to change items one at a time, you may select a number of Fact Boxes and make a change to all of them at the same time. Press the **[CTRL]+[A]** keys. Notice that all of the Fact Boxes are selected.

39. *Double-click on any Fact Box.* The Properties window is now displayed.

40. ***Click the Date Font tab. Then click Italic at the bottom of the Properties window to change all of the dates to italics. Click "OK."*** Notice that all of the dates have been changed to italics.

41. Press the **[CTRL]+[Z]** keys on the keyboard to undo the font change.

42. You previously learned how to create a Fact Box by clicking on the New Fact Box icon on the toolbar. You can also create many Fact Boxes at one time using the Multiple Facts… menu option.

43. ***Click Insert on the menu bar and then click Multiple Facts…*** The Insert Multiple Facts window should now be displayed. Notice that there are two columns, Date & Time and Fact Text. You can now enter a number of items at one time. TimeMap will automatically create a separate Fact Box for each entry.

44. ***Click Cancel in the Insert Multiple Facts window*** to close it.

45. ***Click Tools.*** Notice that one of the options is Spelling. This allows you to run a spell check on your document. ***Click anywhere outside of the drop-down menu*** to make it disappear.

This concludes Lesson 1. ***Click File and then click Exit.*** You do not want to save your changes, so ***click No.***

LESSON 2: CREATING A NEW TIMELINE IN TIMEMAP

This lesson allows you to create a completely new timeline, and assumes that you successfully completed Lesson 1.

1. Start Windows. Then, ***double-click the LexisNexis CaseMap 7 icon on the desktop, or click the Start button on the Windows desktop, point with the mouse to Programs or All Programs, point to the LexisNexis CaseMap Suite, and then click LexisNexis TimeMap4.*** LexisNexis TimeMap 4 will then start.

2. Intermittently, when you start TimeMap you may see a small window in the middle of the screen that says "TimeMap" with some additional information about a grace period. If you get this is message, ***click Continue in the TimeMap window.*** If you do not get this message, go to the next step.

3. Your screen should now look similar to TimeMap Exhibit 1. On the right side of the screen is the Getting Started task pane.

4. ***In the Getting Started task pane click "Horizontal visual" under New.***

5. A blank time map should be displayed.

6. ***Double-click "Double-click to add title"*** at the top of the page. Edit the text box so it says **Samantha Dale Zoning Dispute** and then ***click OK*** to enter the title in the Text Box.

7. Using the Multiple Facts… command ***(click Insert on the menu bar and then click Multiple Facts…).*** Enter the following fact boxes:

Date & Time	Fact Text
01/03/08	Application for Zoning Change Filed
03/01/08	Additional Plats Filed
03/15/08	Initial Zoning Comm. Hrg
03/17/08	Opposition to Zoning Change Filed by Blue Hills Homeowners Assoc.

04/17/08	Resp. to Opp. to Zoning Change Filed
05/01/08	Front-Page Newspaper Story on Zoning Change
05/15/08	Town Hall Mtg. Blue Hills Homeowners
06/01/08	Zoning Change on County Commission Agenda
06/15/08	Zoning Commission Votes to Deny Change

Click OK in the Insert Multiple Facts window.

8. Your screen should now look similar to TimeMap Exhibit 3.

9. Press the **[CTRL]+[A]** keys on the keyboard to select all of the Fact Boxes. Then, ***double-click on any Fact Box*** and format the Date Font, Colors and Lines, and Boxes to your liking.

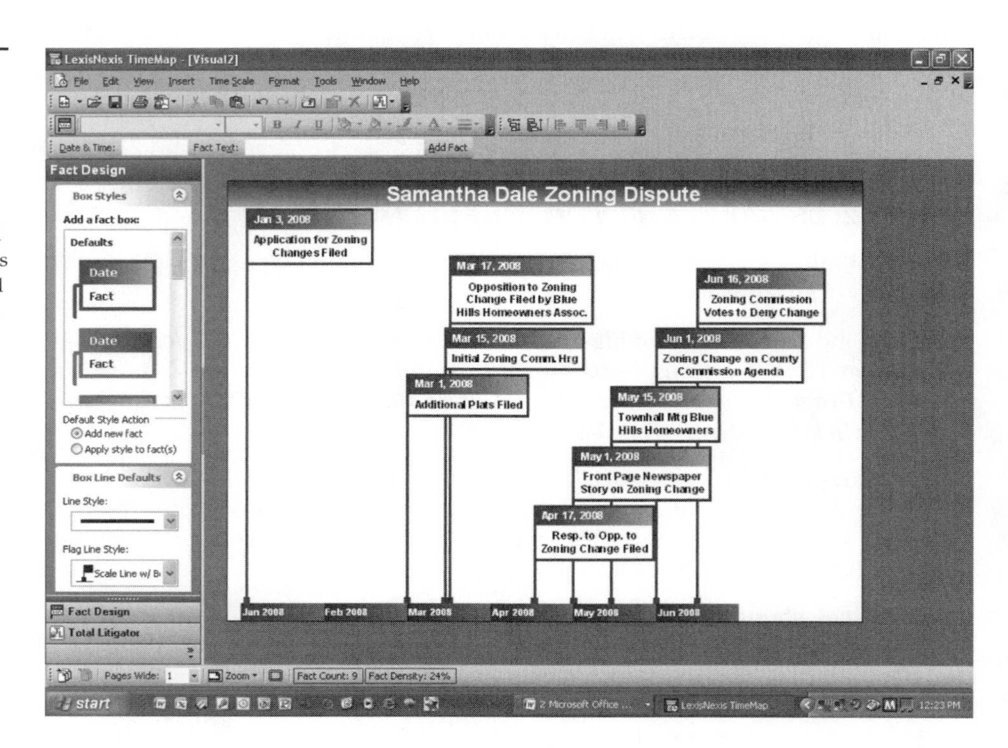

TimeMap Exhibit 3

LexisNexis and the Knowledge Burst logo are registered trademarks of Reed Elsevier Properties Inc. HotDocs is a registered trademark of Matthew Bender & Company. TimeMap and CaseMap are registered trademarks of LexisNexis CourtLink, Inc. Used with the permission of LexisNexis.

10. Experiment with the features discussed in Lesson 1 to manipulate your timemap, including Expand/Compress Scale Width, Increase/Decrease Pages Wide, Time Scale Break, Fit to Pages Wide, and Snap Flag Left/Right Side of Line.

11. Print your timeline by ***clicking the printer icon on the toolbar*** or by ***selecting File from the menu bar and then clicking Print.***

12. ***Click File and Save,*** type **yourname TimeMap** (e.g., Jones TimeMap), and then ***click Save.***

13. ***Click File from the menu bar, click Open, and then double-click one of the example timemaps (e.g., tm4sv01.tmv or tm4sv06.tmv).*** *Note*: You can switch between the open timemaps by ***clicking Window on the menu bar and selecting a different TimeMap file.***

14. Use the example files to get ideas for making your timemap more visually appealing. If you make any changes to the sample files, do not save them.

15. When you are done working on your timemap, save it, print it, ***click File, and then click Exit*** to exit TimeMap.

This concludes Lesson 2.

LESSON 3: EXPORTING ENTRIES IN CASEMAP TO TIMEMAP

This lesson shows you how to automatically export entries from CaseMap to TimeMap using the *Smith v. EZ Pest Control Case* (or the Hawkins case) that you entered into CaseMap.

1. Start Windows. Then, ***double-click the LexisNexis TimeMap 4 icon on the desktop, or click the Start button on the Windows desktop, point to Programs or All Programs, point to the LexisNexis CaseMap Suite, and then click LexisNexis TimeMap4.*** LexisNexis TimeMap 4 will then start.

2. Intermittently, when you start TimeMap you may see a small window in the middle of the screen that says "TimeMap" with some additional information about a grace period. If you get this message, ***click Continue in the TimeMap window.*** If you do not get this message, go to the next step.

3. A blank time map should now be displayed. The right side of the screen should have the Getting Started task pane open.

4. You will now start LexisNexis CaseMap so that you can export the CaseMap entries into TimeMap. ***Click start, point to Programs or All Programs, point to the LexisNexis CaseMap Suite, and then click LexisNexis CaseMap7.*** When you load CaseMap you may see a small window in the middle of the screen that says "CaseMap" with some additional information about a grace period. If you see this message, ***click Continue in the CaseMap window.*** CaseMap will then start, with several options listed on the right of the screen. If you do not see this message, go to the next step.

5. ***Under Open a Case in the Getting Started task pane, click Smith.cm7.*** If the file is not there, ***click Hawkins v. Anstar*** under "Open the example case."

6. The Case Log On window should now be displayed. ***Click the down arrow, click Dave Paralegal, and then click OK.***

7. The CaseMap Fact spreadsheet should now be displayed. ***Click File on the menu bar, click Send To, and then click Send to TimeMap (All).***

8. The chronology from CaseMap should now be exported into TimeMap and the Smith time map should be displayed (see TimeMap Exhibit 4).

9. If you loaded the Hawkins case, you may need to select some of the longer entries and edit them down. In any case, you can see how entries in CaseMap can be automatically sent to TimeMap.

10. Note that, instead of sending all entries from CaseMap to TimeMap, you can also choose to send only one entry at a time.

11. ***Click CaseMap*** at the bottom of the screen to switch to CaseMap.

12. ***Right-click any record in the Fact Text field.***

TimeMap Exhibit 4

LexisNexis and the Knowledge Burst logo are registered trademarks of Reed Elsevier Properties Inc. HotDocs is a registered trademarks of Matthew Bender & Company. TimeMap and CaseMap are registered trademarks of LexisNexis CourtLink, Inc. Used with the permission of LexisNexis.

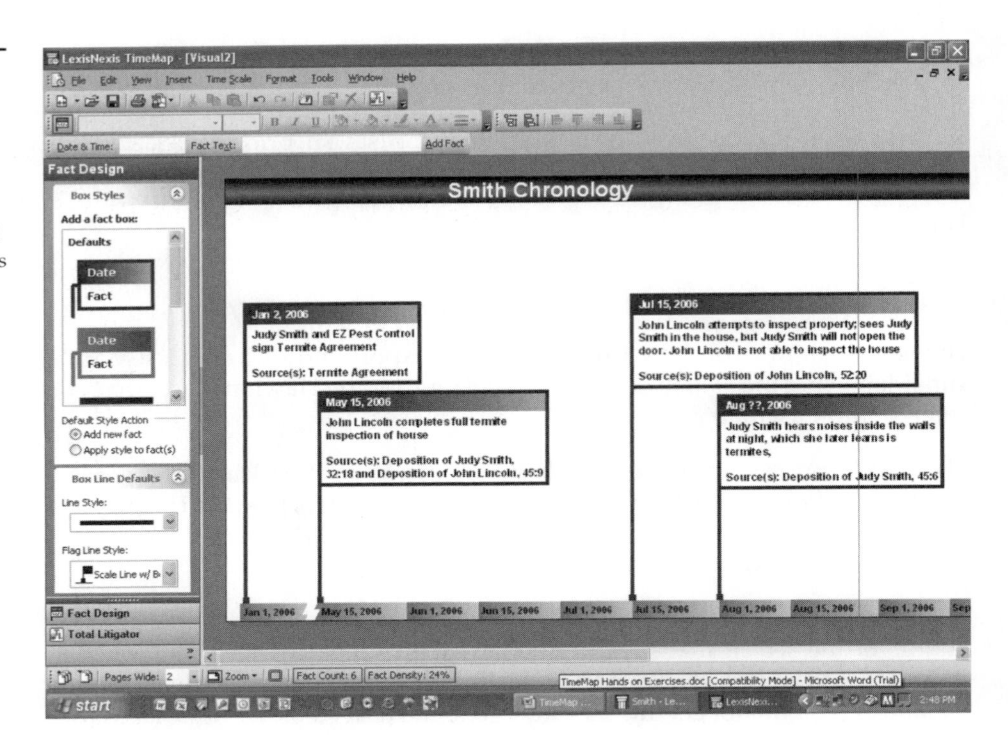

13. ***Point to Send to.*** Notice that one of the options is Send to TimeMap. Using this method you can ***right-click*** on only the specific facts you want to send to TimeMap, instead of all of them.

14. ***Click TimeMap*** at the bottom of the screen to switch to TimeMap.

15. In LexisNexis TimeMap 4, you can export time maps to other programs, such as Microsoft PowerPoint. It works best when Fact Boxes are not split across pages. ***Drag the July 15, 2006 fact box to the left so that it fits on page 1 of the time map. Do the same thing for the Aug ??, 2006 fact box.***

16. ***Click File on the menu bar and then point to Send to.*** Notice that one of the options is Microsoft PowerPoint.

17. If you have Microsoft PowerPoint installed on your computer, ***point to Send to Microsoft PowerPoint.***

18. ***Then, click One Slide Per Page.***

19. Microsoft PowerPoint should now open with the timemap displayed.

20. ***In the Microsoft PowerPoint window, click the Close icon (the "X") to close Microsoft PowerPoint.***

21. ***When a Microsoft PowerPoint dialog box opens, click No because you do not want to save the file.***

22. You can also convert timemaps to PDF files. ***Click File the menu bar, point to Print to PDF, and then click Print to PDF (File).***

23. ***In the Save As dialog box, click Save to accept the default directory and default file name. Then, click Yes to indicate that you would like to open the file.***

24. ***In the PDF Viewer window, click the Close ("X") icon to close PDF Viewer.***

25. The timemap currently spans two pages, but you can only see one page at a time. To see both pages at the same time, ***click View on the menu bar and then click Fit in Window.*** Although the text may be too small to edit in this mode, it does give you a good overview of the timemap for formatting purposes.

26. ***Click View on the menu bar and then point and click Fit Height*** to bring the view back to one page at a time.

27. ***Click View on the menu bar and then click Full Screen*** to see the timemap in full-screen mode.

28. Press the **[ESC]** key to turn off full-screen mode.

29. If you would like, revise the timeline to make it more visually appealing. When you are done working in TimeMap, print the timeline, but do not save it.

30. If you would like additional training on TimeMap, ***click Help on the menu bar and then click TimeMap Webinars***. Several free webinars are available on the Internet that will further assist you in learning TimeMap.

31. ***Click File and then click Exit*** to exit TimeMap.

This concludes the TimeMap tutorial.

CHAPTER 10

THE INTERNET AND ELECTRONIC MAIL

CHAPTER OBJECTIVES

After completing Chapter 10, you should be able to do the following:

1. Explain the different types of services the Internet offers.
2. Discuss problems with using the Internet for research.
3. Explain what a listserv is.
4. Describe the difference between a subject-oriented search engine and a metasearch engine.
5. List resources for finding precise legal information on the Internet.
6. Discuss the pros and cons of using electronic mail in a legal organization.

INTRODUCTION TO THE INTERNET

Internet
One of the world's largest computer networks, known as a network of networks, the information superhighway, or cyberspace. It connects hundreds of millions of computers using telephone lines or other communication techniques. Internet users share email, access the World Wide Web, subscribe to mailing lists (listservs), and access databases around the world.

The **Internet** is one of the world's largest computer networks and is known as a "network of networks," "the information superhighway," or "cyberspace." It connects hundreds of millions of computers and thousands of networks around the world using telephone lines or other communication technologies. Recent reports estimate that there are in excess of 600 million users of the Internet worldwide. Unlike WESTLAW, Lexis, or other online services, no one owns the Internet as a whole or runs it. The Internet is a connection of thousands of computers using the same network protocol or language. Each network on the Internet is independently owned and operated. To access the Internet, all a user needs is a computer, a modem, communication software, a telephone line or other communication technology such as a cable modem, and an account with an Internet access provider.

Services available on the Internet include electronic mail (email), listservs, newsgroups, instant messaging, File Transfer Protocol, Gopher, Telnet, and the World Wide Web.

Connecting to the Internet

Internet Service Provider (ISP)
Provides a user with Internet services such as the World Wide Web, email, listservs, newsgroups, and others.

To connect to the Internet, a user needs a computer, a modem or cable modem, a phone line or wireless connection, Internet software, and an **Internet Service Provider (ISP).** The ISP provides a user with Internet services such as the World Wide Web, email, listservs, newsgroups, and many others. Some of the largest ISPs include America Online (AOL), Yahoo, and AT&T. Users now have many

options for connecting to the "information superhighway." One option is the traditional dial-up service where a user connects to the ISP using a modem and an analog phone line. While the service is relatively inexpensive, the connection is slow, with the bandwidth being typically 56,000 bits per second or slower. (Bandwidth refers to how fast information can flow through the communication pipeline.) Other options for connecting to the Internet include DSL, cable modems, T1, and others. These options, while more expensive, have much larger bandwidths and thus can carry video, sounds, and graphics much faster than using a traditional phone line. Many legal organizations now use these faster options.

Electronic Mail

Electronic mail (email) enables users to send and receive messages almost instantly using a computer. Because the Internet is one of the largest networks of computers in the world, it allows hundreds of millions of users to send email to each other, whether it is across a city or across the world. When a user obtains an Internet account she or he is given an email address, which is the name other people will use to send email to that user. Sending and receiving email is very straightforward; users send messages, receive messages, and manage their mailboxes with a mail program. Email is discussed in more detail later in this chapter.

electronic mail (email)
Enables users to send and receive messages almost instantly using a computer.

Listserv

A **listserv** is an electronic mailing list that allows people on the list to send and receive email messages to and from everyone on the list. To join a listserv (which stands for "list server"), a user sends an email indicating that he or she wants to subscribe. After being added to the listserv, the user will receive copies of any email sent to the listserv. Also, when the user sends an email to the listserv, everyone on the listserv will get a copy of the user's message. A listserv is an easy way for people to communicate through email. There are thousands of listservs on the Internet. Many listservs are organized by topic. You can find listserv mailing lists by searching "listserv" using a search engine (described later in this chapter).

listserv
An electronic mailing list that allows people on the list to send and receive messages to and from everyone on the list via email.

The Legal Assistant Today—Forum (LAT-Forum) listserv is a great way to stay connected, free of charge, to what is going on in the profession. There are thousands of legal assistants that subscribe to the listserv and exchange information every month. Send a blank email to join-lat-forum@lyris.dundee.net to join or go to the Legal Assistant Today website at <http://www.legalassistanttoday.com>.

USENET Newsgroups

A network of computers that contains news and discussion groups (called newsgroups) is known as **USENET.** USENET is an electronic bulletin board service consisting of newsgroups, newsfeeds, and newsreaders. Once you subscribe to a newsgroup, you use a newsreader to access the group's newsfeed. There are thousands of newsgroups, including many on law-related topics.

USENET newsgroups
A network of computers that contains news and discussion groups. USENET is an electronic bulletin board service consisting of newsgroups, newsfeeds, and newsreaders.

Internet Relay Chat

Internet Relay Chat (IRC) allows people all over the world to converse with one another in real time over the Internet. It consists of various separate networks (or "nets") of IRC servers—machines that allow users to connect to IRC. The largest nets often connect more than 15,000 people at once. As you type

Internet Relay Chat (IRC)
Allows people to converse with one another in real time over the Internet.

messages into the computer, other users you are chatting with see them almost immediately. The conversations are organized into channels with each channel representing a different topic. There are thousands of chat channels including many legal chat channels. You can find law-related chat channels by searching for "law chat" in a search engine on the World Wide Web (search engines are discussed later in this chapter). In order to connect to IRC, the user runs a program called a "client" to connect to a server on one of the IRC nets. The server relays information to and from other servers on the same net. Some recommended clients are IRC for Windows, IRCle for the Mac, and IRCII for Unix.

Instant Messaging

> *Instant messaging is about sharing information. It gives users the ability to quickly answer questions, get out messages and receive information they need...Some real advantages [include]: fewer emails and easier, faster communication on time-sensitive matters.*[1]

instant messaging
Allows users to converse in real time with other users who are using the same instant messaging program. As soon as a user connects to the Internet the user will know which of his or her colleagues are signed on and be able to send them a message.

Instant messaging allows users to converse in real time with other users. As soon as a user of an instant messaging program connects to the Internet, he or she will know exactly which colleagues are signed on to the Internet and can send them a message, even if they all use different Internet service providers. The only restriction is that colleagues must use the same instant messaging program that you do. This is different from an Internet Relay Chat (IRC) program, where you do not know who is on the Internet as soon as you connect. In addition, the user must first connect to one of many IRC servers and networks that host many thousands of users from around the world. After the user connects to an IRC server, the user must then join a channel or room to converse with others. A recent survey found that AOL Instant Messenger is used by approximately 80 percent of the legal organizations using instant messaging.

File Transfer Protocol (FTP)

File Transfer Protocol (FTP)
A tool or standard for transferring files over the Internet.

File Transfer Protocol (FTP) is a tool or standard for transferring files over the Internet. In many cases, there are administrators of FTP servers who copy certain files to public directories on FTP servers. Users can then download the files from the FTP servers. There are more than 1,500 FTP sites with access to millions of public files. FTP software allows the user to choose a computer to connect to and then allows the user to upload or download files such as text, pictures, sounds, cases, and statutes. You can download files using an Internet browser or a special FTP program.

Gopher

Gopher
A tool that allows users to access other resources and computers on the Internet.

Gopher is a tool that allows users to access other resources and computers on the Internet. A Gopher server allows users to access information through a main menu and submenus. The menu allows a user to view a document, run other Internet programs, or connect to other Gopher servers.

Telnet

Telnet
An Internet tool that makes one computer a terminal for other computers on the Internet.

Telnet is an Internet tool that makes one computer a terminal for other computers on the Internet. Telnet permits the local user to use a program located on the remote computer. For example, using Telnet a user can remotely access a library catalog and enter commands into the library's computerized catalog to retrieve information.

World Wide Web

The **World Wide Web** is an Internet system, navigation tool, and interface that retrieves information using links to other web pages. To access the Web, a user needs a web browser program such as Microsoft Explorer or Firefox. The Web is a graphical and multimedia interface. Web pages can contain text, graphical images, moving pictures, animation, and sound, and use **hypermedia** or **hypertext links**. If a user is at a web page that references another website and there is a hypermedia or hypertext link, all the user has to do is click the website address to be taken immediately to the new website. There are hundreds of thousands of websites, including many law-related websites. To find information on the Web, the user needs to use a search engine. Whether a user is looking for legal research or non-legal research, there are tricks for how to find the information. Many legal organizations have web pages and intranet/extranet sites. All of these will be covered in detail in this section.

World Wide Web
The World Wide Web is an Internet system, navigation tool, and interface that retrieves information using links to other web pages. To access the Web, a user needs a web browser program such as Microsoft Explorer or Firefox. The Web is a graphical and multimedia interface.

hypermedia or **hypertext links**
Connects web pages together. When a user clicks on a hypermedia or hypertext link, the user is immediately taken to the new website location.

Web Browser Software

To access the World Wide Web, the user needs web browser software. A **web browser** is the interface or program that allows the user to see web pages. The two most popular web browsers are Microsoft Explorer and Firefox. After a web browser has been properly installed, the user simply loads the browser software and the software then connects to the ISP. Once connected to the ISP, the browser software loads the user's home web page.

Everything on the Web has an address known as a **uniform resource locator (URL).**

When a web browser loads, it automatically defaults to the user's home URL. A user can change the home URL any time by entering the new URL in the browser.

Web browsers also have an important feature known as bookmarks. A **bookmark** is a pointer that enables a user to quickly and easily go back to a website.

web browser
The interface or program that allows the user to see web pages.

uniform resource locator (URL)
The address of a web page.

bookmark
A pointer that enables a user to quickly and easily go back to a website.

BLOG

A **blog** or weblog is a website with information contained in posts that are arranged in reverse chronological order. Blogs resemble diary or journal entries, and can contain links to other websites or articles. There are many law-related blogs on the Internet, including specialized blogs on certain types of law and even legal assistant-related blogs (see http://paralegalgateway.typepad.com, and http://estrinlegaled.typepad.com). A good way of finding blogs on the Internet is to use Google's blog search tool, e.g., http://blogsearch.google.com.

blog
A website with information contained in posts that are arranged in reverse chronological order.

> *Law blogs (sometimes called blawgs) and law bloggers are well represented in this new world dubbed the blogosphere. Lawyers and other legal professionals are using blogs for everything from knowledge and information sharing and management, to marketing and anything conceivable in between... The sky is the limit when it comes to possible applications for blogs in the modern law office.*[2]

RSS

RSS is a group of formats that are used to publish and distribute news feeds, blogs and podcasts. RSS allows users to push news, blog updates, and other information to RSS readers and Web pages. Users can subscribe to RSS feeds and access the updated information when it comes in. Free RSS reader programs

RSS
A group of formats that are used to publish and distribute news feeds, blogs, and podcasts.

are widely available on the Internet. There are many legal-related RSS feeds including recent U.S. Supreme Court opinions (http://straylight.law.cornell.edu) and recent copyright information from the U.S. Copyright Office (see www.copyright.gov).

Podcasts

Podcast
An audio recording that is posted on the Internet and is made available for users to download so they can listen to it on a computer or mobile computing device.

A **podcast** is an audio recording (usually in MP3 format) that is posted on the Internet and is typically made available for users to download so they can listen to it on a computer or mobile computing device. Music, lectures, blogs, and other recordings can be made available as a podcast and can also be pushed to users using an RSS format. A good place to start for finding podcasts by subject matter (including legal-related podcasts) is www.allpodcasts.com.

USE OF THE INTERNET IN LEGAL ORGANIZATIONS

The Internet is used by legal assistants for everything from legal research to skip tracing.[3]

Most, if not all, legal organizations are connected to the Internet and are using it in a variety of ways. Some of the most common include performing legal research, performing factual and business research, using email to communicate with clients and colleagues, accessing court records, filing documents electronically, marketing, taking online depositions, and online learning. A recent survey found that 95 percent of legal assistants use the Internet on a daily basis and 97 percent use email on a daily basis to perform their job.

Performing Legal Research on the Internet

A great deal of legal research is available on the Internet. Unfortunately, unlike with WESTLAW and Lexis, it is not available in one place—it is scattered all over the Internet. The positive side of legal research on the Internet is that most of it is free. The resources available include federal case law, federal legislative materials, government regulations, and state case law. However, it is not nearly as comprehensive or as reliable as WESTLAW or Lexis. Where to find legal research on the Internet is explored in more detail later in this chapter.

Performing Factual and Business Research on the Internet

The Internet is better suited to performing factual or business research than it is to performing traditional legal research such as searches for case law and statutes. Factual situations include finding people and information about people, finding expert witnesses, finding evidence useful for impeaching experts and other witnesses, performing research regarding businesses, and looking for other facts in newspaper articles and other sources about cases or witnesses. How to perform factual research on the Internet is discussed in more detail later in this chapter.

Using Email to Communicate with Clients and Colleagues

Email is a very convenient form of communication for legal professionals. It is nearly instantaneous, creates a record for both tracking and saving information, is inexpensive, is easy to use, and is convenient (unlike the telephone, you don't have to play telephone tag with busy callers). Its use is widespread, so many

clients, colleagues, vendors, and others are available for corresponding via email. It even allows users to send or attach documents, such as word processing documents, to the email. The use of email has truly been accepted by the legal community and is now used as much as if not more than, the telephone. Email will be covered in depth later in this chapter.

Accessing Court Records and Filing Documents Electronically

Most courts allow legal professionals to access court records electronically, which is often more convenient than calling clerks or other staff for information. Most courts are also allowing documents to be filed electronically. Electronic filing represents time savings, costs savings, and convenience over filing paper documents.

Law Firm Marketing on the Internet

Law firms have realized that having a web page means marketing the firm 24 hours a day, seven days a week to a potential nationwide and worldwide audience. Law firm web pages are covered in more detail later in this chapter.

Taking Online Depositions

Attorneys can take depositions using an online deposition service (see Exhibit 10–1). A typical online deposition use would be for an attorney to participate in an out-of-state deposition from his or her own office. The online deposition service provides live video and two-way audio on a secure Internet feed. Many services also provide real-time transcription. The attorney is able to see and hear the witness, court reporter, and opposing counsel on his or her computer monitor and ask questions, make objections, and do nearly everything the attorney would do if he or she were at the deposition site. Some services even

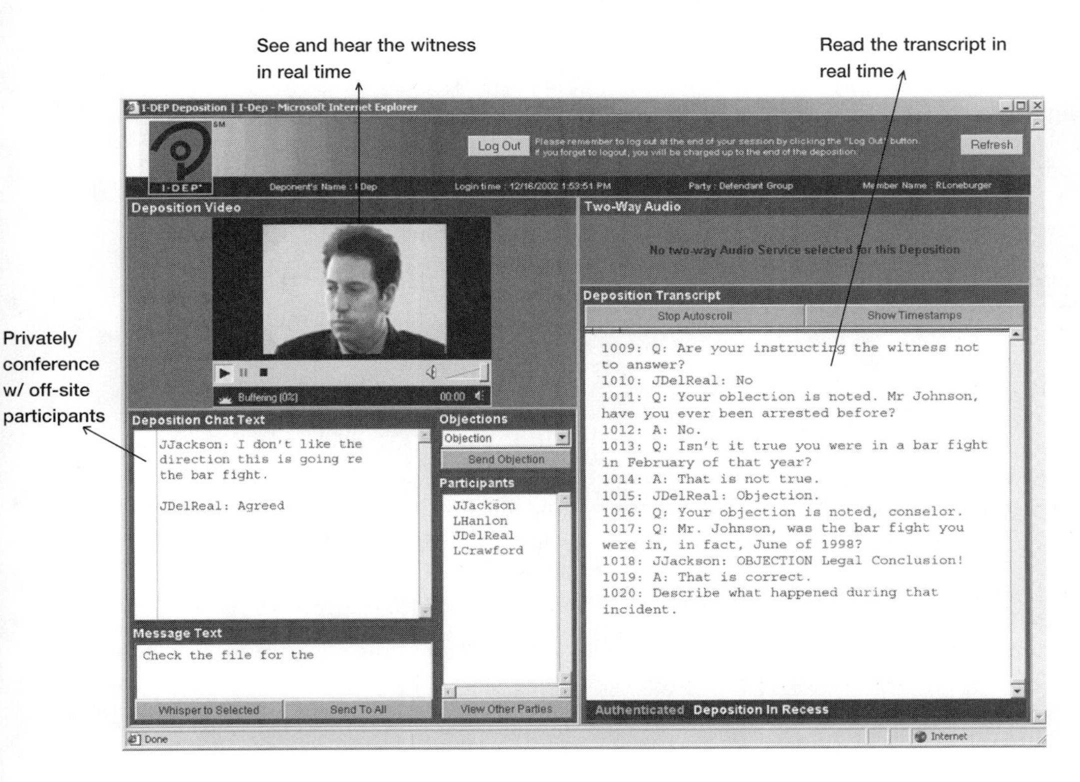

Exhibit 10–1
Online Deposition
I-Dep Deposition Broadcasting Service (Premier Version).

provide private online messaging so that information can be shared between co-counsel.

Online Learning

The Internet is used to deliver online learning seminars in a variety of areas to participants in legal organizations. Legal organizations save thousands of dollars in travel costs and experience productivity increases, since staff members never leave their desks.

Picking a Search Engine

By Genie Tyburski

Want to search the Web, but don't know which engine to use? Have a search engine you like, but sometimes it just doesn't deliver satisfactory results? Use this guide to selecting the "best" finding tool.

LOOKING FOR SOMETHING SPECIFIC
(a home page, a title, a company, a trade association, a government agency, primary law, a court, a person, etc.) Use Google.

LOOKING FOR CURRENT NEWS
(best if news is less than 30 days old) Use AltaVista News, Daypop, Moreover.com, Pandia Newsfinder, Northern Light, or RocketNews.

LOOKING TO SCAN THE WEB
(a general feel for coverage) Use a metasearch service. Find several in the Search Engine Guide on <http://www.virtualchase.com>.

LOOKING FOR A CURRENT DOCUMENT
(documents released or published recently or on the present day) First try Pandia Newsfinder, RocketNews, AltaVista News, or Moreover.com. If people are likely to talk about it, try Google Groups or Daypop. If it's a popular document or press release, try Yahoo Press Releases or Northern Light. If it concerns a social policy issue, try Policy.com. Also, try the home page of the source or the home page of a government agency, trade association, or advocacy group interested in the issue.

LOOKING FOR GOVERNMENT INFORMATION
(primary law, guidance documents, memoranda, reports, etc.) Use Google Uncle Sam or Northern Light. At Northern Light, limit the query to government sites (see Power Search). Also, to locate a government source, try Louisiana State University's U.S. Federal Government Directory or State and Local Government on the Net.

LOOKING FOR STATISTICS
Use a specialty finding aid like the University of Michigan's Statistical Resources on the Web, FedStats, the Census Economic Briefing Room, or American Factfinder. Also consider government agencies devoted to gathering and publishing statistics (e.g., National Center for Education Statistics, National Center for Health Statistics, Census Bureau).

LOOKING FOR A DATABASE
(special literature searches—medical, general, psychological—statistics, public records, etc.) Try guides prepared by librarians like Librarians' Index to the Internet, Resource Discovery Network, Direct Search, INFOMINE, Invisible-Web.net, or the subject guides on <http://www.virtualchase.com>.

LOOKING FOR SUBSTANTIVE STARTING POINT
(broad coverage of a topic) Try guides prepared by librarians or topic experts like Librarians' Index to the Internet, Resource Discovery Network, INFOMINE, Scout Archives, or the subject guides on The Virtual Chase. Also, remember that the websites of government agencies, trade associations, advocacy groups, and special libraries (e.g., National Library of Medicine, National Library of Education, National Agricultural Library) make good general starting points.

Links for this article...

American Factfinder
<http://factfinder.census.gov>

AltaVista News
<http://news.altavista.com>

Census Bureau
<http://www.census.gov>

Census Economic Briefing Room
<http://www.census.gov>

Daypop
<http<http://www.daypop.com>

Direct Search
<http://www.freepint.com>

FedStats
<http://www.fedstats.gov>

Google
<http://www.google.com>

Google Groups
<http://www.google.com/grphp>

Google Uncle Sam
<http://www.google.com/uncle sam>

INFOMINE
<http://infomine.ucr.edu>

Librarians' Index to the Internet
<http://www.lii.org>

Moreover.com
<http://www.moreover.com>

National Center for Education Statistics
<http:/nces.ed.gov>

National Center for Health Statistics
<http://www.cdc.gov/nchs/>

National Agricultural Library
<http://www.nal.usda.gov>

National Library of Education
<http://www.ed.gov>

National Library of Medicine
<http://www.nlm.nih.gov>

News Searching Resources
<http://www.searchengineshowdown.com>

Northern Light
<http://www.northernlight.com>

Northern Light Power Search
<http://www.northernlight.com>

Pandia Newsfinder
<http://www.pandia.com>

State and Local Government on the Net
<http://www.statelocalgov.net>

Policy.com
<http://www.policy.com>

Resource Discovery Network
<http://www.rdn.ac.uk>

RocketNews
<http://www.rocketnews.com>

Scout Archives
<http://scout.cs.wisc.edu>

VirtualChase.com
<http://www.virtualchase.com>

Statistical Resources on the Web
<http://www.lib.umich.edu>

U.S. Federal Government Directory
<http://www.lib.lsu.edu>

Yahoo Press Releases
<http://biz.yahoo.com>

SEARCHING AND FINDING INFORMATION ON THE WORLD WIDE WEB

> *One day at work, I rode the elevator down to the lobby with a partner. Exuberantly, he turned to me and asked, "Which search engine do you think is best?" … I pondered over how to explain in a few seconds that no search engine is above all the best. The engine selected should depend on the information sought.… Many legal professionals have a favorite search engine. Skillful searching, however, demands that you know when—and how—to use a variety of search tools.*[4]

Introduction

Searching the Web for information is one of the most common uses of the Internet for legal assistants. A user who does not have a URL for a website must use a search engine to try to find it. Searching and finding the exact information you are looking for is many times not easy due to the breadth and depth of information on the Web. By some accounts, there are more than nine million different websites and more than one billion web pages on the Internet.

Search Engines

Most search engines use computerized methods called "spiders" to search or "crawl" the Web to compile their databases. Once the spiders find a website, they typically index many of the words on the public pages at the site. Web page owners may also submit their URLs to search engines for crawling and eventual inclusion in their databases. When a user enters a search in a search engine, the user is asking the engine to search its database; it is not actually searching the Web at that moment. In addition, no search engine searches the entire Web. Some studies have shown that no search engine indexed more than 16 percent of the publicly indexable Web. Some search engines are better at finding particular kinds of information than others. Which search engine you use should depend on the particular information you are looking for. There are a number of different types and ways of classifying search engines.

An **individual search engine** compiles its own searchable database. One popular general individual search engine is google.com. In addition to individual search engines that are general in nature, such as Google, there are also **specialty search engines.** A specialty search engine searches only in specific topical areas, such as <http://www.searchgov.com>, which searches government-related websites, or <http://www.findlaw.com>, which searches only law-related websites.

Another kind of search engine is a **metasearch engine.** A metasearch engine does not crawl the Web or compile its own database. Instead, it sends the user's search request to a number of different individual search engines and then eliminates the duplicates and sorts the sites retrieved by rank. Metasearch engines provide a quick overview of a subject and can be used to quickly find which engines are retrieving the best results for the user's particular search. Popular metasearch engines include metacrawler.com and dogpile.com.

A **subject directory** is a site that is maintained by a staff of people who select sites to include in their directory database. A popular subject directory is yahoo.com. Editors organize directory hierarchies into subject categories. The "Web Site Directory" at yahoo.com is an example of this. It should be noted that there is a blurring of the lines between search engines and subject directories, with each sometimes combining both types of search techniques. Many search engines or subject directory sites, such as Yahoo, are also portals. A **portal** is a "jumping off" spot for many things on the Web, offering searching, hierarchical directories, news, sports, shopping, entertainment, and much more. The "portal"

individual search engine
Search engine that compiles its own searchable database.

specialty search engine
Search engine that searches only in specific topical areas.

metasearch engine
Search engine that does not crawl the Web or compile its own database. Instead, it sends the user's search request to a number of different individual search engines and then eliminates the duplicates and sorts the sites retrieved by rank.

subject directory
A site maintained by a staff of people who select sites to include in their directory.

portal
A "jumping off" spot for many things on the Web, offering searching, hierarchical directories, news, sports, shopping, entertainment, and much more.

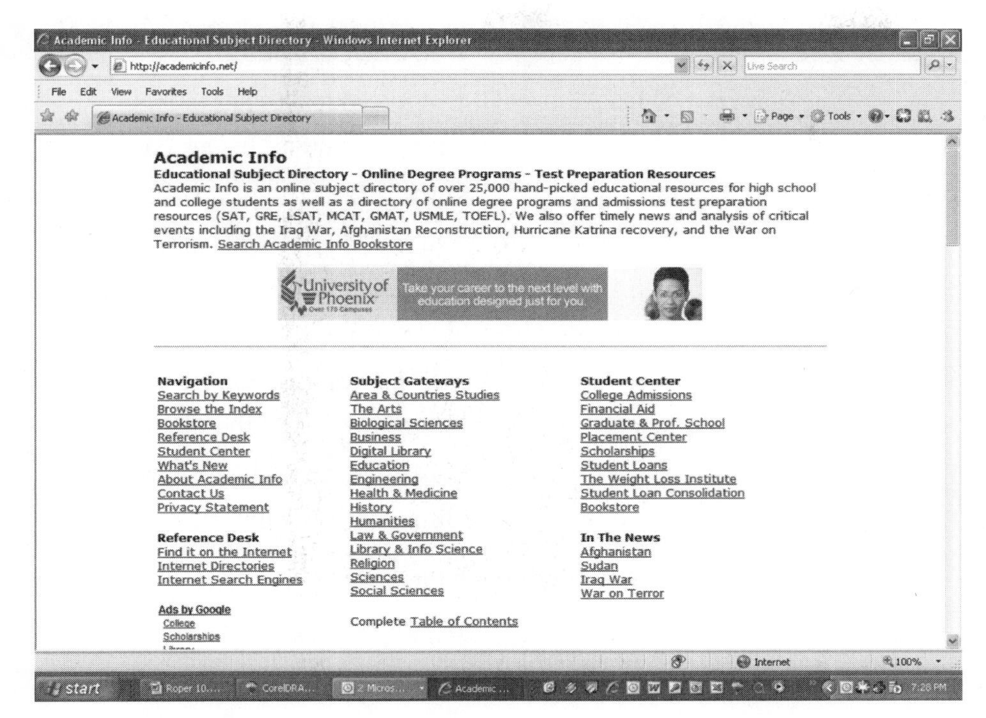

Exhibit 10–2
A Library Gateway
Courtesy of academic info.net

concept is that a user can go to one place on the Web to start and then fan out to a number of other interests/sites from that one starting point. For Example, FindLaw.com is a popular legal portal.

Another way to find information on the Web is to use a gateway site such as a **library gateway.** A library gateway is a collection of databases and information sites arranged by subject. These gateways usually support research and reference needs by pointing the user to recommended, academically oriented pages on the Web. Exhibit 10–2 is an example of a library gateway.

library gateway
A collection of databases and information sites arranged by subject.

Another way to find information on the Web is to use a **subject-specific database.** A subject-specific database is devoted to a single subject. For example, CareerBuilder.com is a subject-specific database that is totally devoted to finding jobs. The open position database in CareerBuilder.com is usually in the hundreds of thousands. There are many such subject-specific databases on the Web.

subject-specific database
A database devoted to a single subject.

The **invisible web** sometimes called the "deep web," refers to the fact that a large portion of the World Wide Web is not accessible to search engine spiders. The search engines cannot access these sites/pages because they may be password protected, in databases, behind firewalls, or otherwise not accessible to the search engines. It is estimated that more than 50 percent of the Web falls into this category. To access "invisible websites" you must point your web browser directly to those sites. For example, a search engine will not find an open position that is listed in careerbuilder.com because it is a database.

invisible web
Refers to the fact that a large portion of the World Wide Web is not accessible to search engine spiders. This includes PDF files, password-protected sites, some databases, documents behind firewalls, and other data.

Exhibit 10–3 shows a variety of websites for search engines, gateways, and databases on the Web.

Search Strategies

The following are a variety of general search strategies for searching the Web.

Think About Your Search Different searches *require* different strategies. If you are looking for general information about a topic, a subject directory search engine such

Exhibit 10–3
List of Search Engines/Gateways/ Databases

NAME OF SITE	WEB URL (ADDRESS)
General Individual/Subject Directory Search Engines	
All The Web	<http://www.alltheweb.com>
AltaVista	<http://www.altavista.com>
Excite	<http://www.excite.com>
Google	<http://www.google.com>
Lycos	<http://www.lycos.com>
MSN Search	<http://search.msn.com>
Northemlight	<http://www.northernlight.com>
WebCrawler	<http://www.webcrawler.com>
Yahoo	<http://www.yahoo.com>
Specialty Search Engines	
Google US Government	<http://www.google.com>
SearchGov (Government)	<http://www.searchgov.com>
SearchEdu (Education)	<http://www.searchedu.com>
SearchMil (Military)	<http://www.searchmil.com>
Pandia Newsfinder (News)	<http://www.pandia.com/news>
Metasearch Engines	
Dogpile	<http://www.dogpile.com
Ixquick	<http://www.ixquick.com>
Kartoo	<http://www.kartoo.com>
Metacrawler	<http://www.metacrawler.com>
qbSearch	<http://www.qbsearch.com>
Library Gateways	
Academic Information	<http://www.academicinfo.net>
Digital Librarian	<http://www.digital-librarian.com>
Infomine	<http://infomine.ucr.edu>
Librarians' Index to the Internet	<http://www.lii.org>
The Internet Public Library	<http://www.ipl.org>
www Virtual Library	<http://www.vlib.org>
Subject Specific Databases	
Careerbuilder.com (employment)	<http://www.careerbuilder.com>
The Invisible Web (database sites)	<http://www.invisibleweb.com>
WebMd (health/medical information)	<http://www.webmd.com>

as Yahoo.com or a metasearch engine such as dogpile (http://www.dogpile.com) are good places to start. However, if you are looking for a more specific piece of information you may want to start with Google.com or AllTheWeb.com, which may have more detailed information. If you are looking for a very narrow piece of information, consider what subject matter it is and use a specialty search engine or a database to find the information. For example, if you were looking for government-related information it would be best to start with a government search engine such as SearchGov (http://www.searchgov.com) or if you were looking for a detailed medical issue it would be best to search MedMD (http://www.medmd.com). The more detailed the information you are looking for, the more detailed your searching engine or database will most likely have to be. See Exhibit 10–3 for a listing of search engines.

Use Advanced Search Options Most search engines have an entry on the title page that refers to advanced search. Advanced search options allow you to tailor your search so that it does not return thousands of documents. For example, in Exhibit 10–4 the user has entered exactly what phrase she is looking for (freedom of speech). She has also directed Google to return files in PDF (Portable Document Format) only. Note that she could have limited it to other file formats as well, such as Word, Excel, or PowerPoint. Notice in Exhibit 10–4 that she limited the search to web pages that had been updated in the past year in the hopes of getting only current articles, and that she limited the search to the title of the page to get articles that were directly on point. Finally, she limited the search to domain names ending with ".gov" to restrict her search to government sites. Using advanced options is a great way to increase efficiency and get better search results more quickly.

Read the Help or Search Guide Files for the Search Engines You Use Different search engines use different syntax for entering searches. *Always* read the

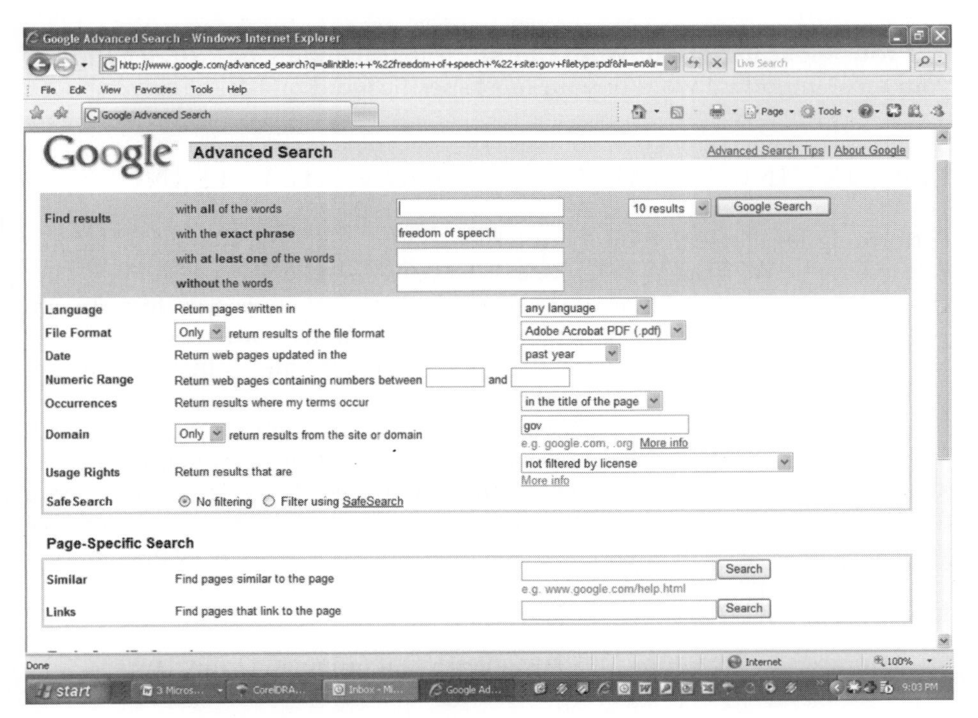

Exhibit 10–4
Advanced Search Options in Google
Courtesy of www.google.com

help file for the search engine(s) you are using to make sure you are entering search commands correctly. It is all too common for a user to assume the commands are the same for different search engines, but later find out the searches were not working properly because the syntax was incorrect for that search engine.

Make Your Search Query Specific To return only relevant documents, make your search query specific. For example, if you are searching for documents about the United States Supreme Court Rules, do not search for just United States Supreme Court. Also, use modifiers to make your search as specific as possible, such as these:

Use + (Plus) and – (Minus) Signs Use plus and minus signs to force a word's inclusion or exclusion in searches. For example, if the search was: *+Roosevelt–Theodore* the search would find documents with Roosevelt but without the word Theodore. If you wanted to find results that included Franklin Roosevelt and not Theodore, the query would be *+Roosevelt +Franklin –Theodore.* The plus and minus signs work in many but not all search engines.

Search for Phrases Using Quotation Marks If you are looking for a specific phrase, put the phrase in quotation marks so that the search engine will retrieve only documents that have the words exactly as they are typed. For example, *"Joint tenant with rights of survivorship"* would retrieve results with exactly those words in that order, not results where the words were scattered all over the document.

Combine Plus and Minus Signs and Phrases You can also combine the plus and minus signs and phrase searching in one query. For example, *"Franklin Delano Roosevelt"–"New Deal" + "World War II"*. This query would list results that had the exact phrase "Franklin Delano Roosevelt" and had the phrase "World War II" but did not have the phrase "New Deal."

Put Your Most Important Words First It is usually the best strategy to put your most important word or your most specific word first in the search.

PERFORMING LEGAL RESEARCH ON THE INTERNET

Performing legal research on the Internet can be done, but it is not at all like researching on WESTLAW or Lexis. In WESTLAW and Lexis, a user can look up, choose, and go to thousands of databases instantly; there is a uniform search engine and uniform Boolean language; and information is formatted neatly, succinctly, and uniformly. Even with all that, it still takes time, training, and experience to be proficient on WESTLAW or Lexis.

In performing legal research on the Internet, little is uniform. You must search for and find information where you can, and you must learn the nuances of many different searching techniques and search languages. There is no one central depository of information. As with any kind of legal research, the more experience you have, the better, but it takes time, training, and experience to be good at it.

You can expect to find the following legal research information on the Internet, by using the sites in Exhibit 10–5:

- Indexes by legal topic (tax law, intellectual property, family law, etc.)
- United States Supreme Court cases (extensive)

Exhibit 10–5
Legal Research Starting Points

SUBJECT	ADDITIONAL INFORMATION	WEB URL (ADDRESS)
	Legal Research Engine/Portal	
All Law	Legal search engine/portal	http://www.alllaw.com
FindLaw	Legal search engine/portal	http://findlaw.com
Lawguru	Legal search engine/portal	http://lawguru.com
Internet Legal Research Group	Legal search engine	http://ilrg.com
	General Starting Points (Federal/State Case Law, Statutes, and Legal Subject Matter)	
CataLaw	General legal related information and indexes	http://www.catalaw.com
Hieros Gamos	Large collection of links to legal resources	http://www.hg.org
Legal Information Institute at Cornell	Large collection of links to legal resources	http://www.law.cornell.edu
Virtual Chase	Large collection of links to legal resources	http://www.virtualchase.com
Law Research	Large collection of links to legal resources	http://www.lawresearch.com
WashLaw Web at Washburn University	Large collection of links to legal resources	http://www.washlaw.edu
World Wide Web Virtual Library: Law at Indiana University	Large collection of links to legal resources	http://www.law.indiana.edu/v-lib
	Federal Government Information, Regulations, Laws, Bills, U.S. Code	
SearchGov	Government search engine	http://www.searchgov.com
FedWorld	Government information	http://www.fedworld.gov
Google US Government	Government search engine	http://www.google.com/ig/usgov
First Gov	Government search engine	http://www.firstgov.com
Code of Federal Regulations	Database for the Code of Federal Regulations	http://www.law.cornell.edu
GPO Access	Wide variety of federal government resources	http://www.gpoaccess.gov
Cornell Legal Information Institute	Wide variety of federal government resources	http://www.law.cornell.edu
Library of Congress	Bills, resolutions, Congressional Record	http://thomas.loc.gov
	Legal Forms	
Internet Legal Resource Guide Forms	Free legal forms database	http://www.ilrg.com/
	Legal Encyclopedia & References	
Law About (from Cornell Law School Legal Information Institute)	Legal encyclopedia	http://www.law.cornell.edu
Legal Dictionary	Legal dictionary	http://www.legal-dictionary.org

continued

Law Dictionary	Legal dictionary	http://dictionary.law.com
Findlaw Legal Dictionary	Legal dictionary	http://dictionary.lp.findlaw.com
	Federal Courts	
Federal Courts Finder	Links to all Federal Courts	http://www.law.emory.edu
Administrative Offices of the U.S. Courts	Links to all Federal Courts	http://www.uscourts.gov
	State Courts	
National Center for State Courts	Information on state (and Federal) courts	http://www.ncsconline.org
	Fee-Based Legal Research	
Westlaw	Full online fee-based legal research	http://www.westlaw.com
Lexis	Full online fee-based legal research	http://www.lexis.com
Lexisone.com	Fee-based legal research for small firms	http://www.lexisone.com
Fastcase.com	Online fee-based legal research	http://www.fastcase.com
Loislaw.com	Online fee-based legal research	http://www.loislaw.com
Versuslaw.com	Online fee-based legal research	http://www.veruslaw.com
Casemaker.com	Online fee-based legal research	http://www.casemaker.us

- Federal appellate court cases (extensive)
- Federal district court cases (partial)
- Federal laws, regulations and legislative bills (extensive—including U.S. Code, Federal Register, Congressional Record, Code of Federal Regulations)
- Federal Rules of Civil Procedures, Federal Rules of Evidence, Uniform Commercial Code, Federal Rules of Criminal Procedure, and Federal Rules of Bankruptcy Procedure
- Executive orders / government sites (extensive)
- State court cases (extensive)
- State statutes (extensive)
- Legal forms
- Legal references (extensive)

Following are some strategies, adapted from *The Legal List—Research on the Internet,* to consider when beginning an Internet legal research project:

1. Decide whether the Internet is an appropriate place to find the legal information

If the user is looking for historic documents, including articles and statutes, or a solid case law background that dates before 1990, the Internet is probably not the place to search. It is better suited for current law, or recent cases or information. In short, the Internet is not a replacement for a traditional law library. With that said, depending on the subject matter, the Internet can have rich treasures of information, but you have to look for them.

A cost-conscious legal researcher should start by researching in any CD-ROM databases and hard-copy books that he or she has, since they are cheap and convenient. The user could then explore the Internet to see what is available on line. Again, this is cheap (actually free) and handy. Finally, the user could go to WESTLAW or Lexis to double-check and confirm the research, fill in any holes, and check citations (Shepardize).

2. Understand your legal project and have a strategy

It is important when doing legal research on the Internet to understand exactly what you are looking for and to have a strategy for finding it. The problem with looking for something on the Internet with no plan in mind is that you can easily spend three to four hours "surfing" from site to site without finding what you are looking for because the amount of information on the Web is so vast. Legal research on the Internet works best if you know exactly what you are looking for (e.g., a new U.S. Supreme Court case, a specific congressional bill, a specific federal regulation, or a specific provision of a state statute).

3. Choose a finding tool

Choose a finding tool or search engine that is suited to the type of information you are looking for. Some tools are better than others for finding specific kinds of information. Exhibit 10–5 includes a number of sites with a variety of finding tools. A user who plans on doing legal research on the Internet should have all of the websites in Exhibit 10–5 bookmarked. The first two sections of Exhibit 10–5 (legal research engine / portals and general starting points) are excellent places to start just about any type of legal research on the Internet.

4. Get help

Not only is the Internet a good source for legal and non-legal information, but it is also a good resource for getting help. It is advantageous to belong to listservs and discussion groups regarding the type of law you work with. When you get stuck or need help on a research project, ask for help. It is possible, if not probable, that others have experienced the same problem you have. You must, of course, be discreet in how you ask for help.

Legal Research on the Internet—An Example

If you wanted to read the U.S. Supreme Court opinion *New York Times Co. v. Sullivan,* 376 U.S. 254 (1964) on the Internet, you could take many avenues to get there. Because an historic case like this is probably available on the Internet, it would be a waste of money (unless you had a flat-rate agreement) to use WESTLAW or Lexis. As indicated previously, you need to determine where your starting point will be. While you could start at FindLaw, Lawguru, or another (legal search engine), it is probable that an important case like this would be on Cornell's Legal Information Institute site (<http://www.law.cornell.edu>). Go to Cornell's site and click "Court opinions," then "Supreme Court Collection," and then "By party—historic decisions." You will see an alphabetical list of historical decisions. Clicking "New York Times Co. v. Sullivan" will display the case on your screen.

If you know what you want and you have an idea where it is (we knew both of these things in this instance), research on the Internet can be done quickly and effectively. However, looking for the unknown or doing research from scratch on a topic you know nothing about can be a long process on the Internet. For example, if you were looking for all of the reported cases in your jurisdiction related to the duty of a property owner toward a trespasser, and were specifically seeking cases where the trespasser slipped and fell while trespassing, the Internet would be a difficult place to conduct this research. WESTLAW or Lexis would both yield far higher quality and much faster results. The free resources on the Internet are just not suited for this type of research yet.

Performing Factual Research on the Internet

> *We use the Internet to research medical conditions, prescription drug information, consumer and commercial product information, and court records to name a few examples. Some paralegals routinely are called on to locate people, such as witnesses, attorneys, and experts, and often quickly become "experts" themselves in any one of the myriad of subjects involved in their caseloads.*[5]

The Internet is best suited for factual research, since there is such a wide variety of information available. Factual research in a law office can cover innumerable situations where the users need information. Here are some typical examples of situations in which a legal assistant might be asked to do factual research.

- You are performing collection work and you need to do a skip trace on a debtor that has left the area.
- Your firm has a client who was adopted, and the client wants your firm to find his birth parents.
- A crucial witness for a case you are working on has disappeared, and you need to find the witness or her relatives or neighbors so you can get a message to her.
- The attorney you are working for has to cross-examine the other party's expert witness and has asked you to find out everything you can about the expert for impeachment purposes.
- Your corporate law department needs to find reputable local counsel to litigate a breach of contract case halfway across the country.
- One of your firm's best clients is considering a merger offer from another company. You have been asked to find out as much as possible about the other company, including looking at SEC filings, annual reports, stock prices, and any news reports on the company for the last year.
- Your firm has a case in an area that it has never handled before. You have been asked to locate another attorney who has national experience in this area and who can either be co-counsel or provide advice to your firm.
- Your firm is considering getting involved in a medical malpractice case and you need to do some general background research regarding a specific type of surgery and medical condition.
- Your client is considering purchasing a piece of real estate and you have been asked to go online and find out as much about the property as you can.
- During litigation the opposing party has made numerous statements to the press and you have been asked to find every occurrence where this took place and document exactly what the person said for impeachment purposes.
- Your client was involved in an auto accident and you have been asked to get a satellite picture of the intersection.

These are all situations where the Internet would be useful for finding information. Exhibit 10–6 shows listings of fact-related websites by subject. Notice that they can help the user find everything from how to find an email address, to who is an inmate in a federal prison, to financial data on a publicly traded company.

Unfortunately, when conducting factual research on the Internet there is no standard or uniform way of entering or finding information. It is a virtual haystack of enormous proportions and finding the needle takes time and effort and the user may have to look in many, many sites to find it, or never find it. If a user finds a site that has a standard way of entering information and which accesses a broad range of information, it will be convenient and less time consuming, but the user will surely have to pay for the information, because that kind of convenience does not come for free.

Exhibit 10–6
Factual Research Starting Points

General Sites

Subject	Additional Information	URL Web (Address)
Dictionary	Dictionary	http://www.dictionary.com
Dictionary	Merriam-Webster	http://www.webster.com
Encyclopedia	Encyclopedia	http://www.reference.com
Encyclopedia	High Beam Encyclopedia	http://www.encyclopedia.com
Encyclopedia	Encyclopedia Britannica	http://www.britannica.com
Encyclopedia	Microsoft Encarta	http://encarta.msn.com
General Factual Research Site	Good starting point for any factual research project	http://www.virtualchase.com
Maps	MapQuest	http://www.mapquest.com
National Lawyer Directory	Martindale-Hubbell	http://www.martindale.com
National Lawyer Directory	FindLaw	http://www.findlaw.com
Satellite Images	Satellite images for major cities	http://www.google.com (maps)
Thesaurus	Thesaurus	http://thesaurus.reference.com
Thesaurus	Thesaurus	http://www.reference.com
Zip Codes	U.S. Postal Service	http://www.usps.gov

Public Records (Free)

Name/Subject	Additional Information	URL Web (Address)
Court Cases/Criminal Cases (Federal)	PACER (Public Access to Court Electronic Records) provides access to an index of filings in federal district, bankruptcy and appellate courts	http://pacer.uspci.uscourts.gov
Criminal Records	Virtual Chase.com—Excellent links to federal and state resources related to criminal records	http://www.virtualchase.com
Criminal Records – Sex Offenders	Sex offender database	http://www.sexoffender.com
Public Record Links and Research Strategies	Virtual Chase.com—Excellent links to public records	http://www.virtualchase.com
Public Record Portal	BRB Public Information Records—Large portal to many sites with public records	http://www.brbpub.com
Real Estate Records	NETR online—Real estate public records	http://www.netronline.com
State Public Records	An excellent source of public records information is available from individual state websites. Many, but not all, states have a standard Web address: www.state.XX.us at XX enter the state's two-letter abbreviation.	

continued

	Example:	
	Florida = www.state.fl.us	
	New York = www.state.ny.us	
Vital Records Information	Births, marriages, deaths, divorces	www.vitalrec.com

Public Records (Fee Based)

Subject	Additional Information	URL Web (Address)
Public Records	Courthouse Direct—Various public information including criminal histories, property ownership, etc. in one place	http://www.courthousedirect.com
Public and Court Records	Court Records.Org—Various public information including criminal histories, property ownership, etc. in one place	http://www.courtrecords.org
Public Records	Search Systems—Wide variety of online information	http://www.searchsystems.net
Public Records	ChoicePoint Auto TrackXp—Wide variety of online information	http://www.autotrackxp.com
Public Records	Accurint—Wide variety of online information	http://www.accurint.com
Public Records	DBT Online—Wide variety of online information	www.dbt.com
Public Records	DCS Information Systems—Wide variety of online information	www.dnis.com
Public Records	Deepdata Access Information Systems—Wide variety of online information	www.deepdata.com
Public Records	Information America—Wide variety of online information	www.infoam.com
Public Records	KnowX—Wide variety of online information	www.knowx.com
Public Records	USDatalink Information Services—Wide variety of online information	www.usdatalink.com
Public Records	BRP—Wide variety of public information	http://www.brbpub.com

Finding People, Addresses, Phone Numbers and Email Addresses

Subject	Additional Information	URL Web (Address)
People, Address, Phone locator	List of links for finding people	http://virtualchase.com
Links and Articles on Finding People	Finding people	http://www.virtualchase.com
People, Addresses, Phone Numbers, Email Addresses, Yellow Pages	Yahoo	www.people.yahoo.com
People, Addresses, Phone Numbers	Database America	www.databaseamerica.com
People, Addresses, Phone Numbers, Email Addresses, Yellow Pages	Bigfoot	www.Bigfoot.com
People, Addresses, Phone Numbers, Email Addresses, Yellow Pages	Infospace	www.infospace.com
Email Addresses	Internet Address Finder	www.iaf.net
People	Classmates.com	www.classmates.com
People	Social networking site	www.facebook.com
People	Social networking site	www.myspace.com

continued

Other Information About People

Subject	Additional Information	URL Web (Address)
Federal Campaign Donors	Federal Candidate Campaign Money Page	www.tray.com
General Information About People (Living and Dead)	Family Finder Index—Includes information from census, marriage, Social Security, and other information	www.familytreemaker.com
Genealogy Links	Genealogy-related website links	http://www.cyndislist.com
Military Personnel	Listing of military personnel (small monthly cost)	www.militarycity.com
Federal Prison Inmates	Federal Board of Prisons	www.bop.gov
Physician List	American Medical Association	www.ama-assn.org
Death Database	Ancestry	www.ancestry.com
Government Record Search	Search of government records for finding people	http://www.governmentrecords.com

News and Directories

Subject	Additional Information	URL Web (Address)
News	Chicago Tribune	www.chicagotribune.com
News	Los Angeles Times	www.latimes.com
News	New York Times	www.nytimes.com
News	USA Today	www.usatoday.com
News	Wall Street Journal	www.wsj.com
News	Directory of News Links	www.newslink.org/menu.html
News	Electronic publications - Exhaustive list of publications available electronically	www.arl.org
News	ABC News	http://abcnews.com
News	CBS News	http://www.cbsnews.com
News	NBC News	http://www.msnbc.msn.com
News	CNN	http://www.cnn.com
News	Fox News	http://www.foxnews.com

Researching Businesses

Subject	Additional Information	URL Web (Address)
Business information	Links to sites with general business information	http://www.virtualchase.com company_information_index.shtml
Business phone/address listings	Bigfoot	http://www.bigfoot.com
Yellow Pages	Bigyellow	http://www.bigyellow.com
Major Corporation Websites		http://www.cio.com
Federal Securities and Exchange Commission	Required public filing for public companies	www.sec.gov/cgi-bin/srch-edgar
Annual Reports for Companies	Public Register's Annual Report Service	www.prars.com
Federal Securities and Exchange Commission	Electronic Data Gathering, Analysis and Retrieval (EDGAR) Database	www.sec.gov

continued

Business Information		www.hoovers.com
Business Information	Business-related information	www.companiesonline.com
Complaint Information	Better Business Bureau	http://www.bbb.org

Finding Expert Witnesses

Expert Witnesses	Claims Providers of America	www.claims.com
Expert Witnesses	Washburn University School of Law	http://www.washlaw.edu/
Expert Witnesses	Technical Advisory Service for Attorneys	www.tasanet.com
Expert Witnesses	Expert witness directory	www.expertpages.com
Expert Witnesses	Expert witness directory	www.ExpertWitnessnetwork.com
Expert Witnesses	Expert witness directory	http://expertwitness.lawinfo.com
Expert Witnesses	Expert witness directory	http://jurispro.com

Medical-Related Information

Subject	Additional Information	Web URL (Address)
Medical Dictionary	Medical dictionary	http://www.medterms.com
Medical Dictionary Online	Medical dictionary	http://www.online-medical-dictionary.org
Medical Conditions Glossary	Medical conditions	http://www.medical-conditions.org
MedLinePlus Medical Dictionary	National Library of Medicine	http://www.nlm.nih.gov mplusdictionary.html
Stedman's Electronic Medical Dictionary	Medical dictionary	http://www.stedmans.com

Searching for information on the Internet is like anything else; becoming good at it takes time and experience. The longer you spend doing it, the better you will become and the more resources and tricks you will learn. Below is additional information regarding factual research on the Internet classified by subject.

General Information

There is a wide variety of general information available on the Internet. General search engines are one excellent way to search for general information on the Internet. The quality and accuracy of this information varies a great deal. Exhibit 10–6 shows Internet sites for dictionaries, encyclopedias, maps, a zip code finder, thesauruses, resources for finding attorneys, and more. One extremely helpful Internet tool for legal organizations is sites providing free access to satellite images of a geographic area. These images are useful in a variety of contents including auto accidents, some criminal matters, and insurance and property casualty litigation.

> *I know your mother's maiden name, your date of birth, your address, and the price you paid for your house. I also know the name of the person who officiated at your wedding, the names of your children (and their dates of birth), the number of times you've been divorced, and how much you inherited from your great aunt. I know the amount of your liens, the type of tattoo you sport (and its location on your body), your political persuasion, and your religion. I even know you are mentally ill… and I've never met you. I know all this because you live in a jurisdiction where public records (state and local) are abundantly free and accessible by anyone with a computer, [time], and an Internet connection.*[6]

Public Records

Searching for public records on the Internet is an art form. In some instances, success requires more luck than science. Generally, public records do not contain personal information about people such as birth dates, social security numbers, and medical or financial information. However, much information is maintained in government records, which are public. Every state, every county, every city can have different rules for what information is public and what is posted online, including what form it takes, what can or cannot be searched, and at what cost. There is little uniformity in national public record searches. It pays for a user to know a lot about the jurisdiction they are seeking the information in. This takes time. It is also important to realize that often information published on the Internet, even when you *can* find it, is not as complete as information maintained at the source such as at a courthouse. By some estimates, only 35 percent of public records are available on the Internet and many of those are incomplete. Therefore, once a user has found a public record that is helpful it is recommended that the user check the actual source to see if other information is available.

The information available in public records is vast. Public record information for specific jurisdiction might include:

- Vital statistics (births, deaths, marriages)
- Corporate records such as secretary of state filings and Securities and Exchange Commission filings
- Court records
- Criminal records
- Licenses (law, medical, nursing, public accounting, insurance, etc.)
- Property-related information
- Sex offenders
- Adoptions
- Bankruptcies
- Judgments / Liens
- Campaign contributions
- Copyrights trademarks, and patents
- Environmental records
- Building permits and zoning
- Motor vehicle records
- Foreclosures
- Corporation commission filings
- Driver's license records

A good place to start is the jurisdiction where the information is kept. Is the information stored by a city, county, state, or federal government? The user needs to know this type of information before doing a meaningful search. For example, suppose you wanted to know the value of a defendant's property holdings in Houston, Texas. You could start at a fee-based public records site, but a better and less expensive way would be to start with the jurisdiction that holds the information. While this sounds easy, it can take some time to track this down if you are not familiar with how it works. In Houston, and in much of the U.S., property is tracked by county, not city. Trying to search for property records for the City of Houston would be futile. However, once you knew that Houston is in Harris County, Texas, you could search for the county in an Internet search engine and be directed to its site. Then, you could find the Harris County Appraisal District website, and use their record search tool to search by the name of the defendant to find all of the defendant's property holdings in Harris County, including the appraised value. The information is all right there.

Some counties in the U.S. even include pictures of the property. However, to find this kind of information, you just cannot Google it. This is how the "invisible web" works. The more a user knows about what they are looking for, where it is stored, and what names or labels it goes by, the better the user will be at trying to find the information the user is looking for.

The Internet is full of websites that charge for public information. Some provide a great value and access to information that would be difficult to find on your own, while others are not worth the time, money and effort. Again, it helps to know exactly what you are looking for. Before using a pay site, ask for references and ask a lot of questions.

Finding People and Information About Them

There is obviously a lot of information about people on the Internet. Sure, a user can "Google" someone by putting their name in a search engine, but many times this doesn't work well. First of all, if the user is conducting a nationwide search for a common name the user will get back thousands of hits. Even if the name is uncommon the user can still expect to get back dozens, if not hundreds, of hits. The more information you have about who you are looking for, the better. When trying to locate someone, it is recommended to start with the obvious, such as searching for their name in Google, Yahoo, and other general search engines listed in Exhibit 10–3, even though doing so will most likely turn up many names.

To cut down on irrelevant hits, it is recommended that you search for exact matches using quotation marks, such as "Cindy Allen," or even better "Cindy J. Allen" or "Cindy Allen" + Tampa. If you do not find who you are looking for, the next step is to use the resources in the "Finding People" section of Exhibit 10–6. This should be done slowly, making sure the name is always spelled correctly and using many variations based on the information you have. Being creative sometimes works, particularly if you know any information about the person that can be used during the search process. If the search is still unfruitful, you may want to use the resources at http://virtualchase.com. There are pages and pages of resources listed on this site and they are usually kept up to date and well maintained. Another alternative would be to try the free public record searches suggested in Exhibit 10–6. The last step would be to try a fee-based site such as http://www.accurint.com or http://www.autotrackxp.com. Both are comprehensive search services that offer access to a wide variety of national public records.

If you still do not locate the individual, old fashioned phone calling, or interviewing neighbors, family and friends, might be successful and provide needed information that can be used in subsequent online searches.

News

The Internet has vast numbers of news-related sites. Sometimes a user may need to find background information related to business dealings or companies. News sites provide broad-based information that is sometimes invaluable (see Exhibit 10–6). Another good tool is to use Google's News Alerts (go to http://google.com, click News, and then click News Alerts). Google News Alerts (see Exhibit 10–7) allow users to have Google automatically conduct searches and emailed the results to them. Notice in Exhibit 10–7 that the user has entered "Ford Explorer" as the search term. The user can then indicate what she would like Google to search (e.g., news, blogs, the Web, newsgroups, listservs, or all of them) and how often. This is a convenient way to stay on top of changing events. For example, if you had a client that was in a crash in a Ford

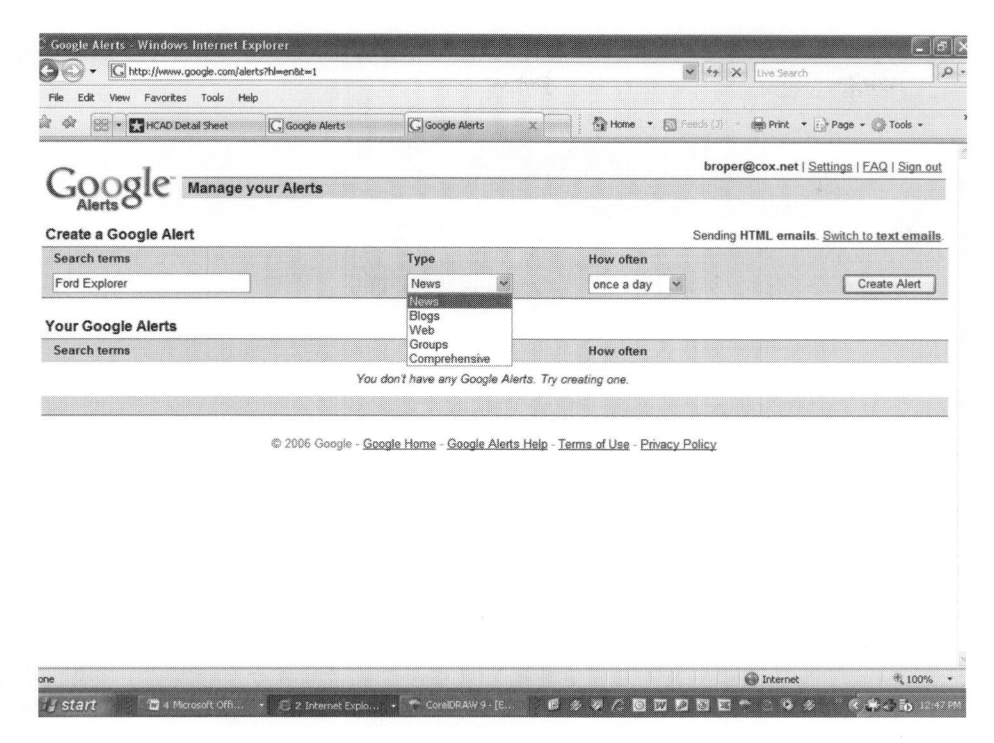

Exhibit 10–7
Google Alerts
Courtesy of www.google.com

Explorer you may want to stay current on information related to the vehicle, such as recalls, other crashes, and so forth. RSS feeds, covered earlier, can also be extremely helpful in staying up to date on news and blogs that are relevant to a case.

Researching Businesses

The Internet is the perfect tool for researching information about companies and businesses. Not only can you find a wealth of information using general search engines and news-related sites, but you can also find out a great deal of other information from more specialized sites. For publicly traded companies the U.S. Securities and Exchange Commission's (SEC) Electronic Data Gathering Analysis and Retrieval (EDGAR) database (http://www.sec.gov) is a good place to start (see Exhibit 10–8). The SEC requires companies to publicly report extensive current information. Corporate websites, press releases, litigation documents, judical decisions, public records such as state attorney general filings, and much more are readily available on the Internet. A good starting point is http://www.virtualchase.com. Virtualchase.com lists more than 100 sources for finding information about companies.

Expert Witnesses

Finding lists of expert witnesses is an easy task using the Internet. There are many sites devoted to this and many general legal sites also offer numerous databases for finding an expert witness on practically any topic (see Exhibit 10–6).

Medical-Related Information

There is much medical related information on the Internet. Exhibit 10–6 shows a few sites.

Exhibit 10–8
The "Find" Feature in Internet Explorer

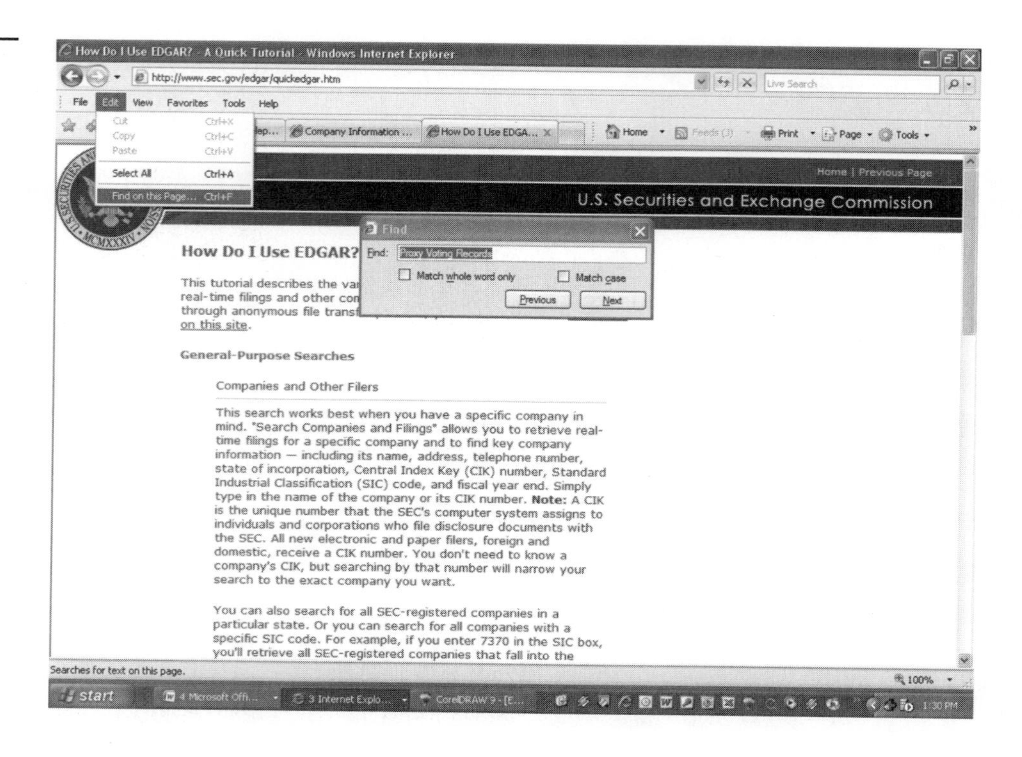

Internet Brower Tools

Internet browsers such as Microsoft Explorer and Firefox have several features that are invaluable when conducting Internet research. The Find feature in Microsoft Explorer [CTRL]+[F] allows the user to search for words on the open web page. It is common when using general search engines to click a link and then be taken to pages and pages of text without being able to see where your search terms were found. Using the Find feature, you can re-enter a search term and be taken directly to its location in the document. Another helpful feature is bookmarks (sometimes called favorites). Bookmarks and favorites allow you to save shortcuts to particular web pages. Not only can users save shortcuts, but they can also arrange the shortcuts into groups by setting up folders such as "news websites," "legal research sites," or "public record sites." Because serious Internet users may have hundreds of bookmarks or favorites, the ability to manage them in folders is critical.

spyware
A general term used for software that tracks a user's movement on the Internet (for ad/marketing tracking), collects personal information about the user, or changes the configuration of the user's computer without the user's consent.

computer viruses
Programs that are destructive in nature and can be designed to delete data, corrupt files, or do other damage.

Spyware and Viruses

Spyware is a general term used for software that tracks a user's movement on the Internet (for ad/marketing tracking), collects personal information about the user, or changes the configuration of the user's computer without the user's consent. Commonly spyware invades a user's computer when they download or install a program. Spyware is sometimes included in a download, but the user is not told about it or the information is buried in the licensing agreement. Whenever you install programs on your computer it is important to carefully read the disclosures, license agreement, and privacy statement. You also should install an anti-spyware program that can remove installed spyware and prevent future spyware programs from attaching.

Computer viruses are programs that are destructive in nature. Viruses can infect a computer when a user opens an attachment that is infected with a virus

or downloads a virus from the Internet. You should install an anti-virus program to prevent viruses from attaching to and infecting computers.

> *For researchers seeking sound information, the Internet presents new challenges. For the first time in history, anyone may disseminate information worldwide almost in an instant .... Can legal professionals avoid falling prey to .... con artists or to fiction masquerading as truth? Yes. But to do so, you must recognize the characteristics of quality in information. Valid information, whether on the Internet or in other various media formats, will usually possess at least the following four attributes: (1) objectivity, (2) timeliness, (3) accuracy, and, (4) authority.*[7]

PROBLEMS WITH RESEARCHING ON THE INTERNET

There are inherent problems with researching on the Internet that legal professionals should consider before beginning.

- *Research on the Internet can take longer to perform.* This is especially true when looking for cases, statutes, and other primary information, because it is spread over so many different sites. It takes experience to know where certain kinds of information reside on the Internet and which sites are better than others, especially for looking for historical cases or data. Users can literally spend hours and hours looking for information and never find it so it is important to have a plan and strategy for conducting Internet research.
- *Research on the Internet must be checked for accuracy and you must be able to give a cite to it.* Unlike WESTLAW, Lexis, and other fee-based information services, it is necessary to make sure that the data you have collected on the Internet is genuine. You must be able to cite the source of the information. Never assume that information on the Web is accurate. It is easy to let your guard down. There is no question that some of the information on the Web is fiction, conjecture, and speculation.
- *There are no added features in Internet information.* The legal researcher needs to remember that cases and other material on the Internet are raw in nature. There are usually no additional features like the case synopsis and keynotes at the beginning of the case that WESTLAW adds. For the most part, the information has not been managed, at least not to the extent that a fee-based service would manage it.

LEGAL ORGANIZATION WEB PAGES

Many legal organizations have created home pages on the Web. There are various reasons for this, many of which revolve around marketing and client relations.

Websites are open 24 hours a day, seven days a week, to local, national, and international customers and clients. A website is a particularly good idea for a legal organization with a specialized practice or a unique niche because it can reach potential clients anywhere in the world. Many organizations have found the marketing potential of a website to be enormous and cost effective when compared to other types of marketing alternatives.

Depending on the information on the website, the organization can also provide timely information to clients and potential clients. Many legal organizations offer legal-related information in their specialty area that would be useful to their clients, thus creating goodwill for the firm. A website can also be used

for recruiting employees such as legal assistants, attorneys, and other staff. Websites can be used by law firms to tell clients who they are and what their practice areas are, offer visitors a resource library of free information that they might find helpful, provide information about their community activities to create goodwill, provide a recruiting site to list open positions and to sell the firm to potential applicants, and provide information about their attorneys' areas of expertise.

Legal organizations have different strategies regarding their websites. Some firms use a brochure-type format much like a hard-copy brochure that presents general information about the firm. Information on the site may include firm history, practice areas, fees for services, staff profiles, geographic location of office and directions, links to other sites, and information that sets their services apart from their competitors. While the site provides information about the firm, it may not "pull" or attract web surfers (also known as potential clients) to the site who do not already know about the firm.

> *The truth is the Internet is the Internet, nothing more and nothing less. It is not a yellow brick road that instantly leads to overnight client-development success stories or hordes of clients that will beat down the door.…[However], through the Internet, lawyers are able to promote their services to prospective clients who were not previously within their reach. Lawyers can also utilize the Internet to enhance their delivery of legal services to existing clients through private websites (extranets). Each lawyer's success or failure with Internet marketing depends on his or her understanding, strategy, and execution in mastering the tools available in this new world of virtual communication.*[8]

Other firms turn their website into information sources and portals, where a vast amount of legal information about certain topical areas is presented. This type of strategy is designed to attract clients to the firm's web page because of the information and expertise shown on the site. Since Internet sites can be expensive to design, program, implement, and maintain, firms need a clear strategy and understanding of what the purpose of the site will be, what image they want to project, who the firm wants to attract, and what visitors will get or will want to find from their site.

Web page development can be done many different ways and can cost a few hundred dollars or tens of thousands of dollars. Some legal organizations hire outside computer companies to design and maintain their website, while others use in-house staff, including legal assistants and attorneys, to do the job.

Legal website design comes down to a just a few important features:

- Design—Good website designs load quickly, are clean and easy to read, have consistent colors and branding, and have a sharp look and feel.
- User-Friendliness—Effective websites are easy to use and intuitive. Users can quickly figure out and navigate their way around the site the first time. They can find what they are looking for without spending a lot of time hunting for it. A search tool should be included for finding detailed information and the site should have an up-to-date site map.
- Current, Relevant Content—It is often said that "content is king." No matter how good a website looks, if the content is not current it will not be successful. The information on the site must also be relevant to the user. So many choices are available on the Internet that often, if the content is not clearly visible within a few seconds of a visitor arriving, the

visitor will go to another site. Content should not only be current but should also be particularized and offer the user a number of helpful resources.

- Interactivity–Great websites are interactive. This means some content should be downloadable, uploadable, printable, and/or dynamic. Exhibit 10–9 shows a number of award-winning legal websites.

Legal Organization	URL
Sonosky, Chambers, Sachse, Endreson & Perry	http://www.sonosky.com
Reed Smith	http://www.reedsmith.com
Osborn Maledon	http://www.osbornmaledon.com
Hunton & Williams	http://www.hunton.com
Goodwin Procter	http://www.goodwinprocter.com
Jenkens & Gilchrist	http://www.jenkens.com
Larry King	http:///www.larrykinglaw.com

Exhibit 10–9
Award-Winning Legal Websites

LEGAL ORGANIZATION INTRANETS AND EXTRANETS

An **intranet** is an internal network designed to provide and disseminate information to internal staff using the look and feel of the World Wide Web. Similar to how the Internet provides information to the public, the intranet provides information to a legal organization's internal users. Users access the organization's intranet by using a web browser.

intranet
An internal network designed to provide and disseminate information to internal staff using the look and feel of the World Wide Web.

Legal organizations use intranets for a variety of purposes but mostly use them to allow people to share internal information, improve knowledge and teamwork, and streamline internal processes. Information usually included on intranets comprises human resources policies, procedural manuals, training information, forms, access to databases, articles, and links to external websites.

> *Intranets and extranets are quickly becoming the standing information and communication tool in the business community as well as the legal profession.... Intranets and extranets are a means of organizing and distributing a firm's knowledge and information base, and will eventually serve as the exclusive interface to the law firm's collection of information and knowledge.*[9]

An **extranet** is a secure web-based site that allows clients to access information about their case and collaborate with the legal professionals that are providing services to them. An extranet employs a variety of security measures to ensure that the general public does not have access to the site, and only clients or other authorized users can view it. Extranets can include document exchanges, case strategies, calendars, updates, forums for collaboration, information sharing, and much more. Extranets are particularly helpful when a legal matter is complex, multiple parties or multiple co-counsel are involved, and sharing of information is critical to the success of the matter. An extranet allows a legal organization to distribute information to one central spot where everyone involved can access it, no matter what their geographic location.

extranet
A secure web-based site that allows clients to access information about their case and collaborate with the legal professionals that are providing services to them.

> *Extranets can be a tool for managing cases and transactions, delivering the collaboration methods needed by internal and external virtual law firms, and fostering partnering arrangements between client law departments and outside counsel.*[10]
>
> *Simply put, an extranet is an online repository that can be enhanced with database features, calendars and a host of other services...Our extranet functions as a storage house for the thousands of documents related to the litigation as well as an area where current developments, deadlines and project information can be accessed. Clients don't lose a day asking us to send them documents or posing questions about whether we have received materials...they can see for themselves right away. To eliminate email traffic with large attachments...[we] use extranets as a distribution platform by posting drafts during a particular transaction and collaborating, making comments and reviewing directly online.*[11]

ELECTRONIC MAIL

Electronic mail (email) allows users to send and receive messages using a computer. When an Internet account is opened, the user is given an email address and can then send and receive messages. Hundreds of millions of people use email every day to communicate.

There are many advantages to using email. Messages can be sent almost instantaneously nearly anywhere in the world; email is very inexpensive; word processing, sound, and graphic files can be attached to email messages; messages can be sent, read, and replied to at the user's convenience; email prevents telephone tag; messages can be sent to groups of people at the same time; users can get their messages from anywhere; and messages can be saved, tracked, and managed electronically. A common client complaint is that legal professionals are often very busy and hard to reach. Email allows legal professionals and clients to communicate with one another quickly and conveniently.

Email in the Legal Environment

Email is now a major means of communicating with clients, other attorneys, and courts, and most legal assistants use email every day in their jobs. In a recent survey of legal assistants approximately 97 percent said they use email daily in their jobs. Email is being used in legal organizations for everything from routine correspondence, to billing, to newsletters, to filing court papers. Most clients now demand email access to their lawyers and legal assistants. The security of email has long been a concern to legal professionals, but in recent surveys the majority of legal organizations indicate that they send confidential or privileged communications/documents to clients via email. The issue of security can be handled a number of ways including requiring clients to provide oral or written consent to sending confidential information via email, adding a confidentiality statement at the end of all emails, using encryption software, or just not using email to send confidential documents. In addition, new uses of email are springing up. Service of process by email has even been approved by a few courts.

Email Software

Sending and receiving email requires email software. Exhibit 10–10 shows the market share of email programs used by legal assistants. According to a recent survey, Microsoft Outlook is used by approximately 87 percent of legal assistants. Email software performs a variety of functions including storing names and email addresses in an address book, retrieving messages, forwarding messages, storing sent messages, and attaching files to messages.

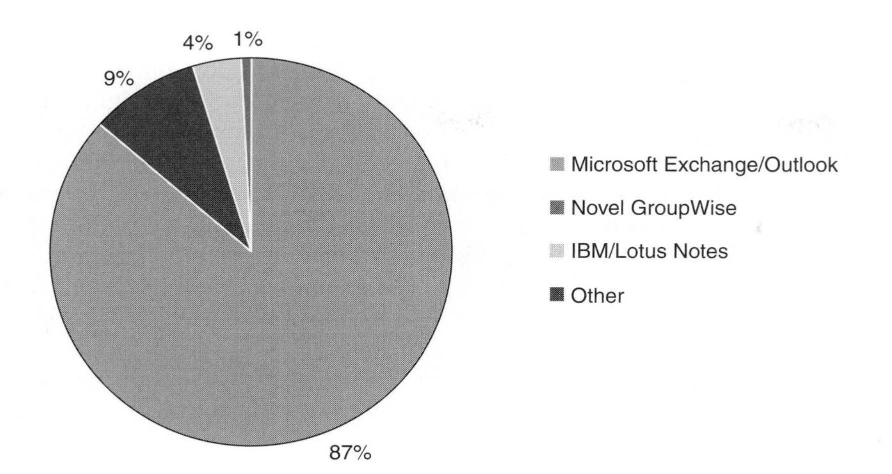

Exhibit 10–10
Legal Organization Email Platforms
This chart was first published in ILTA's 2006 E-Mail Survey and is reprinted here with permission. For more information about ILTA, visit their website at www.iltanet.org.

Spam **Spam** refers to unwanted or unsolicited email messages. It is nearly identical to junk mail. Spam has become quite common, and many laws have been passed to stop spam, but it continues. It is now standard practice to install spam filters on computers (programs that limit the amount of spam that gets through).

spam
Unwanted or unsolicited email messages that are sent to users—nearly identical to junk mail.

Phishing **Phishing** is a type of Internet fraud whereby "phishers" send fraudulent emails in which they impersonate legitimate senders in hopes of gaining personal information from users such as passwords, social security numbers, and bank account information. Many times, the phishers create exact replicas of real sites that look legitimate and authentic. Email and Internet users should always be suspicious of messages that ask for personal information.

phishing
A type of Internet fraud where "phishers" send fraudulent emails in which they impersonate legitimate senders in hopes of gaining personal information from users.

> *The exponential growth of email for client-related exchanges has increased the potential for knowledge management and records management breakdowns. Today's information is spread out in personal inboxes that can't be easily accessed, leveraged, protected, and properly stored. When email that should be part of the client/matter file sits in an email inbox—an unmanaged repository—chances are that the knowledge contained in the email may never be harnessed or, worse yet, could be lost or deleted. Content that constitutes a record may never be properly declared as a record. Allowing email to reside in attorney inboxes is a huge client service and risk management issue. Email system are not storage tools; they were not designed as large capacity repositories.*[12]

Email Record Retention and Destruction

Email has become a de facto standard for client communication. This has caused a number of issues and problems that at first were not anticipated. For example, typical email mailbox sizes can be 500 MB or more. Email mailboxes were never intended to be a place for client storage. In years gone by, legal professionals would send client correspondence via letter and keep a copy of the file. Now, email is so prevalent that hard-copy correspondence is the exception and not the rule. As a way to deal with this change, many legal organizations now have record management software where legal assistants and attorneys can store electronic case-related information in a central networked environment that provides for searching and other capabilities. Now, in many firms, legal professionals must "file" client emails, not in the folders in their email programs, but in the folders of their record management program. By filing the email in the

records management program, it creates a record that others in the firm can access, and create a firm-wide record of the email. In addition, once the email is in the records management program, retention rules can be assigned to the email so that it is properly destroyed according to the retention rules.

Another problem with email left in email folders is that there is no destruction of records; they live on forever. Record retention policies are put in place to limit the amount of information retained based on what the information is. Some legal organizations have moved to automatic deletion of emails in mailboxes (not those stored in record management programs) after a certain number of days (typically 90 or 180 days). This helps manage the amount of storage the email systems continually use, to keep the performance of the email system fast, and to reduce potential liability for retaining records that are not needed but that may contain information harmful to the legal organization.

> *We decided to use our document management system (DMS) as our email repository, so that our users could simply drag and drop email to a DMS folder. The process is based on what they were already doing, but instead of dragging email into an Outlook folder, users can now drag and drop or use the Outlook "file move to folder" feature to place documents directly into a DMS folder ... We then set up auto-profiling so that email placed into a folder adopts the properties of that folder. This prevents the user from needing to profile each email separately [including setting the proper document retention time frame].*[13]

Email Encryption and Digital Signatures

Because email can pass through many network servers before it reaches its destination, it is subject to being read by system administrators, hackers, and others. It is often said that email is more like a postcard than a sealed letter. Some legal organizations use encryption software to protect confidential emails sent to others. Encryption software is used to lock email so that it can be opened only by the intended recipient. There are two types of encryption program designs. One is called symmetric and the other asymmetric (also called public key).

With symmetric encryption, the sender runs the email through the encryption program and a key is created that scrambles the file. Then the sender sends the encrypted email to the recipient and separately transmits the decoding key, which is typically a password or a data file. Running the same encryption program, the recipient uses the decoding key to unscramble the message. Symmetric encryption is fast but not as safe as asymmetric encryption because someone could intercept the key and decode the messages. But because of its speed, it is commonly used for e-commerce transactions.

Asymmetric encryption (also called public key encryption) is more complex, but it is also more secure. Two related keys are required: a public key and a private key. The user makes a public key available to anyone who might send the user encrypted information. That public key can only encode data; it cannot decode it. The private key stays safe with the user. When people wish to send the user encrypted information, they encrypt it using the user's public key (but only the user can decrypt it with the user's private key). Thus, the person sending the user a message has a digital signature file that has been encrypted with the sender's private key. When the user receives the message, the user decrypts it with the private key. Asymmetric encryption is more complex and the process takes longer, but it is safer.

Email Etiquette and Tips

The following email etiquette will help you communicate your messages effectively to the reader.

- *Be succinct and clear, and use short paragraphs.* Whenever possible, keep your emails short and to the point. You should be as clear as possible in your messages so the reader does not have to ask for clarification regarding something you wrote. Use paragraphs liberally. Long paragraphs are hard to read on a computer screen, and it is easy to lose your place, particularly if you have to scroll up and down the message.
- *Spell check and reread your emails.* Most email programs have a spell check function. Use it whenever possible. Many users send emails that are full of spelling and grammar errors that can sometimes change the meaning of the message. Before sending your emails, reread them to make sure they make sense.
- *Be careful to treat email as business correspondence.* Emails cannot be retrieved once they are sent. They are written records that are kept by the recipients, so be extremely careful about what you send and make sure that you can live with the message. When in doubt, do not send it. Also, remember that the recipient cannot see your body language or interpret your tone, so be careful how you phrase things.
- *Do not use ALL CAPS.* Using all caps is equivalent to SHOUTING! Use all caps only when absolutely necessary.
- *If a message is unclear, ask for clarification.* If you are unsure about a message someone has sent you, ask for clarification and do not assume you know the answer.
- *Be careful of Reply All.* Sometimes users get an email with twenty other people copied on it. If the user selects Reply, only the sender of the original email will get a response, but selecting Reply All will send a reply to all twenty of the recipients. Far too often, a user intends to send a personal message to the sender of the email and mistakenly selects Reply All. Before you select Reply All, make sure you really want to send it to everyone on the original message.
- *Check email daily.* If possible, check emails daily and do not allow them to stack up, particularly if clients email you regularly.
- *Do not use email to communicate with clients regarding sensitive information.* For communicating with clients about sensitive information, it is probably better not to use email at all, but if in doubt always ask the client first. Since email can pass through many network servers where the email can be read, it is better not to use email for sensitive information.
- *Double-check the recipient of your email.* Often users intend to send email to one person and accidentally select the wrong person. Always doublecheck the email address to make sure you entered the correct one.
- *Limit each email message to one topic.* It is difficult to decide where to file multiple-topic emails and it is sometimes difficult to follow up on them. There could be multiple follow-up actions buried in one email.
- *Always password protect word-processing and other documents sent to clients.* By password protecting documents you add some degree of security to the attachment with minimal effort.

Problems with Email

While email is inexpensive and convenient, it is not perfect. Keep the following considerations in mind when using email.

- *Do not assume that an email was read just because you sent it.* Like any other form of written communication, email can be lost, the message not opened, or the message accidentally deleted.
- *Email relies on computer technology that fails from time to time.* Email works only if the computer networks are functioning correctly, if the telephone lines or other technology are working, and if a recipient's computer hardware and software are working correctly. If any of these fail, your message will not reach the recipient.
- *Be careful what you say in emails, since they can be forwarded to others.* The nature of an email is that it can be easily forwarded to another person. For example, you may send an email to X about Y, and X may immediately forward it to Y.
- *Email security can be breached.* As noted before, email is not necessarily confidential and email security can be breached in many ways including the following:
  - leaving confidential emails open on your computer screen for others to read over your shoulder
  - leaving your office for lunch or for a break while signed into your email program
  - printing off emails that others find (such as at a network printer)
  - using a password such as "password" or names of family members that would be easy for others to guess

ETHICAL CONSIDERATIONS

There are several ethical considerations regarding the use of the Internet and email. These include the reliability of information on the Internet that you might use to support a client's case, problems regarding marketing on the Internet, the confidentiality of email when corresponding with clients and others, using unsolicited email to market a law firm to others (spam), and making email errors.

Reliability of Information on the Internet

As mentioned earlier in this chapter, the reliability of information on the Internet is not guaranteed. Since anyone can host a website, send emails, post information on listservs and discussion groups, and generally communicate freely on the Internet with little if any oversight, the user cannot assume any information is necessarily accurate. There is a tremendous amount of information on the Internet that is opinion, hearsay, innuendo, and flat-out untruth. The Internet user should adopt a *caveat emptor*—"Let the buyer beware"—philosophy. Whenever possible you should attempt to verify information found on the Internet and develop cross checks to make sure the information is accurate. This is particularly true when using new sites that you have never used before. It is not unlike using *Shepard's* to check the accuracy of cases that you cite to make sure they are still current law.

While there is no specific ethical rule on this subject, attorneys must perform work in a competent manner. See *ABA Model Rules of Professional Conduct* 1.1.

When performing factual or legal research on the Internet for a client's case, legal professionals must do so in a competent and thorough manner so they do not cite inaccurate information.

Marketing on the Internet

Many law firms market their services to clients using the Internet. Attorney advertising and marketing is an area of legal ethics that is heavily regulated by most states due to the potential for abuse.

According to the ABA Model Rules of Professional Conduct, lawyers cannot use false or misleading information; create unjustified expectations, such as publishing recent jury verdicts they received; and cannot solicit clients directly that they do not or have not had a relationship with (ambulance chasing).

The ABA recently updated the *Model Rules* to more closely regulate Internet-based marketing. The new rules apply to all electronic communication including all forms of Internet marketing: law firm web pages, using banner ads, using links, using Internet chat rooms to solicit clients, and using email to solicit prospective clients, among others. States are also taking the lead in regulating Internet-based marketing.

Marketing on the Internet—Spam

As indicated previously, spam is sending unsolicited emails to others. In an infamous case in Tennessee, a lawyer spammed email listservs and discussion groups with a promotion for his immigration practice. The spam was reportedly received by thousands and thousands of people in many countries and resulted in many complaints to the Tennessee disciplinary authority. The attorney was charged with ethical violations including: (a) failing to label his email as advertising; (b) failing to submit a copy of the email to the state bar disciplinary authorities; (c) making reference to himself as an "immigration lawyer," in violation of a rule governing specialization; and others as well. The Tennessee Supreme Court suspended the attorney's license for one year as a result of the spamming.

Email Confidentiality

As discussed earlier, confidentiality while using email to communicate with clients is an important issue. According to the *ABA Model Rules of Professional Conduct,* attorneys must maintain the confidentiality of client-related information.

The ABA issued a formal opinion on this issue (see ABA Standing Committee on Ethics and Professional Responsibility, Formal Opinion No. 99–413, March 10, 1999—Protecting the Confidentiality of Unencrypted email). The committee stated

> *A lawyer may transmit information relating to the representation of a client by unencrypted email sent over the Internet without violating the Model Rules of Professional Conduct because the mode of transmission affords a reasonable expectation of privacy from a technological and legal standpoint. The same privacy accorded U.S. and commercial mail, land-line telephonic transmissions, and facsimiles applies to Internet email. A lawyer should consult with the client and follow her instructions, however, as to the mode of transmitting highly sensitive information relating to the client's representation.*

The ABA found that email affords users a reasonable standard of expectation of privacy and therefore concluded that unencrypted email could be used to communicate with a client. However, the ABA also found that an attorney had a duty to consider the sensitivity of the issue being communicated, what it would mean to the client's representation if the communication were disclosed, and the relative security of the contemplated means of communications. Arguably, the ABA wants legal professionals to use a common sense standard when using email or other forms of communicating with clients. If communication with a client is highly sensitive, then the attorney should consult with the client about whether a more secure form of communication is warranted.

Practical considerations for using email ethically include the following:

- having a policy for the legal organization regarding the use of email and how it will be used to communicate with clients

- consulting clients about what type of information they want to communicate via email, how often the client receives or responds to email, and other information about the particulars of the client's specific email system or habits
- making sure the email addresses are accurately entered so that client communication is not sent to others by mistake
- sending a test email to a client to ensure the right email address is being used
- adding a confidentiality statement to all client emails—this is similar to statements that accompany many fax cover pages that state that the information is intended solely for the recipient and any third party who receives it should immediately forward it or destroy it
- not using email at all for particularly sensitive information

Email Errors

It is important to be careful when using email. Errors can happen several different ways and could result in malpractice claims against the legal organization. Some common errors include the following:

- *Sending an email to a client or others before it is carefully considered*—Unlike a letter placed in the outgoing mailbox that can be retrieved a few hours later, once the user presses the send button, email is gone.
- *Sending email to unintended parties*—It is easy to use the Reply All command to send a private message to a group of people unintentionally, or to click on the wrong email address. Depending on the content of the message, errors like these can damage a client's case, particularly when email is sent to the opposition.
- *Sending the wrong attachments*—Since files can be sent with emails as an attachments, it is particularly important to ensure that the correct file is attached. It is easy to attach the wrong file to an email including one that might be devastating to a client's case. This can be avoided by opening the file after it is attached to the email to make sure it is the correct one.
- *Typing errors*—Typing errors, such as words left out, can substantially change the meaning of a sentence. For example, in a client email you might intend to type "We don't recommend that you do this," but instead you type, "We recommend that you do this." While you have left only one word out, that word could be crucial to how the client proceeds.
- *Don't send out metadata in attachments*—As discussed previously in the text, metadata is information that is included in documents and attachments and that may be seen and read by recipients, such as information which can be found in the Properties and Track Changes sections of Microsoft Office products. Any documents that are sent outside of the legal organization should normally have the metadata checked and removed.

SUMMARY

The Internet is known as the information superhighway. It connects hundreds of millions of computers and thousands of networks around the world. Services on the Internet include email, listservs, newsgroups, Internet Relay Chat, Instant Messaging, File Transfer Protocol, Gopher, Telnet, World Wide Web, blogs, RSS, and podcasts. More than 95 percent of all legal assistants use the Internet on a daily basis in their jobs.

There are several different types of search engines on the Web, including individual search engines that compile their own searchable databases, subject-oriented search engines that organize information into topical menus of subjects, and

INTERNET SITES

Internet sites for this chapter include the following:

General Legal Assistant/Legal Sites on the Internet

Organization	Product/Service	World Wide Web Address
ABA Legal Technology Resource Center	In-depth information related to legal Internet, intranet, and extranet sites	<http://www.abanet.org>
FindLaw	A premier legal research portal/search engine	<http://www.findlaw.com>
Hieros Gamos	Legal portal and legal research resources	<http://www.hg.org>
Internet Legal Resource Guide	Large collection of links to legal resources	<http://www.ilrg.com>
Law and Politics Internet Guide	Large collection of links to legal resources	<http://www.lpig.org>
Legal Information Institute at Cornell Law School	Large collection of legal resources	<http://www.law.cornell.edu>
Virtual Chase	Large collection of legal resources for conducting a variety of legal and factual research on the Internet including manuals on how to conduct such research	<http://www.virtualchase.com>
WashLaw at Washburn University Law School	Large list of links to legal research resources	<http://www.washlaw.edu>

metasearch engines that send a search to multiple search engines. The "invisible web" or "deep web" refers to the fact that approximately 50 percent of the World Wide Web lies behind databases, is password protected, or otherwise is not accessible through search engines. To access those sites the user must go directly to them.

The Internet can be used to perform legal research but it is not at all like using WESTLAW or Lexis. The legal research information is not contained in one central depository. Legal research on the Internet is most efficient when the user knows exactly what he or she is looking for, such as a specific case or statute. The Internet is better suited for factual research than for legal research. The Internet can be used for performing general research, public record searches, finding people or information about people, accessing news information, conducting business research, and finding expert witnesses among others. Spyware and viruses must be avoided if possible, and software can be loaded that prevents or reduces the chances of either of these types of programs attaching to a user's computer. Many legal organizations maintain web pages on the Internet. They represent a 24/7 opportunity for marketing the legal organization.

Approximately 97 percent of legal assistants use email on a daily basis in their jobs. Email is a de facto standard for communication throughout the legal community and between legal professionals and clients. Spam, phishing, and other hazards represent the downside of email.

KEY TERMS

Internet
Internet Service Provider (ISP)
electronic mail
listserv
USENET (newsgroups)
Internet Relay Chat (IRC)
instant messaging
File Transfer Protocol (FTP)
Gopher
Telnet
World Wide Web
hypermedia or hypertext links
web browser
Uniform resource locator (URL)
blog
RSS
podcasts
bookmark
individual search engine
specialty search engine
metasearch engine
subject directory
portal
library gateway
subject-specific database
invisible web
spyware
computer viruses
intranet
extranet
push technology
spam
Phishing

TEST YOUR KNOWLEDGE

1. To connect to the Internet a user needs an ISP. What does ISP stand for?
2. What is another name for an electronic mailing list that allows people on the list to send and receive email to and from everyone on the list?
3. True or False: The Internet has no real use in legal organizations.
4. ____ is a group of formats that are used to publish and distribute news feeds, blogs, and podcasts.
5. True or False: Online learning and Internet depositions are two ways the Internet can currently be used by legal organizations.
6. What is the difference between individual, specialty, and metasearch engines?
7. The fact that search engines like Google and Yahoo can only search about 50 percent of the World Wide Web is referred to as ____________.
8. What tool can users access to better control their searches in search engines such as Google?
9. If a user wanted to search for bikes but not motorcycles in a search engine such as Google, what would the search be?
10. True or False: Performing legal research on the Internet is a lot like using WESTLAW or Lexis.
11. True or False: The Internet is better suited for factual research than for legal research.
12. Name three categories of factual information related to a case that a legal assistant might search for on the Internet.
13. A useful tool in an Internet browser that allows a user to search the contents of a web page is called ______.
14. Name three Internet or email hazards.
15. True or False: In this day and age there is no worry about client confidentiality regarding email; it is perfectly acceptable to send highly sensitive or confidential email to clients.

ON THE WEB EXERCISES

1. Using a general search engine such as Google or Yahoo or an other tool, find three law-related blogs. Write a two-page paper summarizing the content found on the three blogs.
2. Go to http://www.google.com and use the Advanced Search tool to find a current list of the most heavily used search engines on the Web. Specifically, use the date feature to only pull articles that are not more than three months old. Write a short paper regarding the results of your paper, including what the top three most used search engines are.
3. Using a general search engine such as Google or Yahoo or another tool, find one article related to accessing the "invisible" or "deep" web. Write a two-page paper summarizing the contents found in the article.
4. Visit any five websites listed in Exhibit 10–5. Print out the title page of each site and write a two-page summary comparing and contrasting the five sites.
5. Using a general search engine such as Google or Yahoo or another tool, find one article related to accessing public records on the Web. Write a two-page paper summarizing the contents of the article.
6. Visit any five websites listed in Exhibit 10–6. Print out the title page of each site and write a two-page summary comparing and contrasting the five sites.

7. Using the Google Maps feature at http://www.google.com, print out a satellite picture of where you currently live. If a satellite image is not available, print one out of a place you are familiar with.
8. Visit the websites listed in Exhibit 10–10 and write a one-page paper summarizing which website you liked the best and why.
9. Using a general search engine such as Google or Yahoo, find one article on email etiquette. Write a one-page paper summarizing the contents of the article.
10. Locate and print out the *Model Code of Ethics and Professional Responsibility* for the National Federation of Paralegal Associations.
11. Find a list of local legal assistant organization websites that are associated with the National Association of Legal Assistants.
12. Find and print out the American Bar Association's *Model Guidelines for the Utilization of Legal Assistant Services.*
13. Compare the results of at least three separate search engines for finding the website for the Association of Trial Lawyers of America. Which search engine did you like the best and why?
14. Find an email address for any member of Congress from your state. How did you go about finding the email address?
15. Find a list of law-related listservs and subscribe to at least one.
16. Using the Internet, locate the full texts of the U.S. Supreme Court cases of *Bates v. State Bar of Arizona, In re R.M.J., Zauderer v. Office of Disciplinary Counsel,* and *Shapero v. Kentucky Bar Association.* Read the cases, provide a one-paragraph summary of each case, and discuss where and how you found the cases.
17. Using the Internet, find a list of Web resources for immigration law.
18. Find regulations implementing the Family and Medical Leave Act by searching in the Code of Federal Regulations as published online by the U.S. government.
19. Use SEC EDGAR filings and other information to research recent developments regarding the Microsoft Corporation. Use at least five different sources of information. Prepare a one-page summary of the information.

QUESTIONS AND EXERCISES

1. Interview an attorney, legal assistant, or secretary in a legal organization regarding their use of the Internet and email. How has it changed over time?
2. As a new legal assistant in a solo practitioner's office you notice that the office has been slow to embrace technology. The office does not have a high-speed Internet connection and the attorney does not see the need to get one because the Internet is barely used in the office. The office mainly handles personal injury, divorce, and collection cases. Write a one-page memo to the attorney regarding how using the World Wide Web might positively impact the office.

END NOTES

[1] Rick Klau, "Easy Instant Messaging," *Law Practice Management,* October 2002, 12.
[2] Kim Plonsky, "Legal Blogging," *Legal Assistant Today,* May/June 2006, p. 62, 66.
[3] Rod Hughes, "Knowledge is Power," *Legal Assistant Today,* May/June 2002, 54.
[4] Kim Plonsky, "Free Internet Tools for Paralegals," *Legal Assistant Today,* January/February 2007, 41.
[5] Carole Levitt & Mark Rosch, "Forget Privacy," *Law Technology News,* December 2006, 30.
[6] "Genie Tyburski, "Honest Mistakes, Deceptive Facts," *Legal Assistant Today,* March/April 2002, 54.
[7] Edward Poll, *Attorney and Law Firm Guide to The Business of Law,* American Bar Association, 2000, 128.
[8] Edward Poll, *Attorney and Law Firm Guide to The Business of Law,* American Bar Association, 2000, 416.
[9] Eric H. Steele and Thomas Scharbach, "Planning Your Technology Future: Top Trends to Focus on Now," *Law Practice Management,* November/December 2001, 18.
[10] Ari Kaplan, "The Extranet Revolution," *Legal Assistant Today,* November/December 2006, 69.
[11] Tanya Garig, "Getting Organized," *Legal Technology News,* October 2006, 48.
[12] Tanya Garig, "Getting Organized," *Legal Technology News,* October 2006, 48.

HANDS-ON EXERCISES

LEGAL AND FACTUAL RESEARCH ON THE INTERNET

Basic

Number	Lesson Title	Concepts Covered
Lesson 1	Using a Legal Search Engine – Part I	Find practice/subject matters indexes on FindLaw.com, free legal forms in the Internet Legal Research Group, and find free legal-related news articles in Alllaw.com.
Lesson 2	Using a Legal Search Engine – Part II	Find a legal dictionary in Lawguru.com, find a large number of law journals in the Internet Legal Research Group, and find an attorney by subject matter and zip code on Lawguru.com.
Intermediate		
Lesson 3	Conducting Legal Research on the Internet—Part I • U.S. Supreme Court • State/Federal Rules	Find United States Supreme Court Cases, state court rules, and federal court rules.
Lesson 4	Conducting Legal Research on the Internet—Part II • State Statutes • U.S. Code • Code of Federal Regulations	Keyword searching for state statutes, keyword searching in the U.S. Code, and keyword searching in the Code of Federal Regulations.
Lesson 5	Conducting Legal Research on the Internet—Part III • Current Congressional Legislation • Congressional Record • Federal Appeals Court Opinions	Keyword searching current Congressional legislation, keyword searching Federal legislative history in the Congressional Record, and keyword searching Federal appeals court opinions.
Lesson 6	Conducting Factual Research on the Internet—Part I • Expert Witnesses • Attorneys • Satellite Images	Find expert witnesses using ExpertPages.com, find attorneys in particular specialties by city/state using Martindalehubble.com, and find satellite images using Google.
Lesson 7	Conducting Factual Research on the Internet—Part II • Federal Bureau of Prisons Inmate Locator • State criminal records search	Find federal inmates using the Federal Bureau of Prisons Inmate Locator, conduct state criminal background checks.
Lesson 8	Conducting Factual Research on the Internet—Part III • Real estate/appraisal searches • State vital record searches • Federal statistic searches	Find county real estate appraisal records, find state vital records (birth, death, marriage, divorce); and find statistics from the federal government.

continued

Advanced

Number	Lesson Title	Concepts Covered
Lesson 9	Conducting Factual Research on the Internet—Part IV • Securities & Exchange Commission Filings (EDGAR) • Library Gateway—Prescription Drug Search • Library Gateway—Airlines	Find Securities and Exchange Commission Filings using the EDGAR database, find the top 300 prescribed drugs in the U.S. using a library gateway, and find airlines and airport-related information using a library gateway.
Lesson 10	Conducting Factual Research on the Internet—Part V • Annual Reports • Whitepages.com • Salary.com	Find business annual reports on the Internet, find individuals using whitepages.com, and find salary information using salary.com

GETTING STARTED

Introduction

Throughout these lessons and exercises, information you need to type into the program will be designated in several different ways:

- Keys to be pressed on the keyboard will be designated in brackets, in all caps, and in bold (press the: **[ENTER]** key).
- Movements will be designated in bold and italics ***(point to File on the menu bar and click the mouse).***
- Words or letters that should be typed will be designated in bold (type **Training Program**).
- Information that should be displayed on your computer screen is shown in the following style: ***Press ENTER to continue.***

OVERVIEW

These Hands-On Exercises assume that you have a web browser, that you are generally familiar with it, and that you have access to the Internet. The exercises are designed to give you experience using a number of different websites and practice finding different kinds of information. Because the use of web browsers is straightforward and routine, only summary instructions are included in these exercises. **The instructions are current as of this writing, but websites change from time to time, so it is possible that the instructions will not work on sites that have been significantly changed.** If you encounter this problem, just skip that assignment and go to the next.

Basic

LESSON 1: USING A LEGAL SEARCH ENGINE – PART I

Exercise Number	Exercise Objective	Instructions	Comments
1.a.	Find the practice/subject matter indexes on FindLaw.com and find an article related to the State of California and the need for employees to use an organization's internal	• Go to http://www.findlaw.com • Click "For Legal Professionals" at the top of the page • Click "Practice Areas"	Notice that FindLaw has more than forty subject-matter practice areas. Searching subject matter indexes in

continued

Exercise Number	Exercise Objective	Instructions	Comments
	grievance procedures before suing in court	• Click "Administrative Law" • Click "FindLaw Library – Administrative Law Documents, Briefs, Articles and Books" • Click "Judicial Review" • Click on "Decisions Reviewable" • Click "Exhaustion of Administrative Remedies" • Click "California Employers Gain Yet One More Reason for Internal Grievance Policies and Procedures." • Print the article	legal search engines sometimes produces excellent information.
1.b.	Find a free residential lease agreement valid in the state of New York using the Internet Legal Research Group (ilrg.com)	• Go to http://ilrg.com • Click "ILRG Legal Forms Archive" • Click "Leases and Real Estate" • Click "Agreement to Lease (Residential Lease)" • Click "New York" • Scroll down to see/read the "New York Residential Lease Agreement" • Copy the text of the letter and paste it into a word processor • Print the lease agreement	The Internet Legal Research Group has an excellent free forms archive. Many forms on the Internet are for sale, but this site provides many types of forms for free.
1.c.	Find a free legal-related news site using Alllaw.com	• Go to http://www.alllaw.com • Click "Reference & News" • Click "Legal News" • Read and print out the current table of contents	

LESSON 2: USING A LEGAL SEARCH ENGINE – PART II

Exercise Number	Exercise Objective	Instructions	Comments
2.a.	Find a term in a legal dictionary in Lawguru.com's legal search engine	• Go to http://www.lawguru.com • Click "Legal Dictionary" under "Legal Resources" • Search for "Pari Delicto" and print out the definition	
2.b.	Find access to law review articles using the Internet Legal Research Group	• Go to http://ilrg.com • Under ILRG Web Index in the Academia section, click on "Law Journals"	Not only can you see the table of contents for the current Harvard Law Review, but you

Exercise Number	Exercise Objective	Instructions	Comments
		• Scroll down the long list of law journals and click *Harvard Law Review* • Print the table of contents for the current edition	can also click on the articles and read the full text of them.
2.c.	Find an attorney by subject matter and by zip code	• Go to http://www.lawguru.com • Under "LawGuru Tools" click "Find a Lawyer" • Enter your zip code • Under Area of Law select Immigration Law and then click "Search." • Click one of the attorneys' names • Print the listing for the attorney	

Intermediate

LESSON 3: CONDUCTING LEGAL RESEARCH ON THE INTERNET – PART I

Exercise Number	Exercise Objective	Instructions	Comments
3.a.	Find the full text of the United States Supreme Court case of *Faragher v. City of Boca Raton* decided by the Court in 1998 using the Legal Information Institute at Cornell	• Go to http://www.law.cornell.edu/ • Point to "Court opinions" • Click "US Supreme Court Opinions" • Under "Archive of decisions" under "By party" click "1990-present" • Next to "1997–1998" click "1st party" • Click "*Faragher v. City of Boca Raton*" • The syllabus of the court is then displayed, and you can click the HTML or PDF version under "Opinion" to read the full opinion	Notice that when you have a case name and a year and you know the court (particularly if it is a U.S. Supreme Court case) it is easy to find a case on the Internet.
3.b.	Find the Rules of Criminal Procedure for the State of Alaska using Washlaw.edu (search by keyword)	• Go to http://www.washlaw.edu • Click "Alaska" • Under "Courts" click "Rules of Court" • Print the listing of the "Alaska Rules of Court" • Click "Criminal Procedure" to see the Alaska Rules of Criminal Procedure	Notice that the Washlaw site has a large index that includes all fifty states, many federal resources, and that there are many listings for Alaska law. Having so many resources for a state on one page is very convenient.

Exercise Number	Exercise Objective	Instructions	Comments
3.c.	Find the Federal Rules of Civil Procedure using Washlaw.edu	• Go to http://www.washlaw.edu • Under "Federal" click "Court Rules" • Click "Federal Rules of Civil Procedure" • Print the table of contents	Notice that many rules for the Federal courts are listed in one convenient place

LESSON 4: CONDUCTING LEGAL RESEARCH ON THE INTERNET – PART II

Exercise Number	Exercise Objective	Instructions	Comments
4.a.	Access the New Hampshire Revised Statutes using Washlaw.edu and find the statutes related to criminal theft (search by keyword)	• Go to http://www.washlaw.edu • Click on "New Hampshire" • Under "Statutes" click "New Hampshire Revised Statutes" • Under "Full-Text Searching" click "Search" • Search for "criminal theft" • Click "Chapter 637 Theft" • Print out the first page of the statute	When searching for specific state statutes, you can often enter search terms and find the statutes you are looking for. While this works when searching for state statutes, it often does not work when looking for case law (e.g., you may not be able to put in search terms).
4.b.	Access the United States Code (laws made by the U.S. Congress) using the U.S. House of Representatives site (search by keyword)	• Go to http://uscode.house.gov • Click "Search the U.S. Code" • In the "Search Word(s)" field, type "Racketeer-Influenced and Corrupt Organizations" (do not use quotation marks) • Click 18 USC Sec. 1961 (Note: There may be more than one listing) • Print the first page	The US House of Representatives site is an excellent and fast place to search the US Code.
4.c.	Access the Code of Federal Regulations (rules made by federal agencies and executive departments) using FindLaw (search by keyword)	• Go to http://www.findlaw.com • Click "Cases & Codes" • Under "Codes, Statutes and Regulations" click "Code of Federal Regulations (CFR)" • In the Search field type "Family and Medical Leave Act of 1993" • Scroll down to "29CFR825—Part 825 The Family and Medical Leave Act of 1993" and click "TXT" (a text file) or "PDF" • Print the first page	

LESSON 5: CONDUCTING LEGAL RESEARCH ON THE INTERNET – PART III

Exercise Number	Exercise Objective	Instructions	Comments
5.a.	Search for a current bill in Congress using the Library of Congress Thomas site (search by keyword)	• Go to http://thomas.loc.gov • In the "Legislation in Current Congress" section, in the "Search Bill Text" field, type "Tax" (do not type the quotation marks). You will then see all of the bills with "Tax" in the title • Print the first page • Use the Back button • At the Thomas main page under "Browse Bills by Sponsor," select a member of Congress and view the bills that the member sponsored or cosponsored • Print the first page	
5.b.	Search the Congressional Record for legislative research using The Library of Congress Thomas site (search by keyword)	• Go to http://thomas.loc.gov • Click "Congressional Record" on the left side of the page • Click 109 (for the 109th Congress) • Under "Enter Search," type "Pension Protection Act of 2006" (do not type the quotation marks). • Click "PENSION PROTECTION ACT OF 2006 — (Senate — September 05, 2006)" to read a speech by Senator Clinton. • Print the first page	
5.c.	Search Federal Appeals Courts by circuit (search by keyword)	• Go to http://washlaw.edu • Under "Federal" click "10th Circuit Court" • In the search box to the left of "Search 10th Circuit Court Index," type "age discrimination Heslet" (do not type the quotation marks) • Click "05–3177 – Heslet v. Westar Energy Inc. – 04/05/2006." The opinion is then displayed • Print the first page	You can keyword search most federal circuit court opinions going back at least 10 years.

continued

LESSON 6: CONDUCTING FACTUAL RESEARCH ON THE INTERNET – PART I

Exercise Number	Exercise Objective	Instructions	Comments
6.a.	Find a dental expert using ExpertPages.com	• Go to www.expertpages.com • Click "Medical & Surgical Specialties" • Click on "Dentistry and Oral Surgery" • Click your state • Print the first page of the results • Review the experts that are listed by visiting several of the experts' websites	Notice that the site has a wide variety of specialty areas to choose from.
6.b.	Find an attorney in College Station, Texas that specializes in personal injury cases using Martindalehuble.com	• Go to www.martindalehubble.com • Click "Advanced Search" • In the City field, type "College Station" • In the US/State field, click Texas • In the "Areas of Practice" field, click Personal Injury • Click "Search" in the lower right of the screen • Print the first page of the attorneys that were returned • Review the qualifications of several of the attorneys	
6.c.	Find a satellite image of the Golden Gate Bridge	• Go to http://www.google.com • Click Maps • Double-click San Francisco, California • Keep double-clicking the map. The Golden Gate Bridge is north on highway 101 and is toward Richardson Bay. You should also see the Golden Gate National Recreation Area just to the north and west of the bridge • When you can read the words "Golden Gate Bridge," click "Satellite" • Double-click to zoom in on the bridge. You can use the "+" (plus) and "-" (minus) signs to the left to increase and	The satellite map tool is a free and very useful feature in Google. There are many applications where it can be helpful to legal organizations.

Exercise Number	Exercise Objective	Instructions	Comments
		decrease the magnification, and you can use the arrows just above the magnification tools to move the image forward and backward along the stretch of the bridge • Print the page	

LESSON 7: CONDUCTING FACTUAL RESEARCH ON THE INTERNET – PART II

Exercise Number	Exercise Objective	Instructions	Comments
7.a.	Federal inmate search using the Federal Bureau of Prisons	• Go to http://www.bop.gov • Click "Inmate Locator" on the left side of the page • In the "Search By Inmate Name" section under "Last" type: Kaczynski • Under "First" type: Theodore • Under "Race" click: White • Under "Sex" click Male • Click "Start Name Search" • The record for Theodore John Kaczynski (a.k.a. the Unabomber) should be displayed • Print the page	
7.b.	State criminal background searches using tools in VirtualChase.com	• Go to http://www.virtualchase.com • Under "Database of Sources" on the left side, click "Legal Research." • Click "Legal Resources" on the right side of the screen. • Under "Criminal Records" on the right side of the screen, click "State." • Scroll through the list of sites • Notice that some of the information is public while other is not, and that some of the sites are fee-based while some are free • For example, click the link to the "Pennsylvania Access to Criminal History." Users can run a criminal background report in Pennsylvania (because it is deemed a public record), but the cost is $10.00	

continued

Exercise Number	Exercise Objective	Instructions	Comments
		• Close the Pennsylvania Access to Criminal History window to go back to http://www.virtualchase.com • Click the link to the "All States National Sex Offender Public Registry" • Click "I agree" at the Conditions of Use screen. If you are prompted to retype a code that is displayed on your screen, do so. • Enter your zip code, click on your state, and then click "Search" to display a list of registered sex offenders in your area. • Print the page	

LESSON 8: CONDUCTING FACTUAL RESEARCH ON THE INTERNET – PART III

Exercise Number	Exercise Objective	Instructions	Comments
8.a.	Real estate record search using a county website	• Go to http://www.co.shawnee.ks.us • Click on Departments • Click on Appraiser • Click on Commercial Search • Scroll to the bottom of the page and click "Proceed with Regular Search" • In the "Address Search" section under "Number" type 700 • Under "Direction" click "S" • Under "Street Name" type "Kansas" • Click "Search" in the "Address Search" section • Click "700 S Kansas Ave Topeka 66603" • The appraisal record for the property should be displayed. The appraised value along with a digital photograph of the property should be included	

Exercise Number	Exercise Objective	Instructions	Comments
		• Print the page • Click "Building Data" near the top of the screen. You now show see the square feet of the building and other information about the structure(s)	
8.b.	Vital record search (birth, death, marriage, divorce)	• Go to http://www.cdc.gov/nchs/about/major/natality/sites.htm • Click "Minnesota" • Under "Certificates and Records" click "death record." The screen should now display how to get a death certificate. There is usually a small cost involved in getting a birth, death, or marriage certificate, but the information is usually a public record Print the page	
8.c.	Statistical records using Fedstats.gov	• Go to: http://www.fedstats.gov • On the left side of the screen, click the down arrow and select "South Carolina" and then click on "Submit" • Scroll down through the list and look at all of the statistical information regarding the state • Print the list • Click on "back" to go back to http://www.fedstats.gov • On the right side of the screen click the down arrow and select "Labor," then click "Submit" • To the right of "Bureau of Labor Statistics" click "Key Statistics" • Click "Unemployment" • Scroll down and notice on the right side of the screen that the unemployment rate for each state is listed	The Fedstats site gives users access to an enormous amount of data. Finding the data the user needs takes time and patience. If users cannot find the data they need, a quick call to the agency responsible for the information can often shorten the amount of time it takes to find it.

Advanced

LESSON 9: CONDUCTING FACTUAL RESEARCH ON THE INTERNET – PART IV

Exercise Number	Exercise Objective	Instructions	Comments
9.a.	Find current Securities & Exchange Commission filings using EDGAR for Ford Motor Co.	• Go to http://www.sec.gov. • Under "Filings & Forms (EDGAR)" click "Search for Company Filings" • Under "General-Purpose Searches" click "Companies and Other Filers" • At "Company name:" type Ford Motor Co and click "Find Companies" • Click "Ford Motor Co" • Print out the first page of the SEC filings for Ford • Scroll down the list until you come to Form "10-K/A" and then click HTML • Click Form10-KA.htm • Scroll down through the document and you will eventually come to a full financial statement for Ford	Once users get comfortable with In SEC filings there is a tremendous amount of detailed information including compensation plans, detailed financials and other product/sales information.
9.b.	Use the Digital Librarian Library Gateway to find a listing of the top 300 drugs used in the U.S.	• Go to http://digital-librarian.com • Click "Health and Medicine" • Scroll down through the list • Click "RxList: the Internet Drug Index" • Click "Top 300" at the top of the page to see the top 300 drugs dispenses in the U.S. • Print out the first page of the list • Click one of the drugs to see detailed information about the drug	Library gateway sites can offer the user a large number of access points to the web based on topic.
9.c	Use the Digital Librarian Library Gateway to find a listing of major Airlines worldwide and other airline-related information	• Go to http://digitallibrarian.com • Click "Airlines" • Scroll down through the list of airlines to see their web addresses and toll-free phone numbers • Under "Ratings and Safety" and to the right of "Federal Aviation Administration (FAA)," click "Flight Arrivals" • Hover the mouse pointer over an airport; and a brief description of any delays or other information is listed • Click an airport to see additional information related to the airport	

LESSON 10: CONDUCTING FACTUAL RESEARCH ON THE INTERNET – PART V

Exercise Number	Exercise Objective	Instructions	Comments
10.a.	Use AnnualReports.com to find annual reports related to large businesses	• Go to http://www.annualreports.com • Under "Search by Company Name" type: Boeing and then click "Search" • Click "Boeing Company" • Click "Boeing Company Annual Report"	Annual Reports can have a tremendous amount of useful information related to business litigation.
10.b.	Find people using the Internet	• Go to http://www.whitepages.com • Type your name and address in the "People Search" section and then click "Search" • Print the page • Click "Find Neighbors" towards the top of the page (just below the main tabs) • In the "Find Neighbors" section, type the address and then click "Search:"	
10.c.	Find Salary Data	• Go to http://www.salary.com • Under "Enter Job Title" type: Paralegal • At "Zip Code," enter your zip code and then click on "Search" • Click on "Paralegal I" and then print out the report • Click on Paralegal II, III, and IV to see the full range of salaries in your area	

CHAPTER 11

COMPUTER-ASSISTED LEGAL RESEARCH AND CD-ROM LEGAL DATABASES

CHAPTER OBJECTIVES

After completing Chapter 11, you should be able to do the following:

1. Explain why manual research and computerized research compliment one another.
2. Explain what is involved in planning a search query.
3. Formulate simple search queries for WESTLAW or LexisNexis.
4. Identify the advantages and disadvantages of CD-ROM legal databases.

computer-assisted legal research (CALR)
Uses computers to research and retrieve legal information.

CD-ROM legal database
A CD-ROM disk containing a legal database such as a state case law reporter, and searchable like WESTLAW and LexisNexis.

This chapter introduces computer-assisted legal research and CD-ROM legal databases. **Computer-assisted legal research (CALR)** uses computers to research and retrieve legal information. Two of the most common CALR service providers are WESTLAW and LexisNexis. A **CD-ROM legal database** is a CD-ROM disk that has a legal database such as a state case law reporter on it. The CD-ROM legal database can be searched using search techniques similar to those used with WESTLAW and LexisNexis.

INTRODUCTION TO COMPUTER-ASSISTED LEGAL RESEARCH AND CD-ROM DATABASES

In many cases, a combination of manual and computer research is advantageous, particularly in those situations where the user is performing complex research using one of the subscription services, such as WESTLAW or LexisNexis.[1]

I'm convinced that legal researchers who haven't spent time learning how to do book-based research will find themselves at a disadvantage vis-a-vis those who have. The disadvantage arises not from any inherent superiority of books over computer, but from the characteristics inherent in computer-automated text retrieval.

—Christopher G. Wren, Assistant Attorney General, Criminal Appeals Unit, Wisconsin Department of Justice

Legal professionals routinely must conduct legal research, whether it is done using manual methods; Internet-based legal research; computer-assisted legal research with fee-based service providers such as WESTLAW, or CD-ROM legal databases. Each of these methods has advantages and disadvantages. For example, manual legal research methods use a completely different methodology for conducting the research than computer-assisted research. For some legal projects it produces the best results in terms of the quality of research. For other projects, Internet-based legal research can be the least expensive way of finding the research information desired. Because Internet-based legal research information is scattered all over the Web in thousands and thousands of different sites, it tends to work best when the user knows exactly what he or she is looking for, such as a specific case or statute.

> *Internet-based legal research bears little resemblance to computer-assisted legal research using WESTLAW, LexisNexis, LOISLAW, or other fee-based databases.*[2]

Computer-assisted legal research, using on-line fee-based service providers (third-party vendors) such as WESTLAW, LexisNexis, and others, offers yet another alternative. Users subscribe to the service and are given a password for accessing it. Users have a choice of either accessing the service by going through the Internet (with a password) or connecting directly to the service using a modem. Unlike Internet-based legal research, fee-based CALR can be expensive. After a user connects to the CALR service, the user accesses a database to perform legal research. CALR services have thousands and thousands of different databases, so they offer an extremely large pool of information to draw legal research from. The user then searches the database using key words or phrases to find the legal information he or she is looking for.

Another alternative is to use CD-ROM legal databases, where a specific database has been stored on one or more CD-ROM disks. The search techniques used to find information on them are similar to CALR services such as WESTLAW or LexisNexis. The advantage is that they are much cheaper to use than WESTLAW or LexisNexis, but they are not as up-to-date as the online services.

Many legal organizations use a combination of all of these methods to conduct legal research, again, because each has its advantages and disadvantages and each may be the best, depending on the specific situation involved. In most circumstances the best quality of legal research is conducted when a combination of manual and computer-assisted legal research is used.

MANUAL LEGAL RESEARCH

Traditionally, legal research was accomplished using manual methods. Manual legal research is performed in a law library, using books, periodicals, indexes, and digests. Usually, the first step in researching a specific legal issue is to find the appropriate subject heading that covers it in a legal index or digest.

When a relevant case or statute is located in an index or digest, the researcher must pull the bound volume containing the information so that the entire case or statute can be read. Cases and statutes should also be cite checked. **Cite checking** means checking to see that a case or statute is still valid and that the decision has not been overturned or the statute repealed.

cite checking
Checking to see that a case or statute is still valid and that the decision has not been overturned or the statute repealed.

Manual legal research does offer some advantages over computer-based legal research. When conducting computer-based legal research the user becomes the "indexer" and must decide what words or phrases the author

might have used to describe a situation or case the user is looking for. This is important, since the user may not be an expert (and typically is not) in that particular subject matter, so the user is searching for something that he or she may not know much about. The user is also completely dependent on the computer software to perform the search. If the user is inexperienced with the particular program or service, or makes one assumption when the computer makes a different one, cases or material can be overlooked or left out of the results. When conducting manual research, users use manual indexes that have been written by people, typically attorneys, librarians, or experts in indexing. These expert indexers can create sophisticated, conceptually focused indexes that computer searching simply cannot. In addition, manual indexes include not only the exact words of the text indexed but also synonyms, cross-references, summaries, and other analysis that can help the user find what he or she is looking for. Particularly for legal researchers inexperienced in a particular area of the law, manual research provides features that give insight into doctrine, concepts, and analysis that computer-assisted legal research does not. Some studies have shown that when legal researchers have used computer-assisted legal research they have retrieved only 20 to 25 percent of the relevant material when they thought they were retrieving a much higher amount.

> *If I look at this issue from a purely selfish point of view as a practitioner, I hope law students [and legal assistants] will ignore books and other print publications. That gives me a significant competitive advantage: I'll have a broader range of sources to draw on, and I'll know how to use them effectively, and the "newbie" lawyers [and legal assistants] won't. I know that in the areas in which I practice, I can comfortably do most of my work via a computer. But I also know that I'll waste a considerable amount of time if I adopt the same approach when I enter an area of law about which I know little or nothing, and that books will get me to my goal faster.*
>
> *—Christopher G. Wren, Assistant Attorney General,*
> *Criminal Appeals Unit, Wisconsin Department of Justice*

CALR: ONLINE LEGAL DATABASES

CALR searches the words of the cases, statutes, and documents themselves. Legal professionals use their own computers and telecommunications equipment to access legal information services. These services have large databases that contain the full text of federal and state cases, statutes, and legal periodicals. The amount of information available depends on the legal information service.

search query
An instruction to an information service to search a specific database for the occurrence of certain words and combinations of words.

Once connected to a legal information service, the user must select a database and then enter a search query. A **search query** instructs the information service to search a specific database for the occurrence of certain words and combinations of words. The legal information service responds by retrieving all cases or documents that meet the search query. For example, a search query could be formulated to find all occurrences of the words automobile, rollover, and liability in cases for the state of California. The CALR system would then retrieve a list of cases that fulfill the search query.

Because legal information services use the full text of a document, indexes and digests are not needed. Instead, a user simply enters common words that describe the issue, and the system retrieves all cases and documents that meet the request. WESTLAW and LexisNexis are the exception to this general rule. WESTLAW and LexisNexis users can either search the full text of documents (bypassing indexes or digests) or they can use headnotes (an indexing / digesting system). Since the information is stored electronically on large mainframes, the

database can be searched and the documents quickly retrieved. The documents that are retrieved can be read online, sent offline to a printer, or downloaded to a user's computer and then cut and pasted into a word-processing document. **Online** means being connected to an information system and running up charges. **Offline** means no longer being connected to an information service and not accruing charges except possibly a printing or downloading charge. Documents can also be sent via email or facsimile to a particular destination with some services. Alternatively, a list of the appropriate cases or documents can be printed or downloaded so a user can go to a library and examine the hard copy book.

online
Connected to an information service and running up charges.

offline
No longer connected to an information service and not accruing charges except possibly for printing or downloading.

Cite checking can also be done using CALR. Many legal information systems can check the validity of cases or statutes almost instantly.

When CALR is used correctly, it can find or retrieve cases that might not otherwise have been found using manual methods, owing to poor indexing or other errors.

CALR can also be more convenient than manual research. Nearly all legal information services are available 24 hours a day, unlike many law libraries. Also, the research can be done from a legal professional's own office. Further, sources are always available online with CALR.

Another important consideration is that new cases usually are entered into legal information services within a few hours or days of being handed down or decided. Therefore, the information that is available online is almost always more up-to-date than information available in books.

Although CALR is both fast and convenient, it is not free. Commercial legal information services charge yearly subscription fees and fees based on the amount of time connected to their systems. Some legal information services also charge fees for every search that is done on their systems. Some services have connect time charges, which are usually billed by the minute. In addition, some services have a minimum monthly charge, even if the service is not used. Because CALR is so expensive, new users can run up large bills quickly. Therefore, it is particularly important that new users have a thorough understanding of the CALR system they will be using. Some legal organizations bill this expense to their clients, either directly or by incorporating the cost of CALR into their hourly rate.

Some services, such as WESTLAW and LexisNexis, now offer flat-rate billing options as an alternative to paying for connect time. For a flat monthly fee, the firm can have unlimited access to all or certain libraries or databases specified in the package. LexisNexis, for example, offers a program for small law firms called LexisOne where the user can specific what databases to include in the flat rate fee. The more databases included in the package the higher the fee. Regardless of billing method, an attorney or legal assistant can load the needed software on a laptop or home computer and access WESTLAW or LexisNexis from anywhere in the country through a toll-free number or through the Internet.

FEE-BASED COMPUTER-ASSISTED LEGAL RESEARCH SERVICES

> *Today, only retired partners, law firm messengers, and people needing a quiet place to think or write can be found in law libraries, as virtually all legal resources have been digitized and made accessible through electronic data library services. Today, lawyers can access the law wirelessly from their office, or over their Blackberries.*
>
> *-Unknown-*

There are a number of companies that currently provide CALR services to the legal community. WESTLAW and LexisNexis are by far the largest and offer users the most depth in terms of legal and non-legal electronic resources available. Other CALR providers include Loislaw (http://www.loislaw.com), National Law Library (http://www.itislaw.com), Fastcase (http://www.fastcase.com), and Versuslaw (http://versuslaw.com). Exhibit 11–1 shows fee-based CALR providers used by practicing legal assistants. WESTLAW and LexisNexis continue to have the largest share of the market. While users have several options for fee-based CALR, due to the cost involved, users should always plan some basic strategies before going online to do CALR, including knowing which service to use, what database will be accessed, and related information.

Exhibit 11–1
Fee-Based Computer-Assisted Legal Research Used by Legal Assistants
As seen in the May/June 2006 issue of *Legal Assistant Today,* Copyright 2006 James Publishing, Inc. Reprinted courtesy of *Legal Assistant Today* magazine. For subscription information call (800) 394–2626, or visit www.legalassistanttoday.com.

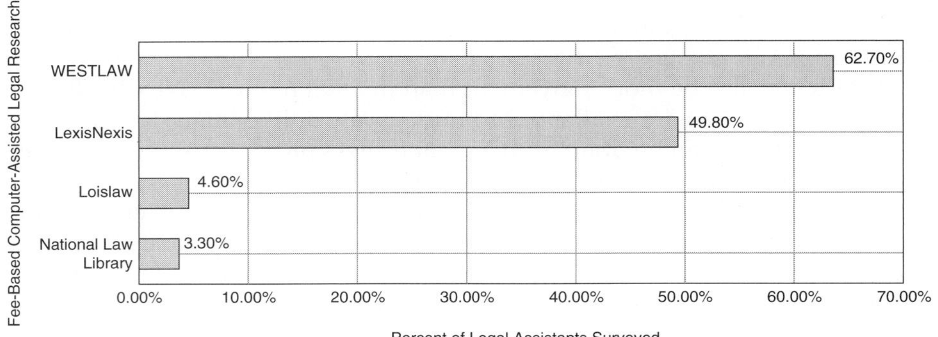

Determine Which CALR Service To Use

Determine which service you would like to use before going online. Many different services are available and each has advantages and disadvantages. Some law firms use WESTLAW exclusively or LexisNexis exclusively, while others subscribe to both providers because each service has different strengths. Some legal organizations bypass both WESTLAW and LexisNexis and instead use free Internet sites for legal research or use relatively low-cost alternatives such as the National Law Library or Loislaw.

Know Which Databases You Want to Access

Always plan which databases you want to search. Most CALR providers have hundreds or even thousands of searchable databases. For instance, if a user wants to search for all cases on a certain topic within the state of New Mexico, he will tell the service to access the New Mexico case law database and begin the search. It is better to know in advance which databases you will be accessing than to decide when the meter is running and costs are being incurred.

Know the Name of the Client the Research Is For

Find out the name of the client the search is being conducted for. About half of all law firms charge clients back for CALR costs, so it is important to know what case the research is for.

Know the Facts and Issues of the Case

It is important for a user to have a good understanding of the facts of the case he or she is working on and specifically what issue or question the user needs to answer by completing the research. It is remarkably easy to spend hours

online haphazardly looking through case after case and incurring costs but not finding what you are looking for, so it it is important to stay focused on the goal of the research. Another reason users must have a good understanding of the factual and legal issues of the case is that often a search must be modified to be more restrictive. (For example, if a query is so broad that 800 cases are returned, there will be far too many cases to skim through). Thus, to effectively restrict a search you must have a good understanding of the issues involved in order to effectively hone the search down to only relevant information.

Know How You Want the Information Delivered

Once you have retrieved the cases or documents you were looking for, it is important to know what format the information should take. WESTLAW and LexisNexis, for example, give several different options for storing the information. You can print the information to a printer, save the document as a PDF file, have the document sent to an email address, download the information to a word-processing file, copy the information to the Clipboard, or have the document sent to a fax machine. Many users will download the information to their word processor, since this gives them many options. Once downloaded, users can read the information at their leisure, cut and paste the information into another document such as a brief or pleading, or print the information.

WESTLAW

This section contains general information about how to use WESTLAW, its many features, how to navigate around the system, and how to use WESTLAW as a research tool. WESTLAW is a full-text computer-assisted legal research service provided by Thomson/West. According to Thomson/West, WESTLAW it is one of the largest law libraries in the world, with more than 17,000 separate databases available for its users. It contains case law from all federal and state courts, statutes from all fifty states, legislative history of acts of Congress, statutes, regulations, case dockets, public records, business and legal news, law reviews, treatises, and much more.

Accessing WESTLAW

WESTLAW can be accessed using either the Internet or a computer with a modem and Westmate software. To access Westlaw via the Internet, a user needs a Web browser, an Internet account, and a Westlaw account. The web address for WESTLAW is http://www.westlaw.com. To enter the WESTLAW site, the user enters a WESTLAW password and a Client ID. The Client ID lets users can track their WESTLAW usage and charge the costs back to specific clients (see Exhibit 11–2).

Welcome to WESTLAW Screen

When WESTLAW is started it typically brings up the "Welcome to Westlaw" page (see Exhibit 11–3). Current news and information about Westlaw is displayed in the screen's main section. Note in Exhibit 11–3 that there are three tabs displayed in the upper left of the screen: "Paralegal," "Westlaw" and "Business & News." The "Westlaw" tab is what is currently displayed in Exhibit 11–3. The tabs are somewhat customizable and are covered in more detail later in the chapter.

KeyCite is WESTLAW'S cite-checking feature. It allows users to check to see if cases and statutes are still good law or if they have been overturned or otherwise negatively affected. KeyCite also allows users to find every time a case or statute has been cited or referenced by other cases. In Exhibit 11–3 there are several references

Exhibit 11–2
Westlaw Sign-on Page
Courtesy of WestLaw.

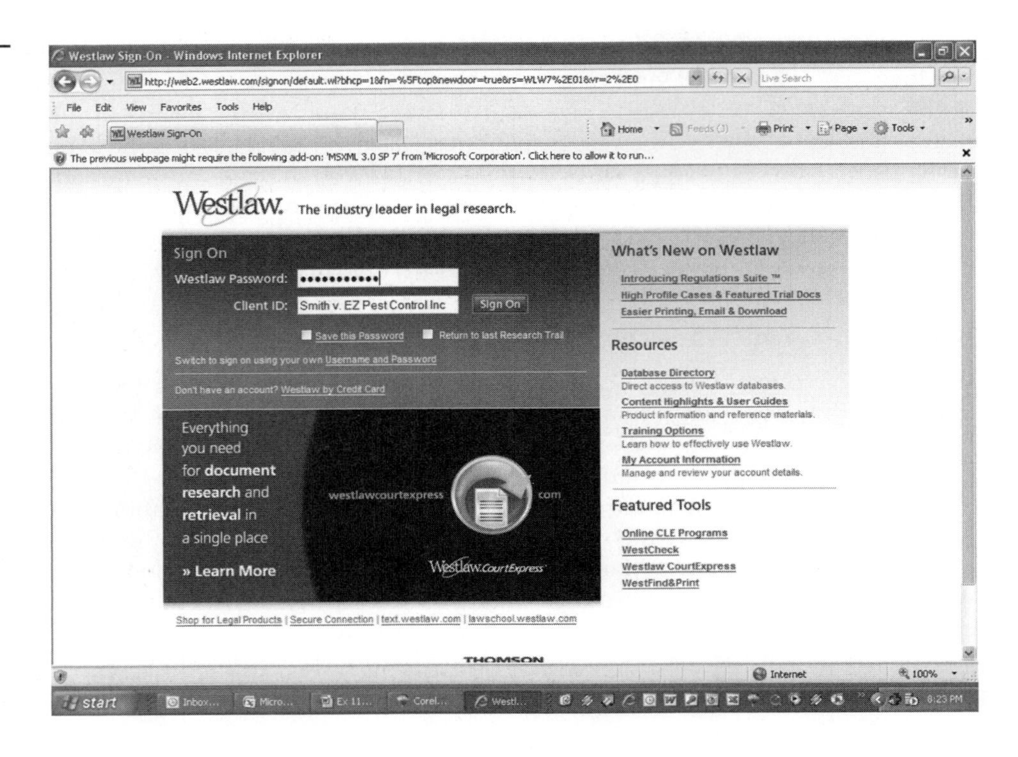

"Find this document by citation" allows a user to enter a case citation and go directly to the case

"Keycite" is WESTLAW'S cite-checking feature where you can see if a case is still good law

Directory of WESTLAW databases

Using Keysearch users can conduct legal research using a topical index list

"Court Docs" allows users to access court dockets and filings

Exhibit 11–3
Welcome to Westlaw Screen
Courtesy of WestLaw.

Tabs

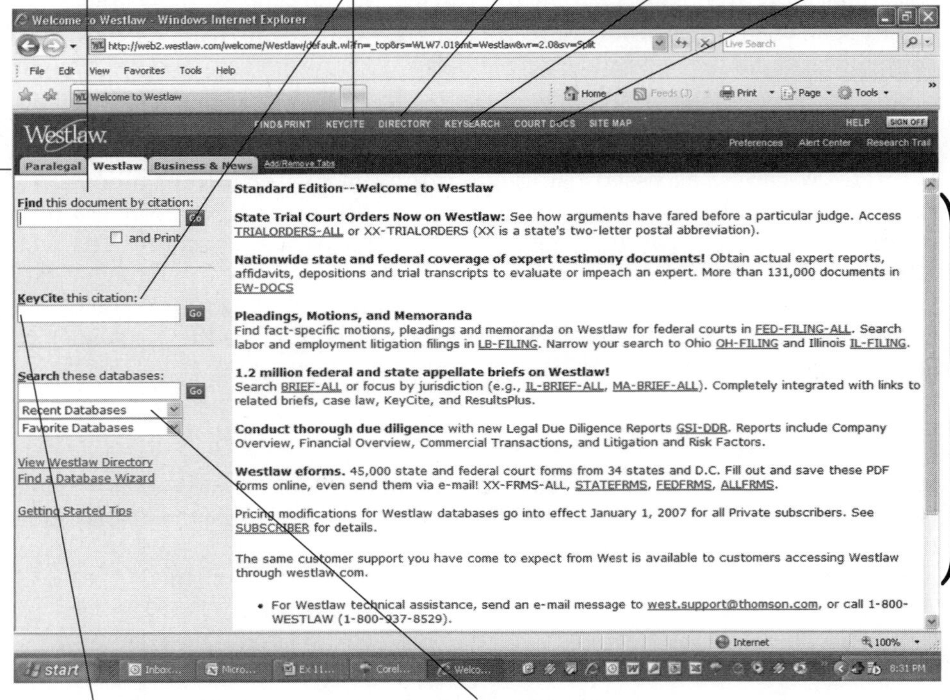

Current news and information about WESTLAW

If a user has a case cite he or she can enter it here and go directly to its history to see if it is still good law

If a user knows the database she wants to use she can go directly to it using this feature

to KeyCite, including a "KeyCite this Citation" field (left center) and the link to "KeyCite" (top center). KeyCite is covered in more detail later in the chapter.

In Exhibit 11–3 the "Find this document by citation:" feature allows a user to enter a citation and then be directly taken to it. For example, if a user entered "451 F.Supp.2d 16" the case would then be automatically displayed without the user having to enter a database or enter a search criteria. The "Directory" link at the top middle of the screen displays a directory of the many Westlaw databases. (Databases are covered later in the chapter.)

The "Search these databases:" feature (see Exhibit 11–3 at bottom left) allows a user to enter a database identifier such as "Allcases" and then go directly to the search screen where search criteria can be entered.

In the top midde of the screen is the link to "KeySearch." KeySearch integrates with the West Key Number System, which identifies key numbers and terms related to legal issues. Using KeySearch a user can conduct legal research by using a topical list of legal issues that has been compiled by Westlaw's attorney-editors. KeySearch is covered in more detail later in the chapter.

Tabs and the Paralegal Tab in Westlaw

Tabs allow a user to directly access a number of Westlaw features, including various databases. Notice in Exhibit 11–4 that there are three tabs near the top left

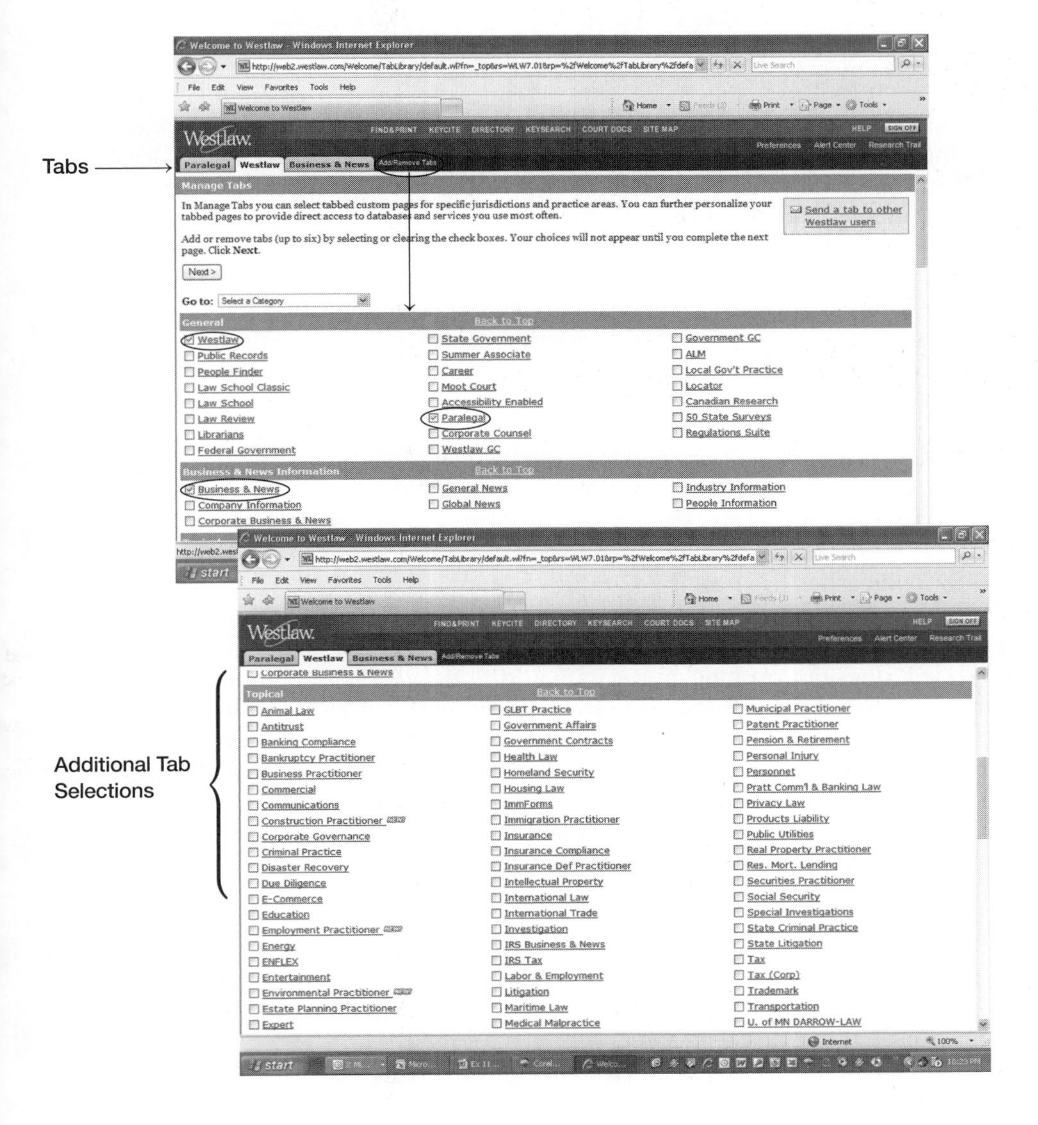

Exhibit 11–4
Creating Tabs in WestLaw
Courtesy of WestLaw.

Exhibit 11–5
The Paralegal Tab
Courtesy of WestLaw.

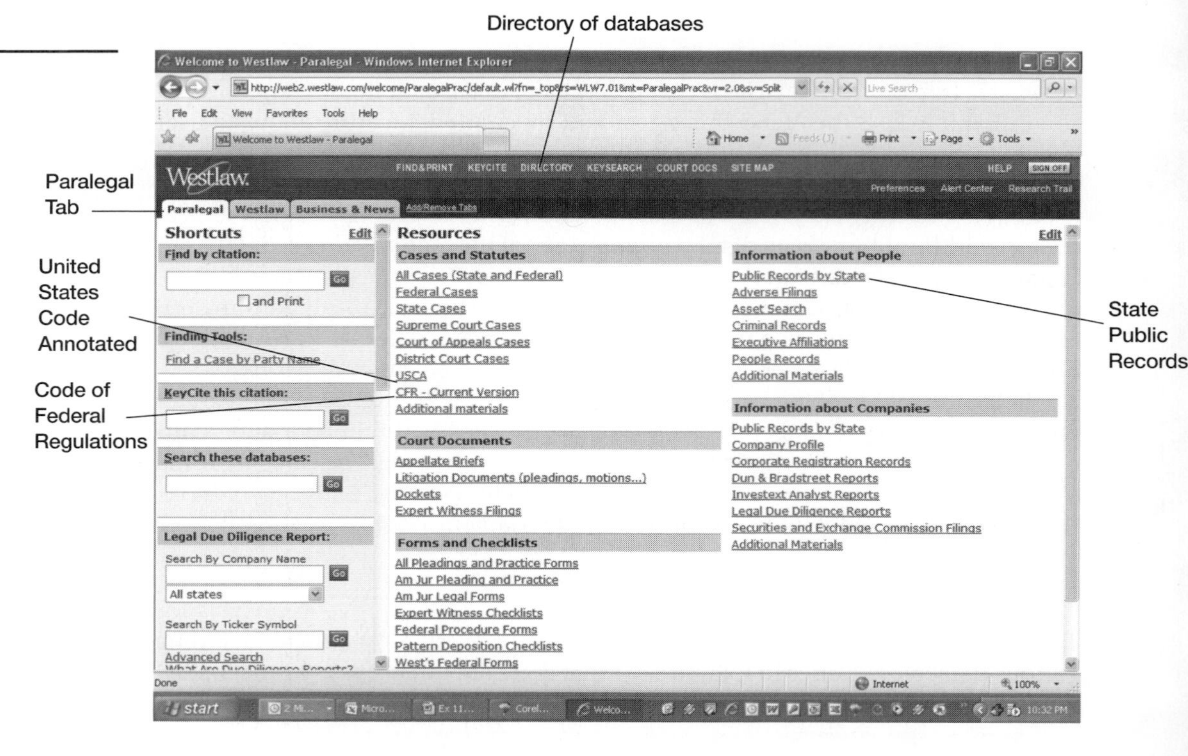

of the screen: "Westlaw," "Paralegal," and "Business & News." In Exhibit 11–4 the user clicked "Add/Remove Tabs" near the top of the screen and then selected each of these three tabs. Notice in Exhibit 11–4 that the user can select from "General", "Business, News and Information," and "Topical tabs." Tabs can also be created for different jurisdictions (e.g., Florida). Tabs are a great way of customizing Westlaw. For example, notice in Exhibit 11–5 that the Paralegal tab is selected.

Exhibit 11–5 shows the screen when the Paralegal tab is selected. Notice in Exhibit 11–5 that many of the tools that paralegals use are now at the user's fingertips. The user can quickly access cases and statutes, public records and information about people, information about companies, court documents, forms and checklists, and other information. The Paralegal tab is a timesaving feature that Westlaw has created specifically for busy paralegals. The Paralegal tab will be used as the primary starting point in Westlaw throughout the remainder of this chapter.

Find by Citation

Find by Citation
A WESTLAW feature that allows a user to immediately retrieve a specific case or statute by entering its citation.

As mentioned earlier, the **Find by Citation** feature allows a WESTLAW user to immediately retrieve a specific case or statute by entering its citation (see the first screen in Exhibit 11–6). The feature is convenient if a user already has a case cite. While it does not provide a user with additional cases or documents, such as happens when a user executes a search query and can look through many other cases, the case itself can be used as a starting point to conduct further research. The Find by Citation feature is also extremely quick because the user does not have to enter a database identifier or a search query. The first screen in Exhibit 11–6 shows the citation being entered in Find by Citation: and the second screen shows the case being retrieved.

Find a Case by Party Name
A Westlaw feature that allows a user to retrieve a case by knowing the name of at least one party and without knowing the citation, or entering a search query.

Find a Case by Party Name

The **Find a Case by Party Name** feature (under Finding Tools in the first screen of Exhibit 11–7) is a WESTLAW feature that allows a user to retrieve a case if they

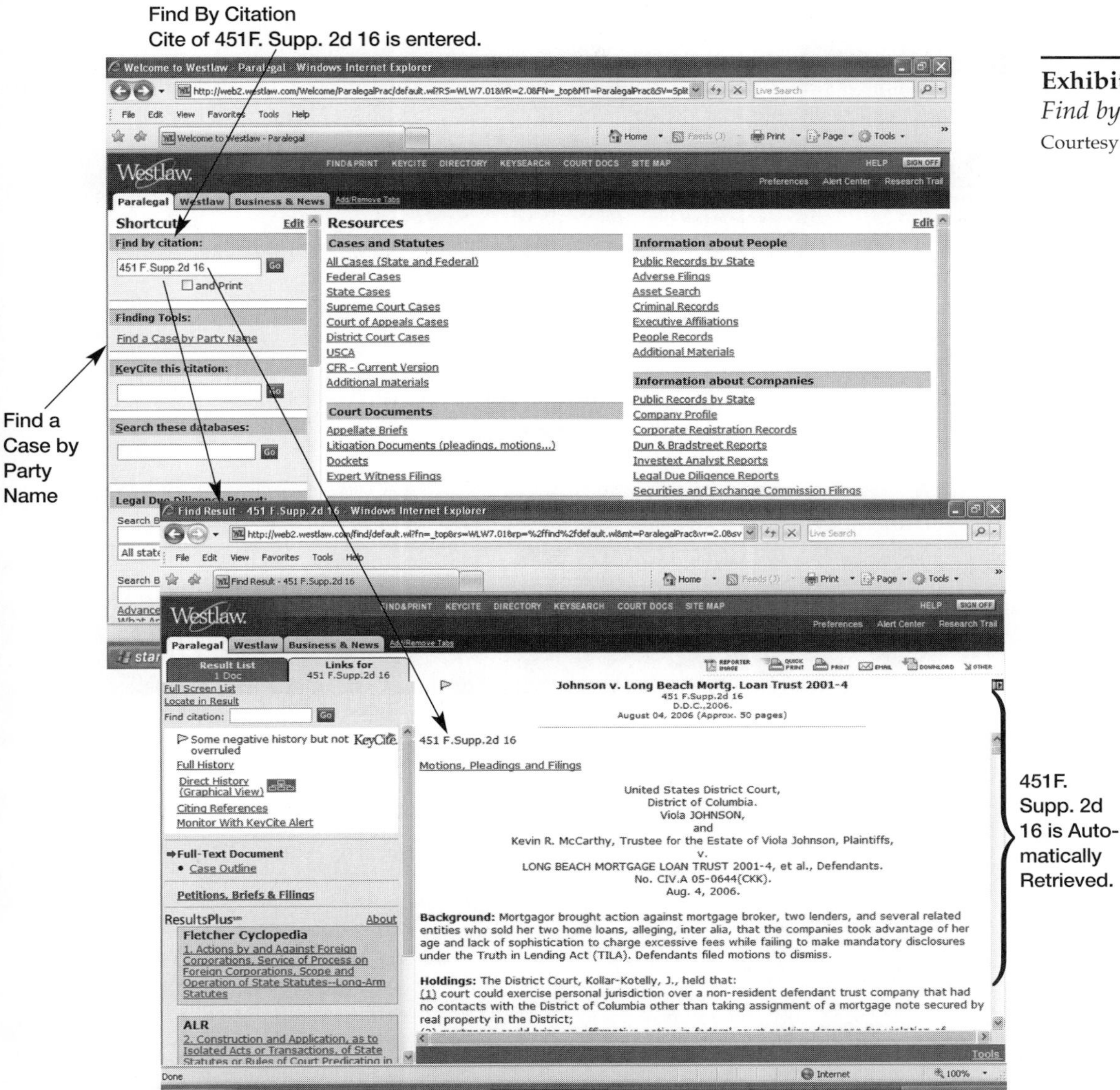
Find By Citation
Cite of 451F. Supp. 2d 16 is entered.
Find a Case by Party Name
451F. Supp. 2d 16 is Automatically Retrieved.

Exhibit 11–6
Find by Citation Feature
Courtesy of WestLaw.

know the name of at least one party; the user need not know the citation or enter a search query. Notice in Exhibit 11–7 (first screen) that the user clicked Find a Case by Party Name, entered the party's name (Viola Johnson), selected a jurisdiction (in this instance All U.S. Federal and State Cases), and selected "Go." A list of possible cases was retrieved (see the second screen of Exhibit 11–7), including the actual case the user was looking for (*Johnson v. Long Beach Mortgage*). While there are other ways to find a case by party name (discussed later in the chapter) the Find a Case by Party Name feature is a convenient feature if the user does not have a full citation for a case and does not know much about a case other than the name.

Westlaw Databases

WESTLAW offers users thousands of databases to search and query. Notice in the Paralegal tab in Exhibit 11–5 under "Resources" that there are many different kinds and types of resources available. All of these resources are databases

Exhibit 11–7
Find a Case by Party Name
Courtesy of WestLaw.

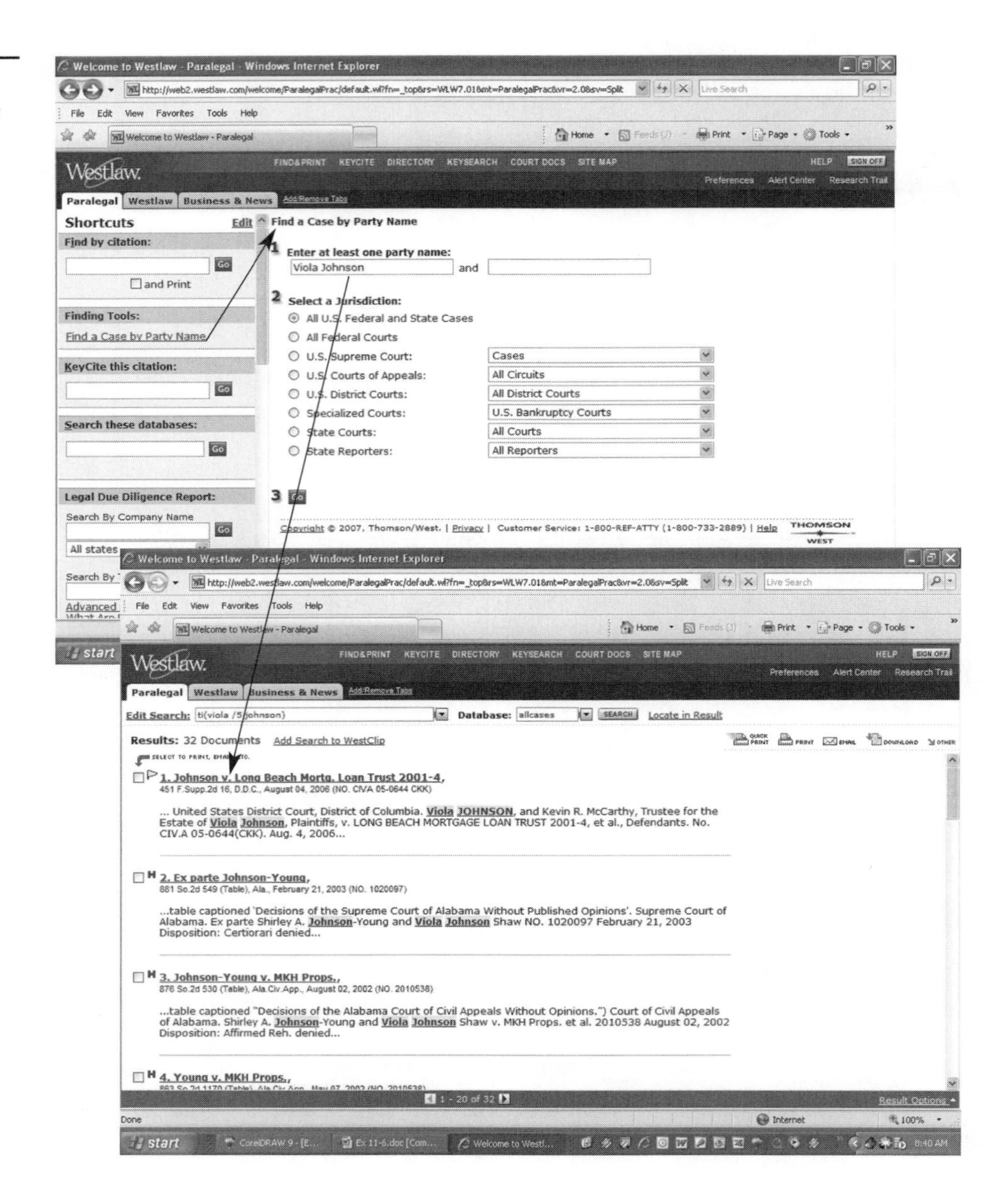

that the user can search. For example, in Exhibit 11–5 under "Cases and Statutes," users can access the All Cases (State and Federal) database, which includes all state and federal cases. Notice in Exhibit 11–5 that users can also access the United States Code Annotated (Federal statutes), the Code of Federal Regulations (federal agency and executive regulations), public records by state, and forms. The Paralegal tab in Exhibit 11–5 shows just a few of the databases that are available in WESTLAW.

Notice in Exhibit 11–5 the word "Directory" in the top middle of the screen. This is a link to the directory database shown in the first screen of Exhibit 11–8. Notice in Exhibit 11–8 the broad scope of databases and other information sources that are available in WESTLAW. This includes a variety of federal and state materials. The second screen in Exhibit 11–8 shows the screen for U.S. State Materials. The U.S. State Materials pages allows users to access the statutes and laws of any state, review court dockets, conduct legislative history research, and access court rules. Notice in the first screen of Exhibit 11–8 that

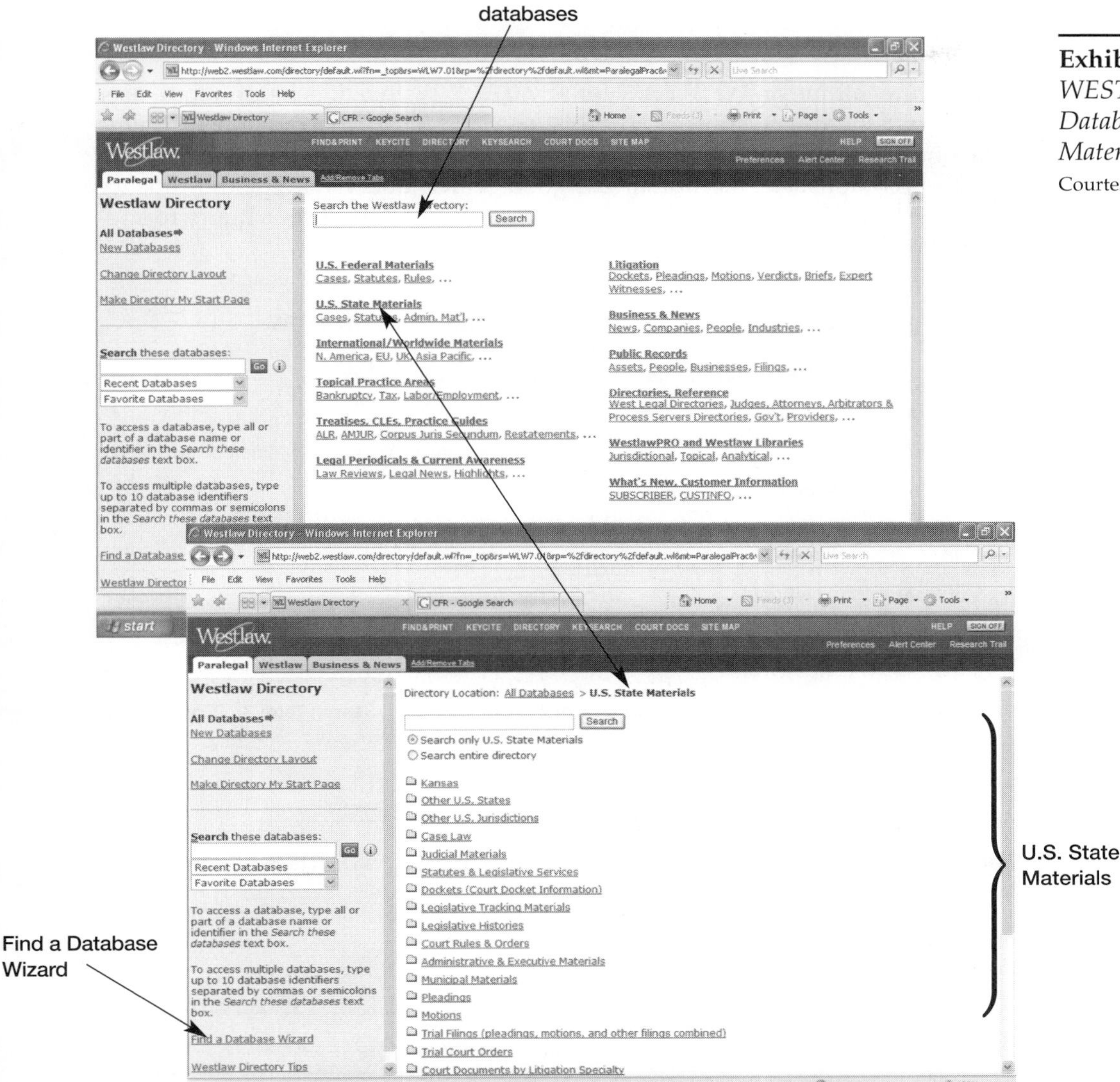

Exhibit 11–8
WESTLAW Directory of Databases and U.S. State Materials
Courtesy of WestLaw.

additional databases covering international law, topical legal areas, treatises, law reviews, business news, public records, and other subjects are available on WESTLAW.

Users can also enter the name of a potential database in the Search the Westlaw Directory: field (see the first screen of Exhibit 11–8). For example, if a user entered "New York Times" in the Search the Westlaw Directory field, WESTLAW would display several databases that were either specific to the *New York Times* (the "NYT" database and larger databases that include the *New York Times*, such as "United States Papers–USNP"). Users can also find a database using the Find a Database Wizard feature (see the second screen in Exhibit 11–8, bottom, left). In this feature, the user answers a series of questions such as "What are you trying to find?" and selects a category from a multiple-choice list. WESTLAW then guides the user to the database.

Creating and Refining Search Queries in WESTLAW

Before going online on WESTLAW, or any CALR system, it is helpful for a user to plan out the query strategy in advance. This limits the time spent online incurring charges. The user must decide what needs to be accomplished and how to accomplish it. Formulating a good search query takes some practice and some time. The query form in Exhibit 11–9 is an example of a query formulation for WESTLAW.

Exhibit 11–9
Computer-Assisted Legal Research Query Plan
Courtesy of WestLaw.

COMPUTER-ASSISTED LEGAL RESEARCH QUERY FORM

Date: *June 1* **Research's Initials:** *TPB* **Client/Case:** *Ward v. United Mortgage*

Estimate Time on Service: *15 min.*

Service to be Used: (Westlaw) Lexis/Nexis LoisLaw Fastcase Versus Law Internet CD/ROM

Database(s) to be searched:

Federal Judicial Circuit District of Columbia (FDDC-ALL)

Type of Search: Natural (Terms and Connectors)

Issues/Question: *Can a Federal court get personal jurisdiction over a non-resident company where the only contact is assignment of a mortgage?*

Search Term 1	Connector 1	Search Term 2	Connector 2	Search Term 3	Connector 3
"personal jurisdiction"	*/s*	*non-resident*	*/s*	*compan!*	*/p*
Synonym(s)					
Search Term 4	**Connector 4**	**Search Term 5**	**Connector 5**	**Search Term 6**	**Connector 6**
mortgage	*&*	*long-arm*			
Synonym(s)					
contract					

Query: *"personal jurisdiction" /s non-resident /s compan! /p mortgage contract & long-arm*

Identify the Keywords to Be Searched and Any Synonyms Always identify the keywords that describe the issue in advance. It is also necessary to identify synonyms of the keywords or alternate spellings of words. Computers cannot think for themselves; users must do this for them. Thus, if a search asks for all cases that have only the word *physician* in them and a relevant case uses the word *doctor,* the system will not retrieve the "doctor" case or cases. Failing to adequately include synonyms in a query can make the query inadequate or incomplete, so relevant cases will be missed.

The query in Exhibit 11–9 deals with whether a court can exercise personal jurisdiction over a defendant that has no contact with the state where the suit is being brought except that the defendant purchased (through assignment) a mortgage from another company who did do business in the state. The questions are whether the plaintiff, who entered into a mortgage with the original mortgage company, can sue the defendant (who purchased the mortgage from the original mortgage company), and whether the defendant has enough contacts with the state to meet the requirements of the long-arm statute and establish jurisdiction.

The keywords that describe the legal issue are *"personal jurisdiction," nonresident, company, assignment,* and *mortgage.* These are words that one might expect to find in a case of this nature. Synonyms for company might be *defendant* or *corporation.* Synonyms for *reassignment* might include *purchase, bought,*

or *buy*. Synonyms for *mortgage* might include *contract*. WESTLAW has a "Thesaurus" feature that can help find synonyms; it is discussed later in the chapter.

Identify the Type of Search to Be Performed WESTLAW offers two different kinds of searching. The first kind is plain-English searching, which WESTLAW calls "Natural Language." The second kind of searching, which WESTLAW calls "Terms and Connectors," is a Boolean logic search method that uses operators such as *and* to connect terms or ideas and *or* when two or more terms or concepts are needed to describe an idea.

Natural Language searching in WESTLAW uses plain English, without the need for complex connectors to search for documents. The advantage of using Natural Language is that it is easier to use; the disadvantage is that the search may not be as precise as a Terms and Connectors search. Searches can be entered in the form of a sentence or question. For example, in Exhibit 11–9 the question in the Issue/Question: field can be entered directly into Westlaw Natural Language (see Exhibit 11–10). In Exhibit 11–10 the user first selected a database by using the Directory feature (Directory > U.S. Federal Materials > All Federal Cases Organized by Circuit of Opinion > D.C. Circuit). The user chose the database called FEDDC-ALL and then selected the Natural Language in

Natural Language
A searching technique that uses plain English, without the need for complex connectors to search for documents.

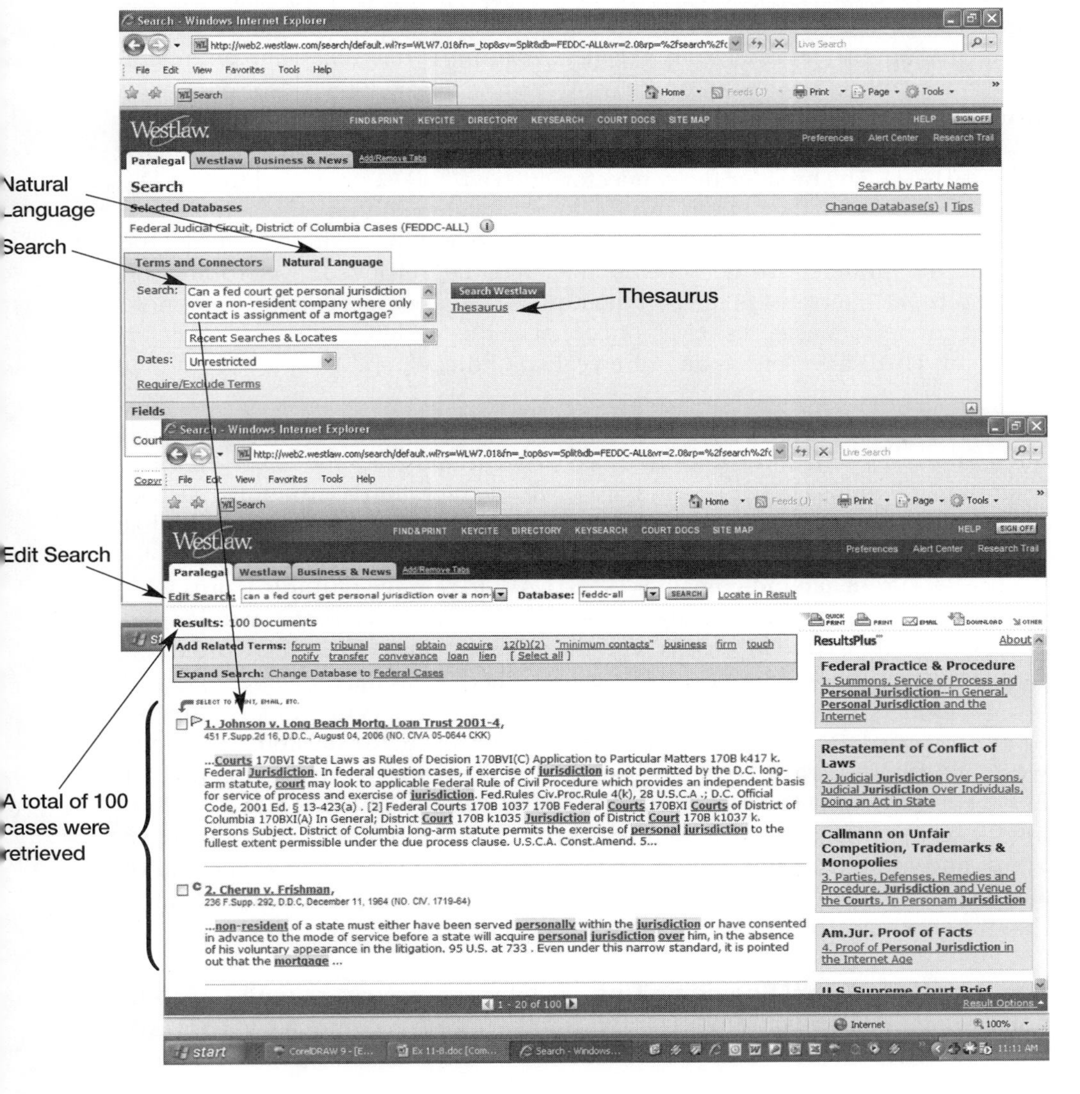

Exhibit 11–10
Westlaw Natural Language Search
Courtesy of WestLaw.

search tab (Exhibit 11–10). The user then entered the search query and selected "Search Westlaw." WESTLAW analyzed the statistical relevance of the terms and retrieved the documents that most closely matched the search requests (see the second screen of Exhibit 11-10).

Terms and Connectors
A searching technique that uses Boolean logic and operators/connectors to connect terms to describe an idea.

Connectors
Characters that show a relationship between the keywords in a search query.

Terms and Connectors searching uses Boolean logic and operators / connectors to connect terms to describe an idea. The final query at the bottom of Exhibit 11–9 shows the Terms and Connectors search in final form.

Once a user has identified the keywords of the search, any synonyms, and that the user will be using Terms and Connectors, the user must next signify the relationships between the terms, using connectors. **Connectors** show a relationship between the keywords in a search query. For example, in Exhibit 11–9, notice the words and symbols in the "Connector" fields. These include the connector "/s," which in WESTLAW means to search for two or more words within the same sentence, "/p," which in WESTLAW means to search for two or more words within the same paragraph, "&," which in WESTLAW means to search for two or more words within a document, and a space, which WESTLAW interprets as OR and which tells WESTLAW to find documents that have either one word or the other (e.g., find documents that use either the word mortgage OR the word contract). The final query in Exhibit 11–9 reads: *"'personal jurisdiction'/s non-resident/s compan!/p mortgage contract & long-arm."* The query tells WESTLAW to search for documents in the selected database (FEDDC-ALL) that have the phrase *"personal jurisdiction"* within the same sentence as the word *"non-resident,"* within the same sentence as *"compan!"* (e.g., *company or companies*) and within the same paragraph as *"mortgage"* or the word *"contract,"* and which also contain the term *"long-arm"* somewhere in the document.

Several different types of connectors are available in WESTLAW (see Exhibit 11–11). The broader the connector, such as "OR" as opposed to "AND," the more expansive the search, and the more documents that will be retrieved. Conversely, the more narrow the connector, such as "/3," (within 3 words) the smaller the number of documents that will be retrieved. Depending on the results of a query, users can edit their query and use more expansive or more narrow connectors as necessary. Notice that in the top left of the second screen of Exhibit 11–10 the user has an option called "Edit Search."

Identify Any Expanders That Might Be Necessary When writing a search query, the user must also take into account variations of the keywords. For example, in Exhibit 11–9, the root word *company* might have variations, such as *company's* or *companies*. Users can include a root expander in the query so that variations of a word will not be missed when the system is searching for relevant cases. A **root expander** enables WESTLAW to retrieve multiple words with the same root. In Exhibit 11–9, the exclamation mark (!) is a root expander that tells WESTLAW to find all words with the root of *compan*. Thus, the words *company, companies,* and *company's* will all be searched for in the database.

root expander
A character that enables a legal information system to retrieve multiple words with the same root.

universal character
A character that represents one letter or number and enables a legal information service to retrieve words with minor variations.

Another type of expander is a **universal character.** A universal character represents one letter or number and enables an information system to retrieve words with minor variations. The asterisk (*) is used as a universal character in WESTLAW. For example, the query "kn*w" would retrieve cases containing the terms *know* and *knew*. A universal character can be placed anywhere a word, and more than one universal character can be used in or at the end of a word (e.g., "test**" would retrieve *test, tests,* and *tested* but not *testify*). Exhibit 11–11 lists common WESTLAW expanders.

Additional WESTLAW Searching Tips Exhibit 11–12 shows a number of additional search tips for using WESTLAW. Another helpful feature for WESTLAW query design is the Thesaurus tool. Notice in Exhibit 11–10 the word "Thesaurus" just under "Search Westlaw." Exhibit 11–13 shows the "Thesaurus" feature in

Exhibit 11–11
Westlaw Connectors and Expanders
Courtesy of WestLaw.

Connector	Definition	Search Query	Documents Found
Space bar	OR	mortgage contract	All documents that have either the word *mortgage* or the word *contract* anywhere in them
&	AND	mortgage & contract	All documents that contain both the word *mortgage* and the word *contract* anywhere in them
/p	Paragraph	mortgage /p contract	All documents that contain the both the word *mortgage* and the word *contract* in the same paragraph
/s	Sentence	mortgage /s contract	All documents that contain both the word *mortgage* and the word *contract* in the same sentence
/n	Words	mortgage /3 contract	All documents that contain both the word *mortgage* and the word *contract* within three words of each other
" "	Phrase	"personal jurisdiction"	All documents where the exact phrase "personal jurisdiction" occurs
+s	Precedes within the same sentence	personal +s jurisdiction	All documents where *personal* precedes *jurisdiction* in the same sentence
+n	Precedes within a number of words	personal +3 jurisdiction	All documents where *personal* precedes *jurisdiction* within three words
%	BUT NOT	R.I.C.O. % "Puerto Rico"	All documents with the word *RICO* (i.e. Racketeer Influenced and Corrupt Organization Act) but not *Puerto Rico*

Expander	Definition	Search Query	Documents Found
!	Root Expander	medic!	All documents that have the words medicine, medical, medicate, or medication
*	Universal character	kn*w	All documents that have the word know or knew in them

WESTLAW. In Exhibit 11–13 the search word "company" is highlighted, and Westlaw provides synonyms such as "association," "business," and "corporation." The Thesaurus tool can be very helpful when formulating search queries.

Exhibit 11–14 shows the terms and connectors search formulated in Exhibit 11–9 and the results of the search. Notice in the first screen of Exhibit 11–14 that one of the fields in the search screen is Dates: and that "unrestricted" currently is shown. Users have many date options in WESTLAW, including limiting searches to documents published in the last thirty, sixty, or ninety days, the last three years, after a user-defined date (e.g., after 1/1/2003), or before a user-defined date (e.g., before 1/1/2006).

Notice in the first screen of Exhibit 11–14 that one of the options is Fields:. Users can limit searches to certain fields or parts of a document, including the title of the case/document, the synopsis, headnote, judge, attorneys, etc. For example, if a user wanted to search for a title of a case, she could either use the Find a Case by Party Name feature discussed previously, or select the down arrow next to Field in the Terms and Connectors query and select Title. The user could then enter a case name such as *Johnson & "Long Beach Mortg."* The completed search would be ti*(Johnson & "Long Beach Mortg")*.

Exhibit 11–12
Westlaw Search Tips
Courtesy of WestLaw.

Tip Number/Description	Explanation
1. The more terms in the query, the fewer cases retrieved	A common problem for new WESTLAW users is that their searches tend to retrieve hundreds of cases, too many to look through. Adding more terms to the query limits the number of cases retrieved.
2. Use singular terms	Westlaw automatically adds plurals (e.g., *"child"* returns *"child's"* and *"children"*). If a user searches the plural (e.g., *"children"*) only the plural is searched for.
3. Use quotes cautiously	Using quotes only search as for exact phrases, so *"statute of limitations"* will not search for *limitations of action* or *limitation period*.
4. Use hyphens	When you do not know how a phrase might appear in a document, use hyphens. *Non-resident* retrieves *"non-resident," "non resident,"* and *"nonresident."*
5. Use periods in acronyms	When you do not know if an acronym might appear with periods or not, use periods. *F.B.I.* will retrieve *"F.B.I.,"* "FBI," and *"F B I"*.

Exhibit 11–13
Using the Thesaurus in WESTLAW
Courtesy of WestLaw.

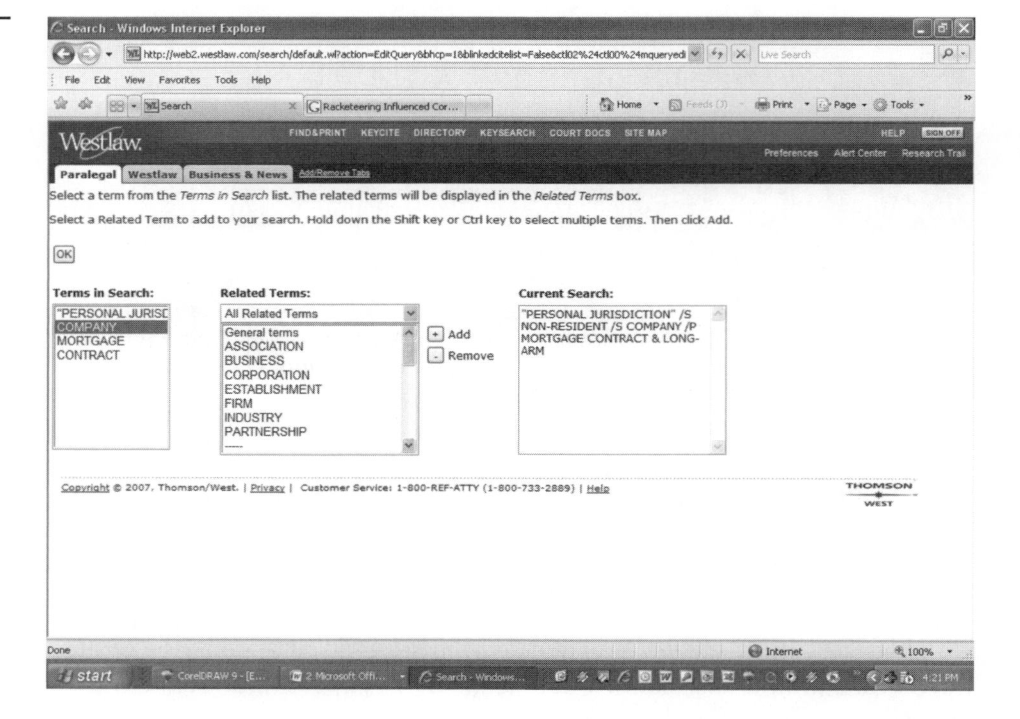

Working with Retrieved Cases in WESTLAW and Expanding a Search

Notice in the second screen of Exhibit 11–14 that two cases *(Johnson v. Long Beach Mortg.,* and *Kopff v. Battaglia)* were initially retrieved. Only a brief summary of each case, showing some of the search terms found, is shown initially. To see the full text of a case, the user would click on the name of the case *(Johnson v. Long*

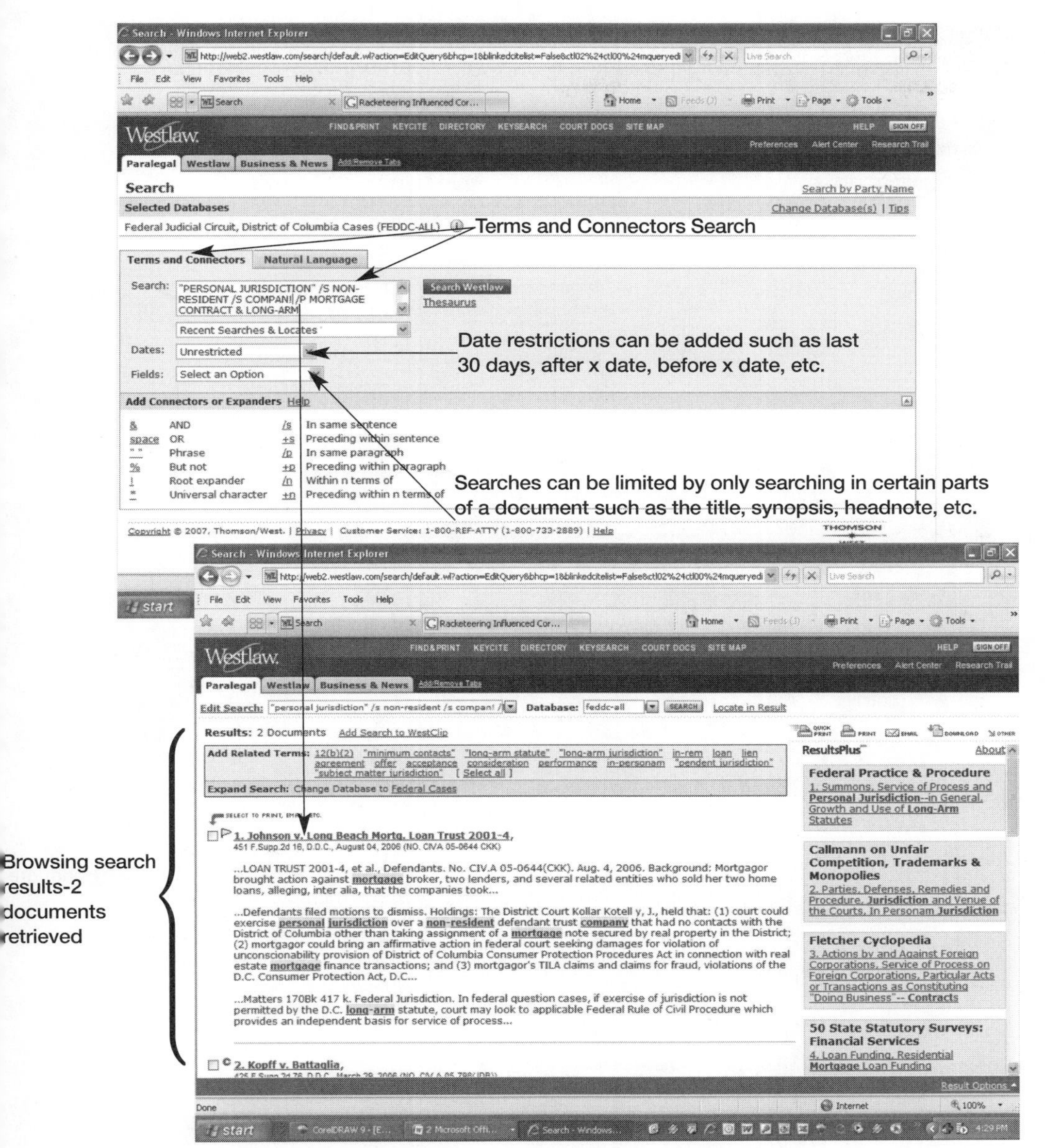

Exhibit 11–14
Terms and Connector Search in Westlaw
Courtesy of WestLaw.

Beach Mortg. in this instance). Exhibit 11–15 (first screen) shows the first page of the *Johnson v. Long Beach Mortgage* case.

The Synopsis Notice in Exhibit 11–15 (first screen) that the background and holdings of the case are displayed. This is called the synopsis of the case. The synopsis of the case was written by WESTLAW research attorneys to help users understand and summarize the case. This is something that many CALR services (other than WESTLAW and LexisNexis) do not offer. By reading the synopsis, the user can evaluate whether or not the case is on point.

Searching Terms and Moving to Additional Cases Exhibit 11–15 (first screen) shows the user's search terms in the synopsis as highlighted. Search terms are always highlighted in the document so the user can clearly see the terms he or she is searching for. Notice that in Exhibit 11–15 (at the bottom of the first screen) the words "Doc 1 of 2" appear and there is a left arrow and a

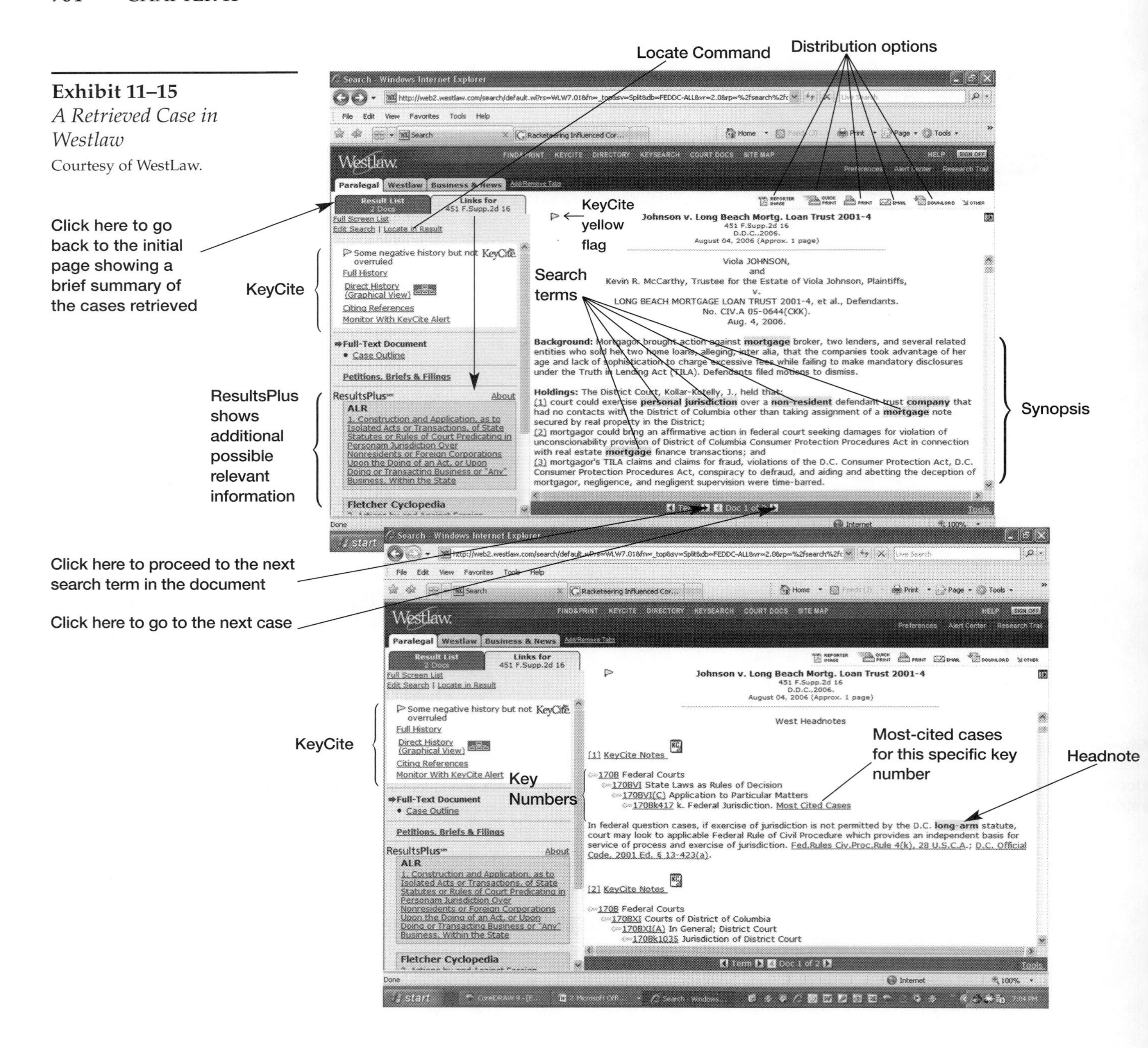

Exhibit 11–15
A Retrieved Case in Westlaw
Courtesy of WestLaw.

right arrow on either side. This shows that the user is currently viewing the first case that was retrieved. To go to the next document, the user would click the right arrow to go to the second case. Notice also in Exhibit 11–15 (at the bottom of the first screen) that the word "Term" is shown with a left arrow and right arrow on either side. To go to his or her next search term, the user would click the right arrow next to "Term." In this manner the user can view all of the search terms in the document to evaluate whether the document is on point or not. If the documents are not relevant, or if too many or too few documents are identified, the user should modify the query. Sometimes when cases are retrieved in WESTLAW there is another option next to "Term" called "Best." In WESTLAW, "Best" means that this is the spot in the case that has the greatest concentration of the user's search terms. Sometimes it is more efficient to use the "Best" option and go straight to the place in the case with the most search terms than to painstakingly go through the case looking at each search term.

Distribution Options After the user has determined that the documents retrieved are relevant, the user has several distribution option to select from (see Exhibit 11–15, top right of the first screen), including "Reporter Image" (which creates a PDF file of the case), "Quick Print" (which quickly prints the case), "Print" (which prints the case with additional options), "email" (which emails the cases to an address supplied by the user), or "download" (which either opens the case or saves it as a word-processing document).

Locate in Result Notice in Exhibit 11–15 (top left of the first screen) the option entitled "Locate in Result." The **Locate in Result** command allows a user to search the retrieved documents for particular terms, whether or not the terms appear in the user's original search. For instance, if the search in the example regarding jurisdiction of the mortgage company had retrieved seventy-five cases, the user could search the retrieved cases for "interstate commerce" or another term to further cull the cases retrieved. This can be particularly helpful when a user retrieves more cases than he can easily look through.

Locate in Result
A command that allows a WESTLAW user to search the retrieved documents for particular terms, whether or not the terms appear in the user's original search.

Results Plus Notice in Exhibit 11–15 (lower left of the first screen) the section that says "ResultsPlus." **ResultsPlus** is an additional feature of WESTLAW that automatically includes other documents (no additional search is needed) such as legal texts, treatises, law review articles, etc., that have a high statistical likelihood of matching the concepts in a user's search. In Exhibit 11–15 an ALR (American Law Reports) article related to isolated acts of nonresidents is suggested as being a possible source of additional information. ResultsPlus suggestions can be extremely helpful and can assist a user in expanding a research project.

ResultsPlus
A WESTLAW feature that automatically includes other documents (no additional search is needed) such as legal texts, treatises, and law review articles related to a user's search.

Headnotes and Key Numbers In the second screen of Exhibit 11–15, West **Headnotes and Key Numbers** are shown. Headnotes summarize each major issue in a case. Most cases include a number of Headnotes. Each Headnote is classified under one or more Topics and Key Numbers in the West Key System. Headnotes and Key Numbers digest the case and break down legal issues into smaller issues that can be tracked and organized. Each Topic and Key Number represents a particular point of law. They allow users to expand their research while still staying on point. In Exhibit 11–15, notice that the Headnote speaks to the issue of the D.C. long-arm statute and the question of gaining jurisdiction over a party. Also, notice in Exhibit 11–15 the Key Number 170Bk417. This is a key number related to the issue at hand. Suppose, for example, that this is the specific legal issue the user needs to research. The user could select this Key Number (170Bk417) to search for other cases with the same Key Number or Headnote (see Exhibit 11–16). In the first screen of Exhibit 11–16 Westlaw has automatically entered the Key Number 170Bk417. In Exhibit 11–16, the user has selected "Most Recent Cases," so the most recent cases are sorted first, and then selected the database to search, which is "U.S. Court of Appeals—D.C. Circuit." The user then clicked "Search" and the second screen of Exhibit 11–16 was displayed, showing the user six cases with the specific Headnote (170BK417) directly on point. The user can now click each case and read it. Headnotes and Key Numbers are a great way to find resources on point.

Headnotes and Key Numbers
Feature in WESTLAW that classifies each legal issue in a case and allow users to search and retrieve other cases with similar Headnotes and Key Numbers.

KeySearch

KeySearch is a Westlaw tool that allows users to find cases in a specific area of law without using terms and connectors or a search query. Users select "Key-Search" at the top of the screen and then select from a list of topics that gradually

KeySearch
A WESTLAW tool that allows users to find documents using a topical index and without the user having to formulate a search query.

Exhibit 11–16
Searching for Similar Headnotes/Key Numbers in WESTLAW
Courtesy of WestLaw.

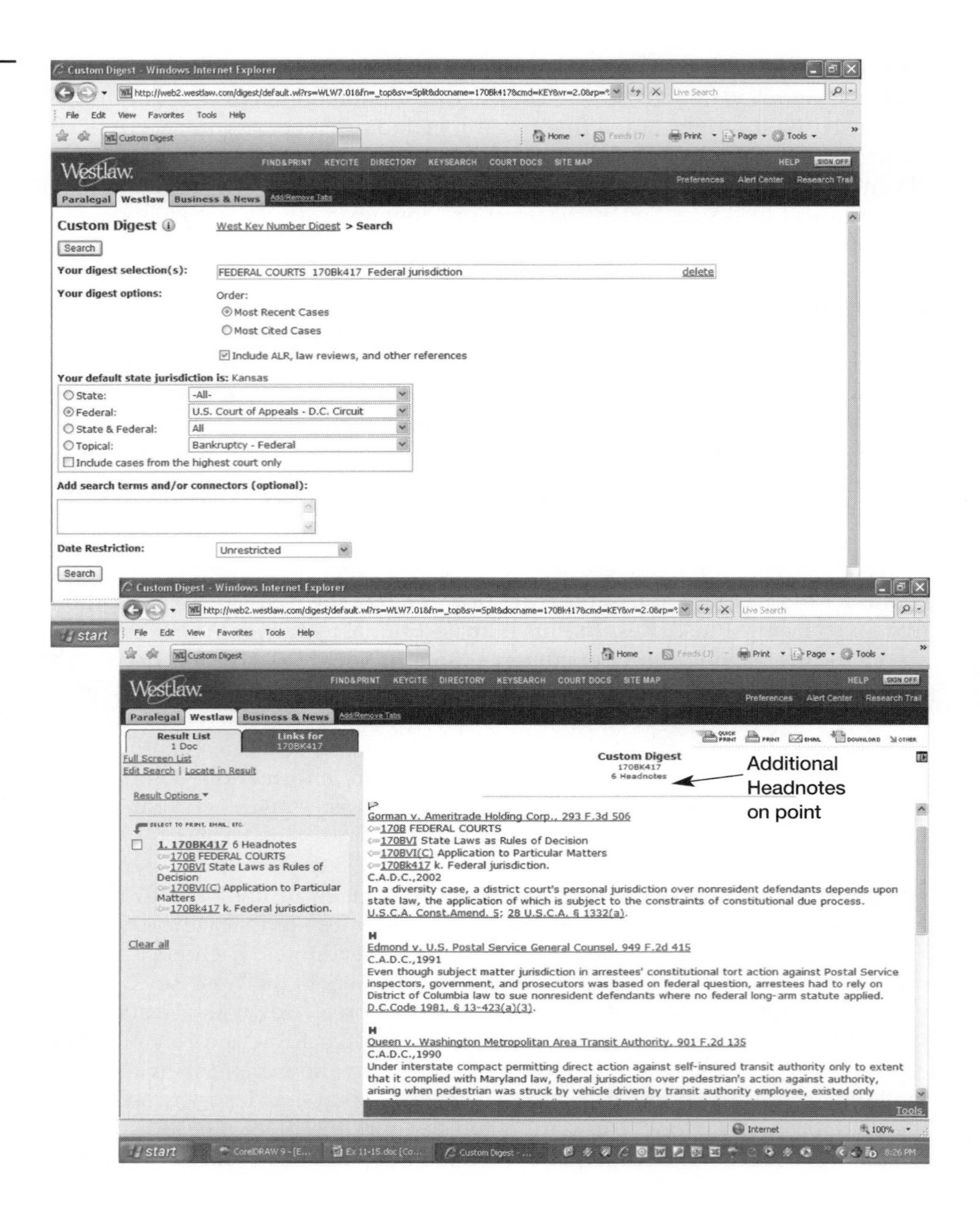

narrow the legal matter down to a specific issue. Notice in Exhibit 11–17 (first screen) that a number of legal issues are listed. In this instance the user selected "Jurisdiction" under "Civil Procedure" and was taken to the next screen. In Exhibit 11–17 (second screen) the user selected "Long-arm Statutes." The user then selected which database to run the KeySearch in. (This detail is not shown in Exhibit 11–17, but the database of the U.S. Court of Appeals—D.C. Circuit was selected) and a list of cases was retrieved (see Exhibit 11–17, third screen). KeySearch allowed the user to find cases on point using a topical index without having to formulate a search query.

KeyCite
Allows WESTLAW users to determine if a case, statute, or other document is good law and allows users to expand their research by finding other sources that have cited the reference.

KeyCite **KeyCite** is WESTLAW'S citation research tool. It allows users to determine if the case, statute, or other document is good law and allows users to expand their research by finding other sources that have cited the reference. Each of these uses will be covered separately.

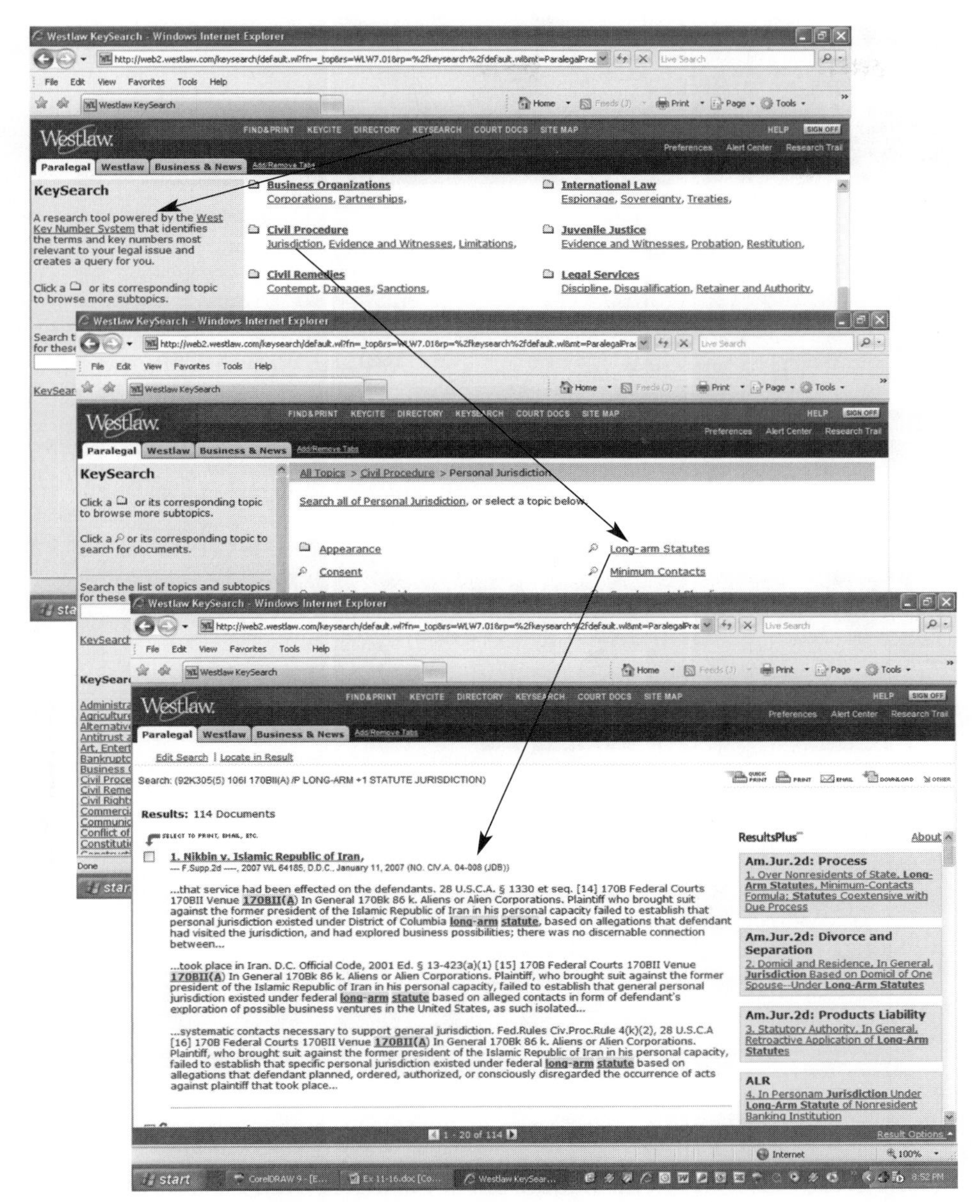

Exhibit 11–17
Conducting Topical Based Research Using KeySearch
Courtesy of WestLaw.

KeyCite: Determining if a Case/Statute is Good Law KeyCite allows WESTLAW users to determine whether a case has been overruled or still is good law, or if a statute has been found unconstitutional or has been repealed. Notice in Exhibit 11–18 (first screen) under "KeyCite this Citation:" that the cite "451 F. Supp. 2d 16" has been entered. Notice in the second screen that the KeyCite results are displayed. KeyCite uses a colored flag system for easily determining whether a case or statute is good law (see Exhibit 11–19). A red flag means that the case is no longer good law for at least one of the points of law it contains. A yellow flag means that the case had had some negative treatment, but has not been reversed or overruled. Notice in the KeyCite listing in Exhibit 11–18 (second screen) for the *Johnson v. Long Beach Mortgage* case that a yellow flag appears next to the title of the case, indicating there has been some negative reference made to the case. Also, notice in the first screen of Exhibit 11–15 that a yellow KeyCite flag is displayed at the beginning of the case. WESTLAW has integrated KeyCite into the full text of documents. Notice also in Exhibit 11–15

Exhibit 11–18
Using WESTLAW'S KeyCite to Determine if a Case is Still Good Law
Courtesy of WestLaw.

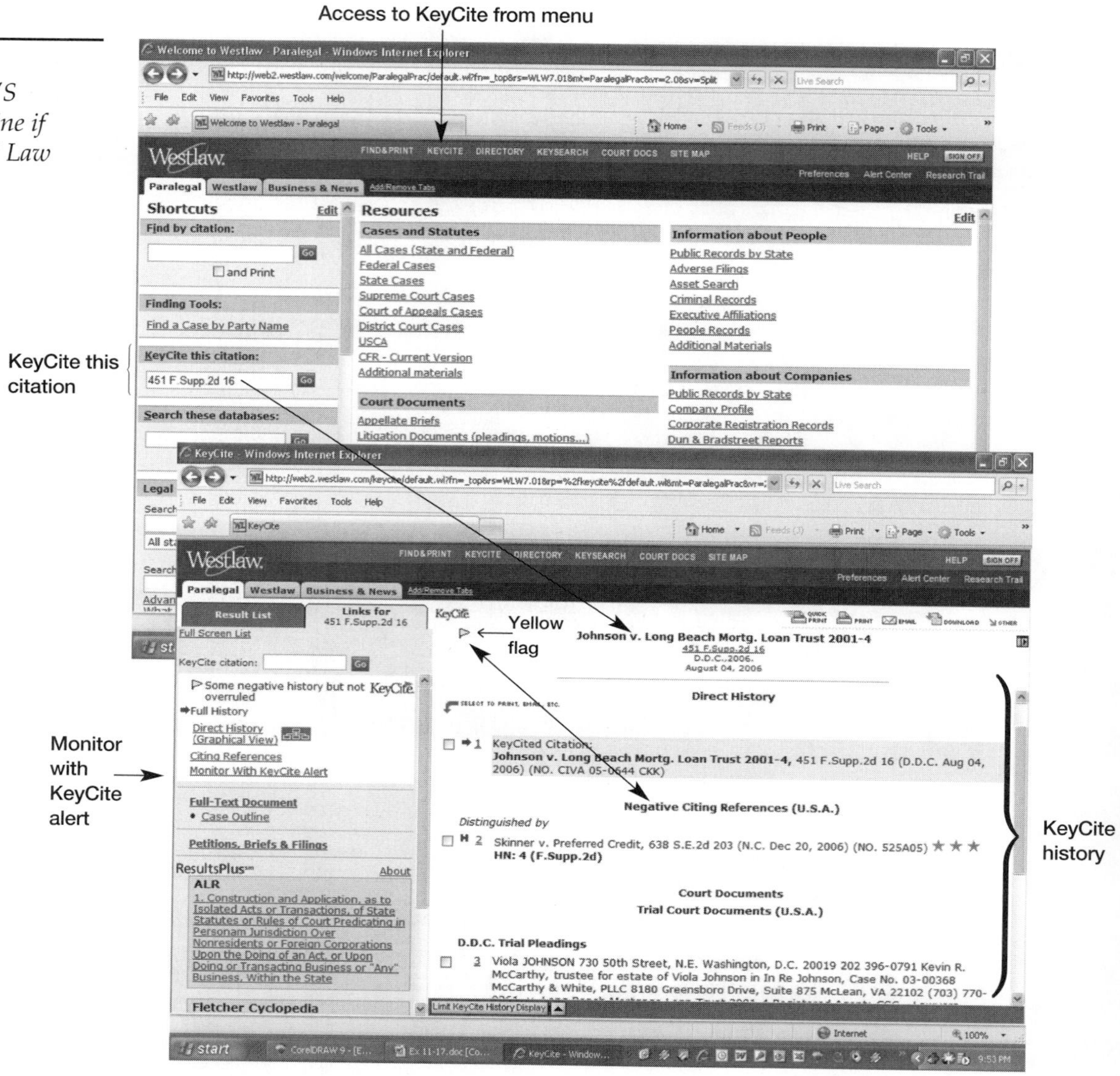

that from the case itself (in the middle left of the first screen) the user can access full KeyCite information for the case, including a full history of the case. Exhibit 11–20 shows an example of a KeyCite report on the Religious Freedom Restoration Act, a Federal statute that was declared unconstitutional. The statute is displayed with a red flag and the history reports a number of cases that recognized it as being unconstitutional (see Exhibit 11–20).

Sometimes it takes years for a case to work its way through the court system. KeyCite Alert is a Westlaw feature that allows a user to be notified (typically through email) when the status of a case changes in KeyCite. Exhibit 11–18 (second screen) shows the Monitor with KeyCite Alert option listed.

KeyCite: Finding Other Sources That Have Cited the Reference KeyCite allows a user to track all of the times a document has been cited by other references. Notice in Exhibit 11–21 (first screen) on the left side of the screen the words "Citing References." The second screen in Exhibit 11–21 shows the "Citing References" information in KeyCite for the case of *Sculptchair, Inc., v. Century Arts, Ltd.* Notice in the second screen of Exhibit 11–21 that the *Sculptchair* case has been cited by 1,110 documents. Notice in Exhibit 11–21 (second screen) that

Exhibit 11–19
KeyCite Symbols

KeyCite Symbol	Explanation
▶ RED FLAG	• In cases and administrative decisions, a red flag warns that the case or administrative decision is no longer good law for at least one of the points of law it contains. In statutes and regulations, a red flag warns that the statute or regulation has been amended by a recent session law or rule, repealed, superseded, held unconstitutional, or preempted in whole or in part.
▷ YELLOW FLAG	• In cases and administrative decisions, a yellow flag warns that the case or administrative decision has had some negative treatment, but has not been reversed or overruled. In statutes and regulations, a yellow flag warns that a statute has been renumbered or transferred by a recent session law; that an uncodified session law or proposed legislation affecting the statute is available (statutes merely referenced, i.e., mentioned, are marked with a green C); that the regulation has been reinstated, corrected or confirmed; that the statute or regulation was limited on constitutional or preemption grounds or its validity was otherwise called into doubt; or that a prior version of the statute or regulation received negative treatment from a court.
H BLUE H	• In cases and administrative decisions, a blue H indicates that there is direct history but it is not known to be negative.
C GREEN C	• A green C indicates that the case/administrative decision has citing references but no direct history or negative citing references. It also indicates that a statute/regulation has citing references, but no updating documents.
★★★★	• Depth of treatment stars indicate how extensively a cited case or administrative decision has been discussed by the citing case. The more stars, the more extensive the coverage. One star, for example, means that the case was only cited.
" QUOTATION MARKS	• Quotation marks indicate that the citing case or administrative decision directly quotes the cited case.

over the first entry listed (*Robert D. Harley Co. v. Global Force*) there are four stars. The four stars are depth of treatment stars (see Exhibit 11–19) and mean that the *Harley* case extensively discussed and considered the Sculptchair case. If the *Harley* case had simply cited the *Sculptchair* case, the *Harley* case would only have one star. Notice also in Exhibit 11–21 that the *Harley*, case has quotation marks in the listing. This means that the *Sculptchair* case was actually quoted in the *Harley* case.

Court Dockets/Documents

WESTLAW has the capability to search many (but not all) Federal and state court dockets. This is sometimes helpful if a user is trying to keep track of a piece of litigation or if a user is trying to find information about a person or company. In Exhibit 11–22 (first screen) the user selected Dockets under Court Documents. The user then selected the database for "Dockets—State and Federal Courts Combined (DOCK-ALL)." While not shown in Exhibit 11–22, the user then

Exhibit 11–20
KeyCite Information on the Religious Freedom Restoration Act (Recognized as Unconstitutional)
Courtesy of WestLaw.

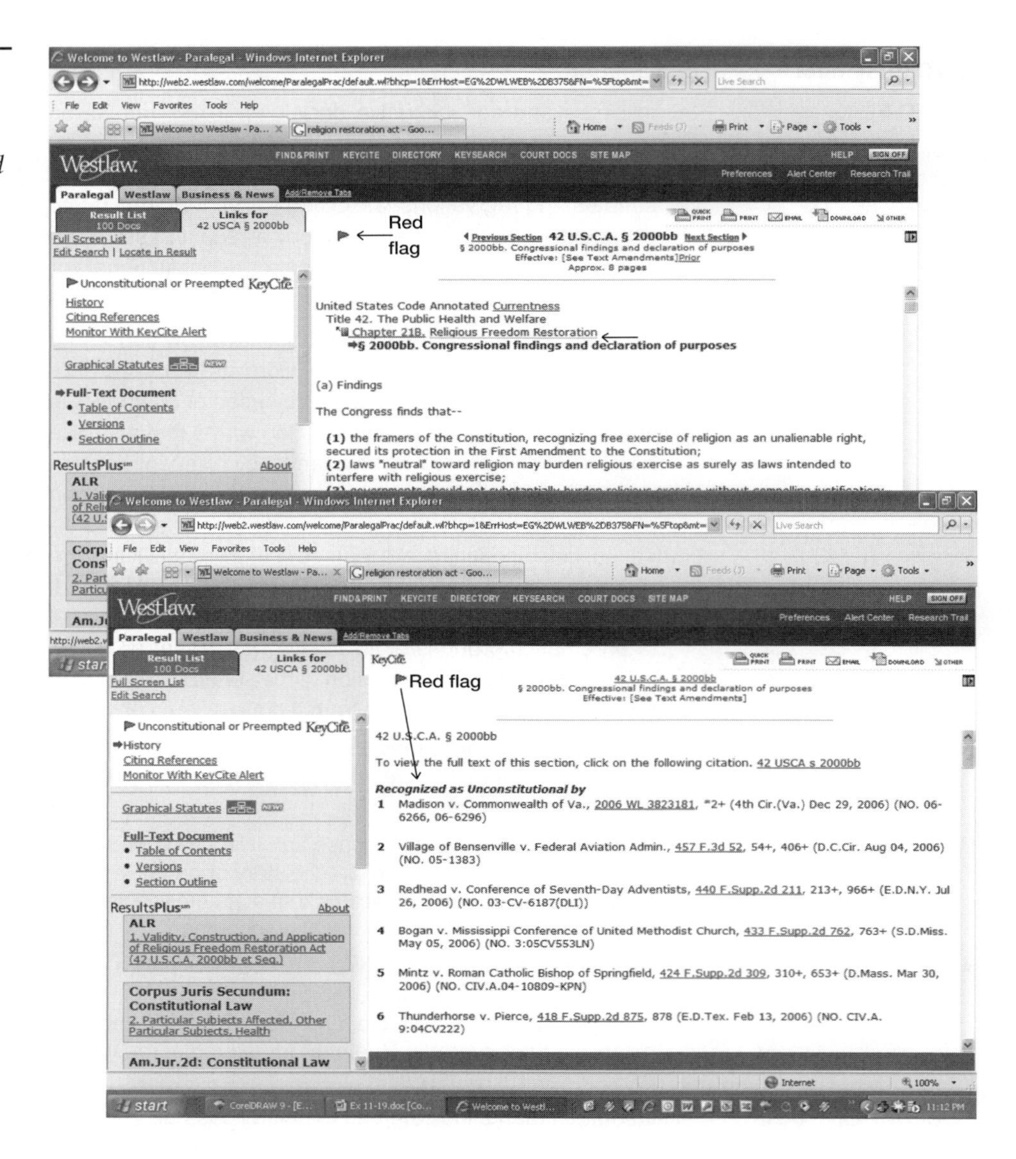

entered WalMart as a party and searched the DOCK-ALL database. The third screen in Exhibit 11–22 shows a docket for a case against WalMart in Broward County, Florida. The docket shows the type of action it is, case number, judge, courthouse and that the status of the case is open.

Public Records Search

WESTLAW allows users to search a number of state public records. While not comprehensive, the search is straightforward and can be quite productive. Notice in the first screen of Exhibit 11–22 (upper right) that one of the options under "Information About People" is "Public Records by State." The first screen in Exhibit 11–23 shows a few of the WESTLAW state public records databases. The second screen of Exhibit 11–23 shows the user searching for John Doe in the City of Los Angeles in the Public Records Combined—California database. The third screen shows a public record that was retrieved. WESTLAW public record searches can be used to find the whereabouts of people and to otherwise find information about people, such as assets, property ownership,

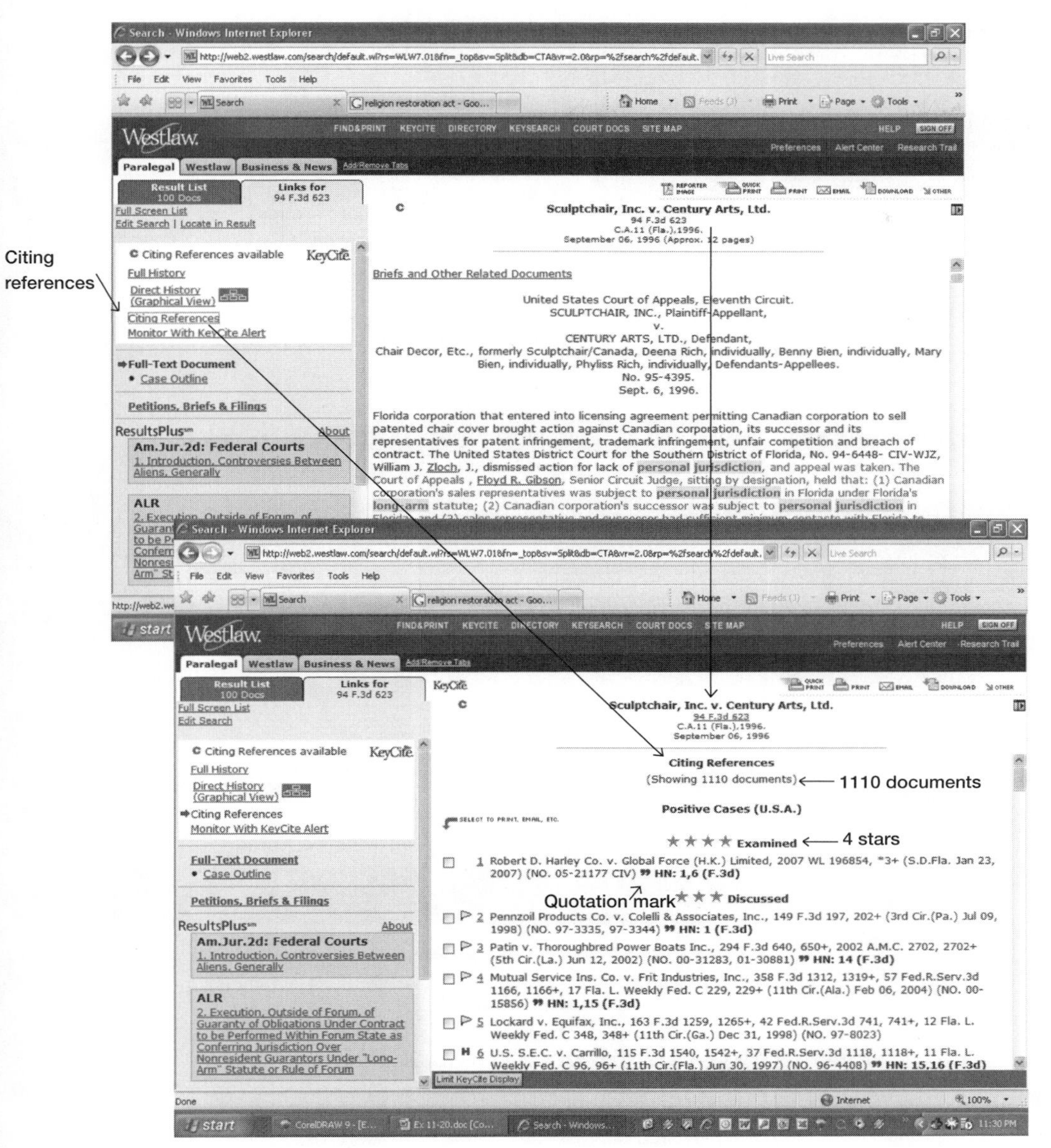

Exhibit 11–21
Citing References for a Case in KeyCite
Courtesy of WestLaw.

and related records. WESTLAW can also access a variety of public records about businesses including company profiles, corporate registration records, and Securities and Exchange Commission Filings, among others.

WESTLAW Training

Like becoming proficient at manual legal research, which requires one to understand the resources available and how to use them effectively, learning to use CALR services such as WESTLAW, takes time. WESTLAW is an extremely powerful research tool and has an enormous number of features, databases, commands, and complexities. To learn to use all of these vast resources takes some time. WESTLAW has a number of excellent tools to assist users in learning how to use the service. At http://www.west.thomson.com/ users can access many different training programs, including free user's guides in PDF format such as the *Westlaw Guide for Paralegals, Litigation Research Guide*, and many others.

Exhibit 11–22
Searching Court Dockets in WESTLAW
Courtesy of WestLaw.

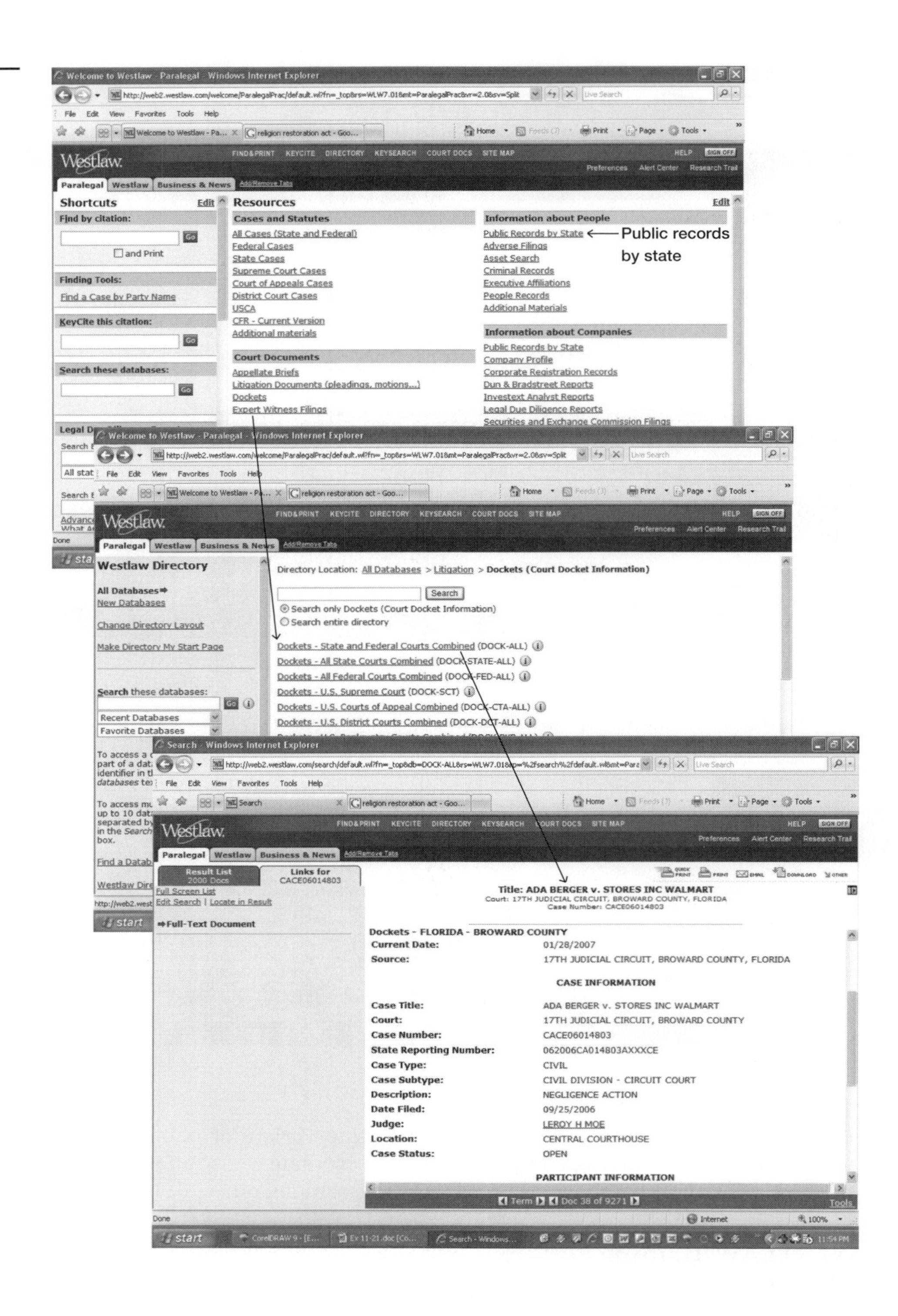

WESTLAW also offers more than 100 web-based trainings. Each one takes approximately five minutes to complete and includes full sound and step-by-step instruction. There is even a program developed specifically for paralegals (see http://www.west.thomson.com/WESTLAW/TRAINING). Users must have a valid WESTLAW password to access the web-based training.

Many other types of training are also available. For example, WESTLAW offers toll-free technical assistance by WESTLAW research attorneys who can advise users on search strategies.

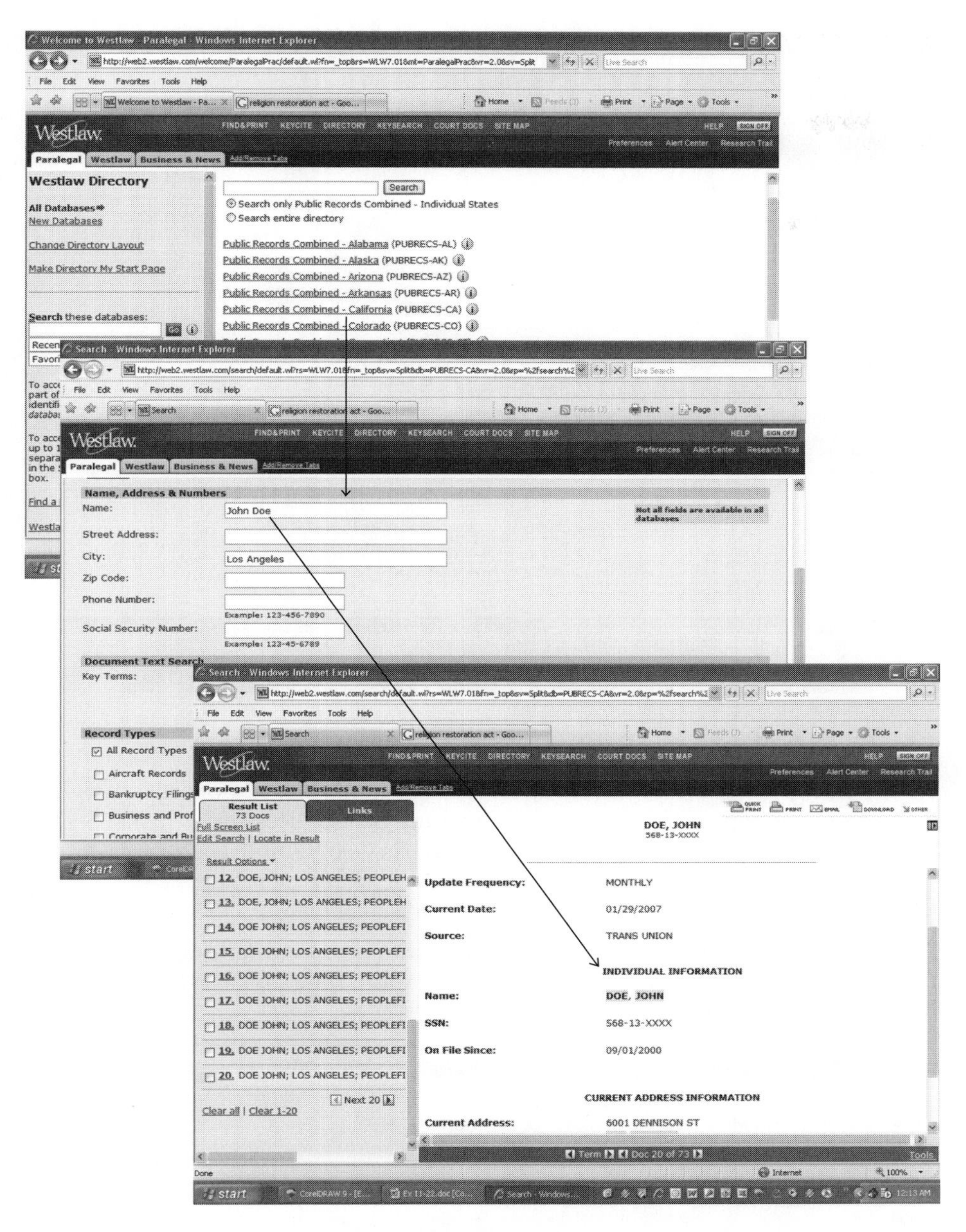

Exhibit 11–23
Public Records Searches in WESTLAW
Courtesy of WestLaw.

LEXIS-NEXIS

LexisNexis is a comprehensive full-text CALR service provider. It was the first online full-text legal information service and is one of the world's largest. This section covers LexisNexis's databases, search/query structure, and other features.

Accessing LexisNexis

LexisNexis can be accessed using either the Internet or a computer with a modem. To access LexisNexis via the Internet, a user needs a web browser, an Internet account, and a LexisNexis account. The web address for accessing LexisNexis is http://www.lexis.com. To enter the LexisNexis site the user enters his or her ID and password (see Exhibit 11–23A).

Exhibit 11–23A
LexisNexis® Sign-On Screen

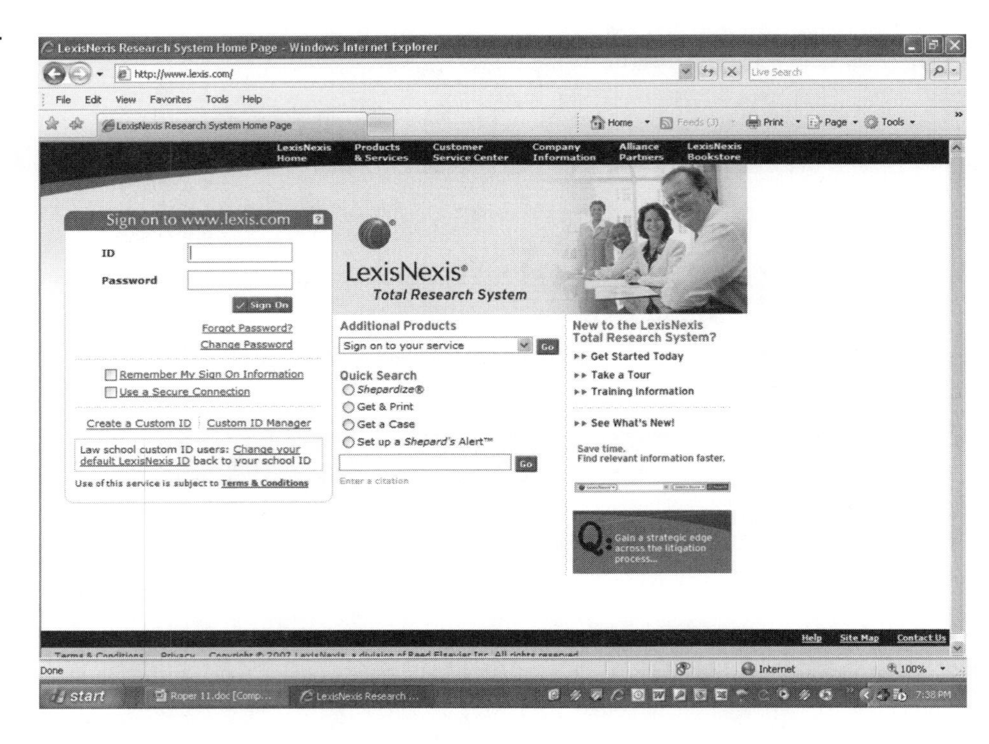

LexisNexis Research System Tabs

LexisNexis gives users a number of research options. The options are shown as tabs across the top of the screen. They include Search, Research, Tasks, Search Advisor, Get a Document, Shepard's, and Alerts (see Exhibit 11–24).

Get a Document

The Get a Document tab allows users to retrieve individual documents from LexisNexis quickly, by entering either the citation, the names of the parties, or the docket number (see Exhibit 11–25).

Exhibit 11–24
Research Options in LexisNexis

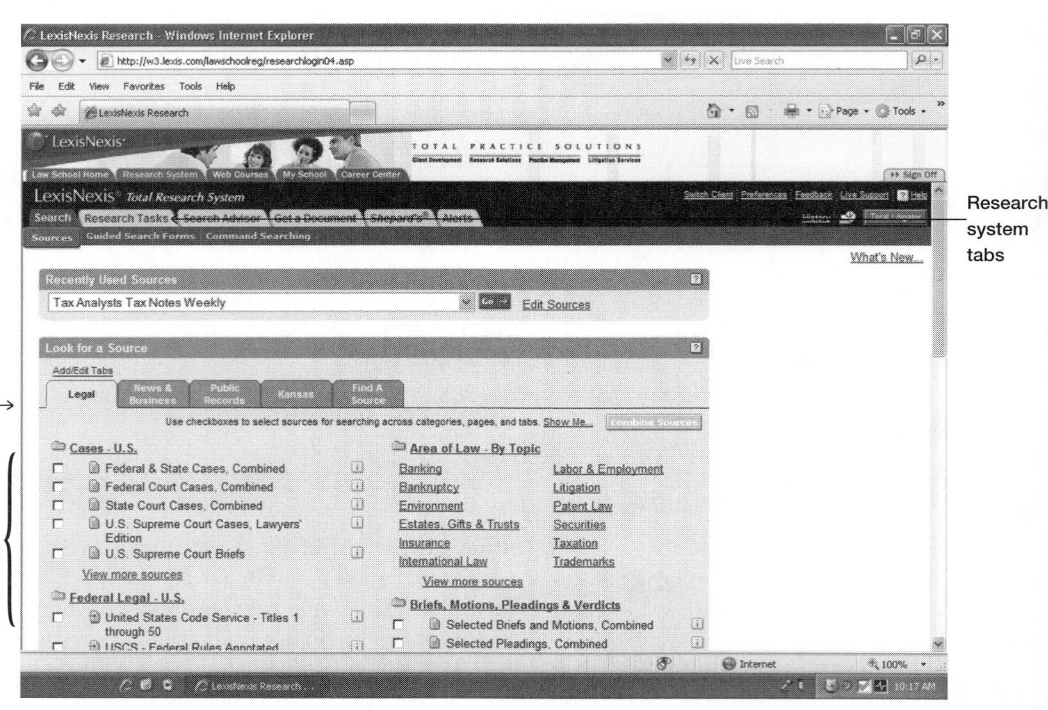

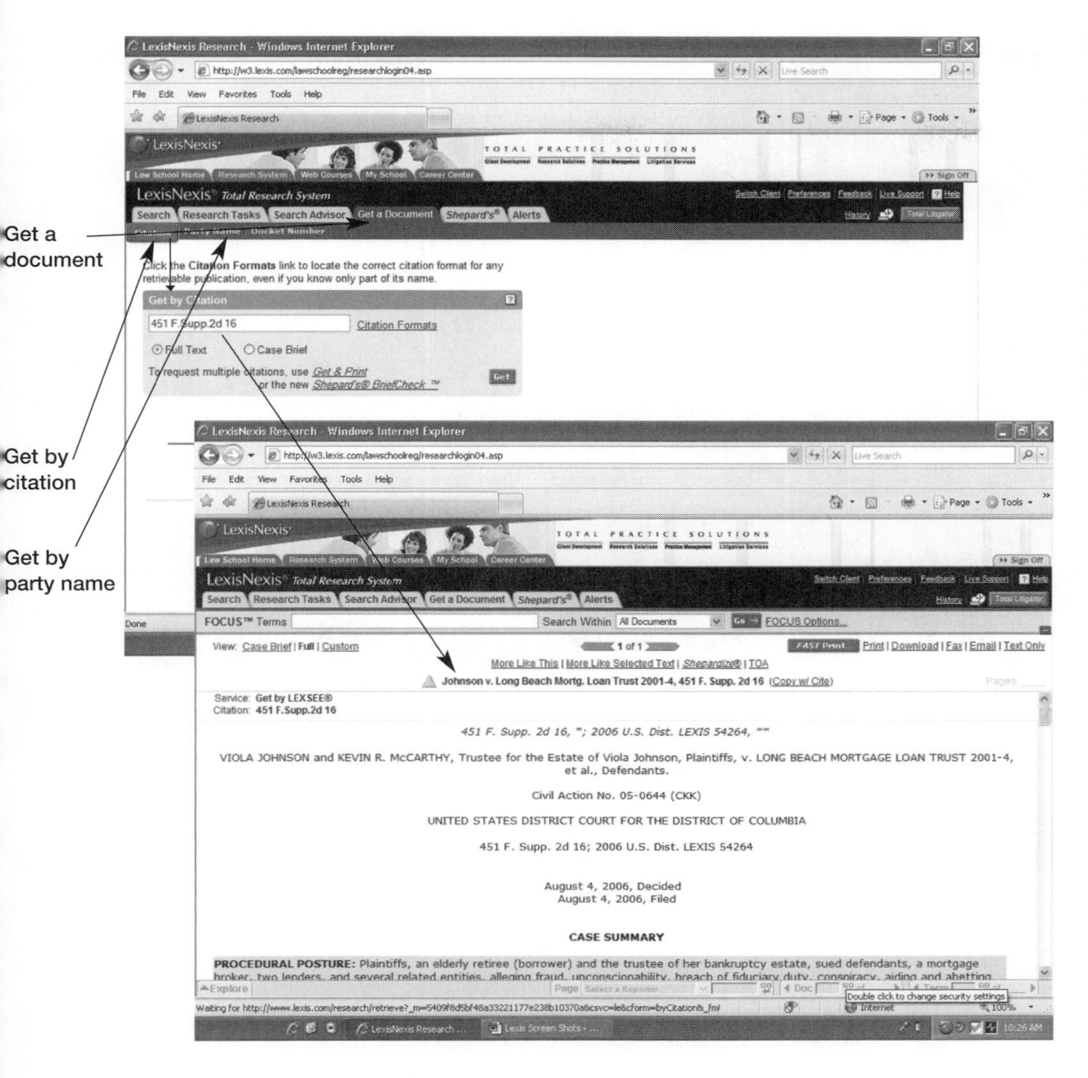

Exhibit 11–25
LexisNexis—Get by Citation

Get by Citation The Get by Citation feature in LexisNexis allows a user to immediately retrieve a specific case or statute by entering its citation. In Exhibit 11–25 (first screen) the user has entered "451 F.Supp.2d 16." LexisNexis automatically retrieved the case without the user having to enter a database or search criteria (see the second screen of Exhibit 11–25). Get by Citation is comparable to Westlaw's Find by Citation.

Get by Citation
Is a LexisNexis feature that allows a user to immediately retrieve a specific case or statute by entering its citation.

Get by Party Name The Get by Party Name feature allows a LexisNexis user to retrieve a document such as a case by entering the name(s) of a party (or parties) (see the first screen of Exhibit 11–26). The user enters a party name, selects the jurisdiction, and then selects "search." The document is then automatically retrieved (see the second screen of Exhibit 11–26) without the user having to enter a full search query. Get by Party Name is a quick and efficient way to find a case if a user just has a party's name. Get by Party Name is similar to Westlaw's Find A Case By Party Name.

Get by Party Name
A feature that allows a LexisNexis user to retrieve a case by entering the name(s) of a party (or parties).

LexisNexis Databases

LexisNexis has approximately 19,000 databases. The database coverage is extremely broad and includes case law, statutes, news, business, medical-related

Exhibit 11–26
LexisNexis—Get by Party Name

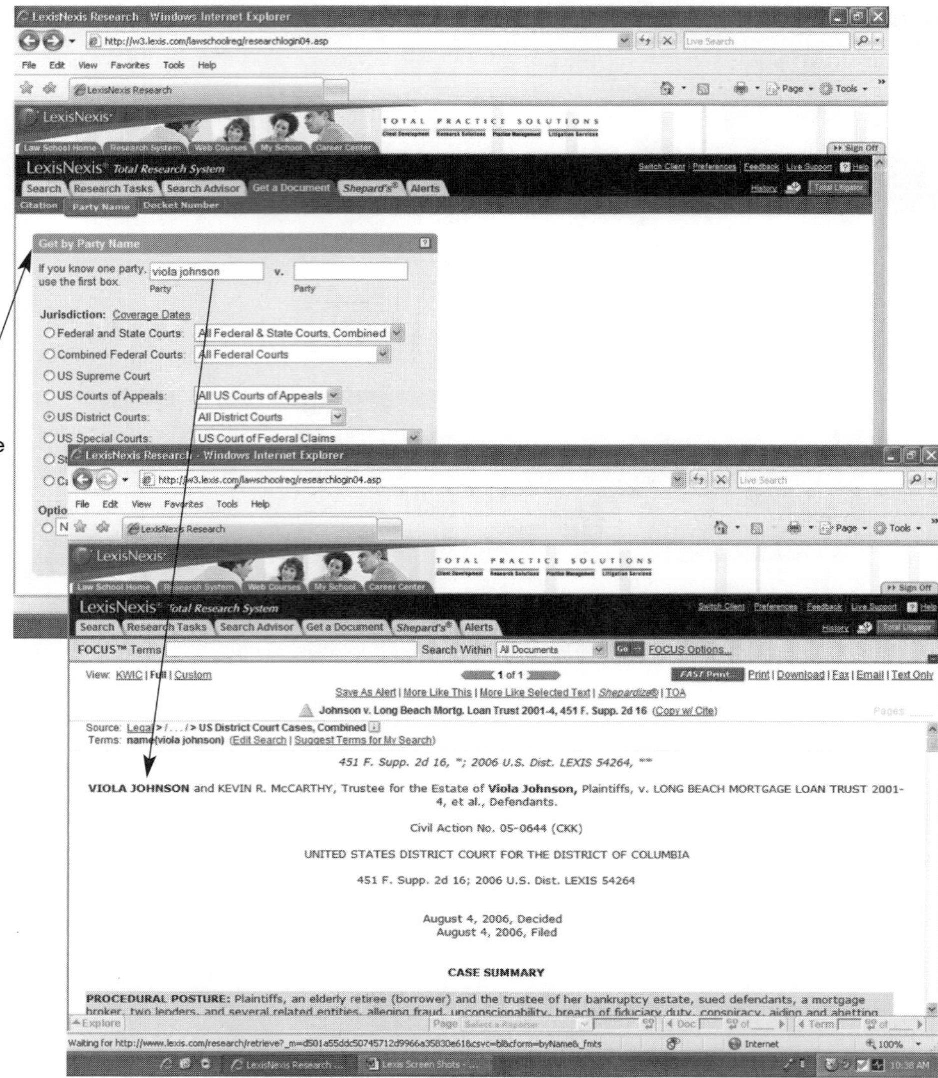

information, public records, and much more. LexisNexis gives users a number of different ways to conduct research.

Search Tab Notice in Exhibit 11–24 that the user is in the Search tab near the top left of the screen. Under Look for a Source the user is in the Legal sub-tab (see Exhibit 11–24). From the Legal sub-tab, the user can access many common databases such as Federal & State Cases, Combined, Federal Court Cases, Combined, United States Code Service, individual state resources (not shown in Exhibit 11–24), and others.

Notice that next to the databases there are open boxes. This is where users select which databases to search in. A user can select multiples boxes / databases at one time and can search in multiple databases with one search. Notice also in Exhibit 11–24 that there are other sub-tabs including News & Business, Public Records, Kansas, and Find A Source. These sub-tabs can be configured by the user depending on his or her needs. Using sub-tabs a user can quickly access a large variety of LexisNexis databases. Users can also browse for databases using the Find A Source sub-tab (see Exhibit 11–27). In Exhibit 11–27 the user selected "U" from the alphabetical list. The user could then browse all of the databases in LexisNexis that start with the letter "U."

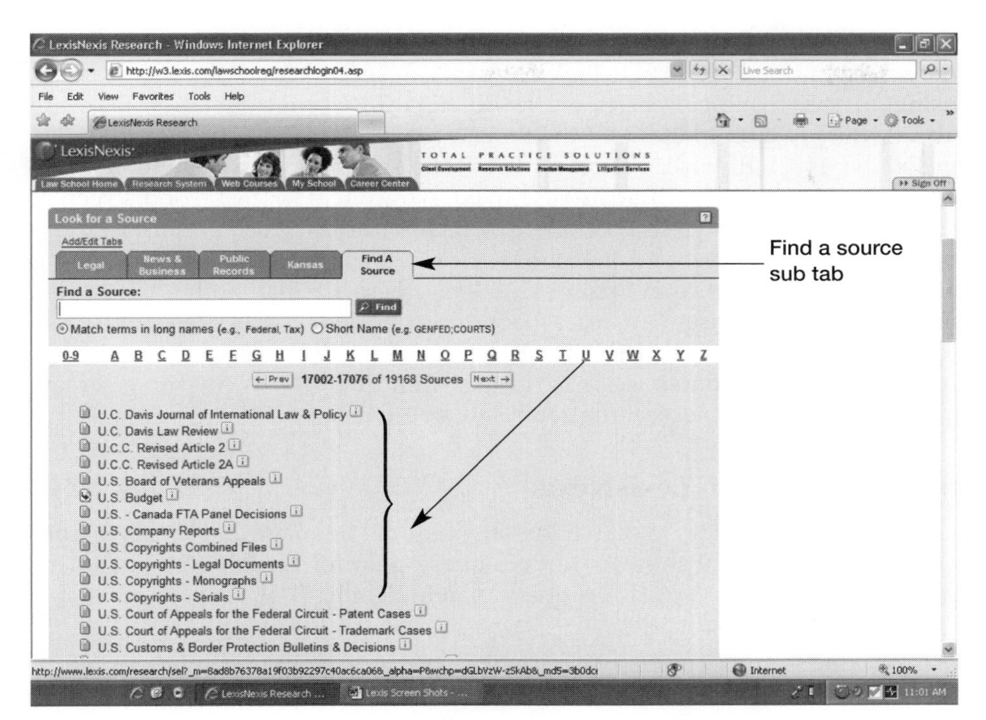

Exhibit 11–27
LexisNexis - Find A Source Sub Tab

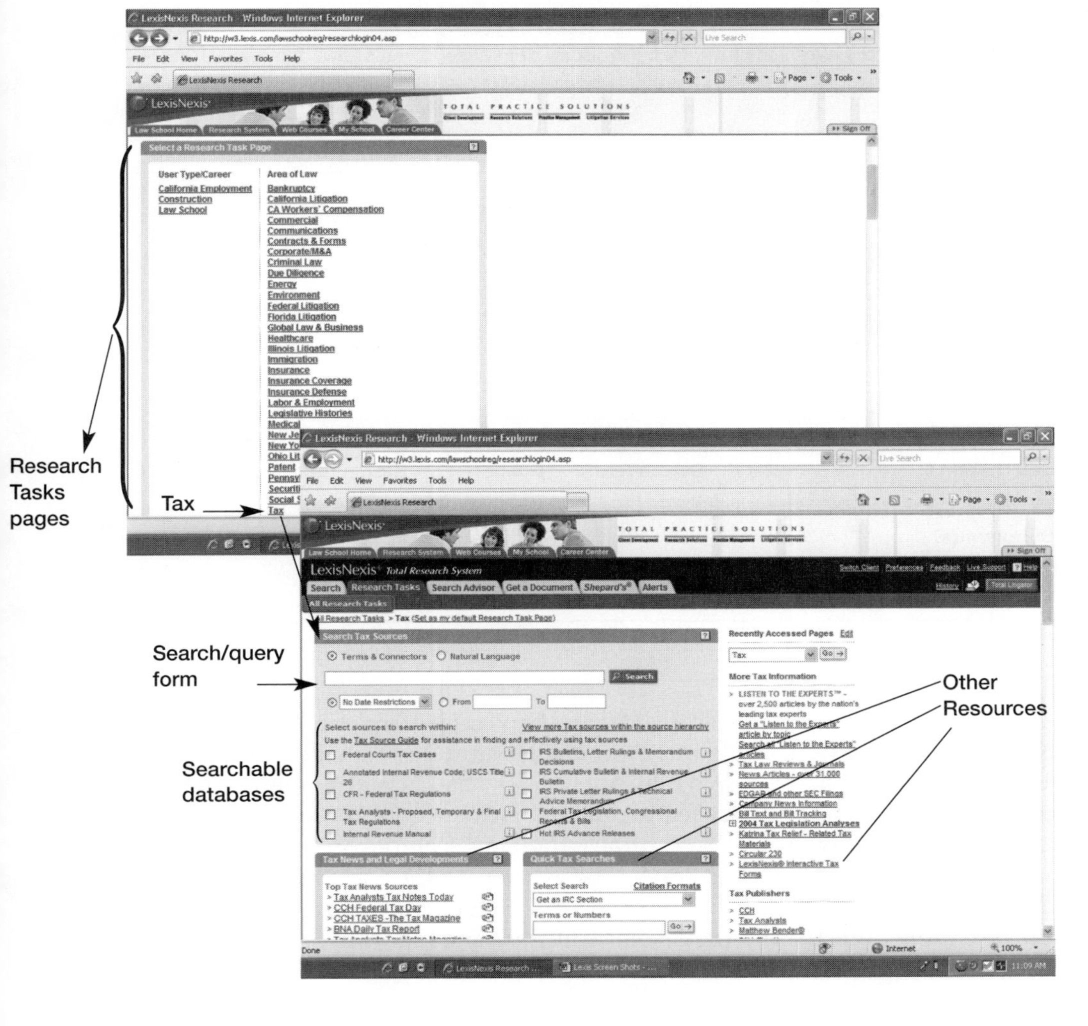

Exhibit 11–28
LexisNexis-Research Tasks Tab

Research Tasks Tab Notice in Exhibit 11–24 the tab is the upper left corner of the screen entitled "Research Tasks." Users can access databases and searches using this tab. Exhibit 11–28 shows the Research Tasks page. Research Tasks are arranged by subject matter (see the first screen of Exhibit 11–28). For example, in Exhibit 11–28 the user selected "Tax." The second screen of Exhibit 11–28 shows the Tax resources that are displayed. Notice that in the second screen of Exhibit 11–28, under "Select sources to search within," LexisNexis lists a number of tax-related databases that the user can search in, either individually or collectively. Also, notice in Exhibit 11–28 that there are many other tax-related resources, that the user can access from this one screen. The Research Tasks feature is convenient because it allows a user to (1) access a number of related LexisNexis databases, (2) run a search query from the same screen, and (3) access other subject matter–related sources.

Search Queries in LexisNexis

LexisNexis allows users to search in both Natural Language and Terms & Connectors. Exhibit 11–29 shows a sample query plan for LexisNexis. The query plan is similar to the WESTLAW query plan in Exhibit 11–9.

Exhibit 11–29

Computer-Assisted Legal Research Query Plan—LexisNexis

COMPUTER ASSISTED LEGAL RESEARCH QUERY FORM

Date: *June 1* **Research's Initials:** *TPB* **Client/Case:** *Ward v. United Mortgage*

Estimate Time on Service: *15 min.*

Service to be Used: Westlaw (Lexis/Nexis) LoisLaw Fastcase Versus Law Internet CD/ROM

Database(s) to be searched:

DC Federal District & State Courts, Combined

Type of Search: Natural (Terms and Connectors)

Issues/Question: *Can a Federal court get personal jurisdiction over a non-resident company where the only contact is assignment of a mortgage?*

Search Term 1	Connector 1	Search Term 2	Connector 2	Search Term 3	Connector 3
"personal jurisdiction"	*/s*	*non-resident*	*/s*	*compan!*	*/p*
Synonym(s)					

Search Term 4	Connector 4	Search Term 5	Connector 5	Search Term 6	Connector 6
mortgage	*AND*	*long-arm*			
Synonym(s)					
contract					

Query: *"personal jurisdiction" /s non-resident /s compan! /p mortgage OR contract AND long-arm*

Natural Language The advantage of using Natural Language is ease of use. The downside is that the search may not be as precise as a terms and connectors search. The Natural Language feature in LexisNexis works like the Natural Language feature in WESTLAW. Natural Language searches (which LexisNexis sometimes refers to as Freestyle) can be entered in the form of a sentence or question. For example, in Exhibit 11–29 the question in the Issue/Question field can be entered directly into LexisNexis Natural Language (see Exhibit 11–30). In Exhibit 11–30 (first screen) the user selected the DC Federal District & State

Courts, Combined, database then selected Natural Language in the search screen (Exhibit 11–30, first screen). The user then entered the search query and entered some terms in the Restrict using Mandatory Terms field including "personal jurisdiction." This means that any case retrieved must have these terms. The user then selected "Search." LexisNexis then analyzed the statistical relevance of the terms and retrieved the documents that most closely matched the search requests. Notice in the second screen of Exhibit 11–30 that the *Johnson v. Long Beach Mortgage* case was retrieved.

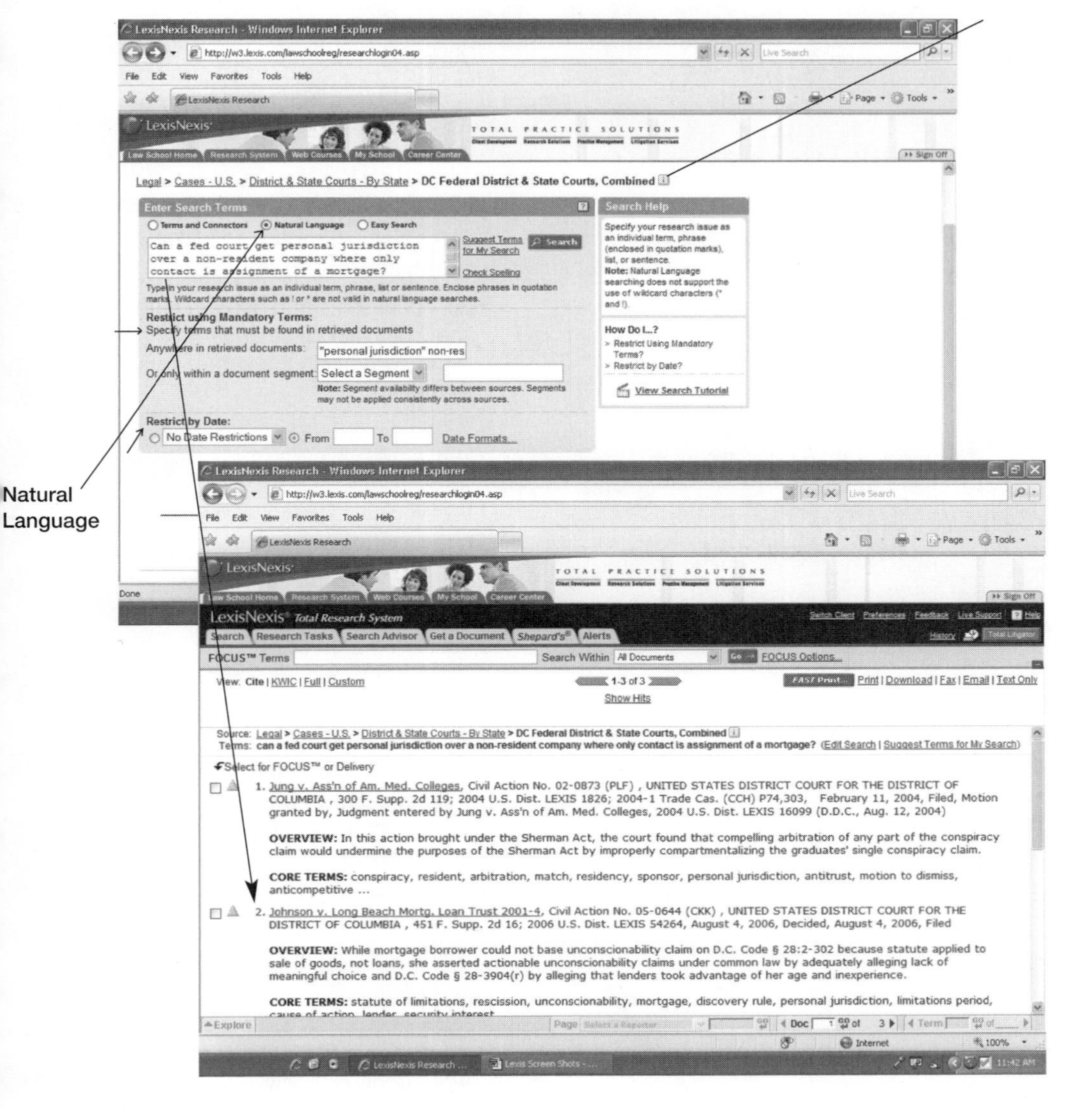

Exhibit 11–30
LexisNexis—Natural Language Search

Terms and Connectors Exhibit 11–31 shows selected connectors and expanders in LexisNexis. LexisNexis automatically searches for plurals of words and most possessive nouns. LexisNexis uses the exclamation mark (!) as a root expander and the asterisk (*) as a universal character, just as WESTLAW does.

LexisNexis includes several types of connectors that for the most part are similar to those in WESTLAW. Connectors in LexisNexis that are the same as WESTLAW include OR, /p, /s, and /n (see Exhibit 11–31, and compare to Exhibit 11–11). Connectors in LexisNexis that are similar, but not identical

Exhibit 11–31
LexisNexis Connectors and Expanders

Connector	Definition	Search Query	Documents Found
OR	OR	Mortgage OR contract	All documents that have either the word *mortgage* or the word *contract* anywhere in them
AND	AND	mortgage AND contract	All documents that contain both the word *mortgage* and the word *contract* anywhere in them
w/p or /p	Paragraph	mortgage w/p contract; or mortgage /p contract	All documents that contain both the word *mortgage* and the word *contract* in the same paragraph
w/s or /s	Sentence	mortgage w/s contract; or mortgage /s contract	All documents that contain both the word *mortgage* and the word *contract* in the same sentence
w/n or /n	Words	mortgage w/3 contract; or mortgage /3 contract	All documents that contain both the word *mortgage* and the word *contract* within three words of each other
" "	Phrase	"personal jurisdiction"	All documents where the exact phrase "personal jurisdiction" occurs
Pre/n	Precedes by n words	personal Pre/3 jurisdiction	All documents where *personal* precedes *jurisdiction* within 3 words
AND NOT	AND NOT	R.I.C.O. AND NOT "Puerto Rico"	All documents with the word *RICO* (i.e., Racketeer Influenced and Corrupt Organization Act) but not *Puerto Rico*

Expander	Definition	Search Query	Documents Found
!	Root Expander	medic!	All documents that have the words *medicine, medical, medicate, or medication*
*	Universal character	kn*w	All documents that have the word *know* or *knew* in them

to those in WESTLAW are AND (which in WESTLAW is represented as "&") and AND NOT (which in WESTLAW is represented as %). In LexisNexis some connectors can be entered more than one way; for example, "/p" can also be entered as "w/p." The final query in Exhibit 11–32 reads "*'personal jurisdiction' /s non-resident/s compan!/p mortgage OR contract AND long-arm.*" This is the same search that was entered in WESTLAW (see Exhibit 11–14). The query tells LexisNexis to search for documents in the selected database (DC Federal

District & State Courts, Combined) that have the phrase *personal jurisdiction* within the same sentence as the word *non-resident,* within the same sentence as *compan! (company or companies),* and within the same paragraph as *mortgage* or *contract,* and which also contain the word *long-arm* somewhere in the document. Notice in Exhibit 11–32 (second screen) that the *Johnson v. Long Beach Mortgage* case is the second case retrieved.

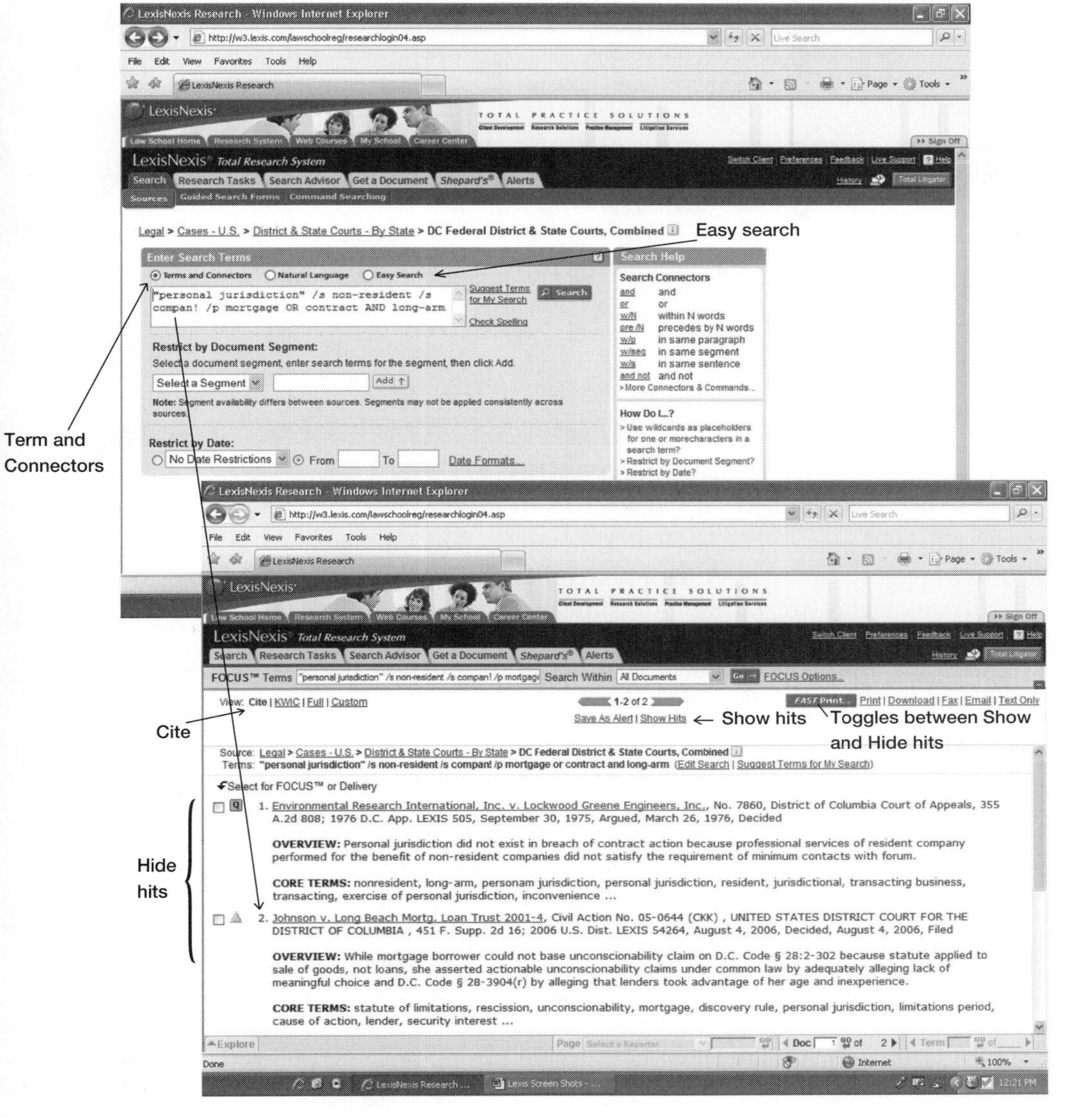

Exhibit 11–32
LexisNexis Terms and Connectors Search

Easy Search Easy Search is a type of search in LexisNexis that only returns the most relevant documents and, according to LexisNexis, is optimized for short search queries that contain only two or three terms. For example, the user could enter "personal jurisdiction non-resident" in Easy Search and LexisNexis would retrieve some leading cases on the subject matter.

Suggest Terms for My Search The Suggest Terms for My Search feature in LexisNexis shows synonyms for search terms in the query (see Exhibit 11–32A). This is a helpful tool for refining searches. The LexisNexis Suggest Terms for my Search feature is similar to WESTLAW's Thesaurus feature.

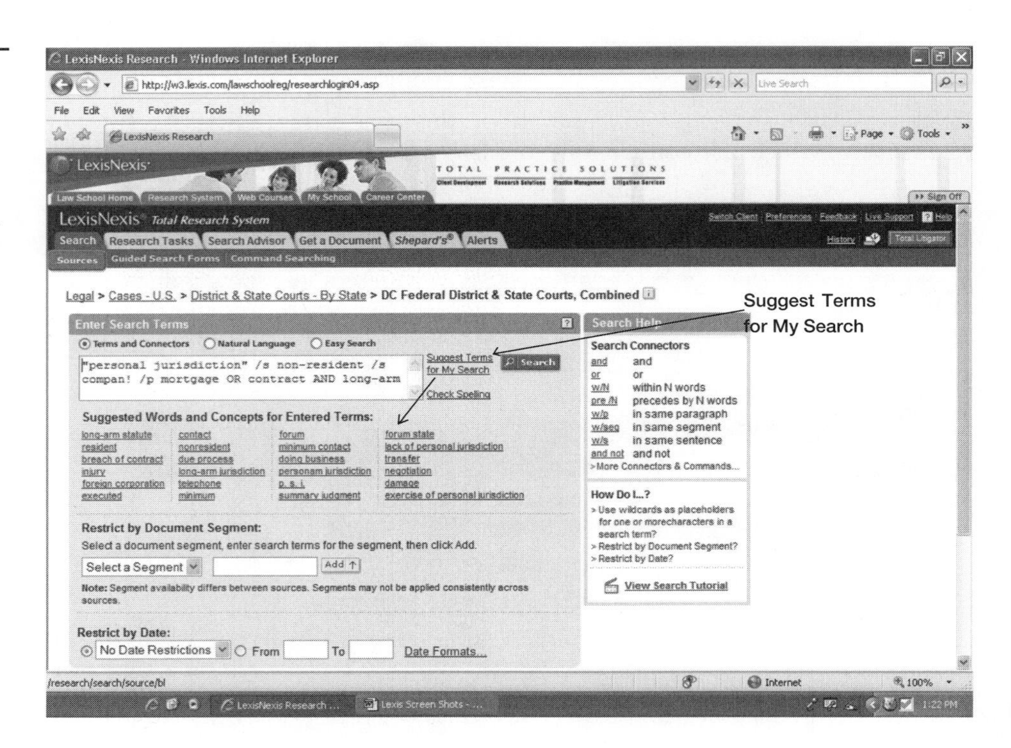

Exhibit 11–32A
LexisNexis—Suggest Terms for My Search

Working with Retrieved Cases in LexisNexis

LexisNexis gives users a number of different options for viewing and working with retrieved documents. After a search has been executed in LexisNexis the system can display the retrieved documents in one of four formats.

Display Formats Once a user has executed a search in LexisNexis there are four main display formats available, including Cite, KWIC, Full, and Custom.

Cite The Cite format shows the user a bibliographic list of the citations retrieved. Cite can either display the search terms or hide the search terms (see Exhibit 11–33, where the "hits" are shown). Notice in the second screen of Exhibit 11–32 to the right of the View: field that Cite is selected in the upper left corner of the screen. A list of the case cites is displayed, including an overview and core terms for each. In Exhibit 11–32 the search term hits are hidden. The second screen of Exhibit 11–32 and Exhibit 11–33 are identical, except that, in 11–32 the hits are hidden and in 11–33 the hits are shown.

When the user clicks Show Hits, the search terms as they appear in the case are now included in the list (see Exhibit 11–33). Users can either display or hide the hits. If the user has the Show Hits option turned on, a lot of information is provided about each case, but it makes it difficult to quickly search through large numbers of cases retrieved. If the user has Hide Hits turned on (see Exhibit 11–32, second screen), the user can see more cases, but in fewer detail. Both options are helpful depending on what the user is trying to accomplish at the time.

KWIC The KWIC option by default shows a twenty-five-word window of text around the user's search terms. KWIC is helpful when the user wants to see the context around his or her search terms but does not want to read the full text of the case.

Full Full shows the user the full text of the document (see Exhibit 11–34).

Custom The user can configure this format to meeting their individual needs.

Case Summaries LexisNexis includes a Case Summary section for each case (see Exhibit 11–34). The Case Summary includes the procedural posture of the

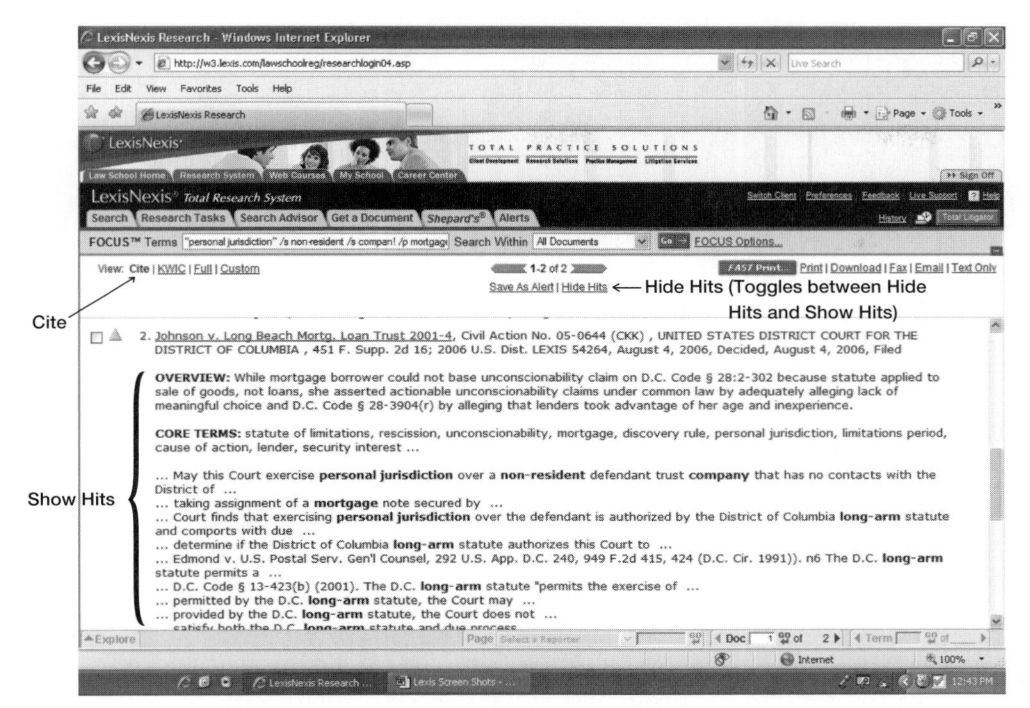

Exhibit 11–33
LexisNexis—Display Format: Cite/Show Hits

case, an overview, the outcome or disposition of the case, and core terms that are used in the case (note that core terms are not shown in Exhibit 11–34). The Case Summary section makes it easy for users to understand the context of a case and its result. LexisNexis's Case Summary feature is similar to WESTLAW's Synopsis feature.

Navigation Frame At the bottom of a retrieved document is the Navigation Frame (see Exhibit 11–34). The Explore feature allows the user to navigate

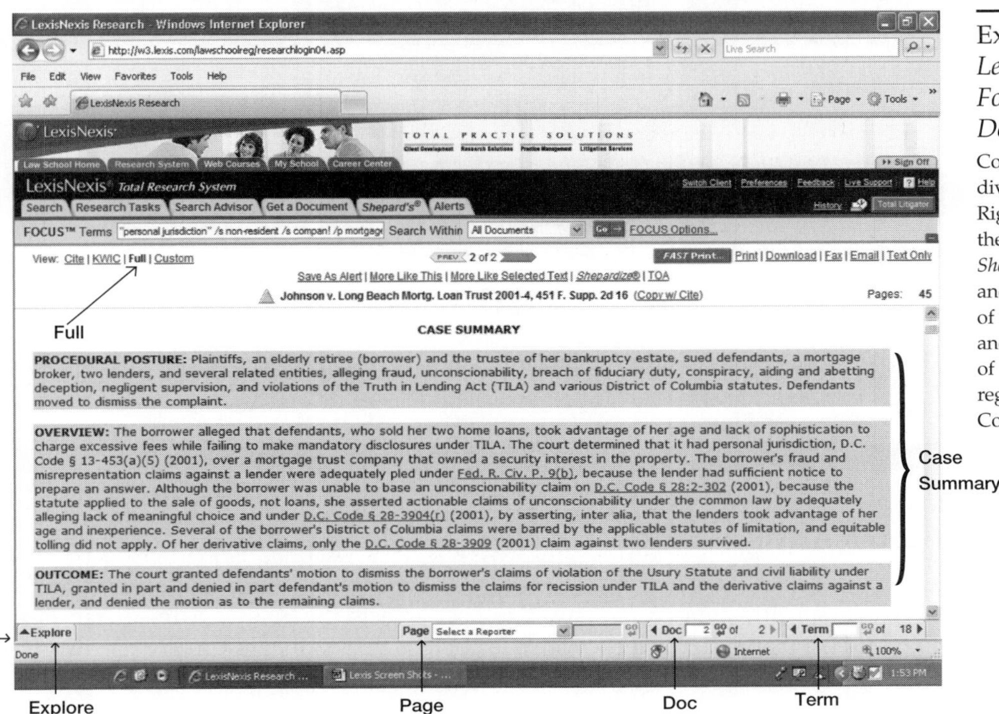

Exhibit 11–34
LexisNexis—Display Format: Full Text of Document

within the document, moving to the top of the document, viewing the dissent, moving to the place in the document where the attorneys are listed, and so forth. The Page feature allows the user to navigate to a specific hard-copy reporter page. The Doc feature allows the user to go to the next or previous document. Alternatively, the user can click in the Doc box, enter a document number, and go to the specific document. The Term feature allows a user to go to the next / previous search term. Viewing the search terms is helpful when a user is trying to evaluate whether the document is on point or not.

FOCUS
A LexisNexis feature that allows a user to search all of the retrieved documents for a term(s), whether or not the term was used in the original search.

FOCUS The LexisNexis **FOCUS** feature allows a user to search all of the retrieved documents for a term(s), whether or not the term was used in the original search. The FOCUS feature allows users to further cull the cases retrieved to find the exact case(s) the user is looking for. The FOCUS feature is similar to WESTLAW's Locate in Result feature.

Headnotes

Headnotes in LexisNexis summarize each major issue in a case (see Exhibit 11–35). Most cases include a number of Headnotes. When a user finds a Headnote on point, the user can select the More Like This Headnote link next to that specific Headnote (see Exhibit 11–35). The More Like This Headnote screen is then displayed (see Exhibit 11–36, first screen). It allows the user to search similar Headnotes in LexisNexis by jurisdiction. In Exhibit 11–36 (second screen) additional cases with similar Headnotes are displayed. Headnotes are a great way for a user to expand his or her research while staying on point.

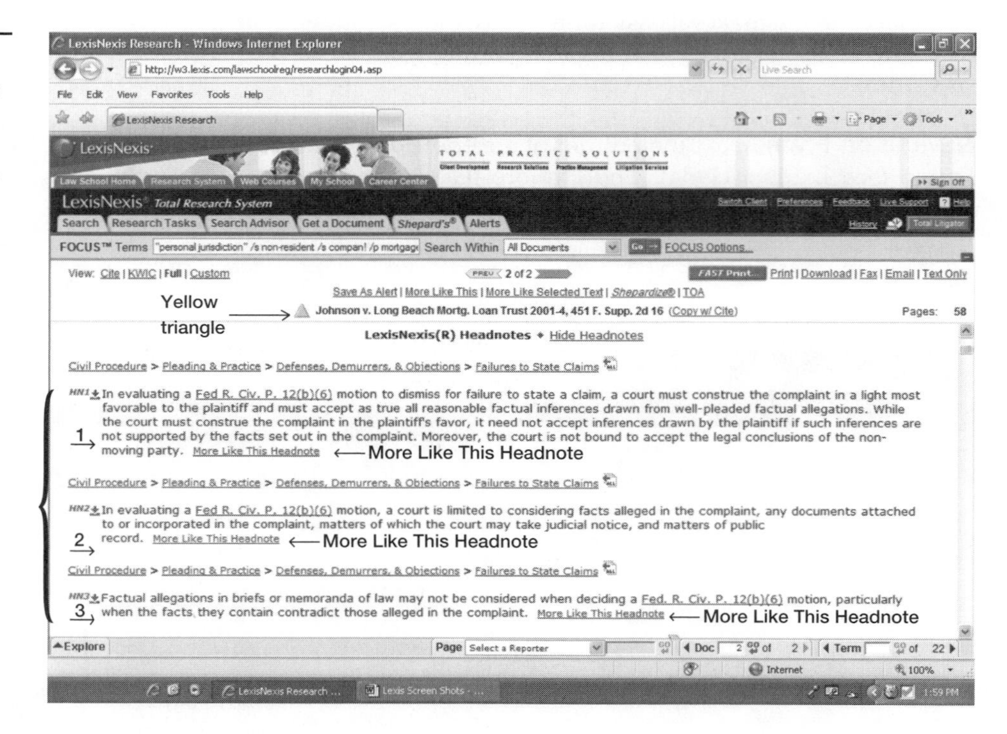

Exhibit 11–35
LexisNexis®—Headnotes

Search Advisor

LexisNexis's Search Advisor feature allows users to search for and find information in a specific area of the law. The user selects the Search Advisor tab (see Exhibit 11–24) and then selects from a list of legal topics that gradually narrow the legal matter down to a specific issue (see Exhibit 11–37). The user then selects the

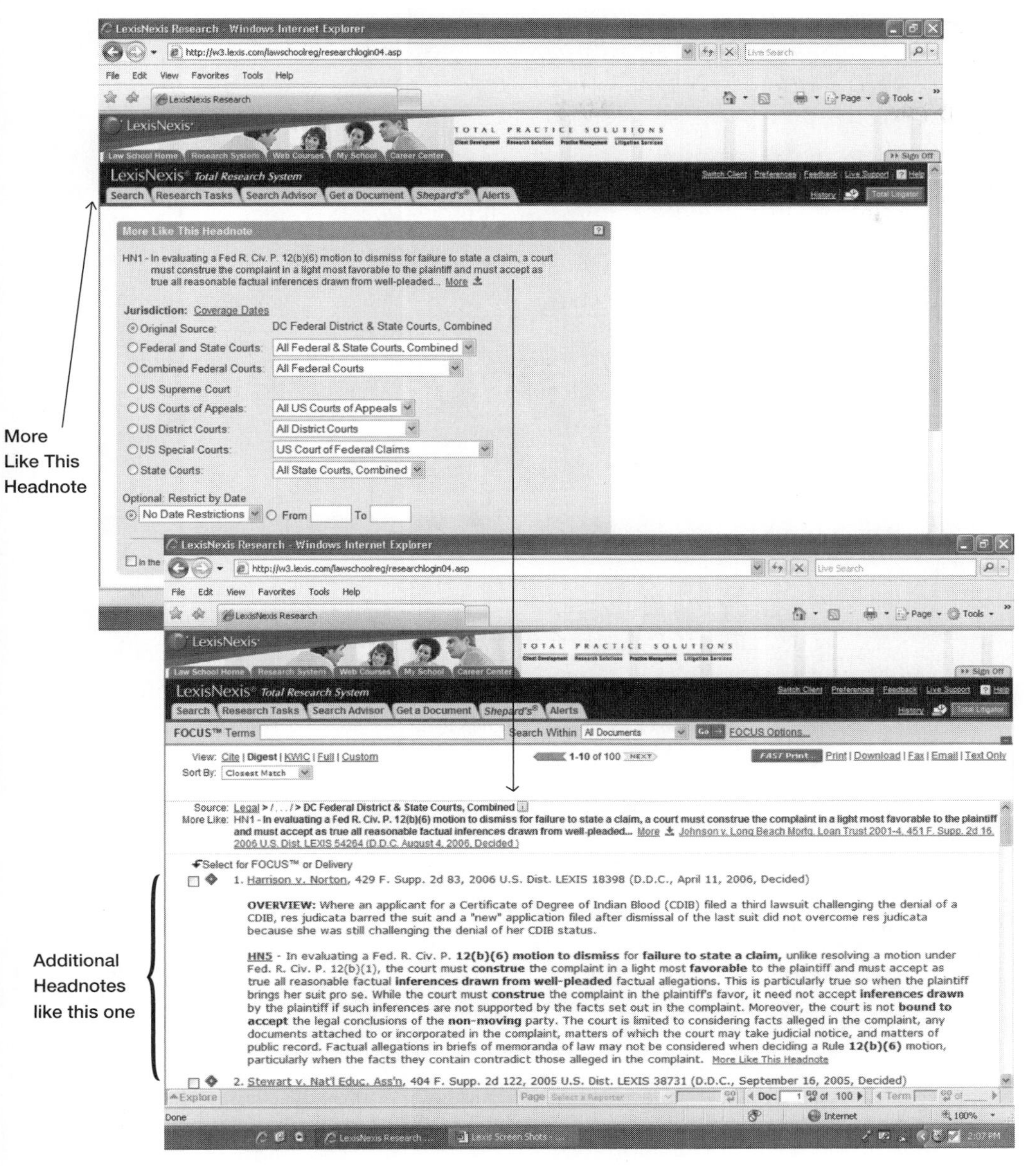

Exhibit 11–36
LexisNexis More Like This Headnote Search

jurisdiction to search and any additional search terms, and LexisNexis retrieves case law and other information related to the subject matter. LexisNexis allows the user to search in cases, statutes and regulations, agency materials, and analytical materials. The Search Advisor feature is similar to WESTLAW's KeySearch.

Shepard's Citations

Shepard's Citations is LexisNexis's citation research tool. It allows the user to determine if a case, statute, or other document is good law and allows the users to expand his or her research by finding other sources that have cited the case. To access *Shepard's* citations, the user selects the *Shepard's* tab (see Exhibit 11–38, first screen). There are actually four separate cite-checking tools on the Shepard's tab. They appear as sub-tabs and include *Shepard's*, Table of Authorities, Auto-Cite, and LEXCITE (see Exhibit 11–38).

Notice in Exhibit 11–38, first screen, that the user has selected the *Shepard's* sub-tab, entered a cite (451 F.Supp.2d 16), selected whether the user wants the

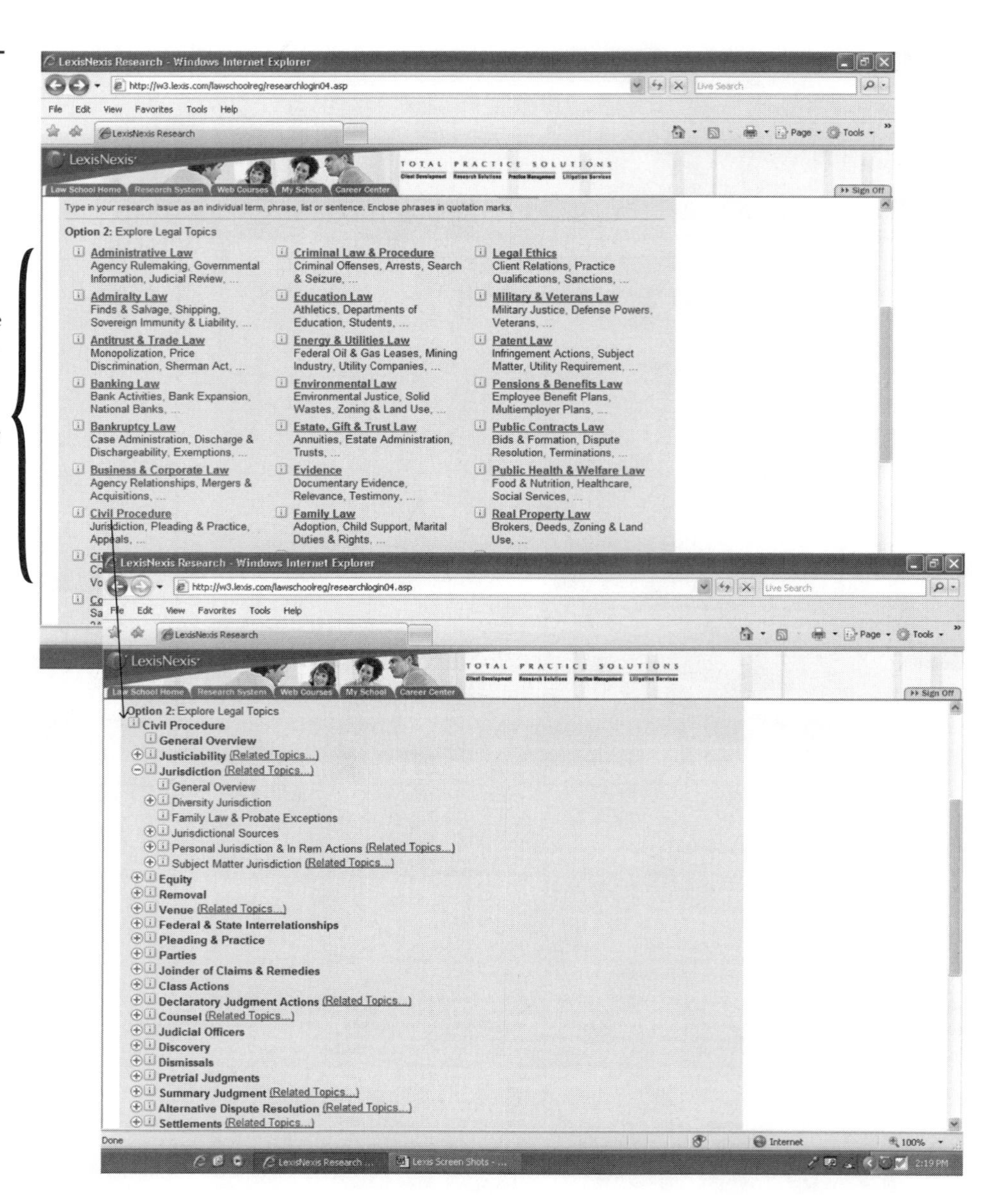

Exhibit 11–37
LexisNexis® Search Advisor

report in the KWIC or FULL format, and then selected "Check." The system returns the case's history and citing references (see Exhibit 11–38, second screen). Notice the yellow triangle at the top of the second screen in Exhibit 11–38. The yellow triangle means that the case has had some negative treatment, but has not yet been reversed or overruled. Notice in the case itself in Exhibit 11–35 that a yellow triangle is displayed near the title of the case. *Shepard's* uses colored shapes so the user can easily determine whether a case or statute is good law (see Exhibit 11–39).

Exhibit 11–40 shows a *Shepard's* report on the Religious Freedom Restoration Act, a federal statute that was declared unconstitutional. Notice in Exhibit 11–40 that the case is shown with a red stop sign next to it. Notice also that there are 549 cites to the case; each cite can be found in the *Shepard's* report (see Exhibit 11–40). Notice also in Exhibit 11–40, that at the top middle of the screen there is a link that says "Save As *Shepard's* Alert." *Shepard's* Alert allows users to be notified, typically through email, when the status of a case changes in *Shepard's*. Notice in Exhibit 11–38 that one of the *Shepard's* sub-tabs is Auto-Cite. Auto-Cite can be used to quickly determine if a case is still good law. *Shepard's* (including Auto-Cite) is similar to WESTLAW's KeyCite.

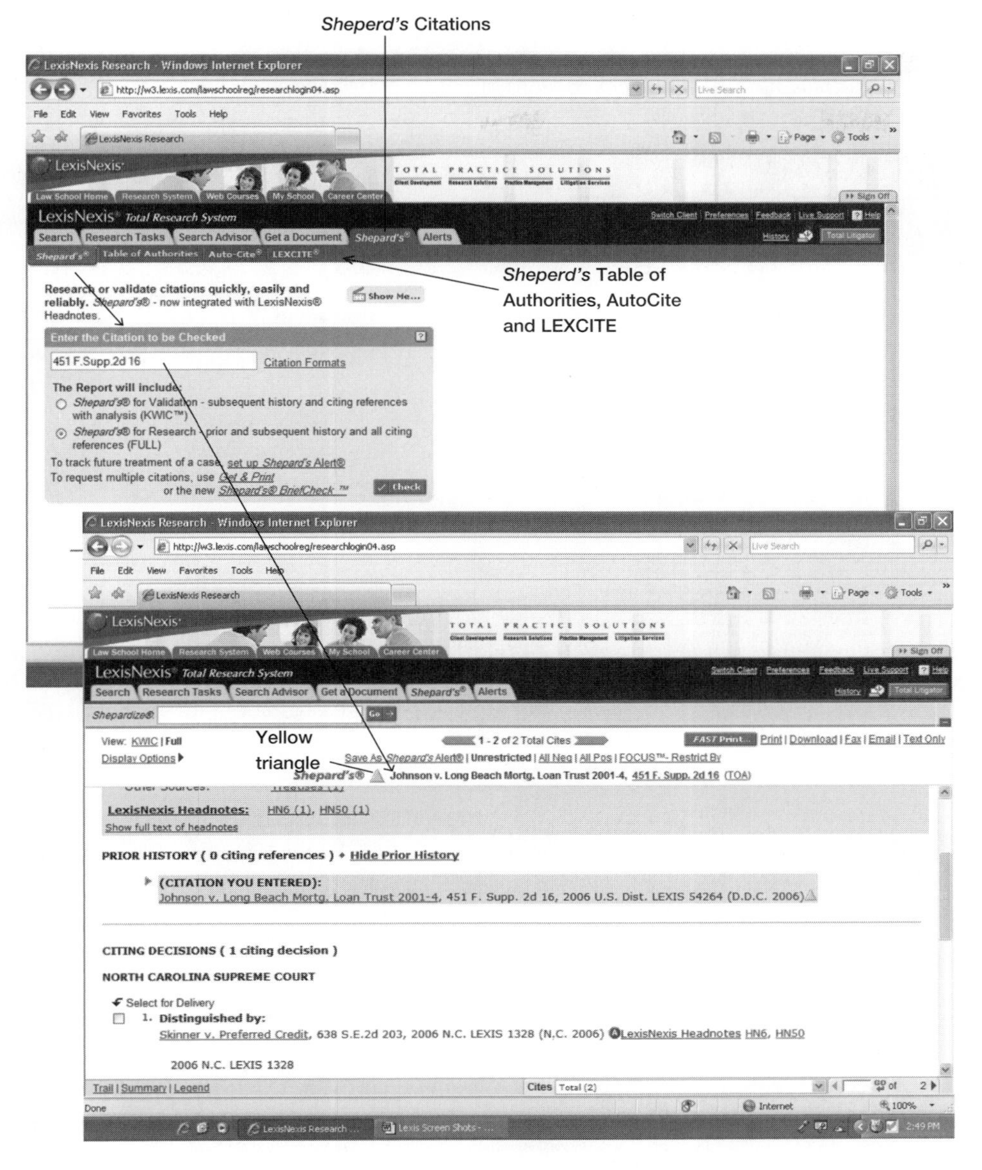

Exhibit 11–38
Using LexisNexis Shepard's® Citations

Shepard's Signal TM Indicators	Explanation
	• Warning: Negative treatment is indicated
	• Questioned: Validity questioned by citing references
	• Caution: Possible negative treatment
	• Positive treatment is indicated
	• Citing references with analysis available
	• Citation information available

Exhibit 11–39
LexisNexis Shepard's Signal ™ Indicators

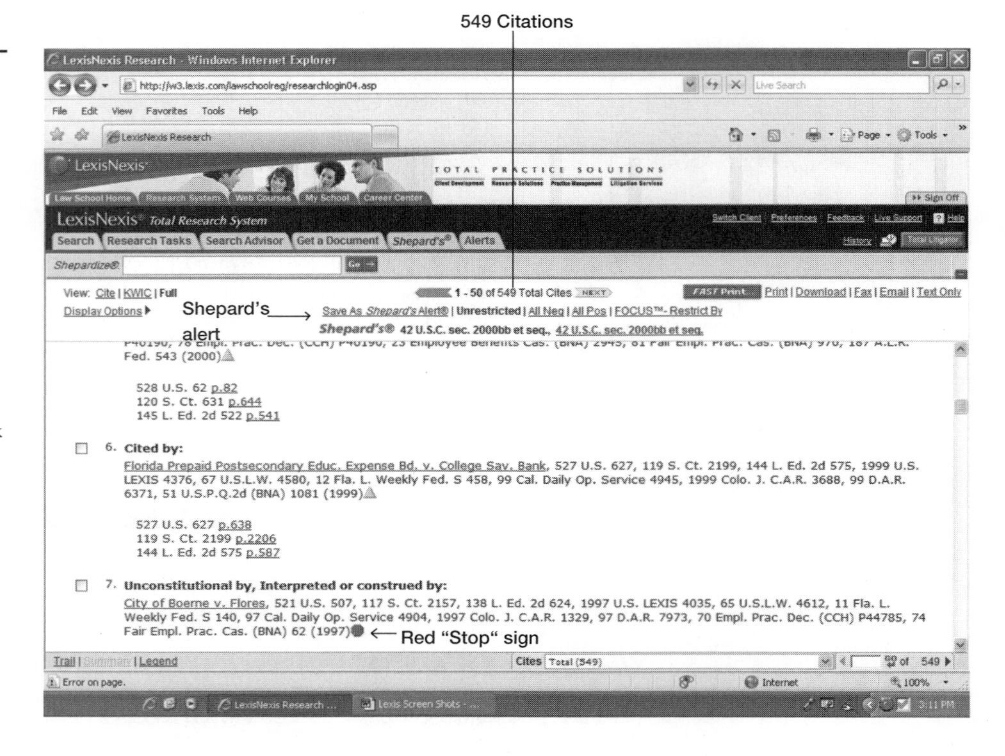

Exhibit 11–40
LexisNexis Shepard's® Citation—Religious Freedom Restoration Act

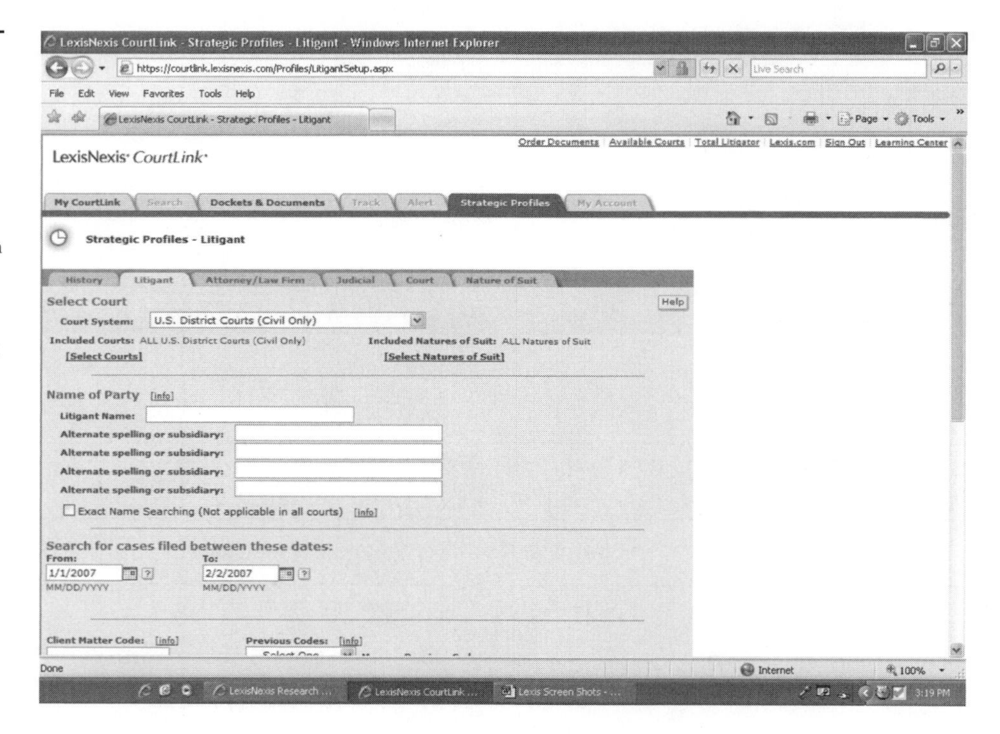

Exhibit 11–41
CourtLink® in LexisNexis®

CourtLink

LexisNexis users can access many federal and state court dockets using CourtLink (see Exhibit 11–41). CourtLink allows users to find information about cases, litigants, and attorneys and law firms, among other things. CourtLinks can also be used to keep track of the current status of litigation.

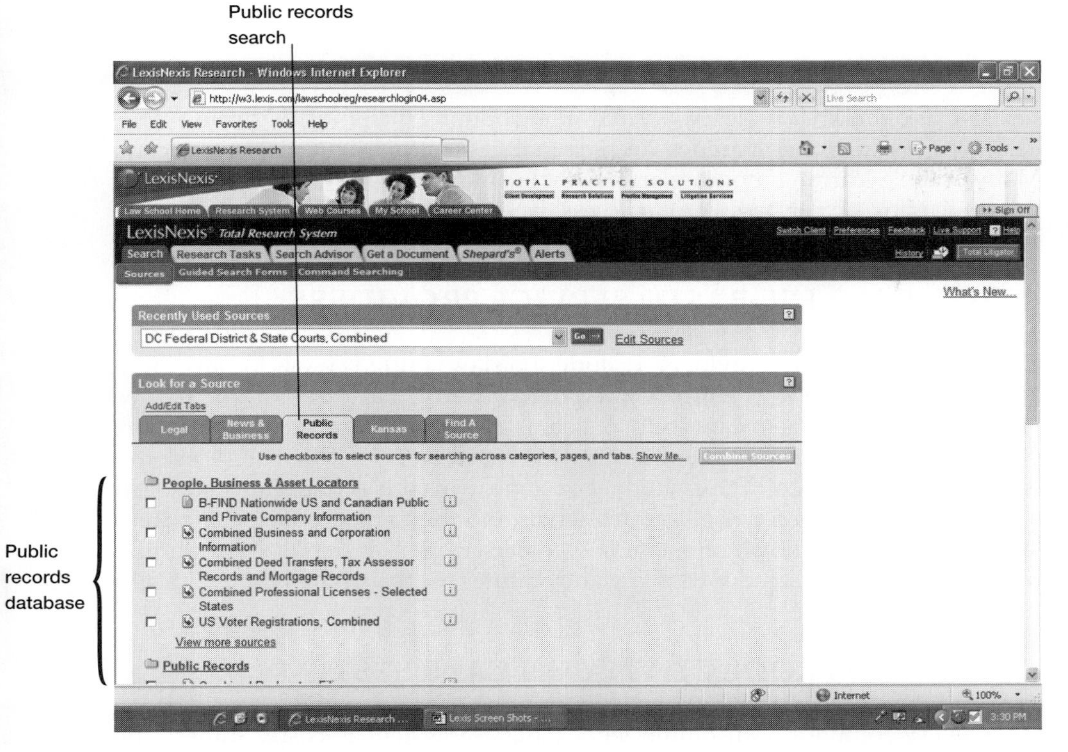

Exhibit 11–42
LexisNexis-Public Records Searches

Public Records Searches

Using LexisNexis, you can access a wide variety of public records databases. Notice in Exhibit 11–24 that there is a sub-tab (on the Search tab) called "Public Records." Exhibit 11–42 shows the databases on the Public Records sub-tab.

Business Information Searches

Using LexisNexis, you can access a wide variety of news and business information. Notice in Exhibit 11–24 that there is a sub-tab called "News & Business" on the Search tab. Exhibit 11–43 shows the databases in the News and Business sub-tab.

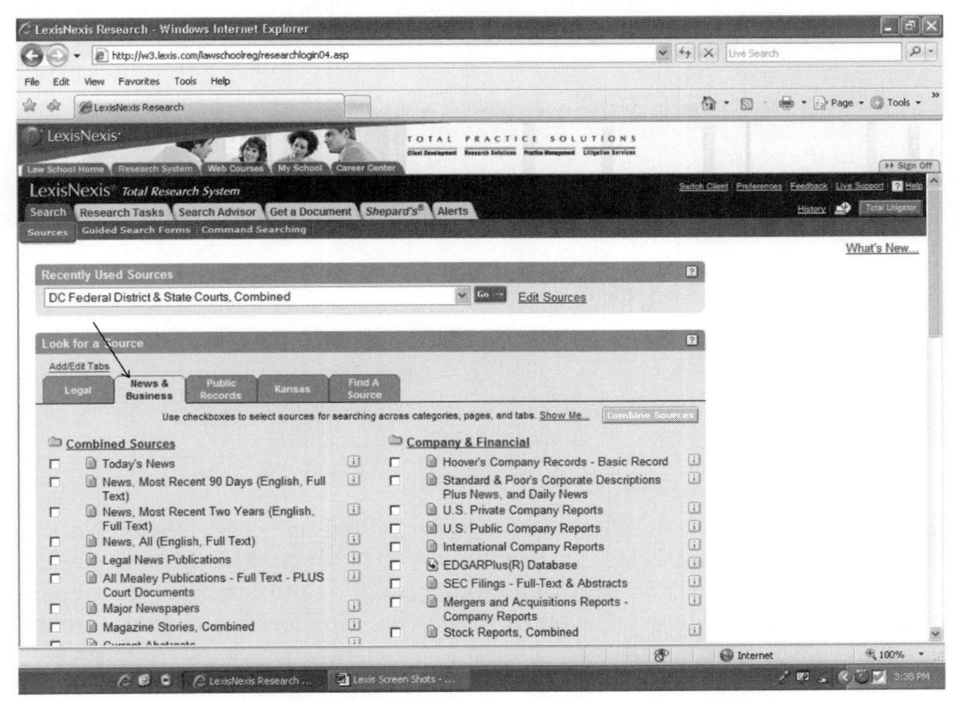

Exhibit 11–43
LexisNexis News and Business Searches

Training

LexisNexis offers are a wide variety of training options, including e-learning modules, webclasses, training guides, and seminars. See http://www.lexisnexis.com. Many of the e-learning modules are available online free of charge, and users do not need a Lexis ID or password to access the e-learning modules.

OTHER CALR FEE-BASED SERVICE PROVIDERS

Other CALR service providers include Loislaw (http://www.loislaw.com), National Law Library (http://www.itislaw.com), Fastcase (http://www.fastcase.com), and Versuslaw (http://versuslaw.com). These service providers compete against WESTLAW and LexisNexis based on price. Their services offer less breadth of electronic information. For some firms this is fine. For example, if a law firm only has a few legal professionals and they practice in specific areas such as divorce, criminal, or estate law, a subscription to one of these service providers that only includes case law and statutes for their state might suffice.

INCREASED PRODUCTIVITY ON CALR SYSTEMS

Since every minute on an online legal database system is costly (unless the organization has negotiated a flat-rate monthly billing option), you can take several precautions to increase your productivity and reduce CALR costs.

Do Not Read Cases Online

In most instances, do not read cases you have found online. If you have the book that the case appears in, simply get the cite, terminate the session, and read the text of the case from the book offline.

If you do not have access to the book, print the case offline or download it. When you are connected to many CALRs, you are incurring several charges, including an access service charge (if you used this method to connect to the service) and a database charge. If you read a case online, you are incurring both types of charges: the access service charge and the database charge.

Do Not Make Typos When Entering the Search

A typo in the search command can cost you several dollars as you wait for the CALR to run the search. Double-check your search command for typos before executing it.

Always Plan the Search

Always carefully plan out your search before going online, and always have several alternative searches ready. This can save your firm hundreds of dollars a month in online charges.

Call the CALR's Research Attorneys

If you have a particularly difficult search, try calling one of the research attorneys provided by many CALR systems. For WESTLAW and LexisNexis, the call is toll-free. The research attorneys are experts at CALR and can help you prepare a successful search. They will even run a search online for you to make sure the search query is correct.

Do Not Consider Alternative Search Queries while Online

If you have run the searches that you prepared while offline and still cannot get what you are looking for, exit the system and think of different alternatives. Remember, in many CALR systems, each time you issue a search command you are incurring another charge. Aimlessly entering search commands will only increase the costs.

CD-ROM LEGAL DATABASES

A CD-ROM legal database is a database like one found on WESTLAW or Lexis-Nexis but is packaged on one or more CD-ROMs. For example, the complete set of Federal Reporters, which contain federal appellate court decisions from 1880 to the present, takes up more than 150 linear feet of shelf space in a law library, and this does not count the indexes necessary to use the reporters. The same Federal Reporters come on twelve CD-ROM disks, take up a few inches of shelf space, and come with a search engine that allows the user to search for needed material. Many CD-ROM publishers also offer connections to the Internet or an online service so that research can be updated.

CD-ROM Legal Libraries

There are hundreds and hundreds of CD-ROM legal libraries currently available. Many books and periodicals published for the legal industry are available on CD-ROM. This includes everything from criminal law and family law to European tax laws, and everything in between. One of the best places to find a listing of law-related CD-ROMs is in a book from Infosources Publishing <http://www.infosourcespub.com> called the *Directory of Law-Related CD-ROMs*. The directory lists more than 1,600 law-related CD-ROM products and is cross-referenced by title, subject, publisher, and computer type. Most of the major legal book publishers, including Thomson/West, BNA, and Matthew Bender, offer a wide variety of CD-ROM products.

CD-ROM Search Engines

Searching CD-ROM legal databases is similar to searching on WESTLAW and LexisNexis. Every CD-ROM legal database uses a search engine, typically either Premise or Folio Views, to perform the search. Users are able to use terms and connectors including proximity searches, wild card searches, and other searches similar to WESTLAW and LexisNexis. Most search engines also have hypertext, which allows a user to go directly to another referenced document immediately (similar to the Internet). For example, if a user is reading a case and another case is referenced, the user can click the mouse on the reference to the second citation, and the computer will immediately take the user to the second case.

Premise Premise is a CD-ROM search engine produced by Thomson/West. Premise is designed to work with Thomson/West CD-ROM libraries. Currently, more than five hundred CD-ROM libraries are available. Premise works much the way WESTLAW does. Users can enter searches using either terms and connectors or natural language. In fact, Premise uses the same terms and connectors as WESTLAW, so WESTLAW users do not have to be retrained to use Premise. Users can also add a variety of different types of personal notes to documents that are retrieved. Premise allows for multiple books to be searched and includes a thesaurus function that can help users develop successful queries. Premise also includes hypertext links and electronic bookmarks, and it offers links to WESTLAW so that research can be updated.

Folio Views Folio Views is a very popular CD-ROM search engine. It was one of the first search engines developed and is currently one of the most widely used. Many, if not most, publishers, including many legal publishers (but excluding Thomson/West) use the Folio Views search engine. It has an easy-to-use interface and comes with hypertext, bookmarks, and the ability to add notes, perform searches using terms and connectors.

Advantages and Disadvantages of CD-ROM Legal Libraries

There are many advantages to using CD-ROM legal libraries:

- *Reduced Space and Reduced Expense Considerations*—CD-ROM legal libraries take up a fraction of the space that similar information in book form would. While most law libraries will want some information in book form, there is much information that can be stored on CD-ROM.
- *Portability*—Unlike books, CD-ROM legal libraries are inherently portable. Users can take the entire body of a state's case law into a courtroom on a laptop computer and have the information at their fingertips. This can prove extremely beneficial to the attorney or legal assistant.
- *Convenience*—Users can access information on their own computers without going to a library or even leaving their office. In addition, information on CD-ROM can be copied into a user's word processor just like information from WESTLAW and LexisNexis.
- *Cost*—The total cost of a CD-ROM legal library is often much less than for hard-copy books or for research on line using WESTLAW or LexisNexis.
- *Maintenance*—The cost of maintaining books and adding and deleting supplements and loose-leaf pages should not be underestimated, particularly in a large law library. It takes library personnel numerous hours to do this, as compared to installing a new CD-ROM to replace an old one. There are, however, some maintenance disadvantages to CD-ROM that will be discussed later in this section. As library personnel maintenance time lessens, productivity should increase in other areas (such as the amount of time library staff can spend to assist customers with research projects).

Disadvantages to CD-ROM legal libraries include the following:

- *Maintenance*—Maintenance of the computer software can be an issue, since most CD-ROM databases have a monthly or quarterly subscription service that must be purchased to keep them up to date. New CD-ROMs and updates must be installed. In addition, search engines must be upgraded to new versions from time to time. Keeping hardware requirements, including RAM and hard disk space, and networking requirements current can also take time. In addition, sometimes the technology involved (including interfacing with a network) is a problem. The systems may not work or may be incompatible. Technical experts must be called in to make modifications, which can be both expensive and time consuming.
- *CD-ROM versus the Internet*—There is some question regarding the long-term validity of CD-ROMs, particularly when compared to the Internet. CD-ROMs must be continually updated, whereas Internet products never need to be updated, because the user connects to the Internet where the product is always current.
- *Switching CD-ROMs*—While there are CD-ROM towers that can handle multiple CD-ROMs, many systems still require users or information system professionals to change CD-ROM disks. This can be inconvenient and time consuming. Some legal organizations copy all their CD-ROMs to large network servers so that CD-ROM towers are not necessary. This also makes accessing the information faster, since server access is much faster than CD-ROM access.
- *Training*—Training users to use CD-ROM legal databases can be a problem when different publishers or search engines are used.

Users Making Their Own CDs

With recordable CD and DVD drives, users can now create their own disks. Storing volumes of research, evidence, memos, briefs, or case files on a user's own CD or DVD can be done easily and cost effectively, and it offers the advantages of portability.

Balancing the Different Types of Computer-Assisted Legal Research

The following strategies can help balance the strengths of the different types of computer-assisted legal research:

1. A legal organization should try to balance on-line services (WESTLAW and LexisNexis), with CD-ROMs, the Internet, and books and periodicals without duplicating information in multiple formats. Some organizations encourage users to research first on CD-ROM and then update the research with WESTLAW or LexisNexis.
2. No matter what format is used, it is imperative that the information be complete, accurate, and of high quality, yet still be as inexpensive as possible.
3. It may make sense to consolidate as much as possible with a single vendor, since this maximizes training and compatibility.

ETHICAL CONSIDERATIONS

There are several ethical considerations regarding computer-assisted legal research, such as taking the time to perform competent legal research; informing the court of cases or information that does not help your client; citing quotes appropriately; and not plagiarizing information.

Performing Competent Legal Research

Performing competent legal research for a client is a fundamental aspect of representing a client in a competent and ethical manner. The *ABA Model Rules of Professional Conduct* at Model Rule 1.1 states that a client must be represented in a competent and adequate manner. A client comes to an attorney to be advised on both the factual and legal nature of the client's legal matter. Since the U.S. system of law is based on legal precedent, it is absolutely essential that an attorney understand the legal aspects of a client's matter. This includes performing the legal research to know how to appropriately represent and advise the client. The Model Rule states that the representation requires "skill," "thoroughness," and "preparation." These are all attributes that go to the heart of good legal research. Sometimes wading through mountains of case law, statutes, legislative history, indexes, legal encyclopedias, treatises, law review articles, regulations, court rules, and other research to support a client's position is like finding a needle in a haystack. It takes skill, thoroughness, and preparation to find the right information and to zealously represent the client's interests. While a client can assist with presenting the facts of a case, the client cannot help regarding the preparation of legal arguments and authorities. This responsibility lies with the attorney and legal assistant.

If an attorney fails to present competent legal arguments based on competent legal research, not only has the attorney failed to perform his ethical duty, but he may have committed legal malpractice. Courts have generally recognized that the attorney has a duty to perform competent legal research. For example, the court in *Gosnell v. Rentokil*, 175 F.R.D. 508, 510 n.1 (N.D. Ill. 1997) considered the question of whether an attorney had a duty to Shepardize a case (e.g., to confirm that the case the attorney was citing was still good law). In *Gosnell* the court stated:

> *It is really inexcusable for any lawyer to fail, as a matter of routine, to Shepardize all cited cases (a process that has been made much simpler today than it was in the past, given the facility for doing so under WESTLAW or LEXIS). Shepardization would of course have revealed that the "precedent" no longer qualified as such.*

Likewise, the court in *DeMyrick v. Quest Quarters Suite Hotels,* No. 93 C1520, 1997 WL 177838, at *1 (N.D. Ill. Apr. 6, 1997), held the following in a similar situation:

> *DeMyrick's motion is particularly distressing under the circumstances. It is not simply that DeMyrick's counsel are highly experienced in Illinois personal injury practice and might therefore be expected to keep themselves current on such issues that are of importance to the conduct of such practice and that arise with some frequency. Beyond that expectancy, no counsel ought to cite a case (such as Comastro in this instance) without Shepardizing that case (or without conducting the equivalent electronic search via WESTLAW or LEXIS). And any such search would immediately have revealed the decision in Roth, which expressly explains Comastro. . . .*

It is important, therefore, to perform thorough legal research to adequately protect the rights and interests of your client.

Informing the Court of Legal Authority That Is Detrimental to a Client

The problem of informing a court of a legal authority that is detrimental to a client is the exact opposite of not doing competent legal research (see above). Here, the attorney or legal assistant competently perform legal research and find the appropriate legal research and authorities but, unfortunately, the research is contrary to the client's position. The *ABA Model Rules of Professional Conduct* at Model Rule 3.3 states that as an officer of the court, the attorney has the duty to disclose to the court legal authority that is controlling in the jurisdiction if it is known to the attorney to be directly adverse to the attorney's client, even if opposing counsel has not done an adequate job of legal research. While this rule may seem unfair to the client, the rule is designed to preserve the integrity of the legal system and to prevent the wasteful use of judicial time.

In *Massey v. Prince George's County,* 907 F. Supp. 138 (D. Md. 1995), the defense counsel in the case deliberately failed to disclose an unfavorable controlling authority during summary judgment proceedings. It was later found that the attorney violated Rule 3.3. *Massey v. Prince George's County,* 918 F. Supp. 905 (D. Md. 1996).

It is important that attorneys and legal assistants competently represent their clients, but it is more important for the judiciary to have all direct relevant authorities from which to make correct legal decisions.

Plagiarizing

Plagiarizing is the act of using another person's writing or ideas and passing it off as one's own. It is important when performing legal research and writing that attorneys and legal assistants do not plagiarize. It can be avoided easily by simply citing the authority that has been used. The *ABA Model Rules of Professional Conduct* at Model Rule 8.4 states that Lawyers may not involve themselves in acts of dishonesty, fraud, deceit, or misrepresentation:

Plagiarism appropriately falls within the purview of dishonesty, fraud, deceit, or misrepresentation. It is dishonest to take credit for the work of another.

In the case of *In Re Petition of John A. Zbiegien for Review of the State Board of Law Examiners' Decision,* 433 N.W.2d 871 (Minn. 1988), a State Board of Law

Examiners recommended that an applicant who applied for admission to the bar not be admitted because of a lack of requisite character and fitness. In that case, the student was a third-year student in law school. The requirements for one of his classes included a research paper. The law student admittedly plagiarized large parts of his paper from the works of other authors. Most of the first twelve pages of the paper were taken verbatim from law review articles and were not properly cited. The law student was given an "F" for the course, not given credit for the course, and lost the tuition he paid for the course. Subsequently, the Board of Law Examiners recommended that he not be admitted to the bar. The Supreme Court of Minnesota held that a single incident of plagiarism in law school, where the person was remorseful and did not hide the matter, did not rise to the level to disqualify the applicant from being admitted to the bar.

In another case, a lawyer was censured by the state's disciplinary administrator for plagiarizing two published works in a thesis that the lawyer wrote to satisfy a requirement for a master's degree. See *In re Anthony Byron Lamberis*, 93 Ill. 2d 222, 443 N.E. 2d 549 (Ill. 1982).

In addition to ethical considerations, plagiarizing can also be a violation of copyright and intellectual property rights. Thus, it is extremely important to appropriately cite and give credit to the author when another person's work is used.

Computer-assisted legal research (CALR) uses computers to research and retrieve legal information. Two of the largest fee-based CALR service providers are WESTLAW and LexisNexis, but there are also less expensive choices available such as Loislaw and the National Law Library.

WESTLAW has more than 17,000 databases and offers an array of features. Find by Citation is a WESTLAW feature that allows a user to enter a cite and be taken directly to the cite without entering a search query or database. WESTLAW's Natural Language is a search system that uses plain English instead of complex connectors to search for documents. WESTLAW's Terms and Connectors search system uses Boolean logic and operators/connectors to connect terms. Common WESTLAW connectors include /s, /p, &, and /n. Root expanders like ! enable WESTLAW to retrieve words with the same root. The "Locate in result" WESTLAW feature allows users to search a retrieved document for particular terms, whether or not the terms appeared in the user's original search. Headnotes and Key Numbers in WESTLAW summarize every major issue in a case and allow users to find additional cases with similar Headnotes and Key Numbers. KeySearch is a WESTLAW tool that allows users to find documents using a topical legal index without users formulating a search query. KeyCite is a WESTLAW citation tool that can be used to find if a case is still good law or to list all the times a source has been listed as a reference in other documents. WESTLAW has many non-legal databases that allow users to search public records, business news, and business-related information.

LexisNexis is a large CALR service provider that, like WESTLAW, controls a large part of the CALR market. LexisNexis offers 19,000 databases and features that are similar to these of WESTLAW. Some LexisNexis features include Get by Citation, Get by Party Name, Natural Language, and *Shepard's* Citations. Terms and connectors in LexisNexis are very similar, but not identical, to terms and connectors in WESTLAW. LexisNexis, like WESTLAW, includes value-added features including case summaries and Headnotes.

CD-ROM legal databases allow users to search for case law using CD-ROMS. CD-ROMS take up much less shelf space than physical books, but are not as up-to-date as online CALR services. CD-ROM legal databases use search engines similar to those of WESTLAW or LexisNexis.

It is important when conducting legal research that it be done competently and without plagiarizing other people's work.

INTERNET SITES

Organization	Product/Service	World Wide Web Address
Fastcase, Inc.	Fastcase, CALR provider	http://www.fastcase.com
ITIS, Inc.	National Law Library, CALR provider	http://www.itislaw.com
Loislaw.com, Inc.	Loislaw, CALR provider	http://www.loislaw.com
Reed Elsevier Inc.	LexisNexis, CALR provider	http://www.lexisnexis.com
Reed Elsevier Inc.	LexisNexis Training	http://www.lexisnexis.com
Thomson/West	WESTLAW, CALR provider	http://www.westlaw.com
Thomson/West	WESTLAW Training	http://west.thomson.com/westlaw
VersusLaw, Inc.	VersusLaw, CALR provider	http://www.versuslaw.com

KEY TERMS

computer-assisted legal research (CALR)
CD-ROM legal database
cite checking
search query
online
offline
Find by Citation
Find a Case by Party Name
Natural Language
Terms and Connectors
connectors
root expander
universal character
Locate in Result
Results Plus
Headnotes and Key Numbers
KeySearch
KeyCite
Get by Citation
Get by Party Name
FOCUS

TEST YOUR KNOWLEDGE

Test your knowledge of the chapter by answering these questions.

1. True or False: It is generally agreed that manual research using books has no place whatsoever in the modern law office.
2. True or False: WESTLAW has a special "tab" or interface designed specifically for paralegals.
3. In WESTLAW, what is the name of the plain-English search feature?
4. When using Terms and Connectors in WESTLAW, a space between two search terms means what?
5. What do the: /s, /p, and /n connectors signify in WESTLAW?
6. What is the root expander character in WESTLAW?
7. What is the universal character in WESTLAW?
8. True or False: When writing a search query in WESTLAW, it is best to not use periods when typing acronyms (e.g., NASA).
9. If a user writes a Terms and Connectors search query in WESTLAW and a large number of cases are retrieved, what action can the user take to reduce the number of cases retrieved?
10. In WESTLAW the Locate in Results feature does what?
11. What does WESTLAW's KeyCite feature do?
12. True or False: WESTLAW has Headnotes but LexisNexis does not.
13. What is the feature in LexisNexis that allows a user to search retrieved cases for additional search terms, whether or not they were in the original search?
14. True or False: WESTLAW's Synopsis and Lexis-Nexis' Case Summary are comparable features.
15. What is the LexisNexis case citation tool called?
16. Both WESTLAW and LexisNexis have Natural Language and Terms and Connectors searching. Which service offers a third searching feature called Easy Search?
17. True or False: /p, /s, /n, and quotation marks all work the same in WESTLAW and LexisNexis.

ON THE WEB EXERCISES

1. Go to http://west.thomson.com/westlaw/ and review at least one WESTLAW training guide. Write a two-page memo summarizing what you learned.
2. Go to http://www.lexisnexis.com/ and take at least one free e-learning module. Write a two-page memo summarizing what you learned.
3. Visit the websites of two other CALR service providers (not WESTLAW or LexisNexis) and compare their products and pricing, if it is available. Which of the services did you like the best, and why? Write a two-page memo summarizing your research.

QUESTIONS AND EXERCISES

1. You are a legal assistant working on a personal injury case where your firm's client had her hand cut off in an accident on the job. The defendant admits liability and is trying to settle the case for an amount that the attorney thinks is too low. The attorney asks you to formulate a search query in WESTLAW or LexisNexis in the hope that you can determine what amount of damages juries have awarded for this type of accident or case.
2. The attorney you work for wants you to immediately research an important issue for him, using a CALR. The attorney is representing a client who worked for a governmental agency. Apparently the client was fired from the agency because the client was arrested for driving under the influence of alcohol while off duty. No formal charges were ever brought. The attorney asks you to formulate a search query plan, using LexisNexis or Westlaw. What is your query?

END NOTES

[1] Judy A. Long, *Computer-Aided Legal Research*, Thomson Delmar Learning, 2003, 1.

[2] Judy A. Long, *Computer-Aided Legal Research*, Thomson Delmar Learning, 2003, 1.

HANDS-ON EXERCISES

WESTLAW
COMPUTER ASSISTED LEGAL RESEARCH

Basic

Number	Lesson Title	Concepts Covered
Lesson 1	Introduction to WESTLAW	Signing-on, introduction to WESTLAW's interface, and working with WESTLAW labs
Lesson 2	Find By Citation, Find by Party Name, And Exploring Retrieved Cases	Find by Citation, Find by Party Name, Star Paging, Reporter Image, KeyCite overview, Case Outline, and Results Plus

Intermediate

Number	Lesson Title	Concepts Covered
Lesson 3	Natural Language Search; Editing Searches; Changing Databases; Using Term, Doc, and Best	Selecting a database, Natural Language search, finding the scope of a database, editing a search, changing to a different database, using date restriction when searching, using the Require / Exclude terms feature, and using the Term, Doc, and Best features
Lesson 4	Terms and Connectors Searching	Terms and connectors searching, using Thesaurus, printing a list of cases, using the Locate in Result tool, and using WestClip
Lesson 5	KeyCite	KeyCite, depth-of-treatment stars, quotes, citing references, Limit KeyCite Display, and Research Trail

Advanced

Number	Lesson Title	Concepts Covered
Lesson 6	KeySearch, Headnotes, and KeyNumbers	KeySearch, Headnotes, KeyNumbers, Most Recent Cases, and Most Cited Cases
Lesson 7	Public Records, Forms, Company Records, And Docket Searches	Public record searches on individuals and businesses, searching for legal forms, and searching court dockets

GETTING STARTED

Introduction

Throughout these lessons and exercises, information you need to type into the program will be designated in several different ways:

- Keys to be pressed on the keyboard will be designated in brackets, in all caps, and in bold (press the: **[ENTER]** key).
- Movements will be designated in bold and italics (***point to File on the menu bar and click the mouse***).
- Words or letters that should be typed will be designated in bold (type **Training Program**).
- Information that should be displayed on your computer screen will be shown in the following style: ***Press ENTER to continue***.

Basic

LESSON 1: INTRODUCTION TO WESTLAW

This lesson introduces you to WESTLAW, and includes instructions for signing-on to WESTLAW, a tour of WESTLAW and the WESTLAW interface, and working with WESTLAW tabs. For an overview of WESTLAW's features, read the WESTLAW section in Chapter 11 of the text.

1. Start Windows.

2. Start your Internet browser. Type **http://www.westlaw.com** in the browser and press **[ENTER]**.

3. Your screen should look similar to WESTLAW Exhibit 1. At the WESTLAW Password field, **enter the WESTLAW password supplied by your instructor.**

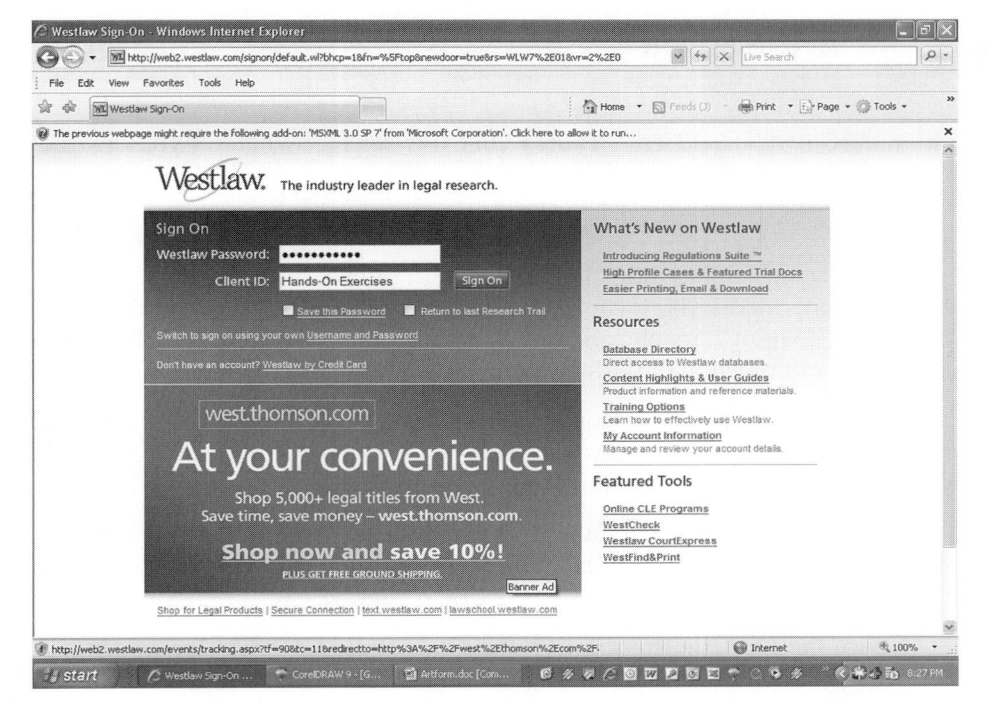

WESTLAW Exhibit 1
Courtesy of WestLaw.

WESTLAW Exhibit 2

Courtesy of WestLaw.

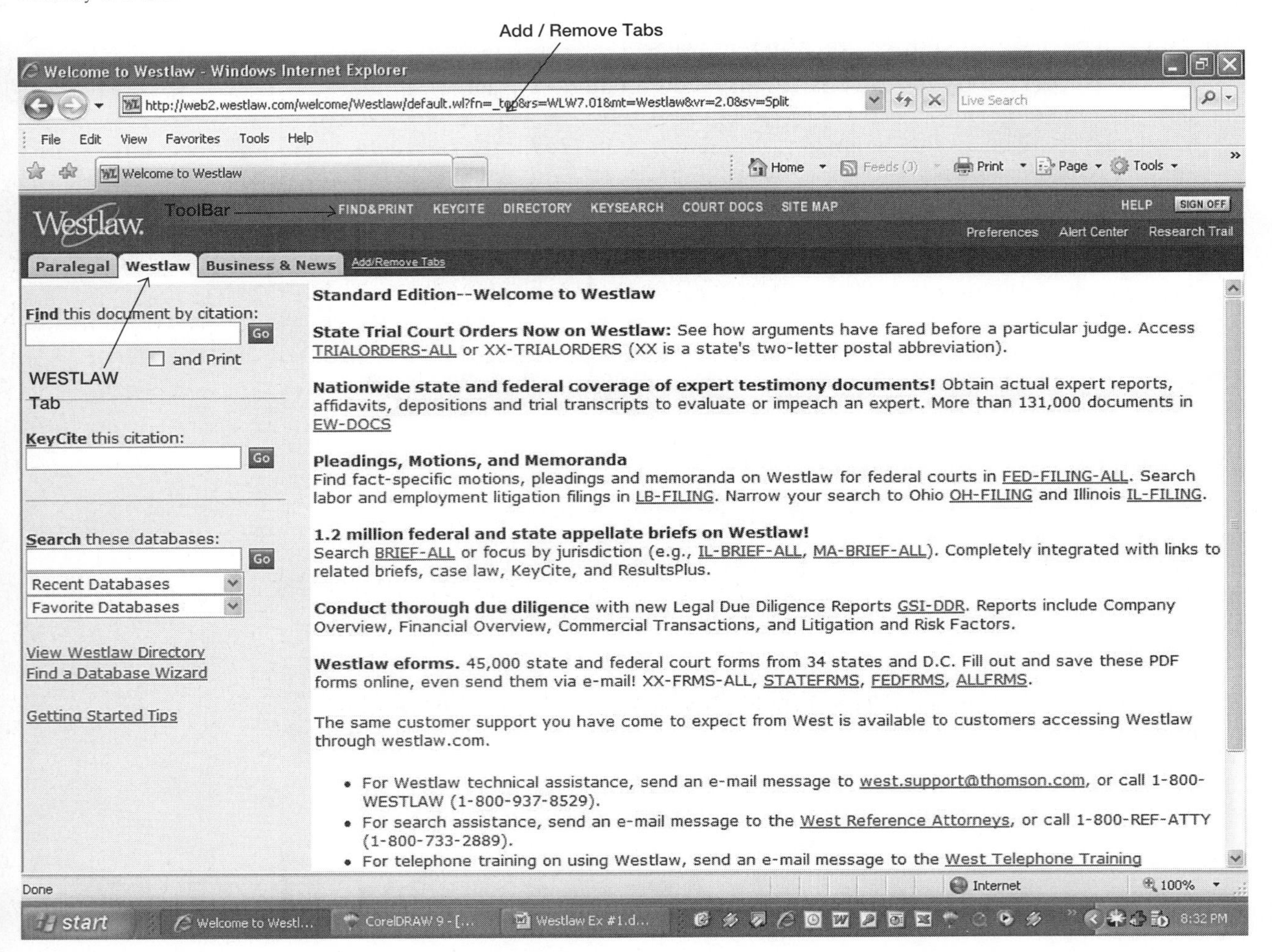

4. In the Client ID field, enter **Hands-On Exercises 1** (or whatever your instructor tells you to enter – see WESTLAW Exhibit 1).

5. ***Click Sign On*** to sign on to WESTLAW.

6. Your screen should now look similar to WESTLAW Exhibit 2. This is the "Welcome to WESTLAW" screen. Note: If your screen does not look like WESTLAW Exhibit 2, try clicking the WESTLAW tab (see WESTLAW Exhibit 2) in the upper left section of the screen.

7. You will now take a brief tour of WESTLAW. In the middle of the Welcome to WESTLAW screen there may be notices or news items about new services or changes to WESTLAW.

8. Notice the **Find this document by citation** field in the upper left section of the screen (see WESTLAW Exhibit 2). This is where you can enter a case or statutory citation and be taken directly to the case or statute.

9. Notice the **KeyCite this citation** field in the middle left of the screen (see WESTLAW Exhibit 2). This is where you can enter a case or statutory citation and have its history displayed, including whether the document is still good law and other documents where the case or statute has been cited.

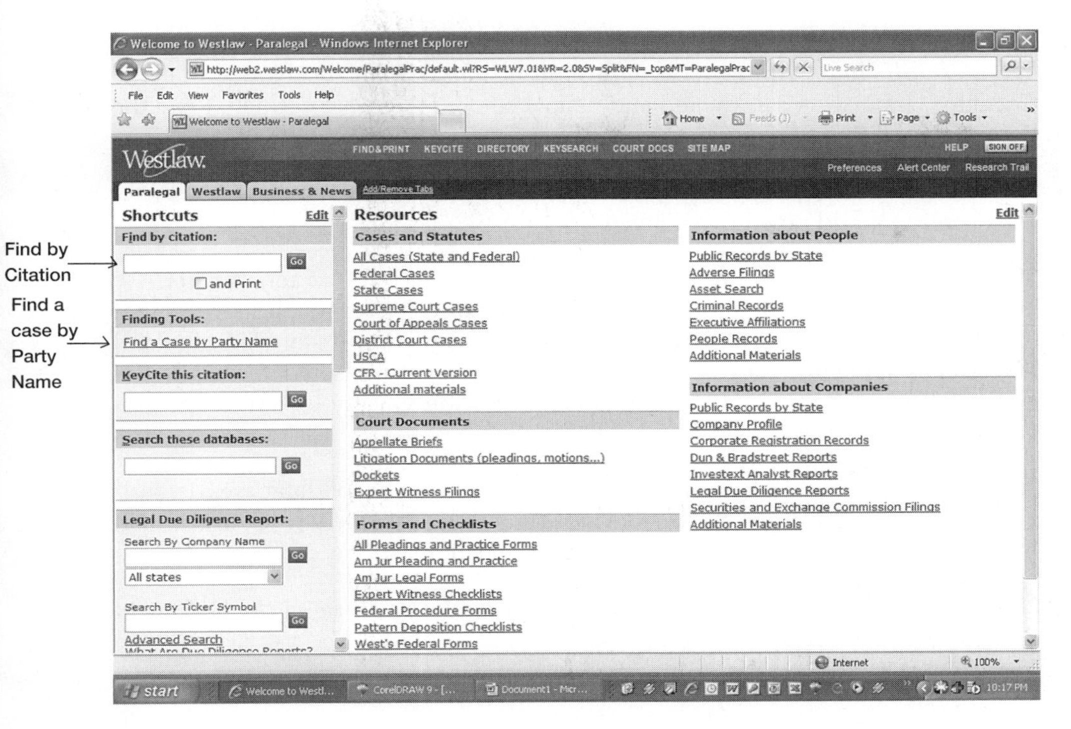

WESTLAW Exhibit 3

Courtesy of WestLaw.

10. Notice the **Search these databases** field in the lower left of the screen (see WESTLAW Exhibit 2). This is where you can enter the name of a specific database and be taken to the database to search or query it.

11. Notice in the lower left of the screen, just below "**Search** these databases," the words "Recent Databases" (see WESTLAW Exhibit 2). ***Click the down arrow next to Recent Databases.*** You may or may not have anything listed, depending on whether you or other users have recently used WESTLAW. If you recently used a database that you want to go back to, you can click here, see the database, select it from the list, and return to it.

12. If a pop-up window appears, press **[ESC]** to make it disappear.

13. Notice the toolbar at the top of the WESTLAW screen (see WESTLAW Exhibit 2). This toolbar is static, meaning it always stays the same, so you can access Find&Print, KeyCite, Directory, KeySearch, Court Docs, Site Map, Help, and SIGN OFF at any time.

14. ***Click Find&Print on the toolbar.*** WESTLAW Find&Print lets you enter multiple citations and automatically send them to a printer, download them to a word processor such as Word or WordPerfect, email the document to whomever you choose, or fax the citation to a fax number you supply. You can also include the citation's KeyCite history or citing references information. Find&Print can be a good tool if you know exactly what you want.

15. ***Click the WESTLAW tab*** (see WESTLAW Exhibit 2). The Welcome to WESTLAW screen should now be displayed.

16. ***Click KeyCite on the toolbar.*** As indicated earlier, KeyCite is WESTLAW's citation tool; using KeyCite, you can get a history of a case, including information on whether the case has been overruled or reversed, or a list of other documents where your case has been cited.

17. You should now be at the KeyCite information screen. ***Use the vertical scroll bar to scroll down through the information about KeyCite.*** Notice that the KeyCite symbols, such as the red and yellow colored flags, are defined. Read the definitions.

18. ***Click the WESTLAW tab*** (see WESTLAW Exhibit 2). The "Welcome to Westlaw" screen should now be displayed.

19. ***Click Directory on the toolbar.*** You should now be at the WESTLAW Directory screen. There should be a search box at the top of the screen that says "Search the Westlaw Directory." Below that it should say "U.S. Federal Materials." The Directory is where you can interactively select from a list of WESTLAW databases. Notice that there is a wide variety of database categories to choose from.

20. ***Click U.S. Federal Materials.*** You should now see a list of databases, including Federal Cases & Judicial Materials, Federal Statutes, Dockets (Court Docket Information), Pleadings, Motions, and other selections.

21. ***Click the Back button on your browser, or click Directory on the toolbar to go back to the directory.***

22. ***Click each of the categories on the directory screen*** (U.S. State Materials, International / Worldwide Materials, Topical Practice Areas, and the other categories). Scroll down through the lists. When you are done with each category, ***click your browser's Back button or click Directory on the toolbar.***

23. ***Click the Westlaw tab.***

24. ***Click KeySearch on the toolbar.*** You should now see a list of legal topics, including Administrative Law, Agriculture, Alternative Dispute Resolution (ADR), Antitrust and Trade Regulation, and others. KeySearch is where you can conduct legal research interactively by selecting specific legal topics.

25. Suppose you were researching the exhaustion of administrative remedies related to administrative law. ***Click "Administrative Law."***

26. Notice that there is a selection entitled "Exhaustion of Administrative Remedies," which might be a good place to start your research. Since you are taking a tour of WESTLAW, you will not do that at this time.

27. ***Click the Westlaw tab.***

28. ***Click Court Docs on the toolbar.***

29. Notice that to the left of the screen it says "Court Docs Databases." This is where you can search for court documents. Notice also that to the left of the screen there are databases for appellate briefs, pleadings, motions, trial court orders, forms, and other items.

30. ***Click the Westlaw tab.***

31. ***Click Site Map on the toolbar.*** The Site Map is a good place to find a WESTLAW feature if you cannot find it anywhere else. Read the selections available under each category.

32. ***Click the Westlaw tab.*** Note: The reason you are clicking the WESTLAW tab instead of going directly to each item on the toolbar is that it is helpful to have a

central starting place from which to access WESTLAW tools and features, at least while you are learning WESTLAW.

33. ***Click Help on the toolbar.*** A WESTLAW Help Center window should now be displayed, including options such as Beginning Your Research, Using a Research Service, and others.

34. ***Click the down arrow under Beginning Your Research.*** Notice that there are specific help topics for adding and removing tabs, entering the client ID, and many others. Press the **[ESC]** key to close the selection box.

35. ***Click the down arrow next to each help category*** (Using a Research Service, "Search Basics," etc.). Be sure to scroll down through all of the choices, including "Pricing."

36. ***Scroll back up to the top of the Help Center window. Click the Support Numbers tab at the top of the Help Center window.*** Notice that toll-free phone numbers are available for WESTLAW Technical Assistance, Research Assistance, and other resources.

37. ***Click the Close icon (a red box with a white "X") in the Westlaw Help Center window.***

38. ***Click the Westlaw tab.***

39. ***Click Add / Remove Tabs just under the toolbar (see WESTLAW Exhibit 2).***

40. To the left of the screen, just under the tabs, it should say "Manage Tabs." This is where you can select the tabs to be displayed in WESTLAW. Tabs in WESTLAW are extremely helpful and you can have many of them if you wish.

41. ***Under the General category, and click the box next to Paralegal. A green check mark should be displayed. If the Paralegal box already has a green check mark next to it, do not click the box.***

42. ***Scroll down through the list, and notice that you can select from a large number of different tabs.*** This includes topical tabs by legal specialty, jurisdictional state choices, jurisdictional federal choices, and others.

43. ***Scroll to the bottom of the screen and click Next.***

44. At the Save Tabs – Step 2 of 2 screen, Paralegal should have a green dot selected next to it. The selection means that when you start WESTLAW, the Paralegal tab will be selected. If the green dot is not next to paralegal, click the radio button next to paralegal to move it there.

45. ***Click Save.***

46. The Paralegal tab should now be selected. The Paralegal tab is a great place to start your research. Throughout the rest of these Hands-on Exercises, you will start at the Paralegal tab. At the top middle of the screen it should say Resources and there should be categories for Cases and Statutes, Court Documents, Forms and checklists, Information about People, and Information about Companies. To the left of the screen, it should say "Shortcuts."

This Concludes Lesson 1 of the WESTLAW Hands-on Exercises. To quit WESTLAW, ***point and click on SIGN OFF. on the Tool Bar,*** or stay in WESTLAW and go on to Lesson 2.

LESSON 2: FIND BY CITATION, FIND BY PARTY NAME, AND EXPLORING RETRIEVED CASES

In this lesson, you will use the following features: Find by Citation, Find by Party Name, Star Paging, Reporter Image, KeyCite overview, Case Outline, and Results Plus. If you did not exit WESTLAW after completing Lesson 1, go directly to step 6 below.

1. Start Windows.

2. Start your Internet browser. Type **http://www.westlaw.com** in the browser and press **[ENTER]**.

3. Your screen should look similar to WESTLAW Exhibit 1. At the Westlaw Password field, **enter the password supplied by your instructor.**

4. In the Client ID field, type **Hands-On Exercise 2** (or whatever your instructor tells you to type).

5. ***Click Sign On*** to sign on to WESTLAW.

6. You should now be at the Paralegal tab (see WESTLAW Exhibit 3). You will now learn how to retrieve a case by entering a citation, using the Find by Citation feature.

7. ***Click in the white box under Find by Citation.*** Enter **189 S.W. 3d 777. *Click Go next to the citation you just entered.***

WESTLAW Exhibit 4
Courtesy of WestLaw.

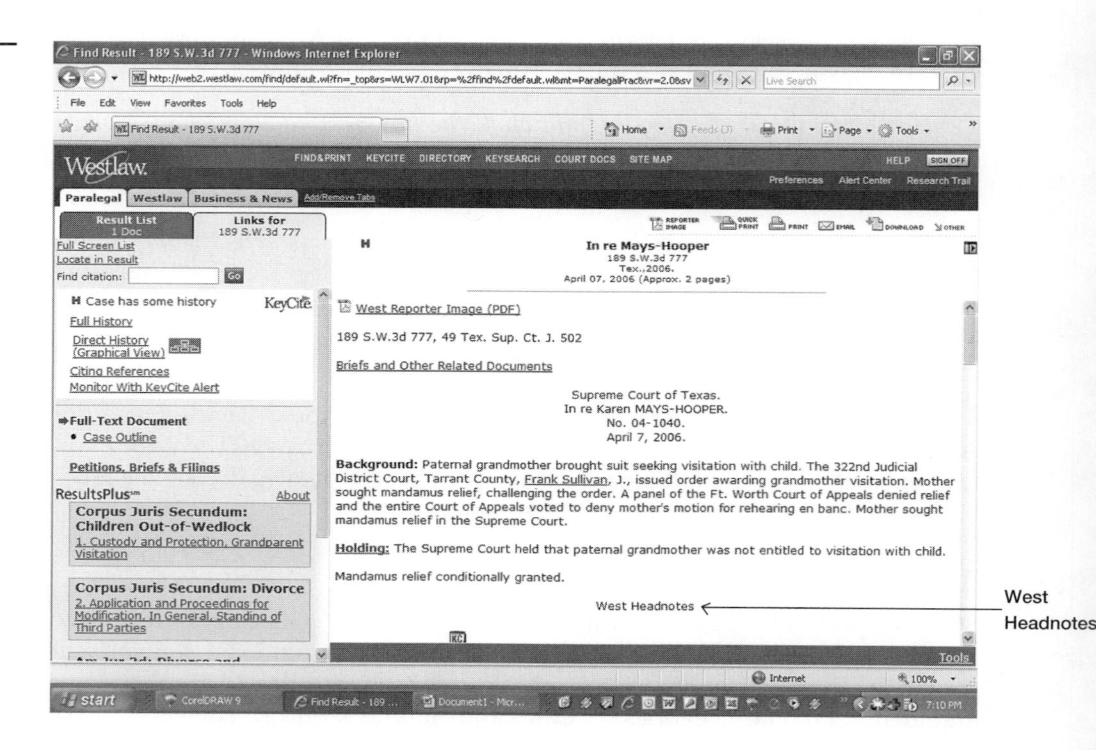

8. The case of *In re Mays-Hooper* should now be displayed (see WESTLAW Exhibit 4). When you know the citation of a case you can enter it in the Find by Citation feature, and WESTLAW will immediately retrieve it without your having to indicate a database or enter a search query.

9. You will now find a case by entering the name of a party. ***Click the Paralegal tab the upper left of the screen.*** You should now be back at the Paralegal tab screen (see WESTLAW Exhibit 3).

10. On the left side of the screen, just below the Find by Citation feature, is the heading "Finding Tools:." ***Click Find a Case by Party Name.***

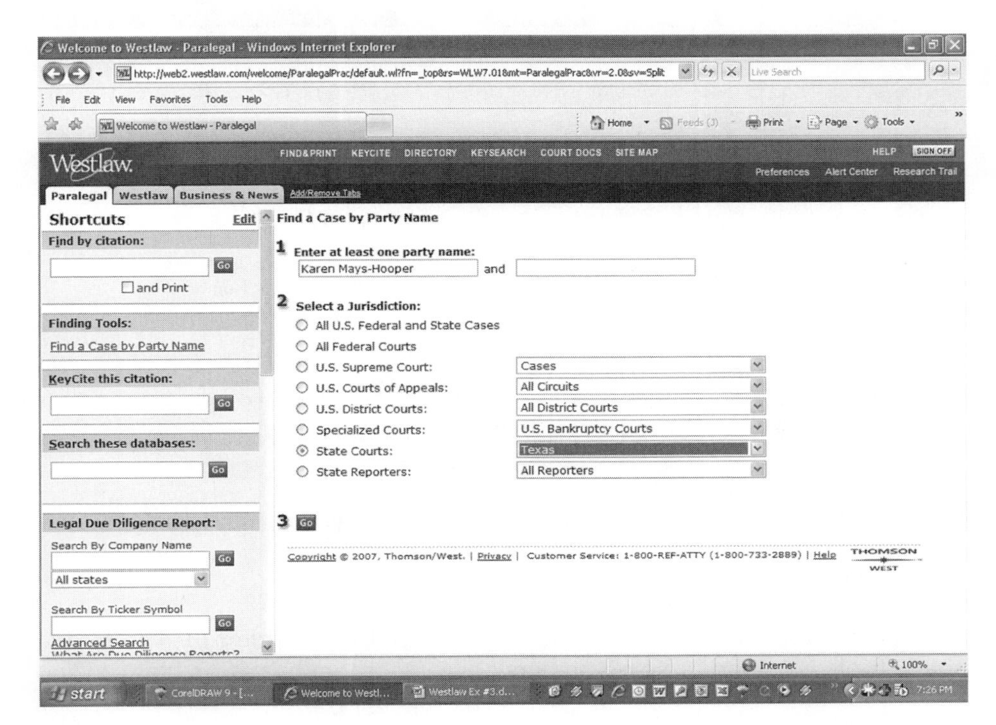

WESTLAW Exhibit 5

Courtesy of WestLaw.

11. The Find a Case by Party Name screen should now be displayed (see WESTLAW Exhibit 5). Just below "1. Enter at least one party name" type **Karen Mays-Hooper** (see WESTLAW Exhibit 5).

12. ***Click the circle to the left of State Courts:*** (see WESTLAW Exhibit 5). ***Click the down arrow next to All Courts and select Texas.***

13. ***Click "Go"*** (see WESTLAW Exhibit 5).

14. A summary of two cases, both with the title In re Mays-Hooper, should now be displayed. ***Click* In re Mays-Hooper, *189 S.W. 3d 777, 49 Tex. Sup.Ct. J. 502.***

15. The *In re Mays-Hooper* case should now be displayed (see WESTLAW Exhibit 4).

16. Notice in the *In re Mays-Hooper* case (see WESTLAW Exhibit 4) that just under the title of the case the background and holding of the case are shown. These elements are called the synopsis of the case. The synopsis of the case is written by WESTLAW research attorneys. This is a value-added feature of WESTLAW that many other CALR services do not offer.

17. Read the background and holding in the case.

18. Notice the heading West Headnotes after the holding of the case (see WESTLAW Exhibit 4). WESTLAW Exhibit 6 shows the Headnotes for the case

WESTLAW Exhibit 6
Courtesy of WestLaw.

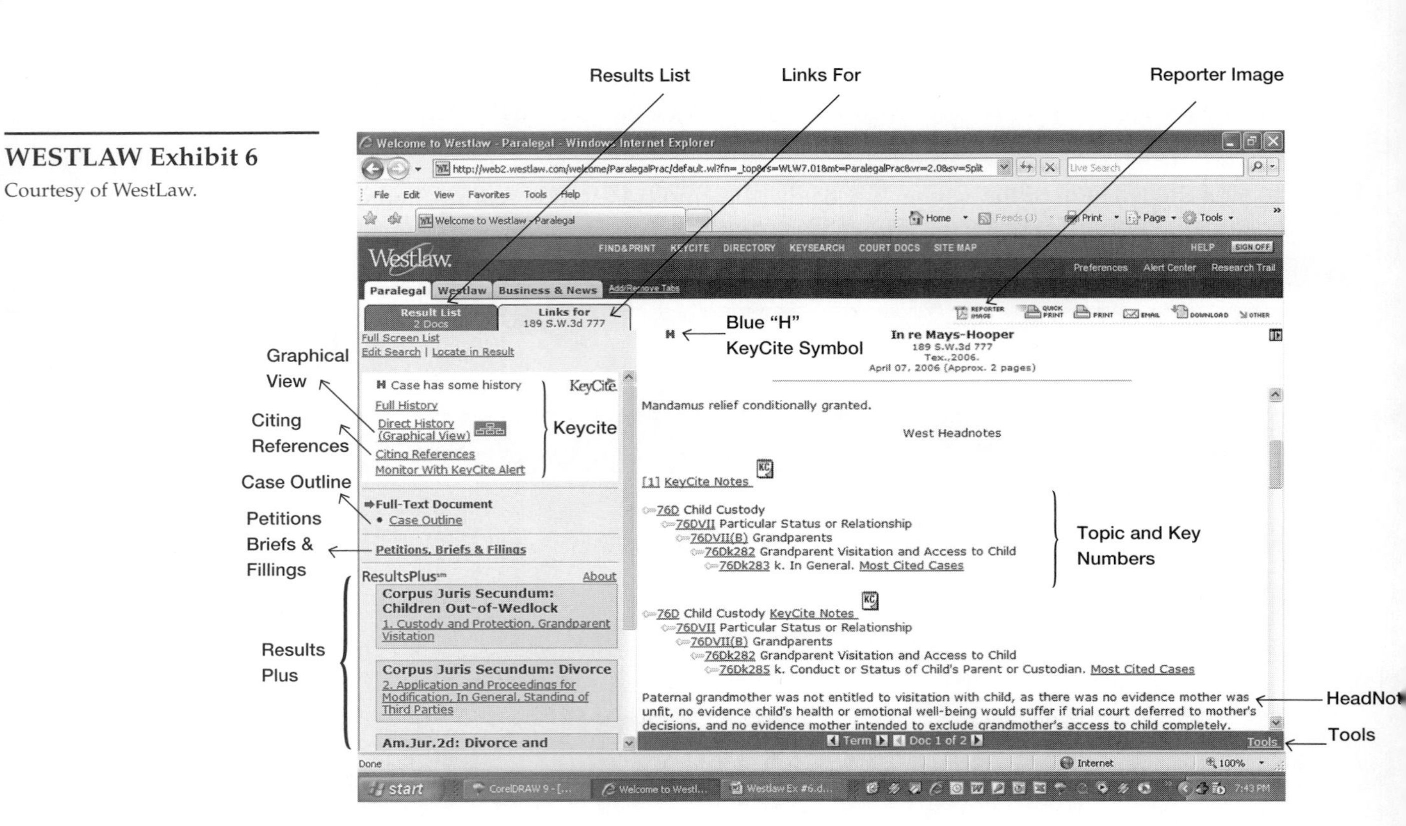

and several Topic and Key Numbers (see WESTLAW Exhibit 6). The Headnotes, Topic Numbers / Key Numbers are also written by research attorneys, and are a value-added feature of WESTLAW that many other CALR services do not offer. These features will be discussed in more detail in later exercises.

19. ***Skim the case by scrolling down through it with the vertical scroll bar.***

20. Press the **[HOME]** key on the keyboard to go back to the beginning of the case.

21. You will next learn how to use WESTLAW Star Paging. Star Paging is a WESTLAW feature that allows you to cite to a specific page of the hard-copy reporter. ***Click Tools in the lower right corner of the screen (see WESTLAW Exhibit 6).***

22. ***Click Go to Star Page.***

23. At the Go to Star Page: screen, type **777.** (This is the beginning page of the case.) Then ***click Go.***

24. Notice that the case is again displayed; look closely the upper left of the screen and you will see "*777" in purple. This tells you that anything after "*777" is on page 777 of the hard copy. So, if you are going to cite anything on this page, you need to cite page 777.

25. ***Scroll down through the case to the paragraph that starts with "The Supreme Court found the trial court's order unconstitutional . . ."*** and notice that on the third line of the paragraph there is a "*778" in purple. This is where page 778 of the hard copy report starts.

26. ***Click Reporter Image at the top center of the screen*** (see WESTLAW Exhibit 6). If the window opens and then automatically closes, you may have a pop-up

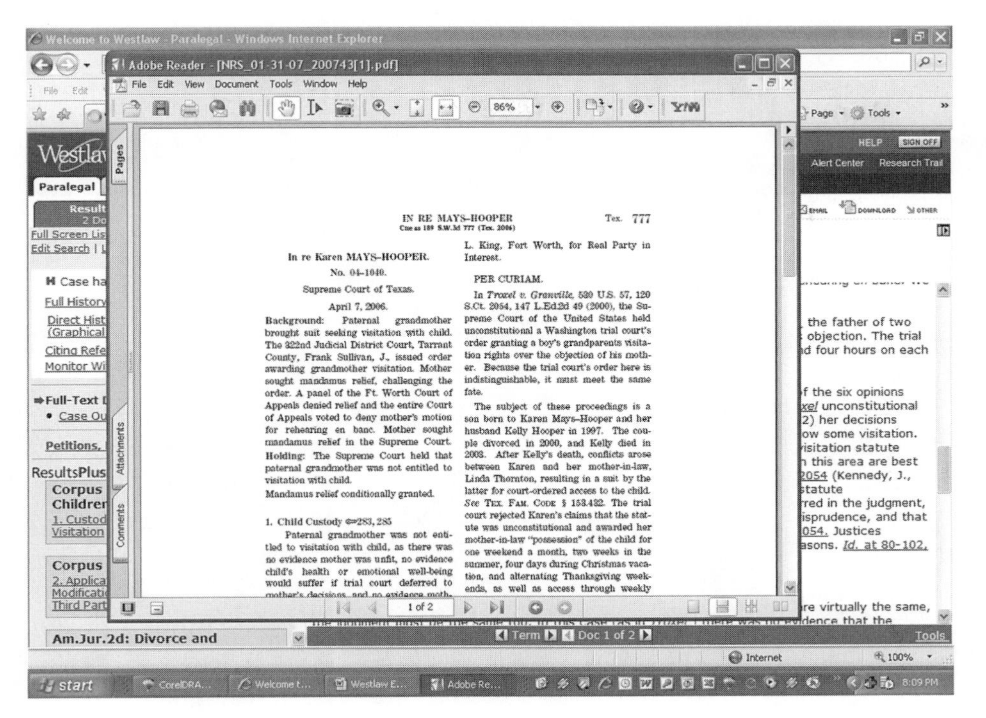

IN RE MAYS–HOOPER Tex. 777
Cite as 189 S.W.3d 777 (Tex. 2006)

In re Karen MAYS–HOOPER.

No. 04–1040.

Supreme Court of Texas.

April 7, 2006.

Background: Paternal grandmother brought suit seeking visitation with child. The 322nd Judicial District Court, Tarrant County, Frank Sullivan, J., issued order awarding grandmother visitation. Mother sought mandamus relief, challenging the order. A panel of the Ft. Worth Court of Appeals denied relief and the entire Court of Appeals voted to deny mother's motion for rehearing en banc. Mother sought mandamus relief in the Supreme Court.

Holding: The Supreme Court held that paternal grandmother was not entitled to visitation with child.

Mandamus relief conditionally granted.

1. Child Custody ⇐283, 285

Paternal grandmother was not entitled to visitation with child, as there was no evidence mother was unfit, no evidence child's health or emotional well-being would suffer if trial court deferred to mother's decisions, and no evidence moth-

L. King, Fort Worth, for Real Party in Interest.

PER CURIAM.

In *Troxel v. Granville*, 530 U.S. 57, 120 S.Ct. 2054, 147 L.Ed.2d 49 (2000), the Supreme Court of the United States held unconstitutional a Washington trial court's order granting a boy's grandparents visitation rights over the objection of his mother. Because the trial court's order here is indistinguishable, it must meet the same fate.

The subject of these proceedings is a son born to Karen Mays–Hooper and her husband Kelly Hooper in 1997. The couple divorced in 2000, and Kelly died in 2003. After Kelly's death, conflicts arose between Karen and her mother-in-law, Linda Thornton, resulting in a suit by the latter for court-ordered access to the child. *See* TEX. FAM. CODE § 153.432. The trial court rejected Karen's claims that the statute was unconstitutional and awarded her mother-in-law "possession" of the child for one weekend a month, two weeks in the summer, four days during Christmas vacation, and alternating Thanksgiving weekends, as well as access through weekly

WESTLAW Exhibit 7

Courtesy of WestLaw; Adobe product screen shot(s) reprinted with permission from Adobe Systems Incorporated.

blocker running. Press the **[CTRL]** key on the keyboard while clicking Reporter Image to bypass the pop-up blocker. At the File Download window, ***click Open.*** (Note: You may need to press the **[CTRL]** key again while clicking Open).

27. If you have a version of Adobe Reader or an other PDF reader installed on your computer, you should now see an image of the hard copy reporter where you can confirm what is on page 777 (see WESTLAW Exhibit 7).

28. ***Click the Close icon (a red square with a white "X") in the Adobe Reader window to close the window.***

29. Notice on the left side of the screen that there are two tabs below the Paralegal tab entitled "Result List" and "Links for" (see WESTLAW Exhibit 6).

30. ***Click Results List.***

31. On the left side of the screen you should now see a short summary of the two cases that were retrieved. The Results List tab allows you to see a summary of the results of your query or search.

32. ***Click Links for.*** Notice that the "Links for" tab includes a KeyCite section (see WESTLAW Exhibit 6). This is where you can find the history of the case. ***Click Graphical View in the KeyCite section on the left side of the screen*** (see WESTLAW Exhibit 6).

33. WESTLAW Exhibit 8 should now be displayed. This is a graphical chart that shows how the case was appealed from the fort Worth Court of Appeals to the Texas Supreme Court.

34. ***Click "Full History (Text)" at the top of the screen.*** You should now see a text-based history of the case.

35. ***Click Graphical View on the left side of the screen to go back to the graphical depiction of the case's history.***

WESTLAW Exhibit 8

Courtesy of WestLaw.

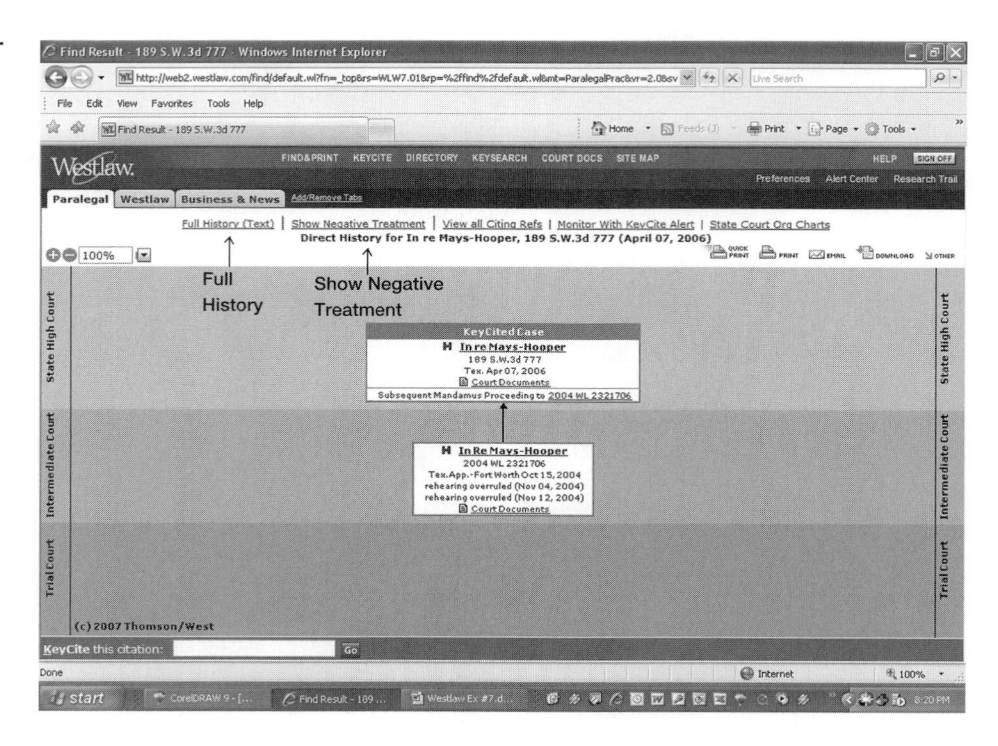

36. ***Click Show Negative Treatment*** (As of the date this exercise was written, there was no negative history).

37. ***Click your browser's Back button to go to the previous screen with the graphical depiction of the case's history.***

38. ***Click "189 S.W.3d 777" (just under the case title "In re Mays-Hooper") to go back to the case.***

39. ***Click Citing References in the KeyCite section*** (on the left side of the screen—see WESTLAW Exhibit 6).

WESTLAW Exhibit 9

Courtesy of WestLaw.

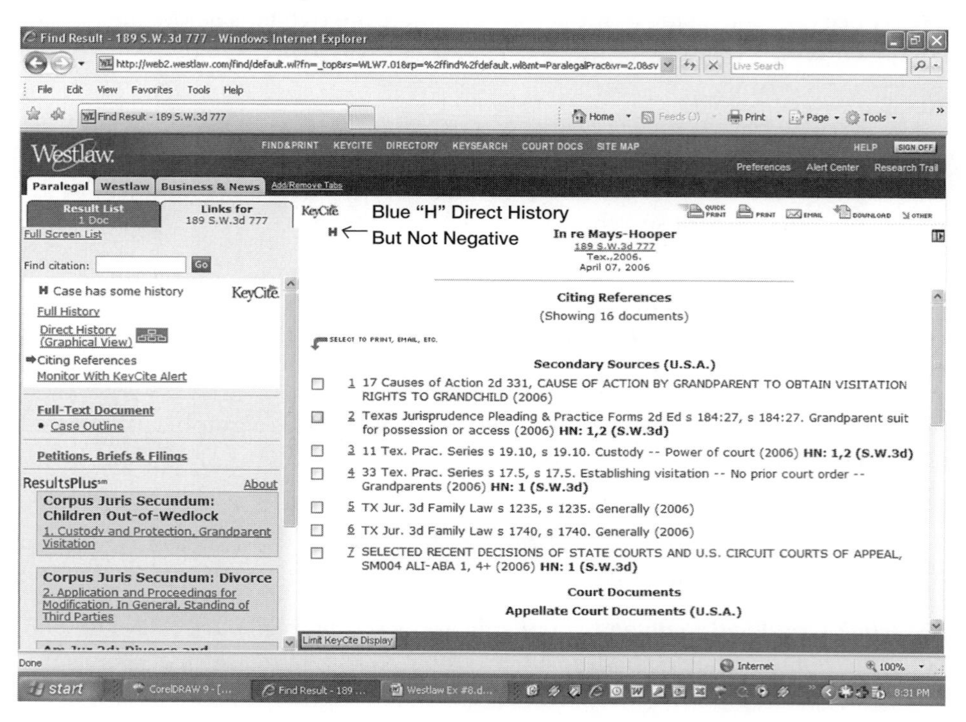

40. A screen similar to WESTLAW Exhibit 9 should be displayed. (*Note:* The screen may look completely different by the time you read this.) This shows all of the times the case has been cited in other cases. Notice the blue "H" in the upper left of the screen (see WESTLAW Exhibit 9). The blue "H" in KeyCite means that there is direct history, but it is not negative. Notice in WESTLAW Exhibit 6 that the blue "H" is also shown on the first page of the case itself.

41. ***Click your browser's Back button to go back to the case.***

42. ***Click Case Outline on the left side of the screen under Full-Text Document*** (see WESTLAW Exhibit 6). You now should see the sections of the case (Synopsis, Headnote(s), and Opinion(s)). This option is particularly helpful when you are reading an extremely long case, because you can jump between the major sections of the case without having to scroll down through each page.

43. ***Click your browser's Back button to go back to the case.***

44. ***Click Petitions, Briefs and Filings on the left side of the screen under Case Outline*** (see WESTLAW Exhibit 6). Notice that a list of the appellate briefs is now shown. If you wanted to read the briefs of the parties, you could do so by clicking the appropriate links.

45. ***Click your browser's Back button to go back to the case.***

46. Notice in the lower left of the screen that there is a section entitled "ResultsPlus." ResultsPlus is where WESTLAW makes suggestions regarding other research that you might find helpful. There are three options listed in the ResultsPlus section.

47. ***Click the option under ResultsPlus that says: Corpus Juris Secundum: Children Out-of-Wedlock (Custody and Protection, Grandparent Visitation).*** You should now see an article from *Corpus Juris Secundum* regarding the issue of grandparent visitation rights.

48. ***Click your browser's Back button to go back to the case.***

49. ***Click the Paralegal tab in the upper left of the screen.*** This concludes Lesson 2 of the WESTLAW Hands-on Exercises. To quit WESTLAW, click Sign Off on the toolbar or stay in WESTLAW and go to Lesson 3.

LESSON 3: NATURAL LANGUAGE SEARCH; EDITING SEARCHES, CHANGING DATABASES; USING TERM, DOC, AND BEST

In this lesson, you will learn how to select a database, run a Natural Language search, find the scope of a database, edit a search, change to a different database, use the date restriction feature when searching, use the Require / Exclude terms feature, and use the Term, Doc, and Best features.

If you did not exit WESTLAW after completing Lesson 2, go directly to Step 6 below.

1. Start Windows.

2. Start your Internet browser. Type **http://www.westlaw.com** in the browser and press **[ENTER]**.

3. Your screen should look similar to WESTLAW Exhibit 1. At the WESTLAW Password field, **type the password supplied by your instructor.**

4. In the Client ID field type **Hands-On Exercise 3** (or whatever your instructor tells you to type).

5. ***Click Sign On*** to sign on to WESTLAW.

6. You should now be at the Paralegal Tab (see WESTLAW Exhibit 3).

7. You will now look for a case in Federal court where an attorney committed fraud by retaining settlement funds of a client in litigation and breached his fiduciary duty to the client.

8. ***Under Cases and Statutes, click Federal Cases.*** The database identifier for this database is ALLFEDS.

WESTLAW Exhibit 10

Courtesy of WestLaw.

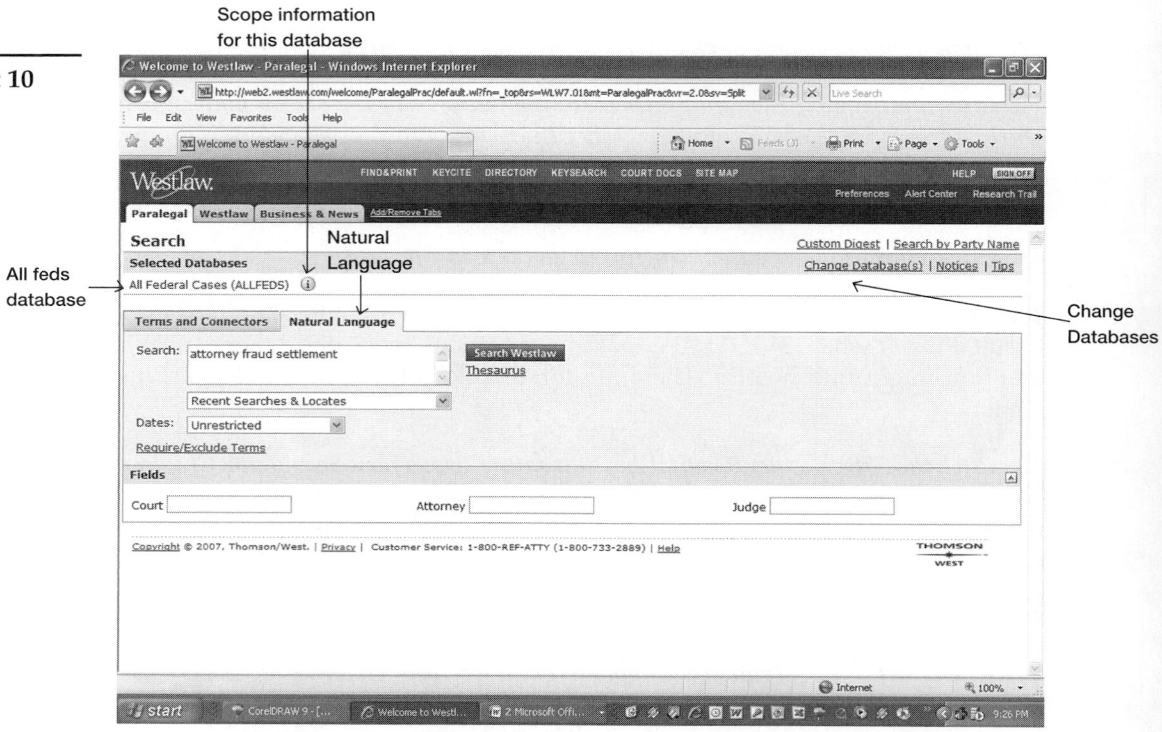

Scope information for this database

Natural Language

All feds database

Change Databases

9. The Search screen should now be displayed (see WESTLAW Exhibit 10).

10. ***Click Natural Language*** (see WESTLAW Exhibit 10). You will now enter a plain-English search into the ALLFEDS database using WESTLAW'S Natural Language feature.

11. In the Search box, type **attorney fraud settlement** and then ***click Search Westlaw*** (see WESTLAW Exhibit 10).

12. Depending on how WESTLAW was set up on your computer, your search will most likely return twenty or more cases. In WESTLAW Exhibit 11, notice that more than one hundred cases were retrieved. This is too many cases to look through.

13. There are two main problems with the search. First, you are searching in an enormous database; and second, you need more search terms listed to lower the number of cases retrieved.

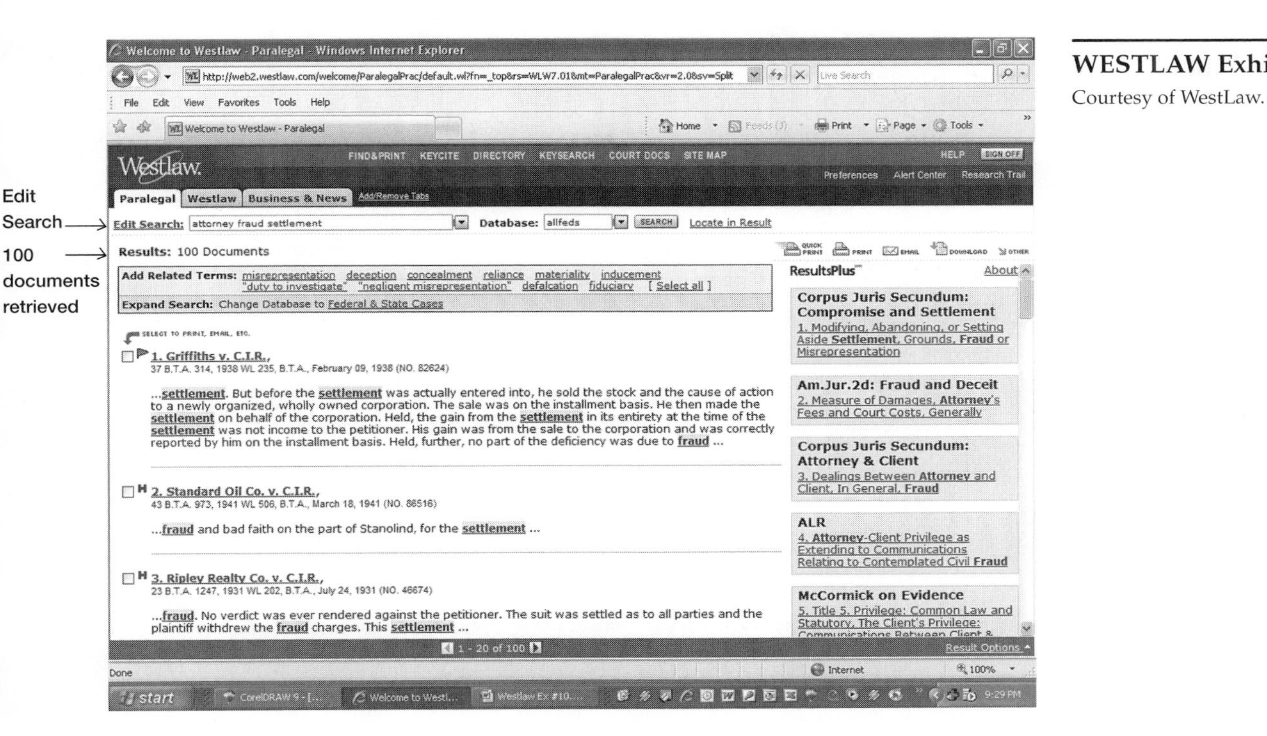

WESTLAW Exhibit 11

Courtesy of WestLaw.

14. ***Click Edit Search just under the Paralegal tab in the upper left of the screen.***

15. You should now be back at the Search screen. You will now look at the scope of the ALLFEDS database to see exactly what database you are searching in.

16. ***Click the "Scope information for this database" symbol, which looks like a round white ball with a lower-case "i" in the middle of it*** (see WESTLAW Exhibit 10).

17. Notice the information listed about the ALLFEDS database, including the "Content Highlights" section, which states "All Federal Cases has all available federal case law with coverage beginning in 1790."

18. ***Scroll down to see just how large the database is.*** The database is extremely large, containing tens of thousands of cases. When you search in a large database like this, you need more search terms.

19. ***Click your browser's Back button to go back to the Search screen.***

20. It can sometimes be more efficient to search in a smaller database than in a larger one. You will now learn how to change your database.

21. ***Click Change Database(s) in the upper right of the Search screen*** (see WESTLAW Exhibit 10).

22. ***Click in the white box under "Add or Delete database(s):" and press the*** **[DELETE]** or **[BACKSPACE]** keys until ALLFEDS has been deleted.

23. Type **DCT4** (see WESTLAW Exhibit 12) ***and then click Run Search.*** DCT4 is the database for U.S. District Court Cases for the Fourth Circuit. This is a much narrower database than ALLFEDS.

24. The search will once again retrieve a large number of cases. Although the database is smaller, the search still needs to be refined and additional search terms added.

WESTLAW Exhibit 12

Courtesy of WestLaw.

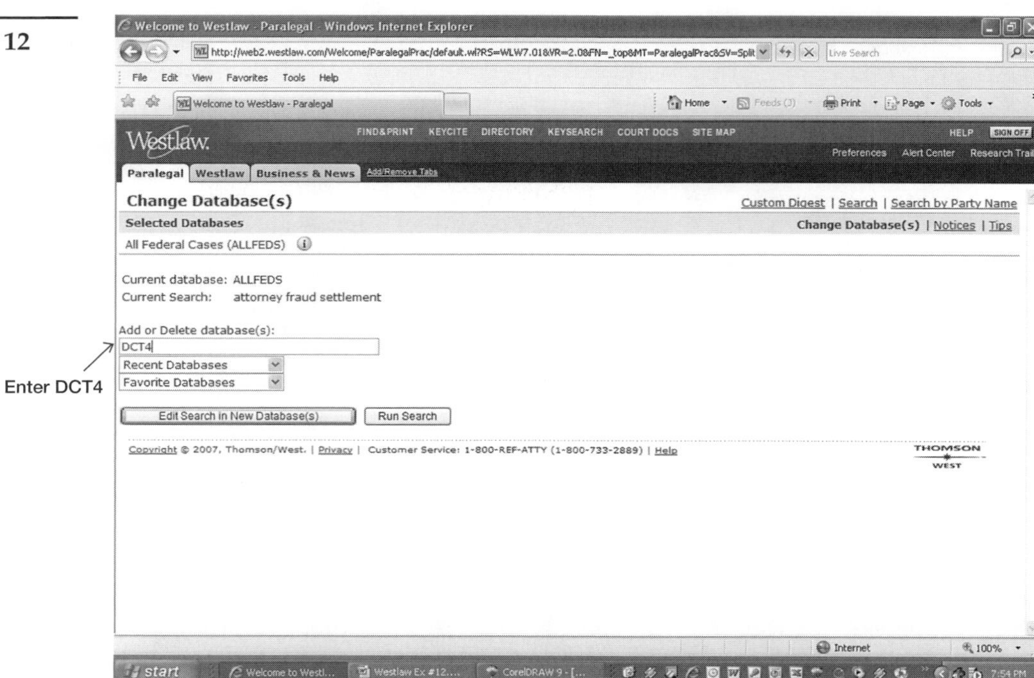

25. ***Click Edit Search in the upper left portion of the screen.***

26. In the Search box, in addition to "attorney fraud settlement," type **"legal malpractice" "fiduciary duty"**. The quotes around "legal malpractice" and "fiduciary duty" force Westlaw to search for these exact phrases.

27. Another way to limit the number of cases retrieved is to restrict the dates of the cases retrieved. ***Click the down arrow next to Dates: Unrestricted in the Search screen*** (see WESTLAW Exhibit 13).

WESTLAW Exhibit 13

Courtesy of WestLaw.

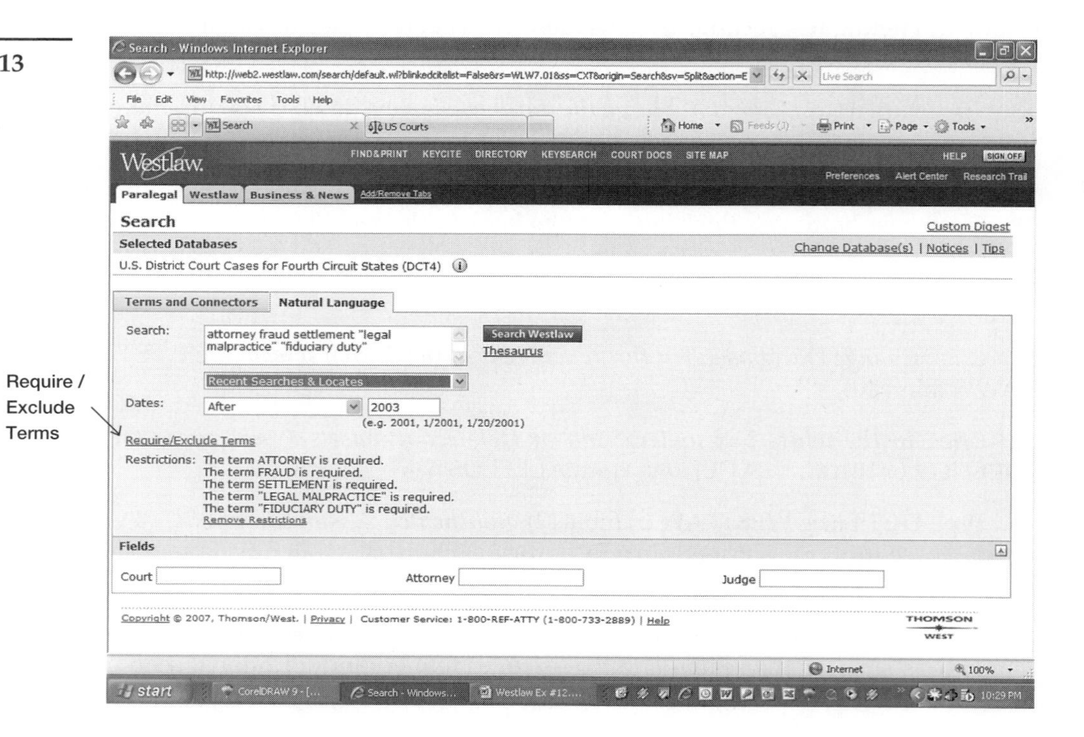

28. ***Click "After."*** In the white box to the right of "After" type **2003** (see WESTLAW Exhibit 13)

29. Still another way to limit the number of cases retrieved is to require all of the terms. ***Click Require / Exclude Terms in the Search screen*** (see WESTLAW Exhibit 13).

30. ***Click the boxes for each of the search terms (attorney, fraud, settlement, "legal malpractice," and "fiduciary duty"), and then click OK.*** Your screen should now look similar to WESTLAW Exhibit 13.

31. ***Click Search Westlaw.***

32. A much smaller number of cases should now be returned. One of the cases that should be retrieved is *Hewlette v. Hovis*, 318 F.Supp. 2d 332 (E.D. Va., May 19, 2004). ***Click the* Hewlette v. Hovis case.**

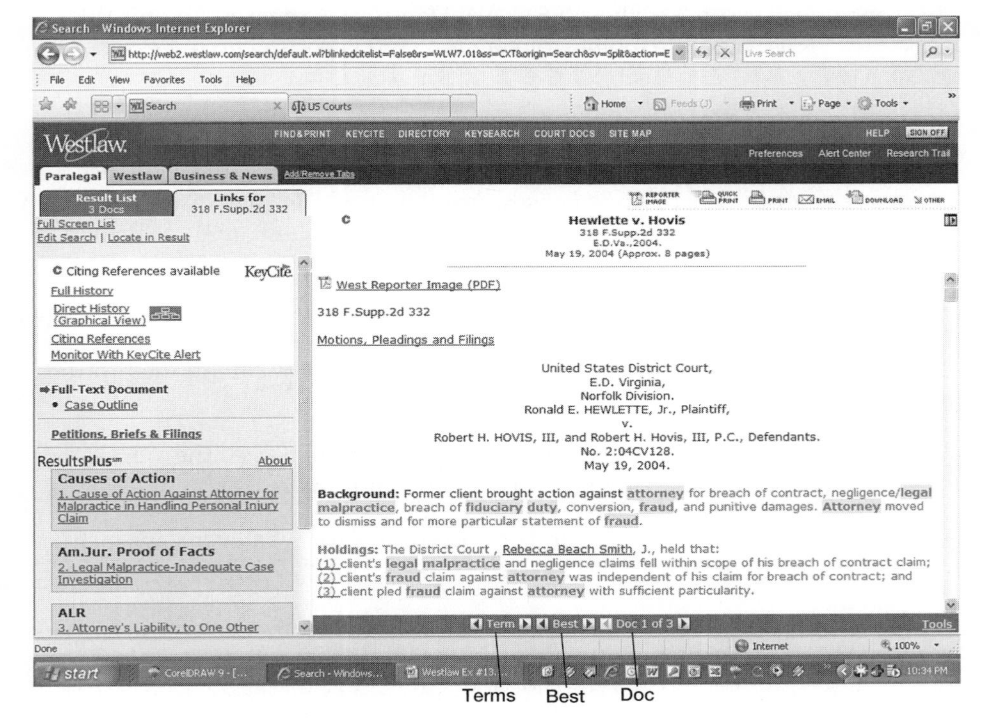

WESTLAW Exhibit 14

Courtesy of WestLaw.

33. The *Hewlette v. Hovis* case should now be displayed (see WESTLAW Exhibit 14).

34. Notice that your search terms are highlighted in the synopsis. ***Click the right arrow to the right of Term at the bottom of the screen.*** Each time you click the right arrow next to Term, Westlaw takes you to the next page where your search terms are listed. You can also go backward in the document looking for your search terms by clicking the left arrow next to Term.

35. ***Click the right arrow to the right of Term to continue to move through the* Hewlette *case.*** Eventually you will move to the next case.

36. The Best feature allows you to go directly to what WESTLAW estimates to be the most relevant part of the case in relation to your search terms. ***Click the left arrow next to Doc at the bottom of the screen to go back to the* Hewlette *case.*** The Doc arrows allow you to move forward and backward through the retrieved cases.

37. You should now be back at the beginning of the *Hewlette* case.

38. Notice that some of the text is in red. ***Scroll down through the case and notice that most (but not all) of the Headnotes are in red.*** The text in red is what WESTLAW considers to the "best" part of the case (the part where the majority of your search terms are located).

39. ***Click the right arrow next to Best at the bottom of the screen.*** WESTLAW should now have taken you to the best part of the next case.

40. ***Click the right arrow next to Doc at the bottom of the screen.*** You should now be at the next document of the search results. Using the left and right arrows next to Doc, you can move between the search results without returning to the list of results.

41. ***Click the Paralegal tab in the upper left of the screen.***
This concludes Lesson 3 of the WESTLAW Hands-on Exercises. To quit WESTLAW click Sign Off on the toolbar, or stay in WESTLAW and go to Lesson 4.

LESSON 4: TERMS AND CONNECTORS SEARCHING

In this lesson, you will learn how to search using terms and connectors, use the Thesaurus feature, print a list of cases, use the Locate in Result tool, and use WestClip. If you did not exit Westlaw after completing Lesson 3, go directly to Step 6 below.

1. Start Windows.

2. Start your Internet browser. Type **http://www.westlaw.com** in the browser, and press **[ENTER]**.

3. Your screen should look similar to WESTLAW Exhibit 1. At the WESTLAW Password field, **type the password supplied by your instructor.**

4. In the Client ID field type: **Hands-on Exercise 4** (or whatever your instructor tells you to type).

5. ***Click Sign On*** to sign on to WESTLAW.

6. You should now be at the Paralegal tab (see WESTLAW Exhibit 3).

7. You will again look for cases in federal court where an attorney committed fraud by retaining settlement funds for a client in litigation and where the attorney breached his fiduciary duty to the client.

8. Under "Search these databases" on the left side of the screen, type **DCT4** and then ***click Go.*** This is the database identifier for U.S. District Court Cases for the states in Fourth Circuit.

9. ***Click Terms and Connectors.***

10. ***Click in the Search box,*** type **attorney /p fraud /p malpractice,** and then ***click Search WESTLAW*** (see WESTLAW Exhibit 15). The "/p" indicates that the terms should be searched for within a paragraph.

11. Westlaw should return fewer than fifty cases, but this is still quite a few, so you should refine your search query. By using "/s" (search within a sentence) and /n (search within a number of words), you can limit the number of cases that are retrieved.

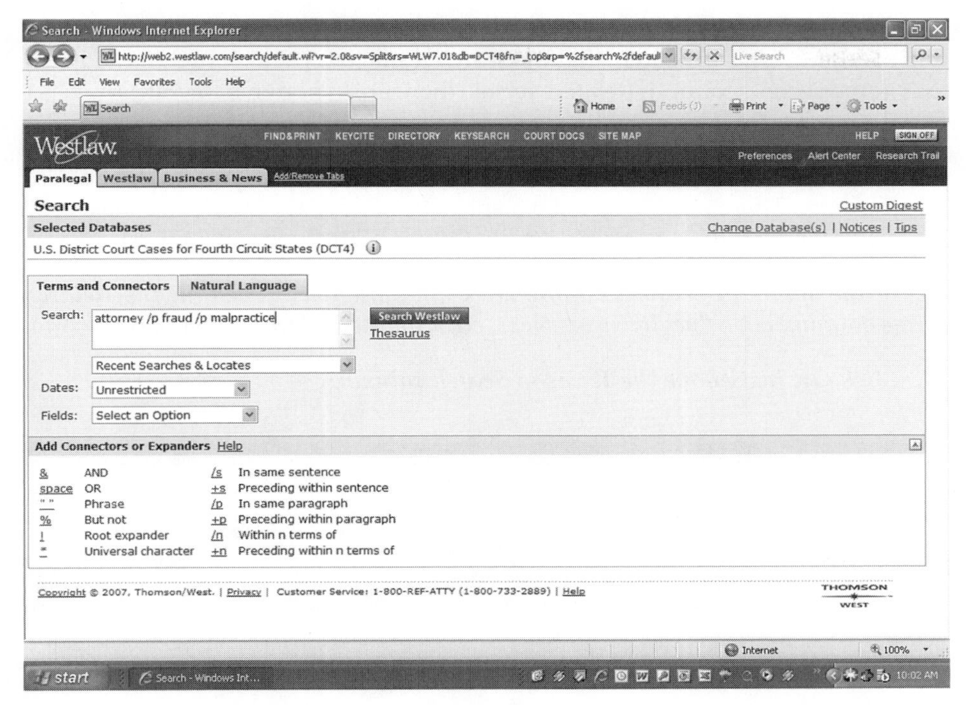

WESTLAW Exhibit 15

Courtesy of WestLaw.

12. *Click Edit Search in the upper left of the screen just under the Paralegal tab.*

13. In the Search box, delete the current query, type **ATTORNEY /S FRAUD /S LEGAL /3 MALPRACTICE /P "FIDUCIARY DUTY"** and then *click Thesaurus* (which is just under "Search Westlaw"). You will use the Thesaurus feature to further refine your search.

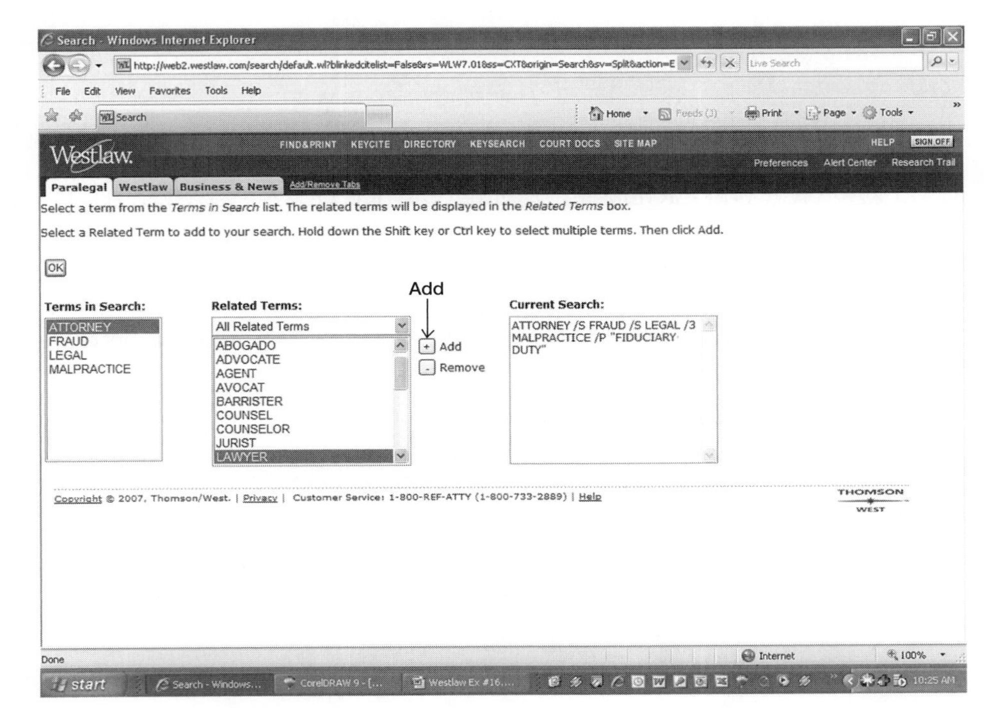

WESTLAW Exhibit 16

Courtesy of WestLaw.

14. You should now see a screen similar to WESTLAW Exhibit 16. Notice in the first column, Terms in Search, that the search term "attorney" is highlighted, and that in the second column, Related Terms, there are synonyms for "attorney."

15. ***In the Related Terms column, scroll down, click "lawyer," and then click the "+" (plus sign) next to Add.*** WESTLAW will then add "lawyer" to the current search query. There should now be a space between "attorney" and "lawyer." WESTLAW interprets the space to mean OR (e.g., attorney OR lawyer).

16. ***In the Terms in Search column, click "malpractice." Then, in the Related Terms column, click "negligence." Next, click on the "+" (plus sign) next to Add.***

17. ***Click OK just above the Terms in Search column.***

WESTLAW Exhibit 17

Courtesy of WestLaw.

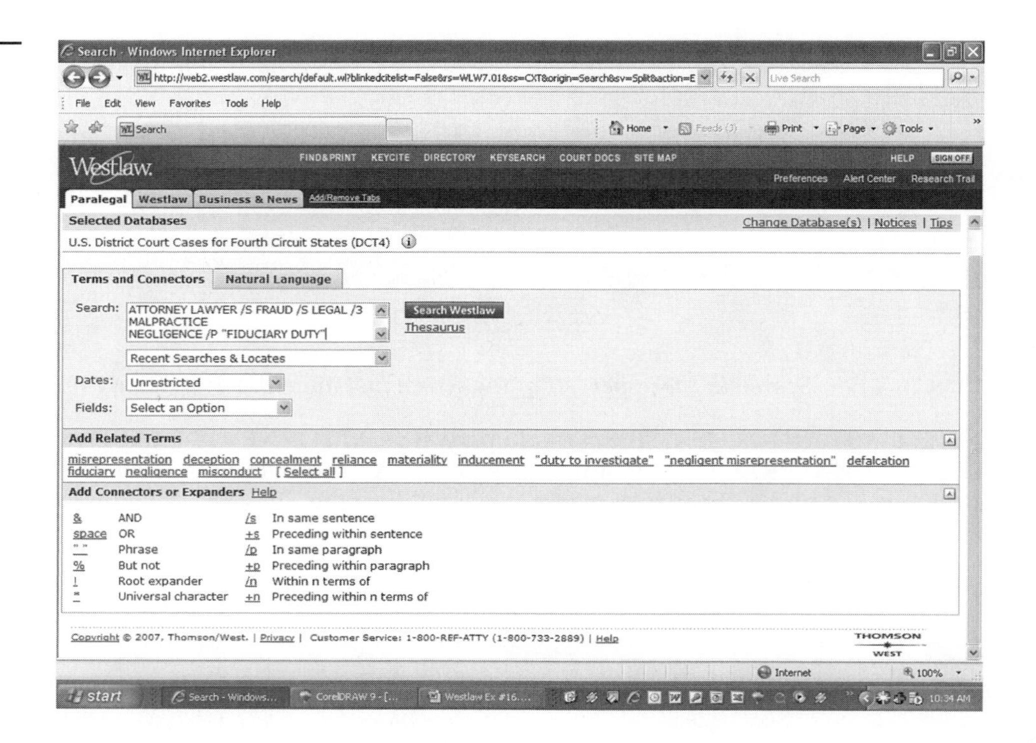

18. The search should now read ATTORNEY LAWYER /S FRAUD /S LEGAL /3 MALPRACTICE NEGLIGENCE /P "FIDUCIARY DUTY" (see WESTLAW Exhibit 17).

19. ***Click Search Westlaw.***

20. WESTLAW should return fewer than fifteen cases, and one of the cases should be the *Hewletter v. Hovis* case.

21. You will now send the results to your printer. ***Click Quick Print in the upper right of the screen.*** The Quick Print window will then appear. After a few seconds the Print window will appear. ***Select the printer you would like to print to, and click Print.***

22. You will now learn how to use the Locate in Result feature. Because your case deals with a settlement, you would now like to search the cases you retrieved for "settlement" to further weed out the cases.

23. ***Click Locate in Result under the tabs at the top of the screen.***

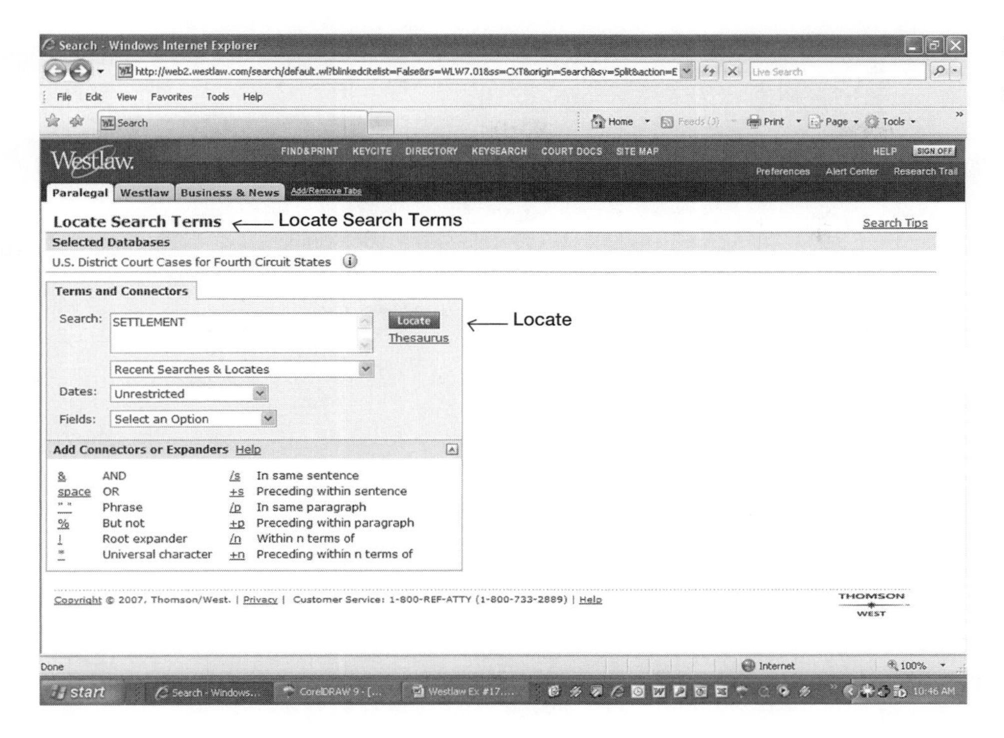

WESTLAW Exhibit 18

Courtesy of WestLaw.

24. Notice that the Search screen is now displayed, but this time the heading says Locate Search Terms (see WESTLAW Exhibit 18).

25. In the Search box, type **SETTLEMENT** and then ***click Locate.***

26. The number of cases should now be reduced. Notice that the word "settlement" is now highlighted, because it was your search term. The *Hewlette v. Hovis* case should be one of the cases that remains.

27. ***Click Cancel Locate to return to the original cases that were retrieved.***

28. You will now learn how to add a search to WestClip. WestClip is a feature that allows you periodically to automatically run a search in WESTLAW.

29. ***Click Add Search to WestClip.*** (It should be near the top left of the screen, just to the right of the number of documents retrieved.)

30. The WestClip: Create Entry screen should be displayed (see WESTLAW Exhibit 19).

31. Notice in WESTLAW Exhibit 19 that your search appears in the WestClip Create Entry screen. There are just a few things left for you to do. If you were going to actually save this search as a WestClip, you would need to enter a name for the search in the "Name of clip:" field. You would also want to edit the delivery settings.

32. ***Click Edit in the upper right of the screen to the right of Delivery Settings.***

33. The WestClip: Edit Delivery Settings screen should now be displayed (see WESTLAW Exhibit 20).

34. ***Click the down arrow next to Daily in the Frequency field.*** Notice that you can run the search at several different frequencies. Press the **[ESC]** key to close the options list.

WESTLAW Exhibit 19

Courtesy of WestLaw.

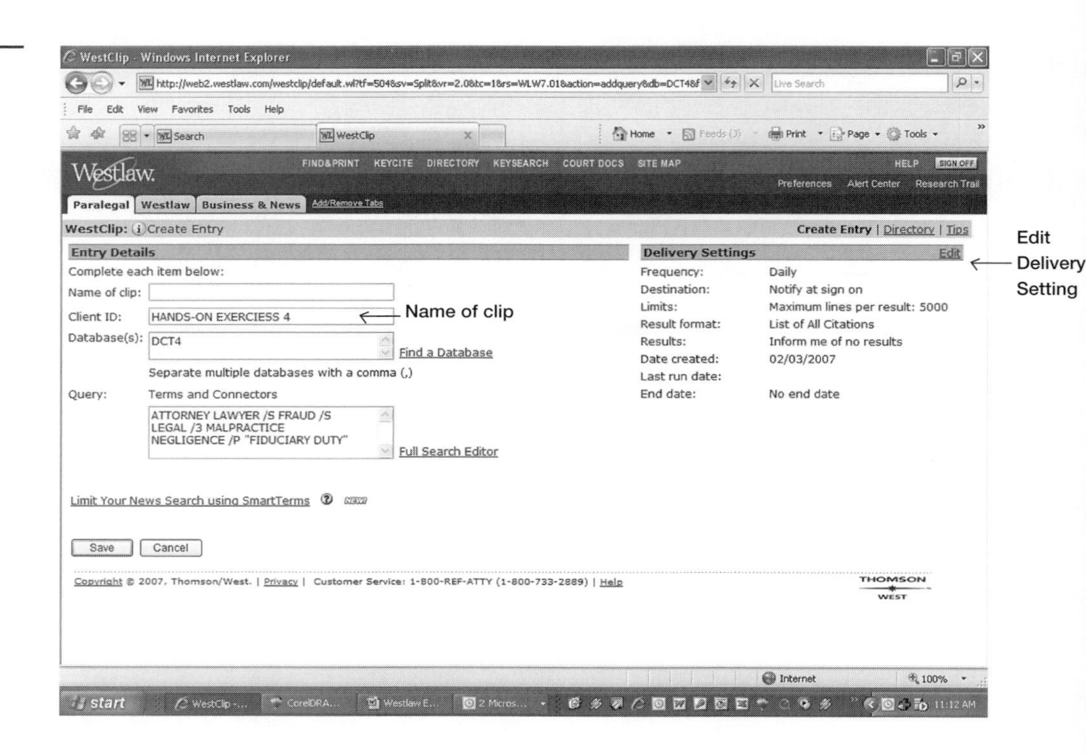

WESTLAW Exhibit 20

Courtesy of WestLaw.

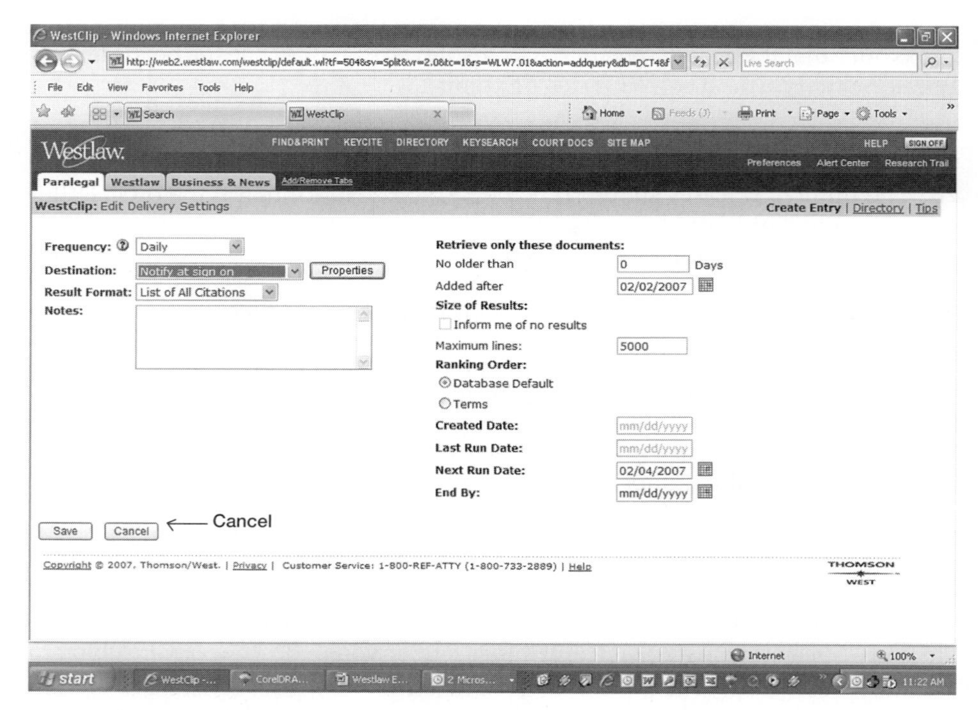

35. ***Click the down arrow next to the Destination field.*** Notice that you can have the result faxed to you, emailed to you, or made available to you when you sign on to WESTLAW.

36. Press the **[ESC]** key to close the options list.

37. Notice that there are a number of other options you can set on the right side of the screen.

38. ***Click Cancel in the lower left of the screen.***

39. You should now be back at the WestClip: Create Entry screen. ***Click Cancel in the lower left of the screen.***

40. You should now be at the Alert Center Directory screen. This is where you can manage a number of different alerts that you can create in WESTLAW.

41. ***Click the Paralegal tab.***

This concludes Lesson 4 of the WESTLAW Hands-On Exercises. To quit WESTLAW, point and click on Sign Off on the toolbar, or stay in WESTLAW and go to Lesson 5.

LESSON 5: KEYCITE

In this lesson, you will learn how to use WESTLAW'S research citation tool, KeyCite. You will also learn about depth-of-treatment stars, quotes, citing references, the Limit KeyCite Display tool, and the Research Trail feature. If you did not exit WESTLAW after completing Lesson 4, go directly to Step 6 below.

1. Start Windows.

2. Start your Internet browser. Type **http://www.westlaw.com** in the browser and press **[ENTER]**.

3. Your screen should look similar to WESTLAW Exhibit 1. At the WESTLAW Password field, **type the password supplied by your instructor.**

4. In the Client ID field type **Hands-on Exercise 5** (or whatever your instructor tells you to type).

5. ***Click Sign On*** to sign on to WESTLAW.

6. You should now be at the Westlaw Paralegal tab (see WESTLAW Exhibit 3).

7. ***Click KeyCite on the toolbar.*** You will now use KeyCite to determine if the *Hewlette v. Hovis* case, which you found in an earlier exercise, is still good law, and you will determine other cases that have cited it in hopes of expanding your research.

8. The KeyCite screen should now be displayed (see WESTLAW Exhibit 21). Take a few minutes and read the narrative in the body of the KeyCite screen. The narrative describes how KeyCite works and what each of the different KeyCite symbols mean.

9. In the "KeyCite this citation" field, type **318 F.Supp.2d 332** (see WESTLAW Exhibit 21). This is the citation for the *Hewlette v. Hovis* case. ***Then, click Go.***

10. Your screen should now look similar to WESTLAW Exhibit 22. Notice in WESTLAW Exhibit 22 that a green "C" is displayed. In KeyCite a green "C" means that the case has been cited as a reference but there is no direct history or negative citing references. This means that the *Hewlette v. Hovis* case has, to date, not been overruled or reversed, and that other cases have not negatively referred to it, and that, at least to date, the case is good law.

11. Let's now use KeyCite to find other cases that have cited the *Hewlette v. Hovis* case. This may assist us in expanding our research to find other cases that will support our position. However, before we do this it would be helpful to look at

WESTLAW Exhibit 21
Courtesy of WestLaw.

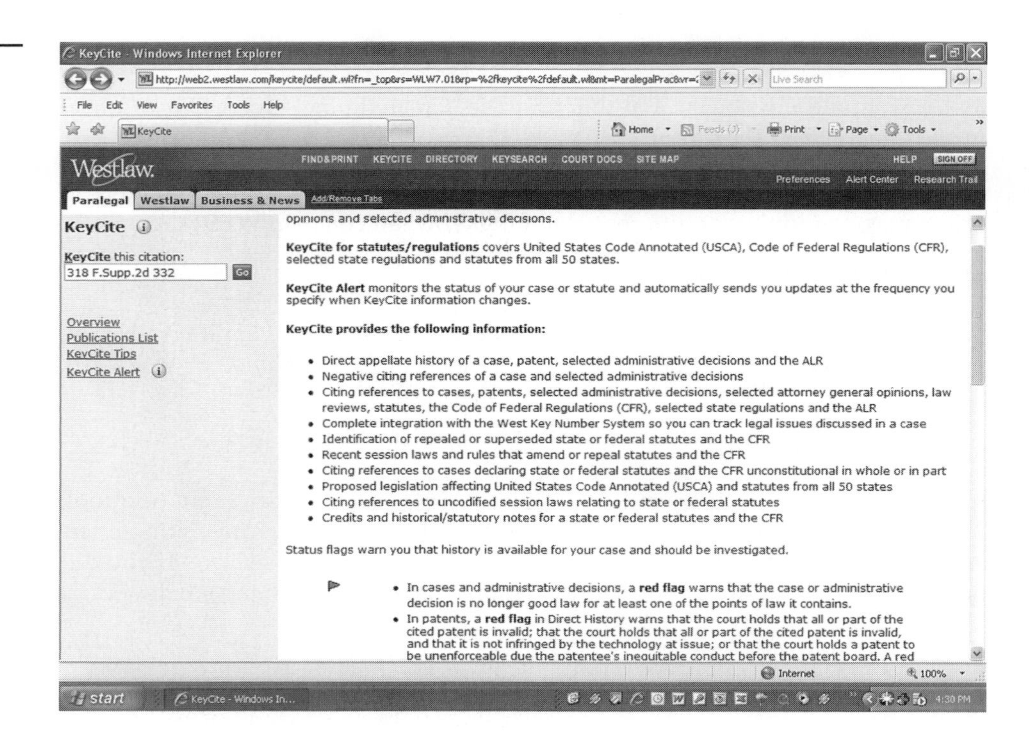

WESTLAW Exhibit 22
Courtesy of WestLaw.

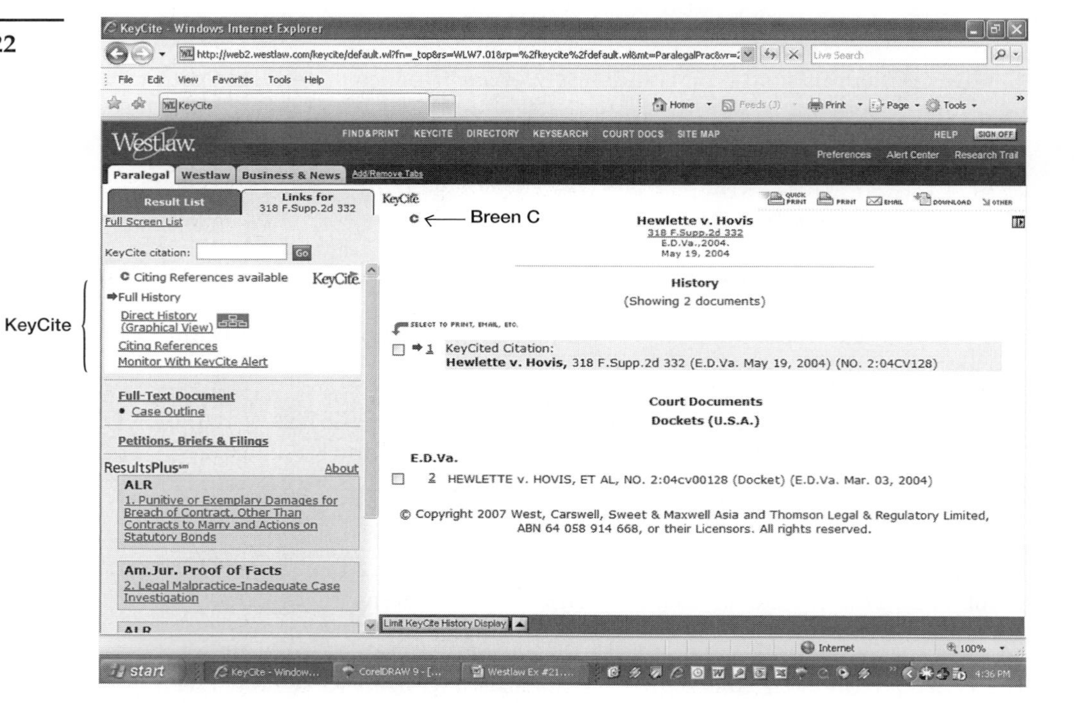

the Headnotes in the *Hewlette v. Hovis* case to know which Headnote is on point for us. In this manner, when we look at additional citing references, we will only look at the references that cite *Hewlette* for the issue we are dealing with.

12. ***Click the "1"*** (see WESTLAW Exhibit 22); this is the decision itself, 318 F.Supp. 2d 332. Notice that a Link Viewer window opens up in the middle of the screen with the decision in it (see WESTLAW Exhibit 23).

HANDS-ON EXERCISES

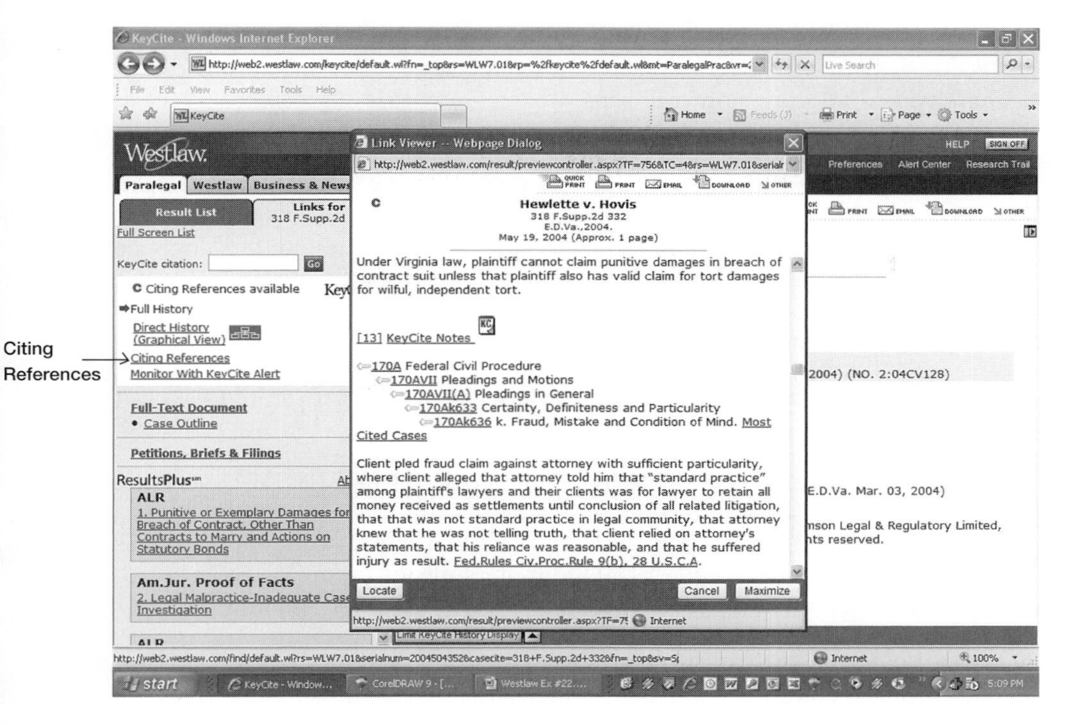

WESTLAW Exhibit 23
Courtesy of WestLaw.

13. ***Scroll to Headnote 13*** (Federal Civil Procedure 170AK636—see WESTLAW Exhibit 23). This is the issue in the case that we are interested in. We now know that we are looking for any references to Headnote 13.

14. ***Click the Close icon (a red square with a white "X") in the Link Viewer window.***

15. ***Click Citing References in the KeyCite section of the page*** (see WESTLAW Exhibit 23).

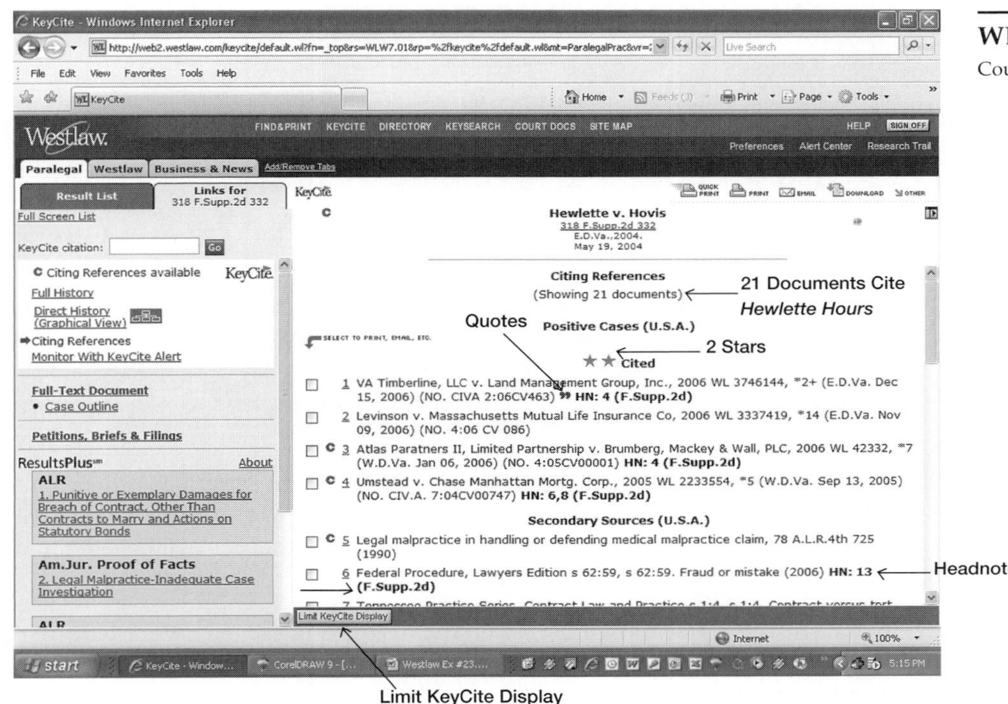

WESTLAW Exhibit 24
Courtesy of WestLaw.

16. Your screen should look similar to WESTLAW Exhibit 24. (As of the time of this writing, there were twenty-one citing references; by the time you read this, there may be more shown on your screen).

17. Notice in WESTLAW Exhibit 24 that HN:13 (Headnote 13) is listed under Secondary Sources in Federal Procedure, Lawyers Edition… ***Find this citation in your list, and then click its number (the number 6 in WESTLAW Exhibit 24) to see the citation.*** Notice that a Link Viewer window opens up with the language in the reference related to Headnote 13. You could then scroll up in the reference and read the whole section in hopes that it would provide additional resources and information related to your issue.

18. ***Click the Close icon (a red square with a white "X") in the Link Viewer window.***

19. Notice in WESTLAW Exhibit 24, just under Positive Cases (U.S.A.), that there are two stars shown. These are depth of treatment stars. The more stars there are, the more references there are for your case. One star means that your case was merely cited with no discussion, while four stars means your case was considered and talked about in the case extensively.

20. Find the first case listed in WESTLAW Exhibit 24 (*VA Timberline, LLC v. Land Management Group, Inc.*) on your screen. Notice the two purple quotation marks. This means that in the *VA Timberline, LLC v. Land Management Group*, the court quotes from the *Hewlette v. Hovis* case related to Headnote 4.

WESTLAW Exhibit 25

Courtesy of WestLaw.

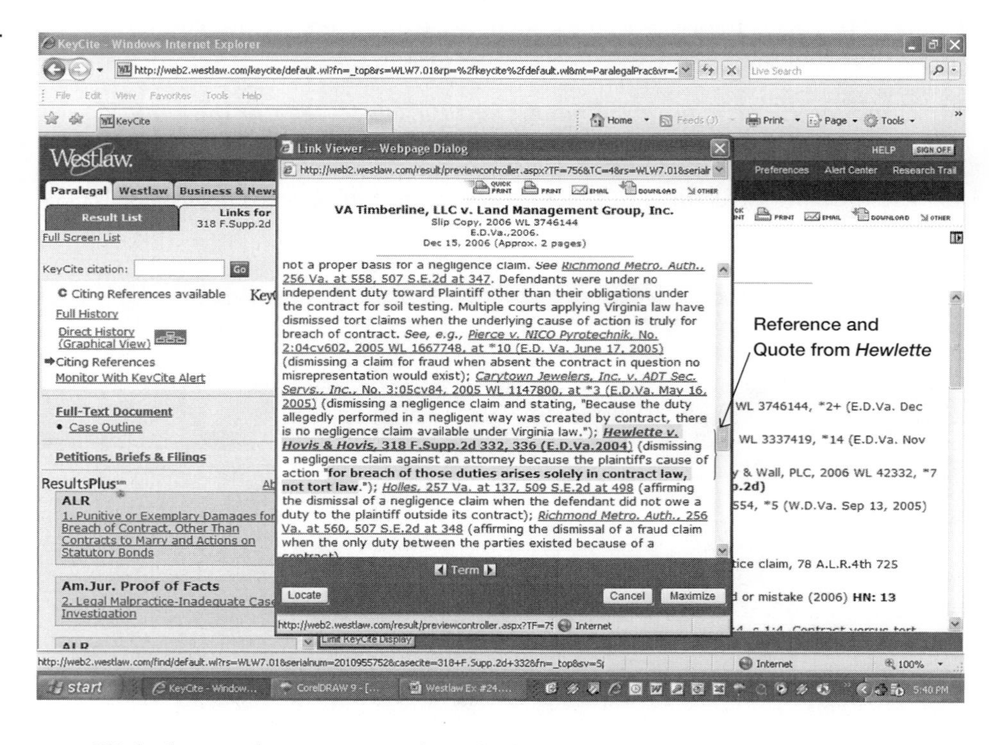

21. ***Click the number associated with the* VA Timberline, LLC v. Land Management Group *case*.** A Link Viewer window should now be displayed that shows where the court in the *VA Timberline* case quoted the *Hewlette* case related to Headnote 4 (see WESTLAW Exhibit 25).

22. Notice in WESTLAW Exhibit 25 that the discussion about the *Hewlette* case in the *VA Timberline* case is relatively short. That is why only two depth-of-treatment stars were shown.

23. ***Click the Close icon (a red square with a white "X") in the Link Viewer window.***

24. You could continue to go down the list of Citing References in WESTLAW Exhibit 24, reading and viewing additional cases related to your Headnote, but there is an easier way to do so if you are looking for a specific Headnote.

25. ***Click Limit KeyCite Display at the bottom of the screen*** (see WESTLAW Exhibit 24).

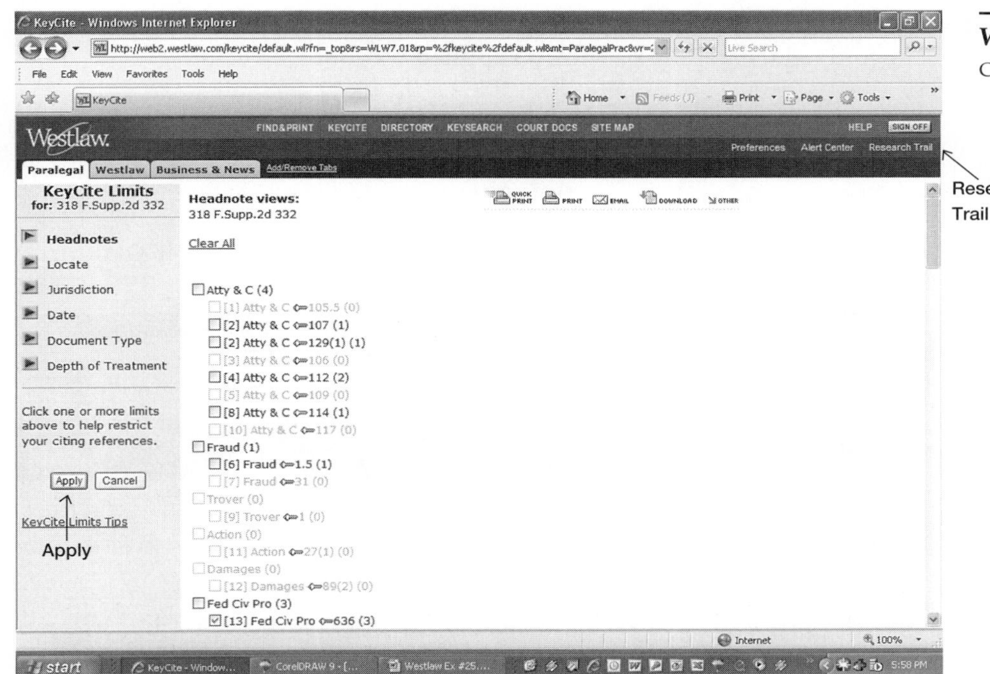

WESTLAW Exhibit 26

Courtesy of WestLaw.

26. The KeyCite Limits window should now be displayed (see WESTLAW Exhibit 26). You will now tell WESTLAW which cites you want to view. ***Click the box next to [13] Fed Civ Pro Key 636(3)*** (see WESTLAW Exhibit 26). ***Then, click Apply.***

27. WESTLAW will respond by only showing you the citations related to Headnote 13. This is a great tool, particularly if you have an important case that has many, many cites and you just want to focus on one aspect of the case.

28. ***Click the Paralegal tab.***

29. Suppose you didn't mean to click the Paralegal tab and that, for whatever reason, the Back button on your Internet browser didn't work, or you accidentally were kicked off or signed off of WESTLAW by mistake. There is a great feature called "Research Trail" that can help you get back to where you were (see WESTLAW Exhibit 26).

30. ***Click Research Trail in the upper right corner of the screen.*** The Research Trail feature shows you where you have been. If you wanted to go back to the *VA Timberline* case, for example, you could just click it in Research Trail.

31. ***Click the Paralegal tab.*** This concludes Lesson 5 of the WESTLAW Hands-on Exercises.

To quit WESTLAW, click Sign Off on the toolbar, or stay in WESTLAW and go to Lesson 6.

LESSON 6: KEYSEARCH, HEADNOTES, AND KEYNUMBERS

In this lesson, you will learn how to use WESTLAW's KeySearch tool, Headnotes and KeyNumbers, and Most Recent and Most Cited Cases features. If you did not exit WESTLAW after completing Lesson 5, go directly to Step 6 below.

1. Start Windows.

2. Start your Internet browser. Type **http://www.westlaw.com** in the browser and press **[ENTER]**.

3. Your screen should look similar to WESTLAW Exhibit 1. At the WESTLAW Password field, **enter the password supplied by your instructor.**

4. In the Client ID field type **Hands-on Exercise 6** (or whatever your instructor tells you to type).

5. ***Click Sign On*** to sign on to WESTLAW.

6. You should now be at the Paralegal tab (see WESTLAW Exhibit 3).

WESTLAW Exhibit 27
Courtesy of WestLaw.

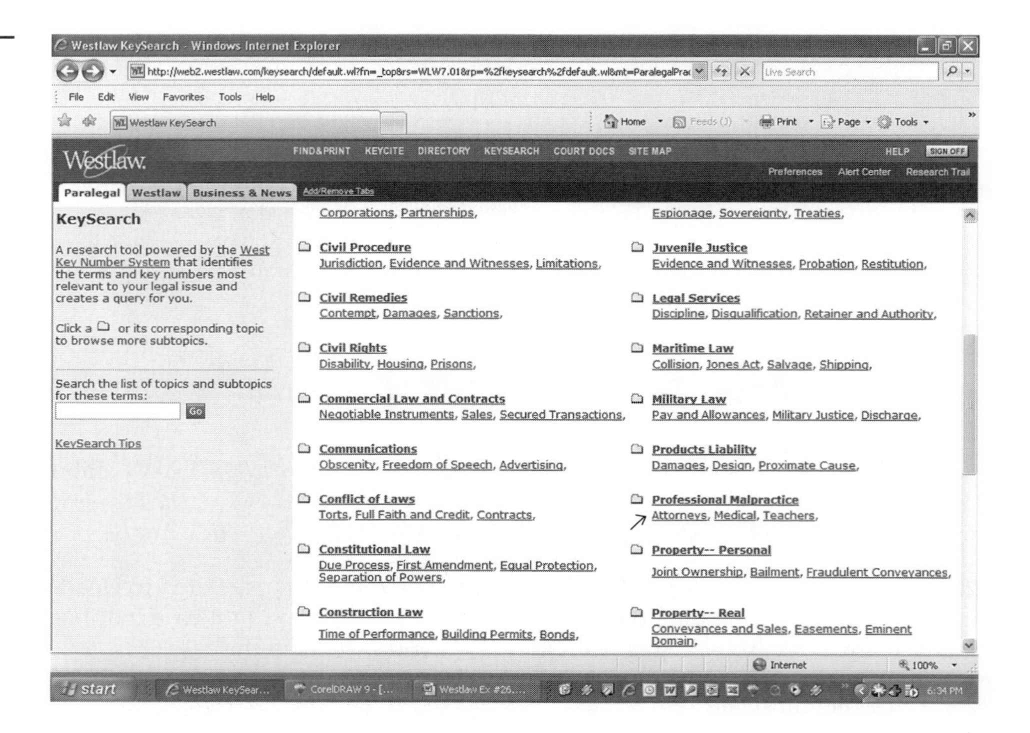

7. ***Click KeySearch on the toolbar.*** Your screen should look similar to WESTLAW Exhibit 27. KeySearch is a good place to begin your research because it provides you with a list of legal topics and subtopics; you do not have to know exactly what you are looking for.

8. ***Click Attorneys under Professional Malpractice.***

9. ***Click Breach of Fiduciary Duty.***

10. Your screen should now look similar to WESTLAW Exhibit 28. ***Select Cases With West Headnotes, click the down arrow next to All Federal Cases, select Fourth Circuit Federal Cases, and then click in the box next to it so that it has a green check mark*** (see WESTLAW Exhibit 28).

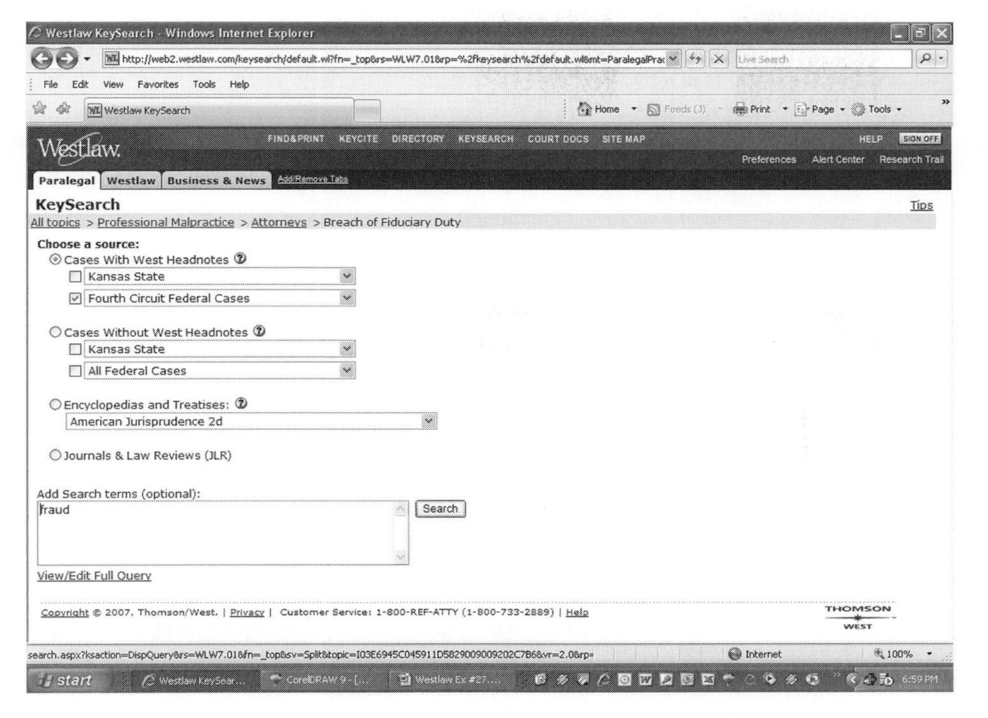

WESTLAW Exhibit 28

Courtesy of WestLaw.

11. In the Add Search terms (optional): field, type **Fraud** and then *click Search* (see WESTLAW Exhibit 28).

12. Your screen should now look similar to WESTLAW Exhibit 29. Notice in the upper left corner of the screen the search query that KeySearch built (see WESTLAW Exhibit 29).

13. *Scroll down the page until you find the* **Hewlette v. Hovis** *case*. In just a few seconds using KeySearch, you were able to find the case we were looking for.

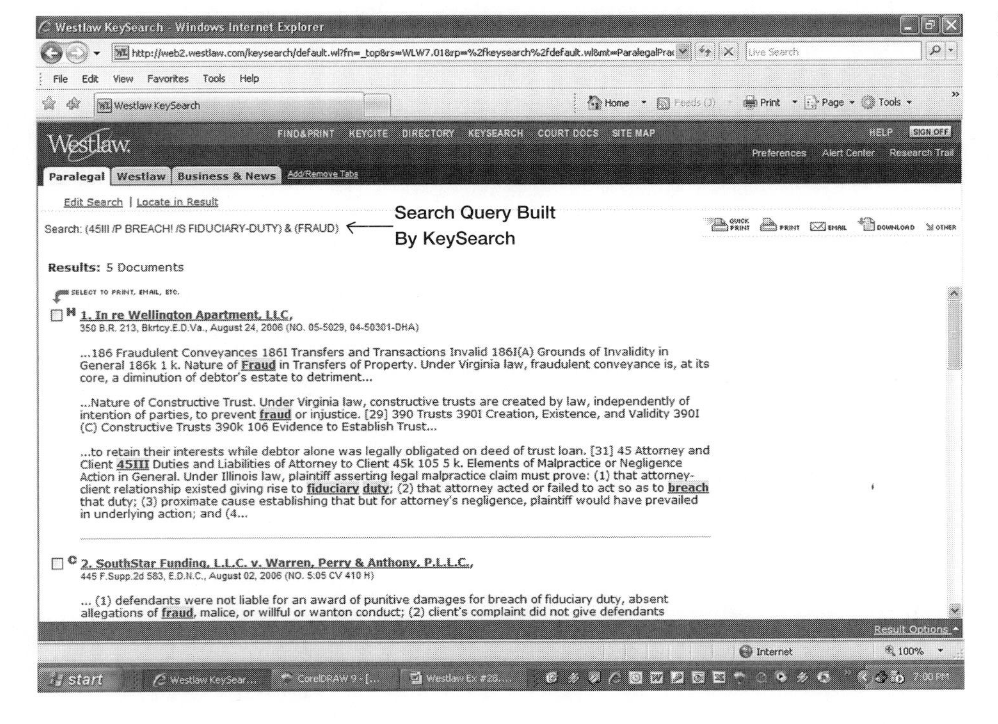

WESTLAW Exhibit 29

Courtesy of WestLaw.

WESTLAW Exhibit 30

Courtesy of WestLaw.

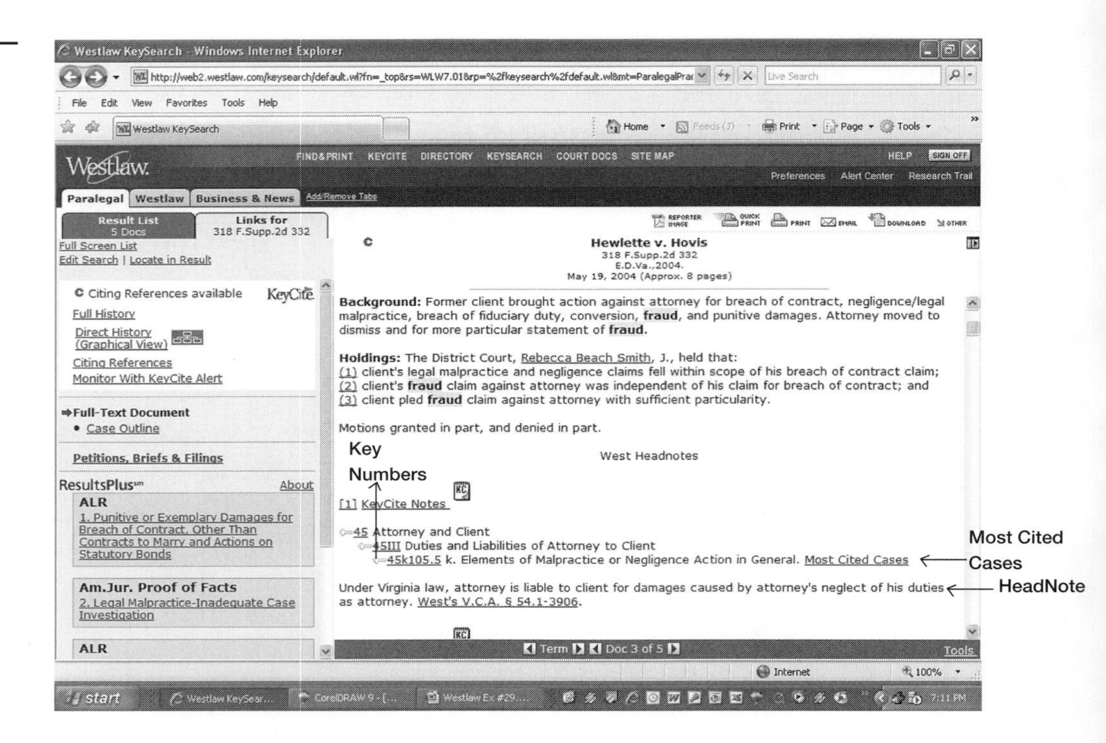

14. *Click the* **Hewlette v. Hovis** *case*. You are now going to find similar cases using the WESTLAW Headnote and KeyNumber system.

15. *In the* **Hewlette v. Hovis** *case, scroll until you come to the first Headnote* (see WESTLAW Exhibit 30). Notice in WESTLAW Exhibit 30 that the most specific KeyNumber in Headnote 1 is 45k105.5. You are now going to search for cases that are similar to Headnote 1 using this KeyNumber.

16. *Click KeyNumber 45K105.5 in Headnote 1.*

WESTLAW Exhibit 31

Courtesy of WestLaw.

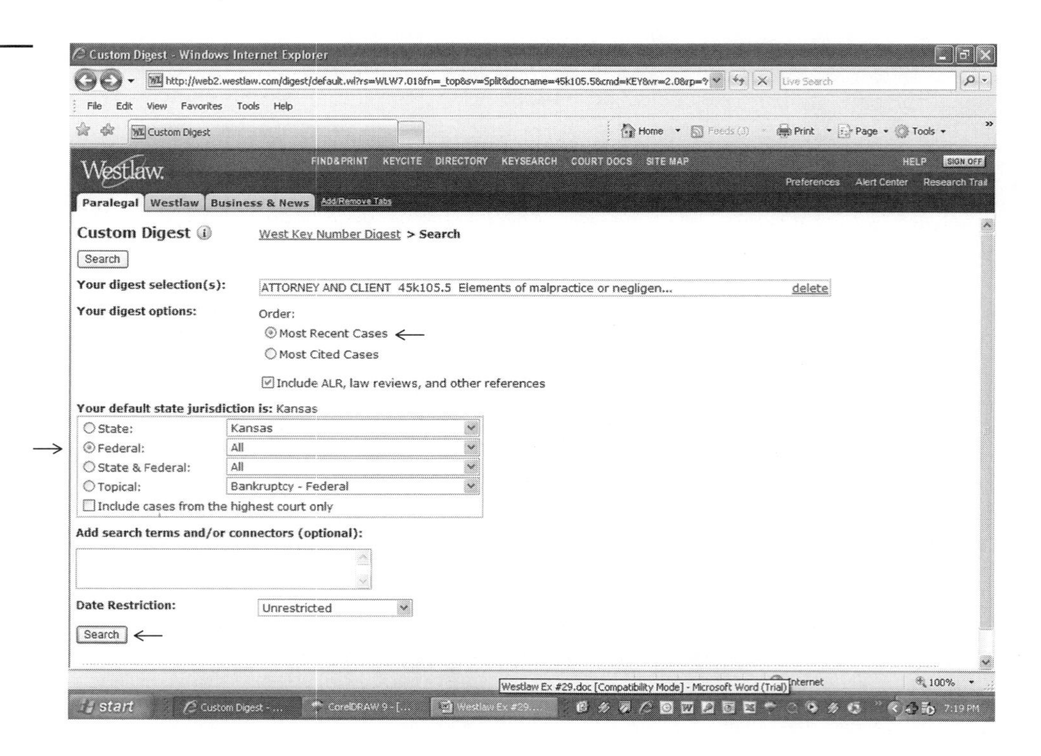

17. The Custom Digest screen should now be displayed (see WESTLAW Exhibit 31). Under "Your digest options:" leave the order as Most Recent Cases. ***In the jurisdiction section, click Federal and leave All selected*** (see WESTLAW Exhibit 31).

18. ***Then, click Search in the bottom left of the screen.*** It may take up to a minute for Westlaw to retrieve all of the cases.

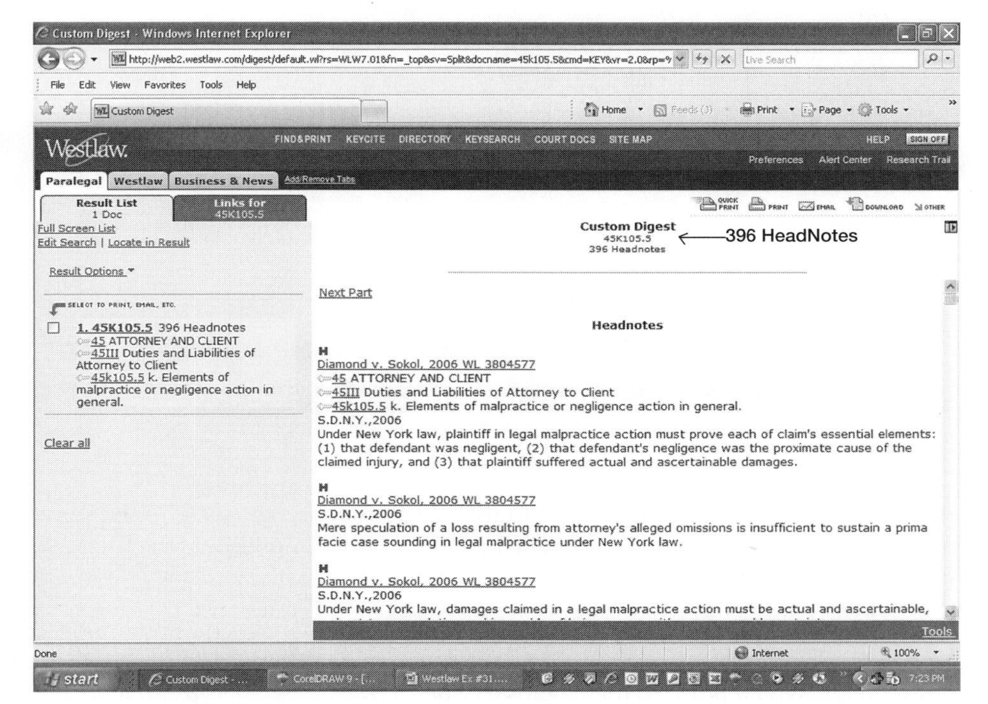

WESTLAW Exhibit 32

Courtesy of WestLaw.

19. Your screen should look similar to WESTLAW Exhibit 32, but your cases will probably be different. ***Scroll down through the list and notice that you have quite a number of Headnotes from which to expand your research.***

20. Remember that the order in which you sorted the cases and headnotes in put the most recent items first. By reading the headnotes, you can get a good understanding of the elements of a claim for legal malpractice.

21. You will next find the cases and headnotes that are most cited (the ones that other, similar cases tend to quote or talk about). This can give you a good idea as to which case(s) is / are the most important.

22. ***Click your browser's Back button twice.*** You should now be back at the *Hewlette v. Hovis* case (see WESTLAW Exhibit 30). If not, click Research Trail in the upper right of the screen, then click on the Hewlette v. Hovis case.

23. ***Scroll to the first Headnote again and click Most Cited Cases at the end of KeyNumber 45K105.5*** (see WESTLAW Exhibit 30).

24. Notice that this is the same screen as in WESTLAW Exhibit 31, except that now Most Cited Cases is selected. ***Click Federal and leave All selected.***

25. ***Click Search in the lower left of the screen.***

WESTLAW Exhibit 33

Courtesy of WestLaw.

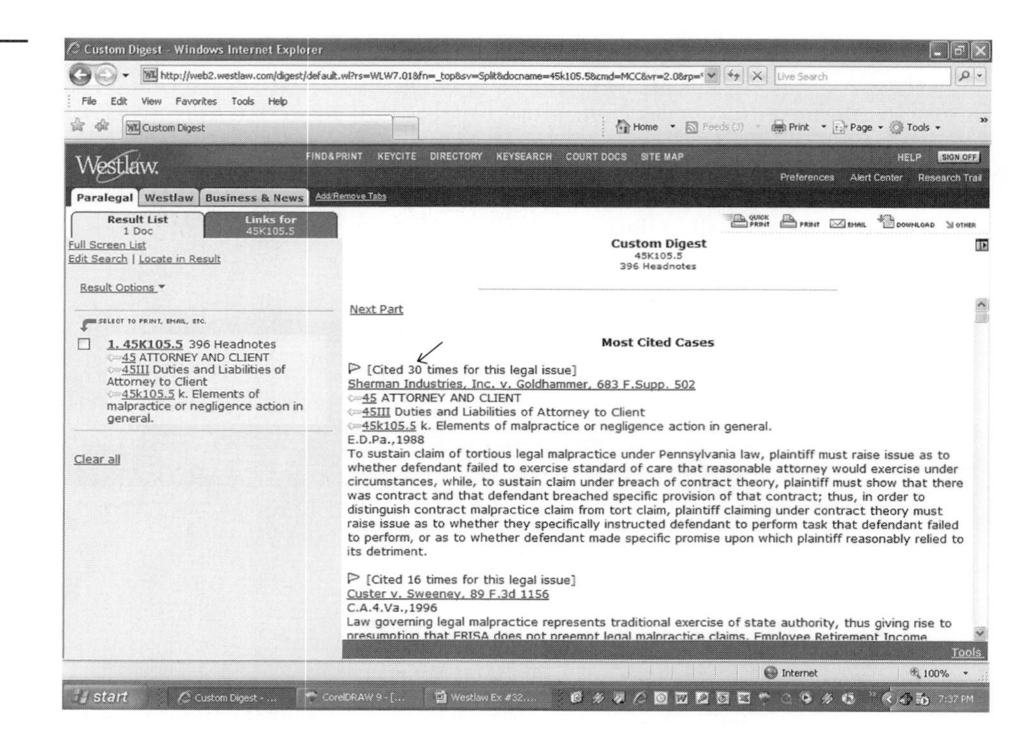

26. Your screen should look similar to (but will probably not include the same cases as) WESTLAW Exhibit 33. In WESTLAW Exhibit 33, notice that the first case states that it has been cited thirty times regarding Headnote 1.

27. ***Scroll down the first ten cases or so on your list.*** Pay particular attention to the KeyCite colors of the flags. You will want to pay specific attention to red and yellow flags, which point to the negative issues in the cases, so you can evaluate how they might apply to your case. This will help you forecast what your opposing counsel may argue.

28. Once you have found a case on point, always look at the Headnote and KeyNumbers, as they can provide you a wealth of additional information.

29. ***Click the Paralegal tab.***

This concludes Lesson 6 of the WESTLAW Hands-On Exercises. To quit WESTLAW click Sign Off on the toolbar, or stay in WESTLAW and go to Lesson 7.

LESSON 7: PUBLIC RECORDS, FORMS, COMPANY RECORDS, AND DOCKET SEARCHES

In this lesson, you will learn how to use WESTLAW to search for public records on people and businesses, search for legal forms, and search court dockets. If you did not exit Westlaw after completing Lesson 6, go directly to Step 6 below.

1. Start Windows.

2. Start your Internet browser. Type **http://www.westlaw.com** in the browser and press **[ENTER]**.

3. Your screen should look similar to WESTLAW Exhibit 1. At the WESTLAW Password field, **type the password supplied by your instructor.**

4. In the Client ID field, type **Hands-on Exercise 7** (or whatever your instructor tells you to type).

5. ***Click Sign On*** to sign on to WESTLAW.

6. You should now be at the Westlaw Paralegal tab (see WESTLAW Exhibit 3).

7. ***Click Public Records by State*** under information About Companies.

8. ***Click Public Records Combined—Florida.***

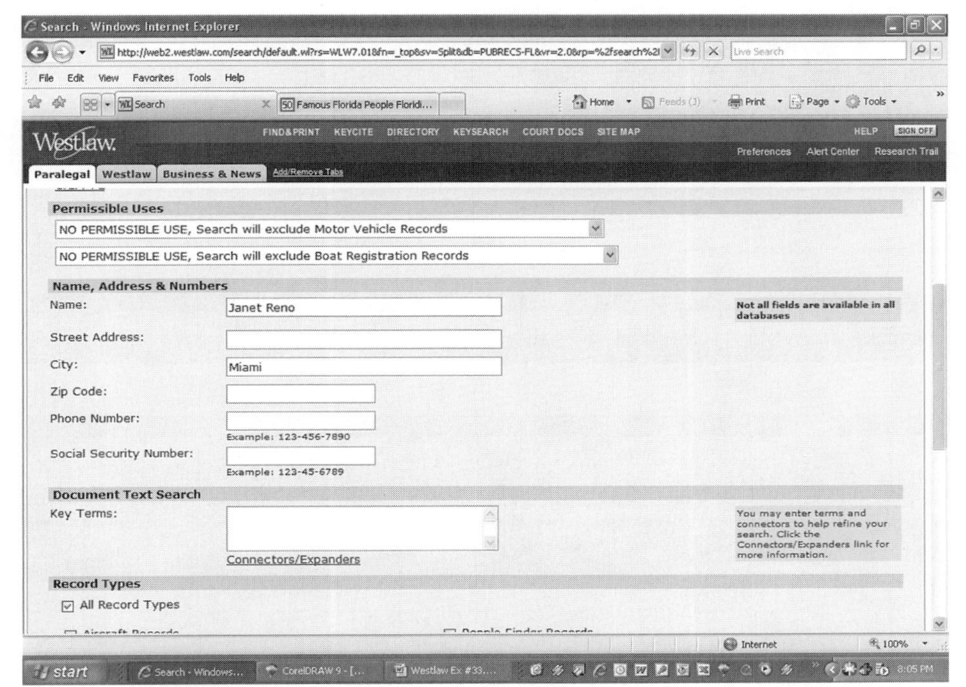

WESTLAW Exhibit 34

Courtesy of WestLaw.

9. Your screen should now appear similar to WESTLAW Exhibit 34. You will now do a public records search for Janet Reno. You will be looking for Ms. Reno's attorney license number.

10. Complete the public records screen as shown in WESTLAW Exhibit 34. Note that under Permissible Uses you must select "NO PERMISSIBLE USE" for motor vehicle and boat registration records, because you do not have a permissible reason for checking these records.

11. ***At the bottom left of the screen, click Search Westlaw.***

12. You should now see a screen similar to WESTLAW Exhibit 35. Notice in Westlaw Exhibit 35 that the eighth record is a professional license for Janet Reno.

13. If you see the record ***RENO JANET; PROFLICENSE—FL, click it.*** This is the public record for Ms. Reno's law license, containing items such as the last time it was updated.

14. ***Click the Paralegal tab.***

15. Your will now look at some public records related to a corporation. ***Click Company Profile under Information about Companies.***

WESTLAW Exhibit 35

Courtesy of WestLaw.

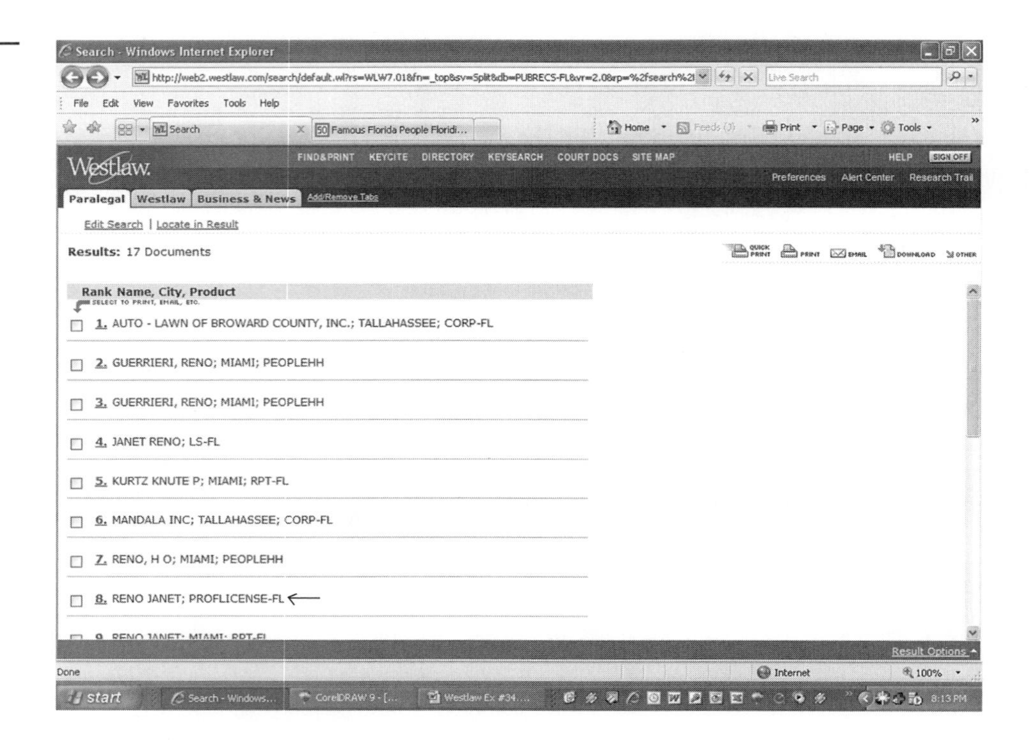

WESTLAW Exhibit 36

Courtesy of WestLaw.

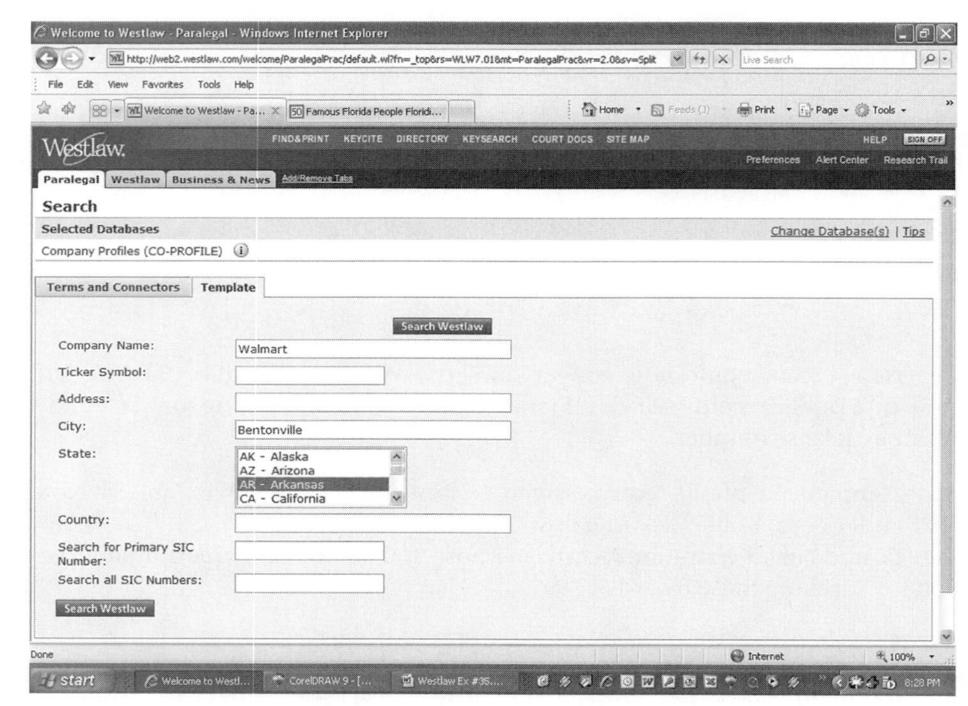

16. You should now see a screen similar to WESTLAW Exhibit 36. Complete the screen as shown in WESTLAW Exhibit 36.

17. *At the bottom left of the screen, click Search Westlaw.*

18. You should now see a number of public records filings for WalMart, including a number of Securities and Exchange Commission filings.

19. *Click the Paralegal tab.*

20. You will now look for a form on WESTLAW. You will look for a special military power of attorney regarding caring for a person's children.

21. ***Click Am Jur Legal Forms under Forms and Checklists.***

22. In the Search field, type **Military Power of Attorney Children** and then *click Natural Language.*

23. ***Click Search Westlaw.*** A number of forms should be retrieved.

24. ***Click 1B Am. Jur. Legal Forms 2d Agency Section 14:174.5.***

25. The form should now be displayed.

26. ***Click the Paralegal tab.***

27. You will now search the federal court dockets for cases involving Microsoft Corporation filed after January 1, 2006.

28. ***Click Dockets under the Court Documents section.***

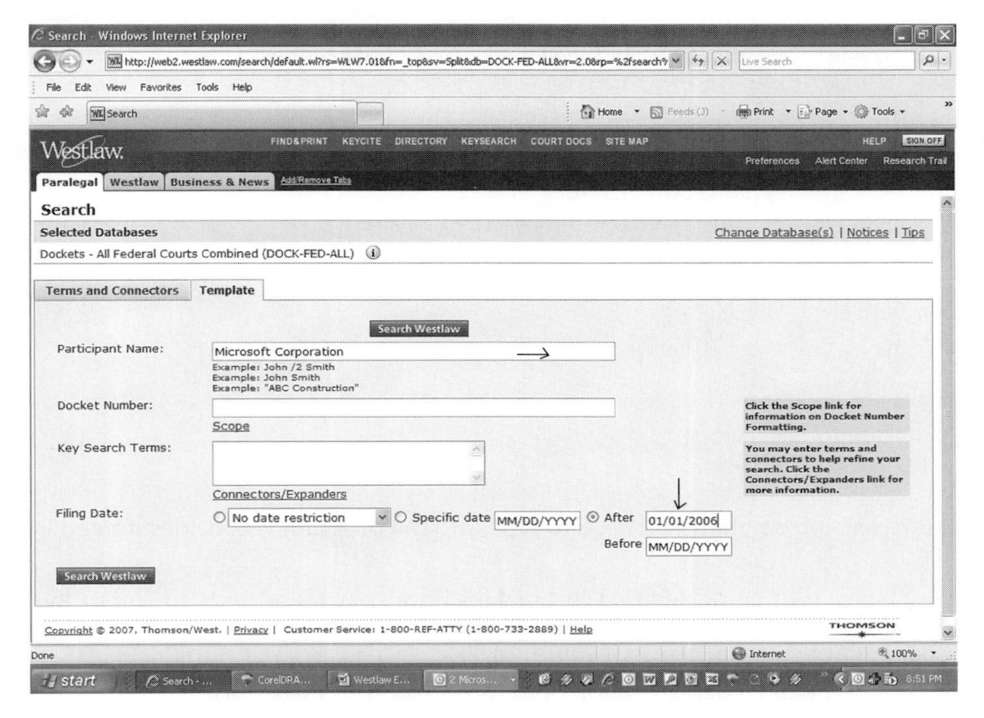

WESTLAW Exhibit 37

Courtesy of WestLaw.

29. ***Click Dockets—All Federal Courts Combined.***

30. ***Complete the search as shown in WESTLAW Exhibit 37 and then click Search Westlaw.***

31. A number of cases should now be displayed, probably in excess of one hundred. ***Click one of the cases*** to review it.

32. ***Click the Paralegal tab.*** This concludes the WESTLAW Hands-on Exercises.

To quit WESTLAW, click on Sign Off on the toolbar.

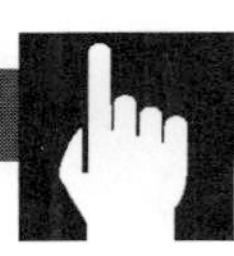

HANDS-ON EXERCISES

LEXISNEXIS
COMPUTER-ASSISTED LEGAL RESEARCH

Basic

Number	Lesson Title	Concepts Covered
Lesson 1	Introduction to LexisNexis	Signing on, introduction to LexisNexis's interface, finding databases, using the Search Advisor, and working with LexisNexis tabs
Lesson 2	Get by Citation, Get by Party Name, and Exploring Retrieved Cases	Get by Citation, Get by Party Name, Cite, KWIC, Full, reporter page numbers, distribution options, and a *Shepard's* overview
Intermediate		
Lesson 3	Natural Language Search, Editing Searches, Changing Databases, Using Doc and Term	Natural Language searching, editing searches, changing databases, using date restriction, requiring and excluding terms, and using the Doc and Term features
Lesson 4	Terms and Connectors Search	Terms and connectors searching, Suggest Terms for My Search, printing a list of retrieved cases and using the FOCUS feature
Advanced		
Lesson 5	*Shepard's* Citations	Shepardizing, Table of Authorities, Auto-Cite, and *Shepard's* Alert

GETTING STARTED

Introduction

Throughout these lessons and exercises, information you need to type into the program will be designated in several different ways:

- Keys to be pressed on the keyboard will be designated in brackets, in all caps, and in bold (press the: **[ENTER]** key).
- Movements will be designated in bold and italics (***point to File on the menu bar and click the mouse***).
- Words or letters that should be typed will be designated in bold (type **Training Program**).
- Information that should be displayed on your computer screen will be shown in the following style: ***Press ENTER to continue.***

BASIC

LESSON 1: INTRODUCTION TO LEXISNEXIS

This lesson introduces you to LexisNexis and includes how to sign on to LexisNexis, a tour of LexisNexis and the LexisNexis interface, finding databases, using the Search Advisor, and working with LexisNexis tabs. For an overview of LexisNexis's features, read the LexisNexis section in Chapter 11 of the text.

1. Start Windows.

2. Start your Internet browser. Type **http://www.Lexis.com** in the browser and press **[ENTER]**.

3. At the ID field, **type the Lexis ID supplied by your instructor.**

4. At the Password field, **type the Lexis password supplied by your instructor.**

5. ***Click Sign On*** to sign on to LexisNexis.

6. ***Click the Research System tab*** (see LexisNexis Exhibit 1).

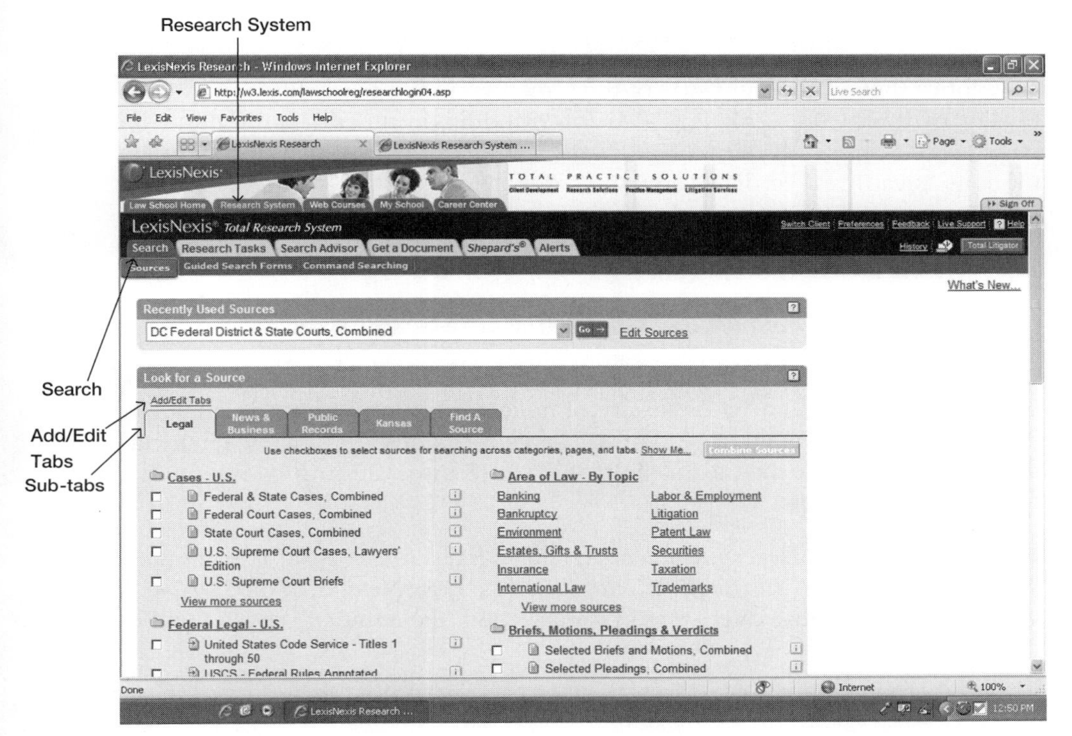

LexisNexis Exhibit 1

Copyright 2007 LexisNexis, a division of Reed Elsevier Inc. All Rights Reserved. Lexis, LexisNexis, the Knowledge Burst logo and *Shepard's* are registered trademarks and *Shepard's Signal* is a trademark of Reed Elsevier Properties Inc. and are used with the permission of LexisNexis. Courtlink is a registered trademark of LexisNexis Courtlink Inc.

7. Your screen should now look similar to LexisNexis Exhibit 1. If your screen does not look like LexisNexis Exhibit 1, click the Search tab. (It is all the way over to the left, just under "LexisNexis Total Research System" (see LexisNexis Exhibit 1)). LexisNexis is highly customizable, so it is possible that your screens might look different than the screens in the Exhibits.

8. You will now take a brief tour of LexisNexis. The Search tab in the upper left of the screen should be selected. (It should have a red background and "Search" should be in white letters—see LexisNexis Exhibit 1).

9. Under "Look for a Source" (see LexisNexis Exhibit 1) a number of sub-tabs should be displayed. The sub-tabs should, at a minimum, include Legal, News & Business, Public Records, and Find a Source (see LexisNexis Exhibit 1).

10. If the Legal sub-tab is not already selected, ***point and click on it***.

11. The Legal sub-tab includes sections such as Cases—U.S. and Federal Legal—U.S. The Legal sub-tab is a good place to start your legal research, because you can access many common databases from this screen.

12. ***Scroll down and click States Legal—U.S. on the left side of the page.*** A list of states should now be displayed.

13. ***Click California.*** You should now see a list of databases and resources for California. If you wanted to search in one of these databases you could click the database name and a search window would open where you could enter your search. If you wanted to search multiple databases at the same time, you could click in the check box next to each database and then select Combine sources. A search window would then open that would allow you to search multiple databases at the same time.

14. ***Click the Legal sub-tab or click your browser's Back button twice.*** You should be back at the Legal sub-tab (see LexisNexis Exhibit 1).

15. Notice that on the right side of the screen you can access different areas of the law by topic (e.g., Banking, Bankruptcy, and Environment). ***Scroll down the page*** and, on the right side of the screen, notice that you can access briefs, motions, pleadings, Verdicts, Court Records from CourtLink, other secondary legal resources, legal news, and other resources.

16. Press the **[HOME]** key to go back to the top of the page.

17. ***Click the News and Business sub-tab*** (see LexisNexis Exhibit 2).

18. Notice that on the left side of the screen, under Combined Sources, LexisNexis gives you a wide variety of general and legal news databases to search. Notice on the right side of the screen, under Company & Financial, that LexisNexis also has a number of resources for finding company and financial information.

19. ***Click the Source Description icon. (It looks like a lower-case "i" in a square and is next to News, all (English, Full Text)*** (see LexisNexis Exhibit 2). *Note:* If you hover your mouse over an icon for a second, the name of the icon will be displayed).

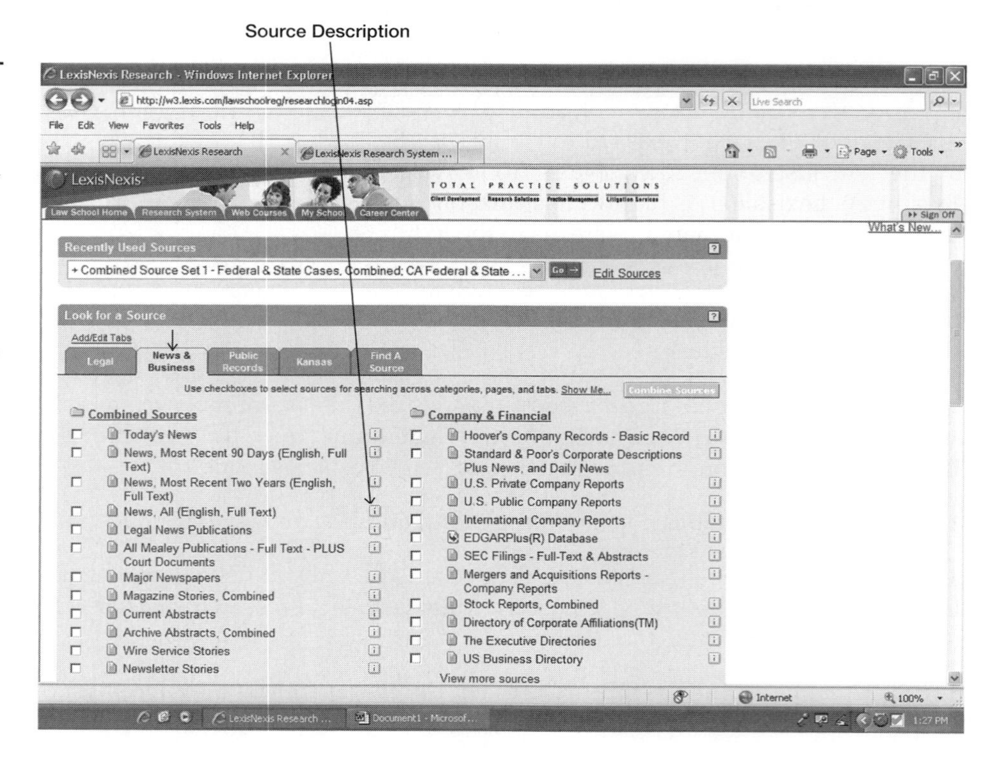

LexisNexis Exhibit 2

20. The Source Information window should now be displayed. ***Scroll down through the list using your mouse or the cursor keys on the keyboard.*** Notice all of the publications covered in this database.

21. ***Click the Close icon (a red square with a white "X") in the Source Information window.***

22. You can use the Source Description icon (a lower case "i" in a square) throughout LexisNexis to discover the scope of a database.

23. ***Click the Public Records sub-tab just to the right of the News & Business sub-tab.*** Notice that a number of public records are available for searching in LexisNexis.

24. ***Click the Find a Source sub-tab.*** In the Find a Source sub-tab you can browse an alphabetical list for a database. Alternatively, you can search for the name of a database in the Find a Source field (see LexisNexis Exhibit 3).

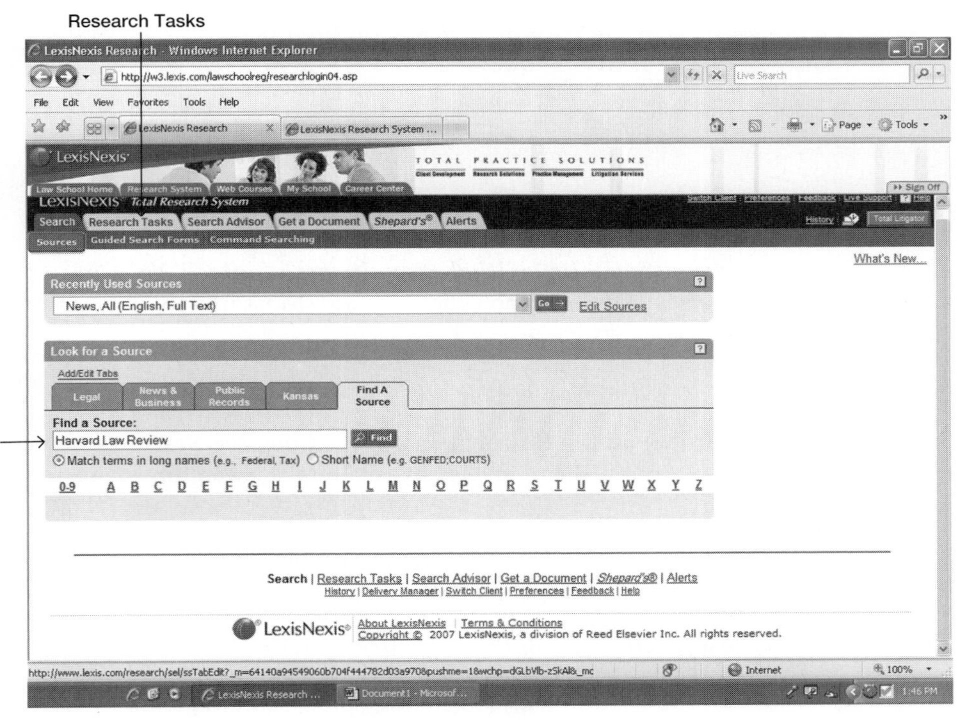

LexisNexis Exhibit 3

25. In the Find a Source field, type **Harvard Law Review** ***and then click Find*** (see LexisNexis Exhibit 3). A list of resources with "Harvard" in the title, including the *Harvard Law Review,* is displayed. You can access the *Harvard Law Review* database by simply clicking it, but for this exercise it is not necessary.

26. ***Click your browser's Back button to go back to the Find A Source page*** (see LexisNexis Exhibit 3).

27. ***Click the Legal sub-tab.*** You can customize the sub-tabs by adding your own jurisdiction or legal topics that you use a lot.

28. ***Click Add/Edit Tabs, which is just over the Legal sub-tab*** (see LexisNexis Exhibit 1).

LexisNexis Exhibit 4

29. Notice that on the left side of the screen a list of states is displayed. ***Scroll down the list and you will see a list of legal specialty areas as well.*** You can add sub-tabs by clicking a selection and then clicking Add. Most users will want to select a tab for their state.

30. ***Click your browser's Back button to go back to the Legal sub-tab.***

31. You will now learn about the Research Tasks tab. ***Click the Research Tasks tab at the top of the screen*** just under LexisNexis Total Research System (see LexisNexis Exhibit 3).

32. The Research Tasks tab allows you to access databases and information by legal subject matter (see LexisNexis Exhibit 4).

33. ***Scroll down the different areas of law and click Labor & Employment.***

34. Notice that from the Labor and Employment Sources screen you can access databases, enter search queries, access employment-related newsletters, and more from one screen. The Research Tasks tab can be a very helpful tool for conducting research in LexisNexis.

35. ***Click your browser's Back button.***

36. You will now learn about the Search Advisor tab.

37. ***Click the Search Advisor tab*** (see LexisNexis Exhibit 5). The Search Advisor tab can help you conduct legal research by allowing you to browse legal topics. It can be a good place to start your research.

38. ***Click Criminal Law & Procedure. Then, click the plus sign ("+") next to Arrests.*** Your screen should now look similar to LexisNexis Exhibit 5. If you were researching Miranda warnings, this would be a good place to start.

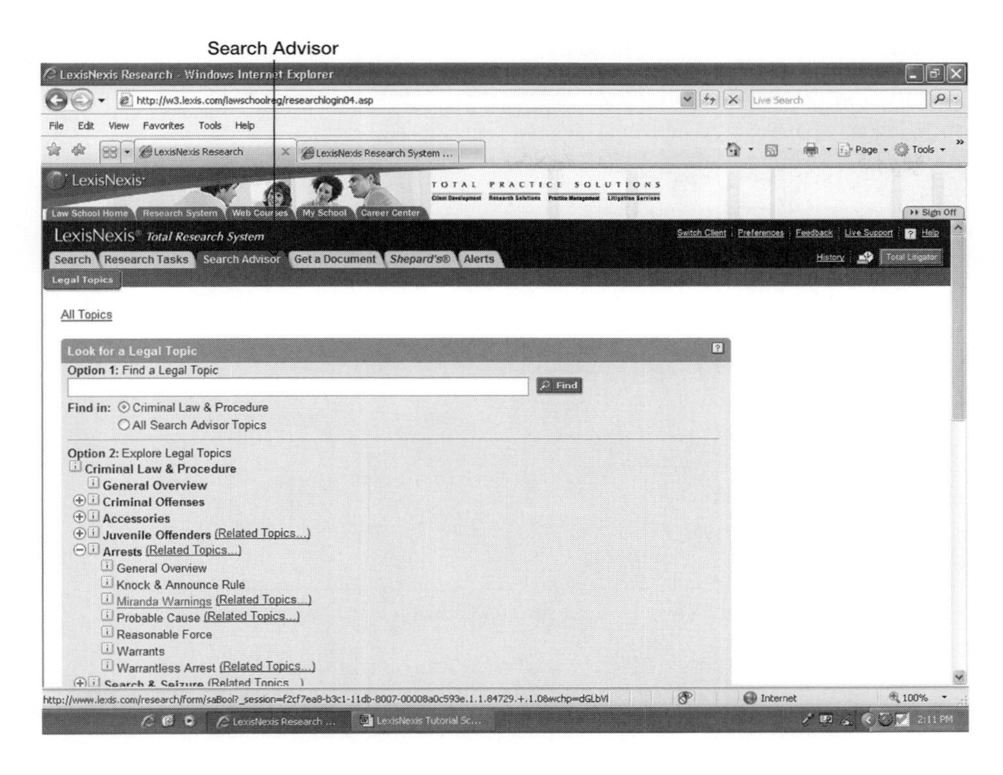

LexisNexis Exhibit 5

39. Press the **[HOME]** key on the keyboard to go to the top of the page.

40. You will now learn about the Get a Document tab. ***Click the Get a Document tab*** (see LexisNexis Exhibit 6). Notice that there are three sub-tabs: Citation, Party Name, and Docket Number.

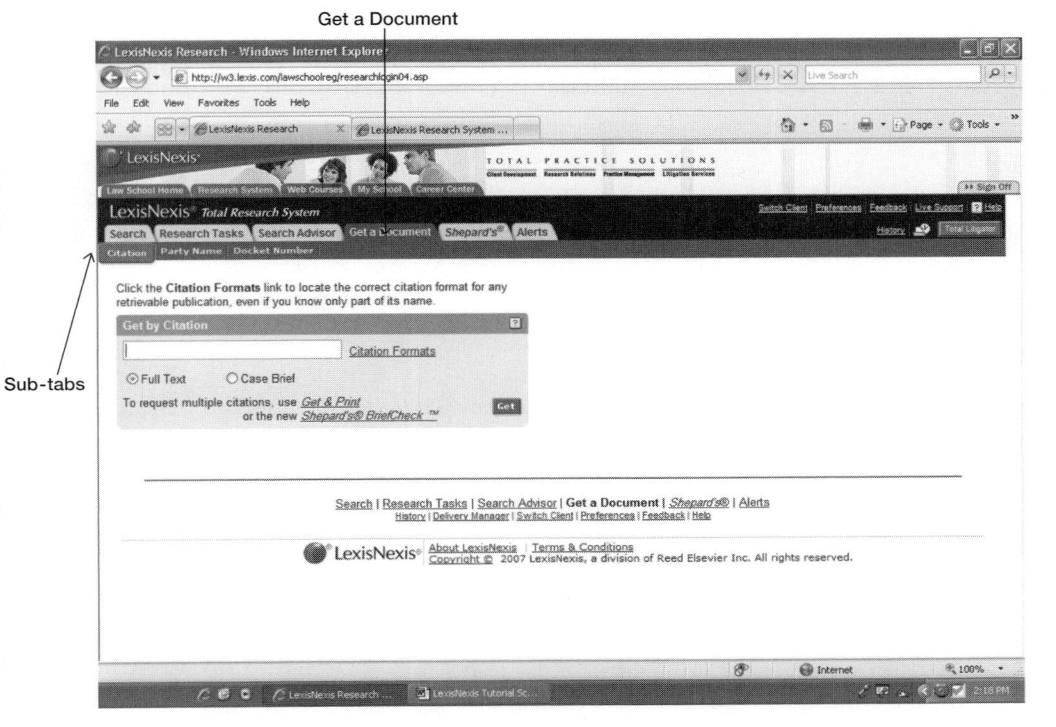

LexisNexis Exhibit 6

LexisNexis Exhibit 7

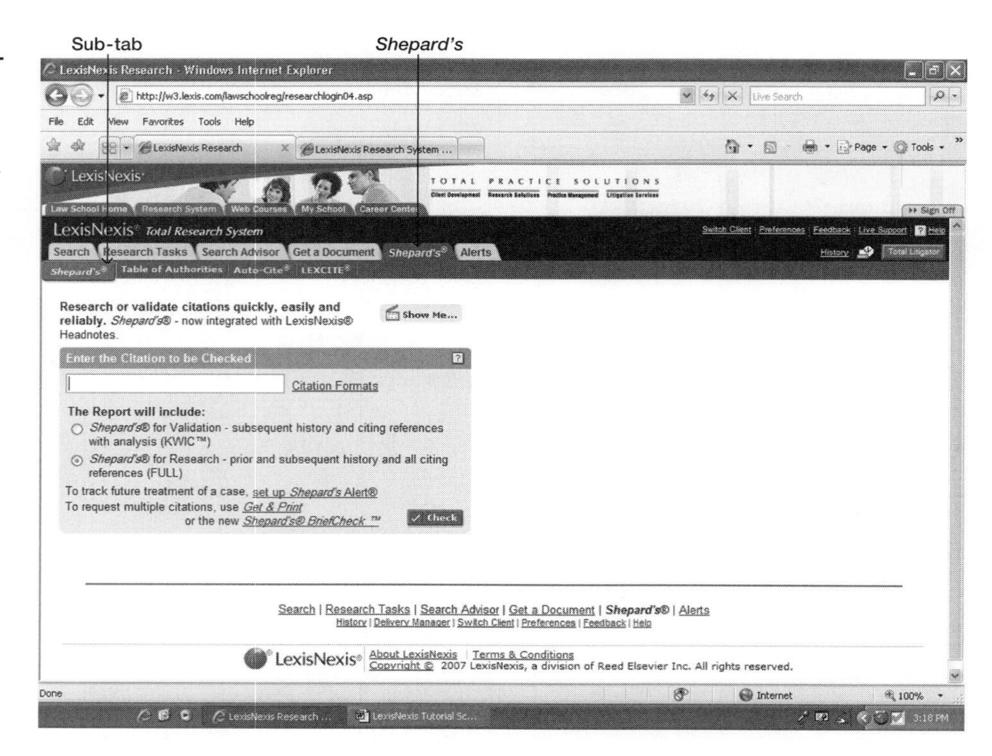

41. ***Click the Citation sub-tab.*** This is where you can go directly to a case, statute, or other document by entering its cite.

42. ***Click the Party Name sub-tab.*** This is where you can retrieve a case by entering a party name.

43. ***Click the Docket Number sub-tab.*** This is where you can retrieve a case by entering its docket number.

44. You will now learn about the *Shepard's* Citations tab. ***Click the Shepard's tab*** (see LexisNexis Exhibit 7). Notice that there are four sub-tabs: *Shepard's*, Table of Authorities, Auto-Cite, and LEXCITE.

45. ***Click the Shepard's sub-tab*** (see LexisNexis Exhibit 7). This is where you can enter a cite and get a comprehensive report of the cases, statutes, secondary sources, and annotations that cite your authority.

46. ***Click the Table of Authorities sub-tab*** (see LexisNexis Exhibit 7). Table of Authorities provides an at-a-glance analysis of the cited references within your case and links to in-depth analysis.

47. ***Click the Auto-Cite sub-tab.*** Auto-Cite verifies the accuracy of your research and gives you a history of your opinion, including cases that refer negatively to your case. Auto-Cite can quickly tell you whether your case or statute is still good law.

48. ***Click the LEXCITE sub-tab.*** LEXCITE allows you to find both reported and unreported cases.

49. ***Click on the Search tab.***

This concludes Lesson 1 of the LexisNexis Hands-on Exercises. To quit LexisNexis, click Sign Off on the toolbar, or stay in LexisNexis and go to Lesson 2.

LESSON 2: GET BY CITATION, GET BY PARTY NAME, AND EXPLORING RETRIEVED CASES

In this lesson you will use the Get by Citation tool, the Get by Party Name feature, Cite, KWIC, Full, reporter page numbers, and distribution options. If you did not exit LexisNexis after completing Lesson 1, go directly to Step 6 below.

1. Start Windows.

2. Start your Internet browser. Type **http://www.Lexis.com** in the browser and press **[ENTER]**.

3. At the ID field, **type the Lexis ID supplied by your instructor.**

4. At the Password field, **enter the Lexis password supplied by your instructor.**

5. ***Click Sign On*** to sign on to LexisNexis.

6. ***Click the Research System tab.***

7. Your screen should now look similar to LexisNexis Exhibit 1. If your screen does not look like LexisNexis Exhibit 1, click the Search tab all the way over to the left, just under LexisNexis Total Research System (see LexisNexis Exhibit 1). LexisNexis is highly customizable, so it is possible that your screens might look different from the screens in the Exhibits.

8. ***Click the Get a Document tab.*** Notice that there are three sub-tabs: Citation, Party Name, and Docket Number. Make sure that the Citation sub-tab is selected.

9. In the Get by Citation field type **189 S.W.3d 777.** Make sure that the Full Text option is selected just under the Get by Citation field (see LexisNexis Exhibit 8).

10. ***Then, click Get.***

11. The case of *In re Karen Mays-Hooper* should now be displayed (see LexisNexis Exhibit 9). If you know the citation of a case, you can enter it in the Get by Citation

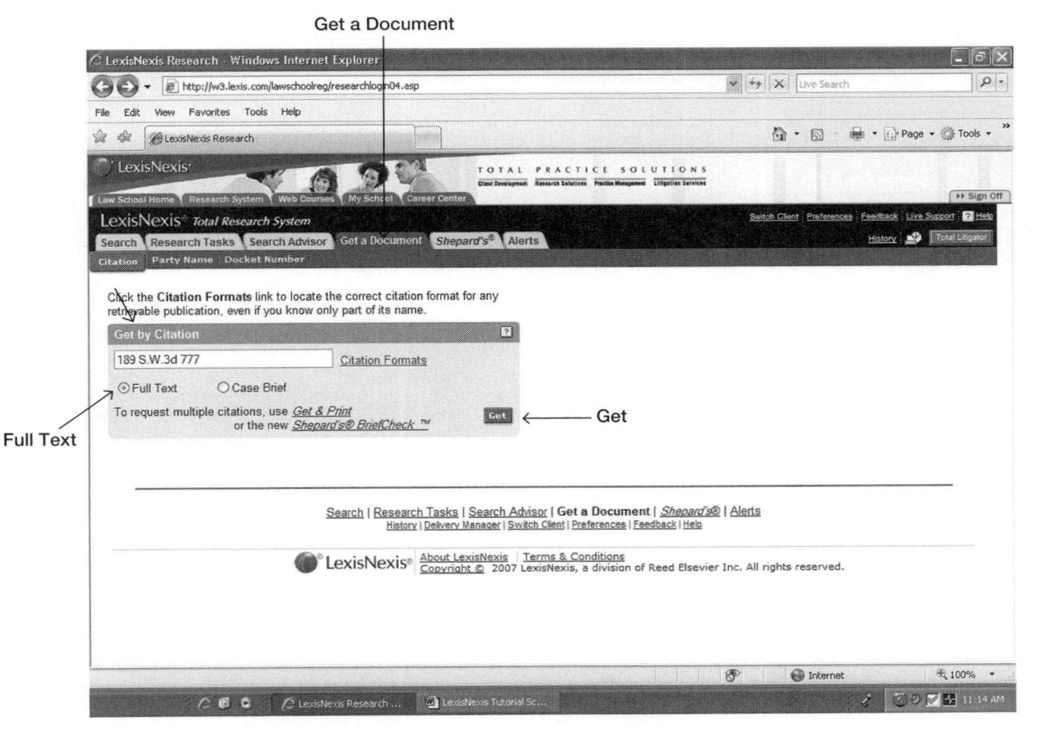

LexisNexis Exhibit 8

LexisNexis Exhibit 9

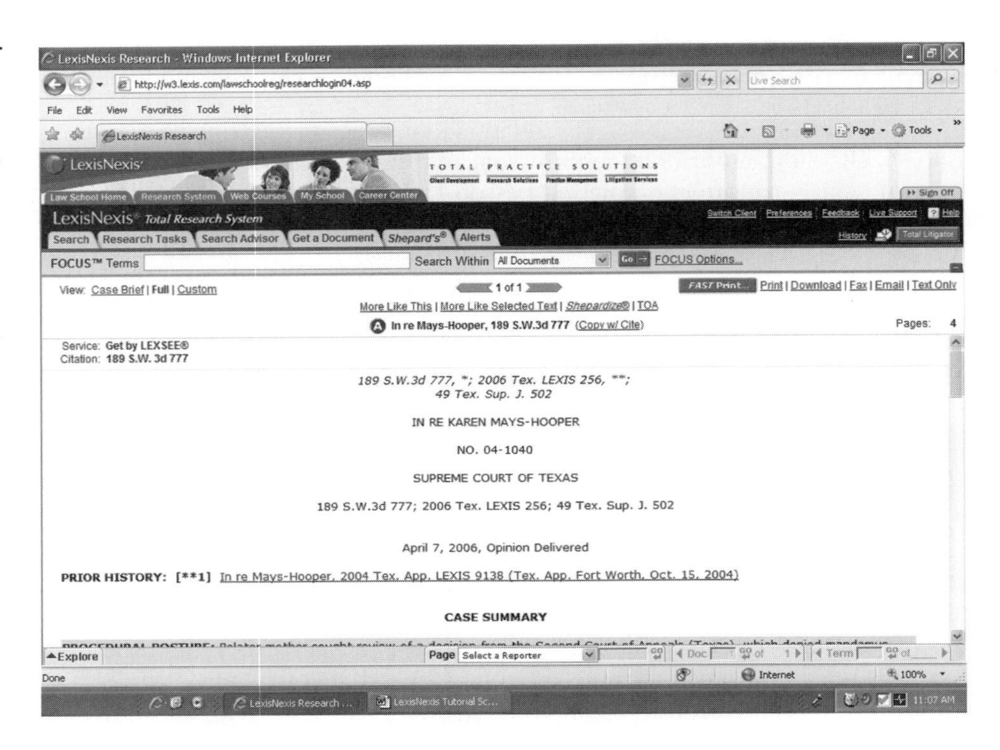

feature and LexisNexis will immediately retrieve it without your having to indicate a database or enter a search query.

12. You will now learn how to find a case by entering the name of a party.
13. ***Click the Get a Document tab.***
14. ***Click the Party Name sub-tab*** (see LexisNexis Exhibit 10).
15. The screen in LexisNexis Exhibit 10 should now be displayed.

LexisNexis Exhibit 10

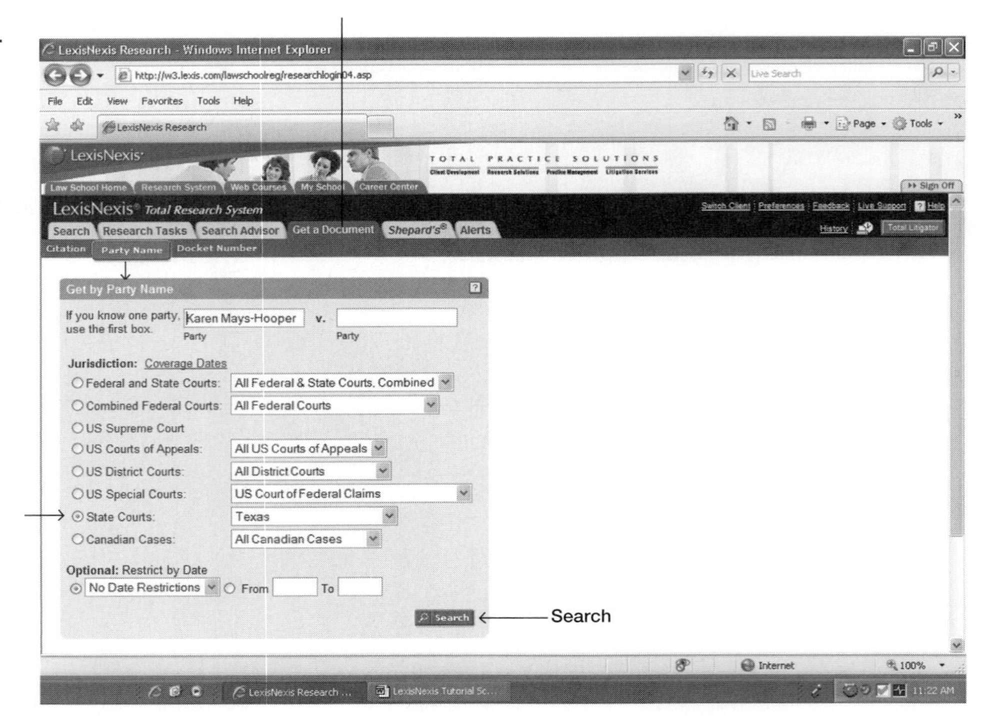

16. In the first party name field, type **Karen Mays-Hooper.**

17. *Click in the circle to the left of State Courts.*

18. *Click the down arrow next to the right of State Courts and select Texas.*

19. *Click Search.*

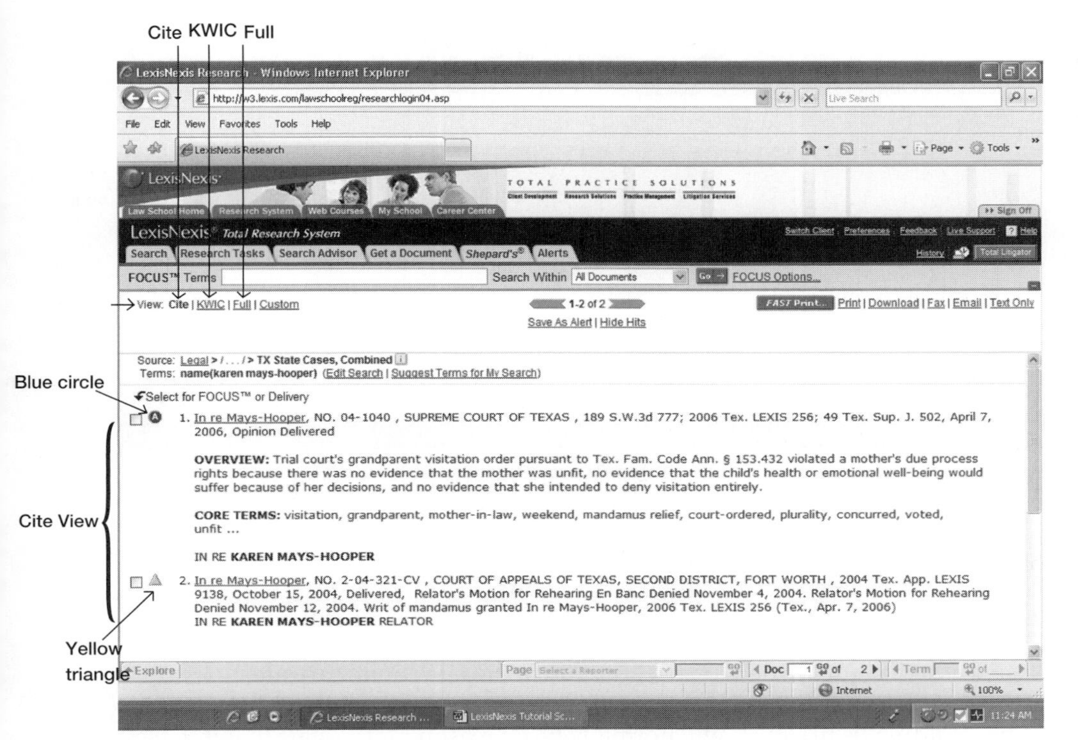

LexisNexis Exhibit 11

20. A summary of two cases, each with the title *In re Mays-Hooper*, should now be displayed (see LexisNexis Exhibit 11).

21. Notice the text "View: Cite, KWIC, Full, Custom" in the upper left of the screen. Notice that Cite is currently selected. These are the different options for how cases can be displayed in LexisNexis.

22. *Click KWIC.* Notice that only the Case Summary of the first case is shown. To go to the next case you would need to select "2 >" in the Doc section of the Navigation Frame at the bottom of the case.

23. *Click Cite.* Notice that there are symbols just to the left of the case names. In the first case there is a blue circle with a white letter "A," and next to the second case there is a yellow triangle. These are *Shepard's* citations symbols. ***Scroll to the bottom of the page, where there is a legend explaining what the symbols mean.***

24. ***Click the first case,* In re Mays-Hooper, *No. 04–1040, Supreme Court of Texas, 189 S.W. 3d 777.***

25. The *In re Mays-Hooper* case should now be displayed (see LexisNexis Exhibit 12).

26. Notice in the *In re Mays-Hooper* case that just under the title of the case are its prior history and a case summary. The case summary is written by LexisNexis

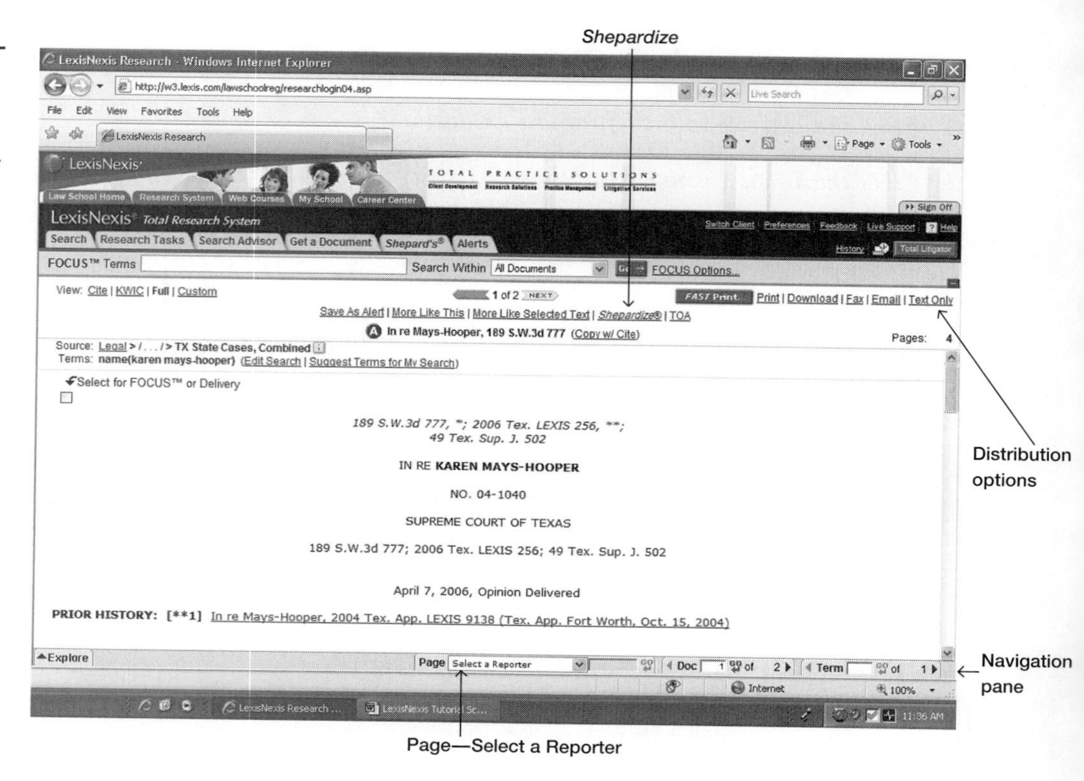

LexisNexis Exhibit 12

research attorneys. This is a value-added service offered by LexisNexis that many other CALR services do not offer.

27. Read the Case Summary.

28. Notice that after the Core Terms section in the Case Summary are LexisNexis Headnotes. Headnote 1 (HN1) states "So long as a parent adequately cares for his or her children (is fit), there will normally be no reason for the state to inject itself into the private realm of the family." The Headnotes are also written by research attorneys and are another value-added service offered by LexisNexis that many other CALR services do not offer. These will be discussed in more detail in later exercises.

29. ***Skim the case by scrolling down through it using the horizontal scroll bar.***

30. When you are finished, press the **[HOME]** key to go back to the beginning of the case.

31. You will next learn how to use the Page command. The Page command in the Navigation Pane allows you to cite to a specific page of the hard copy reporter.

32. ***Click the down arrow next to Page: Select a Reporter in the navigation pane.***

33. ***Click 189 S.W.3d 777.***

34. ***Scroll down; just under the listing of the judge and next to Opinion is the term "[*777]."*** This means that everything after this is on page 777 of the hard copy reporter, so if you need to cite to the exact page you can do so.

35. ***Scroll down through the case to the paragraph that starts with "The Supreme Court found the trial court's order unconstitutional . . ." and notice that on the third line of the paragraph the term "[*778]" appears in red.*** This is where page 778 of the hard copy report starts.

36. Notice the options Fast Print, Print, Download, Fax, Email, and Text Only in the upper right of the screen (see LexisNexis Exhibit 12). These are the distribution options, which define the things that you can do with the case.

37. ***Click Download.*** Notice that the Deliver Documents—Download window is displayed.

38. ***Click the down arrow next to Format: Word (DOC) and notice that in addition to saving the file in Microsoft Word format, you can save the case to WordPerfect, text-only, Adobe (PDF), or a generic format.***

39. ***Click the Close icon (a red square with a white "X" in it) in the Deliver Documents–Download window.***

40. Press **[HOME]** on the keyboard.

41. ***Click* Shepardize *just under the Phrase "1 of 2" at the top middle of the screen*** (see LexisNexis Exhibit 12). A *Shepard's* Summary for the case is now displayed (see LexisNexis Exhibit 13).

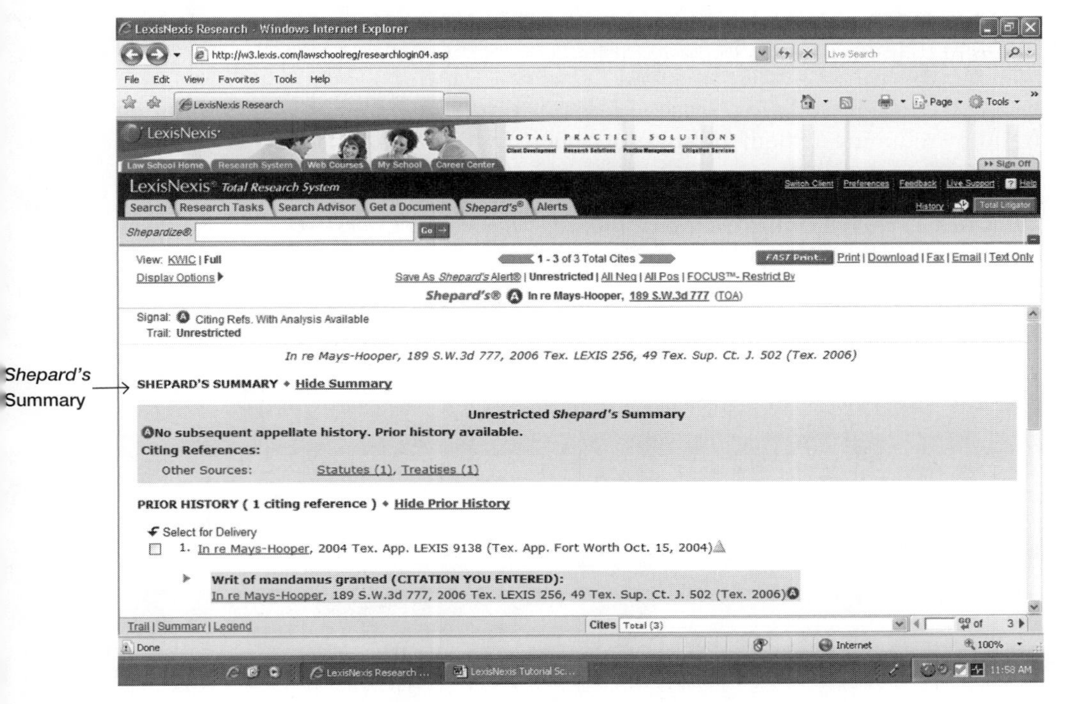

LexisNexis Exhibit 13

42. ***Click your browser's Back button to go back to the* In Re Karen Mays-Hooper *case.***

43. ***Click the Search tab in the upper left corner of the screen.***

This concludes Lesson 2 of the LexisNexis Hands-on Exercises. To quit LexisNexis, click Sign Off on the toolbar, or stay in LexisNexis and go to Lesson 3.

LESSON 3: NATURAL LANGUAGE SEARCH, EDITING SEARCHES, CHANGING DATABASES, USING DOC AND TERM

In this lesson you will learn how to select a database, run a Natural Language search, edit a search, change to a different database, use the date restriction

feature when searching, use the Require/Exclude terms feature, and use the Doc and Term features.

If you did not exit LexisNexis after completing Lesson 2, go directly to Step 6 below.

1. Start Windows.

2. Start your Internet browser. Type **http://www.Lexis.com** in the browser and press **[ENTER]**.

3. At the ID field, **type the Lexis ID supplied by your instructor.**

4. At the Password field, **enter the Lexis password supplied by your instructor.**

5. ***Click Sign On*** to sign on to LexisNexis.

6. ***Click the Research System tab.***

7. Your screen should now look similar to LexisNexis Exhibit 1. If your screen does not look like LexisNexis Exhibit 1, click on the Search tab (all the way over to the left, just under LexisNexis Total Research System (see LexisNexis Exhibit 1)). LexisNexis is highly customizable, so it is possible that your screens might look different than the screens in the exhibits.

8. You will now look for a case in federal court where an attorney committed fraud by retaining settlement funds of a client in litigation and breached his fiduciary duty to the client.

9. ***Click "Federal Court Cases, Combined" under the Cases—U.S. section*** (see LexisNexis Exhibit 1).

10. The LexisNexis search screen (Enter Search Terms) should now be displayed (see LexisNexis Exhibit 14).

LexisNexis Exhibit 14

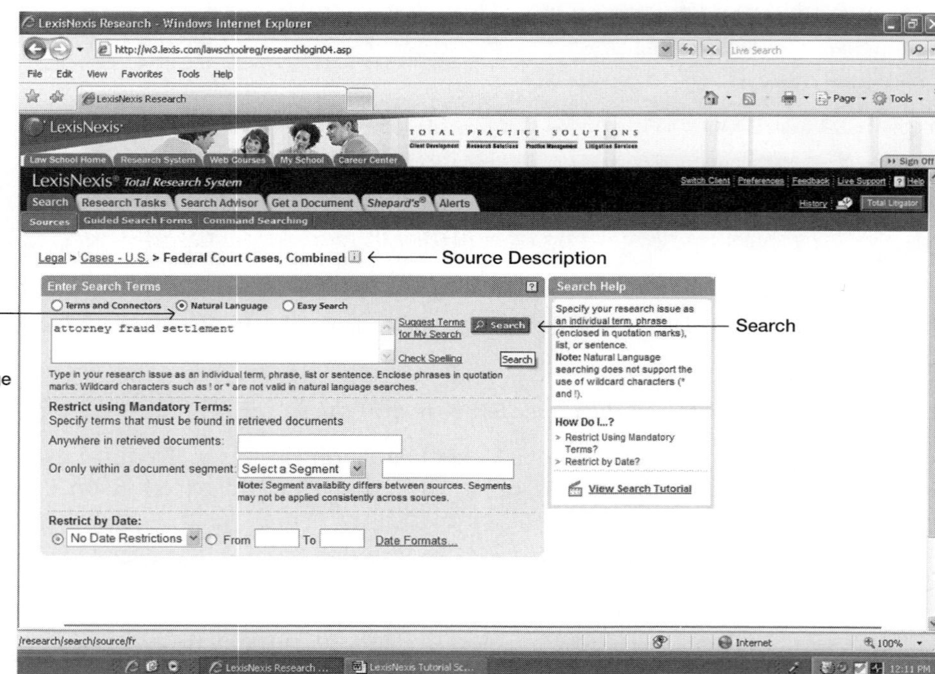

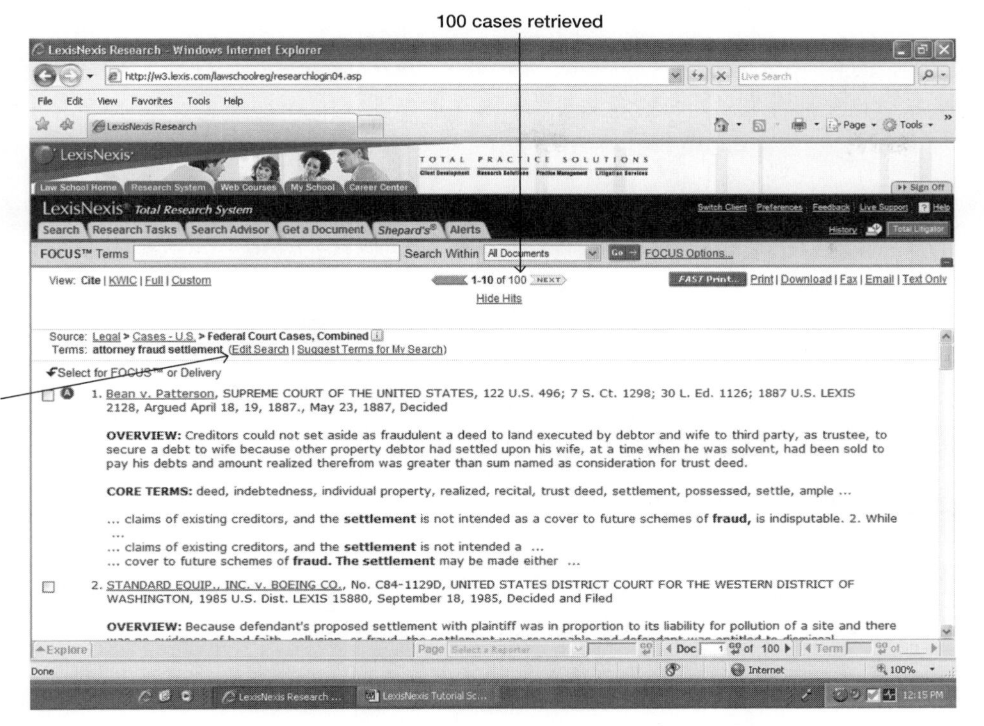

LexisNexis Exhibit 15

11. ***Click Natural Language*** (Exhibit 14). You will now type a plain-English search request into the Federal Court Cases, Combined database using LexisNexis's Natural Language feature.

12. In the search box type **attorney fraud settlement,** ***and then click Search*** (see LexisNexis Exhibit 14).

13. Depending on how LexisNexis was set up on your computer, your search will most likely return twenty or more cases. In LexisNexis Exhibit 15, 100 cases were retrieved. This is too many cases to look through.

14. There are two main problems with the search. First, you are searching in an enormous database; and second, you need to use more search terms to cull the number of cases retrieved.

15. ***Click Edit Search, just above the first case that is listed*** (see LexisNexis Exhibit 15). You should now be back at the LexisNexis Search screen. You will now look at the scope of the database to see exactly what database you are searching in.

16. ***Click the Source Description symbol. (It looks like a white square with a lower-case "i" in the middle of it and is just to the left of "Federal Court Cases, Combined," just above the Search field.)***

17. Notice the information about the database that is listed, including file name, coverage, etc.

18. ***Scroll down to see just how large the database is.*** The database is extremely large and contains tens of thousands of cases. When you search in a large database like this, you need more search terms, not less.

19. ***Click the Close icon (a red square with a white "X") in the Source Information window.***

LexisNexis Exhibit 16

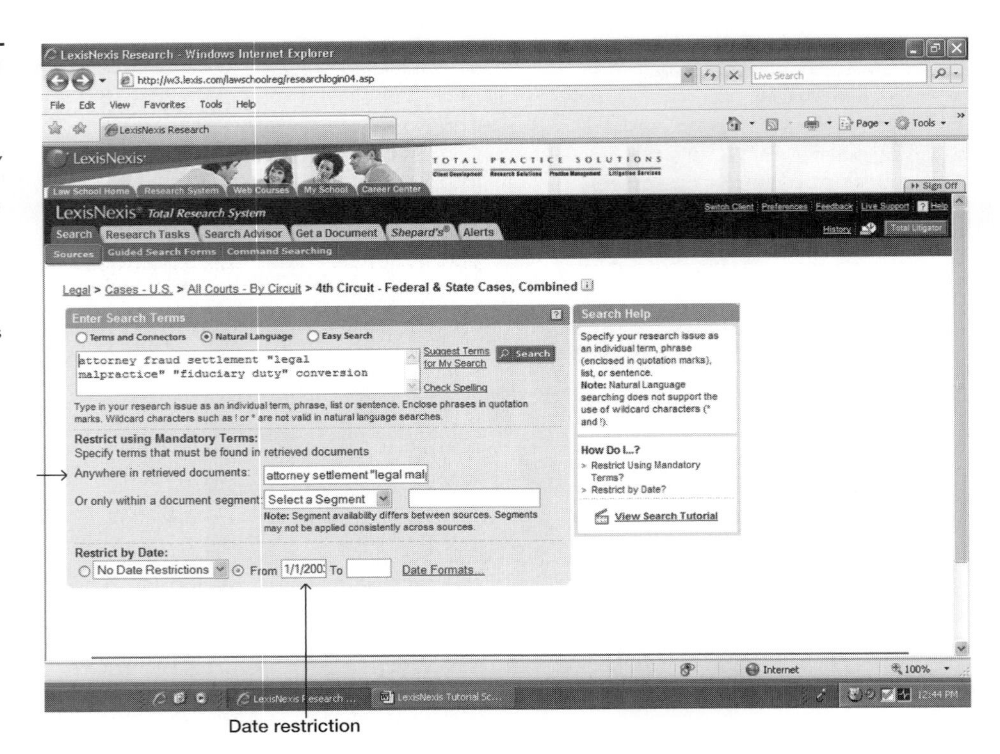

20. It can sometimes be more efficient to search in a smaller database than in a larger one. You will now learn how to change your database.

21. ***Click Cases—U.S., just to the left of Federal Court Cases, Combined.***

22. ***Click All Courts—By Circuit on the right side of the screen.***

23. ***Click on 4th Circuit—Federal and State Cases, Combined.*** You will now be searching state and federal cases just in the Fourth Circuit. This is a narrower database than All Federal Cases.

24. Even with a smaller database, this search would retrieve a large number of cases. The search needs to be refined and additional search terms included.

25. In the search box, in addition to "attorney fraud settlement," type the following: **"legal malpractice" "fiduciary duty" conversion** (see LexisNexis Exhibit 16). The quotes around "legal malpractice" and "fiduciary duty" force LexisNexis to search for these exact phrases.

26. Another way to limit the number of cases retrieved is to restrict the dates of the cases retrieved. In the Restrict by Date section at the bottom of the screen, ***click in the From field and type* 1/1/2003**.

27. Another way to limit the number of cases retrieved is to require some or all of the search terms to appear in the case(s). In the Restrict using Mandatory Terms section, ***click in the "Anywhere in retrieved documents:" field and type* attorney settlement "legal malpractice" "fiduciary duty"**.

28. Double-check that there are no misspellings in your search query.

29. ***Click Search.*** Your screen should now look similar to LexisNexis Exhibit 17.

30. LexisNexis should return a much smaller number of cases. One of the cases that should be retrieved is *Hewlette v. Hovis*, 318 F. Supp. 2d 332 (E.D. Va., May 19, 2004).

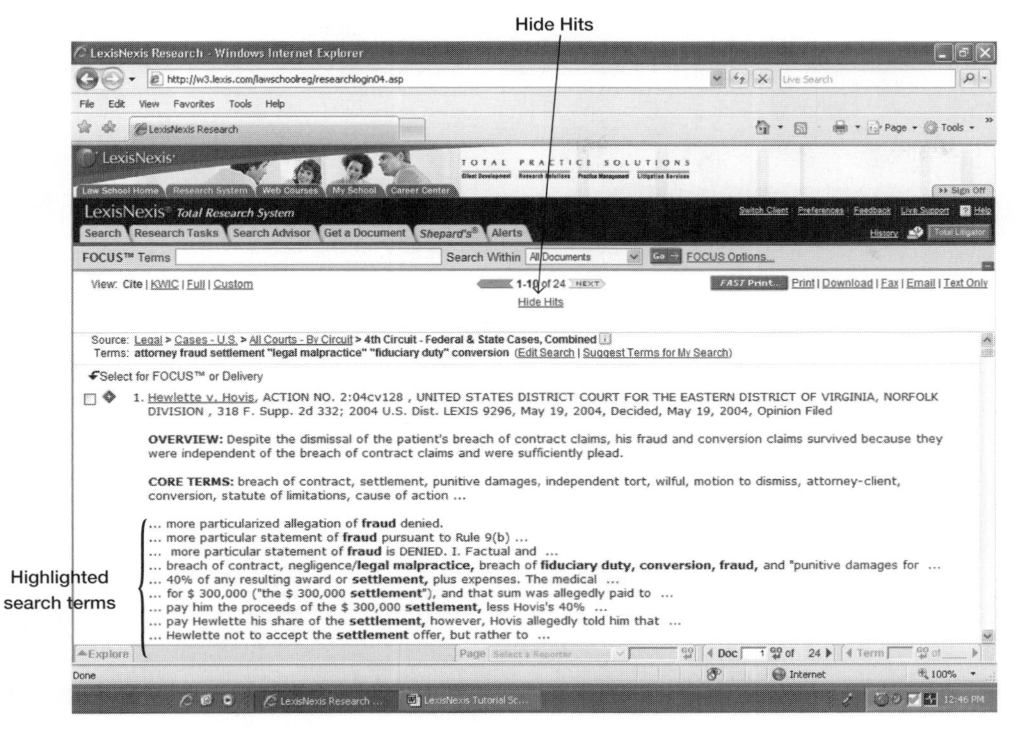

LexisNexis Exhibit 17

31. ***Scroll down through the cases and notice that all of the search terms for the cases are highlighted* (see LexisNexis Exhibit 17).** If you have many cases to look through, this level of detail may or may not be helpful. LexisNexis refers to showing the search terms like this as showing the "hits" (the search terms). You will now use the "Hide Hits" feature to make the search terms disappear so you just see the Overview and Core Terms sections of the case.

32. ***Click the* [HOME] *key to go back to the beginning of the cases.***

33. ***Click Hide Hits in the top middle of the screen.*** Notice that now all of the "hits" have disappeared and have been replaced with the Overview and Core Terms of the case.

34. ***Click the* Hewlette v. Hovis case.**

35. The *Hewlette v. Hovis* case should now be displayed (see LexisNexis Exhibit 18).

36. ***Scroll down and notice that the search terms are highlighted in the Case Summary.***

37. ***Click the right arrow to the right of Term at the bottom of the screen.*** Each time you click the right arrow next to "Term," LexisNexis takes you to the next search term in your case (see LexisNexis Exhibit 18). You could look backwards for your search terms in the document by clicking the left (previous) arrow next to Term.

38. ***Click the right arrow to the right of Term at the bottom of the screen in the Navigation Pane to continue to move through the* Hewlette *case.***

39. ***Click the right arrow next to Doc to go to the next case.*** The Doc arrows allow you to move forwards and backwards through the retrieved cases.

40. You should now be back at the beginning of the *Hewlette* case.

LexisNexis Exhibit 18

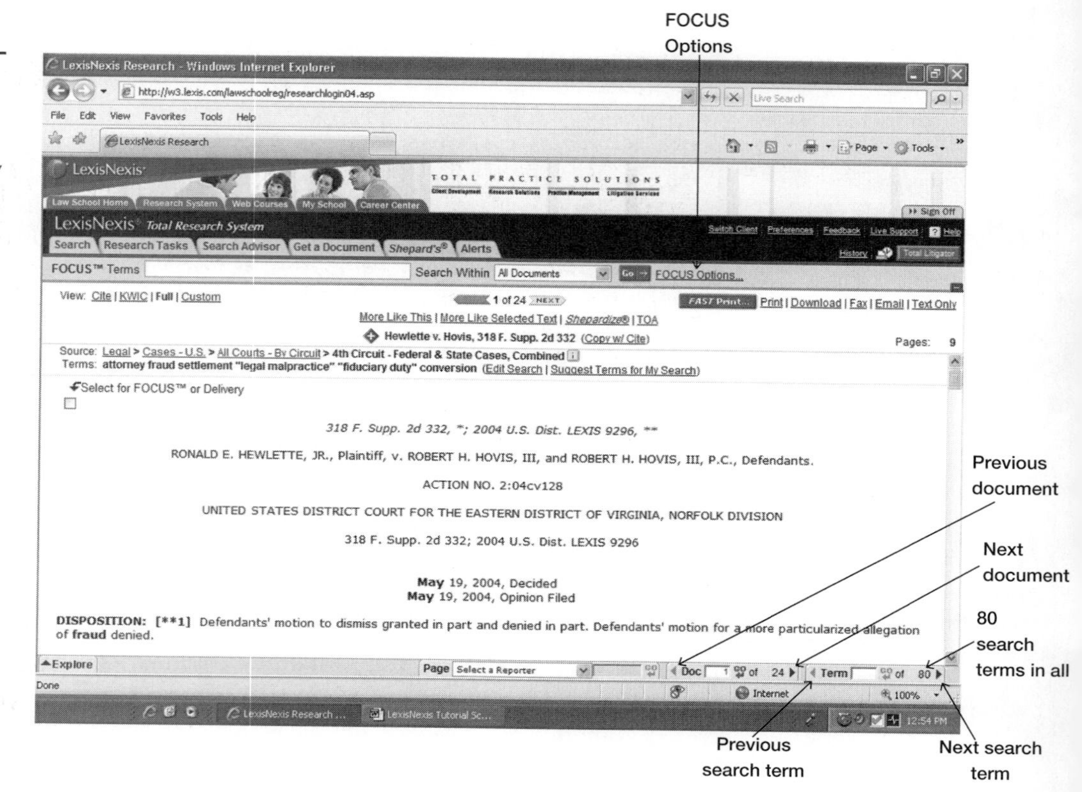

41. *Click the left arrow next to Doc to go back to the* **Hewlette** *case.*

42. *Click the Search tab in the upper left of the screen.*

This concludes Lesson 3 of the LexisNexis Hands-On Exercises. To quit LexisNexis, click Sign Off on the toolbar, or stay in LexisNexis and go to Lesson 4.

LESSON 4: TERMS AND CONNECTORS SEARCH

In this lesson you will learn how to search using terms and connectors, use Suggest Terms for My Search, print a list of cases, and use the FOCUS tool. If you did not exit LexisNexis after completing Lesson 3, go directly to Step 6 below.

1. Start Windows.

2. Start your Internet browser. Type **http://www.Lexis.com** in the browser and press **[ENTER]**.

3. At the ID field, **type the Lexis ID supplied by your instructor.**

4. At the Password field, **enter the Lexis password supplied by your instructor.**

5. *Click Sign On* to sign on to LexisNexis.

6. *Click the Research System tab.*

7. Your screen should now look similar to LexisNexis Exhibit 1. If your screen does not look like LexisNexis Exhibit 1, click the Search tab all the way over to the left, just under LexisNexis Total Research System (see LexisNexis Exhibit 1). LexisNexis is highly customizable, so it is possible that your screens might look different than the screens in the exhibits.

8. You will again look for cases in federal court where an attorney committed fraud by retaining settlement funds for a client in litigation and breached his

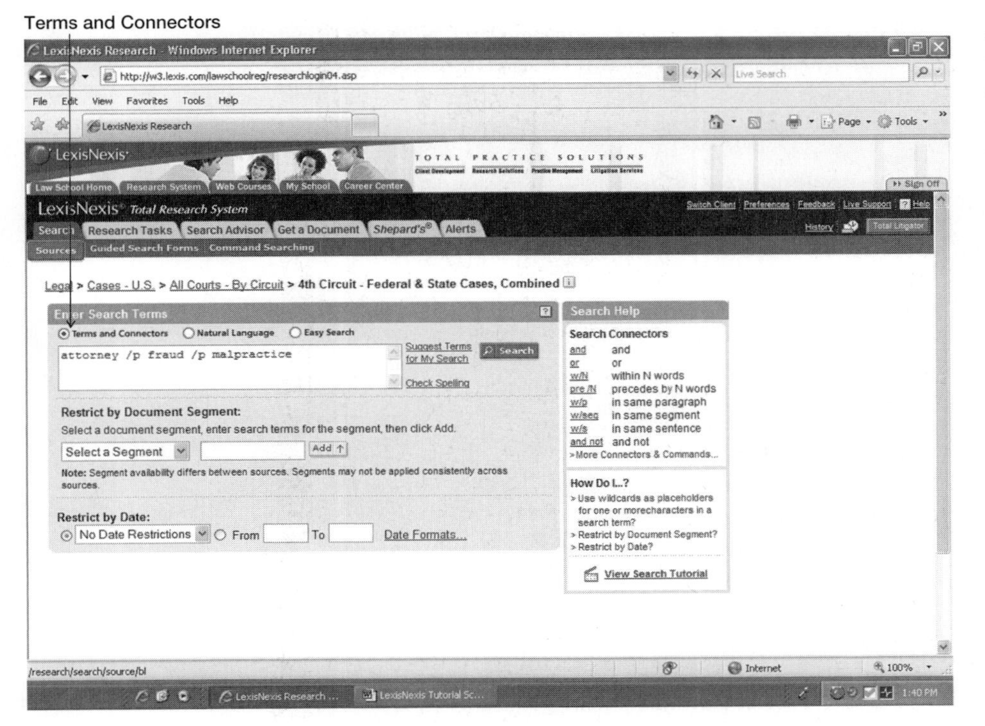

LexisNexis Exhibit 19

fiduciary duty to the client, but this time you will search using Terms and Connectors instead of Natural Language.

9. *Click Cases—U.S.* (see LexisNexis Exhibit 1).

10. *Click All Courts—By Circuit on the right side of the screen.*

11. *Click 4th Circuit—Federal and State Cases, Combined.*

12. *Click Terms and Connectors.*

13. *Click in the search box. Use the [DELETE] key to delete any text in the search box.*

14. *In the search box type* **attorney /p fraud /p malpractice,** *and then click Search* (see LexisNexis Exhibit 19).

15. LexisNexis should return more than two hundred cases. This is too many cases to look through. By using "/s" (within a sentence) and adding search terms, you can limit the number of cases that are retrieved.

16. *Click Edit Search, just above the first case.*

17. *In the search box, modify the query to read* **attorney or lawyer /s fraud /p malpractice /p "fiduciary duty" /p conversion,** *and then click Suggest Terms for My Search* (just to the left of "Search"—see LexisNexis Exhibit 20). You will use this feature to search for synonyms to refine your search.

18. Notice that a number of synonyms are now listed under Suggested Words and Concepts for Entered Terms (see LexisNexis Exhibit 20).

19. *Click in the search field and delete "/p fiduciary duty."*

20. *Next, click "breach of fiduciary duty" under Suggested Words and Concepts for Entered Terms. Add "/p" in front of "breach of fiduciary duty."*

LexisNexis Exhibit 20

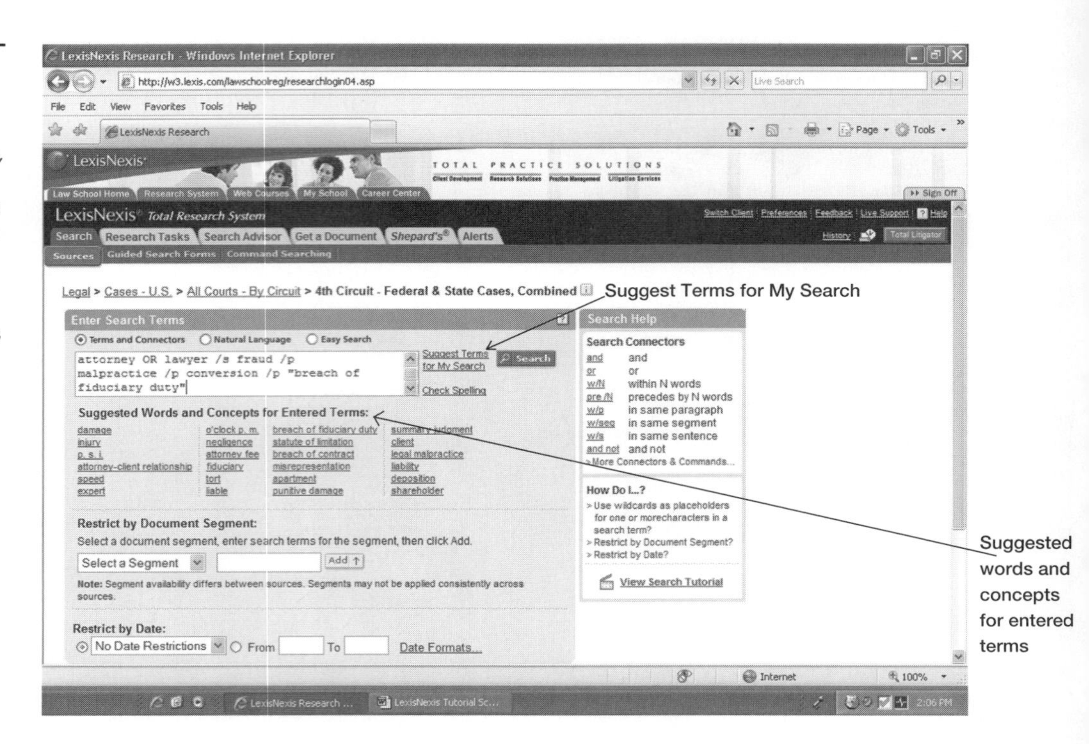

21. Your terms and connector search should now read **attorney OR lawyer /s fraud /p malpractice /p conversion /p "breach of fiduciary duty"** (see LexisNexis Exhibit 20).

22. ***Click Search.***

23. LexisNexis should return with fewer than fifteen cases, and one of the cases should be *Hewlette v. Hovis*.

24. You will now send the results to your printer. ***Click Print*** in the upper right corner of the screen.

25. The Deliver Documents—Print window should now be displayed. ***Select the printer you would like to print to, and then click Print.***

26. You will now learn how to use the FOCUS feature. Because your case deals with a settlement, you would now like to search the cases you retrieved for "settlement" to further cull them. This is particularly helpful when your initial search has retrieved many relevant cases.

27. ***Click "FOCUS Options. . ." just above FAST Print in the upper right corner of the screen (see LexisNexis Exhibit 18).***

28. ***Delete everything in the search field, and then type*** **settlement** (see LexisNexis Exhibit 21).

29. ***Next, in the Search Within field, click the circle next to All Documents*** (see LexisNexis Exhibit 21). ***Then, click FOCUS at the bottom of the screen.***

30. The number of cases should now be reduced. ***Click Show Hits in the top middle of the screen.*** Notice that the word "settlement" is now highlighted, because it was your search term. The *Hewlette v. Hovis* case should be one of the cases that remain.

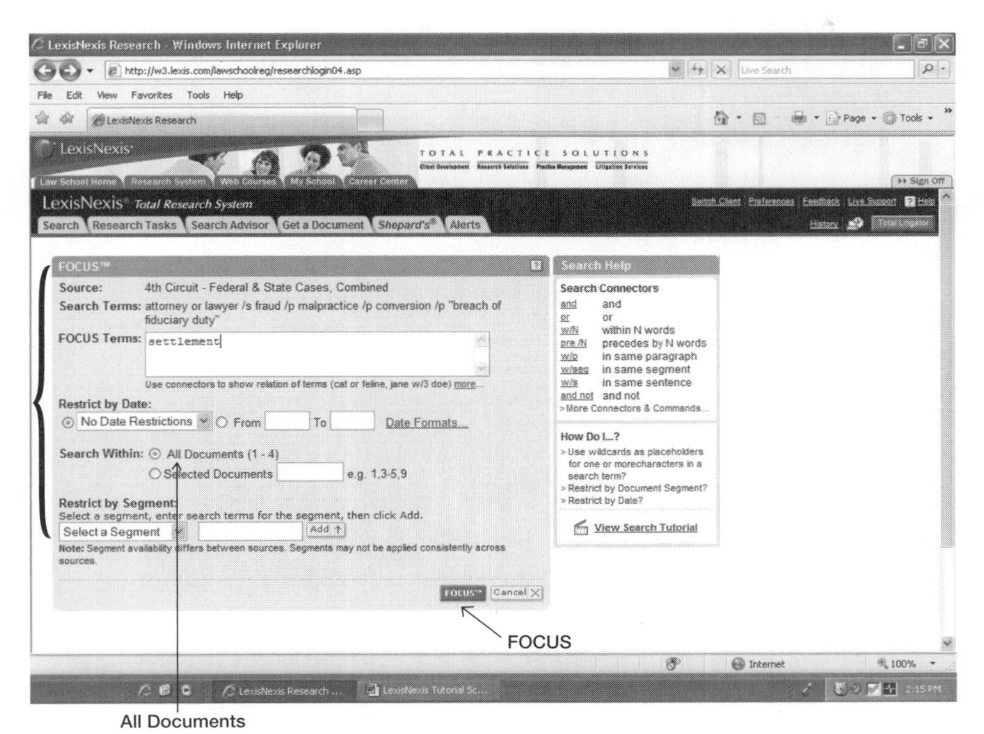

LexisNexis Exhibit 21

31. ***Click Exit FOCUS to the left, just above the first case, to return to the original cases that were retrieved.***

32. *Scroll down and click the* **Hewlette v. Hovis** *case*. Notice that this is the same case that was retrieved using the Natural Language search in the previous hands-on exercise.

33. ***Scroll down just below the Case Summary*** and notice the heading "LexisNexis Headnotes." If you do not see the Headnote, ***click Show Headnotes, just to the right of LexisNexis Headnotes.***

34. You should see eleven Headnotes for the case.

35. Look at Headnote 2 ("In Virginia, under both statutory and common law, an attorney is liable to the client for damages caused by the attorney's neglect of his duties as an attorney" see LexisNexis Exhibit 22).

36. Suppose that this was the issue that you were researching. To expand your research, you could click More Like This Headnote.

37. The More Like This Headnote screen is displayed (see LexisNexis Exhibit 23).

38. ***Click the circle next to Combined Federal Courts: All Federal Courts*** (see LexisNexis Exhibit 23).

39. ***Then, click Search at the bottom of the screen.***

40. Notice that additional cases with similar Headnotes are retrieved. Headnotes are a quick and convenient way of expanding your research.

41. ***Click your browser's Back button twice.*** You should now be back to the screen shown in LexisNexis Exhibit 22.

LexisNexis Exhibit 22

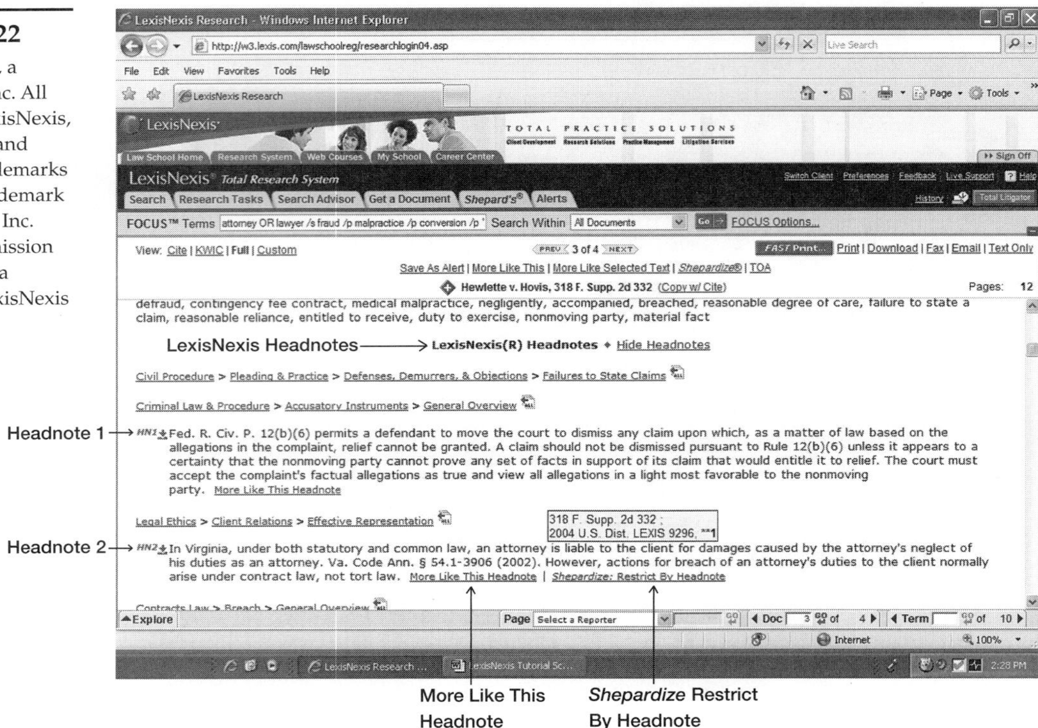

42. *Now, click on* **Shepardize:** ***Restrict by Headnote next to Headnote*** **2 (HN2)** (see LexisNexis Exhibit 22). This feature shows cases that have cited *Heweltte* and that have the same Headnote.

This concludes Lesson 4 of the LexisNexis Hands-on Exercises. To quit LexisNexis, click Sign Off on the toolbar, or stay in LexisNexis and go to Lesson 5.

LexisNexis Exhibit 23

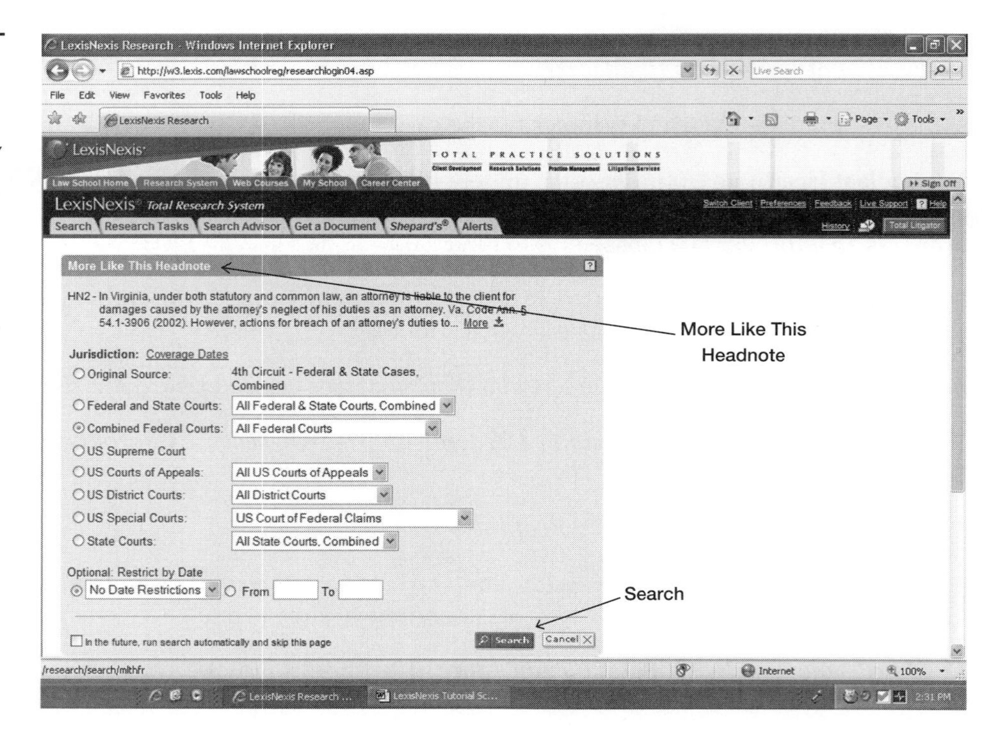

LESSON 5: *SHEPARD'S* CITATIONS

In this lesson, you will learn how to Shepardize a case, and use the Table of Authorities, Auto-Cite, and *Shepard's* Alert features. If you did not exit LexisNexis after completing Lesson 4, go directly to Step 6 below.

1. Start Windows.

2. Start your Internet browser. Type **http://www.Lexis.com** in the browser and press **[ENTER]**.

3. At the ID field, **type the Lexis ID supplied by your instructor.**

4. At the Password field, **type the Lexis password supplied by your instructor.**

5. ***Click Sign On*** to sign on to LexisNexis.

6. ***Click the Research System tab.***

7. Your screen should now look similar to LexisNexis Exhibit 1. If your screen does not look like LexisNexis Exhibit 1, click the Search tab all the way over to the left, just under LexisNexis Total Research System (see LexisNexis Exhibit 1). LexisNexis is highly customizable, so it is possible that your screens might look different than the screens in the exhibits.

8. ***Click the Shepard's tab at the top of the screen.***

9. ***Click the Shepard's sub-tab*** (see LexisNexis Exhibit 24). ***Click the option* Shepard's *For Research*** (see LexisNexis Exhibit 24). The *Hewlette v. Hovis* case, 318 F. Supp. 2d 332, should already be entered, but if it is not, type **318 F. Supp. 2d 332.**

10. ***Then, click Check.***

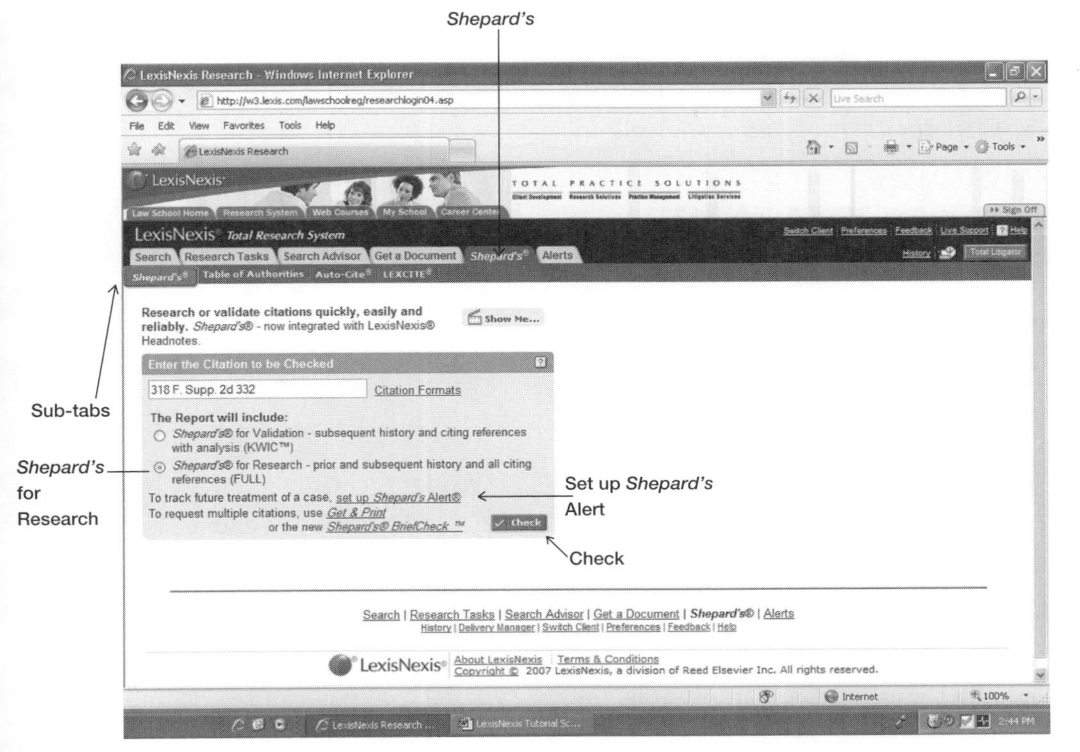

LexisNexis Exhibit 24

LexisNexis Exhibit 25

11. A screen similar to LexisNexis Exhibit 25 should be displayed. Notice in LexisNexis Exhibit 25 that *Shepard's* shows the blue diamond with a white "+"(plus sign) symbol for the *Hewlette v. Hovis* case.

12. ***Scroll down and notice that this symbol means that the* Hewlette *case has had positive treatment.***

13. Also, notice in LexisNexis Exhibit 25 that four other cases have cited the *Hewlette* case.

14. ***Click the Shepard's tab at the top of the page.***

15. ***Click the Table of Authorities sub-tab.***

16. The *Hewlette v. Hovis* case, 318 F. Supp. 2d 332, should already be entered but if it is not, type **318 F. Supp. 2d 332**.

17. ***Then, click Check.***

18. The Table of Authorities feature allows you to see a summary of all of the law cited by your cases by jurisdiction.

19. ***Click your browser's Back button.***

20. ***Click the Auto-Cite sub-tab.***

21. The *Hewlette v. Hovis* case, 318 F. Supp. 2d 332, should already be entered but if it is not, type **318 F. Supp. 2d 332.**

22. ***Then, click Check.***

23. Auto-Cite gives you the procedural history of your case, the full case name, and other information. For example, for the *Hewlette* case you can see its procedural history, including whether it was appealed and other information.

24. ***Click the Shepard's tab, and then click the Shepard's sub-tab.***

25. The *Hewlette v. Hovis* case, 318 F. Supp. 2d 332, should already be entered but if it is not, type **318 F. Supp. 2d 332.**

26. Notice that one of the options just to the left of Check is Set Up *Shepard's* Alert (see LexisNexis Exhibit 24).

27. ***Click Set Up* Shepard's *Alert*** (see LexisNexis Exhibit 24).

28. At the Create a New *Shepard's* Alert screen, ***click Set Up.***

29. You should now see the Set Up a *Shepard's* Alert screen.

30. This allows you to monitor changes in cases as they are appealed and work their way through the court system. You can automatically run a *Shepard's* Alert at stated frequencies, such as weekly or monthly, and have the changes emailed to you or made available to you online.

31. ***Click Cancel.***

32. ***Click the Search tab.***

This concludes the LexisNexis Hands-on Exercises. To quit LexisNexis, click Sign Off on the toolbar.

CHAPTER 

THE ELECTRONIC COURTHOUSE, AUTOMATED COURTROOM, AND PRESENTATION GRAPHICS

CHAPTER OBJECTIVES

After completing Chapter 12, you should be able to do the following:

1. Explain what the "Electronic Courthouse" is.
2. Describe how an automated courtroom works.
3. Describe what presentation graphics software does.
4. Explain how presentation graphics software can be used in the legal environment.

The courthouses of the past, with paper files and manual systems, have changed. Electronic courthouses with the electronic filing of court documents and access to court records, dockets, files, and other data via the Internet are a reality in many jurisdictions. Courtrooms have changed as well. In many jurisdictions, automated courtrooms have evidence display systems including computers and monitors for the judge, attorneys, court reporter, jurors, and the public. In these automated courtrooms presentation graphics and trial presentation software are used to present evidence to the court and jurors electronically, using computers and monitors. The presentations can include text, photographs, video, animation, sound, clip art, recreations, and much more.

THE ELECTRONIC COURTHOUSE

The notion of the local courthouse where legal professionals must mail or hand file documents and access court records and court files using manual methods is rapidly disappearing. In many jurisdictions legal professionals can now instantly file motions, briefs, and other documents electronically and can instantly access court dockets and court records using the Internet. With electronic filing, courts accept electronic versions of legal documents via the Internet or other electronic means instead of requiring the hard copy of the document.

> *Nothing is more certain in the world of court administration than the fact that paper will ultimately vanish and the electronic filing (e-filing) of documents will one day be universal...*[1]

The federal district and bankruptcy courts have been on the cutting edge of this technology for several years. As of this writing, the Case Management/ Electronic Case Filing (CM/ECF) system is used in 98 percent of the federal courts: 92 district courts, 93 bankruptcy courts, the Court of International Trade, the Court of Federal Claims, the Court of Appeals for the eighth Circuit, and the Bankruptcy Appellate Panels for the eighth and tenth Circuits. To date, more than 27 million cases are on the CM/ECF system. More than 250,000 legal professionals have filed documents using the Internet and CM/ECF. The plan is for all United States courts to use CM/ECF in the near future.

> *Implementation of the CM/ECF system significantly changed bankruptcy paralegals' day-to-day duties…E-filing allows [paralegals] to retrieve, view and download pleadings, docket sheets, filed case information, claims registers and activity, party information, calendar events, creditor mailing matrixes, and daily summaries, as well as obtain information on newly filed Chapter 7, 11, and 13 bankruptcy and adversary proceedings.*[2]

Filing documents using the system is easy. The user logs onto a court's website with a court-issued password, enters some general information about the case and the document to be filed, and then submits the document to be filed in Portable Document Format (PDF). Once the PDF file is received, a notice of receipt is generated and sent to the user. Other parties to the action then automatically receive an email notifying them of the filing. The CM/ECF system allows courts the option to make their documents accessible to the public over the Internet.

Another federal system, the Public Access to Court Electronic Records (PACER) program, allows the public to access court-related information (see Exhibit 12–1). PACER is an electronic public access service that allows users to obtain a variety of docket and case-related information regarding federal courts using the Internet. Links to all courts are provided from the PACER website. To access PACER, a user must register with the PACER Service Center, have an Internet connection, and log into the system. There is also a small charge for the service. PACER allows users to request information about an individual or case, including:

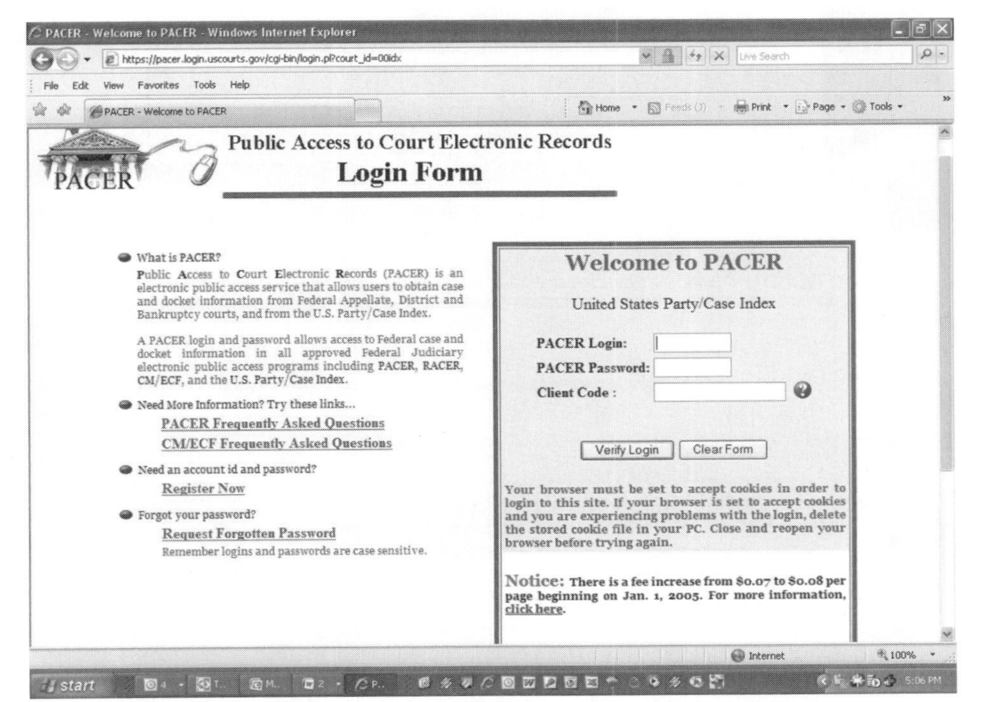

EXHIBIT 12–1
Public Access to Court Electronic Records (PACER)

- Party and participant listings, including attorneys and judges
- General case-related data, including the nature of the lawsuit, the cause(s) of action alleged, and the amount of damages demanded
- A chronology of events/docket items in the case
- The case status
- Judgment(s)

Using PACER, a person can also access the United States Case/Party Index, which allows users to search for party names throughout much of the federal court system. While the federal court system is rapidly nearing the end of its electronic courthouse project, it may take some years for all states to catch up. Some states have completed the move to electronic systems, but many are still in the implementation stages. Traditional roadblocks to these types of systems include cost, standardization issues, security, and obtaining the hardware and software needed to support electronic filing. Like the federal court system, many state courts have selected **Portable Document Format (PDF)** as their standard for filing documents electronically.

Portable Document Format (PDF)
A file format that can be created so the file is read-only, but the file can be printed, saved, and password protected.

The Oklahoma State Courts Network (<http://www.oscn.net>) is a good example of how a state has implemented this technology. The Oklahoma State Courts Network allows users to access court dockets statewide, including the Oklahoma Supreme Court, the Court of Criminal Appeals, the Court of Civil Appeals, and seventy-seven district courts (see Exhibit 12–2).

EXHIBIT 12–2
Internet Access to the Oklahoma State Court Network
Courtesy of the Oklahoma State Court Network.

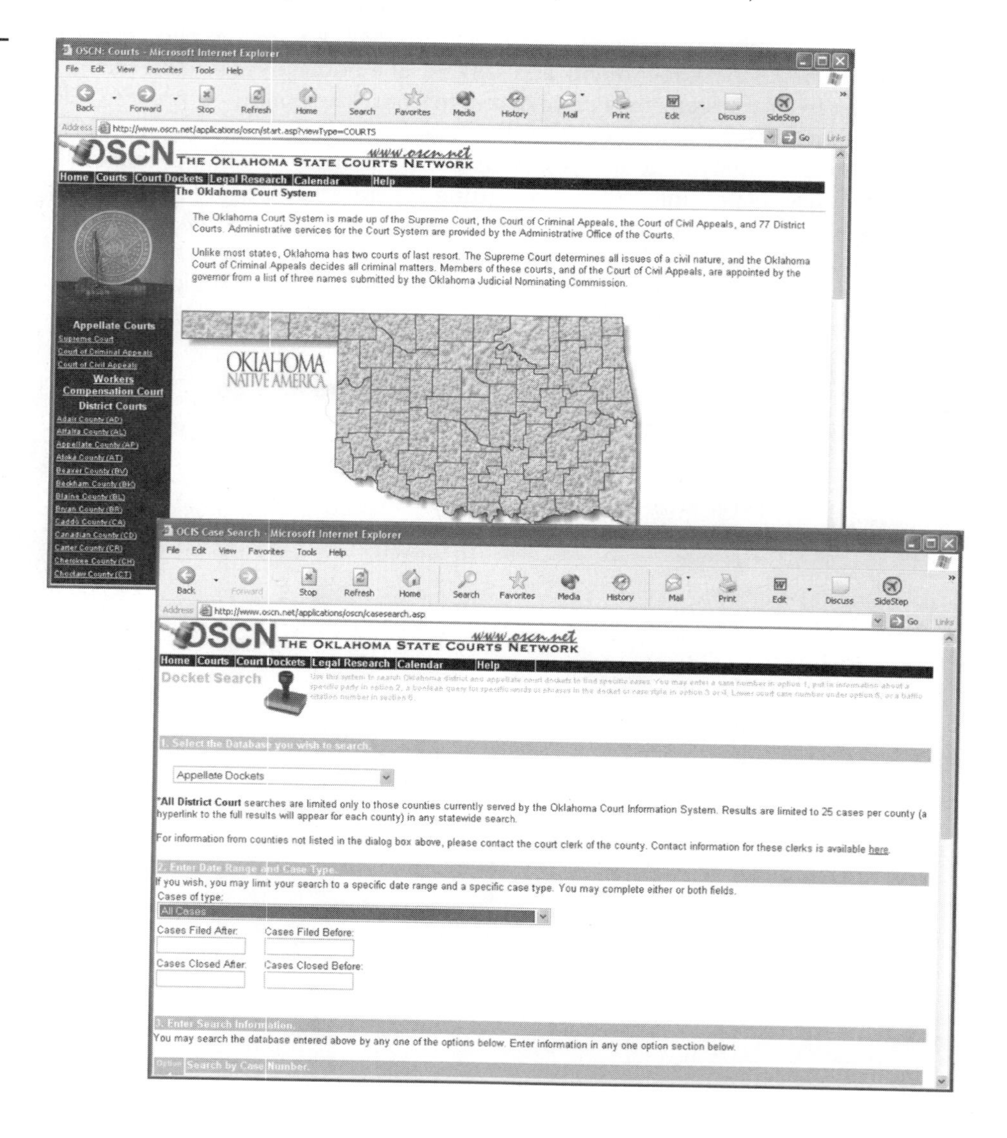

> *I [a practicing legal assistant] have 40 dockets to track in a week and this [Internet access to court dockets/records] works so fast. It probably saves me a couple of hours during my work week... Sometimes I [would] have to sit on the phone for a half hour to speak to a clerk. You used to have to go through hoops to get information. It would take days. Now it's at your fingertips and it takes minutes.*[3]

Electronic services such as WESTLAW and LexisNexis also have access to some court dockets and can electronically track document filings in cases and access court records. Some of these services even automatically alert the legal professional electronically to new filings in cases at intervals such as once a week or twice a week. While a legal organization must pay the vendors for these services (as opposed to getting them free when states or courts implement the program), many legal organizations find it worth the cost.

THE AUTOMATED COURTROOM

In addition to automating access to the courthouse, many courts are also automating their courtrooms (see Exhibit 12–3). Most federal courts have now automated all of their courtrooms nationwide. Most automated courtrooms include evidence display systems, videoconferencing, and real-time court reporting.

EXHIBIT 12–3
The Automated Courtroom
McGlothlin Courtroom, William & Mary Law School Center for Legal and Court Technology.

An **evidence display system** typically provides networked computer monitors to the judge, jurors, court reporter, clerk, attorneys, and the public. The master controls are located at the judge's bench so he or she can control all monitors, sound systems, and/or cameras in the courtroom. The attorneys and/or judge can use the evidence display system to display properly admitted evidence such as images, photographs, video images, animation, and others. Most systems also use a **document camera**, an overhead projector that uses a camera to display hard-copy documents that have not been imaged.

evidence display system
Provides networked computer monitors to a judge, jury, court reporter, clerk, attorneys, and the public.

document camera
An overhead projector that uses a camera to display hard-copy documents that have not been imaged.

Many evidence display systems also support videoconferencing so that if a judge approves the use, an out-of-state witness could testify at a trial and give testimony without being actually present in the courtroom.

Another type of courtroom technology is real-time court reporting. A witness's testimony is transcribed by a court reporter within a few seconds after the witness's testimony. The testimony can be displayed on the courtroom monitors or given to the judge, jurors, or attorneys on a real-time basis.

It is now routine in many trials for attorneys to present opening statements and closing arguments, cross-examine witnesses, and display evidence using electronic means such as presentation graphics and trial presentation software (see Exhibit 12–4). These presentations are made in front of the jury using automated courtroom equipment. The automated courtroom offers many advantages over a manual one. Electronic presentations and evidence can be viewed by everyone in the courtroom simultaneously (so that everyone can see the same thing). Electronic presentations and evidence can simplify complex subjects and add to the ability of judges, jurors, and others to comprehend and understand the issues and facts in a case. For years, educators have known that people remember far more when they can see than when they just hear something. The automated courtroom is also more convenient than manual methods and actually saves court time. For example, if an attorney images all of her exhibits to be admitted for trial, they can then be electronically displayed without having to find and rely on hard-copy documents, which can be lost or misplaced. Computer software that automatically tracks trial exhibits in addition to displaying them using the evidence display system can also save time for everyone involved. In some courts, criminal defendants who are too hostile to appear in court can view the proceedings off site via a live video/audio feed. Using presentation graphics and trial presentation programs, legal professionals are able to get the most out of automated courtroom equipment.

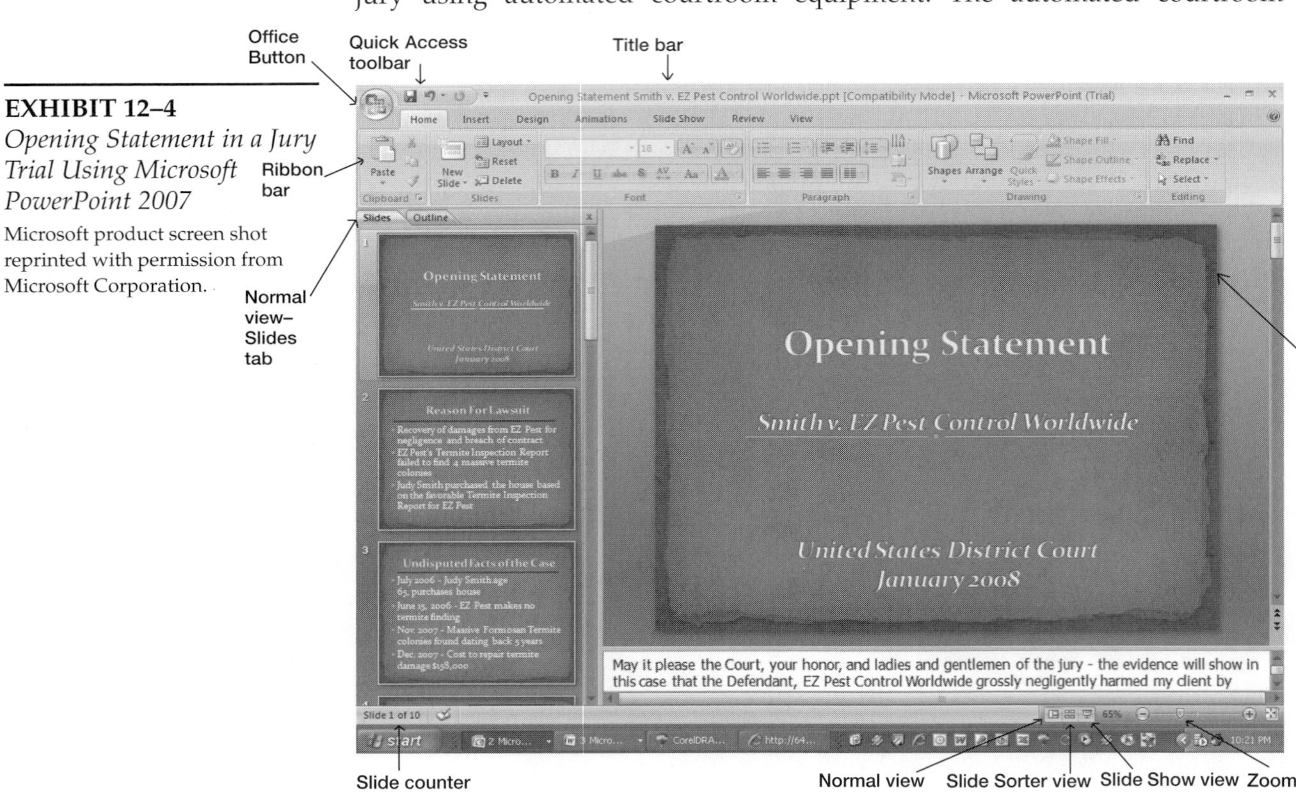

EXHIBIT 12–4

Opening Statement in a Jury Trial Using Microsoft PowerPoint 2007

Microsoft product screen shot reprinted with permission from Microsoft Corporation.

OVERVIEW OF PRESENTATION AND TRIAL PRESENTATION SOFTWARE

Presentation software allows users to create visually interesting electronic presentations. Many legal professionals use generic presentation graphics programs such as Microsoft PowerPoint to create presentations for trials, exhibits, graphs and charts, and presentations for internal training purposes. Presentation software can combine a number of elements to create visually interesting presentations including text, color, video, animation, clip art, graphs, charts, and sound. Presentation software is used to build a presentation by organizing the material involved (evidence, transcripts, images, and/or photographs) into individual slides so the speaker can show it all at one time or control the timing of the presentation slides using a remote control. Most presentation programs also can create outlines and speaker's notes.

presentation software Software that allows users to create visually interesting presentations using graphics, color, sound, video, text, animation, and clip art.

In addition to generic presentation programs, there are also **trial presentation programs** that have been specifically designed to meet the needs of practicing attorneys, particularly those that try cases to juries and courts.

trial presentation programs Presentation graphics programs that are specifically designed to meet the needs of trial attorneys.

Microsoft PowerPoint has a majority of the legal assistant market share for presentation programs. Notice in Exhibit 12–5 that two other programs, TrialDirector and Sanction have a smaller share of the market. Both of these programs are trial presentation programs and are designed specifically for the legal market.

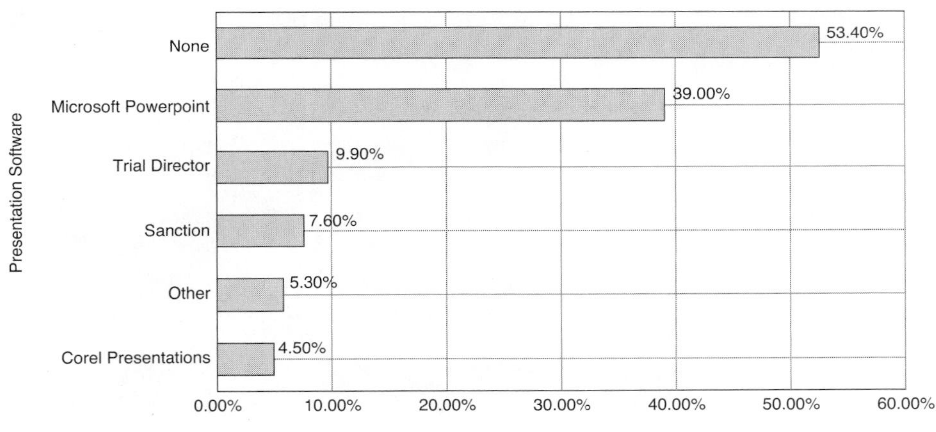

EXHIBIT 12–5
Presentation Software Used by Legal Assistants
As seen in the May/June 2006 issue of Legal Assistant Today, copyright 2006 James Publishing, Inc. Reprinted courtesy of LEGAL ASSISTANT TODAY magazine. For subscription information call (800) 394–2626, or visit www.legalassistanttoday.com.

Trial presentation programs can do much more than just display electronic slides. Some trial presentation programs can manage documents, including maintaining document abstracts and tracking who admitted the document (plaintiff or defendant); the Bates number of the document; the date the document was admitted into evidence; the witness that was on the stand when the document was admitted; the status of the document, including whether the document's introduction was objected to; and other information (see Exhibit 12–6). Even in relatively small cases, managing and tracking documents in a trial, including tracking what documents have been admitted, when they were admitted, whether objections were made, and similar information, can be difficult and time consuming. Trial presentation programs can automate that process in addition to displaying electronic documents.

Trial presentation programs can manage complex tasks, such as creating slides that present video / audio, graphs, and documents into a single slide or individually (see Exhibit 12–7). Trial presentation software also can synchronize the playback of video / audio with a transcript of prior testimony so a fact finder can not only read the words of the transcript but can also see and hear the

EXHIBIT 12–6
Some Trial Presentation Programs Can Manage Documents
inData Corporation.

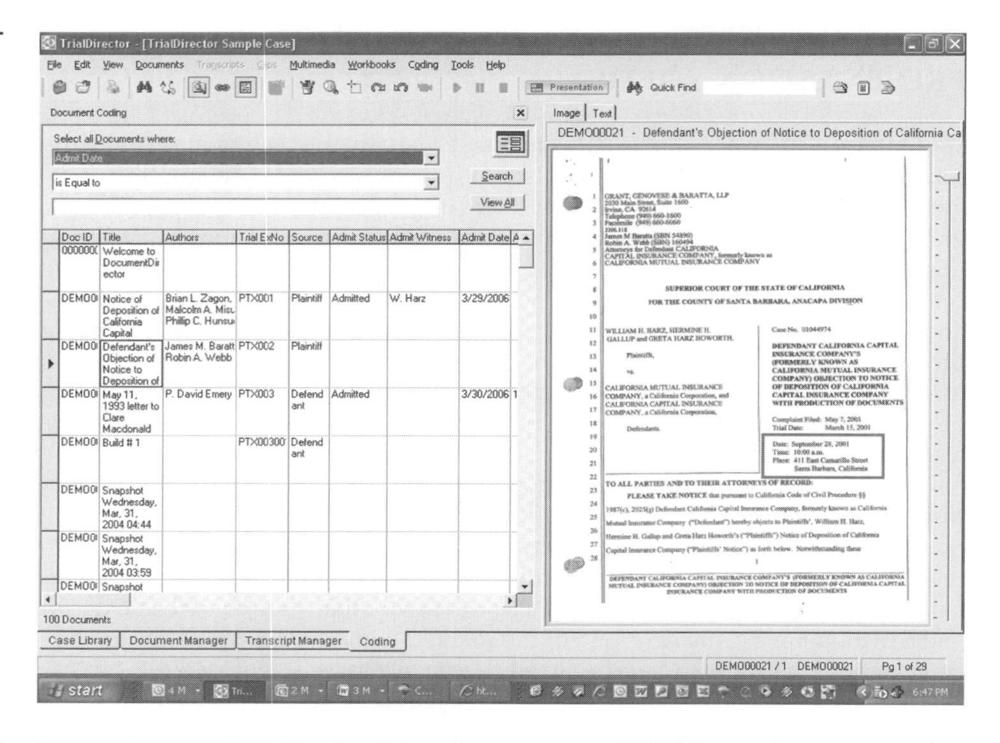

EXHIBIT 12–7
Trial Presentation Software Can Manager Video, Charts and Documents
inData Corporation.

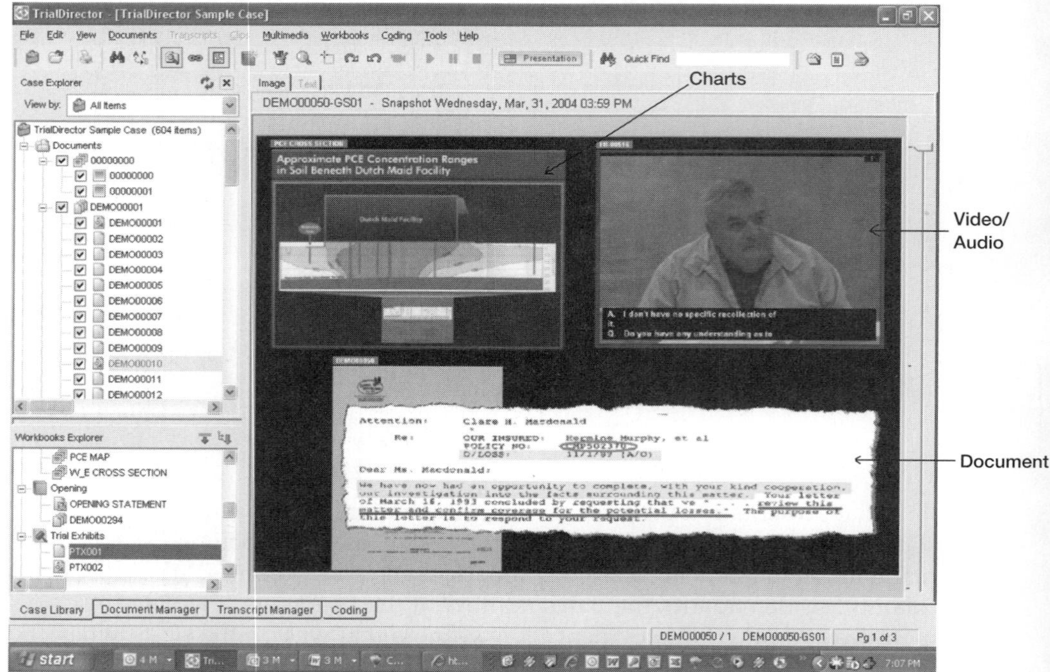

witness speaking the words. This is usually done to discredit a witness when their testimony at trial is substantially different than testimony given during a taped deposition (see Exhibit 12–8). Trial presentation programs can display presentations in applications such as Microsoft PowerPoint (see Exhibit 12–9). Trial presentation programs can also assemble separate presentations for a case into one file or into files that are linked together. Notice that in Exhibit 12–9 the user has created separate presentations for a case, including documents that have been admitted, closing argument, opening statement, trial exhibits, and presentations for each witness. Trial presentation programs allow a user to manage content like this in one convenient place.

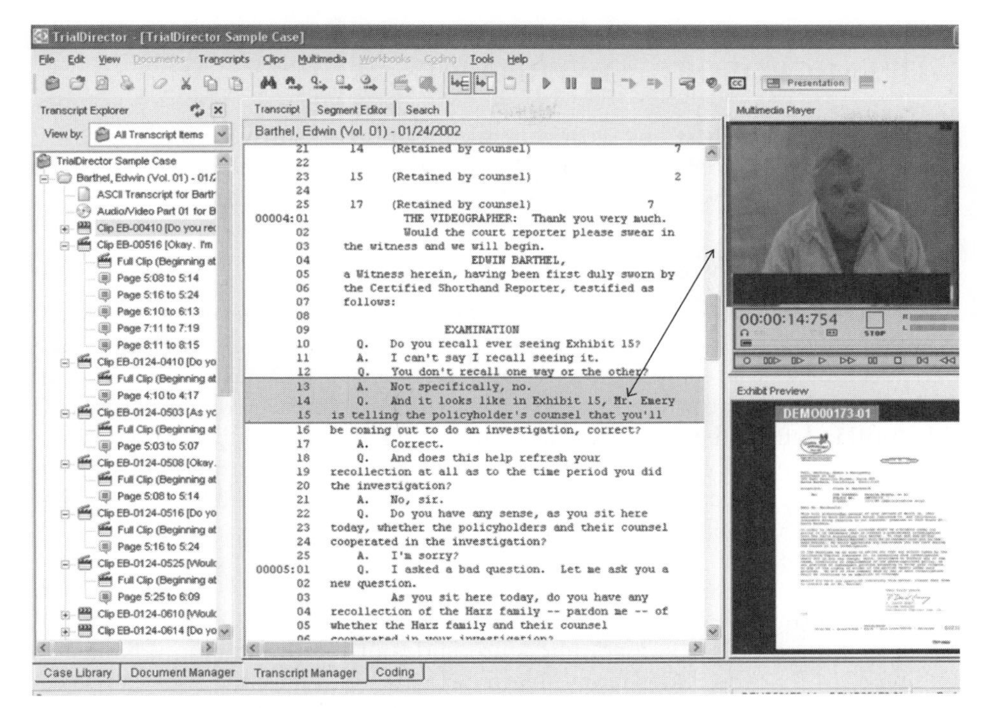

EXHIBIT 12–8
Trial Presentation Software Can Synchronize Transcripts and Video / Audio
inData Corporation.

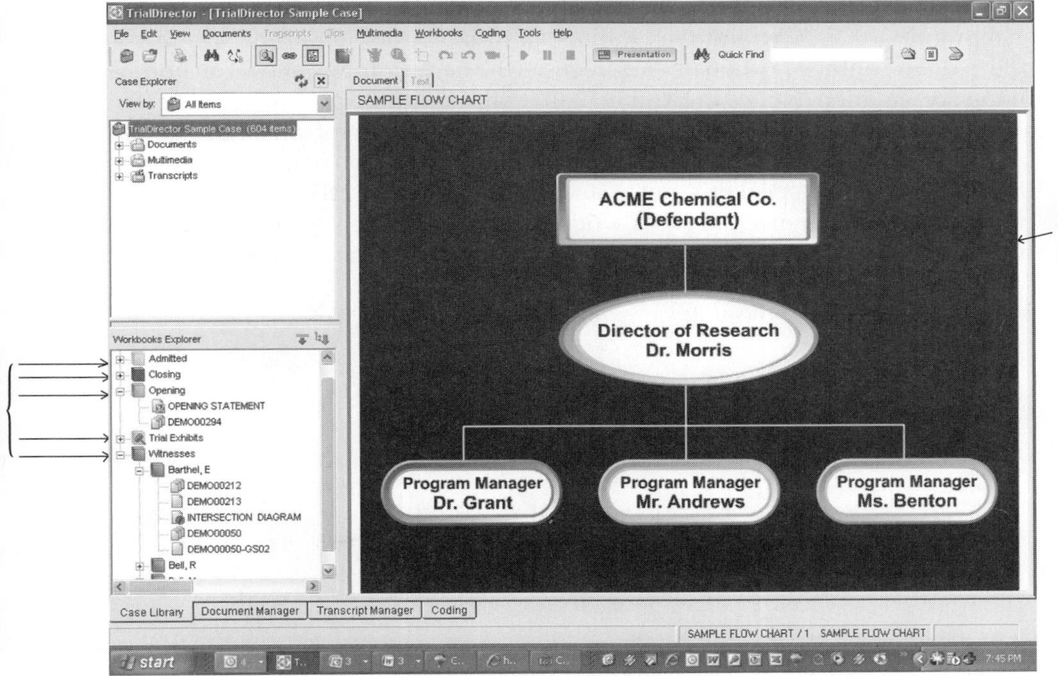

PowerPoint Type Presentation

EXHIBIT 12–9
Trial Presentation Software Can Display Presentations
inData Corporation.

Also, trial presentation programs can access data nonsequentially. PowerPoint works well when everything is linear and goes from beginning to end. However, most trials do not proceed this way. Attorneys need to be able to produce a particular document on a moment's notice. Trial presentation programs can access data quickly and conveniently, unlike PowerPoint. In addition, most trial presentation programs have the ability to search the trial database and access data quickly and efficiently. Generally speaking, trial presentation programs are quite powerful and are generally better suited to most trial purposes than a generic presentation program.

CREATING LEGAL PRESENTATIONS WITH MICROSOFT POWERPOINT

Creating legal presentations with general presentation software like Microsoft PowerPoint is easy to do. In this chapter, an opening statement for a case will be created that will show the interface of Microsoft PowerPoint 2007.

The Screen and Views

Exhibit 12–4 shows the title page for the opening statement presentation. Notice that, as in any Microsoft Office 2007 program, the ribbon bar, Office Button, title bar, and Quick Access toolbar are displayed. In Exhibit 12–4, the slide counter in the lower left of the screen shows that the user is on the first of ten slides. This is helpful in letting the user know at all times where she is in the presentation.

In the lower left corner, three icons are displayed. These three icons represent the different ways the user can view or see this presentation, including Normal view, Slide Sorter view, and Slide Show view.

normal view
Shows the slide that is being created, an outline of the total presentation, and speaker's notes for the slide that is being shown.

Normal View The Normal view for this particular program is shown in Exhibit 12–4. The **normal view** shows the slide that is being created. On the left side of the screen are the first, second, and third slides of the presentation. Notice in Exhibit 12–4 that the Slides tab is selected. In Normal view the user can select either Slides or the Outline display mode (see the upper left of Exhibit 12–4). Exhibit 12–10 shows the second slide of the presentation; this time the slide is shown in Normal view and the Outline tab in the upper left of the window is selected. The outline portion of the screen, as the name implies, shows an outline of the presentation. Notice in Exhibit 12–10 that the outline portion of the screen shows some of the same information contained in the current slide but without any graphic elements. Also, in Exhibit 12–10 there is a section of the screen where the user can enter speaker's notes about that particular slide. These can be printed out for reference purposes when the user is ready to give the presentation. Speaker's notes can be created for each slide of the presentation.

EXHIBIT 12–10
Microsoft PowerPoint: Normal View—Outline mode

Microsoft product screen shot reprinted with permission from Microsoft Corporation.

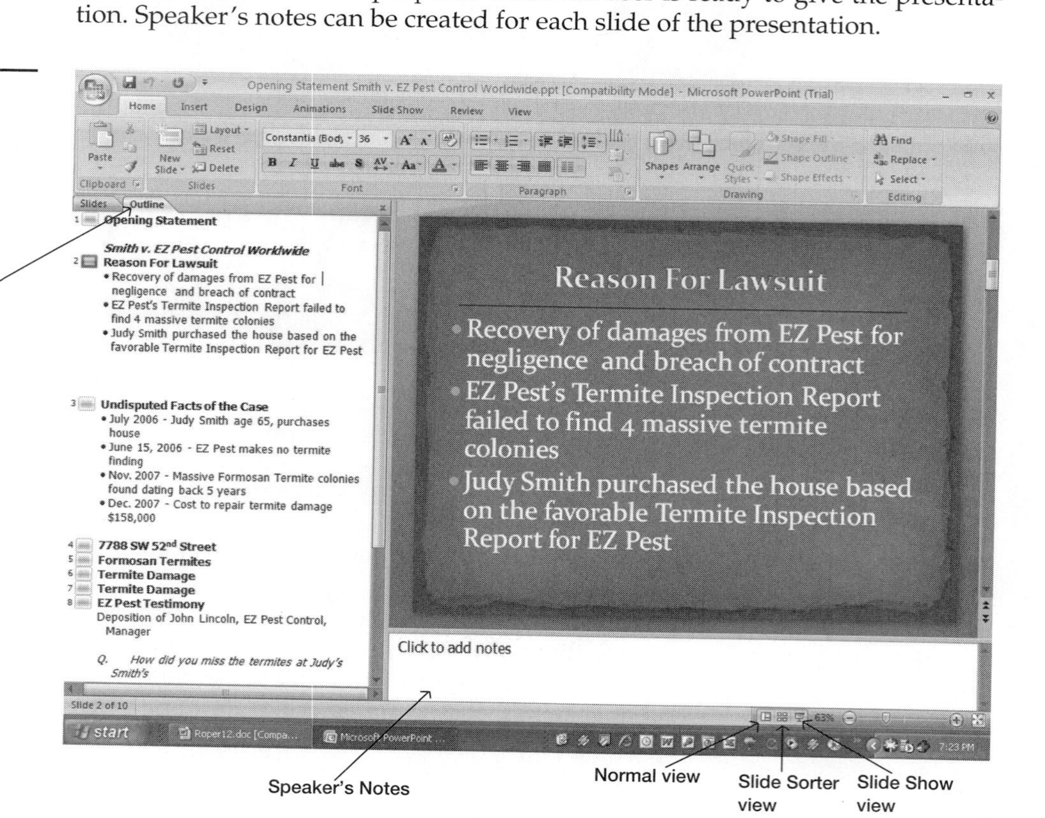

Slide Sorter View The **slide sorter view** shows the slides in the presentation, but in a greatly reduced format. Notice in Exhibit 12–11 that all ten slides of the presentation are shown at one time. The slide sorter view is typically used to change the order of slides. For example, to move slide eight in front of slide three, the user would simply click on slide eight and drag it in front of slide three. The slider sorter view gives the user a big picture of the presentation and allows the user to easily organize or reorganize the presentation.

slide sorter view
Shows the slides in the presentation, but in a greatly reduced format. The slide sorter view is typically used to change the order of slides.

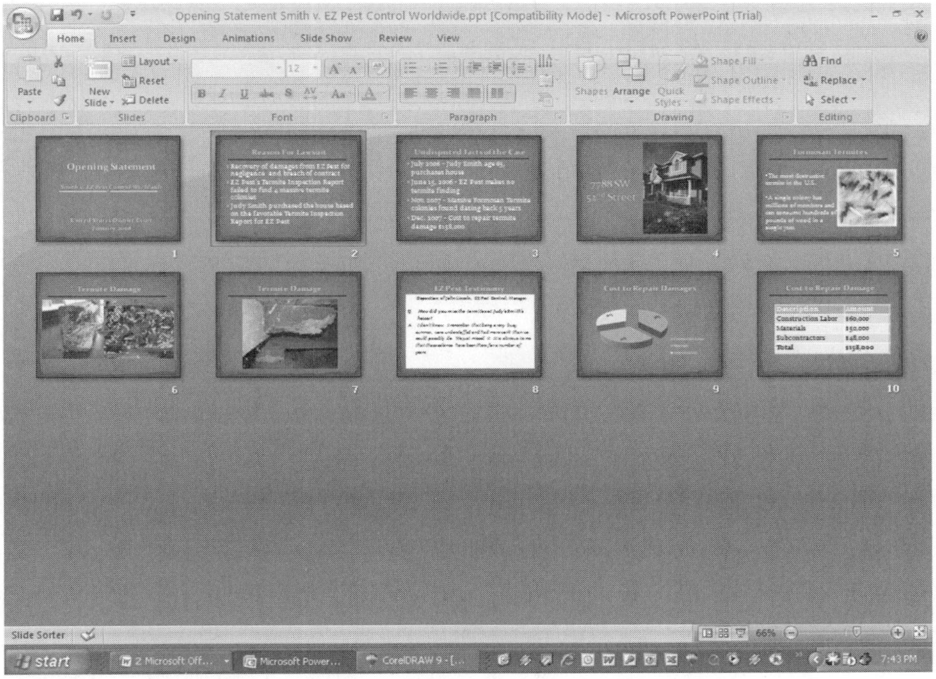

EXHIBIT 12–11
Microsoft PowerPoint:Slide Sorter View
Microsoft product screen shot reprinted with permission from Microsoft Corporation.

Slide Show View The **slide show view** is used during a presentation or when the user is developing the presentation and wants to see how the audience will actually see the slide. Notice in Exhibit 12–12 that the only thing shown on the screen is the slide itself. The program interface, outline, and speaker's notes are not shown.

slide show view
Used during a presentation or when the user is developing the presentation to see how the audience will actually see the slide. Only the current slide is shown on the screen. The program interface, menus, outline view and speaker's notes are not shown.

Backgrounds, Adding Slides, and Formatting a Presentation

The first step in creating a presentation is to select the background. The **background** is the design on which the other elements of the presentation (words, clip art, etc.) will be placed. It is similar to the canvas in a painting. PowerPoint comes with several predesigned backgrounds for users to choose from. Users can also create their own backgrounds or can select backgrounds from Microsoft Office Online.

background
The design on which the other elements of the presentation (words, clip art, etc.) are placed.

The next step in creating a presentation is to add slides. PowerPoint 2007 has a new slide command found on the Home ribbon (see Exhibit 12–13). The new slide command gives the user a menu of different automatic formats for creating a slide (see Exhibit 12–13). These automatic formats make it easy for a user to select a format and then quickly begin entering the information.

Photographs, Clip Art, Word Art, Smart Art

PowerPoint allows users to include clip art, photographs, word art, and smart art in presentations. **Clip art** is predrawn art. Users should be careful in adding clip art to trial and professional legal presentations because some clip art diminishes the professional appearance of the presentation. Notice that the presentation in Exhibit 12–14 includes several clear, high-impact photographs. High-quality

clip art
Predrawn art.

EXHIBIT 12–12
Microsoft Slide Show View
Microsoft product screen shot reprinted with permission from Microsoft Corporation.

Undisputed Facts of the Case

- July 2006 - Judy Smith age 65, purchases house
- June 15, 2006 - EZ Pest makes no termite finding
- Nov. 2007 - Massive Formosan Termite colonies found dating back 5 years
- Dec. 2007 - Cost to repair termite damage $158,000

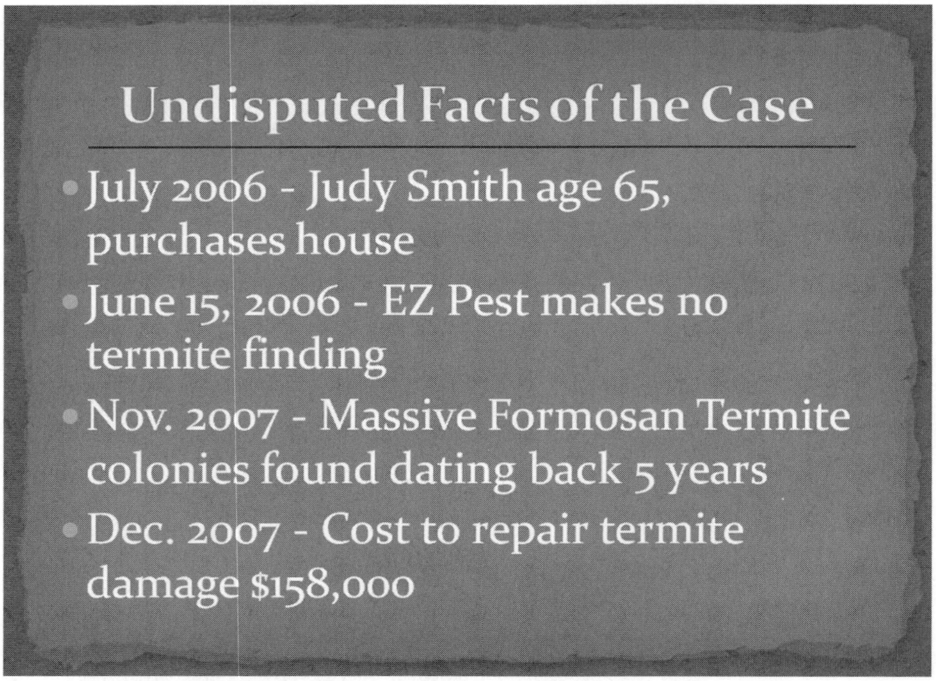

EXHIBIT 12–13
Options for Adding a New Slide
Microsoft product screen shot reprinted with permission from Microsoft Corporation.

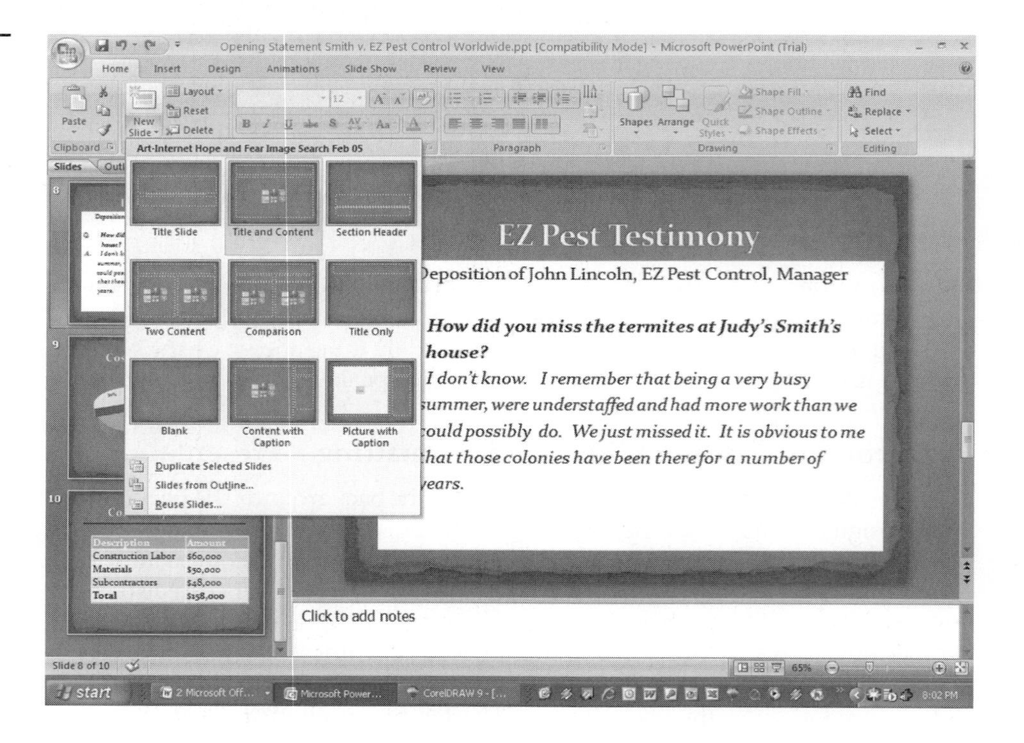

word art
Allows a user to add special formatting to text, including 3-D designs.

smart art
Predrawn graphical elements such as diagrams, process flow charts, and graphical lists.

photographs can enhance the professionalism of a presentation and create visual/impact. **Word art** allows a user to add special formatting to text, including 3-D designs (see Exhibit 12–15). **Smart art** is predrawn graphical elements such as diagrams, process flow charts, and graphical lists (see Exhibit 12–15).

Graphs / Charts

Graphs and charts can also be created in PowerPoint, either as stand-alone elements (such as a graph for a case) or as part of a presentation. Notice in

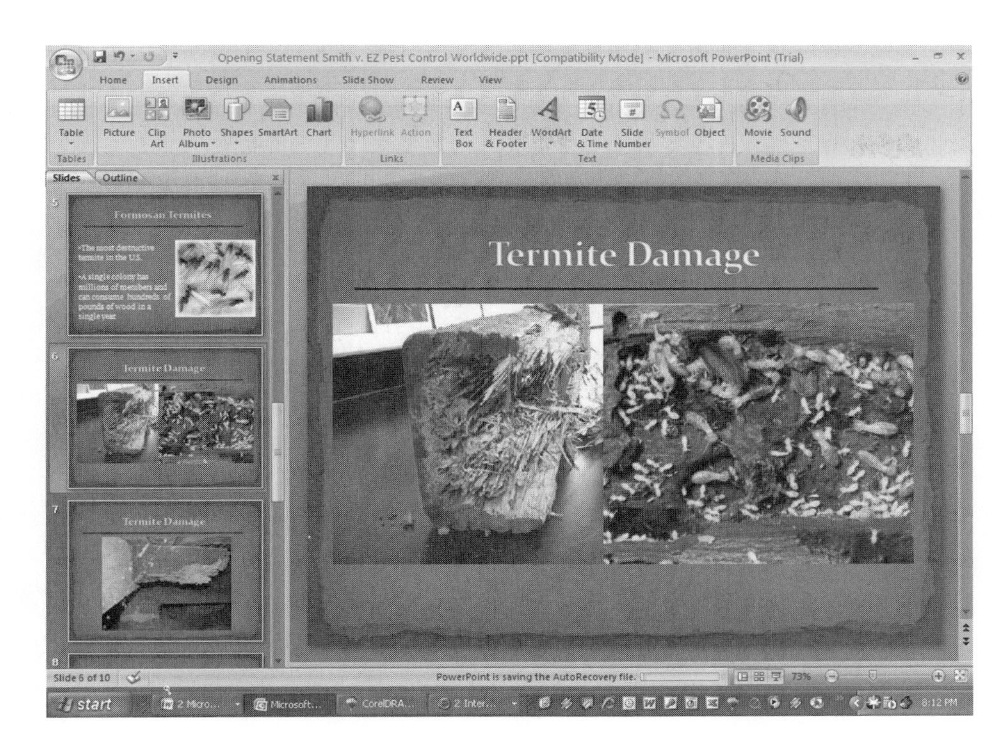

EXHIBIT 12–14
Adding Photographs to a Presentation
Microsoft product screen shot reprinted with permission from Microsoft Corporation.

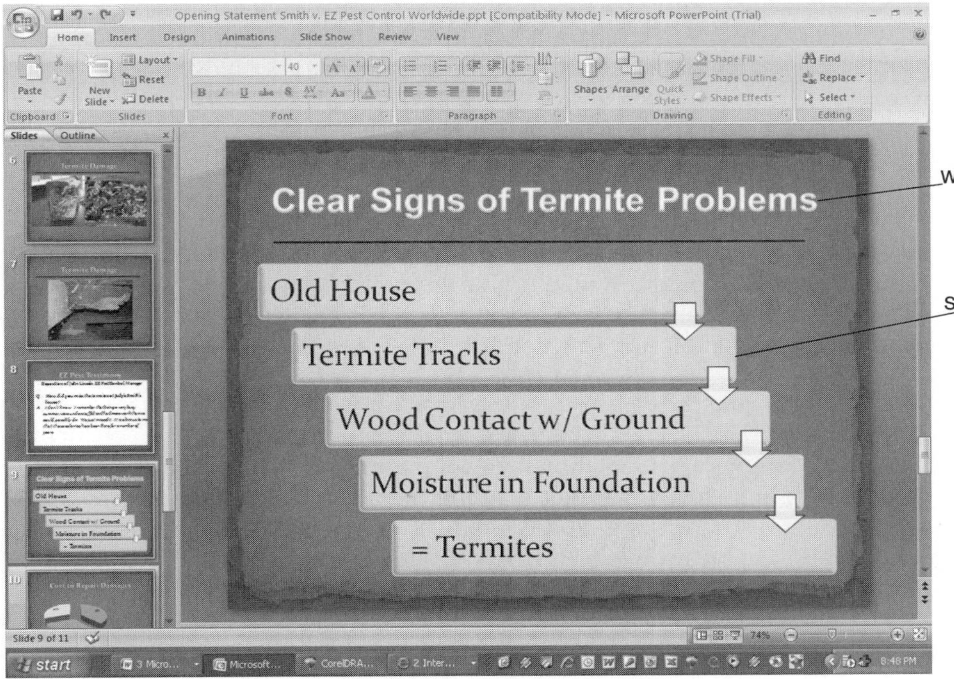

EXHIBIT 12–15
Smart Art & Word Art
Microsoft product screen shot reprinted with permission from Microsoft Corporation.

Exhibit 12–16 that the graph has the same background as the rest of the presentation and that it is in 3-D. PowerPoint provides a wide variety of graphs and charts to choose from, including column charts, bar graphs, and pie charts.

Multimedia, Transition, and Animation Effects

Multimedia effects such as sound files and video clips can also be added to presentations, so that sound and video will run whenever the slide is displayed. This can add interest and excitement to a presentation.

EXHIBIT 12–16
Graph / Charts in PowerPoint
Microsoft product screen shot reprinted with permission from Microsoft Corporation.

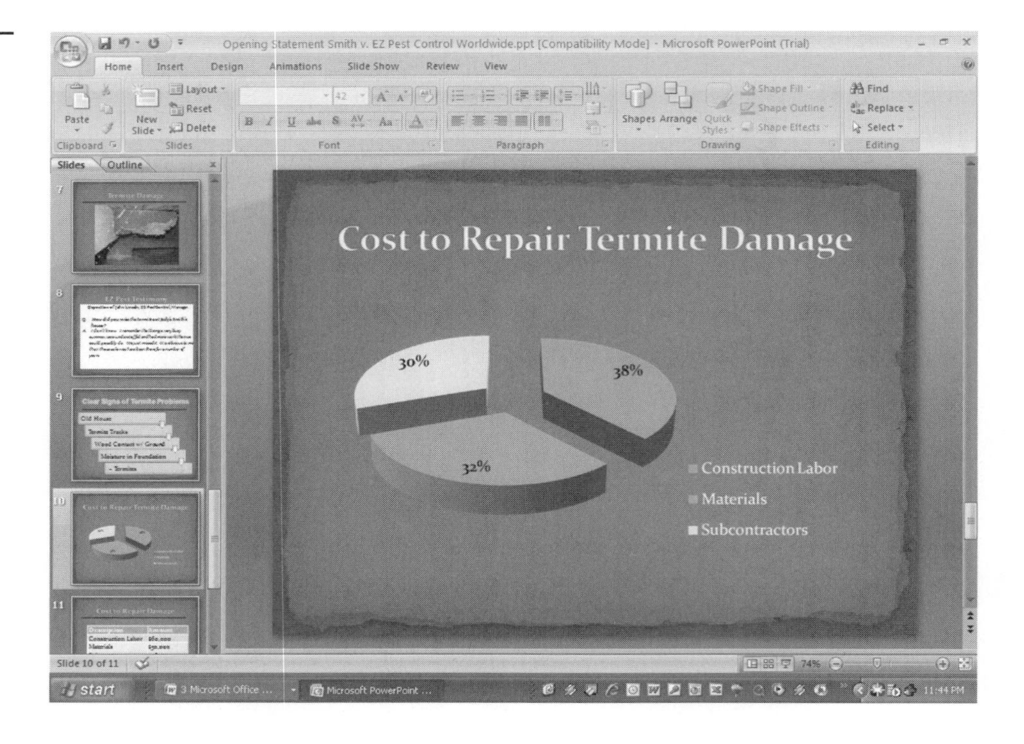

slide transition
Effect that controls how the program proceeds from one slide to another.

Another option is a **slide transition** effect, which controls how the program proceeds from one slide to another. For example, a user could move from slide two to slide three and make slide three appear on the screen much like horizontal blinds being drawn, with each piece sliding onto the screen individually until the slide is complete. "Animation" refers to other effects, such as how bullet points appear on the screen. For example, in Exhibit 12–12, the user could make each bullet point and text fly onto the screen individually, either automatically or when the mouse button was pushed. Animation is similar to slide transitions, but it happens within a slide instead of between slides. Again, users should be careful in using transition and animation affects so as to not diminish the professionalism of the presentation.

Outputting a Presentation

PowerPoint allows a presentation to be output in many different formats. These include slide show presentations, printing the presentation in black and white, printing it in color, printing it onto overhead transparency slides, or exporting it into web-based learning software. In addition, users can print the slides, an outline, speaker's notes, or a combination of these items.

> *You have to make a sales presentation to 12 people who don't want to be there… Do you really want to give every juror an exhibit binder and lose their attention to what you are saying? These are all things I tell my clients when we discuss whether or not they should use courtroom technology.*[4]

COURTROOM PRESENTATION TIPS

In some legal organizations the creation of presentations for trials falls to legal assistants. Creating and designing presentations for trials is different than creating other presentations. In addition, some legal assistants also actually operate

the computer and presentation/equipment during trials to allow the attorney(s) to concentrate on litigation. This section covers a variety of tips and tricks related to preparing and showing courtroom presentations.

Test All Computer Equipment in Advance and Have Staff Support

> *Technology is great when it works and hell on earth when it doesn't… There is nothing that looks worse to a judge or jury than a lawyer fumbling around with technology. Most judges agree that lawyers should have the help of support staff or outside consultants to run the technology.*[5]

It cannot be overstated how important it is for the technology used at trial to actually work when it is supposed to. If the courtroom is equipped with its own equipment, such as a projector and screen, then the user only has to ensure that he or she has the proper cables and other hardware to interface with the court's equipment. If the court is not equipped with the proper electronic equipment, then the user will have to start from scratch and bring a portable projecter, screen, and speakers and set all of this equipment up. Other equipment needed will include a laptop computer, cables, extension cords, and a printer/scanner/copier. It is crucial that all of the hardware and software be tested and retested to make sure that it works. Nothing should be left to chance, and backup equipment should be available if possible. Little things such as testing electrical outlets are critical; just because they are there doesn't mean they work. New, untested equipment should never be added or included at the last minute or until there has been enough time to work out the kinks. Users should thoroughly check out the courtroom several weeks in advance, if possible, to understand the complete layout of the room and what potential problems could occur. Exhibit 12–17 shows a list of potential items to take to court when you provide support for courtroom presentations.

EXHIBIT 12–17
Items to Take When Assisting with A Trial Presentation

Item
Laptop computer
Backup laptop
Thumb drive
Extra blank CDs / DVDs
Surge protector / outlet strip / uninterrupted power supply
Extension cords
Duct tape
Adapter cord for recharging laptop batteries
Ethernet cable
Wireless mouse
Video cords
Software / manuals
Laser pointer
Client data files
Backup hard disk
CDs/DVDs of client data files
Printer/fax/scanner
Speakers

Don't Keep Judges or Juries Waiting—Bring Powerful Technology

Users should always make sure the software they are using can adequately run on the computer hardware they are using. Judges and juries get extremely impatient when a user's computer constantly shows the Windows "hourglass icon." Always bring a laptop with more than enough horsepower to get the job done. The new class of trial presentation software, in particular, has hefty computing needs.

Keep It Simple—Don't Overload Slides with Too Much Information

> *PowerPoint presentations are often overly and poorly used. A jumble of text on a screen doesn't help you.*[6]

Presentations should be professional, clean and simple. A common mistake is to try to put too many bullet points on a slide. This makes it difficult to read. In addition, the font size of slides should be relatively large because some jurors may have trouble reading small fonts.

Use Color Conservatively

It is fine to have some color, but presentation designs should be conservative and professional, no loud extravagant colors. Color should be used to enhance the presentation, not distract the viewer.

Use Animation, Sound and Clip Art Cautiously

Animation, sound clips, and clip art should be used cautiously in trial presentations because they tend to diminish the quality and professionalism of the presentation. It easy for these elements to come off as "cheesy" or just in poor taste.

Use Images, Maps, Video, and Charts/Graphs When Possible

Graphical elements such as images (photographs), maps, video, and charts/graphs should be included in a presentation whenever possible. They add excitement and diversity to text and many times make it easier for jurors to understand the concept the user is trying to convey. Video testimony is particularly important. For example, if a witness states something in open court that was different than given in video deposition, the ability to play the video deposition in front of the jury and impeach the witness's testimony is priceless.

Scan Key Documents and Use Markup Tools

Key documents in a case should be scanned so they can be included in presentations, and important passages of documents should be marked or highlighted for easy identification by the jury.

Include Timelines

> *Don't forget timelines, both on-screen and in a trial exhibit notebook. Jurors absolutely love them. For many judges and jurors, timelines are what bring a case together in a cogent way.*[7]

Timelines are critical in just about every case that goes to trial. They explain what happened in chronological order. Attorneys often present things out of sequence for specific reasons, and witnesses often jump around in their testimony or are unclear regarding dates and times. That's why timelines are crucial for bringing everything together in a case for a jury.

> *On one occasion, a lawyer had a slide presentation prepared for his opening statement and it did not work. He had no backup plan... We finally had to move on with the opening statement without the slide show. It made quite an impression on the jury.*[8]

Always, Always, Always Have a Backup Plan

Always have a backup plan. It is a sad fact that hard disks crash, CDs and DVDs get scratches, software hangs up, computers get unplugged, cables wear out, bright lights wash out computer screens, operator errors occur, and information gets accidentally deleted. It is critical that the user always have a backup plan in case the technology fails. Something—anything—is better than nothing. A presentation that is printed out and can be copied and handed to the judge or jury is better than no presentation at all.

Always Rehearse

Users should always rehearse many times before putting on a presentation to a judge or jury. This is particularly true if a support person will be running the hardware and/or software. Trial presentations take time to prepare and to work out all the kinks and problems. In addition, even if the technology works, it really comes down to the presenter and how well that person presents the information to the judge or jury. Everything must work together and flow well, which takes time and practice.

PRESENTATION GRAPHICS IN THE LEGAL ENVIRONMENT

Presentation graphics software is routinely used in legal organizations for a variety of purposes. Creating electronic presentations for trial purposes is one of the most common uses of presentation graphics programs in legal organizations. For example, Exhibit 12–18 shows an accident scene where a car crossed the double yellow line and struck an oncoming car. Presentation graphics such as are shown in Exhibit 12–18 are often referred to as demonstrative evidence. **Demonstrative evidence** is all evidence other than testimony. Presentation graphics software can be used very effectively to ignite interest in a judge or jury, to underscore and emphasize important aspects of a case, and to clarify complex issues.

demonstrative evidence
All evidence other than testimony.

ETHICAL CONSIDERATIONS

Ethical considerations regarding trial and presentation software and graphics revolve around competency and evidence rules. It is important, when putting together anything that will be used in a client's case, to make sure it is competently done and well thought out. It is certainly not unusual for a legal assistant to be asked to create a chart, graph, table, exhibit or even a full presentation for trial. It is extremely important that these be prepared with a high degree of accuracy and competency.

EXHIBIT 12–18
SmartDraw Legal—Legal Graphics Software
Screen shot created using SmartDraw Legal Edition software.

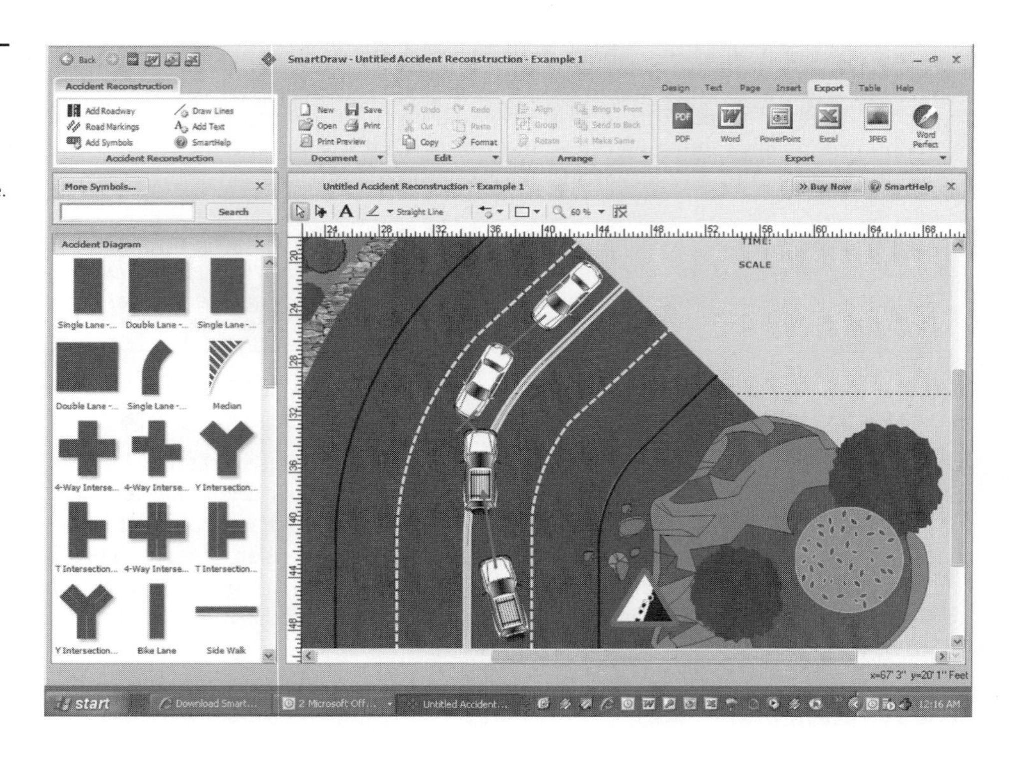

In addition, anything that is presented at trial or to a fact finder will be subject to the rules of evidence and could be objected to by the other party. Charts, graphs, and tables may be viewed as demonstrative evidence. Examples of demonstrative evidence include maps, diagrams, models, charts, and illustrations. The admissibility of demonstrative evidence is largely controlled by the rules of evidence and the judge sitting on the case. Often the arguments between attorneys regarding a piece of demonstrative evidence are about whether it fairly and reasonably depicts the subject matter it covers. Thus, the heart of whether the demonstrative evidence will be admitted depends on the quality and competency of the exhibit itself.

SUMMARY

Electronic courthouses, where legal professionals file documents electronically and have instant access to court information, are becoming a reality. Automated courtrooms with computers and monitors for all participants are also a reality.

Presentation software allows users to create visually interesting electronic presentations. Some of these programs are generic business presentation programs. A trial presentation program is specifically designed to meet the needs of practicing attorneys, particularly those that try cases to juries and courts.

Most presentation graphics programs have several views and display presentations to work with. These may include views such as Normal view, Slide Sorter view, and Slide Show view. Creating new presentations entails creating a background design; adding slides; adding and formatting text; adding photographs, clip art, word art, and smart art; adding graphs and charts; and creating multimedia effects and transition/animation effects.

Designing and presenting trial presentations to judges and juries takes a great deal of preparation and thought. Tips for doing this well include testing

INTERNET SITES

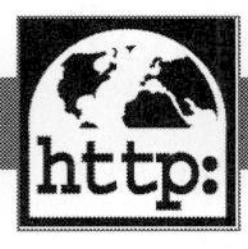

Organization	Software Product	World Wide Web Address
Adobe Acrobat	PDF file creation program	<http://www.adobe.com>
Case Management/Electronic Case Files	The federal courts' case management and electronic case files system	<http://www.uscourts.gov/>
Corel Corp.	Presentations X3 presentation program	<http://www.corel.com>
Doar	Trial presentation services vendor	<http://www.doar.com>
Idea, Inc.	Trial Pro	<http://www.ideaview.com>
InData Software	Trial Director trial presentation program	<http://www.indatacorp.com>
LexisNexis	Timemap—timeline creation software	<http://law.lexisnexis.com/>
Microsoft Corp.	PowerPoint presentation program	<http://www.microsoft.com/>
Public Access to Court Electronic Records	PACER—electronic public access service that allows users to obtain case and docket information from federal appellate, district and Bankruptcy courts, and the U.S. Party/Case Index, via the Internet	<http://pacer.psc.uscourts.gov/>
SmartDraw Legal	Legal graphics software	<http://www.smartdraw.com>
Verdict Systems	Sanction II trial presentation program	<http://www.verdictsystems.com>

computer equipment in advance; keeping slides simple and uncluttered; using color conservatively; cautiously using animation, sound and clip art; using images, maps, video, and charts / graphs when possible; scanning key documents; using markup tools; creating timelines; always having a backup plan; and always rehearsing presentations.

Presentation graphics programs are used in legal organizations for creating internal training programs, public seminars, and presentations for clients; developing evidence for cases; and developing trial presentations.

KEY TERMS

electronic filing
Portable Document Format (PDF)
evidence display system
document camera
presentation software
trial presentation programs
normal view
slide sorter view
slide show view
background
clip art
word art
smart art
slide transition
animation
demonstrative evidence

TEST YOUR KNOWLEDGE

Test your knowledge of the chapter by answering these questions.

1. True or False: The federal courts' Case Management / Electronic Case Filing system only has a few courts / cases / attorneys participating in it.
2. What standard do most courts use for submitting electronic documents?
3. What is a document camera?
4. True or False: Trial presentation programs and generic presentation programs like Microsoft PowerPoint have the same features.
5. Why should users be careful when using clip art and sound files in trial presentations?
6. Name four things to remember when using presentation programs in the courtroom.

ON THE WEB EXERCISES

1. Use a general search engine such as Google or Yahoo! to find several articles regarding using computer presentation programs in the courtroom or before a jury. Write a two-page paper summarizing your research.
2. Use the Internet sites at the end of the chapter and/or a general search engine such as Google or Yahoo! to find two trial presentation programs. Compare the prices, features, support, and training available. Download trial versions of the programs if you can. Write a two-page memo summarizing your research and findings. Include which program you think is best and why.

QUESTIONS AND EXERCISES

1. Contact an attorney, legal assistant, or a court staff member in your area and interview the person regarding their experiences using technology in the courtroom, electronic filing, or accessing electronic court records. Write a two-page memo summarizing your interview.

END NOTES

[1] Sharon D. Nelson, Esq., and John W. Simek, "The State of Paperless Courts," *Law Office Computing*, August / September 2001, 89.
[2] Lynn Penkingcarn, "Electronic Case Filing in Full Swing," *Legal Assistant Today*, May / June 2006, 26.
[3] "Document Retrieval Companies Build Up Services," Mila D'Antonio, *Legal Assistant Today*, September / October 2002, 32.
[4] "Video Summations Gain Popularity in Courtrooms," Lynn Penkingcarn, *Law Office Computing*, December / January 2006, 20.
[5] "A Judicial Perspective of Courtroom Technology," Sharon D. Nelson, Esq. and John W. Simek, *Law Office Computing*, February / March 2006, 79.
[6] "A Judicial Perspective of Courtroom Technology," Sharon D. Nelson, Esq. and John W. Simek, *Law Office Computing*, February/March 2006 79.
[7] "A Judicial Perspective of Courtroom Technology," Sharon D. Nelson, Esq. and John W. Simek, *Law Office Computing*, February/March 2006 79.
[8] "Technology—Who Is...Gerald Bruce Lee," *Law Practice*, July/August 2006, 22.

HANDS-ON EXERCISES

PRESENTATION SOFTWARE

READ THIS FIRST!

1. **Microsoft PowerPoint 2007**
2. **SmartDraw Legal**
3. **Microsoft PowerPoint 2003**

I. Determining Which Tutorial to Complete

To use the PowerPoint Hands-On Exercises, you must already own or have access to Microsoft PowerPoint 2007 or PowerPoint 2003. If you have one of these programs but do not know the version you are using, it is easy to find out. For PowerPoint, 2003, start the program; click Help on the menu bar; then click About Microsoft Office PowerPoint. The program should then tell you what version of it you are using. For PowerPoint 2007, click the Office Button in the upper left of the screen, click PowerPoint Options, and then click Resources the program, and will tell you what version you are using. You must know the version of the program you are using and select the correct tutorial version or the tutorials will not work correctly.

II. Using the PowerPoint Hands-on Exercises

The PowerPoint Hands-on Exercises in this section are easy to use and contain step-by-step instructions. They start with basic skills and proceed to intermediate and advanced levels. If you already have a good working knowledge of PowerPoint, you may be able to proceed directly to the intermediate and advanced exercises. To truly be ready for using presentation software in the legal environment, you must be able to accomplish the tasks and exercises in the more advanced exercises.

III. Accessing the Data

Some of the advanced PowerPoint Hands-on Exercises use documents on Disk 1 provided with this text. To access these files, put the CD in your computer, and click Start, click My Computer, double-click on the appropriate drive, and then double-click the PowerPoint Files folder. You should then see a list of presentations that are available for these exercises.

IV. Installation Questions

If you have installation questions regarding installing the exercise files data from the Disk, you may contact Technical Support at (800) 477–3692.

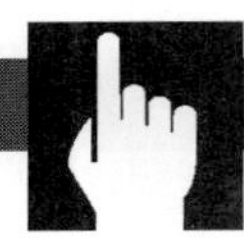

HANDS-ON EXERCISES

HANDS-ON EXERCISES POWERPOINT 2007

Basic Lessons

Number	Lesson Title	Concepts Covered
Lesson 1	Creating a Presentation	Selecting a presentation design, entering text, entering speaker's notes, and saving a file
Lesson 2	Creating Additional Slides	Inserting a new slide, selecting a slide layout, viewing a slide in Slide Show, Outline, and Slide Sorter view, and creating additional slides
Intermediate Lessons		
Lesson 3	Creating a Graph	Creating and entering data in a chart
Lesson 4	Finalizing the Presentation	Using the duplicate slide feature, creating transition effects, creating animation effects, and viewing a final presentation
Advanced Lessons		
Lesson 5	Customizing and Finalizing an Opening Statement Presentation	Inserting a slide from an old presentation into a new presentation while still maintaining the formatting of the new presentation, editing a master slide, creating a table, adding a "grow" animation effect, and adding transition effects to a presentation

GETTING STARTED

Overview

Microsoft PowerPoint 2007 is a presentation graphics program. It allows you to create presentations, charts, graphs, tables, and much more. PowerPoint 2007 is an easy-to-use program.

Please note that during the first four of these exercises, you will be creating a presentation for a legal assistant training program. In the last exercise, you will finalize an opening statement presentation.

Introduction

Throughout these lessons and exercises, information you need to operate the program will be designated in several different ways:

- Keys to be pressed on the keyboard will be designated in brackets, in all caps, and in bold (press the **[ENTER]** key).
- Movements with the mouse will be designated in bold and italics (***point to File on the menu bar and click the mouse***).
- Words or letters that should be typed will be designated in bold and enlarged (type **Training Program**).
- Information that is or should be displayed on your computer screen will be shown in the following style: **Press ENTER to continue.**

LESSON 1: CREATING A PRESENTATION

In this lesson, you will start PowerPoint 2007, select a background design for the legal assistant training program presentation, enter the first slide, view your slide, and save your presentation.

1. Start Windows. Then, ***double-click the Microsoft PowerPoint 2007 icon on the desktop*** to start the program. Alternatively, ***click the Start button, point to Programs or All Programs, click "Microsoft Office," and then point and click on "Microsoft Office PowerPoint 2007."***

2. A blank presentation should be on your screen ***Click the Office Button in the upper left corner of the screen. Then, click New. The New Presentation window should now be displayed.***

3. ***On the left side, under Templates, click Installed Themes. Scroll down and select "Metro." Click Create.***

4. ***A blank title screen should now be displayed.***

5. ***Click "Click to add title."*** Notice that you are now allowed to type your own title. Type **New Legal Assistant Training** (see PowerPoint 2007 Exhibit 1).

6. ***On the Home ribbon tab, click the Center icon in the Paragraph group.***

7. ***Click "Click to add sub-title."*** Type **Johnson Beck & Taylor** (see PowerPoint 2007 Exhibit 1).

8. ***On the Home ribbon tab, click the Center icon in the Paragraph group.***

9. The slide is now created.

PowerPoint 2007 Exhibit 1

Microsoft product screen shot reprinted with permission from Microsoft Corporation.

10. To view your slide, ***click the Slide Show icon in the lower right of your screen*** (PowerPoint 2007 Exhibit 1). *Note:* You will see three icons in the lower right of the screen (for Normal view, Slide Sorter view, and Slide Show view). The Slide Show icon is all the way to the right. Remember, if you point to any icon and hold the mouse pointer there for a second, the title of the icon will be displayed.

11. You should now see your slide displayed full screen on your computer. Notice that the dark background with the light-colored letters makes your slide very readable. This is how your audience will see your slide.

12. Press **[ESC]** to return to editing your presentation.

13. Notice that at the bottom of the screen under the current slide it says "Click to add notes." This is the Speaker's Notes section of the screen. Speaker's Notes are not shown in Slide Show view, but they can be printed so that the presenter has talking points from which to speak.

14. ***Click anywhere in the Speaker's Notes section.*** Now, type **Welcome the new legal assistant(s) and give a short history of the firm** (see PowerPoint Exhibit 1).

15. ***Click the Slide Show icon in the lower right of the screen again.*** Notice that speaker's notes do not appear.

16. Press **[ESC]** to return to editing your presentation.

17. It is a good idea to save your presentation often. To save your presentation, ***click the Office Button. Then, click Save.***

18. Type **New Legal Assistant Training Program,** ***then click Save*** to save the file in the default directory. Be sure to remember where the file is saved so that you can retrieve it in the next lesson.

This concludes Lesson 1.

To Exit PowerPoint

To exit PowerPoint, ***click the Office Button and then click Exit PowerPoint.***

To go to Lesson 2

To go to Lesson 2, stay at the current screen.

LESSON 2: CREATING ADDITIONAL SLIDES

In this lesson, you will add additional slides to the legal assistant training presentation you created in Lesson 1, and you will look at the presentation using several views. If you did not exit PowerPoint from Lesson 1, go to Step 3.

1. Start Windows. Then, ***double-click the Microsoft Office PowerPoint 2007 icon on the desktop*** to start PowerPoint 2007 for Windows. Alternatively, ***click the Start button, point to Programs or All Programs, and then click the Microsoft PowerPoint 2007 icon (or point to Microsoft Office and then click Microsoft Office PowerPoint 2007).*** You should be in a clean, blank document.

2. ***Click the Office Button, then click Open.*** The Open window should now be displayed. ***Navigate to the folder where the file is located. Click New Legal Assistant Training Program and then click Open.*** Alternatively, if you

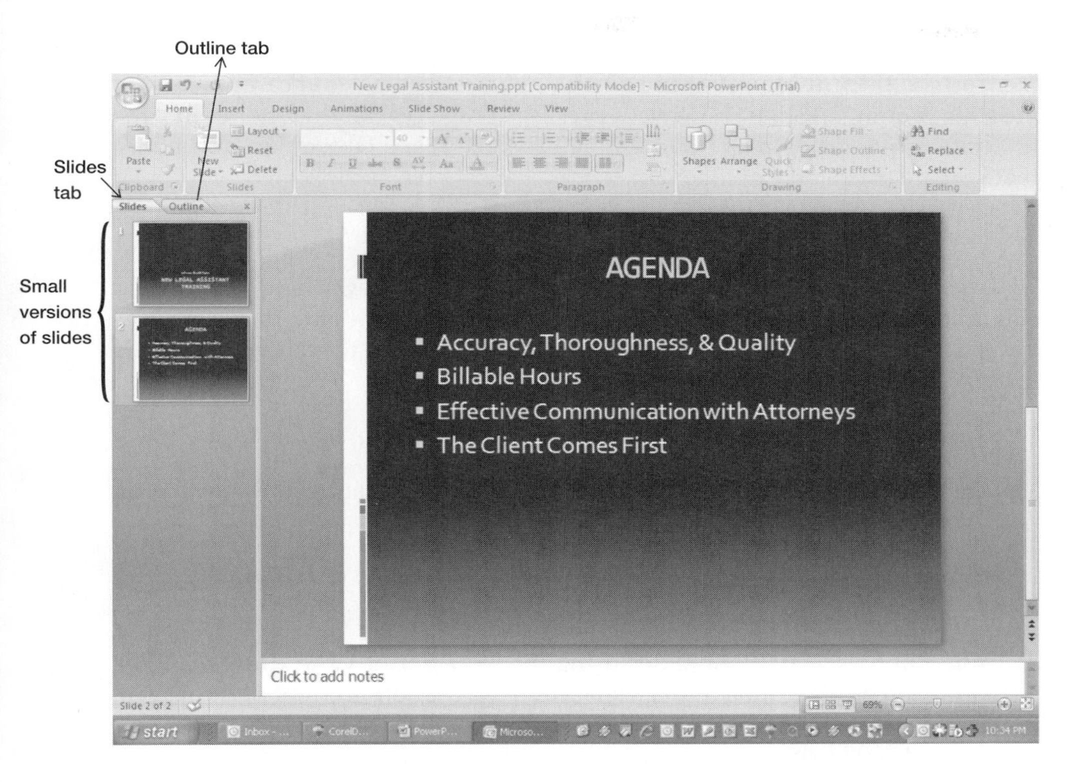

PowerPoint 2007 Exhibit 2

Microsoft product screen shot reprinted with permission from Microsoft Corporation.

click the Office Button recently used files appear on the right side of the menu. Locate your file, and then *click on it*.

3. You should have the "New Legal Assistant Training" slide on your screen. Notice in the lower left of the screen that it says "Slide 1 of 1." This shows you what slide number you are on.

4. To create a new slide, ***on the Home ribbon tab, click the down arrow next to New Slide in the Slides group.*** Notice that the program gives you a number of different layouts.

5. ***Click the Title and Content option.***

6. A new slide is displayed on your screen. The top part of the slide should say "Click to add title" and the bottom section of the slide (next to a bullet) should say "Click to add text." There should also be graphics in the center of the screen.

7. ***Click "Click to add title."*** Type **AGENDA** (see PowerPoint 2007 Exhibit 2).

8. ***On the Home ribbon tab, click the Center icon in the Paragraph group.***

9. ***Click "Click to add text."*** Type **Accuracy, Thoroughness & Quality** and press the **[ENTER]** key**.** Notice that an additional bullet has been created.

10. Type **Billable Hours** and then press the **[ENTER]** key.

11. Type **Effective Communication with Attorneys** and press the **[ENTER]** key.

12. Type **The Client Comes First**.

13. The slide is now created (see PowerPoint Exhibit 2).

14. To view your slide, ***click the Slide Show icon.***

15. You should now see your slide displayed full-screen on your computer. With the slide running in Slide Show view, press the **[Page Up]** key and notice that the first slide is now shown on your screen. Press the **[Page Down]** key and notice that you are back at the second slide.

16. Press **[ESC]** to return to Normal view.

17. You will now look at your presentation using other views. Notice on the left side of the screen that small versions of both of your slides are displayed (see PowerPoint 2007 Exhibit 2). Notice just above the slides that the Slides tab is selected.

18. ***Click the Outline tab just to the right of the Slides tab.***

19. The Outline view is now displayed; notice that you can read the words on both of your slides (see PowerPoint 2007 Exhibit 3).

20. ***Click the Slides tab just to the left of the Outline tab*** to go back to the Slides view.

21. You will now view your slides using the Slide Sorter view. ***Click the Slide Sorter view icon.*** The Slide Sorter view icon is at the bottom right of the screen; the second of the three "View" icons, and has a picture of four small squares (see PowerPoint 2007 Exhibit 1).

22. Notice that you can see all of your slides on the screen at the same time (see PowerPoint 2007 Exhibit 4). This is helpful for getting an overview of your presentation and arranging and rearranging your slide order.

23. ***While you are in Slide Sorter view, point to the second slide, click and drag the mouse pointer (holding down the mouse button) to the left of the first slide, and then release the mouse button.*** Notice that the order of the slides is now changed.

PowerPoint 2007 Exhibit 3

Microsoft product screen shot reprinted with permission from Microsoft Corporation.

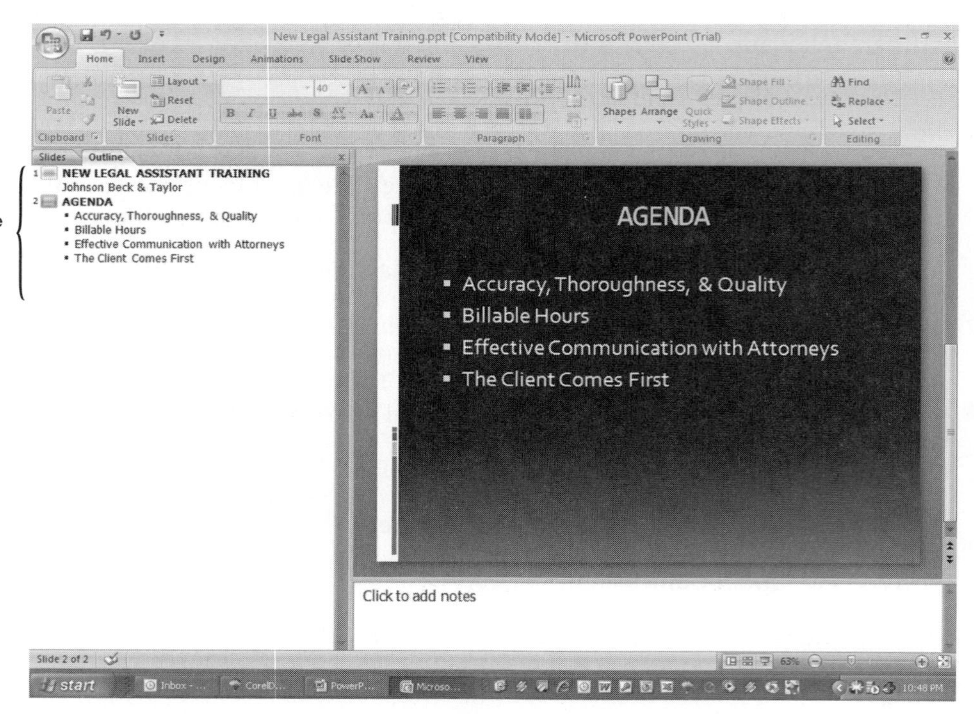

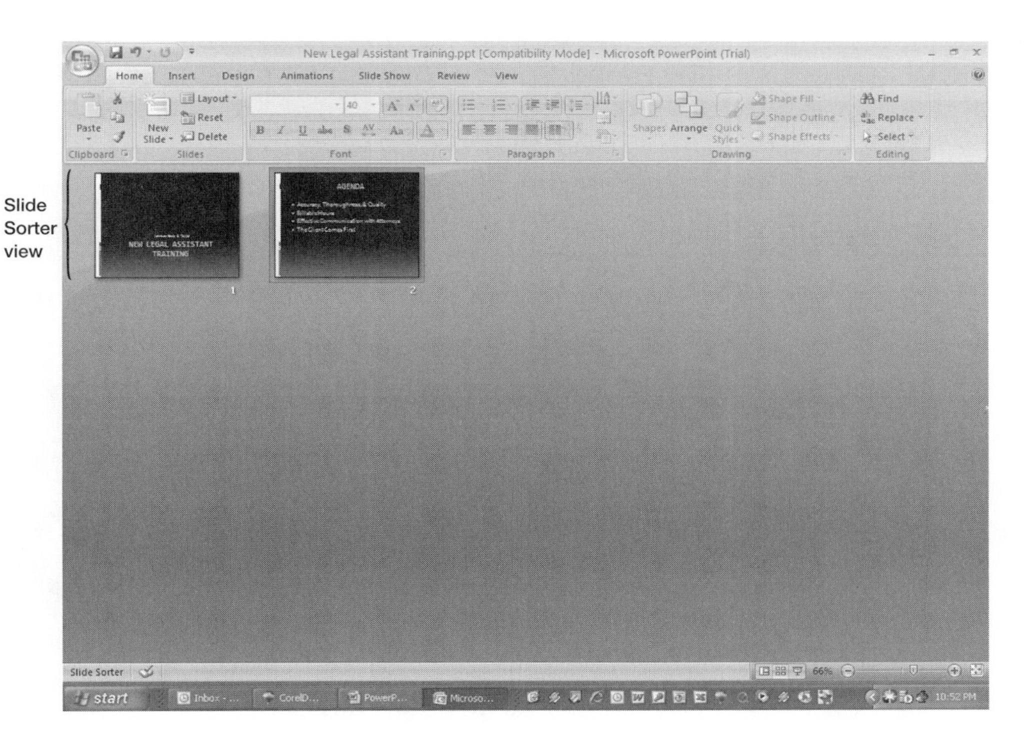

PowerPoint 2007 Exhibit 4

Microsoft product screen shot reprinted with permission from Microsoft Corporation.

24. Press **[CTRL]+[Z]** to undo the move and put the slides back into their original order.

25. ***Click the Normal view icon in the lower right of your screen*** (see PowerPoint 2007 Exhibit 1).

26. You should now have the "AGENDA" slide on your screen. If you are not there, use the **[PAGE DOWN]** key to go there.

27. You are now ready to create another slide. ***On the Home ribbon tab, click the down arrow next to New Slide in the Slides group. Click the Two Content option. A new slide is displayed on your screen.***

28. ***A new slide should now be displayed on your screen.*** The top of the slide should say "Click to add title" and there should be two columns (left and right) that say "Click to add text." There should also be some icons in the middle of the screen.

29. ***Click "Click to add title."*** Type **Accuracy, Thoroughness & Quality** (see PowerPoint 2007 Exhibit 5).

30. ***On the Home ribbon tab, click the Center icon in the Paragraph group.***

31. ***Click the first column,*** "Click to add text." Type **Be careful and complete** and press the **[ENTER]** key.

32. Type **Create forms and systems** and press the **[ENTER]** key.

33. Type **Create checklists**.

34. ***Click the second column, "Click to add text."*** Type **Keep written notes and documentation** and press the **[ENTER]** key.

35. Type **Ask for peer review** and press the **[ENTER]** key.

PowerPoint 2007
Exhibit 5

Microsoft product screen shot reprinted with permission from Microsoft Corporation.

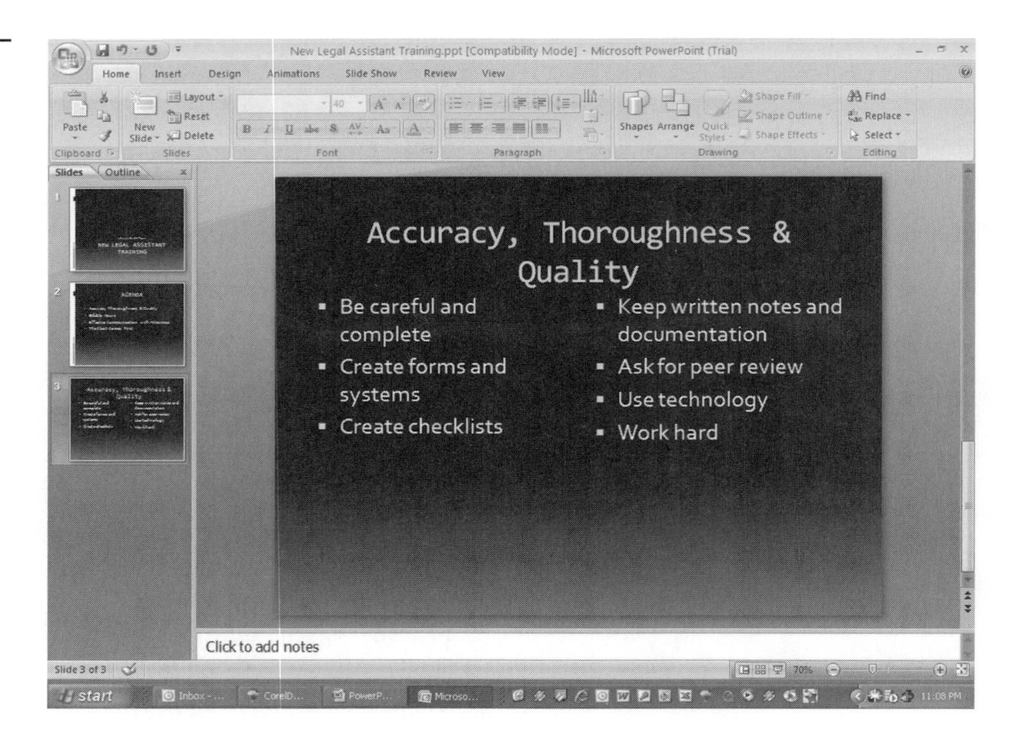

36. Type **Use technology** and press the **[ENTER]** key.

37. Type **Work hard**.

38. Your presentation now has three slides in it.

39. To save your presentation, ***click the Save icon on the Quick Access toolbar. (It looks like a floppy disk and is in the upper left of the screen.)***

This concludes Lesson 2.

To Exit PowerPoint

To exit PowerPoint, ***click the Office Button and then click Exit PowerPoint.***

To go to Lesson 3

To go to Lesson 3, stay at the current screen.

INTERMEDIATE

LESSON 3: CREATING A GRAPH

In this lesson, you will add an additional slide with a graph into the legal assistant training program presentation. If you did not exit PowerPoint from Lesson 2, go to Step 4.

1. Start Windows. Then, ***double-click the Microsoft Office PowerPoint 2007 icon on the desktop*** to start PowerPoint 2007 for Windows. Alternatively, ***click the Start button, point to Programs or All Programs, and then click the Microsoft PowerPoint 2007 icon (or point to Microsoft Office and then click Microsoft Office PowerPoint 2007).*** You should be in a clean, blank document.

2. ***Click the Office Button. Then click Open.*** The Open window should now be displayed. ***Navigate to the folder where the file is located. Click New Legal Assistant Training Program and then click Open.*** Alternatively, if you click the Office Button, recently used files appear on the right side of the menu. Locate your file, and then *click on it.*

3. You should have the New Legal Assistant Training slide on your screen. Push the **[PAGE DOWN]** key until you are on the third slide, "Accuracy, Thoroughness & Quality."

4. You are now ready to create another slide. ***On the Home ribbon tab, click the down arrow next to "New Slide" in the Slides group.***

5. ***Point and click with the mouse on the "Title and Content" option.*** A new slide is displayed on your screen.

6. The top part of the slide should say "Click to add title" and the bottom section of the slide should say "Click to add text." In addition, there are a number of graphical icons in the middle of the screen; one of them is a bar chart.

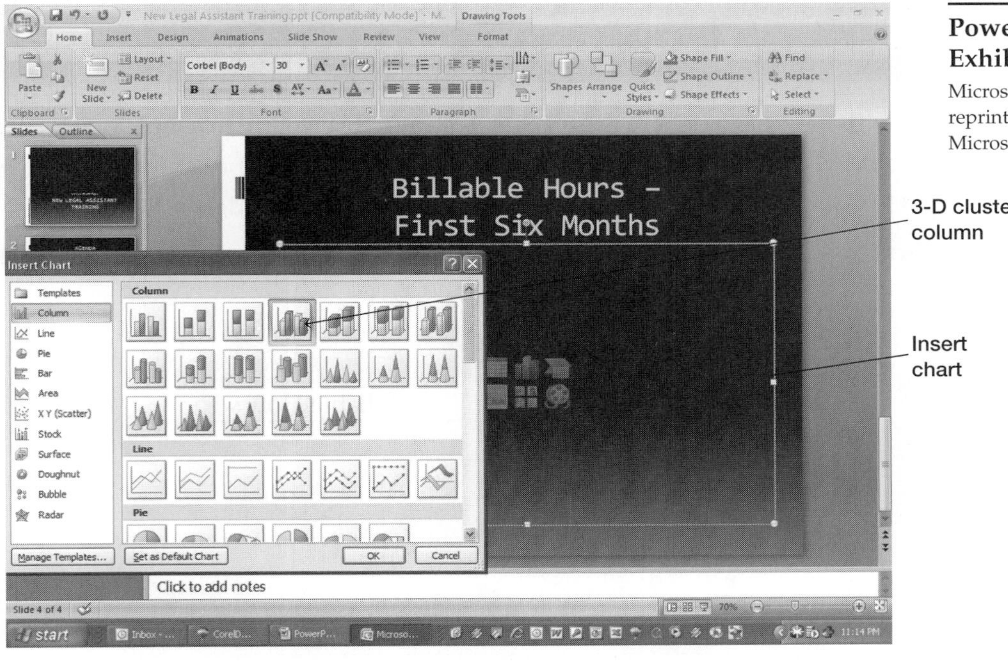

PowerPoint 2007 Exhibit 6

Microsoft product screen shot reprinted with permission from Microsoft Corporation.

7. ***Point and click with the mouse on "Click to add title."*** Type **Billable Hours** and then press the **[ENTER]** key and then type **First Six Months** (see PowerPoint 2007 Exhibit 6). ***From the Home ribbon tab, point and click on the Center icon in the Paragraph group.***

8. Notice in the lower middle of the new slide, there are six graphical icons. ***Point and click with your mouse on the Insert Chart icon (it is in the middle on the first row—it looks like a multicolored vertical bar chart).***

9. The "Insert Chart" window is displayed (see PowerPoint 2007 Exhibit 6). ***Point and click on Column under Templates on the left side of the window. Then, point and click on the "3-D Clustered Column" chart*** (e.g., see PowerPoint 2007 Exhibit 6—it is on the first row, fourth chart from the left).

10. ***Next, click on OK.***

PowerPoint 2007 Exhibit 7

Microsoft product screen shot reprinted with permission from Microsoft Corporation.

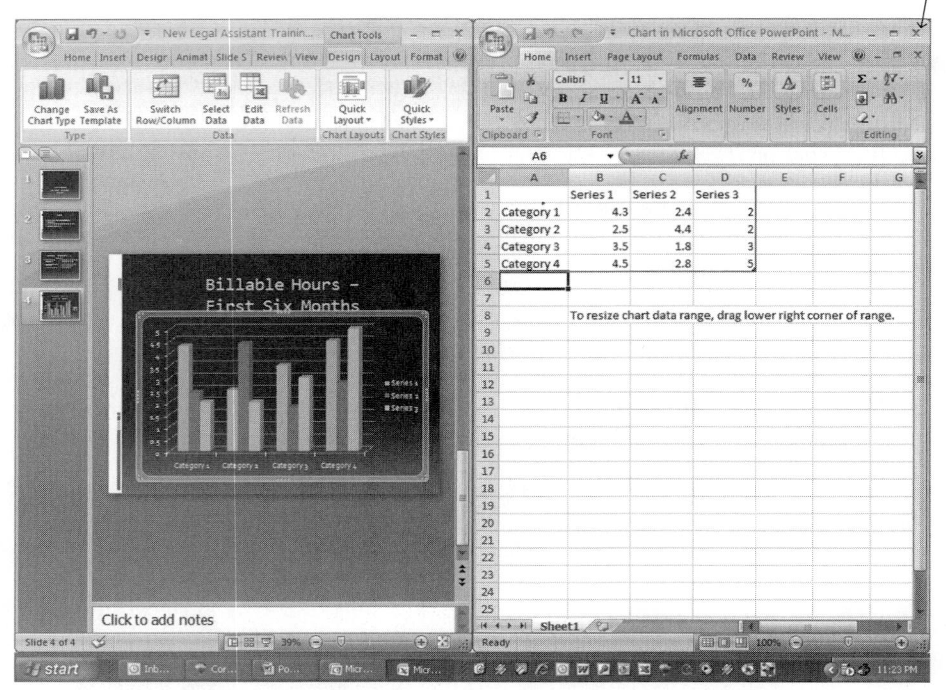

11. Notice that a default chart is displayed on the left and a default spreadsheet is displayed on the right (see PowerPoint 2007 Exhibit 7).

12. You will now add some data and new titles, and also delete some data.

13. Type over the existing data in the spreadsheet for columns A and B as follows (do not do anything with columns C and D yet).

	A	B
1		Billable Hours
2	Mo. 1	80
3	Mo. 2	90
4	Mo. 3	100
5	Mo. 4	100
6	Mo. 5	105
7	Mo. 6	110

14. You will now delete columns C and D since they are not necessary. ***Point to cell C1 and drag the mouse pointer down and to the right so that cell D7 is highlighted.***

15. ***Next, right-click in the highlighted area, point to Delete, and then click Table Columns.***

16. ***A Microsoft Office Excel window will appear saying that the worksheet contains one or more invalid references; click OK.***

17. Your spreadsheet and chart should look similar to PowerPoint 2007 Exhibit 8.

18. ***In the spreadsheet window, click the Close icon (the "X" in the upper right corner; see PowerPoint 2007 Exhibit 8).***

19. The chart should now be displayed (see PowerPoint 2007 Exhibit 9).

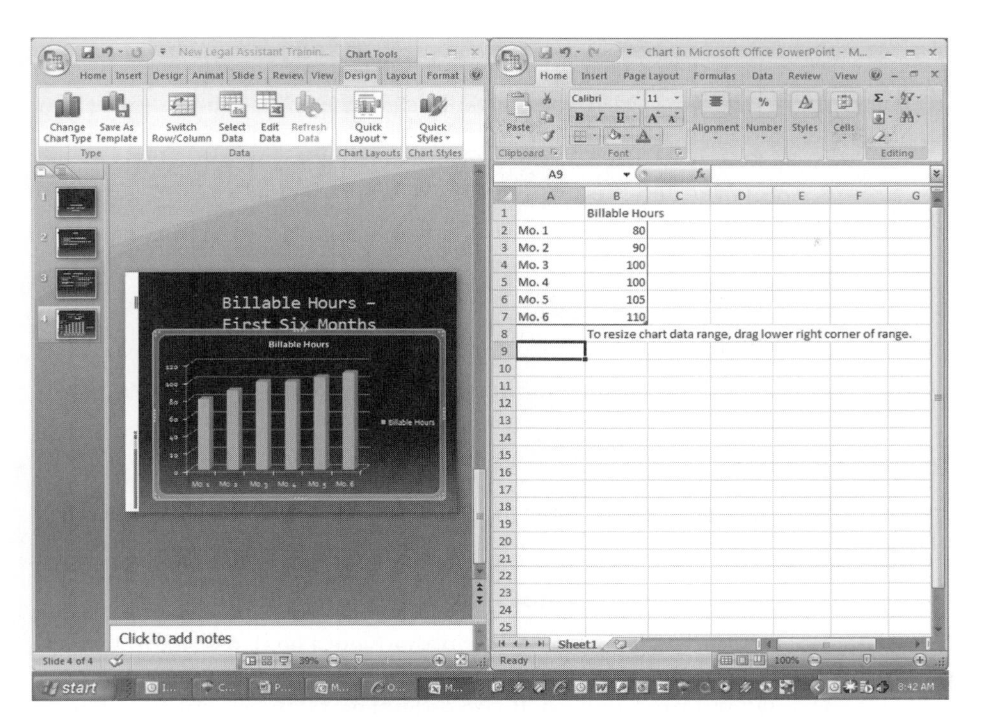

PowerPoint 2007 Exhibit 8

Microsoft product screen shot reprinted with permission from Microsoft Corporation.

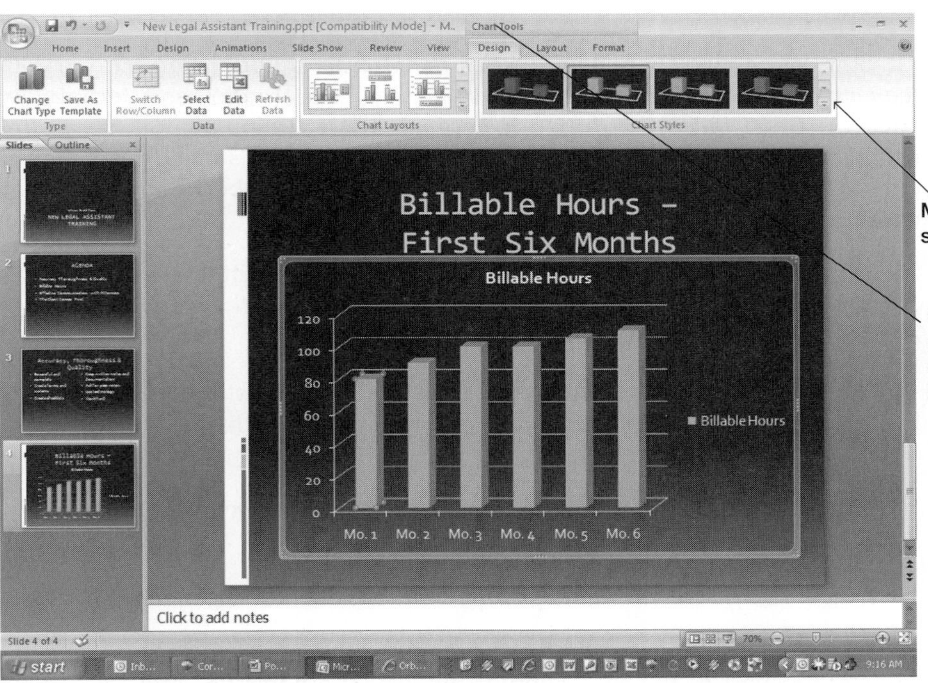

PowerPoint 2007 Exhibit 9

Microsoft product screen shot reprinted with permission from Microsoft Corporation.

20. PowerPoint 2007 gives you many premade chart styles and colors to choose from.

21. ***On the Chart Tools – Design ribbon tab, click the More icon in the Chart Styles group*** **(see PowerPoint 2007 Exhibit 9).** *Note*: You can only access the Chart Tools ribbon when the chart is selected, so ***click the chart if you do not see the Chart Tools ribbon***.

22. Notice that a wide variety of chart styles is now displayed. ***Click any of the charts in the last row;*** these are the 3-D sculpted options.

23. The chart is now complete. To view your chart full-screen, ***click the Slide Show icon.***

24. Press the **[ESC]** key.

25. To save your presentation, ***click the Save icon*** (it looks like a floppy disk) ***on the Quick Access toolbar.***

This concludes Lesson 3.

To Exit PowerPoint

To exit PowerPoint, ***click the Office Button, and then click Exit PowerPoint.***

To go to Lesson 4

To go to Lesson 4, stay at the current screen.

LESSON 4: FINALIZING THE PRESENTATION

In this lesson, you will add more slides to the New Legal Assistant Training presentation, duplicate a slide, enter slide transition effects, create animation effects, and show your presentation. If you did not exit PowerPoint from Lesson 3, go to step 3.

1. Start Windows. Then, ***double-click the Microsoft Office PowerPoint 2007 icon on the desktop*** to start PowerPoint 2007 for Windows. Alternatively, ***click the Start button, point to Programs or All Programs, and then click the Microsoft PowerPoint 2007 icon (or point to Microsoft Office and then click Microsoft Office PowerPoint 2007).*** You should be in a clean, blank document.

2. ***Click the Office Button. Then, click Open.*** The Open window should now be displayed. ***Navigate to the folder where the file is located. Click New Legal Assistant Training Program and then click Open.***

3. You should have the New Legal Assistant Training slide on your screen. Push the **[PAGE DOWN]** key until you are at the fourth slide, which is the bar chart.

4. You are now ready to create another slide. ***On the Home ribbon tab, click the down arrow next to New Slide in the Slides group.***

5. ***Click the Title and Content option.*** A new slide should be displayed on your screen.

6. The top part of the slide should say "Click to add title" and the bottom section of the slide should say "Click to add text."

7. Enter the information shown in PowerPoint 2007 Exhibit 10.

8. You will now create another slide, but this time you will use the Duplicate Slide feature.

9. ***On the Home ribbon tab, click the down arrow next to New Slide in the Slides group.***

10. ***Click the Duplicate Selected Slides icon at the bottom of the menu.***

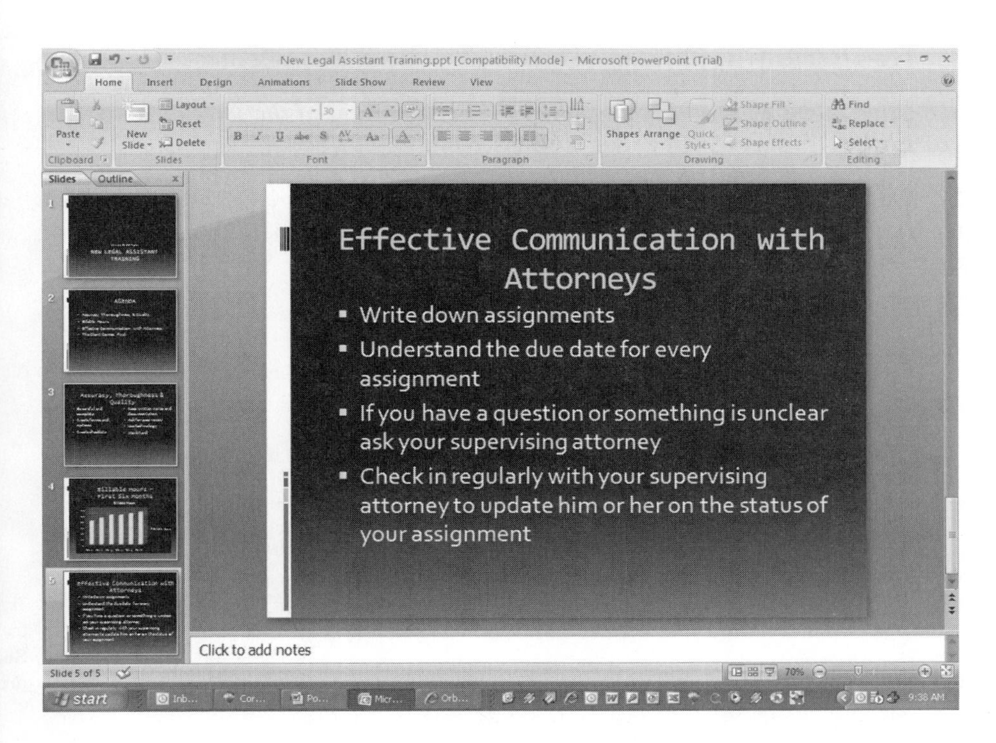

PowerPoint 2007 Exhibit 10

Microsoft product screen shot reprinted with permission from Microsoft Corporation.

11. Notice that another slide has been added that is identical to the previous slide.

12. ***Click in the title of the new slide, then drag the mouse pointer so that all of the text is highlighted.*** Press the **[DELETE]** key. Do the same for the body of the slide.

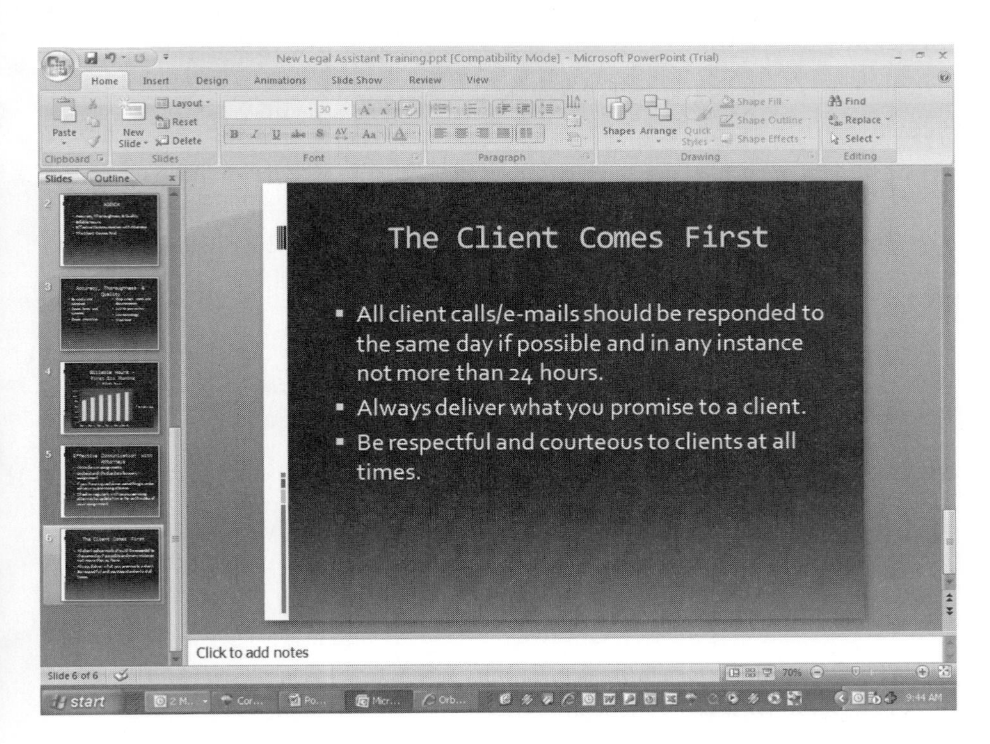

PowerPoint 2007 Exhibit 11

Microsoft product screen shot reprinted with permission from Microsoft Corporation.

13. Enter the information shown in PowerPoint 2007 Exhibit 11.

14. With all of your slides created, you are now ready to begin finalizing the presentation.

15. Press **[CTRL]+[HOME]** to go to the first slide in the presentation.

16. ***Click the Slide Sorter view icon at the bottom right of the screen.*** Notice that you can see all six of your slides on the screen.

17. We will now apply transition effects (effects that take place when you move from one slide to another) and animation effects (effects that take place during display of the slide).

18. ***Click the first slide, "New Legal Assistant Training."***

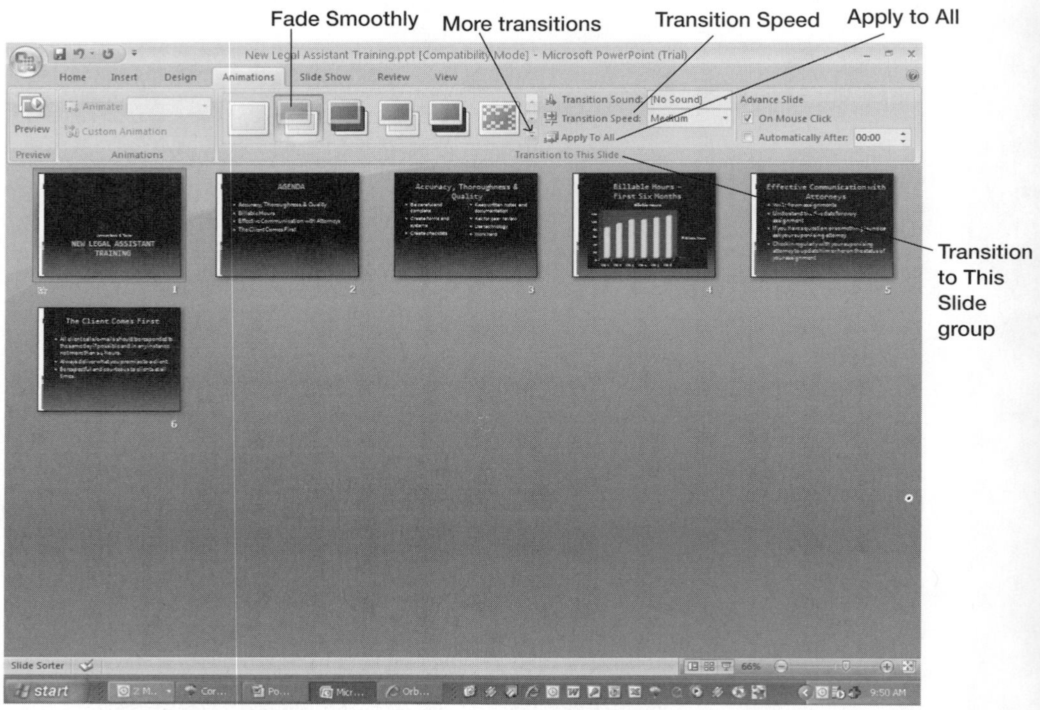

PowerPoint 2007 Exhibit 12

Microsoft product screen shot reprinted with permission from Microsoft Corporation.

19. ***Click the Animations ribbon tab.*** Notice the Transition to This Slide group (see PowerPoint 2007 Exhibit 12). On the left side of the Transition to This Slide group are the different transition choices. To the right are the settings available for each transition.

20. ***On the Animations ribbon tab, click the More icon in the Transition to This Slide group.*** Notice that many types of slide transitions are available.

21. Press the **[ESC]** key to make the "More transitions" list disappear.

22. ***On the Animation ribbon tab, click the Fade Smoothly transition effect in the Transition to This Slide group.*** Notice that after you selected it the slide displayed the transition effect. Fade Smoothly is a professional transition effect that is not distracting, so it is a good one to use in the legal setting.

23. ***On the Animations ribbon tab, click the down arrow next to Transition Speed: Fast and then click Medium.***

24. ***On the Animations ribbon tab, click Apply To All in the Transition to This Slide group.*** This will apply the Fade Smoothly effect to all of the slides in the presentation. Notice that little symbols now appear under all of your slides in the slide sorter; this shows that they have transition effects associated with them.

25. Notice that in the Transition to This Slide group, under Advance Slide, "On mouse click" is selected. This means that the slide will automatically move to the next slide only when the mouse is clicked. You could set it to move to the next slide automatically after a given amount of time, but the current selection is fine for this presentation.

26. ***Click the Slide Show icon at the bottom right of the screen to see your presentation, including the transition effects. Click the mouse button to proceed through the presentation and back to the slide sorter screen.***

27. You will now create an animation effect that determines how the slides with bullet points appear on the screen.

28. ***Double-click the second slide, "AGENDA."***

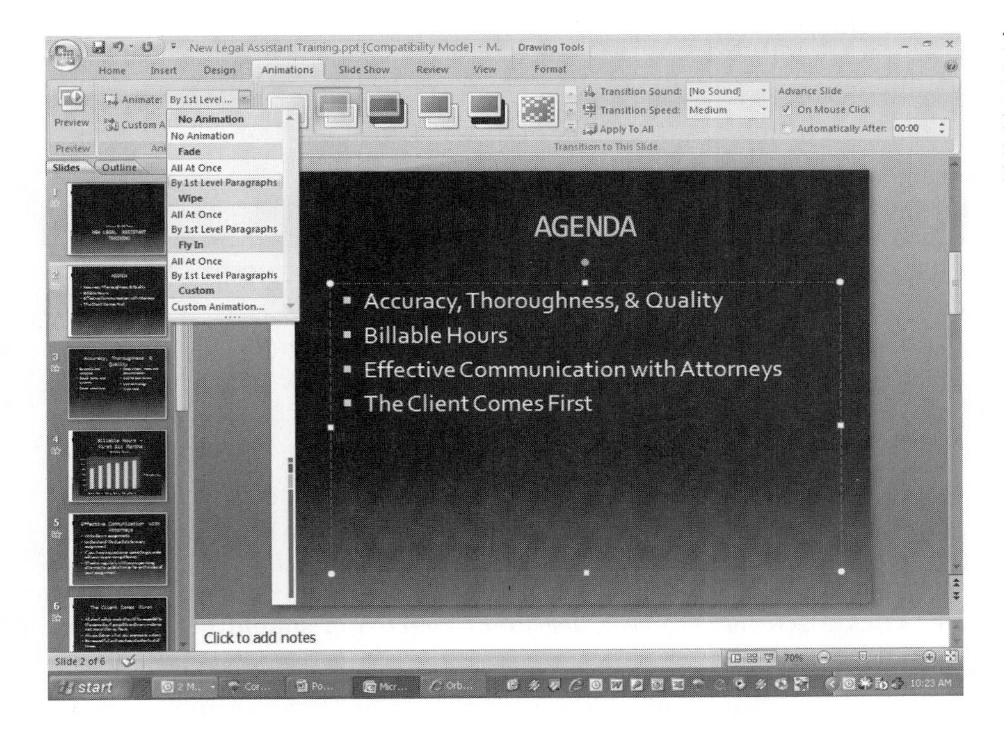

PowerPoint 2007 Exhibit 13

Microsoft product screen shot reprinted with permission from Microsoft Corporation.

29. ***Click anywhere in the lower half of the screen ("Accuracy, Thoroughness, & Quality").***

30. ***Next, on the Animations ribbon tab, click the down arrow next to "Animate: No Animation" in the Animation group*** (see PowerPoint 2007 Exhibit 13).

31. ***Under Fade, click By 1st Level Paragraphs.*** Notice that the animation effect is then demonstrated.

32. ***Repeat this same process for slides 3, 5, and 6.*** *Note:* Because Slide 3 has two columns, you must do each column separately.

33. You are now ready to view your presentation. Press the **[PAGE UP]** key to go to the first slide in the presentation.

34. ***Click the Slide Show icon at the bottom right of the screen.***

35. Your first slide is now shown full-screen size. To proceed to the next slide, press the **[SPACE BAR]** or click the left mouse button. Keep pressing the **[SPACE BAR]** or clicking the left mouse button to proceed with the presentation. Notice on the slides with bullets that you must press the **[SPACE BAR]** or click the mouse to go to the next bullet; this is the animation effect you created.

36. When you get to the end of the presentation, press the **[SPACE BAR]** keyboard or click the left mouse button to go back to editing the presentation.

37. To print your presentation, ***click the Office Button, point to Print, and then click OK.***

38. To save your presentation, ***click the Save icon (it looks like a floppy disk) on the Quick Access toolbar.***

39. ***Click the Office Button, and then click Close.***

This concludes Lesson 4.

To Exit PowerPoint

To exit PowerPoint, ***click the Office Button and then click Exit PowerPoint.***

ADVANCED

LESSON 5: CUSTOMIZING AND FINALIZING AN OPENING STATEMENT PRESENTATION

In this lesson, you will insert a slide from an old presentation into a new presentation while still maintaining the formatting of the new presentation, edit a master slide, create a table, add a "grow" animation effect, and add transition effects to a presentation.

1. Start Windows. Then, ***double-click the Microsoft Office PowerPoint 2007 icon on the desktop*** to start PowerPoint 2007 for Windows. Alternatively, ***click the Start button, point to Programs or All Programs, and then click the Microsoft PowerPoint 2007 icon (or point to Microsoft Office and then click Microsoft Office PowerPoint 2007).*** You should be in a clean, blank document.

2. The next thing you will need to do is open the "Lesson 5A" file from Disk 1 supplied with this text. Ensure that Disk 1 is inserted in the disk drive, ***click the Office Button, and then click Open.*** The Open window should now be displayed. ***Navigate to the drive where Disk 1 is located. Click the PowerPoint Files folder, then double-click to open the Lesson 5A document.***

3. The presentation "Opening Statement—Smith v. EZ Pest Control Worldwide" should now be displayed.

4. The first thing you need to do is to insert a slide from another presentation into this presentation just after the title slide, so make sure you are at the first slide before proceeding.

5. ***On the Home ribbon tab, click the down arrow next to New Slide in the Slides group.***

6. ***Click the bottom option, Reuse Slides.*** Notice that the Reuse Slides task pane is now displayed on the right side of the screen.

7. *Click Browse, and then click Browse File...*

8. *The Browse window should now be displayed. Navigate to the drive where the Disk 1 is located.*

9. *Click the PowerPoint Files folder, then double-click to open the "Lesson 5B" document.*

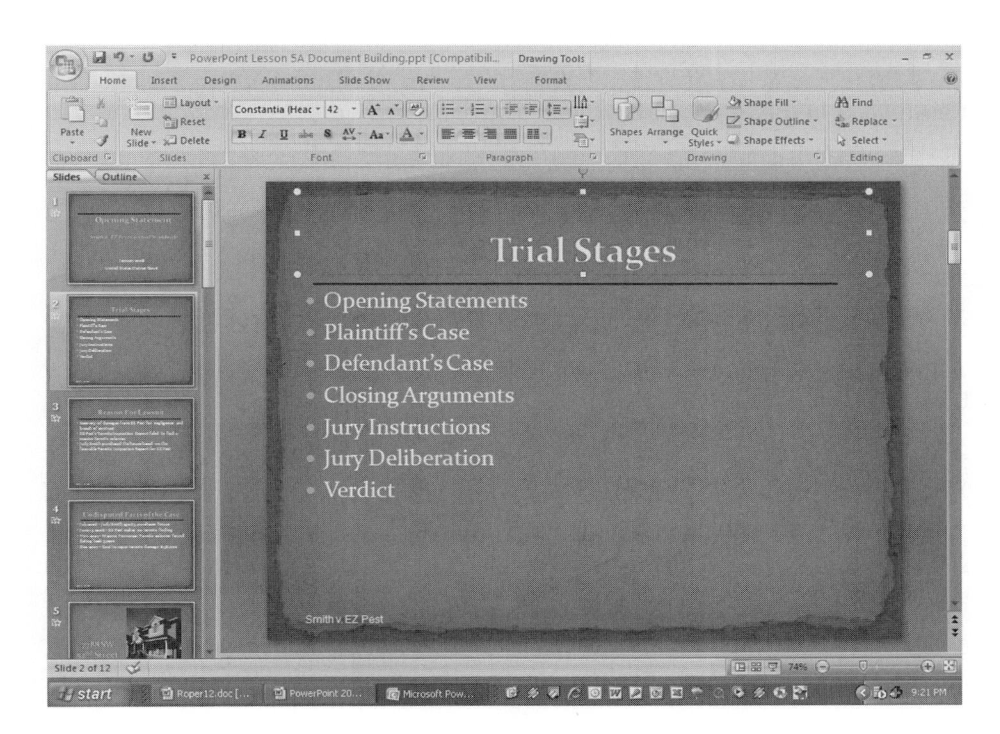

PowerPoint 2007 Exhibit 14

Microsoft product screen shot reprinted with permission from Microsoft Corporation.

10. The Reuse Slides window should again be displayed and the path for the file should now be entered (see PowerPoint 2007 Exhibit 14).

11. Notice that there is one slide shown in PowerPoint 2007 Exhibit 14. There is only one slide in this presentation, but if there were more, they would be displayed. The title of the slide is "Trial Stages."

12. ***Point to the slide.*** Notice that it becomes larger so that you can read it.

13. Notice at the bottom of the Reuse Slides window that there is an option that says "Keep source formatting." If you wanted to insert the existing slide into the new presentation, but you wanted to keep the existing slide's background and style, you could click this option. Because we want the slide we are adding to take the format of our new presentation, we will leave it unchecked.

14. ***Right-click the Trial Stages slide.*** Notice that the options include the ability to insert the single slide or insert all of the slides in the presentation. ***Click Insert Slide to insert the Trial Stages slide into the Opening Statement presentation.***

15. ***Click Close in the Reuse Slides window.***

16. You will now learn how to use the Format Painter feature in PowerPoint.

17. Press **[PAGE DOWN]** to go the third slide. ***Then, click anywhere in the title "Reason For Lawsuit."***

18. ***On the Home ribbon tab, click the Format Painter icon in the Clipboard group (it looks like a paintbrush).*** The Format Painter tool copies the formatting from one piece of text to another. Notice that your cursor is now looks like a paintbrush.

19. Press the **[PAGE UP]** key to return to the Trial Stages slide.

20. ***Click and drag the mouse pointer over the title "Trial Stages" so that it is highlighted and then let go of the mouse button.*** Notice that the format of the title now appears the same as in the third slide.

21. ***With the title "Trial Stages" still selected, on the Home ribbon tab click the Center icon in the Paragraph group.***

22. ***Click anywhere in the slide to make the highlighting disappear.***

23. Press **[PAGE DOWN]** to go the third slide.

24. ***Right-click the black line just under "Reason for Lawsuit" and click Copy.***

25. Press the **[PAGE UP]** key to return to the Trial Stages slide.

26. ***Right-click anywhere in the slide and select Paste.*** A black line should now be visible under "Trial Stages."

27. Notice that the slide now appears in your presentation and that it matches your formatting for the current presentation.

28. Each slide presentation has master slides that control the look and feel of all slides. You will now add something to the master slide so that it appears on all slides in the presentation.

29. ***On the View ribbon tab, click Slide Master in the Presentation Views group.*** Notice that you now see an outline of your slides. If you make changes to font

PowerPoint 2007 Exhibit 15

Microsoft product screen shot reprinted with permission from Microsoft Corporation.

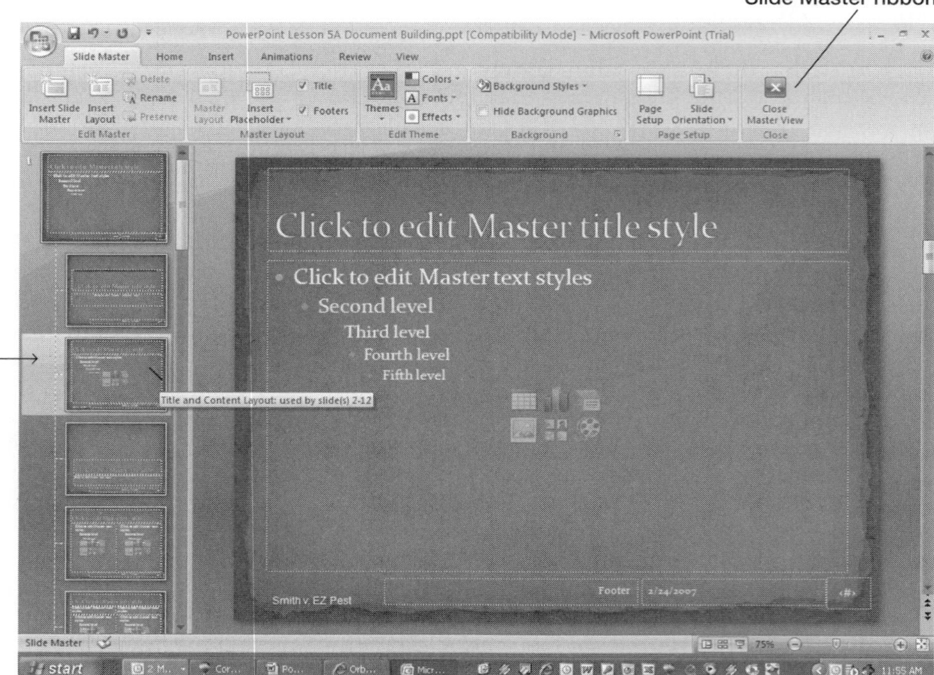

sizes or font colors, or make other changes in the master slide, it will affect all of the other slides that use the master slide you are changing.

30. ***Point to the third slide on the left of the screen; notice that a title appears saying that this slide master is being used by slides 2–12. Click this slide*** (see PowerPoint 2007 Exhibit 15).

31. You will now add a small text box that says *Smith v. EZ Pest* in the lower left of the screen.

32. ***On the Insert ribbon tab, click Text Box in the Text group.*** Your mouse pointer now turns to a gray upside-down cross. You now will draw the text box where your text will go. ***Point to the lower left corner of the screen, and then drag your mouse down and to the right to draw a small rectangular box.*** Make sure that the box is very close to the bottom border, because if it is too high it will interfere with some of the text in the slides.

33. ***On the Home ribbon tab, point to the down arrow on the Font Size icon in the Font group, and select "12."*** Then, type **Smith v. EZ Pest.**

34. ***Click Slide Master on the Ribbon Bar, and then click "Close Master View" in the Close group.***

35. ***Go to slides 2–11 and notice that*** **Smith v. EZ Pest** ***is in the lower left of the screen.***

36. You will now add a new slide with a table. Go to the last slide in the presentation.

37. ***On the Home ribbon tab, click the down arrow next to New Slide in the Slides Group. Select Title Only.***

38. ***Click "Click to add title."*** Type: **Cost to Repair Damage.** ***Use Format Painter to copy the correct title format from the "Reason for Lawsuit" slide to the "Cost to Repair Damage" slide.***

39. The "Cost to Repair" slide should now be ready for additional information to be added to it.

40. You will now add a table showing a breakdown of costs. ***On the Insert ribbon tab, click Table in the Tables group.***

41. ***Drag the mouse so that you have a table that is two columns wide and five rows deep*** (see PowerPoint 2007 Exhibit 16) ***and then press the*** **[ENTER]** ***key.***

42. The table is now displayed. ***Click the outside frame of the table and drag the frame down so it fits properly in the screen.***

43. Enter the information found in PowerPoint 2007 Exhibit 16.

44. When you have finished entering all of the information in the table, ***point to the Description cell and drag the mouse pointer to the "$158,000" cell so that the entire table is highlighted.***

45. ***Then, on the Home ribbon tab, click the down arrow in the Font Size icon in the Font group, and click on "28."***

46. Press the **[ESC]** key to make the highlighting disappear.

PowerPoint 2007 Exhibit 16

Microsoft product screen shot reprinted with permission from Microsoft Corporation.

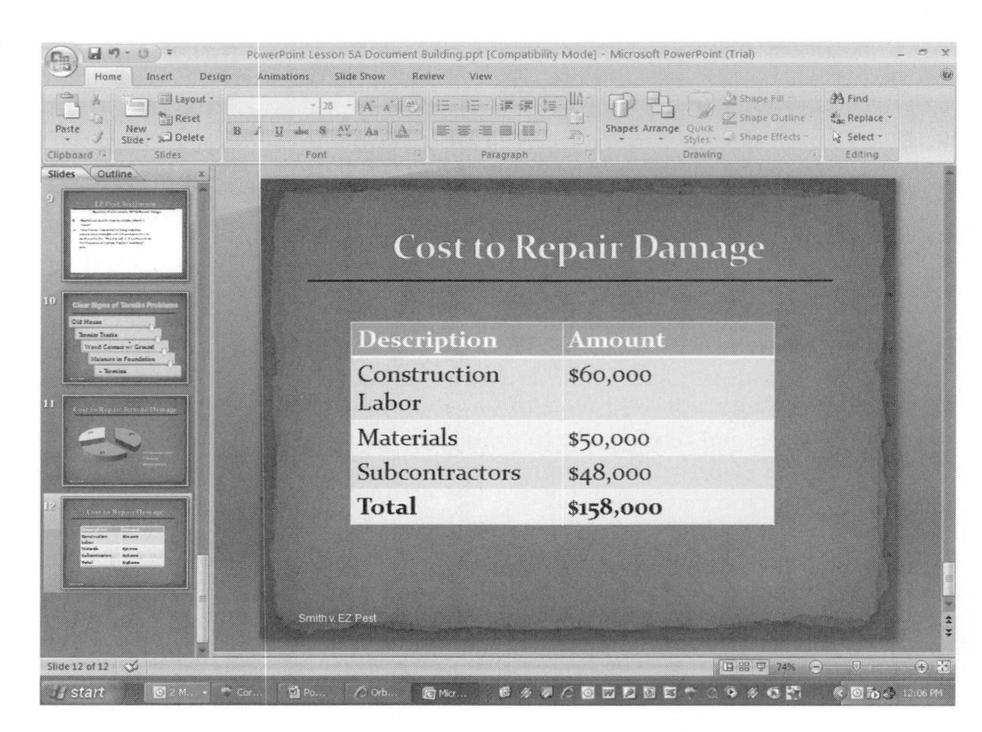

47. *Click in the last cell to the left ("Total") and drag the mouse pointer one cell to the right (to the "$158,000" cell) so that the last two cells in the table are selected. Then, on the Home ribbon bar, click the Bold icon in the Font group.*

48. Your table should now look similar to PowerPoint 2007 Exhibit 16.

49. Press the **[PAGE UP]** key so that you are at the "Cost to Repair Termite Damage" pie chart.

50. You will now add animation to the slide to give it a dramatic effect.

51. *Click anywhere in the pie chart.*

PowerPoint 2007 Exhibit 17

Microsoft product screen shot reprinted with permission from Microsoft Corporation.

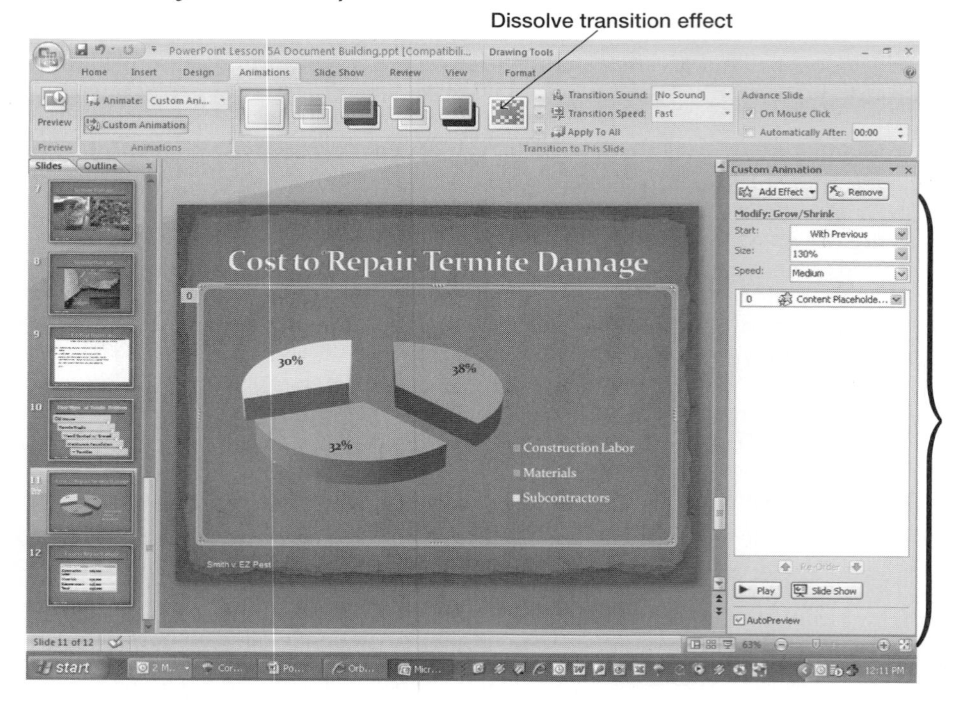

52. ***On the Animations ribbon tab, click Custom Animation in the Animations group.***

53. The Custom Animation task pane should now be displayed (see PowerPoint 2007 Exhibit 17).

54. ***Click Add Effect in the Custom Animation task pane.***

55. ***Point to Emphasis, and then click Grow/Shrink.***

56. ***Click the down arrow next to Start: On Click and then click With Previous.***

57. ***Click the down arrow next to Size: 150%, click Custom and change the size to 130%,*** and then press the **[ENTER]** key. Your screen should now look similar to PowerPoint 2007 Exhibit 17.

58. ***Click Play in the Custom Animation task pane to see the animation effect.***

59. You will now enter a transition effect. ***Click the Animation ribbon tab.***

60. ***On the Animation ribbon tab, click the Dissolve transition effect.***

61. ***On the Animation ribbon tab, click Apply To All in the Transition to This Slide group.*** This will apply the Dissolve effect to all of the slides in the presentation.

62. ***On the Animation ribbon tab, click the down arrow next to Transition Speed: Fast, and then click Medium*** (see PowerPoint 2007 Exhibit 12).

63. ***On the Animation ribbon tab, click "Automatically after" under "Advance slide" in the Slide Transition task pane.***

64. ***Under "Automatically after," change the time to every two seconds (00:02)*** and then press the **[ENTER]** key.

65. ***Click in the "On mouse click" box so that it is unselected.***

66. ***Then, click Apply to All Slides"***

67. ***Click the Slide Sorter icon.*** Notice that it shows the two-second advance on all slides.

68. ***Double-click the first slide.***

69. You are now ready to view your presentation. ***Click the Slide Show icon at the bottom right of the screen to watch your presentation.*** The slides should automatically change every two seconds.

70. When the presentation is completed, ***click the mouse.***

71. To print your presentation, ***click the Office Button, then point to Print and click Print.***

72. ***In the Print window under Print What, click the down arrow and notice that you can print slides, handouts, notes pages, and Outline view.***

73. ***Click Slides, and then click OK.***

74. To save your presentation, ***click the Save icon (it looks like a floppy disk) on the Quick Access toolbar. If a window is displayed regarding compatibility, click Continue.***

This concludes the PowerPoint 2007 Hands-On Exercises. To exit PowerPoint, ***click the Office Button, then click Exit PowerPoint.***

HANDS-ON EXERCISES

SMARTDRAW LEGAL HANDS ON EXERCISES

SmartDraw Legal Presentation Graphics Software Read this first!

I. Introduction – Read this!

The SmartDraw Legal presentation graphics program demonstration version is a full working version of the program with a few limitations. One of the limitations is that the demonstration version times out (quits working) after 120 days. Therefore, it is highly recommended that you not install the program until you are ready to complete the SmartDraw Legal Hands-on Exercises.

II. Using the SmartDraw Legal Hands-on Exercises

The SmartDraw Legal Hands-on Exercises are easy to use and contain step-by-step instructions. Each lesson builds on the previous exercise, so please complete the Hands-on Exercises in order.

III. Installation Instructions

Below are step-by-step instructions for installing the SmartDraw presentation graphics demonstration version on your computer.

1. *Insert Disk 2 supplied with this text into your computer.*

2. When prompted with "What do you want Windows to do?" select "Open folder to view files using Windows Explorer." If your computer does not automatically recognize that you have inserted a CD, double-click the My Computer icon, then double-click the drive where Disk 2 is.

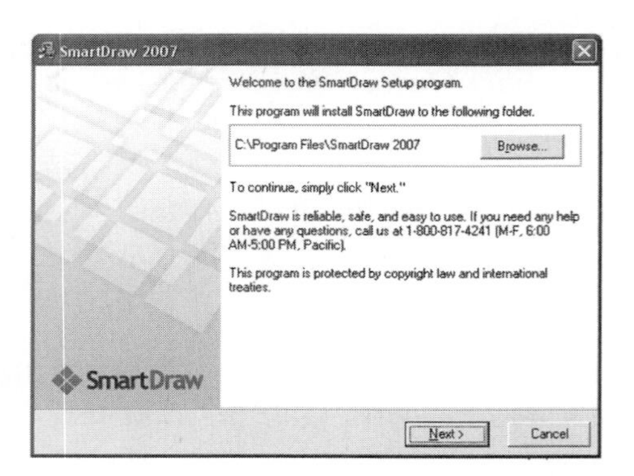

SmartDraw Installation Exhibit 1

Courtesy SmartDraw.

3. Double-click the SmartDraw 2007 folder. Then, double-click the setup.exe file. This will start the SmartDraw installation wizard.

4. The screen in SmartDraw Installation Exhibit 1 should now be displayed.

5. *Click Next to install SmartDraw in the default directory.*

6. The screen in SmartDraw Installation Exhibit 2 should now be displayed. *Click I Accept to accept the license agreement.*

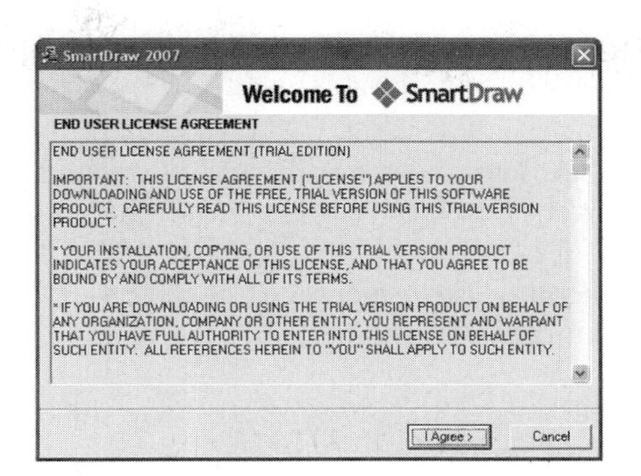

SmartDraw Installation Exhibit 2

Courtesy SmartDraw.

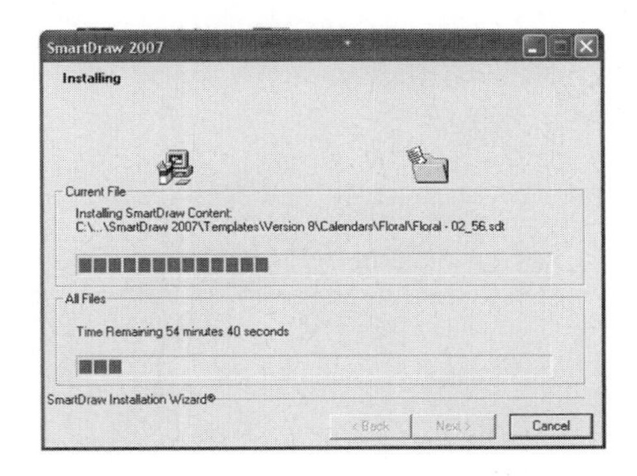

SmartDraw Installation Exhibit 3

Courtesy SmartDraw.

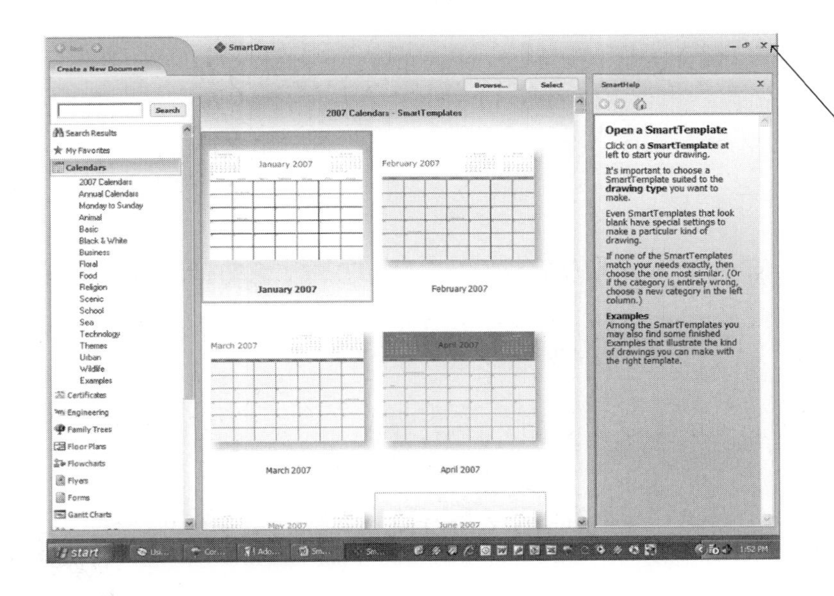

SmartDraw Installation Exhibit 4

Screenshot created using SmartDraw legal edition software.

7. The screen in SmartDraw Installation Exhibit 3 should now be displayed. Files should now be copied on to your computer.

8. When installation is complete, the program will be started. See SmartDraw Installation Exhibit 4.

9. ***Click the Close ("X") icon in the upper right of the SmartDraw screen*** (see SmartDraw Installation Exhibit 4).

10. If you have an Internet connection, your web browser may open Smart-Draw's web page. ***Close your browser.***

IV. Installation Technical Support

If you have problems installing the demonstration version of SmartDraw from the CD-ROM included with this text, please contact Thomson Delmar Learning Technical Support first at (800) 477–3692. Please note that SmartDraw is a licensed product of SmartDraw.com If Thomson Delmar Learning Technical Support is unable to resolve your installation question or if you have a non-installation related question you will need to contact SmartDraw.com directly at (800) 768–3729.

HANDS-ON EXERCISES

SMARTDRAW LEGAL

Basic Lesson

Number	Lesson Title	Concepts Covered
Lesson 1	Introduction to SmartDraw Legal	Understanding the SmartDraw Legal interface, legal templates, tools and features of the program, and the general layout of the screen
Intermediate Lesson		
Lesson 2	Simple Accident Reconstruction Scene	Using SmartTemplate, creating a simple accident reconstruction diagram, selecting items, from various symbol libraries, entering text, using the rotate and flip tools, coloring items, and resizing items
Advanced Lesson		
Lesson 3	More Complex Accident Reconstruction Scene	Creating roadways from scratch, using additional symbol libraries, grouping items, rotating and flipping items, and resizing items

GETTING STARTED

Throughout these exercises, information you need to operate the program will be designated in several different ways.

- Keys to be pressed on the keyboard will be designated in brackets, in all caps, bold and enlarged type (press the **[ENTER]** key).
- Movements with the mouse will be designated in bold and italics (***point to File on the menu bar and click the mouse***).
- Words or letters that should be typed will be designated in bold and enlarged (type **Training Program**).
- Information that is or should be displayed on your computer screen will be shown in the following style: ***Press ENTER to continue.***

LESSON 1: INTRODUCTION TO SMARTDRAW LEGAL

In this lesson, you will learn about the SmartDraw Legal interface, including the different legal templates that come with SmartDraw Legal, and you'll get an overview of the many tools and features in SmartDraw.

1. Start Windows. Then, ***double-click the SmartDraw 2007 icon on the desktop*** to start SmartDraw 2007 for Windows. Alternatively, ***click the Start button, point to Programs or All Programs, point to SmartDraw 2007, and then click SmartDraw 2007.***

2. When you start SmartDraw Legal a screen similar to SmartDraw Legal Exhibit 1 should be displayed. If your screen is different from SmartDraw Legal Exhibit 1, ***click the Legal tab in the top left of the screen and then click Accident Reconstruction on the left side of the screen.***

3. The screen in SmartDraw Legal Exhibit 1 is called the Document Browser. In the Document Browser, you can create a new document or open an existing document. On the left slide of the screen is a list of SmartTemplates. They are templates from which you can start your drawing. As you can see, there are many types of legal SmartTemplates for many different types of cases.

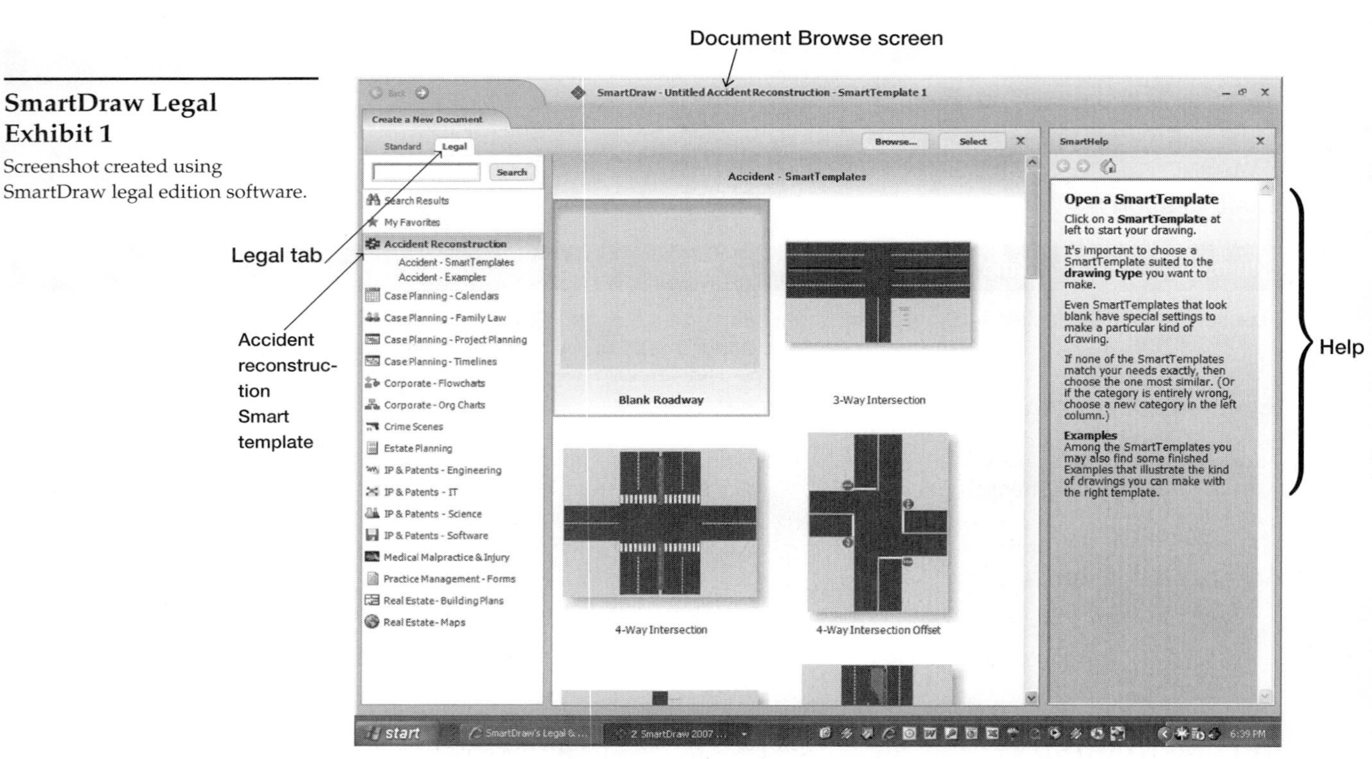

SmartDraw Legal Exhibit 1

Screenshot created using SmartDraw legal edition software.

4. Notice that in the middle of the screen there are several SmartTemplates related to accident reconstruction. ***Use the scroll bar to scroll down the Accident—SmartTemplates list.*** Toward the bottom of the screen there are a number of accident reconstruction examples.

5. ***Click Crime Scenes on the left side of the screen, and then click Crime Scenes Examples.*** Notice that a number of crime scenes are now displayed.

6. ***Scroll down through the crime scene examples.***

7. ***In the task pane on the left, click Medical Malpractice & Injury, and then click Medical Examples.***

8. ***Scroll down through the list of medical examples.***

9. ***In the task pane on the left, click Case Planning—Timelines, and then click Timelines—Examples.***

10. ***Scroll down through the list of timeline examples.*** Notice that some of the timelines are quite colorful and extensive.

11. As you can see, SmartDraw Legal is extremely versatile. On the right side of the screen is a help feature called "SmartHelp," which changes depending on what the user is doing.

12. ***Click Accident Reconstruction on the left side of the screen and then click Accident—Examples.***

13. ***Click the Accident at Curved Point example.***

14. The screen in SmartDraw Legal Exhibit 2 should now be displayed. On the left side of the screen is the Left Panel. This is where the open symbol library is displayed.

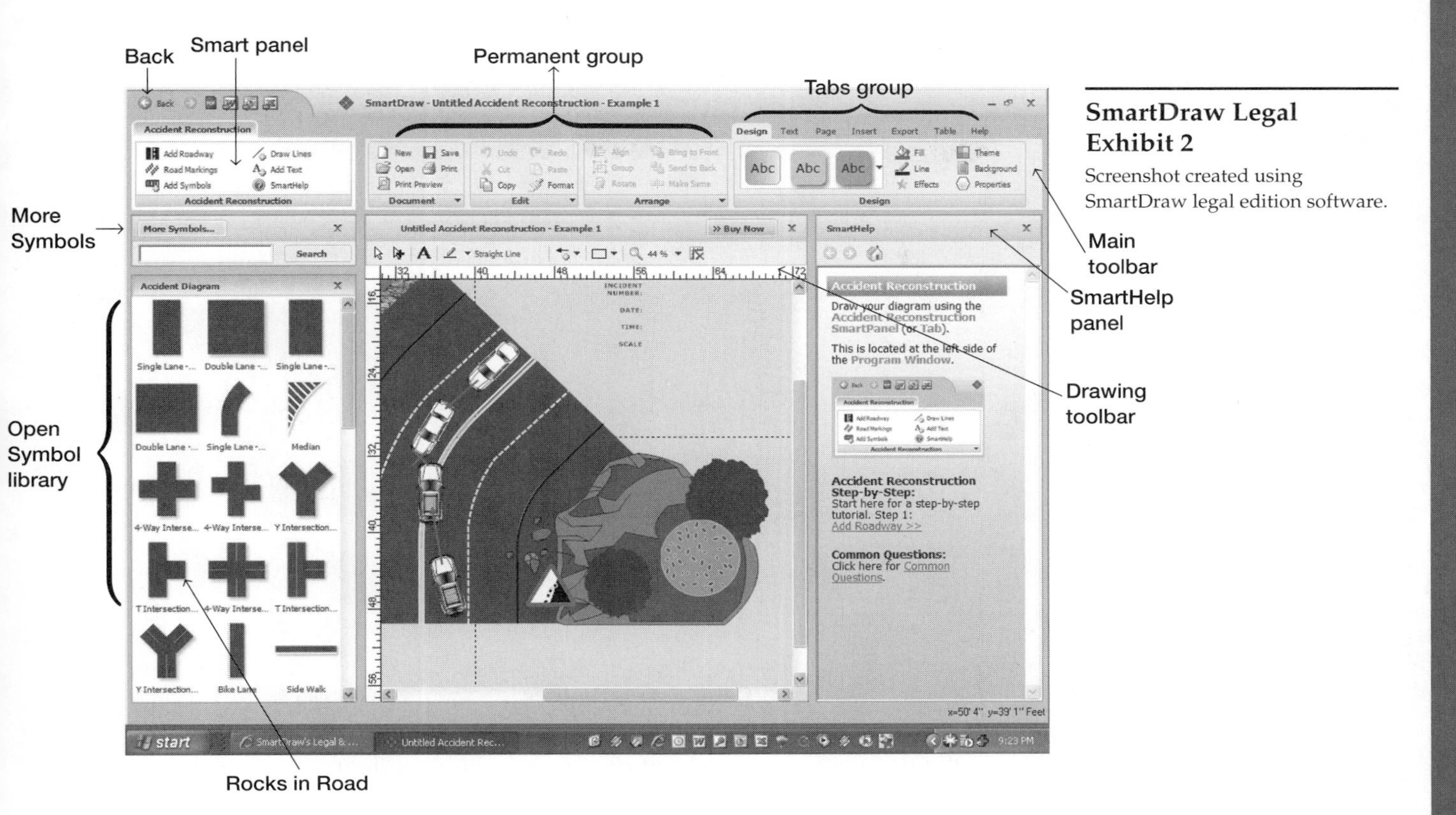

SmartDraw Legal Exhibit 2

Screenshot created using SmartDraw legal edition software.

15. Notice in SmartDraw Legal Exhibit 2 that the Left Panel currently displays different types of roadways.

16. ***Click Road Markings in the upper left of the toolbar.*** Notice that the Left Panel changed to road markings.

17. ***Now, click Add Symbols in the upper left of the toolbar.*** Notice that the Vehicles library now appears in the Left Panel. Notice also that the libraries are stacked on top of one another, and that just above the word "Vehicles" you can see the titles "Road Markings" and "Accident Diagram."

18. ***Click "Accident Diagram" in the Left Panel.*** Notice that the accident diagrams and roadways are now displayed.

19. ***Click "More Symbols..." just above the Left Panel*** (see SmartDraw Legal Exhibit 2).

20. The More Symbols window should now be displayed (see SmartDraw Legal Exhibit 3). Notice that there are many symbol libraries for different kinds of templates, including Accident Reconstruction, Anatomy and Physiology, and Crime Scenes.

21. ***Click the plus sign next to Accident Reconstruction in the More Symbols window.*** Notice that many more symbol libraries are displayed, including Accident Diagram, Articulated Body, Auto Accident, and several others.

22. ***Point to Traffic Signs in the More Symbols window.*** Notice that a small preview of the symbol library is displayed.

23. ***Now, click Traffic Signs and notice that larger versions of the traffic signs are displayed in the right section of the More Symbols window.***

SmartDraw Legal Exhibit 3

Screenshot created using SmartDraw legal edition software.

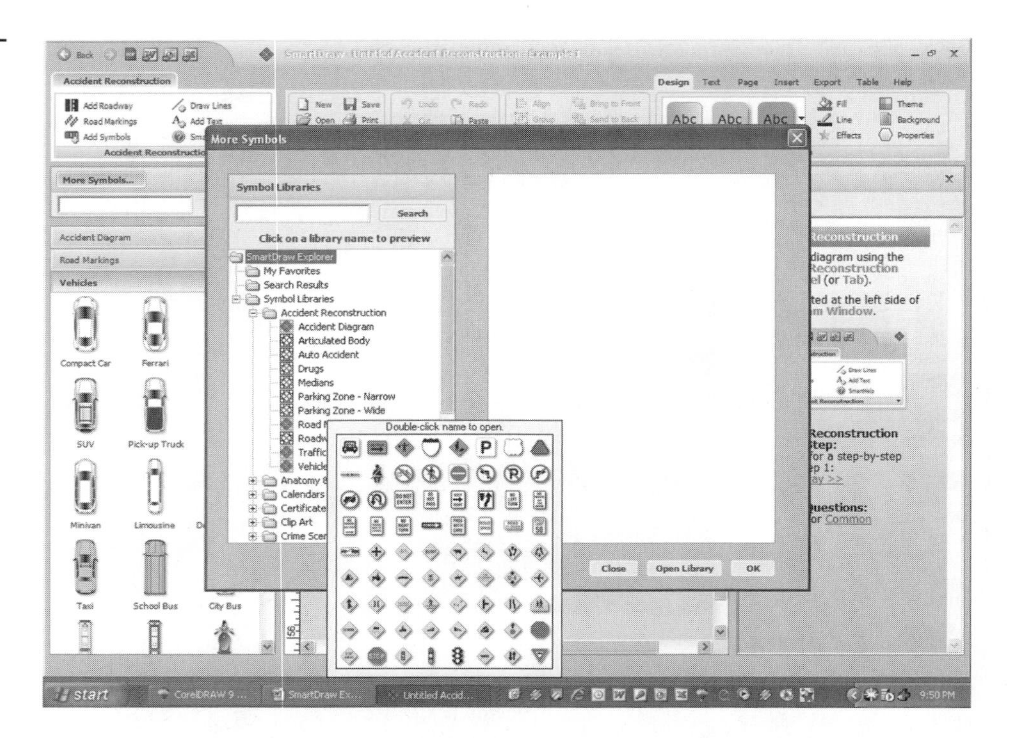

24. ***Click OK in the lower right of the More Symbols window.*** Notice that the Traffic Signs library is now shown in the Left Panel.

25. To close a library, click the Close ("X") icon on the library title. ***Click the Close ("X") icon to the right of the Road Markings library.*** Notice that the Road Markings library disappeared.

26. The SmartDraw Legal toolbar extends across the top of the screen (see SmartDraw Legal Exhibit 2). The SmartDraw Legal toolbar is divided into three sections.

27. The first section is in the upper left and is called the SmartPanel. The SmartPanel contains tools specific to a particular kind of drawing. The tools in the SmartPanel in SmartDraw Legal Exhibit 2 are directly related to accident reconstruction.

28. The second section of the toolbar is the Permanent Group. This is called the permanent group because these tools do not change. They include features such as Document (file, save, print, etc.), Edit (copy, cut, paste) and Arrange (bring to front, rotate, etc.).

29. The third section of the toolbar is the Tab group. The tools in the Tab group change depending on the tab that is selected. Tools on the Tab group include design/color tools, text and font tools, page and margin tools, inserting pictures and tables, etc.

30. The right side of the screen is SmartHelp. This panel can be turned off to give you more room for your drawing.

31. The center panel is where the actual drawing takes place.

32. In the center panel, just above the ruler, there is a Drawing toolbar (see SmartDraw Legal Exhibit 2).

33. The Drawing toolbar includes several important tools and features. ***Point to the letter "A" on the Drawing toolbar.*** Notice that the name of the tool, "Create

or Edit Text," including a short explanation, appears. This tool allows you to add text to your drawing.

34. ***Click Text in the Tab group.*** This is where you can control the size, color, and format of your text.

35. ***Click the down arrow just to the left of Straight Line on the Drawing toolbar.*** This is the Line Type tool. Notice that you are given many choices of different types of lines that you can draw.

36. Press the **[ESC]** key to make the Line Type options disappear.

37. ***Click the Apply Arrowheads tool just to the right of the Line Type Tool.*** The Apply Arrowheads tool allows you to draw lines with arrows.

38. ***Click Left.*** Notice that your mouse pointer turns into a pen. ***Click the tree near the rocks in the road, point mouse to the rocks in the road, and then click the mouse.*** A red line should now be shown pointing to the rocks in the road.

39. ***Click the down arrow in the Add a Shape icon (it looks like a rectangle) on the Drawing toolbar.*** Notice that you can select many types of shapes, including squares, ovals, and circles.

40. Press the **[ESC]** key to make the Shape Type options disappear.

41. ***Click the down arrow next to the Zoom tool (it looks like a magnifying glass).*** This is where you can zoom into or out of your drawing.

42. Press the **[ESC]** key to make the Zoom options disappear.

43. ***Click the Select an Object tool (it is all the way over to the left and looks like an arrow) on the Drawing toolbar.*** This is how you can select and move items in your drawing.

44. ***Click the car that is crossing the double yellow line. Drag the car to the left so that the drawing shows a head-on collision, and then let go of the mouse button.***

45. ***Right-click the same car.*** Notice that many options are displayed, including copy, flip, and rotate.

46. ***Point to Rotate and then click 45.*** Notice that the rotation of the car changed.

47. A very important feature in SmartDraw Legal is the Undo feature (**[CTRL]+[Z]**) which is also found in the Edit group on the toolbar). The Undo feature works on most actions in the program. It allows you to undo something you have just done.

48. Press **[CTRL]+[Z]** to undo the rotation change.

49. ***Click the Back button in the upper left of the screen.*** You should now be back at the Document Browser.

50. ***Click the Close ("X") icon in the upper right of the screen.***

51. ***Click No in the SmartDraw window that asks if you want to save the Untitled Accident Reconstruction—Example 1 file.***

This concludes Lesson 1.

LESSON 2: SIMPLE ACCIDENT RECONSTRUCTION SCENE

In this lesson, you will learn how to use a SmartTemplate and create a simple accident reconstruction diagram. This includes selecting items from the various symbol libraries, entering text, using the rotate and flip tools, coloring items, and resizing items.

1. Start Windows. Then, ***double-click on the SmartDraw 2007 icon on the desktop*** to start SmartDraw 2007 for Windows. Alternatively, ***click the Start button, point to Programs or All Programs, point to SmartDraw 2007, and then click SmartDraw 2007.***

2. You should now be at the Document Browser (see SmartDraw Legal Exhibit 1).

3. Click Accident Reconstruction in the Left Panel, and then click Accident—Smart Templates.

4. ***Click 4-Way Intersection (the second option on the left).*** The four-way intersection template should now be displayed.

5. Notice that it is difficult to see a full view of the intersection. ***Click the Close ("X") icon next to SmartHelp on the right panel of the screen.*** You now have more room to see your drawing.

6. Throughout this lesson, you can use the scroll bars and the Zoom feature on the Drawing toolbar to adjust the view of your drawing.

7. ***Click Add Symbols in the Accident Reconstruction Group section of the toolbar, all the way over to the left.*** Notice that the Vehicle symbols library now appears in the Left Panel.

8. ***Click the Ferrari.*** Notice that your cursor turns into a box; this is a general outline of the current size of the Ferrari. You will need to resize it, but this is the starting size of the graphic.

9. ***Point to the middle of the intersection and click the mouse*** (see SmartDraw Legal Exhibit 4).

10. Notice that the Ferrari is very large compared to the scale of the roadway. This is easy to fix.

11. Notice that there are four squares around the Ferrari. (If there are not four squares, just click the Ferrari.) The squares are called "handles." You can click and drag the handles to change the size and shape of objects.

12. ***Click the left handle at the front of the Ferrari and drag it back and to the right until the Ferrari fits within one of the lanes (see SmartDraw Legal Exhibit 4).***

13. ***Click the Ferrari and drag the mouse pointer to move it so it is entering the intersection.***

14. You will now change the color of the Ferrari. ***With the Ferrari still selected, click Fill on the Design tab in the Tabs group. Then, click any shade of red.*** The Ferrari should now be red.

15. ***Click the Minivan in the Vehicles symbol library and place it in the intersection (do not worry about rotating it yet). Use the same procedures as you used for the Ferrari to resize the minivan using the handles, and place it in the intersection.***

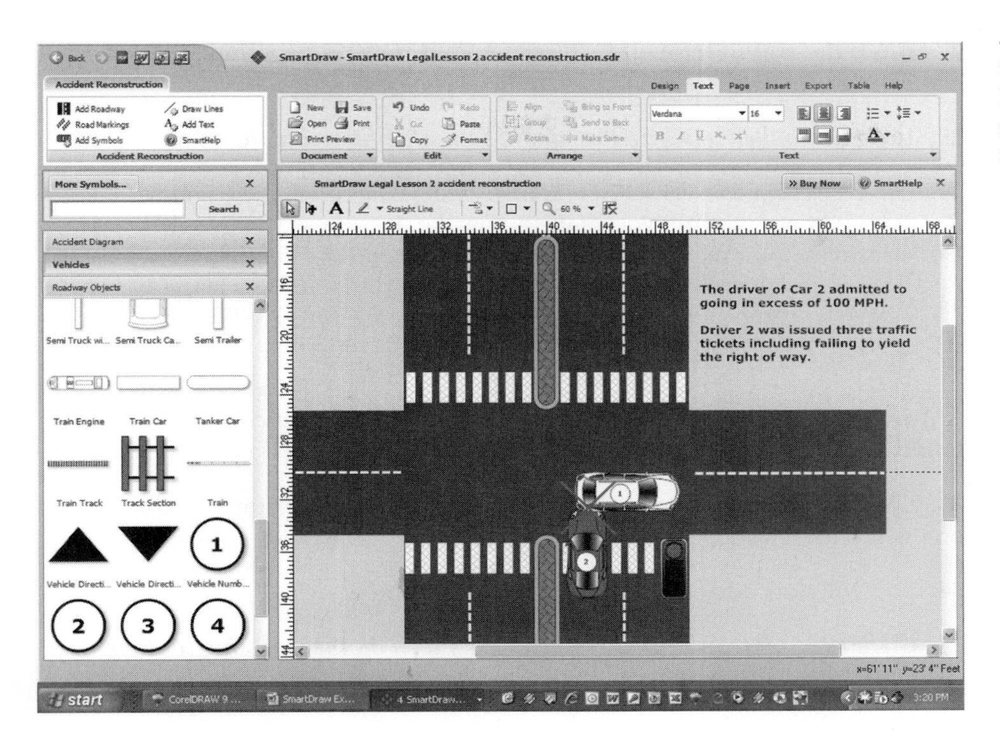

SmartDraw Legal Exhibit 4

Screenshot created using SmartDraw legal edition software.

16. ***To rotate the minivan, right-click the minivan. Then, point to Rotate and click 90.***

17. ***Next, right-click the minivan, point to Flip, and then click Vertical. Place the minivan in the intersection.***

18. You will now add a large red "X" to show the collision. ***Click Accident Diagram in the Left Panel just above the word "Vehicles."***

19. ***Scroll to the bottom of the list and click Damage. Then click the spot where the two vehicles collide.***

20. You will now add a traffic light to the drawing.

21. ***Click More Symbols just above the Left Panel.*** The More Symbols window should now be displayed.

22. ***Click Roadway Objects under Accident Reconstruction. Next, click OK in the More Symbols library.***

23. ***Click Traffic Light—3 in the Left Panel. Then, click the right side of the lane where the Ferrari is*** to place the traffic light there.

24. ***Enlarge the traffic light just a little by clicking the top left handle and dragging the mouse up and to the left.***

25. You will now draw a box to cover the yellow and green lights of the traffic light to illustrate that the traffic light was red (according to eyewitness accounts).

26. ***Click the down arrow next to the Add a Shape icon on the Drawing toolbar, and then select Square.***

27. *Click the traffic light.* The square should now be superimposed over the traffic light.

28. ***Use the handles to resize the square so that it fit inside the traffic light.***

29. ***On the Design Tab, click Fill and then change the color of the square to black.*** Remember, if at any time you make a mistake, just press **[CTRL]+[Z]** or select Undo from the Edit menu on the toolbar to undo the last item(s).

30. You will now add numbers to the cars so you can easily identify them.

31. ***Click the Vehicles symbol library in the Left Panel.***

32. ***Scroll to the bottom, click the number 1 in a circle and click the roof of the minivan.*** The graphic now appears on the minivan.

33. ***Click the number 2 and click the roof of the Ferrari.*** The graphic now appears on the Ferrari.

34. You will now add some explanatory text to the drawing.

35. ***Click the Create or Edit Text (letter "A") icon on the Drawing toolbar.***

36. ***Click the Text tab in the Tab group, click the down arrow in Font Size, and click 16.***

37. ***Click the upper right of the drawing (see SmartDraw Legal Exhibit 4).*** Type **The driver of Car 2 admitted to** and then press the **[ENTER]** key.

38. Type the following text (You must press the **[ENTER]** key at the end of each line):

going in excess of 100 MPH.

Driver 2 was issued three traffic tickets including failing to yield the right of way.

39. When you have typed all of the text, notice that the text is difficult to read. ***Drag the mouse pointer so that all of the text is highlighted, and then click the Bold icon (B) on the Text Tab in the Tab Group.***

40. To save your drawing, ***click Save in the Document group on the toolbar.*** In the File name field, type **SmartDraw Legal Lesson 2** and then ***click Save.***

41. To print your drawing, ***click Print in the Document group, then click Print with watermark.***

42. The Print window should now be displayed. ***Click the option to print it on one page, then click Print.*** *Note:* The demonstration version of SmartDraw Legal only allows you to print a few times before it prohibits further printing, so only print what you need to.

43. ***Click the Back button in the upper left of the screen.*** You should now be back at the Document Browser.

44. ***Click Create a New Document in the top left of the screen.***

This concludes Lesson 2.

To Exit SmartDraw Legal, ***click the Close icon ("X") in the upper right of the screen.***

LESSON 3: MORE COMPLEX ACCIDENT RECONSTRUCTION SCENE

In this lesson, you will build a more complex accident reconstruction drawing. This lesson assumes you have completed Lessons 1 and 2 and that you are generally familiar with the features and tools in those lessons.

1. Start Windows. Then, ***double-click the SmartDraw 2007 icon on the desktop*** to start SmartDraw 2007 for Windows. Alternatively, ***click the Start button, point to Programs or All Programs, point to SmartDraw 2007, and then click SmartDraw 2007.***

2. You should now be at the Document Browser and the drawing you created in Lesson 2 should now be displayed. ***Click Create a New Document at the top of the screen.***

3. ***Click Accident Reconstruction in the Left Panel and then click Accident—Smart Templates.***

4. ***Click Blank Roadway (the first option).***

5. ***Click the Close ("X") icon next to SmartHelp on the right panel of the screen to close the help feature*** so you have additional drawing space.

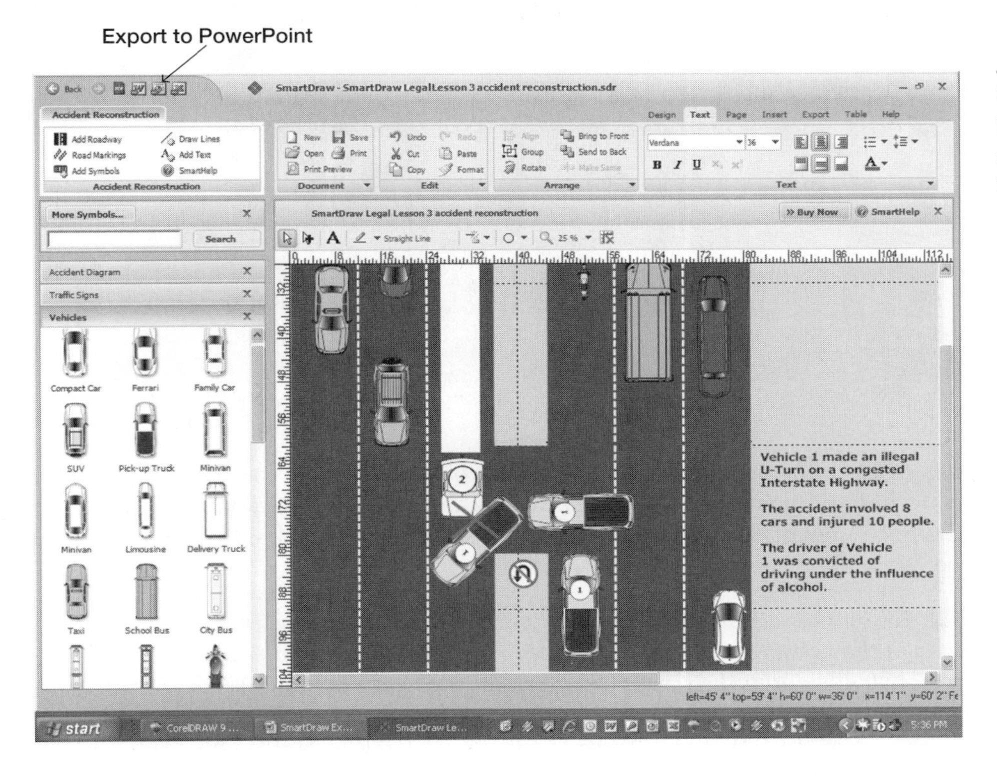

SmartDraw Legal Exhibit 5

Screenshot created using SmartDraw legal edition software.

6. In this lesson, you will create the drawing found in SmartDraw Legal Exhibit 5. You will illustrate an accident that took place on a six-lane highway when a car attempted to do a U-turn in the middle of the highway.

7. The first thing you will do is adjust the zoom to 25 percent so you get an overview of the drawing area when you build the highway. ***Click the down arrow next to the Zoom menu icon (it looks like a magnifying glass) on the toolbar. Click Custom, type 25 in the Set Window Zoom window, and then click on OK.***

8. ***Scroll to the upper left of the drawing by scrolling all the way over to the left and all the way up to the top.***

9. You are now ready to enter the first piece of highway using SmartDraw's Accident Diagram symbol library.

10. ***Scroll down and click the three-lane interstate roadway (it is just above the Shoulder icon in the Accident Diagram symbol library).*** Your cursor should now have a frame of the highway roadway attached to it.

SmartDraw Legal Exhibit 6

Screenshot created using SmartDraw legal edition software.

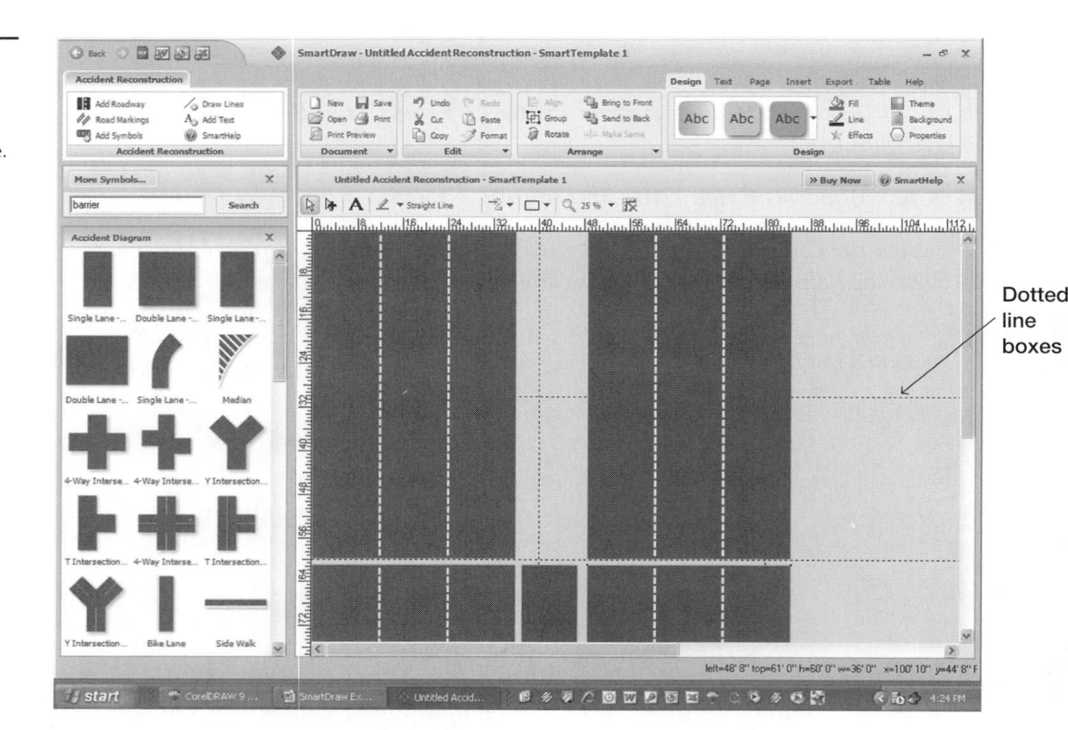

11. ***Click in the upper left of the drawing area*** (see SmartDraw Legal Exhibit 6). *Note:* In Exhibit 6 there are gaps between the pieces so you can see where to lay them, but when you lay the pieces there should be no gaps, the pieces should perfectly align.

12. ***To lay the second piece of roadway, click the three-lane interstate roadway icon in the Left Panel again and put it in line with the first piece so that the highway extends down the screen*** (see SmartDraw Legal Exhibit 6).

13. You will now lay the third piece of roadway, which is the short turn-around lane (this is the lane that is typically used by police and is usually marked with a "No U-Turn" sign on interstate highways).

14. Notice on your screen that the area is divided into boxes with dotted lines. You are going to place the small roadway (piece 3) at the beginning of the third dotted line box and next to the first roadway pieces you laid.

15. ***Scroll up in the Left Panel, and click Single Lane in the Accident Diagram symbol library in the Left Panel. Then, click at the beginning of the third dotted line box and next to the first roadway pieces you laid.*** *Note:* Once you have

clicked the mouse button and placed the piece, you can move it by clicking and dragging the mouse. Also, any graphic that is selected can be "nudged" (moved a small amount) using the cursor keys on the keyboard.

16. You will now lay the other side of the highway – the fourth piece of the highway. ***Click the three-lane interstate roadway piece in the Accident Diagram in the Left Panel.***

17. ***Click so the new road piece is parallel to the very first piece you laid, except that there will be a gap (the width of the U-turn lane—Single Lane piece you just laid.***

18. ***Get another three-lane Interstate piece (the fifth piece) and put it in line with the piece you just laid so that the highway extends down the screen.*** This completes the basic roadway.

19. You will now add a "No U-Turn sign". ***Click More Symbols, just above the Left Panel. In the More Symbols window, click Traffic Signs under Accident Reconstruction.***

20. ***Click OK in the More Symbols window.***

21. ***Scroll down and click No U-Turn in the Traffic Signs symbol library in the Left Panel. Click in the median just before the turn-around lane*** (see SmartDraw Legal Exhibit 5).

22. ***Resize the "No U-Turn" sign so that it is a little larger.***

23. You are now ready to add the vehicles. ***Click Add Symbols in the SmartPanel in the upper left of the screen.*** The Vehicle symbol library should now be displayed.

24. ***Scroll down and click the Semi-Truck with Trailer*** (**Note:** ***The words may be cut off, but it is the long, thin vehicle just to the left of Semi-Truck Cab thin.)***

25. ***Click the inside lane near the turn-around lane*** to place the semi-truck. You will need to flip the semi-truck, around, so after you initially lay it, ***right-click the semi-truck, click Flip, and then click Vertical.***

26. You will now mark the semi-truck as vehicle number 2. ***Scroll down and right-click the "2" in the Vehicles symbol library. Click Edit Symbol. Next, click Automatic Settings so that the check mark disappears. Click "OK."***

27. ***Click the "2" in the Vehicles symbol library and then click the roof of the semi-truck cab.***

28. ***Resize the "2" symbol so that it is a little larger.*** This is a little tricky, because the symbol is small.

29. ***Click the semi-truck.*** Then, hold the **[SHIFT]** key down and ***click the "2" graphic on the cab roof, so that both of the items are selected. Click Group in the Arrange group on the toolbar and then click Group Objects.*** This will connect the two together, so that if you move one you will move the other. If you do not group them together, if you move one of the items, you must then move the other separately unless you remember to select both of them.

30. You will now add the vehicle that was attempting the U-turn. ***Click Pickup Truck.*** You are going to draw several pickups to show how the accident progressed.

31. *Click in the nearest lane just before the U-turn and opposite the semi-truck* (see SmartDraw Legal Exhibit 5).

32. *With the pickup still selected, click Design in the Tab group. Then, click Fill and select yellow* to make it a yellow pickup truck.

33. *Put a "1" on the pickup cab using the same procedure as you did with the semi-truck.*

34. *Click the pickup.* Then, hold the **[SHIFT]** key down and *click the "1" graphic on the cab so that both of the items are selected. Click Group in the Arrange group on the toolbar, and then click Group Objects.*

35. You are now ready to draw the second progression of the pickup, but this time you will just copy the pickup graphic you already placed.

36. *Click Copy in the Edit group on the toolbar.*

37. *Move the cursor up a little bit in front of the existing pickup and click Paste in the Edit group.*

38. *Right-click the second pickup, click Rotate, and then click 90.* The second pickup depicts that it is in the process of attempting to the make the turn to go the other way.

39. You are now ready to create the third pickup in the progression. *Right-click the second pickup and click copy.*

40. *Move the pointer a little way in front of the second pickup, and click Paste in the Edit group.*

41. *Right-click the third pickup, click Rotate, and then click 135.*

42. *Now, point and drag the third pickup so that it is directly in front of the semi* (see SmartDraw Legal Exhibit 5).

43. *Click the Accident Diagram symbol library in the Left Panel, get the Damage marker (a large red "X"), and put it on the spot where the vehicles collide.* Notice that the "X" is thin.

44. *Right-click the red "X." Click Line Thickness, and then click Custom. In the Set Line or Border Thickness window, click Metric Exterior Wall 200 mm and then click OK.* This will make the red "X" damage marker more visible.

45. *Click Vehicles in the Left Panel and add several additional vehicles on the roadway* (see SmartDraw Legal Exhibit 5). Remember, you can right-click the vehicles and select Flip, Vertical if they are not oriented correctly.

46. *Click the Create or Edit Text ("A") icon on the Drawing toolbar, then click the Text tab in the Tab group. Click the down arrow next to Font Size and select 36.*

47. Type the text shown in the right margin of SmartDraw Legal Exhibit 5.

48. *Drag the mouse pointer so that all of the text is highlighted, and then click the Bold ("B") icon on the Text Tab in the Tab Group.*

49. In the top left of the screen (see SmartDraw Legal Exhibit 5), just to the right of the "Back" button, is a Microsoft PowerPoint icon.

50. If you have PowerPoint installed on your computer, ***click the Export to PowerPoint icon.***

51. You should now see the drawing running in PowerPoint. Notice that the drawing appears extremely large and that you can only see a small portion of the drawing. To resize the images, you first need to zoom out of the image. This is done differently depending on the version of PowerPoint you are using.

52. ***If you are using PowerPoint 2007, click the Zoom Out tool in the lower right of the screen until it says 10%. The Zoom Out tool is the minus ("–") sign.***

53. ***If you are using PowerPoint 2003, the Zoom tool is on the toolbar and usually shows a percentage such as 100%. Click the down arrow on the Zoom tool and select 25%.***

54. ***Now, resize the image by clicking in one of the corner handles and dragging the handle toward the middle of the graphic until it fits on the slide.***

55. To view the drawing in a slide show, press **[SHIFT]+[F5]**. The drawing should now be running in the slide show. Press **[ESC]** to exit the slide show, and then click the Close ("X") icon in the upper right corner in PowerPoint. ***Click No when you are asked if you want to save the presentation.***

56. To save your drawing in SmartDraw Legal, ***click Save in the Document group on the toolbar.*** In the File Name field, type **SmartDraw Legal Lesson 3** ***and then click Save.***

57. To print your drawing, ***click Print in the Document group, then click Print with Watermark.***

58. The Print window should now be displayed. ***Click the option to print it on one page, then click Print.*** *Note:* the demonstration version of SmartDraw Legal only allows you to print a few times, and then prohibits you from printing, so only print what you need to.

59. ***Click the Back button in the upper left of the screen.*** You should now be back at the Document Browser.

60. ***Click Create a New Document in the top left of the screen.***

This concludes the SmartDraw Legal Hands-on Exercises. ***To exit SmartDraw Legal, click the Close ("X") icon in the upper right of the screen.***

HANDS-ON EXERCISES

PowerPoint 2003

Basic Lessons

Number	Lesson Title	Concepts Covered
Lesson 1	Creating a Presentation	Selecting a presentation design, entering text, entering speaker's notes, and saving a file
Lesson 2	Creating Additional Slides	Inserting a new slide, selecting a slide layout, viewing a slide in Slide Show, Outline, and Slide Sorter view, and creating additional slides
Intermediate Lessons		
Lesson 3	Creating a Graph	Creating and entering data in a chart
Lesson 4	Finalizing the Presentation	Using the duplicate slide feature, creating transition effects, creating animation effects, and viewing a final presentation
Advanced Lessons		
Lesson 5	Customizing and Finalizing an Opening Statement Presentation	Inserting a slide from an old presentation into a new presentation while still maintaining the formatting of the new presentation, editing a master slide, creating a table, adding a "grow" animation effect, and adding transition effects to a presentation

GETTING STARTED

Overview

Microsoft PowerPoint is a presentation graphics program. It allows you to create presentations, charts, graphs, tables, and much more. PowerPoint is an easy-to-use program.

Please note that throughout this manual you will be creating a presentation for a legal assistant training program. In the last exercise, you will finalize an opening statement presentation.

Introduction to This Training Manual

Throughout this training manual, information you need to operate the program will be designated in several different ways.

- Keys to be pressed on the keyboard will be designated in brackets, in all caps, in bold and enlarged type (press the **[ENTER]** key).
- Movements with the mouse will be designated in bold and italic type ***(point to File on the menu bar and click the mouse).***
- Words or letters that should be typed will be designated in bold and enlarged type (type **Training Program**).
- Information that is or should be displayed on your computer screen is shown in the following style: ***Press ENTER to continue.***

LESSON 1: CREATING A PRESENTATION

In this lesson you will start PowerPoint 2003, select a background design for the legal assistant training program presentation, enter the first slide, view your slide, and save your presentation.

1. Start Windows. Then, ***double-click on the Microsoft Office PowerPoint 2003 icon on the desktop*** to start PowerPoint 2003 for Windows. Alternatively, ***click the Start button, point to Programs or All Programs, and then click the Microsoft PowerPoint 2003 icon (or point to Microsoft Office and then click Microsoft Office PowerPoint 2003).*** You should be in a clean, blank document.

2. A blank document should be on your screen. In the Getting Started task pane on the right side of the screen under Open, ***click Create a new presentation…***

3. Under Templates, ***click On my computer…***

4. In the New Presentation window, ***click the Design Templates tab.*** Notice that a number of templates are now available.

5. ***Click Digital Dots and then click OK.*** If "Digital Dots" is not displayed on your computer, or if you cannot select it, try selecting another design.

6. A title slide should now be displayed on your screen. The top part of the slide should say "Click to add title" and the bottom section of the slide should say "Click to add subtitle."

7. ***Click "Click to add title."*** Notice that you are now allowed to type your own title. Type **New Legal Assistant Training** (See Power Point 2003 Exhibit 1).

8. ***Click "Click to add sub-title."*** Type **Johnson, Beck & Taylor**.

9. The slide is now created.

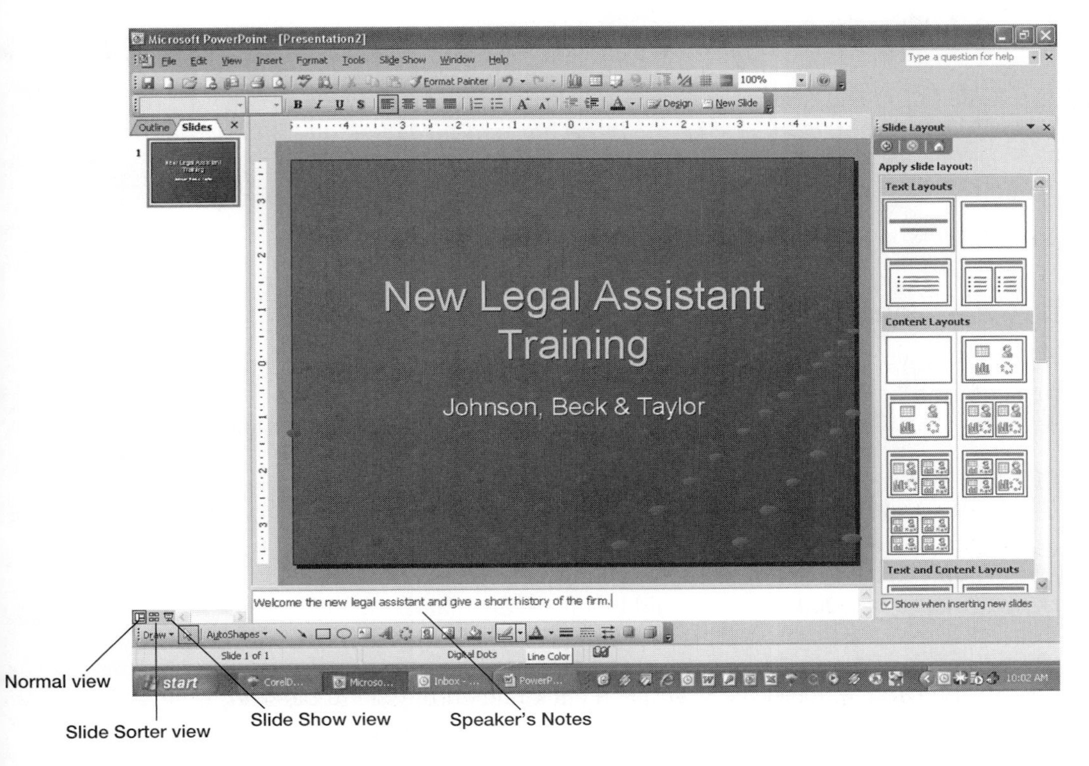

PowerPoint 2003 Exhibit 1

Microsoft product screen shot reprinted with permission from Microsoft Corporation.

10. To view your slide, ***click the Slide Show icon in the lower left corner of your screen.*** *Note:* You will see three icons in the lower left corner of the screen for Normal View, Slide Sorter View, and Slide Show. Slide Show is the icon all the way to the right. Remember, if you point to any icon and hold the pointer there for a second the title of the icon will be displayed.

11. You should now see your slide running full screen on your computer. Notice that the dark background with the white letters makes your slide very readable. This is how your audience will see your slide. Press **[ESC]** to go back to editing your presentation.

12. Notice that at the bottom of the screen under the current slide it says "Click to add notes." This is the Speaker's Notes section of the screen. Speaker's Notes are not shown in the Slide Show view, but they can be printed so that the presenter has talking points from which to speak.

13. ***Click anywhere in the Speaker's Notes section.*** Now, type **Welcome the new legal assistant and give a short history of the firm**.

14. ***Click the Slide Show icon in the lower left corner of the screen again.*** Notice that the speaker's notes do not appear.

15. Press **[ESC]** to go back to editing your presentation.

16. It is a good idea to regularly save your presentation. To save your presentation, ***click File on the menu bar.***

17. ***Then, click Save.***

18. Type **New Legal Assistant Training Program** and press the **[ENTER]** key to save the file in the default directory. Be sure to remember where the file is saved so that you can retrieve it in the next lesson.

This concludes Lesson 1.

To Exit PowerPoint

To exit PowerPoint, ***click File on the menu bar and then click on Exit.***

To go to Lesson 2

To go to Lesson 2, stay at the current screen.

LESSON 2: CREATING ADDITIONAL SLIDES

In this lesson, you will enter additional slides into the legal assistant training presentation you created in Lesson 1, and you will look at the presentation using several views. If you did not exit PowerPoint from Lesson 1, go to Step 3.

1. Start Windows. Then, ***double-click on the Microsoft Office PowerPoint 2003 icon on the desktop*** to start PowerPoint 2003 for Windows. Alternatively, ***click the Start button, point to Programs or All Programs, and then click the Microsoft PowerPoint 2003 icon (or point to Microsoft Office and then click Microsoft Office PowerPoint 2003).*** You should be in a clean, blank document.

2. ***Click File on the menu bar and then click Open. Select your file and then click the Open button.*** Alternatively, you can click File on the menu bar and, if your file is shown at the bottom of the drop-down menu, click it.

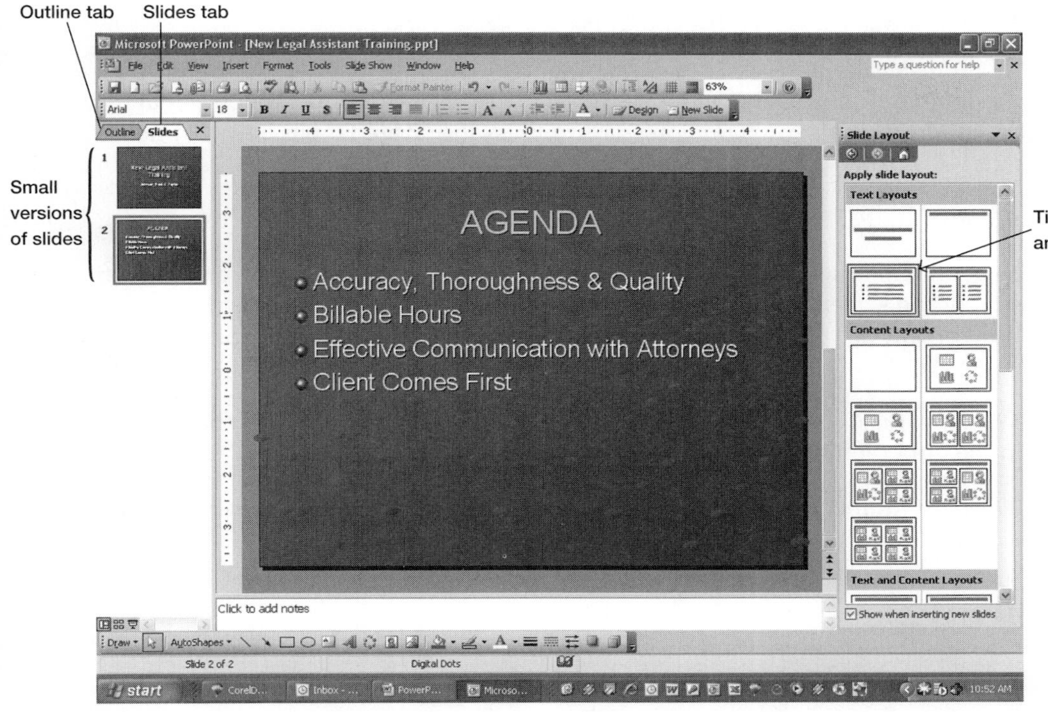

PowerPoint 2003 Exhibit 2

Microsoft product screen shot reprinted with permission from Microsoft Corporation.

3. You should have the "New Legal Assistant Training" slide on your screen. Notice in the lower left of the screen that it says "Slide 1 of 1." This shows you what slide number you are on.

4. To enter another slide, ***click Insert on the menu bar.***

5. ***Click New Slide…***

6. The "Slide Layout" task pane should be displayed on the right side of the screen. The program gives you a number of different Text Layouts, Content Layouts, and Text and Content Layouts. Click several of the choices. Notice that the screen automatically changes.

7. ***Click the "Title and Text" option. (In PowerPoint 2003 Exhibit 2 it is second from the top square on the left; it has four bullets in a column with some squiggly lines).***

8. A new slide is displayed on your screen. The top part of the slide should say "Click to add title" and the bottom section of the slide (next to a bullet point) should say "Click to add text."

9. ***Click "Click to add title."*** Type **AGENDA** (see PowerPoint 2003 Exhibit 2).

10. ***Click "Click to add text."*** Type **Accuracy, Thoroughness & Quality** and press the **[ENTER]** key. Notice that an additional bullet has been created.

11. Type **Billable Hours** and then press the **[ENTER]** key.

12. Type **Effective Communication with Attorneys** and press the **[ENTER]** key.

13. Type **Client Comes First**.

14. The slide is now created.

15. To view your slide, ***click the Slide Show icon.***

16. You should now see your slide running full screen on your computer. With the slide running in Slide Show view, press the **[Page Up]** key and notice that the first slide is now shown on your screen. Press the **[Page Down]** key and notice that you are back at the second slide.

17. Press **[ESC]** to return to Normal view.

18. You will now look at your presentation using other views. Notice on the left side of the screen that small versions of both of your slides are displayed (see PowerPoint 2003 Exhibit 2). Notice just above the slides that the Slides tab is selected.

19. ***Click the Outline tab just to the left of the Slides tab*** (just under the Tool Bar in the upper left of your screen.

20. The Outline view is now displayed; notice that you can read the words on both of your slides (see PowerPoint 2003 Exhibit 3).

PowerPoint 2003 Exhibit 3

Microsoft product screen shot reprinted with permission from Microsoft Corporation.

Outline view

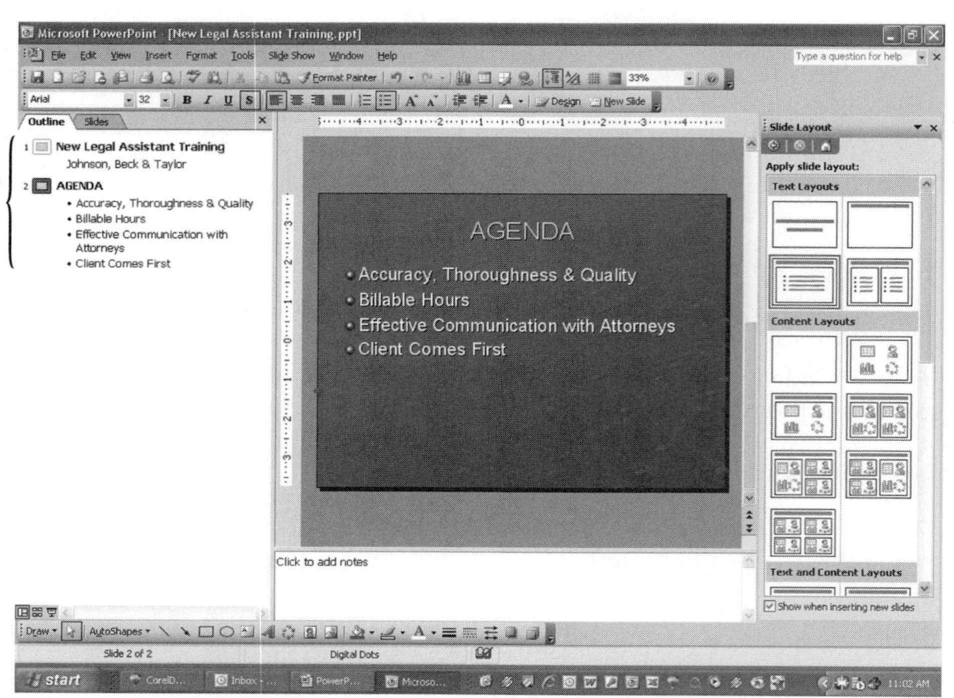

21. ***Click the Slides tab, just to the right of the Outline tab*** to go back to the Slides view.

22. You will now view your slides using the Slide Sorter view. ***Click the Slide Sorter view icon.*** The Slide Sorter View icon is at the bottom left of the screen; it is the icon in the middle, with a picture of four small squares (see PowerPoint 2003 Exhibit 1).

23. Notice that you can see all of your slides on the screen at the same time (see PowerPoint 2003 Exhibit 4). This is helpful to get an overview of your presentation and for arranging and rearranging your slide order.

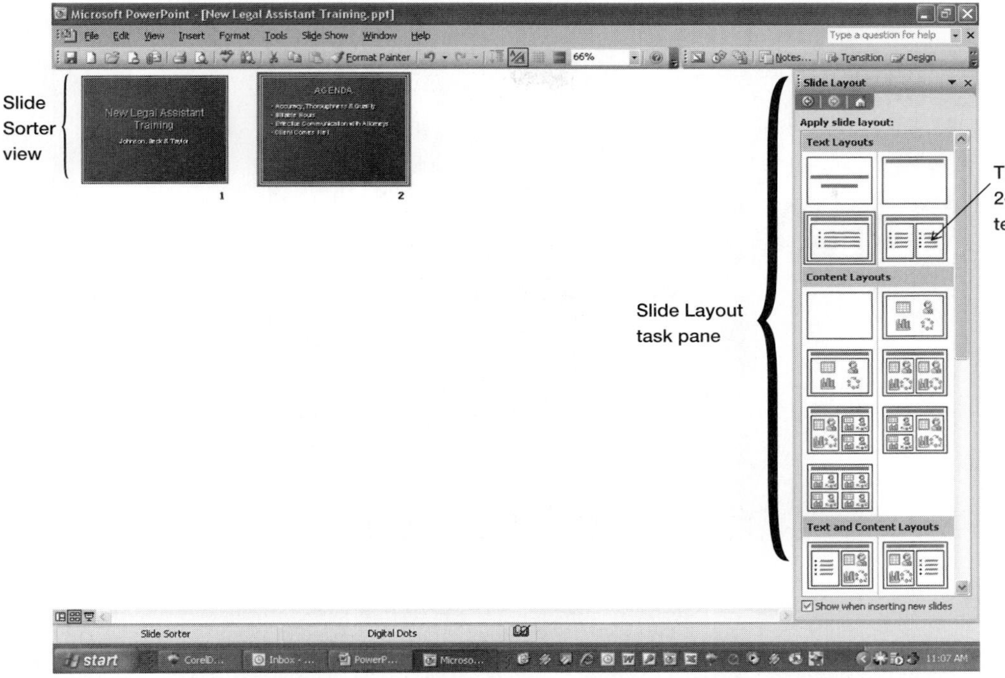

PowerPoint 2003 Exhibit 4

Microsoft product screen shot reprinted with permission from Microsoft Corporation.

24. ***While you are in the Slide Sorter View, click the second slide and drag the mouse pointer (hold down the mouse button) to the left of the first slide, and then release the mouse button.*** Notice that the order of the slides is now changed.

25. Press **[CTRL]+[Z]** to undo the move and put the slides back into their original order.

26. ***Click the Normal view icon in the lower left of your screen*** (see PowerPoint 2003 Exhibit 1).

27. ***You should now have the AGENDA slide on your screen.*** If you are not there, use the **[PAGE DOWN]** key to go there.

28. You are now ready to enter another slide. If the Slide Layout task pane is open, ***right-click the Title and 2-Column Text option.*** **(In PowerPoint 2003 Exhibit 4, it is the square that is second from the top on the right; it has two columns with four bullets and squiggly lines.)** ***Then, click Insert New Slide.*** If the Slide Layout task pane is not open, ***click Insert on the menu bar and click New Slide.*** Then, select the Title and 2-Column Text option.

29. A new slide should now be displayed on your screen. The top of the slide should say "Click to add title" and there should be two columns (left and right) that say "Click to add text."

30. ***Click "Click to add title."*** Type **Accuracy, Thoroughness & Quality** (see PowerPoint 2003 Exhibit 5).

31. ***Point and click with the mouse on the first column*** "Click to add text". Type **Be careful and complete** and press the **[ENTER]** key.

32. Type **Create forms and systems** and press the **[ENTER]** key.

33. Type **Create checklists**.

PowerPoint 2003 Exhibit 5

Microsoft product screen shot reprinted with permission from Microsoft Corporation.

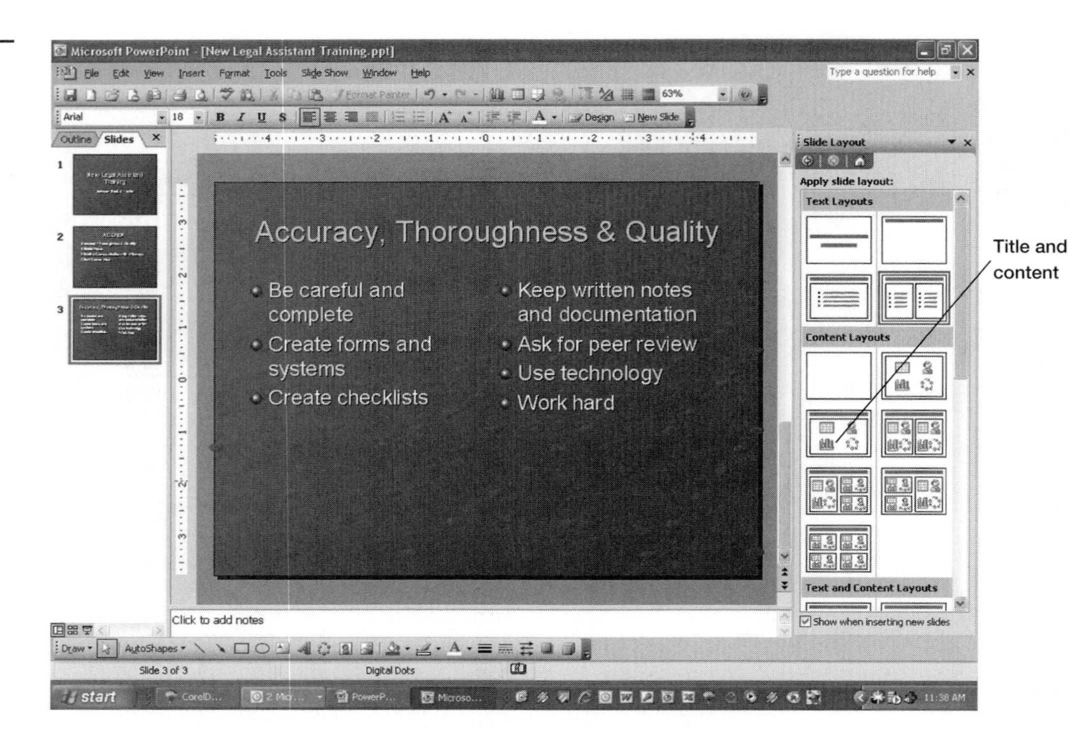

34. *Click the second column, "Click to add text."* Type **Keep written notes and documentation** and press the **[ENTER]** key.

35. Type **Ask for peer review** and press the **[ENTER]** key.

36. Type **Use technology** and press the **[ENTER]** key.

37. Type **Work hard**.

38. Your presentation now consists of three slides.

39. To save your presentation, ***click the Save icon (it looks like a floppy disk) on the toolbar.***

This concludes Lesson 2.

To Exit PowerPoint

To exit PowerPoint, ***click File on the menu bar and then click Exit.***

To go to Lesson 3

To go to Lesson 3, stay at the current screen.

INTERMEDIATE

LESSON 3: CREATING A GRAPH

In this lesson, you will add an additional slide with a graph into the legal assistant training program presentation. If you did not exit PowerPoint from Lesson 2, go to Step 4.

1. Start Windows. Then, ***double-click the Microsoft Office PowerPoint 2003 icon on the desktop*** to start PowerPoint 2003 for Windows. Alternatively, ***click the Start button, point to Programs or All Programs, and then click the Microsoft PowerPoint 2003 icon (or point to Microsoft Office and then click Microsoft Office PowerPoint 2003).*** You should be in a clean, blank document.

2. ***Click File on the menu bar and then click Open. Select your file and then click the Open button.*** Alternatively, you can click File on the menu bar and, if your file is shown at the bottom of the drop-down menu, you can click it.

3. You should have the New Legal Assistant Training slide on your screen. Push the **[PAGE DOWN]** key until you are on the third slide, "Accuracy, Thoroughness & Quality."

4. To add another slide, ***click Insert on the menu bar. Then, click New Slide***. The Slide Layout task pane should be displayed on the right side of the screen.

5. ***Click the Title and Content option.*** (In PowerPoint 2003 Exhibit 5 it is the second from the top square on the left under Content Layouts).

6. A new slide should now be displayed on your screen. The top part of the slide should say "Click to add title" and the bottom section of the slide should say "Click icon to add content."

7. Click ***"Click to add title."*** Type **Billable Hours**, press the **[ENTER]** key, and then type **Goals for Your First Six Months** (see PowerPoint 2003 Exhibit 6).

8. Notice on the lower portion of the slide, just above "Click icon to add content," that there is a box with six icons in it. ***Click the Insert Chart icon.*** (It is in the middle of the first row and looks like a multicolored vertical bar chart.)

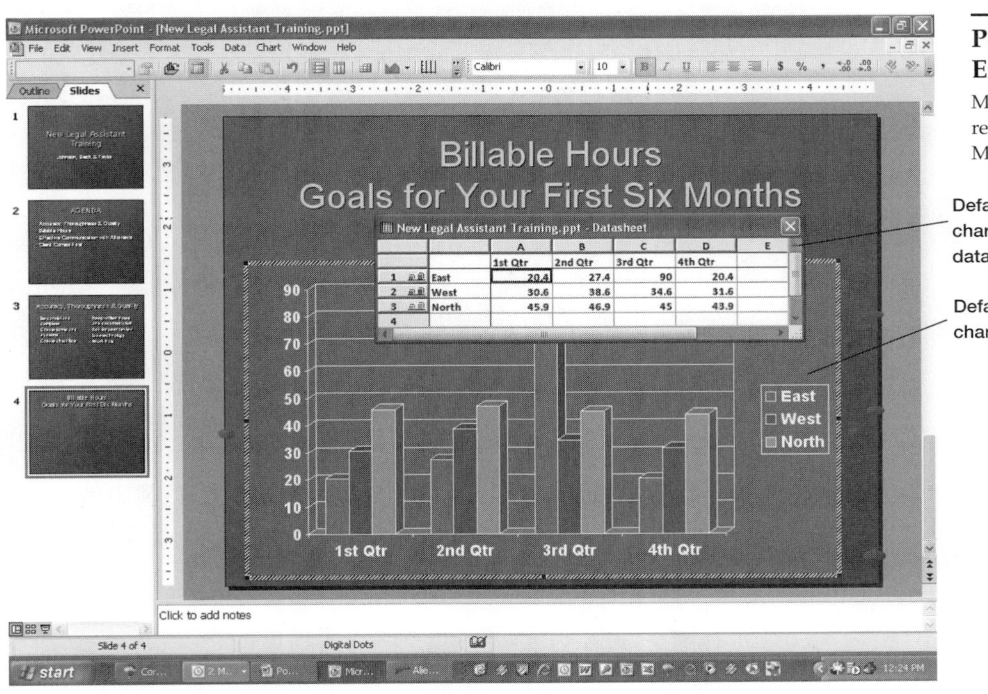

PowerPoint 2003 Exhibit 6

Microsoft product screen shot reprinted with permission from Microsoft Corporation.

9. Notice that a default chart with default data is displayed. Also, notice that a window titled "New Legal Assistant Training – Datasheet" has appeared.

10. To clear the data in the datasheet, ***point to the uppermost cell at the left of the Datasheet window and drag the mouse pointer down and to the right so that all of the data is highlighted,*** and then press the **[DELETE]** key. (Remember, if at any time you make a mistake, you can press **[CTRL]+[Z]** to undo the error.) Notice that the first column has three rows that say 3-D Column. Since we only need one, we will delete the remaining two.

11. ***Click cell A2. Then, right-click and click Delete.***

12. The Delete window should now be displayed. ***Click "Entire Row" and then click OK.*** This will delete that row.

13. Repeat steps 11–12 to delete the next row.

14. Now we are ready to enter the data for the chart. ***Enter the following data in the chart exactly as shown:***

		A	B	C	D	E	F
		Mo. 1	*Mo. 2*	*Mo. 3*	*Mo. 4*	*Mo. 5*	*Mo. 6*
1	*Billable Hours*	*80*	*90*	*100*	*100*	*105*	*110*

15. Your datasheet and chart should look similar to PowerPoint 2003 Exhibit 7.

16. ***To see the chart (without the datasheet), click anywhere outside of the chart, such as in the title of the slide "Billable Hours Goals for Your First Six Months."*** Notice that the chart including the legend, is properly formatted.

17. The chart is now created. To view your chart, ***click the Slide Show icon.***

PowerPoint 2003 Exhibit 7

Microsoft product screen shot reprinted with permission from Microsoft Corporation.

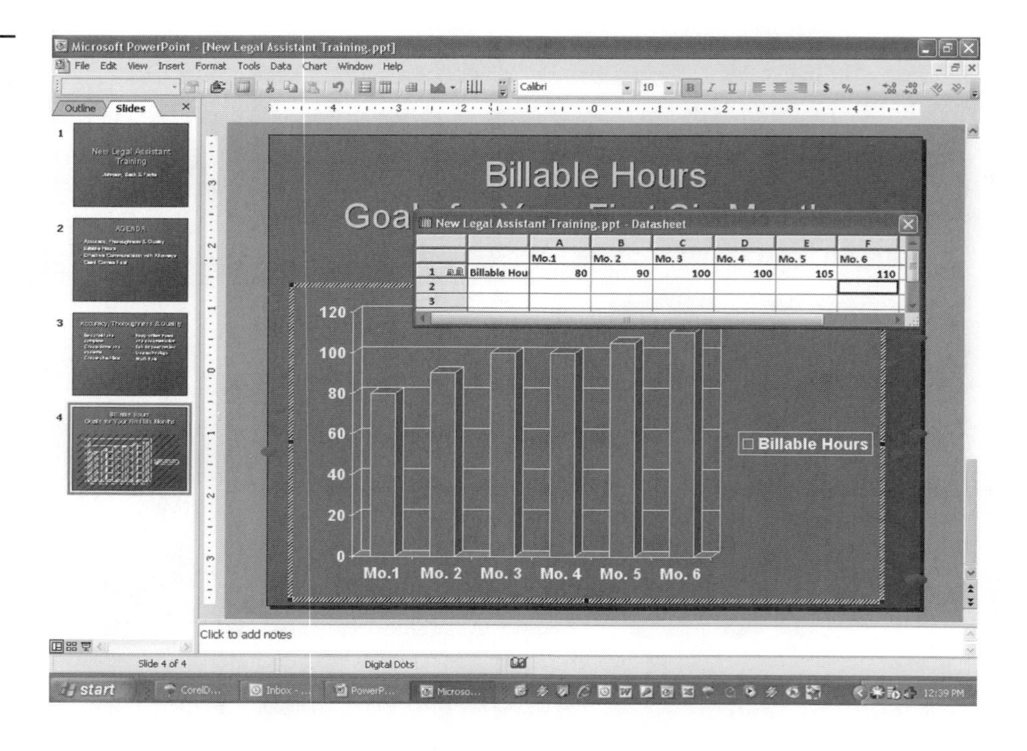

18. Press the **[ESC]** key.

19. To save your presentation, ***click the Save icon on the toolbar. (It looks like a floppy disk.)***

This concludes Lesson 3.

To Exit PowerPoint

To exit PowerPoint, ***click File on the menu bar and then click Exit.***

To go to Lesson 4

To go to Lesson 4, stay at the current screen.

LESSON 4: FINALIZING THE PRESENTATION

In this lesson, you will add more slides to the New Legal Assistant Training presentation, duplicate a slide, enter slide transition effects, create animation effects, and show your presentation. If you did not exit PowerPoint from Lesson 3, go to Step 3.

1. Start Windows. Then, ***double-click the Microsoft Office PowerPoint 2003 icon on the desktop*** to start PowerPoint 2003 for Windows. Alternatively, ***click the Start button, point to Programs or All Programs, and then click the Microsoft PowerPoint 2003 icon (or point to Microsoft Office and then click Microsoft Office PowerPoint 2003).*** You should be in a clean, blank document.

2. ***Click File on the menu bar and then click Open. Select your file and then click the Open button.*** Alternatively, you can click File on the menu bar and, if your file is shown at the bottom of the drop-down menu, you can click it.

3. You should have the New Legal Assistant Training slide on your screen. Push the **[PAGE DOWN]** key until you are at the last slide, "Billable Hours Goals for Your First Six Months."

4. ***Click Insert on the menu bar and then click New Slide.***

5. ***From the Slide Layout task pane click the Title and Text layout (the second box from the top on the left).***

6. Enter the information shown in PowerPoint 2003 Exhibit 8.

7. You will now create another slide, but this time you will use the Duplicate Slide feature.

8. ***Click Insert on the menu bar and then click Duplicate Slide.***

9. Notice that another slide has been added that is identical to the previous slide.

10. ***Click in the title of the slide, then drag the mouse pointer so that all of the text is highlighted.*** Then, click the **[DELETE]** key. ***Do the same for the body of the slide.***

11. Enter the information shown in PowerPoint 2003 Exhibit 9.

PowerPoint 2003 Exhibit 8

Microsoft product screen shot reprinted with permission from Microsoft Corporation.

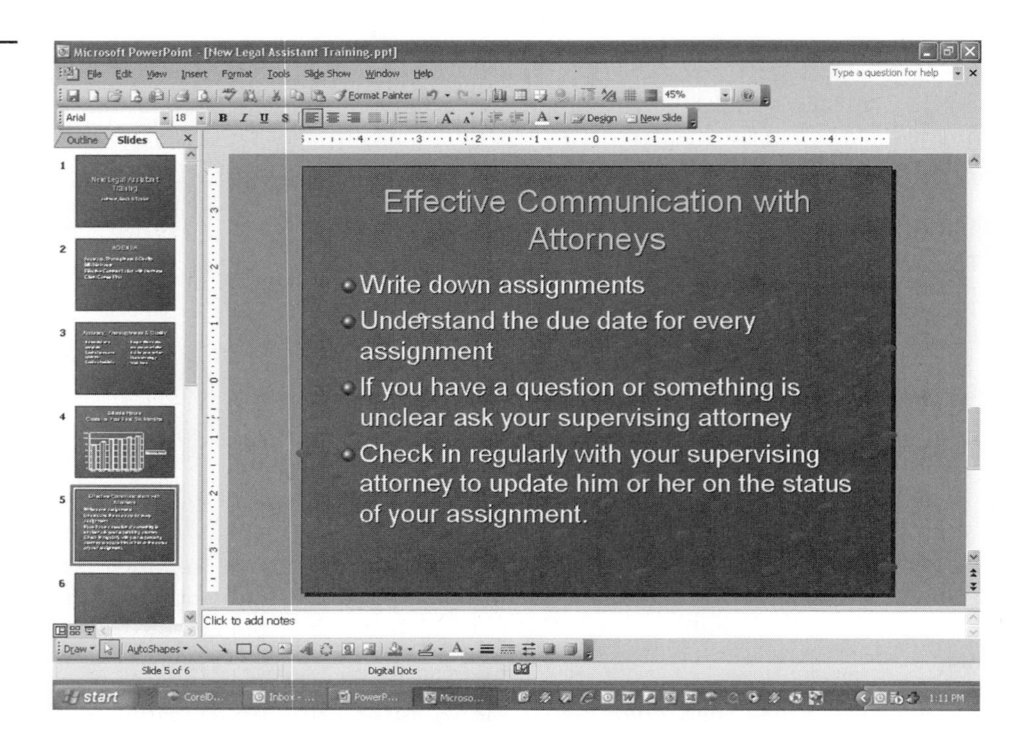

PowerPoint 2003 Exhibit 9

Microsoft product screen shot reprinted with permission from Microsoft Corporation.

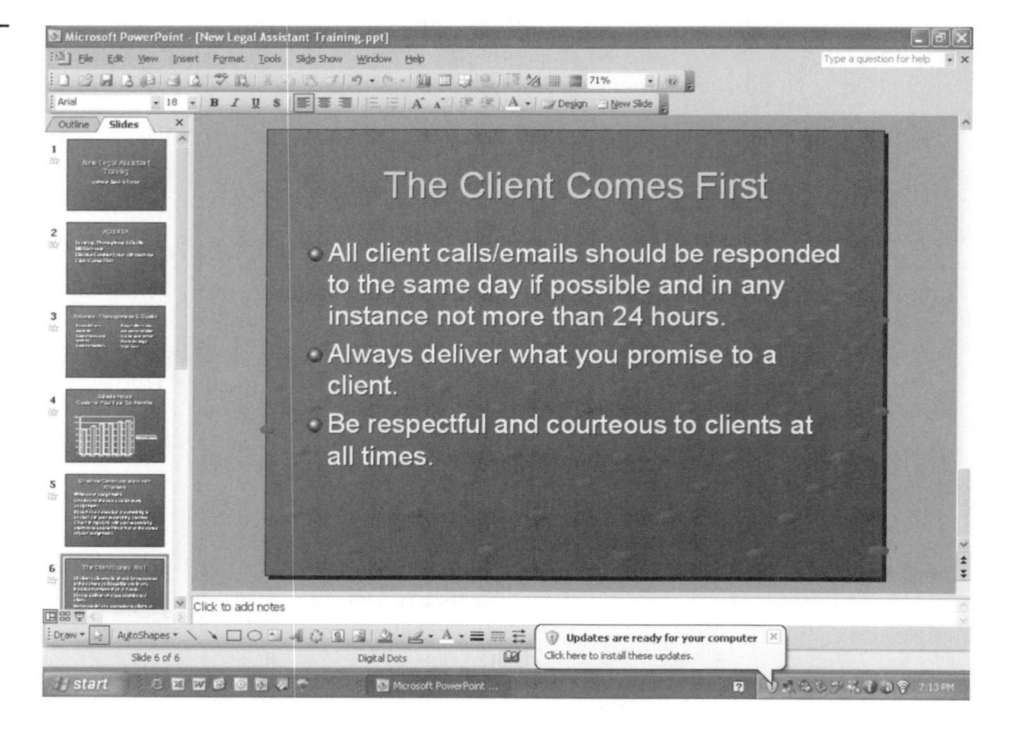

12. With all of your slides created, you are now ready to begin finalizing the presentation.

13. Press **[CTRL]+[HOME]** to go to the first slide in the presentation.

14. ***Click the Slide Sorter view at the bottom left of the screen.*** Notice that you can see all six of your slides on the screen.

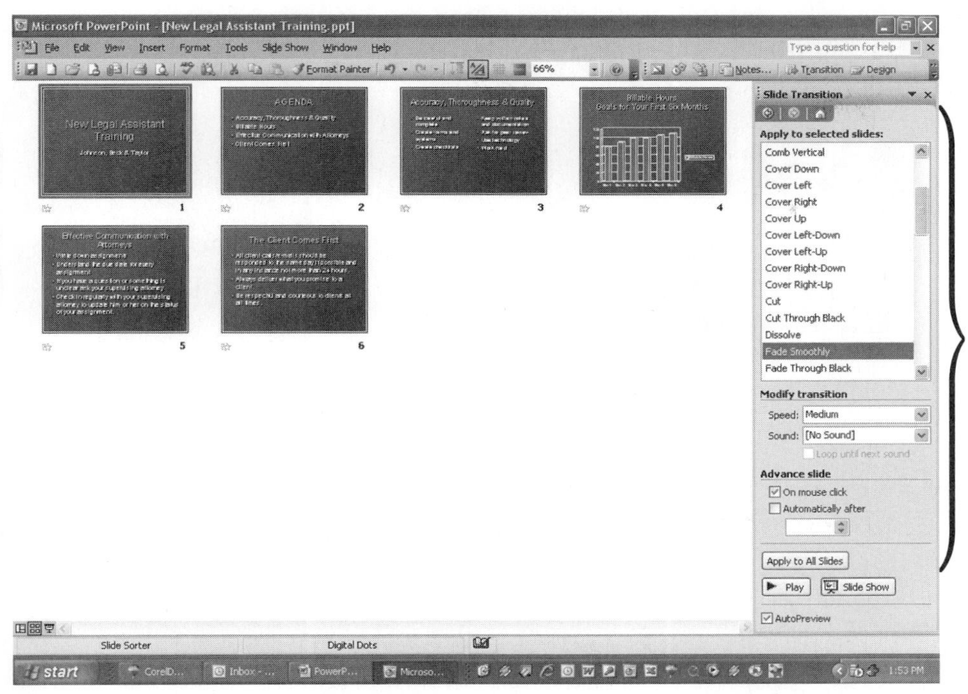

PowerPoint 2003 Exhibit 10

Microsoft product screen shot reprinted with permission from Microsoft Corporation.

15. We will now enter transition effects (effects that take place when you move from one slide to another) and animation effects (effects that take place during display of the slide).

16. ***Right-click on the first slide, "New Legal Assistant Training."***

17. ***Click once on "Slide Transition..."*** (*Note*: There is also an icon at the right of the toolbar that says "Transition." This icon can also be used to enter transition effects.) Notice that the Slide Transition task pane is now displayed on the right side of the screen. There are many transition effects listed (see PowerPoint 2003 Exhibit 10).

18. ***Scroll down and click the Fade Smoothly transition effect.*** Notice that after you selected it, that slide displayed the transition effect. Fade Smoothly is a professional transition effect that is not distracting, so it is a good one to use in a legal setting.

19. ***In the Slide Transition task pane, under Modify transition, click the down arrow next to Fast and select Medium.***

20. Notice in the Slide Transition task pane that under Advance Slide, there is a check mark next to "On mouse click." This means that the slide will automatically move to the next slide when the mouse is clicked. You could set it to move to the next slide automatically after a certain amount of time, but the current selection is fine for this slide.

21. ***In the Slide Transition task pane, click Apply to All Slides near the bottom of the task pane.*** This feature applies the transition effect on this slide to all slides in the presentation.

22. ***Click Slide Show at the bottom of the task pane to see your presentation, including the transition effects.***

HANDS-ON EXERCISES

PowerPoint 2003 Exhibit 11

Microsoft product screen shot reprinted with permission from Microsoft Corporation.

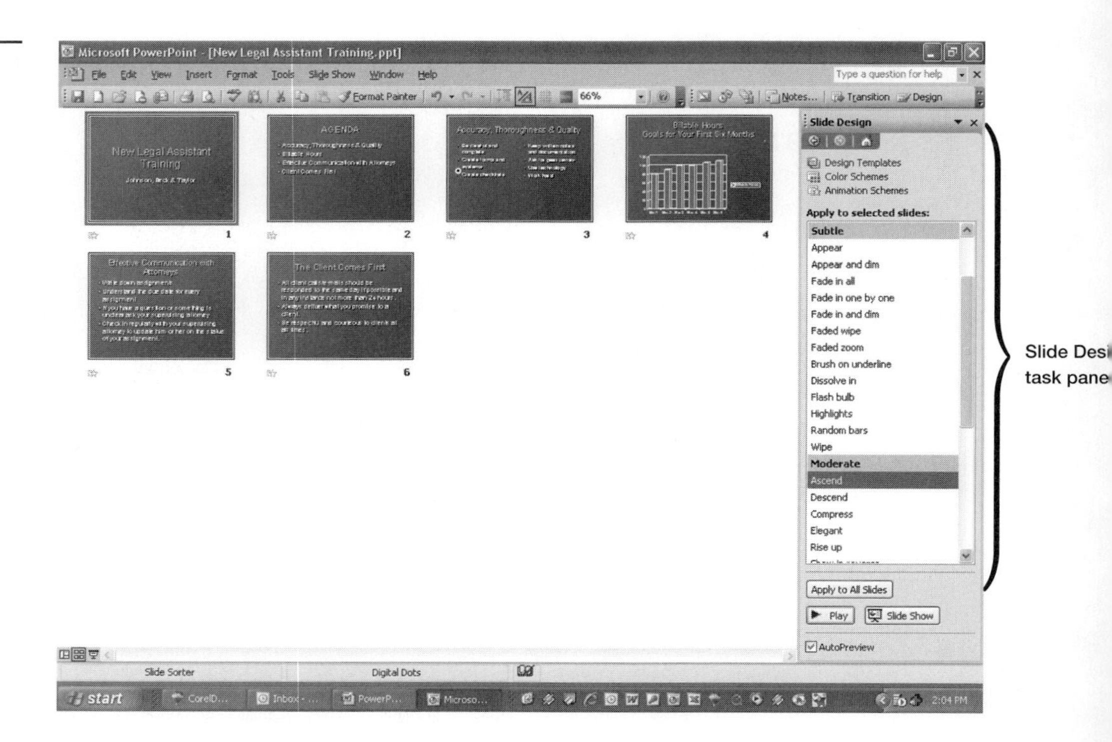

23. *Click to proceed through the presentation and back to slide Sorter view.*

24. *Right-click the second slide, "Agenda."*

25. *Click Animation Schemes.* Notice that the Slide Design task pane is displayed on the right side of the screen (see PowerPoint 2003 Exhibit 11).

26. *Click Ascend under Moderate. Note*: When the slide is shown in a slide show, you will need to click the mouse button to get the next bullet to appear.

27. *Click Apply to All Slides.*

28. You are now ready to view your presentation. *Click the first slide.*

29. *Click the Slide Show icon at the bottom left of the screen.*

30. Your first slide is now shown full screen. To proceed to the next slide, press the **[SPACE BAR]** or *click the left button on the mouse.* Keep pressing the **[SPACE BAR]** or *click the left mouse button to proceed with the presentation.*

31. When you have seen the full presentation, PowerPoint will return to Slide Sorter view.

32. To print your presentation, *click File on the menu bar, click Print and then click OK.*

33. To save your presentation, *click the Save icon on the toolbar* **(It looks like a floppy disk.)**

34. *Click File on the menu bar and then click Close.*

This concludes Lesson 4.

To Exit PowerPoint

To exit PowerPoint, *click File on the menu bar and then click Exit.*

ADVANCED

LESSON 5: CUSTOMIZING AND FINALIZING AN OPENING STATEMENT PRESENTATION

In this lesson, you will insert a slide from an old presentation into a new presentation while maintaining the formatting of the new presentation, edit a master slide, create a table, add a "grow" animation effect, and add transition effects to a presentation.

1. Start Windows. Then, ***double-click the Microsoft Office PowerPoint 2003 icon on the desktop*** to start PowerPoint 2003 for Windows. Alternatively, ***click the Start button, point to Programs or All Programs, and then click the Microsoft PowerPoint 2003 icon (or point to Microsoft Office and then click Microsoft Office PowerPoint 2003).*** You should be in a clean, blank document.

2. The first thing you will need to do is open the "Lesson 5A" file from Disk 1 supplied with this text. Ensure that Disk 1 is inserted in the disk drive, ***click File on the menu bar, and then click Open.*** The Open window should now be displayed. ***Navigate to the drive where Disk 1 is located. Double-click on the "PowerPoint Files" folder, and then double-click on the "Lesson 5A" file.***

3. The presentation "Opening Statement—Smith v. EZ Pest Control Worldwide" should now be displayed.

4. The first thing you would like to do is to insert a slide from another presentation into this one, just after the title slide.

5. ***Click Insert on the menu bar. Then, click Slides from Files.***

6. The Slide Finder window should now be displayed. ***Click Browse.***

7. The Browse window should now be displayed. ***Navigate to the drive where Disk 1 is located.***

8. ***Double-click the "PowerPoint Files" folder and then double-click the "Lesson 5B" file.***

9. The Slide Finder window should again be displayed and the path for the file should now be entered (see PowerPoint 2003 Exhibit 12).

10. Notice that there is one slide shown under "Select slides:" in PowerPoint 2003 Exhibit 12. There is only one slide in this presentation, but if there were more, they would be displayed. You could then decide whether you wanted to insert all of the slides using the Insert All feature in the Slide Finder window, or preferred to choose which slides to insert. Also, notice in the bottom left corner of the Slide Finder window the option that says "Keep source formatting." If you wanted to insert the existing slide into the new presentation, but you wanted to keep the existing slide's background and style, you could click this option. Because we want the slide we are adding to take the format of our new presentation, we will leave it unchecked.

11. ***Click the first slide and then click Insert.*** This is how you can select only certain slides in a presentation to copy to your new presentation.

12. ***Click the Close icon in the Slide Finder window.***

PowerPoint 2003 Exhibit 12

Microsoft product screen shot reprinted with permission from Microsoft Corporation.

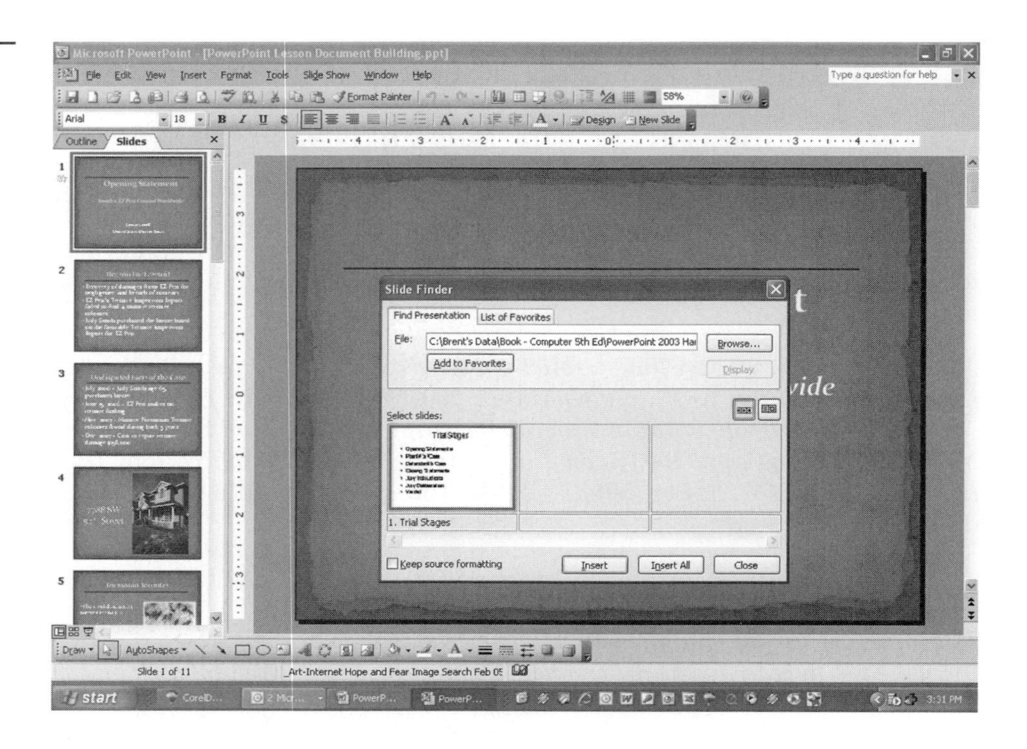

PowerPoint 2003 Exhibit 13

Microsoft product screen shot reprinted with permission from Microsoft Corporation.

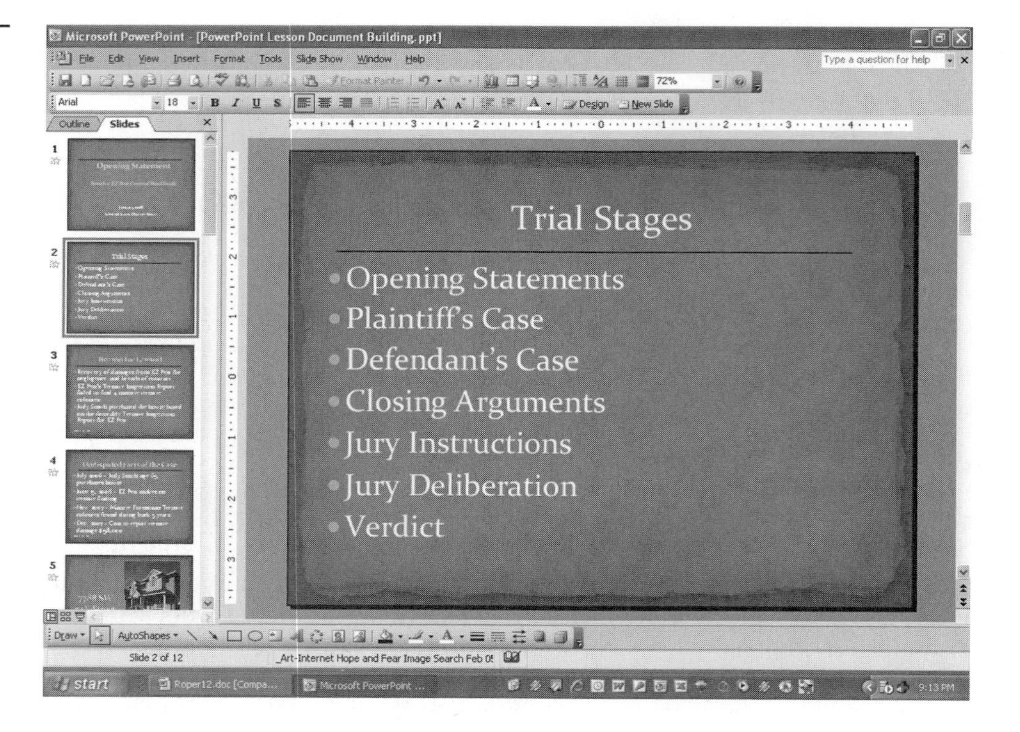

13. Notice that the slide now appears in your presentation, and that it matches your formatting for the current presentation (see Exhibit 13).

14. Each slide presentation has master slides that control the look and feel of all slides. You will now add something to the master slide so that it appears on all slides in the presentation.

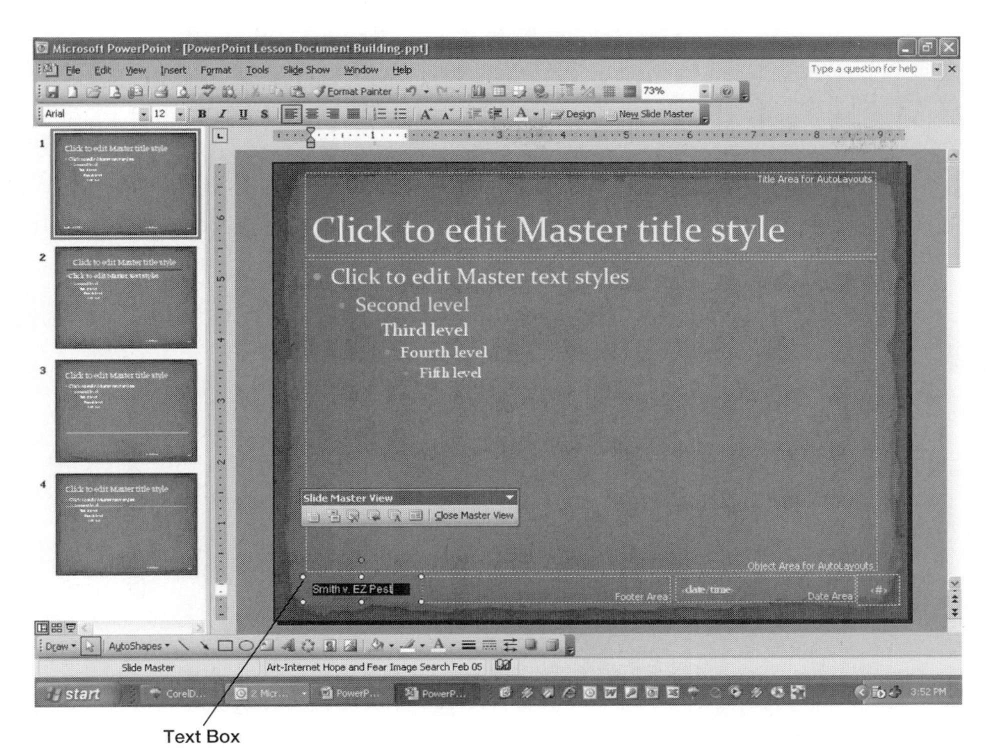

PowerPoint 2003 Exhibit 14

Microsoft product screen shot reprinted with permission from Microsoft Corporation.

15. ***Click View, point to Master, and then click Slide Master.*** Notice that you now see an outline of your slides. If you make changes to font sizes, font colors, or other changes in the Master slide, it affects all of the other slides that use the Master slide you are changing.

16. ***Point to the first slide in the upper left of the screen and notice that a title appears saying that this slide master is being used by slides 3–11. Click this slide*** (see PowerPoint 2003 Exhibit 14).

17. You will now add a small text box in the lower left of the screen that says *Smith v. EZ Pest.*

18. ***Click Insert on the menu bar, and then click Text Box.***

19. Your pointer should now turn into a gray upside-down cross. You now will draw the text box where your text will go. ***Point in the lower left corner of the screen and then drag the mouse pointer down and to the right to draw a small rectangular box*** (see PowerPoint 2003 Exhibit 14).

20. ***Point to the down arrow on the Font Size icon on the toolbar and select "12."*** Then, type **Smith v. EZ Pest**.

21. ***Click Close Master View in the Slide Master View window.***

22. Press the **[PAGE DOWN]** key to go to slide 3 (this is where the Master Slide you revised started). Notice your text box, "Smith v. EZ Pest," in the lower left of the screen. Continue to press **[PAGE DOWN]** until the last slide is displayed.

23. ***Click Insert on the menu bar, and then click New slide. Click the Title Only layout in the task pane on the right side of the screen.***

PowerPoint 2003 Exhibit 15

Microsoft product screen shot reprinted with permission from Microsoft Corporation.

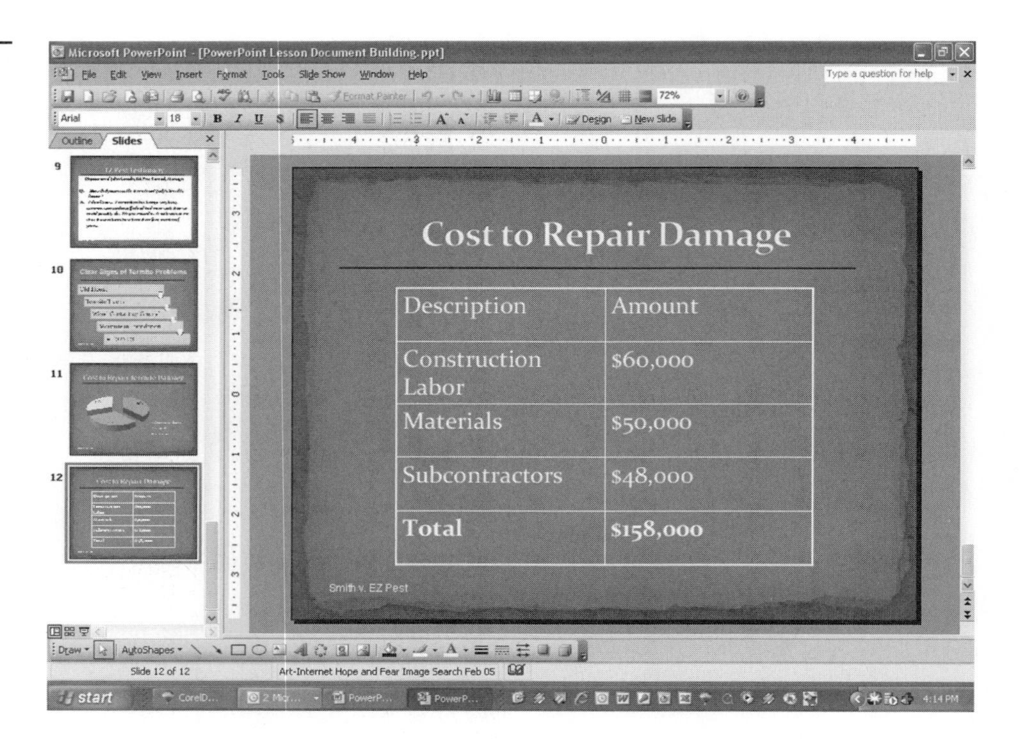

24. *Click "Click to add title."* Type: **Cost to Repair Damage,** and then *click the Center icon on the toolbar.*

25. You will now add a table showing a breakdown of costs.

26. *Click Insert on the menu bar, and then click Table.*

27. The Insert Table window should now be displayed. *Change the Insert Table window so that two columns and five rows are shown, and then click OK.*

28. A frame of the table is now displayed. *Click the outside frame of the table and drag the frame down so it fits properly in the screen* (see PowerPoint 2003 Exhibit 15).

29. Enter the information found in PowerPoint 2003 Exhibit 15.

30. When you have finished entering all of the information in the table, *point to the Description cell and drag the mouse pointer to the "$158,000" cell so that the entire table is highlighted.*

31. *Then, click the down arrow in the Font Size icon on the toolbar and click "28."*

32. *Click in the last cell on the left (Total) and drag the mouse pointer one cell to the right so that the last two cells in the table are selected. Then click the Bold icon on the toolbar.*

33. Your table should now look similar to PowerPoint 2003 Exhibit 15.

34. Press the **[PAGE UP]** key so that you are at the "Cost to Repair Termite Damage" pie chart.

35. You will now add some animation to the slide to give it a dramatic effect.

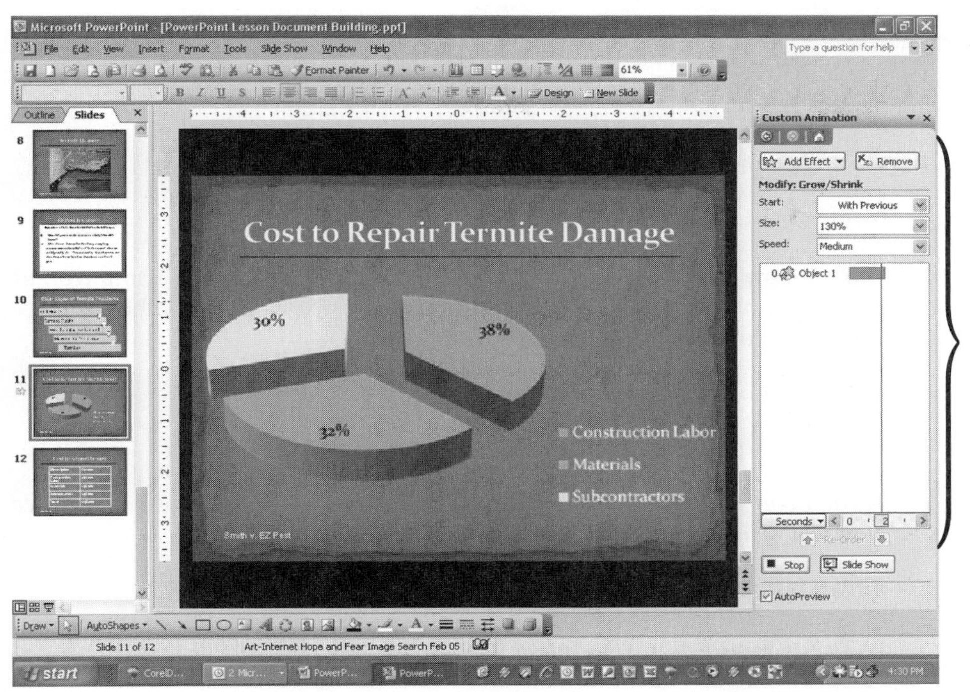

PowerPoint 2003 Exhibit 16

Microsoft product screen shot reprinted with permission from Microsoft Corporation.

36. *Right-click anywhere on the pie chart. Then, click Custom Animation.*

37. The Custom Animation task pane should now be displayed (see PowerPoint 2003 Exhibit 16).

38. *Click Add Effect in the Custom Animation task pane.*

39. *Point to Emphasis and then click Grow/Shrink.*

40. *Click the down arrow next to "Start: On Click" and then click With Previous* (see PowerPoint 2003 Exhibit 16).

41. *Click the down arrow next to Size: 150%, click Custom, change the size to 130%,* and then press the **[ENTER]** key. Your screen should now look similar to PowerPoint 2003 Exhibit 16.

42. *Click Play in the Custom Animation task pane to see the animation effect.*

43. *Click the Slide Sorter view icon at the bottom left of the screen.* Notice that you can see all twelve of the slides.

44. You will now enter a transition effect. *Right-click the first slide.*

45. *Click Slide Transition...*

46. *Scroll down in the Slide Transition task pane, and click Dissolve.*

47. *In the Slide Transition task pane, under Modify Transition, click the down arrow next to Fast and select Medium.*

48. *Click "Automatically after" under "Advance slide" in the Slide Transition task pane.*

49. ***Under "Automatically after," change the time to every (00:02) two seconds*** and then press the **[ENTER]** key.

50. ***Click in the "On mouse click" box so that it is deselected.***

51. ***Then, click Apply to All Slides.***

52. ***Double-click the first slide.***

53. You are now ready to view your presentation. ***Click the Slide Show icon at the bottom left of the screen to watch your presentation.*** The slides should automatically change every two seconds.

54. When the presentation is completed, ***click the mouse.***

55. To print your presentation, ***click File on the menu bar, then click Print.***

56. ***In the Print window under "Print What," click the down arrow and notice that you can print slides, handouts, notes pages, and Outline view.***

57. ***Click Slides, and then click OK.***

58. To save your presentation, ***click the Save icon on the toolbar (it looks like a floppy disk).***

This concludes the PowerPoint 2003 Hands-on Exercises. To exit PowerPoint, ***click File on the menu bar, and then click Exit.***

CHAPTER 13

SPECIALIZED LEGAL SOFTWARE

CHAPTER OBJECTIVES

After completing Chapter 13, you should be able to do the following:

1. Identify the many sources of legal technology information available from the American Bar Association.
2. Identify what the Legal Technology Resource Center (LTRC) is.
3. Explain why legal-specific software might be helpful to legal organizations.
4. Identify what issues should be considered when purchasing legal-specific software.

Most legal organizations have a specialty or a specific area of the law that they practice. Large firms, for instance, may have many specialty areas, having a department for each type of legal matter, such as a tax department, a litigation department, and a probate department, among others. Because most attorneys and legal assistants practice a specific type of law, they can usually benefit from a software program that is designed to handle a specific type of case. This chapter introduces specialized legal software for personal injury law, tax law, criminal law, estate planning law, and more.

INTRODUCTION TO LEGAL-SPECIFIC SOFTWARE

legal-specific software
Software aimed specifically at the legal market.

Legal-specific software is aimed specifically at the legal market. Because the practice of law has become highly specialized, legal-specific software has become quite popular. For example, a lawyer who specializes in tax law might purchase a computer program that is designed to calculate and prepare income tax returns automatically. Legal-specific software can, in many cases, greatly increase the efficiency and productivity of an attorney or a law firm.

WHERE TO FIND LEGAL-SPECIFIC SOFTWARE

Legal-specific software is available but it can be difficult to find if the user does not know where to look. This section contains good places to look for legal-specific software.

American Bar Association

The American Bar Association (ABA) is a leading publisher of legal technology information (see <http://www.abanet.org>). What the ABA lacks in providing a coordinated approach to software and legal technology information, it makes up for in the sheer amount of information available on these topics. The ABA is a good place to start looking for software products and for information on any issue related to legal technology. Below are some of the goods and services that the ABA offers in this area. The ABA also offers many Internet sites related to these issues (see the Internet sites at the end of this chapter).

Legal Technology Resource Center (LTRC) This is a separate project of the ABA that focuses only on legal technology issues. Much of what the ABA publishes comes from the LTRC. Their Internet site address is <http://www.abanet.org/tech/LTRC>.

ABA Books on Legal Technology Issues The ABA publishes more than fifty books covering a wide range of legal technology issues (see <http://www.abanet.org/abapubs/lawoffice.html>). Some of the titles include *The Lawyer's Guide to the Internet, The Lawyer's Quick Guide to Email, Microsoft Word for Windows in One Hour for Lawyers, Winning with Computers,* and *The Lawyer's Guide to Creating Web Pages.*

Legal Organization Technology Surveys The ABA and the LTRC publish regular technology surveys of legal organizations. The surveys cover a wide variety of issues such as what legal organizations are using for computer hardware, application software, the Internet, and legal research. The surveys allow a legal organization to see how other like organizations are using technology and, specifically, what technology they are using.

Internet Discussion Groups on Legal Technology Issues The ABA and LTRC host discussion groups on the Internet. The most popular discussion group is called Lawtech. Legal professionals from all over the country discuss a wide variety of legal technology issues every day. To subscribe to this discussion group, send an email to *listserver@abanet.org* and in the body of the email type SUBSCRIBE LAWTECH [your email address here].

Law Practice The Law Practice Management section of the ABA publishes a monthly magazine titled *Law Practice.* It covers a wide variety of technology issues including monthly columns on the subject, and reviews of software and hardware. The magazine's website is <http://www.abanet.org/pm/magazine>.

ABA Techshow The American Bar Association sponsors an annual legal technology conference and exposition trade show titled Techshow, which attracts more than two thousand attendees and offers education sessions on legal technology issues and a vendor exposition (<http://www.abanet.org/techshow>).

State Bar Associations

Most state bar associations have computer-related sections, which may be a source in your area for information regarding software. In addition, some state bar associations publish their own forms, jury instructions, and other legal documents online or on CD-ROM.

Law Technology News

Law Technology News is published monthly by the New York Law Publishing Company. It focuses on a wide range of legal technology issues and also hosts an Internet site devoted to legal technology issues (<http://www.lawtechnologynews.com>). Law Technology News also publishes a biannual resource guide, which lists legal software vendors and providers by subject.

The Internet

The Internet is one of the best places to look for law-related software. Generic and law-related search engines (see Chapter 10) will provide the user with a wide variety of sites offering information on legal-specific software products.

Directory of Law-Related CD-ROMs

One of the best places to find law-related CD-ROM software is in the *Directory of Law-Related CD-ROMs,* published by Infosources Publishing (201) 836-7072 (<http://www.infosourcespub.com>). This book, which is published annually, lists more than 1,600 law-related CD-ROM products. It is cross-referenced by subject, publisher, and computer type.

Technolawyer.com

Technolawyer.com is a free email newsletter about legal technology issues. Much of the content of the newsletter is written by practicing legal professionals. To subscribe to the newsletter go to <http://www.technolawyer.com.>

OVERVIEW OF SOME LEGAL-SPECIFIC PROGRAMS

There are many different types of legal-specific software on the market. You will be introduced to software for personal injury law, tax law, criminal law, probate law, family law, and more.

Personal Injury Law

Personal injury law deals with cases in which a person has been physically injured. Several programs are specifically geared to personal injury cases. Most of the programs are directed toward attorneys who represent the plaintiff and are case management programs. It is important in personal injury cases, along with other types of cases, that the attorney track the value of each case, as well as tracking dates, deadlines, and the status of the case. The attorney also needs to generate specific form letters and pleadings, track the accounting side of each case, and track evidence, witnesses, and documents.

personal injury law
An area of the law dealing with cases in which a person has been physically injured.

Several personal injury case management systems do all of these tasks (see Exhibit 13–1). Most of these programs have a document generator included with the package that merges the names, addresses, and other client information stored in the program with pre-made form letters, pleadings, and so forth tailored specifically to personal injury cases.

Tax Law

Tax law is another area that is highly specialized. Tax attorneys regularly fill out and compute myriad federal and state income tax forms for individuals,

Exhibit 13–1
Personal Injury Case Management Program
Courtesy of Abacus Data Systems, Inc.

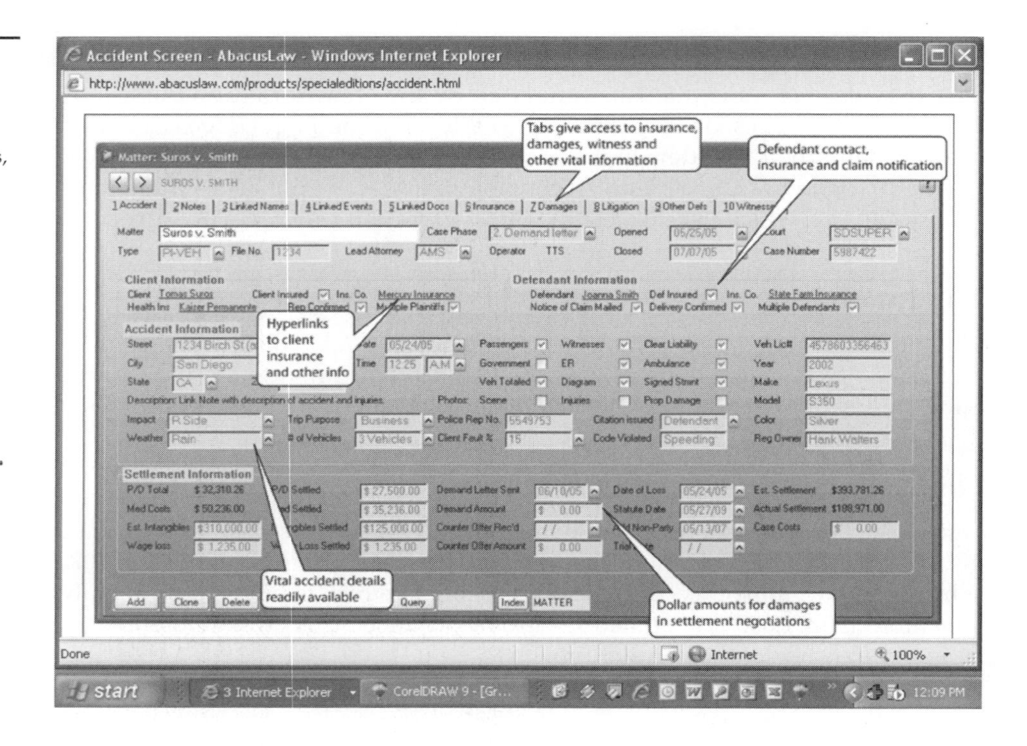

partnerships, corporations, estates, and so forth. Several programs can compute and print out every federal IRS form available. These programs automatically calculate and print out a tax form, which minimizes computing errors. Further, because the forms can be edited on the computer, changes or adjustments can easily be made.

Criminal Law

Criminal law is highly specialized. Because defendants have been charged with a crime, the stakes are very high. Several programs are available to meet the needs of prosecutors and defense attorneys. Exhibit 13–2 shows a program designed to assist prosecutors. Criminal law case management systems, whether tailored to the prosecutor or defense attorney, typically maintain docket and scheduling information, track names and addresses of witnesses, track information about case facts, note whether a bond was required, identify specific counts and crimes charged, and track evidence and documents. Most of the programs offer a document generator to quickly generate form letters, pleadings, and so forth. Some programs also incorporate checklists.

Estate Planning Law

estate planning
An area of the law where lawyers help their clients plan for where they want their property and monies distributed at their death and what tax consequences the plan will have at present and after death.

Attorneys who practice in the **estate planning** field help clients plan where they want their property and monies distributed at their death and what tax consequences the plan will have both presently and at their death. Many different plans and options can be used, including insurance policies, trusts, and wills. Estate planning attorneys determine which plan has the least tax consequences and help the client to put the plan into action.

Several programs help attorneys evaluate and determine the best estate plan. Most programs begin by having the user enter the client's assets and liabilities (including property, insurance, pension benefits, and mortgaged real estate) and whether they are jointly held with a spouse or not. The programs then allow the

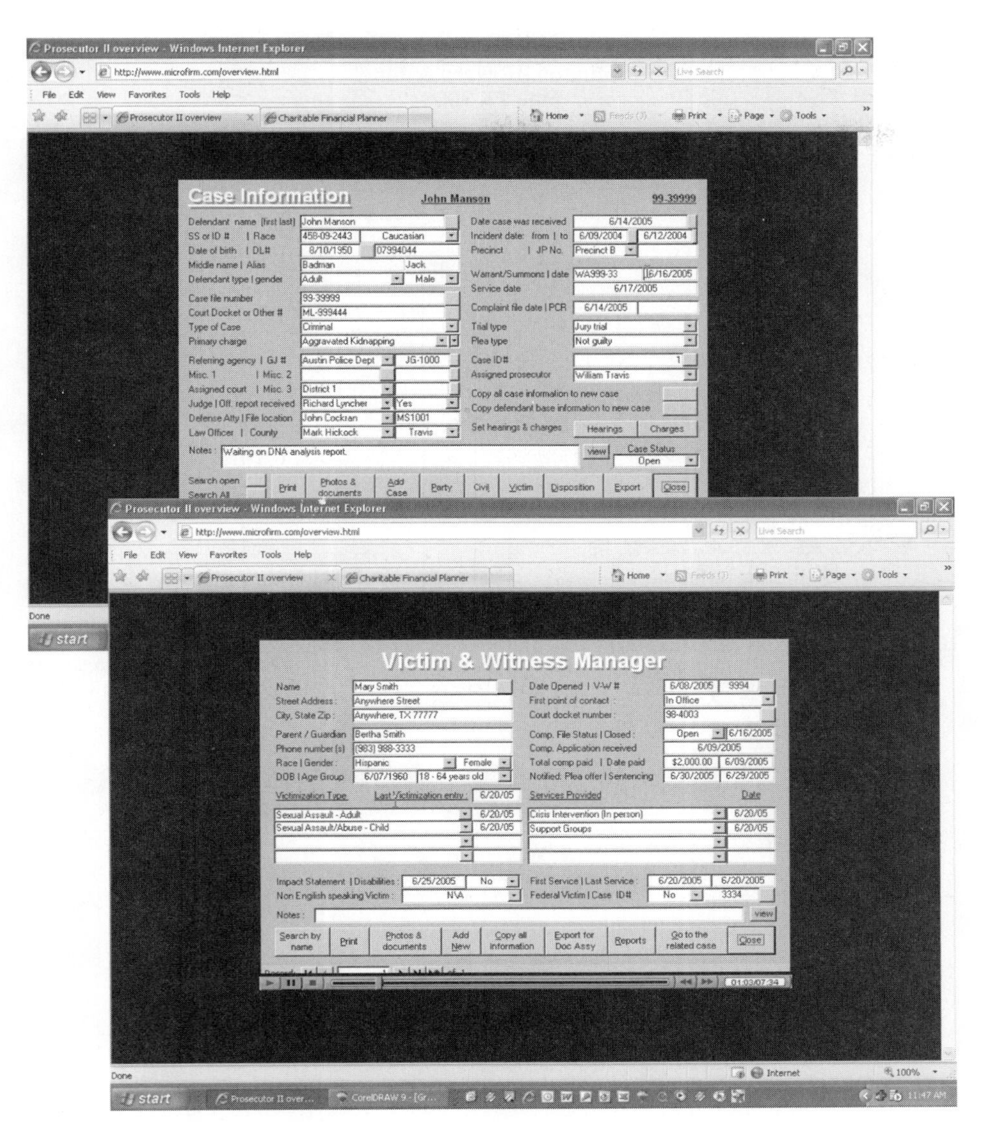

Exhibit 13–2
Criminal Law Software
Courtesy of Microfirm Software Corp.

user to enter several different alternative estate plans for the client. Some programs can then automatically calculate the federal and state estate tax consequences of each of these requests so the attorney can see which alternative has the smallest tax consequence. For example, in Exhibit 13–3 an estate planning program was used to see the effects of an alternate estate plan. Notice the difference in tax liabilities for the two plans, as calculated by the computer. Some systems, in addition to calculating different plans, can actually use artificial intelligence to evaluate a plan a legal professional has designed.

Another facet of practicing estate planning law is drafting and preparing wills and trusts. Once an estate has been properly planned, the attorney must then prepare the documents necessary to put the plan into action. A **will** is an instrument that expresses how a person's property should be distributed at his death. A **trust** is an instrument wherein one party (a trustee) holds property for the benefit of another (a beneficiary).

Wills and trusts can be tedious to draft. Several programs are available to help attorneys draft wills and trusts. These programs can save a lot of drafting and retyping time, and frequently provide checklists and a document generator (see Exhibit 13–4).

will
An instrument that expresses how a person's property should be distributed at his death.

trust
An instrument wherein one party (a trustee) holds property for the benefit of another (a beneficiary).

Exhibit 13–3
Estate Planning Software

Compare Plans — Client Dies First
Johnson, Howard & Janet
May 23, 2008

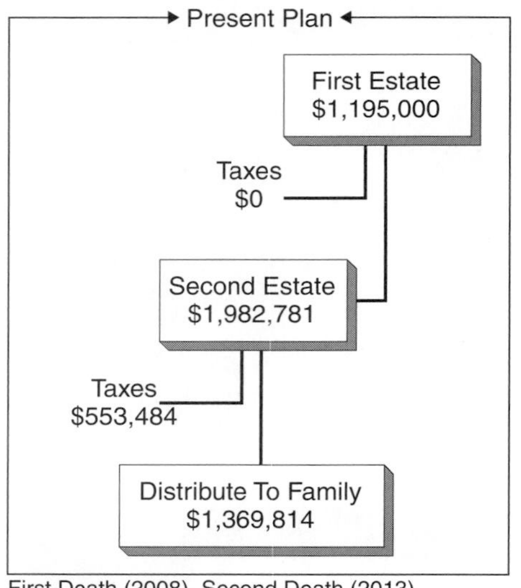

First Death (2008), Second Death (2013)

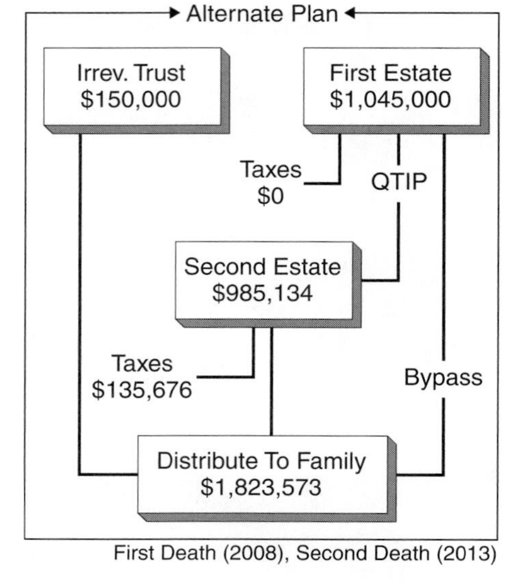

First Death (2008), Second Death (2013)

Exhibit 13–4
Estate Planning—Wills and Trusts Software
National LawForms, Inc., www.nationallawforms.com

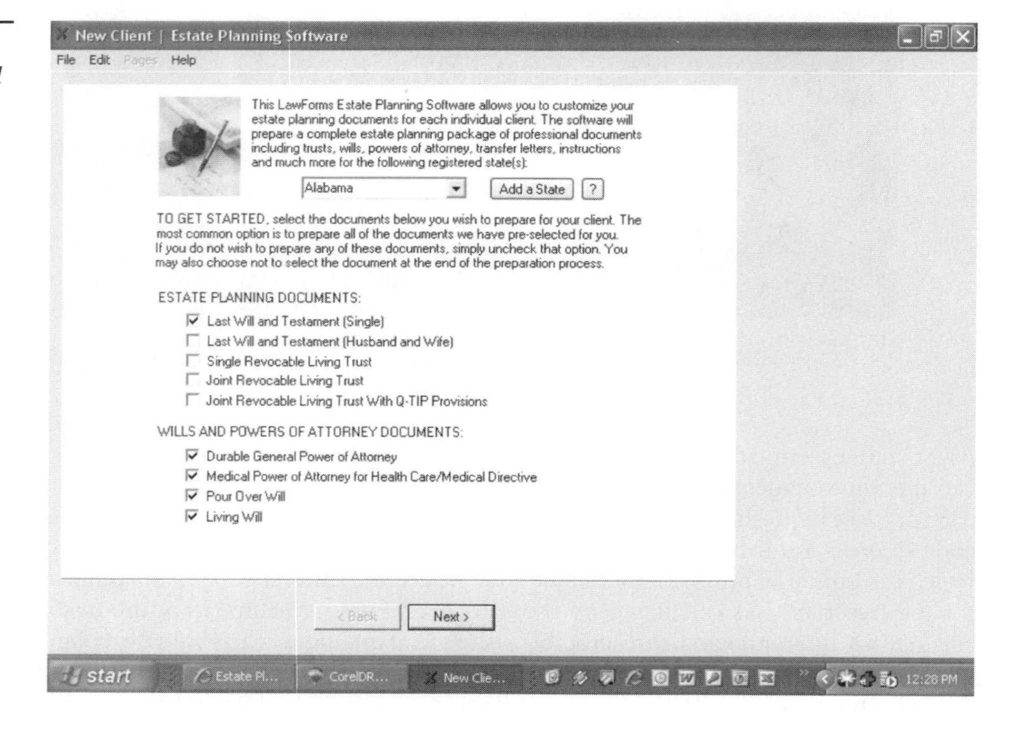

Probate Law

probate law
An area of the law that allows a judge to determine the validity of wills and trusts, the proper beneficiaries or recipients of property, and other like matters.

After a person has died, in many cases a probate case is opened. The purpose of **probate law** (or a probate case) is to allow a judge to determine the validity of wills and trusts, the proper beneficiaries or recipients of property, and other like matters. In addition, the fiduciary must give the judge, the beneficiaries, and the federal and state taxing authorities a proper accounting of what is happening with the estate. Several programs that track all of this information are

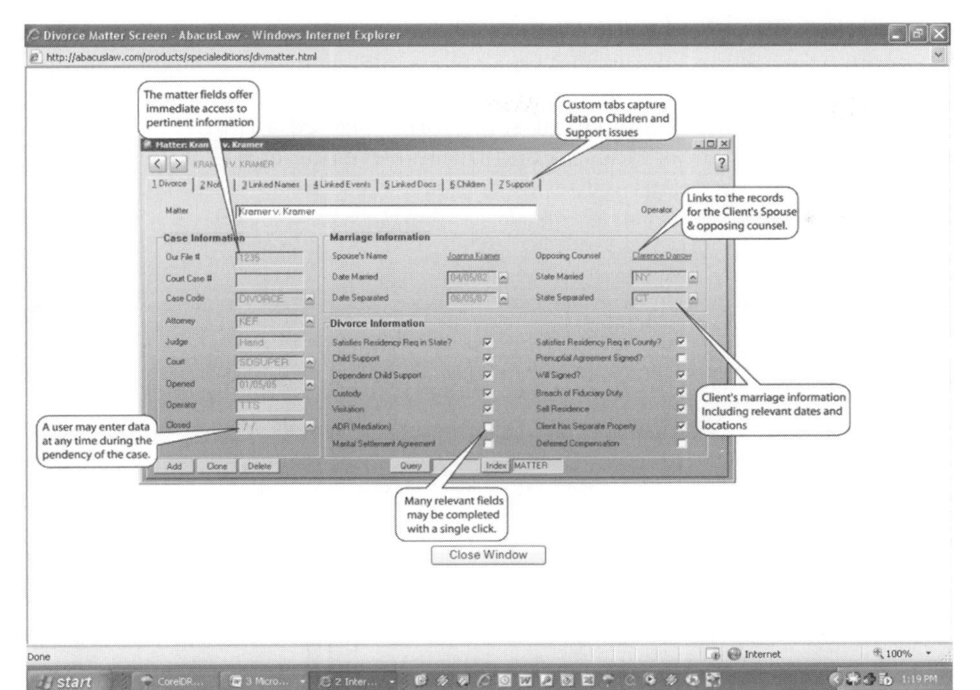

Exhibit 13–5
Family Law Case Management Program
Courtesy of Abacus Data Systems, Inc.

available; some can even fill out the proper IRS tax forms for an estate. In large estates dealing with hundreds of thousands of dollars or more, this type of program can save a lot of time.

Family Law

When a marriage is dissolved by means of a divorce, there are many issues a court must resolve, including division of assets, child support, alimony, custody, and parenting time. Some jurisdictions have computer programs available for purchase that can calculate standard child support and alimony payments based on state law. There are also programs available, such as the program shown in Exhibit 13–5, that can track a wide variety of legal and factual issues in a family law case and then merge that information into word-processing documents.

Real Estate Law

Real estate attorneys deal with the buying and selling of real property (land, houses, buildings, etc.). Nearly all states require that a written agreement be executed when real property is bought or sold. Real estate attorneys regularly draft these types of agreements. They can be quite complicated, since insurance, taxes, utilities, closing costs, and other calculations must be made.

Real Estate Contracts Several real estate programs are available that will automatically draft real estate contracts and help with closings. Most of these programs use a document generator. Some even perform the necessary calculations for computing taxes, insurance, and other items that have been prepaid. For example, the seller of a piece of property may have paid for a year's worth of insurance on the property in advance. If the property is sold during the middle of that year, the seller is usually entitled to recover part of the insurance payment that is prepaid when the buyer takes possession of the property. Some real estate programs will automatically make these calculations.

HUD Forms In some real estate sales, such as when residential property is sold to certain types of buyers, a special type of low-interest loan is available through the federal government. To qualify for such a loan, the buyer must fill out a specific type of form; in residential sales, the form is called a HUD-1 form (HUD stands for Department of Housing and Urban Development) or a RESPA form. Some real estate programs will even generate these forms automatically (see Exhibit 13–6).

Exhibit 13–6
Real Estate HUD-1 Software
National LawForms, Inc., www.nationallawforms.com

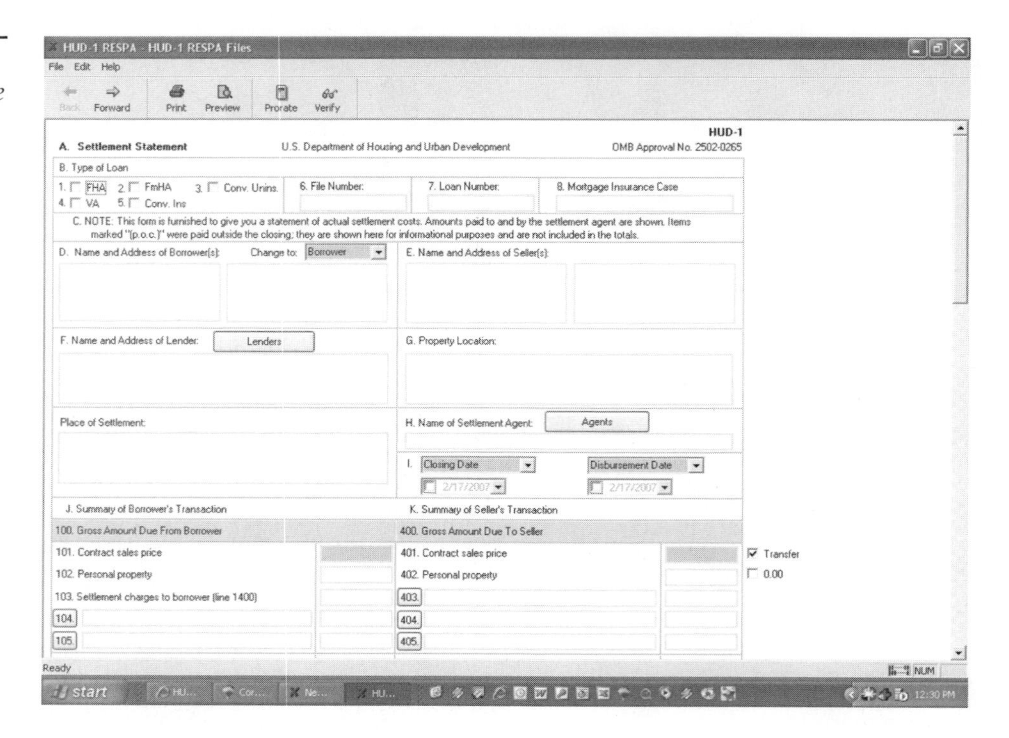

Amortization Schedules Whenever a buyer gets a loan in order to purchase real estate, a schedule of principal and interest payments must be computed. Such a schedule must be generated so that the buyer knows how much the monthly payments are and what part of a payment is going to pay off the principal of the loan and what part is going to pay off the interest on the loan. This is called an amortization schedule. Although amortization schedules can be generated using a spreadsheet, these programs automatically generate them so the user does not have to write the formulas to compute them.

Real Estate Foreclosure In some instances, parties that have purchased a piece of property by obtaining a loan cannot pay the money back and therefore default on the loan. In those cases, it is necessary for the bank or the person who gave the loan to foreclose on the piece of property. A foreclosure action turns the title or ownership of the property back to the bank or the party issuing the loan. Several programs are available that automatically generate the pleadings and other forms necessary in a foreclosure action along with providing a docket system for tracking the litigation.

Business Law

Business lawyers routinely draft business contracts, negotiate sales, set up corporations and partnerships, and so forth. Several business law case management systems help organize and track business law cases. For example, when

setting up a new corporation, articles of incorporation (papers that state what the purpose of the corporation is) must be filed (usually with the state secretary of state's office), bylaws (papers that state how the corporation will be run) must be drawn up, federal and state tax information must be filed, and so forth. Some business law programs automatically generate checklists, track dates in a docket control program, and generate the appropriate forms.

Bankruptcy Law

Bankruptcy attorneys often handle a large number of cases. In addition, a number of different forms, pleadings, deadlines, and other types of data must be tracked. Several bankruptcy programs automate the process of drafting pleadings, tracking deadlines, and otherwise organizing and tracking bankruptcy cases (see Exhibit 13–7). Many of these programs contain a document generator that merges a database of creditors into needed schedules and forms. Some programs will automatically produce budgets and other financial documents for use in the bankruptcy proceedings.

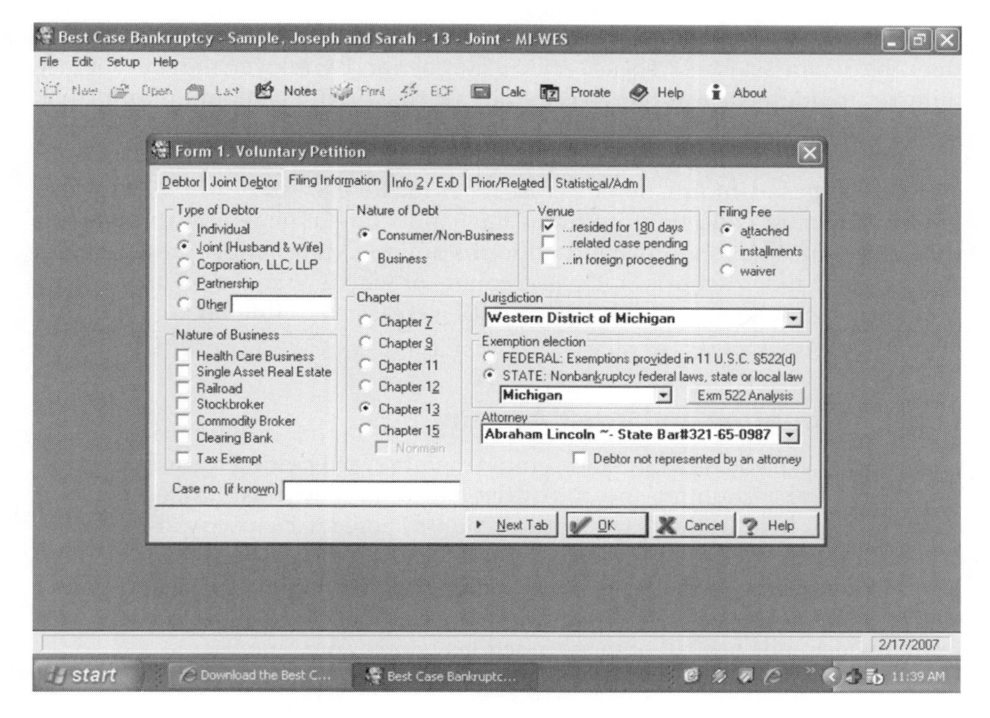

Exhibit 13–7
Bankruptcy Software
Best Case Solutions, a division of Aspen Publishing.

Some of these programs are marketed on the basis of their user-friendliness—trying to take the confusing nature out of the myriad of forms necessary to complete a bankruptcy case. The user answers a few simple questions about the client's situation, and in return the software automatically produces customized bankruptcy forms.

Patent Law

Patent law is another area of the law that is highly technical and specialized and that has its own rules and procedures. Several software programs guide the user in an organized and structured manner throughout a patent case.

Collection Law

collection law
An area of the law that involves suing debtors (persons or businesses that agreed to pay a debt) for the amount of money left unpaid on a bill or debt.

Collection law involves suing debtors (persons or businesses that agreed to pay a debt) for the amount of money left unpaid on a bill or debt. It is practiced by many attorneys and legal assistants. Although the work is usually rather routine, numerous letters, forms, pleadings, and calendar dates, and much account information must be tracked. For example, if a debtor agreed to make monthly payments on a debt, the debt must be calendared each month to make sure the payment is made. If a payment is late, a reminder must be sent. Further, the account history of each debt must be tracked, including principal, amount of interest accruing, payments, expenses (in some states, the debtor must pay for all or part of the expenses incurred in a collection case), and fees. Attorneys usually receive a percentage of the money they recover. Thus, an attorney might receive 30 percent of each dollar collected. All of this information must be carefully tracked.

Several collection software programs are aimed at the collection lawyer. Most collection programs provide for entering new cases, adding transactions (such as entering payments), and tracking when payments are to be made and other types of information using a docket control or tickler program. Most programs also print automatic form letters, pleadings, and so forth. Most programs can automatically calculate interest, balances, and payments. In addition, most programs track the debtor's address, social security number, and employer; the court or case number; if judgment was received in the case; the original amount of principal, interest, and payments; and the balance currently due and owing. Most programs also allow the user to record the contents of phone conversations, promises to pay, and other types of information in a case notes file for each case.

Finally, most collection programs have a document generator that merges the debtor information into standard forms and pleadings. Most programs can also produce many reports, such as accounts of who is to make payments on a certain date and how much is to be paid, as well as generating billing reports to clients and much more.

Legal Accounting and Trust Accounting

Law offices, like any other business, must maintain accounting records. In addition to general accounting records of the law firm, they must also account for client monies held in the firm's trust account. There are many good law office accounting and trust account software programs on the market. Many of these programs combine accounting, trust accounting, and timekeeping and billing into a single program. Since there is overlap in all of these areas, a single program that can perform all of these functions is very convenient.

ISSUES TO CONSIDER WHEN PURCHASING LEGAL-SPECIFIC SOFTWARE

There are several issues to be considered when purchasing legal-specific or generic application software. These include determining your needs and surveying the market, among other things.

Determine Your Needs

The first step before buying any type of software is to determine exactly what you want the software to accomplish. Knowing that will save you time and expense later.

Survey the Market

Make a thorough search or survey of the market to see what types of software are available and whether or not the software will meet your needs. Be sure to check the ABA Legal Technology Resource Center or *Law Technology News* for software reviews on products you are considering, and contact your state bar association or do research on the Internet for other information.

Look for Products with Good Customer Support

Good customer support is an absolute necessity for most legal-specific software. Sometimes, with legal-specific software, the user must pay extra for customer support. Customer support fees can run as high as $300 to $500 a month for some legal-specific systems. Look for companies that provide a toll-free support number along with good documentation.

Do Not Underestimate the Need for Training

Attorneys and law firms are notorious for spending money on complex computer systems and software and then failing to spend the money required to train their staff on how to use them. This is a mistake. Most legal consultants that practice in the area of implementing software systems say that the single most common reason for a successful new software implementation at a law firm is the full training of staff, while the number one reason for systems that fail is inadequate training. It is nearly always a mistake to go cheap on training or to completely leave it out of the implementation process.

Consider Availability and Price

Do not buy a program because "the next version of the program will be great." Consider the program that is currently available, since software companies may intend to put out another version, but in fact may never do so.

Price is a major issue in most software purchases. Unfortunately, legal-specific software can be expensive. Since the legal market is very narrow, software companies must charge much higher prices to earn a profit than when selling a general application program.

Buying legal-specific software can be risky, because some of the companies selling the software can be small and the prices can be very high when compared with those for general office application software.

Determine for Whom the Program Is Designed

Always consider for whom the program is designed. For example, some software companies that sell collection software design the program for collection agencies. In many instances, the software company will also try to sell the program to collection attorneys, even though the software really cannot meet the needs of a collection attorney, since an attorney's needs are completely different. Always ask who is the primary market for the program.

Always Check References

Before you purchase a legal-specific program, always check the company's references. Make sure that the references are attorneys or are within the legal environment and have experience in the particular area. When you call references, do not just ask broad questions, such as "Do you like the system?" Ask specific questions relating to your own needs and wants. Also ask the references how they use the system, if the system has been productive, if the system has

saved them money, if passwords and security devices are built in, if the system can work on a network, and if the manufacturer provides good customer support. Finally, find out about the firm itself. If little similarity exists between your firm and the firm you are calling, call other references until you find one that matches your own. What may work for a large firm may not work at all for a smaller firm. Visit one of the references to see how the program is actually being used.

Determine Whether the Program Has Been Reviewed or Approved by Legal Associations

Always ask whether or not the program has been reviewed by *Law Office Computing* or other magazines, and ask for a copy of the review. Reviews and evaluations are an excellent source for finding out whether the program can really do what it says it will.

Ask for a Demonstration Version of the Program

Always get a demonstration disk, if possible. Many times, a demonstration disk that shows the functions and operations of the program is available free of charge either in the mail or on the company's web page. Even if the disk is not free, if you are considering purchasing the product, get a demonstration disk. It is well worth the investment. You can get a good idea from the demonstration disk of whether or not the program will meet your needs.

Find Out If the Program Has a Money-Back Guarantee

Try to get programs that come with a 30-day or 60-day money-back guarantee. This way, if a program does not meet your needs, you can get your money back. Make sure the money-back guarantee is in writing.

Find Out How Many Copies of the Program Are In Use

Always ask the company how many copies of its program are in use in law offices. This can sometimes give you an idea of how good program is.

Find Out How Old the Company Is

Always ask the company how long it has been in the legal-specific software business. Beware of start-up companies. Look for companies with a solid base in this area.

SUMMARY

Since most attorneys practice in a defined area of the law, it is wise for legal professionals to look for software that will computerize their specialty. Although legal-specific software is on the market, it is often difficult to find. Some good resources for finding legal-specific software include the American Bar Association, the Internet, Law Technology News, and Technolawyer.

Legal-specific software is currently widely available for the following legal specialty areas: personal injury, tax, criminal, estate, probate, family law, real estate, business, bankruptcy, patent, and collections.

When purchasing legal-specific software, users should determine their needs, survey the market, look for products with good customer service, budget for training, consider the availability of the product, check references, and obtain a demonstration version of the program.

INTERNET SITES

Internet sites for this chapter are shown here and on the next page.

Legal Technology Issues

Organization	Product / Service	World Wide Web Address
American Bar Association	Home page	<http://www.abanet.org>
ABA Law Practice Management Section	Information on legal technology issues and products	<http://www.abanet.org/lpm>
ABA Legal Technology Resource Center	Information on legal technology issues and products	<http://www.abanet.org/>
ABA Publications	Books and magazines on a wide variety of legal technology issues	<http://www.abanet.org/>
ABA TechShow	Information on the ABA's annual legal technology conference / exposition	<http://www.abanet.org/>
Infosources Publishing	*Directory of Law-Related CD-ROMs* book	<http://www.infosourcespub.com>
Law Technology News	Magazine on legal technology issues	<http://www.lawtechnologynews.com>
Technolawyer	Legal technology email newsletter	<http://www.technolawyer.com>

Legal-Specific Software

Organization	Software Product	World Wide Web Address
Cornerstone Computer Group	Bankruptcy law	<http://www.cornerstone-computer.com>
EasySoft	Bankruptcy law	<http://www.easysoft-usa.com>
Law Firm Software	Bankruptcy law	<http://www.lawfirmsoftware.com>
Best Case Solutions	Bankruptcy law	<http://www.bestcase.com>
Law Firm Software	Business law	<http://www.lawfirmsoftware.com>
EasySoft	Collection law	<http://www.easysoft-usa.com>
Totality Software	Collections law	<http://www.totalitysoftware.com>
Legal Edge Software	Corporate law department software	<http://www.legaledge.com>
Economic Analysis Group	Corporate law department software	<http://www.case-track.com>
Microfirm Software	Criminal law (Prosecutor II)	<http://www.microfirm.com>
Legal Edge Software	Criminal law	<http://www.legaledge.com>

INTERNET SITES (Cont'd)

Organization	Software Product	World Wide Web Address
Advocate Software	Damages calculation software for personal injury, wrongful death, employment law, and structured settlements	<http://www.advocatesoftware.com>
Brentmark Software	Estate law	<http://www.brentmark.com>
Impact Technologies Group	Estate law	<http://www.impact-tech.com>
EasySoft	Estate law	<http://www.easysoft-usa.com
Law Firm Software	Estate law	<http://www.lawfirmsoftware.com>
Abacus Data Systems	Estate law	<http://www.abacuslaw.com>
Thomson	Estate law	<http://www.west.thomson.com/cowles>
Lapin Agile	Family law	<http://www.kidmate.com>
Abacus Data Systems	Family law	<http://www.abacuslaw.com>
EasySoft	Landlord-tenant law	<http://www.easysoft-usa.com>
Thomson	Patent and trademark law	<http://www.micropatent.com>
Abacus Data Systems	Personal injury law	<http://www.abacuslaw.com>
EasySoft	Real estate law	<http://www.easysoft-usa.com>
Argosy Legal Systems	Real estate law	<http://www.argosylegal.com>
Law Firm Software	Real estate law	<http://www.lawfirmsoftware.com>
Thomson	Tax law	<http://gosystem.thomson.com>
Thomson	Tax law	<http://insource.thomson.com/>
Intuit, Inc.	Tax law	<http://www.proseries.com>
Abacus Data Systems	Workers' compensation law	<http://www.abacuslaw.com>

KEY TERMS

legal-specific software	estate planning	trust	collection law
personal injury law	will	probate law	

TEST YOUR KNOWLEDGE

Test your knowledge of the chapter by answering these questions.

1. True or False: Legal-specific software products are widely available and easy to find for any legal specialty.
2. What is the name of the American Bar Association special project devoted solely to legal technology?
3. What is one of the most important aspects of implementing legal-specific software that attorneys and law firms forget to budget for and do?
4. True or False: When buying legal-specific software, checking references is not that important.

ON THE WEB EXERCISES

1. Go to the American Bar Association's Legal Technology Resource Center on the Internet at <http://www.abanet.org>. Thoroughly review the site. Write a three-page memorandum summarizing what you found on the site.
2. As a legal assistant in a firm that specializes in collection work, you spend most of your day typing form letters and computing interest on debts using a word processor and a spreadsheet. While this is technically "computerized," it is still labor intensive. Use the Internet sites at the end of the chapter and / or a general search engine such as Google or Yahoo! to find three collection programs, preferably designed for attorneys. Compare the prices, features, support, and training available. Download trial versions of the programs if you can. Write a two-page memo summarizing your research and findings. Include which program you think is best and why.
3. You have convinced your employer to purchase a new bankruptcy program. Use the Internet sites at the end of the chapter and / or a general search engine such as Google or Yahoo! to find three bankruptcy programs. Compare the prices, features, support, and training available. Download trial versions of the programs if you can. Write a two-page memo summarizing your research and findings. Include which program you think is best and why.
4. As a legal assistant for a corporation, you have recently seen that there are specific software programs targeted for corporate law departments. Use the Internet sites at the end of the chapter and / or a general search engine such as Google or Yahoo! to find three software programs for corporate law departments. Compare the prices, features, support, and training available. Download trial versions of the programs if you can. Write a two-page memo summarizing your research and findings. Include which program you think is best and why.

QUESTIONS AND EXERCISES

1. Go to your local law library and review whatever titles they have related to legal technology. Prepare a one-page summary of the information you found.
2. Contact an attorney or legal assistant in your area and interview the person regarding the type of software he or she uses in their job. Ask questions related to the types of general office productivity software that he or she uses, as well as any legal-specific programs. Write a two-page memo summarizing your interview.

Glossary

absolute cell reference A cell address in a spreadsheet program formula that does not change when it is copied to a new location.

access rights Network security measure that limits a user's access to only these directories and programs that the user is authorized to access.

access time The amount of time it takes to transfer data between a storage device and RAM.

accounting software An application program that tracks and maintains the financial data and records of a business or an individual.

activity hourly rate A fee based on different hourly rates depending on the type of service or activity performed and the degree of difficulty of the activity.

aged accounts receivable report A report showing all cases that have outstanding balances due and how long these balances are past due.

analytical litigation support programs A type of litigation support program that helps legal professionals analyze a case from a number of different perspectives and to create cause and effect relationships between facts and evidence in a case.

animation Effects that presentation graphics programs use on individual slides, such as how bullet points appear on the screen and are added to a list.

antivirus utility and antispyware Attempts to prevent virus and spyware programs from getting into the computer system and to locate and remove any viruses or spyware that do manage to get into the computer.

application service provider (ASP) A company that provides software or a service application through the Internet directly to the user's computer.

application software Instructions that tell the computer to perform a specific function or task, such as word processing.

arithmetic operators Symbols that tell a spreadsheet how to compute values. Examples include addition signs, subtraction signs, and multiplication signs.

artificial intelligence or expert programs Application programs that use a computer to provide analyses, make decisions, and solve problems based upon a known set of assumptions.

ascending sort A sort criterion that places data in ascending order from beginning to end, from A to Z, or from low numbers to high numbers.

attorney or legal assistant hourly rate A fee based on the attorney's or legal assistant's level of expertise and experience in a particular area.

AutoCorrect A feature that automatically corrects typographical errors as the user types or converts abbreviations to full text as the user types.

automatic page numbering A feature in a word processor (also found in other types of programs) that automatically numbers the pages of a document for the user.

automatic paragraph numbering A feature that automatically numbers paragraphs in word processing documents, including automatically renumbering paragraphs when additions or deletions are made.

AutoText A feature that finishes writing words that a user starts to spell.

auxiliary storage device A device that stores information so that it can be retrieved for later use. Auxiliary storage devices can hold data and retrieve it even after power to the computer has been turned off. Auxiliary storage devices include flash drives, hard disk drives, and others.

background The design on which the other elements of the presentation (words, clip art, etc.) are placed.

backing up Making a copy of a user's computer files.

backup utility Creates a copy of a user's hard disk or other storage device. The backup copy can be restored if the hard disk is damaged or lost.

bar code scanner Reads the special lines on bar codes. Can be used to track documents in litigation as well as office furniture and equipment.

bar graph A graph that consists of a sequence of bars that illustrate numerical values.

Bates stamp Stamps a document with a sequential number and then automatically advances to the next number.

billing The process of issuing bills to collect monies for legal services performed and for expenses incurred.

blended hourly rate fee One hourly rate that is set taking into account the blend or mix of attorneys working on the matter.

bookmark A pointer that enables a user to quickly and easily go back to a website.

blog A website with information contained in posts that are arranged in reverse chronological order.

Boolean logic search A computer search that allows a search request to include or exclude words or other search criteria so that the search is either refined or broadened.

Boolean/logical operator A symbol that instructs a DBMS to search for more than one criterion. Examples include AND, OR, and NOT.

browser A software program that is used to access the World Wide Web (WWW) on the Internet. A browser connects a user to the World Wide Web (remote computers), opens and transfers files, displays text and images, and provides an interface to the Internet and WWW documents.

cable modem A coaxial cable that allows a computer to connect to the Internet through a cable TV provider at much faster rates than normal modems can.

cache memory A high-speed buffer that is used to speed the processing operations of a computer.

calendaring A generic term used to describe the function of recording appointments for any type of business. This includes personal information managers.

case management A legal term that usually refers to functions like docket control, deadlines, Things to do, contact information by case, case notes, document assembly, document tracking by case, integrated billing, and email.

case retainer A fee that is billed at the beginning of a matter, is not refundable to the client, and is usually paid at the beginning of the case as an incentive for the office to take the case.

case type productivity report A report showing which types of cases (i.e., criminal, personal injury, bankruptcy, etc.) are the most profitable.

cash advance Unearned monies that are an advance against the attorney's future fees and expenses.

CD-R (compact disk–recordable) drive A device that permanently stores information on a compact disk.

CD-ROM drive A device that reads information stored on compact disks. CD-ROM drives can typically store up to 650 MB of data on a single disk.

CD-ROM legal database A CD-ROM disk containing a legal database such as a state case law reporter that is searchable like WESTLAW and LexisNexis.

CD-RW (compact disk–Rewritable) drive Similar to a CD-R drive, but the data on the disk can be changed many times, much like a floppy disk or hard disk.

cell An intersection between a row and a column in a spreadsheet.

cell address The row and column location of a cell.

cell pointer The cursor in a spreadsheet program.

cell width The number of characters that can be placed in any given cell in a spreadsheet program.

central processing unit (CPU) The part of a computer that contains the processor chip and main memory. The CPU organizes and processes information in addition to coordinating with peripheral devices.

centralized word-processing system A system where all the word-processing documents for an organization are typed in one single location or by one department (i.e., a word-processing department).

cite checking Checking to see that a case or statute is still valid and that the decision has not been overturned or the statute repealed.

click Point at the item with the mouse and then push one of the mouse buttons.

client hourly rate A fee based on one hourly charge for the client, regardless of which attorney works on the case and what she or he does on the case.

client/server network A network that uses a server to meet the needs of the other computers on the network.

clip art Predrawn art.

close Closes the window and the application that is running in the window.

collection law An area of the law that involves suing debtors (persons or businesses that agreed to pay a debt) for the amount of money left unpaid on a bill or debt.

color printers Typically non-impact printers that use inkjet or laser technologies to print text and graphics in a wide variety of colors.

column An area that extends down a page vertically.

comment The comment feature in a word processor allows a user to annotate and create notes in a document without changing the text of the document.

communication device A device, such as a modem, that allows computers to exchange information.

compare documents The compare documents feature in a word processor allows a user to compare and contrast two documents, either side by side or by blacklining.

compression utility Compresses a file so that it takes up less room when it is saved. Many large files that are downloaded from the Internet are routinely compressed so that it takes less time to complete the download.

computer An electronic device that accepts input data, processes data, outputs data, and stores data electronically (including desktop, laptop, handheld, tablet, and file server).

computer programs Sets of instructions that direct a computer to perform a task.

computer software Step-by-step instructions that direct a computer to perform a task.

computer viruses Computer programs that are destructive in nature and can be designed to delete data, corrupt files, or do other damage.

Computer/Windows Explorer A feature that allows users instant access to drives, documents and files.

computer-aided transcription (CAT) A process that automatically deciphers a court reporter's notes and converts them into a computer-readable format.

computer-assisted legal research (CALR) Using computers to research and retrieve legal information.

connectors Characters that show a relationship between the keywords in a search query.

contingency fee A fee collected if the attorney successfully represents the client, typically a percentage of the total recovery.

Control Panel Allows the user to customize and adjust the settings of the user's Windows environment.

criminal fraud A false representation of a present or past fact made by a defendant.

data filtering The process of searching and culling the data to find relevant information and reduce the overall size of the dataset.

data value One item of information, which is the smallest piece of information in a table.

database A collection of related data items. Databases are created because the information contained in them needs to be accessed, organized, and used.

database management system Application software that manages a database by storing, searching, sorting, and organizing data.

decentralized word-processing system A system where individuals or separate departments in an organization perform their own word-processing.

deduplication or "de-duping" The process of marking or deleting records that are duplicates.

demonstrative evidence All evidence other than testimony.

deposition Oral testimony taken before a court reporter who transcribes the testimony word for word.

descending sort A sort criterion that places data in descending order from end to beginning, from Z to A, or from high numbers to low numbers.

desktop Where windows are placed.

disaster recovery plan A prewritten plan of action in case a disaster befalls the legal organization.

discovery The pre-trial stage of litigation where parties disclose to each other information about their case.

docket control A legal specific term that refers to entering, organizing, tracking, and controlling all the appointments, deadlines, and due dates for a legal organization.

document abstract litigation support system A litigation support system that allows users to enter document abstracts or summaries into a computer and then search and retrieve information contained in those abstracts or summaries.

document assembly software Software that creates powerful standardized templates and forms.

document camera An overhead projector that uses a camera to display hard-copy documents that have not been imaged.

document imaging A litigation support system in which documents are scanned into a computer and the documents' actual images (similar to photographs) are retained in the computer.

document management software Software that organizes, controls, distributes, and allows for extensive searching of electronic documents, typically in a networked environment.

dot-matrix printer An impact printer that prints data by forming rows and columns of dots.

double indenting A feature in a word-processor (also found in other types of programs) that indents text an equal distance from the left and right margins.

double-click Point at an item and press a mouse button twice in rapid succession.

drag Point at an item with a mouse, hold one of the mouse buttons down, move the mouse to another location, and release the button.

DSL (Digital Subscriber Line) A type of digital phone line that is hundreds of times faster than a modem and also allows data and voice to be transmitted on the same line (similar to ISDN, but much faster).

DVD-ROM (digital versatile disk) drive Reads information stored on DVD-ROM or CD-ROM disks.

earned retainer The money the law office or attorney has earned and is entitled to deposit in the office's or attorney's own bank account.

electronic billing Billing clients in a fashion that conforms to standard billing codes and uses a standard electronic format, using means such as the Internet.

electronic discovery The process of producing and retrieving litigation documents in electronic format.

electronic discovery software Software that assists legal professionals in accurately assembling, producing, reading, converting, and searching electronic discovery requests.

electronic filing Where courts accept electronic versions of legal documents via the Internet or other electronic means instead of requiring the hard copy of the document.

electronic mail (email) Allows users to send messages to other people virtually worldwide via the Internet. Email can also be used to send and receive electronic files such as word processing files, spreadsheet files, and database files.

electronically stored information (ESI) The term used by the Federal Rules of Civil Procedure to refer to all electronic data including writings, drawings, graphs, charts, photographs, sound recordings, images, and other data compilations stored in any medium from which information can be obtained and translated.

encryption Running a message through an encoder that uses an encrypting key to alter the characters in the message. Unless the person wanting to read the message has the encryption key needed to decode it, the message appears unreadable.

endnote A numbered reference that is printed at the end of a chapter or document.

estate planning An area of the law where lawyers help their clients plan how they want their property and monies distributed at their death and what tax consequences the plan will have at present and after death.

evidence display system A computerized system that displays evidence via monitors to the judge, jury, counsel, and the public simultaneously.

expense slip A record of each expense item a firm incurs on behalf of the client.

expert witness report A report produced by an expert witness that states the factual basis for the expert's opinion on the matter.

extranet A secure web-based site that allows clients to access information about their case and collaborate with the legal professionals that are providing legal services to them.

fax modem A device that can be used as both a fax machine and a modem.

field A column in a table that contains a category of information.

File Transfer Protocol (FTP) A tool or standard for transferring files over the Internet.

find by citation A WESTLAW feature that allows a user to immediately retrieve a specific case or statute by entering its citation.

find a case by party name A WESTLAW feature that allows a user to retrieve a case by knowing the name of at least one party and without knowing the citation, or entering a search query.

firewall Allows users from inside an organization to access the Internet but keeps outside users from entering the LAN.

flat fee A fee for legal services that is billed as a flat or fixed amount.

flat-file DBMS A DBMS that can work with only one database table at a time.

floppy disk drive An auxiliary storage device that stores data on a plastic magnetic disk called a floppy disk or a diskette.

FOCUS A LexisNexis feature that allows a user to search all of the retrieved documents for a term(s), whether or not the term was used in the original search.

footer Text that appears at the bottom of the pages of a document.

footnote A numbered reference that is printed at the bottom of a page.

form Allows a user to view, enter, and edit data in a custom format designed by the user.

formulas Expressions used in spreadsheet programs to automatically perform calculations on other values.

freeware Computer programs that are distributed to users free of charge.

full-text retrieval litigation support system A litigation support system that enables a user to search and retrieve information contained in the full text of documents stored in the system.

function command A predefined calculation used in a spreadsheet program to speed up the process of entering complex formulas.

Gadget A tool that can be added to the Windows Desktop in the Sidebar.

Gantt chart A timeline of projected begin dates and end dates.

get by citation A LexisNexis feature that allows a user to immediately retrieve a specific case or statute by entering its citation.

get by party name A feature that allows a LexisNexis user to retrieve a case by entering the name(s) of a party (or parties).

Gigahertz (GHz) The clock speed of a computer.

Gopher A tool that allows users to access other resources and computers on the Internet.

graphical user interface (GUI) A user interface used by Windows that utilizes icons, scroll bars, pull-down or pop-up menus, and mouse support.

groupware Allows users on a network to coordinate and manage projects, exchange email, schedule meetings, and manage files.

handheld computer Also called a personal digital assistant (PDA). An extremely portable computer that is small enough to be carried in a user's hand. Features may include email, Internet access, mobile phone service, faxing, and a wide variety of computer applications.

hard disk drive A reliable and fast auxiliary storage device that stores data on a rigid magnetic disk.

hardware The physical equipment of a computer system, as opposed to written programs or software.

harvesting data The process of collecting ESI from the client's information systems.

header A title or heading that appears at the top of the pages of a word processing or other type of document.

Headnotes and Key Numbers Feature in WESTLAW that classifies each legal issue in a case and allows users to search and retrieve other cases with similar Headnotes and Key Numbers.

hourly rate fee A fee for legal services that is billed to the client by the hour at an agreed-upon rate.

hypermedia or **hypertext links** Connects web pages together. When a user clicks on a hypermedia or hypertext link, the user is immediately taken to the new website location.

icon A picture on the screen that represents a particular computer program or feature.

imaging The ability to scan a document into a computer so the user can see the exact image of the document on the computer.

imaging software Converts an image of a hard-copy document (through scanning) into an electronic file such as a PDF (Portable Document Format) file.

impact printer Prints data on paper by physically impacting or striking the paper, as a typewriter does.

in-house computerized litigation support system A litigation support system set up by the firm's or attorney's own staff and computer.

individual search engine Search engine that compiles its own searchable database.

inkjet printer A non-impact printer that sprays very fine ink onto the page.

image format A file structure that shows an image of a document as if it was viewed in the original application without having the original application.

input Data or information that is entered or transferred into a computer (including by keyboard, mouse, scanner, voice, etc.).

input device A device that enters information into a computer.

instant messaging Allows users to converse in real time with other users who are using the same instant messaging program. As soon as a user connects to the Internet the user will know which of his or her colleagues are signed on and be able to send them a message.

integrated software Combines several application functions into one. For example, an integrated program might include a word processing module, a spreadsheet module, and a database module all in one program. In an integrated program, the individual modules are not available separately.

Internet The Internet is one of the world's largest computer networks and is known as a "network of networks." It allows hundreds of millions of users around the world to share information.

Internet depositions Process that allows an attorney to join, monitor, or take a live deposition from a witness from any location with a personal computer, Internet connection, and an Internet deposition provider.

Internet Relay Chat (IRC) Allows people to converse with one another in real time over the Internet.

Internet Service Provider (ISP) Provides a user with Internet services such as the World Wide Web, email, listservs, newsgroup, and others.

interrogatories A series of written questions that are directed to an opposing party in a lawsuit.

intranet An internal network designed to provide and disseminate information to internal staff using the look and feel of the World Wide Web.

invisible web Refers to the fact that a large portion of the World Wide Web is not accessible to search engine spiders. This includes PDF files, password-protected sites, some databases, documents behind firewalls, and other data.

key search A WESTLAW tool that allows users to find documents using a topical index and without the user having to formulate a search query.

KeyCite Allows WESTLAW users to determine if a case, statute, or other document is good law and allows users to expand their research by finding other sources that have cited the reference.

landscape A method of printing that arranges data across the width of a page.

laptop computer Sometimes called a portable or notebook computer. A microcomputer that is portable and easily moved but more powerful than a handheld; can run on batteries or AC power.

laser printer A non-impact printer that uses a laser beam to form characters on a page.

law firm information system A systems approach that uses a combination of computer hardware, computer software, procedures, and human interaction to solve real-life problems in a law office.

legal malpractice An attorney's breach of an ordinary standard of care that a reasonable attorney would have adhered to in that same circumstance.

legal-specific software Software aimed specifically at the legal market.

library gateway A collection of databases and information sites arranged by subject.

line graph A graph that plots numerical values as a time line.

listserv An electronic mailing list that allows people on the list to send and receive messages to and from everyone on the list via email.

Litigation hold When a party reasonably anticipates litigation, the party must invoke a litigation hold on all relevant hard-copy and electronically stored information so that such information is not destroyed.

litigation support service bureau A company that, for a fee, sets up a litigation support system and enters all necessary documents for a case.

litigation support software Software that assists attorneys and legal assistants in organizing, storing, retrieving, and summarizing information that is gathered in the litigation of a lawsuit.

local area network (LAN) A multiuser system that links microcomputers that are in close proximity for the purpose of communication.

Locate in Result A command that allows a WESTLAW user to search the retrieved documents for particular terms, whether or not the terms appear in the user's original search.

lookup option A list of options that a user must choose from when entering information into a table.

macro A previously saved group of commands or keystrokes that, when invoked, replays those commands or keystrokes.

magnetic tape system Storage device that holds data on magnetic tape.

main memory The part of the CPU that stores information that the computer is processing. Main memory consists of read-only memory and random-access memory.

mainframe computer A large and powerful computer that can process and store large volumes of data. Mainframe computers are extremely expensive.

management reports Reports used to help management analyze whether the office is operating in an efficient and effective manner.

Many-to-Many Relationship One record in either table can relate to many records in the other table. The many-to-many relationship is not permitted in most relational databases.

maximize The window will run full screen and take up the entire screen.

memory chips Electronic circuits that store or hold information.

menu bar A bar in some Windows-compatible programs that contains commands that are standard across all Windows programs, as well as commands that are specific to each application program.

merging The process of combining a form with a list of variables to automatically produce a document. Sometimes called document generation.

metadata Electronically stored information that may identify the origin, date, author, usage, comments, or other information about a file.

metasearch engine Search engine that does not crawl the Web or compile its own database. Instead, it sends the user's search request to a number of different individual search engines and then eliminates the duplicates and sorts the sites retrieved by rank.

microcomputer A computer that is cheaper and less powerful than a mainframe computer and is generally referred to as a personal computer.

microprocessors The processor chips found in microcomputers.

minimize The window is running only in the taskbar at the bottom of the screen and is no longer on the user's screen.

modem A device that allows computers in different locations to communicate using a telephone line.

monitor Displays computer output. There are several different types of monitors including cathode-ray-tube (CRT), which is similar to a television, and flat-panel (LCD).

motions and briefs Filed in cases during the litigation to argue whatever position the party is taking on how the case should proceed in court.

mouse An input device that is used to move the cursor on the monitor. As the mouse is moved, the cursor correspondingly moves in the same direction.

multi-function printer A printer that includes printing capabilities as well as added functions such as faxing, scanning, or copying.

multitasking The ability of a computer to run more than one computer program at the same time.

native format A file structure defined by the original creating application.

natural language A searching technique that uses plain English, without the need for complex connectors to search for documents.

network Allows users to see the other computers that are connected to the same network.

network copier/printer A printer that combines the function of a traditional copy machine and a network printer.

network operating system Handles the communication tasks between the computers on the network.

non-impact printer Prints data on paper without physically striking the paper.

normal view Shows the slide that is being created, an outline of the total presentation, and speaker's notes for the slide that is being shown.

objective/bibliographical coding Recording only basic information about documents (document number, document name, date, author, recipient, and so forth) into a document abstract database. The coder makes no subjective characterizations about the document.

offline No longer connected to an information service and not accruing charges except possibly for printing or downloading.

off-the-shelf software Software that has been developed by an individual other than the end user. A person can use off-the-shelf software while knowing nothing about how it was programmed.

office suite A group of individual programs that are packaged together and have similar interfaces.

online Connected to an information service and running up charges.

One-to-One Relationship Each record in the first table contains a field value that corresponds and matches the field value in one record in the other table.

One-to-Many Relationship One record in one table can have many matching records in another table. The table on the "one" side is called the "parent" table and the other is called the "child" table.

operating system program A computer program that directs a computer how to operate its own circuitry and to manage its components.

operating system software Instructions that tell the computer how to operate its circuitry and how to communicate with input, output, and auxiliary storage devices, and that allow the user to manage the computer.

optical character recognition (OCR) A technology that allows the text of documents to be read or scanned into a computer so the text of the document can be searched or brought into a word processor to be edited.

optical storage devices Use laser beams to store data on small laser disks. Optical storage devices can store hundreds of megabytes of data on a single disk.

outline view Shows the presentation in outline format with no graphics or other elements of the presentation added.

output Information or computer results that are produced or transmitted from a computer to a user as a result of the computer's operations (including to monitor, printer, files, etc.).

output device A device that feeds out information from a computer.

outside counsel Term referring to when corporate and government law practices contract with law offices (i.e., outside of the corporation or government entity) to help them with legal matters, such as litigation, specialized contracts, stock/bond offerings, etc.

paperless office Refers to converting all hard-copy documents into an electronic form for storage, processing, and distribution.

passwords Codes entered into a computer system or software that act as a key and allow the user to access the system and the information it contains.

peer-to-peer network A computer network where each computer acts as both a server and a client.

peripheral devices Pieces of equipment that are connected to a computer to perform specific functions such as storing information (auxiliary storage devices), inputting information (input devices), outputting information (output devices), and communicating between computers (communication devices).

personal information manager (PIM) Consolidates a number of different tasks into one computer program. Most PIMs include calendaring, things to do, a contact database that tracks names and addresses of people, note taking, and other tasks as well.

personal injury law An area of the law dealing with cases in which a person has been physically injured.

phishing A type of Internet fraud where "phishers" send fraudulent emails in which they impersonate legitimate senders in hopes of gaining personal information from users.

pie chart A chart that represents each value as a piece or percentage of a total "pie."

Pleading Wizard A word-processing feature that helps legal professionals quickly and easily create a legal pleading by having them answer questions about the pleading to be created.

pleadings Formal documents filed with a court that usually state a party's contentions regarding specific issues.

plug and play A Windows feature that allows a user to add a new piece of hardware by simply plugging it in—Windows automatically recognizes the exact device and loads the appropriate software drivers.

podcasts An audio recording that is posted on the Internet and is made available for users to download so they can listen to it on a computer or mobile computing device.

point Locate an item on the screen by moving the mouse.

Portable Document Format (PDF) A file format developed by Adobe Systems, Inc. for sharing files independently of the application that created the file or the application's operating system. PDFs can be created so the file is read-only, but the file can be printed, saved, and password protected.

portable printer A compact printer that can be connected to a laptop or handheld computing device for printing when the user is away from the office.

portable projector A projector that allows a user to display the image on a computer to an audience.

portal A "jumping off" spot for many things on the Web, offering searching, hierarchical directories, news, sports, shopping, entertainment and much more.

portrait A method of printing that arranges data down the length of a page.

power-on password Password that the computer immediately prompts the user to enter after the machine has been turned on, but before the computer has completely booted the operating system software. If the user does not know the password, the system will not start.

pre-billing report A rough draft version of billings.

presentation software Software that allows users to create visually interesting presentations using graphics, color, sound, video, text, animation, and clip art.

primary file A file that contains the constant information and is usually referred to as a form or template in a merge document.

primary key A field that uniquely identifies each record.

primary sort The first sort criterion that a DBMS uses to sort information.

printer An output device that produces data from the computer on a piece of paper. Many different types and sizes of printers are available.

probate law An area of the law that allows a judge to determine the validity of wills and trusts, the proper beneficiaries or recipients of property, and other like matters.

processor chip The part of the CPU that performs the actual arithmetic computations of the computer.

programmer An individual who writes and develops computer programs.

project management software An application program that allows the user to track the sequence and timing of the separate activities of a larger project or task.

proximity search A computer search that scans a database for words that are in a given proximity to one another.

pure retainer A fee that obligates the office to be available to represent the client throughout the time period agreed upon.

push technology Information that is automatically delivered via email.

query Extracts data from a table based on criteria designed by the user. A query allows a user to search for and sort only the information the user is looking for at that time.

query by example (QBE) A method of querying a database where the user interactively builds a query that will search and sort a database.

Quick Launch Bar Allows a user to quickly launch a program without using the Start button or the desktop.

random (direct) access A device that can go directly to a location of specific data without having to read through all of the data preceding it (like a CD).

random-access memory (RAM) A part of main memory that is temporary and volatile in nature and is erased every time the computer's power is turned off. Application programs and data are loaded into RAM when the computer is processing the data.

read-only memory (ROM) A part of main memory that contains permanent information a computer needs to operate itself. ROM can be read from, but cannot be written to.

real-time court reporting A computerized court reporting system where witness's testimony is immediately converted from a court reporter's notes to a transcript in realtime.

real-time transcription An attorney or legal assistant connects a computer (typically a laptop) with real-time software to the court reporter's transcription machine; within seconds of the testimony being spoken the attorney has a rough-draft version of the transcript.

record A collection of fields that are treated as a unit. It is essentially one row in a table.

recordable DVD drive Device that allows data to be recorded on DVD disks.

recurring entry A calendar entry that recurs.

Recycle Bin Contains files and folders that have been deleted from the computer. Users can use the Recycle Bin to retrieve files that were accidentally deleted.

relational DBMS A DBMS that can work with multiple tables at a time, so long as at least one common field occurs in each table.

relational operator A symbol that expresses data relationships in a database when performing searches. Examples include greater than, less than, and equal to symbols.

relative cell reference A cell address in a spreadsheet program formula that automatically changes to reflect its new location when it is copied.

removable or flash drive A storage device that allows a large amount of data, up to 4 GB to be stored.

report Prints data from a table or query as designed by the user. While forms are designed to be used on the screen, reports are designed to be printed.

report writer Allows the user complete control over how data in the database is printed without affecting the data in the database.

request for admissions A series of questions directed to an opposing party in a lawsuit that must be either admitted or denied.

request for production of documents A series of requests that direct an opposing party in a lawsuit to produce documents that are in its possession or control so that the documents or evidence can be given to or examined by the requesting party.

restore Allows the user to size the window to any height or width needed.

ResultsPlus A WESTLAW feature that automatically includes other documents (no additional search is needed) such as legal texts, treatises, and law review articles related to a user's search.

retainer for general representation A retainer typically used when a client such as a corporation or school board requires continuing legal services throughout the year.

ribbon bar A bar at the top of some Windows programs that contains tools and features instead of menus.

root expander A search technique that increases the scope of a database search by searching for words with a common root.

row An area that extends across a page horizontally.

RSS A group of formats that are used to publish and distribute news feeds, blogs, and podcasts.

sampling data The process of testing data to determine if it is appropriate for production.

scroll bars Bars used to move parts of a document into view when the complete document will not fit in the window.

search box Allows users to search for programs documents, links, and emails directly from the Start button.

search query An instruction to an information service to search a specific database for the occurrence of certain words and combinations of words.

secondary file The file that contains the information that varies in a merge document.

secondary sort The second sort criterion that a DBMS uses to sort information.

sequential access A device that records and reads back data in a sequence (like an audiocassette).

shareware Computer programs that are distributed to users initially at no cost. If the user likes the software program, the user pays the author for it.

single-word search A computer search that scans a database for matches to a single word.

single-user system A system that can accommodate only one person at a time and is not linked to other systems or computers.

slide show view Used during a presentation or when the user is developing the presentation to see how the audience will actually see the slide. Only the current slide is shown on the screen—the program interface, outline, and speaker's notes are not shown.

slide sorter view Shows the slides in the presentation, but in a greatly reduced format. The slide sorter view is typically used to change the order of slides.

slide transition Effect that controls how the program proceeds from one slide to another.

slide view Shows only the current slide that is being developed.

smart art Predrawn graphical elements such as diagrams, process flow charts, and graphical lists.

software Computer programs that instruct the computer hardware how to function and perform tasks (including word processors, email programs, and spreadsheets).

soft deletions Information that has been deleted and is not available to the user, but which nonetheless has not been overwritten. Soft deletions can often be fully restored with complete integrity by forensic experts.

software piracy The unauthorized copying of computer programs.

soundcard A device that enhances the sounds that come out of a computer. Nearly all computers now come with a soundcard.

spam Unwanted or unsolicited email messages that are sent to users—nearly identical to junk mail.

specialty search engine Search engine that searches only in specific topical areas.

speech recognition The ability of a computer to understand speech.

spoliation The destruction of relevant documents in litigation.

spreadsheet A computerized version of an accountant's worksheet or ledger page.

spreadsheet software Programs that calculate and manipulate numbers using labels, values, and formulas.

spyware A general term used for software that tracks a user's movement on the Internet (for ad/marketing tracking), collects personal information about the user, or changes the configuration of the user's computer without the user's consent.

stacked bar graph A graph that depicts values as separate sections in a single or stacked bar.

Start button A button located on the taskbar that is used to start a program, open a document, change system settings, and get help in Windows.

statute of limitations A statute or law that sets a limit on the length of time a party has to file a suit. If a case is filed after the statute of limitations, the claim is barred and is dismissed as a matter of law.

storage Retention of electronic information for future use (using storage devices such as hard disks, CD-ROMs, DVDs, flash drives, and other media).

storage capacity The maximum amount of data that can be stored on a device.

structured query language (SQL) A database programming language used to search for and retrieve information in some DBMSs.

style A named set of formatting characteristics that users apply to text.

subject directory A site maintained by a staff of people who select sites to include in their directory.

subject-specific database A database devoted to a single subject; sometimes called a "vortal."

subjective coding Entering information in the document abstract program about what the document means including what case issues are relevant in the document or notes about the document.

super wildcard search A computer search that scans a database for derivatives of a word both in front of and in back of the root word.

supercomputers The largest, fastest, and most expensive computers in existence.

Switch between Windows A feature that allows a user to switch to a different window while seeing a live view of the windows available.

system A group of interdependent parts that work collectively to accomplish a common task.

table (databases) A collection of related information stored in rows and columns in a database program.

table (word processing) A word processing feature that allows the user to create a table of information using rows and columns.

table of authorities An automated feature in word processors that allows the program to generate an accurate table of authorities.

tape cartridges Small cartridges of magnetic tape on which information is stored.

tape reels Large reels of magnetic tape on which information is stored.

taskbar A feature at the bottom of the screen that shows which programs are running and other Windows-related information.

Telnet An Internet tool that makes one computer a terminal for other computers on the Internet.

terms and connectors A search technique that uses Boolean logic and operators/connectors to connect terms to describe an idea.

text Descriptive data, including headings and titles, that is used for reference purposes in a spreadsheet.

timekeeper Anyone, including partners, associates, and legal assistants, who bills out time.

timekeeper productivity report A report showing how much billable and nonbillable time is being spent by each timekeeper.

timekeeping Tracking time for the purpose of billing clients.

timeslip A slip of paper or computer slip where legal professionals record information about the legal services they provide to each client.

toolbar A Windows tool that contains icons that represent shortcuts to other tools and functions.

touch pad A small rectangular surface that the user slides a finger across. The cursor follows the finger's movement.

trackball Allows the user to control the cursor by rotating a ball that sits on top of the device.

track changes Feature that allows reviewers to recommend changes to a word-processing document that later can be either accepted or rejected by the original author.

trackpoint Device that looks like a pencil eraser positioned in the middle of the keyboard. A finger is used to rotate the trackpoint in the direction the user wants the cursor to move.

trial presentation programs Presentation graphics programs that are specifically designed to meet the needs of trial attorneys.

trial software Programs that help a litigator or a trial team prepare for and present a case to a jury or other fact finder.

trust An instrument wherein one party (a trustee) holds property for the benefit of another (a beneficiary).

trust or escrow account A separate bank account, apart from a law office's or attorney's operating checking account, where unearned client funds are deposited.

unearned retainer Money that is paid up front by the client as an advance against the attorney's future fees and expenses. Until the money is actually earned by the attorney or law office, it actually belongs to the client.

uniform resource locator (URL) The address of a web page.

uninterruptible power supply (UPS) A battery backup device that automatically supplies power to the computer in the event there is any loss of power, no matter how small.

universal character A character that represents one letter or number and enables a legal information service to retrieve words with minor variations.

USENET (newsgroups) A network of computers that contains news and discussion groups. USENET is an electronic bulletin board service consisting of newsgroups, newsfeeds, and newsreaders.

utility software Instructions that help users with the housekeeping and maintenance tasks a computer requires.

validation control The process of controlling and limiting what information is entered into a database for the purpose of ensuring accuracy.

value billing A type of fee agreement that is based not on the time to perform the work but on the basis of the perceived value of the services to the client.

values Numbers that are entered into a spreadsheet program for the purpose of making calculations.

video adapter card Acts as an interface between the monitor and the computer.

videoconferencing A private broadcast between two or more remote locations, with live image transmission, display, and sound.

Voice Over Internet Protocol (VOIP) Functionality that allows users to make telephone calls using a broadband Internet connection instead of a regular analog phone line.

web browser The interface or program that allows the user to see web pages.

"what-if" analysis A feature of spreadsheets that allows the user to build a spreadsheet and then change the data to reflect alternative planning assumptions or scenarios.

wide area network (WAN) A multiuser system that links microcomputers that may be located thousands of miles apart.

wildcard character A search technique that increases the scope of a database search by replacing one character in a word.

wildcard search A computer search that scans a database for derivatives of a word.

will An instrument that expresses how a person's property should be distributed at his death.

window A frame where a particular program is running.

window title A menu title for each window that tells the user what the window contains.

Windows A graphical operating system that was developed by Microsoft for IBM-compatible microcomputers. There are various versions of Windows, including Windows XP and Windows Vista.

Windows-compatible programs Application programs specifically engineered to run under the Windows operating system.

wireless modem Modems that many mobile phones and handheld computers now use to connect to the Internet.

wireless networking Allows computers on the network to communicate with each other using wireless antennas coordinated through a wired access point.

word art Allows a user to add special formatting to text, including 3-D designs.

word-processing software Program used to edit, manipulate, and revise text to create documents.

World Wide Web The World Wide Web is an Internet system, navigation tool, and interface that retrieves information using links to other web pages. To access the Web, a user needs a web browser program such as Microsoft Explorer or Netscape Navigator. The Web is a graphical and multimedia interface.

INDEX

D

E

F

G

H

I

J

K

L

Q

R

S

T

Y

Z

CT Summation

PUTTING LITIGATORS IN COMMAND

CT Summation is an award-winning suite of litigation support tools that provides a comprehensive, end-to-end solution for managing massive volumes of information—from case initiation through final resolution. When you command every aspect of your case, you win.

ALL THE TOOLS YOU NEED, FROM ONE RELIABLE SOURCE

Managing massive volumes of information efficiently and accurately is the key to winning complex cases. CT Summation leads the industry in providing a complete set of tools to organize, find and distill large volumes of disparate information— in one easy-to-use application. All the key evidence you need is at hand during every phase of your case.

A SOLUTION FOR EVERY SITUATION

Only CT Summation offers a complete and comprehensive solution that works for every situation and every member of your legal team—whether the case you're working on is big or small, in-house or hosted.

CT SUMMATION IBLAZE PRODUCT FAMILY

Power and portability are yours with our premium, award-winning litigation support solution. Designed for the desktop or the laptop, this product family helps you efficiently manage case information such as transcripts and documents with the benefits of full-text imaging, PDF support, OCR on-the-fly, electronic evidence support and comprehensive production tools.

CT SUMMATION WEBBLAZE

Our robust, Web-based litigation support application allows you to securely share and access case information via the Internet. Search and organize your case information hosted in CT Summation iBlaze. Use WebBlaze to share information with your litigation team, experts, outside counsel and expert witnesses.

CT SUMMATION ENTERPRISE

The award-winning technology and time-tested functionality of CT Summation iBlaze and CT Summation WebBlaze are combined with the power of Microsoft® SQL Server in this robust product suite. Big cases require powerful support, and CT Summation Enterprise lets you master the massive amounts of information generated by today's voluminous cases.

CT SUMMATION CASEVAULT

Ideal for large cases involving multi-party and multi-district litigation, CT Summation CaseVault is a subscrip-tion-based hosting service that lets you collaborate securely and successfully on a reliable, neutral Web site.

CONCEIVED BY LEGAL PROFESSIONALS, FOR LEGAL PROFESSIONALS

CT Summation pioneered integrated litigation support software in 1988, with input from legal professionals who understand the many facets of litigation. As a result, every member of your legal team is able to work more efficiently. Moreover, you have solutions you can trust to help you navigate virtually any problem or case, efficiently and effortlessly.

CT Summation
800 735 7866 toll free
415 442 0404 tel
www.ctsummation.com

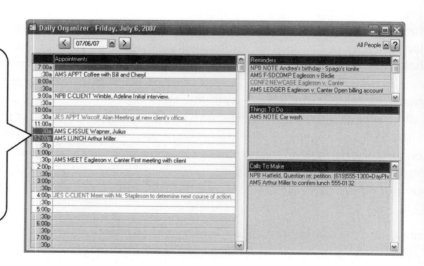

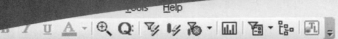

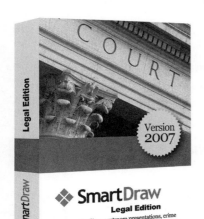

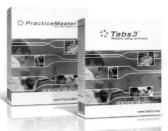